D0202733

Retail Management:
A Strategic Approach

Retail Management:
A Strategic Approach

Seventh Edition

Barry Berman ■ **Joel R. Evans**

Hofstra University **Hofstra University**

Prentice Hall
Upper Saddle River, NJ 07458

Acquisitions Editors: Gabrielle Dudnyk/Donald J. Hull
Assistant Editor: John Larkin
Editorial Assistant: Jim Campbell
Vice President/Editorial Director: James Boyd
Marketing Manager: John Chillingworth
Production Editor: Aileen Mason
Production Coordinator: Carol Samet
Managing Editor: Dee Josephson
Associate Managing Editor: Linda DeLorenzo
Manufacturing Supervisor: Arnold Vila
Manufacturing Manager: Vincent Scelta
Design Manager: Pat Smythe
Interior Design: Levavi & Levavi
Cover Design: Cheryl Asherman
Illustrator (Interior):   A Good Thing, Inc.
Composition: Carlisle Communications, Ltd.
Cover Illustrator: Salem Krieger

Berman, Barry.
   Retail management: a strategic approach / Barry Berman, Joel R.
Evans. — 7th ed.
      p.   cm.
   Includes indexes.
   ISBN 0–13–613829–2
   1. Retail trade—Management.   I. Evans, Joel R.   II. Title.
HF5429.B45   1998   97–38137
658.8'7—dc21   CIP

Prentice-Hall International (UK) Limited, London
Prentice-Hall of Australia Pty. Limited, Sydney
Prentice-Hall Canada, Inc., Toronto
Prentice-Hall Hispanoamericana, S.A., Mexico
Prentice-Hall of India Private Limited, New Delhi
Prentice-Hall of Japan, Inc., Tokyo
Simon & Schuster Asia Pte. Ltd., Singapore
Editora Prentice-Hall do Brasil, Ltda., Rio de Janeiro

Printed in the United States of America

To Linda, Glenna, and Lisa
To Linda, Stacey, and Jennifer

Thank you for your enduring
patience and understanding.

About the Authors

Barry Berman (Ph.D. in Business with majors in Marketing and Behavioral Science) is the Walter H. "Bud" Miller Distinguished Professor of Business and Professor of Marketing and International Business at Hofstra University. He has served as a consultant to such organizations as Fortunoff, Associated Dry Goods, the State Education Department of New York, and professional and trade groups.

Dr. Berman is author or editor of numerous books and articles (including *Marketing Channels*) and is active in various professional associations. He served as the associate editor of the *Marketing Review* for many years. At Hofstra, he has been honored as a faculty inductee in Beta Gamma Sigma honor society and received two Dean's Awards. Dr. Berman is a past recipient of the Teacher of the Year award from the Hofstra M.B.A. Association.

Joel R. Evans (Ph.D. in Business with majors in Marketing and Public Policy) is the RMI Distinguished Professor of Business and Professor of Marketing and International Business at Hofstra University. Before joining Hofstra, he worked for a *Fortune 500* company, owned a retail mail-order business, and taught at Baruch College and New York University. He has also been a consultant for such diverse companies as PepsiCo, Nynex, and McCrory.

Dr. Evans is the author or editor of numerous books and articles and is active in various professional associations. At Hofstra, he has been honored as a faculty inductee in Beta Gamma Sigma honor society and received two Dean's Awards and the School of Business Faculty Distinguished Service Award. Dr. Evans is a past recipient of the Teacher of the Year award from the Hofstra M.B.A. Association.

Barry Berman and Joel R. Evans have worked together for 20 years and are co-authors of several best-selling texts. They are co-founders of the American Marketing Association's Special Interest Group in Retailing and Retail Management, and currently serve on its board. In 1995, they co-chaired the American Marketing Association Faculty Consortium on "Ethics and Social Responsibility in Marketing." Each has a chapter on retailing in the most recent edition of Dartnell's *Marketing Manager's Handbook*. For several years, Drs. Berman and Evans were co-directors of Hofstra's Retail Management Institute and Business Research Institute. Both regularly teach undergraduate and graduate courses to a wide range of students.

Preface

We are delighted by the continuing positive response to this text, as evidenced by adoptions at hundreds of colleges and universities around the world. In this seventh edition, we have set out to retain the coverage and features most desired by professors and students, add new material and features requested by professors and students, introduce applications related to the World Wide Web, keep the book as current as possible, and maintain the length of prior editions.

As always, the concepts of a strategic approach and a retail strategy form the foundation of *Retail Management: A Strategic Approach,* Seventh Edition. With a strategic approach, the "fundamental principle is that the retailer has to plan for and adapt to a complex, changing environment. Both opportunities and constraints must be considered." A retail strategy is "the overall plan or framework of action that guides a retailer. Ideally, it will be at least one year in duration and outline the mission, goals, consumer market, overall and specific activities, and control mechanisms of the retailer. Without a predefined and well-integrated strategy, the firm may flounder and be unable to cope with the environment that surrounds it." The major goals of our text are to enable the reader to become a good retail planner and decision maker and to help focus on change and adaptation to change.

Retail Management is designed as a one-semester text for students of retailing or retail management. In many cases, such students will have already been exposed to marketing principles. We feel retailing should be viewed as one form of marketing and not distinct from it.

THE TRADITION CONTINUES

These significant features have been retained from earlier editions of *Retail Management: A Strategic Approach:*

- Full coverage of all major retailing topics—including consumer behavior, information systems, store location, operations, service retailing, the retail audit, retail institutions, franchising, human resource management, computerization, and retailing in a changing environment.
- A four-color format, with plentiful art and photos throughout.
- A decision-making orientation, with many flowcharts, figures, tables, and photos.
- A real-world approach focusing on both small and large retailers. Among the well-known firms discussed are The Gap, Home Depot, Kinko's, Lands' End, The Limited, McDonald's, Neiman Marcus, J.C. Penney, Sears, Starbucks, Toys "Я" Us, and Wal-Mart.
- Part openers to introduce each section of the text.
- Real-world boxes on current retailing issues in each chapter. These boxes further illustrate the concepts presented in the text by focusing on real firms and situations.

- A numbered summary keyed to chapter objectives, a key terms listing, and discussion questions at the end of each chapter.
- Thirty-nine end-of-chapter cases involving a wide range of retailers and retail practices.
- Eight end-of-part comprehensive cases.
- Up-to-date information from such sources as *Advertising Age, Business Week, Chain Store Age, Direct Marketing, Discount Store News, Dun & Bradstreet, Forbes, Fortune, Journal of Retailing, Progressive Grocer, Stores,* and *Wall Street Journal.*
- A convenient, one-semester format.
- "How to Solve a Case Study," following Chapter 1 in the text.
- An appendix on franchising, following Chapter 4.
- An end-of-text appendix on careers in retailing and another with a detailed glossary.
- Computer-based exercises linked to text concepts.

New to the Seventh Edition

Since the first edition of *Retail Management: A Strategic Approach,* we have worked extremely hard to be as contemporary and forward-looking as possible. We have continually sought to be proactive rather than reactive in our preparation of each edition. That is why we still take this adage of the late Sam Walton so seriously: "Commit to your business. Believe in it more than anybody else."

Accordingly, for the seventh edition, there are many changes in *Retail Management: A Strategic Approach.* We hope you like them:

1. The organization of the text has been revamped.
   a. There are 20 chapters (up from 19 in the sixth edition). There is a new chapter on nonstore and nontraditional retailing.
   b. Many chapters have been reworked substantially so they flow better and truly capture the spirit of retailing as we approach the twenty-first century.
2. These substantive chapter revisions have been made:
   a. Chapter 1 (An Introduction to Retailing) is even more reader-friendly and reflects the diversity of retailing. There is greater discussion of the various perspectives of retailing, retailing's current status, customer service, relationship retailing, the dynamic nature of retailing, and "exciting" consumers. Lands' End is examined in depth.
   b. Chapters 2 and 3 are better integrated. Chapter 2 (Strategic Planning in Retailing: Owning or Managing a Business) focuses on the steps in a retail strategy and the impact of uncontrollable factors. This chapter is theory-oriented.
   c. Chapter 3 (The Contemporary Challenges Facing Retailers) deals with the present-day challenges facing retailers—and how they are dealing with them, including the greater emphasis on category management, channel relationships, the competitive environment, value-based retailing, technology, ethical issues, and international retailing. This chapter is applications-oriented.
   d. Chapter 4 (Retail Institutions by Ownership) now starts with a synopsis that contrasts ownership forms, such as how various formats are positioned and the keys to their success (or lack of it).
   e. Chapter 5 (Retail Institutions by Store-Based Strategy Mix) better melds service retailing into the discussion and also more sharply contrasts the various strategy mixes.
   f. Chapter 6 (<u>New!</u> Nonstore-Based and Nontraditional Retailing) includes such topics as the World Wide Web, direct marketing (including home shopping networks, catalogs on CD-ROM disks, and infomercials), video kiosks, vending technology, and direct selling.
   g. Chapter 7 (Identifying and Understanding Consumers) is more oriented to the unique aspects of consumer behavior in retailing.

    h. Chapter 8 (Information Gathering and Processing in Retailing) has added coverage of data-base management and the roles of different channel members in acquiring data.

    i. Chapters 9 and 10 (Trading-Area Analysis and Site Selection) have even more discussion of technology for site selection (especially geographic information systems) and the uses of computerized census data. We also note the comeback of many downtown areas, the renovations of aging malls, and recent trends in retail sites.

    j. Chapter 11 (Retail Organization and Human Resource Management) has more on the role of women in retailing, labor laws, health care, the minimum wage, employee motivation, and the role of local store managers.

    k. Chapters 12 and 13 (Operations Management) are updated, with Chapter 12 examining the financial dimensions and Chapter 13 the operational dimensions. Store security receives greater attention.

    l. Chapter 14 (Buying and Handling Merchandise) has enhanced coverage of merchandise distinctiveness, relationship marketing with suppliers, computer-aided ordering, direct store delivery, distribution center management, and regular versus opportunistic buying.

    m. Chapter 15 (Financial Merchandise Management) is updated.

    n. Chapter 16 (Pricing in Retailing) better identifies pricing options (and their trade-offs) for retailers, as well as the competitive pricing trends ("value") and why retailers have been unable to abandon frequent sales.

    o. Chapter 17 (Establishing and Maintaining a Retail Image) has more on atmospherics, as well as a better discussion on the various components of store image (with atmosphere being only one of them), the importance of "entertaining" consumers, and the relation of image with store positioning and market segmentation.

    p. Chapter 18 (Promotional Strategy) has enhanced coverage of public relations and the need for a balanced promotion mix. The chapter has a greater retailing flavor (such as the need to balance self-service displays with the proper level of in-store personnel).

    q. Chapter 19 (Planning by a Service Retailer) is updated, more lively in nature, and has more real-life examples.

    r. Chapter 20 (Integrating and Controlling the Retail Strategy) places greater emphasis on integrating the retailing plan and introduces the topics of benchmarking and gap analysis.

    s. Appendix A on careers is updated. Appendix B describes the new Web site that accompanies the text. Appendix C (Glossary) now includes about 525 key terms.

    t. The end papers are totally revamped, with a focus on Web site addresses by topic.

3. The in-chapter boxed material, which is all new, has been made more topical and more focused. Every chapter contains a "Technology in Retailing" box, a "Retailing Around the World" box, and an "Ethics in Retailing" box.

4. All chapter-opening vignettes are new.

5. Almost all of the chapter-ending cases are new or substantially revised. Twenty-one of these cases have a video component; they are denoted by a video symbol in the text.

6. All of the part-ending comprehensive cases are new.

7. A discussion of retailing opportunities and career ladders is in the text-ending Appendix A.

Getting Ready for the 21st Century: A Web Site Keyed to Retail Management: A Strategic Approach

We are really "pumped up" about the new Web site accompanying *Retail Management: A Strategic Approach,* Seventh Edition. This Web site is a dynamic learning, studying, interactive tool that is available to both students and professors. It is easy to use (see Appendix B for more details) and provides hands-on applications. We believe this Web site will be of great value for students as we move into the next century.

The Web site (http://www.prenhall.com/rm__student) has six parts:

- **Interactive Study Guide**—This section contains chapter summaries, chapter-by-chapter listings of key terms, and 20 multiple choice, 20 true–false, and 10 fill-in questions per chapter (with answers and text page references).
- **Web Site Directory**—This section lists hundreds of retailing-related Web sites, divided by chapter and topic. The sites range from search engines to government agencies to retail firms to trade associations, and so forth.
- **Glossary**—This section has all of the key terms cited in *Retail Management*. Terms may be accessed alphabetically by typing in the relevant words.
- **Career Information**—This section includes advice on resumé writing, how to take an interview, jobs in retailing, retail career ladders, and a comprehensive listing of retail employers (about 500 companies). And more!
- **Computer Exercises**—The 16 text-based exercises noted by a computer symbol throughout *Retail Management* may be downloaded from on the Web site, complete with help screens, instructions, and questions.
- **Real-World Software Packages**—This section contains a number of actual software packages used by retailers that may be downloaded. Included are site selection, life-style profiles, and bar coding. And more!

How the Text Is Organized

Retail Management: A Strategic Approach has eight parts. Part 1 introduces the field of retailing, the basics of strategic planning, the decisions to be made in owning or managing a retail business, and retailing's challenging environment. In Part 2, retail institutions are examined in terms of ownership types, as well as store-based, service versus goods, nonstore-based, and nontraditional strategy mixes. The wheel of retailing, scrambled merchandising, and the retail life cycle are also covered. Part 3 focuses on selecting a target market and information-gathering methods, including discussions of the consumer decision process and the retailing information system. Part 4 presents a four-step approach to location planning: trading-area analysis, choosing the most desirable type of location, selecting a general locale, and deciding on a specific site.

Part 5 discusses the elements involved in managing a retail business: the retail organization structure, human resource management, and operations management (both financial and operational). Part 6 deals with merchandise management (buying and handling merchandise, as well as the financial aspects of merchandising) and pricing. In Part 7, the ways of communicating with customers are analyzed, with special attention on retail image, atmosphere, and promotion. Part 8 covers service retailing, and integrating and controlling a retail strategy.

At the end of the text, Appendix A highlights various career opportunities in retailing, Appendix B explains the components of the Web site, and Appendix C is a comprehensive glossary.

A comprehensive teaching package is available for instructors. It includes a detailed instructor's manual, color transparencies, transparency masters, a large test bank, and notes for video lectures. All of the instructional materials have been developed or written by the authors (except for the videos, which we personally selected).

Please feel free to send us comments regarding any aspect of *Retail Management* or its package: Barry Berman (E-mail at MKTBXB@Hofstra.edu) or Joel R. Evans (E-mail at MKTJRE@Hofstra.edu), Department of Marketing and International Business, Hofstra University, Hempstead, N.Y., 11549. We promise to reply to any correspondence.

B.B.
J.R.E.

About the Boxed Material in
Retail Management: A Strategic Approach

As noted earlier in the preface, there are three applications boxes per chapter: "Technology in Retailing," "Retailing Around the World," and "Ethics in Retailing." Through these boxes, a wide variety of thought-provoking situations are presented:

"TECHNOLOGY IN RETAILING" BOXES

"RETAILING AROUND THE WORLD" BOXES

"ETHICS IN RETAILING" BOXES

About the Videos that Accompany *Retail Management: A Strategic Approach*

Retail Management: A Strategic Approach has two video supplements: one for the videos denoted by the symbol in the text and another with four separate video lecture segments.

Every chapter (except Chapter 1) has at least two end-of-chapter cases, 21 of which have optional video components. In addition, a video for Chapter 1, on Lands' End, augments the discussion of that firm; a career-oriented video can be used to complement Appendix A; and a "bonus" video on customer service can be used with several chapters.

These are the cases that have a video component:

Chapter	Case (or Topic)	Text Page Reference
1	Lands' End (chapter discussion)	15
2	Fred Meyer: Using a One-Stop Shopping Strategy and Devising a Corporate Philosophy	56
3	Marks & Spencer: Assessing an International Strategy	93
	Lands' End in England and Japan	94
4	Supervalu: Making It Happen at Retail	122
	Maaco: Evaluating Franchising Opportunities	124
5	Patagonia: An Environmentally Focused Specialty Retailer	162
6	Lands' End and the Web	192
7	Retail Target Marketing Systems	233
8	The Marsh Super Study	266
9	Arby's: Using GIS Mapping Software	310
10	The Mall of America	339
11	Supervalu: Performance Appraisal	377
13	Condiments: Category Management	427
	Sensormatic: Pilferage Control	429
14	Distribution and Marketing Systems Inc. (DMSI): Outsourcing Retail Distribution and Transportation Services	470
15	McKesson's Computerized Financial Merchandise Management Systems for Retailers	502
16	Dahl's Fair Practices	537
17	Gooding's: Atmosphere at the Flagship Store	579
18	Selling at Bon Marche	616
19	Domino's Pizza: Training by a Service Firm	657
20	Fleming Companies: Strategic Planning in Action	688
App. A	Heilig-Meyers Furniture (a career video)	A1
Bonus	Supervalu: Dazzling Service (ties in to many text concepts)	

Besides the video cases, four broad video clips are available so a professor can enhance his or her coverage of these retailing topics:

Video Number	Video Title	Length of Video
1	Franchising	24 minutes
2	Mass Merchandising	17 minutes
3	Retail Site Selection	17 minutes
4	Managing Merchandise Assortments	22 minutes

Full-length lecture notes accompany the preceding videos.

Acknowledgments

Many people have assisted us in the preparation of this book, and to them we extend our warmest appreciation.

We thank these individuals for contributing cases:

Patricia M. Anderson, Quinnipiac College
Anne Heineman Batory, Bloomsburg University
Stephen S. Batory, Bloomsburg University
Howard W. Combs, San Jose State University
Andrew Cullen, The Pennmor Group
Roger Dickinson, University of Texas at Arlington
Jack Eure, Southwest Texas State University
Larry Goldstein, Iona College
Carol Felker Kaufman, Rutgers University, Camden
William W. Keep, University of Kentucky
Gail H. Kirby, Santa Clara University
Richard C. Leventhal, Metropolitan State College
Raymond A. Marquardt, University of Nebraska–Lincoln
Alan R. Miller, Towson State University
Carolyn Predmore, Manhattan College
Stan Rapp, Cross Rapp Consulting Group
Lynn Samsel, University of Nebraska–Lincoln
William R. Swinyard, Brigham Young University

We thank the following reviewers, who have reacted to this or earlier editions of the text. Each has provided us with perceptive comments that have helped us crystallize our thoughts:

M. Wayne Alexander, Moorehead State University
Larry Audler, University of New Orleans
Ramon Avila, Ball State University
Betty V. Balevic, Skidmore College
Stephen S. Batory, Bloomsburg University
Joseph Belonax, Western Michigan University
Ronald Bernard, Diablo Valley College
Charlane Bomrad, Onondaga Community College
David P. Brennan, University of St. Thomas
John J. Buckley, Orange County Community College
David Burns, Youngstown State University

Joseph A. Davidson, Cuyahoga Community College
Peter T. Doukas, Westchester Community College
Jack Eure, Southwest Texas State University
Letty Fisher, Westchester Community College
Myron Gable, Shippensburg University
Linda L. Golden, University of Texas at Austin
James I. Gray, Florida Atlantic University
J. Duncan Herrington, Radford University
Mary Higby, Eastern Michigan University
Charles A. Ingene, University of Washington
Marvin A. Jolson, University of Maryland
Ruth Keyes, SUNY College of Technology
J. Ford Laumer, Jr., Auburn University
Richard C. Leventhal, Metropolitan State College
John Lloyd, Monroe Community College
James O. McCann, Henry Ford Community College
Elizabeth L. Mariotz, Philadelphia College of Textiles
Frank McDaniels, Delaware County Community College
Brian McNeeley, University of Wisconsin—Parkside
Michael Messina, Gannon University
Ronald Michman, Shippensburg University
James R. Odgen, Kutztown University
Howard C. Paul, Mercyhurst College
Roy B. Payne, Purdue University
Dawn Pysarchik, Michigan State University
Curtis Reierson, Baylor University
Barry Rudin, Loras College
Julie Toner Schrader, North Dakota State University
Steven J. Shaw, University of South Carolina
Gladys S. Sherdell, Montgomery College
Jill F. Slomski, Gannon University
John E. Swan, University of Alabama at Birmingham
Anthony Urbanisk, Northern State University
Lillian Werner, University of Minnesota
Kaylene Williams, University of Delaware
Terrell G. Williams, Utah State University

Special thanks and acknowledgment to the Prentice Hall people who have worked on this edition, including our acquisitions editor Gabrielle Dudnyk and production editor Aileen Mason. We also appreciate the efforts of John C. Galloway, Jr. for his computer work; Jack Gifford for his photos; Diane Schoenberg, Marni Shapiro, Richelle Feiner, and Linda Evans for their editorial assistance; and Linda Berman for compiling the indexes.

Barry Berman
Joel R. Evans
Hofstra University

Brief Contents

Contents

Part One

An Overview of Strategic Retail Management

- In Part 1, the field of retailing, basic principles of strategic planning, decisions made in owning/managing a retail business, and contemporary challenges facing retailers are covered.

- Chapter 1 describes retailing's framework, shows why it should be studied, and examines its special characteristics. The value of strategic planning is noted, including a detailed review of Lands' End. The elements of the retailing concept are presented, as well as the nature of the total retail experience, customer service, and relationship retailing. The focus and format of the text are detailed. At the end of the chapter, hints for solving case studies are offered.

- Chapter 2 shows the usefulness of strategic planning for all kinds of retailers. Each aspect of the planning process is examined in depth: situation analysis, objectives, identifying consumers, overall strategy, specific activities, control, and feedback. The controllable and uncontrollable components of a retail strategy are highlighted. Strategic planning is viewed as a series of interrelated steps that are continuously reviewed.

- Chapter 3 looks at the complex environment retailers face. These particular issues are examined: customer relationships and channel relationships, implementing technological advances, ethical behavior, institutional responses, and the international dimensions of retailing. The implications are discussed.

1

An Introduction to Retailing

CHAPTER OBJECTIVES

1. To define retailing, consider it from various perspectives, demonstrate its impact, and note its special characteristics
2. To introduce the concept of strategic planning and apply it
3. To relate the marketing concept to retailing, with an emphasis on the total retail experience, customer service, and relationship retailing
4. To indicate the focus and format of the text

For decades, Sears was the largest U.S. retailer. Then, Wal-Mart and Kmart both whizzed by as Sears lost its touch. It had failed to adapt to the changing competitive and consumer marketplace. In 1992, the firm actually incurred losses of $2 billion! But, just as some industry experts were predicting Sears' ultimate demise, the company turned things around. Since 1993, it has consistently performed better than the retail industry as a whole and regained its profitability.

Much of the credit for the turnaround has been attributed to Sears' current chairman, Arthur Martinez, who was brought in from Saks Fifth Avenue to revitalize Sears. According to Martinez, before he arrived, Sears "didn't have a clear idea who our largest customer was, who our competitors were, or who we were." Subsequent marketing research found that Sears' key customers were working mothers, aged 25 to 54 with household incomes from $25,000 to $54,000. These consumers purchased both apparel and appliances.

Under Martinez's direction, Sears began to carry well-known national brands (besides Sears' own brands), accept major credit cards in addition to the Sears card, and renovate most of its mall-based stores. To highlight its new fashion focus, the "Softer Side of Sears" advertising campaign was devised. The firm closed 113 underperforming stores, ended its 97-year-old general mail-order catalog (but launched two dozen specialty catalogs), and spun off such peripheral businesses as Prodigy and Allstate. It upgraded employee training programs and began to include a customer service dimension in all employee reviews. In 1996, for the first time, only 50 percent of top executives' long-term bonuses was based on financial results; 25 percent was tied to improvements in employee satisfaction and 25 percent to gains in customer satisfaction.

Sears now also targets specific market segments better. For example, it recently developed the "Todo Para Ti" ("Everything for You") campaign for the Hispanic market and became a sponsor of a Gloria Estefan tour. Sears was the first major national retailer to fully test Asian-American marketing efforts. Furthermore, it has expanded its emphasis on the African-American segment.

As a sign of its clearer understanding of the marketplace, Sears recognizes that it should not go after the high end of the consumer market. To continue growing, it wants to attract middle-class baby boomers with young families, as well as 18- to 25-year-olds.[1]

---

[1] Scott McMurray, "Sears Fashions a New Future for Itself," *U.S. News & World Report* (May 13, 1996), pp. 61–62; Cyndee Miller, "Redux Deluxe: Sears Comeback an Event Most Marketers Would Kill For," *Marketing News* (July 15, 1996), pp. 1, 14; and Patricia Sellers, "Sears: The Turnaround Is Ending; The Revolution Has Begun," *Fortune* (April 28, 1997), pp. 106–118.

Retailing consists of those business activities involved in the sale of goods and services to consumers for their personal, family, or household use. It is the final stage in the distribution process.

Retailing today is at an interesting crossroads. On the one hand, retail sales are at their highest point in history. Wal-Mart is the first $100 billion retailer (with its annual revenues reaching that amount in 1996). New technologies are improving retail productivity. There are many opportunities to start a new retail business—or work for an existing one—and to join a franchise. Global retailing possibilities abound. On the other hand, retailers face numerous challenges. Many consumers are bored with shopping or do not have much time for it. Some localities have too many stores (making it harder for these stores to succeed). Retailers often seem to spur one another into frequent price cutting (and lower profit margins). Consumer expectations about customer service are high—while retailers are offering more self-service and automated systems (such as voice mail) to handle customer interactions. At the same time, most retailers are not yet sure what to do with the Internet; even those with web sites often do not know whether to use the Internet for image purposes, customer information and feedback, and/or sales transactions. They also are unsure if the Internet is an opportunity or threat for traditional firms.

Here's the way *Chain Store Age,* a leading retailing publication, recently put it:

> U.S. retailers in the waning years of the twentieth century are confronted with an overstored landscape (about 19 square feet of retail space for every man, woman, and child in the United States, when probably just about one-half to two-thirds of that figure is needed), a mishmash of merchandising that has blurred lines of trade and allowed stores to overlap their products in once noncompetitive fields, an aging population that they largely ignore while still chasing after the youth market, consumers who have lost their "love" of shopping and reduced since 1980 their average number of trips and hours spent in shopping malls by 35 percent and 70 percent, respectively, an increasingly ethnic society whose main pockets of growth are in the Hispanic- and Asian-American markets, each of which has to be addressed individually (e.g., Korean Americans, Chinese Americans), a more polarized society based on incomes, educations, and employment that is squeezing not only the middle class but also inefficient retailers that target that group in favor of more focused and low-cost operators like Wal-Mart, Home Depot, and Albertson's.[2]

Can retailers actually flourish in this setting? You bet! Just look at your favorite restaurant, dry cleaner, and supermarket. Look at the rapid growth of Boston Market, Bed Bath & Beyond, Gymboree, and Old Navy. What do they have in common? A desire to please you—their customer—and a strong niche in the marketplace. To prosper in the long term, they will all need a solid strategic plan and a willingness to adapt to change, both central thrusts of this book.

In this chapter, we will look at the framework of retailing, the importance of developing and applying a sound retail strategy, and the focus and format of the text.

To better understand retailing's role and the range of retailing options that are possible, let us look at it from several perspectives:

■ Suppose we manage a manufacturing firm that makes vacuum cleaners. How should we sell these items to our customers? We could distribute via big chains such as Circuit City or small neighborhood appliance stores, have our own sales force to visit

---

[2]"Seven Pillars to Future Success," *Chain Store Age* (August 1996), Section 2, pp. 9A–10A. See also Gail DeGeorge, Catherine Young, and Geoffrey Smith, "Message from the Mall," *Business Week* (March 24, 1997), pp. 30–33; and Diane Crispell, "Retailing's Next Decade," *American Demographics* (May 1997), pp. 4–10.

people in their homes (as Electrolux does), or set up our own stores (if we have the ability and resources to do so). We could even sponsor TV infomercials or magazine ads, complete with a toll-free phone number.

■ Suppose we have an idea for a new service business, such as a better way to teach first graders to use computer software for spelling and vocabulary. How should we set up the service? We could lease a store in a neighborhood shopping center and run ads in a local paper, rent space in a local Y and rely on teacher referrals, or do mailings to parents and visit children in their homes. In each of these cases, the service is offered in person ("live"). But, today, there is still another option: We could have an animated, talking Internet site to teach children ("online").

■ Suppose we want to open a retail business featuring floral products. What choices do we have? We could operate independently or try to affiliate with FTD or 1-800-Flowers. Our store could be in a neighborhood shopping center or in a big mall. We could concentrate on fresh flowers or a mix of fresh flowers and gift items. We could rely on in-store customers or delivery. We could be open from 7:00 A.M. to 6:00 P.M. or 10:00 A.M. to 9:00 P.M. We could set above-average prices for our first-quality flowers or set discount prices for average-quality flowers. We could use newspaper ads or rely on customer word of mouth.

■ Suppose that we, as consumers, are interested in buying apparel. What choices do we have? We could go to a department store or to a store specializing in apparel. We could shop with a full-service retailer or a discounter (even at a flea market). We could go to a shopping center because of the store variety or order from a catalog to maximize convenience. We could look to retailers with a broad assortment of clothing (if we like to buy complete outfits) or look to retailers with a deep assortment of clothing in one category (if we like to buy items such as shirts and outerwear at different stores). We could zip around the Internet and "visit" the growing list of retailers with Web sites—including ones from around the world.

There is a tendency to think of retailing as primarily including the sale of tangible (physical) goods. However, it is essential to recognize that retailing also encompasses the sale of services. A service may be the shopper's primary purchase (such as a haircut or airline travel) or it may be part of the shopper's purchase of a good (such as delivery or training). Retailing does not have to involve a store. Mail and telephone orders, direct selling to consumers in their homes and offices, Internet transactions, and vending machine sales all fall within the scope of retailing. See Figure 1-1. Lastly, retailing does not have to include a "retailer." Manufacturers, importers, nonprofit firms, and wholesalers act as retailers when they sell goods or services to final consumers. On the other hand, purchases made by manufacturers, wholesalers, and other organizations for their use in the organization or further resale are not part of retailing.

Let us now examine various reasons for studying retailing and its special characteristics.

Reasons for Studying Retailing

Among the reasons for studying retailing are its impact on the economy, its functions in distribution, and its relationship with firms selling goods and services to retailers for their resale or use. These factors are discussed next. A fourth, and important, element for students of retailing is the broad range of career opportunities, described in Appendix A at the end of this book.

The Impact of Retailing on the Economy ❑ Retailing is a major part of U.S. and world commerce. Retail sales and employment are key economic contributors, and retail trends often mirror trends in a nation's overall economy.

According to the Department of Commerce, annual U.S. retail store sales (including some mail-order sales by store retailers) are about $2.5 trillion. Telephone and mail-

Figure 1-1

The Diverse Nature of Retailing

Using state-of-the-art technology and the latest research, Weis Markets, Inc. operates more than 150 stores in Pennsylvania, Maryland, New Jersey, New York, Virginia, and West Virginia. These stores range from traditional supermarkets to food-based super-stores to huge pet supply stores. Its store names include Weis Markets, Mr. Z's Food Mart, King's Supermarkets, Erb's, Scot's Lo Cost, Big Top Market, and SuperPetz.

order sales by nonstore retailers, vending machines, and direct selling generate nearly another $200 billion in yearly revenues. Furthermore, personal consumption expenditures on financial, medical, legal, educational, and other services account for another several hundred billion dollars in annual retail revenues. Outside the United States, retail sales are trillions of dollars per year.

U.S. retail store sales from 1986 to 1995 are presented in Table 1-1. Overall, sales rose by 61.5 percent between 1986 and 1995. This increase was far above the rate of inflation for the period, except during 1990–1991—when the United States (like the rest of the world) was in the midst of a large-scale recession. For the entire 1986–1995 time frame, the sales of durable goods stores increased at a rate that was higher than that for nondurable goods and service stores, mostly due to strong 1992–1995 sales; the performance of furniture and appliance stores, autos, and home centers and hardware stores

Table 1-1 U.S. RETAIL STORE SALES BY KIND OF BUSINESS, 1986–1995 (MILLIONS OF DOLLARS)[a]

Type of Retailing	1986	1987	1988	1989	1990	1991	1992	1993	1994	1995	Average Yrly. % Increase
All retail stores	1,449,636	1,541,299	1,656,202	1,758,971	1,844,611	1,855,937	1,951,589	2,074,499	2,236,966	2,340,817	5.5
Durable goods stores, total	540,688	575,863	629,154	657,154	668,835	649,974	703,604	777,539	880,426	936,212	6.5
Automotive group	326,138	342,896	372,570	386,011	387,605	372,647	406,935	456,890	526,319	560,624	6.3
Furniture and appliance group	75,714	78,072	85,390	91,301	91,545	91,676	96,947	105,728	119,626	129,923	6.6
Lumber, building materials, and hardware group	67,244	72,338	78,690	80,094	82,865	80,344	88,087	95,657	106,950	109,347	6.0
Nondurable goods/services stores, total	911,948	965,436	1,027,048	1,101,817	1,175,776	1,205,963	1,247,985	1,296,960	1,356,540	1,404,605	4.8
General merchandise group	169,397	181,970	192,521	206,306	215,514	226,730	246,420	264,617	282,541	296,904	6.5
Department stores (excluding leased dept.)	134,486	144,017	151,523	160,524	165,808	172,922	186,423	200,494	218,089	230,883	6.2
Variety stores	7,447	7,134	7,458	7,936	8,306	8,341	9,516	9,044	7,891	7,668	−1.0
Apparel group	75,626	79,322	85,307	92,341	95,819	97,441	104,212	107,184	109,603	109,633	4.6
Men's and boy's wear stores	8,646	9,017	9,826	10,507	10,450	10,435	10,197	10,291	12,157	10,091	1.8
Women's apparel, accessory stores	28,600	29,208	30,567	32,231	32,812	32,865	35,750	36,820	34,867	34,576	2.8
Family and other apparel stores	19,336	21,472	23,902	26,375	28,398	30,521	33,222	34,892	37,054	38,869	8.1
Shoe stores	13,947	14,594	15,444	17,290	18,043	17,504	18,122	18,206	18,345	18,758	3.7
Gasoline service stations	102,093	104,769	110,341	122,882	138,504	137,295	136,950	138,299	142,193	148,192	2.7
Eating and drinking places	139,415	153,461	167,993	177,829	190,149	194,424	200,164	213,663	228,351	233,606	6.2
Food group	297,019	309,461	325,493	347,045	368,333	374,523	377,099	385,386	397,800	410,512	3.7
Drug and proprietary stores	50,546	54,142	57,842	63,343	70,558	75,540	77,788	79,645	81,538	84,240	6.0
Liquor stores	19,929	19,826	19,638	20,099	21,722	22,454	21,698	21,567	21,823	22,463	1.4

[a]Includes some mail-order sales for the retail categories shown in the table.

Source: Computed by the authors from *Current Business Reports* (Washington, D.C.: U.S. Department of Commerce), various issues.

The Challenges Facing Retailers in Japan

Japanese retailers are now seeing a new, more complex generation of consumers, known as Dankai Juniors, consisting of 18- to 23-year-olds. Although Japan's baby boomers, known as Dankai, have been rather easy to predict (due to their favoring such status brands as Häagen-Daz ice cream and Louis Vuitton leather goods), the Dankai Junior generation typically hates the "follow the crowd" mentality.

Despite the size and buying power of the Dankai Junior segment (they account for nearly one-tenth of Japan's total population, roughly 12 million consumers), few Japanese retailers understand the buying behavior of this group and have little to specifically offer these consumers. For example, department stores such as Mitsukoshi do not have much that is perceived as attractive to Dankai Juniors. According to the mother of one Dankai Junior, "I feel absolutely safe taking my daughter to Mitsukoshi. I know she's not going to ask me to buy anything for her in there because there's nothing she wants to buy."

One retailer trying to appeal better to Dankai Juniors is Isetan, another department store chain. Isetan has reduced its emphasis on such brands as Gucci and Escada and is now paying more attention to lesser-known designers who are young and hip. As a result, whereas a few years ago, Isetan was viewed as stodgy, it is now viewed as "hot" by Dankai Juniors.

Source: Norihiko Shirouzu, "Twentysomethings in Japan Spurn Haute Couture, Frustrate Retailers," *Wall Street Journal* (April 24, 1995), p. A7B.

were all good. Because of changing shopping patterns and life-styles, family apparel stores, eating and drinking places, and drugstores had above-average sales growth through the decade. For the same reason, variety store sales fell and liquor store sales rose slowly. Some other nondurable goods stores had below-average growth as a result of intense competition and the resultant price cuts.

During 1995, the 100 largest retailers in the world generated $1.4 trillion in revenues. These firms represented 15 different nations and such categories as diversified retailing, supermarkets, specialty stores, department stores, drugstores, convenience stores, mail order, and membership clubs. Forty of the 100 retailers were based in the United States (including three of the top five), 12 in France, 12 in Germany, 11 in Japan, and 10 in Great Britain.[3]

Table 1-2 shows the performance of the 25 largest U.S. retailers for 1995. They accounted for $438 billion in sales—about 19 percent of total U.S. retail store sales—and operated 46,000 stores. The after-tax earnings as a percentage of sales went from +12.2 for The Limited to −6.8 percent for Melville. (The latter firm has since remade itself by selling off Marshalls—clothing, Kay-Bee—toys, and other chains; closing Thom McAn—shoes; and focusing on CVS—pharmacies. It is now named CVS.) Discount and traditional department stores (e.g., Wal-Mart, Kmart, Sears, Dayton Hudson, J.C. Penney), supermarkets (e.g., American Stores, Safeway Stores), membership clubs (e.g., Costco), drugstores (e.g., Walgreen), and specialty chains (e.g., Home Depot, Toys "Я" Us, The Limited) are among the retail types represented in the table.

Retailing is a major source of jobs. U.S. Bureau of Labor Statistics' data show that 21 million people are employed by traditional retailers. Yet this figure understates the true number of people working in retailing because it does not include the several million persons employed by service firms, seasonal employees, proprietors, and unreported workers in family businesses or partnerships. Among the leading retail employers in the United States—and other nations, as well—are eating and drinking places, food stores, general merchandise stores, auto dealers and service stations, apparel and accessory stores, and furniture and home furnishings stores.

[3]"Global Powers of Retailing," *Chain Store Age* (December 1996), Section Three.

Table 1-2   THE 25 LARGEST RETAILERS IN THE UNITED STATES, 1995

Rank	Company	Sales (thousands)	After-Tax Earnings (thousands)	Number of Stores
1	Wal-Mart	$93,627,000	$2,740,000	2,943
2	Kmart	34,389,000	−571,000	2,477
3	Sears Roebuck	28,020,000	1,801,000	2,306
4	Kroger	23,937,795	302,813	2,144
5	Dayton Hudson	23,516,000	311,000	1,029
6	J.C. Penney	20,562,000	838,000	1,883
7	American Stores	18,308,894	316,809	1,650
8	Costco	17,905,926	133,878	240
9	Safeway Stores	16,397,500	326,300	1,059
10	Home Depot	15,470,358	731,523	423
11	Federated Department Stores	15,048,513	74,553	412
12	Albertsons	12,585,034	464,961	764
13	Winn-Dixie	11,787,843	232,187	1,175
14	May Department Stores	10,507,000	752,000	346
15	Walgreen	10,395,096	320,791	2,117
16	Great Atlantic & Pacific (A&P)	10,101,356	57,224	1,014
17	Melville	9,689,062	−657,106	6,657
18	Toys "Я" Us	9,426,874	148,068	1,203
19	Publix	9,400,000	N/A	492
20	Ahold USA	8,335,800	222,000	655
21	Woolworth	8,224,000	−164,000	8,178
22	Food Lion	8,210,884	172,361	1,073
23	The Limited	7,881,437	961,511	5,298
24	Best Buy	7,217,400	48,000	250
25	Montgomery Ward	7,085,000	11,000	398

Note: Retail franchisors are not included in this table. If they were, such firms as McDonald's would be listed.

Source: David P. Schulz, "American Express Top 100 Retailers: The Nation's Biggest Retail Companies," *Stores* (July 1996), pp. 55, 57. Reprinted from STORES Magazine, ©NRF Enterprises, Inc., 1996.

From another perspective—costs—retailing is a substantial field of study. In the United States, on average, nearly 34 cents of every dollar spent in department stores, 44 cents of every dollar spent in specialty stores, and 22 cents of every dollar spent in supermarkets go to the retailers to pay for the operating costs they incur, activities they perform, and profits they earn. Costs include rent, store displays, employee compensation, ads, and store maintenance. Only a small portion of each sales dollar is really retailer profit. In 1995, pre-tax profits of the 25 largest U.S. retailers averaged 2.2 percent of sales.[4] Figure 1-2 shows costs and profits for a typical department store. Thus, a change in retail efficiency would have a great impact on consumers and the economy. Price levels and product assortment are also affected by retailer competence.

Retail Functions in Distribution ❏ Retailing is the last stage in a **channel of distribution,** which comprises all of the businesses and people involved in the physical movement and transfer of ownership of goods and services from producer to consumer. A typical distribution channel is shown in Figure 1-3.

In a distribution channel, retailers play a crucial role as the intermediary between manufacturers, wholesalers, and other suppliers and the final consumer. Here's how: To maximize efficiency, many manufacturers would like to make one basic type of item and sell the entire inventory to as few buyers as possible. Yet, many final consumers want to

[4]Alexandra Moran (Editor), *FOR 1996 Edition* (New York: Wiley, 1996), p. 27; David P. Schulz, "American Express Top 100 Retailers: The Nation's Biggest Retail Companies," *Stores* (July 1996), pp. 55, 57; and authors' computations.

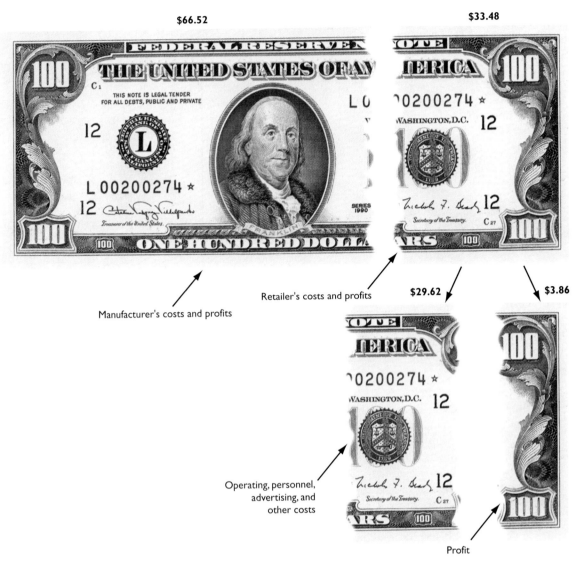

$66.52

$33.48

Manufacturer's costs and profits

Retailer's costs and profits

$29.62

$3.86

Operating, personnel, advertising, and other costs

Profit

Figure 1-2

The High Costs and Low Profits of Retailing—Where the Typical $100 Spent in a Department Store Goes

choose from a variety of goods and services and purchase a limited quantity. So, retailers collect an assortment of goods and services from various sources, buy them in large quantity, and offer to sell them in small quantities to consumers. This is the **sorting process.** See Figure 1-4.

As a result, each manufacturer (wholesaler) becomes more efficient; and final consumers are pleased with the selection available to them. Wide retail assortments allow customers to do one-stop shopping; and they can choose and buy the product version and amount desired. The word *retailing* is actually based on this

Figure 1-3

A Typical Channel of Distribution

Manufacturer → Wholesaler → Retailer → Final consumer

Figure 1-4

The Retailer's Role in the Sorting Process

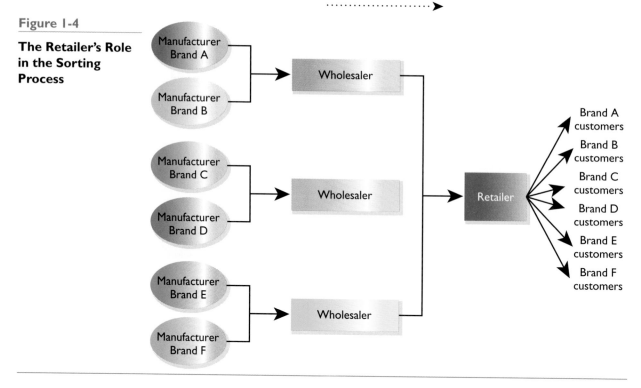

breaking-bulk function. It is derived from the old French word *retailler,* which means "to cut up."

Another distribution function retailers perform is communicating both with their customers and with their manufacturers and wholesalers. Via ads, salespeople, and store displays, consumers are informed about the availability and characteristics of goods and services, store hours, sales, and so on. Manufacturers, wholesalers, and others are informed about sales forecasts, delivery delays to retailers, customer complaints, defective items, inventory turnover (by style, color, and size), and more. Many goods and services have been modified due to feedback to suppliers.

For small manufacturers and wholesalers, retailers can provide assistance by transporting, storing, marking, advertising, and pre-paying for merchandise. However, small retailers may need the same type of help from their suppliers. The number of functions performed by retailers has a direct bearing on the percentage of each sales dollar they need to cover costs and profits.

Retailers also complete transactions with customers. This means striving to fill orders promptly and accurately and often involves processing customer credit via the retailers' or another charge plan. In addition, retailers may provide customer services such as gift wrapping, delivery, and installation.

For these reasons, in most cases, goods and services are sold via retail firms not owned by manufacturers (wholesalers). This lets the manufacturer (wholesaler) reach more customers, reduce costs, improve cash flow, increase sales more rapidly, and focus on its area of expertise.

Such manufacturers as Sherwin-Williams and Ralph Lauren do operate their own retail facilities (besides selling at traditional retailers)—and are excellent at it. In running their stores, these firms complete the full range of retailing functions and compete with conventional retailers. They consider how many final consumers will buy their products, how geographically dispersed those people are, what expenditures are needed to fulfill retailing functions, what level of service is required by consumers, and other factors. Yet, due to the scope of retailing tasks, even strong manufacturers can fail as retailers. As an illustration, Liz Claiborne recently closed its First Issue women's clothing store chain. It had too limited a product assortment, an inadequate number of stores (77 nationally), unexciting decors, and other weaknesses. In short, Liz Claiborne learned that designing clothing and selling it in department stores and specialty stores were not the same as actually operating retail stores. Liz Claiborne really did not know how to be a good retailer. Today, the First Issue brand is sold exclusively through Sears.[5]

The Relationships Among Retailers and Their Suppliers ❑ The complex relationships among retailers and their suppliers must be understood. On the one hand, retailers are part of a distribution channel; thus, manufacturers and wholesalers must be concerned about their retailers' coverage of the consumer market, the caliber of in-store displays, the level of customer services, store hours, and retailers' reliability as business partners. On the other hand, retailers are also major customers of goods and services for resale, store fixtures, data-processing equipment, management consulting, and insurance.

Retailers and their suppliers may have divergent viewpoints that need to be reconciled. Control over the distribution channel, profit allocation, the number of competing retailers handling suppliers' goods and services, in-store display space and locations, promotion support, payment terms, and flexibility in operations are just a few of the issues over which retailers and suppliers may have different priorities and goals. Due to the growing number of regional, national, and global retail chains, retailers now have more power in the distribution channel than ever.[6]

Channel relations are generally smoothest when **exclusive distribution** is involved, whereby suppliers enter into agreements with one or a few retailers that designate the latter as the only companies in specified geographic areas to carry certain brands and/or product lines. This arrangement stimulates both parties to work together in maintaining an image, assigning shelf space, allotting profits and costs, advertising, and so on. Yet, it also usually requires that retailers limit their assortment of goods/services in the product categories covered by the agreement; thus, retailers might have to decline to handle other suppliers' items. From the manufacturers' perspective, exclusive distribution may limit long-run total sales potential.

Channel relations tend to be most volatile when **intensive distribution** is used, whereby suppliers sell through as many retailers as possible. This usually maximizes suppliers' sales, and it enables retailers to offer many brands and product versions. As a result, competition among retailers selling the same items is high. And the retailers may use tactics not beneficial to individual suppliers, as they are more concerned about total store revenues than sales of any one brand. They may allocate shelf space, set prices, and advertise in a way that adversely affects specific brands (by giving them little space, using them as sale items, or not advertising them).

With **selective distribution,** suppliers sell through a moderate number of retailers. This combines aspects of exclusive and intensive distribution. It allows suppliers to have higher sales than in exclusive distribution and lets retailers carry some competing brands. It encourages suppliers to provide advertising and other support, and encourages retailers to give adequate shelf space. However, this middle-ground approach generally has neither the channel cooperation of exclusive distribution nor the sales potential of intensive distribution. See Figure 1-5.

[5]Susan Reda, "First Issue Debut Highlights Sears' Progress in Apparel," *Stores* (December 1996), pp. 34–35.
[6]See Jakki J. Mohr and Robert E. Spekman, "Perfecting Partnerships," *Marketing Management* (Winter–Spring 1996), pp. 35–42; and Nirmalya Kumar, "The Power of Trust in Manufacturer-Retailer Relationships," *Harvard Business Review*, Vol. 74 (November–December 1996), pp. 92–106.

Figure 1-5

Comparing Exclusive, Intensive, and Selective Distribution

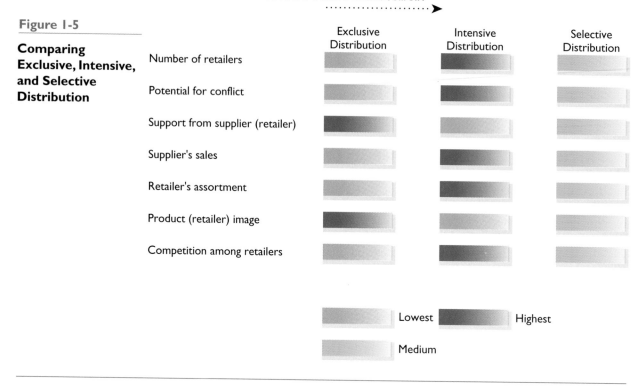

Unless suppliers know retailers' attributes and needs, they cannot have good rapport with them; and as long as retailers have a choice of suppliers, they will select those that best understand and react to their needs. The following illustrate several issues in retailer–supplier relations:

■ Competition in the marketplace—"For a manufacturer to have a factory outlet up in the mountains is a far cry from opening a glitzy new store with state-of-the-art merchandising across the street from a department store with which it has done business for years. Retailers complain that their long-time partners are turning into competitors." As Bloomingdale's chairman put it, "Why should I spend money to build a shop for a brand that is out there opening its own stores?"[7]

■ Product image—Baccarat, the maker of fine crystal, has engaged in a long-running dispute with Ross-Simons, an off-price retailer with store and catalog operations. Ross-Simons carries jewelry and fine housewares with such prestige names as Lenox, Wedgwood, Reed and Barton, Waterford, and Baccarat. However, to protect its high-quality image, Baccarat no longer wants to sell through off-price retailers such as Ross-Simons. As a result, the two firms have been in litigation for a number of years.[8]

■ Slotting allowances—Some large bookstore chains, including Barnes & Noble and Borders, have required publishers to pay slotting allowances for prime store shelf space. This makes the space expensive and difficult to secure for small publishers: "At Barnes & Noble, the 'Discover Great New Writers' program, which assures that a book appears face out in the front of its hundreds of superstores for two or three months and gets a review in a special brochure, cost publishers $1,500 a title, according to the chain's 1996 promotions guide and publishing executives. To have a book featured for one month on a cardboard floor display in front, called a dump, a publisher paid $10,000."[9]

[7]Susan Reda, "When Vendors Become Retailers," *Stores* (June 1995), p. 19.
[8]Michael Hartnett, "Ross-Simons Dispute Raises Antitrust Issues," *Stores* (December 1996), pp. 42–43.
[9]Mary B. W. Tabor, "In Bookstore Chains, Display Space Is for Sale," *New York Times* (January 1, 1996), p. D8.

■ Distribution rights—Until about six years ago, Goodyear sold its tires predominantly through a distribution network of 3,000 independent dealers. Since then, Goodyear has added such major retail chains as Wal-Mart, Sears, and Montgomery Ward. According to the *Wall Street Journal*, this move "alienated many of its bread-and-butter independent dealers that felt they were at a price disadvantage because the big chains received volume discounts for buying in large quantities." To placate the independents, Goodyear now offers them exclusive tire lines and enhanced marketing programs.[10]

Manufacturers of goods that are used in retail businesses should also have a working knowledge of retailing. For example, a fixture manufacturer has to understand the requirements of its retailers. Store layout, the linear feet of shelf space, the use of self-service merchandising, the routing of customer traffic, and storage specifications are some of the criteria retailers use in selecting store fixtures. Both a knowledge of basic retailing principles and the special factors relative to a given type of retailer are necessary for the fixture manufacturer to succeed.

Similarly, firms that sell services, such as insurance, to retailers can benefit from a good understanding of retailing. Inventory valuation, employee job functions, construction costs, crime rates, and depreciation are some relevant factors that must be examined. For example, how should merchandise that has been marked down in price be appraised if there is a fire? Or how much can fire insurance premiums be reduced if new sprinklers are installed in a store?

The Special Characteristics of Retailing

Several special characteristics distinguish retailing from other types of business. Three of them are highlighted in Figure 1-6 and discussed here: The average amount of a sales transaction for retailers is much less than for manufacturers. Final consumers make many unplanned purchases; those who buy for resale or for use in manufacturing products or running a business are more systematic and plan ahead. Most retail customers must be drawn to a store location; salespeople generally visit manufacturers, wholesalers, and other firms to initiate and complete transactions. Each of these factors imposes unique requirements on retail firms.

Average sales transactions are about $54 for department stores, $64 for specialty stores, and $32 for supermarkets. These low amounts create a need to tightly control the

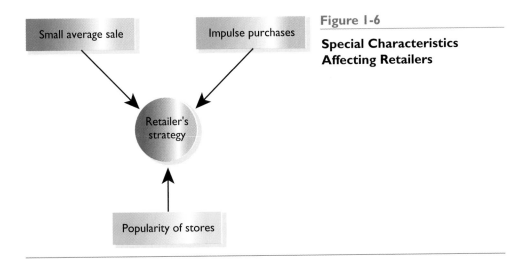

Figure 1-6

Special Characteristics Affecting Retailers

---

[10]"Goodyear to Sell Tires at 350 Montgomery Ward & Co. Outlets," *Wall Street Journal* (June 14, 1995), p. A6.

costs associated with each transaction (such as credit verification, delivery, and bagging); to maximize the number of customers drawn to a store, which may place an emphasis on ads and special promotions; and to increase impulse sales by more aggressive in-store selling. However, low average sales and high costs cannot always be controlled by the retailer. For example, over the last decade, the average amount of a sales transaction in a department store has only gone up by about the rate of inflation. And, despite their high costs, one-half of specialty store sales are on credit.[11]

Because of the many small sales transactions to a large number of different customers, inventory management is often difficult for retailers. As an illustration, in 1995, it took a supermarket 6,500 transactions per week to generate annual sales of $10.5 million.[12] This makes it harder for retailers to determine the levels of existing stock and the popularity of various brands, sizes, and prices of merchandise. For that reason, retailers are expanding their use of computerized inventory systems.

Retail sales often involve unplanned or impulse purchases. For example, surveys have shown that a large percentage of grocery consumers ignore ads before shopping, do not prepare shopping lists in advance (or deviate from lists once in stores), and make purchases that are fully unplanned. This behavior indicates the value of point-of-purchase displays, attractive store layouts, well-organized stores, and store windows. Candy, cosmetics, snack foods, magazines, and other items can be sold as impulse goods if they are placed in visible, high-traffic places in a store. Since consumers buy so many goods and services in an unplanned manner, the retailer's ability to forecast, budget, order merchandise, and have the proper number of personnel on the selling floor is made tougher.

Retail customers usually visit a store, even though mail and telephone sales have increased dramatically in recent years. The large number of final consumers, the interest of many consumers in shopping in person and in comparison shopping among different brands and models, the small average sale size, the unplanned nature of purchases, and consumers' desire for privacy in their homes are just some reasons for the popularity of retail stores. And since people must be attracted to a particular store, the retailer needs to consider such factors as location, transportation facilities, store hours, proximity of competitors, merchandise assortment, parking, and advertising.

THE IMPORTANCE OF DEVELOPING AND APPLYING A RETAIL STRATEGY

A **retail strategy** is the overall plan guiding a retail firm. It influences the firm's business activities and its response to market forces, such as competition and the economy. Any retailer, regardless of size or type, can and should utilize these six steps in strategic planning:

1. Define the type of business in terms of the goods or service category and the company's specific orientation (such as full-service or "no frills").
2. Set long-run and short-run objectives for sales and profit, market share, image, and so on.
3. Determine the customer market to which to appeal on the basis of its characteristics (such as gender and income level) and needs (such as product and brand preferences).
4. Devise an overall, long-run plan that gives general direction to a firm and its employees.
5. Implement an integrated strategy that combines such factors as store location, product assortment, pricing, and advertising and displays to achieve objectives.
6. Regularly evaluate performance and correct weaknesses or problems as they are observed.

---

[11]Moran, *FOR 1996 Edition*, p. 27; and "63rd Annual Report of the Grocery Industry," *Progressive Grocer* (April 1996), p. 42.
[12]Computed by the authors from "63rd Annual Report of the Grocery Industry," pp. 13, 42.

To illustrate these points, the background and strategy of Lands' End—one of the world's foremost retailers—are presented. Then, the marketing concept is defined and applied to retailing.

Lands' End: Where Customer Satisfaction Is Guaranteed. Period.[13]

Company Background ❏ Gary Comer worked at an ad agency for ten years, but felt his true vocation was sailing. So, he left the agency in 1963 and with his sailing partner opened a catalog outlet store in Chicago specializing in sailing equipment and fittings. The name Lands' End (rather than the intended Land's End) was actually the result of a typographical error in an early catalog!

After five years and only moderate success, Gary Comer bought out his partner and began tinkering with the catalog. He added clothing, accessories, and luggage aimed at full-time and weekend sailors. The inaugural full-color catalog (30 pages) appeared in 1975.

1976 saw Lands' End dramatically shift direction. Comer decided to no longer carry sailing equipment; competition was too intense. Instead the firm turned to recreational and informal clothing, accessories, shoes, and soft-sided luggage—and broadened its customer base. Unlike many apparel-based retailers, most Lands' End clothing was (and is) traditionally styled, with only slight seasonal variations. In 1978, headquarters were moved to Dodgeville, Wisconsin and a toll-free 800 phone number established (with 24-hour service commencing in 1980). National ads were introduced in 1981, and the firm went public during 1986. Three specialty catalogs were launched in 1990 (*Coming Home,* with bed and bath items; *Lands' End Kids;* and *Beyond Buttondowns,* with men's apparel). Its first British catalog was sent in 1991; Japanese operations began in 1994. Most recently, the firm opened a World Wide Web site (http://www.landsend.com), complete with an online "Internet Store," "Overstocks," and "Catalog Requests."

Today, Lands' End is a retailing giant. Annual sales (by mail order, phone transactions, outlet stores, and electronic shopping) exceed $1 billion, its U.S. customer base alone is 8.2 million people, and 20 million people are on the firm's mailing list. Nearly 200 million catalogs a year are distributed. Lands' End has 1,100 phone lines and handles 40,000 to 50,000 calls per day (100,000 during December). The Dodgeville distribution center is the size of 12 football fields.

Since late 1994, Michael Smith has been chief executive officer at Lands' End (Gary Comer, the majority stockholder, remains chairman of the board). Smith began with the firm as a college intern, joining full-time as a marketing research analyst after his 1983 graduation from the University of Wisconsin with a major in marketing. He became chief executive at age 33. As one industry observer noted, he "is as unflappable as a Lands' End button-down shirt."

The Lands' End Strategy: Keys to Success ❏ Throughout its 35 years of existence, during the ups and downs facing any retailer, Lands' End has followed a consistent, far-sighted, customer-oriented strategy—one that has paved the way for its long-term achievements. Here are some of Lands' End's keys to a successful strategy:

■ Growth-oriented objectives—The firm is directed to long-run growth. The annual sales growth goal is 10 percent to 15 percent; the actual compound annual growth rate from 1986 through 1995 was 18 percent. To reach the goal, it will seek greater

---

[13]The material in this discussion has been drawn from Lands' End company literature; Robert Berner, "Lands' End Likes Change to Come in a Familiar Package," *Wall Street Journal* (August 30, 1996), p. B3; Susan Chandler, "Lands' End Looks for Terra Firma," *Business Week* (July 8, 1996), pp. 128, 131; Jim Thomas, "Partners in Time," *Distribution* (December 1995), pp. 50–53; Rebecca A. Fannin, "Lands' End Extends Sales in Far East with Local Catalogs," *Advertising Age* (September 30, 1996), p. 54; and Marianne Wilson, "Lands' End Captures Catalog Experience," *Chain Store Age* (March 1997), pp. 140–141.

Wal-Mart: Doing Well By Doing Good

According to a recent study, Wal-Mart (the world's most imposing retailer) has managed to successfully combine its competitive business advantages with a number of symbolic practices, such as charitable and environmental projects.

The study used a phone survey to ascertain consumer attitudes toward Wal-Mart in five markets (Atlanta, Chicago, Dallas, Indianapolis, and Kingston, Canada). Respondents were questioned about which chain performed best on several attributes. Attributes were categorized as performance factors (which store was easiest to reach, had the lowest prices, had the fastest checkouts, and so on), symbolic factors (which store was most concerned about and actively involved in the community at large), and store choice factors (where respondents shop most often).

The study's authors noted, "Wal-Mart is simultaneously the world's largest retailing giant and each neighborhood's own friendly storekeeper. On the one hand, Wal-Mart is an incredibly efficient and sophisticated purchasing, distribution, and technology machine and acts aggressively in its relationships with employees, suppliers, and competitors. These practices let Wal-Mart offer consumers the locational convenience, low price, and wide assortment attributes for everyday, frequently purchased goods. On the other hand, Wal-Mart also engages in a number of symbolic organizational practices that we would normally associate with a locally owned, neighborhood retailer. Promotional flyers describe not only everyday low-priced products but also devote considerable space to describing the charitable, environmental, and community projects engaged in by individually named Wal-Mart 'associates' (Wal-Mart employees)."

Source: Stephen J. Arnold, Jay Handelman, and Douglas J. Tigert, "Organizational Legitimacy and Retail Store Patronage," *Journal of Business Research,* Vol. 35 (March 1996), pp. 229–239.

volume from existing customers and try to get more customers from its data base who have not bought in the last three years to do so. The firm also hopes to gain by expanding its international operations even further (it is adding facilities in Germany, Korea, and elsewhere) and its online Internet Store. See Figure 1-7.

■ Appeal to a prime consumer market—The firm is very strong with 35- to 64-year-old customers, who have a median household income of $55,000. Nearly 90 percent of customers have attended college, and 70 percent are professionals or managers. It focuses on "the top 25 percent of the income spectrum."

■ Outstanding customer service—The firm prides itself on offering the best possible customer service, as exemplified by the "principles of doing business" shown in Figure 1-8. Phone calls are answered in less than two rings, almost all merchandise is always available in stock, and the firm aims to deliver orders within two days of their being placed. Salespeople undergo 80 hours of training when hired, and 24 hours per year thereafter. Trousers are hemmed free of charge and add only one day to an order's delivery. Samples of fabrics are provided free. Lost buttons are replaced and luggage repaired, also for free. Lands' End has the simplest, most comprehensive guarantee in the industry. It has even trademarked the phrase, "GUARANTEED. PERIOD." Customers can return products at any time for any reason.

■ Personalized company image—Unlike traditional mail-order retailers, which show pictures of products, present brief descriptions of them, and cite prices, Lands' End adds a personal touch. For example, an entry for slacks may contain a story on "why the chino slacks may be the best 'hanging out' pants you'll ever put on." The catalog also includes short stories by such notable writers as Gwendolyn Brooks, Ray Bradbury, William Least Heat Moon, David Mamet, and Edward Hoagland. The Lands' End guarantee is stated in each catalog, as is its toll-free number. Shoppers who call are likely to reach full-time, year-round operators, who provide information, answer questions, and process orders. If people have difficult questions, they can talk to "Specialty Shoppers," who are expert in sizing, gift suggestions, and wardrobe coordination.

Figure 1-7

Lands' End's Online Store

Our Internet Store

All products in this site can be ordered on-line using Netscape Navigator® or Microsoft Internet Explorer®. Other ways to order (including from a printed catalog or without a secure web browser).

The Great Gift Wrap Giveaway!
Free kit with any order!
Comes complete with 2 (10 1/2" x 14 1/2" x 2) boxes,
3 sheets of handsome reversible gift wrap, tissue, tape,
seals, fabric ribbon and cards. (Limit 1 per order.)

Kids	Men's Casual	Men's Haber-dashery	Women's	Luggage	Overstocks

etc. Miscellaneous Gifts

Price Differences!

We're making room in our warehouse for spring merchandise. Some items currently in our Store will be heading to Overstocks. If you happen to select any of them, you'll see a lower price when you put it in the shopping basket.

Need gift ideas? The Lands' End Gift Certificate is always appreciated - and always available.

Our Corporate Sales can custom embroider your company or team logo on our products. Shirts, jackets, attaches and more!

Figure 1-8

Lands' End's Business Principles

The Lands' End Principles of Doing Business.

Principle 1.
We do everything we can to make our products better. We improve material, and add back features and construction details that others have taken out over the years. We never reduce the quality of a product to make it cheaper.

Principle 2.
We price our products fairly and honestly. We do not, have not, and will not participate in the common retailing practice of inflating mark-ups to set up a future phony "sale."

Principle 3.
We accept any return for any reason, at any time. Our products are guaranteed. No fine print. No arguments. We mean exactly what we say: GUARANTEED. PERIOD.

Principle 4.
We ship faster than anyone we know of. We ship items in stock the day after we receive the order. At the height of the last Christmas season the longest time an order was in the house was 36 hours, excepting monograms which took another 12 hours.

Principle 5.
We believe that what is best for our customer is best for all of us. Everyone here understands that concept. Our sales and service people are trained to know our products, and to be friendly and helpful. They are urged to take all the time necessary to take care of you. We even pay for your call, for whatever reason you call.

Principle 6.
We are able to sell at lower prices because we have eliminated middlemen; because we don't buy branded merchandise with high protected mark-ups; and because we have placed our contracts with manufacturers who have proven that they are cost conscious and efficient.

Principle 7.
We are able to sell at lower prices because we operate efficiently. Our people are hard-working, intelligent, and share in the success of the company.

Principle 8.
We are able to sell at lower prices because we support no fancy emporiums with their high overhead. Our main location is in the middle of a 40-acre cornfield in rural Wisconsin.

■ Employee relations—At Lands' End, all employees are treasured, "downsizing" is a bad word, and even part-time employees receive full health-care benefits. As Michael Smith says, "If people feel squeezed, they won't treat the customer as well."

■ Extensive promotion program—The firm mails a new catalog every few weeks. It also runs ads in *Fortune, Inc., New York Times Sunday Magazine, Wall Street Journal,* and *USA Today.* Beside the general catalogs, it uses specialty catalogs to appeal to more narrowly defined target markets—to reduce seasonality, as well as total catalog production and mailing costs. It has a strong reputation for product quality and fit.

■ Honest value—The firm states, "Value is more than price. *Value* is the combination of product quality, world-class customer service, and a fair price. Lands' End does not operate retail stores (outside of outlet stores) and works directly with mills and manufacturers, eliminating [intermediaries]. Savings are passed on to customers by offering them the best price possible."

■ Commitment to electronic shopping—The firm is devoted to developing and deploying new technologies that anticipate and cater to the changing marketplace. Lands' End was one of the first retailers to participate in electronic shopping systems, by touch-screen terminals situated in transit stations, office buildings, and hotel lobbies. And as already noted, Lands' End customers can access its World Wide Web site to learn about the company and its services, as well as to place online orders.

■ Efficient operations—Ordering, warehousing, and other operations are highly automated and computerized. The firm has outlet stores in Wisconsin, Illinois, and Iowa. These stores sell returned merchandise or items that have been overordered and must be cleared out.

■ Responsiveness to unsatisfactory performance—In 1993, Gary Comer hired an outsider as Lands' End's chief executive. Unfortunately, employee morale plummeted because of the new, stricter management policies that were enacted. At a company where employees are so highly valued, this was not acceptable. That is why, less than two years later, the "outsider" was dismissed and an "insider" (Michael Smith) replaced him.

The Marketing Concept Applied to Retailing

As just described, Lands' End has a sincere long-term desire to please customers. In doing so, it uses a coordinated, companywide approach to strategy development and implementation; it is value-driven; and it has clear goals. Together, these principles form the marketing concept.

The marketing concept can be transformed into the retailing concept, which should be understood and used by all retailers. See Figure 1-9. The **retailing concept** comprises these four elements:

1. *Customer orientation*—The retailer determines the attributes and needs of its customers and endeavors to satisfy these needs to the fullest.
2. *Coordinated effort*—The retailer integrates all plans and activities to maximize efficiency.
3. *Value-driven*—The retailer offers good value to customers, whether it be a discounter or upscale. This means having prices appropriate for the level of products and customer service.
4. *Goal orientation*—The retailer sets goals and then uses its strategy to attain them.

Unfortunately, the retailing concept is not grasped and applied by every retailer. Some are indifferent to customer needs, plan haphazardly, have prices that do not reflect the value offered, and have unclear goals. Too often, retailers are not receptive to change or new ideas, or they blindly follow strategies implemented by competitors. Some retail-

Figure 1-9

**Applying the
Retailing Concept**

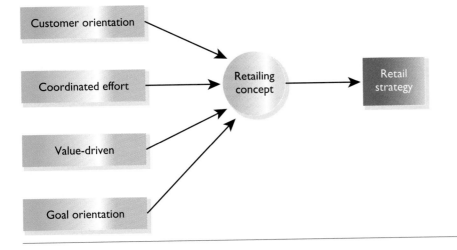

ers do not research their customers or get feedback from them; they rely on supplier reports or their own past sales trends.

The retailing concept is fairly easy to adopt. It requires communicating with consumers and considering their desires critical to a firm's success, developing and enacting a consistent strategy (such as having designer brands, plentiful sales personnel, attractive displays, and above-average prices in an upscale clothing boutique), offering prices perceived as "fair" (a good value for the money) by customers, and working to achieve meaningful, specific, and reachable goals. However, the retailing concept is only a guide to company strategy. It does not deal with a firm's internal capabilities or competitive advantages but offers a broad framework for planning.

Let's look at three issues that relate to a retailer's performance in terms of the retailing concept: the total retail experience, customer service, and relationship retailing.

The Total Retail Experience ❏ While one person may shop at a discount store, another at a neighborhood store, a third at a full-service store, and so on, these diverse shoppers have something crucial in common: They each encounter a total retail experience (including everything from parking to checkout counter) in making a purchase.

The **total retail experience** includes all the elements in a retail offering that encourage or inhibit consumers during their contact with the retailer. Many elements, such as the number of salespeople on the floor, display windows, prices, the brands carried, and inventory on hand, are controllable by a retailer; others, like the adequacy of on-street parking, the timing of deliveries from suppliers, and sales taxes, are not. If some part of the total retail experience is unsatisfactory, consumers may not buy a given good or service—they may even decide not to patronize a retailer again. As one disgruntled shopper recently remarked, "For me, shopping is less enjoyable because the stores are more crowded now, they don't seem to be kept up as well as they used to be, there seem to be longer lines, and kids are running around more."[14]

In planning and enacting a customer-oriented, integrated strategy, a retailer must be sure all of its strategic elements are in place. For the shopper segment to which a particular firm appeals, the total retail experience must be aimed at fulfilling customer expectations—and it must meet those expectations. For example, a discount store should have ample stock on hand when it runs sales, but not plush carpeting on the floor; a neighborhood store should be open late hours, but not have overly trendy products; and a full-service store should have knowledgeable personnel, but not have them perceived as too haughty by customers. See Figure 1-10.

[14]Teresa Andreoli, "Hassle-Free Service Key to Repeat Biz," *Discount Store News* (May 6, 1996), p. 64. See also Paul Goldberger, "The Store Strikes Back," *New York Times Magazine* (April 8, 1997), pp. 45–49.

Figure 1-10

The Total Retail Experience of Cyberplay Computer Exploration Centers

One of the biggest challenges for today's retailers is generating customer "excitement" because many people are bored with shopping or have little time for it. Here is how one firm is doing this:

Amy's Ice Creams, a seven-store chain of premium ice cream shops in Austin and Houston, Texas, sells terrific products and gives excellent service. But that's where the similarity to other scoop shops ends. Visit an Amy's store—the one in Austin's Westbank Market, say, on a Friday night—and you'll see employees performing in a manner you won't forget. That's right: performing. They juggle with their serving spades, toss scoops of ice cream to one another behind the counter, and break-dance on a freezer top. If there's a line out the door, they might pass out samples—or free ice cream to any customer who'll sing or dance or mimic a barnyard animal, or who wins a 60-second cone-eating contest. Employees could be wearing pajamas (Sleep-Over Night) or masks (Star Wars Night); there might be candles (Romance Night) or strobe lights (Disco Night). They wear costumes. They bring props. They pop trivia questions. They create fun.[15]

Customer Service ❏ **Customer service** refers to the identifiable, but sometimes intangible, activities undertaken by a retailer in conjunction with the basic goods and services it sells. It has a strong impact on the total retail experience. Among the factors that comprise a firm's customer service strategy are the store hours, parking access, shopper-friendliness of the store layout, acceptance of credit, level and caliber of salespeople, amenities such as gift wrapping, rest room availability, employee politeness, handling special customer orders, delivery policies, amount of time shoppers spend on checkout lines, and customer follow-up. The list is not all inclusive; and it differs in terms of the value-driven approach taken—discount versus full service. See Figure 1-11.

Consumer satisfaction with a retailer's customer service is influenced by expectations (which relate to the type of retailer involved) and past experience. Furthermore, consumer assessments of customer service depend on perceptions—not necessarily real-

[15]John Case, "Corporate Culture," *Inc.* (November 1996), pp. 42–43.

Figure 1-11

Customer Service at Carson Pirie Scott

This department store chain is so customer-service oriented that its furniture salespeople are equipped with radio-frequency hand-held scanners. This enables them to immediately check on the availability of merchandise, provide faster delivery, and follow up after sales are made.

ity. Different people may evaluate the same customer service levels quite differently. The same consumer may even evaluate a retailer's service level differently at different times, although customer service remains constant.

It is imperative that retailers view customer service as consisting of two components—expected services and augmented services. *Expected services* are those customers want to receive from any retailer, such as basic employee courtesy. Yet, how many employees are trained to always say, "Hello, how may I help you?" and "Thank you for shopping at our store." "Thank you" sometimes seems to be disappearing from the retail vocabulary. Too often, *augmented services*—those that enhance the shopping experience and give retailers a competitive advantage—are stressed without enough attention placed on expected services.

According to many studies, the leading retailer in terms of customer service is Seattle-based Nordstrom. These are two reasons why:

Nordstrom, the department store chain that is often used as a yardstick by which other retailers measure their customer service and convenience programs, has a widely acclaimed personal shopper program steeped in customer convenience. All a customer needs to do is telephone the store requesting a personal shopper and one will be sent to his or her home. Once there, the personal shopper gets a profile of the customer, including shopping history, age, and preferences. The personal shopper then either takes an assortment of merchandise to the person's home or the customer meets with the personal shopper at the store off the sales floor and reviews the items. In addition to this off-site service, Nordstrom's entire merchandise presentation on the sales floor takes into account shoppers navigating by wheelchair.[16]

Some retailers have found that customer service can be improved if they empower personnel. In **employee empowerment,** workers have discretion to do what they believe is necessary—within reason—to satisfy the customer, even if this means bending some company rules. Nordstrom employees are taught, "This is your business. Do your own thing. Don't listen to us in Seattle. Listen to your customer. We give you permission to take care of your customer."[17] At Direct Tire Sales, a salesperson may pay for a cab to

[16]"Best Customer Service," *Business Week* (August 12, 1996), p. 4; and Laura Liebeck, "Shoppers Need Ways to Beat the Clock," *Discount Store News* (May 6, 1996), p. 94.
[17]Seth Lubove, "Don't Listen to the Boss, Listen to the Customer," *Forbes* (December 4, 1995), p. 45.

TECHNOLOGY IN RETAILING

Using High-Tech to Turbocharge the "Art" of Customer Service

More and more small retailers are now automating and better performing various aspects of customer service as a result of the availability of inexpensive PCs and software that can more easily track customer data.

Until recently, Finagle-A-Bagel (a five-store Boston-based bagel chain) had an information system for tracking customer comments and complaints that consisted of sticking Post-It notes to the wall. Today, each time a customer calls, comments are logged into the firm's computerized data base. This data base lets Finagle-A-Bagel employees be more familiar with customers and enables the firm to identify the sources of customer problems and correct them. Thus, a customer who complained salty bagels were not salty enough for him is able to get extra-salty bagels.

Finagle-A-Bagel devised its data-base system to be quite simple. The firm's part-time information systems manager built it in about one hour based on the very basic data base that is part of the firm's word processing program (Microsoft Word).

To monitor sales better at each of its stores, Finagle-A-Bagel has decided to invest in a $50,000 computer system. The system compiles point-of-sale data to ensure that the bagel stores do not run out of stock for key products. It also tracks orders from wholesale customers and retail shops.

Source: Jennifer deJong, "Turbocharging Customer Service," *Inc. Technology* (Number 2, 1995), pp. 35–39.

---

get a stranded customer to his or her destination. Home Depot has built employee empowerment into its way of doing business. Every person on the selling floor gets a minimum of eight weeks training prior to meeting their first customer. Employees have wide latitude in making on-the-spot decisions. Thus, they can freely talk with individual customers and act as consultants and problem solvers.

Despite a desire to provide excellent customer service, a number of outstanding retailers are now wondering if "the customer is always right." Are there limits? Ponder these situations:

> Wal-Mart has abandoned its open-ended return policy and set a 90-day limit for most items. The new policy is designed to combat customers who take their time returning merchandise, such as the shopper who several years ago got a refund for a battered thermos. The store later learned from the manufacturer that the thermos had been bought in the 1950s, before the first Wal-Mart opened. Catalog clothier L.L. Bean, which for years didn't question customers about returns, has decided to crack down. Some shoppers were returning goods they had purchased at garage sales. One even tried to return worn clothes dug out of the closet of a relative who died.[18]

Relationship Retailing ❏ Today's best retailers realize it is in their interest to engage in **relationship retailing,** whereby they seek to establish and maintain long-term bonds with customers, rather than act as if each sales transaction is a completely new encounter with them. This means the retailers must concentrate on the total retail experience, monitor shopper satisfaction with customer service, and stay in touch with customers. Table 1-3 shows a customer respect checklist that retailers could use to assess their relationship retailing efforts.

---

[18]Louise Lee, "Without a Receipt You May Get Stuck with That Ugly Scarf," *Wall Street Journal* (November 18, 1996), p. A1.

Table 1-3 A CUSTOMER RESPECT CHECKLIST

✔ Do we trust our customers? Do we operate our business to effectively serve the vast majority of customers who are honest or to protect ourselves from the small minority who are not?

✔ Do we stand behind what we sell? Are we easy to deal with if a customer has a problem? Is there a sense of urgency to make a customer whole? Are frontline workers empowered to respond properly to a problem? Do we guarantee what we sell? Do we guarantee our service?

✔ Do we stress promise-keeping in our firm? Is keeping commitments to customers—from being in-stock on advertised goods to being on time for appointments—important in our company?

✔ Do we value customer time? Do we anticipate periods of maximum demand for our offerings and staff accordingly to minimize customer waiting? Are our facilities and service systems convenient and efficient for customers to use? Do we prepare new employees to provide efficient, effective service before putting them in front of customers? Do we teach employees that serving customers supersedes all other priorities, such as paperwork or stocking shelves?

✔ Do we communicate with customers respectfully? Are signs informative and helpful? Are our statements clear and understandable? Is advertising above reproach in truthfulness and taste? Are contact personnel professional in appearance and manner? Does our language show respect, such as "I will be happy to do this" and "It will be my pleasure"? Do we answer and return phone calls promptly—with a smile in our voice? Is our voice mail caller-friendly?

✔ Do we respect all customers? Do we treat all customers with respect, regardless of their appearance, age, race, gender, status, or size of purchase or account? Have we taken any special precautions to minimize discriminatory treatment of certain customers?

✔ Do we thank customers for their business? Do we say "thank you" at times other than after a purchase? Do our customers feel appreciated?

✔ Do we respect employees? Do our human resources policies and practices pass the employee-respect test? Do employees, who are expected to respect customers, get respectful treatment themselves? Would employees want their children to work for us when they grow up?

Source: Adapted by the authors from Leonard L. Berry, "Retailers with a Future," *Marketing Management* (Spring 1996), p. 43. Reprinted by permission of the American Marketing Association.

To be effective with relationship retailing, a firm has to keep these two points in mind: First, because it is harder to lure new customers than to make existing ones happy, a "win-win" approach should be enacted. For the retailer to "win" in the long run (lure shoppers, make sales, earn profits, etc.), the customer must also "win" in the long run (receive good value, be treated with respect, feel welcome by the firm, etc.). Otherwise, the retailer loses (shoppers patronize competitors) and customers lose (by having to spend time and money to learn about other retailers). Second, due to the advances in computer technology, it is now much easier to develop a customer data base—complete with information on people's attributes and past shopping behavior. Thus, ongoing customer contact can be better, more frequent, and more focused.

THE FOCUS AND FORMAT OF THE TEXT

There are various approaches to the study of retailing: an institutional approach, which describes the types of retailing and their development; a functional approach, which concentrates on the activities that retailers perform (such as buying, pricing, and personnel practices); and a strategic approach, which involves defining the retail business, setting objectives, appealing to an appropriate customer market, developing an overall plan, implementing an integrated strategy, and regularly reviewing operations.

We will study retail management from each of these perspectives, but focus on the *strategic approach.* Our fundamental principle is that the retailer has to plan for and adapt to a complex, changing environment. Both opportunities and constraints must be considered. Strategic retail management constantly encourages the retailer to study competitors, suppliers, economic factors, changes in consumers, marketplace trends, legal restrictions, and other elements. A firm prospers when its competitive strengths match the opportunities in the environment, weaknesses are eliminated or minimized, and plans look to the future, as well as the past.

This text is divided into eight parts. The balance of Part 1 presents strategic planning in retailing. Each step in the strategic planning process is covered in detail and the contemporary challenges facing retailers are examined. Part 2 characterizes retailing institutions on the basis of their ownership, store-based strategy mix, and nonstore-based and nontraditional retailing format. Goods and service retailing are also contrasted. Part 3 deals with consumer behavior and information gathering in retailing. Parts 4 to 7 discuss the specific elements of a retailing strategy: planning the store location; managing a retail business; planning, handling, and pricing merchandise; and communicating with the customer. Part 8 looks at special strategic considerations in service retailing. It also shows how a retailing strategy may be integrated, analyzed, and improved.

Summary

In this and every chapter in the text, the summary is linked to the objectives stated at the beginning of the chapter.

1. *To define retailing, consider it from various perspectives, demonstrate its impact, and note its special characteristics* Retailing entails the business activities involved in selling goods and services to consumers for their personal, family, or household use. Today, it is at an interesting crossroads, with many challenges ahead.

Retailing may be viewed from multiple perspectives. It includes tangible and intangible items, does not have to use a store, and can be conducted by manufacturers and others—as well as by retail firms.

Annual U.S. store sales are $2.5 trillion, with other forms of retailing accounting for hundreds of billions of dollars in added revenues. The world's 100 largest retailers generate over $1.2 trillion in yearly revenues. About 21 million people in the United States work for traditional retailers, which understates the number of those actually employed in a retailing capacity. Department and specialty stores receive up to 40 cents or more of every sales dollar as compensation for operating costs, the functions performed, and the profits they earn.

Retailing is the last stage in a distribution channel, which contains the businesses and people involved in physically moving and transferring ownership of goods and services from producer to consumer. In a channel, retailers perform valuable functions as intermediaries for manufacturers, wholesalers, and final consumers. They collect product assortments from various suppliers and offer them to customers. They communicate with both customers and other channel members. They may ship, store, mark, advertise, and pre-pay for items. They complete transactions with customers and often provide customer services.

Retailers and their suppliers have complex relationships because the retailers serve two roles. They are part of a distribution channel aimed at the final consumer; and they are major customers for their suppliers. Channel relations are smoothest with exclusive distribution; they are most volatile with intensive distribution. Selective distribution combines aspects of both in an attempt to balance sales goals and channel member cooperation.

Retailing has several special characteristics. The average sales transaction is small. Final consumers make many unplanned purchases. Most customers visit a store location.

2. *To introduce the concept of strategic planning and apply it* A retail strategy is the overall plan guiding the firm. It has six basic steps: defining the business, setting objectives, defining the customer market, developing an overall plan, implementing an integrated strategy, and evaluating performance and making necessary modifications. Lands' End's strategy has been particularly well designed and carried out.

3. *To relate the marketing concept to retailing, with an emphasis on the total retail experience, customer service, and relationship retailing* The marketing concept (known as the retailing concept when applied to re-

tailing situations) should be understood and used by all retailers. This concept requires a firm to have a customer orientation, use a coordinated effort, and be value-driven and goal-oriented. Unfortunately, despite its ease of use, many firms do not adhere to one or more elements of the retailing concept.

The total retail experience consists of all the elements in a retail offering that encourage or inhibit consumers during their contact with a given retailer. Some elements are controllable by a retailer; others are not. Customer service includes identifiable, but sometimes intangible, activities undertaken by a retailer in association with the basic goods and services sold. It has an effect on the total retail experience, and

consists of two components—expected services and augmented services. In relationship retailing, a firm seeks long-term bonds with customers, rather than acting like each sales transaction is a totally new encounter with them.

4. *To indicate the focus and format of the text* Retailing may be studied by using an institutional approach, a functional approach, and a strategic approach. Although all three approaches are utilized in this text, the focus will be on the strategic approach. The underlying principle is that a retail firm needs to plan for and adapt to a complex, changing environment.

Key Terms

retailing (p. 3)
channel of distribution (p. 8)
sorting process (p. 9)
exclusive distribution (p. 11)

intensive distribution (p. 11)
selective distribution (p. 11)
retail strategy (p. 14)
retailing concept (p. 18)

total retail experience (p. 19)
customer service (p. 20)
employee empowerment (p. 21)
relationship retailing (p. 22)

Questions for Discussion

1. Which of these involve retailing? Explain your answers.
   a. A travel agency targeting college students.
   b. An appliance retailer selling to hospitals.
   c. An insurance company specializing in automobile insurance.
   d. A restaurant.
2. Describe the sorting process from the manufacturer's perspective. From the retailer's.
3. What kinds of information do retailers communicate to customers? To suppliers?
4. What are the pros and cons of a firm such as Ralph Lauren having its own retail facilities, as well as selling through traditional retailers?
5. Why would one retailer seek to be part of an exclusive distribution channel while another seeks to be part of an intensive distribution channel?
6. Describe how the special characteristics of retailing offer unique opportunities and problems for music stores.
7. What is a retail strategy? Could it be utilized by a small neighborhood stationery store? Why or why not?

8. On the basis of the chapter presentation on Lands' End, present five suggestions that a new retailer should consider.
9. Explain the retailing concept. Apply it to a delicatessen.
10. Define the term *total retail experience*. Then, describe a recent retail situation where you were dissatisfied and state why.
11. Differentiate between expected and augmented customer services. Relate your answer to the concept of employee empowerment.
12. How could a small retailer engage in relationship retailing?
13. What checklist item in Table 1-3 do you think would be most difficult for a retailer to address? Why?
14. Distinguish among these approaches to the study of retailing:
    a. Institutional.
    b. Functional.
    c. Strategic.

Web-Based Exercise:
NATIONAL RETAIL FEDERATION (http://www.nrf.com)

Questions

1. Read the cover story of the most recent issue of *Stores* magazine (this is available on the Web site). Prepare a one-page summary of the implications of this article to a retailer.
2. a. Describe a recent "hot issue" affecting retailers.
   b. How should a small local retailer respond to this issue?
   c. How should a large nationally-based retailer respond to this issue?
3. Outline the services that the NRF provides to its members.
4. Assess the Web site in terms of the value of the information provided, ease of use, and creative impact. Then, offer concrete suggestions for improving the site in each of these areas.

HOW TO SOLVE A CASE STUDY

This discussion is intended to give you insights into case-study analysis. A case study is a collection of facts and data based on a real or hypothetical business situation.

The goal of a case study is to develop your ability to solve complex business problems, using a logical framework. The issues in a case are generally not unique to a specific person, firm, or industry, and they often deal with more than one retail strategy element. Sometimes, the material presented in a case is in conflict. For example, two managers may disagree about a strategy; statistics may be contradictory; or there may be several interpretations of the same facts.

In all case studies, you must analyze what is presented and state which specific actions best resolve major issues. These actions must reflect the information in the case and the environment facing the firm.

STEPS IN SOLVING A CASE STUDY

Case studies revolve around the identification of the key issues and the enumeration and evaluation of proposed courses of action. Analysis should include these sequential steps:

1. Presentation of the facts surrounding the case.
2. Identification of the key issues.
3. Listing of alternative courses of action that could be taken.
4. Evaluation of alternative courses of action.
5. Recommendation of the best course of action.

Presentation of the Facts Surrounding the Case

It is helpful to read a case until you are comfortable with the information in it. Rereadings often are an aid to comprehending facts, possible strategies, or questions that need clarification and were not apparent earlier. Pay particular attention to exhibits, tables, charts, and diagrams. And data may be more revealing when translated into percentages or compared with prior years.

In studying a case, assume you are a retail consultant hired by the firm. While facts should be accepted as true, statements, judgments, and decisions made by the individuals in a case should be questioned, especially if not supported by facts—or when one individual disagrees with another.

During your reading of the case, you should

■ Underline crucial facts.
■ Interpret all figures and charts.
■ Critically review the comments made by individuals.
■ Judge the rationality of past and current decisions.
■ Develop questions whose answers would be useful in addressing the key issue(s).

Identification of the Key Issue(s)

Many times, the facts surrounding a case point out the key issue(s) facing a retailer, such as new opportunities, a changing environment, a decline in competitive position, poor profits, and/or excess inventories. Identify the characteristics and ramifications of the issue(s) and examine them, using the material contained in the case and in the text. In some instances, you must delve deeply because the key issue(s) and their characteristics may not be immediately obvious.

Listing Alternative Courses of Action That Could Be Taken

Next, alternative courses of action pertaining to the key issue(s) in the case, identified in the prior step, are listed. Consider these courses of action based on their appropriateness to the firm and the situation. Thus, the advertising strategy for a small neighborhood stationery store would not be appropriate for a large gift store located in a regional shopping center.

Proposed courses of action should take into account such factors as

■ The business category.
■ Goals.
■ The customer market.
■ The overall strategy.
■ The product assortment.
■ Competition.
■ Legal restrictions.
■ Economic trends.
■ Marketplace trends.
■ Financial capabilities.
■ Personnel capabilities.
■ Sources of supply.

Evaluation of Alternative Courses of Action

Evaluate each potential course of action, according to the facts surrounding the case, the key issue(s), the retail strategy concepts in the text, and the firm's environment. Specific criteria should be used and each alternative analyzed on the basis of these criteria. The ramifications and risks associated with each course of action should also be considered. Important data not included in the case should be mentioned.

Recommendation of the Best Course of Action

Be sure your analysis is not just a case summary. You will be critiqued by your professor on the basis of how well you identify key issues or problems, outline and assess alternative courses of action, and reach realistic conclusions (that take the retailer's size, competition, image, and so on into consideration). You need to show a good understanding of both the principles of strategic retail management and the dynamics of the case.

Be precise about which alternative is more desirable for the retailer in its current context. Remember, the purpose of your analysis is to apply a logical reasoning process to retailing. A written report must demonstrate this process.

Note: The cases in *Retail Management* have questions to guide you. However, your analysis should not be limited by them.

2

Strategic Planning in Retailing: Owning or Managing a Business

Donley's Old West Steakhouse and Buffet, located in Union, Illinois, is run by brothers Randy and Mike Donley. The restaurant abuts Donley's Wild West Town, a museum and theme village founded by Randy and Mike's father. The huge 270-seat restaurant, reminiscent of a saloon, was an immediate hit with both tourists and local residents when it opened in 1994. Yet, even though restaurant revenues were close to $2 million in 1995 and it was usually crowded, the Donleys lost money. According to Randy, "The busier we were, the more we lost." The losses, amounting to $250,000 in 1995, occurred despite the two brothers each working 18-hour days.

Only after hiring a restaurant consulting firm, did the Donleys begin to better grasp the reasons for their losses and revamp their strategy. By enacting several tactics recommended by the consultant, they reduced annual food costs by $280,000. The tactics included offering cheaper cuts of meat on the buffet (saving $2,500 per week), homemade desserts instead of ready-made (saving $500 per week), and decorating the buffet with unused kale, a type of cabbage, instead of throwing it out (saving $2,000 per year). The consulting firm also recommended that employees purchase their meals at cost (rather than be given free meals as a fringe benefit), that supply cabinets and freezers be locked to control employee theft, and that the food purchasing contract be renegotiated.

In addition to cost controls, the Donleys learned to refine their overall business skills. They now screen job applicants better (e.g., they will no longer hire temperamental chefs). Also they are more aware of the value of human relations skills in managing employees.

As a result of these changes, the restaurant turned its first monthly profit ($12,000) in March 1996. This compared quite favorably with losses of $25,000 in March 1995. It was really nice that the profit was earned without the restaurant having to substantially raise prices (only the price of a Sunday buffet was increased—from $10.95 to $11.95).

Now that cost controls and a more professional management style have been implemented, the brothers plan to boost revenues by attracting additional customers from the Chicago suburbs with such features as a casino night or a cigar night. They are also considering opening two new units.[1]

CHAPTER OBJECTIVES

1. To show the value of strategic planning for all types of retailers
2. To explain the steps in strategic planning for retailers: situation analysis, objectives, identification of consumers, overall strategy, specific activities, control, and feedback
3. To examine the individual controllable and uncontrollable elements of a retail strategy
4. To present strategic planning as a series of integrated steps

---

[1]Stephanie N. Mehta, "Restaurant Novices Learn to Turn Popularity into Profit," *Wall Street Journal* (August 9, 1996), pp. B1–B2.

OVERVIEW

As noted in Chapter 1, a ***retail strategy*** is an overall plan or framework of action that guides a retailer. Ideally, it will be at least one year in duration and outline the mission, goals, consumer market, overall and specific activities, and control mechanisms of the retailer. Without a predefined and well-integrated strategy, the firm can flounder and be unable to cope with environmental factors.

The process of strategic retail planning has several attractive features. First, it provides a thorough analysis of the requirements for different types of retailing. Second, it outlines the objectives of the retailer. Third, a firm learns how it can differentiate itself from competitors and develop an offering that appeals to a group of customers. Fourth, the retailer studies the legal, economic, and competitive environments. Fifth, the company's total efforts are coordinated. Sixth, crises are anticipated and often avoided.

Strategic planning can be conducted by the owner of the firm, professional management, or a combination of the two. As a person moves up the retail career ladder, a key indicator of performance and advancement potential is whether increased planning responsibility is undertaken and how well it is completed. According to recent research, even among family businesses, 56 percent of high-growth companies have strategic plans.[2]

The steps in planning and enacting a retail strategy are interdependent; and a firm often starts with a general plan that becomes more specific as options and payoffs become clearer. In Chapter 2, we cover the development of a comprehensive, integrated retail strategy, as shown in Figure 2-1.[3] In Chapter 3, we look at the challenging environment retailers are facing as they conduct strategic planning.

SITUATION ANALYSIS

Situation analysis is the candid evaluation of the opportunities and potential problems facing a prospective or existing retailer. It seeks to answer two general questions: What is the firm's current status? In which direction should the firm be heading? For a retailer, situation analysis means defining and adhering to an organizational mission, evaluating ownership and management options, and outlining the goods/service category to be sold.

During this stage, especially for a new retailer or one thinking about making a major strategy change, an honest, in-depth self-assessment is needed. It is all right for a person or company to be ambitious and aggressive; but overestimating one's abilities and prospects can be harmful—if the result is entry into the wrong retail business, inadequate resources, and misjudging competitors.

Organizational Mission

An ***organizational mission*** is a retailer's commitment to a type of business and to a distinctive role in the marketplace. It is reflected in the firm's attitudes toward consumers, employees, suppliers, competitors, government, and others. A clear organizational mission lets a firm gain a customer following and distinguish itself from competitors. See Figure 2-2.

One key decision a retailer must make is whether to base its business around the goods and services sold or around consumer needs. For example, a retailer entering the hardware business must decide if a line of bathroom vanities should be stocked, in

---

[2]"Family Businesses on the Go," *Inc.* (January 1996), p. 86.

[3]For interesting articles on strategic planning, see Amar Bhide, "The Questions Every Entrepreneur Must Answer," *Harvard Business Review*, Vol. 74 (November–December 1996), pp. 120–130; Jeffrey S. Conant, Denise T. Smart, and Roberto Solano-Mendez, "Generic Retailing Types, Distinctive Marketing Competencies, and Competitive Advantage," *Journal of Retailing*, Vol. 69 (Fall 1993), pp. 254–279; and "How to Succeed in Business in 4 Easy Steps," *Inc.* (July 1995), pp. 31–42.

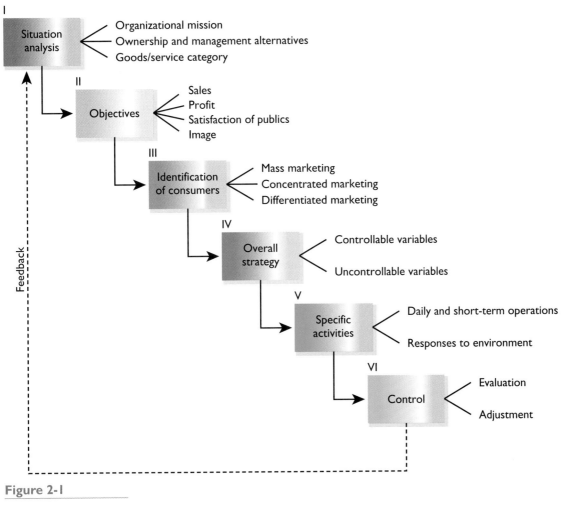

Figure 2-1

Elements of a Retail Strategy

Figure 2-2

Neiman-Marcus' Organizational Mission

"We've grown from a small Texas store to a fashion icon with 29 stores specializing in exclusive apparel for men, women, and children, gifts, fine china, glassware, furs, precious jewelry, and cosmetics. Our image has become global, but one Neiman-Marcus factor remains unchanged—a commitment to providing our customers with unequaled service."

addition to hardware products. A traditionalist retailer would probably opt not to carry vanities because they seem unconnected to the perceived business. But, a firm viewing a hardware store as a do-it-yourself home improvement center sees the vanities as a logical part of its product mix. The latter would carry any merchandise that the consumer, not the storekeeper, desires.

A second major decision for a retailer is whether it wants a place in the market as a leader or a follower. The firm could seek to offer a unique strategy, such as Taco Bell becoming the first national quick-serve Mexican food chain. Or it could emulate standard practices of competitors in its category but do a better job in executing them, such as a neighborhood fast-food Mexican restaurant offering 5-minute guaranteed service and a cleanliness pledge.

A third basic decision involves a firm's market scope. Large chains often seek a broad customer base (due to their resources and name recognition). However, it is usually best for small retailers—and most startups—to focus on a narrower customer base. By doing so, they can compete better with bigger firms; the latter tend not to adapt strategies as well to local markets.

Although the development of an organizational mission is the first step in a retailer's planning process, the mission should be continually reviewed and adjusted to reflect changing company goals and a dynamic retail environment.

Following is a well-conceived organizational mission, paraphrased from Ross Stores' Web site (http://www.rossstores.com). The company operates Ross Dress for Less stores:

> Ross Stores began in 1982 with six San Francisco area stores. Ross now has over 300 stores in eight states. As an off-price retailer, Ross stocks first-quality, in-season, brand-name apparel, accessories, and footwear for the entire family at savings of 20 percent to 60 percent off regular department and specialty store prices, as well as similar savings on fragrances, gift items, and linens for the home. Target customers are value conscious men and women between the ages of 25 and 54 with middle- to upper-middle-class incomes. Ross customers define value both in terms of brands and strong discounts in contrast to full-price retailers. Ross Stores' mission is to offer competitive values to customers by focusing on the following principles:
>
> ■ Offer an appropriate level of brands and labels at strong discounts throughout the store.
> ■ Meet customer needs on a more regional basis.
> ■ Deliver an in-store shopping experience that reflects the expectation of the off-price customer.
> ■ Manage real estate growth in key markets to maintain dominance or achieve parity with the competition.

Ownership and Management Alternatives

An essential aspect of situation analysis is assessing ownership and management alternatives. Ownership options include whether to operate as a sole proprietorship, a partnership, or a corporation—as well as whether to start a new business, buy an existing business, or become a franchisee. Management options include owner-manager versus professional manager and centralized versus decentralized structures. As two legal experts commented, "People dealing with a firm may not notice whether it's a sole proprietorship, a partnership, or a corporation. The firm chosen, though, can make a big difference when it's time to pay taxes, respond to a law suit, or split up the business."[4]

A **sole proprietorship** is an unincorporated retail firm owned by one person. All benefits, profits, risks, and costs accrue to the single owner. A sole proprietorship is simple to

---

[4]Steven C. Bahls and Jane Easter Bahls, "In Good Form," *Entrepreneur* (September 1996), pp. 75–79.

form, fully controlled by the owner, operationally flexible, easy to dissolve, and subject to single taxation by the government. It makes the owner personally liable to legal claims from suppliers, creditors, and others, and it can result in limited capital and expertise.

A **partnership** is an unincorporated retail firm owned by two or more persons, each of whom has a financial interest. Partners share benefits, profits, risks, and costs. A partnership allows responsibility and expertise to be divided among multiple principals, provides a greater capability for raising funds than a proprietorship, is simpler to form than a corporation, and is subject to single taxation by the government. It, too, makes owners personally liable to legal claims from suppliers, creditors, and others; can be dissolved due to a partner's death or a disagreement; binds all partners to actions made by any individual partner acting on behalf of the firm; and usually has less ability to raise capital than a corporation.

A **corporation** is a retail firm that is formally incorporated under state law. It is a legal entity apart from individual officers (or stockholders). Corporate status means funds can be raised by the sale of stock, legal claims against individuals are not usually allowed, ownership transfer is relatively easy, the firm is assured of long-term existence (even if a founder leaves, retires, or dies), the use of professional managers is encouraged, and unambiguous operating authority is outlined. It is subject to double taxation (company earnings and stockholder dividends), faces more government rules than other ownership forms, can require a complex and costly process when established, can be viewed as impersonal, and can separate ownership from management. A closed corporation is typically operated by a limited number of persons, who control ownership; stock is not available for public purchase. In an open corporation, stock is widely traded and available for public purchase.

Sole proprietorships account for 74 percent of all retail firms in the United States that file tax returns, partnerships for 4 percent, and corporations for 22 percent. However, in terms of sales volume, sole proprietorships account for 10 percent of total U.S. retail store sales, partnerships for 3 percent, and corporations for 87 percent.[5]

Starting a new business—being entrepreneurial—offers a retailer flexibility in location, operating style, product lines, customer markets, and other factors; and it lets a strategy be fully tailored to the owner's desires and strengths. It can also mean having construction or renovation costs, having a time lag until the business is ready to open and then until profits are earned, beginning with an unknown name and image, and having to form supplier relationships and amass an inventory of goods. Figure 2-3 presents several factors to consider when starting a business.

Buying an existing business allows a retailer to acquire an established company name, a customer following, a good location, trained personnel, and standing facilities; to operate immediately; to generate ongoing sales and profits; and possibly to get good lease terms or financing (at favorable interest rates) from the seller. It also means fixtures may be older, there is less flexibility in developing and enacting a strategy tailored to the new owner's desires and strengths, and the growth potential of the business may be limited. Figure 2-4 provides a checklist of questions to consider when purchasing an existing retail business.

By becoming a franchisee, a retailer can combine independent ownership with franchisor management assistance, thorough strategic planning, a known company name and a loyal customer following, cooperative advertising and buying, and a regional, national, or global (rather than local) image. It also means a contractual agreement may specify rigid operations standards, limit the product lines sold, and restrict the choice of suppliers; the franchisor usually receives continuous payments (royalties); advertising fees may be required; and there is a possibility of termination by the franchisor if the agreement is not followed satisfactorily.

[5]*Statistical Abstract of the United States 1996* (Washington, D.C.: U.S. Department of Commerce, 1996), p. 533.

Figure 2-3

Selected Factors to Consider When Starting a New Retail Business

Source: Adapted by the authors from *Small Business Management Training Instructor's Guide: No. 109* (Washington, D.C.: U.S. Small Business Administration).

NAME OF BUSINESS_____

A. SELF-ASSESSMENT AND BUSINESS CHOICE
 1. Evaluate your strengths and weaknesses.
 2. Commitment paragraph: Why should you be in business for yourself? Why open a new business rather than acquire an existing one or become a member of a franchise chain?
 3. Describe the type of retail business that fits your strengths and desires. What will make it unique? What will the business offer for customers? How will you capitalize on the weaknesses of competitors?

B. OVERALL RETAIL PLAN
 1. State your philosophy of business.
 2. Choose an ownership form (sole proprietorship, partnership, or corporation).
 3. State your long- and short-run goals.
 4. Analyze your customers from their point of view.
 5. Research your market size and store location.
 6. Quantify the total retail sales of your goods /service category in your trading area.
 7. Analyze your competition.
 8. Quantify your potential market share.
 9. Develop your retail strategy: store location and operations, merchandising, pricing, and store image and promotion.

C. FINANCIAL PLAN
 1. What level of funds will you need to get started and to get through the first year? Where will they come from?
 2. Determine the first year profit, return on investment, and salary that you need/want.
 3. Project monthly cash flow and profit-and-loss statements for the first two years.
 4. What sales will be needed to break even during the first year? What will you do if these sales are not reached?

D. ORGANIZATIONAL DETAILS PLAN (ADMINISTRATIVE MANAGEMENT)
 1. Describe your personnel plan (hats to wear), organizational plan, and policies.
 2. List the jobs you like and want to do and those you dislike, cannot do, or do not want to do.
 3. Outline your accounting and inventory systems.
 4. Note your insurance plans.
 5. Specify how day-to-day operations would be conducted for each aspect of your strategy.
 6. Review the risks you face and how you plan to cope with them.

From a strategic perspective, the management format chosen also has a dramatic impact. In an owner-manager system, planning tends to be less formal and more intuitive, and many tasks tend to be reserved for the owner-manager (such as employee supervision and cash management). With a professional manager system, planning tends to be more formal and systematic. However, a professional manager is usually more constrained in his or her authority than an owner-manager. In a centralized structure, planning authority is limited to top management or ownership; for a decentralized structure, managers in individual departments have major input into decisions. Regardless of management format, a retailer is best able to prepare and enact a proper strategy only if there is ample information and communication.

A comprehensive discussion of independent retailers, chains, franchises, leased departments, vertical marketing systems, and consumer cooperatives appears in Chapter 4.

Goods/Service Category

Before a prospective retail firm can fully design a strategic plan, it selects a **goods/service category**—the line of business—in which to operate. Figure 2-5 shows the diver-

Figure 2-4

A Checklist for Purchasing an Existing Retail Business

NAME OF BUSINESS _____

These questions should be considered when purchasing an existing retail business:

1. Why is the seller placing the business up for sale?

2. How much are you paying for goodwill (the cost of the business above its tangible asset value)?

3. Have sales, inventory levels, and profit figures been confirmed by your accountant?

4. Will the seller introduce you to his/her customers and stay on during the transition period?

5. Will the seller sign a statement that he/she will not open a directly-competing business in the same trading area for a reasonable time period?

6. If sales are seasonal, are you purchasing the business at the right time of the year?

7. In the purchase of the business, are you assuming existing debts of the seller?

8. Who receives proceeds from transactions made prior to the sale of the business but not yet paid by customers?

9. What is the length of the lease if property is rented?

10. If property is to be purchased along with the business, has it been inspected by a professional engineer?

11. How modern are the storefront and store fixtures?

12. Is inventory fresh? Does it contain a full merchandise assortment?

13. Are the advertising policy, customer service policy, and pricing policy of the past owner similar to yours? Can you continue old policies?

14. If the business is to be part of a chain, is the new unit compatible with existing units? How much trading-area overlap is there with existing stores?

15. Has a lawyer examined the proposed contract?

16. What effect will owning this business have on your life-style and on your family relationships?

---

sity of goods/service categories from which a retailer may choose. Chapter 5 examines the attributes of food-based and general merchandise store retailers, as well as the differences between goods and service retailing. Chapter 6 focuses on nonstore and nontraditional retailing. Chapter 19 looks at the special strategic features of service retailing.

At this stage of planning, it is advisable (for most retailers) to specify both a general goods/service category and a niche within that category. For example, Jaguar dealers are luxury auto retailers that cater to upscale customers. Wendy's is an eating and drinking chain that is famous for its quality fast food, with a menu emphasizing hamburgers. Motel 6 is a hotel chain whose forte is inexpensive rooms with few frills.

When selecting the goods/service category, the potential retail business owner should select a type of business that will allow him or her to match personal abilities, financial resources, and time availability with those required by the kind of business.

Personal Abilities ❏ Personal abilities depend on an individual's aptitude—the preference for a type of business and the potential to do well; education—formal learning about retail practices and policies; and experience—practical learning about retail practices and policies.

A person should have an aptitude for the business to be entered. Thus, an individual who wants to run a store, likes to use initiative, and has the ability to react quickly to competitive developments will be suited to a different type of situation from a person who depends on others for advice and does not like to make decisions. The first individual could be an independent operator, in a dynamic business like apparel; the second might seek partners or a franchise and a business that is stable, like a stationery store. In addition, some people enjoy personal interaction with their customers; they would dislike the impersonality of

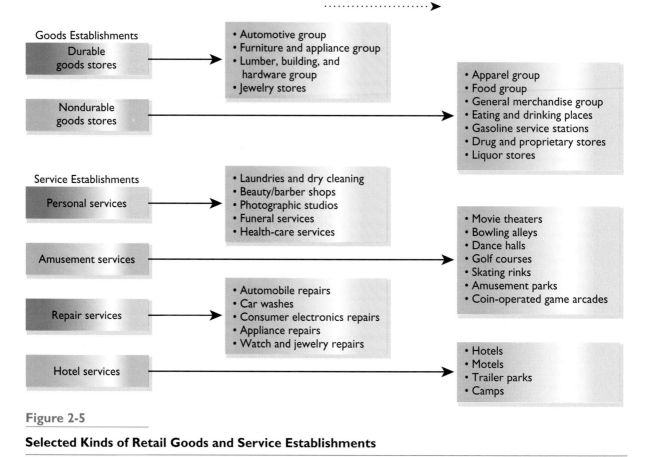

Figure 2-5

Selected Kinds of Retail Goods and Service Establishments

a pure discount or self-service operation. Still others enjoy the relative impersonality of mail-order or Internet retailing.

In certain fields, education and experience requirements are specified by federal or state laws. Insurance brokers, stockbrokers, real-estate brokers, barbers, beauticians, certified public accountants, pharmacists, and opticians represent a cross section of the kinds of retailers who must satisfy educational or experience standards to demonstrate professional competency. For instance, real-estate brokers have to be licensed. This involves examining the individuals' ethical character, as well as their knowledge of real-estate practice and law. (Yet, the designation "broker" does not depend on the ability to sell or have a customer-oriented demeanor.)

Some skills can be learned by education or experience; others are inborn. Accordingly, potential retail owners have to review their personal skills and match them with the demands of a given business. This is a hard process that involves insight into oneself and careful reflection. Strengths and weaknesses must be weighed in this matching process. Partnerships may arise when two or more parties possess complementary skills. A person with extensive selling experience may join with someone having the operating skills necessary to open a store. Each partner would have valued skills but may be unable to operate a retail entity without the expertise of the other.

Financial Resources ❑ Another primary factor in selecting the goods/service category for a retail business is the level of financial resources required. Many enterprises, especially new, independent ones, fail because the owners do not adequately project the financial resources needed to open and operate the firm. Table 2-1 outlines some of the typical investments for a new retail venture.

Table 2-1 SOME OF THE TYPICAL FINANCIAL INVESTMENTS FOR A NEW RETAIL VENTURE	
Use of Funds	**Source of Funds**
Land and building (lease or purchase)	Personal savings, bank loan, commercial finance company
Inventory	Personal savings, manufacturer credit, commercial finance company, sales revenues
Fixtures (including display cases, storage facilities, signs, lighting, carpeting, etc.)	Personal savings, manufacturer credit, bank loan, commercial finance company
Equipment (including cash register, marking machine, office equipment, computers, etc.)	Personal savings, manufacturer credit, bank loan, commercial finance company
Personnel (including salespeople, cashiers, stockpeople, etc.)	Personal savings, bank loan, sales revenues
Promotion	Personal savings, sales revenue
Personal drawing account	Personal savings, life insurance loan
Miscellaneous: Equipment repair Credit sales (bad debts) Professional services Repayment of loans	Personal savings, manufacturer and wholesaler credit, bank credit plan, bank loan, commercial finance company

Note: Collateral for a bank loan may be a building, fixtures, land, inventory, or a personal residence.

Novice retailers frequently underestimate the need for a personal drawing account. This is used for the daily, weekly, and monthly living expenses of the owner and his or her family over the early, unprofitable stage of a business. Because few new ventures are immediately profitable, the budget must include such expenditures. The costs of renovating an existing facility are also often miscalculated by new retailers. Underfunded firms tend to initially invest in only essential renovations. Other improvements wait until the firms are prospering, and alterations are paid from profits. This practice reduces the initial investment, but it can give the retailer a poor image.

Merchandise assortment, as well as the types of goods and services sold, impact on the financial outlay required of a new retailer. The use of a partnership, corporation, or franchise agreement will also affect the initial investment.

Table 2-2 shows the financial requirements for a hypothetical used-car dealer. Table 2-3 shows inventory costs and revenues. The initial personal savings investment of $300,000 to enter the business would force many potential owners to rethink the choice of product category, as well as the intended format of the organization. First, the plans for a 40-car inventory reflect this owner's desire for a balanced product line. If the firm concentrates on subcompact, compact, and intermediate cars, it can be more specialized and reduce inventory size. This would lead to a lower investment. Second, an entering used-car dealer can also reduce the initial investment by seeking a location whose facilities do not have to be modified, like the site of a previous used-car dealer. Third, fewer of one person's financial resources are needed if he or she enters into a partnership or corporation with others, which allows costs—and profits—to be shared.

The federal Small Business Administration assists businesses by guaranteeing well over 50,000 loans per year. In addition, such private companies as Wells Fargo and American Express now have financing programs specifically aimed at small businesses.[6]

Time Demands ❏ Time demands on retail owners (or managers) differ significantly by goods or service category. They are influenced both by the consumers' shopping patterns and by the owners' or managers' ability to automate operations or delegate activities to others.

[6]Karen Axelton, "Under Inspection," *Entrepreneur* (December 1996), p. 19; Daniel Immergluck, "Business as Usual?" *Inc.* (February 1996), pp. 23–24; and I. Jeanne Dugan, "Small Business Is Big Business," *Business Week* (September 30, 1996), p. 117.

Table 2-2 FINANCIAL REQUIREMENTS FOR A USED-CAR DEALER

Total investments (first year)	
Lease (10 years, $60,000 per year)	$ 60,000
Beginning inventory (40 cars, average cost of $10,000)	400,000
Replacement inventory (40 cars, average cost of $10,000)[a]	400,000
Fixtures and equipment (includes painting, paneling, carpeting, lighting, signs, heating and air-conditioning system, electronic cash register, service bay)	60,000
Replacement parts	75,000
Personnel (one mechanic)	45,000
Promotion (brochures and newspaper advertising)	35,000
Drawing account (to cover owner's personal expenses for one year; all selling and operating functions except mechanical ones performed by the owner)	40,000
Accountant	15,000
Miscellaneous (including loan payments)	60,000
Profit (projected)	40,000
	$1,230,000
Source of funds	
Personal savings	$ 300,000
Bank loan	400,000
Sales revenues (based on expected sales of 40 cars, average price of $13,250)	530,000
	$1,230,000

[a]Assumes that forty cars are sold during the year. As each type of car is sold, a replacement is bought by the dealer and placed in inventory. At the end of the year, inventory on hand remains at forty units.

Many retailers must have weekend and evening hours—and be open on holidays—to serve today's busy consumer. Gift shops, toy stores, housepainters, and others have extreme seasonal shifts and keep long hours during prime seasons. Yet, mail-order firms and those selling through the Internet (which can process orders during any part of the day) have more flexible hours.

The ability or inability to automate operations or delegate duties also affects the number of hours worked. Some businesses require less owner involvement, including gas stations with no repair or maintenance services, coin-operated laundries, movie theaters, and motels. The emphasis on automation, self-service, standardized goods and services, and financial controls lets the owners reduce time investments. Other businesses require active owner involvement. Hair salons, TV repair stores, butcher shops, restaurants, and jewelry stores are time-consuming businesses.

Table 2-3 ANALYSIS OF BEGINNING INVENTORY COSTS AND EXPECTED FIRST-YEAR SALES REVENUES BY TYPE OF CAR FOR A USED-CAR DEALER

Type of Car	Number of Cars in Beginning Inventory	Average Cost	Average Selling Price	Cost of Beginning Inventory	Total Annual Revenue[a]
Subcompact	8	$ 7,000	$ 8,750	$ 56,000	$ 70,000
Compact	11	8,000	10,400	88,000	114,400
Intermediate	12	10,500	14,500	126,000	174,000
Full-size/luxury	5	16,400	22,000	82,000	110,000
Minivan/station wagon	4	12,000	15,400	48,000	61,600
	40	$10,000	$13,250	$400,000	$530,000

[a]Forty cars are sold during the year. As each type of car is sold, a replacement is bought by the dealer and placed in inventory. At the end of the year, inventory on hand remains at forty units.

Intensive owner participation can be due to several factors. First, the owner may be the key worker, with consumers attracted by his or her skills (the major competitive advantage of the firm). In that case, delegating work to others will diminish consumer loyalty. Associated with this situation are the attention and expertise only an owner can give to certain customers. Second, some types of retailing, such as personal services, are not easy to automate. In these instances, owner involvement is necessary to provide the services. Third, because a lot of small retailers are underfunded, the owner and his or her family must undertake all aspects of the business; there is not enough money to hire employees. According to one study, spouses work in 40 percent of family-owned businesses and children in 37 percent of them.[7] Fourth, in a business that operates on a cash basis and has weak financial controls, the owner must be around to avoid being cheated. For a firm with poor inventory procedures, it may be difficult to match sales with inventory levels, making it easy for employees to pocket cash sales if not watched by the owner.

It is sometimes assumed that a person running a retail firm works only when it is "open for business." However, off-hours activities are often essential. A butcher must go to a meat wholesaler at least once a week to make purchases. (That is why these wholesalers are busiest very early in the morning.) At a restaurant, some foods must be prepared in advance of the posted dining hours. An antique dealer spends nonstore hours hunting for goods. A small storekeeper cleans, stocks shelves, and does the books during the hours the firm is not serving customers.

A prospective retail owner also has to examine his or her time preferences regarding stability versus seasonality (some would rather work 40-hour weeks, 48 weeks a year; others would rather work 80-hour weeks for 6 months and relax the other 6 months); ideal working hours (days and times); and personal involvement (absentee ownership or on-site management).

OBJECTIVES

After situation analysis, a retailer sets **objectives,** the long-run and short-run performance targets it hopes to attain. Stating clear objectives helps mold a strategy and translates the organizational mission into action. A firm can pursue one or more of these goals: sales (including growth, stability, and market share); profit (including level, return on investment, and efficiency); satisfaction of publics (including stockholders and consumers); and image (including customer and industry perceptions). Each of the preceding is sought by many retailers. Some strive to fully achieve all of the goals; others attend to a few and want to achieve them really well.

Sales

Sales objectives are related to the volume of goods and services a retailer sells. Growth, stability, and market share are the sales goals most often sought by retailers.

Some retailers set sales growth as a top priority. Thus, they look to expand operations and increase revenues. There is less emphasis on short-run profits. The assumption is that investments in the present will yield profits in the future. A small or large retailer that does well often becomes interested in opening new units and enlarging revenues. Yet, too active a pursuit of expansion can result in problems. Many retailers successful in their current business fail as they open new units. Management skills and the personal touch are sometimes lost with improper expansion. Sales growth is a legitimate goal, but it should not be too fast or preclude considering other objectives.

Stability in annual sales and profits is the goal of a wide range of retailers that place emphasis on maintaining their sales volume, market share, price lines, and so on. Small retailers often seek stable sales that enable the owners to make a satisfactory living every year, without the pressure of sharp downswings or upsurges. And certain retailers develop

[7]Arthur Andersen & Co.'s Enterprise Group, "All in the Family," *Crain's New York Business* (May 24, 1993), p. 18.

a loyal customer following and are intent not on expanding but on continuing the approach that attracted the original consumers.

For some firms, market share—the percentage of total retail-category sales contributed by a given company—is another goal. In retailing, it is often an objective only for large retailers or retail chains. The small retailer is more concerned with competition across the street or down the block than with total sales in a metropolitan area.

Sales objectives may be expressed in dollars and units. To achieve dollar goals, a retailer can engage in a discount strategy (low prices and high unit sales), a moderate strategy (medium prices and medium unit sales), or a prestige strategy (high prices and low unit sales). In the long run, using sales units as a performance target is important. Dollar sales over a several-year period may be difficult to compare due to changing retail prices and the rate of inflation; but unit sales are easier to compare from year to year. A firm with sales of $350,000 in 1990 and $500,000 in 1997 might assume it is doing well, until unit figures are computed: 10,000 in 1990 and 8,000 in 1997.

Profit

With profitability objectives, retailers seek at least minimum profit levels during designated time periods, usually a year. Profit may be expressed in dollars or as a percentage of sales. For a firm having yearly sales of $5 million and total yearly costs of $4.2 million, pre-tax dollar profit is $800,000 and profits as a percentage of sales are 16 percent. If the goal is equal to or less than $800,000, or 16 percent, the retailer is satisfied. If the goal is greater than $800,000, or 16 percent, the company has not attained the minimum desired level of profits and is dissatisfied.

Firms with substantial capital expenditures in land, buildings, and equipment often set return on investment (ROI) as a goal. ROI is the relationship between company profits and investment in capital items. It is used similarly to any profit statistic: A satisfactory rate of return is predefined and then compared with the actual rate of return at the end of the year or other designated period. For a retailer with annual sales of $5 million and expenditures (including monthly long-term payments for capital items) of $4 million, the yearly profit is $1 million. If the total investment to the retailer for land, buildings, and equipment is $10 million, then ROI equals $1 million/$10 million, or 10 percent per year. The goal must be 10 percent or less for the retailer to be satisfied.

Increased operating efficiency is many retailers' goal. It may be expressed as 1 − (operating expenses/company sales); the higher the figure, the more efficient the firm. A retailer with sales of $2 million and operating costs of $1 million has a 50 percent efficiency rating ([1 − ($1 million/$2 million)]). Of every sales dollar, 50 cents go for such nonoperating costs as merchandise purchases and to profits, and 50 cents go for operating expenses. The retailer might set a goal to increase operating efficiency to 60 percent. On sales of $2 million, operating costs would have to drop to $800,000 ([1 − ($800,000/$2 million)]). Sixty cents of every sales dollar would then go for nonoperating costs and profits; and 40 cents for operations. The elevated efficiency would lead to better profits. Nonetheless, a firm must be careful; if expenses are cut too much, customer service may decline and this would probably lead to a sales decline and a resulting profit drop.

Satisfaction of Publics

A retailer may strive for satisfaction of publics' objectives. Publics include stockholders, consumers, suppliers, employees, and government.

Stockholder satisfaction is a vital goal for any publicly owned retail firm. It is up to top management to set and attain goals consistent with stockholder wishes. Many companies follow policies leading to small annual increases in sales and profits (because these goals can be sustained over the long run and indicate good management), rather than

At The Container Store: POS Terminals Do More Than Check Out

The Dallas-based The Container Store is the category leader in the storage and organization segment of the housewares industry. The chain has 15 stores. These stores average 23,000 square feet of space and generate annual sales volume of $5 million per unit.

Like other progressive retailers, The Container Store wants its point-of-sale (POS) terminals to help frontline employees provide customer service capabilities for shoppers that previously were associated with a separate customer service department. According to the chain's director of information technology, "The core function of the staff in the store is service first, cashiering second. Every sales associate sells—no one is just a cashier. We don't want the customer service effort to stop at the point of sale."

The Container Store regards the customer's checkout experience as the perfect opportunity to sell additional merchandise. For example, to increase related-item selling, The Container Store's salesclerks are encouraged to use the POS terminals to verify the availability of stock in the firm's warehouse locations.

The POS terminals perform many functions that were once done manually, such as completing forms to ship merchandise and preparing gift certificates. During the checkout, the terminals also produce vital managerial reports on sales by product category, unit sales, and cashier performance.

Source: Bruce Fox, "Service, Not Transactions, Drives POS," *Chain Store Age* (April 1996), pp. 101–106.

---

ones introducing innovative ideas possibly leading to peaks and valleys in company sales and profits (indicating poor management). Stable earnings for firms lead to stable dividends for stockholders.

Customer satisfaction with the total retail experience is a goal most firms target today, although some have awakened to this only recently. It is crucial to satisfy consumers and not have a policy of caveat emptor ("Let the buyer beware"). Retailers must listen to criticism and adapt appropriately. They can do this by gearing their overall mission and goals to customer satisfaction. If shoppers are pleased, other goals are more easily reached. Yet, despite so many retailers including customer satisfaction as a stated objective, the importance of this goal ranks too low for many, large and small alike. For them, the other objectives cited rate higher in the list of priorities.

Good supplier relations is also a key goal. Retailers must understand and work together with their suppliers if favorable purchase terms, new products, good return policies, prompt shipments, and cooperation are to be received. Good relations are particularly important for small retailers due to the many functions suppliers carry out for them.

Cordial labor relations is another major goal—often basic to retailers' performance, whether they are small or big. Good employee morale means less absenteeism, better customer treatment, and lower turnover. Relations can be improved by effective selection, training, and motivation.

Because all levels of government impose rules affecting retailing practices, a significant goal may be to understand and adapt to their policies. In some cases, firms can influence these rules by acting singly or as members of large groups, such as trade associations or chambers of commerce.

Image (Positioning)

A major goal for virtually any retailer is to create and maintain the image it feels is proper for the specific type of business involved. An **image** represents how a given retailer is perceived by consumers and others. A firm may be seen as innovative or conservative, specialized or broad-based, discount-oriented or upscale. The key to a successful image is that consumers view the retailer in the manner the latter intends.

Through **positioning,** a retailer devises its strategy in a way that projects an image relative to its retail category and its competitors, and elicits consumer responses to that image. Thus, a firm selling women's apparel could generally position itself as an upscale or midpriced specialty store, a department store, a discount department store, or a discount specialty store, and it could specifically position itself with regard to any nearby retailers carrying women's apparel.

For some retailers, such as McDonald's, Hertz, or the market-leading drugstore chain in your area, industry leadership (which may be local) is a positioning goal. This leadership often results in two major benefits for a firm. First, it may enhance company image because consumers are apt to place the leader on a higher pedestal than its competitors. Second, other retailers may follow the pricing and other strategies of the leader rather than their own innovative approaches—a form of imitation that is the best kind of flattery. A subsidiary benefit is the internal morale boost that accompanies being "number one," and this motivates all to work harder.

Two opposite positioning philosophies have gained in popularity during recent years: mass merchandising and niche retailing. **Mass merchandising** is a positioning approach whereby retailers offer a discount or value-oriented image, a wide and/or deep merchandise assortment, and large store facilities. (For example, Wal-Mart has a wide, deep merchandise mix while Sports Authority has a narrower, deeper assortment.) These retailers want to appeal to a broad customer market, attract high levels of customer traffic, and generate high stock turnover. Because mass merchants have relatively low operating costs, achieve economies in operations, and appeal to value conscious people, their continuing popularity is forecast.

In **niche retailing,** retailers identify customer segments and deploy unique strategies to address the desires of those segments. The retailers concentrate their efforts on a specific segment or segments and not the mass market. Niching creates a high level of loyalty and shields the retailers from more conventional competitors. This approach will

Figure 2-6

The Distinctive Niche Positioning of Shades of California

also have a large future presence because it lets many retailers stress factors other than price in their strategies and encourages a more specialized focus by firms such as department stores. The growth of boutique-type stores and compartmentalized department stores should continue. See Figure 2-6.

Because both mass merchandising and positioned retailing are popular, some observers are calling this the era of **bifurcated retailing.** According to these observers, it means the decline of middle-of-the-market retailing. Firms that are not competitively priced nor particularly individualistic may have difficulty competing.

Let us further illustrate the concept of positioning by presenting some results from a recent major study of the women's fashion market in Chicago.[8] The study involved more than 2,000 female apparel shoppers. It was conducted by Babson College and sponsored by 15 firms:

■ Figure 2-7 shows a positioning map with 27 retailers depicted. The map highlights consumer perceptions regarding the comparative position of each chain on a "value scale" and on a "fashion scale." Value is based on both the caliber of clothing and the shopping experience relative to product prices. Fashionability is based on the freshness, styling, and assortment of clothing. Respondents commented only on the stores at which they actually shopped.

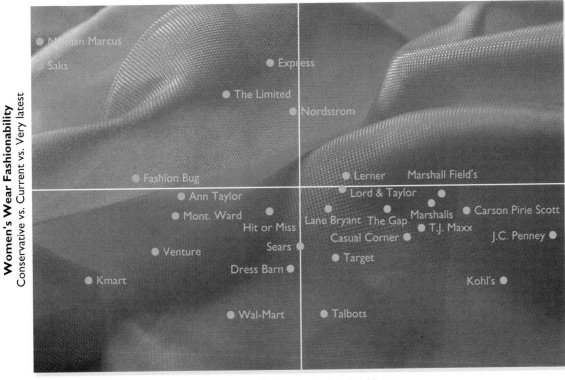

Women's Wear Value for the Money

Worst value (left)   Best value (right)

Figure 2-7

How Chicago Retailers Are Positioned in the Women's Fashion Market

[8]"Shopping Chicago: Who Fills Women's Apparel Needs?" *Chain Store Age* (October 1996), Section Three; and James Mammarella, "Value Rules Apparel Decisions as Battle for Market Share Sharpens," *Discount Store News* (October 7, 1996), pp. 21–29.

Figure 2-8

The Strengths and Weaknesses of Selected Retailers in the Chicago Women's Fashion Market

Carson Pirie Scott

Strengths: Always in stock, with the right sizes and colors, and at the right price; however, when compared with other chains, it does not win outright on very many dimensions.

Weaknesses: Chain has a lot of scores in the 20s shows it has a significant number of weaknesses despite currently being the market leader. It is not a "fun" place to shop, it does not carry unique items, decor and design are not particularly appealing, the lighting is weak, and, much more significantly, so is the service. The chain also is perceived as not having a clear fashion position.

Compagnie Internationale **EXPRESS**

Strengths: Contemporary fashion, particularly for the under-25 set, offering good displays that help customers pull outfits together; also wins high marks for having the right sizes and colors in the latest fashion wear. Positioned at the middle- to upper-end of the fashion market for young women.

Weaknesses: Areas for improvement include product quality, service levels, advertising (never a high priority for any division of The Limited), lack of business casual clothing and, most importantly, needs to build a stronger value position.

GAP

Strengths: Young women find The Gap a friendly place in which to shop for casual, weekend wear, attracted by the displays that show how outfits can be pulled together, and by the good fashion posters. They respond to the easy-to-shop layout and the neat and organized displays, and how they are generally assured of finding the right sizes and colors in the right price ranges.

Weaknesses: Limited selection, included lack of "business casual" wear (already identified elsewhere as a major opportunity for the chain), plus could be some price resistance as well as concerns about merchandise quality.

KOHL'S

Strengths: Overall market winner when it comes to being seen by its customers as offering the best value and the right price ranges; very strong too when it comes to being in stock with the right colors and sizes; customers love its advertised specials and promotions.

Weaknesses: Despite its current market strength, survey responses show Kohl's has a number of areas of vulnerability. Customers complain of its weak overall fashion assortment, lack of service, weaknesses in store design, plus it appears positioned at the very bottom of the fashion spectrum. Kohl's needs to take another look at adding more current, up-to-date fashion to its assortments, and it wouldn't hurt to try and build more customer loyalty through taking a more active role in the community.

LANE BRYANT

Strengths: This chain stands way above all the rest when it comes to most effectively meeting the needs of the large-sized market (confirmed by its score of 91% as being perceived by its primary shoppers as being the best source for "half sizes or large sizes" (the next best score is 29% for Sears). Also customers appreciate the friendly service as they shop for the right in-stock sizes and colors.

Weaknesses: Stores could be a great deal better when it comes to all aspects of layout and decor, coupled with a perceived lack of a real fashion position; such weaknesses could make the chain vulnerable to a well-organized rival coming on strong with its own large-size fashion strategy.

Lord & Taylor

Strengths: Somehow manages to exude strong age appeal for both the 24 to 44 and the 45 to 54 age cohorts; maybe that's because of its perceived strength in offering conservative and classic clothing, in the right sizes, colors and price ranges, in-stock, and at the "best value for the money," including special promotions and sales. Petites also like it because of the good range of merchandise it carries.

Weaknesses: Could do a better job when it comes to store design (including signage and lighting, and adding just plain fun), providing more unique merchandise, heightened community involvement, more effective advertising, and improved levels of service. Customers claim offering more large-size merchandise would be good too (which also makes sense giving its strong appeal to slightly older consumers). However, even without fixing these weaknesses Lord & Taylor's significant strengths indicate it could benefit from having one or two more stores in the market area.

■ The benefits sought by consumers differ dramatically by type of retailer. For example, shoppers look to mass merchandisers for low prices, convenient locations, and a good returns/exchange policy; at specialty stores for up-to-date fashions; at upscale department stores for high-quality fashions and the best salespeople; and at traditional department stores for the largest assortment and current fashions.

■ Positioning encompasses both the perceived strengths *and* the perceived weaknesses of various retailers in contrast to other firms: "By carefully examining their own strengths and weaknesses and those of their competition, and through carefully observing other shifts in consumer behavior and preference, retailers may identify significant opportunities for not only increasing their own market share, but also their overall sales and profitability. Such returns would appear to be well worth the effort."[9] Figure 2-8 indicates the strengths and weaknesses for six of the retailers examined in this study.

Selection of Objectives

The combination of objectives a retailer selects will greatly influence the development of an overall strategy. A firm that clearly defines objectives and devises a strategy to achieve them improves its chances of success.

[9]"Shopping Chicago: Who Fills Women's Apparel Needs?" p. 20B.

An example of a retailer with clear goals and a proper strategy to attain them is Hannaford Bros., which has over 140 stores in Maine, New Hampshire, Vermont, Massachusetts, upstate New York, Virginia, and the Carolinas. According to its Web site (http://www.hannaford.com):

A publicly held company since 1971, Hannaford stock is traded on the New York Stock Exchange. In 1995, Hannaford marked the forty-seventh consecutive year that dividends were paid on its common stock and the thirty-third consecutive year that the dividend increased. We're known for our discipline in managing expenses and have moved much of our business on to the *productivity loop*—constantly lowering our cost structure by working smarter, employing technology more effectively, then lowering prices to drive sales, which makes us even more efficient. This has helped keep our earnings growing and our sales increasing faster than most other companies in our industry. Our store formats include combination stores, conventional supermarkets, and conventional supermarkets with pharmacy. Well over half of the stores have in-store pharmacies.

Hannaford is a preferred employer, offering competitive wages and valuable benefits to its associates, who are empowered to make decisions and take on greater responsibility. The policy of promoting from within opens career opportunities to interested associates, and the company's strong training and development programs help associates gain the skills they need to succeed. Hannaford is also a leader in environmental activities. The company's award-winning Earth Matters programs improve the environment and substantially cut our waste stream and costs.

IDENTIFICATION OF CONSUMER CHARACTERISTICS AND NEEDS

The retailer or prospective retailer next must identify consumer characteristics and needs. The customer group that a retailer seeks to attract and satisfy is called the **target market.** In selecting its target market, a firm may use one of three techniques: **mass marketing,** selling goods and services to a broad spectrum of consumers; **concentrated marketing,** zeroing in on one specific group; or **differentiated marketing,** aiming at two or more distinct consumer groups, with different retailing approaches for each group.

Conventional supermarkets and drugstores and traditional shoe stores are examples of retailers defining their target markets broadly. They have a wide assortment of medium-quality items sold at popular prices. In contrast, a small upscale men's shoe store or a fruit and vegetable store exemplifies the retailer selecting a well-defined and specific consumer group and offering a narrow, deep product assortment at above-average prices (or in other cases, below-average prices). A retailer aiming at one segment does not try to appeal to everyone.

Department stores are among the retailers seeking multiple market segments. They cater to several customer groups and provide unique goods and services for each. Accordingly, men's apparel may be sold in a number of distinctive boutiques in the store. Also, large retail chains frequently have divisions that appeal to different market segments. Dayton Hudson Corporation operates traditional department stores for customers interested in full-service and discount department stores for customers interested in low prices.

The choice of target market and the approach for attracting it give direction to a retailer's strategic decisions. See Table 2-4. In addition, a firm can then determine appropriate competitive advantages and allocate financial resources. Most importantly, the value of **competitive advantages**—the distinct competencies of a retailer relative to competitors—must not be overlooked. Why? The selection of a target market and its satisfaction by a unique retail offering are necessary for a retailer's goals to be achieved. Some examples will demonstrate this.

Table 2-4 TARGET MARKETING TECHNIQUES AND THEIR STRATEGIC IMPLICATIONS

TARGET MARKET TECHNIQUES

Strategic Implications	Mass Marketing	Concentrated Marketing	Differentiated Marketing
Retailer's Location	Near a large population base	Near a small or medium population base	Near a large population base
Goods and Service Mix	Wide assortment of medium-quality items	Deep assortment of high-quality or low-quality items	Distinct goods/services aimed at each market segment
Promotion Efforts	Mass advertising	Direct mail, subscription	Different media and messages for each segment
Price Orientation	Popular prices	High or low	High, medium, and low—depending on market segment
Strategy	One general strategy directed at a large homogeneous (similar) group of consumers	One specific strategy directed at a specific, limited group of customers	Several specific strategies, each directed at different (heterogeneous) groups of consumers

Tiffany defines its target market as upper-class, status-conscious consumers. Thus, it situates stores in prestigious shopping areas, offers high-quality products, uses elegant print ads, has extensive customer services, and charges relatively high prices. Kmart describes its target market as middle-class, value-conscious consumers. Thus, it locates in midrange shopping centers and districts, offers national brands and Kmart brands of medium quality, features good values in its ads, maintains some customer services, and charges below-average to average prices. Off-price stores aim at extremely price-conscious consumers. Many locate in discount strip shopping centers or districts, offer national brands (sometimes manufacturer overruns or merchandise not sold by other retailers) of average to below-average quality merchandise, emphasize low prices in ads, offer few or no customer services, and set very low prices. The key to the success of each of these retailers lies in its ability to define customers and cater to their needs in a distinctive manner.

A retailer is better able to select a target market and satisfy customer needs if it has a good understanding of consumer behavior. This topic is discussed in Chapter 7.

OVERALL STRATEGY

After completing a situation analysis, setting objectives, and selecting the target market, a retailer is ready to develop an in-depth overall strategy. This involves two components: those aspects of business the firm can directly affect (such as hours of operation and sales personnel) and those to which the retailer must adapt (such as competition, the economy, and laws). The former are called **controllable variables,** and the latter are called **uncontrollable variables.** See Figure 2-9.

Figure 2-9

Developing an Overall Retail Strategy

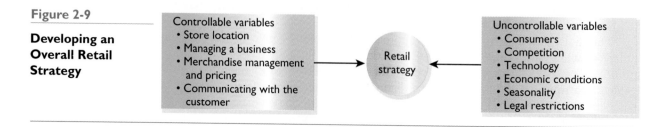

Controllable variables
- Store location
- Managing a business
- Merchandise management and pricing
- Communicating with the customer

Retail strategy

Uncontrollable variables
- Consumers
- Competition
- Technology
- Economic conditions
- Seasonality
- Legal restrictions

A strategy must be prepared with both kinds of variables in mind. The ability of retailers to grasp and predict the effects of controllable and uncontrollable variables is greatly aided by the use of suitable data. In Chapter 8, information gathering and processing in retailing are described.

Controllable Variables

The controllable parts of a retail strategy consist of the basic categories shown in Figure 2-9: choosing a store location, managing a business, merchandise management and pricing, and communicating with the customer. A good strategy integrates these areas so a unified plan is devised and followed. These elements are comprehensively covered in Chapters 9 to 19.

Choosing a Store Location
❏ A retailer has several store location decisions to make. The initial one is whether to use a store or nonstore (e.g., mail-order) format. Next, for store-based retailers, a general location and a specific site are determined. Competitors, transportation access, population density, the type of neighborhood, nearness to suppliers, pedestrian traffic, and store composition are among the factors to be considered in picking a location.

The terms of tenancy (such as rent, operating flexibility, and length of contract) are reviewed and a build, buy, or rent decision made. The locations of multiple outlets, an increasing phenomenon today, may be considered if expansion is a goal. Each of these aspects of location can cause problems if inadequately defined in the strategy phase.

Managing a Business
❏ The second area of strategic planning, managing a business, entails two major elements: the retail organization and human resource management, and operations management. Tasks, policies, resources, authority, responsibility, and rewards are outlined by a retail organization structure. Practices regarding employee hiring, training, compensation, supervision, and so on are instituted by human resource management. Job descriptions and functions are detailed and communicated, along with the authority and responsibility of all personnel and the chain of command.

ETHICS IN RETAILING

At J.C. Penney: A Lack of Oversight Costs It Dearly

Despite earning $56,000 a year as a buyer for J.C. Penney, Jim Locklear had supplemented his earnings with as much as $1.5 million in bribes and kickbacks over a four-year period. Upon being discovered, Locklear admitted to selling the promise of large orders, as well as granting favored accounts such crucial yet confidential information as competitors' bid prices. According to the lawsuit that was filed against him, Locklear even threatened to take business away from one manufacturers' representative and award it to a competitor unless he received a kickback.

Several facets of the Locklear situation are unusual. One, it is relatively rare for the government to prosecute a retail buyer because many retailers are reluctant to bring charges out of fear of adverse public-ity. Two, despite his acceptance of bribes, Locklear was viewed as a first-rate housewares buyer. Under Locklear, J.C. Penney's annual sales of tabletop merchandise rose from $25 million to $45 million. Third, J.C. Penney has not treated suppliers that bribed Mr. Locklear as innocent victims. Instead, J.C. Penney has refused to conduct any additional business with the firms paying monies to him.

Even after this incident, J.C. Penney does not plan a major overhaul of its ethics code beyond a recent revision prohibiting buyers from accepting hunting or fishing trips as gifts. In contrast, Wal-Mart's ethical code does not even allow a buyer to accept a cup of coffee from a vendor.

Source: Andrea Gerlin, "How a Penney Buyer Made Up to $1.5 Million on Vendors' Kickbacks," *Wall Street Journal* (February 7, 1995), pp. A1, A16.

Operations management requires efficiently and effectively performing the tasks and policies necessary to satisfy customer, employee, and management goals. The financial dynamics of operations involve asset management, budgeting, and resource allocation. Other specific aspects of operations management include store format and size, space allocation, personnel use, store maintenance, energy management, inventory management, store security, insurance, credit management, computerization, and crisis management.

Merchandise Management and Pricing ❏ The third aspect of strategic planning deals with merchandise management and pricing. In merchandise management, the general quality of the goods and services offered is determined. Decisions are made as to the width of assortment (the number of different product categories carried) and the depth of assortment (the variety of products carried in a given category).

Policies are set with respect to how innovative the retailer is going to be in introducing new items. Criteria for buying decisions (how often, what terms, which suppliers, and so on) are established. Forecasting, budgeting, and retail accounting procedures are outlined, as is the level of inventory for each type of merchandise carried. Finally, the retailer devises procedures to assess the success or failure of each item sold.

With regard to pricing, a retailer chooses from among several pricing techniques (such as leading/following, cost-plus/demand-oriented, and so on); and it decides what range of prices to charge, consistent with the firm's image and the quality of goods and services offered. The number of prices within each product category is determined, such as how many prices of candy to carry. Psychological pricing may be used. And the use of markdowns is planned in advance.

Communicating with the Customer ❏ The fourth area of planning involves building and maintaining a distinctive image, as well as the promotion techniques deployed. As mentioned earlier, image is critical for retailers. Therefore, a distinctive and desirable (by the target market) image is sought. This image can be created and sustained by applying several techniques.

The physical attributes, or atmosphere, of a store and its surrounding area greatly influence consumer perceptions of a retailer. The impact of the storefront (the building's exterior) should not be undervalued, as it is the first part of a store seen by the customer. Inside the store, layouts and displays (the arrangement and positioning of merchandise), wall and floor colors, lighting, scents, music, and the kind of sales personnel also contribute to store image.

Customer services and community relations generate a favorable image for the retailer. Customer services are such things as parking, gift wrapping, a liberal return policy, extended hours in busy seasons, layaway plans, alterations, credit, and phone and mail sales. Community relations are enhanced by involvement in civic activities, donations to charity, and so on.

The right use of promotional techniques enhances a firm's sales performance. Techniques can range from inexpensive flyers for a supermarket or take-out restaurant to an expensive national ad campaign for a franchise chain. Three forms of paid promotion are available: advertising, personal selling, and sales promotion. In addition, a retailer can obtain free publicity when stories about the firm are written, televised, or broadcast.

The preceding discussion outlined the basic controllable portions of a retail strategy. Yet, uncontrollable variables must also be kept in mind while setting up a strategy. A discussion of these variables is next, and Chapter 3 examines the challenging environment facing retailers.

Uncontrollable Variables

The uncontrollable parts of a retailing strategy are composed of the factors shown in Figure 2-9: consumers, competition, technology, economic conditions, seasonality, and legal restrictions. Farsighted retailers monitor the external environment and adapt the controllable parts of their strategies to take into account elements beyond their immediate control. The uncontrollable nature of these variables is explained next.

Consumers ❑ Once a target market is picked, a firm's strategy is set accordingly. A skillful company knows it cannot alter demographic trends or life-style patterns, impose tastes, or "force" goods and services on people. Rather, that firm learns about its target market and forms a strategy consistent with consumer trends and desires. Selecting a target market is within a retailer's control; but the firm cannot sell goods or services that are beyond the price range of its customers, not wanted, or not displayed or advertised in the proper manner.

Competition ❑ After the type of business and store location are chosen, there is little most retailers can do to limit the entry of competitors. In fact, a retailer's success may encourage the entry of new firms or cause established competitors to modify their strategies to capitalize on the popularity of that retailer. An excessive increase in competition would lead a company to re-examine its strategy, including the definition of its target market and its merchandising focus, to ensure that it sustains a competitive advantage. An error too many retailers make is assuming that being first in a location is a sufficient advantage in fighting off new entrants. Yet, a continued willingness to satisfy the target market better than any competitor is fundamental.

Technology ❑ In today's world of retailing, technology is advancing rapidly. Advanced computer systems are available for inventory control and checkout operations. Electronic surveillance may be used to reduce shoplifting. Bar coding, in growing use, is revolutionizing merchandise handling and inventory control. There are more efficient ways for warehousing and transporting merchandise. Toll-free 800 numbers are more popular than ever before for consumer ordering. And, of course, there is the Internet. Nonetheless, some advancements are expensive and may be beyond the reach of small retailers. For instance, although small firms may be able to use computerized checkouts, they will probably be unable to use fully automated inventory systems or toll-free numbers. As a result, their efficiency may be less than that of larger competitors. They must adapt by giving more personalized service (because prices may be above average to reflect operating costs).

Economic Conditions ❑ Economic conditions are beyond any retailer's control, no matter how large. Inflation, consumer unemployment, interest rates, tax levels, and the annual Gross Domestic Product (GDP) are just some economic factors with which a retailer copes and which it cannot change. In delineating the controllable aspects of its strategy, a retailer needs to consider and adapt to forecasts about international, national, state, and local economies.

Seasonality ❑ A constraint on certain retailers is the seasonality of goods and services and the possibility that unpredictable weather will play havoc with sales forecasts. Retailers selling sports equipment, clothing, fresh food, travel services, and car rentals cannot control the seasonality of consumer demand or bad weather. A solution to this uncontrollable part of planning may be for such retailers to diversify offerings, such as carrying a goods/service mix with items that are popular in different seasons of the year. For instance, a sporting-goods retailer can emphasize ski equipment and snowmobiles in the winter, baseball and golf equipment in the spring, scuba equipment and fishing gear in the summer, and basketball and football supplies in the fall. The impact of seasonality and weather are reduced by adapting the controllable part of the retail strategy.

Legal Restrictions ❑ All retailers should be familiar with the legal restrictions they face. Table 2-5 shows how each of the four controllable aspects of a retail strategy is affected by the legal environment. A discussion of legislation at the different levels of U.S. government follows.

Table 2-5 THE IMPACT OF THE LEGAL ENVIRONMENT ON RETAILING[a]

Controllable Factor Affected	Selected Legal Constraints on Retailers
Store Location	Zoning laws—Restrict the potential choices for a location and the type of facilities that may be constructed. Blue laws—Restrict the days and hours during which retailers may operate. Environmental laws—Limit the retail uses of certain sites. Door-to-door (direct) selling laws—Limit the hours and manner of business to protect consumer privacy. Local ordinances—Involve fire, smoking, outside lighting, capacity, and other rules. Leases and mortgages—Require parties to abide by stipulations in tenancy documents.
Managing a Business	Licensing provisions—Mandate minimum education or experience requirements for personnel in certain retail businesses. Personnel laws—Involve nondiscriminatory hiring, promoting, and firing of employees. Antitrust laws—Limit mergers and expansion. Franchise agreements—Require parties to abide by legal precedents with regard to purchase terms, customer service levels, etc. Business taxes—Include real-estate and income taxes. Recycling laws—Mandate that retailers participate in the recycling process for various containers and packaging materials. Delivery laws—Penalties for late deliveries are imposed in some states.
Merchandise Management and Pricing	Trademarks—Provide retailers with exclusive rights to the brand names they develop. Licensing agreements—Allow retailers to sell goods and services created by others in return for royalty payments. Merchandise restrictions—Forbid some retailers from carrying or selling specified goods or services. Product safety laws—Prohibit retailers from selling items that have been inadequately tested or that have been declared unsafe. Product liability laws—Allow retailers to be sued if they sell defective products. Warranties and guarantees—Must adhere to federal standards. Lemon laws—Specify consumer rights if products, such as autos, require continuing repairs. Sales taxes—In most states, consumers required to pay state or local taxes on items, in addition to the prices set by retailers. Unit-pricing laws—Require price per unit to be displayed (most often applied to supermarkets). Price-marking laws—Specify that discounted and sale items must be marked properly. Dual pricing—Occurs when the same item has different prices on different containers (to reflect the higher prices of new goods). In some areas, this is not permitted. Collusion—Retailers not allowed to discuss selling prices with competitors under any circumstances. Sale prices—Defined as a reduction from the retailer's normal selling prices. Calling anything else a sale is illegal. Minimum-price and loss-leader laws—Require that certain items not be sold for less than their cost plus a markup to cover retail overhead costs. Price discrimination—Suppliers generally not allowed to offer unjustified discounts to large retailers that are unavailable to smaller ones. Item-price-removal laws—Mandate that prices be marked on each item, as well as on store shelves.
Communicating with the Customer	Truth-in-advertising and -selling laws—Require retailers to be honest and not omit key facts in ads or sales presentations. Truth-in-credit laws—Require that consumers be fully informed of all terms when buying on credit. Telemarketing laws—Intended to protect the privacy and rights of consumers with regard to telephone sales transactions. Comparative advertising—Retailers expected to provide complete documentation when making claims about their offerings versus competitors (e.g., lower prices). Bait-and-switch laws—Make it illegal to lure shoppers into a store to buy low-priced items and then to aggressively try to switch them to higher-priced ones. Inventory laws—Mandate that retailers must have sufficient stock when running sales. Labeling laws—Require merchandise to be correctly labeled and displayed. Cooling-off laws—Allow customers to cancel completed orders, often made by in-home sales, within three days of a contract date. Other restrictions—Prohibit some goods and services from being advertised in certain media (e.g., no tobacco ads on radio or television).

[a]This table is broad in nature and omits a law-by-law description. Many laws are state or locally oriented and apply only to certain locations; the laws in each place differ widely. The intent here is to give the reader some understanding of the current legal environment as it affects retail management. For more specifics, contact the sources named in the chapter.

At the federal level, legislation began in 1890 with the Sherman Act, which was designed to reduce monopolies and restraints of trade. The Clayton Act was enacted in 1914 to strengthen the Sherman Act. Also in 1914, the Federal Trade Commission was formed to deal with unfair trade practices and consumer complaints. The 1930s saw the Robinson-Patman and Miller-Tydings Acts, both aimed at protecting small retailers after the Depression. The Robinson-Patman Act was enacted due to the special discounts the A&P supermarket chain got in purchasing its products. The Miller-Tydings Act (fair trade) sought to limit discounting on the part of some retailers by forcing all retailers to sell fair-traded items at the same prices. This law is no longer in effect.

The Anti-Merger Act was passed in 1950 to limit mergers between large firms. The 1960s and 1970s saw numerous consumer protection acts in such areas as door-to-door sales, product labeling, product safety, packaging, consumer credit, and warranties and guarantees. Although the acts are mostly oriented to manufacturers, they affect retailers using deceptive selling practices and/or selling private-label items. The 1980s were a period of federal deregulation and self-regulation, allowing retailers greater freedom in their operations. The 1990s have seen somewhat more federal activity with the enactment of the Telephone Consumer Protection Act, new Food and Drug Administration rules for food labeling, and the Telecommunications Act of 1996.

At the state and local levels, retailers have many restrictions with which to deal. Zoning laws prohibit firms from operating at certain sites and demand that building specifications be met. Blue laws limit the days or hours during which retailers can conduct business. Construction, fire, elevator, smoking, and other codes are imposed on retailers by the state and city. The licenses to operate some businesses are under state or city jurisdiction. Minimum-price laws sometimes require that specified items not be sold for less than a floor price. Other ordinances restrict direct-selling practices. Many states and municipalities engage in consumer protection; they police retailers from this vantage point. And a number of states and cities have stepped up their efforts to restrict unfair or socially undesirable retailing practices.

A strategy must be pursued in a manner satisfying all levels of government. In the long run, a firm voluntarily adhering to the spirit and letter of the law will maintain a consumer following and be less apt to attract adverse government attention. For more information, contact the Federal Trade Commission (http://www.ftc.gov), state and local

The Implications of NAFTA for Retailers

Supply Chain Directions for a New North America, a report published by the Council of Logistics Management, sees several benefits to retailers from NAFTA—the North American Free Trade Agreement among the United States, Canada, and Mexico. These benefits include reduced import and export barriers, and the standardization of customs procedures.

The report also reminds retailers of the special challenges in servicing the Mexican market. Specifically mentioned are shipper selection criteria and the complexities in meeting legal requirements. Thus, in selecting shippers in Mexico, retailers need to carefully evaluate their ability to safeguard goods while in transit, and poor road conditions in some parts of the country mean that shippers use heavy-duty cushioning.

Retailers need to pay careful attention to Mexican legal restrictions. They must present a Certificate of Origin for each product before it enters Mexico. Goods without a Certificate of Origin are subject to a tariff or can be held up for long periods in Customs. In addition, U.S. products must meet all Mexican labeling regulations to be sold there. Labels have to include in Spanish each item's generic name, trade name, manufacturer, country of origin, and a description of any risk to consumer users. Retailers must adhere their own labels, if manufacturer labels do not provide this information.

Source: Julie Ritzer Ross, "NAFTA: Transforming the Supply Chain," *Stores* (April 1996), p. 64.

regulatory agencies, the National Retail Federation (http://www.nrf.com), the Better Business Bureau (http://www.bbb.org), or a specialized group such as the Direct Marketing Association (http://www.the-dma.org).

Integrating Overall Strategy

At this point, the retailer has finished devising an overall strategy. It has chosen an organizational mission, an ownership and management style, and its goods/service category. Worthwhile long-run and short-run goals have been set. A consumer market has been designated, and its attributes and needs studied. General decisions have been made about store location, managing the business, merchandise management and pricing, and communications efforts. These elements must be coordinated to have a consistent, integrated strategy—and the uncontrollable variables affecting a firm (consumers, competition, technology, economic conditions, seasonality, and legal restrictions) systematically accounted for in the strategy.

The company is ready to perform the specific chores to carry out its strategy productively.

SPECIFIC ACTIVITIES

Short-run decisions are now made and enacted for each controllable part of the retail strategy in Figure 2-9. These actions are known as **tactics** and encompass a retailer's daily and short-term operations. They must be responsive to the uncontrollable environment. Here are some tactical moves a retailer may make:

■ Store location—Trading-area analysis gauges the geographic area from which a firm draws its customers. The level of saturation in a trading area is studied regularly. Relationships with nearby retailers are optimized. Lease terms and provisions are negotiated and fulfilled. A chain carefully decides on the sites of new outlets. Facilities are actually built or modified.

■ Managing a business—There is a clear chain of command from senior managers to entry-level workers. An appropriate organizational structure is set into place. Personnel are hired, trained, and supervised. Asset management tracks assets and liabilities. The budget is spent properly (and throughout the year). Systematic operating procedures are used and adjusted as required.

■ Merchandise management and pricing—The assortments within departments and the space allotted to each department require constant decision making. Innovative firms look for new merchandise and are willing to clear out slow-moving items. Purchase terms may have to be negotiated often, and new suppliers sought. Selling prices reflect the firm's image and target market. Price alternatives can offer consumers some choice. Adaptive actions are needed to sell slow-moving items, respond to higher supplier prices, and react to competitors' prices.

■ Communicating with the customer—The storefront and display windows, store layout, and merchandise displays need constant attention. These elements help gain consumer enthusiasm, present a fresh look, introduce new product categories, and reflect changing seasons. Ads are designed and then placed during the proper time and in the appropriate media. The deployment of sales personnel varies by merchandise category and season.

Consumer demand, competitor actions, economic conditions, technological advances, seasonality, and legal restrictions especially need to be weighed when making tactical decisions. The essence of excellence in retailing is building a sound strategy and fine-tuning it as the environment changes. A retailer that stands still is often moving backward. Tactical decision making is discussed in much greater detail in Chapters 9 through 19.

As noted, a firm's strategy and tactics should be evaluated and revised continuously. In **CONTROL** the **control** phase, a semiannual or annual review of the company takes place (Step VI in Figure 2-1), with the strategy and tactics (Steps IV and V) that have been developed and implemented being evaluated against the business mission, objectives, and target market (Steps I, II, and III) of the firm. This procedure is called a retail audit, which is a systematic process for analyzing the performance of a retailer. The retail audit is covered in Chapter 20.

A retailer's strengths and weaknesses are revealed as performance is assessed. The aspects of a strategy that have gone well stay in place; those that have gone poorly are revised, consistent with the mission, goals, and target market. If possible, minor adjustments are made, because major ones may confuse customers. The adjustments are reviewed in the firm's next retail audit.

During each stage in a strategy, an observant management receives signals or cues, **FEEDBACK** known as **feedback,** as to the success of that part of the strategy. Refer to Figure 2-1. Positive feedback includes high sales, no problems with the government, and low employee turnover. Negative feedback includes falling sales, government sanctions (like fines), and high turnover.

Retail executives look for positive and negative feedback so they can determine the causes and capitalize on opportunities or rectify problems.

Summary

1. *To show the value of strategic planning for all types of retailers* A retail strategy is the overall plan or framework of action that guides a firm. It consists of situation analysis, objectives, identification of a customer market, broad strategy, specific activities, control, and feedback. Without a well-conceived strategy, a retailer can stumble and be unable to cope with environmental factors.

2. *To explain the steps in strategic planning for retailers* Situation analysis is the candid evaluation of the retailer's opportunities and potential problems. It looks at the firm's current position and where it should be heading. This analysis consists of defining and adhering to an organizational mission, evaluating ownership and management options, and outlining the goods/service category. An organizational mission is a commitment to a type of business and a place in the market. Ownership/management options include sole proprietorship, partnership, or corporation; starting a business, buying an existing one, or being a franchisee; owner management or professional management; and being centralized or decentralized. The goods/service category depends on personal abilities, financial resources, and time resources.

Objectives are the retailer's long- and short-run goals. A firm may pursue one or more of these objectives: sales (growth, stability, and market share), profit (level, return on investment, and efficiency), satisfaction of publics (stockholders, consumers, and others), and image/positioning (customer and industry perceptions).

Next, consumer characteristics and needs are determined, and a retailer selects a target market. A firm can sell to a broad spectrum of consumers (mass marketing); zero in on one customer group (concentrated marketing); or aim at two or more distinct groups of consumers (differentiated marketing), with separate retailing approaches for each.

A broad strategy is then formed. It involves controllable variables (aspects of business a firm can directly affect) and uncontrollable variables (factors a firm cannot control and to which it must adapt).

After a general strategy is set, a firm makes and implements short-run decisions (tactics) for each controllable part of that strategy. These actions must be forward-looking and responsive to the external environment.

Through a control process, strategy and tactics are evaluated and revised continuously. A retail audit systematically reviews a strategy and its execution on a regular basis. Strengths are emphasized and weaknesses minimized or eliminated.

An alert firm seeks out signals or cues, known as feedback, that indicate the level of performance at each step in the strategy.

3. *To examine the individual controllable and uncontrollable elements of a retail strategy* There are four major controllable factors in retail planning: store location, managing a business, merchandise management and pricing, and communicating with the customer. The principal uncontrollable variables affecting retail planning are consumers, competition, technology, economic conditions, seasonality, and legal restrictions.

4. *To present strategic planning as a series of integrated steps* Each of the stages in a retail strategy needs to be performed, undertaken sequentially, and coordinated in order to have a consistent, integrated, unified strategy.

Key Terms

retail strategy (p. 30)
situation analysis (p. 30)
organizational mission (p. 30)
sole proprietorship (p. 32)
partnership (p. 33)
corporation (p. 33)
goods/service category (p. 34)
objectives (p. 39)

image (p. 41)
positioning (p. 42)
mass merchandising (p. 42)
niche retailing (p. 42)
bifurcated retailing (p. 43)
target market (p. 45)
mass marketing (p. 45)
concentrated marketing (p. 45)

differentiated marketing (p. 45)
competitive advantages (p. 45)
controllable variables (p. 46)
uncontrollable variables (p. 46)
tactics (p. 52)
control (p. 53)
feedback (p. 53)

Questions for Discussion

1. Why is it necessary to develop a thorough, well-integrated retail strategy? What could happen if a firm does not develop such a strategy?
2. How would situation analysis differ for a small retailer and a large retailer?
3. What are the pros and cons of starting a new business versus buying an existing one?
4. Develop a checklist to help a prospective retailer choose the proper goods/service category in which to operate. Include personal abilities, financial resources, and time demands.
5. Why do retailers frequently underestimate the financial and time requirements of a business?
6. Draw and explain a positioning map showing the kinds of retailers selling bicycles.
7. Differentiate between mass merchandising and niche retailing. Why is it possible for both approaches to succeed?
8. Discuss local examples of retailers applying mass marketing, concentrated marketing, and differentiated marketing.
9. Marsha Hill is a maitre d' at a popular French restaurant. She has saved $100,000 and wants to open her own restaurant. Devise an overall strategy for Marsha, including each of the controllable factors listed in Figure 2-9 in your answer.
10. A competing retailer has a better location than yours. It is in a modern shopping center with a lot of customer traffic. Your store is in an older neighborhood and requires customers to travel a great distance to reach you. How could you use a merchandising, pricing, and communications strategy to overcome your disadvantageous location?
11. How could each of these minimize the effects of seasonality?
   a. Outdoor furniture store.
   b. Mail-order fruit business.
   c. College bookstore.
12. Describe how a retailer can use fine-tuning in strategic planning.
13. How are the control and feedback phases of retail strategy planning interrelated?
14. Should a service-oriented firm (such as a bank) use the strategic planning process differently from a goods-oriented firm (such as a home appliance firm)? Why or why not?

Web-Based Exercise:

BETTER BUSINESS BUREAU (http://www.bbb.org)

Questions

1. Describe the range of services offered by the Better Business Bureau for final consumers. For retailers.
2. An apparel retailer has been able to purchase 500 cashmere coats from a major designer. As part of the negotiations, the retailer has agreed not to state the designer's brand or suggested list price in any advertising. However, the manufacturer is free to list the coat's comparative value. What must the retailer do to comply with the Better Business Bureau's code of advertising with regard to comparative value?
3. Develop a policy for effectively handling consumer complaints for a furniture retailer. Most of the complaints involve either late delivery of goods (due to a manufacturer's late shipment) or defective furniture.
4. What are the pros and cons of the Better Business Bureau's alternative dispute resolution program for cars?

**CASE I
Dolphin Bookstore: Development of a Goods/ Services Strategy***

Dolphin Bookstore was founded in 1946 in Port Washington, New York, an affluent Long Island suburb. The store, located on the town's main shopping street, was purchased in 1972 by Dorothea Vunk, an employee of the store's original owners. She ran the store with the part-time assistance of her husband and two daughters.

Although Vunk was able to pay off the loan for the store after 5 years of ownership, it was never a financial success. Much of the reason for the store's continued existence was the long hours worked by Dorothea Vunk and her family members. Yet, she had little understanding of the basics of buying, cash flow management, promotion, and strategic planning. She ran the store primarily to "make friends and sell a few books along the way."

In January 1982, Patty Vunk purchased the store from her parents upon their retirement. Unlike her parents, who had an eclectic selection of titles, Patty Vunk sought to rationalize the store's stock. All goods purchased had to fit into one of four basic categories: a personalized selection of book titles, children's books, distinctive cards and stationery items, and specialized gift items that convey feelings. Patty Vunk sought to stock only book titles that she could recommend to customers. She reasoned that if she read and then liked a particular title, she could better communicate its contents to her customers. She also planned to have a strong selection of children's books, an area neglected by many large chain-based bookstores. In addition to children's books, Patty stocked plush toys that coordinated with very popular books. This strategy enabled Vunk to receive higher profit margins from the sale of toys, to attract additional customers, and to increase customer purchases. A third focus was on a handpicked, unique selection of greeting cards, holiday items, and correspondence items. Lastly, Patty Vunk wanted to sell gift items that conveyed emotional thoughts or feelings. The store's atmosphere was renovated to reflect its products and new target market.

Unfortunately, the building was sold just as Patty Vunk was completing renovation on the store's interior. The new owners informed her that they would not renew the lease and that they did not understand why she was doing all this work when her lease expired in a little over 2 years. Vunk then knew she had a little over 2 years to build her business to the point where the profits could sustain a significant increase in rent at another site. She began to focus her energies on finding a new store location in Port Washington.

It took close to 2 years for Patty Vunk to find new retail space in town that met her criteria regarding minimum store size, pedestrian traffic, parking facilities, and rental costs. When she found the new space, she immediately envisioned how the new store should be laid out. In 1989, she moved to the new location, which was three blocks from her original store, just as the lease on the original store expired.

*This case was prepared and written by Professor Carolyn Predmore, Manhattan College.

CASE 1
(Continued)

Patty Vunk's current store builds on the goods/services of the previous store. In addition, she has instituted a well thought-out promotional strategy that consists of regular advertising in Port Washington's local weekly newspapers, the hosting of book signings and author discussions, and direct mail promotions. For example, she runs four special promotions per year to a targeted group of customers. This approach is so successful that it results in purchases from 7 percent to 8 percent of the targeted population. Patty is now thinking of developing a Web site.

Patty Vunk has been so successful that she has expanded her store twice (it is now three times larger than it was in 1989 and ten times larger than the original location). The store has also managed to withstand the competition from both a discount bookstore and a Barnes & Noble chain store unit (that features a wide selection of books, discounted prices, an in-store Starbucks coffee bar, and a "stay and read for as long as you want" philosophy).

Questions

1. Evaluate the appropriateness of the Dolphin Bookstore's four-point goods/service category definition.
2. How can Patty Vunk lower the time demands associated with her running a bookstore?
3. How can Dolphin Bookstore better compete against a Barnes & Noble store that offers low prices, long store hours, and an in-store coffee bar?
4. Should Patty develop a Web site? Explain your answer.

CASE 2
Fred Meyer: Using a One-Stop Shopping Strategy and Devising a Corporate Philosophy[†]

When Fred G. Meyer founded his company in the 1920s, one of the great ideas he implemented involved the one-stop shopping format. Today, the average Fred Meyer store has over 225,000 items including such diverse products as produce, frozen foods, diamond rings, home electronics, fashion apparel, home and garden supplies, and housewares. And the company has a state-of-the-art Web site (http://www.fred-meyer.com).

The terms *supermarket, drugstore, department store, home improvement center,* and *specialty store* can all be applied to some portion of a typical Fred Meyer store. Unlike discount department stores, each department within a Fred Meyer store has a broad and deep product mix that features both manufacturer and private brands. However, in a strategy similar to many discount department stores, Fred Meyer stores encourage cross-shopping between departments, and utilize a self-service format with a common checkout. Although some discount department stores have separate departmental managers, most departments in Fred Meyer stores are managed by a single manager ("store director"). This manager has the authority to tailor his or her store's merchandise selections to the needs of a community.

Fred Meyer, based in Portland, Oregon, is the dominant retailer in one of the fastest-growing regions of the United States. Even though close to 500 new competitors' stores have opened in its trading areas in the past five years, Fred Meyer's current management believes that its stores are less vulnerable to new competitors because no single competitor can affect the entire store. Fred Meyer's one-stop shopping approach is also an important competitive advantage for single-parent households and families where both spouses work.

[†]The material in this case is drawn from *Fred Meyer 1995 Annual Report*; and *Fred Meyer 10K for the Fiscal Year Ended February 3, 1996*.

CASE 2
(Continued)

Fred Meyer plans to stay dominant in the Pacific Northwest (which is comprised of Oregon, Washington, Utah, Alaska, Idaho, Montana, and California) by opening an average of 5 new one-stop shopping stores per year over the next several years. In 1996, it had 102 one-stop stores and 34 specialty stores (mostly jewelry stores located in regional shopping malls).

Fred Meyer constantly strives to improve its efficiency. For example, through improvements in distribution and in marketing information systems, it is now able to carry 225,000 different products in its current 150,000 square foot prototype stores. In contrast, its 1991 prototype store needed a 190,000 square foot structure to accommodate the same number of items. The smaller store size format lets Fred Meyer reduce its energy costs, lower its rental costs, and be able to sublease owned properties. For example, as a result of increased distribution efficiencies, Fred Meyer has been able to increase its tenant revenues by over 80 percent since 1991.

In 1995, Fred Meyer's total sales were $3.43 billion, up 9.6 percent from 1994; its net income increased to $30.3 million from $17.1 million for the corresponding time period. And during 1995, Fred Meyer opened 6 additional stores, remodeled 8 older ones, opened a new 600,000 square foot distribution center, and upgraded its marketing information system.

Table 1 outlines Fred Meyer's present corporate philosophy. It parallels the philosophy of Fred G. Meyer, who was active in running the business until his death in 1978. According to Fred G. Meyer, "Always strive to offer Customers the service, selection, quality, and price that satisfies them, for by doing that we will serve our Customers well and continue to prosper and grow."

Table 1   THE FRED MEYER CORPORATE PHILOSOPHY

At Fred Meyer we are governed by the beliefs that:

■ Customers are essential, for without them we would have no business. Customers shop most where they believe their wants and needs will be satisfied best.

■ Satisfactory profits are essential, for without profits our business can neither grow nor satisfy the wants and needs of our Customers, employees, suppliers, shareholders, or the community.

■ Skilled, capable, dedicated employees are essential, for the overall success of our business is determined by the combined ideas, work, and effort of all Fred Meyer employees.

Based on these beliefs we are committed to:

■ Serving customers so well that after shopping with us they are satisfied and want to shop with us again.

■ Operating our business efficiently and effectively so we earn a satisfactory profit today and in the future.

■ Providing an environment that encourages employees to develop their abilities, use their full potential, and share ideas that further the success of the business so they gain a sense of pride in their accomplishments and confidence in their abilities.

We believe that by following this philosophy we will satisfy Customers and earn their patronage, provide for the profitable growth of the company, and enrich the lives of Fred Meyer employees and their families.

Source: Fred Meyer 1995 Annual Report, inside cover page.

CASE 2
(Continued)

Questions
1. Evaluate Fred Meyer's corporate philosophy statement.
2. Although Fred Meyer opened his first store in the 1920s, the chain became a public corporation in 1960. Discuss the pros and cons of the corporate form of ownership.
3. Describe Fred Meyer's positioning strategy.
4. What are Fred Meyer's competitive advantages?

Video Questions on Fred Meyer
1. Discuss the other retail innovations created by Fred G. Meyer.
2. How did Fred Meyer adapt to a changing environment between the 1920s and 1990s?

3

The Contemporary Challenges Facing Retailers

As the U.S. sales growth of Ben & Jerry's super premium ice cream has tapered off, sales in Japan have soared. Yet, when a major distributor offered to expand operations even further in Japan, he was rebuffed. Why? Ben & Jerry's board of directors believed the distributor lacked a strong reputation in backing social causes. According to the president and chief executive officer of Ben & Jerry's, "The only clear reason to take the opportunity was to make money."

In recent years, the firm's managers have also openly debated whether to expand efforts in France due to the French government's use of the South Pacific for nuclear testing. One of the company's co-founders wanted to stay out of France unless Ben & Jerry's ads in that country took a stand against the government's nuclear testing. Although Ben & Jerry's eventually entered the French market (without the antitesting ads), some analysts regarded the effort as half-hearted due to its overall concern for social issues.

CHAPTER OBJECTIVES

1. To review the broad challenges facing today's retailers—and show the crucial nature of both customer relationships and channel relationships in a highly competitive marketplace
2. To consider the challenge of implementing technological advances in retailing
3. To discuss the ethical challenges in retailing
4. To study how retail institutions are evolving in response to the challenges they face
5. To look at the challenging international dimension of retailing

Some retailing experts feel the Japanese distributor and French market entry examples highlight the major struggle that has existed within Ben & Jerry's board of directors. On one side of the struggle are Ben Cohen and Jerry Greenfield, the co-founders who collectively own 42 percent of the voting stock. They are both active in social causes and openly favor slower growth so as not to harm their local community or employee relations. On the other side are the top executives who receive much of their overall compensation from stock options, newly hired professional managers, and stockholders who favor faster growth.

The new professional managers have instituted cost controls, budgets, and a new product development department. Nonetheless, Ben & Jerry's is still far from a traditional company. Ben and Jerry drive Harley-Davidson motorcycles to work, many employees favor T-shirts, and the firm gives three free pints of ice cream a day to each of its employees. Ben & Jerry's has also maintained its very progressive, socially minded agenda. The firm, for instance, donates 7.5 percent of its pre-tax profits to social causes, purchases higher-cost milk and cream from Vermont dairies to foster local employment, and uses organic fruits and nuts, whenever possible. While in the past it limited the chief executive's compensation to no more than 7 times the lowest-paid worker's, it recently upgraded this compensation to 14.5 times the lowest-paid worker's.[1]

---

[1]Paul C. Judge, "Is It Rain Forest Crunch Time?" *Business Week* (July 15, 1996), pp. 70–71; and Joseph Pereira, "Ben & Jerry's Finds New CEO in Gun Industry," *Wall Street Journal* (January 3, 1997), pp. B1, B3.

OVERVIEW

To succeed in the long run, a retail strategy must anticipate and adapt to the changing business environment. As such, a good firm fully analyzes emerging opportunities and threats—its challenges. **Opportunities** are the marketplace openings that exist because other retailers have not yet capitalized on them. Ikea does well because it is the pioneer firm in offering a huge selection of furniture at discount prices. **Threats** are environmental and/or marketplace factors that can adversely affect retailers if they do not react to them (and sometimes, even if they do). Single-screen movie theaters have virtually disappeared in some areas because they have been unable to fend off inroads made by multiscreen theaters.

A firm needs to spot and adapt to trends early enough to satisfy its target market and stay ahead of competitors, yet not so early that the target market is unready for changes or that false trends are perceived. A late response to trends could mean a firm might miss out on profitable opportunities but minimize its risks. Proper strategic planning takes into account the nature of environmental factors in terms of their certainty of occurrence and magnitude of change, their effect on a retailer's business, and the time required for a retailer to react properly.

Marketplace challenges vary in terms of certainty of occurrence. For example, population size can be forecast more accurately than average household income because the former relies on birth- and deathrates (which can be estimated with relative precision), while the latter depends on the unemployment rate, labor productivity, the level of inflation, the amount of imports, and other factors (which are tougher to predict). When forecasts are accurate, future planning is simplified; with uncertain forecasts, retailers need to be more careful in their strategies.

Greater strategy modifications are needed if a marketplace factor's magnitude of change is high. Thus, beauty salons are enacting significant strategy revisions to adjust to the steady rise in working women. And hardware and other retailers are reacting to the rise in do-it-yourselfers.

The time a retailer requires to react to marketplace challenges depends on the aspect of its strategy needing modification. Merchandising strategy shifts—such as stocking an unexpectedly popular fad item—are much more quickly enacted than adjustments in a firm's overall locational, pricing, or promotion strategy. In addition, a new retailer can adapt to trends more readily than existing ones with established images, ongoing leases, and space limitations.

Although the marketplace is often especially challenging for small retailers, ones that prepare well can stand up to the competition from larger firms:

> Chris Zane's competitors don't like him much. While his business is still small ($1.5 million in annual sales), Zane is already New Haven, Connecticut's largest independent bicycle dealer. He's confident. ("Let Wal-Mart come—I'm ready," he boasts.) He's combative. ("I'll put you out of business," he's said to other dealers.) And, most important, he'll do almost anything to attract and keep customers. ("I'll give you lifetime service, guarantee you the lowest price, fix you a cappuccino.") He'd better. Like similar retailers all over America, Zane's Cycles is under siege. Superstores and chains have taken over, leaving specialty bike retailers with only one out of every four sales. "The smaller guys are fading away because they won't get into the game and compete at a higher level," says Craig Seeger, a sales representative who services Zane's. Far from fading, however, Chris Zane has *gained* market share—growing business 25 percent a year by putting into practice every customer-winning tactic he can think up, adapt, or steal. He has read management tomes, sought out gurus, picked suppliers' brains, and studied customer behavior in his store and elsewhere. He aims not to sell to customers but to *own* them.[2]

[2]Donna Fenn, "Leader of the Pack," *Inc.* (February 1996), p. 31.

This chapter looks at these challenges facing retailers and their strategic implications: customer and channel relationships, technological advances, ethical issues, institutional trends, and international retailing.

In Chapter 1, we introduced the concept of relationship retailing, whereby retailers seek to form and maintain long-term bonds with customers, rather than act as if each sales transaction is a new encounter with them. But for relationship retailing to work properly, enduring relationships are needed with other channel members, as well as with customers. Both jobs are challenging.

THE CHALLENGE OF RELATIONSHIP RETAILING

Customer Relationships

More retailers than ever before realize loyal customers are the backbone of their business. Here's why: "In general, the longer a customer stays with a firm, the more that customer is worth. Long-term customers buy more, take less of a company's time, are less price sensitive, and bring in new shoppers. Best of all, there is no acquisition cost. Good long-standing customers are worth so much that sometimes reducing customer defections by as little as five points—from, say, 15 percent to 10 percent yearly—can double profits."[3] Nonetheless, for many retailers, this comment still rings true: "As fast as we bring in new customers, old ones are going out."[4]

When applying relationship retailing, there are three central factors to keep in mind: the customer base, loyalty programs, and defection rates. Let's explore these next.

After the target market is selected, retailers must regularly analyze their customer base in terms of population and life-style trends, the reasons for shopping, the level of loyalty, and the mix of newly sought versus loyal customers:

■ In the United States, the population is aging, a fourth of all households have only one person, a sixth of the populace moves annually, most people live in urban and suburban areas, the number of working women is growing, household income has been rather stagnant for the past 25 years, and the African-American, Hispanic-American, and Asian-American segments are expanding. As a result, gender roles are changing, shoppers are more demanding, market segments are more diverse, there is less interest in shopping, and time-saving goods and services are desirable.

■ According to a recent survey of a cross section of *retailers*, the three leading consumer-oriented factors contributing to retail success are saving customers time and energy, the service and assortments offered, and the uniqueness of the retail experience—with pricing ranked fifth. Yet, while these factors are critical to shoppers, recent *consumer* surveys indicate prices rank higher in prominence. Apparel customers cited "best value for money" first among a long list of shopping criteria and supermarket customers rated "low prices" second among 45 items (after "cleanliness").[5]

■ All consumers are not equal. Some are more worth nurturing long relationships with than others; they represent the retailer's **core customers.** They should be singled out in a firm's data base: "The most practical way to get started is by

[3]Frederick R. Reichheld, "Learning from Customer Defections," *Harvard Business Review*, Vol. 74 (March–April 1996), p. 57.

[4]Jerome A. Colletti and Wally Wood, "Hold On!" *Across the Board* (June 1996), p. 27.

[5]King-Casey, "Retail Success Factors," *Stores* (September 1996), p. 104; "Shopping Chicago: Who Fills Women's Apparel Needs?" *Chain Store Age* (October 1996), Section Three, p. 11B; and "63rd Annual Report of the Grocery Industry," *Progressive Grocer* (April 1996), p. 43. See also Ian P. Murphy, "Study: Apparel Shoppers' Pulse Has Quickened," *Marketing News* (April 14, 1997), p. 34.

answering three overlapping questions. First, which of your customers are the most profitable and the most loyal? Look for those who spend more money, pay their bills more promptly, are reasonable in their service requests, and seem to prefer stable, long-term relationships. Second, which customers place the greatest value on what you have to offer? Some customers will have found that your merchandise, services, and special strengths are simply the best fit for their needs. Third, which of your customers are worth more to you than your competitors? Some customers warrant extra effort and investment. Conversely, no company can be all things to all people. Customers who are worth more to a competitor will eventually defect."[6]

■ A retailer's desired mix of newly sought versus loyal customers depends on that firm's stage in its life cycle, goals, and resources, and its competitors' actions. A mature firm is more apt to rely on core customers, supplementing revenues with new shoppers. An entrepreneur faces the dual tasks of attracting shoppers and building a loyal following; it cannot do the latter without the former. If goals are growth-oriented, the customer base must be expanded by new stores or new non-store efforts, greater advertising, and so on; the challenge is to do this in a way that does not unduly deflect attention away from core customers. It is more costly to attract new customers than to serve existing ones; this does not mean core customers are cost free. When competitors try to take away a firm's existing customers through price cuts and special promotions, the firm may feel it necessary to pursue competitors' customers in the same fashion. Again, it must be careful not to alienate its own core customers.

Customer loyalty (frequent shopper) programs are intended to reward a retailer's best customers, the ones with whom it wants to form long-lasting relationships. To work, they must be well-conceived and complement a sound retail strategy (and not be expected to overcome a poor strategy):

> Because it seems so simple, relationship retailing programs—also called frequency or loyalty programs—are popping up everywhere. These days, it seems, no self-respecting retailer is without one. Spend $100 at Waterstone's Books & Music, get a $10 gift certificate. Purchase a tall espresso at Starbucks in the morning, come back in the afternoon and get the next size larger for the price of a tall. Rack up 20,000 points in the Frequent Diners Club at Lettuce Entertain You restaurants in Chicago, Minneapolis, Phoenix, and Seattle, and receive two round-trip tickets to Honolulu, plus five nights in a hotel. Do relationship retailing programs also work for smaller businesses? Yes, no, and maybe. Relationship retailing is a strategy, not a short-term program. Firms implementing a system of rewards but neglecting to develop a companywide devotion to customer service internally, fail. Businesses believing a generic "Dear Preferred Customer" letter is all it takes to communicate with high-value clientele, fail. Only those retailers delivering genuine benefits based on intimate knowledge of their best customers and creating a "customer-first" mentality at all levels of their organization reap the ultimate benefit: greater customer loyalty leading to greater share of customer.[7]

What do good customer loyalty programs have in common? Their rewards are useful and appealing to customers, and they are attainable in a reasonable time frame. The programs honor shopping behavior (the greater the purchase amounts, the greater the benefits). A data base tracks behavior (it "keeps score"). The programs have features that are unique to the particular retailers and not redeemable elsewhere. There is a range of

[6]Reichheld, "Learning from Customer Defections," p. 61.
[7]Mary Connors, "Dear Preferred Customer," *Dividends* (May 1996), pp. 13–14.

Figure 3-1

Adopting a Frequent Shopper Program

With the Advanced 2000 software system from Innovative Computer Consultants, retailers can easily offer a frequent shopper program. Customer registration and record-keeping functions are performed at the checkout register. The system monitors purchases, so that bonus certificates can be mailed to customers when they have accrued enough points.

prizes to stimulate both short-run and long-run purchases. Communications with customers are personalized. Frequent shoppers are made to feel special. The rules of participation are publicized and rarely changed. The programs are well-promoted and membership is encouraged.[8] See Figure 3-1.

Of those U.S. adults who are members of frequent shopper programs, 56 percent say their decision as to which firm to patronize is affected; and one-fifth of them say their purchases are influenced almost all of the time. Forty-eight percent of U.S. adults have

[8]See Stephanie Seacord, "Who's Been Sleeping in Our Beds?" *Marketing Tools* (March–April 1996), pp. 58–65; Louise O'Brien and Charles Jones, "Do Rewards Really Create Loyalty?" *Harvard Business Review,* Vol. 73 (May–June 1995), pp. 75–82; Joe Brancatelli, "More Bang for Frequent-Flier Bucks," *Fortune* (September 30, 1996), pp. 278–279; and Patricia A. Murphy, "Frequent Shopper Programs Top Quarter of Supermarket Sales," *Stores* (May 1997), pp. 44–46.

participated in a food store loyalty program, 32 percent in a car wash program, and 25 percent in an oil change program.[9]

Let's return to our Zane's Cycle example and see how Chris Zane applies relationship retailing. Zane gives away parts (such as chain links) that would otherwise be priced at $1 or less: "We're not going to chase the pennies. We're looking at the long-term effect. You should see the look on people's faces." He gives five $1,000 scholarships annually to seniors at the local high school, financed by candy machines around town: "We're doing something our competitors aren't and the category killers aren't. If people see that we're taking care of the community, they're more likely to come to us." Zane often lectures to children on bicycle safety and sells helmets at cost. He has a glossy catalog that includes biking tips: "People will come in with things circled several weeks after it comes out." The store markets free cellular phones to customers signing up for Bell Atlantic service activations, highly unusual for a bicycle store—which also has a mahogany coffee bar and a play area for children. And Zane provides a lifetime service guarantee and a 90-day price guarantee program: "Now we can say, 'Buy the bike, ride it, and if you find it for less, we'll take care of it.' Our pricing gained credibility."[10]

Studying customer defections, by tracking data-base statistics or conducting consumer surveys, contributes valuable information. Such analysis shows the firm how many customers it is losing and (with surveys) why they are no longer patronizing a given retailer. Customer defections may be expressed in absolute terms—people who no longer buy from the firm at all—or in relative terms—people who are shopping less frequently with the firm.

Each retailer must determine what its acceptable defection rate is. As previously noted, not all customers are "good" customers. Thus, it may better serve a retailer if shoppers who always look for sales, return items without sales receipts, expect fee-based services to be free, and so on, become defectors. Nonetheless, it is imperative for retailers to avoid the kinds of complaints cited in Table 3-1; they invariably lead to customer defections.

The more knowledge a retailer gathers from defecting customers, the more it can learn and, thus, the better it can serve current and future customers. Unfortunately, too few retailers actually review customer defection data or survey defecting customers, due to the complexity of doing so and an unwillingness to hear bad news.

Channel Relationships

The members of a distribution channel (manufacturers, wholesalers, and retailers) jointly represent a **value delivery system,** which comprises all of the activities needed to develop, produce, deliver, and sell and service particular goods and services. This concept has several ramifications for retailers:

- Each channel member is dependent on the other. When consumers shop with a certain retailer, they often do so because of both the characteristics of that retailer and the products it carries.
- Every value delivery system activity must be enumerated and responsibility assigned for them.
- Small retailers may have to work with suppliers outside of the normal distribution channel in order to acquire the products they want and gain adequate support from suppliers. For example, while large retailers may be able to buy directly from manufacturers, smaller retailers may have to buy through wholesalers that handle small accounts.

[9]Jennifer Fulkerson, "It's in the Customer Cards," *American Demographics* (July 1996), pp. 44–47.
[10]Fenn, "Leader of the Pack," pp. 34–38.

Table 3-1 COMMON CUSTOMER SERVICE COMPLAINTS: TACTICS TO AVOID

True Lies: Blatant dishonesty or unfairness, such as service providers selling unneeded services or purposely quoting fake, "low-ball" cost estimates.

Red Alert: Providers who assume customers are stupid or dishonest and treat them harshly or disrespectfully.

Broken Promises: Service providers who do not show up as promised. Careless, mistake-prone service.

I Just Work Here: Powerless employees who lack the authority—or the desire—to solve basic customer problems.

The Big Wait: Waiting in a line made long because some of the checkout lanes or service counters are closed.

Automatic Pilot: Impersonal, emotionless, no-eye-contact, going-through-the-motions nonservice.

Suffering in Silence: Employees who don't bother to communicate with customers who are anxious to hear how a service problem will be resolved.

Don't Ask: Employees unwilling to make any extra effort to help customers, or who seem put out by requests for assistance.

Lights On, No One Home: Clueless employees who do not know (will not take the time to learn) the answers to customers' common questions.

Misplaced Priorities: Employees who visit with each other or conduct personal business while the customer waits. Those who refuse to assist a customer because they're off duty or on a break.

Source: Adapted by the authors from Leonard L. Berry, "Retailers with a Future," *Marketing Management* (Spring 1996), p. 43. Reprinted by permission of the American Marketing Association.

■ A value delivery system is as good as its weakest link. No matter how well a retailer performs its activities, it will still have unhappy shoppers if suppliers deliver products late, refuse to deal with that retailer, or do not adequately honor warranties.

■ The nature of a given value delivery system must be related to target market expectations. For example, discount shoppers are less interested in lavish store interiors and more interested in name brands, self-service, and low prices, while upscale shoppers are less concerned with low prices and more concerned with personal service, high-quality private brands, and a pleasing store environment.

■ Channel member costs and functions are influenced by each party's role in a value delivery system. Long-term cooperation and two-way information flows foster efficiency.

■ Value delivery systems are more complicated than in the past because of the vast assortments carried by retail superstores, the many forms of retailing, and the use of multiple channels of distribution by some manufacturers.

■ Nonstore retailing (by mail order, phone transactions, and the Internet) requires a different kind of value delivery system than store retailing. Though there is no "store" as such, shoppers have high hopes as to the caliber of catalogs and Web pages, delivery times, product assortments, convenience, and customer service.

■ Due to conflicting goals as to profit margins, shelf space, and so on, some channel members are adversarial—to the detriment of the value delivery system and channel relationships. In recent years, there has been a move toward greater channel power by large retail chains.

When they forge strong channel relationships, members of a value delivery system can better serve each other and the final consumer. According to several industry experts, here's why:

By working together as partners, retailers and their suppliers can provide the greatest value to customers at the lowest possible cost. Take the supermarket industry, in which adversarial relationships still prevail. Industry experts believe seamless partnerships between manufacturers and supermarkets would accelerate the deployment of sophisticated systems such as just-in-time delivery, electronic data interchange, and so-called efficient-consumer-response systems that permit manufacturers to monitor sales in stores and to produce and ship their goods in response to actual consumer demand. Such cooperative systems could squeeze $30 billion in excess costs out of the industry by eliminating superfluous inventory, duplicate functions, and various intermediaries. Moreover, the results witnessed when manufacturers and supermarket chains do cooperate suggest that both sides could increase sales volume by working together to customize offerings at different stores and for different end users. Cooperation between Kraft Foods and supermarket chains such as Publix Super Markets in Florida and Wegmans Food Markets in upstate New York has generated significant returns for both sides.[11]

Though the term *channel partnership* has been used to designate a variety of relationships between buyers and sellers, we define it as an ongoing relationship between a retailer and an independent supplier in which the parties agree on objectives, policies, and procedures for ordering and physical distribution of the supplier's products. Some partnerships also include agreements for packing, price marking, new product development and testing, and joint sales promotion activities, but the primary focus is almost always on ordering and physical distribution. Thus, channel partnerships might also be called *supply partnerships.*[12]

If a retailer and a supplier agree to work as partners, there is a dramatic change in the way they deal with each other, as Richard Bravmen of Symbol Technologies described at a conference: "Traditionally, the relationship between retailers and suppliers (and between those suppliers and their further upstream sources) was, at best, arm's length, if not at times downright adversarial. The manufacturer's objective was to move the greatest possible volume of goods at the highest price. The retailer's goal was to negotiate the lowest price for those goods. Competitive pressures led to the development of a new paradigm. It focused on a simple idea: make sure the right product at the right price is on the shelf when the customer enters the store, while maintaining the lowest possible inventory at all points in the pipeline running from suppliers to retailer. Since this strategy has to do with managing the pipeline of merchandise flow, it requires cooperation between retailers and their upstream suppliers."[13]

One relationship-oriented technique that some manufacturers and retailers are trying to use, especially supermarket chains, is known as **category management.** With this approach, channel members collaborate to maximize product category performance by offering product assortments and prices that better address consumer needs. Products are managed by overall category rather than by individual item. Category management is still in its infancy. It requires a lot of time to implement and analysis can be complicated.

For retailers, category management is based on these principles. First, rather than just buy goods and services, retailers listen more to customers and stock what they really want. Second, profitability is improved because inventory on hand follows demand patterns closer. Third, by being better focused, each product department can become a destination category for shoppers. Fourth, retail buyers are assigned broader responsibilities and more accountability for categorical performance. Fifth, retailers and their suppliers must share data and be more computerized. Sixth, retailers and their suppliers must plan together for the best product assortments.[14] Category management is discussed further in Chapter 13.

Figure 3-2 lists various elements that contribute to effective channel relationships.

[11]Nirmalya Kumar, "The Power of Trust in Manufacturer-Retailer Relationships," *Harvard Business Review,* Vol. 74 (November–December 1996), p. 95.

[12]Robert D. Buzzell, "Channel Partnerships Streamline Distribution," *Sloan Management Review,* Vol. 36 (Spring 1995), p. 86.

[13]Ibid.

[14]Jeanne Whalen, "Category Insight Bonds Marketers to Retailers," *Advertising Age* (October 16, 1995), pp. 24, 26; Pete Hisey, "Category Management: Retail's New Change Maker," *Discount Store News* (May 1, 1995), pp. 22, 43; Carol Radice, "Taking Ownership of Category Management," *Progressive Grocer* (July 1996), pp. 120–124; and Carol Radice, "Moving to Customer Category Management," *Progressive Grocer* (April 1997), pp. 69, 72.

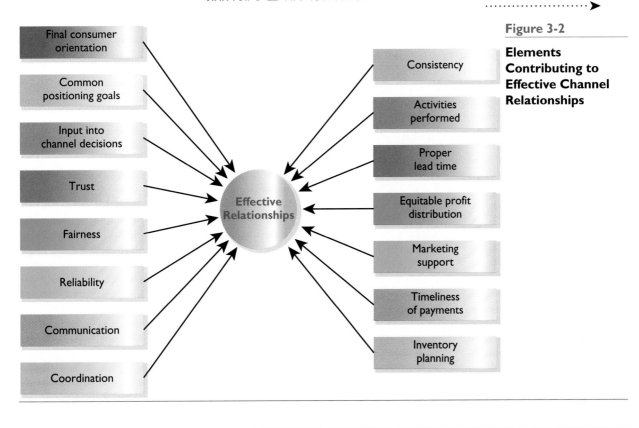

Figure 3-2

Elements Contributing to Effective Channel Relationships

Technological advances are beneficial when the result is an improved information flow between retailers and their suppliers, as well as between retailers and their customers; smoother customer transactions; more efficient operations; faster, more insightful decision making; better inventory management; and greater employee productivity. However, the challenge for retailers is that technology may change rapidly, making it hard to select a new system; it may be difficult to meld new technologies with ones that are already in use, which could even be incompatible; some advances far outpace consumers' readiness for them (such as in-home banking by computer); technological performance may not be as promised by the vendor ("hypeware"); and the advent of the Internet is intimidating to many store-based retailers, which are unsure how to react. In addition, for some small retailers, vendor after-sales support may be lacking and off-the-shelf technology and software may be all that it can afford. Large retailers get better support and more often buy customized technology and software.

This comment neatly sums up the complexities of and concerns about technology:

THE CHALLENGE OF TECHNOLOGY IN RETAILING

Why isn't anyone correct about technological predictions? Because an important new technology changes the standard. It's not a matter of the old world, plus something new. It's a matter of a whole new world. The automobile, telephone, and television all redid the world (and the world of retailing!). Today's information technologies are redoing the world in ways we can't predict, save to say that they're going to be mighty important. And technology creates instant dependency, a panic-stricken feeling of loss when it doesn't work. As a retailer or consumer, have you ever put a card into an ATM machine, and the machine refused to give you the card back? Even though you're sophisticated and educated, you still get that unmistakable surge of technology-induced panic.[15]

[15]James R. Rosenfield, "Technology: Terrific When It Works, Really Awful When It Doesn't," *Direct Marketing* (November 1995), pp. 38–39.

OmniLink and CareMax: Helping Pharmacies Cope with the Managed Care Environment

McKesson is the largest pharmaceutical wholesaler in the United States and Canada. It provides independent pharmacies with a wide variety of services to help them better compete for consumers who are members of managed care networks.

Independent pharmacies participating in McKesson's CareMax program can electronically connect to McKesson via its OmniLink computer network. Here's how the OmniLink network operates. A McKesson-affiliated pharmacy dials in by its PC modem and enters basic data. OmniLink then instantly looks up the consumer's medical plan to determine specific requirements of his or her managed care plan. These often relate to whether a generic drug must be dispensed if available, the initial quantity dispensed, and the number of allowed refills. If requirements are met by the pharmacy, the transaction is sent directly to the managed care provider for processing. If requirements are not met, the pharmacy is alerted so a correction can be made (or the consumer informed that the care plan will not cover a prescription as written). Each participating pharmacy pays $400 to sign up for CareMax. The continuing cost is about 12 cents per transaction.

Besides enabling consumers to continue patronizing their independent pharmacies, the CareMax program provides patients with refill reminders by contacting them if they are more than five days late on a refill. CareMax also gives patients information on new brands and generic equivalents for their specific conditions.

Source: Allene Symons, "McKesson Debuts OmniLink, CareMax Compliance Network," *Drug Store News for the Pharmacist* (March 1996), pp. 47–48.

In general, these four points should be taken into account in studying the application of technological advances in retailing. One, the prices of new technology are constantly falling. Not long ago, only large retailers could truly afford the state-of-the-art equipment then on the market. Now, regardless of their size, virtually every firm can afford a high-powered PC, retail-based computer software, a Web site, and other basic technology. Two, more technology specifically for retailers is available, from software that plans store interiors to data-base management systems to bar coding devices that prepare product labels to energy-saving thermostats. Three, in each firm, the roles of technology and "humans" must be clear and consistent with the organizational mission and style of business. And although technology can be a great aid in providing a high level of customer service, it can also become overloaded and break down (and it is viewed as impersonal or "cold" by some consumers). Setting up new technology needs to be as smooth as possible, with minimal disruptions to suppliers, employees, and, of course, customers. Four, customers expect certain technological advances to be in place, so they can rapidly complete credit transactions, get feedback on product availability, and so on. Retailers have to deploy some advances (such as the two just mentioned) simply to be competitive. By enacting other advances, they can carve out differential advantages—consider the paint store with computerized paint-matching equipment for customers who want to touch up old jobs and the stationery store with an interactive video kiosk that allows people to customize greeting cards.

Throughout *Retail Management,* in the "Technology in Retailing" boxes and chapter discussions, we devote a lot of attention to technological advances. In this chapter, we discuss technology's impact in terms of electronic banking, customer interactions, and retail operations.

Electronic Banking

Electronic banking involves both the use of automatic teller machines (ATMs) and the instant processing of retail purchases. It allows centralized record keeping and lets customers complete transactions 24 hours a day, 7 days a week at a variety of bank and non-bank locations.

At present, in the United States alone, there are 125,000 ATMs (up from 18,500 in 1980 and 60,000 in 1985) and people make 10 billion ATM transactions per year (up from 3.6 billion in 1985), numbers that are sure to keep growing.[16] ATMs are located in banks, shopping centers, department stores, supermarkets, convenience stores, hotel lobbies, and airports; on college campuses; and at various other sites. With "sharing systems," consumers can make transactions at ATMs outside their local banking areas. For instance, the Cirrus and Plus networks each make it possible for consumers to have access to tens of thousands of ATMs worldwide.

Besides its use in typical financial transactions (such as check cashing, deposits, withdrawals, and transfers), electronic banking is increasingly being used in retailing situations. More retailers (especially those previously accepting only cash or check payments, such as supermarkets) are accepting some form of electronic debit payment plan, whereby the purchase price is immediately deducted from a consumer's bank account by computer and transferred into a retailer's account. There are now nearly 1 billion such electronic transfers at U.S. retail stores each year (up from 14 million in 1985), versus about 7.5 billion transactions with traditional credit cards.[17]

One highly touted, but thus far limited in use, new version of debit payment is called the "smart card" by industry observers. The "smart card" being tested in the United States by Visa and MasterCard is similar in approach to the pre-paid phone card, whereby consumers buy computer-coded cards in denominations of $10, $20, $50, $100, and more. Then, as they shop, retail card readers deduct the purchase amounts from the cards. After being used up, the cards are thrown away or they can be recoded. One big limitation for consumers is that few retailers currently handle smart card transactions. Unlike cash payments, retailers pay a fee for smart card transactions. In the future, "smarter" smart cards are expected to be more permanent and embedded with more information (such as frequent shopper points).[18]

The role of individual retailer credit cards is declining due to the popularity of such financial services providers as Visa and MasterCard, which together have 160 million cardholders (many of whom have both cards). Yet, numerous retailers will still stress their own credit programs since they believe they may lose their identities if these programs are used less frequently by customers.

Customer Interactions

Technology is changing the nature of retailer–customer interactions. If applied well, benefits accrue to both parties. If not, there are negative ramifications. Here are several illustrations.

Point-of-sale scanning equipment is widely utilized by supermarkets, department stores, specialty stores, membership clubs, and others—hundreds of thousands of firms in all. Why? By electronically scanning merchandise (rather than having cashiers "ring up" each product), retailers can quickly complete customer transactions, amass sales data, reduce costs, and adjust inventory figures. But there is a serious downside to scanning: the error rate. And this issue can be quite upsetting to consumers. According to a recent study by the Federal Trade Commission (FTC), scanner errors in reading prices occurred 9.2 percent of the time in department stores, 6.3 percent of the time in drugstores, 5.4 percent of the time in home centers, 4.6 percent of the time in discount stores,

---

[16]*Statistical Abstract of the United States 1996* (Washington, D.C.: U.S. Bureau of the Census, 1996), p. 517.

[17]Susan Harrigan, " 'Smart Cards' Are Coming Your Way," *Newsday* (September 29, 1996), p. F8.

[18]Nikhil Deogun, "The Smart Money Is on 'Smart Cards,' But Electronic Cash Seems Dumb to Some," *Wall Street Journal* (August 5, 1996), pp. B1, B8; Richard Cross, "Smart Cards for the Intelligent Shopper," *Direct Marketing* (April 1996), pp. 30–34; and Amy Cortese, "The Ultimate Plastic," *Business Week* (May 19, 1997), pp. 119, 122.

Figure 3-3

**Using Sophisticated
Scanning-System Displays to
Reassure Customers**

3.5 percent of the time in food stores, and 1.8 percent of the time in toy stores. Yet, although consumer perceptions are that errors always lead to overcharges, the FTC found that undercharges were more likely than overcharges.[19] One way to reassure consumers about scanner accuracy is to display more information at the point of purchase. See Figure 3-3.

A novel experiment now underway involves self-scanning, a concept whose future success is by no means certain. Here's how it works:

> Rite Aid (the drugstore chain) is testing a self-checkout system in the Philadelphia market. The system, from Stores Automated Systems, Inc., is stationary, unlike the hand-held scanners Safeway is rolling out in Britain. Rite Aid has placed a single "eXPRESS" self-checkout unit between two conventional POS stations in one store. A second test installation is planned shortly. Shoppers scan their goods across a scanner and place them into a bag positioned on a scale. The total weight of the bagged items is compared to the total weight of the scanned items, ensuring the shopper has indeed scanned all the items bagged. A signature-capture device allows shoppers to pay for purchases by credit or debit card without needing a cashier. A SASI spokeswoman said Rite Aid is testing the system to shorten peak lunch hour and evening rush lines. The Rite Aid test is the first for the SASI system, but she said SASI is negotiating with a supermarket chain interested in using the stations to speed express checkouts.[20]

---

[19]"Department Stores Trail Supermarkets in Scanner Accuracy," *Chain Store Age* (December 1996), p. 125.
[20]"Rite Aid Testing Self-Checkout," *Chain Store Age* (August 1996), p. 76.

Figure 3-4

A Self-Checkout Station

Figure 3-4 shows a SASI eXPRESS station.

Other technological innovations are also influencing how retailers and their customers conclude transactions:

■ With signature capture, shoppers sign their names right on a computer screen. At Sears, "the cardholder uses a special pen to sign a paper receipt—which becomes the cardholder copy—on top of a pressure-sensitive pad that captures the signature, stores it, and displays it on the checkout terminal screen so a clerk can compare it with the one on the back of the credit card. Sears has a brochure explaining the procedure is entirely voluntary and electronic signatures are not stored separately and can be printed only along with the entire sales receipt."

■ At some restaurants, when dinner is over, "The waiter brings the check—and a sleek box that opens like the check presentation folder used by many restaurants, revealing buttons and a miniscreen. He (she) brings it over and disappears discreetly. Following instructions on the screen, you verify the tab, select the payment type (credit card or ATM card), insert the card into a slot, and enter your personal identification number, or PIN, if using an ATM card. You then enter the tip—a specific amount or, if you want the device to figure the tip, a percentage. Completing the transaction triggers a blinking light. Thus summoned, the waiter removes the device; your receipt is printed out from another terminal."

■ "It never fails. You're late, and the customer ahead of you keeps the whole line waiting while he or she slowly fills out a check. That's not a problem at Wal-Mart, where the register has a built-in check printer. A customer hands a blank check to the clerk, who inserts it into the machine. It comes out imprinted with the store's name, the date, and the amount in numbers and text, ready to sign. Other retailers, including Waldenbooks, The Container Store, and Hechinger's, a Maryland-based home improvement chain, do likewise."[21]

[21]Margaret Mannix, "Checkout Tech," *U.S. News & World Report* (February 27, 1995), pp. 71–72.

■ In-home ordering systems rely on three basic formats: TV programming, interactive computer programming, and merchandise catalogs. With a TV-based system, the consumer watches special programming that appears on commercial or cable television and places an order by a toll-free 800 phone number. With an interactive computer-based system, a shopper uses a PC and modem to view graphic or pictorial presentations of goods and services, accompanied by text descriptions and ordering procedures. The person orders by entering a product code number into the PC and indicating the quantity desired. For a merchandise video catalog, the retailer can reproduce (with special video clips inserted) its printed shopping catalog on a videocassette or CD and send it to targeted customers. Shoppers then watch the catalog on a TV and phone orders to the retailer. These formats are covered in more detail in Chapter 6.

One other technological advance, still in its infancy, may be appealing to retailers and consumers—if it works both easily and inexpensively. It involves custom-made clothing:

A person would strip down to underwear and step into a booth equipped with six light projectors and six video cameras. Light would be projected to produce a pattern of horizontal black and white lines on the person. In seconds, the result would be almost 1.4 million data points in three-dimensional space. The measurements would be linked to a garment pattern, which would then be modified. The resulting information would be sent by computer to a laser at an apparel maker, which would custom cut the cloth. Envisioned is a smaller retail space, with most stock consisting of samples people could examine and touch before ordering custom garments based on their body scans. Tied to agile factories, able to switch rapidly from one product to another, the retailer would be able to have the garment ready for a consumer in a few days.[22]

Computerization of Operations

Retailers are computerizing more of their operations, due to better technology, productivity gains, and the affordability of PCs and computer networks. Let us present a variety of examples.

Videoconferencing is being used by retailers such as Home Depot, Wal-Mart, Caldor, and J.C. Penney. It allows them to link store employees with central company headquarters, as well as communicate with vendors. Videoconferencing can be deployed via satellite technology and by PC (using special hardware and software). In both cases, audio/video communications are used to train workers, spread news, stimulate employee morale, and so on.

Wireless telephone communications are aiding retail operations by offering low-cost, secure in-store transmissions. SpectraLink Corporation markets five-ounce pocket phones that let personnel talk to one another anywhere in a store. There are no airtime charges or monthly fees because the SpectraLink system is linked to the retailer's existing phone system. See Figure 3-5.

Through PC-based software such as Retail Pro, many firms are using computerized inventory control. Retail Pro is simple to use and aimed at independent retailers: "With a keystroke, data on stock levels for each store, committed quantities (layaways or special orders), and open purchase orders are instantly displayed. Whether purchasing, receiving, transferring, or selling merchandise, the retailer always has up-to-date inventory information."[23] See Figure 3-6.

---

[22]John Holusha, "Producing Custom-Made Clothes for the Masses," *New York Times* (February 19, 1996), p. D3.

[23]Retail Technologies International company brochure.

Figure 3-5

The SpectraLink Pocket Communications System

Retailers are also using technology to schedule employee work hours, maintain financial records, determine when to discount prices, and otherwise improve their productivity. As one expert noted, "technology done well enhances speed and reliability and reduces opportunities for employee incompetence. Remembering things—that's what computers do better than people. It used to be the salesperson who recognized you. Now a store's electronic systems do."[24]

The ethical challenges facing retailers fall into three interconnected categories: ethics, social responsibility, and consumerism. Ethics relates to the moral principles and values of the firm. Social responsibility has to do with acting to benefit society. Consumerism entails the protection of consumer rights. "Good" behavior is based on not only the firm's practices, but also on the norms and expectations of the community in which it does business.

ETHICAL CHALLENGES IN RETAILING

Ethics

In dealing with their constituencies (customers, the general public, employees, suppliers, competitors, and others), retailers have a moral obligation to act ethically. Furthermore, due to the heightened societal and media attention now paid to firms' behavior and the high expectations people have today, a failure to be ethical may very well lead to adverse publicity, lawsuits, the loss of customers, and a lack of self-respect among company employees. Each of these events happened to Sears several years ago after it was discovered the firm was overcharging auto repair customers because of the overzealous and deceptive sales practices of its employees.

[24]Faye Brookman, "Drug Retailers Turn to Automated Pharmacy Systems," *Stores* (November 1996), p. 36.

Figure 3-6

Retail Pro: Computerized Inventory Control

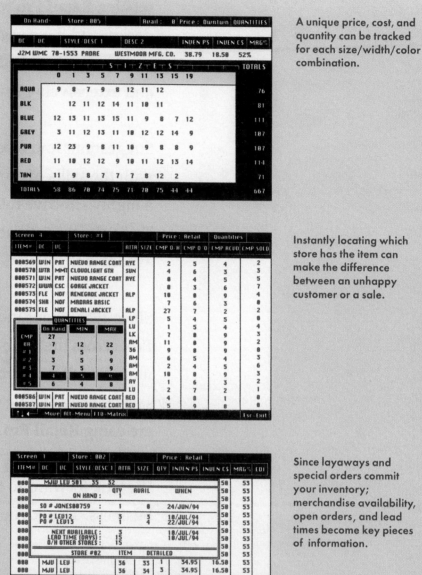

A unique price, cost, and quantity can be tracked for each size/width/color combination.

Instantly locating which store has the item can make the difference between an unhappy customer or a sale.

Since layaways and special orders commit your inventory; merchandise availability, open orders, and lead times become key pieces of information.

When a retailer has a sense of **ethics,** it acts in a trustworthy, fair, honest, and respectful manner with each of its constituencies.[25] For this to occur, the firm's executives must clearly articulate to employees what kinds of behavior are acceptable and which are not—and how unacceptable behavior will be treated. Often, society may deem certain behavior to be unethical but laws may not forbid it. Most observers would agree that practices like these are unethical (and sometimes illegal, too):

■ Raising prices on scarce products after a natural disaster such as a hurricane or earthquake.
■ Not having adequate stock when a sale is advertised.

[25]N. Craig Smith, "Ethics and the Marketing Manager" in N. Craig Smith and John A. Quelch (Editors), *Ethics in Marketing* (Homewood, Illinois: Irwin, 1993), pp. 3–34.

■ Charging high prices in low-income neighborhoods because consumers there do not have the transportation mobility to shop out of their neighborhoods.

■ Selling alcohol and tobacco products to children.

■ Having a salesperson pose as a market researcher when engaged in telemarketing.

■ Defaming competitors.

■ Selling refurbished merchandise as new.

■ Pressuring employees to push high-profit items to shoppers, even if they are not best for them.

■ Selling information from a customer data base.

The best way to avoid unethical acts is for firms to have written ethics codes, clearly communicate them to employees, monitor behavior, and punish poor behavior—and for top managers to be highly ethical in their own conduct.

Many trade associations promote ethics codes to member firms. For example, the Direct Marketing Association (DMA) has a code of ethics that members are encouraged to follow. Here are some of the provisions of the DMA's code:

■ Article 1—All offers should be clear, honest, and complete.

■ Article 5—Disparagement of any person or group on grounds of race, color, religion, national origin, gender, marital status, or age is unacceptable.

■ Article 7—Offers suitable for adults only should not be made to children.

■ Article 9—All direct marketing concepts should disclose the name of the sponsor and each purpose of the contact. No one should make offers or solicitations in the guise of research or a survey when the real intent is to sell goods or services or to raise funds.

■ Article 17—Sweepstakes prizes should be advertised in a clear, honest, and complete way so the consumer may know the exact nature of the offer.

■ Article 28—Merchandise should not be shipped without first receiving customer permission.

■ Article 38—Telemarketers should remove the name of any customer from their telephone lists when requested by the individual.

■ Article 42—Direct marketers should adhere to Better Business Bureau standards and all applicable government laws.[26]

Social Responsibility

A retailer exhibiting **social responsibility** acts in the best interests of society—as well as itself. The challenge is to balance corporate citizenship with a fair level of profits for stockholders, management, and employees. Some forms of social responsibility are virtually cost-free to the firm, such as having employees participate in community events or disposing of waste products in a more careful way. Some are more costly, such as making financial donations to charitable organizations or giving away goods and services to a school. And still others mean going above and beyond the letter of the law, such as having free loaner wheelchairs for disabled persons in addition to the legally mandated wheelchair accessibility to the retailer's premises.

Most retailers know socially responsible acts do not go unnoticed by consumers. Though the acts may not stimulate greater patronage for firms with weak strategies, they can be a customer inducement for retailers otherwise viewed as "me too" entities. It may also be possible to directly profit from good deeds. Consider this: If a retailer donates excess inventory to a charity that cares for the ill, poor, or infants, it can take a tax deduction equal to the cost of the goods plus one-half the difference between the cost

---

[26]*Direct Marketing Association Guidelines for . . . Ethical Business Practices* (New York: Direct Marketing Association n.d.).

Bringing Modern Banking Practices to Poor Communities

In the past, many banks assumed that 80 percent of the South African population was too poor (due to the effects of apartheid) to be profitable customers for them. Today, with the fall of apartheid, most of these banks are aggressively courting the South African mass market. None of them is as focused as E Bank (E for "easy" or for the Xhosa word for "OK").

E Bank keeps its overall costs down by staying away from expensive buildings with fancy lobbies. It has simplified the banking process, offers accounts that require little effort to handle, and concentrates on the most desirable services (such as providing an easy, safe, and economical way to store cash). E Bank also stays away from services that are not required or not easily understood by this segment (such as certificates of deposit or checking accounts). As a result, small accounts cost very little to process.

By using modern automated teller machines, E Bank operates more than thirty branches throughout South Africa, with six of these in small townships. It has about 175,000 clients, many of whom are illiterate. In contrast, as of 1994, only a few hundred upper-middle-class Blacks in all of South Africa had bank accounts. E Bank, as a result, is being watched as a possible prototype for banks in other developing countries.

Source: Ken Wells, "Its New ATMs in Place, a Bank Reaches Out to South Africa's Poor," *Wall Street Journal* (June 13, 1996), pp. A1, A10.

and the retail price of the goods. To apply the rule, the retailer must be a corporation and the charity must use the goods and not sell or trade them.[27]

This is what a cross section of retailers are doing to be socially responsible. McDonald's founded the Ronald McDonald House program, which serves people around the world. Families can stay at a low-cost Ronald McDonald House instead of a more costly hotel when their seriously ill children receive medical treatment outside their own community. Target Stores no longer carries cigarettes; and A&P has removed cigarette vending machines from its supermarkets to reduce sales to minors. Wal-Mart is experimenting with environmental demonstration stores that carry equipment and materials that lessen pollution and conserve energy: "By building and operating these stores, we're performing a real-world test to determine which ideas will help protect our planet and keep energy as efficient for all of us." J.C. Penney requires domestic and foreign suppliers to sign a code of conduct stipulating that underage labor is not used.[28]

The pledge at Hannaford Bros.' Web site (http://www.hannaford.com/community) sums up the role of a socially involved retailer:

Hannaford strongly encourages all associates to participate in events and organizations that make a difference in their communities. You'll find Hannaford associates running United Way and other fund-raising campaigns, leading school and community groups, and contributing time, as well as dollars, to local organizations. Our company policies also reflect our commitment to the community. Wherever we do business, we seek to enhance the quality of life, whether through our Hannaford Charitable Foundation, our sponsorship of organizations and events like museum

[27]Nancy Scarlato, "Give and Take," *Entrepreneur* (December 1996), p. 68.
[28]"The Ronald McDonald House of LI—The House That Love Built," *LIBNews* (April 15, 1996), p. 10; "Target to Stop Selling Cigarettes," *Newsday* (August 29, 1996), p. A65; "A&P Butts Out," *Chain Store Age* (August 1996), p. 37; Marianne Wilson, "Wal-Mart Refines Green Prototype," *Chain Store Age* (March 1996), pp. 30, 32; and Bob Ortega, "Conduct Codes Garner Goodwill for Retailers, But Violations Go On," *Wall Street Journal* (July 3, 1995), pp. A1, A14.

exhibits or performing arts, our nationally recognized environmental programs, or store-giving programs. Our goal is to create a better, healthier, more prosperous future for all of us.

Consumerism

Consumerism involves the activities of government, business, and independent organizations that are designed to protect individuals from practices infringing upon their rights as consumers.[29] This definition is based on the premise that consumers have basic rights and that they should be safeguarded. As stated by President Kennedy 35 years ago, consumers have the right: to safety (protection against hazardous goods and services), to be informed (protection against fraudulent, deceptive, and incomplete information, advertising, and labeling), to choose (access to a variety of goods, services, and retailers), and to be heard (consumer feedback, both positive and negative, to the firm and to government agencies).

Retailers need to avoid business practices violating these rights, and do all they can to understand and protect them. Here are some reasons why:

■ Retailing is so competitive that people will be more apt to patronize firms perceived as customer-oriented and not to shop with ones seen as greedy.

■ Because consumers are more knowledgeable and selective than in the past, retailers must offer fair value, provide detailed information, and be prepared to handle questions and complaints.

■ Consumers are becoming more price-conscious. The popularity of off-price retailing is also heightening consumer awareness of prices.

■ Large retailers are sometimes viewed as indifferent to consumers. They may not provide enough personal attention for shoppers or may have inadequate control over employees (resulting in poor practices and a lack of uniformity from one branch outlet to the next).

■ The use of self-service is increasing, and it can cause frustration for some shoppers.

■ The rise in new technology is unsettling to many consumers, who must learn new shopping behavior (such as how to use automated teller machines).

■ Retailers are in direct customer contact, so they are frequently blamed for and asked to resolve problems actually caused by manufacturers (such as defective products and unclear operating instructions). Thus, retailers must reconcile the interests of their suppliers and their customers. In addition, retailers can pass on safety, information, and other recommendations to suppliers.

Consider the negative consumer feelings about this practice:

Law enforcement officials say each link in the wholesale used-car chain—manufacturer, auto auction, and dealer—can easily shirk liability for meeting requirements for lemon disclosure because enforcement ends at state lines. Since California and Connecticut led the way in 1982, all states have adopted lemon laws. Generally, buyers are allowed to return new vehicles during the warranty period if a defect has not been corrected after four attempts or if the vehicle is out of service for 30 days for any combination of defects. But there are big differences among states about how much information must be disclosed to subsequent buyers of such vehicles.[30]

---

[29]Peter D. Bennett (Editor), *Dictionary of Marketing Terms,* Second Edition (Chicago: American Marketing Association, 1995), p. 62.
[30]Andrea Adelson, "Pushing Lemons Over State Lines," *New York Times* (August 27, 1996), p. D4.

Figure 3-7

Voluntary Product Testing at Target Stores

Target's Responsibility
At Target, toys are an important part of our business. We want the toys you buy to meet Target's and the U.S. Government's high standards of quality, value, and safety. Therefore, we abide by all U.S. Consumer Product Safety Regulations. Target also utilizes an independent testing agency. They test samples of all toys we sell to help ensure your child's safe play.

All toys sold at Target are tested to be certain they are free from these dangers:

Sharp edges

Toys of brittle plastic or glass can be broken to expose cutting edges. Poorly made metal or wood toys may have sharp edges.

Small parts

Tiny toys and toys with removable parts can be swallowed or lodged in child's windpipe, ears, or nose.

Loud noises

Noise-making guns and other toys can produce sounds at noise levels that can damage hearing.

Sharp points

Broken toys can expose dangerous points. Stuffed toys can have barbed eyes or wired limbs that can cut.

Propelled objects

Projectiles and similar flying toys can injure eyes in particular. Arrows or darts should have protective soft tips.

Electrical shock

Electrically operated toys that are improperly constructed can shock or cause burns. Electric toys must meet mandatory safety requirements.

Wrong toys for the wrong age

Toys that may be safe for older children can be dangerous when played with by little ones.

Accordingly, many retailers have devised programs to protect consumer rights without waiting for government or consumer pressure to do so. Following are examples of these actions:

J.C. Penney adopted the "Penney Idea" in 1913 and still adheres to its seven basic concepts:

To serve the public, as nearly as we can, to its complete satisfaction; to expect for the service we render a fair remuneration and not all the profit the traffic will bear; to do all in our power to pack the customer dollar full of value, quality, and satisfaction; to continue to train ourselves and our associates so the service we give will be more and more intelligently performed; to improve constantly the human factor in our business; to reward men and women in our organization via participation in what the business produces; and to test our every policy, method, and act in this way—"Does it square with what is right and just?"[31]

[31]J.C. Penney.

In the 1970s, Giant Food, a leading supermarket chain, hired Esther Peterson (once President Johnson's consumer-affairs advisor) at a rank equal to vice-president. It then devised a consumer bill of rights, patterned on President Kennedy's, to which it has adhered ever since:

1. Right to safety—Giant's product safety standards, such as age-labeling toys, go far beyond those required by government agencies.
2. Right to be informed—Giant has a detailed labeling system and utilizes unit pricing, open dating, and nutritional labeling.
3. Right to choose—Consumers who want to purchase possibly harmful or hazardous products (like cigarettes and foods with additives) can do so.
4. Right to be heard—A continuing dialog with reputable consumer groups is in place.
5. Right to redress—There is a money-back guarantee policy on all products.
6. Right to service—Customers should receive good in-store service.[32]

A number of retailers have voluntarily enacted their own product-testing programs, whereby merchandise is tested for such attributes as value, quality, misrepresentation of contents, safety, and durability before being placed for sale. Sears, J.C. Penney, A&P, Macy's, Target Stores, Montgomery Ward, and Giant Food are just a few of those doing testing. See Figure 3-7.

Among the other consumerism activities undertaken by various retailers are setting clear procedures for handling customer complaints, reviewing advertising-message clarity, sponsoring consumer education programs, and training personnel on how to interact properly with customers.

Consumer-oriented actions are not limited to large chains; small firms can also be involved. A local toy store can separate toys by age category. An independent supermarket can have special displays featuring environmentally safe detergents. A neighborhood restaurant can cook foods in low-fat vegetable oil and emphasize menu items with reduced sodium. A sporting-goods store can give a money-back guarantee on exercise equipment, so people can try it out in their homes.

HOW RETAIL INSTITUTIONS ARE EVOLVING IN RESPONSE TO THE CHALLENGES

The challenges noted in this chapter are having an impact on the nature of retail institutions. Progressive firms know their individual strategies must be modified as retail institutions evolve over time. Complacency is not desirable. For example, many retailers have witnessed shrinking profit margins due to intense competition and consumer interest in lower prices. This drop has put pressure on the firms to tighten internal cost controls and to promote higher-margin goods and services while eliminating unprofitable items.

Here's one view of the institutional challenge:

Until recently, the retailing industry was characterized by lines of trade and retail formats that were easily distinguished due to their pricing and service strategies, but especially because they had distinctive product offers. Consumers went to drugstores for prescription drugs and supermarkets for food. People's expectations about the nature of the shopping experience in each type of store were fairly standard. Today, distinctions among retail sectors have blurred as firms expand their offerings to meet customers' needs for convenience, generate more traffic, and try to get a larger share of customers' pocketbooks. We see increased competition for a number of product categories that once were the exclusive or primary domain of a particular store type. In the current slow-growth environment with increasing constraints on expansion in the number of stores, retailers will continue to look for opportunities to

[32]Giant Food.

Table 3-2 A RETAILING EFFECTIVENESS CHECKLIST

Answer yes or no to each of the following questions. For "no" answers, you should analyze your performance in these areas and determine how to improve efforts.

1. Is a clear long-term organizational mission articulated? _____
2. Is the current status of your firm taken into consideration when setting future plans? _____
3. Is your firm's role in the business system understood? _____
4. Are sustainable competitive advantages identified and pursued? _____
5. Are company weaknesses identified and minimized? _____
6. Is your management style compatible with the firm's way of doing business? _____
7. Is there a logical short-run and long-run approach to your firm's chosen goods/service category (line of business)?
8. Are there specific, realistic, and measurable short- and long-term goals? _____
9. Do these goals guide strategy development and resource allocation? _____
10. Are the characteristics and needs of your target market known? _____
11. Is the strategy tailored to the chosen target market? _____
12. Are systematic plans prepared for each element of your strategy mix?
    a. Location _____
    b. Managing the business _____
    c. Merchandise management and pricing _____
    d. Communicating with the customer _____
13. Are the following uncontrollable factors monitored?
    a. Consumers _____
    b. Competition _____
    c. Technology _____
    d. Economic conditions _____
    e. Seasonality _____
    f. Legal restrictions _____
14. Is your overall strategy integrated? _____
15. Are short-, moderate-, and long-term plans compatible? _____
16. Does your firm know where each merchandise line, for-sale service, and business format stands in the marketplace? _____
17. Are tactics carried out in a manner consistent with the strategic plan? _____
18. Are your strategic plan and its elements adequately communicated? _____
19. Is unbiased feedback regularly sought for each aspect of the strategic plan? _____
20. Is information about new opportunities and threats sought out? _____
21. After a strategic plan is enacted, are company strengths and weaknesses, as well as successes and failures, studied on an ongoing basis? _____
22. Are results studied in a way that reduces your firm's chances of overreacting to a situation? _____
23. Are strategic modifications made when needed? _____
24. Are strategic plans modified before crises occur? _____
25. Does your firm avoid strategy flip-flops (which confuse customers, employees, suppliers, and others)? _____

Source: Adapted by the authors from Joel R. Evans, "Strategic Planning in Retailing: A Necessity in the 1990s," *Retail Strategist* (Number 2, 1991), p. 19.

sell more to the customers they already have. The need to gain a strong differential competitive advantage is greater than ever. Retailers must broaden their perception of who competitors are and act accordingly.[33]

The use of a **retailing effectiveness checklist,** which lets a firm systematically assess its preparedness for the future, can be quite helpful in planning. An illustration of such a checklist is shown in Table 3-2. If a retailer answers no to any of the questions raised in the table, it needs to adjust its strategy to prosper in the future.

Let us see how firms are reacting to the formidable environment by mergers, diversification, and downsizing; cost containment and value-driven retailing; and adaptation tactics.

[33]Linda Hyde, "Cross Competition Escalates Battle for Market Share," *Chain Store Age Executive* (August 1993), pp. 11A–13A.

Mergers, Diversification, and Downsizing

Some firms have used mergers and diversification to sustain sales growth in a highly competitive environment (or when the institutional category in which they operate matures). For stronger firms, this trend is expected to carry over into the future.

Mergers involve the combination of separately owned retail firms. Diversification mergers take place between retailers of different types, such as the ones between J.C. Penney (the department store chain) and Thrift Drug and Eckerd (drugstore chains). Specialization mergers occur between similar types of retailers, such as two local banks or two department store chains (as took place when Federated Department Stores acquired R.H. Macy). By merging, retailers hope to jointly maximize resources, enlarge their customer base, improve productivity and bargaining power, limit weaknesses, and gain competitive advantages. This is a way for resourceful retailers to grow more rapidly and for weaker ones to enhance their long-term prospects for survival (or gain some return on investment by selling assets).

With **diversification,** retailers become active in businesses outside their normal operations—and add different goods and/or service categories. For example, to expand beyond its core business, The Limited, Inc. has developed these and other store formats: Structure (for men), Limited Too (for girls), Cacique (French lingerie), and Bath & Body Works (toiletries). In addition, it has acquired Victoria's Secret (a mail-order and store-based lingerie business), Henri Bendel (upscale women's clothing), and Penhaligon's (a London-based perfumery), among others.

Because of mergers and diversification, the size of many retail chains has grown dramatically. They have not all done well with that approach. As in the manufacturing sector, even though stronger firms are expanding, we are also now witnessing **downsizing**—whereby unprofitable stores are closed or divisions are sold off—on the part of retailers dissatisfied with performance. Because Kmart's diversification did not meet expectations, the firm closed or sold off virtually all of its ventures outside the discount department store field (including Office Max, the Pay Less drugstore chain, and Sports Authority). And McDonald's exited the children's play center arena, after deciding Leaps & Bounds was too far outside its main business.

For several reasons, the interest in downsizing is expected to continue. One, various retailers have overextended themselves and do not have the resources or management talent to succeed without retrenching. Two, in their quest to open new stores, certain firms have chosen poor sites (because they have already saturated the best locations). Three, retailers like Barnes & Noble are becoming more interested in operating fewer, but much larger, stores. Four, retailers such as supermarkets are finding they can do better if they focus attention regionally rather than nationally. Five, diversified firms like Kmart have decided to return more to their roots.

This means many "retailers have grown accustomed to shifts in what the consumer wants and are well acquainted with economic cycles. Even as they shutter unprofitable stores, they are opening newer, profitable formats and converting existing units to these formats." As Woolworth's former chief executive put it: "[Downsizing] is consistent with our long-standing strategy to restructure, reformat, and revitalize businesses that can meet our financial objectives within a reasonable time span—and to redeploy assets away from those businesses which cannot. We expect this program, as well as other recent steps, will move the company closer to its goal of being a low-cost, customer-driven organization." To implement this philosophy, a new chief executive was hired in late 1994; and during 1995 alone, the firm sold or closed more than 700 stores and three distribution centers, while opening 300 new stores in its various Foot Locker chains and its Northern Group of apparel stores.[34]

---

[34]"Retailing: Current Analysis," *Standard & Poor's Industry Surveys* (January 27, 1994), pp. 70–71; and *Woolworth Corporation 1995 Annual Report.*

Cost Containment and Value-Driven Retailing

With a cost-containment approach, retailers strive to hold down both their initial investment costs and the ongoing operating costs. In recent years, more firms have enacted this fundamental principle because of the intense competition from discounters, the need to control complicated chain or franchise operations, high land and construction costs, the volatility of the economic environment, and the desire to maximize productivity.

Cost containment can be accomplished by one or more of these strategy-mix decisions:

■ Standardizing operating procedures.
■ Standardizing store layouts, size, and product offerings.
■ Using secondary locations, freestanding units, and locations in older strip centers and by occupying sites abandoned by others (second-use locations).
■ Placing stores in smaller communities where building regulations are less strict, labor costs are lower, and construction and operating costs are reduced.
■ Using inexpensive construction materials, such as bare cinder block walls and concrete floors.
■ Using plainer fixtures and lower-cost displays.
■ Buying refurbished equipment.
■ Joining cooperative buying and advertising groups.
■ Encouraging manufacturers to finance inventories.

A major driving force behind cost containment is the quest to provide good value to customers. According to one study, 35 percent of consumers now shop at least once a week with a discount store. The challenge, though, is this: "Value goes beyond price. Today, value relates to a broader picture involving the entire shopping experience. The price one pays for a product is evaluated against the entire purchase experience. While consumers enjoy getting products at the lowest possible price, there is evidence they will pay more if the experience meets their related needs and expectations. Retailers must come to grips with the fact that everyday fair pricing will be the critical expectation for a majority of shoppers and that price alone will not be a sufficiently attractive, persuasive motivator for most people. The total shopping experience will dominate as the consumer navigates his or her way through a maze of distribution alternatives."[35]

Adaptation Strategies

One of the most important challenges for any retailer is to get people to perceive it as a **destination retailer,** whereby consumers believe a particular firm is worth a special shopping trip (whether the destination be a store, a catalog, or a Web site), and to hold on to this perception:

The key for retailing entities—from mass merchandisers to specialty stores to entire malls to nonstore retailers—is to view, define, and position themselves as shopping destinations. They must strive to be destinations for consumers to consciously seek, rather than places for consumers to wander into. If a retailer stakes out and captures a consumer's "share of mind" in its chosen category, it has accomplished differentiation.[36]

[35]Private Label Manufacturers Association, "Discount Shopping Frequency," *Stores* (June 1996), p. 90; and Dawn Wilensky, "A Delicate Balance: Price Vs. Value," *Discount Store News* (May 6, 1996), p. 56.
[36]Roger Seibert, "Retailing's Five Most Important Trends," *Arthur Andersen Retailing Issues Letter* (March 1991), p. 4.

A good example of a retailer with a destination image is Home Depot, the fast-growing, industry-leading chain: "In some cases we have 25,000 to 30,000 people walking through a store in a week, 50 percent of whom are women. We could sell them anything. If we wanted to put panty hose up at the front register, we'd sell a fortune in panty hose. But we don't. We don't want the customer to think we're a discounter, a food store, a toy store, or anything else, because it would confuse him or her. The perception of the consumer always has to be, when they think of a do-it-yourself project, they think of Home Depot." As one retailing expert said, "Home Depot succeeds where other do-it-yourself chains stumble because it staffs stores with knowledgeable sales help, not the kid who can tell you only that Sheetrock is in aisle seven. If a customer is thinking of putting up, say, a stockade fence in the yard, a Home Depot salesperson can explain how many sections to order, what kinds of posts are needed to reinforce the fence, and even what size nails to use."[37]

Here are illustrations of how three retailers are using adaptation strategies to prepare for the future. Wal-Mart is opening stores in more affluent communities, having saturated its traditional markets with about 3,000 outlets: Midas is promoting itself as a full-service retailer, not just one that fixes mufflers, "Repairing a car is like basic math. Once you master the basics, then you can build on them." Ukrop's, in Richmond, Virginia, has cafes in many of its supermarkets. The cafes are open for breakfast, lunch, and dinner—and serve such items as grilled salmon fillets: "After decades of standing by and letting the McDonald's of the world gobble up consumers' food dollars, supermarket operators like Ukrop's are fighting back. They are strengthening deli departments, revamping menus, and devoting more space to showcase a wider selection of prepared foods. Some are installing food courts that bear a striking resemblance to ones found in shopping malls, with ample seating, separate checkout counters, and colorful signs."[38]

THE CHALLENGING INTERNATIONAL ENVIRONMENT OF RETAILING

The international environment of retailing encompasses both U.S. firms operating in foreign markets and foreign retailers operating in U.S. markets. More retailers are becoming international in scope, building on the robust recent trend in this direction:

Retailers in significant numbers are spreading out around the world to secure their positioning. As markets mature in their homelands, companies are thinking "international" for three reasons. First, they have to. In the United States, for instance, the industry is overstored, as shopping center space has doubled since 1987. When adjusted to 1987 real dollars, square-foot productivity is about half what it was 10 years ago. Announcements have been made that some 3,500 stores have closed in the last year and a half. Around the world, most of the surviving retailers already have stores in just about every viable market in their own country. So if they are to grow, they will have to venture into formerly "uncharted" lands. Second reason, many firms have mature concepts that are ready to be exported, presumably with incremental profit. Third, retailers need customers and many are living beyond their companies' original boundaries. In the case of U.S. retailers, for instance, there is a strong incentive in the fact that 95 percent of the world's population lives outside the United States. China is now the world's third-largest economy and is projected to grow threefold, to become number one by the year 2020.[39]

In embarking on an international retailing strategy, firms should consider the factors shown in Figure 3-8.

[37]Susan Caminiti, "The New Champs of Retailing," *Fortune* (September 24, 1990), pp. 86, 90, 100.
[38]Louise Lee, "Discounter Wal-Mart Is Catering to Affluent to Maintain Growth," *Wall Street Journal* (February 7, 1996), pp. A1, A8; Leah Haran, "Midas Wants Motorists to Look Beyond Mufflers," *Advertising Age* (March 11, 1996), p. 3; and Eleena De Lisser, "Catering to Cooking-Phobic Customers, Supermarkets Stress Carryout, Add Cafes," *Wall Street Journal* (April 5, 1993), p. B1.
[39]"Global Powers of Retailing," *Chain Store Age* (December 1996), Section Three, p. 9B.

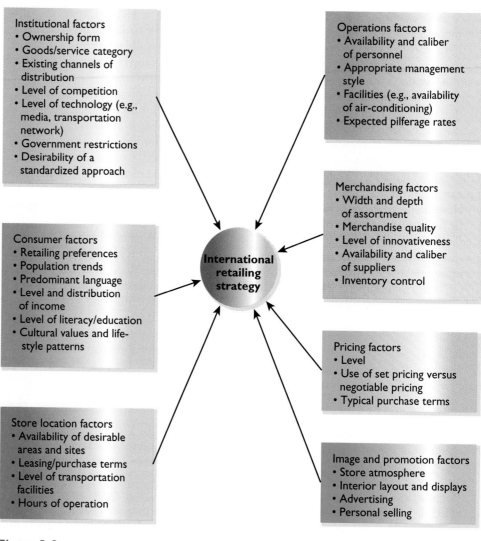

Figure 3-8

Factors to Consider When Engaging in International Retailing

Opportunities and Risks in International Retailing

For participating firms, there are wide-ranging opportunities and risks in international retailing.

Opportunities may exist for several reasons. One, foreign markets may represent better growth opportunities (because of population and other trends). Two, domestic markets may be saturated or stagnant. Three, a retailer may be able to offer goods, services, or technology not yet available in foreign markets. Four, competition may be less in foreign markets. Five, foreign markets may be used to supplement, not replace, domestic sales. Six, there may be tax or investment advantages in foreign markets. Seven, due to worldwide governmental and economic shifts, many countries are now more open to the entry of foreign firms.

Risks may also exist for several reasons. One, there may be cultural differences between domestic and foreign markets. Two, management styles may not be easily adaptable. Three, foreign governments may place restrictions on some operations. Four, personal income may be poorly distributed among consumers in foreign markets. Five, distribution systems and technology may be inadequate (for example, poor roads, lack of refrigeration, and a weak mail system). Six, institutional formats may vary greatly among countries.

Shopping Comes of Age in Brazil

Since the adoption of its 1994 economic plan, *plano real*, Brazil has created a more stable currency, dramatically reduced inflation, and substantially boosted sales of imported products. Yet even with the rapid economic growth, Brazil's total retail sector still accounts for only 8 percent of its gross domestic product (compared with 14 percent in Argentina and 18 percent in Chile). This means there's a lot of retailing potential there, especially with a population in excess of 160 million.

Brazil's new economic stability and market growth make it a much more attractive market for retailers than before. Lojas Americanas, one of Brazil's largest department store chains, plans to expand from 100 to 200 stores by the year 2000. Supermarkets are also adding stores, upgrading merchandise, and improving the services offered to consumers. France-based Carrefour, for example, ran 38 large hypermarkets (which combine general merchandise and food in one store) in Brazil as of 1996; it plans to double the number of Brazilian stores by 1999.

Retailing experts predict that many new facilities will be opened by discounters and huge category killers, and that urban locations with large population bases will be favored. Currently, most of Brazil's best shopping centers are in São Paulo and Rio de Janeiro. Yet, there are ten other cities in Brazil with populations of more than 1 million. Plentiful opportunities are also forecast for electronics (such as TVs and computers) and private-label goods.

Source: Coopers & Lybrand, "Brazil: With Stability Comes Opportunity," *Chain Store Age* (April 1996), Section 2, pp. 9–10.

When developing an international strategy, a retailer must pay particular attention to the concept of **standardization.** Can the strategy followed in a firm's home market be standardized and directly applied to foreign markets, or do personnel, the physical structure of facilities, operations, advertising messages, product lines, and other factors have to be adapted to local conditions and needs? Table 3-3 shows some retailing-related differences in various nations.

Consider this,

Compared to the 50 states [in the United States], with their principal language of English and overall federal law and tax systems, Europe is a jigsaw of cultures, languages, and nationalistic differences that are not instantly diluted by the removal of internal trade barriers. This patchwork includes those who have a general suspicion of financial institutions and thus a low use of credit (the French); a nation of families who wouldn't dream of driving out to breakfast on a Sunday morning (the British); a nation with longer trading hours than the 10:00 A.M. to 10:00 P.M. of the United States, but where a majority of shops close for three hours in midday (Spain); and Europe's most economically powerful country, whose citizens are notoriously price-conscious and do much of their food shopping in no-frills discount stores (Germany).[40]

Generally speaking, several factors can affect the level of success of an international retailing strategy:

■ Timing—"Being first in a market doesn't ensure success, of course, but being there before the serious competition does increase one's chances."
■ A balanced international program—"While timing is important, market selection is even more critical. One factor firms must consider is the stability of a nation's currency and government."

[40]Ian Waddell, "Global Challenges Set the Scene for 1992," *Chain Store Age Executive* (May 1990), p. 190. See also Len Lewis, "Going Global," *Progressive Grocer* (March 1997), pp. 28–34.

Table 3-3 SELECTED RETAILING-RELATED DATA BY COUNTRY

Country	Average Weekly Hours of Operation	Employees' Minimum Number of Paid Vacation Days and Holidays	Level of Competition	Quality of Infrastructure	Entry Barriers	Urban Per-Capita Income
Canada	68	19	High	High	Moderate	High
France	51	36	High	High	High	High
Germany	58	40	High	Moderate	High	High
Great Britain	56	31	High	High	High	High
Italy	66	42	Moderate	Moderate	High	High
Japan	54	23	Moderate	High	High	High
Mexico	54	17	Low moderate	Low moderate	Moderate	Low
Netherlands	57	28	High	High	High moderate	High
Spain	66	44	High moderate	High moderate	High	Moderate
United States	72	15	High	High	Low	High

Sources: Adapted by the authors from *Going Global: International Opportunities for Retailers* (New York: Ernst & Young, 1993), various pages; and Coopers & Lybrand, "Retailing in the 21st Century: A Global Perspective," *Chain Store Age Executive* (1993), Special Issue, various pages.

■ A growing middle class—"A rapidly growing middle class means expendable income, which translates into sales."

■ Matching concept to market—"In *developed* retail markets, where quality and fashion are more appreciated, specialty operations are entering with success. On the other hand, when entering *developing* markets, discount/combination (food and general merchandise) retailers have been successful. Consumers in these markets are more interested in price, assortment, value, and convenience."

■ Solo or partnering—"When establishing a presence in many countries, retailers have often chosen the route of joint ventures with local partners. The joint venture appeases countries and populations whose cultural sensitivity is particularly acute. The joint venture makes it easier to establish government contacts and learn the ways of getting things done."

■ Store location and facilities—"Foreign retailers often have to adapt their concepts to different real-estate configurations in other markets." Shopping malls may be rare in some places.

■ Product selection—"Consumers in most parts of the world would be overwhelmed by the product assortment in North American stores."

■ Service levels—"Consumers in some areas do not expect anything close to the level of service American shoppers have come to demand." This can be a real point of distinction.[41]

U.S. Retailers and Foreign Markets

Here are examples of U.S. retailers with high involvement in foreign markets.

Toys "Я" Us has been active internationally for years, and now has more than 400 stores abroad (up from about 75 in 1990). Among the 20 or so nations in which it has well-established stores are Australia, Canada, France, Germany, Great Britain, Japan, Singapore, Spain, and Sweden. In 1994, it signed its first foreign franchising agreements,

[41]"Global Powers of Retailing," Section Three, pp. 10B–13B. See also Debra Hazel, "U.S. Development Comes to the World," *Chain Store Age* (February 1997), pp. 131–133.

Figure 3-9

Toys "Я" Us Around the World

thus entering the United Arab Emirates and other Middle Eastern nations. During 1996, it moved into Indonesia, Italy, South Africa, and Turkey. Why the new emphasis on franchising? As its Web site (http://www.tru.com) indicates, "Their local knowledge of the retail market combined with the Toys "Я" Us expertise in the management of children's megastores should provide a powerful combination to fully cover the potential of the market and increase the availability of toys." See Figure 3-9.

Many of the world's leading mail-order retailers are U.S.-based, including American Express, Avon, Citicorp, Franklin Mint, and Reader's Digest. These firms are efficient and have a clear handle on customers and distribution methods. However, as of now, total worldwide mail-order sales (for both U.S. and foreign firms) outside the United States are only a fraction of those in the United States. Thus, there is great growth potential in foreign markets.

Blockbuster Entertainment is on an aggressive pace to "make the American couch potato a worldwide phenomenon." Blockbuster plans to grow from 1,500 stores outside the United States in 1995 to 2,000 by the year 2000. Besides blanketing Europe, Australia, and Japan with stores, Blockbuster is opening outlets throughout Latin America. The first one in São Paulo, Brazil, achieved the highest one-month sales level in company history.[42]

For the past decade, the majority of McDonald's new restaurants have opened outside the United States. Today, sales at 7,500 outlets in 95 foreign nations account for nearly one-half of total systemwide revenues. Besides Western Europe, McDonald's also has outlets in such places as Argentina, Brazil, Brunei, Canada, Costa Rica, Czech Republic, Hungary, Japan, Mexico, New Zealand, the Philippines, Poland, Russia, Venezuela, and Yugoslavia. The new restaurant in India is one of its most unique: "In coming to this predominantly Hindu nation, where cows are sacred and most people don't eat beef, McDonald's ditched the Big Mac for an Indian stand-in, the Maharaja

[42]Geraldine Fabrikant, "Blockbuster Seeks to Flex Its Muscles Abroad," *New York Times* (October 23, 1995), p. D5; and Jeffery D. Zbar, "Blockbuster's Fast Forward," *Advertising Age* (September 18, 1995), p. I-32.

Mac. That's two all-mutton patties, special sauce, lettuce, cheese, pickle, and onions, all on a sesame seed bun. Although McDonald's restaurants in other countries adapt to local tastes—serving pork burgers in Thailand, for example—the outlet in New Delhi is the first to shun beef outright. The purveyor of billions and billions of burgers worldwide hopes to sway this country of vegetarians with such offerings as Vegetable McNuggets and Vegetable McBurgers."[43]

Avon recognizes that in the United States and other developed industrial nations, its traditional direct-selling approach has been losing popularity (http://www.avon.com):

> While Avon has been selling overseas for decades, today it is emphasizing expansion into countries with emerging or developing economies. The company has entered 14 new markets since 1990. The fastest-growing international markets include Brazil, Argentina, the Philippines, and Malaysia. Leading expansion markets include China, the number-one growth opportunity, Central Europe (Poland, Hungary, the Czech Republic, and Slovakia), and Russia. Avon started selling in India and South Africa in 1996. It also is investigating markets such as Romania, Ukraine, Bulgaria, and Vietnam. These emerging markets typically have strong demand for Western-quality products and an underdeveloped retail infrastructure. They also require only modest capital investment because Avon sells through independent sales representatives. Importantly, they have large populations of entrepreneurial women who seek earnings opportunities. In 1995, Avon generated 38 percent of total sales from developing markets and 64 percent of sales from all international markets, both developing and developed. Avon has operations in 41 countries, and Avon products are also available in an additional 84 countries by licensing and distribution agreements.

Foreign Retailers and the U.S. Market

A large number of foreign retailers have entered the United States, to appeal to the world's most affluent mass market. Here are three examples.

Ikea is a Swedish-based home furnishings retailer with stores in over 25 countries; in 1985, Ikea opened its first U.S. store in Pennsylvania. Since then, it has also opened stores in such areas as California, Maryland, New Jersey, New York, and Washington, D.C.—more than a dozen U.S. stores in all. The company features durable, stylish ready-to-assemble furniture at "rock-bottom prices." Because Ikea positions itself as a dominant furniture retailer, its stores are large and have enormous selections. For instance, the outlet in Elizabeth, New Jersey (the U.S. flagship store) is 270,000 square feet and has a playroom for children and other customer amenities. The firm generates nearly 90 percent of its sales from international operations, including several hundred million dollars at its U.S. stores.[44]

Germany's Aldi is a supermarket chain that ranks among the world's top 20 retailers (with $23 billion in annual sales). There are hundreds of Aldi stores in the United States, mostly in the West: "The stores don't advertise; they aren't even in the phone book. Stores are located away from costly real estate such as strip malls. They generally measure 8,000 square feet, one-third the size of a typical grocery store. Aldi situates mostly in farm towns or blue-collar neighborhoods. It likes dealing with big working-class families that eat at home and eat heartily."[45]

---

[43]Dan Biers and Miriam Jordan, "McDonald's in India Decides the Big Mac Is Not a Sacred Cow," *Wall Street Journal* (October 14, 1996), p. A14.

[44]"Coopers & Lybrand's Global Powers of Retailing," *Chain Store Age* (December 1995), Section Two, pp. 5, 8; and Richard W. Stevenson, "Ikea's New Realities: Recession and Aging Consumers," *New York Times* (April 25, 1993), Section 3, p. 4.

[45]"Global Powers of Retailing," Section Three, p. 4B; and Marcia Berss, "Bag Your Own," *Forbes* (February 1, 1993), p. 70. See also Steve Weinstein, "Foreign Affairs," *Progressive Grocer* (November 1996), pp. 26–32.

Table 3-4 SELECTED ACQUISITIONS OF U.S. RETAILERS BY FOREIGN FIRMS

U.S. Retailer	Principal Business	Foreign Acquirer	Country of Acquirer
Brooks Brothers	Apparel	Marks & Spencer	Great Britain
Burger King	Restaurants	Grand Metropolitan	Great Britain
Capezio	Apparel	Luxottica	Italy
Carvel	Ice cream	Investcorp	Bahrain
Citgo	Gasoline distribution	Petroleus de Venezuela	Venezuela
Edwards	Supermarkets	Royal Ahold	Netherlands
Finast	Supermarkets	Royal Ahold	Netherlands
Food Lion	Supermarkets	Delhaize "LeLion"	Belgium
Great Atlantic & Pacific (A&P)	Supermarkets	Tengelmann	Germany
Hannaford Bros.	Supermarkets	Sobey Parties	Canada
Hardee's Food System	Fast Food	Imasco	Canada
International House of Pancakes (IHOP)	Restaurants	Wienerwald	Switzerland
Kay Jewelers	Jewelry	Ratners Group	Great Britain
LensCrafters	Optical stores	Luxottica	Italy
Motel 6	Economy motels	Accor	France
Saks Fifth Avenue	Department stores	Investcorp	Bahrain
7-Eleven (Southland)	Convenience stores	Ito-Yokado	Japan
Shaw's Supermarkets	Supermarkets	J. Sainsbiny	United Kingdom
Spiegel	Mail-order and specialty stores	Otto Versand-Handelsgruppe	Germany
Stop & Shop	Supermarkets	Royal Ahold	Netherlands
Talbots	Apparel	Jusco Ltd.	Japan

The Body Shop is a British-based chain that specializes in natural cosmetics and lotions such as Colourings cosmetics, Banana Shampoo, and Peppermint Foot Lotion—"products that cleanse, beautify, and soothe the human form." There are 1,400 Body Shop stores in 46 countries, including the United States. The firm has 275 U.S. stores (nearly 60 percent of which are franchised), which generate roughly $100 million of Body Shop's sales.[46]

Besides extending their traditional businesses into the United States, a number of foreign firms have acquired major ownership interests in American retailers. Sales of U.S.-based retailers owned by foreign firms are difficult to measure, but probably exceed $100 billion annually. Foreign ownership in U.S. retailers is highest for general merchandise stores, food stores, and apparel and accessory stores. Some of the U.S. acquisitions made by foreign firms over the last two decades are shown in Table 3-4.

Both U.S. retailers operating in foreign markets and foreign firms operating in the U.S. market need to be careful in their approach:

Being nimble is perhaps the most important of all managerial traits for global managers. Successful retail organizations need to be structured for nimbleness to respond appropriately and quickly to changes in the market. There are few retail markets that aren't changing. America is aging, and the "silver streakers" are changing the way we do business. Consumers have less time to shop, yet they want better, more personalized service. Information moves so quickly that fashion trends that once took months to travel from Paris to New York to Dallas now fly halfway around the world overnight. A failure to spot changes that make old ideas worthless can be the management equivalent of putting on blinders and almost always results in markdowns, unsold merchandise, or even business failure.[47]

[47]Lou Grabowsky, "Globalization: Reshaping the Retail Marketplace" *Arthur Andersen Retailing Issues Letter* (November 1989), p. 5.

Summary

1. *To review the broad challenges facing today's retailers—and show the crucial nature of both customer relationships and channel relationships in a highly competitive marketplace* A long-term view means retailers anticipate and plan for a changing world, with its attendant opportunities and threats. Opportunities exist because other retailers have not yet capitalized on them. Threats can adversely affect retailers if they do not react to them. A firm needs to spot and adapt to trends early enough to satisfy its customers and stay ahead of competitors, yet not so early that people are unready for changes or false trends are perceived.

For relationship retailing to work properly, enduring relationships are needed with other channel members, as well as with customers. Both jobs are challenging. More retailers than ever now realize loyal customers are the backbone of their business. In applying relationship retailing, there are three central factors to keep in mind: the customer base, loyalty programs, and defection rates. All consumers are not equal. Some are more worth nurturing long relationships with than others; they are a retailer's core customers. They should be singled out in a firm's data base. Consumer loyalty (frequent shopper) programs are intended to reward a retailer's best customers. Studying customer defections shows the firm how many customers it is losing and (with surveys) why they are no longer patronizing a given retailer.

The members of a distribution channel (manufacturers, wholesalers, and retailers) jointly represent a value delivery system, which comprises all of the activities needed to develop, produce, deliver, and sell and service particular goods and services. When they forge strong channel relationships, members of a value delivery system can better serve each other and the final consumer. One technique that some manufacturers and retailers are attempting to use is known as category management, whereby channel members collaborate to maximize product category performance by offering product assortments and prices that better address consumer needs. Products are managed by overall category rather than by individual item.

2. *To consider the challenge of implementing technological advances in retailing* Technological advances are advantageous when they lead to an improved information flow between retailers and their suppliers, as well as between retailers and their customers; smoother customer transactions; more efficient operations; faster, more insightful decision making; better inventory management; and greater employee productivity. The challenge is that technology may change rapidly, be difficult to meld with equipment that is already in use, outpace consumers' readiness for it, be overhyped, and be intimidating to many retailers.

Electronic banking involves both the use of automatic teller machines (ATMs) and the instant processing of retail purchases. It allows centralized record keeping and lets customers complete transactions 24 hours a day, 7 days a week at a variety of bank and nonbank locations. Technology is also changing the nature of retailer–customer interactions through point-of-sale scanning equipment, signature capture, check printers, in-home ordering systems, and other breakthroughs. Retailers are computerizing more of their operations, due to better technology, productivity gains, and the affordability of PCs and computer networks.

3. *To discuss the ethical challenges in retailing* These challenges fall into three related categories: ethics, social responsibility, and consumerism. Ethics relates to a firm's moral principles and values. Social responsibility has to do with benefiting society. Consumerism entails the protection of consumer rights. "Good" behavior is based on not only the firm's practices, but also on the norms and expectations of the community in which it does business.

Ethical retailers act in a trustworthy, fair, honest, and respectful way with each of their constituencies. Firms are more apt to avoid unethical behavior if they have written ethics codes, communicate them to employees, monitor and punish poor behavior, and have ethical senior executives. Retailers perform in a socially responsible manner when they act in the best interests of society—as well as themselves—through recycling and conservation programs, and other efforts. Consumerism activities involve government, business, and independent organizations. Four consumer rights are considered basic: to safety, to be informed, to choose, and to be heard. Many retailers have enacted voluntary plans to aid consumers.

4. *To study how retail institutions are evolving in response to the challenges they face* Many retail institutional changes are occurring due to the evolving marketplace. For individual firms, a retailing effectiveness checklist can aid in rating future preparedness.

Each of these approaches has been popular for different firms, depending on their strengths, weaknesses, and goals: mergers—by which separately owned retailers join together, diversification—by which a retailer becomes active in businesses outside its normal operations, and downsizing—whereby unprofitable stores are closed or divisions are sold. Sometimes, single companies use all three approaches. More firms are also utilizing cost containment and value-driven retailing. They strive to hold down initial investment costs, as well as operating costs. There are many ways to do this. A challenge for any firm is to be perceived as a destination retailer, thereby worth a special shopping trip.

5. *To look at the challenging international dimension of retailing* International retailing, comprising U.S. firms in foreign markets and foreign firms in U.S. markets, is rapidly gaining stature. In entering a new market, a retailer must consider institutional, consumer, location, operations, merchandising, pricing, and image and promotion factors. Opportunities and risks must be assessed, as well as the applicability of standardization. A firm must decide how much of its domestic strategy should be modified to address foreign needs and legal requirements.

Key Terms

opportunities (p. 60)
threats (p. 60)
core customers (p. 61)
customer loyalty (frequent shopper)
  programs (p. 62)
value delivery system (p. 64)

category management (p. 66)
electronic banking (p. 68)
ethics (p. 74)
social responsibility (p. 75)
consumerism (p. 77)
retailing effectiveness checklist (p. 80)

mergers (p. 81)
diversification (p. 81)
downsizing (p. 81)
destination retailer (p. 82)
standardization (p. 85)

Questions for Discussion

1. Comment on this statement: "Proper strategic planning takes into account the nature of environmental factors in terms of their certainty of occurrence and magnitude of change, their effect on a retailer's business, and the time required for the retailer to react properly."
2. Why should a retailer devote special attention to its core customers? How should it do so?
3. Devise a customer loyalty program for a local movie theater.
4. What is a value delivery system? How may it be improved?
5. What are the pros and cons of ATMs? As a retailer, would you want an ATM in your store? Why or why not?
6. Will the time come when most consumer purchases are made with self-scanners? Explain your answer.
7. Describe three unethical, but legal, acts on the part of retailers that you have encountered. How have you reacted in each case?

8. Differentiate between social responsibility and consumerism from the perspective of a retailer.
9. What is a retailing effectiveness checklist? How could a small retailer use it? A large retailer?
10. Explain how a retailer could utilize all three of these approaches at the same time: mergers, diversification, and downsizing.
11. Describe the advantages and disadvantages of cost containment in retailing.
12. What is a destination retailer? How is this concept relevant for nonstore retailers, as well as store-based ones?
13. How could a standardized strategy on the part of a U.S. retailer fail when introduced into Canada, a country with many similarities to the United States?
14. What are the opportunities and risks facing a U.S. retailer that enters Latin America?
15. Why do you think so many foreign-based firms have acquired U.S. retailers?

Web-Based Exercise:

MARKS & SPENCER (http://www.marks-and-spencer.co.uk)

Questions

Answer each of these questions based only on the information contained in the firm's Web site. Do not refer to the material in Case 1 below.

1. Describe Marks & Spencer's scope of retail activity.
2. Identify the major elements of Marks & Spencer's retail strategy.

3. Describe Marks & Spencer's financial services. What are the synergies between Marks & Spencer's traditional business and its financial services business?
4. What are Marks & Spencer's major opportunities and threats?

CASE 1
Marks & Spencer: Assessing an International Strategy*

According to a recent survey by *Management Today,* for the third year in a row, Marks & Spencer was voted as Great Britain's most admired company. Affectionately called "Marks & Sparks" by consumers throughout the country, it is Great Britain's leading retailer accounting for 35 percent of Great Britain's lingerie sales and 10 percent of the women's shoe market. Marks & Spencer's 1996 sales were 7.23 billion pounds ($12.07 billion dollars), and net income after tax was 9.0 percent of sales. Its Web site is (http://www.marks-and-spencer.co.uk).

Marks & Spencer's overall retail strategy is based on offering consumers a good value for clothing and food products, as well as on securing high growth for its retail operations. The firm applies its strategy by purchasing items directly from manufacturers, bargaining hard, and constantly being concerned about product quality—and by pursuing worldwide growth from both internal expansion and acquisitions.

Because Marks & Spencer accounts for such a large percent of its suppliers' overall sales (as much as 90 percent for some suppliers), the retailer can be tough in bargaining, while at the same time holding suppliers accountable for high-quality standards. Many Marks & Spencer's products feature the firm's private brand, St. Michael, which began in 1927. Seventy-seven percent of the goods sold by Marks & Spencer worldwide are made in Great Britain. Most items made outside Great Britain are from producers owned by its long-standing British suppliers.

Although in the past, Marks & Spencer was most successful with clothing, it now combines apparel and food retailing into a traditional department store format. Its food business today generates about 35 percent of the company's annual revenues and Marks & Spencer is Great Britain's leading seller of sandwiches and take-out meals. Specialty foods are sold at its department stores and at its British food-only stores. As with clothing, the firm uses a distribution approach for food that bypasses wholesalers and gets high-quality products direct from suppliers.

Compared with other British stores, Marks & Spencer stores have a spartan, but efficient, appearance. For example, storefronts are plain, and to reduce the dependence on sales help, the chain stresses self-service merchandising. It deliberately uses clear labeling on food products so sales assistance is not needed to explain a food's preparation or ingredients to a customer.

Marks & Spencer operates 368 stores, 280 of them in Great Britain and an additional 72 franchised outlets in the Philippines, Singapore, Indonesia, Malaysia, Thailand, and other

---

*The material in this case is drawn from "A Hard Core of Six Keep a Stranglehold on the Top in the Free-For-All," *Management Today* (December 1995), p. 46; "British Retailer on a Roll," *Asian Business* (April 1996), pp. 66–67; *Marks & Spencer 1996 Annual Report;* "Rivals Target M&S Position," *Marketing* (May 30, 1996); and Patrick J. Spain and James R. Talbot (Editors), *Hoover's Handbook of World Business 1995–1996* (Austin, Texas: Reference Press, 1995), pp. 328–329.

nations. Revenues outside Great Britain account for 15 percent of Marks & Spencer's companywide revenues. The firm has been in Canada since the early 1970s, through its purchase of People's (a general merchandise chain which it sold in 1992), D'Allaird's (a women's clothing chain), and Walker's (a clothing shop whose stores were later renamed Marks & Spencer). Marks & Spencer purchased Brooks Brothers (an upscale U.S. men's and women's clothing retailer) and Kings Super Markets (a New Jersey-based regional chain) in 1988. It recently opened stores in Hungary, Vienna, Spain, Hong Kong, and Turkey. Marks and Spencer also has stores in France, Holland, Belgium, and Spain. It has recently targeted expansion opportunities in Korea, Taiwan, Australia, and China (where it opened a representative office). All stores, regardless of location, carry very similar lines of merchandise. However, size distributions in each country reflect that country's population (such as smaller sizes in Hong Kong).

Questions
1. Evaluate Marks & Spencer's overall retailing strategy.
2. Does Marks & Spencer practice relationship retailing? Explain your answer.
3. What technological advances did Marks & Spencer adopt? Why?
4. What criteria would you use to determine if Marks & Spencer is an ethical retailer?

Video Questions on Marks & Spencer
1. Evaluate Marks & Spencer's strategy of expanding into foreign markets.
2. Describe the pros and cons of Marks & Spencer's long-term partnering relationships with its key vendors.

Lands' End is a mail-order based retailer of informal clothing for men, women, and children. In addition, it sells shoes, soft luggage, and bed-and-bath items. Unlike other mail-order firms, most of Lands' End's offerings stress traditional-styled "classic apparel" that "does not mimic the changing fads of the fashion world." Its Web site is (http://www.landsend.com).

Lands' End's strategy for growth consists of increasing sales from its regular U.S.-based catalogs, the use of targeted mailings for specialty catalogs, and greater sales to foreign markets. Like other mail-based retailers, Lands' End has begun to court international markets as a means of increasing its sales and profit growth. Although the firm does not separate out foreign sales and profits, industry analysts assume that Lands' End's foreign sales constituted about 10 percent of its total 1996 revenues. Let's now look at Lands' End's international operations, with a particular focus on England and Japan.

Lands' End started its international operations in Canada in 1987 (due to the closeness to the United States and the language similarity), but it was not until September 1991 that it introduced its first Great Britain-based catalog. Like all of its other internationally-based catalogs to come, this catalog featured prices in a nation's home currency. However, Lands' End wrongly assumed too much about the similarities between U.S. English and British English. As a consequence, the first British catalogs were developed in the United States, using American copywriters. These catalogs created quite a stir in Great Britain. For example, while "pants" refers to slacks in the United States, this term means men's underwear in Great Britain. Likewise, the term "thongs" in the United States usually refers to beach shoes; in Great Britain, "thongs" are skimpy bathing suits. To overcome the potential semantic problems and the differences in spelling in the United States and Great Britain, Lands' End decided to produce its later catalogs in Great Britain using British nationals.

[†]The material for this case is drawn from David A. Heenan, "The Rise of a World-Wide Cybermarket," *Journal of Business Strategy* (May–June 1995), pp. 20–21; *Lands' End 1996 Annual Report; Lands' End 10K for Fiscal Year Ending April 30, 1996;* and Patrick J. Spain and James R. Talbot (Editors), *Hoover's Handbook of American Business 1996,* (Austin, Texas: Reference Press, 1996) pp. 862–863.

CASE 2
(Continued)

In 1993, Lands' End opened a telephone order and distribution facility (staffed by 170 people) outside London. This British location enables Lands' End to reduce delivery times through local fulfillment of orders. In 1994, that facility began to serve the French, German, and Netherlands markets. Each country's catalogs are in its native language and prices are listed in the national currency of that nation.

To further its international expansion, Lands' End launched its catalog business in Japan in 1994. Although Lands' End had its initial operations in Japan in 1994, it was not until fiscal year 1996 that it mailed out six issues of its Japanese language, yen-denominated catalog. To ensure excellent customer service, Lands' End took great care in developing its customer service, inventory management, and distribution facilities. Lands' End operates its own phone center and administrative offices in Japan, but subcontracts warehouse operations in Japan to a third party.

Lands' End has adapted its marketing strategies and tactics to be successful in Japan. For example, a popular advertising medium in Japan is a four-page, four-color newspaper insert that is typically crowded with hundreds of items. Lands' End does not use newspaper inserts in the United States and favors the use of an uncluttered format, with large pictures and lots of copy. Thus, to appeal to the Japanese market, Lands' End decided to use the newspaper inserts, but with its uncluttered format style. Lands' End has also changed its payment system to reflect the Japanese custom that customers pay for goods after receiving them.

The Lands' End catalog operation in Japan began to be profitable within two years of opening for business. Nonetheless, Lands' End must deal with extensive current and potential competition. For instance, Japan currently accounts for 70 percent of L.L. Bean's foreign sales.

Questions

1. What are the pros and cons of Lands' End's pursuing an international strategy versus further developing its specialty catalog operation in the United States?
2. Evaluate Lands' End's international strategy in England.
3. Appraise Lands' End's international strategy in Japan.
4. Assess Lands' End's overall international strategy.

Video Questions on Lands' End

1. How could Lands' End have been better aware of its problems with Queen's English?
2. Comment on Lands' End's criteria for entering international markets.

Retailers with a Future*

INTRODUCTION

Over the last 30 years, square footage for U.S. shopping centers has more than doubled—four times the growth in retail sales during this period. Many retailers operating in America today are casualties waiting to happen, poised to be among the thousands of retail failures that occur annually in the United States (12,952 in 1995). Mediocre retailers need to fear competition the most. High-performance retailers—retailers with a future—just keep growing while mediocre ones, with no special competence, struggle to survive. Retailers with a future know they must compete on value, not price. The single biggest mistake many retailers are making today is assuming that value and price mean the same thing to customers. They do not. Price is only a part of value.

To consumers, value is the benefits received for the burdens endured. Potential benefits include quality merchandise, caring personal service, pleasant store atmosphere, convenience, and peace-of-mind. Burdens include both monetary costs (price) and nonmonetary costs, such as store employees who know little about merchandise and don't care, slow checkout, inadequate parking facilities, and sloppy, unattractive, or poorly merchandised stores. Retailers become successful with a strong benefits-to-burdens offer. They maximize key benefits to customers and minimize the most critical burdens. They compete on value, not solely on price—or not on price at all.

COMPETING ON VALUE

Price is price; value is the total experience. If customer service is generally poor and merchandise looks the same from one store to another, most consumers will want the lowest price because they have no reason to pay more. But offer them a better shopping experi-

ence and you build a company with a future. That's what Home Depot does. And Victoria's Secret. And Starbucks Coffee. And Pier 1 Imports. And Sears, resurrected at the 11th hour by new leadership.

None of these firms competes strictly on price. Home Depot gives customers the confidence to be do-it-yourselfers. Victoria's Secret turns an awkward category into a romantic, sexy one called "intimate apparel." Starbucks has transformed coffee into a fashion beverage. With exciting products from all over the world, Pier 1 turns each store visit into an adventure. And Sears didn't start its comeback with a price message; it invited consumers to try the "softer side of Sears."

Retailers with a future are led by executives who have a good answer to the question: "What do we want to be famous for with customers?" Great retailers are famous with customers for delivering a valuable bundle of benefits, a bundle that customers depend on receiving. Competitors might match the prices, but they won't be able to duplicate the entire bundle.

To compete on value, retailers need to offer at least five benefits: (1) a dominant merchandise assortment, (2) fair prices, (3) respect for customers, (4) time and energy savings, and (5) fun.

DOMINANT ASSORTMENTS

One of the most powerful forces for change in retailing is the emergence of category killers—retailers that stock a complete merchandise assortment for the category in which they compete. Category killers like CompUSA, Office Depot, and Bed, Bath & Beyond offer people a one-stop shopping alternative to limited-assortment competitors. In effect, the influence of category killers has raised customers' expectations of retail merchandising practices.

A used-car lot with 50 or 75 vehicles for sale is acceptable until a customer visits CarMax, which offers over 500 used cars. The mall bookstore with 15,000–20,000 titles is fine until a book lover sees a Barnes & Noble superstore with more than 100,000 titles. The department store appears to have an adequate lingerie selection until Victoria's Secret opens in the same mall and presents new possibilities. The

*The material in this case was adapted by the authors from Leonard L. Berry of Texas A&M University, "Retailers with a Future," *Marketing Management* (Spring 1996), pp. 39–46. Reprinted by permission of the American Marketing Association.

traditional pet store with a few thousand items looks and feels like a pet store should until a PetsMart store arrives in the market with 25,000 square feet of bright, airy shopping space, 12,000 SKUs (stock-keeping units), an in-store kiosk with another 80,000 SKUs, and a full range of in-store services, such as pet grooming, a veterinarian clinic, and a pet adoption center.

Retailers with a future invest in category dominance with maximum merchandise breadth and depth for their chosen business. They don't just dominate with vast assortments but dramatize the dominance with sensory merchandising, interactive technology, unique departments, and special services. When consumers enter Victoria's Secret, they experience an impressive visual display of merchandise, sensuous aroma, and sounds of the London Philharmonic Orchestra. At CarMax, shoppers sit at a computer with a salesperson to identify the cars on the lot that meet their needs.

Retailers with a future use assortment dominance to generate in-store excitement, offer so much merchandise that customers can comparison shop without going to another store, and have the best in-stock performance of all competitors. By carrying goods and services complementary to the core line, they sell a total solution to a customer's problem. Home Depot sells material for building a deck, the know-how to build it, and the plants and fertilizer to landscape it.

Becoming an assortment dominator is more about attitude than store size or format. For example, a 3,000-square-foot bookstore can reinvent itself as a seller of children's books, videos, and educational toys and become an assortment dominator. The attitude is that no competitor will have a better selection or present it in a more compelling manner. Sears is expanding separate specialty store chains to sell furniture and hardware, a strategy that frees up more of the existing department store space for apparel and housewares—the "softer side of Sears." This strategy is letting Sears achieve more assortment dominance in both soft goods and hard goods.

Assortment dominators are first-choice outlets for one or more categories of merchandise. Although specialists in each category they sell, they aren't specialty stores in the traditional sense. They are killers—big stores, medium stores, small stores, catalog firms—no matter what the case.

PRICING FAIRNESS

Many retailers engage in unfair and confusing pricing practices that erode credibility and drain profits. The three-level "strawman" pricing scheme is typical of such practices: A phony "regular price" to be quickly lowered, the "sale price" at which most items are ex-

pected to be sold, and deeper markdowns to clear slow-selling merchandise. In one survey, 75 percent of respondents said department stores purposely priced merchandise high only to mark it down for an advertised sale. Retailers with a future reject trickery and price products at an everyday level that represents good value for customers. Their prices earn the customer's trust, not destroy it.

Pricing fairness does not have to mean *lowest* price. Though some successful retailers promise everyday lowest prices in their promotions, very few actually use this strategy because it means a cost structure much lower than that of competitors. Most firms know they can't back up this kind of promise because a competitor with a lower price always lurks around the corner.

Instead, many retailers with a future follow the principles of everyday *fair* pricing:

- Most merchandise is sold at regular (nonsale) prices that represent a good value for customers. The retailer strips waste from operations and gives customers their money's worth.
- Sales events are legitimate, meaning the merchandise on sale is marked down from the regular price, rather than being marked down from an inflated, phony price.
- Prices are easy for customers to understand.
- Prices are communicated in a simple, straightforward manner without any hidden charges.

Taco Bell, which brought value pricing to the fast-food sector, is an everyday fair-pricer. Its strategy is to offer the best value fast meal whenever and wherever customers are hungry. To apply this strategy, Taco Bell discarded traditional business approaches that gave the consumer only 27 cents worth of food for each dollar. Through machine-made tacos, off-site production, more training, and greater employee empowerment and less supervision, Taco Bell now gives customers more than 40 cents worth of food per dollar.

As recently as 1990, Taco Bell assigned one supervising manager for every five restaurants. Multiple field management layers have since been eliminated and today supervising managers are responsible for 30 or more points of distribution. Store construction and operating costs have been significantly reduced by centralizing food preparation and reconfiguring restaurants from 70 percent kitchen/30 percent seating to 70 percent seating/30 percent kitchen.

Everyday fair pricing works best when combined with other strong benefits. Barnes & Noble superstores have a dominant assortment, innovative store designs, comfortable interiors, good customer service, front-of-store parking, coffee bars, and fair pricing. Pricing is straightforward—10 percent off the publisher's list price on all hardback books, 20 percent off paperbacks on the *New York Times* bestseller list, and 30 percent off hardbacks on the *Times* list.

RESPECT FOR CUSTOMERS

Having formally studied quality of service in America for more than 12 years, I [Leonard L. Berry] am convinced that a *customer-respect deficit* exists in U.S. service businesses, including retailing. Customers are the lifeblood of every retailer, yet all too often they are treated badly. Something as basic as respect can influence a company's competitiveness because it sends a clear message to customers: Respectful service signals customers that a firm is worthy of their loyalty; disrespectful service signals that they should take their business elsewhere.

Disrespectful service is so common that customers notice, and remember, when a company treats them well. Retailers with a future respect their customers' time; desire for a courteous, professional service experience; and demand for fair treatment. By investing in respectful service and making it a priority, retailers with a future turn a business basic into a customer draw.

Tattered Cover ❏ One of America's most successful independent book retailers, Tattered Cover has two Denver stores. The main one is in a four-story, 40,000-square-foot building. People love the store because it feels like home, with wooden bookshelves, antique furniture and desks, and comfortable chairs and couches. People are encouraged to touch the books and may sit and read all day if they wish.

Tattered Cover's culture is to put customer and book together. On a slow day, it handles 300 special orders; on a fast day, up to 650. "Diligence and doggedness are what we do best," says owner Joyce Meskis. "We search for the elusive title." General manager Linda Millemann adds: "Managers from other stores say, 'You're big enough to do that,' but that is how we got big."

Employees are trained to be nonjudgmental about customer purchases. "People buy sensitive books. It's the customer's right to read what he or she wants," floor manager Sidney Jackson explains. This nonjudgmental attitude is reinforced by the wide variety of publications in stock—about 220,000 different books and approximately 1,300 newspapers and magazines.

Tattered Cover's competitive advantage is the atmosphere of trust and community that pervades the stores. Check-writing customers are not asked to furnish identification and all employees get a key to the store on their first day of work. The key symbolizes to employees that Tattered Cover is their store. Employees also are allowed to borrow any of the books in inventory, a policy that creates more informed personnel and symbolizes complete trust. The respect shown employees encourages the respect they provide to customers, which fosters intense loyalty to the store. Indeed, it is the way human beings are treated at Tattered Cover that sets it apart.

Royers' Round Top Cafe ❏ Round Top, Texas, a town with 55 residents, is not exactly a prime setting for a retail success story. Yet, Royers', a 38-seat restaurant, attracts 300 to 400 customers on a typical Saturday, many traveling from Houston, 50 miles away. The draw is wonderful food, world-class pies (it's a nickel extra if you don't have ice cream with the pie), and respectful service.

Customers wait for tables on a front porch, where they partake of beer and wine on an honor system. Once seated, customers are never rushed through a meal. "Eating's an event that should be enjoyable and relaxing," says owner Bud Royer. "I won't let floors be swept until customers at the last table walk out the door. I don't want the last table to feel we're rushing them because we want to go home." Royers' accepts no credit cards but does not turn away people without cash. The customer eats, takes the bill home, and mails in a check. No one has failed to pay the bill yet.

The customer-respect deficit in retailing creates an opening for retail companies that are prepared to treat customers well. Size of company is not important; size of commitment is.

SAVE CUSTOMER'S TIME AND ENERGY

Studies report that people feel free time is dwindling. In studies by the *Americans' Use of Time Project*, adults were asked if they "always," "sometimes," or "almost never" felt rushed to do the things they have to do. Thirty-eight percent said they "always" felt rushed, up from 22 percent in 1971. The perception of time poverty is greatest for people combining work, marriage, and parenthood. Two-thirds of working mothers reported always being rushed. And time scarcity contributes to stress. According to a study in *American Demographics*, 60 percent of Americans feel under great stress at least once a week; 19 percent feel this way almost every day.

These factors have a negative impact on personal energy levels, which is not conducive to a leisurely visit to the shopping mall. Consumers now visit malls less often and visit fewer stores in less time when they do go. Yankelovich Partners asked consumers what they would do on a free Saturday or Sunday. Sixty-nine percent said they would watch TV and 46 percent said they would take a nap. A hidden competitor for stores is the increasingly appealing idea of staying home. In Yankelovich's annual *Monitor* study, consumers are asked what is important in deciding where to shop. "Makes it easy to shop" is now rated important by two-thirds of respondents.

Retailers with a future save customers time and energy. They invest in making their stores easy to get to and easy to get through and/or making shopping possible without going to a store at all. They compete on convenience, offering maximum access, one-stop or no-stop shopping, logical store design, quick transactions, and no-hassle returns.

Walgreen ❑ With nearly $500 in sales per square foot (compared to an industry average of $300), the largest U.S. drugstore chain focuses on making stores easy to get to and get through. Walgreen's customer is the high-frequency shopper who visits a drugstore more than five times a month. They represent just 10 percent of the population, but account for 50 percent of Walgreen's sales.

High-frequency customers buy general merchandise, as well as pharmaceuticals in drugstores. The key attraction is convenience. Walgreen blankets markets with freestanding stores that are easily accessible on the "corner of Main and Main"—with ample parking, drive-through pharmacy windows, wide aisles, low shelves, excellent in-store signs, and scanner-based checkouts. Once a person's name, address, and prescription data are put into the Intercom computer system, a label and receipt are printed automatically. Refills require no new information and Intercom can supply customers a printout of prescription purchases for their tax and insurance records.

Intercom, which links all Walgreen stores, keeps prescription records for use in emergencies. Where state law allows, customers can get a refill at any Walgreen store. A person from Texas who forgets her medicine on a trip to Arizona need only visit an Arizona store for a refill. Walgreen customers can reach a pharmacist 24 hours a day by a toll-free 800 number, and the firm will send a prescription by overnight mail. With Intercom, Walgreen can provide patient prescription records to hospital emergency rooms—at any time of day.

FUN TO SHOP

Selective consumers are unlikely to shop in lackluster stores. Retail dullness—merchandise sameness, boring displays, worn and tired stores, and an absence of in-store events—is a losing strategy in today's and tomorrow's marketplace.

The pace of sensory stimulation is so great that many people are easily bored. Their reality is global travel, 50-plus TV channels in the home, multimedia computers, online access to virtually any kind of material on the Internet, innovative marketing campaigns from firms such as Nike, and innovative retailing from companies such as Warner Brothers Studio Stores. Consumers today are used to being entertained and they expect it in exchange for their time, effort, and money. As the worlds of retailing and entertainment continue to merge, dull retailers will fade into oblivion.

West Point Market ❑ An outstanding specialty food store in Akron, Ohio, West Point Market is the perfect sensory retailer. Flowers are everywhere, in front of the store, in the parking lot, at the entrance, and in the aisles. The property has more than 50 trees. The delivery truck is painted with dancing vegetables. Merchandise signs are hand-drawn in soft colors by an artist. Exits are marked by hand-carved wooden signs; and colorful balloons decorate the entire store. And there's more:

- Information and recipe tags on store shelves educate shoppers on how to use the products: "This creamy mild cheese with caraway seeds slices well for ham sandwiches on hearty rye."
- The market's "Customers of Tomorrow" program includes kiddie shopping carts and cookie credit cards (good for a free cookie on each store visit).
- Rest rooms feature classical music, almond soap, indirect lighting, and fresh flowers.
- Product tasting and in-store demonstrations are common.

Everyone in this store is smiling—customers and employees alike—because West Point Market makes food shopping fun.

Barnes & Noble ❑ Customers frequently take their time strolling through this bookseller's superstores, perusing the well-stocked magazine section, sitting in a chair to read or people-watch, enjoying a coffee at the in-store Starbucks, perhaps meeting a friend, and then finally purchasing some books. At Barnes & Noble, customers can have a literary and social experience in one store visit.

As Leonard Riggio, Barnes & Noble's chief executive, has said, "The store is the principal message. Too many retailers devote too much attention to ads, instead of creating great stores. Bookstores never again will be considered sleepy places."

VALUE COMPELS

America's consumers, increasingly selective and expectant, can find many sources of compelling retail value. They have no reason to patronize mediocre retailers that offer nothing special. Every retailer needs to ask and honestly answer this question: If our company were to disappear from the landscape overnight, would customers really miss us? For retailers with a future, the answer is a resounding "yes." Like salt, they have no satisfying substitute.

Questions

1. Cite three specific practices a retailer could enact to better ensure its future.
2. Relate these concepts to the case: total retail experience, customer service, and employee empowerment.
3. How could a small retailer be an "assortment dominator"?
4. What goals should a firm have if it wants to pursue everyday fair pricing?
5. How is store location both a controllable and an uncontrollable factor?
6. Where do small retailers fit in a value delivery system? Large retailers?
7. How important is ethical behavior to a retailer with a future? Explain your answer.

Part Two

- In Part 2, the organizational missions, ownership and management alternatives, goods/service categories, and objectives of a broad range of retail institutions are presented. By understanding the unique attributes of these institutions, prospective and ongoing retailers are better able to develop and adapt their own strategies.

- Chapter 4 examines the characteristics of retail institutions on the basis of ownership type: independent, chain, franchise, leased, vertical marketing, and consumer cooperative. The methods used by manufacturers, wholesalers, and retailers to obtain control in a distribution channel are also discussed. An end-of-chapter appendix has added information on franchising.

- Chapter 5 describes retail institutions in terms of strategy mix. Three key concepts are introduced: the wheel of retailing, scrambled merchandising, and the retail life cycle. Several store-based strategy mixes are then studied, with food and general merchandise retailers reviewed separately. The chapter ends by contrasting service and goods retailers' strategies.

- Chapter 6 focuses on nonstore retailing and nontraditional retailing approaches. Direct marketing, direct selling, vending machines, the World Wide Web, video kiosks, and video catalogs are among the topics included.

Chapter 4

Retail Institutions by Ownership

CHAPTER OBJECTIVES

1. To show the ways in which retail institutions can be classified
2. To study retailers on the basis of ownership type and examine the characteristics of each
3. To explore the methods used by manufacturers, wholesalers, and retailers to exert influence in the distribution channel

Even the best and most experienced franchisors admit that some of their firms' best ideas, such as McDonald's Big Mac sandwich, have originated with their franchisees. A key reason for the prominence of franchisees in new-product ideas is their closeness to the consumer. In some cases, franchise contracts actually give franchisees some leeway to change the business format formula. Other times, franchisees knowingly break the rules to try their innovations. Let's look at the role of franchisees in new-product innovation at four fast-food franchises: McDonald's, International Dairy Queen, IHOP (International House of Pancakes), and KFC.

Herbert Peterson, a McDonald's franchisee in Santa Barbara, California, developed the Egg McMuffin (an English muffin with egg, Canadian bacon, and cheese) in 1971. According to Peterson, although Ray Kroc, the McDonald's Corporation's chief executive, quickly approved the new product, the Egg McMuffin initially met resistance from some fellow franchisees who did not want to open for breakfast. Now, of course, the Egg McMuffin is a McDonald's mainstay.

Another classic example involves the development of Blizzards, the best-selling product at International Dairy Queen and now a required item at all franchised units. Sam Temperato, a St. Louis franchisee, devised the product (a mixture of coconut, bananas, pecans, and vanilla frozen dessert) in 1984. After his franchised units' sales increased by more than 10 percent, Temperato urged the parent company to approve the product. When a new-product development committee almost rejected the Blizzard (its members feared the product was too labor intensive), Temperato hired a bus, at his expense, and went to show the committee members first-hand how the product was made and how well it sold. The committee approved the product!

When IHOP, a franchisor with nearly 700 restaurants, had a request from a franchisee to add T-bone steak to the menu, the company was quite skeptical. However, it authorized a test anyway. Sales of the product at the test location were so positive that IHOP decided to allow all franchises to sell the steak. IHOP units now sell 3 million pounds of T-bone steak annually.

To acknowledge the importance of franchisees in new-product development, KFC recently created a 10-member Chef's Council to screen new menu items. The council is staffed with six franchisees and four officials from KFC's Miami headquarters. Already, the council has approved several new products, including a chicken pot pie.[1]

---

[1]Stephanie N. Mehta, "Restaurant Novices Learn to Turn Popularity into Profit," *Wall Street Journal* (August 9, 1996), pp. B1–B2.

The term **retail institution** refers to the basic format or structure of a business. In the United States, about 2.2 million different firms are defined as retailers by the Bureau of the Census, and they operate more than 2.6 million establishments.

OVERVIEW

An institutional study shows the relative sizes and diversity of different kinds of retailing, enables firms to better understand and enact their own strategies, and indicates how various types of retailers are affected by the external environment. In particular, institutional analysis is important in these phases of strategic planning: selecting an organizational mission, choosing an ownership alternative, defining the goods/service category, and setting objectives.

In the next three chapters, retail institutions are viewed from these perspectives: ownership (Chapter 4), store-based retail strategy mix (Chapter 5), service versus goods retail strategy mix (Chapter 5), and nonstore-based retail strategy mix and nontraditional retailing (Chapter 6). Figure 4-1 contains a breakdown of each category. The classifications are not mutually exclusive; that is, a retail institution may be correctly placed in more than one category. For example, a department store unit may be part of a chain, have a store-based strategy, sell services—as well as goods, accept mail-order sales, and have an Internet site.

It is vital that the data in Chapters 4 to 6 be interpreted carefully. Because some institutional categories are not mutually exclusive, care should be taken in combining statistics to aggregate data so double counting does not occur. And while data are as current

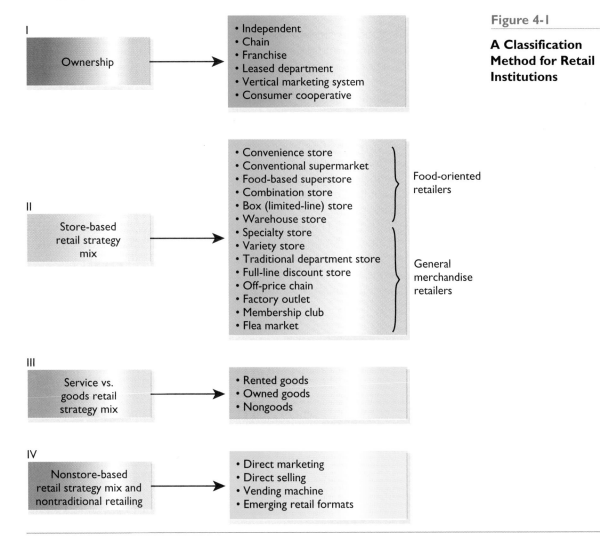

Figure 4-1

A Classification Method for Retail Institutions

I

Ownership →
- Independent
- Chain
- Franchise
- Leased department
- Vertical marketing system
- Consumer cooperative

II

Store-based retail strategy mix →
- Convenience store
- Conventional supermarket
- Food-based superstore
- Combination store
- Box (limited-line) store
- Warehouse store
} Food-oriented retailers

- Specialty store
- Variety store
- Traditional department store
- Full-line discount store
- Off-price chain
- Factory outlet
- Membership club
- Flea market
} General merchandise retailers

III

Service vs. goods retail strategy mix →
- Rented goods
- Owned goods
- Nongoods

IV

Nonstore-based retail strategy mix and nontraditional retailing →
- Direct marketing
- Direct selling
- Vending machine
- Emerging retail formats

as possible, not all information corresponds to a common date and (as of this writing) the last fully published U.S. government retailing census is the *1992 Census of Retail Trade.*

RETAIL INSTITUTIONS CHARACTER-IZED BY OWNERSHIP

Retail firms may be independently owned, chain-owned, franchisee-operated, leased, owned by manufacturers or wholesalers, or consumer-owned.

Although retailers are primarily small (80 percent of all retail stores are operated by firms with only one outlet and over one-half of all firms have two or fewer paid employees), there are also very large retailers. In 1995, the five leading U.S. retailers totaled more than $200 billion in sales and employed 1.6 million people.

Opportunities in retail ownership abound. For example, according to the National Foundation for Women Business Owners, 42 percent of all U.S. retail businesses are owned by women. This compares with just 17 percent of all manufacturing businesses being owned by women.[2]

From positioning and operating perspectives, each ownership format serves a marketplace niche and presents certain advantages and disadvantages. Retail executives must not lose sight of this, playing up their strengths and working around their weaknesses:

- Independent retailers should capitalize on their targeted customer base and do all they can to please shoppers in a friendly, folksy way. Word-of-mouth communication is important. These retailers should not try to serve too many customers or enter into price wars.
- Chain retailers should capitalize on their widely known image, make sure each store lives up to that image, and take advantage of economies of scale and mass promotion possibilities. They should not become too inflexible in adapting to the changes in the marketplace.
- Franchisors should capitalize on the vastness of their geographic coverage—made possible by franchisee investments—and the motivation of franchisees as owner-operators. They should not get bogged down in policy disputes with franchisees or charge excessive royalty fees.
- Leased departments should enable store operators and outside parties to join forces and offer an enhanced shopping experience, while sharing expertise and expenses. They should not hurt the image of the store or place too much pressure on the lessee to bring in store traffic.
- A vertically integrated channel should give a firm greater control over sources of supply, but it should not provide the consumer with too little choice of products or too few outlets. The opposite is true for a nonintegrated channel.
- Cooperatives should provide members with significant price savings. They should not expect too much involvement on the part of members or add facilities that raise costs too much.

Independent

An **independent** retailer owns only one retail unit. In the United States, there are 2 million independent retailers. They account for about 40 percent of total U.S. store sales. About one-half of all independents are run entirely by the owners and/or their families; these firms generate just 3 percent of total U.S. store sales (averaging $65,000–$70,000 in annual revenues) and have no paid workers (there is no payroll).

The high number of independent retailers is associated with the **ease of entry** into the marketplace. Due to low capital requirements and no, or relatively simple, licensing provisions, entry for many kinds of small retail firms is easy. The investment per worker

[2]Paula Mergenhagen, "Her Own Boss," *American Demographics* (December 1996), pp. 37–41.

in retailing is usually much lower than for manufacturers. Retailer licensing, although somewhat more stringent in recent years, is still pretty routine. Each year, tens of thousands of new retail businesses, most independents, open in the United States.

The ease of entry into retailing is reflected in the low market shares of the leading firms in many goods/service categories as a percentage of total category sales. For example, in two retail categories where large chains are quite strong (drugstores and grocery stores), the five largest drugstore retailers and the five leading grocery retailers account for only about 28 percent and 20 percent of sales in their respective categories.[3]

Since a great deal of competition is due to the relative ease of entry into retailing, it is undoubtedly an essential factor in the high rate of retail business failures among newer firms. The Small Business Administration estimates that one-third of new U.S. retailers do not survive their first year and two-thirds do not continue beyond their third year. Most of these failures involve independents. Because the decade of the 1980s was relatively good economically for the United States, failure rates were comparatively low. In the early 1990s, failure rates were higher—as a result of the economic slowdown. When the economy recovered in 1993, failure rates again fell. Nonetheless, in 1995, nearly 13,000 retailers (of all sizes) filed for bankruptcy protection, in addition to the thousands of small retailers that just closed their doors.

Competitive Advantages and Disadvantages of Independents ❑

Independent retailers have a variety of advantages and disadvantages. Among their advantages are flexibility, low investments, specialized offerings, direct control of strategy, image, consistency, independence, and entrepreneurial drive.

There is a great deal of flexibility in choosing retail formats and locations, and in devising strategy. Because only one store location is involved, a detailed list of specifications can be set for the best location and a thorough search undertaken. Uniform location standards are not needed, as they are for chain stores, and independents do not have to worry about being too close to other company stores. In setting strategy, independents have great latitude in selecting target markets. Because many independents have modest goals, small segments of the overall customer market may be selected rather than the mass market. Product assortments, prices, store hours, and other factors are then set consistently with the market.

Inasmuch as independents run only one store, investment costs for leases, fixtures, workers, and merchandise can be held down. In addition, there is no duplication of stock or personnel functions. Responsibilities are clearly delineated within a store.

Independents often act as specialists and acquire skills in a niche of a particular goods/service category. They are then more efficient and can lure shoppers interested in specialized retailers.

Independent retailers exert strong control over their strategies because only one store must be managed, and the owner-operator is typically on the premises. Decision making is usually centralized, and the layers of management personnel are minimized.

There is a certain image attached to independents, particularly small ones, that chains find difficult to capture. This is the image of a personable retailer providing a comfortable atmosphere in which to shop.

Independents are able to sustain consistency in their efforts since only one geographic market is served and just one strategy (store hours, product assortment, prices, sales personnel, promotion, and so on) is carried out. For example, there cannot be problems due to two branch stores selling identical items at different prices.

Independent retailers have "independence." Owner-operators tend to be in full charge and do not have to fret about stockholders, board-of-directors meetings, and labor unrest. Independents are often free from union work and seniority rules. This can enhance labor productivity.

[3]"Retailing Basic Analysis," *Standard & Poor's Industry Surveys* (May 9, 1996), pp. R90–R98; and David P. Schulz, "The Nation's Biggest Retail Companies," *Stores* (July 1996), pp. 55–57.

Goodwin's Market: Devising a Retail Operations System for Small Firms

Goodwin's Market is an independent supermarket located in southern California. Its annual sales are about $10 million.

A few years ago, despite his lack of formal computer training, Martin Goodwin (the firm's vice-president) recognized that the software he was using at home was better integrated than the much more costly package he had purchased for his business. As a result, Goodwin switched to inexpensive Microsoft software for the store's point-of-sale (POS) and accounting applications.

At the point of sale, Goodwin's Market uses Microsoft's Access program to perform price lookup for the 30,000 or so items it regularly stocks. To guard against earthquakes, each POS computer is self-contained. Thus, even if the firm's server was disrupted, each register would still function. Goodwin's Market runs its general ledger, accounting, payroll, and other applications on a modified version of Microsoft's Office Professional package. The firm uses Excel spreadsheets to generate management reports and Word (word-processing software) to create and mail promotional material.

Martin Goodwin says his system has reduced hardware maintenance costs by $15,000 per year and lowered checkout equipment costs by 30 percent. He is so proud of his system that he has begun to market it to other retailers.

Source: "Using Technology to Achieve Critical Success Factors," *Chain Store Age* (October 1995), pp. 8A–11A.

As a last major advantage, owner-operators usually have a strong entrepreneurial drive. They have personal investments in their businesses, success or failure has substantial implications, and there is a high degree of ego involvement.

Among the disadvantages of independent retailing are limits in bargaining power, few economies of scale, labor intensiveness, reduced access to media, overdependence on the owner, and little time and few resources for planning.

In bargaining with suppliers, independents may not have much power as they often buy in small quantities. They may even be bypassed by suppliers or limited in the merchandise selection made available to them. Reordering may also be tough if minimum order requirements are too high for them to qualify. To overcome this problem, a number of independents, like hardware stores, have formed buying groups to increase their power in dealing with suppliers.

Independents typically cannot gain economies of scale (low per-unit costs due to the handling of many units at one time) in buying and maintaining inventory. Due to financial constraints, small assortments of items are bought several times per year rather than large orders once or twice per year. This means transportation, ordering, and handling costs per unit are high.

Operations for many independents are very labor intensive, with little computerization. Ordering, taking inventory, marking merchandise, ringing up sales, and bookkeeping may be done manually. Such procedures are less efficient than computer tabulations (which are expensive for some small firms in terms of the initial investment in hardware and software—although such costs are falling significantly). In many cases, owner-operators are unwilling to spend time learning how to set up and implement computerized procedures.

By virtue of the relatively high costs of TV ads and the large geographic coverage of magazines and some newspapers (too large for firms with one outlet), independents are limited in their access to advertising media and may pay higher fees per infrequent ad compared to regular users. Yet, there are various promotion tools available for creative independents (see Chapter 18).

A crucial problem for many independents—particularly small, family-run ones—is an overdependence on the owner. Often, all decisions are made by this person, and there is no continuity of management when the owner-boss is ill, on vacation, or retires.

Figure 4-2

Talbots: A Leading Apparel Chain

The Talbots, Inc. operates hundreds of apparel stores for women and children. These stores generate $1 billion in revenues annually.

According to one study of family-owned businesses, the leading worries at those firms involved identifying successors, the role of nonfamily workers, and management training for family members.[4] Long-run success and employee morale can be affected by overdependence on the owner.

Another serious issue for independent retailers is the limited amount of time and resources allocated to long-run planning. Since the owner is intimately involved in the daily operations of the firm, responsiveness to new legislation, new products, and new competitors often suffers.

Chain

A **chain** retailer operates multiple outlets (store units) under common ownership; it usually engages in some level of centralized (or coordinated) purchasing and decision making. In the United States, there are roughly 80,000 retail chains which own about 550,000 establishments.

The relative strength of chains is great and their popularity is rising, even though the number of retail chains is small (under 4 percent of all U.S. retail firms). Chains today operate more than one-fifth of retail establishments, and because stores in chains tend to be considerably larger than those run by independents, chains account for 60 percent of total store sales and employment.

While the vast majority of chains have 4 or fewer outlets, the several hundred firms with 100 or more outlets account for greater than one-third of U.S. retail sales. Forty or so U.S. retailers have at least 1,000 outlets each (not including franchises like McDonald's). See Figure 4-2.

---

[4]Arthur Andersen & Co.'s Enterprise Group, "Family Worries," *Crain's New York Business* (May 24, 1993), p. 19.

The dominance of chains varies greatly by type of retailer. For example, in these categories, chains operating 2 or more outlets generate 75 percent or more of total retail sales: department stores, variety stores, and grocery stores. On the other hand, stationery, beauty salon, furniture, and liquor store chains (with 2 or more outlets) generate far less than 50 percent of total retail sales in their categories. Figure 4-3 shows selected data by retail store category for chains with 11 or more outlets.

Competitive Advantages and Disadvantages of Chains ❑ There are abundant competitive advantages for chain retailers: bargaining power, wholesale function efficiencies, multiple-store efficiencies, computerization, access to media, well-defined management, and long-range planning.

Many chains have bargaining power in dealing with suppliers because of the volume of the chains' annual purchases. As a result, these chains receive new items as soon as introduced, have reorders promptly filled, get proper service and selling support from suppliers, and obtain the best prices possible. In addition, large chains may gain exclusive rights to selling certain items and may have suppliers make goods under the retailers' brands. For example, Sears has manufacturers produce appliances with the retailer's Kenmore name and tools with its Craftsman name.

Chain retailers can achieve cost efficiencies by performing wholesaling functions themselves. Buying directly from manufacturers and in large quantities, shipping and storing goods, and attending trade shows sponsored by suppliers to learn about new offerings are just some wholesaling activities that can be fulfilled by chains. By doing so, they can sometimes bypass wholesalers, and the result is lower supplier prices to the retailers. Thus, prices paid by chains are often less than those paid by independents, without violation of the Robinson-Patman Act.

Efficiency in multiple-store operations can be gained by shared warehousing facilities; volume purchases of standardized store fixtures, employee uniforms, and so on; centralized purchasing and decision making; and other factors. Chain retailers typically

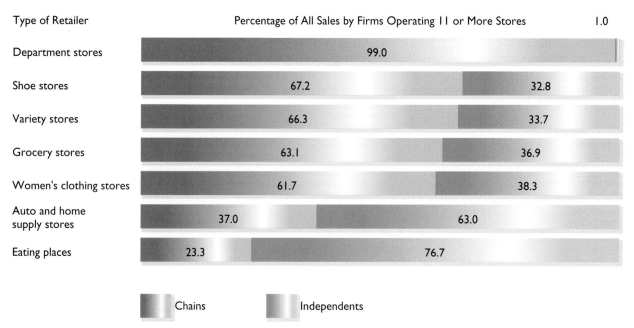

Chains   Independents

Figure 4-3

The Popularity of Chains for Selected Types of Retailer

Source: Computed by the authors from *Statistical Abstract of the United States 1996* (Washington, D.C.: U.S. Department of Commerce, 1996), p. 766.

give headquarters executives broad authority for overall personnel policies, as well as for buying, pricing, and advertising decisions.

Chain retailers, because of their resources and number of transactions, are well able to use computers in ordering merchandise, taking inventory, forecasting, ringing up sales, and bookkeeping. This increases efficiency and reduces overall costs.

Chains, particularly national or regional ones, can take advantage of a variety of media, from TV to magazines to traditional newspapers. Large sales volume and geographic coverage of the market allow chains to utilize all forms of media.

Most chains have well-defined management philosophies, whether centralized or decentralized. There tend to be detailed overall strategies, and employee responsibilities are clearly outlined. In addition, continuity is usually ensured when managerial personnel are absent or retire because there are personnel to fill in and succession plans in place.

Finally, many chain retailers expend considerable time and resources in long-run planning. Frequently, specific personnel are assigned to long-term planning on a permanent basis. Opportunities and threats are also carefully monitored.

Chain retailers do have a number of disadvantages: inflexibility, high investments, reduced control, and limited independence.

Once chain retailers are established, their flexibility is limited. Additional nonoverlapping store locations may be hard to find. Consistent strategies must be maintained throughout all branches—prices, promotions, and product assortments must be similar for each store. For chains that use centralized decision making, there may be difficulty in adapting to local needs, such as taking into account differences in life-styles among city, suburban, and rural customers.

Chains' investment costs may be high. Multiple-store leases, fixtures, product assortments, and employees are involved. The purchase of any merchandise may be costly because a number of store branches must be stocked.

Managerial control can be hard for chains, especially for those with geographically dispersed branches. Top management cannot maintain the control over each branch that independent owners have over their single outlets. Lack of communication and time delays in making and enacting decisions are two particular problems.

Personnel in large chains may have limited independence in their jobs. In many cases, there are several layers of management, unionized employees, stockholders, and boards of directors. Thus, some chain retailers are empowering their personnel to give them more independence—so they can better address special customer needs as they arise.

Franchising

Franchising involves a contractual arrangement between a franchisor (which may be a manufacturer, a wholesaler, or a service sponsor) and a retail franchisee, which allows the franchisee to conduct a given form of business under an established name and according to a given pattern of business. In a typical arrangement, the franchisee pays an initial fee and a monthly percentage of gross sales in exchange for the exclusive rights to sell goods and services in a specified geographic area. Franchising represents a retail organizational form in which small businesspeople can benefit by being part of a large, multiunit chain-type retail institution.

There are two broad types of franchising arrangements: product/trademark and business format. In **product/trademark franchising,** franchised dealers acquire the identities of their suppliers by agreeing to sell the latter's products and/or operate under suppliers' names. Dealers operate relatively autonomously from suppliers. Although they must adhere to certain operating rules, they set store hours, choose locations, determine store facilities and displays, and otherwise run the stores. Product/trademark franchising represents about two-thirds of all retail franchising sales. Examples are auto dealers and many gasoline service stations.

Is the U.S. Postal Service Being Fair to Private Postal Franchises?

The U.S. Postal Service (USPS) tested new Pack and Send services at more than 200 post offices around the country, including San Diego, Orlando, Las Vegas, and Atlanta. As a result, the owners of privately owned mail and parcel franchises were furious. Among the Pack and Send services being tested were packaging services and the sales of telephone debit cards, and under consideration were high-volume copying services and banking.

Private mail and parcel franchisors and franchisees expressed concern about the fairness of their new competition. As noted by the director of the Coalition Against Unfair USPS Competition, a trade association of private postal-service operators, the USPS does not pay any federal, state, or local income taxes, or even sales taxes. In addition, the USPS can under-price competitors because, legally, it is only allowed to break even on its operations; it cannot make a profit. Lastly, the USPS has a monopoly on first-class mail and a virtual monopoly on third-class mail.

The USPS saw its new venture as perfectly fair. According to a USPS spokesperson, the decision to offer the services "was based on what was best for our customers and what made sense for us as a business." Some industry analysts believed the USPS interest in broadening its services was due to greater competition from such electronic forms of communication as fax machines and the Internet.

Because of the controversy, USPS decided to terminate the Pack and Send program, rather than go through the approval process for full-scale use of the service.

Sources: Janean Chun, "Fair Play," *Entrepreneur* (October 1996), pp. 187–188; and Janean Chun, "Packing Up," *Entrepreneur* (May 1997), p. 184.

With **business format franchising,** there is a more interactive relationship between franchisors and franchisees. The franchisees receive assistance on site location, quality control, accounting systems, startup practices, management training, and responding to problems—besides the right to sell goods and services. The use of prototype stores, standardized product lines, and cooperative advertising let these franchises achieve a level of coordination previously found only in chains. In recent decades, most growth in franchising has involved business format arrangements, which are common for restaurants and other food outlets, real estate, and service retailing. Due to the small size of many franchisees, business format franchising accounts for more than 75 percent of all franchised outlets (though just one-third of total sales).[5]

Though variations in franchising exist, McDonald's is a good example of a business format franchise arrangement. The firm provides each new franchisee with intensive training at its "Hamburger U," a detailed operations manual (complete down to the most minute facets of running machinery), regular visits by field service managers, and repeat trips to Hamburger U for brush up training. In return for a twenty-year franchising agreement with McDonald's, a conventional franchisee invests several hundred thousand dollars (over 90 percent of which goes to suppliers of kitchen equipment, signs, seating, and decor, and for pre-opening expenses) and pays royalty fees totaling at least 12.5 percent of gross sales directly to McDonald's.[6]

Size and Structural Arrangements ❑ Retail franchising began in the United States in 1851, when Singer Sewing Machine first franchised dealers. It did not become

---

[5]Surinder Tikoo, "Assessing the Franchise Option," *Business Horizons,* Vol. 39 (May–June 1996), pp. 78–82; and *Answers to Frequently Asked Questions About Franchising* (Washington, D.C.: International Franchise Association, 1996).
[6]"18th Annual Franchise 500," *Entrepreneur* (January 1997), pp. 242–243; McDonald's franchising literature; and Jennifer Waters, "McD's Puts New Priority on Speed," *Advertising Age* (April 14, 1997), p. 49.

Table 4-1 1995 RETAIL FRANCHISE SALES

Type of Retailer	Sales (billions)	Percentage of Total Sales
Auto and truck dealers	$464.1	51.6
Gasoline service stations	138.6	15.4
Restaurants (all types)	122.4	13.6
General merchandise stores	42.3	4.7
Hotels and motels	35.1	3.9
Automotive goods and services stores	21.6	2.4
Convenience stores	18.9	2.1
Other food stores	15.3	1.7
Rental services firms	10.8	1.2
Real-estate firms	9.9	1.1
Personal and household services firms	9.9	1.1
Recreation, entertainment, and travel businesses	6.3	0.7
Educational goods and services firms	2.7	0.3
Miscellaneous firms	2.1	0.2
Total	$900.0	100.0

Sources: Estimated by the authors from *Franchising in the Economy: 1989–1992* (Washington, D.C.: International Franchise Association Educational Foundation, Inc., and Arthur Andersen & Co., 1992), various pages; and numerous other sources. Because of the scarcity of 1995 statistics by retailer category, the authors have extrapolated from earlier data, using the 1995 total franchising sales figure of $900 billion.

popular until the early 1900s as underfinanced auto makers started using franchising to expand their distribution systems. Although auto and truck dealers still provide more than one-half of all U.S. retail franchise sales, there are few retail sectors that have not been affected by franchising's growth. In the United States, there are now 3,000 retail franchisors doing business with 250,000 franchisees. They operate 600,000 franchisee- and franchisor-owned U.S. outlets, employ 8 million people, and generated retail sales of $900 billion in 1995, well over one-third of total store sales. In addition, hundreds of U.S.-based franchisors currently have foreign operations, with tens of thousands of outlets.[7] Table 4-1 shows 1995 U.S. retail franchise sales by goods/service category.

For the United States, about 85 percent of franchising sales and franchised outlets entail franchisee-owned units; the rest are from franchisor-owned outlets. If franchisees operate only one outlet, they are classified as independents by the U.S. Department of Commerce; franchisees that operate two or more outlets and franchisor-owned stores are classed as chains. Today, a large and growing number of franchisees operate as chains. See Figure 4-4.

Three types of structural arrangements dominate retail franchising. Figure 4-5 presents examples of each:

■ Manufacturer-retailer—A manufacturer gives an independent businessperson the right to sell goods and related services (subject to conditions) through a licensing agreement.
■ Wholesaler-retailer
  a. Voluntary—A wholesaler organizes a franchise system and grants franchises to individual retailers.
  b. Cooperative—A group of retailers sets up a franchise system and shares the ownership and operations of a wholesaling organization.
■ Service sponsor-retailer—A service firm licenses individual retailers to let them offer specific service packages to consumers.

---

[7]Albert J. Rosenthal, "Franchising Fellowship," *Marketing Management* (Fall 1995), pp. 4–6; and Leonard N. Swartz, *Worldwide Franchising Statistics: A Study of Worldwide Franchise Associations* (Chicago: Arthur Andersen, 1995).

Figure 4-4

McDonald's: The World's Leading Franchisor

Of McDonald's nearly 20,000 restaurants around the world, about 80 percent are operated by franchisees.

Competitive Advantages and Disadvantages of Franchising ❏ Franchisees receive several benefits by investing in successful franchise operations. First, individual businesspeople can own and operate retail enterprises with relatively small capital investments. Second, franchisees acquire well-known names and goods/service lines. Third, standard operating procedures and management skills may be taught to the franchisees. Fourth, cooperative marketing programs are often employed (e.g., national advertising)

Figure 4-5

Structural Arrangements in Retail Franchising

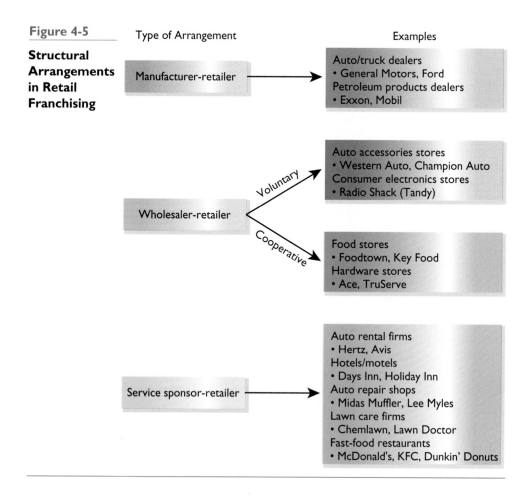

that could not otherwise be afforded. Fifth, franchisees obtain exclusive selling rights for specified geographical territories. Sixth, franchisee purchases may be less expensive per unit due to the volume represented by the overall firms.

Some potential problems do exist for franchisees. First, oversaturation could occur if too many franchisees are in one geographic area; the sales and profits of each unit would then be adversely affected. Second, due to overzealous selling by some franchisors, the income potential and required managerial ability, initiative, and investment of franchised units may be incorrectly stated. Third, franchisees may be locked into contract provisions whereby purchases must be made through franchisors or certain approved vendors. Fourth, cancellation provisions may give franchisors the right to void individual franchises if any provisions of franchise agreements are not met. Fifth, in some industries, franchise agreements are of short duration. Sixth, under most franchise contracts, royalties are a percentage of gross sales, regardless of franchisee profits. These six factors contribute to **constrained decision making,** whereby franchisors can exclude franchisees from or limit their involvement in the strategic planning process.

To curb unfair franchisor sales practices, the Federal Trade Commission (FTC) has a disclosure requirements and business opportunities rule. It applies to all U.S. franchisors and is intended to provide adequate information to potential franchisees prior to making investments. Though the FTC does not regularly review disclosure statements, about 15 states do check them and may require corrections. Also, a number of states have fair practice laws that stipulate franchisors may not terminate, cancel, or fail to renew franchisees without just cause. Arizona, California, Indiana, New Jersey, Virginia, Washington, and Wisconsin are among the states with fair practice laws. Furthermore, many states require that franchise offerings be registered.

Franchisors accrue lots of benefits by having individual franchisees. First, a national (or international) presence can be developed more quickly and with smaller investments on the part of franchisors. Second, qualifications for franchise ownership can be set and enforced. Third, money is obtained when goods are delivered rather than when they are sold. Fourth, agreements can be drawn up requiring the franchisees to abide by stringent regulations set by the franchisors. Fifth, because franchisees are owners and not employees, they have a greater incentive to work hard. Sixth, after franchisees have paid for their franchised outlets, the franchisors also receive royalties and may sell products to the individual proprietors.

Franchisors also face potential problems. First, franchisees could harm a firm's overall image and reputation if they do not maintain company standards. Second, a lack of uniformity could adversely affect customer loyalty. Third, intrafranchise competition is not desirable. Fourth, the resale value of individual units is injured if franchisees perform poorly. Fifth, ineffective franchised units directly injure their franchisors' profitability from selling services, materials, or products to the franchisees and from royalty fees. Sixth, franchisees, in greater numbers, are seeking their independence from franchisor rules and regulations.

Additional information on franchising is contained in the appendix that follows the cases at the end of this chapter.

Leased Department

A **leased department** is a department in a retail store—usually a department, discount, or specialty store—that is rented to an outside party. The proprietor of a leased department is usually responsible for all aspects of its operations (including fixtures) and normally pays the store a percentage of sales as rent. The store imposes various requirements on the leased department to ensure overall consistency and coordination.

In most situations, leased departments are used by existing store-based retailers to broaden their merchandise or service offerings into product categories requiring highly

Figure 4-6

Meldisco: A Leader in Leased Departments

specialized skills or knowledge not possessed by the retailers themselves. Thus, leased departments often operate in categories that tend to be on the fringe of the store's major product lines. They are most common for in-store beauty salons, banks, photographic studios, and millinery, shoe, jewelry, cosmetics, watch repair, and shoe repair departments. Leased departments are also gaining popularity in shopping center food courts. They account for $12 billion to $15 billion in annual department store sales. Unfortunately, data on current overall leased department sales are not available.

Meldisco Corporation is a leading operator of leased departments. It runs leased shoe departments in more than 2,400 stores and has annual sales of $1.3 billion.[8] Many of its leased departments are at Kmart stores, as illustrated in Figure 4-6. In these departments, Meldisco owns the inventory and display fixtures, staffs and merchandises the departments, and pays fees for the space occupied. The stores where Meldisco has its leased departments cover the costs of utilities, maintenance, advertising, and checkout services.

Competitive Advantages and Disadvantages of Leased Departments ❑ From the stores' perspective, having leased departments has a number of benefits. Store personnel might otherwise lack the merchandising ability to handle and sell certain goods and services. The leased department operators pay for inventory and personnel expenses, thus reducing store costs. The market can be enlarged by providing

[8]Meldisco information sheet.

one-stop customer shopping. Personnel management, merchandise displays, the re-ordering of items, and so on are undertaken by the lessees. A percentage of revenues is received regularly.

There are also some potential pitfalls, from the stores' perspective. Leased departments may use operating procedures that conflict with those of the stores. Lessees may adversely affect stores' images. Customers may blame problems on the stores rather than on the lessees.

For leased department operators, there are these advantages: Existing stores are usually well known, have a large number of steady customers, and generate immediate sales for leased departments. Some expenses are reduced because of shared facilities, such as security equipment and outside display windows. There are economies of scale (volume savings) through pooled ads. Lessees' images are aided by their relationships with popular stores.

Lessees face these possible problems: There may be inflexibility as to the hours they must be open and the operating style they must utilize. The goods/service lines they are allowed to offer will usually be restricted. If lessees are successful, the stores may raise the rent or may not renew leases when they expire. The in-store locations may not generate the sales expected.

A leased department may be viewed from two perspectives: as an element in a shopping center and as a part of a franchise system. In the shopping center context, a leased department operator is renting an area with a given traffic flow to conduct its business. The lessee must examine the character of the traffic flow and its relationship to the chosen target market; the lessor must examine the extent to which the leased department will either create added traffic or be a parasite and live off the traffic generated by other parts of the store. The franchise analogy relates to a leased department's ability to blend with the merchandise philosophy of another retailer and the need to set a broad policy for all departments, so an entire store's image is not injured by one operator.

An example of a prosperous long-term lease arrangement is one shared by the CPI Corporation and Sears. For nearly 40 years, CPI (http://www.cpicorp.com) has had photo studios in Sears stores. In exchange for the use of 300 square feet of space in 910 Sears stores, CPI pays Sears 15 percent of its gross sales. CPI's annual sales per square foot are much higher than Sears' overall average. CPI has a five-year licensing agreement with Sears that has been renewed several times. Its yearly revenues via leased departments in Sears outlets exceed $280 million.

Vertical Marketing System

A **vertical marketing system** consists of all the levels of independently owned businesses along a channel of distribution. Goods and services are normally distributed through one of these types of vertical marketing systems: independent, partially integrated, and fully integrated. See Figure 4-7.

In an independent vertical marketing system, there are three levels of independently owned businesses: manufacturers, wholesalers, and retailers. Such a system is most often used if manufacturers and retailers are small, intensive distribution is sought, customers are widely dispersed, unit sales are high, company resources are low, channel members want to share costs and risks, and task specialization is desirable. Independent vertical marketing systems are used by many stationery stores, gift shops, hardware stores, food stores, drugstores, and a number of other businesses. They are the leading form of vertical marketing system.

With a partially integrated vertical marketing system, two independently owned businesses along a channel perform all production and distribution functions without the aid of the third. The most common form of this system is when a manufacturer and a retailer complete transactions and shipping, storing, and other distribution functions in the absence of an independently owned wholesaler. A partially integrated system is most

Figure 4-7

Vertical Marketing Systems: Functions and Ownership

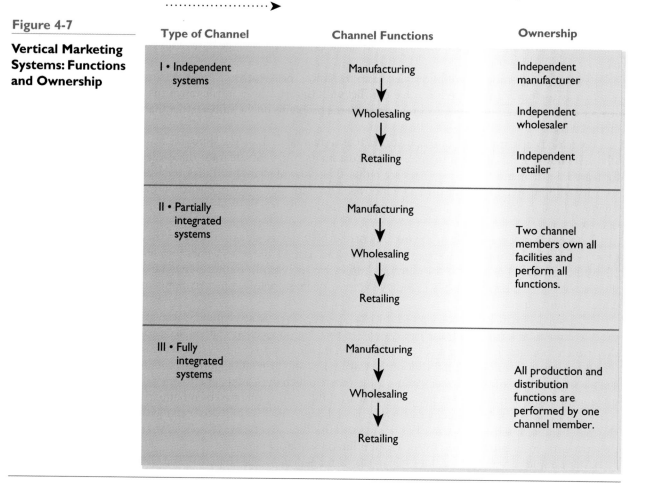

Type of Channel	Channel Functions	Ownership
I • Independent systems	Manufacturing → Wholesaling → Retailing	Independent manufacturer / Independent wholesaler / Independent retailer
II • Partially integrated systems	Manufacturing → Wholesaling → Retailing	Two channel members own all facilities and perform all functions.
III • Fully integrated systems	Manufacturing → Wholesaling → Retailing	All production and distribution functions are performed by one channel member.

apt if manufacturers and retailers are large, selective or exclusive distribution is sought, unit sales are moderate, company resources are high, greater channel control is desired, and existing wholesalers are too expensive or unavailable. Partially integrated systems are often used by furniture stores, appliance stores, restaurants, computer retailers, and mail-order firms.

Through a fully integrated vertical marketing system, a single firm performs all production and distribution functions without the aid of any other firms. In the past, this system was usually employed only by manufacturers, such as Avon, Goodyear, Sherwin-Williams, and major gasoline refiners. At Sherwin-Williams, the paint manufacturer, its 2,150 company-owned stores account for 65 percent of company sales.[9] Today, more retailers have fully integrated systems for at least some of their products. For example, Kroger (the food retailer) produces dairy items, baked goods, ice cream, and other items; and Sears has ownership shares in an appliance maker, a paint and detergent maker, an apparel maker, and others.

A fully integrated vertical marketing system enables a firm to have total control over its strategy, have direct contact with final consumers, have higher retail markups without raising prices (by eliminating channel members), be self-sufficient and not rely on others, have exclusivity over the goods and services offered, and keep all profits within the company. For example, by making many of the products sold in its stores, Ben & Jerry's (the ice cream firm) maximizes product visibility, trains and supervises store per-

[9]David P. Schulz, "Sherwin-Williams Steps Up Effort in Consumer Paint Market," *Stores* (November 1996), pp. 39–42.

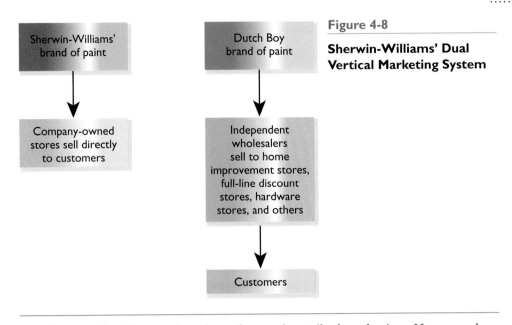

Figure 4-8

Sherwin-Williams' Dual Vertical Marketing System

sonnel, has exclusivity over brands, and controls retail ads and prices. However, there may be some difficulties with a fully integrated system, including high investment costs and a lack of expertise in both manufacturing and retailing.

Some firms (including many of those cited in this section) use a **dual vertical marketing system,** whereby they are involved in more than one type of distribution arrangement. Thus, Sherwin-Williams has a fully integrated system for its Sherwin-Williams paints and sells them only at company-owned stores. Sherwin-Williams also sells its Dutch Boy paints in home improvement stores, full-line discount stores, hardware stores, and others by an independent vertical marketing system (which includes wholesalers). This means Sherwin-Williams can appeal to different consumers, increase revenues, share some of its costs, and maintain a good degree of control over its strategy. See Figure 4-8.

Besides partially or fully integrating a vertical marketing system, a firm can exert power in a distribution channel because of its economic, legal, or political strength; superior knowledge and abilities; customer loyalty; or other factors. **Channel control** occurs when one member of a distribution channel can dominate the decisions made in that channel by the power it possesses. Manufacturers, wholesalers, and retailers each have a combination of tools to improve their positions relative to one another.

Manufacturers can exert control by franchising, whereby franchisees' marketing programs come under close scrutiny; developing strong brand loyalty, wherein retailers have to stock merchandise because of consumer demand; pre-ticketing merchandise, thereby designating suggested list or selling prices; and exclusive distribution, where retailers voluntarily agree to adhere to given standards in exchange for sole distribution rights in given geographic areas.

Wholesalers have the ability to exert influence over manufacturers and retailers in these situations: If wholesalers are large, their businesses are important and they can put pressure on suppliers and buyers. They can introduce their own private brands and circumvent manufacturers. A franchise system and/or brand loyalty can be developed to control the distribution system. The wholesalers can become the most efficient members in the channel for the functions they perform, such as shipping and processing reorders.

Retailers can exert clout with other channel members in these instances: a large proportion of a supplier's output is sold to one retailer, private branding is employed, or economic power (large gross sales) exists.

When one retailer represents a large percentage of a manufacturer's sales volume, channel control may be applied. For example, there are a number of independent companies from which Sears purchases a large proportion of its output. One such company is Whirlpool Corporation, the maker of major appliances, which produces Sears' Kenmore brand of appliances. As a result, Sears has a strong bargaining position.

Private brands (labels) or store brands can enable retailers to have channel control, improve competitive positioning, and raise profit margins. For instance, over one-half of the apparel purchased by national chains and about one-fifth of the apparel bought by specialty retailers involve private-label goods. In a typical supermarket, private-label goods (including "no-name" generics) account for 15 percent to 20 percent of purchases. At Sainsbury, a British-based supermarket chain, two-thirds of the products it buys are private-label items.

With private labeling, retailers can gain significant power over wholesalers and manufacturers by attaining brand loyalty for their own products, converting brand loyalty to store loyalty, and requiring that items be made to specifications. Private labeling lets retailers switch vendors (sellers) with no impact on their own customer loyalty, as long as the same product specifications are used. Just the threat of switching vendors (with no offsetting impact on private-brand sales) is often adequate action to get a supplier in line on a retailer's price, delivery, or terms request.

Clearly established channel roles often have significant advantages for all parties. Long-term relationships allow for scheduling efficiencies and let retailers receive supplier financing and vendors obtain bank loans (due to pre-sold inventories). Some economies result because activities are eliminated, simplified, or shared. Advertising, financing, and billing are dramatically simplified, and many tasks, such as merchandise marking, can be performed by the manufacturer.

Consumer Cooperative

A **consumer cooperative** is a retail firm owned by its customer members. In a cooperative arrangement, a group of consumers invests in the company, receives stock certificates, elects officers, manages operations, and shares the profits or savings that accrue. In the United States, there are several thousand consumer cooperatives, ranging from small buying clubs to Recreational Equipment Inc. (REI) with $450 million in annual

St. Petersburg Association: A Russian Consumer Cooperative

Vladimir Ershov is president of the St. Petersburg Association of consumer cooperatives, the largest food distribution company in St. Petersburg, Russia. It operates 41 retail stores, a warehouse, and 15 farmers' markets. Ershov has made a number of trips to the United States in an attempt to develop stronger ties with U.S. food wholesalers. He currently buys products from Green Giant, Pillsbury, Land O' Lakes, and Skylark (meats).

When the cooperative was originally founded, Russian consumers were amazed by the large selection in its stores; but they soon became used to the variety. The stores today even carry 20 different types of spaghetti. According to Ershov, "Whatever they [Russian consumers] can afford, they buy. Whatever we don't have, we order."

Russian consumers especially like American canned goods such as corn, beans, and green peas. And because the St. Petersburg growing season is short, most fresh vegetables have to be imported. Before the imported vegetables were stocked, farmers' markets were only open during the growing season. They are now open year-round.

Ershov believes there are too many sellers and not enough farmers. As a result, many small retail businesses have begun to purchase goods from his warehouse and then resell these goods to final consumers at prices slightly below the cooperative's regular retail prices. At the same time, farm production has been stymied due to lack of governmental support.

Source: Chad Rubel, "Russian Grocery Store Exec Seeks U.S. Imports," *Marketing News* (May 20, 1996), p. 2.

sales. Consumer cooperatives have been most popular in food retailing. However, the 500 or so U.S. food cooperatives account for only a fraction of 1 percent of total retail store sales (and less than 1 percent of total grocery sales).

Consumer cooperatives exist for these basic reasons: Some consumers feel they can operate stores as well as or better than traditional retailers. They believe existing retailers are inadequately fulfilling customer needs as to healthful, environmentally safe products. They also assume existing retailers often make excessive profits and that they can sell merchandise for lower prices.

This is how REI operates: It sells outdoor recreational equipment, such as backpacks and bicycles, to 1.4 million active members. It has 4,000 employees in 44 stores, runs a mail-order business, and has a Web site (http://www.rei.com). Unlike other cooperatives, REI is operated by a professional staff that adheres to the policies set by the member-elected board. There is a $15 one-time membership fee, which entitles customers to shop at REI, elect people to the board of directors, and share in profits (based on the amount spent by each member). REI's goal is to distribute a 10 percent dividend to members.[10]

Cooperatives have not grown beyond their current level because they involve a lot of consumer initiative and drive; consumers are usually not expert in buying, handling, and selling goods and services; cost savings and low selling prices have not been as expected in many cases; and consumer boredom in running or working for the cooperatives frequently sets in. Traditional retailers are also now doing a better job of appealing to consumer niches in categories such as grocery products.[11]

[10]REI literature; and "Single Version of the Truth Rescues a Tough Year for REI," *Chain Store Age* (September 1996), p. 77.
[11]See Steve Weinstein, "Assets and Liabilities," *Progressive Grocer* (May 1996), p. 163.

Summary

1. *To show the ways in which retail institutions can be classified* There are 2.2 million retail firms in the United States operating 2.5 million establishments. They can be classified on the basis of ownership, store-based strategy mix, service versus goods strategy mix, and nonstore-based strategy mix and nontraditional retailing. These categories are not mutually exclusive; many retailers can be placed in more than one category. This chapter deals with retail ownership. Chapters 5 and 6 report on the other classifications.

2. *To study retailers on the basis of ownership type and examine the characteristics of each* Eighty percent of U.S. retail establishments are run as independents, with each operating only one store. This number is mostly due to ease of entry. Among the competitive advantages of independents are their flexibility, low investments, specialized offerings, direct strategy control, image, consistency, independence, and entrepreneurial spirit. Disadvantages include limited bargaining power, few economies of scale, labor inten-

siveness, reduced media access, overdependence on the owner, and limited planning.

Retail chains consist of multiple stores under common ownership, usually with some centralized purchasing and decision making. They account for a fifth of retail establishments, but 60 percent of U.S. retail sales. Chains have these advantages: bargaining power, wholesale function efficiencies, multiple-store efficiencies, computerization, media access, well-defined management, and long-range planning. They face these potential problems: inflexibility, high investments, reduced control, and limited independence.

Franchising embodies contractual arrangements between franchisors (manufacturers, wholesalers, or service sponsors) and franchisees that let the latter conduct given businesses under established names and according to specified rules. It accounts for over one-third of U.S. store sales. Franchisees have these benefits: small investments, well-known company names, standardized operations and training, cooperative marketing efforts, exclusive selling rights, and volume purchases. They can face constrained decision making by oversaturation, lower than promised profits, strict contract provisions, cancellation clauses, short-term contracts, and continuing royalty payments. Franchisors benefit by more quickly and cheaply developing large businesses, setting franchisee qualifications, improving cash flow, outlining operating procedures, gaining high franchisee motivation, and receiving ongoing royalties. They can suffer if individual franchisees hurt the company image, do not operate uniformly, compete with one another, lower resale values, and seek greater independence.

Leased departments are in-store sites rented to outside parties. They usually exist in categories on the fringe of their stores' major product lines. Stores gain these advantages: expertise of lessees, reduced costs, greater traffic, merchandising support, and revenues. Potential disadvantages are conflicts with lessees and adverse effects on store image. Benefits for lessees are well-known store names, steady customers, immediate sales, reduced expenses, economies of scale, and an image associated with the store. Potential problems are inflexibility, restrictions on items sold, lease nonrenewal, and poorer results than expected.

Vertical marketing systems consist of all the levels of independently owned firms along a channel of distribution. In independent systems, there are separately owned manufacturers, wholesalers, and retailers. In partially integrated systems, two separately

owned firms, usually manufacturers and retailers, perform all production and distribution functions without the aid of a third. In fully integrated systems, single firms do all production and distribution functions. Some firms use dual vertical marketing systems, whereby they are involved in more than one type of system.

Consumer cooperatives are retail firms owned by their customers, who invest, receive company stock, elect officers, manage operations, and share savings or profits. They account for a tiny fraction of retail store sales. Cooperatives are formed when consumers believe they can perform retailing functions, offerings of traditional retailers are inadequate, and traditional retailers' prices are too high. They have not grown because consumer initiative is required, expertise may be lacking, expectations have frequently not been met, and boredom occurs.

3. *To explore the methods used by manufacturers, wholesalers, and retailers to exert influence in the distribution channel* Even without an integrated vertical marketing system, channel control can be exerted by the most powerful firm(s) in the channel. Manufacturers, wholesalers, and retailers each have ways to increase their impact in a channel. Retailers' influence is greatest when they represent a large percentage of their vendors' sales, private branding is used, and economic power due to order volume exists.

Key Terms

retail institution (p. 103)
independent (p. 104)
ease of entry (p. 104)
chain (p. 107)
franchising (p. 109)

product/trademark franchising
  (p. 109)
business format franchising (p. 110)
constrained decision making (p. 113)
leased department (p. 113)

vertical marketing system (p. 115)
dual vertical marketing system
  (p. 117)
channel control (p. 117)
consumer cooperative (p. 118)

Questions for Discussion

1. What are the characteristics of each of the ownership forms discussed in this chapter?
2. How may a retailer be categorized by more than one ownership form? Give two examples.
3. Why does the concept of ease of entry usually have a greater impact on independent retailers than on chain retailers?
4. How can an independent retailer overcome the problem of overdependence on the owner?
5. What difficulties might an independent encounter if it tries to expand into a chain?

6. What competitive advantages and disadvantages do regional chains have in comparison with national chains?
7. Do you expect retail chains with 100 or more outlets to continue to increase their percentage of U.S. retail sales? Explain your answer.
8. What are the similarities and differences between chains and franchising?
9. From the franchisee's perspective, under what circumstances would product/trademark franchising be advantageous? When would business format franchising be better?

10. Why would a department store want to lease space to an outside operator rather than run a business, such as shoes, itself? What would be its risks in this approach?

11. What are the pros and cons of Sherwin-Williams' using a dual vertical marketing system?

12. At many retail apparel chains, store brands account for more than 50 percent of sales. What are the pros and cons of this strategy from a channel control perspective?

13. How could a small independent gift store increase its channel control?

14. Why have consumer cooperatives not expanded much in recent years? What would you recommend to change this?

Web-Based Exercise:

FEDERAL TRADE COMMISSION (http://www.ftc.gov/bcp/franchise)

Questions

1. Summarize the major lessons to be learned by a prospective franchisee in the *Consumer Guide to Buying a Franchise.* (http://www.ftc.gov/bcp/franchise/franchiz.htm)

2. Describe how the FTC Franchise Rule protects a prospective franchisee. (http://www.ftc.gov/bcp/franchise/netrule.htm)

3. Summarize the major implications of three recent FTC enforcement cases involving franchising. (http://www.ftc.gov/bcp/franchise/caselist.htm)

4. Discuss how franchise disclosure laws differ in two states that are close to your college or university. What are the ramifications of these differences to franchisors? To franchisees? (http://www.ftc.gov/bcp/franchise/netdiscl.htm)

**CASE 1
Supervalu:
Making it
Happen at
Retail***

Supervalu is the second-largest food distributor in the United States, after Fleming. It supplies about 4,100 supermarkets in 48 states (most of which are independently owned and operated) with grocery and nongrocery items such as produce, meat, dairy products, housewares, and paper goods. Through Supervalu, the independent supermarkets receive economies of scale that better enable them to compete against large chains. In addition, Supervalu operates about 280 corporate-owned stores under several formats including superstores, food and drug combination stores, limited assortment stores, and traditional supermarkets (under these names: Cub Foods, Shop' n Save, Bigg's, Save-A-Lot, and Laneco). Its Web site is (http://www.supervalu-intl.com).

Retail customers served by Supervalu range in size from small convenience stores to large supercenters (that are 200,000 square feet in size) and everything in between (such as traditional supermarkets, food and drug combination stores, and limited assortment stores). Its customers also include both independents and chain store operators.

Supervalu believes one way to grow as a wholesaler is to "grow its customers." It, therefore, offers a wide variety of services to enhance the marketability of its customers. These include a private-label program, cost reduction programs, merchandising assistance, and site location planning. Let's look at these programs.

Supervalu's private-label sales to its retail food store customers accounted for about 10 percent of its overall wholesale food sales in 1996. Its private-label products include

*The material in this case is drawn from Michael Garry, "GIS: Finding Opportunity in Data," *Progressive Grocer* (June 1996), pp. 61–69; Ryan Mathews, "Wanted: Low-Cost Distribution," *Progressive Grocer* (January 1996), pp. 39–40; Larry Partridge, "The Deli's Best Friend," *Progressive Grocer* (January 1996), p. 95; Glenn Snyder," 'Smoking' the Competition," *Progressive Grocer* (March 1996), pp. 122–123; *Supervalu 1996 Annual Report; Supervalu 10K for the Year Ended February 24, 1996;* and Patrick J. Spain and James R. Talbot (Editors), *Hoover's Handbook of American Business 1996* (Austin, Texas: Reference Press, 1996), pp. 1366–1367.

CASE 1
(Continued)

frozen foods, dairy, grocery items, bakery products, and general merchandise. Besides making these products available to its retail food store customers, Supervalu plans and implements private-label sales events, provides in-store merchandising materials, and conducts special personnel training programs for these stores. Supervalu knows its private-label assistance for retailer customers builds store loyalty (through loyalty toward the private-label brand).

In 1992, Supervalu began its ADVANTAGE restructuring program, designed to make the company's food distribution system more efficient. Through the ADVANTAGE program, every buying decision, delivery, and transaction was rated as a way of eliminating unnecessary functions. The main goal of ADVANTAGE has been to reduce costs to Supervalu's supermarket customers, even if this means goods are shipped directly from a vendor to a retail store (bypassing Supervalu's distribution center). The ADVANTAGE program has separate logistics systems for goods with low and high inventory turnover, with small and large volumes, and with low and high values. It also relies on consolidating orders from multiple distribution centers to increase Supervalu's bargaining power. The ADVANTAGE program is so comprehensive that some retail analysts predict that it will change the way in which food is distributed in the United States.

To illustrate Supervalu's merchandising assistance, let us look at the work of Bob Beckerman, Supervalu's director of delicatessen operations. Beckerman views his job to be a consultant to Supervalu's retail operators. As part of his duties, he regularly meets with Supervalu's major delicatessen suppliers to devise local, regional, and nationally-based merchandising programs. Training programs are even developed by Supervalu for individual operators and transmitted through satellite broadcasts.

Supervalu also helps its retailer customers better plan their new store location strategies. Supervalu extensively uses geographic information systems (GIS) software to generate maps showing vital data on customer demographics, sales, and competitor locations. By using GIS software, Supervalu better evaluates potential sites in terms of the number of shoppers who live in given areas, their spending power, and the closeness to other stores. Supervalu also uses GIS software to recommend a specific store format for a given market area.

Questions
1. "Supervalu provides its retailer customers with the benefits of chain ownership." Evaluate this statement.
2. Should Supervalu utilize constrained decision making? Explain your answer.
3. What type of vertical marketing system does Supervalu represent?
4. Analyze Supervalu's distribution system from the perspective of channel control.

Video Questions on Supervalu
1. Discuss Supervalu's design and construction services.
2. What other services does Supervalu offer its retailer customers?

Maaco Auto Painting and Bodyworks was founded in 1972 by Anthony A. Martino, who created Aamco Transmissions in the 1950s. After Martino sold his interest in Aamco in the 1960s, he observed that another segment of the auto after-market was ripe for franchising—auto paint and collision repair. At the time, auto body and painting service businesses were fragmented, with thousands of small independent body shops, one national company that performed cheap jobs, and custom shops that specialized in restoring expensive vehicles.

As Martino saw it, the low- and high-priced ends of the market were saturated, while the huge middle market was underrepresented. So, he devised the methods, manuals, and systems for an auto painting and collision repair franchise business by a pilot shop he opened in Wilmington, Delaware. Today, there are 500 independently owned and operated Maaco franchises in 43 states and Canada. And during 1997, Maaco painted its 10 millionth vehicle.

Maaco is the only national firm in the $24 billion a year paint and collision business. It repaints cars three to seven years old, restores rust-damaged cars, and repairs cars that have been involved in accidents. Although it offers paint jobs for as low as $199, Maaco is most involved with the middle-market price range of $300 to $500 paint jobs. According to Anthony Martino, "Maaco's strategy of painting 40 cars a week at $500 per car is more profitable than painting three or four cars a week at $1,200." The success of Maaco is due to its positive image, the consistency and uniformity of operations, and the support programs provided to franchisees.

Maaco is the best-known U.S. auto paint and collision repair chain. Its strong reputation is based on the quality of work conducted by its local franchisees and a nationally accepted limited warranty. The image is reinforced by a national advertising program and public relations conducted by Maaco, as well as local ads and public relations activities by franchisees.

Maaco instills consistency and uniformity throughout all of its franchised locations. Each location uses the same manner of operation (that includes hand and machine sanding, chemical washing, proper masking, painting in a modern spray booth, and baking in a temperature-controlled oven) and the same caliber supplies. Each franchisee also receives four weeks of formal training at corporate headquarters and three weeks of on-site training.

Maaco's customer support team works with franchisees on financing assistance, site selection, installation of equipment, lease negotiations, placing ads for crews, crew training, and problem solving. During training, franchisees receive operations, sales, advertising, and promotional manuals; and they meet and discuss their store opening with department heads from each major support area. After store openings, Maaco provides ongoing support for sales and marketing, public relations, purchasing, operations, weekly reports, and quality control. The firm's training process is an ongoing one.

The total costs for a Maaco franchise are about $200,000 ($60,000 is the minimum cash required, the balance is financed). This includes all equipment, an initial inventory of supplies, a $30,000 franchise fee, and take-home pay for the franchisee for his or her first year of business. In addition, franchisees pay a royalty fee of 8 percent of sales to Maaco and are obligated to spend $750 per week in local advertising. Some franchisees pool their budgets to advertise on TV.

Maaco's objectives call for each franchised unit to have an annual net profit of $130,000. Although the costs (based on rents and local labor rates) and income (based on the number of paint jobs, the percent of insurance claim work, and the percent of fleet business) differ by location, Maaco's profit expectations are based on an average franchise location repairing and painting 25 to 30 cars per week. Maaco also assumes that each

CASE 2
Maaco: Evaluating Franchising Opportunities[†]

[†]The material in this case is drawn from Maaco's Web site (http://www.maaco.com); *Maaco: The Franchise* (King of Prussia, Pennsylvania: 1990); *The Maaco Story: 1972 to the Present* (King of Prussia, Pennsylvania: n.d.); and telephone interviews with Maaco staff.

CASE 2
(Continued)

franchised outlet can convert 60 percent of its estimates into completed business with an average price of $450 per car, including bodywork.

The average franchise has weekly sales of between $12,000 and $15,000 for all but the first three months of each year, when business is slower on a nationwide basis. Franchisees generally run special sales during the winter season to keep their full-time work crews busy.

Questions

1. What are the pros and cons of an individual becoming a Maaco franchisee rather than opening an independent auto paint and body shop?
2. Develop a checklist of factors a person should consider in evaluating a Maaco franchising opportunity.
3. What additional information, besides that provided in the case, should a prospective franchisee acquire before purchasing a Maaco franchise? Cite sources that he or she could use to acquire this information.
4. Evaluate the financial data provided in this case from the perspective of a potential franchisee.

Video Questions on Maaco

1. Describe the challenges and opportunities that Maaco faces in the future.
2. Assess the video as a means of attracting potential franchisees.

APPENDIX ON FRANCHISING

This appendix is presented because of the rapid growth of franchising and its exciting possibilities. For example, in 1986, the Serruya brothers (Aaron, Michael, and Simon—who then ranged in age from 14 to 20) opened their first Yogen Früz frozen yogurt stand in a Toronto mall. Today, because of the Serruyas' aggressively franchising their concept, Yogen Früz has 2,600 outlets, only 9 of which are company-owned, under three different trade names—including the recently acquired I Can't Believe It's Yogurt (ICBIY) and Bresler's. Annual revenues are in the hundreds of millions of dollars (U.S.). They have blanketed the United States and Canada, with several outlets in Asia and Latin America. None of this would have been possible without the use of franchising (and a great concept, of course).[1]

In this appendix, we go beyond the discussion of franchising in Chapter 4. We provide information on managerial issues in franchising and on the relationships between franchisors and franchisees.

Since 1980, annual U.S. retail franchising sales have tripled. As noted in the chapter, 600,000 retail establishments in the United States are affiliated with 3,000 franchisors and employ 8 million full- and part-time workers (including the proprietors). Many large business format franchisors have at least 1,000 outlets. The U.S. Department of Commerce predicts that retail franchising will continue to grow sharply for at least the next decade.

U.S. franchisors are now situated in over 100 countries worldwide, a number that keeps on rising. This trend is due to these factors: U.S. franchisors recognize the growth potential in foreign markets. Franchising is becoming accepted as a retailing format in more nations. Trade barriers among nations have been reduced due to such pacts as NAFTA—the North American Free Trade Agreement—that is making it easier for U.S.-, Canada-, and Mexico-based firms to operate in the others' marketplaces.

[1]Holly Celeste Fisk, "Just Desserts," *Entrepreneur* (September 1996), p. 179.

Franchising appeals to many owners and potential owners (franchisees) of small busi- **MANAGERIAL**
nesses for a variety of reasons. Most franchisors have easy-to-learn, standardized oper- **ISSUES IN**
ating methods they have perfected over the years. This means new franchisees do not **FRANCHISING**
have to learn from their own trial-and-error methods, which may be costly and time-
consuming. Franchisors often have training facilities where franchisees are taught how
to operate equipment, manage employees, maintain records, and improve customer relations; they usually follow up with field visits by a service staff.

A new outlet of a nationally advertised franchise (such as Subway fast food, Fantastic
Sams hair salons, or Midas auto service stores) can develop a large customer following
rather quickly and easily because of the reputation of the firm. And not only does franchising result in good initial sales and profits, it also reduces franchisees' risk of failure *if
the franchisees affiliate with strong, supportive franchisors.*

The investment and startup costs for a franchised outlet can be as low as a few thousand dollars for a personal service business and as high as several million dollars for a hotel. In return for its expenditures, any franchisee usually gets exclusive selling rights for
a geographic area; a business format franchisee also gets training, store equipment and
fixtures, and assistance in picking out a store site, negotiating with suppliers, advertising, and so on.

What kind of individual is best suited to being a franchisee? This is what one expert
believes:

> Owning a franchise is not for everyone. The right person in the wrong program can
> lead to profound unhappiness. Because the time investment can involve one's life
> savings and a long-term legal commitment, this is not a step that should be taken
> lightly. Fiercely independent entrepreneurs are rarely happy in the franchise world.
> If one is interested in running and designing every aspect of an operation, he or she
> should think twice before buying a franchise. That person may be better off with an
> independent business. Most franchising programs impose a strict regimen on fran-
> chisees, dictating everything from how to greet customers to how to prepare and pre-
> sent the product or service. If one chafes at any restrictions, he or she may find fran-
> chise life too confining. But for a person used to the security of a full-time job, being
> a franchisee can offer the support needed to make a transition to entrepreneurship.
> These days, many downsized middle managers are bringing a wealth of business
> savvy to the franchise world. Thousands are at that stage in their careers where they
> have some capital to invest and are not interested in inventing a new (and risky) busi-
> ness concept, yet are attracted to the dream of self-employment.[2]

According to a study of more than 200 franchise companies, the typical franchisee
has attended college (over 40 percent have at least a bachelor's degree), is between the age
of 35 and 50, and earns an annual income of $67,000 plus. More than one-third previ-
ously worked in professional or executive positions.[3] A Gallup poll of retailing franchisees found that

■ 94 percent of the franchisees said they were very or somewhat successful.
■ 75 percent of the franchisees said their businesses met or exceeded their expectations.
■ 63 percent of the franchisees expressed greater satisfaction with their franchising experience than with their prior business experience.

[2]Andrew A. Caffey, "Opportunity Knocks," *Entrepreneur Magazine's Buyers Guide to Franchise & Business
Opportunities 1997*, p. 3.
[3]Dan Fost and Susan Mitchell, "Small Stores with Big Names," *American Demographics* (November 1992),
pp. 52–58.

Table I   THE COSTS OF BECOMING A NEW FRANCHISEE WITH SELECTED FRANCHISORS (as of 1997)

Franchising Company	Franchise Fee	Startup Costs	Royalty Fee as a % of Sales	Franchisee-Owned Outlets as a % of All Outlets
Aamco Transmissions	$30,000	$114,000	7	99+
Dunkin' Donuts	$40,000	$70,300–$484,300	4.9	93
Fantastic Sams	$25,000	$83,600–$120,800	$191/week fee	99+
Great American Cookies	$25,000	$105,800–$600,500	7	69
Jazzercise	$325–$650	$1,360–$16,850	up to 20	99+
Lawn Doctor	$35,500	$6,000	10	100
McDonald's	$45,000	$363,000–$601,000	12.5 and up	79
Medicine Shoppe	$10,000–$18,000	$46,850–$89,450	5.5	99+
Miracle Ear Hearing	$28,000 and up	$73,000 and up	$44/aid	97
Molly Maid	$9,900 and up	$15,000–$30,000	3–6	99
Moto Photo	$35,000	$134,800 and up	6	88
Nevada Bob's Discount Golf	$37,500–$57,500	$189,500–$240,500	2	89
Petland	$25,000	$131,500–$455,000	4.5	99+
Super 8 Motels	$21,000	$240,000–$2,200,000	5	100
Wicks 'N' Sticks	$25,000	$138,550–$224,300	6	98

Source: Compiled by the authors from "18th Annual Franchise 500," *Entrepreneur* (January 1997), various pages.

■ 79 percent of the franchisees rated the relationship with their franchisors as good or excellent.

■ 75 percent of the franchisees said they would again buy an outlet from the same franchisor if they had the opportunity to do so.[4]

An illustration of how inexpensive franchising can be is Novus Windshield Repair, a Minneapolis-based firm with 2,600 franchised outlets. A typical franchisee makes an initial payment of $25,000 to $40,000 (including equipment and supplies) and ongoing royalty payments of about 8 percent of sales. The franchisees engage in the repair of vehicle windshields.[5]

Table 1 shows the franchise fees, startup costs, and royalty rates for new franchisees at 15 leading franchisors in a wide variety of business categories. At present, financing support is offered by almost one-third of U.S. franchisors, including Burger King, Mail Boxes, Etc., 7-Eleven, Subway, and Thrifty Rent-A-Car. Sixty percent of the firms cited in Table 1 either provide financing or arrange third-party financing. In addition, by various programs, the U.S. Small Business Administration is one of the best financing options for prospective franchisees. Some banks also offer special interest rates for franchisees affiliated with established franchisors.

Besides receiving fees and royalties for allowing franchisees to run one or more outlets, franchisors may sell goods and services to their franchisees. Sometimes, this is required; more often, for legal reasons, such purchases are at the franchisees' discretion (subject to franchisor specifications). Each year, franchisors sell billions of dollars worth of items to franchisees.

Franchisors can set detailed standards covering every aspect of the business, such as signs, product freshness, merchandise selection, the level of involvement expected of franchisees, and employee uniforms. About one-half of U.S. business format franchisors require franchisees to be owner-operators and work full-time at the business. The franchisors' stan-

[4]Michael H. Seid, "Franchising Thrives in the '90s," *Stores* (May 1993), p. 74.
[5]"18th Annual Franchise 500," *Entrepreneurship* (January 1997), pp. 212–213.

1.	What are the required franchise fees: initial fee, advertising appropriations, and royalties?
2.	What degree of technical knowledge is required of the franchisee?
3.	What is the required investment in time by the franchisee? Does the franchisee have to be actively involved in the day-to-day operations of the franchise?
4.	What is the extent of control of a franchise by a franchisor in terms of materials purchased, sales quotas, space requirements, pricing, the range of goods to be sold, required inventory levels, and so on?
5.	Can the franchisee accept the regimentation and rules of the franchisor?
6.	Are the costs of required supplies and materials purchased from the franchisor at market value, above market value, or below market value?
7.	What degree of name recognition do consumers have of the franchise? Does the franchisor have a meaningful advertising program?
8.	What image does the franchise have among consumers and among current franchisees?
9.	What are the level and quality of services provided by the franchisor to franchisees: site selection, training, bookkeeping, human relations, equipment maintenance, and trouble-shooting?
10.	What is the franchisor policy in terminating franchisees? What are the conditions of franchise termination? What is the rate of franchise termination and nonrenewal?
11.	What is the franchisor's legal history?
12.	What is the length of the franchise agreement?
13.	What is the failure rate of existing franchises?
14.	What is the franchisor's policy with regard to company-owned and franchisee-owned outlets?
15.	What policy does the franchisor have in allowing franchisees to sell their business?
16.	What is the franchisor's policy with regard to territorial protection for existing franchisees? With regard to new franchisees and new company-owned establishments?
17.	What is the earning potential of the franchise during the first year? The first five years?

dards must be adhered to by franchisees. Thus, franchisor concerns about systemwide consistency and franchisee desires to conduct their own business sometimes lead to conflicts.

Franchised outlets can be purchased (leased) directly from franchisors, master franchisees, or existing franchisees. Franchisors sell either new locations or company-owned outlets (some of which may have been taken back from unsuccessful franchisees). They sometimes sell the rights to develop outlets in geographic regions or counties to master franchisees, which then deal with individual franchisees. Existing franchisees usually have the right to sell their units if they first offer them to their franchisor; if potential purchasers meet all financial and other criteria; and/or if purchasers undergo comprehensive training. Of particular interest to prospective franchisees is the emphasis a company places on franchisee-owned outlets versus franchisor-owned ones. This helps indicate the commitment of the firm to franchising. As indicated in Table 1, leading franchisors typically have a small percentage of company-owned outlets.

One last point regarding managerial issues in franchising concerns the failure rate of new franchisees. For many years, it was believed that becoming a success as a franchisee was virtually a "sure thing"—and much safer than starting a business from scratch—due to the franchisor's well-known name, its years of experience, its training programs, and so on. More recently, research has shown that becoming a franchisee may be at least as risky as opening a new business. Why? Some franchisors have oversaturated the market with stores and not provided the promised support, and unscrupulous franchisors have preyed on unsuspecting investors.[6]

With the preceding in mind, Figure 1 has a checklist by which potential franchisees can assess opportunities. In using this checklist, franchisees should also obtain full prospectuses and financial reports from all franchisors under consideration; and they should talk to existing franchise operators and customers. For more information, check out "Franchises and Business Opportunities" (http://www.ftc.gov.bcp/franchise/net-fran.htm).

FRANCHISOR-FRANCHISEE RELATION-SHIPS

Many franchisors and franchisees have good relationships because they share goals regarding company image, the way the business is operated and managed, the goods and/or services offered, cooperative advertising, and sales and profit growth. This two-way relationship is shown by the actions of Taco John's, a franchisor with 420 franchised Mexican restaurants:

> Say you're looking to buy a fast-food franchise. So you send away for marketing brochures, including one from Taco John's International. Initially, the Taco John's material reads no differently from everything else you have spread out across your kitchen table. The literature is peppered with pat references to "Taco John's and You" and even quotes satisfied customers, and (no kidding) restaurant critics. Standard fare. Then you get to the following passage: "[The Taco John's] Franchise Agreement is one of the most progressive in the industry, the first ever to be developed cooperatively with a franchisee association." Big deal. Actually, it is. In most franchise systems, the franchisee signs an agreement that boils down to this: either you do what the franchisor says or you stuff someone else's tacos. Taco John's chose to get franchisees more involved.[7]

Yet, for several reasons, tensions do exist between various franchisors and their franchisees. These are just some of the reasons why:

■ The franchisor–franchisee relationship is not one of employer to employee. Franchisor controls are often viewed as rigid.

■ Many franchise agreements are considered too short in duration by franchisees. Nearly one-half of U.S. agreements are 10 years in duration or less (one-sixth are 5 years or less), usually at the franchisor's request.

■ For the franchisees that lease their outlets' property from their franchisors, the loss of a franchise license generally means eviction; and the franchisee receives nothing for "goodwill."

■ Some franchisees feel franchisors want to buy back their units due to higher profit potential.

■ Some franchisors believe their franchisees do not reinvest enough in their outlets and that this results in a poor image for the firm.

[6]See Timothy Bates, "Look Before You Leap," *Inc.* (July 1995), pp. 23–24.
[7]Christopher Caggiano, "The Collectively Bargained Franchise Agreement," *Inc.* (November 1995), pp. 73–75.

- Franchisees may not be concerned enough about overall company image and the consistency of operations from one outlet to another.
- Franchisors may not give adequate territorial protection to franchisees and may open new outlets near existing ones.
- Franchisees may refuse to participate in cooperative advertising programs.
- Franchisees may offer substandard service.
- Some franchisors use minor contract infractions to oust franchisees.
- Franchised outlets that are put up for sale must usually be offered first to franchisors, which also have approval of sales to third parties.
- Some franchisees believe franchisor marketing support is low.
- Franchisees may be prohibited from operating competing businesses.
- Restrictions on purchases and suppliers may cause franchisees to pay higher prices and to have limited product assortments.
- Franchisees may band together to force changes in policies and exert pressure on franchisors.
- Sales and profit expectations may not be realized.

Tensions can lead to conflicts—even litigation. Potential negative franchisor actions include terminating agreements; reducing promotional and sales support; and adding unneeded red tape for orders, information requests, and warranty work. Potential negative franchisee actions include terminating agreements, adding competitors' product lines, refusing to promote goods and services, and not complying with franchisor information requests.

Each year, business format franchisors terminate the contracts of 10 percent of the franchisee-owned stores that opened within the prior five years; and the American Arbitration Association is asked to mediate hundreds of franchising disputes—at the request of both franchisors and franchisees. Since 1990, the number of franchisee complaints to the Federal Trade Commission about poor business franchisors on the part of their franchisors has grown at a 50 percent annual rate.[8]

Although franchising has historically been characterized by franchisors' possessing more power than franchisees, this inequality has been reduced in several ways. First, a number of franchisees affiliated with specific franchisors have joined together to increase their power. For example, the National Coalition of Associations of 7-Eleven Franchisees represents more than 2,000 franchisees running 7-Eleven convenience stores. Second, a number of large umbrella organizations representing franchisees, like the American Franchisee Association and the American Association of Franchisees Dealers, have been formed.

Third, many franchisees now operate more than one outlet, so they have greater clout. For instance, the major oil producers fear multiunit gasoline stations can amass enough power to buy from independent suppliers.[9] Fourth, there has been a substantial rise in litigation between franchisors and franchisees. As an example, an association representing franchisees that operated 3,100 KFC outlets filed suit against the franchisor after the latter sought to eliminate a clause in their franchise agreements stipulating that no new outlets could be built within 1.5 miles of existing ones. After several years of legal maneuvering, in 1996, KFC agreed to restore the protective radius for U.S. franchisees.[10] Fifth, when dissatisfied, some franchisee groups have sought to purchase their franchisors. For instance, a franchisee group at Straw Hat Pizza acquired their franchisor.

---

[8]See Andrew E. Serwer, "Trouble in Franchise Nation," *Fortune* (March 6, 1995), pp. 115–129.
[9]See Nicole Harris and Mike France, "Franchisees Get Feisty," *Business Week* (February 24, 1997), pp. 65–66.
[10]Jeffrey A. Tannenbaum, "PepsiCo's KFC Unit Reinstates Territorial Protection," *Wall Street Journal* (February 27, 1996), p. B2.

Improved communication and better cooperation are necessary to resolve these issues. One innovative approach to doing so is used by AlphaGraphics Printshops of the Future, a chain with 325 franchised outlets. At AlphaGraphics, "the franchisor no longer decides by itself how every penny of royalties will be used. Instead, 25 percent of royalty fees are set aside for services of each franchisee's choosing, such as help from computer consultants or promotional mailings." In return, "franchisees must keep current with royalty payments, submit monthly financial statements, and prepare annual budgets."As AlphaGraphics' chief executive said, "It's very difficult to help franchisees improve their business unless you have timely financial statements."[11]

Another progressive approach is the new code of ethics devised by the International Franchise Association. If the IFA's 32,000 franchisor, franchisee, and supplier members adhere to this voluntary code, the conflicts between franchisors and franchisees will decline substantially. These are some of the standards of conduct recommended in the IFA code:

■ Franchisors' offering circulars shall be complete, accurate, and not misleading.
■ Franchisors and franchisees shall deal with each other in an honest, ethical, and mutually respectful manner.
■ Franchisors shall not prohibit franchisees from forming, joining, or participating in any franchisee association.
■ Franchisee agreements may only be terminated for good cause. Franchisees shall be given a reasonable opportunity to remedy their shortcomings before they are actually terminated.
■ Prior to opening new outlets, franchisors shall consider the potential impact of those outlets on existing franchisees if the new outlets would be in close proximity to them.[12]

As one observer summed things up:

To attract more qualified franchisees, purchase arrangements must be more flexible. To increase franchisee satisfaction, a more balanced partnership between franchisor and franchisees is needed. To maximize the prospects for financial success for both parties, operating arrangements should take into account individual circumstances. Therefore, more franchisors will adopt, or at least experiment with, restructured franchise arrangements. This restructuring will affect both the terms of purchasing a franchise and the ongoing franchisor-franchisee relationship.[13]

[11]Jeffrey A. Tannenbaum, "To Pacify Irate Franchisees, Franchisers Extend Services," *Wall Street Journal* (February 24, 1995), pp. B1–B2.
[12]*IFA Code of Principles and Standards of Conduct* (Washington, D.C.: International Franchise Association).
[13]Bruce J. Walker, "Retail Franchising in the 1990s," *Arthur Andersen Retailing Issues Letter* (January 1991), p. 4.

Chapter 5

Retail Institutions by Store-Based Strategy Mix

CHAPTER OBJECTIVES

1. To describe the wheel of retailing, scrambled merchandising, and the retail life cycle and show how they help explain the performance and evolution of retail strategy mixes

2. To examine characteristics of a wide variety of retail institutions involved with store-based strategy mixes (divided into food-oriented and general merchandise groupings)

3. To contrast service-based retailing with goods-based retailing

Some Wall Street analysts tend to favor one of two strategies for specialty retailers. With the first approach, the retailer successfully focuses on a niche market with a unique offering. In the second, the specialty retailer is able to translate the niche concept into a strategy that is successful with the mass market. Urban Outfitters, an apparel marketer catering to the young "funky" market, clearly practices the first approach. According to the president of Urban Outfitters' newest division, Anthropologie, "We just don't believe that big is necessarily good."

Anthropologie concentrates on the sale of contemporary apparel and household items (such as Moroccan tea cups and French bed covers) to the former Urban Outfitters shopper who is now over 25 years of age. Nonetheless, Anthropologie's president says, "As forward as we are with fashion is as conservative as we are fiscally." For example, Anthropologie grew from one store in 1992 to only six stores in 1996. Although some observers predict there will eventually be 50 Anthropologie stores, its president makes a more cautious projection of 35 stores. Anthropologie's slow record of store openings is shared by its parent company. Urban Outfitters opened its first store in 1970 in Philadelphia; twenty-five years later, it had just grown to 27 stores—with $133 million in annual sales. In contrast, The Gap opened 225 stores in 1995 alone.

Some retailing experts respect the firm's slow-growth plans as being prudent. Others question why the firm's excellent management has not given investors the growth they desire. Urban Outfitters executives counter these objections by showing that earnings have grown by 44 percent during the past four years. Over this period, profit margins at Urban Outfitters have averaged 33 percent, a high figure for a specialty clothing retailer. Company executives also state that Wall Street analysts often fail to acknowledge the difficulties associated with rapid growth, such as the failure of operating systems to monitor growth or the preoccupation with new store locations at the expense of existing store units.

Some attribute part of the firm's overall profitability to its smart decision making in selecting appropriate retail locations. Urban Outfitters executives acknowledge that since their stores have a limited market potential they cannot successfully place new stores into mall locations that would be perfectly appropriate for more traditional clothing retailers.[1]

[1] Jennifer Steinhauer, "Retail Reality: A Success Not Obsessed by Expansion," *New York Times* (May 8, 1996), pp. D1, D4.

OVERVIEW

In Chapter 4, retail institutions were described by type of ownership arrangement. In this chapter, we discuss three key concepts in planning retail strategy mixes: the wheel of retailing, scrambled merchandising, and the retail life cycle. We then study the basic strategies of a broad range of store-based retail institutions. The chapter concludes by contrasting service versus goods retailing. Chapter 6 deals with nonstore-based strategies and nontraditional retailing.

CONSIDER-ATIONS IN PLANNING A RETAIL STRATEGY MIX

A retailer may be classified by its **strategy mix**. This mix is a firm's particular combination of these factors: store location, operating procedures, goods/services offered, pricing tactics, store atmosphere and customer services, and promotional methods.

Store location refers to the use of a store or nonstore format, placement in a geographic area, and the kind of site (such as a shopping center versus an isolated store). Operating procedures include the kinds of personnel employed, management style, store hours, and other factors. The goods/services offered may encompass several product categories or just one; and quality may be low, medium, or high. Pricing refers to a retailer's comparative strategy: prestige pricing (creating a quality image through high prices); competitive pricing (setting prices at the level of rivals); or penetration pricing (underpricing other retailers to attract value-conscious consumers). Store atmosphere and customer services are reflected by a firm's physical facilities and the level of personal attention provided, credit, return policies, delivery, and other factors. Promotion involves the retailer's activities in such areas as advertising, displays, personal selling, and sales promotion. By combining these elements, a retailer can develop a unique strategy.

To thrive in today's environment, a retailer should strive to be dominant in some aspect of its strategy. The firm may then be able to reach **power retailer** status—whereby consumers view the company as distinctive enough to become loyal to it and go out of their way to shop there. We tend to link dominant with large. Yet, both small and large retailers can dominate in their own way. There are several ways to be a power retailer:

1. Be price-oriented and cost-efficient to appeal to price-sensitive shoppers.
2. Be upscale to appeal to full-service, status-conscious consumers.
3. Be convenience-oriented to appeal to consumers interested in shopping ease, nearby locations, or long store hours.
4. Offer a dominant assortment with an extensive selection in the product lines carried to appeal to consumers interested in variety and in-store shopping comparisons.
5. Be customer service-oriented to appeal to people who are frustrated by the decline in retail service—as they perceive it.
6. Be innovative or exclusive and provide a unique method of operations (such as video kiosks at airports) or carry products/brands not stocked by other firms to appeal to customers who are innovators, bored, or looking for items not in the "me too" mold.

Combining two or more of these approaches can yield even greater power.[2]

Before we look at specific retail strategy mixes, three significant concepts that help explain the performance and evolution of these mixes are presented: the wheel of retailing, scrambled merchandising, and the retail life cycle. These concepts are quite useful in describing existing retailers' performance, predicting new retail institutions, determining the impact of new institutions on existing firms, and forecasting how existing retailers are apt to respond to change.

---

[2]Joel R. Evans and Barry Berman, "Power Retailing: Not Just for Large Firms," *Tips for Better Retailing,* Vol. 1 (Number 1, 1995).

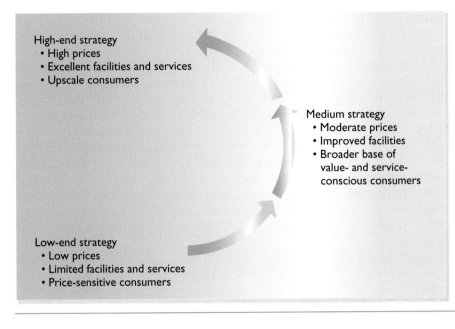

Figure 5-1

The Wheel of Retailing

As a low-end retailer upgrades its strategy, to increase sales and profit margins, a new form of discounter takes its place.

The Wheel of Retailing

According to the **wheel of retailing** theory, retail innovators often first appear as low-price operators with a low-cost structure and low profit-margin requirements. Over time, these innovators upgrade the products they carry and improve their facilities and customer services (by adding better-quality items, locating in higher-rent sites, accepting exchanges and allowing refunds, providing credit and delivery, and so on), and prices rise. As the innovators mature, they become vulnerable to new discounters with lower cost structures; hence, the wheel of retailing.[3] See Figure 5-1.

The wheel of retailing is grounded on four basic premises:

1. There are many price-sensitive shoppers willing to trade customer services, wide selections, and convenient locations for lower prices.
2. Price-sensitive shoppers are often not loyal and are willing to switch to retailers with lower prices. Other, prestige-sensitive customers like shopping at retailers with high-end strategies.
3. New institutions are frequently able to have lower operating costs than existing institutions.
4. As retailers move up the wheel, they typically do so to increase sales, broaden the target market, and improve store image.

For example, in the 1950s and again in the 1970s, traditional department store prices rose to levels that spurred the growth of two new institutional forms: the full-line discount store and the retail catalog showroom. These firms could stress low prices because

[3]The pioneering works on the wheel of retailing are Malcolm P. McNair, "Significant Trends and Developments in the Postwar Period" in A. B. Smith (Editor), *Competitive Distribution in a Free High Level Economy and Its Implications for the University* (Pittsburgh: University of Pittsburgh Press, 1958), pp. 17–18; and Stanley Hollander, "The Wheel of Retailing," *Journal of Marketing*, Vol. 25 (July 1960), pp. 37–42. For a more recent analysis of the concept, see Stephen Brown, "The Wheel of Retailing: Past and Future," *Journal of Retailing*, Vol. 66 (Summer 1990), pp. 143–149; and Stephen Brown, "Postmodernism, the Wheel of Retailing, and Will to Power," *International Review of Retail, Distribution, and Consumer Research*, Vol. 5 (July 1995), pp. 387–414.

of such cost-cutting techniques as having a small sales force, situating in lower-rent store locations, using inexpensive fixtures, emphasizing high stock turnover, and accepting only cash or check payments for goods.

As full-line discount stores and retail catalog showrooms succeeded, they typically sought to move up along the wheel. This meant enlarging the sales force, improving locations, upgrading fixtures, carrying lower-turnover merchandise, and granting credit. These improvements led to higher costs, which, in turn, led to higher prices. In the 1980s, the wheel of retailing again functioned as newer types of discounters, such as off-price chains, factory outlets, and permanent flea markets, expanded to satisfy the needs of the price-conscious consumer. The 1990s have seen the emergence of a retail institution known as the "category killer" store (a huge discount-oriented outlet specializing in one or a few product categories), which appeals to consumers who are interested in low prices and a large selection in the product line(s) carried. The category killer store's size lets it both buy merchandise and operate very efficiently.

As indicated in Figure 5-1, the wheel of retailing reveals three basic strategic positions: low end, medium, and high end. The medium strategy may have some difficulties if retailers in this position are not perceived as distinctive by consumers. Figure 5-2 shows the opposing alternatives a retailer faces in considering a strategy mix. Through this dichotomy, one can differentiate between the two extreme cases of strategic emphasis: low end and high end. The wheel of retailing suggests that established retailers should be cautious in adding services or in converting their strategy from low end to high end. Because price-conscious shoppers are not usually store loyal, they are likely to switch to lower-priced firms. Furthermore, retailers may be eliminating the competitive advantages that have led to profitability. As will be discussed shortly, this occurred with the retail catalog showroom, which is now a defunct format in the United States.

ETHICS IN RETAILING

Will Superstores Change Consumer Perceptions About Buying Used Cars?

Over the past few years, a number of major retailers, including Circuit City with its CarMax superstores, have entered the used-car business. Some retailing analysts expect other leading retailers (possibly even Wal-Mart) to enter the used-car business in the near future.

Unlike traditional new- and used-car dealers, the new megadealers typically offer consumers a very wide variety of vehicles from which to choose (some have as many as 1,000 late-model cars and trucks), let consumers preview the inventory (using sophisticated computer software that contains a photo and a list of features for each vehicle in stock), and have friendly, low-pressure sales personnel. And in further contrast to most traditional car dealerships, megadealers usually do not permit bargaining.

Many traditional car dealers publicly say they are not worried about the megadealers. They are quick to point out that firms such as CarMax charge $200 to $500 more per vehicle than they do. And the large inventories stocked by megadealers would also be a tremendous financial liability during a recession.

There is much at stake in the battle for market share in the used-car business. Industry experts agree the sales of used cars often account for one-half or more of a traditional new-car dealer's overall profits. The megadealers also feature low-mileage, late-model cars (often returned from leases) that traditional car dealers favor.

Sources: Kathleen Kerwin, Thane Peterson, Keith Naughton, Bill Vlasic, and Gail DeGeorge, "Autos: Used-Car Fever," *Business Week* (January 22, 1966), pp. 34–35; and Kathleen Kerwin, Gail DeGeorge, David Greising, Keith Naughton, Bill Vlasic, and Larry Armstrong, "Hurricane Huizenga," *Business Week* (February 24, 1997), pp. 88–93.

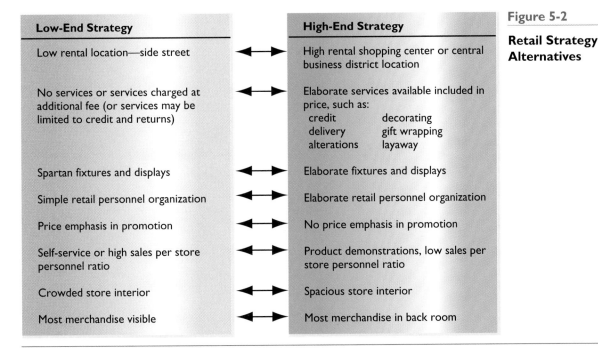

Figure 5-2

Retail Strategy Alternatives

Low-End Strategy	High-End Strategy
Low rental location—side street	High rental shopping center or central business district location
No services or services charged at additional fee (or services may be limited to credit and returns)	Elaborate services available included in price, such as: credit / decorating; delivery / gift wrapping; alterations / layaway
Spartan fixtures and displays	Elaborate fixtures and displays
Simple retail personnel organization	Elaborate retail personnel organization
Price emphasis in promotion	No price emphasis in promotion
Self-service or high sales per store personnel ratio	Product demonstrations, low sales per store personnel ratio
Crowded store interior	Spacious store interior
Most merchandise visible	Most merchandise in back room

Scrambled Merchandising

Whereas the wheel of retailing focuses on strategy changes based on product quality, prices, and customer service, scrambled merchandising involves a retailer's increasing its width of assortment (the number of different product lines carried). **Scrambled merchandising** occurs when a retailer adds goods and services that are unrelated to each other and to the firm's original business. See Figure 5-3.

The great popularity of scrambled merchandising today is due to a number of factors: retailers are interested in increasing overall sales volume; goods and services that are fast-selling and have high profit margins are usually the ones added; consumers may make more impulse purchases; consumers are attracted to one-stop shopping; different target markets may be reached; and the effects of seasonality and competition may be reduced. In addition, a retailer's original product line(s) may be declining in popularity, causing that firm to scramble just to hold onto its customer base. This is what is happening with Blockbuster Entertainment, due to the advent of pay-per-view and premium movie channels on cable TV. Blockbuster, which once functioned solely as a video rental and sales firm, now carries compact discs, CD-ROM diskettes, magazines, movie merchandise, candy, video games and game players, and more.[4]

Scrambled merchandising is quite contagious. For example, drugstores, bookstores, florists, and photo-developing firms are all affected by scrambled merchandising on the part of supermarkets. About 11 percent of total U.S. supermarket sales are from general merchandise, health and beauty aids, and other nongrocery items, such as pharmacy products, books and magazines, flowers, and seasonal merchandise.[5] In response, the aforementioned retailers are compelled to use scrambled merchandising to fill the void in their sales caused by the supermarkets. They have added unrelated items, like toys and gift items, greeting cards, batteries, and cameras. This then creates a void for other retailers, which are also forced to scramble.

[4]Sally Goll Beatty, "Blockbuster Ads Will Play Down Video Rentals," *Wall Street Journal* (December 30, 1996), pp. B1, B3; Peter Newcombe, "Peanut Butter and Pearl Jam," *Forbes* (February 10, 1997), p. 152; and Eben Shapiro, "Blockbuster Bid Stars Viacom Top Guns," *Wall Street Journal* (May 7, 1997), pp. B1, B14.

[5]"1995 Supermarket Sales Manual," *Progressive Grocer* (July 1996), p. 34.

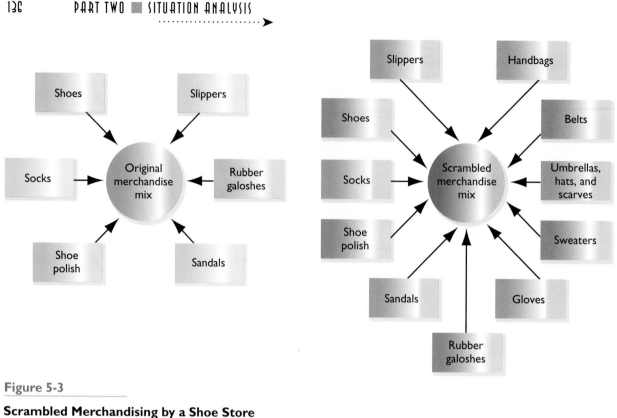

Figure 5-3

Scrambled Merchandising by a Shoe Store

The prevalence of scrambled merchandising means that competition among different types of retailers is increasing and that distribution costs for manufacturers are affected as sales are dispersed over more retailers. There are other limitations to scrambled merchandising, such as the potential lack of retailer expertise in buying, selling, and servicing items with which they are unfamiliar; the costs associated with a broader product assortment (including lower inventory turnover); and the potential damage to a retailer's image if scrambled merchandising is ineffective.

The Retail Life Cycle

A third key concept in understanding the performance and evolution of diverse retail strategy mixes is the **retail life cycle**. It asserts that retail institutions—like the goods and services they sell—pass through identifiable life cycle stages: innovation, accelerated development, maturity, and decline.[6] The direction and speed of institutional changes can be interpreted from this theory. Table 5-1 summarizes the stages of the retail life cycle.

[6]William R. Davidson, Albert D. Bates, and Stephen J. Bass, "The Retail Life Cycle," *Harvard Business Review,* Vol. 54 (November–December 1976), pp. 89–96. See also Stanley C. Hollander and Glenn S. Omura, "Chain Store Developments and Their Political, Strategic, and Social Interdependencies," *Journal of Retailing,* Vol. 65 (Fall 1989), pp. 299–325; Ronald Savitt, "Looking Back to See Ahead: Writing the History of American Retailing," *Journal of Retailing,* Vol. 65 (Fall 1989), pp. 326–355; Albert D. Bates, "The Extended Specialty Store: A Strategic Opportunity for the 1990s,"*Journal of Retailing,* Vol. 65 (Fall 1989), pp. 379–388; "The Discipline of Market Leaders," *Chain Store Age* (April 1995), p. 38; "Seven Pillars to Future Success," *Chain Store Age* (August 1996), Section Two, pp. 9A–15A; Gary E. Hoover, "What Happens After All the Categories Are Killed?" *Arthur Andersen Retailing Issues Letter* (July 1996), pp. 1–4; and James R. Lowry, "The Life Cycle of Shopping Centers," *Business Horizons,* Vol. 40 (January–February 1997), pp. 77–86.

Table 5-1 THE RETAIL LIFE CYCLE

Area or Subject of Concern		STAGE IN THE LIFE CYCLE			
		Innovation	Accelerated Development	Maturity	Decline
Market characteristics	Number of competitors	Very few	Moderate	Many direct competitors; moderate indirect competition	Moderate direct competition; many indirect competitors
	Rate of sales growth	Very rapid	Rapid	Moderate to slow	Slow or negative
	Level of profitability	Low to moderate	High	Moderate	Very low
	Duration of stage	3–5 years	8 years	Indefinite	Indefinite
Appropriate retailer actions	Investment/ growth/risk decisions	Investment minimization; high risks accepted	High level of investment to sustain growth	Tightly controlled growth in untapped markets	Marginal capital expenditures and only if essential
	Central management concerns	Concept refinement through adjustment and experimenting	Establishing a pre-emptive market position	Excess capacity and overstoring; prolonging maturity and revising the business concept	Engaging in a run-out strategy
	Use of management-control techniques	Minimal	Moderate	Extensive	Moderate
	Most successful management style	Entrepreneurial	Centralized	Professional	Caretaker

Source: Adapted by the authors from an exhibit in William R. Davidson, Albert D. Bates, and Stephen J. Bass, "The Retail Life Cycle," *Harvard Business Review*, Vol. 54 (November–December 1976), p. 92. Reprinted with permission of the *Harvard Business Review.* Copyright 1976 by the President and Fellows of Harvard College; all rights reserved.

From an industrywide perspective, in the United States:

The initial retail era focused on merchandise. Money was made when goods were bought. Stores located in the inner city. Market reach was limited and local. Advertising was mostly by word of mouth or in local media. This era came to an end with the Great Depression.

The next retail era hit its growth phase in the post-World War II era. It was expansion-oriented. Opening new stores was the focus of management. Money was made when goods were sold. Stores followed their customers to the suburbs and the regional mall was born. Market reach was national, as was advertising. The beginning of the end for this era was the 1987 stock market crash and the collapse of Campeau (then owner of Federated Department Stores).

The new era in retail development reflects the informationalization of the industry. It represents a shift in management focus from market expansion to information intensification, from geography to communication-focused technologies, from return on investment to return on customers, from sales growth to profit growth, from increasing individual transactions to establishing long-term customer relationships. Third-wave retailers share these attributes: global focus, obsession with technology, and organizational restructuring around the customer.[7]

Let us now study the stages of the retail life cycle as they apply to individual institutional formats and show specific examples. During the first stage of the cycle (innovation), there is a strong departure from the strategy mixes of existing retail institutions. A firm in this stage significantly alters at least one element of the strategy mix from that of traditional competitors. Sales and then profits often rise sharply for the first firms in a category. Yet, there are risks that new institutions will not be accepted by consumers, and there may be large initial losses due to heavy investments. At this stage, long-run success is not clear.

An example of an institution never making it past the innovation stage in the United States was the hypermarket—a huge (220,000+ square feet) combination economy supermarket and discount department store. It sought people interested in low prices and one-stop shopping. Although popular in Europe for over 40 years, due to the otherwise small stores there, it only recently came to the United States. These were among the problems hypermarkets encountered during their U.S. introduction: per-unit sales for most stores were not large enough to earn reasonable profits; revenues were too great for low-margin food items and too low for higher-margin general merchandise; the high amount of customer traffic needed to break even was not attained; and American consumers found the initial stores to be too large and, thus, too inconvenient to shop in quickly. Noted one analyst: "The stores were somewhat cumbersome. They were too big for U.S. consumers."[8] In 1994, the leading European hypermarket retailer, France's Carrefour, exited the U.S. market and closed its two Philadelphia stores.

In the second stage (accelerated development), both sales and profits of a retail institution exhibit rapid growth. Existing firms expand their geographic bases of operations, and newer companies of the same type enter the marketplace. Toward the end of accelerated development, cost pressures (to cover a larger staff, a more complex inventory system, and extensive controls) may begin to affect profits.

The book superstore—which carries up to 150,000 titles, occupies 50,000 to 60,000 square feet of space, carries CDs, discounts many hardcover titles, often includes cafes, and more—is an institution in the growth stage. In less than a decade, this superstore has come to dominate bookselling. Although there were 700 U.S. book superstores in 1996, some experts believe the United States can support 1,500 such stores. They predict significant expansion at least until the year 2000. As of late 1996, 142 U.S. metropolitan markets still did not have a book superstore, a sure indicator of significant growth potential.[9]

The third stage (maturity) is characterized by a slowdown in total sales growth for the institutional type. As such, even though overall sales may continue going up, that rise is at a much lower rate than during the introduction and growth stages. It also means profit margins may have to be reduced to stimulate purchases. Maturity is brought on by saturation of the market due to the high number of firms in an institutional format, competition from newer institutions, changing societal interests, and management skills that

[7]Carl Steidmann, "Third-Wave Retailers Find New Way to Do Business," *Chain Store Age Executive* (August 1993), p. 9A.

[8]Emily DeNitto, "Hypermarkets Seem to Be Big Flop in U.S.," *Advertising Age* (October 4, 1993), p. 20.

[9]Michael Hartnett, "Barnes & Noble Reshapes Book Market with Superstore Success," *Stores* (April 1996), pp. 40–41; Patrick M. Reilly, "Where Borders Group and Barnes & Noble Compete, It's War," *Wall Street Journal* (September 3, 1996), pp. A1, A8; and Hardy Green, "Superstores, Megabooks—and Humongous Headaches," *Business Week* (April 14, 1997), pp. 92–94.

may be inadequate to lead mature or larger firms. Once maturity is reached, the goal is to sustain it as long as possible and not fall into decline.

The liquor store, a form of specialty store, is an institution currently in the maturity stage of the retail life cycle; sales are rising, but very slowly compared to earlier years. As noted in Chapter 1, U.S. liquor store sales went up by only 1.4 percent annually from 1986 through 1995—far less than the overall rate for all U.S. retailers. The slowdown in sales has been due to competition from other institutions, such as membership clubs, mail-order wine retailers, and supermarkets (in states allowing wine or liquor sales by supermarkets); changing American life-styles and attitudes with regard to liquor; the lifting of the drinking age from 18 to 21 in all fifty states; and the limitations on the nonalcoholic items that liquor stores are permitted to sell in some areas.

The final stage in the retail life cycle is decline, whereby industrywide sales and profits for the retail format fall off, many firms abandon the format, and newer formats attract consumers previously committed to that retailer type. In some cases, a decline may be hard or almost impossible to reverse. In others, it may be avoided or postponed by repositioning the institution.

The retail catalog showroom's U.S. popularity peaked in the mid-1980s. With a catalog showroom, consumers selected items from a catalog, shopped in a warehouse setting, and wrote up sales orders. By the end of 1996, the U.S. catalog showroom business had virtually vanished. Of the big three catalog firms, Best Products and Consumers Distributing went out of business and Service Merchandise switched to a more traditional store format. Why? Many other retailers aggressively cut costs and prices, so showrooms were no longer low-price leaders. Showrooms had a tough time reacting to price cuts by competitors because catalogs had to be printed so far in advance. Due to the need to reach more consumers, advertising expenses rose. Too many items were slow-sellers and/or had low profit margins. Some consumers found showrooms too crowded and disliked writing up orders, the lack of displays reduced browsing time, and the paucity of apparel goods also held down revenues.[10] On the other hand, conventional supermarkets have slowed their decline by placing new units in suburban shopping centers, redesigning interiors, lengthening store hours, having low prices, expanding the use of scrambled merchandising, closing unprofitable smaller units, and converting to larger outlets.

The retail life cycle concept is valuable in indicating the proper retailer response as institutions evolve. Expansion should be the focus in the initial stages, administrative skills and operations become critical in maturity, and adaptation is essential at the end of the cycle: "No matter how successful an organization has been in the past, that is no guarantee of future success. If anything, past greatness creates a barrier to future change. For retailers that understand the changes which are taking place in their business environment, the future represents an unprecedented landscape of opportunity."[11]

RETAIL INSTITUTIONS CATEGORIZED BY STORE-BASED STRATEGY MIX

Selected aspects of the strategy mixes of 14 store-based retail institutions are presented in this section and highlighted in Table 5-2. These strategy mixes are divided into food-oriented and general merchandise groupings. Though not all-inclusive, the strategy mixes do provide a fairly comprehensive overview of store-based retailing strategies.

Food-Oriented Retailers

Six key strategy mixes are used by food-oriented retailers: convenience store, conventional supermarket, food-based superstore, combination store, box (limited-line) store, and warehouse store. Each is discussed in the following subsections.

[10]Karen Hsu, "Service Merchandise Turns the Page on Its Catalog Past," *Wall Street Journal* (August 25, 1995), p. 4; Michael Hartnett, "Best Products Tries Specialty Road to Recovery," *Stores* (October 1996), pp. 70–72; and "Best Products Calls It Quits," *New York Times* (November 1, 1996), p. D16.
[11]Steidmann, "Third-Wave Retailers Find New Way to Do Business," p. 11A.

Table 5-2 SELECTED ASPECTS OF STORE-BASED RETAIL STRATEGY MIXES

Type of Retailer	Location	Merchandise	Prices	Atmosphere and Services	Promotion
Food-Oriented					
Convenience store	Neighborhood	Medium width and low depth of assortment; average quality	Average to above-average	Average	Moderate
Conventional supermarket	Neighborhood	Extensive width and depth of assortment; average quality; national, private, and generic brands	Competitive	Average	Heavy use of newspapers, flyers, and coupons; self-service
Food-based superstore	Community shopping center or isolated site	Full assortment of supermarket items, plus health and beauty aids and general merchandise	Competitive	Average	Heavy use of newspapers and flyers; self-service
Combination store	Community shopping center or isolated site	Full selection of supermarket and drugstore items or supermarket and general merchandise; average quality	Competitive	Average	Heavy use of newspapers and flyers; self-service
Box (limited-line) store	Neighborhood	Low width and depth of assortment; few perishables; few national brands	Very low	Low	Little or none
Warehouse store	Secondary site, often in industrial area	Moderate width and low depth; emphasis on national brands bought at discounts	Very low	Low	Little or none
General Merchandise					
Specialty store	Business district or shopping center	Very narrow width of assortment; extensive depth of assortment; average to good quality	Competitive to above-average	Average to excellent	Heavy use of displays; extensive sales force
Traditional department store	Business district, shopping center, or isolated store	Extensive width and depth of assortment; average to good quality	Average to above-average	Good to excellent	Heavy ad and catalog use; direct mail; personal selling
Full-line discount store	Business district, shopping center, or isolated store	Extensive width and depth of assortment; average to good quality	Competitive	Slightly below-average to average	Heavy use of newspapers; price-oriented; moderate sales force
Variety store	Business district, shopping center, or isolated store	Good width and depth of assortment; below-average to average quality	Average	Below-average	Heavy use of newspapers; self-service

Table 5-2 *(CONTINUED)*

Type of Retailer	Location	Merchandise	Prices	Atmosphere and Services	Promotion
Off-price chain	Business district, suburban shopping strip, or isolated store	Moderate width, but poor depth of assortment; average to good quality; low continuity	Low	Below-average	Use of newspapers; brands not advertised; limited sales force
Factory outlet	Out-of-the-way site or discount mall	Moderate width, but poor depth of assortment; some irregular merchandise; low continuity	Very low	Very low	Little; self-service
Membership club	Isolated store or secondary site (industrial park)	Moderate width, but poor depth of assortment; low continuity	Very low	Very low	Little; some direct mail; limited sales force
Flea market	Isolated site, racetrack, arena, or parking lot	Extensive width, but poor depth of assortment; variable quality; low continuity	Very low	Very low	Limited; self-service

Convenience Store ❑ A **convenience store** is usually a food-oriented retailer that is well located, is open long hours, and carries a moderate number of items. This type of retailer is small (only a fraction the size of a conventional supermarket), has average to above-average prices, and average atmosphere and customer services. The ease of shopping at convenience stores and the impersonal nature of many large supermarkets make convenience stores particularly appealing to their customers, many of whom are male. See Figure 5-4.

Forty years ago, there were 500 convenience stores and industry sales were under $200 million. As of 1995, there were 75,000 convenience stores (excluding the thousands of stores where food was a very small fraction of revenues); and total annual sales at those stores were $90 billion (including gasoline). Today, U.S. convenience stores account for 7 percent of retail grocery sales, 5 percent of fast-food sales, and 20 percent of gasoline sales.[12]

Figure 5-4

Convenience Store Retailing at Service Stations

Thousands of service stations include convenience stores on their premises. Shown here is a Phillips 66 station in Albuquerque, New Mexico, which features a Kicks convenience store.

[12]*State of the Industry Report* (Alexandria, Virginia: National Association of Convenience Stores, 1996); and authors' estimates.

Items such as milk, eggs, and bread once represented the major portion of sales; now, sandwiches, tobacco products, snack foods, soft drinks, newspapers and magazines, beer and wine, video rentals, lottery tickets, and a car wash are also often key items. In addition, gasoline generates 20 percent to 40 percent or more of total sales at many stores; at one time, virtually no convenience stores carried gasoline. A number of convenience stores have installed ATMs and expanded nonfood offerings to remain attractive to shoppers.

7-Eleven, Circle K, Super America Group, and National Convenience Stores are the largest food-based convenience store chains in the United States, with 7-Eleven alone having 5,500 outlets. Texaco's Food Mart and Amoco's Food Shops are among the convenience store chains operated by oil companies at their gas station locations.

The convenience store's natural market advantages are its usefulness for fill-in merchandise when a consumer does not want to travel to or spend time shopping at a supermarket, the ability of customers to buy gas and fill-in merchandise at the same time, the use of drive-through windows, and the long store hours. Most of the items sold by a convenience store are used within thirty minutes of purchase. Many customers shop there at least two or three times a week and the average sales transaction is small. Due to limited shelf space, stores receive multiple weekly deliveries and prices reflect the small sale amounts and the high handling costs. Because customers are less price-sensitive than those shopping at other food-oriented retailers, gross margins are much higher than those of conventional supermarkets.

Lately, the industry has faced various problems: some areas are saturated with stores; supermarkets are providing more competition due to longer hours and better stocking of nonfood items; a number of stores have become too big, making shopping less expeditious; the traditional target market (35-year-old blue-collar workers) has been shrinking; and several chains have had financial difficulties, including 7-Eleven, Circle K, and National Convenience Stores.

Conventional Supermarket ❏ The Food Marketing Institute defines a **supermarket** as a self-service food store with grocery, meat, and produce departments and minimum annual sales of $2 million. Included in the definition are conventional supermarkets, food-based superstores, combination stores, box (limited-line) stores, and warehouse stores.

A **conventional supermarket** is a departmentalized food store that emphasizes a wide range of food and related products; sales of general merchandise are rather limited. This institution started in the 1930s when it was recognized that only a large-scale operation would enable a retailer to combine volume sales, self-service, and low prices. Self-service allowed supermarkets to cut costs, as well as increase volume. Personnel costs were reduced, and impulse buying increased. The car and the refrigerator contributed to the supermarket's success by lowering travel costs and adding to the life span of perishables. Easy parking and lower prices (for consumers buying in bulk) were tactics used by the supermarket to exploit these inventions.

Since the early 1960s, overall supermarket sales have stabilized at about 75 percent of total U.S. grocery sales, with conventional supermarkets now responsible for 45 percent of total supermarket sales. In 1995, there were 18,425 conventional supermarkets with sales amounting to $142 billion.[13] Chains account for a majority of sales, with the leaders being Kroger, American Stores, Safeway, Albertson's, and Winn-Dixie. Most independent supermarkets are affiliated with cooperative or voluntary organizations, such as IGA and Supervalu.

Conventional supermarkets have generally relied on high inventory turnover (volume sales). Their profit margins are low. In general, average gross margins (selling prices

---

[13]"63rd Annual Report of the Grocery Industry," *Progressive Grocer* (April 1996), p. 13.

The Netherlands' Royal Ahold: Expanding in the United States

With the acquisition of Stop & Shop (and its 176 stores), Netherlands-based Royal Ahold is now the fifth-largest operator of supermarkets in the United States (up from eighth place). In addition to Stop & Shop, Ahold owns these supermarket chains: Tops Markets, Bi-Lo, Edwards, Finast, and Giant Food. Although Ahold's stores extend from New England to the Carolinas on the East Coast, its strength is greatest in the Northeast, where it has a 20 percent market share.

As part of its overall U.S. strategy, Ahold is working to extend its operating efficiencies by fostering cooperation among the various units and by centralized purchasing, distribution, and store design. Ahold recently centralized purchasing and distribution functions for Tops, Bi-Lo, Edwards, Finast, and Giant at a location near Tops' Buffalo headquarters. Similarly, it has consolidated all information services at one location. It is now seeking to use a common vendor for pilferage control and for labor scheduling.

Ahold has enacted similar productivity improvements at its Netherlands stores, where it has a 30 percent market share. In the Netherlands, for example, four distribution centers efficiently move all goods among Ahold's 600 supermarkets. The firm also prepares its own bakery and meat products. It even has a 50 percent interest in the world's largest producer of sherry wines.

Sources: Martin Du Bois, "Ahold Succeeds with Growth Strategy," *Wall Street Journal* (April 2, 1996), p. A10; and Julie Ritzer Ross, "Ahold Steps Up Drive for East Coast Markets," *Stores* (July 1996), pp. 58–64.

less merchandise costs) are 22 percent or so of sales and net profits are 1 percent to 2 percent of sales.

Conventional supermarkets are seeing intense competition from other types of food stores: convenience stores offer greater customer convenience; food-based superstores and combination stores have more product lines and greater variety within them, as well as better gross margins; and box and warehouse stores have lower operating costs and prices. Membership clubs (discussed later in the chapter), with their discount prices, also provide competition—especially now that they have aggressively expanded their food lines. Thus, over the last two decades, thousands of conventional supermarkets have closed and many others have changed their strategy mix to another format. Variations of the conventional supermarket are covered next.

Food-Based Superstore ❑ A **food-based superstore** is larger and more diversified than a conventional supermarket but usually smaller and less diversified than a combination store. This format originated in the 1970s as supermarkets sought to stem sales declines by expanding store size and the number of nonfood items carried. Some supermarkets merged with drugstores or general merchandise stores, but more grew into food-based superstores. There were 6,300 food-based superstores in the United States during 1995, with sales of nearly $101 billion.[14]

The typical food-based superstore occupies 25,000 to 50,000 square feet of total space and obtains 20 percent to 25 percent of revenues from general merchandise items, such as garden supplies, flowers, small household appliances, wine, and film developing. It caters to consumers' complete grocery needs and offers them the ability to buy fill-in general merchandise.

Like combination stores, food-based superstores are efficient, offer people a degree of one-stop shopping, stimulate impulse purchases, and feature high-profit general

[14]Estimated by the authors from "63rd Annual Report of the Grocery Industry," p. 13.

Figure 5-5

Vons: A Food-Based Superstore

This California Vons has an enormous selection of food and related products.

merchandise. But they also offer other advantages: It is easier and less costly to redesign and convert supermarkets into food-based superstores than into combination stores. Many consumers feel more comfortable shopping in true food stores than in huge combination stores. Management expertise is better focused in food-based superstores.

In the last decade, all the leading U.S. supermarket chains have turned more to food-based superstores. They have expanded and remodeled existing supermarkets and built numerous new stores. Many independent supermarkets have also converted facilities to food-based superstores. See Figure 5-5.

Combination Store ❑ A **combination store** unites supermarket and general merchandise sales in one facility, with general merchandise typically accounting for 25 percent to 40 percent of total store sales. The introduction of food-based combination stores can be traced to the late 1960s and early 1970s, when common checkout areas were developed for independently owned supermarkets and drugstores or supermarkets and general merchandise stores. A natural offshoot of this was to fully integrate the two operations under one management. In 1995, there were 1,700 U.S. combination stores (including supercenters), and annual sales were $34 billion.[15]

Combination stores are popular for the following reasons. They are very large, from 30,000 up to 100,000 or more square feet. This leads to operating efficiencies and cost savings. Consumers like one-stop shopping and will travel further to get to the store. Impulse sales are high. Many general merchandise items have better gross margins than traditional supermarket items. Supermarkets and drugstores have many commonalities in the customers served and the kinds of low-price, high-turnover items sold. Drugstore and general merchandise customers are drawn to the store more frequently than they would be otherwise.

A **supercenter** is a special type of combination store that blends an economy supermarket with a discount department store. It is the U.S. version of the hypermarket (the

[15]Ibid.

European institution that did not succeed in the United States). At least 40 percent of supercenter sales are from nonfood items. These stores usually range from 75,000 to 150,000 square feet in size and they stock up to 50,000 and more items, much more than the 30,000 or so items carried by other combination stores.[16]

Among the firms operating combination stores are Meijer, Fred Meyer, Wal-Mart, Kmart, and Albertson's.

Box (Limited-Line) Store ❏ The **box (limited-line) store** is a food-based discounter that focuses on a small selection of items, moderate hours of operation (compared to supermarkets), few services, and limited national brands. There are usually less than 1,500 items, little or no refrigerated perishables, and few sizes and brands per item. Price marking is on the shelf or on overhead signs. Items are displayed in cut cases. Customers do their own bagging. Checks are usually not accepted. Box stores depend on aggressively priced private-label brands. They aim to price merchandise 20 percent to 30 percent below supermarkets.

The box-store concept originated in Europe around 1970 and was exported to the United States in the mid-1970s. The growth of these stores has not been as anticipated, as sales have gone up modestly in the 1990s. Other food stores, in some cases, have matched box-store prices. Many people are loyal to national brands and box stores cannot fulfill one-stop shopping needs.

There were 850 box stores in the United States in 1995, with sales of $2.8 billion.[17] The leading box operator is Aldi.

Warehouse Store ❏ A **warehouse store** is a food-based discounter offering a moderate number of food items in a no-frills setting. Unlike box stores, warehouse stores appeal to one-stop food shoppers. These stores concentrate on special purchases of national brands. They use cut-case displays, provide little service, post prices on shelves, and locate in secondary sites (like industrial districts).

Warehouse stores began in the late 1970s. As of 1995, there were 2,525 U.S. stores with nearly $33 billion in sales.[18] There are three warehouse store formats in terms of size: 15,000 to 25,000 square feet, 25,000 to 35,000 square feet, and 50,000 to 65,000 square feet.

The largest store is known as a super warehouse. There are 425 of them in the United States. They have annual sales exceeding $20 million each and contain a variety of departments, including produce. High ceilings are used to accommodate pallet loads of groceries. Shipments are made directly to the store. Customers pack their own groceries. Super warehouses can be profitable at gross margins that are far lower than those for conventional supermarkets. Major super warehouse chains include Food 4 Less (Fleming Companies), Sun Food Market (A&P), and Cub Foods (Supervalu).

A potential problem, which has limited the growth of warehouse stores, is the lack of brand continuity. Because products are bought by the stores when special deals are available, brands may be temporarily or permanently out of stock. In addition, many consumers do not like shopping in warehouse settings.

Table 5-3 shows selected operating data for convenience stores, conventional supermarkets, food-based superstores, combination stores, box stores, and warehouse stores.

---

[16]See "The Squeeze Is On: Wal-Mart and Kmart Supercenters Put the Squeeze on Supermarkets," *Chain Store Age Executive* (August 1995), Section Three; Michael Hartnett, "Studies Probe Appeal of Supercenters," *Stores* (December 1995), pp. 22–23; and Zina Moukheiber, "The Great Wal-Mart Massacre, Part II," *Forbes* (January 22, 1996), pp. 44–45.
[17]Estimated by the authors from "63rd Annual Report of the Grocery Industry," p. 13.
[18]Ibid.

Table 5-3 SELECTED TYPICAL OPERATING DATA FOR FOOD-ORIENTED RETAILERS, 1995

Factor	Convenience Store[a]	Conventional Supermarket	Food-Based Superstore	Combination Store[a]	Box (Limited-Line) Store	Warehouse Store
Number of stores	75,000	18,425	6,300	1,700	850	2,525
Total annual sales	$90 billion	$142 billion	$100.8 billion	$34 billion	$2.4 billion	$32.8 billion
Average annual sales per store	$1.2 million	$7.7 million	$16.0 million	$20.0 million	$2.8 million	$13.0 million
Average store selling area (sq. ft.)	5,000 or less	15,000–20,000	25,000–50,000	30,000–100,000+	5,000–9,000	15,000+
Number of checkouts per store	1–3	6–10	10+	10+	3–5	5+
Gross margin	25–30%	18–22%	20–25%	25%	10–12%	12–15%
Number of items stocked per store	3,000–4,000	12,000–17,000	20,000+	30,000+	Under 1,500	2,500+
Major emphasis	Daily fill-in needs; dairy, sandwiches, tobacco, gas, beverages, magazines	Food; only 5% of sales from general merchandise	Positioned between supermarket and combo store; 20–25% of sales from general merchandise	One-stop shopping; general merchandise is 25–40% of sales	Low prices; few or no perishables	Low prices; variable assortments; may or may not stock perishables

[a]Convenience store data include some outlets owned by oil companies and gas stations where nongasoline sales represent a major part of the business, but not those where food is only a tiny percent of sales. Combination store data include supercenters.

Sources: "63rd Annual Report of the Grocery Industry," *Progressive Grocer* (April 1996); and authors' estimates.

General Merchandise Retailers

There are eight store-based general merchandise retail strategy mixes shown in Table 5-2; each is covered in the following subsections: specialty store, traditional department store, full-line discount store, variety store, off-price chain, factory outlet, membership club, and flea market.

Specialty Store ❑ A **specialty store** concentrates on selling one goods or service line, such as apparel and its accessories, toys, furniture, or muffler repair. In contrast to a mass marketing approach, specialty stores usually carry a narrow, but deep, assortment of goods or services in their chosen goods/service category and tailor their strategy to selective market segments. This enables specialty stores to maintain better selections and sales expertise than competitors, which are often department stores. It also lets them control investments and have a certain amount of flexibility.

Consumers often shop at specialty stores because of the knowledgeable sales personnel, the variety of choices within the goods/service category, the customer service policies, the intimate store size and atmosphere (although this is not true of the category killer store), the lack of crowds (also not true of category killer stores), and the absence of aisles of merchandise unrelated to their purchase intentions—they do not have to go through several departments looking for the desired product. While some specialty stores have elaborate fixtures and upscale merchandise for affluent shoppers, others are discount-oriented and aim at price-conscious consumers.

Total specialty store sales are difficult to estimate because they sell almost all kinds of goods and services, and aggregate specialty store data are not compiled by the U.S. Department of Commerce. However, annual specialty store sales in the United States are hundreds of billions of dollars. During 1995, the top 100 specialty store chains had sales of $142 billion and operated nearly 80,000 outlets. Among these 100 chains, about one-quarter were involved with apparel. Specialty store leaders include Toys "Я" Us (toys), The Limited, Inc. (apparel), and Circuit City (consumer electronics).[19]

As noted earlier in the chapter, a new type of specialty store, the category killer, is now gaining strength. A **category killer store** is an especially large specialty store. It features an enormous selection in its product category and relatively low prices; and consumers are drawn from wide geographic areas. Toys "Я" Us, The Limited, The Gap, Sam Goody, and Barnes & Noble are among the many specialty store chains that are opening new category killer stores to complement existing stores. Blockbuster, Sports Authority, Home Depot, and Staples are among the specialty store chains fully based on the category killer store concept. For example, Sports Authority stores average 42,000 square feet of selling space. With annual company sales of over $1 billion, it is the world's largest specialty store chain for sporting goods. In a U.S. environment with 65,000 sporting goods stores, Sports Authority is moving fast. Its stores are "emporiums stacked floor to ceiling with basketballs, bats, golf clubs, hockey pucks, fishing rods, sneakers, and skis in just about every conceivable shape, size, and quality. The stores are so densely stocked that it's practically impossible to walk out without whatever you were looking for."[20]

Nonetheless, smaller specialty stores (even ones with under 1,000 square feet of space) can prosper if they are focused, offer strong customer service, and avoid being imitations of larger firms. Many consumers do not like shopping in huge stores: "People say they have less time to shop. Cavernous cat-killer stores take a lot of time to navigate, and they aren't just around the corner. If you're shopping for fun, you might head for Bed Bath & Beyond to buy a soap dish. If you're in a hurry, the five varieties available at a local hardware shop may suffice."[21]

[19]Computed by the authors from David P. Schulz, "Top 100 Specialty Stores," *Stores* (August 1996), pp. S3–S23.
[20]Esther Wachs Book, "Here Comes a Cat Killer," *Forbes* (April 22, 1996), pp. 49, 52.
[21]Gretchen Mortgenson, "Too Much of a Good Thing?" *Forbes* (June 3, 1996), pp. 114–119.

Table 5-4 SELECTED OPERATING RESULTS FOR SPECIALTY STORES, 1995	
Percent of total revenues from owned departments	99.7
Percent of total revenues from leased departments	0.3
Percent of total revenues from cash transactions	54.0
Percent of total revenues from credit transactions	46.0
Annual sales per square foot	$256
Annual sales per employee	$98,317
Size of average transaction	$64
Gross margin as a percent of net sales	43.5
Operating expenses as a percent of net sales	40.1
Earnings from operations as a percent of net sales	3.4

Source: Alexandra Moran (Editor), *FOR 1996 Edition* (New York: Wiley, 1996), pp. 8–9. © John Wiley & Sons, Inc. Reprinted by permission.

Any size specialty store can be adversely affected by seasonality or a decline in the popularity of its product category because its offering is so focused. This type of store may also fail to attract consumers interested in one-stop shopping for multiple product categories.

Table 5-4 shows selected 1995 operating data for specialty stores participating in the National Retail Federation's annual survey.

Traditional Department Store ❏ A **department store** is a large retail unit with an extensive assortment (width and depth) of goods and services that is organized into separate departments for purposes of buying, promotion, customer service, and control. It has the greatest selection of any general merchandise retailer, often serves as the anchor store in a shopping center or district, has strong credit card penetration, and is usually part of a chain. To be defined as a department store by the U.S. Bureau of the

Despite the Glitz: The Universe Wasn't Very Incredible

When Tandy introduced its first Incredible Universe store in 1992, retailing analysts, as well as consumers, welcomed its fresh approach. The store had a theme park atmosphere (including laser shows and karaoke contests) and a huge selection. Tandy counted on Incredible Universe and its new Computer City superstore chain to quickly profit and expand.

However, in 1995, the two new divisions had combined losses of $50 million. So, the same retailing analysts began to question Incredible Universe's "bigger is better" strategy. Although they initially assumed the stores would attract consumers from great distances, many people disliked shopping in a store the size of two football fields. In addition, Incredible Universe had a tough time maintaining customer traffic after the novelty of newness passed.

In an attempt to revive the chain, Tandy replaced some executives, reduced store expansion plans (from 10 to 2 new stores in 1996), and revised its advertising strategy (placing more emphasis on products than on the store concept). Still, 55 percent of Incredible Universe's revenues came from slow-growth categories (such as large appliances and consumer electronics).

Finally, after Incredible Universe sustained substantial losses in 1996 (estimated to be as much as $50 million), Tandy decided to shutter the chain in 1997.

Luckily for Tandy, as Incredible Universe declined, Radio Shack stores saw renewed vigor. Consumers like the more intimate size and more focused product mix.

Sources: Evan Ramstad, "Tandy to Shed Incredible Universe Chain," *Wall Street Journal* (December 31, 1996), pp. 3–4; and "Incredible Universe Goes on the Block," *Discount Store News* (April 14, 1997), pp. 6, 59.

Figure 5-6

Parisian: A Department Store Chain with an Apparel Emphasis

Census, a store has to meet four criteria. First, it must employ at least fifty people. Second, apparel and soft goods (nondurables) must account for at least 20 percent of total sales. Third, the merchandise assortment must include some items in each of these lines: furniture, home furnishings, appliances, and radio and TV sets; a general line of apparel for the family; and household linens and dry goods. Fourth, if annual sales are under $10 million, no more than 80 percent can be from any one line. If sales are at least $10 million, there is no limitation on the percentage from a line, as long as combined sales of the smallest two lines are at least $1 million.

Two types of retailers satisfy the Bureau of Census definition: the traditional department store (introduced by Macy's, Wanamaker, and others in the 1860s) and the full-line discount store (introduced by firms such as Kmart, Target, and Wal-Mart in 1962). Together, they accounted for $232 billion in sales in 1995—excluding leased departments. This was almost 10 percent of U.S. retail store sales. The traditional department store is discussed here; the full-line discount store is examined in the following subsection.

At a **traditional department store,** merchandise quality ranges from average to quite good. Pricing is moderate to above average. Customer service ranges from medium levels of sales help, credit, delivery, and so forth to high levels of each. For example, Macy's strategy is aimed at middle-class shoppers interested in a wide assortment and moderate prices, whereas Bloomingdale's aims at upscale consumers through more trendy merchandise and higher prices. Some traditional department stores (such as Dayton's and Rich's) sell textile products, family wearing apparel, and furniture and appliances. Others (such as Nordstrom and Saks Fifth Avenue) place greater emphasis on apparel and do not carry major appliances. See Figure 5-6.

Over its history, the traditional department store has been responsible for many innovations, such as advertising prices, enacting a one-price policy (whereby all shoppers pay the same price for the same good or service), developing computerized checkout facilities, offering money-back guarantees, adding branch stores, decentralizing management, and moving into suburban shopping centers.

However, during the last several years, industrywide sales growth of traditional department stores has lagged behind that of full-line discount stores; and long-time chains such as Gimbels, Abraham & Straus, and Wanamaker have gone out of business, leading various observers to ask "will the traditional department store survive?"[22] Today,

---

[22]See "Philadelphia Keeps Strawbridge Name But Loses a Retail Tradition," *New York Times* (July 22, 1996), p. A13; and Robert Berner, "Dayton Hudson's Once-Fashionable Stores Tread Water," *Wall Street Journal* (August 1, 1996), p. B4.

traditional department store sales, which were $94 billion in 1995, represent less than one-half of total department store sales. These are some reasons for this institution's difficulties:

- ▪ They no longer have brand exclusivity for a lot of the items they sell; manufacturers' brands are available at specialty and discount outlets.
- ▪ Many firms have been too passive with private-label goods. Instead of creating their own brands, they have signed exclusive licensing agreements with fashion designers to use the latter's names. This perpetuates customer loyalty to the designer and not the store.
- ▪ There are more price-conscious consumers than ever before and they are attracted to discount retailers.
- ▪ The popularity of shopping malls has aided specialty stores since consumers can accomplish one-stop shopping through several specialty stores in the same mall or shopping center.
- ▪ Large specialty chains have strong supplier relations and extensive advertising campaigns; department stores do not dominate the smaller stores around them as they once did.
- ▪ Many discounters, which did not previously, now accept credit cards.
- ▪ Customer service has deteriorated and store personnel are not as loyal, helpful, or knowledgeable as before.
- ▪ Some stores are too large and have too much unproductive selling space and low-turnover merchandise.
- ▪ The scrambled merchandising of food retailers has drawn away sales.
- ▪ Unlike specialty stores, many department stores have had a weak focus on customer market segments and a fuzzy image. Too often, departments have been organized by supplier brand name rather than according to customer needs.
- ▪ Such chains as Sears have repeatedly changed strategic orientation, confusing consumers as to their image. (Is Sears a traditional department store chain or a full-line discount store chain?)
- ▪ Chain management has sometimes been too decentralized; thus, there have been different merchandising strategies in branch stores (which blur image).
- ▪ Some companies are not as innovative in their merchandise decisions as they were; they react to suppliers rather than make suggestions to them.
- ▪ Specialty stores often have better assortments in the lines they carry. No department store has the toy selection of Toys "Я" Us or the sporting goods assortment of Sports Authority.
- ▪ Leveraged buyouts saddled several chains with significant debt, causing a poor cash flow; limited funds for store renovations, advertising, and (in some cases) adequate merchandise assortments; and adverse publicity.

To overcome these problems, traditional department stores need to clarify their niche in the marketplace (retail positioning); place greater emphasis on customer service and sales personnel; present more exciting, better-organized store interiors and displays—and change them frequently; use space better by downsizing stores and eliminating slow-selling, space-consuming items (such as J.C. Penney dropping consumer electronics products); and open outlets in smaller, underdeveloped towns and cities (as Sears has done). They can also centralize more buying and promotion functions, do better research, and reach customers more efficiently (by such tools as targeted mailing pieces). As one expert noted,

> Traditional department stores, all but written off for dead, have been showing signs of life lately. They have moved forcefully to clean up their acts. They have dropped money-losing lines and adopted the purchasing and inventory practices that help make discounters successful. Furthermore, many department store chains have

Table 5-5 SELECTED OPERATING RESULTS FOR TRADITIONAL DEPARTMENT STORES, 1995

Percent of total revenues from owned departments	96.8
Percent of total revenues from leased departments	3.2
Percent of total revenues from cash transactions	28.9
Percent of total revenues from credit transactions	71.1
Annual sales per square foot	$204
Annual sales per employee	$123,535
Size of average transaction	$54
Gross margin as a percent of net sales	33.5
Operating expenses as a percent of net sales	29.6
Earnings from operations as a percent of net sales	3.9

Source: Alexandra Moran (Editor), *FOR 1996 Edition* (New York: Wiley, 1996), pp. 5–6. © John Wiley & Sons, Inc. Reprinted by permission.

strengthened their balance sheets. Sloppy financial management—especially ill-conceived leveraged buyouts—played as big a role in triggering problems as did weak operating results. These factors are helping traditional department stores to recapture market share, especially from specialty apparel stores.[23]

Table 5-5 shows selected 1995 operating results for traditional department stores. Data in this table can be compared with those in Table 5-4 (operating results for specialty stores). In general, traditional department stores had more dependence on leased departments, more credit transactions, lower sales per square foot and revenues per transaction, higher sales per employee, lower margins and operating costs, and higher earnings than specialty stores.

Full-Line Discount Store ❏ A **full-line discount store** is a type of department store with these features:

■ It conveys the image of a high-volume, low-cost, fast-turnover outlet selling a broad merchandise assortment for less than conventional prices.
■ Centralized checkout service is provided.
■ Customer service is not usually provided within store departments, but at a centralized area. Products are normally sold by self-service with minimal assistance in any single department.
■ A catalog order service is often not available.
■ The nondurable (soft) goods carried are typically private brands, whereas the durable (hard) goods are well known manufacturer brands.
■ Hard goods often account for a much greater percentage of sales than at traditional department stores, with more emphasis on such items as auto accessories, gardening equipment, and housewares. Less fashion-sensitive merchandise is carried.
■ Buildings, equipment, and fixtures are less expensive; and operating costs are lower than for traditional department stores and specialty stores.
■ There is somewhat less emphasis on credit sales than in full-service stores.

For 1995, full-line discount store revenues were $138 billion (excluding supercenters), about 57 percent of all U.S. department store sales. Together, three chains (Wal-Mart, Kmart, and Target) operated 5,000 full-line discount stores with $97 billion

[23]Gregory A. Patterson, "Department Stores, Seemingly Outmoded, Are Perking Up Again," *Wall Street Journal* (January 4, 1994), pp. A1, A6.

Table 5-6 SELECTED OPERATING RESULTS FOR FULL-LINE DISCOUNT STORES, 1995

Product Category	Total Industry Sales (billions)	Average Percent of Store Sales	Average Annual Sales per Square Foot	Average Annual Stock Turns	Percentage Initial Markup	Percentage Gross Margin
Apparel	$37.9	25.1	$134	3.1	34.2	33.6
Food	13.1	8.6	761	7.5	25.8	19.2
Consumer electronics	11.9	7.9	446	2.8	26.3	16.5
Housewares	10.7	7.1	280	3.2	39.4	29.1
Health and beauty aids	9.4	6.2	341	3.9	26.7	19.8
Domestics	8.1	5.4	144	2.6	43.7	33.9
Toys	7.8	5.2	205	2.5	36.0	28.1
Lawn/garden	6.1	4.0	143	3.6	39.0	28.2
Sporting goods	5.4	3.6	180	2.2	34.0	27.2
Stationery	5.3	3.5	199	2.9	46.0	40.4
Pharmacy	4.8	3.2	515	9.0	28.5	24.6
Furniture	4.7	3.1	232	2.9	41.6	32.2
Household cleaners	4.6	3.0	255	5.4	26.0	19.6
Hardware	4.5	3.0	279	2.4	41.4	34.2
Automotives	4.0	2.7	377	3.0	29.7	22.0

Source: Pete Hisey, "Annual Productivity Report on Full-Line Discount Stores," *Discount Store News* (August 5, 1996), p. 46. Reprinted by permission.

in sales during that year. Overall, about a dozen full-line discount chains had sales of at least $1 billion in 1995.[24]

The success of full-line discount stores is due to a variety of factors. They have a clear customer focus: middle-class and lower-middle-class shoppers looking for good value. The stores feature popular brands of average- to good-quality merchandise at competitive prices. They have aggressively added new goods and service categories and often have their own, well-advertised brands. Firms have worked hard to improve their image and made more customer services available. The average outlet tends to be smaller than a traditional department store, which improves productivity. Sales per square foot are often higher than in traditional department stores. A number of full-line discount stores are located in small towns, where competition is reduced. Chains have been well managed, with standardized branch outlets and good employee relations. Full-line discount store facilities are newer than those of many traditional department stores.

The greatest challenges facing full-line discount stores are the strong competition from other retailers (particularly lower-priced discounters and new store formats, such as category killers), too rapid expansion of some firms, saturation of prime locations, and the dominance of Wal-Mart, Kmart, and Target. As a result, the industry has had a number of consolidations, bankruptcies, and liquidations involving such chains as Zayre, Ames, Bradlees, Caldor, Hills, Lechmere, S.E. Nichols, and Heck's. Some of these firms have since reorganized and recovered.

Table 5-6 shows selected 1995 operating results for full-line discount stores by product category. Note the high overall sales of apparel, the high sales per square foot of food, the high turnover rate for pharmacy items, and the high gross margins of stationery.

Variety Store ❑ A **variety store** handles a wide assortment of inexpensive and popularly priced goods and services, such as stationery, gift items, women's accessories,

[24]"The DSN Top 200," *Discount Store News* (July 1, 1996), p. 41.

health and beauty aids, light hardware, toys, housewares, confectionery items, and shoe repair. Transactions are often on a cash basis. There are open displays and few salespeople. Variety stores do not carry full product lines, may not be departmentalized, and do not deliver products.

In 1995, variety store sales were $7.7 billion, about 0.3 percent of total U.S. retail store sales. McCrory, with 500 variety stores (after many closings), is the leading firm in this store category.

Over the past twenty years, variety stores have shown the poorest performance of any existing store category. This is due to heavy competition from specialty stores and discounters, the older facilities of many stores, the low profit margins associated with some of the items carried, and the decision of firms such as Woolworth to diversify. At one time, Woolworth had 1,200 variety stores, with annual sales reaching $2 billion. Unfortunately, as one analyst noted, Woolworth's variety stores "have tried to sell everything from pin cushions to beach chairs to ab flexers, and it just doesn't work." After unsuccessfully seeking to revamp its 120-year-old chain, in mid-1997, Woolworth decided to exit the variety store business in the United States.[25]

One interesting spin-off of the conventional variety store has been taking place. Dollar discount stores and closeout chains are becoming more prevalent. These stores often sell similar kinds of items as traditional variety stores, but in plainer surroundings and at much lower prices. Dollar General and Family Dollar are leading dollar discount store chains and Consolidated Stores (with its Odd Lots/Big Lots stores) and Pic 'N' Save are two major closeout chains.

Off-Price Chain ❑ An **off-price chain** features brand-name (sometimes designer label) apparel and accessories, footwear (primarily women's and family), linens, fabrics, cosmetics, and/or housewares and sells them at everyday low prices in an efficient, limited-service environment. It frequently has community dressing rooms, centralized checkout counters, no gift wrapping, and extra charges for alterations. Merchandise is bought opportunistically, when special deals occur. Other retailers' canceled orders, manufacturers' irregulars and overruns, and end-of-season merchandise are often purchased for a fraction of their original wholesale prices.

Off-price chains usually aim at the same type of shoppers as traditional department stores, but at prices up to 40 percent to 50 percent lower. And as a T.J. Maxx executive once noted, shoppers are lured by the promise of new merchandise on a regular basis: "Every T.J. Maxx store gets thousands of items of new, quality merchandise in every week."[26] In addition, various off-price shopping centers now appeal to people's interest in one-stop shopping.

The most crucial aspect of the strategy of off-price chains involves buying merchandise and establishing long-term relationships with suppliers. To succeed, the chains must secure large quantities of merchandise at reduced wholesale prices and have a regular flow of goods into the stores. Their stock turnover is far higher than that of department stores.

Sometimes, manufacturers seek out off-price chains to sell samples and products that have not done well (this generally occurs three to four weeks after the beginning of a season) and merchandise remaining on hand near the end of a season. In this way, manufacturers have access to quick cash, gain a market for closeouts and discontinued items, and have relationships with retailers promising not to mention brands or prices in ads (to not alienate department store or specialty store clients). Off-price chains tend to be less demanding than department stores in terms of the advertising support requested from suppliers, do not return products, and pay promptly.

---

[25]Laura Bird, "Hamsters Get Heave-Ho in New Five-and-Tens," *Wall Street Journal* (September 26, 1996), pp. B1, B10; and Jennifer Steinhauer, "Woolworth Says Goodbye to the Dime Store," *New York Times* (July 18, 1997), pp. A1, D6.

[26]Alice Z. Cuneo, "T.J. Maxx Fashions Ads to Battle Off-Price Pack," *Advertising Age* (September 16, 1996), p. 20.

Other times, off-price chains employ a more active buying strategy. Instead of waiting for closeouts and canceled orders, they convince manufacturers to make merchandise such as garments during off-seasons and pay cash for items before they are produced (or delivered).

In 1995, the total sales of U.S. off-price apparel stores were more than $15 billion, and the four leading chains had sales of $9.2 billion and operated 1,600 stores.[27] The leaders are T.J. Maxx, Marshalls, Burlington Coat Factory, and Ross Stores.

Off-price chains have faced some marketplace pressures because of growing competition from other institutional formats (such as department stores running special sales throughout the year), the discontinuity of their merchandise, poor management at some firms, insufficient customer service for some upscale shoppers, and the shakeout of some underfinanced companies.

Factory Outlet ❏ A **factory outlet** is a manufacturer-owned store selling a manufacturer's closeouts, discontinued merchandise, irregulars, canceled orders, and, sometimes, in-season, first-quality merchandise. Manufacturers' interest in outlet stores has increased for four basic reasons. First, a manufacturer can control where its discounted merchandise is sold. By placing outlets in out-of-the-way locations, depressed areas, or areas with low sales penetration of the firm's brands, factory outlet revenues are unlikely to affect a manufacturer's key customers (which may be specialty and department stores). Second, these outlets can be profitable despite prices up to 60 percent less than customary retail prices. This is due to low operating costs—as a result of few services, low rent, limited displays, and plain store fixtures. In addition, the manufacturer does not have to pay wholesalers or retailers. Third, at factory outlets, manufacturers can decide upon store visibility, set promotion policies, remove labels, and be sure that discontinued items and irregulars are disposed of properly. Fourth, since many specialty and department stores are increasing their use of private labels, manufacturers may need revenue from outlet stores to sustain their own growth.

In recent years, more factory outlet stores have been locating in clusters or in outlet malls to expand customer traffic and use cooperative ads. Large outlet malls are in Connecticut, Florida, Georgia, New York, Pennsylvania, Tennessee, and a number of other states. In 1995, there were 12,000 U.S. factory outlet stores—many in the 340 outlet malls nationwide; and they accounted for $14 billion in sales.[28] Manufacturers with factory outlets include Bass (footwear), Champion (apparel), The Gap (apparel), Harry & David (fruits and gift items), Levi's (apparel), Liz Claiborne (apparel), Pepperidge Farm (food), Perfumania (fragrances), Phillips-Van Heusen (clothing), Samsonite (luggage), and Totes (rain gear). See Figure 5-7.

When determining whether to enter into or expand factory outlets, manufacturers need to be cautious. They must evaluate their expertise in retailing, the dollar investment costs, the impact on existing retailers that buy from them, and the response of final customers. Certainly, manufacturers will not want to jeopardize their products' sales at full retail prices.

Membership Club ❏ A **membership club** appeals to price-conscious consumers, who must be members to shop there. It straddles the line between wholesaling and retailing. Some members of a typical club are small business owners and employees who pay a nominal annual fee (such as $35 each) and buy merchandise at wholesale prices; these customers make purchases for use in operating their firms or for personal use. They yield 60 percent of total club sales. The bulk of members are final consumers who buy exclusively

---

[27]"The DSN Top 200," p. 61.
[28]Edwin McDowell, "America's Hot Tourist Spot: The Outlet Mall," *New York Times* (May 26, 1996), Section 1, pp. 1, 18; and Susan Reda, "Mills Find Cure for Outlet Doldrums by Focusing on Entertainment Theme," *Stores* (April 1997), pp. 106–107.

Figure 5-7

**Factory Outlets:
The Phillips-Van
Heusen Way**

Phillips-Van Heusen is a
manufacturer that is a big
believer in factory outlet
stores as a way to sell
overruns, out-of-season
merchandise, and irregu-
lars. It has a number of
such stores around the
United States.

for their own use; they represent 40 percent of overall club sales. These consumers also usually pay a nominal membership fee and must belong to a union, be municipal employees, work for educational institutions, or belong to other specified groups to become members (in reality, eligibility is defined so broadly as to exclude few consumers). Sometimes, their prices are slightly higher than those paid by business customers.

The membership club is a derivative of the membership-based discount retailer popular in the 1950s and 1960s in the United States and the giant European warehouse outlet catering to small food and drugstore retailers. The operating strategy of the current membership club began in the mid-1970s and centers on large store facilities (up to 100,000 or more square feet), inexpensive isolated or industrial park locations, opportunistic buying (with some merchandise discontinuity), a fraction of the items stocked by full-line discount stores, little or no advertising, plain fixtures, wide aisles (to give forklift trucks access to shelves), concrete floors, limited or no delivery, fewer credit options than in many other stores, goods sent directly from manufacturers to stores, and very low prices.

A membership club sells three kinds of goods: general merchandise, such as appliances, computers, housewares, consumer electronics, tires, and apparel (35 percent to 60 percent of sales); food (20 percent to 35 percent of sales); and sundries, like health and beauty aids, tobacco, liquor, and candy (15 percent to 30 percent of sales). Today, it may also have a pharmacy, photo developing, a car-buying service, and other items formerly viewed as frills for this format. Its stock turnover rate is several times that of a department store.

In 1995, there were more than 950 membership clubs. The retail aspect of these clubs accounted for sales of $18 billion to $20 billion, up from $2.5 billion in 1985. Together, the two leading firms, Sam's Club and Costco (formerly PriceCostco), generate 90 percent of industry sales.[29]

The major retailing challenges faced by membership clubs relate to the limited size of their final consumer market segment, the allocation of efforts between business and final consumer accounts (without antagonizing one group or the other, and without presenting a blurred store image), the lack of interest by many consumers in shopping at warehouse-type stores, the power of the two industry leaders, and the potential for saturation caused by overexpansion.

[29]"The DSN Top 200," p. 79.

Flea Market ❑ A **flea market** has many retail vendors offering a range of products at discount prices in plain surroundings. It is rooted in the centuries-old tradition of street selling—shoppers touch, sample, and haggle over the prices of items. Once, flea market vendors sold only antiques, bric-a-brac, and assorted used merchandise. Today, they also frequently sell new goods, such as clothing, cosmetics, watches, consumer electronics, housewares, and gift items. Many flea markets are located in nontraditional sites not normally associated with retailing: racetracks, stadiums, arenas, and drive-in movie parking lots. Others are at sites abandoned by supermarkets and department stores. They may be indoor or outdoor.

At a flea market, individual retailers rent space on a daily, weekly, or seasonal basis. For example, a large flea market might rent twenty-foot by forty-foot spaces for $30 to $50 or more per day, depending on the location. Some flea markets impose a parking fee or admission charge on consumers shopping there.

There are a few hundred major flea markets in the United States—such as the Rose Bowl Flea Market in Pasadena, California—but overall sales data are not available. The improved credibility of permanent flea markets (which have been operating for a long time and are open year-round), consumer interest in bargaining, the prevalence of Sunday shopping, the broadened product mix, the availability of some brand-name merchandise, and consumers' heightened price sensitivity have all contributed to the appeal of this retail institution. For example, the Rose Bowl Flea Market has 1,500 vendors and attracts 20,000 shoppers on a typical day (it is open the second Sunday of every month). Flea World in Sanford, Florida, has 1,200 vendors and is open Friday through Sunday throughout the year. At any flea market, price haggling is encouraged, cash is the predominant currency, and many vendors gain their first real experience as retail entrepreneurs.[30] *Goodridge's Guides to Flea Markets* lists more than 6,000 flea markets, big and small, around the United States.

Some traditional retailers are not happy about flea markets. They believe flea markets represent an unfair method of competition because the quality of merchandise may be misrepresented or overstated, consumers may purchase items at flea markets and then return them to other retailers for refunds that are higher than the prices paid, suppliers are often unaware their products are sold there, state and federal taxes can be easily avoided, and operating costs are quite low. Furthermore, flea markets may cause traffic congestion.

The high total sales volume from off-price chains, factory outlets, membership clubs, and flea markets can be explained by the wheel of retailing. All of these institutions are low-cost operators appealing to price-conscious consumers who are not satisfied with other retail formats—which have upgraded merchandise and customer services, raised prices, and moved along the wheel.

RETAIL INSTITUTIONS CATEGORIZED BY SERVICE VERSUS GOODS STRATEGY MIX

Given consumers' heightened interest in services and the extent of scrambled merchandising in retailing, it is now more important than ever to understand the differences between the strategy mixes involved with services and those for goods. The following discussion applies to both store-based and nonstore-based retailers, as well as to both firms offering only services and those offering goods *and* services. There are substantial distinctions in the way services are marketed from the manner in which goods are marketed.

Service retailing involves transactions between companies or individuals and final consumers where the consumers do not purchase or acquire ownership of tangible products. **Goods retailing** focuses on the sale of tangible (physical) products.

Some retailers engage in either service retailing (such as travel agencies) or goods retailing (such as hardware stores); others offer a combination of the two (such as video stores that rent, as well as sell movies). The latter format is the fastest-growing. Consider

---

[30]Marla Matzer, "Country Grunge," *Forbes* (June 6, 1994), pp. 114–116.

how many pharmacies offer film developing, how many department stores have beauty salons, how many computer stores run fee-paid training classes, how many stationery stores sell lottery tickets, how many hotels have gift shops, how many golf driving ranges sell equipment, and so on.

As noted in Chapter 1, total U.S. service retailing sales are several hundred billion dollars annually. Service retailing is far reaching and encompasses such diverse businesses as hotels and motels, personal services, auto repair and rental, and amusement and recreational services. There are three kinds of service retailing: **rented-goods services,** in which consumers lease and use goods for specified periods of time; **owned-goods services,** in which goods owned by consumers are repaired, improved, or maintained; and **nongoods services,** in which intangible personal services (rather than goods) are offered to consumers—who experience the services rather than possess them.

Some examples of rented-goods service retailing are Hertz car rentals, carpet cleaner rentals from a supermarket, and video rentals at a 7-Eleven. In each case, a tangible good is leased for a fee for a fixed time duration. The consumer may enjoy the use of the item, but ownership is not obtained and the good must be returned when the rental period is up.

Owned-goods service retailing illustrations include repair of a watch mainspring, lawn care to eliminate weeds, and an annual air conditioner tune-up to maintain performance. In this grouping, the retailer providing the service never owns the good involved.

In nongoods service retailing, personal services, involving the use of the owner's or an employee's time in return for a fee, are offered; tangible goods are not involved. Some examples are stockbrokers, tutors, travel agents, real-estate brokers, and personal trainers. In each case, the seller offers personal expertise for a specified time period.

Because the characteristics of services differ significantly from those of goods, as shown by the following list, these distinctions must be incorporated into strategic retail planning:

■ The buyer is often called a *client,* not a *customer.*
■ Services can provide a differential advantage for goods-based retailers that carry the same product lines as competitors.
■ Surpluses cannot be inventoried; thus, some services can be very perishable.
■ Standards are not precise because many services cannot be mass produced.
■ Service performance may vary from one customer to another and from one experience to another.
■ Rental firms have to get used to investing in inventory and earning back their investment little by little, rather than as goods are sold.
■ Service prices are sometimes expressed as rates, fees, admissions, charges, tuition, and so on.
■ It may be hard to apply the economic concepts of supply and demand, and costs are also difficult to assign because of the intangible nature of services.
■ Until recently, few service chains existed (but this is changing rapidly—examples are Century 21 for real estate and H&R Block for tax services), and the concentration of firms in the service sector is relatively small.
■ Many service retailers do not understand that their services must be promoted; being available does not guarantee business.
■ Symbolism derives from how well a service is performed rather than from ownership of a good.
■ Many services are performed in a professional or formal manner.
■ In some cases, consumers may decide to bypass retailers and complete services themselves.
■ Some service firms (like the public library) are nonprofit in nature.

The complexity of service retailing can be summed up in this example: "Ace Hardware, which calls its rental program 'Ace Rental Place,' tells its member stores that

.... ➤

Figure 5-8

Ace Hardware: Selling *and* Renting Products

rental departments create a new revenue stream, attract new customers, build traffic, and can create add-on sales. On the down side, rental departments may not be as productive as space used for some merchandise categories. There is also the cost of investment in tool inventory. The Ace program was introduced five years ago; there are now more than 150 retailers participating in the effort. The basic inventory ranges from ladders to hand trucks to all sorts of small hand and power tools. Some dealers have added major specialty items such as jackhammers, chippers/shredders, and trenchers."[31] See Figure 5-8.

It should also be mentioned that although several services have not been commonly considered a part of retailing (such as medical, dental, legal, and educational services), they should be when they entail a transaction with a final consumer.

Chapter 19 presents an in-depth discussion of strategic planning concepts as they apply to service retailing.

[31] David P. Schulz, "Independents Find Growth Through Rental Business," *Stores* (December 1996), p. 45.

Summary

1. *To describe the wheel of retailing, scrambled merchandising, and the retail life cycle and show how they help explain the performance and evolution of retail strategy mixes* In Chapter 4, retail institutions were examined by type of ownership. This chapter views retailing from two strategy perspectives: store-based and service versus goods. A retail strategy mix involves a combination of factors: location, operations, goods/services offered, pricing, atmosphere and customer services, and promotion. To flourish, a firm should strive to be dominant in some aspect of its strategy and thus reach power retailer status.

Three important concepts help explain the performance and evolution of various retail strategy mixes. According to the wheel of retailing, retail innovators often first appear as low-price operators with a low-cost structure and low profit-margin requirements. Over time, these firms upgrade their offerings and customer services and raise prices accordingly. They then become vulnerable to new discounters with lower-cost structures which take their place along the wheel. Scrambled merchandising occurs as a retailer adds goods and services that are unrelated to each other and the firm's original business to increase overall sales and profit margins. Scrambled merchandising is contagious, and retailers often use it in self-defense. The retail life cycle assumes that retail institutions pass through identifiable stages of innovation, development, maturity, and decline. Attributes and strategies change as institutions mature.

2. *To examine characteristics of a wide variety of retail institutions involved with store-based strategy mixes* Retail institutions may be classed by store-based strategy mix and divided into food-oriented and general merchandise groupings. In all, 14 store-based strategy mixes are covered in the chapter.

These are the food-oriented store-based retailers: A convenience store is well located, is open long hours, and offers a moderate number of fill-in items at average to above-average prices. A conventional supermarket is departmentalized and carries a wide range of food and related items; little general merchandise is stocked; and prices are competitive. A food-based superstore is larger and more diversified than a conventional supermarket but smaller and less diversified than a combination store. A combination store unites supermarket and general merchandise sales in a large facility and sets competitive prices; the supercenter is a type of combination store. The box (limited-line) store is a discounter focusing on a small product selection, moderate hours, few services, and few national brands. A warehouse store is a discounter offering a moderate number of food items in a no-frills setting that can be quite large (for a super warehouse).

These are the general merchandise store-based retailers: A specialty store concentrates on one goods or service line and has a tailored strategy; the category killer is a special kind of specialty store. A department store is a large retailer that carries an extensive assortment of goods and services. The traditional one has a range of customer services and charges average to above-average prices. A full-line discount store is a department store with a low-cost, low-price strategy. A variety store has an assortment of inexpensive and popularly priced items in a simple setting. An off-price chain features brand-name items and sells them at low prices in an austere environment. A factory outlet is manufacturer-owned and sells that firm's closeouts, discontinued merchandise, and irregulars at very low prices. A membership club appeals to price-conscious shoppers, who must be members to shop there. A flea market has many retail vendors offering a range of goods at discount prices in nontraditional store settings.

3. *To contrast service-based retailing with goods-based retailing* Due to consumers' heightened interest in services and the extent of scrambled merchandising, it is more important than ever to understand the differences between the strategy mixes involved with services and those for goods. Service retailing involves transactions between companies or individuals and final consumers where the consumers do not purchase or acquire ownership of tangible products. Goods retailing entails the sale of tangible (physical) products. Some firms engage in either service retailing or goods retailing; others offer a combination of the two. The latter approach is the fastest-growing. There are three kinds of service retailing: rented goods, owned goods, and nongoods. Chapter 19 examines strategic planning for service retailing.

Key Terms

strategy mix (p. 132)
power retailer (p. 132)
wheel of retailing (p. 133)
scrambled merchandising (p. 135)
retail life cycle (p. 136)
convenience store (p. 141)
supermarket (p. 142)
conventional supermarket (p. 142)
food-based superstore (p. 143)
combination store (p. 144)

supercenter (p. 144)
box (limited-line) store (p. 145)
warehouse store (p. 145)
specialty store (p. 147)
category killer store (p. 147)
department store (p. 148)
traditional department store (p. 149)
full-line discount store (p. 151)
variety store (p. 152)

off-price chain (p. 153)
factory outlet (p. 154)
membership club (p. 154)
flea market (p. 156)
service retailing (p. 156)
goods retailing (p. 156)
rented-goods services (p. 157)
owned-goods services (p. 157)
nongoods services (p. 157)

Questions for Discussion

1. Describe how a small firm could be a power retailer.
2. Explain the wheel of retailing. Is this theory applicable today? Why or why not?
3. Develop a low-end retail strategy mix for a gift store. Include location, operating procedures, goods/services offered, pricing tactics, and promotion methods.
4. The gift store in Question 3 wants to upgrade to a high-end strategy. Outline the changes that must be made in the firm's strategy mix. What are the risks facing the retailer?
5. How could these retailers best apply scrambled merchandising? Explain your answers.
   a. Florist.
   b. Home cleaning company.
   c. Movie theater.
   d. Restaurant.
6. Contrast the strategy emphasis that should be followed by institutions in the innovation and growth stages of the retail life cycle with the emphasis by institutions in the maturity stage.

7. What alternative approaches are there for institutions that are in the decline phase of the retail life cycle?
8. Contrast the strategy mixes of convenience stores, conventional supermarkets, food-based superstores, and warehouse stores. Is there room for each? Explain your answer.
9. Do you think supercenters will succeed in the long run? Why or why not?
10. Contrast the strategy mixes of specialty stores, traditional department stores, and full-line discount stores.
11. What must the off-price chain do to succeed in the future?
12. Do you expect factory outlet stores to keep growing? Explain your answer.
13. One retailer sells cars; another firm rents them. Develop a strategy mix for each and compare these mixes.
14. What factors should a goods-based retailer keep in mind if it decides to add rentals to its product mix?

Web-Based Exercise:

THE GAP, INC. (http://www.gap.com)

Questions

1. Summarize The Gap, Inc.'s overall retail strategy based on the information provided at its Web site.
2. Evaluate the Gapstyle feature component of the Web site and present specific suggestions for improving this feature.

3. Evaluate The Gap's advertising campaign component of the Web site and offer specific suggestions for improving it.
4. What other components/features could be added to this Web site? Explain your answer.

CASE 1

Patagonia: An Environmentally Focused Specialty Retailer*

Patagonia was founded by Yvon Chouinard in 1957 in Ventura, California, as an outlet for the sale of his handmade mountain climbing equipment. In 1972, Chouinard began to manufacture, distribute, and sell apparel items aimed at consumers who had a passion for mountaineering, skiing, snowboarding, and other outdoor sports. From the firm's beginning, Chouinard insisted that his clothing be as technically sound as his climbing gear. The firm prides itself on field-testing its products under extreme conditions. Today, Patagonia has a large mail-order operation, with 15 company-owned U.S. stores, 3 in Europe, and 5 in Asia/Oceania. Its Web site is (http://www.patagonia.com/menu.html).

**This case was prepared and written by Professor Gail H. Kirby, Santa Clara University. The material is drawn from Melissa Dowling, "Patagonia Raises Cotton-Pickin' Prices," *Catalog Age* (May 1996), p. 10; Meryl Davids, "Wanted: Strategic Planners," *Journal of Business Strategy* (May–June 1995), pp. 31–36; Polly LaBarre, "Patagonia Comes of Age," *Industry Week* (April 3, 1995), pp. 42–48; Fleming Meeks, "The Man Is the Message," *Forbes* (April 17, 1989), pp. 148–152; *Organic Cotton Store, Patagonia Inc. 1995*; and Edward O. Welles, "Lost in Patagonia," *Inc.* (August 1992), pp. 44–57.*

CASE 1
(Continued)

Chouinard believes Patagonia exists to serve as a model for corporate responsibility. His long-standing philosophy has been to run the firm along "self-sustaining" principles. In 1984, Patagonia began tithing—distributing 10 percent of pre-tax profits (now about 1 percent of sales) to preserving and restoring the natural environment through a program it calls an "earth tax." Grants are distributed twice a year, generally to small grassroots groups that seek to protect a part of a forest, a stretch of river, or a specific species. Chouinard adds that "no one can wait for government to impose a levy, because by then the planet will be beyond repair." Chouinard foresees an era when people "will consume less but consume better."

Patagonia is a classic ecologically aware, socially progressive, entrepreneurial firm. Its unique mission can be seen from the job description for a new chief executive officer (CEO) that appeared in the *Wall Street Journal*. The ad said the firm required a CEO who could surf and kayak, was committed to open communication and high product quality, who agreed that Patagonia should continue to pledge 1 percent of sales to controversial environmental and social causes, wanted slow growth, and was committed to reducing environmental pollution. Ultimately, Patagonia decided to divide the responsibilities among a four-member team with each member responsible for their area, but with major decisions made collectively.

Beginning in spring 1996, Patagonia made a commitment to use only organically grown cotton in its cotton garments. The company switched to organic cotton because it believed the pesticides, herbicides, and other chemicals used in growing traditional cotton are detrimental to our soil, air, and groundwater. This affects not only humans, but also birds and wildlife. In contrast, its certified organic cotton is grown using such natural methods as the introduction of beneficial bugs that eat harmful insects, the use of cover crops to control weeds, and the use of compost and other natural fertilizers. These methods are rarely used in place of traditional chemicals.

The change to organic cotton has its costs. Organic farming is not only more labor-intensive, but also additional costs are incurred in the ginning, spinning, and knitting or weaving of organically grown cotton due to the small runs. These higher costs forced Patagonia to raise the prices of its cotton apparel items by $2 to $10. Patagonia devoted several pages of its spring 1996 catalog explaining its switch from traditional to organic cotton.

Besides the switch to organic cotton, Patagonia has an Internal Environmental program, where two-thirds of its waste is reused (through reusing boxes, recycling paper, and having composts at its main offices). Patagonia has even created a fabric recycling program, including the development of a post-consumer recycled cloth.

A quick flip through a Patagonia catalog reveals differences between it and most other apparel catalogs. For example, the Patagonia catalog contains broad product descriptions of the fabrics, the construction of inner and outer layers, the applicability for given activities (such as mountaineering, skiing, and snowboarding), and weight of each good. The environmental influence is immediately apparent. Organic cotton goods and post-consumer recycled fabrics are clearly labeled. And a two-page spread on the inside front cover of a recent catalog, for example, was devoted to describing toxic chemicals that were released from a hazardous waste dump and their effect on local residents' quality of life.

Questions

1. What factors in our physical environment have been important in shaping Patagonia's marketing strategies? Comment on Patagonia's approach.
2. Assess Patagonia's decision to utilize company-owned specialty stores as its major store-based retailing channel.

CASE 1
(Continued)

3. Discuss the pros and cons of Patagonia's selling selected lines of merchandise through department stores.
4. Describe the pros and cons of Patagonia's establishing factory outlets for excess stock and off-season merchandise.

Video Questions on Patagonia

1. What are the pros and cons of Patagonia's hiring personnel that have a serious passion for outdoor sports?
2. Discuss the pros and cons of Patagonia's no-growth marketing strategy.

CASE 2
Old Navy: A New Tune for an Old Sailor[†]

Despite the success of The Gap, Inc.'s traditional stores (which include The Gap, GapKids, babyGap, and Banana Republic stores), the firm's top executives recently determined that the firm still did not serve a large proportion of its potential customers. For example, The Gap, Inc.'s research showed that middle-market shoppers (with an annual income of $20,000 to $50,000) rarely buy in regional shopping malls, where Gap has most of its stores. As a result, The Gap, Inc. was unsuccessful in attracting the middle-market apparel market, one that spends about $75 billion a year on clothing and accessories.

Thus, in 1994, The Gap, Inc. (whose Web site is http://www.gap.com) opened its first Old Navy Clothing stores. The stores were positioned to combine the style and quality of the chain's The Gap stores, with the low prices and large selection of an apparel-based discounter. Old Navy aimed at consumers who traditionally shopped at either department stores (such as Sears and J.C. Penney), or at discounters (such as Wal-Mart, Target, and Marshalls). The Gap, Inc. initially converted 48 underperforming Gap stores around the country to Old Navy stores, as a market test of this concept. The test not only convinced the firm that its initial belief about a large untapped market was correct, but also taught it some valuable lessons about the middle-market shopper. For example, the popularity of multiple-item purchases of basic commodities (such as socks and underwear in bulk), led to Old Navy's bundling these items in packages of three or more and to providing shopping carts.

At first glance, a typical Old Navy Clothing store resembles many other apparel-based discounters with its concrete flooring, exposed duct work and insulation, shopping carts, and central checkout counters. However, upon a closer look, several key differences are apparent. Old Navy's clothing is displayed in a manner more similar to The Gap and Banana Republic stores or Ralph Lauren/Polo and Tommy Hilfiger sections in department stores. Old Navy's layout includes high school lockers that are stripped to bare metal. The lockers, with several doors missing, serve as attractive display cases. Old Navy conceals its overhead storage space with canvas flaps that lend a somewhat nautical quality to the store. The checkout counters are made from polished press board and galvanized metal, instead of Formica plastic-laminated surfaces that are so popular at discounters. Unlike much apparel that is usually sold in this price range, Old Navy clothing is more distinctively styled. It also uses many more sales promotions than The Gap, Inc.'s other chain units. Thus, Old Navy might offer customers a gift with each purchase, such as a baseball hat or dog tags with the Old Navy logo.

Old Navy uses less costly fabrics, wider production allowances, and lower rental costs to enable it to reduce its costs and its prices. Although acrylic and wool blends are

[†] This case was prepared and written by Professor Richard C. Leventhal, Metropolitan State College. The material is drawn from Susan Caminiti, "Will Old Navy Fill the Gap?" *Fortune* (March 18, 1996), pp. 59–62; *The Gap, Inc. 1995 Annual Report; The Gap, Inc. 10K for the Year Ended February 3, 1996;* and Shari Sanders, "Sailing into the Mass Market," *Discount Store News* (March 4, 1996), pp. A35–A37.

popular for sweaters at Old Navy, The Gap and Banana Republic stores sell mostly wool sweaters. The seam allowances at Old Navy are less consistent, so a shopper may have to try on several pairs of jeans in the same style and size to find one that fits best. Store rental costs are also reduced by situating in shopping strips or "power" centers, built around a Wal-Mart or a Home Depot, rather than in more expensive regional shopping center locations. As a result, Old Navy's price points can be as much as 40 percent lower than at The Gap.

A potential threat to The Gap, Inc. is that Old Navy may cannibalize (take away) sales from The Gap, Inc.' s other retail units, particularly The Gap and Banana Republic. To protect against such cannibalism, The Gap, Inc. has worked hard to reposition The Gap and Banana Republic.

As of 1996, there were 139 Old Navy stores in 27 states. The Gap, Inc. plans to add between 50 to 100 new Old Navy stores each year for the next several years. Although The Gap, Inc. does not separate sales and profit data by division, some retail analysts estimate that Old Navy generated sales of $400 million for the fiscal year ending in 1996, with profits of around $20 million.

Questions

1. What are Old Navy's competitive advantages and disadvantages versus full-line discount stores such as Wal-Mart, Kmart, and Target?
2. Should Old Navy participate in scrambled merchandising? If yes, how? If no, why not?
3. Has Old Navy defined its target market adequately? Explain your answer.
4. How can The Gap, Inc. prevent Old Navy from cannibalizing sales from its other store units?

6

Nonstore-Based and Nontraditional Retailing

CHAPTER OBJECTIVES

1. To look at the characteristics of the three major retail institutions involved with nonstore-based strategy mixes: direct marketing, direct selling, and vending machines—with an emphasis on direct marketing

2. To consider these nontraditional forms of retailing: the World Wide Web, video kiosks, and video catalogs

German-based Otto Versand-Handelsgruppe (Otto) is the largest mail-order firm in the world with $16.5 billion in sales. Through its 36 mail-order companies (including Spiegel and Eddie Bauer) in 16 nations (in Western Europe, Asia, and North America), Otto accounts for a growing share of global mail-order sales. Most of its companies sell apparel or home furnishings.

More than one-half of Otto's sales are in its home market of Germany. Otto's success there is partly due to German laws that drastically limit retail stores' hours of operation. As a consequence, many Germans prefer to purchase through mail-order-based retailers. Germans, on average, annually spend $352 per capita on mail orders versus $252 per capita in the United States and $17 per capita in Italy (largely due to Italy's less reliable mail system).

Otto has a $25 million direct marketing advertising budget in Germany. This enables the firm to send between 8 million and 10 million mailings per year. These mailings range from reminder postcards (for consumers who have not purchased any products from Otto in the past 3 years) to one of 20 specialty catalogs (such as those that feature clothing for children or for older women who wear large sizes). Otto has special expertise in logistics and in electronic data processing, which provide effective competitive advantages. For example, in Germany, Otto uses its own distribution system to deliver clothing on hangers to customers' homes within 24 hours of orders being received. Items are delivered until 9:00 P.M.

In industrialized nations, Otto's expansion strategy has been to acquire successful mail-order retailers and slowly take them into other markets. Thus, the firm bought Spiegel in 1982. This acquisition gave Otto a strong mail-order presence in the United States, as well as in-depth knowledge of Spiegel's ability to target specific consumer segments. Spiegel, Otto's largest non-German business, has been largely U.S.-based; it entered Canada in 1996. Otto purchased Eddie Bauer in 1988. Eddie Bauer began operating in Europe and Japan during 1994. Otto planned to have 15 Eddie Bauer stores as of the end of 1996 and to open 2 more stores in Germany.

With developing countries, where there are few, if any, such mail-order companies to acquire, Otto normally takes a majority stake through a joint venture arrangement with an established retailer, such as its recent successful joint venture in India.[1]

---

[1]Dagmar Mussey, "Otto Expands Family-Owned Catalog Empire," *Ad Age International* (September 1996), p. i4.

In this chapter, we examine both nonstore-based retailing and several emerging types of **OVERVIEW** nontraditional retailing. These formats are influencing the strategies of current store-based retailers, as well as newly formed retail businesses. Thus, the discussion in Chapter 6 builds on the material covered in Chapter 5.

Retailers engage in **nonstore retailing** when they use strategy mixes that are not store-based to reach consumers and complete transactions. It occurs by direct marketing, direct selling, and vending machines. Some retailers, such as J.C. Penney and L.L. Bean, combine both store and nonstore activities to expand their customer markets and sales potential. Others, such as Mary Kay and QVC, stick to nonstore retailing to better target segments and hold down operating costs. Overall nonstore retailing sales are nearly $200 billion yearly, with more than 70 percent of that from direct marketing (hence, the direct marketing emphasis in this chapter). See Figure 6-1.

Nontraditional retailing encompasses a variety of newer techniques that do not neatly fit into the long-standing conventional types of retailing considered as "store-based" or "nonstore-based." These include the use of the World Wide Web, video kiosks, and video catalogs. Sometimes, the formats operate as an aspect of store-based retailing; other times, they do not. What they have in common is their departure from traditional retailing, which makes a separate discussion of these formats valuable.

Direct marketing is a form of retailing in which a customer is first exposed to a good **DIRECT** or service through a nonpersonal medium (such as direct mail, conventional or cable **MARKETING** TV, radio, magazine, newspaper, or computer) and then orders by mail or phone (usually with a toll-free number)—sometimes, by computer. Annual U.S. sales to final consumers are $145 billion (excluding charitable contributions of $57 million), and over 100 million people make one or more direct marketing purchases during a typical year. Japan, Germany, Great Britain, France, and Canada are the leaders in direct marketing

Figure 6-1

Nonstore Retailing and Cyberplay Computer Exploration Centers

Through the World Wide Web, Cyberplay promotes its child-oriented computer learning services, such as classes on how to use a PC and how to access the Internet. Web visitors can take a "virtual tour" of its facilities. At its exploration center in Winter Park, Florida (shown here), Cyberplay provides the actual "edutainment."

revenues outside the United States. Among the products bought most frequently are gift items, apparel, magazines, books and records/CDs, sports equipment, home accessories, and insurance.[2]

In the United States, direct marketing customers are more apt to be married, upper middle class, and over 45 years of age. Mail shoppers are more likely to live in areas far from malls. Phone shoppers are more likely to live in upscale metropolitan areas and to dial in orders to avoid traffic and save time. Although the share of direct marketing purchases made by men is small, it is growing. For instance, 25 percent of catalog shoppers are now men, up from less than 20 percent a few years ago. Since 1987, the number of male catalog shoppers has risen by 60 percent, compared with 40 percent for females.[3]

Although direct marketing is one of the largest and fastest-growing retail institutions in the United States, it is also one of the most misunderstood. According to an industry expert, "It used to be easy to spot direct marketers. We were the ones who used to put all those envelopes and catalogs in the mail. But yesterday's mavens of direct mail are now becoming masters of multimedia, as we access a large and rapidly expanding arsenal of technological tools."[4] Nonetheless, direct marketing is quite different from store-based retailing: "In the retail store business, you buy an inventory and sell it off. In the direct marketing business, you create a demand and fill it." And store-based retailers "tend to be burdened by real estate."[5]

Direct marketers can be divided into two broad categories: general and specialty. General direct marketing firms offer a full line of products and sell everything from clothing to housewares. J.C. Penney (via its mail-order business) and QVC are examples of

Figure 6-2

Spiegel: A Leading Specialty Direct Marketer

Spiegel's direct marketing apparel sales are over $1 billion, mostly via its specialty catalogs. Customers may place mail orders or talk to well-trained telephone operators (who are represented here).

[2]"Highlights of the Mail Order Marketplace," *Direct Marketing* (August 1996), pp. 48–57; and Susan Thorne, "Unified Europe May Boost Catalog Sales," *Shopping Center Today* (May 1997), pp. 156, 168.
[3]Mediamark Research Inc., "Where Americans Shop from Home," *U.S. News & World Report* (July 8, 1996), p. 21; and Calmetta Y. Coleman, "Catalog Shopping, Favored by Women, Is Finally Making Inroads Among Men," *Wall Street Journal* (March 25, 1996), p. A9B.
[4]Howard C. Kraft, "The Destiny of Direct: A New Perspective on the Future of Direct Marketing," *Journal of Direct Marketing*, Vol. 7 (Autumn 1993), p. 65.
[5]Holly Klokis, "Catalog Options: Mail-Order or Store Traffic?" *Chain Store Age* (May 1985), p. 31; and Susan Reda, "Formula for the Future," *Stores* (October 1993), p. 74.

general direct marketers. Specialty firms focus on more narrow product lines, like their specialty store counterparts. Spiegel, L.L. Bean, Publishers Clearinghouse, and Franklin Mint are among the thousands of U.S. specialty direct marketers. See Figure 6-2.

Direct marketing has a number of strategic business advantages:

■ Many costs are reduced—startup costs can be rather low; reduced inventories can be held; no fixtures or displays are needed; a prime site is unnecessary; regular store hours do not have to be kept; a sales force is not needed; and a firm may be run out of a garage or basement.

■ It is possible for a firm to offer lower prices (due to reduced costs) than store-based retailers carrying the same items. A very large geographic area can be covered inexpensively and efficiently.

■ Customers are given a convenient method of shopping; there are no crowds, parking congestion, or lines at cash registers.

■ People do not have to be concerned about the safety of store shopping early in the morning or late at night.

■ Specific consumer segments can be pinpointed through mailings.

■ Sometimes, consumers can legally avoid paying sales tax by purchasing from direct marketers not operating retail facilities in the consumer's state (however, a number of states are interested in eliminating this loophole).

■ A store-based retailer can supplement its regular business and expand its geographic trading area (even becoming a national or international firm) without adding outlets.

There are some limitations to direct marketing, but they are not as critical as those facing direct selling firms. First, products cannot be examined prior to purchase by a consumer. Thus, the range of items sold is usually more limited than that sold in stores, and direct marketers need liberal return policies to attract and keep customers. Second, prospective direct marketers may underestimate entry costs. Catalogs can be expensive to design, and printing and mailing may be several dollars per catalog. A computer system may be required to track shipments, monitor purchases and returns, and keep mailing lists current. A 24-hour phone staff may be needed.

Third, since most catalogs are delivered by standard mail (formerly called third-class mail), the profitability of direct marketers is highly sensitive to postal rates and to the costs of paper stock. The U.S. Postal Service has raised the rates charged for standard mail with some regularity, although, beginning in 1996, firms (mostly large-volume mailers) were given a rate reduction for better mail preparation. In 1995, due to paper shortages, U.S. paper costs rose by 50 percent, causing some companies to switch to lighter paper or trim the size of their catalogs. Paper prices have stabilized since then. Fourth, even the most successful catalogs draw purchases from less than 10 percent of recipients. The high costs and relatively low response rates have caused some merchants to charge for their catalogs (with the fee usually reimbursed after the first order is placed) or to limit catalogs to customers previously meeting minimum purchase amounts. Fifth, direct marketing clutter exists. In 1995, about 15 billion catalogs were mailed—more than 55 apiece for every man, woman, and child in the United States. Sixth, some unscrupulous direct marketers have given the industry a poor image due to delays in delivery and shipping damaged goods. Seventh, because catalogs are prepared several months to a year in advance, prices and styles may be difficult to plan.

The "30-day rule" is a U.S. federal regulation that greatly affects direct marketers. It requires firms to ship orders within 30 days of their receipt or notify customers of delays. If an order cannot be shipped in 60 days, the customer must be given a specific delivery date and offered the option of canceling the order and getting a refund or continuing to wait for the order to be filled. The rule includes orders placed by mail, phone, fax, and computer.

Despite the limitations it faces, long-run growth for direct marketing is projected for several reasons. Consumer interest in convenience and the difficulty in

Direct Marketing's Emerging International Opportunities

Retailers seeking to utilize direct marketing in foreign markets have to fully appreciate each market's unique culture, language, and accepted selling practices. To succeed, direct marketers need the skill to adapt their messages by using culture-specific techniques and personalized letters. Hiring mailing list providers that understand foreign cultures, as well as their rules and regulations, is also beneficial.

Although this is gradually changing, selling goods and services through direct marketing in Japan has been difficult because many Japanese consumers rely on individual introductions from friends and colleagues. Furthermore, Japanese consumers must be assured that the products advertised will actually meet their high standards.

Japanese consumers often require high levels of customer service and after-sale support. They also tend not to purchase products unless they know they are able to reach an individual at the selling firm to complain, if necessary.

Asian consumers also strongly prefer that letters be tailored to them. For example, in Korea, the family name of the consumer is not as important as his or her first name or middle initial. Direct marketers must be careful in translating foreign addresses or in placing addresses in a deliverable format.

Direct marketing materials that incorporate pictures of the firm's corporate executives are also favored in Asia. These pictures enhance the consumer's long-term relationship with the firm.

Source: Steven Soricillo, "Going Direct into Overseas Markets," *Direct Marketing* (March 1996), pp. 53–54.

setting aside time for shopping are expected to continue. More direct marketers will be operating 24-hour service for orders. Product standardization and the prominence of well-known brands are reducing consumer perceptions of risk when buying on the basis of a catalog or other nonpersonal description. Direct marketers have rapidly improved their skills and efficiency; they are much more effective than before. Technological breakthroughs and new direct marketing approaches, like in-home computerized ordering systems, are expected to encourage more consumer shopping.

Due to its vast current scope and its long-run retailing potential, our detailed discussion of direct marketing is intended to give the reader an in-depth look into this important, evolving, and formidable retail institution. The next sections cover the domain of direct marketing, emerging trends, the steps in a direct marketing strategy, and key issues facing direct marketers.

The Domain of Direct Marketing

As defined at the beginning of this chapter, direct marketing is a form of retailing in which a consumer is exposed to a good or service through a nonpersonal medium and then orders by mail or phone or computer. It may also be viewed in this manner:

> Direct marketing is an interactive system of retailing that uses one or more advertising media to effect a measurable response and/or transaction at any location, with this activity stored on a data base.[6]

Accordingly, we *do* include these as forms of direct marketing: any catalog; mail, TV, radio, magazine, newspaper, telephone directory, or other advertisement; computer-based transaction; or other nonpersonal contact that stimulates customers to place orders by the mail, telephone, or computer.

[6]*Direct Marketing.* This definition appears in every issue of the monthly magazine.

We *do not* include these as forms of direct marketing:

■ Direct selling—Consumers are solicited through in-home (and in-office) personal selling efforts or seller-originated telephone calls. In both cases, the company uses personal, rather than nonpersonal, communication to initiate contact with consumers.
■ Conventional vending machines—Consumers are exposed to nonpersonal media but do not usually complete transactions by mail or phone or computer. These people do not really interact with the firm, and a data base cannot be generated and kept.

Direct marketing *is* involved in many video kiosk transactions; when items are mailed to consumers, there is interaction between the firm and the customer, and a data base can be formed. Direct marketing is also in play when consumers originate telephone calls based on catalogs or ads they have seen.

The Customer Data Base: Key to Successful Direct Marketing

Because direct marketers initiate the contact with customers (in contrast to many store shopping trips that are initiated by the consumer), it is imperative that they develop and maintain a comprehensive customer data base. By doing so, they can pinpoint their best customers, make offers targeted specifically at customers' needs, avoid costly mailings to nonresponsive shoppers, and track changing behavior and sales trends by customer. A good data base is the major asset of most direct marketers, and *every* thriving direct marketer has a strong customer data base.

Data-base retailing is a way of collecting, storing, and using relevant information on customers. Such information typically includes the person's name, address, background data, shopping interests, and purchase behavior (including the amounts bought, how often, and how recently). Though customer data bases are often associated with large computerized information systems, they may also be used by small firms that are not overly computerized.

Here's how data-base retailing can be beneficial:

In many situations, a version of the 80-20 principle probably applies, whereby 80 percent of sales are made to 20 percent of customers. With data-base retailing, a firm could identify those 20 percent and better satisfy them through superior product selection, announcements of special sales, more personalized correspondence, etc. In addition, the firm could identify and place heightened emphasis on the next 40 percent of its customers, a group that has often been ignored by companies. Through data-base marketing, a retailer could also learn which people no longer patronize it and which shop less often. In these instances, people may be called or sent letters—in a cordial manner—to see why they are no longer shopping (or shopping less). Based on the reasons given, a retailer could undertake special promotions geared directly to those customers. What's the key to successful data-base retailing? It must be viewed in a positive way as a beneficial tool—not as an unwelcome and burdensome chore. Knowledge is power and power leads to profits.[7]

Emerging Trends

Several emerging trends are relevant to direct marketing: the evolving attitudes and activities of direct marketers, changing consumer life-styles, the increased competition among firms, the greater use of dual distribution channels, newer roles for catalogs and TV, technological advances, and mounting interest in international direct marketing.

[7]Joel R. Evans and Barry Berman, "Using Data-Base Marketing to Target Repeat (Loyal) Customers," *Tips for Better Retailing,* Vol. 1 (Number 3, 1995).

Table 6-1 DIRECT MARKETING PRACTICES: THE VIEW FROM THE FIELD (BASED ON A STUDY OF 3,000 DIRECT MARKETING PROFESSIONALS)

■ When selling their goods and services, direct marketers have specific goals in mind and engage in certain strategies to meet them. They frequently focus on improving customer retention, reactivating customers, and improving customer purchase frequency. Three-quarters or more say they currently are doing more along these lines than they were five years ago, and that they plan to do more in the next five years.

■ About 80 percent think lifetime customer value is a more significant operating principle today than it was five years ago, and that it will be even more so five years from now.

■ Three-quarters think frequency programs are effective means to obtain buyer loyalty and that there will be more of them in the next two years. Yet, two-thirds say they currently are not using such programs.

■ Over one-half indicate their companies usually take a product-driven approach, while 44 percent take a market-driven approach. Of those taking a more market-driven approach, 87 percent say this is more than they did five years ago. Moreover, 80 percent expect their firms will have a more market-driven approach in the next two years.

■ Sixty-one percent of firms use direct mail, 39 percent catalogs, 25 percent package/statement stuffers, and 25 percent magazines.

■ Fifty-seven percent have had a marketing data base for four years or more, 24 percent for two to three years, and 19 percent for one year or less. Sixty-eight percent say their firm's marketing data base is centralized in their organization.

■ Thirty-one percent indicate their firm spent under $100,000 to build their marketing data base (this includes hardware, software, internal resources, external consulting, development time, and external data), 28 percent spent between $100,000 and $499,999, and 18 percent spent $500,000 or more. Twenty-three percent did not provide an estimate.

■ In maintaining their data base, 35 percent spend under $50,000 annually, 16 percent spend between $50,000 and $99,999, and 14 percent spend between $100,000 and $249,999. Twenty-one percent did not provide estimates.

■ Of those who have not enacted data-base management programs, 39 percent say it was due to lack of appropriate professional staff, 28 percent to lack of appropriate software, and 23 percent to expense.

■ Customer service remains an important issue—61 percent think customers expect more service from direct marketing than from stores. Ninety-two percent feel service will become more critical in the future.

■ To grow their businesses and keep pace with new technologies, catalog merchants and retailers are diversifying. The top three diversification methods are retailers selling through catalogs, catalog merchants making their own products, and catalog merchants selling by the Internet and commercial online services. Two-thirds consider diversifying through new media to be a major industry trend, with 28 percent saying it is a likely direction their firm will pursue.

Source: Direct Marketing Best Practices (New York: Direct Marketing Association, 1996). Reprinted by permission of the DMA Marketing Council.

Evolving Attitudes and Activities of Direct Marketers ❑ In 1996, the Direct Marketing Association (DMA) (http://www.the-dma.org) conducted a comprehensive study of direct marketing professionals and published the results in a 42-page book entitled *Direct Marketing Practices and Trends*. The DMA looked at current practices, plans for the future, and opinions regarding industry trends. In all, 3,000 direct marketing professionals participated in the research project.

Table 6-1 reports some of the DMA's findings.

Changing Consumer Life-Styles ❑ From a direct marketing perspective, the life-styles of American consumers have shifted dramatically over the last 25 years, mostly due to the large number of women who are now in the labor force and the longer commuting time to and from work for suburban residents. Today, many consumers do not have the time or the inclination to shop at retail stores. They are attracted by the convenience and ease of purchases through direct marketing.

Because consumers are now more satisfied with their experiences than in the past (owing to improved company performance), direct marketing sales should continue to be strong. These are some factors consumers consider in selecting a direct marketing firm with which to deal:

■ Company reputation (image).
■ Types of goods/services offered.
■ Assortment.

- Brand names carried.
- Availability of a toll-free telephone number for ordering.
- Credit card acceptance.
- Promised delivery time.
- Comparable store prices.
- Satisfaction with past purchases.

Increased Competition Among Firms ❏ As direct marketing sales have risen, so have the number of competitors. And although there are a number of big firms, like J.C. Penney and Spiegel, there are also thousands of small ones. According to the Direct Marketing Association, there are over 10,000 U.S. mail-order companies.

The high level of competition has occurred because entry into direct marketing is far easier and less costly than entry into store retailing. A direct marketer does not need a store location; can function with a limited staff; and can place inexpensive, one-inch ads in the back of leading magazines, send out brochures to targeted customers, and have a low-cost Web site on the Internet. It can keep minimal inventory on hand and place orders with suppliers after people have paid for items (as long as the firm abides by the 30-day rule of the Federal Trade Commission).

The "Marketplace" section of *Runner's World* (a magazine with several hundred thousand readers) further illustrates the ease of entry into direct marketing. It costs about $600 for a one-inch ad. Among the mail-order items advertised in that section are running shoes, rowing machines, sports watches, contact lenses, sports apparel, and heart rate monitors.

Since direct marketing lures many small firms that may inadequately define their market niche, offer nondistinctive goods and services, have limited experience, underestimate the effort required, have trouble with supplier continuity, and receive a large share of consumer complaints, it is estimated that one out of every two new direct marketers fails. Nonetheless, according to a *Consumer Reports* survey of 88,000 readers, nearly three-quarters of shoppers said they were very satisfied or completely satisfied with their mail-order experiences.[8]

Greater Use of Dual Distribution Channels ❏ Another contributor to the intense direct marketing competition is the expanded use of dual distribution channels by firms. In the past, most stores used ads to draw customers to their locations. Now, many stores supplement revenues by using ads, brochures, and catalogs to obtain mail-order and phone sales. They see that direct marketing is efficient, targets specific segments, appeals to people who might not otherwise shop there, and needs a lower investment to reach other geographic areas than opening branch outlets. Various store- and catalog-based retailers are also using Web sites to gain new shoppers and be more convenient for customers. See Figure 6-3.

Bloomingdale's and Nordstrom are examples of store-based retailers that have successfully entered into direct marketing. Bloomingdale's by Mail was established in 1982 and has seen sales grow rapidly since then, as the customer data base has grown to 750,000 people. Annually, it issues dozens of catalogs and has sales of $115 million. Nordstrom's The Catalog was started in 1994. It capitalizes on the firm's legendary reputation for customer service: toll-free 24-hour shopping, same-day shipments for orders placed before 11:00 A.M., second-day air delivery via Federal Express, and complementary gift boxes.[9]

These comments sum up direct marketing's appeal to store-based firms: "The two formats are clearly complementary to each other, rather than conflicting." "I don't know anyone who buys everything by mail. People who buy by mail and phone also buy a lot in our stores." "In terms of growth potential, with direct marketing, we can grow faster than the three years it takes to build a new store." "Anytime we go into a new area and open a store, we already have a whole set of customers there from the catalog."[10]

---

[8]"Mail-Order Shopping: Which Catalogs Are Best?" *Consumer Reports* (October 1994), pp. 621–627.

[9]*Federated Department Stores Annual Report 1996*; and Cyndee Miller, "Catalogs Alive, Thriving," *Marketing News* (February 28, 1994), p. 9.

[10]Cara S. Trager, "Retailers, Catalogers Cross Channels," *Advertising Age* (October 26, 1987), pp. S-9–S-10.

Figure 6-3

L.L. Bean: Adding Online Shopping to Its Retail Portfolio

L.L. Bean is one of the world's leading catalog firms. It also has a popular store in its hometown of Freeport, Maine. And today it offers interested customers the added convenience of shopping online at its Web site (http://www.llbean.com).

Newer Roles for Catalogs and TV ❑ Direct marketers have been recasting the ways in which they use their catalogs, as well as their approach to TV retailing. Here's how.

With regard to catalogs, firms are revamping the ways in which they use their catalogs in three basic areas. First, many companies now print "specialogs"—in addition to or instead of the annual catalogs that feature all of their offerings. Each year, such firms as Spiegel, L.L. Bean, and Talbots send out dozens of catalogs, including separate specialogs for petite women, gifts, shoes, intimate apparel, and other goods. By using a **specialog,** firms cater to specific needs of customer segments, emphasize a limited number of items, and reduce their catalog production and postage costs (as a specialog may be 8 to 50 pages in length, compared to hundreds of pages for a general catalog). As a Lands' End spokesperson noted, "We found that specialty catalogs fetch a better response. The bigger the book, the less productive it is."[11]

Second, to help defray their catalog costs, these days, some companies accept ads from noncompeting firms that are compatible with their own images. For instance, Bloomingdale's by Mail has had ads for cognac, Lincoln Continental, and Club Med. Overall, catalog ads provide several million dollars in revenues for direct marketers.

Third, both to stimulate sales and to defray costs, some catalogs are sold in bookstores, supermarkets, and airports. Thus, thousands of stores carry an assortment of the catalogs made available to them. The percentage of consumers buying a catalog who actually make a product purchase is many times higher than that for those who get catalogs sent via the mail.

TV retailing has two components: shopping networks and infomercials. On a shopping network, the only regular programming involves merchandise presentations and their sales (usually by phone). The two biggest players are the cable giants QVC and Home Shopping Network (HSN), with combined annual revenues of $2.7 billion. Each channel has access to a TV audience of 50 million to 60 million house-

[11]Sunita Wadekar Bhargava, Stephanie Anderson Forest, and Lois Therrien, "After the Big Book, The Big Race," *Business Week* (September 20, 1993), p. 106.

holds. Only 5 percent of U.S. consumers bought goods through TV shopping programs in 1988; more than twice as many are doing so today. The popularity of TV-based home shopping is expected to rise as the number of channels increases and as interactive shopping technology (which lets people browse through channels and ask for data and advice) becomes available. Once regarded as a medium primarily for shut-ins and the lower middle class, the typical TV-based shopper is now younger, more fashion-conscious, and as apt to be from a high-income household as the overall U.S. population.[12]

The strategies of HSN and QVC are similar. Both firms feature jewelry, women's clothing, and personal-care products, and do not emphasize nationally recognized brands. Most items must be purchased from HSN and QVC during the limited time the products are advertised. This practice encourages consumers to act immediately, but it also forces some consumers to watch programs for long hours in the hope that specials are repeated.

An **infomercial** is a program-length TV advertisement (most often, 30 minutes in length) for a specific good or service that airs on cable television or on broadcast television at a fringe time. As they watch the infomercial, consumers call in their orders, which are then delivered directly to them. Infomercials are particularly worthwhile for products that benefit from visual demonstrations. Good infomercials work because they present detailed information on the product, include customer testimonials, are entertaining, and are divided into neatly timed segments (since the average viewer watches only a few minutes of the "show" at a time)—with ordering information flashed on the screen in every segment.

It is estimated that infomercials (which first appeared in the mid-1980s) now account for over $1 billion in annual U.S. revenues. Over their airings, the infomercials for these products have all generated at least $80 million in revenues: Nordic Track exercise equipment, Juiceman juice makers, Victoria Jackson cosmetics, Soloflex exercise equipment, Pro Form Crosswalk treadmills, Susan Powter exercise videos, Tony Robbins motivational tapes and books, Popiel food dehydrators, and Tony Little exercise videos. In general, infomercial shoppers are "less risk averse, more price-conscious, and more convenience-seeking than nonshoppers. They are also more brand-conscious, innovative, impulsive, and variety-seeking than nonshoppers."[13]

Technological Advances ❑ Direct marketing is in the midst of a technological revolution that is improving operating efficiency and offering enhanced sales opportunities. These are just some advances taking place:

■ Market segments can be better targeted. Through "selective binding," 300-page catalogs can be sent to the best customers and 100-page catalogs to new prospects.[14]

■ Firms can inexpensively use computers to enter customer mail and phone orders, arrange for shipments, and monitor inventory on hand.

■ It is now relatively easy for direct marketers to set up and maintain computerized data bases.

■ Huge, automated distribution centers can more efficiently accumulate and ship out orders.

■ Customers can dial toll-free phone numbers to place orders and get information. The cost per call for the direct marketer is quite low.

---

[12]"Shopping by Television," *Consumer Reports* (January 1995), pp. 8–12.

[13]Naveen Donthu and David Gilliland, "Observations: The Infomercial Shopper," *Journal of Advertising Research*, Vol. 36 (March–April 1996), pp. 73–76.

[14]Jane Hodges, "Happier Holidays Ahead in '96?" *Advertising Age* (November 4, 1996), p. 22.

- Consumers can conclude transactions from many more locations, including by phones on airlines that have automatic links to particular direct marketers.
- Cable TV programming lets consumers view 24-hour shopping channels and place phone or mail orders.
- In-home/at-office PC-based shopping transactions can be conducted by consumers who have computers and modems (to interface with the seller)—sometimes through special software programs and mostly through the World Wide Web (Internet).

Due to their importance, these three technological advances are given separate coverage later in this chapter: the World Wide Web, video kiosks, and video catalogs.

Mounting Interest in International Direct Marketing ❑ Many more retail firms have become involved with international direct marketing over the last several years because of the opportunities in foreign markets and the growing consumer acceptance of nonstore retailing in those countries. Among the booming number of U.S.-based direct marketers with a significant international presence are Neiman Marcus, Eddie Bauer, Sharper Image, and Williams-Sonoma.

Outside the United States, annual mail-order sales (by both domestic and foreign firms) from final consumer transactions are nearing $100 billion. German and Japanese consumers account for well over one-half of total non-U.S. spending.[15]

Consider this:

> The United States is the most advanced direct marketer in the world today, with Europe close behind and Japan learning quickly. When one considers the enormous impact direct marketing has had on U.S. commerce, the prospects in developing countries are exciting. Small companies will be able to afford to do business across international lines, competing with the largest rivals. Mail-order firms whose catalogs currently draw 1 or 2 percent response in the United States may get 10 to 20 percent in other countries where competing products aren't available or catalog glut isn't a problem. Before these efforts can become reality, however, several major obstacles need to be overcome. These include major gaps in addressing information, a lack of standards, different currencies, wide variations in national postal rates and procedures, and the need for uniformity that can ensure the smooth flow of mass mailings the world over.[16]

The Steps in a Direct Marketing Strategy

A direct marketing strategy has eight stages: business definition, generating customers, media selection, presenting the message, customer contact, customer response, order fulfillment, and measuring results and maintaining the data base. See Figure 6-4.

Business Definition ❑ First, a company makes these two decisions regarding its business definition:

- Is the firm going to be a pure direct marketer or is it going to engage in a dual distribution channel (involving both store-based and direct marketing)? If the firm chooses the latter, it must clarify the role of direct marketing in its overall retail strategy.
- Is the firm going to be a general direct marketer and carry a broad product assortment, or is it going to specialize in one goods/service category? Either way, a merchandising approach must be conceived.

[15]"Highlights of the Mail Order Marketplace," p. 57.
[16]"Mail-Order Marketing: A Worldwide View," *Direct Marketing* (May 1996), pp. 31–32.

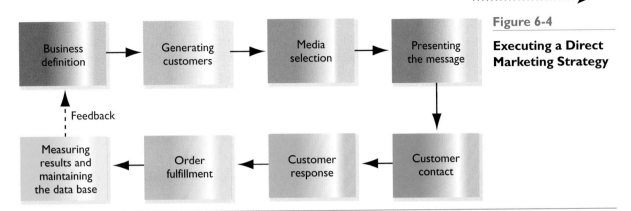

Figure 6-4

Executing a Direct Marketing Strategy

Generating Customers ❑ A mechanism for generating customers is devised next. Several options are available. A direct marketer can

■ Purchase a mailing list from a list broker. For a single mailing, a list usually costs from $50 to $100 or more per 1,000 names and addresses (depending on the mailing size); it is supplied in mailing-label format. List brokers annually rent or sell billions of names and addresses to direct marketers—which can buy broad lists or ones broken down by gender, location, occupation, and so on. In purchasing a mailing list, the direct marketer should check its currency.

■ Buy a PC-based list on a CD-ROM disk from a firm such as American Business Information, which sells a CD for $59.95 with data on 88 million U.S. households (at http://www.abii.com). With such a disk, the direct marketer can use the list multiple times, but it is responsible for selecting names and printing labels.

■ Send out a blind mailing to all the residents in a particular area. This method can be expensive and may receive a very low response rate.

■ Advertise in a newspaper, magazine, Web site, or other medium and ask customers to order by mail, phone, or online through a PC.

■ Contact consumers who have previously shopped with the firm or requested information. As an example, for years, J.C. Penney has managed a multimillion customer data base. This is the most efficient means, but it takes a while to develop a data base. And if a company wants to grow, it cannot rely solely on these consumers.

Media Selection ❑ Several media are available to the direct marketer. They include

■ Printed catalogs.
■ Direct-mail ads and brochures.
■ Inserts with monthly credit card and other bills ("statement stuffers").
■ Freestanding displays with coupons, brochures, or catalogs (such as magazine subscription cards at the supermarket checkout counter).
■ Ads or programs in the mass media: newspapers, magazines, radio, TV.
■ Online computer services.
■ Video kiosks.
■ Video catalogs.

In choosing among these alternatives, the direct marketer should consider costs, ease of distribution, lead time required, and other factors.

Presenting the Message ❑ At this point, the firm develops and presents its message in a way that engenders consumer interest, creates (or maintains) the proper image, points out compelling reasons for a purchase, and provides data about the goods or services offered (such as prices, sizes, and colors). The message must also contain complete ordering instructions, including a method of payment, how to designate the items purchased, shipping charges, and the firm's address/phone number/Web site.

The direct marketer should plan a message and the medium in which it is presented in the same way a traditional retailer plans a store. The latter uses a storefront, lighting, carpeting, the store layout, and displays to foster a particular atmosphere and image. In direct marketing, the headlines, message content, use of color, paper quality, personalization of letters to customers, space devoted to each item, and order in which items are presented are among the elements affecting a firm's shopping atmosphere and image.

Customer Contact ❏ Next, for each campaign it runs, a direct marketer decides whether to contact all customers in its data base or to seek specific market segments (with different messages and/or media aimed at each). It can classify prospective customers as *regulars* (those having bought from the firm on a continuous basis); *nonregulars* (those having bought from the firm on an infrequent basis); *new contacts* (those having never been sought before by the firm); and *nonrespondents* (those having been contacted before but never making a purchase).

Regulars and nonregulars are the most apt to respond to any future offerings of a company. Furthermore, a direct marketer can better target its efforts to these people because it has purchase histories on them. Thus, customers who have bought clothing in the past are prime prospects for specialized apparel catalogs.

New contacts probably know little about the firm. Messages to them must create interest, accurately portray the firm, and present meaningful reasons for consumers to purchase. This group is important if growth is sought.

Nonrespondents who have been contacted repeatedly by a firm without making purchases are highly unlikely to buy in the future. Unless a firm can present a message in a vastly different way, it is inefficient to continue seeking this group. Yet, firms such as Publishers Clearinghouse annually send millions of mailings to people who have never bought; in their case, this is proper because they are selling inexpensive impulse items and need only a small response rate to succeed.

Customer Response ❏ Customers can respond to direct marketers in one of three ways:

■ They can buy through the mail, phone, or computer.
■ They can request further information, such as a catalog.
■ They can ignore the message.

In general, purchases are made by no more than 2 percent to 3 percent of the people contacted. This rate is higher for specialogs, mail-order clubs (e.g., for books or music), and firms focusing on repeat customers.

Order Fulfillment ❏ A firm needs a system to process orders. When they are received by mail, the firm must sort them, determine if payment is enclosed, check whether the requested product is in stock, mail announcements if items cannot be sent on time, coordinate shipments, and replenish inventory. When orders are placed by phone, the firm must have a trained sales staff available during the hours in which people may call. Salespeople answer questions, make suggestions, enter orders, note the payment method, see whether items are in stock, coordinate shipments, and replenish inventory. When orders are placed by PC, there must be a mechanism for handling credit card transactions, issuing customer receipts, and sending order requests to the warehouse in a prompt, efficient way. In all cases, names, addresses, and purchase data are added to the data base for future reference.

During peak seasons, additional warehouse, shipping, order-processing, and sales personnel are needed to supplement regular employees. Direct marketers that are highly regarded by consumers fill orders promptly (usually within two weeks), have knowledgeable and courteous personnel, do not misrepresent product quality, and provide liberal return policies.

Measuring Results and Maintaining the Data Base ❏ The last step in a direct marketing strategy is analyzing results and maintaining the data base. Most forms of direct marketing yield such clearly measurable results as these:

- Overall response rate—It can be determined what number or percentage of the people reached by a particular brochure, catalog, Web site, and so on actually make a purchase.
- Average purchase amount—This can be analyzed by customer location, gender, and so on.
- Sales volume by product category—Sales can be related to the space allotted to each product in brochures, catalogs, and so on.
- Value of list brokers—The revenues generated by various mailing lists can be compared.

After measuring results, the direct marketer reviews its customer data base and makes sure new shoppers are entered, address changes have been noted for existing customers, purchase and customer background information is current and available in various segmentation categories, and nonrespondents are purged from the data base (when feasible).

This stage provides feedback for the direct marketer as it plans for each new campaign.

Key Issues Facing Direct Marketers

In planning and enacting their strategies, direct marketers must keep these points in mind.

A large number of households still dislike one or more aspects of direct marketing. The greatest levels of consumer dissatisfaction deal with late or nondelivery, deceptive claims, items broken or damaged in transit, wrong items being delivered, and the lack of information provided. Yet, as already noted, in most cases, the leading direct marketers are highly rated by consumers.

Most U.S. households report that they open all direct mail, but many would like to receive less of it. Since the average American household is sent 150 or so catalogs a year, besides hundreds of other direct-mail pieces, firms have to be concerned about marketplace clutter. It is hard to be distinctive in this kind of environment and to increase customer response rates.

Many consumers are concerned about their names and background information being sold by list brokers, as well as by some direct marketers to other direct marketers. They feel the practice is an invasion of privacy and that the decision to make a direct marketing purchase does not constitute permission to pass on personal information. To counteract this, the direct marketing industry has agreed to remove people's names from mailing list circulation if they make a request to the Direct Marketing Association. As the president of the National Retail Federation noted, "Consumer privacy is one of the most far-reaching issues our industry will ever tackle. It pierces the heart of customer data-base management and target marketing efforts that retailers have spent the last decade building and expanding, and it threatens to cause expensive and disruptive changes." In 1996, the European Community issued a *Directive on Privacy* for its member nations, which "calls for full disclosure to consumers of all potential

Privacy Issues and the World Wide Web

According to some experts, although technical advancements and legal reforms make privacy abuse more difficult on the Internet and the World Wide Web than before, potential areas for such abuse still exist. Here are three of the issues:

■ *Ease of monitoring consumer purchases:* It is now very simple for firms to record consumer purchases by using bar code scanners and monitoring credit card purchases.
■ *Utilization of data bases beyond their original intent:* Network data bases that are compiled as people connect to online Web sites can be sold to firms at other Web sites.
■ *Reduction in the cost of solicitations to prospects:* Because the expense of sending messages over the Internet and the World Wide Web is so low, firms can now send messages to everyone, re-

gardless of their interest. Given the low cost of distributing information, Internet junk mail will soon be extensive.

With over 35 million consumers worldwide predicted to use online services as of the year 2000, there is a real need to resolve these important privacy issues. One leader in privacy protection is New Zealand. That country's privacy law requires that firms seek consumer authorization to collect marketing-related data, and all such data must be acquired directly from the individual himself or herself. Other nations, including Holland and Germany, have similar laws.

Sources: James Morris-Lee, "Privacy: It's Everyone's Business Now," *Direct Marketing* (April 1996), pp. 40–43; and Lorna Pappas, "The Web: It's Becoming a Safer Place to Shop," *Chain Store Age* (January 1997), pp. 122–128.

uses of information. In many cases, it requires full prior consent by the individual."[17] Clearly, U.S. direct marketers will have to address this issue more squarely in the near future.

Dual distribution retailers need to sustain a consistent image for both their store-based and direct marketing efforts. They must also recognize both the similarities and the differences in the strategies for each approach. According to an industry expert, "One is centralized and one is decentralized. Catalog is a case of you shout to the person in the next cubicle to solve a problem. With retail, you have to go 200 miles down the Amtrak line to talk to people. Of the catalogs that have gone into retail, I'd guess less than 50 percent have been successful."[18]

The steady increase in postal rates has made the mailing of catalogs, brochures, and other promotional materials expensive for some firms. Thus, many direct marketers are turning more to newspapers, magazines, and cable TV—and the Web.

Finally, direct marketers must carefully monitor the legal environment. They must be aware that, in the future, more states will probably require residents to pay sales tax on out-of-state direct marketing purchases; the firms would have to remit the tax payments to the affected state.

DIRECT SELLING

Direct selling includes both personal contact with consumers in their homes (and other nonstore locations such as offices) and phone solicitations initiated by a retailer. Cosmetics, jewelry, vitamins, household goods and services (such as carpet cleaning), vacuum cleaners, dairy products, and magazines and newspapers are among the items

[17]Susan Reda, "Retailers Respond to Growing Privacy Debate," *Stores* (December 1996), pp. 20–30; and Len Lewis, "Up in Smoke," *Progressive Grocer* (February 1997), pp. 31–32.
[18]N. R. Kleinfield, "Even for J. Crew, the Mail-Order Boom Days Are Over," *New York Times* (September 2, 1990), Section 3, p. 5.

Table 6-2 A SNAPSHOT OF THE U.S. DIRECT SELLING INDUSTRY

Percent of Sales by Major Product Groups

Personal-care products (cosmetics, jewelry, skin care, etc.)	38.8 %
Home/family care products (cleaning products, cookware, cutlery, etc.)	34.4 %
Services/miscellaneous/other	10.3 %
Wellness products (weight loss products, vitamins, etc.)	9.2 %
Leisure/educational products (books, encyclopedias, toys/games, etc.)	7.3 %

Place of Sales (as a percent of sales dollars)

In the home	59.0 %
Over the phone	15.9 %
In a workplace	14.8 %
At a public event (such as a fair, exhibition, shopping mall, theme park, trade show, etc.)	4.3 %
Other locations	6.0 %

Sales Approach (method used to generate sales, as a percent of sales dollars)

Individual/one-to-one selling	64.9 %
Party plan/group sales	32.1 %
Customer placing order directly with firm	1.6 %
Other	1.4 %

Demographics of Salespeople (as a percent of all salespeople)

Independent contractors/Employees	99.8 %/0.2 %
Female/Male/Couples and two-person teams	70.4 %/19.3/10.3 %
Part-time/Full-time (30 hours and up per week)	88.9 %/11.1 %

Source: Fact Sheet: 1996 Direct Selling Industrywide Growth & Outlook Survey (Washington, D.C.: Direct Selling Association, 1997). Reprinted by permission.

sometimes sold in this manner. In 1995, direct selling accounted for $18 billion in U.S. sales and employed 7.2 million people (most on a part-time basis).[19] Table 6-2 shows an industry overview.

The strategy mix for direct selling emphasizes convenience in shopping and a personal touch. Many times, detailed demonstrations can be made. Consumers are often more relaxed in their homes than in stores. They are also likely to be attentive and are not exposed to competing brands (as they are in stores). For some shoppers, such as older consumers and parents with young children, in-store shopping is difficult to undertake because of limited mobility. For the retailer, direct selling has lower overhead costs because store locations and fixtures are not necessary.

Nonetheless, direct-selling revenues in the United States have risen relatively slowly over the last several years. Here are some reasons why:

■ More women now work, and they may not be interested in or available for in-home purchases.

■ Improved job opportunities in other fields and the interest in full-time career-oriented positions have reduced the pool of people interested in direct-selling jobs.

■ A firm's market coverage is limited by the size of its sales force. Many firms are able to reach fewer than one-half of potential customers.

■ Sales productivity is low because the average transaction is small and most consumers are unreceptive to this type of selling—many will not open their doors to salespeople or talk to telephone sales representatives.

■ Sales force turnover is high. The bulk of employees are poorly supervised part-timers.

[19]*Fact Sheet: 1995 Direct Selling Industrywide Growth & Outlook Survey* (Washington, D.C.: Direct Selling Association, 1996).

Figure 6-5

Direct Selling and Mary Kay

Throughout the world, Mary Kay Cosmetics employs 400,000 direct-sales "consultants," who mostly visit customers in their homes and account for $1 billion in revenues.

■ To stimulate sales personnel, compensation is usually 25 percent to 50 percent of the revenues they generate. This means average to above-average prices.

■ Various legal restrictions are in effect due to deceptive or high-pressure sales tactics. There are stringent requirements with respect to telemarketing under the FTC's new Telemarketing Sales Rule (described at http://www.ftc.gov/bcp/telemark/rule.htm); in particular, telemarketers must promptly disclose their identity, that the purpose of the call is to sell goods or services, the nature of the goods or services, and that no purchase or payment is necessary to win a "free" prize.

■ A poor image is associated with the term *door-to-door;* hence, the industry preference for the term *direct selling.*

Firms are responding to these issues in various ways. For example, Avon is placing greater emphasis on workplace sales, which today account for one-third of its total direct-selling revenues; is offering free training to sales personnel (it used to charge a fee); is rewarding the best workers with better territories; and is rapidly expanding internationally (which now accounts for nearly two-thirds of its total revenues). Mary Kay and Tupperware use community residents as salespeople and have a party atmosphere rather than a strict door-to-door cold-canvassing approach; this requires networks of family, friends, and neighbors. Inasmuch as Fuller Brush salespeople reach two-thirds of U.S. households, it uses mail-order catalogs to reach the other one-third. It also advertises for sales positions in the catalogs. Kirby salespeople make evening in-home presentations to contact working women. On the other hand, after decades of door-to-door selling in the United States, Encyclopaedia Britannica decided to abandon those efforts and concentrate instead on direct mail, catalogs, telemarketing, and the Internet: "The revenues from our in-home sales efforts in North America no longer justified the costs." Its $1,500 books also could no longer compete with CD-ROM disks selling for well under $100.[20]

---

[20]Linda Corman, "Closing the Book," *Sales & Marketing Management* (September 1996), pp. 80–86; and Tara Parker-Pope and Lisa Bannon, "Avon's New Calling: Selling Barbie in China," *Wall Street Journal* (May 1, 1997), pp. B1, B5.

Among the leaders in direct selling are Avon and Mary Kay (cosmetics), Amway (household supplies), Tupperware (plastic food containers), Shaklee (vitamins and health foods), Fuller Brush (small household products), Kirby (vacuum cleaners), and Welcome Wagon (at-home greetings for new residents sponsored by groups of local retailers). Some department stores, such as J.C. Penney, also use direct selling. Penney's decorator consultants sell a complete line of furnishings, not available in its stores, to consumers in their homes. See Figure 6-5.

A **vending machine** is a retailing format that involves the coin- or card-operated dispensing of goods (such as beverages) and services (such as life insurance sales at airports). It eliminates the use of sales personnel and allows for around-the-clock sales. Machines can be placed wherever they are most convenient for consumers—inside or outside a store, in a motel corridor, at a train station, or on a street corner.

VENDING MACHINES

According to the National Automatic Merchandising Association (http://www.vending.org/home.htm), the major industry organization, "In the United States, vending is generally conceded to have begun in 1888 when Thomas Adams of the Adams Gum Company installed penny gum dispensing machines on the New York elevated train platforms." Today, a range of products "are vended from simple to highly-sophisticated vending machines by many thousands of companies nationwide, and worldwide for that matter."

Although many attempts have been made to "vend" clothing, magazines, and other general merchandise, 93 percent of the $30 billion in 1995 U.S. vending machine sales involved hot and cold beverages, food items, and cigarettes. Because of various health-related issues, between 1980 and 1995, cigarettes' share of vending machine sales fell from 25 percent to just 6 percent. With the heavy concentration of vending machine revenues in beverages and foods, the greatest sales volume is achieved in factory, office, and school lunchrooms and refreshment areas; public places such as service stations are also popular sites for machines. Newspapers on street corners and sidewalks, various machines in hotels and motels, and cigarette machines in restaurants and at train stations are highly visible aspects of vending, but they account for a small percentage of U.S. vending machine sales.[21] Two of the leading vending machine operators are Canteen Corporation and ARA Services.

Items priced above $1.50 have not sold well in vending machines because too many coins are required for each transaction, and fewer than one-quarter of U.S. vending machines are equipped with dollar bill changers. Furthermore, many consumers have been reluctant to purchase more expensive items that they cannot see displayed or have explained. However, consumers' expanded access to and use of debit cards (whereby customer bank balances are immediately reduced to reflect purchases) are expected to have a major impact on resolving the payment issue, and the new video kiosk-type of vending machine lets people see product displays and get detailed information (and then place a credit card or debit card order). Well-known brands and standardized nonfood items are best suited to increasing sales via vending machines.

To improve productivity and customer relations, vending machine operators are deploying a variety of innovations. For instance, machine malfunctions have been reduced by the application of electronic mechanisms to coin-handling and dispensing controls. Microprocessors track consumer preferences, trace malfunctions, and record receipts. Some machines even have voice synthesizers that are programmed to say such phrases as "Thank you, come again" or "Your change is 25 cents."

Operators must still deal with these issues: theft, vandalism, stockouts, above-average prices, and the perceptions of a great many consumers that vending machines should be patronized only for fill-in convenience items.

[21] *Vending Times Census of the Industry* (1996); and authors' estimates.

NON-TRADITIONAL FORMS OF RETAILING

In recent years, the world of retailing and how people shop have witnessed enormous changes from the days when retailing meant simply visiting a store, shopping from a printed mail-order catalog, greeting the Avon lady in one's home, or buying a piece of candy from a vending machine. Who would have thought that a consumer could "surf the Web" in search of bargains, interact with a video kiosk that can show products in 3D (with animation), or pop a CD-ROM mail-order catalog into a PC and watch it at one's leisure? Well, these events are all real and they're already with us. Let's take a look at them.

The World Wide Web

Let us begin this section by defining two terms that seem to cause a lot of confusion: Internet and World Wide Web. The **Internet** is a global electronic superhighway of computer networks that use a common protocol and are linked by telecommunications lines and satellite. It functions as a single, cooperative virtual network and is maintained by universities, governments, and businesses. The **World Wide Web (WWW)** is one way of accessing information on the Internet, whereby people work with easy-to-use Web addresses (sites) and pages. WWW users see words, colorful charts, pictures, and video, and hear audio—turning their PCs into interactive multimedia centers. They can easily move from one site to the next by pointing at the proper spot on a computer screen and clicking a mouse button. Web browsing software, such as Netscape and Microsoft Internet Explorer, facilitate "surfing the Web."[22]

For our purposes, both "Internet" and "World Wide Web" convey the same central theme: online interactive retailing. However, since almost all online interactive retailing is done by the Web, the term World Wide Web appears in our discussion, which is comprised of these topics: the purpose of online interactive retailing, its present scope, characteristics of Web users, points to consider in deciding whether to have a Web site, and examples of Web retailers.

From the perspective of the retailer, the World Wide Web can serve one or more of these purposes:

■ Enhance the retailer's image.
■ Reach geographically dispersed consumers, including foreign ones.
■ Provide information to the consumer—as to product categories carried, store locations, usage information, answers to common questions, customer loyalty programs, and so on.
■ Promote new products and fully explain and demonstrate their features.
■ Furnish customer service in the form of E-mail "hot links" and communications.
■ Be more "personal" with consumers by letting them point and click on topics they choose.
■ Obtain customer feedback.
■ Give special offers and send coupons to Web customers.
■ Describe employment opportunities.
■ Make sales.

The purpose(s) chosen by a given retailer depend(s) on whether its major goal is to interactively communicate with consumers or to sell goods and services, whether it is predominantly a traditional retailer that wants to have a Web presence or a newer firm

---

[22]For further information on these concepts, see Pallab Paul, "Marketing on the Internet," *Journal of Consumer Marketing*, Vol. 12 (Number 4, 1996), pp. 27–39; Thomas L. Ainscough and Michael G. Luckett, "The Internet for the Rest of Us: Marketing on the World Wide Web," *Journal of Consumer Marketing*, Vol. 13 (Number 2, 1996), pp. 36–47; and "Wired Kingdom," *Chain Store Age* (January 1997), pp. 1A–19A.

TECHNOLOGY IN RETAILING

Auto-By-Tel: Selling New Cars Through the Internet

Buying a new car has become easier thanks to Web-based new-car buying services. One of these car services, Auto-By-Tel (http://www.autobytel.com) gets price quotes from participating new-car dealers, based on the customer's specific purchase request. Auto-By-Tel has 1,400 dealers that are members of its service. Each one pays Auto-By-Tel an annual fee of $1,400, plus an additional fee of between $250 and $1,500 per month for referrals.

Auto-By-Tel lets shoppers quickly determine the best selling price and the availability of a specific model. It also enables them to avoid going to dealers advertising specials that are not in stock when the customer arrives and to avoid price haggling. For car dealers, Auto-By-Tel provides a base of car buyers who are truly interested in purchasing.

In addition to Auto-By-Tel, several other online services are available for prospective car buyers. DealerNet (http://www.dealernet.com), for example, has links to about 500 dealers and 1,600 new-car models. It recently added a data base on 20,000 used cars and now consumers can apply for General Motors Acceptance Corporation (GMAC) credit on the Web. DealerNet charges dealers between $1,495 and $2,495 to develop their Web sites and $495 to $695 a month to maintain them. Unlike Auto-By-Tel, DealerNet only shows a suggested retail price for each car.

Source: Edward Baig, "Kicking Tires on the Web," *Business Week* (April 29, 1996), p. 130.

that wants to derive most or all of its revenues from Web transactions, and the level of resources the retailer is willing to commit to Web site development and maintenance. As of 1997, there were millions of Web sites overall, with tens of thousands of Web sites being retail-related (estimates ranged from 50,000 such sites to more than 100,000 of them). More retail sites are added every day. Hundreds of large store-based retail chains—in addition to thousands of nonstore Web specialists—already have Web sites or are actively working on them.

Why are sales noted last in the preceding list? It is because retailers should not get their hopes too high that Web-based sales can drive their revenues up significantly in the near future, despite the massive number of people accessing the WWW. Let us look at some U.S. statistics showing the Web's scope (keeping in mind that data are mostly rough estimates at this time): In 1996, 15 million people surfed the Web from home at least once per week, a figure expected to rise to 40 million by the year 2000; retail sales were about $575 million, an amount projected to go to $6.6 billion by the year 2000; 1 percent of Americans made a Web purchase; and the leading Web shopping sectors were computer products, travel services, publications, apparel, gifts and flowers, food and drink, event tickets, and entertainment. Thus, the Web accounted for only a tiny fraction of 1 percent of total retail sales, which will still be true in the year 2000![23]

Web users have these characteristics:

- Age and gender—Over 60 percent of users are male. Those ages 18 to 54 (male and female) are the most likely to be users.
- Income—Nearly 40 percent of users have an annual household income of at least $50,000.

[23]Sales Automation Association, "Weekly Dose," *Sales & Marketing Management* (June 1996), *SMT* supplement, p. 11; MasterCard International, "Internet Shopping: New Competitor or New Frontier?" *Stores* (February 1996), supplement; John Simons, "The Web's Dirty Secret," *U.S. News & World Report* (August 19, 1996), p. 51; Len Lewis, "Shopping the Net," *Progressive Grocer* (September 1996), pp. 35–40; Jane Hodges, "Web Won't Ring with Gift Shopping," *Advertising Age* (December 2, 1996), p. 53; Zina Moukheiber, "Plus ç Change," *Forbes* (February 10, 1997), pp. 46–47; and Betsy Spethmann, "Wired for Sales," *Promo* (March 1997), pp. 51–56.

- ■ Education—Fifty-seven percent of users have attended college.
- ■ Reasons for using the Web—People seek information, entertainment, and interactive communications.
- ■ Time spent on the Web—Four-fifths of users are on the Web for four hours or less per month.
- ■ Online purchases—Those 18 to 29 years of age and people earning $25,000 to $49,999 are the most apt to already have made a Web-based purchase.[24]

In general, the WWW offers many positive features for retailers: It is inexpensive to have a Web site. The potential marketplace is huge and dispersed, yet relatively easy to reach. Web sites can be quite exciting, with all types of "bells and whistles," due to their multimedia capabilities. People can visit Web sites at any time, and their visits can be as short or long as they desire. Information can be targeted, so that, for example, a person visiting a toy store's Web site could opt to click on the icon labeled "Educational Toys—ages three to six." A customer data base can be established and customer feedback obtained. The WWW also has negative features for retailers: If consumers do not know a firm's Web address, it may be cumbersome to find. Most people are not yet willing to buy online, for privacy, security, and other reasons. There is tremendous clutter with regard to the number of retail Web sites, and it is sure to get worse. Because Web surfers are easily bored, a firm must regularly update its Web site to ensure repeat visits. The more multimedia features a Web site has, the slower it may be for people to access. Some firms have been overwhelmed with customer service requests and questions through Web-based E-mail. Improvements are needed to coordinate store-based and Web-based transactions. There are few standards or rules as to what may be portrayed at Web sites. Consumers expect online services to be free and are very reluctant to pay for them.

Here is how the best Web retailers are doing online business:

What is the magic formula that successful pioneers have discovered? These firms haven't invented unique types of businesses—they're doing what everyone else is: selling products, selling advertising, and selling information. But with a difference. Instead of plowing huge sums into their sites, most are operating on tiny budgets. That has forced them to focus on how to reach and serve customers, rather than, say, pumping money into fancy graphics that look good in management meetings but wind up slowing down Web sites and turning off consumers. "We've had a focus on controlling costs, which others haven't had to do," says one entrepreneur. "It's simply the discipline of having to be profitable to survive." Even more important, successful Web players are not simply replicating existing firms in the new online medium but are taking full advantage of the unique, interactive nature of the Net. The hottest stores on the Web don't just provide convenience and low prices—though those are essential ingredients. Across the board, successful Web retailers have created virtual "communities." At their sites, like-minded cybernauts congregate, swap information, buy something, and come back. Above all, Web trailblazers share the ability to adapt—to scrap what's not working and improvise a new plan on the fly. It is increasingly common for Web businesses to have hybrid strategies: Online stores end up taking ads; publishers go into retail sales looking for ways to get subscription revenue.[25]

As highlighted in Table 6-3, a retailer has many decisions to make if it wants to utilize the World Wide Web. A firm cannot just put up a fancy site and wait for consumers to visit it in droves. For a small retailer, setting up a very simple Web site does not have

---

[24]Thomas E. Weber, "Who Uses the Internet?" *Wall Street Journal* (December 9, 1996), p. R6; and MasterCard International, "Internet Shopping: New Competitor or New Frontier?"

[25]Kathy Rebello, Larry Armstrong, and Amy Cortese, "Making Money on the Net," *Business Week* (September 23, 1996), p. 106.

Table 6-3 RETAILER DECISIONS IN UTILIZING THE WORLD WIDE WEB

■ What are the company's Web goals?
■ What budget will be allocated to developing a Web site and maintaining it?
■ Who will develop and maintain the Web site, the retailer itself or an outside specialist?
■ Should the firm set up an independent Web site for itself or should it be part of a "cybermall"?
■ What features will the Web site have?
■ What information will the Web site provide?
■ How will the goods and services assortment differ at the Web site from the firm's store?
■ Will the Web site offer benefits not available elsewhere?
■ How fast will the user be able to download the text and images from the Web site, and point and click from screen to screen?
■ How often will Web site content be changed?
■ What staff will handle Web inquiries and transactions?
■ How fast will turnaround time be for Web inquiries and transactions?
■ Will shoppers have to call a toll-free number to conclude a transaction after seeing an item on the Web?
■ How will online orders be processed?
■ What online payment methods will be accepted?
■ What search engines (such as Yahoo, Infoseek, and Magellan) will list the retailer's Web site?
■ How will the Web site be promoted: (a) on the WWW and (b) by the company?
■ How will Web data be stored and arranged?
■ How will Web success be measured?
■ How will the firm determine which Web shoppers are new customers and which are customers who would otherwise visit a company store?
■ How will the firm ensure secure (encrypted) transactions?
■ How will consumer privacy concerns be handled?

to be costly or time consuming. There are software programs such as WebPublisher, that sell for under $100: "WebPublisher provides 20 basic Web page themes, designed by professional artists, that you can enhance with text, graphics, and hyperlinks, also called 'hot links' (highlighted words that, when selected, send the viewer to another relevant screen for more information)." There are part-time Web page designers who charge $100 to $300 to set up a site. And there are professional firms that charge thousands of dollars to design and regularly modify sophisticated Web sites: "Asking what a Web site will cost to produce is like asking how much a house will cost. Building a site with an outside vendor generally ranges from $4,000 for a home page with 5 to 7 additional pages, to $120,000 for a full-blown Web site with 80 to 100 pages." Once a Web site is designed, the retailer must have it listed in "search engines" (the Web's equivalent to phone directories), promoted (hot linked) at other sites, and noted in all of its literature, ads, and so on; and there are monthly fees to be paid to an Internet service provider (ISP).[26]

These two examples show the diversity of retailing on the World Wide Web:

Soon after opening a small retail shop called Hot Hot Hot in Pasadena, California, Perry Lopez and Monica Bosserman Lopez were eager to broaden sales of their specialty hot sauces and foods. Since first-year sales were on track to reach $150,000, they couldn't afford to experiment. Their site had to crank out business. Step one was to decide which of their 450 products they would serve up online. "We could have added all kinds of information and products," says Monica, "but that costs

[26]Jerry Fisher, "Net Results," *Entrepreneur* (December 1996), pp. 98–101; Robert McKim, "Constructing Criticism: How to Build a Better Web Site," *Promo* (January 1996), pp. 67–68; Barry Silverstein, "The Internet: It's Not a Proven Direct Marketing Medium . . . Yet," *Direct Marketing* (January 1996), pp. 30–33; Richard Cross and Janet Smith, "The New Value Equation," *Marketing Tools* (June 1996), pp. 20–24; Rusty Warner, "Making the Most of the New Media," *Marketing Tools* (October 1996), pp. 66–70; and Kim W. Bayne, "Is Your Site a Success?" *Marketing Tools* (March–April 1996), pp. 68–72.

money. Does it increase sales or just create more pages for the user to weed through?" The partners chose to list 125 products, organized alphabetically and by heat level, country of origin, and ingredients. Working closely with Presence (a Web service firm), they developed a 20-page site in three months, which included testing to make sure users could find the information they wanted quickly and easily. Presence's fee for devising the site was $20,000; and the retailer pays 5 percent of online receipts monthly, which covers transaction processing (Presence sends orders directly to Hot Hot Hot's small warehouse) and an hour of labor monthly to make changes to the Web site. The payback has been quick. The 1,000-plus daily visitors who drop by Hot Hot Hot's site (http://www.hot.presence.com or http://www.hothothot.com) generate 25 percent of the firm's total sales—now over $300,000.[27] See Figure 6-6.

Wal-Mart launched into cyber-retailing in 1996 with the introduction of online shopping services on its Wal-Mart and Sam's Club Web sites (http://www.wal-mart.com). The sites offer Wal-Mart a way to expand its customer base. It plans to offer upscale products at hefty discounts, items that never found a home on store shelves due to low demand from core shoppers, who are quite price-conscious. While the sites will never carry a full Wal-Mart offering, they do have 1,500 Wal-Mart items

Figure 6-6

Hot Hot Hot: What Makes a Good Web Site

At a lot of sites, you can get lost; there's no visual continuity. It needs to be simple to move around in, like a catalog, where it's easy to flip back to page two if you want. So there's a graphic on each page to keep the continuity going—like the heat level appearing again at the top of this page. You know you're still in the same catalog. And the icons at the bottom make it easy to get back to where you were.

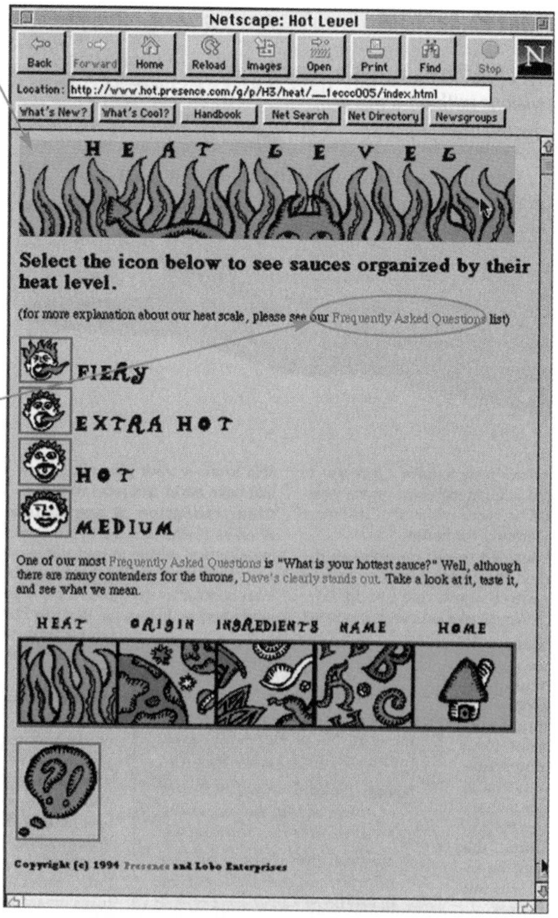

Hypertext links are what people use to navigate the Web, jumping from page to page by clicking on the highlighted text. You can add hypertext links to external sites as much as you want. But then you're sending people away from your site instead of involving them in your catalog. The one or two external links we use are specifically related to our product, rather than just a cool site users might want to see. Internally, we'd like customers to be able to use a hypertext link to go directly to the order form from anywhere in our site. This is one change we'll be making.

[27]Phaedra Hise, "The Well-Merchandised Web Site," *Inc.* (October 1995), p. 83; and "Heating Up Sales," *SMT* (March 1997), p. 33.

and 2,000 separate products through Sam's Club, almost none available in Wal-Marts and Sam's Clubs. Wal-Mart spokeswoman Stacey Webb says, "Over time, we expect to see growth in the number of products available. But we don't want to overwhelm people with hordes of products. We're going to keep to items customers love."[28]

Video Kiosks

The **video kiosk** is a freestanding, interactive computer terminal that displays products and related information on a video screen; it often uses a touchscreen for consumers to make selections. Although some video kiosks are located in stores to enhance customer service, others enable consumers to place orders, complete transactions (typically with a credit card), and arrange for products to be shipped. Video kiosks can be situated practically anywhere (from the lobby of a college dormitory to an airport), require little or no personnel besides maintenance workers, and are an entertaining and easy way for people to shop.

According to Northern Communications (http://www.kioskstore.com), a kiosk manufacturer, "'Kiosk' is derived from a Turkish word, referring to an open summerhouse or pavilion; it first became popularized in France in the 1870s, when tall columns, often housing newsstands and bearing posters advertising galleries and theaters, began to emerge on the streets of Paris. Today, an electronic kiosk is distinguished by several minimum characteristics: a powerful CPU, often networked to a proprietary telecommunications system or the Internet, with full-motion video and audio, usually with MPEG hardware, a receipt printer, and magstripe card reader. Kiosks are appearing in bewildering variety now, with high-resolution laser printers, video teleconferencing, fingerprint and barcode readers, smart cards, and more. The line is beginning to blur between kiosks and ATMs, as the demand for public access to cyberspace begins to grow."

As of 1996, there were about 150,000 video kiosks in use throughout the United States. One estimate is that there will be nearly 1 million kiosks by 2001. One-half of video kiosks are involved with retail sales transactions, though accurate sales estimates are not available.[29]

Video Catalogs

A **video catalog** is a retail catalog that appears on a CD-ROM disk and is viewed on a computer monitor. After observing the catalog, the consumer typically phones in an order to the retailer. At one time, video catalogs were issued in videotape format. But today, virtually all of them are in CD-ROM format, which has many more multimedia possibilities, stores greater information, lets viewers more easily select what items they want to access, and is cheaper to produce and mail. Over 10 million Americans now have CD-ROM drives in their home computers, and this number is rising rapidly. According to Spiegel, 18 percent of its print catalog customers have CD-ROM capabilities.[30]

While the Web has gained more attention, there are advantages to video catalogs. CD-ROM disks process data fast, which means instant viewing and hearing video clips, elaborate graphics, and sound bites that take several seconds to minutes to download on the Web. Video disks are better organized, so shoppers can readily pick products. Retailers gain greater visibility than they do as one of the legion of firms on the Web. Like the Web, CD-ROM disks have point and click capabilities. In contrast to print catalogs,

---

[28]Pete Hisey, "Wal-Mart Seeks Shoppers with Online Service," *Discount Store News* (August 19, 1996), pp. 1, 54.

[29]Paul Karon, "Beating an Electronic Path to Government with Online Kiosks," *Los Angeles Times* (August 25, 1996).

[30]Calmetta Y. Coleman, "Spiegel Catalog to Publish CD-ROM Version . . . Again," *Wall Street Journal* (February 15, 1996), p. B4.

costs may be less. Spiegel says the creative costs of a CD-ROM catalog are $150,000 versus $3,000 per page for a paper one.[31]

One of the leaders in CD-ROM retailing is 2Market, which has distributed millions of catalogs (most at $3.95 per copy). Each of its disks has a select group of retailers. One recent disk included Eddie Bauer, Warner Brothers, Starbucks, Godiva, 1-800-Flowers, Tower Records, PC & Mac Connection, F.A.O. Schwarz, Hammacher Schlemmer, Sharper Image, and Nature Company. 2Market estimates that 4 percent to 8 percent of customers order from its catalogs, a percentage much higher than for paper catalogs.[32]

[31]Ibid.
[32]"In Internet's Shadow, a Niche for CD-ROM," *Chain Store Age* (June 1996), pp. 60, 64.

Summary

1. *To look at the characteristics of the three major retail institutions involved with nonstore-based strategy mixes: direct marketing, direct selling, and vending machines—with an emphasis on direct marketing* Firms employ nonstore retailing when they use strategy mixes that are not store-based to reach customers and complete transactions. Such retailing encompasses direct marketing, direct selling, and vending machines.

In direct marketing, a consumer is first exposed to a good or service through a nonpersonal medium and then orders by mail or phone or computer. The 1995 U.S. retail sales by direct marketing were $145 billion. Direct marketers fall into two broad categories: general and specialty. Among the business strengths of direct marketing are its reduced operating costs, large geographic coverage, customer convenience, targeted segments, and more. Among the limitations of direct marketing are the consumer's inability to examine items before purchase, the costs of printing and mailing, the low response rate, the marketplace clutter, and more. Under the "30-day rule," there are stipulations to the policies a firm must follow as to shipping speed. The long-run prospects for direct marketing are strong because of consumer interest in reduced shopping time, 24-hour ordering, the stocking of well-known brands, improvements in operating efficiency, and technological breakthroughs.

The key to successful direct marketing is the customer data base, with data-base retailing being a way of collecting, storing, and using relevant information on customers. Several trends are also vital to direct marketers: their evolving attitudes and activities, changing consumer life-styles, increased competition, greater use of dual distribution channels, newer roles for catalogs and TV, technological advances, and the growth in international direct marketing. Specialogs and infomercials are just two tools being utilized more often by direct marketers.

There are eight stages in a direct marketing strategy: business definition, generating customers, media selection, presenting the message, customer contact, customer response, order fulfillment, and measuring results and maintaining the data base. Direct marketers also need to consider that many consumers still dislike shopping in this way, feel overwhelmed by the amount of direct mail they receive, and are concerned about their privacy.

Direct selling includes both personal contact with consumers in their homes (and other nonstore sites) and phone solicitations by the seller. It generated $17 billion in 1995 U.S. retail sales, covering a wide range of goods and services. The strategy mix emphasizes shopping convenience, a personal touch, demonstrations, and more relaxed consumers. Yet, U.S. sales have not gone up much due to the rise in working women, the labor intensive nature of the business, sales force turnover, government restrictions, and the poor image of some firms.

A vending machine involves coin- and card-operated dispensing of goods and services. It eliminates sales personnel, permits 24-hour sales, and may be placed at any site convenient for consumers. Hot and cold beverages, food items, and cigarettes represented 93 percent of the $30 billion in 1995 U.S. vending revenues. Efforts to branch into other product categories have met with customer resistance, and items priced above $1.50 have not done well.

2. *To consider these nontraditional forms of retailing: the World Wide Web, video kiosks, and video catalogs* The Internet is a global electronic superhighway that acts as a single, cooperative virtual network. The World Wide Web (WWW) is one way of accessing information on the Internet, whereby people turn their PCs into interactive multimedia centers. From the retailer's perspective, the

Web can serve one or more purposes, from enhancing a firm's image to making sales. The purpose chosen depends on the goals and focus. Firms should not get their hopes too high that Web sales can drive revenues up much in the near future. The Web will still generate less than 1 percent of total retail sales in the year 2000.

The WWW offers these positive features for retailers: It is inexpensive to have a Web site. The potential marketplace is huge and dispersed, yet relatively easy to reach. Web sites can be quite exciting. People can visit Web sites at any time. Information can be targeted. A customer data base can be established and customer feedback obtained. Yet, if consumers do not know a firm's Web address, it may be hard to find. Most people are not yet willing to buy online. There is clutter with regard to the number of retail Web sites. Because Web surfers are easily bored, a firm must regularly update its Web site to ensure repeat visits. The more multimedia features a Web site has, the slower it may be to access. Some firms have been overwhelmed with customer service requests. Improvements are needed to coordinate store- and Web-based transactions. There are few standards or rules as to what may be portrayed at Web sites. Consumers expect online services to be free and are very reluctant to pay for them.

The video kiosk is a freestanding, interactive computer terminal that displays products and other information on a video screen; it often uses a touch-screen for people to make selections. Although some kiosks are in stores to upgrade customer service, others let consumers place orders, complete transactions, and arrange for shipping. Kiosks can be put almost anywhere, require little or no personnel, and are an entertaining and easy way for people to shop.

A video catalog appears on a CD-ROM disk and is viewed on a PC screen. The consumer typically phones in an order to the retailer. Although the Web has garnered more attention, there are advantages to video catalogs. The disks process information quickly, which means immediate viewing and listening. The disks are better organized, so people can readily choose products. Retailers gain greater visibility than as one of the legion of firms on the Web. Disks feature point and click capabilities. In contrast to print catalogs, costs may be lower.

Key Terms

nonstore retailing (p. 165)
direct marketing (p. 165)
data-base retailing (p. 169)
specialog (p. 172)

infomercial (p. 173)
direct selling (p. 178)
vending machine (p. 181)
Internet (p. 182)

World Wide Web (WWW) (p. 182)
video kiosk (p. 187)
video catalog (p. 187)

Questions for Discussion

1. Why would a retailer want to use nonstore retailing rather than store-based retailing?
2. Do you agree that nonstore retailing will continue to grow? Explain your answer.
3. Why is direct marketing one of the most misunderstood retailing institutions in the United States?
4. How would you increase a direct marketer's response rate from 2 percent of those receiving a mail catalog to 5 percent?
5. Explain the "30-day rule" for direct marketers.
6. What is data-base retailing?
7. What are the two main decisions to be made in the business definition stage of planning a direct marketing strategy?
8. How should a small direct marketing firm handle consumer concerns about their privacy?
9. Differentiate between direct selling and direct marketing. What are the strengths and weaknesses of each?
10. As an industry consultant, what would you propose to increase sales volume by direct selling?
11. Select a product not heavily sold through vending machines and present a brief plan for doing so.
12. From a retailer's perspective, what are the advantages and disadvantages of having a World Wide Web site?
13. What must retailers do to stimulate greater shopping interest on the World Wide Web?
14. What future role do you see for video kiosks? Why?
15. Why are CD-ROM video catalogs an underappreciated retail format?

Web-Based Exercise:

PEAPOD (http://www.peapod.com)

Questions

1. Describe Peapod's overall retail strategy based on the information provided at its Web site.
2. What are the pros and cons of Peapod's services? Base your answer on the "Tour the Peapod" site feature.

3. To which market segments should Peapod appeal? Explain your answer.
4. Discuss the pros and cons to a local supermarket chain of having a long-term relationship with Peapod.

**CASE I
Williamson-Dickie: Using Dual Channels in the Apparel Industry***

For years, there seemed a belief existed that a manufacturer distributing through traditional retail stores could not also market products by direct marketing. More recently, however, manufacturers' use of dual channels (traditional retailers and direct marketing) has become a standard practice in the sale of such diverse goods and services as computer hardware and software, financial services, hotels, and airline travel. IBM and Compaq, for example, sell their computers through direct channels at the same prices as their traditional retailers. A dual distribution strategy lets a manufacturer directly target key customers, stimulates repeat purchasing activity through special offers to loyal customers, and builds long-term relationships.

Williamson-Dickie (W-D), the maker of Dickies brand of work clothes, has effectively made the transition from just using indirect distribution through retailers to a dual channel strategy (that includes direct marketing). Steve Lefler, W-D's president, reasoned that besides boosting domestic sales, a good catalog would stimulate international sales. The catalog would also reduce reliance on W-D's superstore-based customers, many of whom only stock W-D's best-selling lines. Although W-D's smaller stores still stock a full product line, their importance has dropped.

In the early 1990s, W-D faced a series of problems in developing its mail-order operation. When W-D initially planned its mail-order catalog operation, this strategy was seen by its small independent retailers as a form of unfair competition. Furthermore, W-D needed to generate and maintain a final customer data base to successfully pursue its direct marketing strategy.

The first W-D catalog, mailed in 1991, was an unattractive piece sent to consumers who had requested additional product information. Soon thereafter, W-D realized the need to reorganize its phone call center, add additional operators, and totally redesign the catalog. Lefler soon noticed that the number of customer inquiries it typically received was insufficient to support the expense of an attractive four-color catalog. W-D had to devise and maintain a customer data base.

Lefler and his colleagues decided to use W-D's carton labels, packing slips, and inspection forms to communicate the existence of the firm's mail-order catalog. Although the inside pocket of each W-D garment always contained an inspection slip, in the past nothing else was ever communicated on the reverse side of the slip. So, W-D added the statement: "Ask your dealer about other Dickies products or call (toll-free number) for a free catalog." This simple tactic resulted in W-D's compiling a data base of nearly 400,000 names. W-D even runs an annual sweepstakes (in which winners are drawn from 3 million entry blanks that are inserted in garments and from entry blanks available at 6,000 displays in retail locations) to build and update its data base. W-D currently mails out 270,000 catalogs at a time, with a 6 percent response rate.

*The material in this case was prepared and written by Stan Rapp, Cross Rapp Consulting Group; and Professor Jack Eure, Southwest Texas State University.

CASE 1
(Continued)

Of the retailers that resented W-D's move to a dual distribution strategy, many were small firms that were already hard-pressed by giant superstore competitors. Thus, W-D took special care in dealing with these retailers. For example, Lefler sent each complaining retailer a letter explaining how the company was not taking sales from its small dealers. The letter explained that W-D's mail-order prices were slightly higher than at traditional retailers. In addition, W-D explained that its mail-order customers are first referred to a local retailer if W-D's inventory management system verifies that this retailer has recently ordered the purchaser's preferred style and color in the buyer's size. According to Lefler, 98 percent of the callers do not order from the catalog, but are inspired to go to their local store to try on a new item.

According to a retail consultant, even though W-D's dual distribution strategy can be easily adapted to other firms, few companies are now taking advantage of this opportunity.

Questions
1. Comment on W-D's decision to use a dual distribution strategy. What should its goals be? Why?
2. Describe the steps W-D should have gone through in planning and implementing its direct marketing strategy.
3. Did W-D do an adequate job of reassuring retailers that dual distribution could benefit them?
4. What other steps should W-D take to deal with disgruntled retailers?

CASE 2
Lands' End and the Web[†]

Lands' End's print promotional media consist of a monthly core catalog and several specialized catalogs sent to different market segments. The "core" catalog, with its 155 pages per issue, focuses on the firm's basic product lines of clothing and accessories for men, women, and children. It also offers seasonal merchandise such as swimsuits, holiday gifts, and outerwear. The core catalog accounts for two-thirds of Lands' End's annual sales. Specialized catalogs focus on children's clothing (six catalogs per year), bedding and bath items (nine catalogs per year), and men's and ladies' tailored clothing and accessories (four catalogs per year for men and two for women). Lands' End also mails out two end-of-season clearance catalogs, interim catalogs, and a smaller version of its core catalog to prospective customers.

In recent years, Lands' End has been placing more emphasis on alternate technologies for reaching customers, including the World Wide Web. Its customers can now order any item in any one of its U.S. catalogs directly from Lands' End's Web site (http://www.landsend.com). Table 1 highlights the features of its Web site. Several aspects of the World Wide Web make it particularly attractive to Lands' End: the match of Web user demographics with those of Lands' End customers, better control over printing and distribution costs, the reduced need for customer support staff, better timeliness, and the ability to attract an international clientele.

Web browsers are upscale with similar demographics to Lands' End's customers. For example, Lands' End research indicates 49 percent of its customers are in the 35 to 45 age group, 62 percent have household incomes of $50,000 or more, and 90 percent have attended or graduated from college. This profile compares favorably with studies showing that the average U.S. Web user has a household income higher than the national average, and that 57 percent have either attended or graduated from college. The only major difference is that while two-thirds of Lands' End's U.S. orders are placed by females, females comprise about one-third of overall U.S. Web users.

[†]The material in this case is drawn from David A. Heenan, "The Rise of a Worldwide Cybermarket," *Journal of Business Strategy*, Vol. 16 (May–June 1995), pp. 20–21; *Lands' End 1996 Annual Report*; *Lands' End 10K for the Fiscal Year Ending April 30, 1996*; and Thomas E. Weber, "Who Uses the Internet?" *Wall Street Journal* (December 9, 1996), p. R6.

CASE 2
(Continued)

Table I   SELECTED FEATURES OF THE LANDS' END WEB SITE

- Consumers can order any item in any Lands' End U.S. catalog.
- Customers can mix and match selections from the print catalogs with items in the Web store's Overstocks section.
- The site does not contain a lot of video. Lands' End wants its customers to be able to quickly access its screens.
- The site has a similar "feel" to a Lands' End paper catalog.
- Tips for care of garments and determining the correct size of garments are provided.
- A number of "hot links" are provided. Thus, a consumer can easily access any Lands' End specialty catalog from multiple screen locations.
- An "order processor" automatically determines if the ordered items are in stock. If not, other products, sizes, or colors are immediately suggested.
- The total costs of an order (including gift box charges, monogramming costs, and shipping costs to anywhere in the world) are automatically tabulated.
- To protect shoppers from credit card fraud, the online order form is encrypted.
- Customer excitement and return site visits are stimulated by having an overstock listing, which is modified weekly.
- Customers can E-mail comments and suggestions directly to Lands' End.
- Current and potential investors can secure financial data on Lands' End.

Using the Web also frees direct marketers from the costs of printing and distributing catalogs, as well as the risk of increased paper and postage costs. Because Lands' End can add product descriptions to its Web site without increasing printing and distribution costs, its Web site is also typically more copy-intensive than its catalog. In addition, the Lands' End Web site lessens the need for customer support staff. Why? Land's End customers can now correspond with Lands' End (by E-mail), determine the correct size, order merchandise, and even verify a product's availability in a given size and color without ever talking to a customer representative.

Traditional paper catalogs must be ordered months before they are actually shipped. Thus, the goods in a catalog may not be available as indicated or the price listed may not reflect competitive conditions or changes in costs. In contrast, Web prices and availability can be modified on a daily basis.

Lastly, the Web attracts an international clientele. People residing in nations not receiving Lands' End catalogs can "shop" at Lands' End without incurring long-distance telephone charges.

Questions

1. Explain the relationship between direct marketing and the World Wide Web.
2. How can Lands' End better coordinate its Web and catalog promotions?
3. Describe how Lands' End can use its Web site to improve its customer service.
4. Should Lands' End offer a special discount to consumers who place orders through its Web site (versus those who use phone or mail) to reflect its cost savings? Explain your answer.

Video Questions on Lands' End

1. Describe the pros and cons of Lands' End including video in its Web site.
2. Discuss Lands' End's credit card security strategy for its Web sales.

Part Two ▪ Comprehensive Case

Starting and Growing a Retail Business*

INTRODUCTION

Nothing I have ever done has been as demanding, challenging, and rewarding as starting my own gift, clothing, and accessory business. I began in 1990 by opening a kiosk in a mall where I sold handblown glass during peak holiday seasons. I didn't make enough profit to pay for my time, but I found I absolutely loved retailing. The next year, I continued my business by sharing a permanent mall space with two other retailers. Growing weary of long hours and high rental fees at a regional mall, in 1993, I opened Morgan Fitzgerald's in a 2,000-square-foot remodeled space in a strip center. Since then, I have learned more retailing lessons than I thought possible.

CUSTOMERS RESPOND TO CREATIVE SELLING AND SERVICE

Mall specialty stores and large department stores have inventories greatly exceeding the size of my inventory. But my customers, who are primarily thirty-five plus, say they don't like to shop at the mall. The racks of clothes pressed tightly together and a lack of salespeople available to help make shopping in mall stores confusing for them. My customers tell me the salespeople don't seem to have much product knowledge. Customers also complain about the distances they must walk just to get to the stores where they want to shop.

Morgan Fitzgerald's offers what the big stores don't—convenience, product knowledge, and personal customer service. For easy access and more convenience, customers park at our front door; if a customer needs help, we go to her car. As a customer enters the store, we look at her size, body shape, and color palette. We mentally scan the store for clothing that will fit.

After greeting a customer, we try to find how we can help. "Just looking" to us means "show me some-

thing I'll be interested in," and we do. Selling is more than ringing the cash register. It is determining the customer's needs and matching these needs with our products. That means our staff not only has to know our products and their features, but also must listen to what our customer says. What looks good on the hanger may not look good on a particular customer. Nothing is as frustrating to a customer as trying on garment after garment and having nothing look good. That's one way our personal service helps. We analyze our customer's body type. A woman with protruding stomach and slightly rounded shoulders needs nowaist shifts with a little extra shoulder pad lift. We have trained ourselves to look at customers and determine sizes before they have to tell us. This allows us to mentally pinpoint garments that will probably fit well.

To make a garment seem complete, it needs accessories. Personal service means showing the customer what accessorizes an outfit. While she is trying on clothes, we pull accessories to show her. Accessories should enhance a garment and be appropriate and functional for the customer. If the customer prefers clip earrings, we convert pierced earrings to clip. If she has arthritis, we suggest a velcro or button scarf that attaches easily. We probably have sold more scarves than any other store in the market, including major department stores. Why? Because we put a scarf around just about every customer's neck who will let us, and our customers like it.

We try not to pester a customer who wants to browse, but recognize that unless we show the products, a customer may miss or fail to appreciate appealing product features. As a woman nears an item with particular selling features, we demonstrate the product and place it in her hands.

We have a notebook listing customers' special requests. But we also jot down names and phone numbers of those who really like particular garments but do not buy them. If the garments go on sale, we call the customers, providing personal service for customers, and sales for us.

No store can be all things to all people, but our store personnel will help customers find items that we

*The material in this case was adapted by the authors from Nancy Pride, owner of Morgan Fitzgerald's, "Lessons of a Retailing Novice," *Arthur Andersen Retailing Issues Letter* (July 1995), pp. 1–5. Reprinted by permission.

don't have at Morgan Fitzgerald's. If a customer has gone to the trouble of visiting us to find a product and we don't have it, we call other local stores to help her locate it. Our calling provides a service for our customer, lets her know we really want to help, and gives her time to look at our items as we call. (The calls have an interesting side effect: other stores reciprocate.)

It is critical for our business to develop relationships with customers. While chatting with a customer, our salespeople learn more about her, and thus when she returns, will give her faster and more accurate service. For us, retailing is not just business; it is an interpersonal business.

LISTEN TO EVERYONE

When we first started, we had to listen to our customers. We didn't have much merchandise and didn't know enough about what customers wanted. Fortunately for us, we are in the habit of listening now and avoid mistakes because of it. Then and now, we ask each customer to fill out a form including name, address, birth month and day, anniversary month and day, sizes, color and style preferences, and interests. This serves two purposes: it facilitates further customer contact and lets us know about customer wants and preferences. For example, our customers told us what they could not find in town. Older customers wanted bright colors because neutrals made them look older. They wanted classic garments that could be worn year after year. They wanted garments fitting their body shapes. Many of our elderly customers have mild osteoporosis, causing higher waistlines and rounded shoulders that require gathering or pleating from shoulders. Their arms and legs may have age spots, varicose veins, or wrinkles, requiring garments with longer hems and long sleeves, even in summer. All waistbands need some elastic for comfort.

Although we must listen to our customers, their requests must fit within the overall goal of the store. We had one large customer who told us there was a market for better large women's clothing. We followed her advice and, for the size of our store, ordered a high percentage of large sizes. She is indeed a loyal and excellent customer. However, within the first year she lost 95 pounds. We still have a few too many 2X garments waiting for the right customer. By stocking those sizes, we learned there are a number of large women, mostly in the 1X size, that look to us for clothing; and they tend to prefer a moderately priced casual line.

Sales representatives have a tremendous amount of knowledge and are willing to share it. We invite and appreciate suggestions on ways to merchandise better, and have received a remarkable amount of advice that has actually worked. No jacket should be shown without a blouse under it. Why? It shows off the jacket while subtly suggesting to the buyer what to wear with it. We have sold several "total outfits" because our customer saw the entire picture and liked it. Put a jacket on the customer before she sees the price tag. She may just fall in love with it.

When you find a vendor that fits your needs and provides good service, buy heavily. That vendor will have a reason to make sure your service continues to be good. Judge your sales representatives' advice by their honesty on all matters. If they have been truthful about which of your competitors carries or has carried your lines, if they have identified the garments that have "checked well," and not labeled slow-movers as "the sellers," you can probably trust their advice. Ask the vendors you trust for names and phone numbers of owners of similar businesses in noncompeting regions. Call them and ask for their advice. They recognize how difficult retailing is and are usually very gracious about sharing information on successful lines, selling techniques, or supply sources. Before you add a major new fixture, for example, talk to other owners. We learned that our three-way mirror needs to be hinged, and it needs to be out in the store instead of in the dressing room. When the mirror is not in the dressing room, the customer comes out in the store where we see what is wrong with the fit. We can suggest another garment with a better fit.

Your own employees may be an untapped resource. Elaine, who has helped give birth to Morgan Fitzgerald's, has been in retailing for more than 40 years. Her experience and knowledge help her predict what is important to the customer. I encourage her input and will often rely on her advice when making buying decisions. Besides helping me, she has ownership in the decisions.

ALTERNATE COMMUNICATION CHANNELS CAN PRODUCE RESULTS ECONOMICALLY

Mass media are necessary. But for a retailer starting out with severe demands on capital or a firm trying to reduce costs, there are alternative, less costly ways to communicate with customers. We attract new customers by letting local groups know we will give free programs. When we do fashion shows, we get our models from the group asking us to give the show. The models come to the store, become familiar with our clothing, wear garments they like, and exude enthusiasm while modeling. They return to us later and often buy something they have modeled.

Programs given at nursing homes yield loyal customers. Department stores often ignore older ladies who require more service and who are very particular about the type of garments they want. If a store provides that extra service and attention, the older customers return.

Signage communicates. Our outdoor signage communicates with its subtitle, "Gifts, Clothing and Accessories." When we asked how our customers heard about us during our first year, they frequently responded, "I saw your sign." An owner of a neighboring needlecraft store seemed puzzled that her mat and frame sales increased dramatically from her previous location. Her sign read simply, "The Stitchery" with subtitle "Mats & Frames." The sign at the prior site did not mention mats and frames. A main sign must clearly reflect what a store offers.

Temporary signs communicate particularly well for special events. Spend the extra money for a banner that says, "Scarf workshop today," "Sale," or "Trunk show today." It creates excitement while it communicates. It also works. I have watched people who are stopped at the traffic light read the sign and turn into the parking lot.

Use your windows to communicate. Beautiful display windows do attract attention; however, a simple suction cup stuck to the inside of the glass that displays a new outfit each day communicates what is in the store, what has just arrived, or what is on sale.

The telephone works. Customers don't want to be pestered, but they usually appreciate a call when something new in their size arrives. Ninety percent of the time, our calls bring customers into the store because they know we know their size and their color and style preferences.

It is a lot easier to keep existing customers than to attract new ones. An accurate customer mailing list is the number one communication tool for us. Every person who comes in the door is a potential long-term customer. If a person leaves without filling out a form, the communication channel closes. Ninety-nine percent of our customers choose to fill out a data form; the rate is high because if they resist, we tell them that not only are they helping us buy the right garments, but the information on the form will enable us to send a birthday card with a 10 percent discount coupon. We also use the information sheet to identify customers who may have a particular interest in new shipments and then notify them by personal note. If customers receive handwritten notes, they know they are special. They are not just sale receipt numbers. We

have a high response rate to such notes. Some people respond immediately, some two or three weeks after receiving the note, and some after receiving three or four cards. By sending cards, our store name is on our customers' minds, indicating that we are ready and waiting when they need something.

Newspapers need news. If you can creatively show a reporter an angle that makes your business newsworthy, you may just get free coverage. In our case, as I looked out at neighboring businesses, I realized that 90 percent of them were owned by women. The editor liked the angle and we got front-page coverage.

GOOD PAPERWORK IS ESSENTIAL

Record keeping is not particularly fun. Yet, if you do it accurately and consistently, you will be more successful. Some retailers feel paperwork belongs only to the accountant who prepares the financial statements and myriad government forms. Paperwork actually can be the nerve center for the business. An apparel store must have suppliers or there is nothing to sell. All too often, a store owner doesn't monitor the suppliers effectively or doesn't pay the suppliers promptly. The order copy should become a work sheet, not a file sheet. The retailer learns when goods are to be shipped—what sizes, styles, and colors. When you order, have a stamp made to list your requirements for purchases, such as shipping complete orders, or having no substitutions.

Comparing items ordered to items received within the specified completion date can save money. If a manufacturer ships beyond the completion date or ships different sizes, colors, or styles, you may refuse the shipment or ask for a percentage off. If items are still saleable, the reduced cost improves your margins. Double check the cost of goods on the invoice with the cost listed on the order sheet. Also double check the cost listed on the packing list with your invoice. If you use the packing list to mark your retail prices and the packing list prices are not the same as your invoice, you may price your goods below your necessary markup. If you agree to pay for shipping charges only (not shipping and handling), weigh packages on arrival and log the amount. Most companies don't overcharge, but some do.

Keeping a clear paper trail of returned goods is important because many manufacturers do not keep such good records. Promptly contact the manufacturer after receiving flawed goods, ship them back as soon as authorization is given, and keep a record of the cost of the return shipment. You need to deduct the shipping fee from payment. If you don't keep accurate records, suppliers will not remind you. You will end up returning faulty goods and still paying for them.

Keeping a log of shipments received by date and amount due lets you be aware of payment due dates and deduct prompt payment discounts. A retailer's payment reputation spreads quickly among manufacturers. Manufacturers' work is as difficult as retailers'. Slow payment by the retailer makes manufacturers look for other retailers with better pay reputations.

A retailer also needs to know specific information about inventory without having to go back to every invoice. To help with this, a code should be placed—either by electronic means or manually—to indicate the cost and the date placed into inventory. The code can help determine when to place an item on sale and how much to mark it down.

I dislike record keeping and am not proficient at it. Likewise, my employees' key weakness is in this area. I needed to set up systems to make it easier and farm out (outsource) some of the work. I cannot delegate all record keeping, but I can assign some that isn't essential for me to do.

BE EVER MINDFUL OF INNOVATION

While attending an apparel show shortly after opening my store, I sat next to a woman who had a successful dress shop. I asked her advice and she said, "You'll do fine as long as you keep it exciting." Even if I carried different lines than she does and have a different type of customer; in her opinion, my store would succeed if I kept it exciting. The customer enjoys excitement, and generating it can be as simple as rearranging a display, calling customers when new items arrive, conducting in-store "shows," having a designer visit the store, or decorating for the holidays.

Innovation includes consistently looking for new lines and better ways to serve customers. Would my customers respond to a birthday high tea held at our store each month? Would a "rolling store" that travels to nursing homes be effective? Would a July sales representative's sample show bolster sales during the slowest month of the year? Would discount coupons handed out by salespeople wherever they go bring in new customers? Innovation needn't be original. If you see a creative display elsewhere, use it in your store. Read trade publications for ideas.

LESSONS I'VE LEARNED

As I think over the various retailing lessons I've learned and paired them with the various customer comments I have heard, I have concluded that there are things that both large and small apparel stores can do to better serve their customers.

TIPS FOR LARGER STORES

- Create a less threatening or confusing store environment. Use stores within stores. Having a self-contained space with clothing and accessories integrated increases cross-selling and helps the customer. Sales personnel should be assigned so customers know someone they have worked with will be available when they shop. Have store personnel at major entrances who can direct customers to the products they seek.
- Improve store signage. If clerks are not available to help, signs can direct. Consider directional signs (like decorative street signs) to help customers find the various departments.
- Train sales staff to identify body shapes and the clothing that looks best on those body shapes.
- Have a parking lot train or van to pick up customers at their cars to increase convenience.
- If you sell clothing for older customers, have older buyers help select it. They will probably be more sensitive to the particular needs of the older customer.

TIPS FOR SMALLER STORES

- Differentiate your products from other stores. You can be more diverse and interesting because you do not have to buy in large amounts. Shop competitors to avoid head-to-head competition.
- Determine your market niche, for one store cannot offer inventory to suit all tastes.
- Choose a location that has easy access and high visibility.
- Look for products with selling features. Not only will you sell more, but you will have a built-in reason to demonstrate to the customer.
- Develop strong employee and customer relationships.
- Plan events to add excitement.
- Allocate enough advertising dollars to one medium to make a statement rather than diminishing your impact by spreading your dollars too thinly over too many different media.
- Define your strengths and pay others to do the rest. You and your employees cannot do it all.

I have often heard there is no silver bullet that guarantees successful retailing. I understand this better after learning some of retailing's lessons. There is no one silver bullet because a person with determination, creativity, and sensitivity can create his or her own bullet, fashioned by his or her own style, interests, and personality. It is not just common themes that come from the retailing lessons that create success, it is the retailer's individuality.

Questions

1. How should a prospective new retailer react to this statement? "Nothing I have ever done has been as demanding, challenging, and rewarding as starting my own gift, clothing, and accessory business."
2. How could a small retailer act as a power retailer?
3. Under what circumstances should the owner of a small retail business consider becoming a franchisee in the same line of business?
4. How heavily involved with scrambled merchandising should a small retailer become? Explain your answer.
5. Should a small retail store engage in direct marketing? Why or why not?
6. Will the Web's popularity undermine the popularity of small store-based retailers? Explain your answer.
7. Cite five concepts that any retailer could learn from by reading this case.

Part Three

Targeting Customers and Gathering Information

- In Part 3, various techniques for identifying and understanding consumers, and selecting a target market, are first presented. Information-gathering methods—which can be used in selecting a target market, as well as in developing and implementing an overall strategy—are then described.

- Chapter 7 discusses why it is necessary for a retailer to determine and respond properly to its target market, the customer group that the firm tries to satisfy. Consumer demographics, life-styles, and decision making are all examined and related to retailing. Throughout the chapter, relevant retail implications are noted.

- Chapter 8 deals with information gathering and processing in retailing. First, the difficulties that may arise from basing a retail strategy on nonsystematic research are considered. The retail information system, its components, and recent advances in information systems are then reviewed in depth. The chapter concludes by outlining and describing the marketing research process, with particular emphasis on the characteristics and alternative kinds of secondary data and primary data.

7

Identifying and Understanding Consumers

CHAPTER OBJECTIVES

1. To discuss why it is important for a retailer to properly select, identify, and understand its target market

2. To enumerate and describe a number of consumer demographic and life-style factors, and explain how these concepts can be applied to retailing

3. To examine the consumer decision process and its stages: stimulus, problem awareness, information search, evaluation of alternatives, purchase, and post-purchase behavior

4. To differentiate among different types of consumer decision making

5. To present several retail applications regarding consumer characteristics and behavior

According to one expert, U.S. supermarkets need to market food products more from the perspective of "home meal solutions" and less from the perspective of "separate food ingredients." These are among the factors that are making the market for meal solutions so attractive: the increased consumption of take-out and restaurant-based meals, the significance of convenience in food preparation, and the large percentage of working mothers.

Take-out food and food consumption away from the home now account for about two-fifths of the average U.S. consumer's food budget. Expenditures on take-out food and restaurant meals have grown by over 25 percent during the past fifteen years. Most of the spending on food cooked outside the home involves either pizza (48 percent) or chicken (36 percent).

According to a recent study, convenience, speed, and ease of use are the most important factors for two-thirds of the consumers who prepare food daily. And 42 percent of consumers said they are willing to pay more for food with these attributes. Interestingly, over 40 percent of people stated that as of 4:00 P.M. on a given day they have no idea what they would eat for dinner that evening.

Over 70 percent of mothers work, and nearly three-quarters of this group work full time. This creates a desire for time-saving food preparation strategies.

Supermarkets are in a unique position to market a meals solution strategy because two-thirds of female shoppers visit the supermarket an average of twice per week. In addition, most membership clubs and mass merchandisers do not stock a sufficient assortment of foods to provide consumers with a variety of meal-based solutions. Despite these competitive advantages, supermarkets currently account for only 12 percent of take-out food spending.

An effective example of a meals solution strategy was a promotion sponsored by Pathmark, a Northeast regional supermarket chain. The promotion featured a number of frozen pasta varieties, along with a variety of ingredients that could be prepared in different ways. Each meal required just six minutes of cooking time. Besides advertising that provided hints on meal preparation, Pathmark facilitated the shopping experience by placing these items together in each of its supermarkets. Instead of having consumers go through the entire store to separately stock up on pasta, vegetables, and pasta sauce, Pathmark grouped these products together near the front of the store for easy access. The items were also available for home delivery.[1]

[1] Christopher W. Hoyt, "Meal Solutions Are Supermarkets' Salvation," *Promo* (July 1996), p. 25.

A retailer's ability to devise and apply a sound strategy depends on how well that firm se- **OVERVIEW**
lects, identifies, and understands its customers. This entails selecting the type of target
market to reach, identifying the characteristics and needs of the firm's specific target
market, and understanding how consumers make decisions:

> Retailers have long depended on their ability to size up people when they walk in
> the door. Customers give themselves away by their clothing, speech, and man-
> nerisms. While gut instinct still works for some retailers, the era of successful
> scrutiny has passed. You can no longer pigeonhole at a glance because increasing
> consumer diversity has made stereotyping futile. You now need a more systematic
> way to understand your customers. In 1800, a typical American had access to
> fewer than 300 products on sale in his or her hometown, one retail establishment
> (a country store), and about 500 feet of retail space. In contrast, a typical
> American in a city of a million people now has access to over a million consumer
> products, thousands of merchants, and (in 1997) nearly 20 million square feet of
> selling space.[2]

> Many of today's retailers have a general perception of consumers. But they still
> do not really understand them. We have confused consumers with too many
> choices. It is overwhelming. Most retailers need to selectively get out of some
> kinds of merchandise. We need to stock the products people want to buy as op-
> posed to the products owners want to sell. The information is there. Retailers
> need to use it to think about their customers in a different manner in terms of
> what they offer them, how they offer it, and most importantly, how they value
> the customers.[3]

A **target market,** as defined in Chapter 2, is a customer group a retailer seeks
to satisfy. With mass marketing, a firm like a supermarket or a drugstore sells
goods and services to a broad spectrum of consumers; it does not really focus efforts on any one kind of customer. In concentrated marketing, a firm tailors its
strategy to the needs of one distinct consumer group, such as young working
women; it does not attempt to satisfy people outside that segment. With differentiated marketing, a firm aims at two or more distinct consumer groups, such as
men and boys, with a different strategy mix for each segment; it can do this by operating more than one kind of outlet (such as separate men's and boys' clothing
stores) or by having distinct departments grouped by market segment in a single
store (as a department store might do). In deciding the type of target market to
reach, a firm would consider its goods/service category and goals, competitors'
actions, the size of consumer segments, the relative efficiency of each target market alternative for the particular retailer, the resources required, and other factors.
See Figure 7-1.

After the retailer chooses a target market method, it identifies the characteristics and
needs of those customers to whom it wants to appeal and tries to understand how they
make purchase decisions. Consumer characteristics include demographic and life-style
factors. Consumer needs relate to a firm's store location, goods/service assortment,
prices, and so on. Purchase decisions may be made impulsively or may encompass a detailed thought process. In this chapter, we examine consumer characteristics and needs
and the way purchase decisions are made.

[2]Marvin Nesbit and Arthur Weinstein, "How to Size Up Your Customers," *American Demographics* (July
1986), p. 34; and James H. Snider, "Consumers in the Information Age," *Futurist* (January–February
1993), p. 15.
[3]"Open Forum: Focus on the Changing Consumer," *Chain Store Age* (October 1996), pp. 12D–13D.

Figure 7-1

Selecting a Target Market

Because of the diversity of the marketplace, retailers have many choices in deciding upon their target markets. Firms must gear their strategy mixes toward satisfying the needs of the target markets they select.

IDENTIFYING CONSUMER CHARACTER-ISTICS AND NEEDS

Consumer characteristics and needs can be identified by studying demographic and life-style factors. A retailer can then develop a target market profile by combining two or more factors.

Demographics are objective and quantifiable population data that are easily identifiable and measurable. **Life-styles** are the ways in which individual consumers and families (households) live and spend time and money.

Consumer Demographics

Consumers can be identified in terms of such demographic variables as these: population size, household size, marital and family-status, income, retail sales, age, birthrates, mobility, place of residence, gender, employment status, occupation, education level, and ethnic/racial background.

First, a retailer should have some basic knowledge of the overall demographics of the U.S. population. Next, it would determine the demographic attributes of its own target market.

A Demographic Snapshot of the United States[4] ❏ Table 7-1 shows selected U.S. demographic data by region. These data are a useful starting point for retailers, since most firms are local and regional. Following is a demographic overview of the United States.

There are now 270 million people living in 100 million households. The four most-populated regions are the South Atlantic, East North Central, Pacific, and Middle Atlantic. The greatest proportion of single-person households reside in the Middle Atlantic, West North Central, New England, and East North Central regions.

Three-fifths of the adult population is married; but one-half of marriages end in divorce. The average age at first marriage is 26 for men and 24 for women. About 70 percent of all households (a "household" has one or more persons living in a housing unit, whether related or not) consist of families (a "family" has two or more related persons living together).

The typical American family has a total annual after-tax income of about $40,000. The top one-sixth of families have yearly incomes of $75,000 or more; but the lowest one-sixth earn under $15,000 per year. When earnings are high, consumers are more apt to have **discretionary income**—money left after paying taxes and buying necessities. People in the New England, Middle Atlantic, and Pacific regions have the highest median incomes.

The average annual U.S. retail expenditures per household are about $25,000. Together, the South Atlantic, East North Central, Pacific, and Middle Atlantic regions account for two-thirds of all U.S. retail sales.

The median age of the U.S. population is 35. The average is lowest in the West South Central, Mountain, and Pacific regions. The national annual birthrate is 15 births per thousand people. It is highest in the Pacific, West South Central, and Mountain regions.

About 15 percent to 20 percent of the U.S. population changes residences each year; 60 percent of all moves are in the same county. People in the Middle Atlantic, New England, East North Central, and East South Central regions are the most apt to have lived in the same place for at least five years.

About 80 percent of all people reside in urban or suburban areas. Urbanization is highest in the Pacific and Middle Atlantic regions. The fastest-growing cities and states are in the Mountain, Pacific, West South Central, South Atlantic, and Southwest regions. See Figure 7-2.

Nationwide, there are 6 million more females than males, and three-fifths of females aged 16 and older are in the labor force (many full time). Female participation in the labor force is greatest in the West North Central and New England regions.

Most U.S. employment—male and female—is in services. Also, there are now more professionals and white-collar workers and fewer blue-collar and agricultural workers.

More adults have attended some level of college than ever before. And one-fifth of all U.S. adults aged 25 and older have at least graduated from a four-year college. The

[4]The data presented in this section are from *Statistical Abstract of the United States 1996* (Washington, D.C.: U.S. Department of Commerce, 1996), various pages.

Table 7-1   SELECTED U.S. DEMOGRAPHICS BY REGION (AS OF 1996)

Region	Percent of U.S. Population	Persons Per Household	Percent of U.S. Household Income	Percent of U.S. Retail Sales	Percent of Population 18 to 34 Years Old
New England	5.0	2.66	5.8	5.2	25.7
Middle Atlantic	14.4	2.71	15.8	13.4	24.4
East North Central	16.5	2.69	16.7	17.1	24.3
West North Central	7.0	2.62	6.7	7.5	23.7
South Atlantic	17.9	2.63	17.8	18.9	24.8
East South Central	6.1	2.67	5.4	5.8	24.0
West South Central	11.0	2.78	10.0	10.6	25.1
Mountain	6.0	2.71	5.6	6.2	24.3
Pacific	16.1	2.87	16.3	15.2	26.2

Region	Percent of Population 65 and Older	Annual Births Per 1,000 People	Percent of Population Living in Metropolitan Areas	Population Per Square Mile of Land Area	Percent Change in Population 1990–1995
New England	14.0	14.3	89.4	211.9	+ 0.8
Middle Atlantic	14.2	15.2	91.2	383.6	+ 1.5
East North Central	12.8	15.5	79.4	178.4	+ 3.4
West North Central	13.7	14.5	59.0	36.1	+ 3.9
South Atlantic	13.7	15.5	79.1	176.5	+ 7.9
East South Central	12.6	14.9	57.5	89.9	+ 5.8
West South Central	11.1	17.7	76.6	67.6	+ 8.0
Mountain	11.3	17.5	72.2	18.3	+ 14.5
Pacific	11.2	18.8	91.5	46.9	+ 7.2

New England = Connecticut, Maine, Massachusetts, New Hampshire, Rhode Island, Vermont

Middle Atlantic = New Jersey, New York, Pennsylvania

East North Central = Illinois, Indiana, Michigan, Ohio, Wisconsin

West North Central = Iowa, Kansas, Minnesota, Missouri, Nebraska, North Dakota, South Dakota

South Atlantic = Delaware, District of Columbia, Florida, Georgia, Maryland, North Carolina, South Carolina, Virginia, West Virginia

East South Central = Alabama, Kentucky, Mississippi, Tennessee

West South Central = Arkansas, Louisiana, Oklahoma, Texas

Mountain = Arizona, Colorado, Idaho, Montana, Nevada, New Mexico, Utah, Wyoming

Pacific = Alaska, California, Hawaii, Oregon, Washington

Sources: Computed by the authors from U.S. Bureau of the Census data; except for household income and retail sales data, which are from "1996 Survey of Buying Power," *Sales & Marketing Management* (1996), p. 54.

highest percentages of adults with college degrees are in the New England and Pacific regions. Young males and females are now graduating from college in roughly equal numbers.

The population comprises a number of different ethnic and racial groups. For example, in the United States, there are 35 million African-Americans, 28 million Hispanic-Americans, and 10 million Asian-Americans. These groups represent large potential target markets.

Relating Demographic Factors to the Choice of a Target Market ❏
Although the preceding data give a good picture of the United States as a whole and by region, consumer demographics vary within areas. Even in the same state or city, some locales have larger populations and more affluent, older, and better-educated residents

The Evolving Consumer Marketplace in Poland

Since the end of Communism in 1989, Polish consumers have developed more of a desire for goods and services generally associated with middle-class U.S. consumers. According to a recent survey of over 1,000 adults, 95 percent of Polish households now own a refrigerator, 88 percent have a color TV, 62 percent have a washing machine, and 53 percent have a VCR. And well over 10 percent of these households want to purchase mountain bicycles, CD players, video cameras, and home computers.

One analyst estimates that 10 percent to 15 percent of Poland's 39 million population should be classified as middle class in terms of income (between $800 and $1,600 per month for a household of four with two incomes). However, if the middle class is defined in terms of attitude, that analyst places the size as over 20 percent of the population.

The rapid growth of the Polish middle class means opportunities for retailers that cater to this segment. Ikea, with four stores in Poland, has seen a large increase in demand for kitchens and home furnishings. Part of the surging interest in furnishings is due to the bigger average size of new apartments (966 square feet versus 818 square feet for those built in 1989).

Sources: Jane Perlez, "A Bourgeoisie Blooms and Goes Shopping," *New York Times* (May 14, 1996), pp. D1, D6; and "Global Retailing: Assignment Eastern Europe," *Chain Store Age* (January 1997), Section 3, pp. 14–15.

than others. Because most retailers are local or operate in only parts of particular regions, they must compile data about the people living in their particular trading areas and those most likely to patronize them. A firm would use the demographic information to develop a profile of its specific target market.

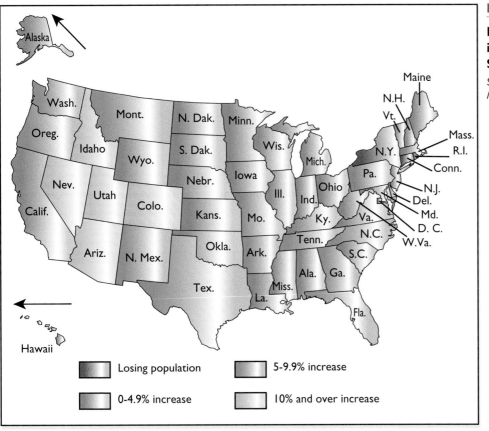

Figure 7-2

Population Growth in the United States, 1996–2001

Source: Sales & Marketing Management.

Losing population

0-4.9% increase

5-9.9% increase

10% and over increase

A firm could identify its target market in terms of some combination of these demographic factors, and plan its retail strategy accordingly:

■ Market size—How many consumers are in the target market?
■ Household size—What is the average size of the household?
■ Marital and family status—Are consumers single or married? Do families have children?
■ Income—Is the target market lower income, middle income, or upper income? Is discretionary income available for luxury purchases?
■ Retail sales—What is the retail sales potential for the retailer's goods/service category?
■ Age—What are the prime age groups to which the firm appeals?
■ Birthrates—How important are birthrates for the retailer's goods/service category?
■ Mobility—What percentage of the target market moves each year (into and out of the trading area)?
■ Where people live—How large is the trading area from which customers can realistically be drawn?
■ Gender—Is the target market predominantly male or female, or are they equal in proportion?
■ Employment status—Does the target market contain working women, retirees, and so on?
■ Occupation—In what industries and occupations are people working? Are they professionals, office workers, or of some other designation?
■ Education—Are customers college-educated?
■ Ethnic/racial background—Does the target market consist of a distinctive racial or ethnic subgroup?

Consumer Life-Styles

Consumer life-styles are based on both social and psychological factors. They are greatly affected by people's demographic backgrounds.

As with demographics, a retailer should first have some basic knowledge of various consumer life-style concepts. Then, the retailer would determine the life-style attributes of its own target market.

Social Factors ❏ These social factors are key elements in identifying consumer life-styles: culture, social class, reference groups, social performance, family life cycle, and time utilization.

A **culture** is a distinctive heritage shared by a group of people. It influences the importance of family, work, education, and other concepts by passing on a series of beliefs, norms, and customs. In the United States, there is an overall culture, which stresses individuality, success, education, and material comfort, as well as different subcultures for various demographic groups (such as Hispanic and Asian) due to the many countries from which residents have come.

A **social class** system is an informal ranking of people in a culture based on their income, occupation, education, dwelling, and other factors. There are people with similar values and life-styles in each social class category. See Table 7-2.

Reference groups influence people's thoughts and/or behavior. They may be categorized as aspirational, membership, and dissociative. An aspirational group is one to which a person does not belong but wishes to join, such as a higher social class, a professional club, or a fraternity. A membership group is one to which the person does belong, such as the current social class, his or her family, or a union. A dissociative group is one to which the person does not want to belong, such as a lower social class or an unpopular club. Those reference groups that are face-to-face, such as families, have the greatest im-

Table 7-2 SOCIAL CLASSES IN THE UNITED STATES

Class	Size	Characteristics
Upper Americans		
Upper-upper	0.3%	Social elite. Inherited wealth. Exclusive neighborhood. Summer home. Children attend best schools. Money not important in purchases. Secure in status.
Lower-upper	1.2%	Great earned wealth. Newly rich. Often business leaders and professionals. College educated. Seek the best for children. Active socially. Insecure. Conspicuous in consumption. Money not important in purchases.
Upper-middle	12.5%	Career-oriented. Successful business executives and professionals. Earnings over $60,000 per year. Status tied to occupation and earnings. Most educated in society, not from prestige schools. Demanding of children. Quality products purchased. Attractive home. Socially involved. "Gracious living."
Middle Americans		
Middle class	32.0%	"Typical Americans." Average-earning white-collar workers and the top group of blue-collar workers. Many college educated. Respectable. Conscientious. Try to do the right thing. Home ownership sought. Do-it-yourselfers. Family focus.
Working class	38.0%	The remaining white-collar workers and the bulk of blue-collar workers. "Working class" life-style. Some job monotony. Seek job security more than advancement. Usually high-school educated. Close-knit families. Brand loyal and interested in name brands. Not status-oriented.
Lower Americans		
Upper-lower	9.0%	Employed, mostly in unskilled or semiskilled jobs. Poorly educated. Low incomes. Hard to move up the social class ladder. Protective against lower-lower class. Standard of living at or slightly above poverty. Reside in affordable housing.
Lower-lower	7.0%	Unemployed or menial jobs. Poorest income, education, and housing. The "bottom layer." Present-oriented. Impulsive as shoppers. Overpay. Use credit.

Sources: This table is derived by the authors from Richard P. Coleman, "The Continuing Significance of Social Class in Marketing," *Journal of Consumer Research,* Vol. 10 (December 1983), pp. 265–280; James F. Engel, Roger D. Blackwell, and Paul W. Miniard, *Consumer Behavior,* Eighth Edition (Orlando, Florida: Dryden, 1995), pp. 677–707; and Wayne D. Hoyer and Deborah J. MacInnis, *Consumer Behavior* (Boston: Houghton Mifflin, 1997), pp. 325–347.

pact on people. In addition, within reference groups, there are opinion leaders whose views are respected and sought.

Social performance refers to how well a person does his or her roles as worker, citizen, parent, consumer, and so on. A person's performance determines acceptance by peers and influences the types of goods and services bought. Thus, a poor performer can emulate peers in an attempt to win approval, withdraw and become a loner, or buy expensive goods to "show off."

The **family life cycle** describes how a traditional family evolves from bachelorhood to children to solitary retirement. It is shown in Table 7-3. At each stage, a family's needs, purchases, and income change. Besides planning for the traditional life cycle, retailers need to be responsive to the large number of adults who never marry, divorced adults, single-parent families, childless couples, and so on. That is why more attention is being paid to the **household life cycle,** which incorporates the life stages of both family and nonfamily households.

Time utilization refers to the types of activities in which a person is involved and the amount of time allocated to them. Some of the broad categories of time utilization are work, transportation, eating, recreation, entertainment, parenting, sleeping, and (retailers hope) shopping. Today, many consumers allocate much less time to shopping activities than in the past.

Psychological Factors ❏ These psychological factors are key components in identifying consumer life-styles: personality, class consciousness, attitudes, perceived risk, and the importance of the purchase.

Table 7-3   APPLYING THE TRADITIONAL FAMILY LIFE CYCLE TO RETAILING

Stage in Cycle	Characteristics	Relevance for Retailing
Bachelor (male or female)	Independent. Young. Early stage of career. Entry-level earnings.	Clothing. Car. Stereo. Travel. Restaurants. Entertainment. Appeal to status.
Newly Married	Two incomes. Relative independence. Present- and future-oriented.	Furnishing apartment. Travel. Clothing. Durables. Appeal to enjoyment and togetherness.
Full Nest I	Youngest child under 6. One to one-and-a-half incomes. Limited independence. Future-oriented.	Goods and services geared to child. Family-use items. Practicality of items. Durability. Safety. Appeal to economy.
Full Nest II	Youngest child over 6, but dependent. One-and-a-half to two incomes. At least one spouse established in career. Future-oriented.	Savings. Home. Education. Family vacations. Child-oriented products. Some interest in luxuries. Appeal to comfort and long-range enjoyment.
Full Nest III	Youngest child living at home, but independent. Highest income level. Independent. Thoughts of retirement.	Education. Expensive durables for children. Replacement and improvement of parents' durables. Appeal to comfort and luxury.
Empty Nest I	No children at home. Independent. Good income. Thoughts of self and retirement.	Retirement home. Travel. Clothing. Entertainment. Luxuries. Appeal to self-gratification.
Empty Nest II	Retirement. Limited income and expenses. Present-oriented.	Travel. Recreation. Living in new home. Health-related items. Little interest in luxuries. Appeal to comfort at a fair price.
Sole Survivor I	Only one spouse alive. Actively employed. Present-oriented. Good income.	Immersion in jobs and friends. Interest in travel, clothing, health, and recreation areas. Appeal to productive citizen.
Sole Survivor II	Only one spouse alive. Retired. Some feeling of futility. Lower income.	Travel. Recreation. Health-related items. Security. Appeal to economy and social activity.

A **personality** is the sum total of an individual's traits, which make that individual unique. Personality traits include a person's levels of self-confidence, innovativeness, autonomy, sociability, emotional stability, assertiveness, and so on. Together, these attributes have a great impact on a consumer's life-style.

Class consciousness is the extent to which a person desires and pursues social status. It helps determine a consumer's use of reference groups and the importance of prestige purchases. A class-conscious person values the social status associated with particular goods, services, and retailers. A person who is not class conscious is more interested in pleasing himself or herself; actual goods/service/retailer quality, not status, is essential.

Attitudes (opinions) are the positive, neutral, or negative feelings a person has about the economy, politics, goods, services, institutions, and so on. They are also the feelings consumers have toward an individual retailer, its location, its personnel, the goods and services offered, the prices charged, and the displays and ads used. Of special concern to a retailer is whether the consumer believes its strategy is desirable, unique, and fairly priced.

Perceived risk is the level of risk a consumer believes exists regarding the purchase of a specific good or service from a given retailer, whether or not that belief is factually correct. There are six types of perceived risk: functional (Will a good or service perform as expected?); physical (Can a good or service hurt me?); financial (Can I really afford the

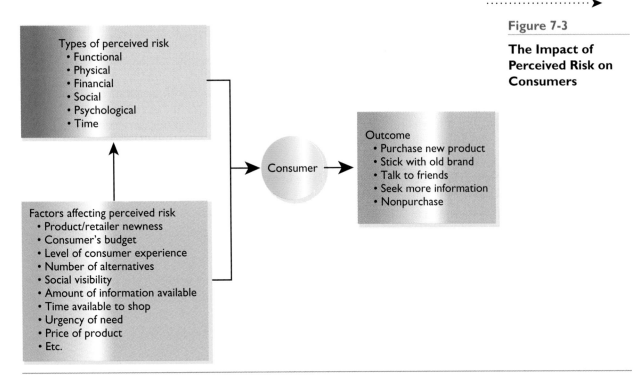

Figure 7-3

The Impact of Perceived Risk on Consumers

purchase?); social (What will peers think of my shopping with this retailer?); psychological (Am I doing the right thing?); and time (How much effort must I exert to make a purchase?).[5] Perceived risk will be highest if the retailer or the brands it carries are new, a person has a tight budget, a person has little experience, there are many alternatives from which to choose, a purchase is socially visible or complex, and so on. See Figure 7-3. Retailers must work to reduce perceived risk by providing ample information.

The importance of the purchase to the consumer affects the amount of time that person will spend in making a decision and the range of alternatives considered. If a purchase is viewed as important, perceived risk tends to be higher than if it is viewed as unimportant; and the retailer must act accordingly.

Relating Life-Style Concepts to the Choice of a Target Market ❑ A retailer could develop a life-style profile of its target market by analyzing these concepts:

■ Culture—What cultural values, norms, and customs are most important to the target market?

■ Social class—Are consumers lower, middle, or upper class? Are they socially mobile?

■ Reference groups—To whom do people look for purchasing advice? Does this differ by goods or service category? How can a firm target opinion leaders?

■ Social performance—Are people high or low performers? How is shopping affected by this?

■ Family (or household) life cycle—In what stage(s) of the cycle are the bulk of customers?

■ Time utilization—How do people spend time? How do they view the time spent shopping?

■ Personality—Do customers have identifiable personality traits?

[5]Leon G. Schiffman and Leslie Lazar Kanuk, *Consumer Behavior*, Sixth Edition (Upper Saddle River, New Jersey: Prentice Hall, 1997), pp. 183–185.

- Class consciousness—Are consumers status conscious? What does this signify for purchases?
- Attitudes—How does the target market feel about the retailer and its offerings in terms of specific strategy components?
- Perceived risk—Do customers feel risk in connection with the retailer? Which goods and services have the greatest perceived risk?
- Importance of the purchase—How important are the goods/services offered by the retailer to the target market?

Specific Retailing Implications of Consumer Demographics and Life-Styles

Retailers need to consider demographic and life-style factors from several perspectives. Following are some illustrations. By no means do the examples cover the full domain of retailing.

Gender Roles ❑ The increasing number of working women, who may put in an average of 60 to 70 hours (or more) each week between their job and home responsibilities, is altering life-styles significantly.

Compared to women who have not worked, working women tend to be more

- Self-confident and individualistic.
- Adept at handling their social environment.
- Concerned with the convenience and ease of performing household duties.
- Interested in sharing household and familial tasks with their husbands.
- Cosmopolitan in taste, and knowledgeable and demanding as consumers.
- Interested in leisure activities and travel.
- Concerned with improving themselves and their educational background.
- Appearance-conscious (concerned with the way they dress).
- Interested in maintaining a youthful posture.
- Interested in equal rights.
- Indifferent to small price differences among stores or merchandise.
- Uninterested in leisurely shopping trips.

Due to the trend toward more working women, the life-styles of American males are also changing. Large numbers of men now take care of children, shop for food, do laundry, wash dishes, cook for the family, vacuum the house, and clean the bathroom. Today, 30 percent of U.S. supermarket sales (in dollars) are accounted for by male shoppers.[6] See Figure 7-4.

The future will see still more changes in men's and women's roles (and in their conflicts over them). Furthermore, the authority and duties of husbands and wives will be shared with greater frequency than before. Retailers need to understand and adapt to this trend.

Consumer Sophistication and Confidence ❑ Consumer life-styles will reflect increased levels of education. For example, by the year 2000, more than one-half of all Americans 25 years of age and older will have completed at least one year of college; and over one-quarter will have four-year degrees. For younger adults, education levels will be even higher.

Thus, many U.S. consumers will be more knowledgeable and cosmopolitan; more aware of national and worldwide trends in tastes, styles, and goods and services; and

[6]See Susan Mitchell, *The Official Guide to American Attitudes* (Ithaca, New York: New Strategist Publications, 1996).

Figure 7-4

Blurring Gender Roles

Due to changing life-styles, more husbands and wives shop together.

more sophisticated. Furthermore, nonconforming behavior will be more widely accepted since increased education will lead to the self-assurance that shoppers require to reduce their need for conformity, while providing an appreciation of available choices. Confident shoppers depend less on brands and labels and are more willing to experiment, but more educated consumers also insist on detailed information about goods and services.

As a result, "Because today's consumers are well-educated and skeptical, they're also more apt to see through hollow claims. Consumers will exhibit a sharply stronger demand for quality in goods and services. One thing retailers have to do is go into their own stores as a mystery shopper. Does their store really provide customer service—does it make the shopping experience fun? As a shopper will you wait in line at the register for 3.5 minutes, or will you be forced to stand in the middle of the store and ask, 'Does anyone really want my money?' Retailers have got to ask themselves if they would shop at their own stores."[7]

Poverty of Time ❑ For some households, the increased number of working women, the desire for personal fulfillment, the longer distances between the locations of work and home, and the greater number of people working at second jobs contribute to a **poverty of time.** According to this concept, an interest in financial security may result in less rather than more free time since the alternatives competing for consumers' time rise considerably. Many customers are thus apt to place a high value on goods and services minimizing time expenditures.

There are various ways for retailers to respond to the poverty-of-time concept. They can

■ Describe, label, and identify goods and services more clearly in advertising and displays. Popular brands also facilitate customer shopping.

[7]Bill Kelley, "The New Consumer Revealed," *Sales & Marketing Management* (May 1993), p. 51; and Teresa Andreoli, "Pinpointing Shifting Shoppers," *Discount Store News* (April 3, 1995), p. 31.

■ Carry pre-packaged products, which can be selected by self-service.
■ Set up specialized departments by goods/service category within the store.
■ Maintain adequate inventory to avoid running out of stock.
■ Increase the number of branch stores to limit customer travel time.
■ Have longer hours of operation, including evening and weekend openings.
■ Add on-floor sales personnel.
■ Reduce checkout time.
■ Use mail-order and telephone selling.

Self-Fulfillment ❏ Of importance to retailers is the concept of **self-fulfillment,** whereby

> Consumer behavior is becoming more individualistic and less defined by reference to easily identified social groups. Americans are piecing together "component life-styles" for themselves, choosing goods and services that best express their growing sense of uniqueness. The consumer of the 90s is likely to head to a discount chain store to get the best price on socks and T-shirts, move to a deep-discount drugstore for shampoo and toothpaste, and then head to a supermarket to buy store-brand bread and cookies. But the last stop may be a small specialty shop where she [he] selects an expensive figurine of blown crystal to add to her [his] collection.[8]

These are some ways in which different consumers seek to fulfill themselves. They may

■ Emphasize physical health, fitness, and exercise.
■ Search for meaningful careers.
■ Emphasize or de-emphasize material possessions and status symbols.
■ Become more or less interested in romanticism.
■ Turn to or away from life-style simplicity.
■ Try for self-improvement.
■ Attain individuality ("Do your own thing").

Consumer interest in self-fulfillment will continue to expand in the future.

Shopper Profiles ❏ Considerable research has been aimed at describing overall consumer shopping profiles, as well as more specific ones.

One research study of heavy catalog consumers identified six major overall shopper profiles (market segments): loyalist shoppers, value shoppers, fashionable shoppers, diverse shoppers, recreational shoppers, and emotional shoppers. The profiles are highlighted in Figure 7-5.

A study comparing 18- to 29-year-old women with those aged 30 to 49 found that "women in their twenties are not yet loyal to one store, and instead go to whatever shopping outlet is best at the moment. In contrast, baby boom women ages 30 to 49 are more likely to say they've already set retail preferences and are more apt to visit the same store. The one exception to this trend is drugstores, where the majority of younger women have already formed strong bonds that go beyond mere convenience."[9]

After surveying 2,000 motorists, Mobil was able to divide them into five gasoline segments:

■ Road warriors—Generally higher-income, middle-aged men who drive 25,000 to 50,000 miles a year, buy premium with a credit card, purchase sandwiches and drinks from the convenience store, will sometimes wash their cars at the car wash. 16 percent of buyers.

[8]"31 Trends Shaping the Future of American Business," *The Public Pulse,* Vol. 2 (Number 1, 1988), p. 1; and Michael J. McDermott, "Retailing," *Adweek* (September 11, 1989), p. 124. See also Peter F. Drucker, "Retailing in a Post-Capitalist Society," *Stores* (August 1993), pp. RB1–RB4.
[9]"Quick Takes," *Promo* (October 1996), p. 6.

Decision Making Style | **Description/Size**

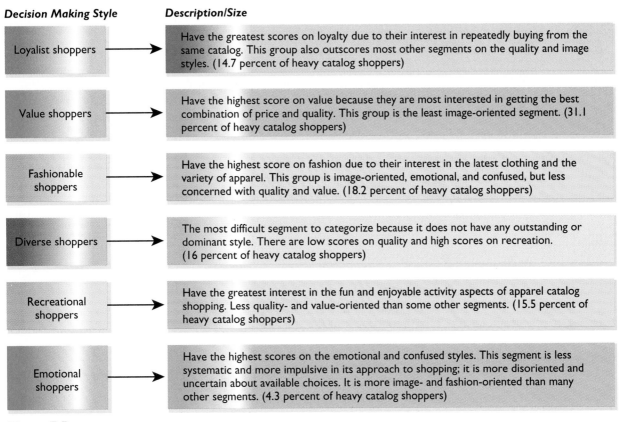

Figure 7-5

Decision-Making Styles for Heavy Catalog Shoppers of Apparel (611 Respondents)

Note: The percentages do not equal 100.0 due to small rounding errors.

Source: William J. McDonald, "The Roles of Demographics, Purchase Histories, and Shopper Decision-Making Styles in Predicting Consumer Catalog Loyalty," *Journal of Direct Marketing,* Vol. 7 (Summer 1993), pp. 55–65. Reprinted by permission of John Wiley & Sons.

■ True blues—Usually men and women with moderate to high incomes, who are loyal to a brand and sometimes to a particular station, frequently buy premium gasoline and pay in cash. 16 percent of buyers.

■ Generation F3 (for fuel, food, and fast)—Upwardly mobile men and women, half under 25 years of age (who are constantly on the go), drive a lot and snack heavily from the convenience store. 27 percent of buyers.

■ Homebodies—Usually housewives who shuttle their children around during the day and use whatever gasoline station is based in town or along their route of travel. 21 percent of buyers.

■ Price shoppers—Generally aren't loyal to either a brand or a particular station, and rarely buy the premium line, frequently on tight budgets, efforts to woo them have been the basis of marketing strategies for years. 20 percent of buyers.[10]

In-Home Shopping ❑ Over the years, about a dozen in-home shopping studies have uncovered some insightful results. The in-home shopper is not always a captive audience. Shopping is often discretionary, not necessary. Convenience in ordering one item, without traveling for it, is important. In-home shoppers are often also active store shoppers, and they are affluent and well-educated. Many in-home shoppers are self-confident, younger,

[10]Allana Sullivan, "Mobil Bets Drivers Pick Cappuccino Over Low Prices," *Wall Street Journal* (January 30, 1995), pp. B1, B8.

Distinguishing Between Trusting and Skeptical Consumers

In a study of ethical practices in retailing, consumers reacted to an 18-item scale on "customer-related situations." The respondents were asked how frequently they thought each situation or practice occurred in retail stores. Most of the situations or practices were unethical retailer tactics—such as "sales clerk gives incorrect change to a customer on purpose" and "retailer charges full price for a sale item without the customer's knowledge." A few were unethical consumer practices—such as "customer damages product while in the store, then wants a markdown" or "retailer takes a return from customers when the item should not be returned." Study participants were also asked to provide demographic data.

A statistical analysis of the data revealed two distinct groups of consumers. For each practice or situation, consumers in group one ("trusting consumers") felt retailers acted unethically less often than those in group two ("skeptical consumers") believed.

Trusting customers were more likely to be older, female, and married, and to have higher incomes (between $50,000 and $75,000) than skeptical consumers. The data further suggested that trusting consumers are more apt to be either high school graduates or college graduates and skeptical consumers are more apt to have either no high school degree or have completed some graduate study (a real dichotomy!).

Source: James L. Thomas, Faye S. McIntyre, and Faye W. Gilbert, "Retail Ethics: An Exploratory Examination of Consumer Perceptions" in Brian T. Engelland and Denise T. Smart (Editors), *1995 Southern Marketing Association Proceedings* (Evansville, Indiana: Southern Marketing Association, 1995), pp. 155–158.

and venturesome. They like in-store shopping but have low opinions of local shopping conditions. For some catalog shoppers, time is not an important shopping variable. In households with young children, in-home shopping is more likely if the female is employed part time or not at all than if she works full time.

To appeal to in-home shoppers, a retailer should remember the differences between in-home and store purchases. In-home shoppers often have a limited ability to comparison shop; may not be able to touch, feel, handle, or examine products firsthand; are concerned about customer service (such as returns); and may not have a salesperson from whom to acquire information.

Outshopping ❑ **Outshopping** (out-of-hometown shopping) is important for both local and surrounding retailers to study. The former want to minimize this behavior, whereas the latter want to maximize it. Research on outshopping has been conducted for more than 25 years.

Outshoppers are often male, young, members of a large family, and new to the community. Income and education vary by situation. Outshoppers differ in their lifestyles from those who patronize neighborhood or hometown stores. They enjoy fine foods, like to travel out-of-town, are active, like to change stores, and read out-of-town newspapers more than hometown shoppers. They also downplay hometown stores and compliment out-of-town stores. This is important information for suburban shopping centers.

Outshoppers have the same basic reasons for patronizing out-of-town shopping areas whether they reside in small or large communities. Among these reasons are easy access, liberal credit terms, store diversity, product assortments, prices, the presence of large chain outlets, entertainment facilities, customer services, and product quality.

Addressing Consumer Needs

While developing an in-depth profile of its target market, the retailer should also identify the most important consumer needs. These are just a few of the questions that could be considered:

- How far will customers travel to get to the retailer?
- How important is convenience?
- What store hours are desired? Are evening and weekend hours required?
- What level of customer services is preferred?
- How extensive a goods/service assortment is desired?
- What level of goods/service quality is preferred?
- How important is price?
- What retailer actions are necessary to reduce perceived risk?
- Do different market segments have special needs? If so, what are they?

When the retailer gears its strategy toward satisfying consumer needs, it is appealing to their **motives,** the reasons for their behavior. The better the firm addresses the most desired needs of its target market, the more motivated (likely to purchase) the customers will be.

For example, it is important for retailers to know that only about one-half of U.S. consumers enjoy shopping for clothes or for food and that the average time spent in a mall is down a lot from a decade ago; yet, more people like to shop if they feel they have the time. Almost twice as many women as men feel shopping is a great way to relax. Two-thirds of U.S. consumers like "watching for sale advertisements from their favorite stores and shopping for bargains." Yet, "value alone, while still important to today's consumer, is not enough. Rather, the '90s shopper is seeking out the right combination of quality, selection, price, and service. This shift is hitting many retailers hard and rewarding others."[11]

Here are two illustrations of how specific retailers are addressing the needs of various target markets:

- Middle class and blue collar—At Consolidated Stores' Odd Lots and Big Lots close-out stores, "Our customers are divided into two primary types. First come the customers who shop Consolidated because of economic need. With low or fixed incomes, they have to stretch every penny to the maximum, and at Big Lots they can stock up on staples and splurge on occasional luxuries at the lowest prices possible. We see these regular shoppers, week after week, stocking up on everything they need. A second group of customers includes those who can afford to shop at more expensive stores but see no reason to pay more for the same brand-name merchandise they can get at Consolidated's closeout prices. These treasure hunters shop us regularly without any specific item in mind, but with the idea of picking up whatever they can find that's a great bargain. They almost never leave without finding something that's priced too low to pass up."[12]
- African-American—"Discount department stores are the most popular retail outlets for virtually all Americans, including blacks. Yet blacks are a little less likely than their white counterparts to say they shop at stores like Wal-Mart and Kmart at least once a month. Seven in ten white Americans ages 16 and older say they go to a discount store at least once a month, compared with six in ten blacks. One possible reason for the difference is that many blacks patronize discounters' upscale competitors. Blacks are more likely than whites to say they shop at a department store and specialty stores once a month or more. The propensity of blacks to favor department and specialty stores isn't lost on retailers, including J.C. Penney, Sears, and Nordstrom. 'We recognize that our customers come from every community, and it is important that we serve all the communities where we do business,' says Paula Stanley, public affairs coordinator for Seattle-based Nordstrom. 'It's part of our corporate commitment to diversity.' That

[11]Laura Richardson, "Consumers in the 1990s: No Time or Money to Burn," *Chain Store Age* (August 1993), pp. 15A–17A; Barry Berman, "The Changing U.S. Consumer: Implications for Retailing Strategies," *Retail Strategist*, Vol. 1 (Number 1, 1991), pp. 17–18; "Shopping Still a 'Favorite' Pastime," *Promo* (February 1993), p. 52; "Retailing: Basic Analysis," *Standard & Poor's Industry Surveys* (May 9, 1996), pp. R79–R81; and Langer Associates, "Everyday People," *MarketingTools* (May 1996), pp. 27–30.
[12]*Consolidated Stores 1996 Annual Report.*

commitment includes increasing minority representation in employment and management, and doing business with women and minority vendors. 'Also, one-third of the models we use represent ethnic diversity, and we regularly advertise in minority-owned media and do community outreach programs,' Stanley says."[13]

UNDER-STANDING HOW CONSUMERS MAKE DECISIONS

In addition to identifying the characteristics of its target market, the retailer should have an understanding of how customers make decisions. This requires knowledge of **consumer behavior,** which involves the process by which people determine whether, what, when, where, how, from whom, and how often to purchase goods and services. Such behavior is influenced by a person's background and traits.

The retailer must really grasp the consumer's decision process from two different perspectives: (a) what good or service the consumer is thinking about buying and (b) where the consumer is going to make the purchase of that item (if the person opts to buy). The consumer can make these two decisions separately or jointly. If made jointly, the person relies on the retailer for support (information, assortments, knowledgeable sales personnel, and so on) over the entire decision process. If the decisions are made independently—what to buy versus where to buy—the person then gathers information and advice before entering a store and views the retailer more simply as a place of purchase (and probably more interchangeable with other firms).[14]

In choosing whether or not to purchase a particular item ("what"), the consumer considers such factors as features, durability, distinctiveness, value, ease of use, fashion, and so on. In choosing which retailer to patronize for that item ("where"), the consumer considers such factors as store location, assortments, credit arrangements, sales help, hours, customer service, and so on. Thus, the manufacturer and retailer have distinct challenges: The manufacturer wants the consumer to buy its brand ("what") at any location that carries it ("where"). The retailer wants the consumer to buy the product, not necessarily the manufacturer's brand ("what"), at its store or nonstore location.

Please keep this in mind as you review the stages in the consumer's decision process: As he or she moves through the process, that consumer determines *what* product to buy and *where* to buy it. The best retailers are those that assist the consumer at each stage in the process from stimulus (newspaper ads), problem awareness (stocking new models that are better than existing ones), information search (point-of-sale displays and good salespeople), evaluation of alternatives (clearly marked differences among products), purchase (acceptance of major credit cards), and post-purchase behavior (extended warranties and money-back returns). The greater the role a retailer assumes for itself in the consumer's decision process, the more loyal the consumer will become to that retailer, which is then viewed as indispensable.

The Consumer Decision Process

The **consumer decision process** consists of two parts: the process itself and the factors affecting the process. The decision process has six basic steps: stimulus, problem awareness, information search, evaluation of alternatives, purchase, and post-purchase behavior. Factors that affect the process are a consumer's demographics and life-style. The complete consumer decision process is shown in Figure 7-6.

Each time a person buys a good or service, he or she goes through a decision process. In some cases, all six steps in the process are utilized; in others, only a few of the steps are employed. For example, a consumer who has previously and satisfactorily bought lug-

---

[13]Christy Fisher, "Black, Hip, and Ready to Shop," *American Demographics* (September 1996), pp. 52–58; and Alice Z. Cuneo, "New Sears Label Woos Black Women," *Advertising Age* (May 5, 1997), p. 6.
[14]See Philip A. Titus and Peter B. Everett, "The Consumer Retail Search Process: A Conceptual Model and Research Agenda," *Journal of the Academy of Marketing Science,* Vol. 23 (Spring 1995), pp. 106–119.

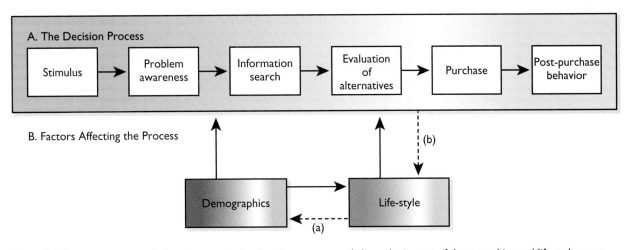

A. The Decision Process

Stimulus → Problem awareness → Information search → Evaluation of alternatives → Purchase → Post-purchase behavior

B. Factors Affecting the Process

Demographics → Life-style

(b)

(a)

Note: Solid arrows connect all the elements in the decision process and show the impact of demographics and life-style upon the process. Dashed arrows show feedback. (a) shows the impact of life-style on certain demographics, such as family size, location, and marital status. (b) shows the impact of a purchase on elements of life-style, such as social class, reference groups, and social performance.

Figure 7-6

The Consumer Decision Process

gage at a local store may not use the same extensive process as a person who has never bought luggage.

The decision process outlined in Figure 7-6 assumes the end result is the purchase of a good or service by the consumer. It is important to realize that at any point in the process, a potential customer may decide not to buy; the process then stops. The good or service may be unnecessary, unsatisfactory, or too expensive.

Before we consider the different ways in which the consumer uses the decision process, the entire process depicted in Figure 7-6 is explained.

Stimulus ❑ A **stimulus** is a cue (social or commercial) or a drive (physical) meant to motivate or arouse a person to act. When one talks with friends, fellow employees, professors, and so on, a social cue is received. Such cues may activate behavior. This is an example of a social cue: "Gee Ed, I hear the Tivoli Theater has a good movie. Let's go." It is a hint at arousing some action, which the person on the receiving end may ignore, treat as unimportant, or follow up on. The special attribute of a social cue is that it comes from an interpersonal, noncommercial source.

A second type of stimulus is a commercial cue. It is a message sponsored by a retailer, a manufacturer, a wholesaler, or some other seller. The objective of a commercial cue is to interest a consumer in a particular retailer, good, or service. Ads, sales pitches, and point-of-purchase displays are commercial stimuli. For example, "Our store is going out of business. If you are thinking about a winter coat, *now* is the time for a bargain." Although the intent of a commercial cue is to create excitement about a retailer, a good, or a service as the first step in the consumer decision process, such cues may not be regarded as highly as social ones by consumers because the messages are seller-controlled. A consumer may receive a cue differently when a friend, rather than a salesperson, makes a suggestion.

A third type of stimulus is a physical drive. It occurs when one or more of a person's physical senses are affected. Hunger, thirst, cold, heat, pain, or fear could cause a physical drive. A strong drive normally impels some type of action. However, if the stimulus is weak, it may be ignored. This is an example of a physical drive: "We've been driving for five hours, and I am really thirsty. We'd better stop for a soda before my mouth gets too dry." In the scenario, the person's physical senses are affected, and there is some desire to act to rectify the situation. However, the remaining steps in the decision process help determine whether a person will really act or just think about doing so.

A potential consumer may be exposed to any or all three stimuli for any good or service. If a person is aroused (motivated), he or she will go to the next step in the decision process. If a person is not sufficiently aroused, he or she will ignore the stimulus—thus terminating the decision process for the given good or service.

Problem Awareness ❑ At **problem awareness,** the consumer not only has been aroused by social, commercial, and/or physical stimuli, but also recognizes the good or service under consideration may solve a problem of shortage or unfulfilled desire. It may sometimes be difficult to learn why a consumer is motivated enough to move from the stimulus stage to problem awareness. This is especially so because many people shop at the same store or buy the same good or service for different reasons (convenience, price, image, quality, service, durability, and so on); people may not know their own motivation (it may be subconscious); and people may not tell a retailer their real reasons for shopping there or buying a certain item.

Recognition of shortage occurs when a consumer discovers a good or service may need to be repurchased. A good could wear down beyond repair (automobile, refrigerator, watch, clothing), or the consumer might run out of an item (milk, bread, tissues, hair spray). Service may be required when a good can be repaired (automobile, refrigerator, watch) or a service wears out (hair cutting, lawn mowing, car washing). In each case, the consumer would see a possible need to replenish a good or service. Here is an example of a stimulus interacting with problem awareness (recognition of shortage): "The sun is strong today. I'll need eye protection (*stimulus*), but my old sunglasses are broken (*recognition of shortage*)."

Recognition of unfulfilled desire takes place when a consumer becomes aware of a good or service that has not been purchased before—or a retailer that has not been patronized before. A good or service may improve the person's life-style, self-image, status, looks, and so on in a new, untried way (contact lenses, Caribbean vacation, diet center), or it may offer new, unheard-of performance characteristics (self-cleaning oven, pot-cleaning dishwasher, voice-activated computer). In this case, the person is aroused by an urge to improve himself or herself and considers the necessity of fulfilling these desires. This is an example of a stimulus interacting with problem awareness (recognition of unfulfilled desires): "Our friends eat at good restaurants and have fine meals at least once a week, but we eat at fast-food places (*stimulus*). Once in a while, I'd like to go into a restaurant, have a maitre d' show us to a table, drink a bottle of fine wine, and enjoy a delicious meal (*recognition of unfulfilled desire*)." Most consumers are more hesitant to react to unfulfilled desires than to shortages. There are greater risks, and benefits can be harder to determine. This is especially true if the consumer has had substantial satisfactory experience with the good or service to be replaced.

Whether a person becomes aware of a shortage or an unfulfilled desire, he or she will act only if it is seen as a problem worth solving. Otherwise, the decision process will end. A strong stimulus does not always mean the presence of a worthy problem. For instance: "The sun is strong today. I'll need eye protection. My old sunglasses are broken, but I can tape the frame together."

Information Search ❑ Once a person decides a shortage or unfulfilled desire is worth further consideration, information is sought. An **information search** has two parts: (1) determining the alternative goods or services that will solve the problem at hand (and where they can be bought) and (2) ascertaining the characteristics of each alternative.

First, the consumer compiles a list of various goods or services that address the problem encountered in the previous step of the decision process. This list does not have to be very formal nor even in written form. It can simply be a group of alternatives the consumer thinks about. The key is that the person enumerates potential solutions to the problem and perhaps thinks about where the items could be purchased. This aspect of information search may be internal or external.

A consumer with a lot of purchasing experience (in the specific area) will normally utilize an internal search of his or her memory to determine the goods or services (and retailers) that would be satisfactory for solving the current problem. A typical thought process of this type is: "It's raining (*stimulus*). My old raincoat is torn; I need a new one (*problem awareness*). The question is: Will I buy a London Fog, a Botany, or a Harbor Master raincoat? And what store should I go to: Macy's, The Limited, or Sears (*internal search for listing alternatives*)?"

A consumer with little purchasing experience will often use an external search to develop a list of goods or services and retailers that would solve the current problem. Thus, the consumer seeks information outside his or her memory. An external search can involve commercial sources (mass media, retail salespeople), noncommercial sources (*Consumer Reports*, government publications), and social sources (family, friends, colleagues). Here is an example of how an information source may be used in listing alternatives: Consumer: "It just cost me $400 for a new transmission. I am worried my car will cause me more problems (*stimulus*). Now is the time to look for a new car before this one breaks down again (*problem awareness*)." Car salesperson: "Here is a brochure that lists every new car model we carry. Why don't you look it over and then walk around the lot. I'll be right behind you, but stay out of your way for now (*commercial source for listing alternatives*)."

Second, the consumer gathers information relating to the characteristics of each alternative. Once the list of possible alternatives is known, the consumer must determine their attributes. This kind of information may be obtained internally (memory) or externally, in much the same manner as the list of alternatives is generated. An experienced consumer will search his or her memory for the attributes (pros and cons) of each good or service alternative. A consumer with little experience or a lot of uncertainty will search externally for information about each alternative under consideration. Commercial, noncommercial, and social sources are available for the collection of information about good or service attributes. For example, "My wife and I want to go to Europe for a vacation (*stimulus* and *problem recognition*). Your ad mentioned six different packages (*list of alternatives*). Please explain the details and costs of each one (*commercial source for characteristics of alternatives*)."

The extent to which a consumer searches for information depends, in part, on that person's perception of the risk attached to the purchase of a specific good or service. Risk varies among individuals and by situation. For some, it is inconsequential; for others, it is quite important.

The retailer's role in a consumer's search process is to provide enough information for him or her to feel comfortable in making decisions, thereby reducing the consumer's perceived risk. Point-of-purchase advertising, product displays, and knowledgeable sales personnel help provide consumers with the information they need to make decisions.

Once the consumer's search for information is completed, he or she must decide whether the current shortage or unfulfilled desire can be met by any of the alternatives. If one or more are satisfactory, the consumer moves to the next step in the decision process. However, the consumer will discontinue the process should no satisfactory goods or services be found. For example, when all big-screen televisions are perceived as too expensive or all diet centers are unappealing, the consumer will not continue the purchase process.

Evaluation of Alternatives ❏ At this point, the consumer has enough information to select one good or service alternative from the list of choices. Sometimes, this is quite easy—if one alternative is clearly superior to the others across all attributes. An alternative that is of excellent quality and has a low price will be the easy choice over more expensive, average-quality ones.

A choice is often not that simple, and the consumer must carefully engage in an **evaluation of alternatives** before making some decisions. If two or more options seem attractive, the person will determine which criteria (attributes) to evaluate and the relative importance of them. Then the alternatives will be ranked, and a choice will be made.

The criteria for a decision are those good or service attributes that the consumer considers to be relevant. These criteria may include price, quality, fit, color, durability, warranty, and so on. The consumer sets standards for these characteristics and evaluates each alternative according to its ability to meet the standards. The importance of each criterion is also determined by the consumer. And the attributes of a good or service are usually of different importance to each person. Thus, for some people, the initial price may be more important than the operating costs (as measured by electrical consumption) of a new air conditioner. In selecting an air conditioner brand, this type of consumer will choose a less expensive product that consumes a lot of energy over a more expensive, more efficient product.

Next, the consumer ranks the alternatives under consideration (from most favorite to least favorite) and selects one from among the list. This illustration shows the entire process of evaluating alternatives: "Judy and Larry talked about visiting California for quite a while. This year they finally decided they would leave Vermont for the first time and go to California. They talked with friends, read magazines and newspapers, and consulted a travel agent. They zeroed in on three alternatives: a 14-day bus trip, a 17-day car trip, and a 10-day plane trip. Judy and Larry agreed their choice of a trip would depend on cost, time available for sightseeing, and the quality of sightseeing. Cost was important, but the time available for sightseeing and the sightseeing itself were more important. The bus trip was the cheapest; the plane trip was the most expensive. The car trip left the least time for sightseeing; the plane trip provided the most. The car trip offered the best-quality sightseeing because it was so flexible; the bus trip provided the worst because it included a fixed itinerary. Judy and Larry decided that, on the basis of their criteria and the order of these criteria, the plane trip was the best available alternative. The bus trip was the worst."

For some goods or services, it is especially hard for consumers to evaluate the characteristics of the available alternatives because the items are technical, intangible, new, or poorly labeled. When this occurs, consumers often use price, brand name, or store name as an indicator of quality, and choose an alternative based on this criterion.

Once a consumer examines the attributes of alternatives and ranks them, he or she chooses the good or service that is most satisfactory. In situations where no alternative proves adequate, a decision not to purchase is made.

Purchase ❏ Following the choice of the best alternative, the consumer is ready for the **purchase act**—an exchange of money or a promise to pay for the ownership or use of a good or service. Important decisions are still made during this step in the process. From a retailing perspective, the purchase act can be the most crucial aspect of the decision process because the consumer is mainly concerned with three factors: place of purchase, terms, and availability. See Figure 7-7.

The consumer must determine where to buy the good or service. The place of purchase may be a store or a nonstore location. Many more items are bought at store locations (such as department, drug, and furniture stores) than at nonstore locations (such as home, work, and school). The place of purchase is evaluated in the same manner as the good or the service itself: alternative places of purchase are listed; their characteristics are defined; and they are ranked. The most desirable place of purchase is then chosen.

Criteria for selecting a store-based retailer include such factors as store location, store layout, customer service, sales help, store image, and level of prices. Criteria for selecting a nonstore retailer include such factors as image, customer service, level of prices, hours, interactivity, and convenience. A consumer will shop with the store or nonstore retailer that offers the best combination of criteria, as defined by that consumer.

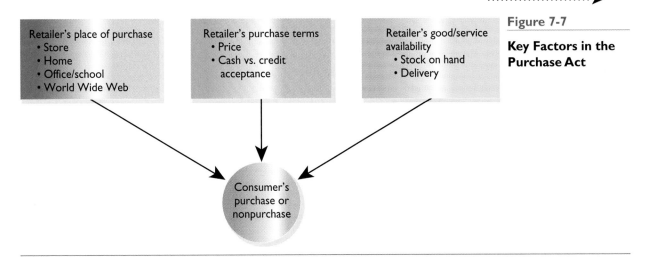

Figure 7-7

Key Factors in the Purchase Act

The consumer is also interested in purchase terms and the availability of the good or service. Purchase terms include the price and method of payment. Price is the dollar amount a person must pay to achieve ownership or use of a good or service. Method of payment is the way the price may be paid (cash, short-term credit, long-term credit). Availability relates to stock-on-hand and delivery. Stock-on-hand is the amount of an item that a place of purchase has in inventory. Delivery is the time span between the order and the receipt of an item and the ease with which an item is transported to its place of use.

If the consumer is pleased with these three components of the purchase act, the good or service will be bought. If there is dissatisfaction with the place of purchase, the terms of purchase, or availability, the consumer may not buy the good or service, although there is contentment with the item itself. Here are examples of each situation:

Jenny wanted to buy a sofa to complete her living-room set. She already had two chairs and a coffee table, but until now, Jenny could not afford a new sofa. She knew exactly what she wanted, a SuperSofa convertible (Model 155). The questions were where to buy the sofa, how to pay for it, how soon it could be delivered, and how it would be delivered. Jenny selected the Living Room Store from among four possible stores and bought the sofa. She never considered buying by telephone or mail because she didn't trust nonpersonal shopping. The Living Room Store provided Jenny with what she wanted. She received good service at a convenient location and a special discount was given for paying cash. Because the sofa was in stock, it was delivered within one week. Delivery was included in the sofa's price.

Ken wanted to buy a stereo system. He knew which system to get and had saved $100 for a down payment. But, after a month of trying to buy the stereo, Ken gave up in disgust. He explained why: "The system I wanted was sold in only three stores in my area and through an online retailer. Two of the stores overpriced the stereo by about $75. The third store had a really good price, $599, but the owner insisted that I pay in cash. In addition, I would have had to drive to their warehouse, twenty miles away, and pick up the system myself. The Web-based company had a really good deal—low price, credit, and delivery. But they ran out of the model I was interested in and told me the wait would be four months. After I heard that, I just gave up. My portable CD player will have to suffice."

Post-Purchase Behavior ❑ After buying a good or service, a consumer may engage in **post-purchase behavior.** Such behavior falls into either of two categories: further purchases or re-evaluation. In some situations, buying one good or service leads to further purchases. For instance, the purchase of an automobile leads to buying insurance. The purchase of a new suit may be accompanied by the purchase of a new shirt and tie. Buying a stereo system will require tapes or CDs to play on it. Therefore, these purchases provide the impetus for others, and consumer decisions continue until the last purchase is made. Just as in the decision process for the original item, the characteristics of the supplementary items are noted and the alternatives ranked. A retailer that utilizes scrambled merchandising by stocking unrelated items may also stimulate a shopper to make further purchases, once the primary good or service is bought.

A warning: Retailers should carefully evaluate their expansion of product lines (related or nonrelated). The skills necessary to obtain a supplemental customer purchase may not be similar to those required for the major good or service category. For example, real-estate transactions and property insurance sales involve different skills; TV sales and service contracts require different retailer activities; and muffler repairs and auto painting are quite dissimilar.

The consumer may also re-evaluate the purchase of a good or service. Does it perform as promised? Do its actual attributes match the expectations the consumer had of these attributes? Has the retailer done as expected? Satisfaction may lead to customer contentment, a repurchase when the good or service wears out, and favorable conversations with friends interested in the same item. Dissatisfaction may lead to unhappiness, brand or store switching when the good or service wears out, and unfavorable conversations with friends interested in the same item.

The latter situation (dissatisfaction) may result from **cognitive dissonance,** that is, doubt that the correct decision has been made. The consumer may regret that the purchase was made at all or may wish that another alternative from the list had been chosen. To overcome cognitive dissonance and dissatisfaction, the retailer must realize that the consumer decision process does not end with a purchase. Customer after-care (by a phone call, a service visit, or an ad) may be as important as anything the retailer can do to complete the sale. When items are expensive or important to a consumer, after-care takes on added significance because the person really wants to be right. In addition, the more alternatives from which to choose, the greater the doubt after a decision is made and the more the importance of after-care.

Many retailers know that consumers often have doubts and second thoughts about recent purchases. Decades ago, department stores pioneered the concept of a money-back guarantee, so customers could return merchandise if doubts or second thoughts became too great.

Realistic sales presentations and advertising campaigns can also minimize dissatisfaction because consumer expectations do not then exceed reality. If overly high expectations are created, a consumer is more apt to become unhappy because a good or service does not perform at the level promised. The coupling of an honest sales presentation with good after-care of the consumer should reduce or eliminate cognitive dissonance and dissatisfaction.

Types of Consumer Decision Making

As noted earlier, every time a consumer purchases a good or service or visits a retailer, he or she uses a form of the decision process described in the preceding subsections. Often, the process is used subconsciously, and a person is not even aware of its use. Also, as indicated in Figure 7-6, the decision process is affected by the characteristics of the consumer.

For example, older consumers may not spend as much time as younger ones in making purchase decisions because of their experience. Well-educated consumers may search out many information sources before making a decision. Upper-income consumers may spend little time making a decision because they can afford to buy again if a purchase is unsatisfactory. In a family with children, each member may have an input into a decision, thereby lengthening the process. Class-conscious consumers may be more interested in social sources than in commercial or noncommercial ones. Consumers with low self-esteem or high perceived risk may use all of the steps in the decision process in detail. People who are under time pressure may skip steps in the process to save time.

The decision process is used differently in dissimilar situations. One situation (such as the purchase of a new home) may require the thorough use of each step in the process; perceived risk will probably be high regardless of the consumer's background. Another situation (such as the purchase of a magazine) may enable the consumer to skip certain steps in the process; perceived risk will probably be low regardless of the person's background.

There are three types of decision processes: extended decision making, limited decision making, and routine decision making. They are explained next.

Extended Decision Making ❑ **Extended decision making** occurs when a consumer makes full use of the decision process shown in Figure 7-6. A considerable amount of time is spent gathering information and evaluating alternatives (both "what" to buy and "where" to buy it) before a purchase is made. After a purchase is completed, the potential for cognitive dissonance is great. In this category are expensive, complex goods and services with which the consumer has had little or no experience. Perceived risk of all kinds is high. Examples of items requiring extended decision making are a house, a first car, and a life insurance policy.

At any point in the purchase process, a consumer can stop, and for expensive, complex items, this occurs quite often. Consumer characteristics (such as age, education, income, marital status, time utilization, and class consciousness) have their greatest impact with extended decision making.

Because their customers tend to use extended decision making, retailers like real-estate brokers and auto dealers should emphasize personal selling, printed materials, and other methods of communication to provide as much information as possible. A low-key approach should be enacted, so shoppers feel comfortable and not threatened. In this way, the consumer's perceived risk can be minimized.

Limited Decision Making ❑ **Limited decision making** occurs when a consumer uses each of the steps in the purchase process but does not need to spend a great deal of time on each of them. This type of decision making requires less time than extended decision making because the consumer typically has some experience (with both the "what" and "where" of the product). In this category are items the person has purchased before, but not regularly. Risk is moderate and the consumer will spend some time shopping. The thoroughness with which the decision process is used depends mostly on the person's prior experience. Priority would probably be placed on evaluating known alternatives according to the person's desires and standards, although information search is also important for some. Examples of goods and services requiring limited decision making are a second car, clothing, a vacation, and gifts.

Consumer characteristics have an impact on decision making, but the effect lessens as perceived risk falls and experience rises. Income, the importance of the purchase, and motives play very strong roles in the uses of limited decision making.

This form of consumer decision making is most relevant to retailers like department and specialty stores that cater to in-store shopping behavior and carry goods and services that people have bought before. The interior environment and assortment of the store are very important. Sales personnel should be available for questions and to differentiate among brands or models.

Routine Decision Making ❑ **Routine decision making** takes place when the consumer buys out of habit and skips steps in the purchase process. The person wants to spend little or no time shopping, and the same brands are usually repurchased (often at

Relationship Retailing: The Value of Knowing the Customer

By compiling and using customer data bases, retailers can provide a level of personalized service to consumers that was unthinkable just a few years ago. This kind of service is often called one-to-one relationship retailing. And it means giving individual attention to each customer, as well as significantly improving the productivity of shoppers' time.

For example, because of the vast information in its data base, Silverman's (a three-store men's apparel chain in North and South Dakota), can ascertain a customer's size, the amount he has spent in the store to date, the number of times he purchased something in the store, and his clothing style and brand preferences. As a result, even a new salesperson can easily learn about a customer's preferences—virtually the

moment the customer arrives in the store. The data base has also been used to better target Silverman's direct-mail promotions.

The customer profiles in Silverman's data base are also ideal in helping friends or spouses with gift suggestions that are sure to please. The gift giver, knowing the recipient shops at Silverman's, is able to discover his size and brand, style, and color preferences.

Silverman's reports that its customers have responded well to the personalized attention that its data base lets it provide. Furthermore, since Silverman's started using relationship retailing, the average sale at its three stores has increased by 80 percent!

Source: Stephen M. Silverman, "Retail Retold," *Inc. Technology* (Summer 1995), pp. 23–25.

---

the same stores). In this category are items that are purchased regularly. These goods and services have little risk for the consumer because of experience. The key step for this type of decision making is problem awareness. When the consumer realizes that a good or service is needed, a repurchase is often automatic. Information search, evaluation of alternatives, and post-purchase behavior are less likely than in limited or extended decision making. These steps are not undertaken as long as a person is satisfied. Examples of goods and services often requiring routine decision making are weekly groceries, newspapers, and haircuts.

Consumer characteristics have little impact on purchases in routine decision making. Problem awareness almost inevitably leads to a purchase.

This type of decision making is most relevant to retailers like supermarkets, dry cleaners, and fast-food outlets. For them, these strategic elements are crucial: a good location, long hours, clear in-store displays, and, most important, product availability. Ads should be reminder-oriented. The major task for store personnel would be completing the transaction quickly and precisely.

Specific Retailing Implications of the Consumer's Decision Process

Both the individual components of the consumer decision process and the level of decision making have been applied in many different retail settings. Here are several illustrations.

Problem Awareness ❏ A survey of teens who patronize shopping centers found that 44 percent go to the centers for shopping with no specific products in mind and 38 percent go to be with friends. According to another study, adult men are significantly more likely than women to know exactly what they're going to buy when they go on a shopping trip.[15]

[15]"The Survey Says: Teenagers Want to Shop 'Til They Drop'," *Chain Store Age* (November 1994), p. 96; and "Shopping Still a 'Favorite' Pastime," *Promo* (February 1993), p. 52.

Information Search ❏ When seeking information, many consumers like to get word-of-mouth communication from their peers: 49 percent seek the advice of others in selecting a car mechanic, 47 percent look to others for information on doctors, 38 percent talk to others about where to eat out, 28 percent ask others what movie to see, 22 percent ask advice on what car to buy, and 20 percent ask others where to get a personal loan.[16]

Among women apparel shoppers, these are the top five information sources (in rank order):

- Going shopping in the store.
- Looking through catalogs.
- Observing what other women wear.
- Sales promotions/flyers.
- Newspaper fashion advertising.[17]

Evaluation of Alternatives ❏ An important aspect in the consumer's evaluation of alternatives is the criteria set by that person. For example, research on women apparel shoppers determined that they rate these store attributes as most important in comparing outlets (in the order of importance): best value for money, good sales/markdowns, largest assortment, easiest one to get to, and highest-quality fashions. Likewise, supermarket shoppers rate cleanliness, low prices, all prices clearly labeled, accurate and pleasant clerks, and freshness dates marked on products as keys. Older shoppers are more interested in a good meat department and helpful managers. Younger shoppers are more attracted by one-stop shopping, a good deli, hot take-out foods, and long hours.[18]

Surveys of parents and their children have found that children have great impact in choosing the clothing, breakfast cereal, toys, ice cream and soft drinks, and videos to be purchased. They have little impact on the choice of a PC or a car.

Purchase Behavior ❏ Consumer purchase behavior has been researched from various perspectives. Surveys show that consumer enthusiasm for shopping has fallen in recent years. Far more people say they spend less time shopping today than in 1990, and they visit fewer stores on each shopping trip.

Overall surveys of supermarket shoppers show Thursday, Friday, and Saturday are the most popular days for the major store visit (yielding 51 percent of those trips). However, among people working full time, two-thirds of their major shopping trips are on Friday, Saturday, or Sunday. On average, during a typical week, 42 percent of all supermarket shoppers visit stores in the morning, 33 percent in the afternoon, 22 percent in the evening, and 3 percent in late evening.[19]

In-store behavior is affected by merchandise stockouts. According to one study, if the brand they wanted was not on a store shelf, 42 percent would buy another brand, 28 percent would buy nothing and leave, and 30 percent would switch stores to buy the desired brand.[20]

Many consumers are "channel surfers," who patronize different retail formats over the year. For example, A.C. Nielsen data show that while virtually all U.S. households visit a supermarket during a year, 93 percent visit drugstores, 88 percent department stores, 51 percent convenience stores, 37 percent toy stores, 29 percent pet stores, and 8 percent delicatessens.[21]

Figure 7-8 shows how retailers can affect shoppers' in-store behavior.

---

[16]Chip Walker, "Word of Mouth," *American Demographics* (July 1995), pp. 38–44.
[17]"Chicago Apparel Study," *Chain Store Age* (October 1996), Section Three, p. 23B.
[18]Ibid., p. 11B; and "63rd Annual Report of the Grocery Industry 1996," *Progressive Grocer* (April 1996), p. 43.
[19]"63rd Annual Report of the Grocery Industry 1996," p. 44.
[20]Meyers Research, "Convenience vs. Loyalty," *Promo* (February 1996), p. 28.
[21]"Channel Surfers," *Progressive Grocer* (June 1996), pp. 37–42.

Figure 7-8

Influencing Purchase Behavior

Retailers can have a great impact on people's purchase behavior, their mood while in the store, the length of the shopping trip, the extent of impulse purchases, and other factors. Well-planned store interiors can facilitate shopping and generate a sense of excitement. Shown here are the customer-friendly layouts of a food store (upper left), a full-line discount store (upper right), and an off-price store (lower left).

Consumer Satisfaction/Dissatisfaction ❏ Retailers are quite attentive to the causes of consumer satisfaction and dissatisfaction because they want to optimize their strategies. A study of mall shoppers discovered that people are most satisfied with the variety of merchandise, friendly employees, good sales prices, and quality merchandise. They are least satisfied with the convenience of the location, ease of parking, and the excitement of the shopping experience.[22]

A study of consumer dissatisfaction (involving grocery shopping, auto repair, medical care, and banking services) was able to segment people into four major groups. Passives are unlikely to state complaints to retailers or to take any other actions if unhappy. Voicers are most apt to complain to the retailer if dissatisfied; they do not usually complain to friends or outside parties, nor do they switch patronage. Irates are quite likely to complain to friends and switch patronage; they are not apt to contact parties such as the Better Business Bureau. Activists are quite likely to complain to friends, switch patronage, and contact parties such as the Better Business Bureau, the local newspaper, and others.[23]

In doing customer satisfaction research, "One of the major faults that companies have is that they only focus on what's important to them. There's only a 40 percent overlap between what management says is important to customers and what customers say is important."[24]

Level of Consumer Decision Making ❏ Three of the concepts relevant to retailers that have been investigated with regard to the level of consumer decision making are shopping and travel time, impulse purchases, and store loyalty.

When a consumer uses extended or limited decision making, he or she is more apt to spend time shopping and traveling to a retailer than if routine decision making is involved. However, the type of decision making used depends on the consumer segment. Some people simply like to shop more than others. The former might say that "This shopping trip was truly a joy for me," while the latter might say, "This was a good store visit because it was over very quickly."[25]

A study of U.S. adults ages 45 and older was able to divide shoppers into three main groups:

- Routine managers (51 percent) specialize in time management by a daily routine of activities. This means more efficient organization and a moderate sense of purpose. They spend 3.1 hours per week shopping, with 0.3 search, 2.6 purchase, and 0.2 post-purchase hours.
- Aimless wanderers (37 percent) have the lowest overall time perceptions score profile. They have the lowest scores on a sense of purpose, are the least organized and routine-oriented, and appear less efficient at organizing time during daily activities. They spend the most time shopping at 8.2 hours per week, with the majority in search at 4.1 hours and the remainder in purchase and post-purchase, 3.3 and 0.8 hours, respectively.
- Purposeful organizers (12 percent) have a strong sense of purpose in their daily lives. They are also effective organizers who accomplish goals and complete tasks and are routine-oriented. This group reports spending the least amount of time shopping, 2.5 hours per week, including 0.1 search, 2.3 purchase, and 0.1 post-purchase hours.[26]

[22]Stanley D. Sibley and Soo Young Moon, "Testing Satisfaction Models with the Mall Shopper" in Paul C. Thistlethwaite, Rolf Hackmann, and Charles Pettijohn (Editors), *Midwest Marketing Association 1993 Proceedings* (Macomb, Ill.: Western Illinois University, 1993), pp. 157–163.

[23]Jagdip Singh, "A Typology of Consumer Dissatisfaction Response Styles," *Journal of Retailing,* Vol. 66 (Spring 1990), pp. 57–99.

[24]Shelly Reese, "Happiness Isn't Everything," *Marketing Tools* (May 1996), pp. 52–58.

[25]Barry J. Babin, William R. Darden, and Mitch Griffin, "Work and/or Fun: Measuring Hedonic and Utilitarian Shopping Value," *Journal of Consumer Research,* Vol. 20 (March 1994), p. 649.

[26]William J. McDonald, "Time Use in Shopping: The Role of Personal Characteristics," *Journal of Retailing,* Vol. 70 (Winter 1994), pp. 358–359.

Generally, as noted earlier, retailers must emphasize a unique product selection, good salespeople, competitive prices, a pleasant shopping atmosphere, and goods/service guarantees to encourage consumers to spend more time with them and to travel a greater distance to shop. Consumers are apt to patronize nearby stores unless there are compelling reasons to do otherwise. **Geographic mapping** is a good technique for a retailer to use in evaluating the trading area of a store. With it, a firm learns the distances people are likely to travel to get to a store, the population density of the geographic area surrounding the store, and the travel patterns and times from various sites. A map is then drawn showing these factors. This is covered more in Chapter 9.

Impulse purchases occur when consumers purchase products and/or brands they had not planned on buying before entering a store, reading a mail-order catalog, seeing a TV shopping show, tuning to the WWW, and so on. With impulse purchases, at least part of consumer decision making is influenced by the retailer. There are three kinds of impulse shopping:

■ Completely unplanned—A consumer has no intention of making a purchase in a goods or service category before he or she comes into contact with a retailer.
■ Partially unplanned—A consumer intends to make a purchase in a goods or service category but has not chosen a brand before he or she comes into contact with a retailer.
■ Unplanned substitution—A consumer intends to buy a specific brand of a good or service but changes his or her mind about the brand after coming into contact with a retailer.

With partially unplanned and substitution kinds of impulse purchases, some decision making takes place before a person interacts with a retailer. In these cases, the consumer may be involved with any type of process (extended, limited, or routine). Completely unplanned shopping is usually related to routine decision making or limited decision making, there is little or no time spent shopping, and the key step is problem awareness. Impulse purchases are more susceptible to in-store displays than pre-planned purchases.

According to a recent supermarket study, on a given shopping trip, about 70 percent of brand purchases are unplanned and the average shopper spends 12 percent more than planned. The comparable numbers are 74 percent and 5 percent for mass merchants.[27]

When **store loyalty** exists, a consumer regularly patronizes a particular retailer (store or nonstore) that he or she knows, likes, and trusts. Such loyalty lets a person reduce decision making because he or she does not have to invest time in learning about and choosing the retailer from which to make purchases. Over the years, research has addressed various aspects of store loyalty: Store-loyal consumers tend to be time-conscious, use the entertainment media, enjoy shopping locally, be fashion leaders, not rely on credit, and not be engaged in outshopping. In a service setting, such as an auto repair shop, customer satisfaction with service quality often leads to store loyalty; price has little bearing on decisions.

In today's competitive marketplace, it is a real challenge for a retailer to gain store loyalty, and the greatest asset any firm can have. Applying all facets of the retail concept certainly enhance a firm's chances of gaining and keeping loyal customers: customer orientation, coordinated effort, value-driven, and goal orientation. Practicing relationship retailing helps also!

---

[27]"POPAI's 1995 Study: 'More Purchase Decisions Made in Store,' " *Promo* (October 1995), p. 15. See also Dennis W. Rook and Robert J. Fisher, "Normative Influences on Impulsive Buying Behavior," *Journal of Consumer Research*, Vol. 22 (December 1995), pp. 305–313.

Summary

1. *To discuss why it is important for a retailer to properly select, identify, and understand its target market* To properly develop and apply a strategy, a retailer must determine which type of target market to reach, identify the characteristics and needs of the specific chosen target market, and understand how consumers make decisions.

2. *To enumerate and describe a number of consumer demographic and life-style factors, and explain how these concepts can be applied to retailing* Consumer characteristics and needs can be identified by studying demographic and life-style factors. Demographics are easily identifiable and measurable population statistics; life-styles are the ways in which consumers live and spend time and money.

People can be described in terms of these demographic factors: population size, household size, marital and family status, income, retail sales, age, birthrates, mobility, place of residence, gender, employment status, occupation, education level, and ethnic/racial background. Based on these factors, this chapter presents a demographic overview of the United States and relates demographics to a retailer's identification of a target market.

Consumer life-styles are comprised of social and psychological elements and are greatly affected by demographics. Social factors include culture, social class, reference groups, social performance, the family life cycle, and time utilization. Psychological factors include personality, class consciousness, attitudes, perceived risk, and the importance of a purchase. As with demographics, a retailer can generate a life-style profile of its target market by analyzing these concepts.

When a retailer gears its strategy toward satisfying consumer needs, that firm is appealing to their motives—the reasons for behavior. The better a company addresses the needs of its customers, the more likely they are to make purchases.

3. *To examine the consumer decision process and its stages* Retailers require a knowledge of consumer behavior—the process whereby individuals decide whether, what, when, where, how, from whom, and how often to purchase goods and services. In particular, the retailer must grasp the consumer's decision process from two different perspectives: (a) what good or service the consumer is thinking about buying and (b) where the consumer is going to make the

purchase of that item. The consumer can make these two decisions separately or jointly. If made jointly, the person relies on the retailer for support over the entire decision process. If the decisions are made independently—what to buy versus where to buy—the person gathers information and advice before entering a store and views the retailer more as a place of purchase (and probably more interchangeable with other firms).

The consumer decision process has six basic steps: stimulus, problem awareness, information search, evaluation of alternatives, purchase, and post-purchase behavior. The process is influenced by a person's background and traits.

A stimulus may be a social or commercial cue or a physical drive meant to motivate a person to act. At problem awareness, the consumer not only has been aroused by a stimulus, but further recognizes that the good or service under consideration may solve a problem of shortage or unfulfilled desire. Next, an information search determines the available alternatives and the characteristics of each. The alternatives are then evaluated and ranked. In the purchase act, a consumer considers the place of purchase, terms, and availability. After a purchase is made, there may be post-purchase behavior in the form of additional purchases or re-evaluation. The consumer may have cognitive dissonance if there is doubt that a correct choice has been made.

4. *To differentiate among different types of consumer decision making* Every time a consumer makes a purchase, he or she uses a form of the decision process. However, the process may be used subconsciously, and it is affected by consumer characteristics. Extended decision making occurs if a person makes full use of the six steps in the decision process. In limited decision making, each step is used, but not in great depth. Routine decision making takes place when a person buys out of habit and skips steps in the purchase process.

5. *To present several retail applications regarding consumer characteristics and behavior* Retail applications provide insights into various aspects of consumer demographics, life-styles, and decision making, such as gender roles, consumer sophistication and confidence, poverty of time, self-fulfillment, shopper profiles, in-home shopping, outshopping information search, impulse purchases, and store loyalty.

Key Terms

target market (p. 201)
demographics (p. 202)
life-styles (p. 202)
discretionary income (p. 203)
culture (p. 206)
social class (p. 206)
reference groups (p. 206)
family life cycle (p. 207)
household life cycle (p. 207)
personality (p. 208)
class consciousness (p. 208)

attitudes (opinions) (p. 208)
perceived risk (p. 208)
poverty of time (p. 211)
self-fulfillment (p. 212)
outshopping (p. 214)
motives (p. 215)
consumer behavior (p. 216)
consumer decision process (p. 216)
stimulus (p. 217)
problem awareness (p. 218)
information search (p. 218)

evaluation of alternatives (p. 220)
purchase act (p. 220)
post-purchase behavior (p. 221)
cognitive dissonance (p. 222)
extended decision making (p. 223)
limited decision making (p. 223)
routine decision making (p. 223)
geographic mapping (p. 228)
impulse purchases (p. 228)
store loyalty (p. 228)

Questions for Discussion

1. Comment on this statement: "Retailers have long depended on their ability to size up people as they walk in the door. Today, you need a more systematic way to understand customers."

2. Contrast the mass-market approach used by a supermarket with the concentrated marketing approach used by a bakery featuring expensive pastries and breads. Could a retailer combine these two approaches? If so, how?

3. How can a national fast-food chain use the demographic data presented in the chapter?

4. Develop demographic profiles for two different market segments to which a hardware store could appeal.

5. Contrast the family life cycle concept with the household life cycle concept. What is the value of each?

6. Explain how a retailer selling do-it-yourself furniture (with pre-cut wood) could reduce the six types of perceived risk.

7. Distinguish between in-home shopping and outshopping. In each case, what should be the strategic emphasis of retailers?

8. What two different perspectives should a retailer have in studying the consumer decision process? Why is this useful?

9. Describe how the consumer decision process would operate for these goods and services. Include "what" and "where" in your answers: a new PC, concert tickets, and a used car.

10. For each item cited in Question 9, which elements of the decision process are most important to retailers? Develop appropriate strategies.

11. What criteria could a consumer use in deciding which bank to patronize? How would these criteria differ by market segment?

12. Why should a real-estate broker care whether clients have cognitive dissonance? The seller moves after a transaction and the buyer will not be in the market for another house again until a great many years have elapsed.

13. Differentiate among the three types of impulse purchases. Give an example of each.

14. How does store loyalty benefit both the retailer and the consumer?

Web-Based Exercise:

MICROVISION BY EQUIFAX (http://www.ends.com/low/lifequiz.html)

Questions

1. Print out the MicroVision life-style segments for two zip codes (one for your home zip code and one for a zip code near your college or university).

2. Describe the differences in life-style between the two areas.

3. Using the MicroVision data, develop a retail strategy for (a) a restaurant with branches in each zip code and (b) an appliance retailer with branches in each zip code.

4. How would you assess the accuracy of the MicroVision segments?

Clay Dickinson is the owner of Green and Growing Nursery, a retail garden center located in Collegevale, a midwestern city of 200,000. Three years ago, Dickinson moved to Collegevale to purchase the garden center from its retiring owner. When he bought the nursery, it had an adequate supply of annuals, perennials, shrubs, and seeds, as well as a good assortment of houseplants. Although Dickinson had many good ideas to revitalize the center's overall appearance and improve its product mix, he got so busy running the store that many of these plans have not been implemented.

Now, Clay Dickinson is faced with increased competition from other nursery stores, in addition to several specialty and discount retailers. According to a retail analyst familiar with the Green and Growing Nursery, "if only the firm's profits were as green as its plants!"

Collegevale has three other nursery retailers: Cameron's, A Daisy A Day, and Fisk's. Each has a different overall retail strategy. Cameron's is a three-store chain that focuses on quality products, has a well-trained staff, and offers a broad assortment of merchandise, including the largest tree nursery in the region. Cameron's is well-regarded in the community, but has a reputation for charging somewhat higher prices. A Daisy A Day, part of a national chain, has two outlets in Collegevale. Unlike Cameron's, A Daisy A Day focuses its offerings on popular plants and products, and sells them at low prices. Lastly, while Fisk's specializes in supplying horticultural products to professional landscapers, it also sells nursery products to final consumers. As a consequence of its target market strategy, Fisk's is located in an out-of-the-way site, is open at times and days to accommodate its professional customers (for example, it is closed on Sunday), and rarely advertises in mass media.

Besides these garden centers, several specialty and discount retailers (including a local hardware store, a Kmart, and a Wal-Mart) sell plants and gardening supplies (such as vegetable seedlings and fertilizer) on a seasonal basis. Though Clay Dickinson is confident that his merchandise and services are of better quality, Kmart and Wal-Mart offer lower prices, one-stop shopping, and the convenience of being open seven days per week.

A recent report sponsored by the American Association of Nurserymen's Horticultural Research Institute (HRI), on consumer perceptions of garden centers, has given Dickinson a lot to think about. The HRI report indicates that people visit nurseries an average of ten trips a year, and while they mainly go to browse, two-thirds of them purchase something on their average visit.

For final consumers, garden centers/nurseries are the major sources of supply for annual plants, perennial plants, houseplants, trees, shrubs, and chemicals and fertilizer applied by someone in the household. On the other hand, sod, landscape design advice, landscape installation and maintenance, and yard improvement items were purchased less often, meaning that these areas represented unrealized opportunities for garden centers. The HRI study found that although consumers said they made some transactions for the latter products in garden centers, the average amount purchased was lower than through some other channel (such as hiring a service firm). Garden centers were also poorly evaluated as sources of lawn mowing and fertilizer application services. The study suggests that expanded offerings in these areas would not only increase dollar volume sales, but also permit a center to offer one-stop shopping for yard products and services. Lastly, the study found the most important factors that people consider in the purchase of garden products and services are product quality, product prices, a large assortment or selection, knowledgeable salespeople, and excellent customer service.

After reviewing the HRI report, Clay Dickinson met with Carol Stacey, his store manager. He remarked: "How can we use the findings of this report to improve traffic and increase profits? We need to do something to recapture market share." Ms. Stacey suggested

CASE 1
Green and Growing Nursery*

---

*The material in this case was prepared and written by Lynn Samsel, doctoral candidate, and Professor Raymond A. Marquardt, University of Nebraska–Lincoln.

CASE 1
(Continued)

they analyze their merchandise mix in light of the competition and the report findings. She had also been thinking about adding landscape services to their offerings and thought this would be the ideal time to suggest it to Clay Dickinson.

Questions

1. Identify three different market segments that exist for gardening and landscape services. How well does Green and Growing Nursery do in appealing to each segment?
2. Explain how the consumer decision process can be applied to the purchase of nursery products and landscape services. Include "what" and "where" in your answer.
3. What types of nursery products can be most effectively sold in a Wal-Mart? Explain your answer using the extended, limited, and routine decision-making processes.
4. How can Green and Growing Nursery increase its impulse sales of vegetable seedlings? Develop specific strategies using the concepts of completely unplanned, partially unplanned, and unplanned substitution.

CASE 2
Retail Target Marketing Systems[†]

Retail Target Marketing Systems (RTMS) is a software consulting firm that specializes in analyzing the final consumer buying habits for its retailer accounts. RTMS (http://www.rtms.com) was founded in 1986. Some of its retailer customers include Sears Canada, Filene's Basement, Carson Pirie Scott, Mercantile Stores, and Family Bookstores.

Through its Archer data base, RTMS provides retailers with the tools to determine who are their most important customers, what goods these customers purchase, when these goods are purchased, and where these goods are purchased. These types of information enable firms to better appeal to individual customers (through one-on-one retailing programs)—as well as to key market segments—by more targeted merchandising, payment, and promotional programs.

Although Archer can perform a number of consumer behavior analyses for retailer clients, three crucial reports relate to the buying activities of selected customers, customer penetration, and advertising effectiveness.

▪ Prospect Buying and Summary Reports—Archer can evaluate a customer data base to identify the shoppers "most likely to buy" selected kinds of merchandise. These prospects may be chosen based on purchases made on a specific date or within a range of dates (for example, a buyer of a major appliance is a good candidate for an extended warranty), purchases in a specific merchandise category (to identify heavy purchasers of clothing, for example), or total store or chain purchases (to identify loyal customers). Because Archer's reports are generated at the individual customer level, a retailer can use it to generate cost-effective mailing lists.

▪ Customer Penetration Report—Archer can assess customer purchases based on zip code, city, and/or state of residence. From these reports, Archer can prepare reports of customer penetration and sales by zip code. These reports can also be integrated with mapping software so these relationships are depicted on an actual map. Thus, a map may indicate that although a retailer has successfully attracted customers from the east side of a town, it has been unsuccessful in the west region (due to poor road conditions). The retailer could then choose to better focus on potential customers in the west by increased use of mail-order catalogs, local media, or perhaps even an additional store location.

▪ Advertising Effectiveness Reports—The data in Archer can be used to analyze the results of an advertising campaign to determine its effect on sales of the promoted item(s), sales of the promoted item(s) plus add-on purchases (such as batteries and

[†]The material in this case is drawn from data supplied by Retail Target Marketing Systems.

CASE 2
(Continued)

external speakers for a portable stereo unit), and a retailer's total sales (including items that have not been advertised). This type of analysis realizes the value of both the direct and indirect effects of a promotion. For example, while a good promotion may affect the sales of advertised goods only, an excellent promotion should benefit either the entire department's sales or the store's overall sales. To reduce potential bias, Archer compares the increased sales levels from a promotion to a control group of stores that have had no increased promotion during the test period. This promotional module can even determine the cumulative effects of multiple promotions, the effectiveness of one promotion versus another, or the results from different media.

The RTMS retail data-base system is carefully monitored to reduce false reporting of transactions due to the existence of duplicate records for the same customer (such as F. Smith and Frank Smith, both at the same address). Name and address records are compared with listings in a national street data base so incorrect addresses are amended. Addresses are also periodically updated when a customer moves from one location to another. These steps reduce unnecessary catalog preparation and mailing costs for retailer clients.

Questions
1. What are the pros and cons of Archer's prospect buying and summary reports from a consumer behavior analysis perspective?
2. What are the pros and cons of Archer's advertising effectiveness reports from a consumer behavior analysis perspective?
3. For which type of consumer decision making (extended, limited, or routine) are Archer's advertising effectiveness reports most suited? Explain your answer.
4. Evaluate the overall benefits of Archer. What are its limitations? Why?

Video Questions on Retail Target Marketing Systems
1. Describe the services offered by RTMS.
2. Develop a list of criteria to evaluate RTMS as a retail service provider.

Chapter 8

Information Gathering and Processing in Retailing

CHAPTER OBJECTIVES

1. To show why retailers should systematically collect and analyze information when developing and modifying their strategies

2. To examine the role of the retail information system, its components, and the recent advances in such systems

3. To describe the marketing research process: problem definition, secondary data search, generating primary data (if needed), data analysis, recommendations, and implementing findings

4. To discuss the characteristics and types of secondary data and primary data, including the retailer's data collection role

Shopping center developers and managers have begun to extensively deploy marketing data bases by using "club cards." For example, the Oaks and North Country Fair, two Southern malls owned by the Hahn Company, started the nation's first mall-based database system designed to track sales made at the point of purchase. The system, called the Shoppers Advantage Program, let the centers' merchants target and track mall customers in terms of who they are, how much they spend, where they shop, and how often they shop.

Here's how the Shoppers Advantage Program works: It is a joint venture between the Hahn Company and retailer tenants. Consumers are invited to sign up for their Shoppers Advantage card through a traditional variety of media (direct mail, newspaper ads, and radio ads). In addition, each mall has special fund-raising events in which schoolchildren, parents, and teachers are encouraged to sign up people. A customer application includes such data as the person's and spouse's birth and anniversary dates, income range, and home and business phone numbers.

The Shoppers Advantage card offers consumers special "Advantage" discounts and offers at dozens of stores, an opportunity to win theater and movie tickets, and advance notification of new store openings. Each purchase made by a Shoppers Advantage Program member is scanned, and the availability of special offers is based on the card's usage.

The data-base information, which is downloaded each evening from every store to the center's marketing department, provides merchants with immediate access to sales data. The center generates sales reports that are tabulated by individual store, store category, and the entire mall. Reports generally include such data as the number of Advantage customers to date, customer rewards, and data-base opportunities. Weekly promotions are planned using the data base. These promotions have included theater ticket giveaways, reduced car rental rates, and exclusive offers and gifts. During the first months, 12,000 customers became members and more than 135 merchants joined the Advantage program.

Store promotions by merchants that target a select group of Advantage members have had 10 percent to 30 percent response rates, leading to between 3 percent and 10 percent in additional store sales. As a result, Hahn plans to use the Shoppers Advantage Program in other shopping centers.[1]

[1]Diane Brandes, "Marketing Data Base Helps Build Businesses at Malls," *Direct Marketing* (July 1996), pp. 18–20.

Whether a retailer is developing a new strategy or modifying an existing one, information gathering and processing can be quite valuable. Such aspects of a retail strategy as the attributes and purchase behavior of current and potential customers, alternative store and nonstore locations, store management and operations, goods and service offerings, pricing, and store image and promotion can be studied—so as to make the best possible strategic decisions. Illustrations of research in these and other areas are provided throughout this chapter. **OVERVIEW**

Acting on the basis of good information reduces a retailer's chances of making wrong decisions. Without proper information, a firm's risk of poor performance is higher because it may act on the basis of too little knowledge or on knowledge gained nonsystematically. The extent of research activity should, to a large degree, be determined by the level of risk involved in a decision. For instance, there is considerable risk for a department store considering a new branch-store location. There is much less risk if a retailer is deciding whether a store should carry a new line of sweaters. In the branch-store situation, thousands of dollars for research and many months of study may be proper. In the case of the new sweaters, limited research may be sufficient.

Information gathering and processing should be conducted in an ongoing manner, yielding enough data for planning and control. Unless information is obtained on a regular basis, it may focus on short-run problems (crises), rather than the firm's long-range strategy-planning needs.

In this chapter, the shortcomings of nonsystematic research are noted. The retail information system and the marketing research process (with an emphasis on secondary data and primary data) are then discussed in detail.

Retailers are often tempted to rely on nonsystematic or incomplete ways of obtaining information in developing and evaluating their strategies due to time constraints, cost constraints, and the lack of research skills. Here are examples of nonsystematic ways of information gathering and processing: **RETAIL STRATEGIES BASED ON NON-SYSTEMATIC RESEARCH**

- Using intuition (e.g., "My gut reaction is to order 100 dozen quartz watches and sell them for $75 each as Christmas gifts.")
- Continuing what was done before (e.g., "I have never sold jewelry on credit. Why should I do so now?")
- Copying a successful competitor's strategy (e.g., "Bloomingdale's has had great success with the sale of gourmet foods. We should stock and promote those products.")
- Devising a strategy after speaking to a few individuals about their perceptions (e.g., "My friends Bill and Mary feel our prices are too high. We ought to lower them to improve sales and profits.")
- Assuming that past trends will continue into the future (e.g., "The wholesale prices of CD players have fallen 25 percent in the last year. So, we can wait another six months to make a purchase and get a very low price. We can then underprice competitors who are buying now.")

Let us now look at the negative ramifications of the decisions made by several retailers that have not obtained information in a systematic way and analyze their strategic errors.

A movie theater charges $6 for tickets throughout the entire week. The manager cannot understand why attendance is poor during weekday afternoons. That manager feels because all patrons are seeing the same movie, prices should be the same for a Monday matinee as a Saturday evening show. Yet, by looking at data stored in the theater's retail information system, the manager would learn attendance is much lower on Mondays than on Saturdays, indicating that because people prefer Saturday evening performances, they are willing to pay $6 to see a movie then. On the other hand, weekday customers have to be lured, and a lower price is a way to do so.

A toy store orders conservatively for the holiday season because the previous year's sales were weak. The store sells out two weeks before the peak of the season, and additional merchandise cannot be delivered to the store in time for holiday sales. The toy store uses a technique employed by many firms: incremental budgeting. Under that policy, a percentage is added to or subtracted from the prior year's budget to arrive at the present year's budget. In this case, the store owner assumed the previous year's poor sales would occur again. However, a survey of consumers would have revealed a new degree of optimism and an increased desire to give gifts. A research-based retailer would have planned its inventory accordingly.

A chain bookstore decides to open a new branch unit seventy miles from its closest current store. The decision is based on the growing population in the area and the present absence of an outlet there by the chain. After a year, the new store is doing only 40 percent of its expected business. A subsequent study by the chain reveals that the store name (and image) was relatively unknown in the area and the choice of advertising media was incorrect. In planning the new branch, these two important factors were not researched.

A mail-order retailer is doing well with small appliances, portable TVs, and moderately priced cameras. The firm has developed a good reputation in its traditional product lines and attracted loyal customers. It wants to add other product lines to capitalize on its name and customer goodwill. Yet, recent expansion into furniture and stereo systems has yielded poor results because the firm did not first conduct research on the consumer behavior of mail-order customers: People will readily buy standard, branded merchandise via the mail; but they are more reluctant to buy most furniture and stereos that way. The latter items must be experienced or tried out before a purchase.

A florist cuts the price of two-day-old flowers from $4 to $1 because they have a shorter life expectancy as of the time they are purchased by customers; but they don't sell. The florist assumes bargain-hunting consumers will want them as gifts or for floral arrangements. What the florist does not know (due to no research) is that people perceive the older flowers to be of very poor quality, color, and smell. The reduced price is actually too low and turns off customers!

The conclusion to be drawn from these examples is that nonsystematic or incomplete means of collecting and analyzing information can cause a firm to enact a bad strategy.

THE RETAIL INFORMATION SYSTEM

Proper data gathering and analysis should not be approached as a one-shot resolution of a single problem or issue. They should be viewed as key parts in an ongoing, well-integrated process or system. A **retail information system** anticipates the information needs of retail managers; collects, organizes, and stores relevant data on a continuous basis; and directs the flow of information to the proper retail decision makers.

In the following subsections, these topics are covered: building and using a retail information system, data-base management, and gathering information through the UPC and EDI.

Building and Using a Retail Information System

Figure 8-1 presents a general retail information system. With such a system, a retailer begins by clearly stating its business philosophy and objectives. The philosophy and

Figure 8-1

**A Retail
Information System**

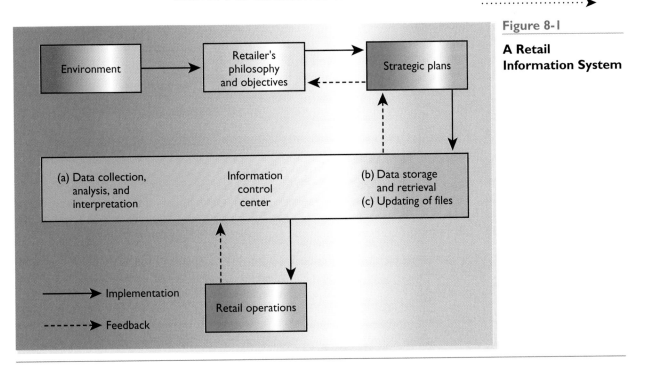

objectives are influenced by environmental factors (such as competitors, the economy, and government).

The retailer's philosophy and objectives provide very broad guidelines, which direct strategic planning. Some aspects of strategic plans are routine and, in the long run, may require little re-evaluation. Other aspects are nonroutine and will require careful evaluation each time they arise.

Once the retail strategy is outlined, the data needed to implement it are collected, analyzed, and interpreted. If the data are already available, they are retrieved from storage in the company's files. Each time new data are acquired, the files are updated. All of this takes place in the firm's information control center. Based on the data in the control center, decisions are then made and put into operation.

After decisions are operationalized, performance results are fed back into the information control center and compared with pre-set standards. Data are retrieved from files, or further data are collected. Routine adjustments are implemented immediately. Regular reports and, when needed, exception reports (explanations of deviations from expected performance) are fed back to the appropriate managers. If needed, a retailer may have to react to performance results in a way that affects its overall philosophy or goals (like revising the firm's image if it is perceived as old-fashioned or sacrificing short-run profits to introduce a new, computerized checkout counter).

All types of information should be stored in the control center for future and ongoing use, and the control center should be integrated with the short- and long-run planning and operations of the company. Information should not be gathered sporadically and haphazardly, but systematically—consistent with management objectives, plans, and operations.

Having a retail information system offers several advantages. First, information collection is organized and broad (companywide) in perspective. Second, data are continuously collected and stored. Therefore, opportunities can be foreseen and crises avoided. Third, the elements of retail strategy can be coordinated. Fourth, new strategies can be developed more quickly. Fifth, quantitative results are obtainable, and cost-benefit analysis can be done. However, devising a retail information system may not be easy. It may require high initial time and labor investments. Complex decision making may be necessary to set up and follow through on such a system.

Recent studies of department stores, mass merchants, specialty stores, and supermarkets have found that retail information systems have these attributes:

■ Retailers typically spend one-half or one percent to one and one-half percent of sales on their information systems efforts.
■ Many firms have set up information systems departments.
■ Formal, written annual plans are often produced for information systems departments.
■ Microcomputers are used by most companies using information systems analysis.
■ Substantial growth in the use of retail information systems is expected.
■ There are differences among retailers, based on sales and type of stores operated.[2]

As computer technology has become more sophisticated and less expensive, greater numbers of retailers (of all types) have developed comprehensive information systems. For example, in 1978, only 200 supermarkets used computerized scanning systems; now, 26,000 supermarkets (90 percent of all stores) have installed such systems.[3] In the mid-1970s, most computerized systems were used only to reduce clerical cashier errors and improve inventory control. Today, computers often form the foundation for a retail information system and are involved in consumer surveys, ordering, transfers of merchan-

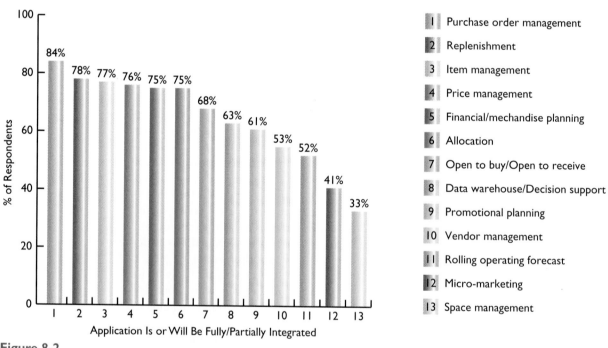

Figure 8-2

How Retailers Rate Their Level of Integration of Computerized Systems

Source: Reprinted by permission from "Ernst & Young's 15th Survey of Retail Information Technology," *Chain Store Age*, p. 31. Copyright Lebhar-Friedman, Inc., 425 Park Avenue, New York, NY 10022.

[2]"Ernst & Young's 15th Survey of Retail Information Technology," *Chain Store Age* (September 1996), Section II.
[3]Rebecca Piirto Heath, "Wake of the Flood," *Marketing Tools* (November–December 1996), pp. 58–63.

Figure 8-3

**Retail Pro
Management
Information
Software**

Screen 1	Store: CMP	YEAR: 1993			ANALYZED: 22/OCT/93	TOTALS $

STYLE:		WDC DMH S330			LDR: 18/OCT/93	LDS: 16/OCT/93
	AVGI #	SOLD #	SOLD P$	SOLD M$	SOLD %	STK/SL	STHRU%	TURN	GMROI
JAN	127.52	23.00	1286.85	688.85	53.5	8.9	11.2	2.2	2.49
FEB	112.96	33.00	1846.35	988.35	53.5	5.5	18.1	3.5	4.04
MAR	99.13	28.00	1416.95	688.95	48.6	6.6	15.1	3.4	3.21
APR	93.50	19.00	956.73	462.73	48.4	8.3	12.1	2.4	2.28
MAY	96.19	27.00	1585.06	803.06	53.4	7.1	14.1	3.4	3.85
JUN	96.30	31.00	1680.57	802.57	49.9	5.3	18.7	3.9	3.85
JUL	69.94	34.00	1776.42	892.42	50.2	4.8	21.0	5.8	5.89
AUG	65.52	39.00	1989.05	975.05	49.0	4.2	23.8	7.1	6.87
SEP	84.00	24.00	1342.80	718.80	53.5	8.0	12.6	3.4	3.91
OCT	143.55	86.00	4576.68	2340.68	51.1	1.9	51.5	7.2	7.53
NOV									
DEC									
AVG	97.61	35.43	1885.20	964.14	51.1	5.1	19.7	4.4	4.56
YTD		344.00	18305.46	9361.46	51.1	1.2	80.9	4.4	4.56

LAST ANALYZED	ON HAND	COMMITTED	ON ORDER	DAYS SUPPLY:	26
QUANTITY:	81	1	54	BASIS:	30
PRICE:	4531.95	55.95	3021.30	TOTAL PO'S:	1
COST:	2106.00	26.00	1404.00	NEXT PO#:	DMH12
MARGIN $:	2425.95	29.95	1617.30	QTY DUE:	54
MARGIN %:	53.53%	53.53%	53.53%	SHIP:	11/JUL/93

〈Select〉 Compare Year Days Graph Toggle Watch Decimals Range PO Print 〈Esc=Exit〉

Information on receiving, on-hand and sales is expressed month by month, in either numerical or graphical form, clearly showing important market trends.

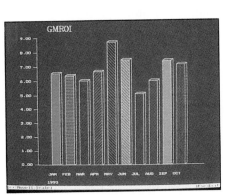

Five primary statistics are constantly monitored and always available: GMROI, Turn, Stock to Sales, Sell-through and Days of Supply.

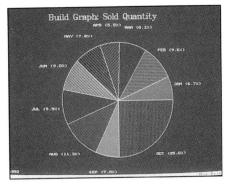

Information graphically displayed helps you quickly interpret the real situation.

dise between stores, and other diverse activities. Figure 8-2 shows just some of the kinds of functions that retailers are integrating into their computerized retail information systems. These applications are being used by both small and large retailers. According to one study of small- and medium-sized retailers, 80 percent have computerized financial management, 70 percent analyze sales electronically, and 60 percent have computerized inventory management systems.[4]

These are illustrations of how retailers are placing greater emphasis on computerizing their information systems. Retail Technologies International (http://www.retailpro.com) has developed Retail Pro management information software that it markets to retailers. This software is already in use at 9,000 stores in 26 countries. Retail Pro software appeals mostly to smaller retailers such as Golf Discount in St. Louis, The Sock Company in New Jersey, and General Surplus in Ohio. Retail Pro has these features, as depicted in Figure 8-3:

[4]IBM, "Retail Technology Applications," *Stores* (July 1996), p. 92. See also David P. Schulz, "Smaller Chains Look for Growth Through Improved Information Systems," *Stores* (May 1997), pp. 70, 72.

Despite the fact that most retailers have great instincts for what people want to buy, all too often they have to make important management decisions without sufficient information. Retail Pro's comprehensive report and analysis capabilities provide the retailer with clarity and insight into all aspects of the business. Every inventory control and point-of-sale function generates key information that can be filtered and summarized into a wide variety of reports and graphs. Aside from a large selection of standard reports, Retail Pro comes with a built-in report designer that allows you to create your own reports and reproduce them anytime desired. Also Retail Pro interfaces with popular report writer software, providing unlimited possibilities. Producing routine reports is effortless using Retail Pro's automated batch report feature. You simply define a script that produces a custom series of reports. Retail Pro can then automatically play that script at any time (during the night, for example) and produce the specific reports you desire. All reports can be displayed on the screen or sent directly to the printer. Retail Pro gets you the information you need, when you need it, so that you can make tough decisions with confidence.[5]

MicroStrategy (http://www.strategy.com) is another software designer that works with retailers (typically larger ones) to prepare computerized information systems. Its clients include Mervyn's, Victoria's Secret, Hannaford Bros., Thrifty PayLess, Kmart, CVS, and Federated Department Stores. MicroStrategy calls itself an online analytical processing (OLAP) vendor. One of its leading products is DSS Agent, which is highlighted in Figure 8-4:

DSS Agent is a decision support interface created to bring integrated query and reporting, powerful analytics, and decision support work flow to every desktop. For end users, DSS Agent provides an arsenal of features for online analysis of their corporate data. Even complex reports are easy to create; they can be viewed in a host of presentation formats, polished into production reports, distributed to other users, and extended through a host of ad hoc features including Drill Everywhere and Data Surfing. DSS Agent is designed with the interests of an enterprisewide deployment in mind. Reports, and all the discrete business elements they comprise, are created and dispatched as personal, user group, or global objects. The interface itself is customizable to different users' skill levels. A set of meta-data manipulation tools allows for the central creation and management of decision support systems, further reducing information technology costs. DSS Agent provides an opportunity to roll out, at low cost and risk, an analytical business reporting lens in a comprehensive DSS environment that is powerful, intuitive, and secure.[6]

Calgary Co-op is North America's largest retail cooperative, just ahead of REI. Its annual sales are $500 million, from 15 stores; and it stocks groceries, hardware, building supplies, pharmaceuticals, apparel, and auto items. In 1990, Calgary Co-op realized it needed better technological capabilities to track its performance. So, it came up with a software application that captured weekly product sales from its stores. Soon after, it began working with a prototype executive information system (EIS) to enhance data analysis and reporting. However, the firm still had trouble analyzing product sales at the level of detail it wanted. Calgary Co-op then turned to Unisys to develop a program that could link existing systems and improve the retailer's ability to manage information. The proposal included: "providing a 'quick-look monitor board' to highlight the best, worst, and acceptable product performers as measured against established criteria; forecasting sales performance over time to reveal business trends not easily discerned from traditional

[5]*Retail Pro: Because It Works for You* (Carmichael, California: Retail Technologies International, Inc., 1996).
[6]*DSS Agent* (Vienna, Virginia: MicroStrategy, Inc., 1996).

Figure 8-4

**DSS Agent: Online
Analytical
Processing Software
(OLAP)**

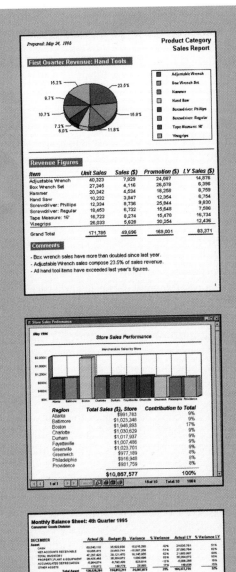

Production Report Writing

DSS Agent delivers the industry's first three-tier OLAP report writer. By combining the analytic power of an OLAP server with the simplicity of a report writer, DSS Agent brings the best of both worlds to the desktop of every end user.

Rich Formatting Capabilities

You have complete control over the look and feel of your reports, including the ability to customize headers, fonts, layout, and background. Horizontal and vertical totals and subtotals are easily added to any report. A wide selection of customizable number and date formats ensure that your reports conform to any standard throughout the world.

Easily Developed Reports

DSS Agent simplifies the report development process, letting you create and deploy reports that meet even the most difficult presentation requirements. Use DSS Agent's powerful report design mode to specify and retrieve information from your data warehouse. Then switch to the design application to adjust the layout, format the data, graph the results, and add your own personalized comments.

Advanced Analytical Library

Extend your reports with a standard library of statistical, arithmetical, date, and string functions. For example, display the mean, median, standard deviation, maximum, and minimum profit margin for all stores during the first quarter. The function builder interface even lets you construct your own functions, which you can then apply to any data series for display in report writer mode.

hard-copy reports; drilling down to the lowest level of detail to provide answers to questions highlighted by the monitor boards and graphs; and ensuring consistent decision making by using the same set of criteria and information across all Calgary Co-op business units." The new systems have been a great success.[7]

Sports Authority is taking still another approach with its retail information system, one intended to enable employees and others to better share information. Sports

[7]"New Executive Info System Keeps Calgary Competitive," *Chain Store Age* (March 1996), p. 40.

Authority is taking advantage of a technology known as "groupware." This is how the groupware approach functions: "At any given time, data bases residing on Sports Authority's mainframe computer can be accessed by many different employees, thus facilitating decision making and follow-through. The technology that makes this possible is called groupware, a tool that allows for file-sharing and project collaboration among employees and outside business partners. Groupware is gaining ground in retail and other industries, say analysts, because much of the network infrastructure required for client/server applications is finally in place. Sports Authority moved to groupware after deciding electronic mail, which had been the chain's primary communications vehicle, did not support the 'teamwork' approach needed to support rapid growth."[8]

Data-Base Management

Data-base management is the procedure used to gather, integrate, apply, and store information related to specific subject areas. It is a key element in a retail information system and may be employed with customer data bases, vendor data bases, product-category data bases, and so on. For instance, a retailer may compile and store data on the characteristics and purchase behavior of customers, compute and store sales figures by vendor, and maintain historical records by product category. Each of these would represent a separate data base. According to research, 65 percent of retailers use their data bases for customer frequency programs and for customer research, 60 percent for promotion evaluation, 50 percent for store trading area analysis and for joint promotions with manufacturers, 40 percent for media planning, and one-third for customer communications.[9]

Grassfield's, an upscale men's clothing store in Denver, is one of the many retailers (small and large alike) now placing more emphasis on data-base management. Grassfield's calls its system "Invitational Marketing," because its primary purpose is to invite customers' business:

> It's not the products; it's their relationships with the retailer and the salesclerks that keep people coming back to a fine store. Max Grassfield has been aware of this for a long time. Several years ago, he asked himself, "What can we do to make Grassfield's unique?" The answer, which he evolved after much study, research, and effort, was to develop methods to know his customers "better than the other stores know their customers." For the last ten years, Grassfield's has been collecting a data base of information, voluntarily provided by its customers. Originally, the data included customer names, addresses, telephone numbers, sizes, birthdays, and—because wives are often heavily involved in their husbands' clothing purchases—the names of their wives. Max collected information on all his customers—cash, check, and charge card—not just those who opened a Grassfield charge account. He evolved a group of regularly written, one-to-one communications with customers. Each letter incorporates the customer's first name or nickname (as the customer prefers), his sizes, his wife's name, his product preferences, and references to what he bought in the previous season. Most communications are programmed to include messages designed only for the particular customer addressed: "I've been keeping my eyes on the 44 Long suits...." Every letter is personally signed by a salesperson who waited on the recipient during a past visit to the store. For personal notes, Max created a special half-sheet (5-inch by 8-inch) letterhead bearing the Grassfield's two-color logo in an A-2

[8]Julie Ritzer Ross, "Groupware Gains Ground as Retailers Profit from Information-Sharing Advantages," *Stores* (December 1996), pp. 49–50.
[9]Donnelley Marketing, "Retail Data-Base Marketing Programs," *Stores* (October 1995), p. 81.

For Woolworth in Great Britain: Data Warehousing Pays Off

Woolworth's initial British data warehouse, built in 1993, was linked to Woolworth's point-of-sale (POS) cash registers in 200 of its stores. Although not all of the company's stores were hooked up to the system, Woolworth extrapolated sales data for all of its stores on the basis of the sample. A major difficulty with the original system was its inability to break out sales performance on a store-by-store basis, and that system was not powerful enough to do the types of analyses requested by management.

Woolworth's new British data warehouse became operable just in time for the 1995 Christmas season, a vital time for Woolworth (as well as other retailers) to earn strong profits. As described by Woolworth's systems director, the new data warehouse better enabled the retailer to control the distribution of goods to its stores, identify underachieving store units, and manage orders. As a result, for Christmas 1995, the data warehouse helped Woolworth achieve a 35 percent increase in profitability (largely due to a 9 percent sales growth and the limited use of markdowns).

At first, access to the data warehouse was restricted to a small Woolworth team, comprised of individuals from systems, merchandising, and supply-chain management. Recently, Woolworth expanded warehouse access to 80 users.

Source: "Britain's Woolworth Embraces Data Warehousing," *Chain Store Age* (October 1996), pp. 87–90.

envelope. To display Grassfield's merchandise, he developed an oversized (6-inch by 9-inch) glossy photo postcard in full color. The text for the letters and postcards is printed on the store's laser printer.[10]

One of the newest advances in data-base management is known as **data warehousing,** whereby copies of all the data bases in a company are maintained in one location and can be accessed by employees at any locale. A data warehouse "is a huge repository separate from the operational data bases set up to support specific departmental applications. Since information from the individual operational data bases is copied into the data warehouse at regular intervals, anyone in a retailer's organization can access information from the data warehouse without disrupting the often critical applications the donor data bases were designed to support." There are four components to a data warehouse: the data warehouse itself, where the data are physically stored; software that copy original data bases and transfer them to the warehouse; graphical software that allows inquiries to be processed; and a guide (directory) to items kept in the warehouse.[11]

Sears, Wal-Mart, Lands' End, and Federated Department Stores are among the scores of leading retailers that have adopted data warehousing. At Lands' End, weekly data from its order-processing and customer-mailing systems are placed into the retailer's data warehouse: "Detailed information is kept on some 20 million customers, enabling decision makers to find and analyze data by customer, product, and transaction. The transaction information available through the data warehouse includes not only purchases, but also requests for catalogs, shipping dates, and orders for merchandise that was not in stock. The data warehouses used by Lands' End and other retail companies represent the latest answer to a difficult, decade-long search by firms to give top management and other decision makers access to data stored in corporate mainframes."[12]

[10]Arthur Middleton Hughes, "A Tailor-Made Program," *Marketing Tools* (July–August 1996), pp. 10–17.
[11]"The Dallas Summit," *Chain Store Age* (September 1996), pp. 3B–6B; Ramon Barquin, Steve Crofts, and Alan Paller, "Data Warehousing: The Road to Knowledge Production," *Fortune* (November 11, 1996), pp. S1–S9; "Data Warehouse Managers," *Chain Store Age* (January 1997), pp. B1–B15; and Julie Ritzer Ross, "Data Warehousing Surges as Retailers of All Sizes Fuel Growth," *Stores* (April 1997), pp. 72–76.
[12]Gary Robins, "Data Warehousing," *Stores* (September 1995), pp. 19, 24.

Data-base information can come from internal and external sources. A retailer can develop its data bases internally by keeping detailed records and arranging them properly. To illustrate, a firm could generate data bases containing such information as this:

■ By customer—frequency of purchases, goods and services bought, average purchase amount, demographic background, and typical method of payment.
■ By vendor—total purchases by the retailer per time period, total sales to customers per time period, the most popular items, the retailer's profit margins, average delivery time, and quality of service.
■ By product category—total category's sales per time period, each model's sales per time period, the retailer's profit margins, and the percentage of items sold at a discount.

There are also a number of firms that compile data bases and make them available (for a fee) to retailers. One is Donnelley Marketing (http://www.liststore.com/whois.htm). It offers several different data bases, including these: *DQI*^{2} is the most powerful consumer information resource available. It includes consumer data on over 150 million U.S. consumers and 97 million U.S. households. A retailer can select from over 1,600 demographic, life-style, and purchase behavior variables such as age, income, dwelling type, length of residence, and 1990 Census data. *SHARE FORCE* is a life-style data base with information on nearly 17 million mail-responsive individuals who have filled out and returned detailed surveys on their buying behavior, life-styles, and leisure activities. *New Movers Data Base* is a compilation of individuals and families who have moved over the last two years. Updated monthly, it is compiled from private-sector sources and is good for demographics, mobility (e.g., when moved, distance moved, etc.), and socio-economic status data.

With either internally or externally generated data bases, a retailer can identify opportunities and problems, and undertake the best actions (which may be customized due to the information provided by the data bases) to address them. The retailer must be sure its data bases are kept current, the privacy of customers and vendors is not violated, and the effectiveness of actions aimed at various data bases is regularly reviewed. As Williams-Sonoma, the home products retailer, notes, "Our sophisticated systems—many of them unique to our firm—eliminate unprofitable names, cross-market all of our catalogs to promising customers, and target mail to specific geographic areas. At the same time, we are sensitive to our customers' privacy concerns and use manual, as well as computer-matching, methods to verify names and addresses and minimize duplicate mailings."[13]

Gathering Information Through the UPC and EDI

To gather and process data more efficiently for use in their information systems, a growing number of retailers now rely on the Universal Product Code (UPC) and electronic data interchange (EDI).

With the **Universal Product Code (UPC),** products (or tags attached to them) are marked with a series of thick and thin vertical lines, representing each item's identification code. UPC-A labeling—the preferred format—also includes numbers, as well as the lines. The vertical lines are "read" by optical scanning equipment at checkout counters. Cashiers do not have to enter transactions manually—although they can, if needed. Because the UPC is not readable by humans, the retailer or vendor must attach a ticket or sticker to every product specifying its size, color, and other information (if these data are not on the package or the product itself). Because the UPC does not include price information, this too must be added by a ticket or sticker.

[13]*Williams-Sonoma 1992 Annual Report*, p. 9.

Figure 8-5

State-of-the-Art Uses of UPC Technology

As this photo montage shows, Symbol Technologies has devised a host of scanning products (some of which are wireless) that make UPC data capture and processing quite simple. For example, Symbol products can be used at the point of sale to enter transaction data and transmit them to a central office, at product displays to verify shelf prices, at storage areas to aid in taking physical inventories, at receiving stations to log in the receipt of new merchandise, and at delivery points to track the movement of customer orders.

By using UPC-based technology, retailers are able to record information instantaneously on a product's model number, size, color, and other factors when an item is sold, and to transmit the information to a computer that monitors unit sales, inventory levels, and other factors. Retailers' goals are to generate better merchandising data, improve inventory management and control, speed up transaction time, increase productivity, reduce clerical errors in processing transactions, and coordinate the flow of information. Over the years, UPC technology has substantially improved. Today, it is the accepted industry standard for both food retailers and general merchandise retailers (including specialty stores). Figure 8-5 illustrates how far UPC technology has come with regard to information gathering and processing.

Initially, the UPC was widely accepted by food retailers (due to their volume of routine transactions and the impact of this on inventory management) and not popular among general merchandise retailers. But today, UPC technology is utilized by general merchandisers, specialty stores, and others. Virtually every time a sales transaction or inventory data is scanned by computer, UPC technology is involved. About 150,000 manufacturers and retailers worldwide belong to the Uniform Code Council (UCC), an association that has taken the lead in setting and promoting inter-industry product identification and communication standards (http://www.uccouncil.org). The UPC is discussed further in Chapter 15 ("Financial Merchandise Management").

Through **electronic data interchange (EDI),** retailers and their suppliers regularly exchange information via their computers with regard to inventory levels, delivery times, unit sales, and so on, of particular items. As a result, both parties enhance their decision-making capabilities, better control inventory levels, and are more responsive to consumer demand trends.

This is how Black & Decker and its online retailers are applying EDI: "At checkout, a clerk scans in a tool's bar code. Information from the scanning is sent from the store's computer to Black & Decker mainframes at company headquarters in Towson, Maryland, automatically generating a purchase order for new tools to replace those sold. The tool manufacturer gains invaluable forecasting and merchandising information. Black & Decker's major retailer customers typically provide weekly EDI, point-of-sale reports."[14]

The use of the UPC greatly facilitates EDI. Accordingly, a growing number of retailers that are involved with UPC-based technology have also embraced some form of EDI with their suppliers. According to some estimates, between 60,000 and 80,000 U.S. firms—retailers and manufacturers—already use EDI. This topic is covered further in Chapter 13 ("Operations Management: Operational Dimensions").

THE MARKETING RESEARCH PROCESS

Marketing research in retailing entails the collection and analysis of information relating to specific issues or problems facing a retailer. At farsighted firms, marketing research is just one element in a thorough retail information system. At other firms, marketing research may be the only type of information gathering and processing that is done.

The **marketing research process** embodies a series of activities: defining the issue or problem to be studied, examining secondary data, generating primary data (if needed), analyzing data, making recommendations, and implementing findings. It is not a single act. The use of this process lets a retailer conduct research systematically, rather than haphazardly, and make better decisions.

Figure 8-6 outlines the research process. Each activity is done sequentially. Thus, secondary data are not examined until after an issue or problem is defined. The dashed line around the primary data stage means these data are generated only if the secondary data search does not yield enough information to make a decision. Components of the research process are described next.

Issue (problem) definition involves a clear statement of the topic to be studied. What information does the retailer want to obtain in order to make a decision? Without a clear understanding of the topic to be researched, potentially irrelevant and confusing data could be collected. Here are two examples of issue (problem) definitions for a downtown shoe store:

1. "Of three potential new store locations, which should we choose?"
2. "How can we improve the sales of our men's shoes?"

[14]Thomas J. Wall, "The ABCs of EDI," *Sales & Marketing Management* (June 1996), *SMT* supplement, pp. 30–33.

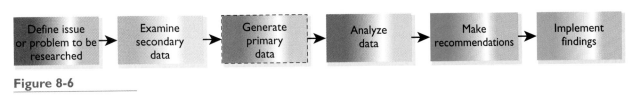

Figure 8-6

The Marketing Research Process in Retailing

It should be discerned from these examples that research issues (problems) may differ in nature. Whereas the first one relates to a comparison of three locations and is fairly structured, the second one is much more open-ended.

After the research issue (problem) has been defined, secondary data sources are examined. **Secondary data** are those that have been gathered for purposes other than addressing the issue or problem currently under study. Secondary data may be internal (such as company records) or external (such as government reports and trade publications). Secondary data are described in more depth in the next section.

Primary data are those collected to address the specific issue or problem under study. This type of data may be generated via surveys, observations, experiments, and simulation. Primary data are discussed more fully later in this chapter.

Sometimes secondary data are relied upon; other times, primary data are crucial. Still other times, both are important. Three points are noteworthy. First, the diversity of possible data collection (types and costs) is great. Second, only data relevant to the problem or issue under investigation should be amassed. Third, as indicated earlier, primary data are usually acquired only if the secondary data search yields insufficient information (hence, the dashed box in Figure 8-6).

By gathering secondary or primary data, these kinds of information can be compiled for the two shoe store issues (problems) that were just stated:

Issue (Problem) Definition	Information Needed to Solve Issue (Problem)
1. Which store location?	1. Data on access to transportation, traffic, consumer profiles, rent, store size, and types of competition are gathered from government reports, trade publications, and observation by the owner for each of the three potential store locations.
2. How to improve sales of shoes?	2. Store sales records for the past five years by product category are gathered. A consumer survey in a nearby mall is conducted.

After secondary and/or primary data are gathered, **data analysis** is performed to assess that information and relate it to the defined issue or problem. Alternative solutions are also clearly outlined. For example:

Issue (Problem) Definition	Alternative Solutions
1. Which store location?	1. Each site is ranked for all of the criteria (access to transportation, traffic, consumer profiles, rent, store size, and types of competition).
2. How to improve sales of shoes?	2. Alternative strategies to boost shoe sales are analyzed and ranked.

The advantages and disadvantages of each alternative are then enumerated. See Table 8-1.

Table 8-1   RESEARCH-BASED RECOMMENDATIONS

Issue (Problem)	Alternatives	Pros and Cons of Alternatives	Recommendation
1. Which store location?	Site A.	Best transportation, traffic, and consumer profiles. Highest rent. Smallest store space. Extensive competition.	Site A: the many advantages far outweigh the disadvantages.
	Site B.	Poorest transportation, traffic, and consumer profiles. Lowest rent. Largest store space. No competition.	
	Site C.	Intermediate on all criteria.	
2. How to improve sales of shoes?	Increased assortment.	Will attract and satisfy many more customers. High costs. High level of inventory. Reduces turnover for many items.	Lower prices and increase ads: additional customers offset higher costs and lower margins; combination best expands business.
	Drop some lines and specialize.	Will attract and satisfy a specific consumer market. Excludes many segments. Costs and inventory reduced.	
	Slightly reduce prices.	Unit sales increase. Markup and profit per item decline.	
	Advertise.	Will increase traffic and new customers. High costs.	

At this point, **recommendations** are made as to the strategy the retailer should enact to best address its issue or problem. Of the available options, which is best? Table 8-1 shows recommendations for the shoe store issues (problems) discussed throughout this section.

Last, but not least, is the **implementation** of the recommended strategy. If research is to replace intuition in developing and enacting a retail strategy, a decision maker must follow recommendations from research studies, even if they seem to contradict his or her own ideas.

SECONDARY DATA

Advantages and Disadvantages

In the marketing research process, secondary data (information collected for other purposes) have several advantages over primary data. The assembly of data is inexpensive. Company records, trade journals, and government publications are all rather inexpensive to use. No data collection forms, interviewers, and tabulations are needed.

Secondary data can be gathered quickly. Company records, library sources, and Web sites can be accessed immediately, whereas the generation of primary data can take up to several months. When a firm keeps past reports and other materials in its retail information system, secondary data are often stored in an easy-to-find and organized manner.

For many retailing issues, there are several sources of secondary data. These let a firm gain many perspectives and lots of data. In a primary study, there are limited data and one perspective.

A secondary source may possess information the retailer would otherwise be unable to get. For example, government publications often have statistics no private company could acquire on its own. Furthermore, the data contained in government literature may be more honest and accurate than those a private company could collect.

When secondary data are assembled by a source such as *Progressive Grocer*, A.C. Nielsen, *Business Week*, or the federal government, the results are believable. Each of these sources has a high level of credibility and a reputation for thoroughness.

A retailer may often have only a rough idea of the topics it wants to investigate. In this instance, a search of secondary data may help that firm to define issues (problems) more specifically. In addition, background information about a given issue or problem can be gathered from secondary sources before a primary study is undertaken.

Although secondary data have many advantages, there are several potential disadvantages. Available data may not suit the purposes of the current study because they have been collected for other reasons. As an illustration, the units of measurement may be different. A retailer normally needs local demographic and other types of information. Yet, neighborhood statistics may not be found in secondary sources (which typically contain federal, state, and city statistics). Data may also be categorized in an unusable fashion. For instance, a service station owner might be interested in the number of local citizens having cars. He or she would want this information broken down by year, model, and mileage driven, so as to stock parts. A motor vehicle bureau could provide statistics on the models but not the mileage driven.

Secondary data may be dated. Because information was assembled for another purpose, it may also have outlived its usefulness. Conclusions reached five or even two years ago may not be valid today. As an example, the *Census of Retail Trade* is conducted every five years. The last fully published retail census is based on data gathered in 1992, and many statistics contained in that census are outdated. Furthermore, there is often a long time delay between the completion of a census and the release of that information to the public. Some of the data from the 1992 retail census were not actually distributed until 1996.

The accuracy of secondary data must be carefully evaluated. The retailer needs to decide whether data have been compiled in an unbiased, objective way. The purpose of the original research, the data collection techniques used, and the method of analysis should each be examined for bias—if they are available for review. This is crucial if research has been done by a firm with a stake in the findings. Supporting evidence (raw data) should be read, as well as summary reports.

The source of secondary data can be a disadvantage, as well as an advantage. A partisan, profit-making firm tends not to provide competitors with access to data that will hurt it (or help the competitors). Thus, generalities and omissions should be noted. Some sources are also known for poor data collection techniques; they should be avoided. If conflicting data are found, the source with the best reputation for accuracy should be relied on. Conflicting results presented by equally accurate sources may lead a retailer into primary research (the collection of its own data).

Lastly, the reliability—the ability to replicate a study and get the same outcome—of secondary data is not always known. In retailing, many research projects are not retested and the user of secondary data has to hope results from one narrow study are applicable to his or her firm.

In sum, a retailer desiring information to resolve an issue (problem) has many criteria to consider in contemplating the use of secondary data. In particular, low costs, speed, and access to materials must be weighed against improper fit, out-of-date statistics, and data accuracy.

Whether secondary data resolve the retailer's issue (problem) or not, their low cost and immediate availability require that primary data not be collected until after searching secondary data. Only if secondary data are unsatisfactory or incomplete should primary data be collected.

A variety of secondary data sources for retailers are now detailed.

Sources

There are various sources and types of secondary data. The major distinctions are between internal and external sources. **Internal secondary data** are available within the company, sometimes from the data bank of a retail information system. **External secondary data** are available from sources outside the firm.

Internal Secondary Data ❏ Before spending time and money searching for external secondary data or primary data, the retailer should look at information available inside the firm. Among the major sources of internal secondary data are budgets, sales reports, profit-and-loss statements, customer billing reports, inventory records, prior company research reports, and written reports on company performance.

At the beginning of the year, most retailers develop budgets for the next 12 months. These budgets, based on sales forecasts, outline planned expenditures for that year. A firm's budget and its performance in attaining budgetary goals (adhering to an outlined plan of expenditures) are good sources for secondary data.

Retailers often use sales reports as indicators of performance. For many, this information is accurately and rapidly available by point-of-sale registers. In studying sales by store, department, item, and salesperson and comparing them with prior periods, a firm gets a sense of growth or contraction. But this feeling, and overdependence on sales data, may be misleading. Higher sales do not always mean higher profits. To be valuable, sales data should be used in conjunction with profit-and-loss data.

A firm's profit-and-loss statements may provide a lot of information. If profit goals are set, actual achievements can be measured against them. Trends in company success can be viewed over time. Profits can be assessed by store, department, item, and employee. A detailed breakdown of profits and losses can show strengths and weaknesses in operations and management and can lead to improvements.

Customer billing reports provide a host of information. A retailer could learn about inventory movement, sales made by different personnel, peak selling times, and sales volume. For credit customers, the retailer could review sales by geographic area, outstanding debts, length of repayment time, and types of purchases. Company invoices could show the retailer its own past purchase history and allow the firm to evaluate that performance against budgetary or other goals.

Inventory records show the levels of merchandise carried by a firm throughout the year and the movement of these items. Knowledge of the lead time needed to place and receive orders from suppliers and of the amounts of safety stock (extra merchandise kept on hand to prevent running out) held at different times during the year can aid in inventory planning. These are valuable sources of secondary data.

If a firm does primary research, the resultant report should be kept for future use (hopefully in the information control center of a retail information system). When a research report is used initially, it involves primary data. Later reference to that report is secondary in nature (because the report is no longer used for its "primary" purpose). A detailed report should have some validity in the future unless conditions change drastically, although the date of the report must be noted.

Written reports on company performance are another source of internal secondary data. The reports may be composed by senior executives, buyers, sales personnel, or stockroom workers. Sales personnel turnover and customer responses to in-store displays are the kinds of information available through written reports. With proper direction, all phases of retail management can be improved through formal report procedures.

External Secondary Data ❏ After checking internal sources, a retailer should consult external secondary data sources—if internal information is not sufficient for a decision to be made as to a defined issue (problem). External secondary data sources are comprised of government and nongovernment categories.

To use either source of external secondary data properly, one should be familiar with the appropriate reference guides. Such guides contain listings of written (sometimes computer-based) materials for a specified time. These listings are usually by subject or topic heading. Here are several reference guides (including computerized data bases), chosen because of their retailing importance. They are available in any business library or other large library:

- *ABI/INFORM* (data base). Covers hundreds of journals in business and management. Articles are indexed, classified by subject, and abstracted.
- *Business Index.* Monthly. Completely indexes hundreds of periodicals, including newspapers. Selectively indexes another 900 periodicals.
- *Business Periodicals Index.* Monthly, except for July. Cumulations quarterly, semi-annually, and annually. Subject index of hundreds of English language periodicals.
- *Census Catalog and Guide* (Washington, D.C.: U.S. Bureau of the Census). Cites the programs and services of the Census Bureau. Lists reports, diskettes, microfiche, and maps.
- *Dialog Information Retrieval Service* (data base). Contains hundreds of data bases covering a wide variety of disciplines. Information on public companies, economic data, financial news, and business news.
- *Predicasts F&S Index: Europe.* Monthly, with quarterly and annual cumulations. Covers industries and companies.
- *Predicasts F&S Index: International.* Monthly, with quarterly and annual cumulations. Covers industries and companies.
- *Predicasts F&S Index: United States.* Weekly, with monthly, quarterly, and annual cumulations. Covers industries and companies.
- *Wall Street Journal Index.* Monthly, with quarterly and annual cumulations.

The government distributes a wide range of statistics and written materials. Here are several publications, chosen because of their retailing importance. They are available in any business library or other large library:

- *Census of Retail Trade.* Every five years ending in 2 and 7. Detailed statistics by store classification and metropolitan region. Data include multiple ownership, employment, goods/service categories, and sales.
- *Census of Service Industries.* Every five years ending in 2 and 7. Similar to *Census of Retail Trade* but covers service industries organized by SIC code.
- *Combined Annual and Revised Monthly Retail Trade.* Compiled annually. Ten-year statistics on retail sales and retail inventories by kind of business for specified areas and cities.
- *Monthly Retail Trade Survey.* Monthly. Retail sales, inventories, and other data by kind of retail store.
- *Statistical Abstract* (Washington, D.C.: U.S. Superintendent of Documents, Government Printing Office, annual). Detailed summary of U.S. statistics.
- *Survey of Current Business.* Monthly, with weekly supplements. On all aspects of business, as reported by the U.S. Department of Commerce.
- *Other.* Registration data (births, deaths, automobile registrations, etc.). Available through a variety of federal, state, and local agencies.

Government agencies, such as the Federal Trade Commission (http://www.ftc.gov), provide pamphlets and booklets on topics like franchising, unit pricing, deceptive ads, and credit policies. The Small Business Administration (http://www.sbaonline.sba.gov) helps smaller retailers, providing literature and managerial advice. Pamphlets and booklets are either distributed free of charge or sold for a nominal fee. The Bureau of the Census maintains a detailed Web site (http://www.census.gov), at which it provides some free data and some fee-based.

Nongovernment secondary data come from various sources, many of which are listed in reference guides. Four major nongovernment sources are regular periodicals; books, monographs, and other nonregular publications; other channel members; and commercial research houses.

Table 8-2 SELECTED SOURCES OF EXTERNAL SECONDARY DATA: REGULAR PERIODICALS

Advertising Age (http://www.adage.com). Weekly, with applications to retailing.

American Demographics (http://www.demographics.com). Monthly, with articles on important population trends affecting retailers.

Business Week (http://www.businessweek.com). Weekly, with articles on all phases of business.

Chain Store Age (http://www.chainstoreage.com). Monthly, focuses on chain store and shopping center information.

Direct Marketing (http://ourworld.compuserve.com/homepages/petehoke/homepage.htm). Monthly, with articles on all aspects of the field.

Discount Store News (http://www.discountstorenews.com). Includes *Apparel Merchandising*. Biweekly, with articles on industry developments and apparel merchandising.

Drug Store News (http://www.lf.com/pubs/drsnseg.htm). Biweekly, with articles on current trends, health and beauty aids, and productivity statistics.

Fortune (http://pathfinder.com/fortune). Semimonthly, with articles on all phases of business.

Journal of the Academy of Marketing Science (http://www.sagepub.com/sagepage/sitemap.htm). Quarterly, with articles in all areas of marketing.

Journal of Advertising Research (http://www.arf.amic.com/publish.htm). Bimonthly, includes articles on advertising in retailing.

Journal of Consumer Marketing (http://www.mcb.co.uk/portfolio/home.htm#J). Quarterly, with applied articles on all aspects of marketing.

Journal of Direct Marketing (http://journals.wiley.com/wilcat-bin/ops). Quarterly, with articles on all aspects of direct marketing.

Journal of Marketing (http://www.ama.org/pubs/jminfo). Quarterly, with articles in all areas of marketing.

Journal of Marketing Channels. Quarterly, with articles on distribution systems.

Journal of Marketing Research (http://www.ama.org/pubs/jmr/index.html). Quarterly, with articles on research developments in all areas of marketing.

Journal of Retailing (http://www.haas.berkeley.edu/~jr). Quarterly, with articles on theories and developments in all aspects of retailing.

Journal of Services Marketing (http://www.mcb.co.uk/portfolio/home.htm#J). Quarterly, with articles on all aspects of service marketing.

Marketing News (http://www.ama.org/pubs/mn/pub2.htm). Biweekly, covers all aspects of marketing.

Progressive Grocer (http://www.pgshowdaily.com/index.htm). Monthly, with emphasis on food retailing trends.

Promo (http://www.mediacentral.com/Promo.). Monthly, covers all aspects of sales promotions.

Restaurant Business (http://www.restaurantbiz.com). Eighteen times per year, covers developments in the restaurant field.

Retail Business Review. Bimonthly, with focus on credit, store security, and inventory management.

Retail Technology (http://www.retailtech.com). Monthly, with focus on computer-related technology.

Sales & Marketing Management (http://www.smmmag.com). Monthly, of interest to retailers: annual survey of buying power by county (based on income, retail sales, and population in each country).

Standard & Poor's Industry Surveys: Retailing Basic Analysis (http://www.stockinfo.standardpoor.com/faqs/indsfaq.htm). Yearly (and periodic updates), with information on all aspects of retailing.

Stores (http://www.stores.org). Monthly, with emphasis on department stores, specialty stores, and off-price retailing.

Supermarket Business (http://www.supermarketbusiness.com). Monthly, with articles on supermarket retailing.

Supermarket News (http://www.supermarketnews.com). Weekly, includes articles on market share, changes in markets, and financial data on the industry.

Wall Street Journal (http://wsj.com). Five times weekly, with articles on all aspects of business.

Women's Wear Daily (http://www.wwd.com). Five times weekly, with emphasis on fashion information.

Regular periodicals are widely available in printed versions at most libraries or by personal subscriptions. A growing number of such publications are also now online through Web sites. Some of the sites provide considerable free information; a few are fee-based. Table 8-2 contains a lengthy, but not all encompassing, list of regular periodicals that are relevant to retailers. For every title, there is a brief description; and if available, Web sites for the publications are also noted.

Periodicals may be quite broad in scope (such as *Business Week* and *Fortune*) and discuss a great many business topics; or they may have specialized coverage (such as *Chain Store Age* and *Stores*) and deal mostly with topics of concern to retailers. Solutions to retail problems can be found in both the broad and the narrow publications. It is imperative for readers of periodicals to know the differences in orientation and quality among various publications. These examples are intended to provide an overview of the diversity of information available in the periodic literature:

- Store location—Articles have appeared on computer-based models for site selection, location theories, small-town sites, shopping centers, specialty shopping areas, and factory outlets.
- Operations—Articles have appeared on different management styles, customer-conscious employees, drug testing of employees, cost control, store remodeling, and shoplifting.
- Merchandising—Articles have appeared on the retail product mix, fads versus trends, the buyer's role, vendor selection, and inventory management.
- Pricing—Articles have appeared on consumers' use of information, laws, everyday low prices, discounts, one-price stores, direct marketing prices, and coping in price-sensitive times.
- Store image and promotion—Articles have appeared on how store image is developed, store atmosphere, the promotion mix, merchandise promotions, and customer service.
- Evaluating the strategy—Articles have appeared on company mergers, strategy execution, attaining goals, and competitive distinctiveness.

A number of organizations publish books, monographs, and other nonregular literature on retail topics. Some, like Prentice Hall (http://www.prenhall.com/phbusiness), are traditional publishers that produce textbooks and practitioner-oriented books. Others, such as the American Marketing Association (http://www.ama.org), the Better Business Bureau (http://www.bbb.org), the International Franchise Association (http://www.franchise.org), and the National Retail Federation (http://www.nrf.com), have distinct goals in publishing their materials.

One type of organization (such as the American Marketing Association) distributes information to increase the level of knowledge of readers on various topics. A second type (such as the Better Business Bureau) wants to improve the public's image of business and expand the role of industry self-regulation. These associations provide literature to familiarize firms with efficient and legal practices. A third type (such as the International Franchise Association and the National Retail Federation) describes current industry practices and emerging trends, and acts as a spokesperson and lobbyist to advocate the best interests of member firms. All these groups distribute materials for moderate fees or free (to members). Besides the associations cited, others can be uncovered by consulting Gale's *Encyclopedia of Associations* in the library.

Retailers can often obtain information from channel members: advertising agencies, franchise operators, manufacturers, and wholesalers. Whenever any of these firms undertake research for their own purposes (such as determining the most effective kind of advertising message, the type of consumer most likely to buy a particular product, or the sort of retailer the consumer will patronize in making a purchase) and then presents some or all of the findings to their retailers, external secondary data are involved. Channel members will pass on findings to enhance their sales and relations with retailers. They usually do not charge retailers for the information.

The last external secondary data source is the commercial research house that conducts ongoing studies and makes the results of those studies available to many clients for a fee. The fee can be rather low, or it can range to thousands of dollars, depending on the complexity of the issue or problem examined. This type of research is secondary when the retailer acts as a subscriber and does not request specific studies pertaining only to itself.

Rewarding the Best Customers and "Firing" Cherry Pickers

According to a retail consultant who spent six months visiting at 83 major supermarket chains, few stores collect data concerning their customers. A second study by *Progressive Grocer* confirmed that although 18 percent of supermarket operators have frequent-shopper programs, only a small percentage tailor their programs based on customer-specific sales data.

The offering of specials to loyal shoppers rewards those who purchase a large percentage of their products in one supermarket and reduces "cherry pickers," shoppers who purchase only specially priced goods. Milwaukee-based MegaMart and Virginia-based Ukrops are among the supermarket chains now offering specials to frequent customers based on their purchase history in a given category. Thus,

a consumer who buys toothpaste every six weeks or so at Megamart will not receive an offer until five weeks after his or her last purchase of toothpaste; and to encourage consumers to revisit the store, some coupon offers are good for only three hours. In contrast, Ukrop's sends its "Ukrops Valued Customers" a monthly newsletter with coupons tailored individually for each cardholder.

Some supermarkets with customer-specific marketing programs have even begun to replace their traditional newspaper-based ads with regular direct-mail offers to their most loyal customers.

Sources: Murray Raphel, "Customer Specific Marketing," *Direct Marketing* (June 1996), pp. 22–27; Michael Garry, "The Best and the Brightest," *Progressive Grocer* (March 1996), pp. 65–68; and Julie Ritzer Ross, "Frequent-Shopper Programs Becoming Entrenched in Supermarket Industry," *Stores* (February 1997), pp. 32–35.

Among the large commercial houses specializing in secondary data for retailers are R.H. Donnelley, Information Resources Inc., A.C. Nielsen, R.L. Polk, and Standard Rate & Data Service. They provide a host of subscription services at much lower costs (and probably with greater expertise) than the retailer would incur if the data were collected only for its primary use.

PRIMARY DATA

Advantages and Disadvantages

After a firm has exhausted the available secondary data, its defined issue or problem may still not be resolved. In this instance, primary data (those collected to resolve a specific topic at hand) are necessary. In cases where secondary data research is sufficient, primary data are not collected.

There are several advantages associated with primary data. They are collected to fit the specific purposes of the retailer. The data are current. The units of measure and the data categories are designed to address the issue or problem under investigation. In addition, the retailer either collects the data itself or hires an outside party to do so. Thus, the source is known and controlled, and the methodology is constructed for the specific study. There are no conflicting data from different sources, and the reliability of the research can be determined, if desired. When secondary data do not resolve an issue or problem, primary data are the only alternative.

There are also several possible disadvantages often associated with primary data. They are normally more expensive to obtain than secondary data. The collection tends to be more time-consuming. Some types of information cannot be acquired by an individual firm. If only primary data are collected, the perspective may be limited. Irrelevant information may be collected if the issue is not stated specifically enough.

A retailer desiring information to resolve an issue or problem has many criteria to consider in evaluating the use of primary data. In particular, specificity, currentness, and reliability must be weighed against high costs, time, and limited access to materials. The benefits of primary research must be weighed against the limitations.

A variety of primary data sources for retailers are discussed next.

Figure 8-7

Survey Research at Food Lion

At Food Lion, a leading supermarket chain, surveys are regularly used to obtain shopper feedback on customer service, product displays, and other topics. As shown here, company employees are often involved as interviewers.

Sources

The first decision to be made in collecting primary data is who will undertake it. A retailer can gather the data itself (internal) or hire a research firm (external). Internal data collection is usually quicker and cheaper. External data collection is usually more objective and formalized.

Second, a sampling methodology would be specified. Instead of gathering data from all stores, all products, all customers, and so on, a retailer can obtain accurate information by studying a sample of stores, products, or customers. Sampling saves time and money. There are two broad sampling approaches: With a **probability (random) sample,** every store, product, or customer has an equal or known chance of being chosen for study. In a **nonprobability sample,** stores, products, or customers are chosen by the researcher—based on judgment or convenience. A probability sample is more accurate but is also more costly and difficult to undertake. A further discussion of sampling is beyond the scope of this book.

Third, the retailer must choose among four basic types of primary data collection: survey, observation, experiment, and simulation. All of these methods are capable of generating data for each element of a retail strategy.

Survey ❑ The **survey** is a research technique whereby information is systematically gathered from respondents by communicating with them. Surveys may be used in a variety of retail settings. For instance, Circuit City surveys thousands of customers each month to determine their satisfaction with each aspect of the selling process. Spiegel combines an in-house computer-assisted telephone interviewing system (CATI) with mail questionnaires, small-group personal surveys, and on-site shopper surveys (at its Eddie Bauer stores) to regularly determine customer tastes and needs. Food Lion uses in-store surveys to find out how satisfied its customers are and what their attitudes are on various subjects. See Figure 8-7.

A survey may be conducted in person, over the phone, or through the mail. In almost all cases, a questionnaire is used. A personal survey is face-to-face, flexible, and able to elicit lengthy responses; and any question ambiguity can be explained. It may be costly, and interviewer bias is possible (such as interviewers inadvertently suggesting ideas to respondents). A telephone survey is fast and relatively inexpensive. Yet, responses are usually short and nonresponse may be a problem. It must be verified that the desired respondent is contacted. A mail survey can reach a wide range of respondents, has no interviewer bias, and is relatively inexpensive. Slowness of return, high nonresponse rates, and participation by incorrect respondents are the major potential problems. The technique chosen depends on the goals and requirements of the research project.

Figure 8-8

A Nondisguised Survey on Apparel Shopping

Interest, Activity or Attitude	Disagree	Neutral	Agree
Women are now wearing slacks to work quite often.	3%	25%	72%
In the future, I will most likely continue to shop at the stores where I buy my clothing now.	3	28	70
I want my fashion store to take anything back, no questions asked.	5	26	69
Classic means "timeless"—you can wear it forever.	7	25	68
I prefer classic looks to more trendy looks in clothes.	7	28	65
I often say positive things to other people about the stores where I shop for my clothing.	5	32	63
I am willing to sacrifice attractive store decor and fancy fixtures for real savings on my clothing.	7	32	61
When I look at an item of clothing, and then the price, I know whether or not it's a good value for the money.	5	34	60
In more and more jobs, dressing casually is now acceptable.	5	36	59
I don't mind paying more for clothing if it will last a long time.	4	38	58
I like to shop at clothing stores where I can get in and out quickly.	5	37	58
I buy more clothing on sale than I do at regular prices.	8	34	58
I am buying a lot of basic, solid colors so that I can mix and match my wardrobe.	5	40	55
I am willing to pay a bit more for quality.	4	41	55
Even when I buy more expensive clothing, I buy it only when it's on sale.	12	34	54
I prefer to have all alterations included in the price of clothing (such as suits, slacks, etc.)	17	29	54
I buy most of my clothes very close to the time I actually need them rather than buying for the future.	12	35	53
I am very cost-conscious when it comes to clothes.	8	39	53
My primary fashion store is one where I can obtain all the clothes that I need.	18	30	52
I am increasingly buying underwear, socks, hosiery, exercise wear, etc. at discount stores.	27	23	50
I don't buy clothes that make me stand out from everyone else.	14	36	50

It must also be decided if a survey is nondisguised or disguised. In a **nondisguised survey,** the respondent is told the real purpose of the study. Figure 8-8 shows how a nondisguised survey of more than 2,000 Chicago women could be used to design a lifestyle profile for apparel retailers. With this survey, respondents (those agreeing or disagreeing with the statements) are told the true purpose of the study, and a questionnaire is used to enter answers. In a **disguised survey,** the respondent is not told the study's real purpose. Otherwise, the person may answer what he or she thinks a firm wants to hear. Disguised surveys can use word associations, sentence completions, cartoon analysis, or projective questions (such as "Do your friends like shopping at this store? Do they find the styles to be in fashion?").

The **semantic differential**—a listing of bipolar adjective scales—is a survey technique that may be disguised or nondisguised, depending on whether the respondent is told the study's true purpose. The respondent is asked to rate one or more retailers on several criteria; each criterion is evaluated along a bipolar adjective scale, such as unfriendly-friendly or untidy-neat. By computing the average rating of all respondents for each criterion, an overall store profile can be developed. A semantic differential comparing two furniture retailers appears in Figure 8-9. Store A is a prestige, high-quality store and Store B is a medium-quality, family-run store. The semantic differential reveals the overall images of the stores and graphically portrays them.

A survey-related tool gaining popularity is **multidimensional scaling,** a technique by which attitudinal data are collected for several attributes in a manner that allows data analysis to produce a single overall rating of a retailer (rather than a profile of individual characteristics). A further description of the technique is beyond the scope of this text, but Figure 8-10 shows how multidimensional scaling can be used to construct single overall ratings. In this example, service level, product assortment, and price level are the

Please check the blanks that best indicate your feelings about Stores A and B.

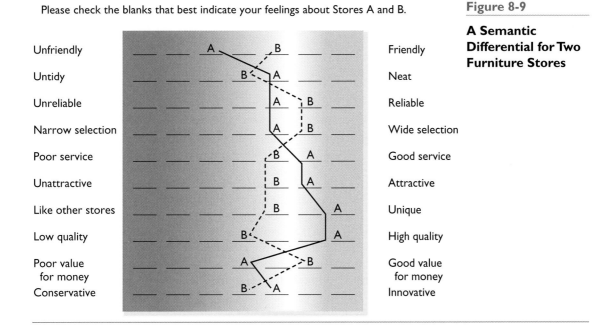

Figure 8-9

A Semantic Differential for Two Furniture Stores

criteria used to create profiles for four competing drugstores. These ratings reveal consumer perceptions of the stores, show the stores' strengths and weaknesses, and aid in strategy development and modification.

From Figure 8-10, these conclusions can be reached: Drugstore A is rated as good on all three criteria; it is the best-liked store. Drugstore B is equal to A in terms of service level and product assortment; it is viewed as having high (bad) prices. Drugstore C is equal to A in terms of product assortment and price level; it is viewed as providing bad

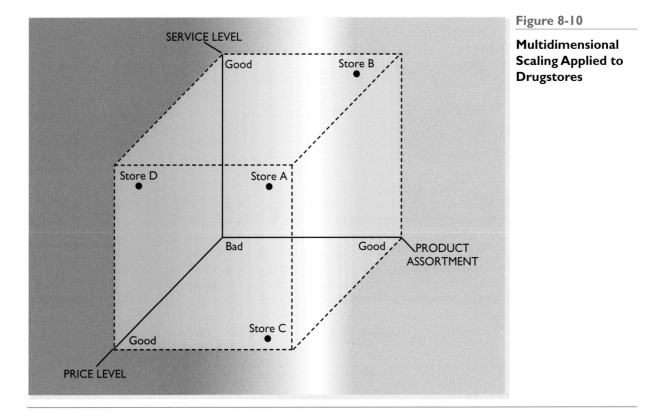

Figure 8-10

Multidimensional Scaling Applied to Drugstores

service. Drugstore D is equal to A in terms of service level and price level; it is viewed as having a bad product assortment. Drugstores B, C, and D need to improve their strategies to compete with A.

Other types of survey-related techniques also can be utilized, but those described should demonstrate the usefulness of this primary data tool.

Observation ❏ **Observation** is a form of research in which present behavior or the results of past behavior are observed and recorded. People are not questioned in a survey format. Observation may not require the cooperation of respondents, and interviewer or question biases are minimized. In many instances, observation can be used in actual situations, eliminating the influences of artificial environments. The major disadvantage of using observation (by itself) is that attitudes cannot be obtained.

For example, retailers can use observation to determine the quality of sales personnel presentations (by having researchers pose as shoppers), to monitor related-item buying by consumers, to determine store activity by time of day and day of week, to make pedestrian and vehicular traffic counts (to measure the potential of new locations), and to determine the proportion of shopping center patrons using public transportation.

With **mystery shoppers,** retailers hire people to pose as customers and observe their operations, from sales presentations to how well displays are maintained to in-home service calls. One marketing research firm, National Shopping Service in Los Angeles, has a nationwide pool of 10,000 mystery shoppers. This is how mystery shopping works:

> Most companies today realize that to stay in business, they must continually upgrade, or at least maintain, an acceptable level of quality and service. That's where mystery shoppers come into play: They offer businesses an inside view of their employees' performance and their customers' satisfaction. In a sense, mystery shoppers can be thought of as just normal customers with unbiased opinions. They shop at stores and eat at restaurants just like you and I. The only difference is, they enter these establishments with a single purpose in mind—to evaluate and observe what goes on around them. Mystery shoppers pay attention to such details as the condition of the establishment and its rest rooms, the attitude and dress of the employees, and the efficiency of the transaction. They know ahead of time what to look for because they are prompted by the client to focus on specific details about the business. When they're done "shopping," they fill out an evaluation form, which is later analyzed and compiled with evaluations from other shoppers into a report for the client. The data collected by mystery shoppers are used to improve product quality, prevent and deter fraud, improve employee morale, monitor the competition, and employ a proactive approach to assessing problem areas of a business.[15]

When observation is utilized, decisions are necessary as to whether it should be natural or contrived, disguised or nondisguised, structured or unstructured, direct or indirect, and human or mechanical.

Natural observation occurs if a real, ongoing situation is involved—such as actual customers being viewed entering, shopping in, and leaving a store. Contrived observation takes place under more artificial conditions, such as mystery shoppers posing as customers to determine a salesperson's "pitch" or "dummy" displays being set up to see shoppers' reactions.

In disguised observation, the shopper or company employee is not aware he or she is being watched. A two-way mirror or hidden camera provides disguised observation. In nondisguised observation, the participant knows he or she is being observed—such as a department manager's observing the behavior of a cashier.

Structured observation calls for the observer to watch for and note specific behavior. Unstructured observation requires the observer to watch and note all actions performed

[15]Charlotte Mulhern, "Under Cover," *Entrepreneur* (September 1996), p. 204. See also Paula Kephart, "The Spy in Aisle 3," *Marketing Tools* (May 1996), pp. 16–21.

by the person being studied, such as a researcher's watching the total in-store behavior of customers to determine the actions they take and the items they buy.

With direct observation, the observer watches the present behavior of people. With indirect observation, the observer examines evidence of past behavior. Food products in consumer pantries are examples of items that could be analyzed by indirect observation.

Human observation is carried out by people and is flexible. It may be disguised, but the observer may enter biased notations or interpretations and may miss behavior. Mechanical observation eliminates viewer bias and does not miss any behavior. A video camera that films in-store consumer activity is an example of mechanical observation.

Experiment ❏ An **experiment** is a type of research in which one or more elements of a retail strategy mix are manipulated under controlled conditions. An element may be, for example, an item's price, the layout of a department in a store, a shelf display, or store hours. In an experiment, just the element under investigation is manipulated; all others remain constant. For instance, if a retailer is interested in finding out the effects of a price change on a brand's unit sales, only the price of that brand is varied (such as making this week's price $0.99 and next week's $1.19, and then comparing unit sales for each week). The other elements of the retail strategy remain the same. This way, only the effect of the price change is measured.

An experiment may utilize survey or observation techniques to record data. In a survey, questions are asked about the experiment: Did you buy Brand Z because of its new shelf display? Are you buying extra ice cream because it's on sale? In observation, behavior is watched during the experiment: The revenues of Brand Z increase by 20 percent when a new display is used. Ice cream sales go up by 25 percent during a special sale.

Surveys and observations are experimental in nature if they occur under closely controlled situations. But when surveys ask broad attitudinal questions or observations of unstructured behavior occur, experimental procedures are not involved. In a retail setting, an experiment can be hard to undertake since many factors beyond the command of the retailer (such as weather, competition, and the economy) may influence results. On the other hand, a well-controlled experiment can provide a lot of good, specific data.

The major advantage of an experiment lies in its ability to show cause and effect (for instance, a lower price equals higher sales). It is also systematically structured and implemented. The major potential disadvantages are high costs, contrived settings, and uncontrollable factors.

Simulation ❏ A **simulation** is a type of experiment whereby a computer-based program is used to manipulate the elements of a retail strategy mix rather than test them in a real setting. Two types of simulations are now being employed in retail settings: those based on mathematical models and those involved with "virtual reality."

For the first type of simulation, a mathematical model of the expected controllable and uncontrollable factors (and their interactions) facing the retailer is first constructed. These factors are then manipulated by a computer so their effects on the overall retail strategy and specific elements of it are learned. No consumer cooperation is needed, and many different factors and combinations of factors can be manipulated in a controlled, rapid, inexpensive, and rather risk-free manner. This kind of simulation is becoming more popular for retailers because their level of mathematical and computer sophistication is rising and appropriate software is becoming available. However, it is still somewhat difficult to use.

For the second type of simulation, the retailer must devise or purchase interactive software that enables participants to simulate actual behavior in a format that is as realistic as possible. While this approach is more futuristic than mathematical simulations,

J.C. Penney: Building Information Partnerships

Standardized communications standards, such as the Voluntary Interindustry Commerce Standards (VICS), and the existence of more compatible computer system architecture both let retailers and their vendors easily share information. The major benefit of an information partnership is that it makes it simpler for merchants and their suppliers to understand each other's business in depth.

Information partnerships result in shorter delivery times, reduced stockouts, and lower distribution costs—which benefit suppliers *and* their retailer partners. Furthermore, these partnerships can lead to more contacts between retailers and suppliers at all levels of their organizations, not just between a vendor's salespeople and a retail buyer.

Despite the number of information partnerships, some industry analysts feel that there is still considerable distance to go before the maximum benefits of such partnerships can be obtained. According to David Evans, J.C. Penney's senior vice-president of planning and information systems, "We're not completely there yet as far as openness and trust are concerned, but better software and hardware are certainly propelling us in the right direction." J.C. Penney now shares point-of-sale data on a regular basis with several thousand suppliers. Evans notes that "letting them know how their products are doing in our stores enables them to make better production decisions, which, in turn [enhances] our own sales."

Source: Julie Ritzer Ross, "Are Partnerships for Real?" *Stores* (September 1996), pp. 24–30.

there is interest in creating a "virtual shopping environment." These are some of the exciting possibilities through virtual-reality simulations:

> Recent advances in computer graphics and three-dimensional modeling promise to bring simulated test marketing to a much broader range of companies, products, and applications. How? By allowing the marketer to re-create—quickly and inexpensively—the atmosphere of an actual retail store on a computer screen. A consumer can view shelves stocked with any kind of product. The shopper can "pick up" a package from the shelf by touching its image on the monitor. In response, the product moves to the center of the screen, where the shopper can use a three-axis track ball to turn the package so that it can be examined from all sides. To "purchase" the product, the consumer touches an image of a shopping cart, and the product moves to the cart. Just as in a physical store, products pile up in the cart as the customer shops. During the shopping process, the computer unobtrusively records the amount of time the consumer spends shopping in each product category, the time the consumer spends examining each side of a package, the quantity of product the consumer purchases, and the order in which items are purchased. The virtual store duplicates the distracting clutter of an actual market. Consumers can shop in an environment with a realistic level of complexity and variety.[16]

It should be noted that, at present, there is limited software for virtual-reality simulations and people must be trained in how to use the software. See Figure 8-11.

The Data Collection Role of Retailers in a Distribution Channel

Retailers can have a key role in collecting primary data due to their position at the last stage in a distribution channel. Of all the firms in a channel, often only retailers have direct contact with and easy access to shoppers.

---

[16]Raymond R. Burke, "Virtual Shopping: Breakthrough in Marketing Research," *Harvard Business Review,* Vol. 74 (March–April 1996), pp. 120–131.

Figure 8-11

Simul-Shop: A Virtual-Reality Simulation

These are some ways in which retailers can assist other channel members in collecting primary data. They can

- Provide informal feedback on supplier prices, ads, and so on, based on their past experience.
- Allow data to be gathered on their premises. Many marketing research firms seek to conduct interviews at shopping centers because a large, broad base of people is available.
- Gather specific information requested by suppliers, such as how shoppers are reacting to prescribed in-store displays.
- Pass along information on the characteristics of consumers buying particular brands, models, and so on. Because, for many retailers, credit transactions account for a major portion of sales, these retailers can link purchases with consumer age, income, occupation, and other factors.
- Participate in single-source data collection by allowing their stores to have specially equipped computerized checkouts. In **single-source data collection,** a research firm (like Information Resources Inc.) develops a sample of consumer households, determines the demographic and life-style backgrounds of those households through surveys, observes television viewing behavior through in-home cable hookups to the firm's computers, and monitors shopping behavior by having people make purchases in designated stores. At these stores, consumers present an identification card similar to a credit card; all items bought are then recorded by computerized scanning equipment. This system is more accurate than multisource data collection (whereby the people surveyed are often different from those whose behavior is observed). It is a relatively new and somewhat expensive way of amassing data, and it has thus far been mostly limited to purchases in supermarkets.

Summary

1. *To show why retailers should systematically collect and analyze information when developing and modifying their strategies* Whether developing a new retail strategy or modifying an existing one, good information is necessary. Acting on the basis of proper information reduces a retailer's chances of making incorrect decisions. Retailers relying on nonsystematic or incomplete methods of research, such as intuition, increase their probabilities of failure.

2. *To examine the role of the retail information system, its components, and the recent advances in such systems* Acquiring useful information should be viewed as an ongoing, well-integrated process. Thus, a retail information system anticipates the information needs of retail managers; continuously collects, organizes, and stores relevant data; and directs the flow of information to the proper retail decision makers. Such a system has several components: environment, retailer's philosophy, strategic plans, information control center, and retail operations. The most important component is the information control center. It directs data collection, stores and retrieves data, and updates files.

Data-base management is the procedure used to collect, integrate, apply, and store information related to specific topics (such as customers, vendors, and product categories). One of the newest advances in data-base management is data warehousing, whereby copies of all the data bases in a firm are maintained in one location and can be accessed by employees at any locale. It is a huge repository separate from the operational data bases set up to support specific departmental applications. Data-base information can come from internal—company-generated—and external—purchased from outside firms—sources.

In recent years, retailers have greatly increased their use of computerized retail information systems, and the Universal Product Code (UPC) has become the dominant technology for recording and processing product-related data. Through electronic data interchange (EDI), the computers of retailers and their suppliers regularly exchange information.

3. *To describe the marketing research process* Marketing research in retailing involves a process consisting of a series of activities: defining the issue or problem to be researched, examining secondary data, gathering primary data (if needed), analyzing the data, making recommendations, and implementing findings. It is systematic in nature and not a single act. The steps should be undertaken sequentially.

4. *To discuss the characteristics and types of secondary data and primary data, including the retailer's data collection role* Secondary data (information gathered for other purposes) are inexpensive, can be collected quickly, may have several sources, and may provide otherwise unattainable information. Some sources are quite credible. And when the problem is ill defined, a secondary data search can clarify it. There are also potential pitfalls to secondary data: they may not suit the purposes of the study; units of measurement and categories of data may not be specific enough; information may be old or inaccurate; a source may be disreputable, and different sources may have conflicting results; and data may not be reliable.

Secondary data should always be consulted before primary data are obtained. Internal secondary data are available within the firm. External secondary data are available from government and nongovernment sources outside the company. Reference guides, regular periodicals, nonregular publications, channel members, and commercial research houses all provide external secondary data. Many sources have Web sites.

Primary data (those gathered for the resolution of the specific topic at hand) are collected when secondary data do not adequately address the issue or problem at hand. Primary data are precise and current; the data are collected and categorized with the measures desired; the methodology is known; there are no conflicting results; and the level of reliability can be determined. When secondary data do not exist, primary data are the only alternative. The potential disadvantages of primary data are the costs, time, limited access, narrow perspective, and amassing of irrelevant information.

Primary research may be done internally or externally. Four types of primary data collection are available: survey (personal, telephone, or mail), observation (mystery shoppers, natural-contrived, human-mechanical), experiment, and simulation. Each technique has its own advantages and disadvantages.

Retailers often have a vital role in collecting primary data due to their position at the final stage in a distribution channel. They can provide informal feedback to suppliers, allow data to be gathered on their premises, assist in monitoring consumer behavior, pass along information on consumer characteristics, and participate in single-source data collection.

Key Terms

retail information system (p. 236)
data-base management (p. 242)
data warehousing (p. 243)
Universal Product Code (UPC)
  (p. 244)
electronic data interchange (EDI)
  (p. 246)
marketing research in retailing
  (p. 246)
marketing research process (p. 246)
issue (problem) definition (p. 246)

secondary data (p. 247)
primary data (p. 247)
data analysis (p. 247)
recommendations (p. 248)
implementation (p. 248)
internal secondary data (p. 250)
external secondary data (p. 250)
probability (random) sample
  (p. 255)
nonprobability sample (p. 255)
survey (p. 255)

nondisguised survey (p. 256)
disguised survey (p. 256)
semantic differential (p. 256)
multidimensional scaling (p. 256)
observation (p. 258)
mystery shoppers (p. 258)
experiment (p. 259)
simulation (p. 259)
single-source data collection (p. 262)

Questions for Discussion

1. At the beginning of this chapter, several unsuccessful strategies were described. What types of information gathering and processing would you recommend for each of the following retailers?
   a. Toy store.
   b. Chain bookstore.
   c. Mail-order retailer.
   d. Florist.

2. How could a small retailer devise a retail information system?
3. How could a large retailer be involved with data warehousing?
4. What are the value of the Universal Product Code (UPC) and electronic data interchange (EDI) with regard to the retail information systems of general merchandise retailers?

5. How do the terms *retail information system* and *marketing research in retailing* differ?

6. What are the steps in the marketing research process? May any of these steps be skipped? Why or why not?

7. Cite the major advantages and disadvantages of secondary data.

8. As a sporting-goods store owner, what kinds of secondary data would you want to obtain from Nike or Reebok?

9. Under which circumstances should a retailer collect primary data?

10. Describe the major advantage of each method of gathering primary data: survey, observation, experiment, and simulation.

11. What are the benefits and risks of using nondisguised consumer surveys?

12. Develop a ten-item semantic differential for a local restaurant to judge its image. Who should be surveyed? Why?

13. Why would a retailer use mystery shoppers rather than other forms of observation? Are there any instances when you would not recommend their use? Why or why not?

14. Discuss some problems a retailer could face in conducting an in-store display experiment.

15. Comment on "virtual shopping" as a research tool for retailers.

Web-Based Exercise:

RETAIL PRO—A DECISION SUPPORT SYSTEM (http://www.retailpro.com)

Questions

1. Describe the major decision support features of the Retail Pro point-of-sale system.

2. What are the pros and cons of purchasing versus leasing Retail Pro?

3. Develop criteria to evaluate Retail Pro in comparison to other point-of-sale systems.

4. Determine the costs and potential savings of using Retail Pro versus a manual system.

CASE 1
ShopKo: Providing Information to Suppliers Through the Internet*

ShopKo, a 130-store regional full-line discount chain with $2 billion in annual sales, recently decided to overhaul its retail information system when research indicated that the value of its reports was limited because of their slow response time to queries and the inflexibility in presentation formats. A noteworthy element of its new information system is ShopKo's providing access to certain point-of-sale data by key suppliers through the Internet.

Unlike smaller retailers, ShopKo's retail information system requirements are complex. ShopKo carries 200,000 SKUs (stock-keeping units), has multiple departments (including hard goods, soft goods, pharmacy, and optometry)—each of which has distinct needs, reviews sales statistics on a daily basis, and seeks to store data for a two-year time period. Thus, ShopKo wants its new information system to have the flexibility to evaluate sales data on several levels (from the daily sales of a specific style in a specific store to the monthly sales of all jeans in a given geographic region). And it wants a retail information system that can generate sales analysis, inventory management, forecasting, and profitability reports.

ShopKo's system was devised in conjunction with MicroStrategy (http://www.strategy.com), a vendor whose software became the basis for ShopKo's decision support system. For its part in helping ShopKo meet its goals, MicroStrategy was selected ShopKo's 1996 "Vendor of the Year." MicroStrategy's system for ShopKo has two major components: DSS Agent and DSS Web.

The DSS Agent software enables ShopKo executives to obtain answers to specific questions, as well as to develop customized reports, to alter the level of detail (such as

*The material in this case is drawn from Julie Ritzer Ross, "ShopKo Initiative Overhauls System for Data Analysis," *Stores* (September 1996), pp. 44–47; and MicroStrategy press releases.

individual store, region, or country sales data), and to alert ShopKo's management to out-of-stock or faster than anticipated selling situations. This gives ShopKo's managers a better understanding of sales trends, and of the contribution of specific lines of merchandise to a store's overall profitability.

According to ShopKo's director of information services, Gene Klawikowski, "The information is presented within a matter of minutes, is easier to understand than before, and has [proven] comprehensive enough to support the most critical decision-making." These qualities better enable ShopKo to match goods stocked to a consumer's actual purchasing patterns. For example, the retail information system now provides the means for ShopKo to determine whether consumers only buy goods on sale, add a few additional goods, or purchase their weekly needs at the same time. This information better enables ShopKo to plan its use of specials.

DSS Agent software also played an important part in the growth of ShopKo's managed health services business from $13 million to $350 million in a recent two-year period. ShopKo's ProVantage subsidiary uses DSS Agent to handle claims processing for pharmacies and prescription benefit management services for firms. The ProVantage network has connections to more than 40,000 member pharmacies.

The second key part of ShopKo's retail information system is DSS Web software. This component allows vendors to log onto ShopKo's World Wide Web page with a standard browser (such as Netscape or Internet Explorer) and thereby determine how well their products are selling. According to Klawikowski, "By being the first retailer to link up with suppliers in this way, we're enhancing our vendor partnership and bringing more value to our customers." The Web component of its retail information system gives ShopKo suppliers remote access to the same data used by ShopKo when it evaluates each vendor. These data include current sales, sales compared to prior periods, and profitability rankings (such as bottom 10 and top 10 items). All DSS Agent data and reports can be immediately accessed through DSS Web. Like DSS Agent, a supplier can prepare reports based on finer or broader levels (such as product line, time, or number of stores). DSS Web significantly reduces the need to use special software or to maintain data at client machines; these two responsibilities have involved considerable expense with other systems.

Questions
1. Describe the benefits of DSS Agent software for ShopKo.
2. What reports would you suggest that ShopKo generate using DSS Agent software?
3. Discuss the benefits of ShopKo's providing DSS Web access to its suppliers from the suppliers' perspective. From ShopKo's perspective.
4. Should ShopKo charge its suppliers for access to DSS Web? Explain your answer.

Marsh Supermarkets (http://www.marsh.net) is an Indianapolis-based chain that operates 271 food stores in five different formats. In the early 1990s, Marsh Supermarkets conducted a classic two-part consumer behavior study that has been viewed by some industry experts as "the most detailed shopper profile analysis ever compiled."

In the study's first phase, Marsh recorded all customer transactions in five of its stores (located in upscale metropolitan, blue-collar metropolitan, and county-seat rural areas) using scanner-equipped point-of-sale equipment. These data were employed to analyze sales, profit, and productivity relationships. For example, by varying advertising during the study, Marsh was able to determine the impact of different promotions on sales.

---

†The material in this case is drawn from *Marsh Supermarkets, Inc. 1996 Annual Report;* Robert E. O'Neill, "Customer Behavior: Seeing is Believing," *Progressive Grocer* (January 1993), pp. 57–62; and Glenn Snyder, "Shedding Light on Bulb Sales," *Progressive Grocer* (June 1993), p. 117.

CASE 2
(Continued)

The second phase of the study tracked 1,600 shoppers in two Marsh test stores over a three-week period. One outlet was a combination store with a large general merchandise department and a pharmacy. The other was a conventional supermarket with general merchandise integrated into the grocery store. This phase was designed to determine how many shoppers use lists, where shoppers go in the store, how many shoppers talk with employees, and how long typical shoppers spend in a supermarket. To avoid influencing shopper behavior, trackers used walkie-talkies to communicate with each other as they observed customers from catwalks located above the store. Behavior was recorded from 7 A.M. to 7 P.M. on Wednesdays, Fridays, and Saturdays with consumers divided into three groups based on their behavior: fill-in shoppers, routine shoppers, and stock-up shoppers. Fill-in shoppers, who comprised 43 percent of the test stores' total customers, bought 10 or fewer items on a given shopping trip. The average fill-in shopper spent $12.51 weekly at the supermarket, completed a shopping trip in 11 minutes, and bought 5 items per trip. Routine shoppers, who accounted for 41 percent of the test stores' total customers, bought 11 to 35 items per shopping trip. The average routine shopper spent $39.40 per trip, completed a shopping trip in 23 minutes, and bought 20 items per trip. Stock-up shoppers, who accounted for only 16 percent of the test stores' total customers, bought 36 or more items per shopping trip. On average, stock-up shoppers spent $85.30 weekly, stayed in the store for 39 minutes, and bought 48 items.

Two other significant findings of the Marsh study relate to pass-buy ratios. In general, average department "pass rates"/penetration (the percentage of shoppers who pass through a given department) is highest for the first department encountered in a store's traffic-flow pattern and then declines for each department that is farther from the first department. In the Marsh study, meat, produce, and dairy products were passed by 74 percent, 56 percent, and 47 percent of shoppers, respectively. The "buy" ratio (the percentage of shoppers who buy a good in a given department) also varies by department. Only 10 percent of the departments studied had buy ratios higher than 50 percent. One-third had ratios between 26 percent and 50 percent, and 56 percent had buy rates of 25 percent or less.

The Marsh Super Study also reported specific findings for a number of different product categories. As an example, for lightbulbs, consumer demographics, the selling season, and a store's marketing program all had a great impact on sales. The upscale metropolitan store had lightbulb sales of $1.59 per $1,000 of total sales, versus $1.06 and $1.41 per $1,000 in the blue-collar metro and county-seat rural stores, respectively. Lightbulb sales were highest during the third and fourth quarters when days were shortest. Temporary price reductions, newspaper advertising, and displays were effective in generating lightbulb sales. Although a temporary price reduction alone generated a 9.6 percent increase in sales; the combined effect of price, advertising, and displays resulted in a 430.1 percent increase in sales.

Questions

1. To a retailer using the Marsh Super Study as secondary data, what are the strengths and weaknesses of the methodology employed in the study?
2. What could a nonsupermarket retailer learn from the Marsh study?
3. What other kinds of primary and secondary data could a supermarket use in researching the behavior of shoppers? Explain your answer.
4. Describe how Marsh could integrate its shopper study into its retail information system.

Video Questions on Marsh Super Study

1. Discuss the Marsh Super Study findings for lightbulbs.
2. How should a supermarket owner or manager use these findings to increase sales and profitability?

Part Three
Comprehensive Case

Developing Customer- and Information-Based Retailing Strategies*

INTRODUCTION

In-store cafes, interactive signs that talk, child-friendly environments, and so on, are all part of the aggressive programs used by retailers to keep customers coming back. That's not to mention "free" Cannes trips. This is retailing today, and some programs are actually inspiring people to spend more. Yet, success is not universal. Stunned by Wal-Mart's success, Kmart, one of the big three U.S. retailers (along with Wal-Mart and Sears) has had a serious identity crisis.

WAL-MART'S UP, KMART'S DOWN

"Everyone can make a comeback. But for Kmart to make real progress, it must decide who it is," said Jeffrey Hill, managing director of Meridian Consulting Group—which has worked with both Wal-Mart and Kmart. "It must establish a competitive point of difference. Wal-Mart has a very focused strategy. When you think of Wal-Mart, you think of value. With Kmart there's no clear answer." Kmart's philosophy was growth by diversification. It gobbled up Borders bookstores, Sports Authority, and Office Max. "Unfortunately, executives took their eyes off the base business and focused on too many things. Wal-Mart took advantage of that. Now, the main business is ill; and management has had to focus on it and sell off many of these distractions."

While Kmart gained a reputation for operational woes, Wal-Mart spent years developing technology that allowed quick response and just-in-time delivery. That translated to significantly lower costs in taking products to consumers and a higher likelihood of being in stock. Wal-Mart also capitalized on its reputation for value to create what Hill calls a "halo effect" for private-label goods. It uses hot prices to get con-

sumers in the door and converts them to private-label items. "Now they own the consumer and the consumer is buying Wal-Mart products."

In addition, Wal-Mart has benefited from a consistency of management that Hill contends let the chain weather the loss of founder Sam Walton. In contrast, Kmart finds itself still in transition after CEO Joseph E. Antonini's departure. "Kmart will be mired in transition mode for a long time," Hill said. "The loss of momentum is immeasurable." Kenneth Watson, Kmart's executive vice-president for marketing and product development, has acknowledged consumer complaints and said the firm is working harder to have merchandise in stock and improve customer service.

Many grocery retailers are finding themselves embroiled in a similar battle, as Wal-Mart, Kmart, and Target open more supercenters, a hybrid store format combining a mass merchandise store and a supermarket. Recently, Babson College conducted a study of supercenters in Victoria, Texas, and Gainesville, Georgia. Wal-Mart and Kmart both have supercenters in the cities, but are encountering different competitive scenarios. In Victoria, the leading competitors are two large H.E. Butt stores and a midsized Albertson's. In Gainesville, there are several regional players and a local firm called J&J. According to the study, Wal-Mart was the price leader for manufacturer brands in both markets—an ominous sign for grocery retailers. "If U.S. food retailers are going to stand by and let Wal-Mart march into their markets and establish low-price leadership, they deserve the same fate as Kmart," Babson marketing professor Douglas Tigert said in the report.

In Victoria, Super Kmart and H.E. Butt were "trying hard to stay below the consumer threshold of noticeability" (in comparison to Wal-Mart's lower prices), which the report estimated to be at 3 percent to 4 percent. Prices at Albertson's were 9 percent higher. In Gainesville, the price spread across the seven chains was almost 22 percent, which Tigert said was about the highest ever measured in a single market. The big surprise was that Food Lion, which built its reputation as a low-price leader, was 16 percent

*The material in this case was adapted by the authors from Cyndee Miller of *Marketing News*, "Retailers Do What They Must to Ring Up Sales," *Marketing News* (May 22, 1995), pp. 1, 10. Reprinted by permission of the American Marketing Association.

higher than Wal-Mart, and its meat and produce prices were 28 percent higher. The only serious price competitor to Wal-Mart in the market was J&J, with just one store.

THE CHALLENGE OF STIMULATING TODAY'S CONSUMERS

Although some products have been hot during holiday seasons, in recent years, many retailers have been forced to resort to serious price slashing to get consumers to even look at clothing. And according to Ann Hunt, president of a media marketing firm, "I don't think things are going to get too much better. There are too many stores out there with too many clothes."

Hunt, who surveyed 1,000 opinion leaders for their views on apparel and how it is marketed, advised those in the fashion business to get real: "Women have had it. They've been vocal, but ignored. Now, they're putting down their foot and not buying." Almost two-thirds of the women surveyed said they were spending less on fashion-related merchandise than in previous years.

Hunt pointed a finger at advertising, which is "based on thinking of 25 years ago, of women sitting at home, leafing through a paper, wondering, 'Well, where will I shop today?' " Two-thirds of those her firm surveyed said current ads did not stimulate their interest in clothing. "Ads are not the problem, and they're not the solution; but if advertising was better, it could boost sales."

Hunt had kind words for Macy's "10 to Count On" ads, which gave a rundown on the latest trends; and she commended the Target discount chain for "almost upscale advertising for the price points they're in; yet they're very realistic and accessible." Dillard's has done well by showing items and how they're worn. "When women are making a decision to buy something, they want to see a whole outfit. That arty photography where everything is in the shadows is a real turnoff."

Hunt said retailers could take a hint from the home furnishings industry, presenting apparel as a reflection of how people live, instead of shoving designer trends down their throats. "Most women have become secure about what they want to buy. If they see something that fits them, they'll buy it. What they're not listening to is, 'Designers say bare midriffs this year.' They just tune that out. Retailers have let designers, who aren't in touch with real women, dictate."

Retail consultant Wendy Leibmann, president of WSL Marketing, agreed that a fundamental change in the way consumers buy apparel is a "potential bombshell." "People just aren't buying as much apparel, and the clothing they are buying is more casual and is at lower price points." So while many retailers are pushing the return of glamour and stocking shelves with patent leather minis and stiletto heels, it's sweatshirts and khakis that people are actually buying.

That's good for J.C. Penney, which Liebmann said is successfully established as a strong midmarket player and "really well-positioned for a downturn in the way consumers are shopping for apparel." It's bad for The Gap—now battling both discounters and department stores invading its turf. "There's the potential for Gap stores to get really squeezed." Furthermore, Gap stores may be losing their cachet with younger consumers. "They've lost their hip factor. That's a problem you face if you're on every corner. There's no point of difference. People are still comfortable with the clothes, but they don't get excited about going there anymore."

The Gap's lower-priced Old Navy clothing stores are picking up some of the slack, "but The Gap doesn't want to cannibalize its own business, so it has to be careful where it puts stores," Leibmann said. "It has to continue establishing Old Navy as a separate entity."

WHAT THE CONSUMER IS SPENDING ON NOW

While apparel sales may be a bit threadbare, consumers are showing interest in other areas. Anything for the home has been hot. It seems that, in the stressed-out 1990s, people view the home as a haven from the big, bad world. Successful niche players, like Bed Bath & Beyond, are successfully cashing in on the trend; yet no category killer has really shown up on the scene.

But department stores are moving in. Dayton Hudson opened two Marshall Field's Home Stores in Chicago during 1996, and Carson Pirie Scott opened three standalone home furnishings stores there. Some department stores, such as Rich's in Atlanta and Burdines in Miami, have set up separate furniture shops at malls they're already occupying.

Not to be left out, Sears has employed a national advertising campaign for its freestanding Homelife furniture stores. The theme is, "It's everything you need to bring your home to life." Leibmann said this could be a good approach for Sears. Crate & Barrel and Pottery Barn are more upscale and trendy. "But aside from Ikea, which is more modern, there aren't many low- to midlevel furniture stores anymore. So it's an opportunity for Sears if it can promote it that way."

Turning to another challenge for retailers, Leibmann said, "What we've learned in the 1990s is that people won't overpay for anything ever, ever again. If the perception is that they're not getting what they paid for, they won't shop there anymore. That doesn't mean the lowest price; but when they walk out of a store, they want to be comfortable with what they paid." Leibmann added that she sees the same trend in Europe, with sales becoming more common and discount perfumeries and drugstores in vogue. And U.S. firms with value positioning will see opportunities in markets like China and Eastern Europe, where consumers are starting to get money.

Leibmann also sees more consumers shopping for exactly what they want rather than just settling for acceptable products. As such, they will trek to a variety of stores, knowing they'll eventually get what they want: "If they're looking for tools, do they go to a local discount store which might have what they need? Or, do they make a trip to Home Depot where they're assured to find what they want? What this says to retailers is that if they're going to offer a range of merchandise, they better offer breadth and width in the categories in which they want to succeed."

REACHING CONSUMERS IN NEW WAYS

Leibmann also forecasts growth in "alternative forms of shopping," including catalogs, home shopping, and online services. But that doesn't mean the demise of the store. "If anything, it's going to nibble at everyone. People aren't going to spend more, they're just spreading it around." Home Shopping Network has felt the bite, with some quarterly losses and erratic sales—despite a revamped strategy that brought in new products and private-label designer goods.

Leibmann predicts the alternative forms of shopping will be an extension of the traditional store: "It's another way to reach the customer, not one versus another. The four-wall entities—Wal-Mart, Bloomingdale's—need to let people shop any way they want," be it at the actual store or by personal shopping service, catalog, or online service. Many are already doing that. Food retailers, including Safeway and A&P's Food Emporium, as well as such drugstore retailers as Eckerd Drug, have offered customers the option of shopping by phone, fax, or computer.

Retailers also are conjuring up creative ways to entice people into stores. At some Giorgio Armani's A/X shops, consumers pick out some "absolutely fab" outfits and dine on Italian cuisine at the cafes conveniently located in the stores. "People are getting a little burnt out on shopping," said Anne Brixner, marketing director at The Retail Group, a strategic planning and design firm. "Thus, retailers are frequently needing to turn into entertainers just to get shoppers in the door."

That doesn't mean stores have to go Hollywood. It may just mean placing interactive signs at the end of an aisle. In Pet Food Warehouse, if people press a customer-service button (marked by a sign with a huge paw print), they hear the sound of a dog barking and a call for assistance. "It makes it more memorable and gets people to spend more time in the store," said Brixner.

That's especially necessary for retailers trying to target the "been-there-done-that" Generation Xers: "They get bored quickly. If it looks like it's the same merchandise as a week ago, they get in and out fast," according to Brixner. So when The Retail Group consulted on the design for a new Megamart consumer electronics store, it made sure to include lots of fun stuff for "Xers" to play with, including a listening bar and a comfy seating area to check the home-theater equipment.

Manufacturers also are influencing the retail design scene. "In the old days, manufacturers developed products and shipped them to the retailer. Now, more have a say in where products are placed, how they're sold, what signage will say," Brixner noted. "Or, they're going for total control and opening their own stores." With fewer department stores left and retailers looking to push private-label brands, manufacturers are showing more interest in that idea than ever before.

Everyone from Speedo to Sony has opened shops devoted to their brands. While traditional retailers pick and choose what parts of a line they want to carry, these stores stock the whole line. Designed to make a statement about the brand, showcase stores are stylish affairs. Speedo's store has mannequins that appear to be diving from a ceiling done in swimming pool tiles. As Brixner said, "It creates brand awareness so when people see it in the department store, they recognize it. That's almost like an advertising vehicle." The risk is that brand stores might cannibalize sales at other stores. "I've heard both sides. My belief is that initially a brand store takes away sales since it's new and hot and people are anxious to see it. After a while, it just helps build awareness."

Stride Rite is a manufacturer selling to department and specialty stores, and running its own concept and outlet stores. It also has boutiques in areas leased by department stores. According to Dennis Garrow, president of the firm's retail division, traditional retailers shouldn't see a dramatic drop in sales due to the opening of concept stores. "There appear to be two different types of customers. There's some cannibalization, but it's not anywhere near as great as you might think."

Stride Rite's plan "calls for more retail concepts. There will be a lot of experimentation," Garrow said. Stride Rite has a new concept store for toddlers up to 8-year-olds. Designed to be more "child-friendly," the firm moved play areas out of corners and into more central locations so kids can whoop it up in parents' eyesight. In the store center, there's a 7-foot glass column with multicolored gears and pulleys that children activate with a button. Stride Rite plans to open several more of these stores and to renovate many older stores. Also recognizing that it "tends to lose children after age five," the firm came up with Great Feet superstores targeting the tastes of 6- to 8-year-olds. The boy's area looks like an outdoor basketball court. Stride Rite is even opening more stores devoted to its Keds brand. It currently operates one in the Mall of America, as well as outlets that are in its kids stores. Garrow described the Keds stores as "very casual in nature, well beyond whatever people know Keds to be, which is usually the little white sneaker."

ZEROING IN ON TARGET CUSTOMERS

Some firms are trying to tap into all the data they've amassed. "The retail industry is catching up with what other industries have known for years—the value of customer information. Because the more in tune they are with customers, the better they can target marketing efforts," said Scott Bryden, marketing resources manager at Intelligent Marketing Systems, which handles customer retention programs, event management, and marketing research for malls.

According to Bryden, "Retailers were doing the front end, in terms of promotions and mailings, but it's only been over the last four or five years that they've started to do the back end, collecting information and trying to monitor customers and track purchases to see how to target future efforts." The incentive for action was simple: "There has been a downturn in mall traffic. People are just not visiting the mall as much." And they don't spend as much time when they are there or visit as many stores per trip. As a result, more malls are using campaigns to promote "cross-shopping" by offering incentives to get a shopper who usually visits the mall for women's apparel to go out for electronics. Bryden estimated that over a one-year period, a campaign could lead to an average 17 percent increase in people shopping at stores they didn't normally visit.

Some malls are hoping to build traffic through customer loyalty programs, rewarding frequent shoppers with prizes or discounts on merchandise sold in the mall. That program also is popular with individual retailers. Neiman Marcus has had a loyalty program for more than a decade. Sears kicked off its Best Customer program in 1992; and Macy's, Dayton Hudson, J.C. Penney, and Nordstrom have launched tests or full programs. Grocery stores, home improvement chains, and bookstores are also trying to recruit customers for their loyalty programs. As Rick Barlow, president of Frequency Marketing, said, frequency marketing can "build a genuine relationship between the store and the customers based on information they provide."

In keeping with its tony image, Neiman Marcus bestows awards on big spenders that may be quite lavish. Those spending $3,000 with its charge card automatically become InCircle members. They are eligible to earn a free, 10-day vacation on the French Riviera by spending an additional $250,000 within a year. And to stay ahead of the pack, Neiman Marcus enhanced member amenities. "We're doing quite well with our Neiman Marcus card and our InCircle program. This is just a way to take it to the next level. It also lets us cast a wider net with our regular credit card," said Billy Payton, vice-president for marketing and customer programs at Neiman Marcus.

The retailer has added benefits to its regular credit card, including opportunities to receive benefits early (when customers open the account) and at lower spending levels. Neiman's also introduced a new gold card, available for $50, that allows holders to earn double points for the first $1,500 charged with the card. There's also a new platinum level in the retailer's InCircle program. After forking over the annual fee of $500, platinum customers earn double points on the first $30,000 in purchases per year. Customers accumulate one InCircle point for every dollar in purchases made at Neiman Marcus, but only if they use the store's own credit card. The only other card honored companywide is American Express.

"We are in an age where retailers are not out there promoting their own credit cards, and at the same time they're accepting other credit cards," Payton said. "That means they're losing contact with customers. They don't know their addresses, so they can't reach them through direct mail. We don't think that's the best way to grow customers and build relationships with them." He dismissed concerns that the program might be missing out on loyal shoppers who opt not to use the Neiman Marcus card. "We know we have a group of customers who prefer to use the InCircle card and receive the perks and privileges," he said. "Obviously, we wouldn't continue if it wasn't working well."

Payton said he didn't expect Neiman Marcus to be affected by the debut of other retailers' loyalty programs "because of the solid foundation we've built." He added that the program offers "real benefits" that "aren't all self-serving," such as free trips on American Airlines. The program is being promoted through in-store visuals and on billing statements. Neiman Marcus has also run an ad in *Worth* magazine and launched an even more extensive advertising campaign.

Questions

1. From a target market perspective, why has Wal-Mart leaped ahead of Kmart in many customers' hearts and minds?
2. What target market should Kmart now go after? With what strategy?
3. How should today's retailers be reacting to the consumer's poverty of time, outshopping, and impulse purchases?
4. Comment on this statement: "What we've learned in the 1990s is that consumers won't overpay for anything ever, ever again."
5. How can a retailer use an information system to better serve its customers, as well as to expand its customer base?
6. Devise a brief customer survey that Stride Rite could use to assess its Great Feet superstores.
7. Should Neiman Marcus utilize mystery shoppers? If yes, how? If no, why not?

Part Four

- Once a retailer conducts a situation analysis, sets goals, and identifies consumer characteristics and needs, it is ready to develop and enact an overall strategy. In Parts 4 through 7, the major elements of such a strategy are examined: choosing a store location, managing a business, merchandise management and pricing, and communicating with the customer. Part 4 concentrates on store location.

- Chapter 9 discusses the crucial nature of store location for retailers and outlines a four-step approach to location planning. Step 1, trading-area analysis, is covered in this chapter. Among the topics studied are the use of geographic information systems, the size and shape of trading areas, how to determine trading areas for existing and new stores, and major factors to consider in assessing trading areas. Several data sources are described.

- Chapter 10 deals with the last three steps in location planning: deciding on the most desirable type of location, selecting a general location, and choosing a particular site within that location. Isolated store, unplanned business district, and planned shopping center locales are contrasted. And criteria for evaluating each location are outlined and detailed.

....

Trading-Area Analysis

CHAPTER OBJECTIVES

1. To demonstrate the importance of store location for a retailer and outline the process for choosing a store location
2. To discuss the concept of a trading area and its related components
3. To show how trading areas may be delineated for existing and new stores
4. To examine three major factors in trading-area analysis: population characteristics, economic base characteristics, and competition and the level of saturation

During the 1986 to 1995 time period, U.S. multitenant shopping space increased from under 4 billion square feet to close to 5 billion square feet. As a result, many retailing analysts believe the United States is now overstored; and they frequently cite Standard & Poor's Corporation data showing a drop in retailer profit margin from 6.9 percent of sales for the 1985 to 1989 period (when there were 17 square feet of retail space per person) to 5.8 percent of sales in the 1990s (when per capita footage increased to 19 square feet).

Despite repeated warnings about overstoring, strong retailers continue to expand at the expense of their weaker competitors. According to one real-estate research firm, 86 million square feet of new multitenant retail space was added in the United States in 1996. Chains with aggressive store-opening plans include May Department Stores (it is in the midst of a five-year plan to add 125 stores), Dillard's, and Wal-Mart.

Dallas, with 26 feet of shopping space per person, is one of the clearer examples of the overstoring problem. With 26 malls already open, five more malls and an additional 115.5 million square feet of space were planned for 1996. Recently, Nordstrom opened a new store unit at Dallas-Fort Worth's Galleria Mall, despite the area's already having at least 10 large department stores (including Macy's, Marshall Field, and Saks Fifth Avenue at the Galleria and Sears, Dillard's, J.C. Penney, and Foley's at a mall directly across the street from the Galleria). Yet Nordstrom thinks that its Dallas store will bring in $100 million in sales, a first-year record for any new Nordstrom store. According to Daniel Nordstrom, one of Nordstrom's six co-presidents, "If you are doing something exciting, fresh, and interesting, you can motivate the consumer to buy."

Retailers seek out Dallas-Fort Worth because of the area's population of 4.5 million people and its growing economy. Many, like Daniel Nordstrom, say "If we do a really good job, customers will respond regardless of the amount of retail square footage."

A major concern among regional planners is that additional retail units merely take sales away from existing stores, rather than expand an area's total sales. They feel such overexpansion leads to bankruptcies for less effective retailers, a high store vacancy rate in certain locales, and retail blight.[1]

---

[1] Robert Berner, "Retailers Keep Expanding Amid Glut of Stores," *Wall Street Journal* (May 28, 1996), pp. A21, A26.

OVERVIEW

Since more than 90 percent of retail sales are made at stores, the selection of a store location is one of the most consequential strategic decisions a typical retailer makes. This chapter and Chapter 10 explain why the choice of the proper store location is so crucial; and they describe the steps a retailer should take when choosing a location for a store and deciding whether to build, lease, or purchase facilities.

THE IMPORTANCE OF LOCATION TO A RETAILER

The importance of store location to a retailer should not be underestimated. Decision making can be complex, costs can be quite high, there is typically little flexibility once a location has been chosen, and the attributes of a location have a strong impact on the retailer's overall strategy. In general, a good location may let a retailer succeed even if its strategy mix is rather mediocre. Thus, a hospital gift shop may do very well, although its merchandise assortment is limited, prices are above average, and it does not advertise. On the other hand, a poor location can be such a liability that even the most able retailer may be unable to overcome it. A small mom-and-pop grocery store may not do well if it is situated across the street from a food-based superstore; although the small firm features personal service and long hours, it cannot match the product selection and prices of the superstore. Yet, at a different site, it might do quite well.

The selection of a store location generally requires extensive decision making by the retailer because of the number of criteria to be considered. These include the size and characteristics of the surrounding population, the level of competition, access to transportation, the availability of parking, the attributes of nearby stores, property costs, the length of the agreement, population trends, legal restrictions, and other factors.

A store location usually requires a sizable financial investment and a long-term commitment by the retailer. Even a firm seeking to minimize its investment by leasing (rather than owning a building and land) can have a major investment. Besides lease payments that are locked in for the term of an agreement, a retailer must spend money on lighting, fixtures, the storefront, and so on.

Although leases of less than 5 years are common in less desirable retailing locations, leases in good shopping centers or shopping-district locations are often 5 to 10 years or more. It is not uncommon for a supermarket site to be leased for 15, 20, or 30 years. Department stores and large specialty stores, which are on major downtown thoroughfares, have been known occasionally to sign leases longer than 30 years.

Due to its fixed nature, the amount of the investment, and the length of lease agreements, store location is the least flexible element of a retailer's strategy mix. A firm such as a department store cannot easily move to another site or be converted into another type of retail operation. In contrast, advertising, prices, customer services, and the goods/service assortment can be modified rather quickly if the environment (consumers, competition, the economy, and so on) changes. Furthermore, if a retailer breaks a lease, it may be responsible for any financial damages incurred by the property owner. In some instances, a retailer may be prohibited from subleasing its location to another party during the term of an agreement.

A retailer owning the building and land on which it is situated may also find it difficult to change locations. It would have to find an acceptable buyer, which might take several months or longer; and it may have to assist the buyer in financing the property. It may incur a financial loss, should it sell during an economic downturn.

Any retailer moving from one location to another faces three potential problems. First, some loyal customers and employees may be lost; the greater the distance between the old and the new locations, the greater the loss. Second, a new location may not possess the same characteristics as the original one. Third, the store fixtures and renovations at an old location often cannot be transferred to a new one; their remaining value is lost if they have not been fully depreciated.

Store location has a strong impact on a retailer's long-run and short-run planning. In the long run, the choice of a location affects the firm's overall strategy. The retailer needs to be at a store site that will be consistent with its organizational mission, goals, and target market for an extended period of time. The firm also needs to regularly study and monitor the status of its location in terms of population trends, the distances people travel to the store, and the entry and exit of competitors—and to adapt long-run plans accordingly.

In the short run, store location influences the specific elements of a retail strategy mix (product assortment, prices, promotion, and so on). For example, a firm located in a downtown area populated by office buildings may have little pedestrian traffic on weekends. Therefore, it would probably be inappropriate to sell items such as major appliances at this location (because these items are generally purchased jointly by husbands and wives). The retailer would have to either close on weekends and not stock certain types of merchandise or remain open on weekends and try to attract customers to the area by using extensive promotion or aggressive pricing. If the retailer closes on weekends, it is adapting its strategy mix to the attributes of the location. If it stays open, it must invest additional resources in advertising to attempt to alter consumer buying habits. A retailer trying to overcome its location, by and large, faces greater risks than one adapting to its site.

In choosing a store location, retailers should follow these four steps:

1. Evaluate alternate geographic (trading) areas in terms of the characteristics of residents and existing retailers.
2. Determine whether to locate as an isolated store, in an unplanned business district, or in a planned shopping center within the geographic area.
3. Select the general isolated store, unplanned business district, or planned shopping-center location.
4. Analyze alternate sites contained in the specified retail location type.

This chapter concentrates on Step 1. Chapter 10 details Steps 2, 3, and 4. The selection of a store location is a process involving each of these four steps.

TRADING-AREA ANALYSIS

A **trading area** is "a geographical area containing the customers of a particular firm or group of firms for specific goods or services."[2] It is also defined as

> A district the size of which is usually determined by the boundaries within which it is economical in terms of volume and cost for a marketing unit or group to sell and/or deliver a good or service.[3]

The first step in the choice of a retail store location consists of describing and evaluating alternate trading areas and then deciding on the most desirable one. After a trading area is picked, it should be scrutinized regularly.

A thorough analysis of trading areas provides the retailer with several benefits:

■ The demographic and socioeconomic characteristics of consumers can be detailed. Government and other published data can be utilized to obtain this information. For a new store, the study of proposed trading areas reveals market opportunities and the retail strategy necessary for success. For an existing store, it can be determined if the current retail strategy still matches the needs of consumers.

---

[2]Peter D. Bennett (Editor), *Dictionary of Marketing Terms,* Second Edition (Chicago: American Marketing Association, 1995), p. 287.
[3]Ibid., p. 289.

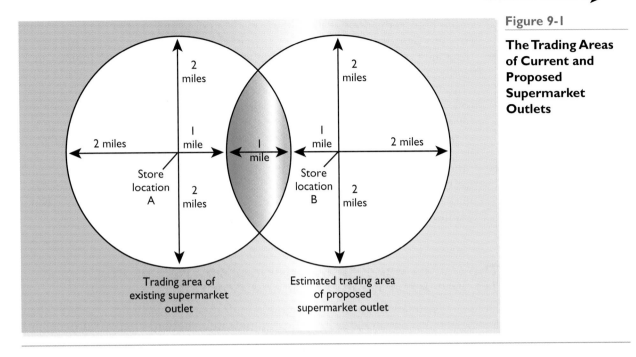

Figure 9-1

The Trading Areas of Current and Proposed Supermarket Outlets

■ The focus of promotional activities can be ascertained. For example, a retailer finding that 95 percent of consumers live within a three-mile radius of a store location would find it inefficient to advertise in a newspaper with a citywide audience. To avoid wasted circulation, the firm could look at media coverage patterns of proposed or existing locations.

■ It can be determined whether the location of a proposed branch store will service new customers or take away business from existing stores in a chain or franchise. Suppose a supermarket chain currently has an outlet in Jackson, Mississippi, with a trading area of two miles. The chain is considering adding a new store, three miles from the Jackson branch. Figure 9-1 shows the distinct trading areas and expected overlap of the two stores. The shaded portion represents the **trading-area overlap** between the stores, in which the same customers are served by both branches. The chain needs to find out the overall net increase in sales if it adds the proposed location shown in Figure 9-1 (total revised sales of existing store + total sales of new store − total previous sales of existing store).

■ Chain management can anticipate whether competitors want to open stores at nearby locations if the firm does not expand there itself. That is why TJX is willing to have two of its chains, T.J. Maxx and Marshalls, situate within 1½ miles of each other in more than 100 markets throughout the United States, even though they are both off-price apparel chains. The firm feels this strategy limits competitive entries into its market areas.[4]

■ The proper number of outlets operated by a chain retailer in a geographic region can be calculated. How many outlets should a bank, a travel agency, and so on situate in a region to provide adequate service for customers (without raising investment costs too much or having too much overlap)? For instance, when CVS entered the Atlanta market in 1996, it decided to open nine new stores in one day. This enabled it to have enough coverage of the city to properly service the residents there, without placing stores too close together. A major competitive advantage for Canadian Tire

[4]*TJX Companies, Inc. 1995 Annual Report.*

Corporation is that four-fifths of the Canadian population live within a 15-minute drive of a Canadian Tire store.[5]

■ Geographic weaknesses can be highlighted. Suppose a suburban shopping center conducts a trading-area analysis and discovers that a significant number of people residing south of town do not shop there, and a more comprehensive study then reveals residents are afraid to drive past a dangerous railroad crossing on the southern outskirts of town. As a result of its research, the shopping center could exert political pressure to make the crossing safer, thus leading to a lot of shoppers from south of town.

■ Other factors can be described and evaluated. Competition, availability of financial institutions, transportation, availability of labor, location of suppliers, legal restrictions, projected growth, and so on can each be determined for the trading area being examined.

The Use of Geographic Information Systems in Trading-Area Delineation and Analysis

Increasingly, retailers are using geographic information systems software in their trading-area delineation and analysis. **Geographic information systems (GIS)** combine digitized mapping with key locational data to graphically depict such trading-area characteristics as the demographic attributes of the population, data on customer purchases, and listings of current, proposed, and competitor locations. Thus, GIS software enables retailers to easily research the attractiveness of alternative locations and to present the findings on computer-screen maps. Prior to the widespread introduction of GIS software from private companies, retailers often placed different color pins on paper-based maps to represent current and proposed locales—as well as competitor sites—and had to do their own data collection and analysis.[6]

For the most part, GIS software programs are extrapolated from the 1990 *Census of Population* and the U.S. Census Bureau's national digital map, which is known as TIGER (topologically integrated geographic encoding and referencing). TIGER incorporates all streets and highways in the United States. GIS software programs can be accessed in two ways: by downloading the maps from Web sites or by purchasing CD-ROM disks.

TIGER maps may be downloaded for free from the TIGER Map Service Web site (http://tiger.census.gov). These maps can be tailored to reflect census tracts, railroads, highways, waterways, and other physical attributes of any area in the United States. However, TIGER maps do not include retail facilities, other commercial entities, population characteristics, and so on; the site can be cumbersome to use; and since 25,000 to 30,000 maps daily are downloaded from the TIGER site, service may be slow.[7] Figure 9-2 shows a sample from the TIGER Map Service.

Private companies offering GIS mapping software on the World Wide Web include Environmental Systems Research Institute (ESRI) (http://www.esri.com), Autodesk (http://www.mapguide.com), and MapInfo (http://www.mapinfo.com). Their soft-

---

[5]Faye Brookman, "CVS Touts Beauty, Convenience in Bid to Build Front-End Sales," *Stores* (January 1997), p. 74; and *Canadian Tire Corporation, Limited 1995 Annual Report.*

[6]See Michael Garry, "GIS: Finding Opportunity in Data," *Progressive Grocer* (June 1996), pp. 61–69; Berna Miller, "Where in the World Is Hallcrest Dr.?" *Marketing Tools* (January–February 1996), pp. 18–22; Kazumi Tanaka, "Putting Your Business on the Map," *Inc. Technology* (Number 2, 1996), pp. 94–99; "Budget Data Bases," *Marketing Tools* (May 1996), p. 34; and Susan Reda, "New Software Tool Aids Supermarket Site Selection," *Stores* (February 1997), pp. 42–43.

[7]Thomas G. Exter, "Taming the TIGER for 2000," *Marketing Tools* (June 1996), pp. 10–13.

The Power of Low-Cost Desktop Geographic Mapping

Until 1994, only one desktop-mapping software package was available for less than $500. There are now at least three products priced at about $100. Each of these geographic-mapping packages lets a retailer plot out a competitor's business locations and see where potential customers live in relation to a proposed location. These packages can also convert a retailer's address data-base records to symbols on a map. The low software price, the ease of use, and the ability to run the software on inexpensive PCs all make the use of desktop-geographic-mapping software much more appealing to small retailers.

BusinessMap, a $99 Windows-based product, enables firms to select and load specific state maps individually. Thus, a firm can save hard disk space by only loading the state data it is currently using. BusinessMap includes five maps (United States, Mexico, Canada, Europe, and the world), with information on zip code boundaries and census demographic data for the United States. Other $100 packages include Select Street (which can overlay a data base on a street map) and Map-Linx (which reads data stored in an ACT! data base).

According to one industry expert, these packages level the playing field. "Now people outside of research departments and the *Fortune* 500 will be able to use data collected by the U.S. government and sold by private market-research companies for their own market research projects."

Source: Laura Lang, "Easy Street," *Marketing Tools* (May 1996), pp. 12–15.

ware has many more enhancements than TIGER. The companies often give free demonstrations, but expect to be paid for current applications.[8]

Among the firms producing GIS software on CD-ROM disks are Decisionmark (http://www.decisionmark.com), the Caliper Corporation (http://www.caliper.com/mtudinfo.htm), Tetrad Computer Applications (http://www.tetrad.com/pcensus/pcensus.html), GeoSystems (http://www.geosys.com), and Claritas (http://www.claritas.com). A montage of GIS software appears in Figure 9-3.

Although GIS software programs differ by vendor (many of which offer trading-area consulting services, besides selling software), CD-ROM software generally can be bought for as little as a few hundred dollars to several thousand dollars each, is designed to work with PCs, and allows for some manipulation of trading-area data. Claritas even markets Profiler software with prices starting as low as $50 for a metropolitan area or $99 for all zip codes in a state.

GIS software can be applied in a variety of ways. For instance, a chain retailer could use GIS software to learn which of its stores have trading areas containing households with a median annual income of more than $50,000. That retailer could derive the sales potential of proposed new-store locations and those stores' potential effect on sales at existing branches. The firm could utilize GIS software to learn the demographic attributes of customers at its best locations, and then dervive a model to enable it to scan locations throughout the nation to find the ones with the most desirable trading-area attributes. A retailer could even use GIS software to find the chain's market penetration by ZIP code and to pinpoint its geographic areas of strength and weakness.

Many firms are now employing GIS software in their retail trading-area delineation and analysis. Here are some examples:

■ PepsiCo uses GIS technology to help pinpoint the best locations for new KFC, Pizza Hut, and Taco Bell outlets.
■ A&P Canada uses GIS software to determine how many customers come from within one, two, and three miles of each store. The software even draws a border to

[8]Laura Lang and Vicki Speed, "Mapping Cyberspace," *Marketing Tools* (September 1996), pp. 8–13.

Figure 9-2

The TIGER Map
Service

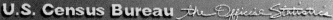

TIGER Mapping Service
The "Coast to Coast" Digital Map Database.

Welcome to the home page for the TIGER Map Service, a project sponsored by the U.S. Bureau of the Census. The goal of this service is to provide a public resource for generating high-quality, detailed maps of anywhere in the United States, using public geographic data.

Try out <u>TMS Version 2.5</u>, **now with additional layers! (requires table support)**

If your browser doesn't support tables, you can still use <u>TMS Version 1.3.1</u>, which draws good maps as well.

For more information...

- □ <u>Background and General Information</u> about the TMS project
- □ <u>Technical Details & Credits</u>
- □ <u>Frequently Asked Questions (FAQ)</u>
- □ The <u>TIGER home page</u>
- □ <u>Applications and Links from Other Sites</u> that use TMS
- □ <u>Current Features and Future Plans</u> for the TMS
- □ How to <u>Request TMS maps directly</u> from your own HTML web pages or CGI script.
- □ <u>Cyber Awards</u> for TMS has more information about the Tiger data and products.
- □ <u>Ordering</u> and Product Information.
- □ <u>GIS Gateway</u> page.

Please email general comments and suggestions to: <u>TMS@Census.GOV</u>

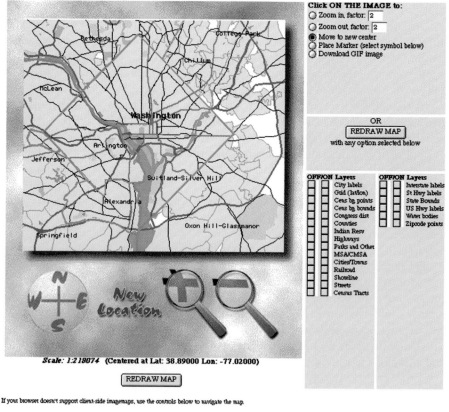

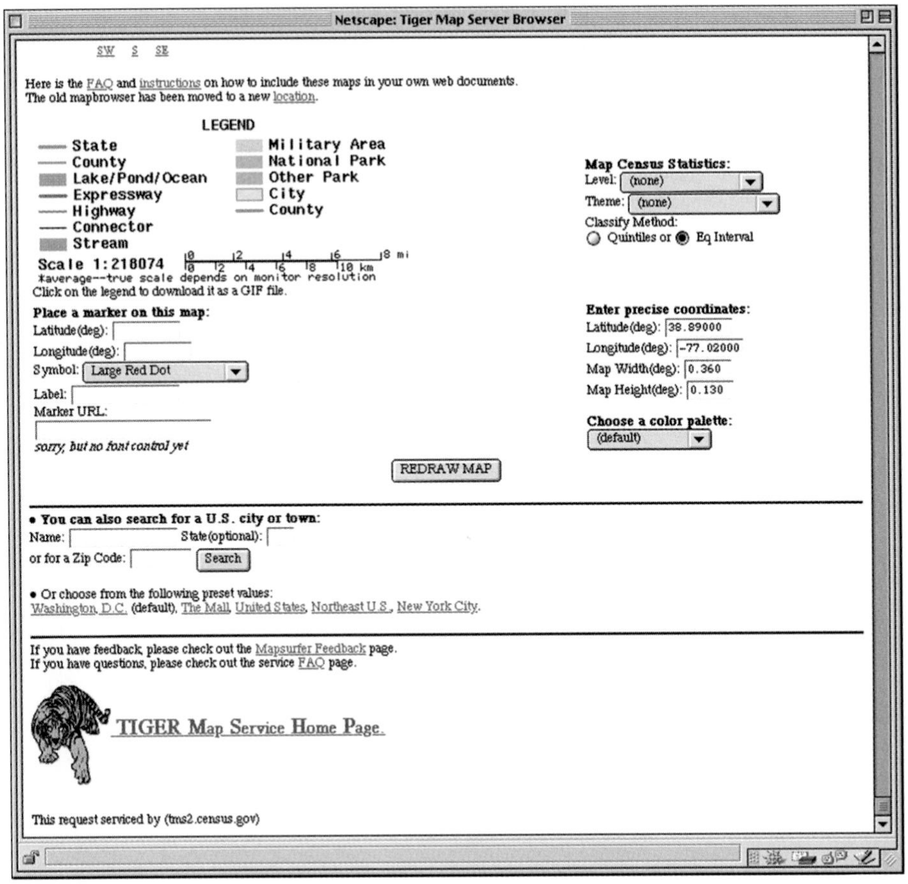

Figure 9-2

(Continued)

show where 70 percent of each store's customers reside. A&P Canada also looks to see whether its advertising media coverage matches each store's trading area; and it can learn each store's relative attractiveness for specific market segments via GIS computer mapping.[9]

■ At the new Rack 'n Sack store in Richmond, Virginia (a division of the Farm Fresh company of food stores), business has been satisfactory; but Farm Fresh wants to know where business is coming from: "Such information has traditionally been gleaned from focus groups, telephone solicitations, and customer spottings. However, GIS provides a lot more information on the market around the store. We can see who's shopping and learn about their demographics and life-styles. We can see where we're making inroads and where we're not."[10]

■ Western Auto (a division of Sears) uses GIS software to establish the appropriate demographics for proposed locations, to help prepare direct-marketing campaigns, and to better adjust the merchandising mix to the characteristics of each trading area. According to Sears' corporate planning manager, the use of GIS software has let Western Auto reduce the time needed for new stores to break even. It now takes 6 months to break even on operating expenses, down from 18 months before.[11]

[9]Gary Robins, "Retail GIS Use Growing," *Stores* (January 1993), p. 46.
[10]Garry, "GIS: Finding Opportunity in Data," p. 69.
[11]Rick Tetzeli, "Mapping for Dollars," *Fortune* (October 18, 1993), p. 92.

Existing Customers

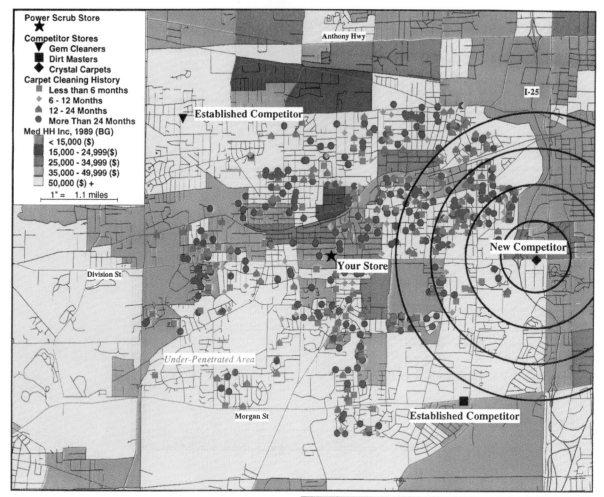

This map demonstrates Proximity's ability to:
- Display the location of all your customers
- Segment the list according to information specific to each customer (Carpet Cleaning History)
- Show an under-penetrated area without nearby competitors
- Display the location of a new competitor's store that threatens a segment of your customer base

A direct mail campaign can be designed to communicate to individuals within each segment.

DECISIONMARK
1-800-365-7629

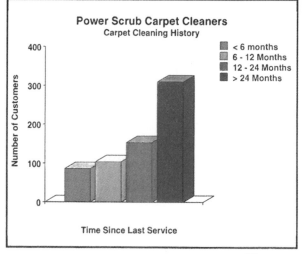

Proximity™

Figure 9-3

GIS Software in Action

When delineating and analyzing trading areas, their characteristics need to be studied and compared. Through geographic information systems (GIS) software, such as that represented here, retailers can learn about many trading-area characteristics and then choose the most appropriate area(s) in which to situate.

MAPTITUDE®
Geographic Information System for Windows

Finalist
Best Applications Software

The Intelligent Mapping Solution for Business, Government, and Education.

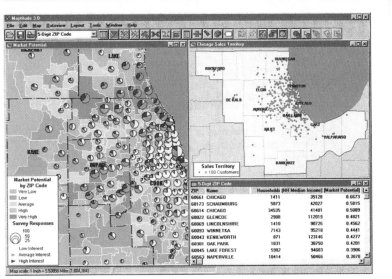

FEATURES:

- MapWizard® Automatic Mapping Technology
- Maps at Any Scale
- Map Editing and Customization
- Integrated Maps and Charts
- Statistics
- Shortest and Fastest Routes
- OLE 2.0 Support
- Built-In Database Engine
- ODBC Links to DBMS
- Page Layout and Drawing Tools
- Pin Mapping by Address, ZIP Code, and More
- Built-In Geographic Data Translators

THE MAPTITUDE DATA LIBRARY

Maptitude comes with an extensive data library for map making and applications development. Included at no extra cost are:

- U.S. Streets
- Cities and Towns
- States and Counties
- Census Tracts
- 3 and 5-Digit ZIP Codes
- Highways
- MSAs, ADIs, and DMAs
- Countries of the World
- Detailed Census Demographic Data

Many other compatible data files are available from Caliper, government sources, and leading data vendors.

Increase Your Maptitude™

Maptitude Geographic Information System (GIS) for Windows brings maps to life – vivid, intelligent maps that help you see and understand patterns in the data that drive your work. Maptitude is a powerful combination of software and geographic data that provides everything you need to realize the benefits of computerized mapping and spatial analysis in a single, cost-effective package. With Maptitude you can:

- Enhance reports and presentations with maps that clearly illustrate your message
- Reveal spatial trends that cannot be seen in database tables and spreadsheets
- Answer geographic questions that affect your operations
- Create shared geographic data resources for your workgroup, department, or organization

Maptitude goes well beyond the limited functions of other street atlas and desktop mapping products by providing features and functions that let you edit maps, analyze data, and connect to corporate databases.

A World of Data on Your Desktop

Maptitude provides a wealth of US Bureau of the Census geographic and demographic data, plus abundant geographic data from around the world. These data sets, conveniently packaged using a compact geographic data format, let you start making maps immediately. You can create maps at any scale, from all the countries of the world to streets around a single address.

The Easy Way to Make Maps

Maptitude makes it easy to create effective map presentations. With a few clicks of the mouse, MapWizard® automatic mapping technology helps you create color and pattern coded maps, dot-density maps, scaled symbols maps, and maps with integrated pie charts and bar charts. You can work with a wide selection of colors, patterns, and symbols to enhance your presentation, and use a complete set of graphic editing and drawing tools to customize maps to match your needs.

Figure 9-3

(Continued)

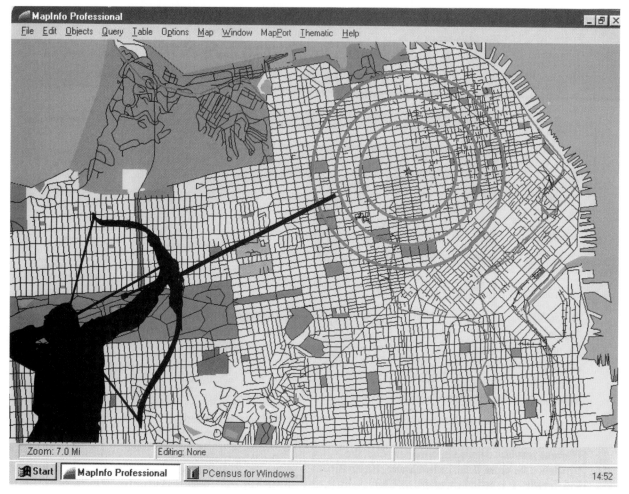

PCensus For Windows
Demographic Analysis Made Easy!

PCensus lets you define areas with circles or polygons to give demographic reports. It also displays demographics for standard areas: states, counties, places, census tracts, block groups or Zip codes.

PCensus uses databases containing the most detailed census data with over 3,000 items. You can compare study areas and export census variables to databases or spreadsheets. There are no per-use or annual fees.

"PCensus is straight forward and user friendly. We have found their staff friendly and willing to go out of their way to be helpful."
Mr. George Stone
Senior Research Analyst
DALLAS MORNING NEWS

Who uses PCensus: Retailers, Planners, Healthcare providers, Real Estate agents and developers, Utilities - anyone who needs to know about the population in an area.

MapInfo works with PCensus to define the study areas and create thematic maps.

"We are very happy with how PCensus interfaces with MapInfo. It's well organized and easy to learn. I would recommend it to anyone."
Mr. Phil Shinbein
Transportation Planer
CITY OF EL PASO

EQUIFAX NATIONAL DECISION SYSTEMS
MARKET PARTNERS

PCensus also offers regular updates based on the scientific analysis of population trends and economic climates through EQUIFAX and The WEFA Group: Current-Year Estimates and Five-Year Projections, MicroVision Market Segments, Consumer-Facts, with household spending on over 400 goods and services, and Business-Facts with daytime population and businesses.

 Expand your markets to all of North America. Statistics Canada's most recent census data is available for PCensus.

"We've used PCensus since the late 80's. Our people have it on their laptops in the field so we can react better and much quicker."
Mr. Greg Soucie
Real Estate Manager Western Canada
McDONALD'S RESTAURANTS OF CANADA LTD.

Figure 9-3

(Continued)

The Size and Shape of Trading Areas

Each trading area consists of three parts: primary, secondary, and fringe. The **primary trading area** encompasses 50 percent to 80 percent of a store's customers. It is the area closest to the store and possesses the highest density of customers to population and the highest per capita sales. There is little overlap with other trading areas (both intracompany and intercompany).

The **secondary trading area** contains an additional 15 percent to 25 percent of a store's customers. It is located outside the primary area, and customers are more widely dispersed. The **fringe trading area** includes all the remaining customers, and they are the most widely dispersed. For example, a store could have a primary trading area of four miles, a secondary trading area of five miles, and a fringe trading area of eight miles. The fringe trading area typically includes some outshoppers, who are willing to travel greater distances to patronize certain stores.

Figures 9-4 and 9-5 contain illustrations of trading areas and their segments. In reality, trading areas do not usually follow such concentric or circular patterns. They adjust to the environment. The size and shape of a trading area are influenced by a large variety of factors, among them: store type, store size, the location of competitors,

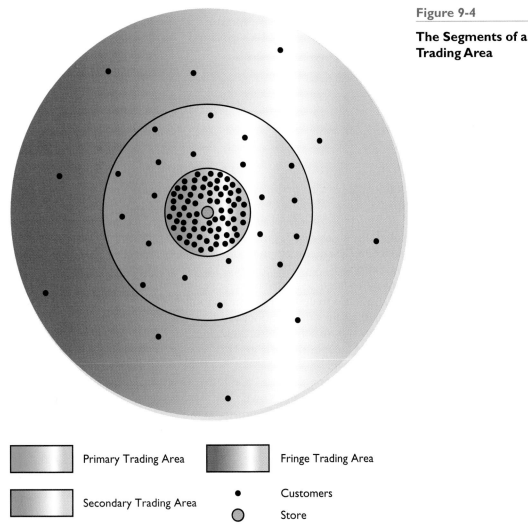

Figure 9-4

The Segments of a Trading Area

Primary Trading Area

Secondary Trading Area

Fringe Trading Area

• Customers

◉ Store

Figure 9-5

Delineating Trading-Area Segments by Customer Willingness to Travel

Through its DQI[2] data base (which was discussed in Chapter 8), Donnelly Marketing can help retailers identify customers and where they live in relation to where they shop. Patterns of cross-shopping between adjacent stores can also be identified. Thus, as indicated here, retailers can accurately determine their primary, secondary, and fringe trading areas.

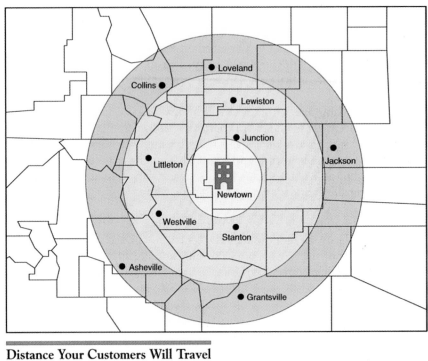

Distance Your Customers Will Travel

- 79% will travel 0 - 5 miles
- 15% will travel 5 - 10 miles
- 6% will travel 10+ miles

residential housing patterns, travel time and traffic barriers (such as toll bridges or poor roads), and availability of media. These factors are discussed next.

Two types of stores can have different-sized trading areas although they are both located in the same shopping district or shopping center. One store could offer a better merchandise assortment in its product category(ies), promote more extensively, and create a stronger image. This store—known as a **destination store**—would have a trading area much larger than that of a competitor with a less unique appeal to consumers. As an illustration, situated in the same shopping center could be an outlet of a leading apparel specialty chain with a distinctive image and shoppers willing to travel up to thirty miles and a shoe store perceived as average and shoppers willing to travel up to ten miles. That is why, in comparing itself to other retailers, Dunkin' Donuts has used the slogan, "It's worth the trip."

Another type of outlet, called a **parasite store**, does not create its own traffic and has no real trading area of its own. The store depends on people who are drawn to the location for other reasons. A magazine stand in a hotel lobby and a snack bar in a shopping center are both parasites. Customers are not drawn to a location because of them but patronize these stores while they are there.

The extent of a store's trading area is affected by its own size. As a store gets larger, its trading area usually increases. This relationship exists because the size of a store generally reflects the assortment of goods and services provided for customers. Yet, trading-area size does not rise proportionately with increasing store size. As a rule, trading areas for supermarkets are much greater than those for convenience stores; because of their size, supermarkets have a better product selection and convenience stores appeal to consumers' needs for fill-in merchandise. In a regional shopping center, department stores typically have the largest trading areas, followed by apparel stores. Gift stores in such a center have comparatively small trading areas.

The locations of a retailer's competitors determine their impact on the size of its trading area. Whenever potential customers are situated between two stores, the size of the trading area is often reduced for each; and the size of each store's trading area normally increases as the distance between them grows (the target markets then do not overlap as much). On the other hand, when stores are situated very near one another, the size of each trading area would not necessarily be reduced because of competition. In this case, the grouping of stores may actually increase the trading area for each store because more consumers would be attracted to the general location due to the variety of goods and services. However, it is important to recognize that each store's market penetration (the percentage of total retail sales in the trading area) may be low with this type of competition. Also, the entry of a new store may change the shape and/or create gaps in the trading areas of existing stores.

Residential housing patterns affect a store's trading area. In many urban communities, people are clustered in multiunit housing near the center of commerce. With such population density, it is worthwhile for a retailer to locate quite close to consumers; and trading areas tend to be small because several shopping districts (in close proximity to one another) are likely to exist and prosper, particularly for the most densely populated cities. In many suburban communities, people live in single-unit housing, which is more geographically spread out. Accordingly, to generate sufficient sales volume, a retailer would need to attract shoppers from a greater distance.

Travel or driving time has an influence on the size of a trading area that may not be clear from a study of the geographic distribution of the population. Physical barriers (such as toll bridges, tunnels, poor roads, rivers, railroad tracks, and one-way streets) usually reduce trading areas and contribute to their odd shapes. Economic barriers (such as differences in sales taxes between two towns) also affect the size and shape of trading areas. If one town has much lower taxes than another, it may entice consumers to travel longer in return for saving on purchases.

The size of a trading area is often affected by a retailer's promotion efforts. Therefore, in a community where a newspaper or other forms of local advertising media are available, a retailer could easily afford to use these media and enlarge its trading area. However, if local media are not available in a community, the retailer would have to weigh the costs and probable waste of advertising in citywide or countywide media against the possibilities of increasing the trading area.

Delineating the Trading Area of an Existing Store

The size, shape, and characteristics of the trading area for an existing store (or shopping district or shopping center) can usually be delineated quite accurately. Store records (secondary data) or a special study (primary data) can be used to measure the trading area. In addition, as noted earlier in the chapter, many firms offer computer-generated data and maps based on census and other statistics. This information can be tailored to individual retailers' needs.

Store records can reveal the addresses of both credit and cash customers. Addresses of credit customers can be obtained through a retailer's billing department; addresses of cash customers can be acquired by analyzing delivery tickets, cash sales slips, store contests (sweepstakes), and check-cashing operations. In both instances, the analysis of addresses is relatively inexpensive and quick because the data were originally collected for other purposes and are readily available.

Since many big retailers have their own computerized credit card systems, they can delineate trading areas by studying the addresses of these customers. Primary, secondary, and fringe trading areas can be described in terms of

■ The frequency with which people from various geographic localities shop at a particular store.
■ The average dollar purchases at a store by people from given geographic localities.
■ The concentration of a store's credit card holders from given geographic localities.

Though it may be easy to get data on credit card customers, conclusions drawn from these data might not be valid if cash customers are excluded from analysis. Credit use may vary among customers from different localities, especially if consumer characteristics in the localities are dissimilar. Thus, an evaluation of only credit customers may overstate or understate the total number of shoppers from a particular locality. This problem is minimized if data are collected for both cash and credit customers.

A retailer can also collect primary data to determine the size of a trading area. It can record the license plate numbers of cars parked near a store, find the general addresses of the owners of those vehicles by contacting the state motor vehicle office or the local treasurer's office, and then note them on a map. For a few thousand dollars or less, a retailer could have R.L. Polk (a marketing research company) record the license plate numbers and determine the general owner addresses and demographics of parked vehicles. In either case, only general addresses (zip code and street of residence, but not the exact house number) are given out, to protect people's privacy. When using license plate analysis, nondrivers and passengers must not be omitted. Customers who walk to a store, use public transportation, or are driven by others should be included in research. To collect data on these customers, questions must often be asked (survey).

If a retailer desires still more detailed demographic and life-style data about consumers in particular localities, it can purchase those data from such firms as Claritas. PRIZM is the computerized system devised by Claritas for identifying communities by life-style clusters. Sixty-two different types of neighborhoods have been identified and described using names like "Gray Power," "Starter Families," and "Suburban Sprawl." PRIZM initially was based on zip codes; it now is also based on census tracts, block groups and enumeration districts, phone exchanges, and postal routes. Standard PRIZM reports can be bought for as little as $99 each; costs are higher if the reports are tailored to the individual retailer.[12]

No matter which way a trading area is delineated, the retailer should realize a time bias may exist. A downtown business district is patronized by different customers during the week (people who work there) than on weekends (people who travel there to shop). Special events may attract customers from great distances for only brief periods of time; after the events are over, the size of the trading area may drop. Therefore, an accurate estimate of the size of a store's trading area can be obtained only through complete and continuous investigation.

After any trading area is delineated, a retailer should map out the locations and densities of customers. This may be done in either of two ways: manually or with a geographic information system. In the manual method, a paper map of the area surrounding a store is used. Different colors of dots or pins could be placed on this map to represent population locations and densities, incomes, and other factors. Customer

---

[12]*PRIZM Life-Style Segmentation* (Arlington, Virginia: Claritas, Inc., 1995).

locations and densities are then indicated; and the primary, secondary, and fringe trading areas are noted by zip code. Customers can be reached by promotions aimed at particular zip codes. With a geographic information system, key customer data (such as the frequency of purchases and the amounts purchased) are combined with other information sources (such as census data) to yield computer-generated digitized maps that depict primary, secondary, and fringe trading areas.

Delineating the Trading Area of a New Store

A new store opening in an established trading area can use the methods just detailed. This section refers more to a trading area with less well-defined shopping and traffic patterns.

Prospective trading areas for a new store must frequently be evaluated by judging market opportunities rather than current customer patronage and traffic (pedestrian and vehicular) patterns. Since the techniques used in delineating the trading area of an established store are often insufficient, additional tools must be utilized.

Trend analysis and/or surveys can be employed. Trend analysis—estimating the future based on the past—involves examining government and other data concerning predictions about population location, auto registrations, new housing starts, mass transportation, highways, zoning, and so on. Consumer surveys can gather information about the time and distance people would be willing to travel to various possible retail locations, the features attracting people to a new store, the addresses of the people most apt to visit a new store, and other topics. Either or both of these techniques may provide a basis for delineating alternate new-store trading areas.

On a more advanced level, there are three basic types of computerized trading-area analysis models that could be used to assess new store locations: analog, regression, and gravity. An **analog model** is the simplest and most popular trading-area analysis model. Potential sales for a new store are estimated on the basis of existing store revenues in similar areas, the competition at a prospective location, the new store's expected market share at that location, and the size and density of the location's primary trading area. A **regression model** develops a series of mathematical equations showing the association between potential store sales and various independent variables at each location under consideration. The impact of such independent variables as population size, average income, the number of households, nearby competitors, transportation barriers, and traffic patterns are studied. A **gravity model** is based on the premise that people are drawn to stores that are closer and more attractive than competitors'. Such factors as the distance between consumers and competitors, the distance between consumers and a given site, and store image are included in this model.

Computerized trading-area analysis models offer several benefits to retailers: They operate in an objective and systematic manner. They can offer insights as to how each locational attribute should be weighted. They are useful in screening a large number of locations. They can be used to assess management performance by comparing forecasts with results.

Several more specific methods for delineating new trading areas are described next.

Reilly's Law ❑ The traditional means of trading-area delineation, devised by Reilly in 1929, is called **Reilly's law of retail gravitation**.[13] The law's purpose is to establish a point of indifference between two cities or communities, so the trading area of each can be determined. The **point of indifference** is the geographic breaking point between two

[13]William J. Reilly, *Method for the Study of Retail Relationships,* Research Monograph No. 4 (Austin: University of Texas Press, 1929), University of Texas Bulletin No. 2944.

cities (communities)—at which consumers would be indifferent to shopping at either. According to Reilly's law, more consumers will be attracted to the larger city or community because a greater amount of store facilities (assortment) will exist there, making the increased travel time worthwhile.

The law may be expressed algebraically as[14]

$$D_{ab} = \frac{d}{1 + \sqrt{P_b/P_a}}$$

where

D_{ab} = limit of city (community) A's trading area, measured in miles along the road to city (community) B

d = distance in miles along a major roadway between cities (communities) A and B

P_a = population of city (community) A

P_b = population of city (community) B

Based on this formula, a city with a population of 90,000 (A) would draw people from three times the distance as a city with 10,000 (B). If the cities are 20 miles apart, the point of indifference for the larger city is 15 miles, and for the smaller city, it is 5 miles:

$$D_{ab} = \frac{20}{1 + \sqrt{10,000/90,000}} = 15 \text{ miles}$$

City A–
90,000
population   15 miles   5 miles   City B–
                                                                                   10,000
                                                                                   population

Point of indifference

Reilly's law rests on these major assumptions: (1) two competing areas will be equally accessible from the major road; and (2) retailers in the two areas will be equally effective. Other factors (such as the dispersion of the population) are held constant or ignored.

The law of retail gravitation is an important contribution to trading-area analysis because of its ease of calculation and the research that has been conducted on it. Reilly's law is most useful when other data are not available or when the costs of compiling other data are too great. By combining this technique with others, a retailer could generally determine if the most appropriate trading area is being considered.

Despite its usefulness, Reilly's law has at least two key limitations. First, distance measurement is confined to major thoroughfares and does not involve cross streets; yet, many people will travel shorter distances along these slower cross streets. Second, actual distance to a store may not correspond with consumer perceptions of distance.[15] A store offering few customer services and crowded aisles is likely to be a greater perceived distance from the customer than a similarly located store with a more pleasant shopping environment.

Huff's Law ❑ In the 1960s, Huff isolated several variables (rather than just one, as Reilly had done) and related them to trading-area size. **Huff's law of shopper attraction** delineates trading areas on the basis of the product assortment (of the items desired

[14]Richard L. Nelson, *The Selection of Retail Locations* (New York: F.W. Dodge, 1959), p. 149.
[15]See Priya Raghubir and Aradana Krishna, "As the Crow Flies: Bias in Consumers' Map-Based Distance Judgments," *Journal of Consumer Research*, Vol. 23 (June 1996), pp. 26–39.

by the consumer) carried at various shopping locations, travel times from the consumer's home to alternative shopping locations, and the sensitivity of the kind of shopping to travel time. The assortment variable is measured by the total square feet of selling space a retailer expects all firms at a shopping location to allocate to a product category. Sensitivity to the kind of shopping entails the purpose of a trip (restocking versus shopping) and the type of goods/service sought (such as furniture versus clothing versus groceries).[16]

Huff's law is expressed as

$$P_{ij} = \frac{\dfrac{S_j}{(T_{ij})^\lambda}}{\displaystyle\sum_{j=1}^{n}\dfrac{S_j}{(T_{ij})^\lambda}}$$

where

P_{ij} = probability of a consumer's traveling from home i to shopping location j

S_j = square footage of selling space in shopping location j expected to be devoted to a particular product category

T_{ij} = travel time from consumer's home i to shopping location j

λ = a parameter used to estimate the effect of travel time on different kinds of shopping trips

n = number of different shopping locations

λ must be determined through research or a computer program.

This formula may be applied as follows: Assume a leased-department operator is studying three possible shopping locations with 200, 300, and 500 total square feet of store space expected to be allocated to men's cologne (by all retailers in the areas). A group of potential customers lives 7 minutes from the first location, 10 minutes from the second, and 15 minutes from the third. From previous research, the operator estimates the effect of travel time to be 2. Therefore, the probability of consumers shopping for men's cologne is 43.9 percent at Location 1; 32.2 percent at Location 2; and 23.9 percent at Location 3:

$$P_{i1} = \frac{(200)/(7)^2}{(200)/(7)^2 + (300)/(10)^2 + (500)/(15)^2} = 43.9\%$$

$$P_{i2} = \frac{(300)/(10)^2}{(200)/(7)^2 + (300)/(10)^2 + (500)/(15)^2} = 32.2\%$$

$$P_{i3} = \frac{(500)/(15)^2}{(200)/(7)^2 + (300)/(10)^2 + (500)/(15)^2} = 23.9\%$$

As a result, if 200 males live 7 minutes from Location 1, about 88 of them will shop there.

These points should be considered in using Huff's law:

[16]David L. Huff, "Defining and Estimating a Trading Area," *Journal of Marketing*, Vol. 28 (July 1964), pp. 34–38; and David L. Huff and Larry Blue, *A Programmed Solution for Estimating Retail Sales Potential* (Lawrence: University of Kansas, 1966). For further information, see Christophe Benavent, Marc Thomas, and Anne Bergue, "Application of Gravity Models for the Analysis of Retail Potential," *Journal of Targeting, Measurement, and Analysis for Marketing*, Vol. 1 (Winter 1992–1993), pp. 305–315; and Eric Cohen, "Miles, Minutes, & Custom Markets," *Marketing Tools* (July–August 1996), pp. 18–21.

■ To determine the overall trading area for Location 1, the same type of computations would have to be made for consumers living 5, 10, 15, 20 minutes, and so on, away. The number of consumers at each distance who would shop there are then summed. In this way, the stores in Location 1 would be able to estimate their total market, the size of the trading area, and the primary, secondary, and fringe areas for a particular product category.

■ If new retail facilities (square feet of selling space) in a product category are added to a locale, the percentage of people living at every travel time from that location who shop there goes up.

■ The probability of consumers shopping at a particular location is highly dependent on the effect of travel time for the product category. In the previous example, if the product is changed to a more important item, such as men's dress watches, consumers would be less sensitive to travel time. A λ value of 1 would result in these probabilities: Location 1, 31.1 percent; Location 2, 32.6 percent; and Location 3, 36.3 percent. Location 3 becomes much more attractive for this product category because of its assortment.

■ All the variables are rather hard to calculate; and for mapping purposes, travel time needs to be converted to distance in miles. In addition, travel time depends on the transportation form used.

■ On different shopping trips, consumers buy different items. That means the trading area would vary from trip to trip.

Other Trading-Area Research ❏ Over the years, a number of other researchers have examined trading-area size in a variety of settings. They have introduced additional factors and sophisticated statistical techniques to explain the consumer's choice of shopping location.[17] For example, in his model, Gautschi added to Huff's analysis by including shopping-center descriptors (such as center design and hours of operation) and transportation conditions (such as cost, performance, and safety).[18] Weisbrod, Parcells, and Kern studied the attractiveness of shopping centers on the basis of expected population changes, expected store characteristics, and the evolving transportation network.[19] Ghosh developed a consumer behavior model that takes into consideration multipurpose shopping trips.[20] Young and Calantone developed a model to assess customer perceptions of destination attractiveness, the distance to locations, retailer-to-retailer accessibility, customer interchange, and access to competing locales.[21] LeBlang demonstrated that consumer life-styles could be used to predict sales at new department store locations.[22] Drezner found that the market share captured by a new or existing retail facility was sensitive to both facility location and attractiveness.[23] Rust and Donthu looked at ways to reduce the effects of omitted variables in retail store choice models.[24]

[17] A good summary of the research up to the early 1980s is C. Samuel Craig, Avijit Ghosh, and Sara McLafferty, "Models of the Retail Location Process: A Review," *Journal of Retailing*, Vol. 60 (Spring 1984), pp. 5–36.

[18] David A. Gautschi, "Specification of Patronage Models for Retail Center Choice," *Journal of Marketing Research*, Vol. 18 (May 1981), pp. 162–174.

[19] Glen E. Weisbrod, Robert J. Parcells, and Clifford Kern, "A Disaggregate Model for Predicting Shopping Area Market Attraction," *Journal of Retailing*, Vol. 60 (Spring 1984), pp. 65–83.

[20] Avijit Ghosh, "The Value of a Mall and Other Insights from a Revised Central Place Model," *Journal of Retailing*, Vol. 62 (Spring 1986), pp. 79–97.

[21] Mark R. Young and Roger J. Calantone, "Advances in Spatial Interaction Modeling of Consumer-Retailer Interaction" in William Bearden, Rohit Despande, and Thomas J. Madden, et al. (Editors), *1990 AMA Educators' Proceedings* (Chicago: American Marketing Association, 1990), pp. 264–267.

[22] Paul LeBlang, "A Theoretical Approach for Predicting Sales at a New Department-Store Location Via Life-Styles," *Direct Marketing*, Vol. 7 (Autumn 1993), pp. 70–74.

[23] Tammy Drezner, "Optimal Continuous Location of a Retail Facility, Facility Attractiveness, and Market Share: An Interactive Model," *Journal of Retailing*, Vol. 70 (Spring 1994), pp. 49–64.

[24] Roland T. Rust and Naveen Donthu, "Capturing Geographically Localized Misspecification Error in Retail Store Choice Models," *Journal of Marketing Research*, Vol. 32 (February 1995), pp. 103–110.

CHARACTER-ISTICS OF TRADING AREAS

After the size and shape of various alternative trading areas (existing or proposed) have been determined, the retailer should study the characteristics of those areas. Of special interest are the attributes of residents and how well they match with the retailer's definition of its target market. Thus, an auto repair franchisee may compare the opportunities available in several areas by examining the number of car registrations; a hearing aid retailer may evaluate the percentage of the population 65 years of age or older; and a bookstore retailer may be concerned with the educational level of residents.

Among the trading-area factors that should be studied by most retailers are the population size and characteristics, availability of labor, closeness to sources of supply, promotion facilities, economic base, competition, availability of locations, and regulations. The **economic base** refers to an area's industrial and commercial structure—the companies and industries that residents depend on to earn a living. The dominant industry (company) in an area is very important because its drastic decline may have adverse effects on a large proportion of the area's residents. An area with a diverse economic base, where residents work for a variety of nonrelated industries, is more secure than an area dependent on one major industry. Table 9-1 summarizes a number of the major factors to consider in evaluating retail trading areas.

Much of the information necessary to describe an area can be obtained from the U.S. Bureau of the Census, the *Survey of Buying Power, Editor & Publisher Market Guide, Rand McNally Commercial Atlas & Market Guide, American Demographics, Standard Rate & Data Service,* regional planning boards, public utilities, chambers of commerce, local government offices, shopping-center owners, and renting agents. In addition, GIS software programs provide data on the potential buying power in an area, the location of competitors, and highway access. Both consumer demographic and life-style information are also included in these programs.

Although the yardsticks noted in Table 9-1 are not equally important in all retail location decisions, each should be considered (to prevent an oversight). The most important yardsticks should be viewed as "knockout" factors: if a location does not meet minimum standards on key measures, it should be immediately dropped from further consideration.

These are examples of desirable trading-area attributes, according to a diverse retailer mix:

■ Finish Line, a sports apparel and shoe chain, looks for sites in mid-sized markets. It evaluates the market areas, shopping mall locations, consumer traffic, competition, and the costs associated with opening new stores. It likes to be in enclosed shopping centers.[25]

■ Heilig-Meyers, the largest U.S. home furnishings chain, has most of its stores in towns with fewer than 50,000 people, at least 25 miles from major markets, and within 200 miles from existing or planned distribution centers. Since a distribution center needs 30 to 40 stores to be efficient, the chain tries to expand within each distribution center's zone of market coverage. It has a small percentage of stores in areas such as Chicago, Cleveland, and Atlanta.[26]

■ Western Beef situates many of its stores in ethnic, minority, and working-class neighborhoods often overlooked (or abandoned) by larger supermarket chains.[27]

■ Saks Fifth Avenue is introducing a new "Main Street" store format, with stores of 35,000 to 50,000 square feet each (compared to its typical 200,000-square-

[25]*Finish Line 1995 Annual Report.*
[26]*Heilig-Meyers Company 1996 Annual Report.*
[27]*Western Beef 1995 Annual Report.*

Table 9-1 MAJOR FACTORS TO CONSIDER IN EVALUATING RETAIL TRADING AREAS

Population Size and Characteristics

■ Total size and density
■ Age distribution
■ Average educational level
■ Percentage of residents owning homes
■ Total disposable income
■ Per-capita disposable income
■ Occupation distribution
■ Trends

Availability of Labor

■ Management ⎤
■ Management trainee ⎬──Analysis of
■ Clerical ⎦

    a. High school and college graduates
    b. Outmigration of graduates
    c. Average wages in the area vs. average wages in the United States

Closeness to Sources of Supply

■ Delivery costs
■ Timeliness
■ Number of manufacturers and wholesalers
■ Availability and reliability of product lines

Promotion Facilities

■ Availability and frequency of media
■ Costs
■ Waste

Economic Base

■ Dominant industry
■ Extent of diversification
■ Growth projections
■ Freedom from economic and seasonal fluctuations
■ Availability of credit and financial facilities

Competitive Situation

■ Number and size of existing competitors
■ Evaluation of strengths and weaknesses for all competitors
■ Short-run and long-run outlook
■ Level of saturation

Availability of Store Locations

■ Number and type of locations
■ Access to transportation
■ Owning versus leasing opportunities
■ Zoning restrictions
■ Costs

Regulations

■ Taxes
■ Licensing
■ Operations
■ Minimum wages
■ Zoning

The Ambitious Expansion Plans of McDonald's

Through its ambitious expansion plans, McDonald's planned to open between 2,500 and 3,200 new units in both 1996 and 1997. Why is that? "McDonald's is the largest and best-known global food-service retailer, with more than 19,200 restaurants in 95 countries (as of 1996). Yet on any day, even as the market leader, McDonald's serves less than one percent of the world's population. The Company plans to expand its leadership position by adding restaurants and by increasing sales and profits via excellent operations, superior marketing, and cost efficiencies."

Two-thirds of the new units were set for foreign markets. According to one market analyst, "McDonald's has just recognized a wide-open opportunity to do two things: Gain first-move advantage in a lot of new markets, and grab market share from other operators out there who are no match." Noting McDonald's advan-

tage over its weaker competitors, another analyst said, "It's a market-share game, and McDonald's has a 'take no-prisoners' approach."

Most of the foreign units involve full-sized traditional restaurants; but as many as 600 of these new domestic units are to be satellite units. These mini-McDonald's units are placed in Wal-Marts and other retailers or developed in association with gas stations by a co-branding arrangement (such as with Amoco and Chevron). The decision to vastly expand store openings comes at a time when same-store sales (for stores open more than one year) have declined for McDonald's U.S. units. Some franchisees fear the new domestic units will take sales away from existing stores.

Sources: "McDonald's Chairman Announces Management Realignments to Further Focus Leadership in Global Growth Arenas," *McDonald's Press Release* (October 8, 1996); and Richard Gibson, "McDonald's Accelerates Store Openings in U.S. and Abroad, Pressuring Rivals," *Wall Street Journal* (January 18, 1996), p. A3.

foot department stores). The idea is to have "compact versions of full-line stores, featuring merchandise specifically tailored to customers in a tight geographic radius" in affluent downtown areas like Greenwich, Connecticut, and Austin, Texas.[28]

■ Gottschalks, a department store chain, prefers to concentrate in secondary cities, where there is strong demand for nationally advertised items but less competition. In locating, Gottschalks studies the demographic characteristics of the surrounding population, the economic conditions within trading areas, and the extent of competition. It is aware the current economic climate has had a greater effect on its California stores than on other geographic areas.[29]

■ The Syms off-price apparel chain seeks locations near major highways or thoroughfares in suburban areas that are populated by at least 1 million persons and that are readily accessible to customers by car. In certain areas, where there is a population of over 2 million people, Syms has opened more than one store.[30]

Several stages of the process involved in gathering data to analyze retail trading areas are shown by the flowchart in Figure 9-6. This chart incorporates not only the characteristics of residents, but also those of the competition. By studying both these factors, a retailer can determine how saturated an area is for its type of business.

We next discuss three factors in trading-area selection: population characteristics, economic base characteristics, and the nature of competition and the level of saturation.

[28]Susan Reda, "New Saks Store Tests Appeal of Smaller 'Main Street' Format," *Stores* (January 1997), pp. 125–126.
[29]*Gottschalks, Inc. 1995 10K.*
[30]*Syms Corporation 1996 Annual Report.*

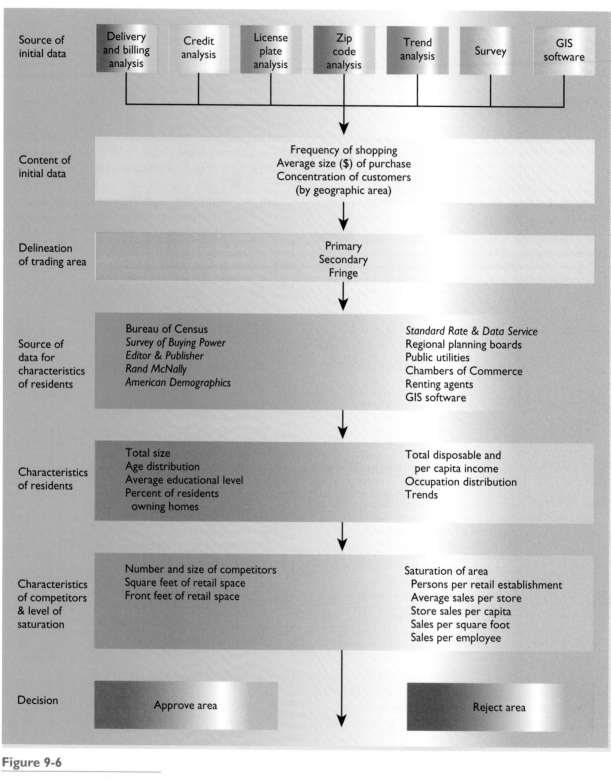

Figure 9-6

Analyzing Retail Trading Areas

Characteristics of the Population

A lot of knowledge about a trading area's population characteristics can be gained from secondary sources. These sources can provide data about an area's population size, number of households, income distribution, education level, age distribution, and more. Because the *Census of Population* and the *Survey of Buying Power* are such valuable sources, each will be briefly described.

Census of Population ❏ The **Census of Population** supplies a wide range of demographic data for all U.S. cities and surrounding vicinities. Such data are organized on a geographic basis, starting with blocks and continuing to census tracts, cities, counties, states, and regions. As a rule, fewer data are available for blocks and census tracts than for larger units because of concerns about individuals' privacy. The major advantage of census data is that they provide valuable demographic information on small geographic units.

After a retailer has outlined the boundaries of a trading area, it can use census data to gather information for each of the geographic units contained in the area and then study aggregate demographics. A major breakthrough for retailers occurred with the 1970 census, when the U.S. Bureau of the Census created a computer file for the storage and retrieval of population data by geographic area. The 1980 census added useful data categories for retailers interested in segmenting the market—including racial and ethnic data, small-area income data, and commuting patterns. An online computer system was also introduced to make census data more accessible.

The 1990 census further expanded the availability of detailed information via computer formats—such as computer tapes, floppy disks, CD-ROM (compact disk-read only memory), and online services. But the biggest advance with the 1990 census involved the introduction of TIGER (topologically integrated geographic encoding and referencing) computer tapes, which contain the most detailed physical breakdowns of U.S. areas ever produced. TIGER computer tapes comprise a computer-readable data base that contains digital descriptions of geographic areas (such as area boundaries and codes, latitude and longitude coordinates, and address ranges). Because TIGER tapes must be used in conjunction with population and other data, GIS software is necessary. As noted earlier in this chapter, many private firms have devised computer-based location-analysis programs, based in large part on TIGER. These firms also usually project data to the present year and into the future.

The major drawbacks of the *Census of Population* are that it is undertaken only once every ten years and that all data are not immediately available when they are collected. For example, information from the 1990 *Census of Population* was released in phases from 1991 through 1993. Census material can thus be out of date and inaccurate, particularly several years after collection. Therefore, supplementary sources, such as municipal building departments or utilities, state government offices, other U.S. Bureau of the Census reports (including the *Current Population Survey*), and computerized projections by firms like Dun & Bradstreet must be used to update *Census of Population* data.

The value of actual census tract data (available from the *Census of Population* and updated to 1995 by computerized projections by Dun & Bradstreet) to retailers can be shown through an illustration of Long Beach, New York, a city of 35,000 residents located 30 miles east of New York City on Long Island's south shore. Long Beach encompasses six census tracts, numbers 4164, 4165, 4166, 4167.01, 4167.02, and 4168. See Figure 9-7. Although census tract 4163 is contiguous with Long Beach, it represents Atlantic Beach, another community.

Table 9-2 contains a variety of population statistics for each of the census tracts in Long Beach. The characteristics of the residents in each tract differ markedly; thus, a retailer might choose to locate in one or more tracts but not in others.

Suppose a growing bookstore chain is evaluating two potential trading areas. Area A corresponds roughly with census tracts 4165 and 4166. Area B is similar to census tracts

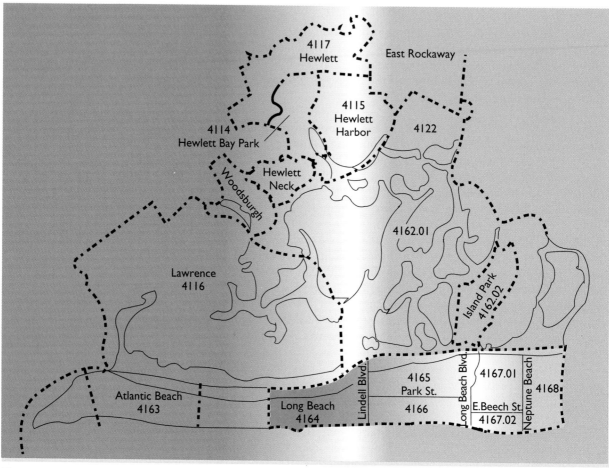

Figure 9-7

The Census Tracts of Long Beach, New York

4167.01, 4167.02, and 4168. The population data for these two areas have been extracted from Table 9-2 and are presented in Table 9-3. Some interesting comparisons can be made.

Area A is different from Area B, despite their geographic proximity and similar physical size:

■ The population in Area B is 29 percent larger than the population in Area A.
■ Although both areas increased in population from 1990 to 1995, the rate of population growth was greater in Area A.
■ The number of Area B residents aged 25 and older with college degrees is almost two times greater than that of Area A.
■ The annual median incomes in Area A and Area B are roughly equal.
■ The percentage of workers who are managers or are in professional specialty occupations is greater in Area B than in Area A.

The management of the bookstore chain would probably select Area B since its residents have more of the attributes desired for the target market; but Area A is also strong in some regards. Thus, the chain might also have to consider the proximity of the sites available in Area A and Area B relative to the locations of its existing stores, before making a final decision.

Table 9-2 SELECTED CHARACTERISTICS OF LONG BEACH, NEW YORK, RESIDENTS BY CENSUS TRACT, 1990 AND 1995

	TRACT NUMBER					
	4164	**4165**	**4166**	**4167.01**	**4167.02**	**4168**
Total population:						
1990	7,082	5,694	5,613	4,162	4,479	6,480
1990 population						
25 and older	5,315	3,331	4,306	3,003	3,620	5,074
1995	6,925	5,815	6,274	4,375	4,832	6,388
Number of households:						
1990	2,735	1,812	2,219	1,465	2,295	3,066
1995	2,676	1,834	2,516	1,547	2,479	3,010
Education:						
College graduates (% of population 25 and older), 1990	15.2	13.1	17.8	17.1	20.4	19.5
Income:						
Median household income, 1990	$45,245	$42,621	$38,642	$47,297	$33,891	$42,471
Median household income, 1995	$49,735	$48,158	$44,492	$53,164	$38,287	$48,333
Selected occupations:						
Managerial and professional specialty occupations (% of employed persons 16 and older), 1990	17.3	12.2	17.3	14.6	17.8	19.6

Sources: Census of Population and Housing (Washington, D.C.: U.S. Bureau of the Census, 1990), Census Tracts Nassau-Suffolk New York Standard Metropolitan Statistical Area; *Market Profile Analysis: Consumer and Business Demographic Reports: Nassau-Suffolk NY DMSA* (Dun & Bradstreet Information Services, 1995/1996 Edition), p. 22; and authors' computations.

Survey of Buying Power ❑ The *Survey of Buying Power*, published yearly by *Sales & Marketing Management* magazine, reports current demographic data on metropolitan areas, cities, and states. It also provides some information not available from the *Census of Population,* such as total annual retail sales by area, annual retail sales for specific product categories, annual effective buying income, and five-year population and retail sales projections.

Table 9-3 SELECTED POPULATION STATISTICS FOR LONG BEACH TRADING AREAS A AND B

	Area A (Tracts 4165 and 4166)	**Area B (Tracts 4167.01, 4167.02, and 4168)**
Total population, 1995	12,089	15,595
Population change, 1990–1995	+6.9%	+3.1%
Number of college graduates, 25 and older, 1990	1,203	2,242
Median household income, 1995	$46,040	$45,855
Managerial and professional specialty occupations (% of employed persons 16 and older), 1990	14.5%	17.8%

Table 9-4 SELECTED DATA FROM *SURVEY OF BUYING POWER* RELATING TO THE AUTOMOBILE MARKET IN THREE ILLINOIS COUNTIES, 1995

	COUNTY		
	Du Page	**Kane**	**Lake**
December 31, 1995			
Total population	865,400	360,000	575,000
Number of people 18 and over	634,300	251,600	414,000
Percentage of population 18 and over	73.3	69.9	72.0
Number of households	309,400	120,400	194,400
Total effective buying income (EBI)	$19,346,570,000	$5,788,019,000	$13,537,206,000
Median household EBI	$53,821	$42,102	$52,509
Per-capita EBI	$22,356	$16,078	$23,543
Percentage of households with $35,000–$49,999 EBI	19.0	21.2	17.7
Percentage of households with $50,000+ EBI	55.2	39.1	52.8
Total retail sales	$11,049,386,000	$3,087,969,000	$6,604,528,000
Buying power index (%)	0.4500	0.1396	0.2983
Percentage of U.S. EBI	0.4880	0.1460	0.3415
Percentage of U.S. retail sales	0.4691	0.1311	0.2804
Percentage of U.S. population	0.3267	0.1359	0.2171
Automobile retail sales, 1995	$3,038,459,000	$670,540,000	$1,922,796,000
Projections for December 31, 2000			
Total population	938,300	397,300	625,800
Percentage of change in population, 1995–2000	8.4	10.4	8.8
Total EBI	$24,701,086,000	$7,084,716,000	$17,991,870,000
Percentage change in total EBI, 1995–2000	27.7	22.4	32.9
Total retail sales	$14,277,621,000	$3,724,196,000	$8,883,714,000
Percentage change in total retail sales, 1995–2000	29.2	20.6	34.5
Buying power index (%)	0.4728	0.1410	0.3243

Source: Adapted from *Sales & Marketing Management: 1996 Survey of Buying Power* (1996), pp. 54, 82, 171, 172. Reprinted by permission of Sales & Marketing Management Inc. © 1996, S&MM Survey of Buying Power.

The most important disadvantage of the *Survey* is its use of broad geographic territories. These territories may not correspond with a store's trading area (they are often much larger than a trading area) and cannot be broken down easily.

The value of the *Survey of Buying Power* can be seen by showing how a prospective new-car dealer could apply it during trading-area analysis for a store location. This dealer is investigating three counties near Chicago: Du Page, Kane, and Lake. Table 9-4 lists selected relevant 1995 population and retail sales data, as well as projections for the year 2000, for each county under consideration. The *Survey* updates these data each year.

To fully understand the information in Table 9-4, two key terms used in the *Survey of Buying Power* must be defined.[31] **Effective buying income (EBI)** is personal income (wages, salaries, interest, dividends, profits, rental income, and pension income) minus federal, state, and local taxes and nontax payments (such as personal contributions for social security insurance). EBI is commonly known as disposable personal income.

[31]"Glossary," *Sales & Marketing Management: 1996 Survey of Buying Power* (1996), p. 216.

Table 9-5   COMPUTATIONS OF BUYING POWER INDEXES: DU PAGE, KANE, AND LAKE COUNTIES, 1995[a]

Du Page County
Buying power index   =   0.5 (0.4880%) + 0.3 (0.4691%) + 0.2 (0.3267%)
                     =   0.4500%

Kane County
Buying power index   =   0.5 (0.1460%) + 0.3 (0.1311%) + 0.2 (0.1359%)
                     =   0.1396%

Lake County
Buying power index   =   0.5 (0.3415%) + 0.3 (0.2804%) + 0.2 (0.2171%)
                     =   0.2983%

[a]BPI = 0.5 (area's % of U.S. effective buying income) + 0.3 (area's % of U.S. retail sales) + 0.2 (area's % of U.S. population)

The **buying power index (BPI)** is a single weighted measure combining effective buying income, retail sales, and population size into an overall indicator of an area's sales potential, expressed as a percentage of total U.S. sales:

Buying power index   =   0.5 (the area's percentage of U.S. effective buying income)

+ 0.3 (the area's percentage of U.S. retail sales)

+ 0.2 (the area's percentage of U.S. population)

Each of the three criteria in the index is assigned a weight, based on its relative importance.

The buying power indexes for Du Page, Kane, and Lake counties are computed in Table 9-5. The BPI of Du Page is over three times greater than that of Kane and 50 percent greater than that of Lake. As the data in Table 9-4 indicate, Du Page has a larger population and more people 18 and older than either Kane or Lake. These are vital statistics for an auto dealer. In addition, 74.2 percent of Du Page's residents have effective buying incomes of $35,000 or better, compared to 60.3 percent of Kane's residents and 70.5 percent of Lake's. In 1995, automobile sales were $3 billion in Du Page, compared to $671 million in Kane and $1.9 billion in Lake.

A Cadillac dealer using *Survey of Buying Power* data might select Du Page and a Chevrolet dealer might select Kane. But, because *Survey* statistics are broad in nature, several subsections of Kane may be superior choices to subsections in Du Page (based on census data) for the Cadillac dealer. And the level of competition in each area also must be noted.

Different retailers require different kinds of information about an area's population. The location decision for a bookstore or an automobile dealer usually requires more data than are needed for a fast-food franchise. For a fast-food franchisor, the prime criterion in trading-area analysis is often population density. Thus, many fast-food franchisors seek communities having a large number of people living or working within a three- or four-mile radius of their stores. On the other hand, bookstore owners and automobile dealers cannot locate merely on the basis of population density. They must consider a more complex combination of population attributes in evaluating areas and should look at the sources of data described in this chapter.

Economic Base Characteristics

It is imperative to study the characteristics of each area's economic base. This base reflects the commercial and industrial infrastructure of a community and the sources of income for its residents. A retailer seeking stability normally prefers an area with a diversified economic base (one with a large number of nonrelated industries and financial institutions) to one with an economic base keyed to one major industry. The latter area is more affected by a strike, declining demand for one product line, and cyclical fluctuations.

In evaluating a trading area, a retailer should investigate such economic base factors as the percentage of the labor force in each industry or trade grouping, the transportation network, banking facilities, the potential impact of economic fluctuations on the area and particular industries, and the future of individual industries (firms). These data can be obtained from *Editor & Publisher Market Guide,* regional planning commission studies, regional industrial development organizations, chambers of commerce, and other sources.

Editor & Publisher Market Guide provides considerable economic base data for cities on a yearly basis, including principal sources of employment, transportation networks, bank deposits, auto registrations, the number of gas and electric meters, newspaper circulations, and major shopping centers. It also contains statistics on population size and total households by city. Like the *Survey of Buying Power, Editor & Publisher Market Guide* has one serious drawback for retailers. Data cover broad geographic areas and are hard to disaggregate.

The value of *Editor & Publisher* can be shown by examining some important economic base data from the 1997 description of Sacramento, California. Sacramento is the capital of California. Among its principal industries are retail and wholesale trade, manufacturing, farming, food processing, lumber products, government, construction, transportation and public utilities, insurance and real estate, and other services. More specifically, Sacramento is involved with U.S. aircraft repair and modification, aerospace, and mobile home manufacturing; and even has an Army depot and training center. It has a large transportation system involving several railroads, motor freight carriers, intercity bus routes, and airlines. The population of several hundred thousand has access to 22 different commercial banks, 11 different savings and loan associations, 28 credit unions (each with at least one Sacramento branch), and 1 newspaper; and residents own 594,958 passenger autos. There are a number of major shopping centers and retail outlets.[32]

The bookstore chain noted earlier would find *Editor & Publisher* information on shopping centers and retailers to be quite helpful in analyzing cities. The auto dealer would find *Editor & Publisher* information on the transportation network, the availability of financial institutions, and the number of passenger cars to be very useful. In trading-area analysis, *Editor & Publisher Market Guide* is best used to supplement census and *Sales & Marketing Management* statistics.

The Nature of Competition and the Level of Saturation

A retailing opportunity in an area cannot be accurately assessed unless the competitive structure is studied. Although a trading area may have residents who match the retailer's desired market and may have a strong economic base, it may be a poor location for a new store if competition is too extensive. Similarly, an area with a small population and a narrow economic base may be a good location if competition is minimal.

While examining competition in an area, such factors as these should be analyzed: the number of existing stores, the size distribution of existing stores, the rate of new-store openings, the strengths and weaknesses of all stores, short-run and long-run trends, and the level of saturation. These factors should be evaluated in relation to an area's population size and growth, not just in absolute terms.

For example, over the past decade, many retailers have expanded into states in the Southeast and Southwest due to their growing populations. Thus, Tiffany, Saks Fifth Avenue, Gumps, Target, Marshall Field, Lord & Taylor, and Macy's are among the retailers that have entered the New Orleans, Dallas, Orlando, and/or Phoenix markets to be in areas with expanding populations. However, there is some concern that localities such as

---

[32]"Sacramento," *Editor & Publisher Market Guide 1997,* Section 2, p. 44.

these may become oversaturated because of the influx of new stores. Furthermore, while the population in the Northeast has been declining relative to the Southeast and the Southwest, one of its major strengths—population density—should not be disregarded by retailers. According to the U.S. Bureau of the Census, population density (as expressed by the number of persons residing per square mile) in the Northeast is much higher than in the Southeast and Southwest. In New Jersey, there are 1,070 people per square mile; in Massachusetts, 775; in Louisiana, 100; in Texas, 72; in Florida, 262; and in Arizona, 37.

The level of retail saturation in a trading area can be defined as understored, overstored, or saturated. An **understored trading area** has too few stores selling a specific good or service to satisfy the needs of its population. An **overstored trading area** has so many stores selling a specific good or service that some retailers will be unable to earn an adequate profit. A **saturated trading area** has the proper amount of retail facilities to satisfy the needs of its population for a specific good or service, as well as to enable retailers to prosper.

Despite the large number of areas in the United States that are overstored, there still remain plentiful opportunities in understored communities:

> As suburbs become saturated with stores, underserved minority neighborhoods stand out as major opportunities for growth. With high-profile inner-city projects such as the Harlem USA development in New York and Baldwin Hills Crenshaw Plaza in Los Angeles raising awareness and attention, retailers, financiers, and developers are showing increasing interest in ethnically oriented shopping centers. Both central city areas, home to middle-class African-Americans and fast-growing Hispanic and Asian communities, are being assessed for their commercial retail potential, as major national retailers learn how to expand in this market. Unlike traditional ethnic shopping districts jammed with small, local merchants catering to a single nationality, the projects being evaluated today feature a broad mix of national retailers in an enclosed mall or power center development. Until recently, these neighborhoods have been largely ignored by mainstream retailers that favored developments in suburban areas. With those areas being saturated, however, neighborhoods with high concentrations of African-Americans, Hispanics, Asians, and other groups are emerging as a new opportunity in today's fiercely competitive retail climate.[33]

Measuring Trading-Area Saturation ❑ When measuring the level of retail saturation in a trading area, this premise should be kept in mind: any trading area can support only a given number of stores or square feet of selling space per goods/service category. The ratios cited in this subsection attempt to quantify retail store saturation. These ratios are meaningful only if norms are set; the saturation level in a trading area can then be measured against a standard set by the retailer, or it can be compared with that of other trading areas.

For example, the owner of a chain of auto accessory stores might find that his current trading area is saturated by computing the ratio of auto accessory sales to household income. On the basis of this calculation, the owner would then decide to expand into a nearby metropolitan area with a lower ratio rather than adding another store in the more established trading area.

Among the ratios that retailers most often use to determine a trading area's level of retail saturation are the

■ Number of persons per retail establishment.
■ Average sales per retail store.
■ Average sales per retail store category.

---

[33]Susan Reda, "Ethnically Oriented Centers Draw New Retailer, Developer Interest," *Stores* (January 1997), pp. 122–124.

ETHICS IN RETAILING

Revitalizing the Inner City: A Retailing Perspective

According to Professor Michael Porter of Harvard, a sustainable economic base can be created in the inner city by identifying and exploiting its competitive advantages. Porter says there are four main competitive advantages to an inner-city location:

■ Strategic location—close to downtown amenities.
■ Local market demand—that is underserved by existing businesses.
■ Integration with regional clusters—located near to regional concentrations of businesses.
■ Human resources—dedicated employees seeking moderate-wage employment.

Two of these advantages particularly affect retailing: local market demand and human resources.

Although other geographic market areas may be oversaturated, many inner-city markets are undersaturated. For example, in Los Angeles, the inner city's degree of market penetration as contrasted with the rest of the city is 35 percent for supermarkets and 40 percent for department stores. The inner city also represents a major market for retailers that can enact a micromarketing strategy aimed at residents. Thus, Goldblatt Brothers successfully rebuilt itself as an inner-city retailer in Chicago offering residents products at closeout prices. And the inner city has a large labor pool of people who favor working near their homes. In contrast to suburban areas, inner-city retailers may be better able to attract employees for entry-level positions.

Source: Michael E. Porter, "The Competitive Advantage of the Inner City," *Harvard Business Review,* Vol. 73 (May–June 1995), pp. 55–71.

■ Average store sales per capita or household.
■ Average sales per square foot of selling area.
■ Average sales per employee.

The data to compute these and other ratios can be obtained from a company's records on its own performance, city and state license and tax records, phone directories, personal visits to locales, consumer surveys, economic census data, *Dun & Bradstreet* reference books, *Editor & Publisher Market Guide, County Business Patterns,* trade association publications, and other sources. Retail sales by product category, the population size, and the number of households per market area can be found in the *Survey of Buying Power.*

While investigating an area's level of saturation for a specific good or service, saturation ratios must be interpreted carefully. Variations among areas sometimes may not be reliable indicators of differences in saturation. For instance, car sales per capita are usually different for a suburban area than for an urban area because suburban residents have a much greater need for their cars. Thus, each area's level of saturation should be evaluated against different standards—based on optimum per capita sales figures in that area.

In calculating the saturation level in an area based upon sales per square foot of selling space, the retailer must remember to take its proposed new store into account. If that proposed store is not part of the calculations for the level of saturation, the relative value of each trading area may be distorted; sales per square foot of selling area decline the most when new outlets are added in small communities. Furthermore, the retailer should consider whether a new store will expand the total consumer market for a specific good or service category in a trading area or just increase the firm's market share in that area without expanding the total market.

Table 9-6 shows 1995 background data and selected measures of trading-area saturation for the supermarket industry (including conventional supermarkets, food-based superstores, and so on) in three major Texas market areas: Dallas, Houston, and San Antonio. The market areas depicted in the table are quite broad because they include the

Table 9-6 BACKGROUND DATA AND SELECTED MEASURES OF TRADING-AREA SATURATION FOR SUPERMARKETS (OF ALL TYPES) IN THREE MAJOR TEXAS MARKETS, 1995

	Dallas	Houston	San Antonio
Background Data:			
Total supermarket sales (mil)	$8,727	$6,230	$6,258
Total population (in 000s)	6,600	5,107	4,802
Total number of households (in 000s)	2,476	1,842	1,629
Total number of supermarkets	800	528	438
Total square footage for all supermarkets (in 000s)	28,357	18,014	15,255
Average square footage per supermarket	35,446	34,117	34,829
Measures of Trading-Area Saturation:			
Number of persons/supermarket	8,250	9,672	10,963
Average sales per supermarket (in 000s)	$10,909	$11,799	$14,288
Average supermarket sales per capita	$1,322	$1,219	$1,303
Average supermarket sales per household	$3,523	$3,380	$3,839
Average supermarket sales per square foot	$308	$346	$410

Source: "For the Record," *Progressive Grocer* (April 1996), pp. 53–57; and authors' computations.

cities noted, as well as the cities, suburbs, and communities surrounding them. Note: Average sales per employee data were not available in the *Progressive Grocer* study used in this discussion.

Dallas is the least saturated on the basis of one of the five ratios: average sales per capita. It also has the largest population. San Antonio is the least saturated in terms of the number of persons per supermarket, average sales per supermarket, average supermarket sales per household, and average sales per square foot. There are far fewer supermarkets in San Antonio than in the other areas, which accounts for the greater number of people per supermarket. While Houston does not lead on any measure, it is second (ahead of Dallas) for three of them. Thus, all three areas offer some positive and negative attributes for prospective supermarkets, and the choice of an area must be linked to saturation factors deemed most critical by a particular retailer.

Summary

1. *To demonstrate the importance of store location for a retailer and outline the process for choosing a store location* The choice of a store location is significant because of the complex decision making involved, the high costs, the lack of flexibility once a site is chosen, and the impact of a site on a retailer's strategy. A good location may let a retailer succeed even if its strategy mix is relatively mediocre.

The selection of a store location consists of four steps: (1) evaluating alternative trading areas; (2) determining the most desirable type of location; (3) picking a general site; and (4) settling on a spe-

cific site. This chapter looks at Step 1. Chapter 10 details Steps 2, 3, and 4.

2. *To discuss the concept of a trading area and its related components* A trading area is the geographical area from which a retailer draws its customers. When two or more shopping locales are near to one another, they may have trading-area overlap.

Today, many retailers are utilizing geographic information systems (GIS) software to delineate and analyze their trading areas. This software combines digitized mapping with key locational data to graphically depict trading-area characteristics, thereby allowing retailers to research alternative locations and display the findings on computer screen maps. Several vendors market GIS software (via Web sites and CD-ROM disks), based on enhancements to the TIGER topological program of the U.S. government.

Every trading area has primary, secondary, and fringe components; the farther consumers live from a shopping area, the less apt they are to travel there. The size and shape of a trading area depend on store type, store size, competitor locations, housing patterns, travel time and traffic barriers, and media availability. Due to their distinctiveness, destination stores have much larger trading areas than parasite stores.

3. *To show how trading areas may be delineated for existing and new stores* The size, shape, and characteristics of the trading area for an existing store or group of stores can be identified quite accurately. A retailer can gather data from store records, sponsoring contests, recording license plate numbers and linking them to customer addresses, surveying consumers, buying specialized computer-generated data, and so on. Time biases must be considered in amassing data. Results should be mapped and customer densities noted.

Alternate trading areas for a new store must often be described in terms of opportunities, rather than current patronage and traffic patterns. Trend analysis and consumer surveys may be used. There are three computerized trading-area models that could be used for planning a new store location: analog, regression, and gravity. These models offer several benefits.

Two techniques for delineating new trading areas are Reilly's law of retail gravitation, which relates the population size of different cities to the size of their trading areas; and Huff's law of shopper attraction, which is based on each area's shopping assortment, the distance of people from various retail locales, and the sensitivity of people to travel time.

4. *To examine three major factors in trading-area analysis: population characteristics, economic base characteristics, and competition and the level of saturation* Once the size and shape of each possible trading area have been determined, these key factors should be studied in depth. The best secondary sources for population data are the *Census of Population* and the *Survey of Buying Power,* which have complementary strengths and weaknesses for retailers. Census data are the most detailed and specific for retailers; they become dated. A buying power index is available through the *Survey of Buying Power;* but it reports on broader geographic areas.

A trading area's economic base reflects a community's commercial and industrial infrastructure, as well as its residents' income sources. A retailer should look at such economic base factors as the percentage of the labor force in each industry grouping, the transportation network, banking facilities, the potential impact of economic fluctuations on the area, and the future of individual industries. *Editor & Publisher Market Guide* is a good source of data on economic base characteristics.

A trading area cannot be properly analyzed without studying the nature of competition and the level of saturation. An area may be understored (too few retailers), overstored (too many retailers), or saturated (the proper number of retailers). Store saturation may be measured in several ways, such as the number of persons per retail establishment, the average sales per retail store, the average store sales per capita or household, average sales per square foot of selling space, and average sales per employee.

Key Terms

trading area (p. 276)
trading-area overlap (p. 277)
geographic information systems (GIS) (p. 278)
primary trading area (p. 285)
secondary trading area (p. 285)
fringe trading area (p. 285)
destination store (p. 285)
parasite store (p. 286)

analog model (p. 289)
regression model (p. 289)
gravity model (p. 289)
Reilly's law of retail gravitation (p. 289)
point of indifference (p. 289)
Huff's law of shopper attraction (p. 290)
economic base (p. 293)

Census of Population (p. 297)
Survey of Buying Power (p. 299)
effective buying income (EBI) (p. 300)
buying power index (BPI) (p. 301)
Editor & Publisher Market Guide (p. 302)
understored trading area (p. 303)
overstored trading area (p. 303)
saturated trading area (p. 303)

Questions for Discussion

1. If a retailer has a new 20-year store lease, does this mean the next time it studies the characteristics of its trading area should be 15 years from now? Explain your answer.
2. What is trading-area overlap? Are there any advantages to a chain retailer's having some overlap among its various stores? Why or why not?
3. Describe three ways in which a music chain could use geographic information systems (GIS) software in its trading-area analysis.
4. How could an off-campus store selling small appliances situated near a college campus determine its primary, secondary, and fringe trading areas? Why should the appliance store obtain this information?
5. Why do few trading areas look like concentric circles?
6. How could a parasite store increase the size of its trading area?
7. Explain Reilly's law. What are its advantages and disadvantages?
8. Use Huff's law to compute the probability of consumers traveling from their homes to each of three shopping areas: square footage of selling space—Location 1, 4,000; Location 2, 6,000; Location 3, 8,000; travel time—to Location 1, 10 minutes; to Location 2, 15 minutes; to Location 3, 30 minutes; effect of travel time on shopping trip—2. Explain your answer.
9. What are the major advantages and disadvantages of *Census of Population* data in delineating trading areas?
10. Describe the kinds of retail information contained in the *Survey of Buying Power*. What is its most critical disadvantage?
11. Look at the most recent buying power index in the *Survey of Buying Power* for the area in which your college is located. What retailing-related conclusions do you draw?
12. Look at the most recent issue of *Editor & Publisher Market Guide* and study the economic base characteristics for the area in which your college is located. What retailing-related conclusions do you draw?
13. If a retail area is acknowledged to be "saturated," what does this signify for existing retailers? For prospective retailers considering this area?
14. Calculate several supermarket saturation ratios for cities A and B, based on these data:

	City A	City B
Total supermarket sales (millions)	$7,000	$6,100
Total population (thousands)	8,000	5,000
Total households (thousands)	3,000	2,300
Total supermarkets	700	570
Total supermarket employees	34,000	30,000

Which city is better to locate a new store? Explain your answer.

Web-Based Exercise:

ESRI INTERNET MAPPING SOLUTIONS (http://www.esri.com)

Questions

1. Use the ESRI Live Internet Demo (specifically the MapObjects Internet Map Server). Prepare a thematic map of the state where your college/university is located. Use as many demographic variables as possible to study the characteristics of the county where your college/university is located. Describe the county using the ESRI data.
2. What types of retailers are most appropriate for this county? Explain your answer.
3. Compare the demographic characteristics of your college/university's county to an adjacent county.
4. A bookstore has units in both counties you have studied. Make specific recommendations as to how the bookstore should amend its retail strategies for each county.

CASE 1
The Prince of Cruises: Choosing a Location *

Michael Charlotte has been a travel agent for over 15 years. For the last seven, he has worked as an outside agent specializing in cruise travel and tours, primarily for groups (such as members of senior citizen groups, fraternal organizations, and religious-based organizations). As an outside agent, Charlotte operates as an independent contractor for the travel agency, Go Somewhere Vacations. Charlotte and his agency divide the commissions on bookings he generates, generally about 10 percent of the vacation price. In contrast, an inside agent is an employee of the agency and is usually paid on the basis of a salary.

Go Somewhere Vacations is the largest travel agency in Bel Air, Maryland, which is a residential town located about 30 miles north of Baltimore. The agency is on the main street in Bel Air's central business district.

Recently, Charlotte decided he wanted to fulfill his lifelong dream of operating his own agency. He has a moderate base of clients who he feels would continue to book their vacations through him. In addition, Charlotte feels he can expand his client base. As in the past, he plans to continue specializing in cruise travel and tours. He wants to call his agency The Prince of Cruises.

Charlotte is considering three alternative types of locations for his new agency: a home/office arrangement (in which the agency would be operated out of a converted garage space in his home), leasing a store site in a local Bel Air shopping center (about one-quarter mile from Go Somewhere Vacations' current location), or renting space in an office building in downtown Bel Air. Regardless of the location chosen, each alternative would require approximately a $17,500 investment for office furniture and furnishings, computer equipment and modem hookups, and telephone systems and wiring. However, each alternative has totally different characteristics in terms of its trading area and customer traffic.

By operating the agency out of his house, Charlotte would save rental expenses. The home/office arrangement would also enable him to conduct business on weekends and in the evenings, when most agencies are closed. However, the ability to attract walk-in clients would be severely limited due to the absence of signs, the lack of pedestrian traffic, and the need to comply with Bel Air's strict residential zoning regulations. The home/office setup would also require an additional $7,000 expense to properly wire, panel, and insulate Charlotte's former two-car garage. Lastly, Charlotte would have to develop an arrangement with an authorized travel agency to be able to sell airline tickets from a home office.

Although the home/office alternative would take him a longer time to develop a new client base, Charlotte's expenses would be lowest under this alternative. Charlotte projects commissions of $40,000 for the first year if he operates out of his home, half of which would be derived from his existing client base. Once the minimum required client base is developed, he could then move to another location.

Secondly, Charlotte could rent retail space in a local Bel Air shopping center at an amount of approximately $4,000 a month. The agency would have to be open seven days a week and evenings (under shopping center rules). This facility would require at least two agents and a receptionist-office manager. Charlotte forecasts that this location could generate 100 walk-ins per day, of which five could be converted to bookings. He also feels that bookings will be higher at this location than at any other due to the ability to attract street traffic, closeness to other stores, and the trading areas of adjacent stores.

The third option is to rent an office in the downtown business district. This office would be open during the week, Monday through Friday. An additional staff of at least two would be necessary, an agent and a receptionist-office assistant, with resulting salary and benefit expenses of $50,000 a year. Rent and other office expenses would run approximately $2,500 a month. It is projected that 50 visitors a week would walk into the

*This case was prepared and written by Professor Allan R. Miller, Towson State University.

office. Mike feels he can convert three of these walk-ins. This type of location would be ideal in attracting business travelers, but the average commission on domestic air travel is significantly less than on cruises.

CASE 1 (Continued)

Questions
1. Develop a methodology for estimating the trading area of each of these locations.
2. Which location could be considered a parasite store? Explain your answer.
3. Describe how Charlotte could assess the level of saturation of Bel Air in terms of travel agents.
4. Which location do you recommend? Explain your answer.

**CASE 2
Arby's: Using GIS Mapping Software**[†]

Since the early 1980s, inexpensive geographic information systems (GIS) mapping software for personal computers has been available. One new product, Atlas Select, now integrates more than two gigabytes of geographic and demographic information on just a single CD-ROM disk. Unlike the other GIS systems, Atlas Select (from Claritas, http://www.claritas.com) enables users to select any geographic area or data variable by name, instead of using a file name or code to access information. Atlas Select sells for $1,295; this price includes customer access to 1990 census data, zip code boundaries, U.S. highway designations, and the ability to look up street addresses.

In using Atlas Select and similar GIS products, retailers can now easily generate maps or reports by selecting from a list of folders and files that contain important information on competitive businesses, consumer demographics and life-style data, and geographic data (based on zip codes, census maps, county, and state-based locations). Reports can be generated on a retail site's trading area characteristics, after the retailer "points and clicks" a PC mouse to identify the borders of a site's trading area.

Atlas GIS (from ESRI, http://www.esri.com) reports provide details on a trading area's characteristics. These data can be analyzed in a variety of ways. For example, a retailer user may wish to determine the total population within a given number of miles (such as 3, 5, and 8 miles) from a specific site. A trading area's current population can also be contrasted with its population in 1990 or with a year 2000 forecast population.

One user of Atlas GIS is Arby's, a fast-food franchisor that specializes in selling fresh, hot roast beef. Prior to using the Atlas GIS software, Arby's denoted its current locations by first placing a dot on a road map and then drawing a circle around it. Market surveys of competition were done in a similar fashion.

Conducting trading-area analysis with Atlas GIS software has several advantages for Arby's. First, it avoids the tedious process of producing handmade maps. Second, maps can easily be related to a data base, such as the number of residents within a given distance of each site. Third, a larger number of potential sites can be identified based on desirable trading-area characteristics. And fourth, "what if" scenarios—such as the impact of a new franchise location on an existing unit's sales—can be more easily determined. According to an Arby's executive, "You can imagine what they'd have to go through to make a change [in the manual method]."

In employing Atlas GIS software for its trading-area analysis, Arby's works with two urban geographers. It can easily determine the trading areas for existing, as well as new

[†]The material in this case is drawn from "Claritas Press Release," (May 10, 1996); "Claritas Press Release," (May 29, 1996); Mitch Betts, "Use Drive Times to Build Trading Areas and Marketing Segments," *Marketing News* (May 10, 1993), p. 2; "Better Strategic Mapping Eyes New Road," *Computerworld* (June 6, 1994), p. 30; "Electronic Mapping Software Can Aid Business," *Information Today* (February 1996), p. 24; and "SMI's Atlas Select Simplifies File Management," *Bank Marketing* (March 1996), p. 54.

CASE 2
(Continued)

locations, evaluate the trading-area characteristics of potential sites, and examine the level of saturation in each area. Through this software, Arby's has found that 75 percent of its customers usually travel 11 minutes or less from their home or workplace to a location. The firm has also learned each store's primary, secondary, and fringe trading areas on the basis of travel time (less than 5 minutes, 5 to 10 minutes, and 10 to 15 minutes). The analysis is based on a detailed data base of road characteristics (which outline each road's normal traffic speed and the distance of a location to an entrance or exit ramp of an interstate highway). These drive times have been placed into an Atlas GIS program to develop maps based on driving times from every Arby's location.

Arby's is using these findings to segment the market for its food services by travel time to each outlet. Customers located less than 5 minutes from an existing Arby's represent a good target market for the firm's quick-service message or for programs that increase a customer's frequency of purchase. On the other hand, for customers who live or work more than 15 minutes from an existing store, Arby's would use a marketing program that stresses the fresh preparation and sliced-to-order benefits of its roast beef.

Questions

1. Compare the pros and cons of Atlas software versus manual systems for describing the characteristics of trading areas to Arby's.
2. Develop specific criteria that Arby's can use to evaluate a GIS software vendor.
3. In deciding whether to open a second outlet in a particular trading area, what criteria should Arby's use? How could Arby's use Atlas software to aid its decision making in this situation?
4. Would you recommend the use of Atlas or similar software for a retailer with one store? Explain your answer.

Video Questions on Strategic Mapping

1. The video lists five functions for Atlas Select. Explain each of them.
2. Give three trading-area applications of Atlas Select for Arby's that are not cited in the video.

10

Site Selection

CHAPTER OBJECTIVES

1. To thoroughly examine the types of locations available to a retailer: isolated store, unplanned business district, and planned shopping center

2. To note the decisions necessary in choosing a general retail location

3. To describe the concept of the one-hundred percent location

4. To discuss several criteria for evaluating general retail locations and the specific sites within them

5. To contrast alternative terms of occupancy

Many retailing analysts say airports are becoming the new shopping malls. They are especially attractive in that, unlike a typical regional shopping mall, airport sites rarely have slow periods. An airport's retail facilities may be busy from 6:30 A.M. to 10:00 P.M., making an airport store's retail staff very efficient. In addition, airport locations are good for attracting busy businesspeople. Although many businesspeople are not available for shopping at traditional malls during weekdays, they are a captive audience while waiting for a flight. Lastly, airport stores do not require advertising expenditures to draw customers, as they are already there.

Some airports are designing retail facilities to resemble a traditional shopping center. At the Denver International Airport, "each concourse has a central core building with an atrium kind of like a mall." The Denver Airport has about 140,000 square feet of total retail space (out of a total area of 5.5 million square feet). It already has 95 tenants, including The Body Shop, Tie Rack, and The Nature Company.

Pittsburgh's current airport facilities, which opened in 1993, have 80,000 square feet of store space. Not only is the retail portion 100 percent leased, but there are plans to build an additional 15,000 square feet. Including food and beverage concessions, retailers at Pittsburgh International Airport average annual sales per square foot of $1,000 (some retailers have reported sales of as high as $2,500 per year).

Rents in airports tend to be higher than in regional malls, and tenants must be able to effectively utilize smaller locations than their standard prototype. For example, a typical The Nature Company unit averages between 4,000 and 4,500 square feet; its airport stores are generally about 1,400 square feet.

Airport locations can work for almost any type of retailer with a high degree of store awareness. Examples of retailers that would be inappropriate for airport locations are category killers that could not downsize their stores, or discounters. As with any shopping center, however, a developer needs to research each market's needs and the demographics of airport travelers. A retail study was conducted among commuters at Stapleton Airport (the former Denver Airport facility). This study provided input to planning the retail mall at the new Denver International Airport.[1]

---

[1] "Are Airports Becoming the New Malls?" *Chain Store Age Executive* (May 1995), pp. 78, 80; and Shelly M. Reese, "Airport Retailing Takes Off?" *Stores* (September 1996), pp. 74, 76.

OVERVIEW   After a retailer investigates alternative trading areas (Step 1), it then determines what type of location is desirable (Step 2), selects the general location (Step 3), and evaluates alternative specific store sites (Step 4). Steps 2, 3, and 4 are discussed in this chapter.

TYPES OF LOCATIONS   There are three basic location types a retailer should distinguish among: the isolated store, the unplanned business district, and the planned shopping center. Each type has its own characteristics relating to the composition of competing stores, parking facilities, nearness to nonretail institutions (such as office buildings), and other factors.

Step 2 in the location process is a determination of which type of location to use.

The Isolated Store

An **isolated store** is a freestanding retail outlet located on either a highway or a street. There are no adjacent retailers with which this type of store shares traffic.

The advantages of this type of retail location are many:

- There is no competition.
- Rental costs are relatively low.
- There is flexibility.
    1. No group rules must be abided by in operation.
    2. Larger space may be attained.
    3. Location is by choice.
- Isolation is good for stores involved in one-stop or convenience shopping.
- Better road and traffic visibility is possible.
- Facilities can be adapted to individual specifications.
- Easy parking can be arranged.
- Cost reductions are possible, leading to lower prices.

There are also various disadvantages to this retail location type:

- Initial customers may be difficult to attract.
- On an ongoing basis, many people will not travel very far to get to one store.
- Most people like variety in shopping.
- Advertising costs may be high.
- Operating costs cannot be shared, such as outside lighting, security, maintenance of grounds, and trash collection.
- The prior existence of other retailers and community zoning laws may restrict access to desirable locations.
- Often, a store must be built rather than rented.
- Generally, unplanned business districts and planned shopping centers are much more popular among consumers; they generate the bulk of retail sales.

The difficulty of attracting and holding a target market is the major reason large retailers (such as Wal-Mart) or convenience-oriented retailers (such as 7-Eleven) are usually those best suited to isolated locations. For example, a smaller specialty store would probably not be able to develop a customer following at this type of location because people would be unwilling to travel to or shop at a store not having a very large assortment of products (width and/or depth) and a strong image for merchandise and/or prices.

Years ago, when discount operations were frowned on by traditional retailers, numerous shopping centers forbade the entry of discounters. This forced various discounters to become isolated stores or to build their own centers, and they have been successful. Today, diverse retailers operate in isolated locations, as well as at business district and shopping center sites. Examples of retailers using a mixed location strategy are Kmart,

Figure 10-1

Site Selection and McDonald's

McDonald's situates its restaurants in all kinds of locations, from isolated sites to unplanned business districts to planned shopping centers—even in many Wal-Mart stores.

Kinney Shoes, McDonald's, Carvel, Sears, Toys "Я" Us, Wal-Mart, and 7-Eleven. Some retailers, such as many gas stations and convenience stores, continue to emphasize isolated locations.[2] See Figure 10-1.

The Unplanned Business District

An **unplanned business district** is a type of retail location where two or more stores situate together (or in close proximity) in such a way that the total arrangement or mix of stores in the district is not the result of prior long-range planning. Stores locate based on what is best for them, not the district. Thus, four shoe stores may exist in an area with no pharmacy.

There are four kinds of unplanned business districts: the central business district, the secondary business district, the neighborhood business district, and the string. A brief description of each follows.

Central Business District ❑ A **central business district (CBD)** is the hub of retailing in a city. It is the largest shopping area in that city and is synonymous with the term *downtown*. The CBD exists in the part of a town or city with the greatest concentration of office buildings and retail stores. Vehicular and pedestrian traffic are highly concentrated. The core of the CBD usually does not exceed a square mile, with cultural and entertainment facilities surrounding it. Consumers are drawn from the whole urban area and include all ethnic groups and all classes of people.

The CBD has at least one major department store and a broad grouping of specialty and convenience stores. The arrangement of these stores follows no format; it depends on history (first come, first located), retail trends, and luck.

Here are some of the strengths that enable CBDs to attract a large number of shoppers and potential shoppers:

---

[2]See Michael Hartnett, "Stand-Alone Specialists Create Big-Box Market Niche," *Stores* (January 1996), pp. 70–73; and "Sears Finds a HomeLife for Hard Lines," *Chain Store Age Executive* (November 1996), p. 70.

■ Excellent goods/service assortment.
■ Access to public transportation.
■ Variety of store types and images within one area.
■ Wide range of prices offered.
■ Variety of customer services.
■ High level of pedestrian traffic.
■ Nearness to commercial and social facilities.

In addition, chain headquarters stores are often situated in CBDs.

These are some of the inherent weaknesses of the CBD:

■ Inadequate parking.
■ Traffic and delivery congestion.
■ Travel time for those living in the suburbs.
■ Age of many of the retail facilities.
■ Declining condition of some central cities relative to their suburbs.
■ Relatively poor image of central cities to some potential consumers.
■ High rents and taxes for the most popular sites.
■ Movement of some popular downtown stores to suburban shopping centers.
■ Discontinuity of offerings (such as four shoe stores and no pharmacy).

Although the CBD remains a major force in retailing, over the past four decades, its share of overall store sales has fallen substantially, compared to the planned shopping center. Besides having the weaknesses just cited, much of the CBD's decline has been due to the continuing suburbanization of the population. In the first half of the twentieth century, most urban workers lived right near their jobs, and central cities had a large well-balanced mix of income, racial, and cultural groups. But gradually, many people (especially middle-class and upper-income ones) have moved to the suburbs—where they are served by planned shopping centers.[3]

Nonetheless, a number of CBDs are doing quite well and others are striving to return to their former stature. Many are using such tactics as modernizing storefronts and equipment, forming cooperative merchants' associations, fixing sidewalks and adding brighter lighting to create "atmosphere," building vertical malls (with several floors of stores), improving transportation networks, closing streets to vehicular traffic (with sometimes, disappointing results), bringing in "razzmatazz" retailers such as Niketown and Warner Bros. Studio Stores, and integrating a commercial and residential environment known as mixed-use facilities.

There are signs of turnarounds and continuing strong retail developments in numerous cities: "The most successful downtowns throughout America are those that are moving back to what they were in the beginning," said Doyle Hyett, chairman of an urban renewal consulting firm. "They are moving back to much more of a neighborhood feel, as original city centers. 'Pedestrianization' as we define it today is not to close off cars; it is to make it easy to move through." Instead, say other planners: "Most shoppers who arrive downtown in their cars want to park near their shopping area or have easy drop-off access to stores. Pedestrian malls offer neither. Birds and trees are perfectly nice, but no one really goes shopping to see them."[4]

[3]Mitchell Pacelle, "Some Urban Planners Say Downtowns Need a Lot More Congestion," *Wall Street Journal* (August 7, 1996), pp. A1, A6.

[4]Jennifer Steinhauer, "When Shoppers Walk Away from Pedestrian Malls," *New York Times* (November 5, 1996), pp. D1, D4. See also Michael Hartnett, "Booming Northwest Draws Strong Retail Growth," *Stores* (November 1996), pp. 64–68; and Mitchell Pacelle, "More Stores Spurn Malls for the Village Square," *Wall Street Journal* (February 16, 1996), pp. B1, B3.

One of the best examples of a strong CBD is Chicago, where the business community has worked hard to strengthen the central city to make it more competitive with suburban shopping centers and to stimulate office construction.

Retailers are flocking to downtown Chicago, in the process writing an exciting new chapter in the story of this city's economic growth. The retail revival of the Windy City has been spurred by an influx of companies that have traditionally been associated more with regional malls and power centers in the suburbs than with downtown locations. "Chicago is the capital of the Midwest. The city draws visitors from an eight-state area, who love to vacation here. And there is not only the built-in tourist trade and convention trade, we have a healthy, thriving downtown with a lot of young singles and young families who choose to live in this urban environment," says David P. Bossy, founding principal of the Chicago-based Mid-America Real Estate Group. New retail tenants include Borders Books, Filene's Basement, Victoria's Secret, Toys "Я" Us, Bed Bath & Beyond, The Gap, The Cheesecake Factory, Office Max, and multiple locations for Trak Auto and Super Trak Auto. "While people were busy putting up cookie cutter stores in the suburbs and creating regional shopping hubs, I think there has been a slow awakening to the fact that urban hubs have a huge amount of purchasing power that is underserved," says Bruce A. Kaplan, president of Northern Realty Group of Chicago. "Through the recession, real estate became relatively cheap. Some of these urban areas became fairly reasonable. But the biggest reason behind this growth in retail is population density. In the Clybourn corridor of Lincoln Park, for example, retailers can get triple the traffic they get in the suburbs, which is creating a natural evolution back to an area that had been overlooked," he explains.

Three areas of the city are noted most often as the hub of new retail: State Street and the Loop area; Michigan Avenue—the "Magnificent Mile," and Lincoln Park. Stanley Nitzberg, a principal at Mid-America, describes the three areas this way: "State Street and the Loop area are continuing to grow with service- and convenience-type uses, as well as selected big box and specialty stores primarily in ready-to-wear. It is likely there will be more entertainment-type uses here—such as restaurants, books, records, and tapes. This is still primarily a Monday-through-Friday, office-type environment. The Magnificent Mile has a very eclectic group of flagship-type stores across all categories. The stores are larger and finished out in a more upscale way like the Crate & Barrel store on Michigan Avenue. Lincoln Park is similar to the Flatiron district of Manhattan, and Soho in lower Manhattan. Because of its population density and income levels, this is an area that is attracting chain stores, but you will not find a Tiffany store here. Crate & Barrel and Borders Books are planning to build here."[5]

Faneuil Hall in Boston (http://www.bostonian.com/faneuil/doc/facts.htm) is a different type of successful CBD renovation. When developer James Rouse took over the 6.5-acre site containing three 150-year-old, block-long former food warehouses, it had been abandoned for almost ten years. Rouse creatively used landscaping, fountains, banners, open-air courts, informal entertainment (street performers), and colorful graphics to enable Faneuil Hall to capture a festive spirit. Faneuil Hall combines shopping, eating, and watching activities and makes them fun. Today, Faneuil Hall has over 70 shops, 14 full-service restaurants, 40 food stalls, and a popular comedy nightclub. It attracts millions of shoppers and visitors yearly.

[5]Michael Hartnett, "Chicago Shopping Revival: It's a Retailer's Kind of Town," *Stores* (December 1996), pp. 56–57.

Figure 10-2

Revitalized Central Business Districts

Large business districts rely on the customer traffic drawn by office buildings, as well as cultural and entertainment facilities. Two popular, revitalized districts are depicted here: The Gallery at Harborplace in Baltimore (top) and South Street Seaport in New York (bottom).

Other major CBD projects include Tower City Center (Cleveland), Pioneer Place (Portland), The Gallery at Harborplace (Baltimore), Union Station (Washington, D.C.), Circle Centre (Indianapolis), St. Louis Centre, South Street Seaport and Metropolis Times Square (New York City), Horton Plaza (San Diego), New Orleans Centre, and Underground Atlanta. See Figure 10-2.

Secondary Business District ❑ A **secondary business district (SBD)** is an unplanned shopping area in a city or town that is usually bounded by the intersection of two major streets. Cities—particularly larger ones—often have multiple SBDs, each having at least a junior department store (which may be a branch of a traditional department store or a full-line discount store), a variety store, and/or some larger specialty stores, in addition to many smaller stores. This type of location has grown in importance as cities have increased in population and "sprawled" over larger geographic areas.

The kinds of goods and services sold in an SBD mirror those in the CBD. However, an SBD has smaller stores, less width and depth of assortment, and a smaller trading area (consumers will not travel as far) and sells a higher proportion of convenience-oriented items.

The major strengths of the SBD include good product assortments, access to thoroughfares and public transportation, less crowding and more personal service than the CBD, and placement nearer to residential areas than the CBD. The SBD's major weaknesses include the discontinuity of offerings, the sometimes high rent and taxes (but not as high as in a CBD), traffic and delivery congestion, aging facilities, parking difficulties, and fewer chain store outlets than in the CBD. These weaknesses have generally not affected the SBD to the extent they have affected the CBD—and parking problems, travel time, and congestion are less for the SBD.

Neighborhood Business District ❑ A **neighborhood business district (NBD)** is an unplanned shopping area that appeals to the convenience shopping and service needs of a single residential area. An NBD contains several small stores, such as a dry cleaner, a stationery store, a barber shop and/or a beauty salon, a liquor store, and a restaurant; the leading retailer is typically a supermarket, a large drugstore, or a variety store. This type of business district is situated on the major street(s) of its residential area.

An NBD offers consumers a good location, long store hours, good parking, and a less hectic atmosphere than a CBD or an SBD. On the other hand, there is a limited selection of goods and services, and prices (on the average) tend to be higher because competition is less than in a CBD or an SBD.

String ❑ A **string** is an unplanned shopping area comprising a group of retail stores, often with similar or compatible product lines, located along a street or highway. There is little extension of the shopping area onto streets perpendicular to the string street. A string may start as an isolated store, success then breeding competitors. Car dealers, antique stores, and clothing stores are examples of stores commonly situating in strings.

A string location possesses many of the advantages associated with an isolated store site (such as lower rent, more flexibility, better road visibility and parking, and lower operating costs), along with some of its disadvantages (such as the limited variety of products, the increased travel time for many consumers, higher advertising costs, zoning restrictions, and the need to build premises). Unlike an isolated store, a string store has competition at its location. This attracts more customer traffic to the string area and allows for some sharing of common costs among firms. It also leads to less control over prices and lower store loyalty for each outlet there. But an individual store's increased traffic flow, due to locating in a string rather than an isolated site, may be greater than the customers lost to competitors. This may explain why four gas stations will locate on opposing corners.

Figure 10-3 shows a map depicting the various forms of unplanned business districts and isolated locations.

The Planned Shopping Center

A **planned shopping center** consists of a group of architecturally unified commercial establishments built on a site that is centrally owned or managed, designed and operated as a unit, based on balanced tenancy, and surrounded by parking facilities. Its location, size, and mix of stores are related to the trading area being served.[6] A typical shopping center has one or more anchor, or generator, stores and a diversity of smaller stores. Through **balanced tenancy,** the stores in a planned shopping center complement each

---

[6]*Statistical Abstract of the United States 1996* (Washington, D.C.: U.S. Bureau of the Census, 1996), p. 772.

Figure 10-3

Unplanned Business Districts and Isolated Locations

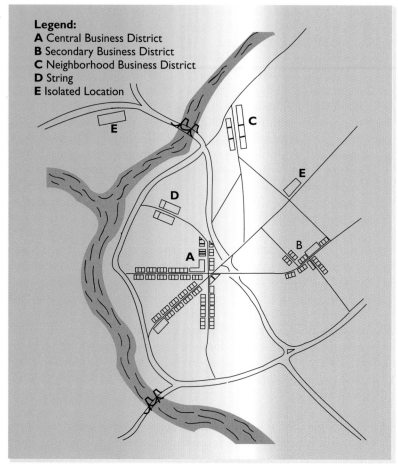

Legend:
A Central Business District
B Secondary Business District
C Neighborhood Business District
D String
E Isolated Location

other in the quality and variety of their product offerings, and the kind and number of stores are linked to the overall needs of the surrounding population. To ensure balanced tenancy, the management of a planned shopping center usually specifies the proportion of total space to be occupied by each kind of retailer, limits the product lines that can be sold by each of the various retailers, and stipulates what kinds of firms can acquire unexpired leases. At a well-run center, a coordinated and cooperative long-run, centerwide retailing strategy is adhered to by all member stores.

There are several positive attributes associated with the planned shopping center. Here are some of them:

■ Well-rounded goods and service assortments because of long-range planning.
■ Strong suburban population.
■ Interest in one-stop, family shopping.
■ Cooperative planning and sharing of common costs.
■ Creation of distinctive, but unified, shopping center images.
■ Maximization of pedestrian traffic for individual stores.
■ Access to highways and availability of parking for consumers.
■ Declining appeal of city shopping for some consumers.
■ Generally lower rent and taxes than CBD stores (except for most enclosed regional mall sites).
■ Generally lower theft rates than central business district stores.
■ Popularity of malls.
　1. Open (shopping area closed to vehicular traffic).

KL LinearCity: The New Face of Retailing in Malaysia

KL LinearCity, the combined office building, condominium, and shopping mall project that is planned for Kuala Lumpur, Malaysia, will be the world's longest multiuse building. The 10-story tubelike structure, to be built along the Kelang River, is so long (1.24 miles) that a canal is planned for the seventh floor (80 feet above the ground) to transport consumers and workers throughout the complex.

The overall project is so extensive that its total planned completion time is 24 years. Construction will be done on a modular basis. Key components include a 5-mile-long monorail to be built throughout Kuala Lumpur, a 10,000 car parking garage, 10 million square feet of commercial space, and the cleaning up of the Kelang River. The complex will also have a wide variety of attractions, including a rollerblade arena and an artificial rain forest (complete with robotic dinosaurs).

The government of Malaysia, with a total population of 20 million people, favors the project as a reflection of the country's increased prosperity. After adjusting for inflation, Malaysia's economy has grown at more than 8 percent per year for the past 8 years. Proponents of the project note the importance of cleaning up the polluted Kelang River and transforming this area into a transportation and commercial hub. Detractors are concerned over such environmental issues as flood control and traffic congestion.

Source: Raphael Pura, "Will This Great Mall Top China's Wall?" *Wall Street Journal* (July 11, 1996), p. A10.

2. Closed (shopping area closed to vehicular traffic and all stores under one temperature-controlled roof).

■ Growth of discount malls and other newer types of shopping centers.

Despite this overwhelming list of positive qualities for the planned shopping center, there are also some limitations with this arrangement:

■ Landlord-imposed regulations that reduce each retailer's operating flexibility, such as required store hours.

■ Generally higher rent than for an isolated store location (with some regional shopping centers being quite expensive).

■ Restrictions as to the goods/services that can be sold by each store.

■ Competitive environment within the center.

■ Required payments for items that may be of little or no value to an individual retailer, such as membership in a merchants' association.

■ Too many malls in a number of areas (some observers call this "the malling of America").

■ Rising consumer boredom with and disinterest in shopping as an activity.

■ Aging facilities of some older centers.

■ Domination by large anchor stores.

The importance of planned shopping centers is evident from the following. First, according to the International Council of Shopping Centers (http://www.icsc.org), 35 years ago, there were fewer than 1,000 U.S. shopping centers; now, there are 42,000-plus (with 5 billion square feet of leasable footage), 10 percent of which are closed shopping malls. Shopping center revenues exceed $935 billion annually and account for almost 40 percent of total U.S. retail store sales (including automobiles and gasoline). Nearly 11 million people work in shopping centers. Second, many shopping center customers are active. Nine out of ten Americans over age 18 visit some type of center at least once each year. Third, individual retail chains have a large shopping center presence. The Limited, Inc., Dillard's, and J.C. Penney are among the vast number of chains with substantial sales and profits from shopping center outlets.

Fourth, some big retailers have been involved in shopping center development. Typically, these firms buy a site of their choosing, years in advance, and contact another major retailer (depending on the center's size). They then bring in a developer, who builds, owns, and leases the center and connects it to the anchor stores. For instance, Sears has participated in the construction of dozens of shopping centers, and Publix Super Markets operates centers with hundreds of small-store tenants. Fifth, each year, numerous new centers of all kinds and sizes are built and tens of millions of square feet of retail space are added to existing centers.

To sustain their long-term growth, shopping centers are engaging in such practices as these:

■ Several older centers have been or are being renovated, expanded, or repositioned. The Mall at Short Hills in New Jersey; Woodfield Mall in Schaumburg, Illinois; King of Prussia in Pennsylvania; Belle Promenade in New Orleans; County East Mall in Antioch (a San Francisco suburb); Newmarket North Center in Hampton, Virginia; Roosevelt Field in Long Island, New York; Speedway Center in Indianapolis; and the Promenade in Fort Lauderdale are among the 10- to 30-year-old centers that have recently been revitalized. As one developer noted, "Over the last five years, a lot of us have determined there are some properties that are inherently strong and deserve attention; and that is where investments are going in this company—not to properties that must be saved, but to those whose value must be enhanced."[7]

■ Certain derivative types of centers are being used to foster consumer interest and enthusiasm. Two of these, megamalls and power centers, are discussed later in this chapter.

■ Shopping centers have been responding to shifting consumer life-styles: "Changing shopper demands are playing a major role in reshaping development patterns. The shifts in tastes that have weakened many specialty retailers of ladies' ready-to-wear have been a bonanza for stores selling entertainment-related products, including books, tapes, sporting goods, and foods. In recent years, there has been a shift in shopping center dominance from apparel to life-style stores like Disney, Warner Bros., Crate & Barrel, Williams-Sonoma, Grand Cuisine, and The Right Start. For the first time, in 1995, less than 50 percent of our space [the Taubman Company, a leading developer] was devoted to apparel and related accessories. Most of it was in furnishings, kitchen, health, and entertainment."[8]

■ The retailer mix is broadening at many centers to attract people interested in one-stop shopping. In particular, more centers than before are apt to include such service-oriented businesses as banks, stockbrokers, dentists, doctors, beauty salons, TV repair outlets, and/or car-leasing offices. Many centers are also heavily involved with "temporary tenants." These are retailers who lease space (usually in mall aisles or walkways) and sell from booths or moving carts. The tenants benefit from the lower rent and short-term commitment; the shopping centers benefit by creating more excitement and diversity in shopping. This way, customers often happen upon new vendors in unexpected places.[9]

■ There is renewed interest by shopping center management in providing convenience and customer service for patrons. As an example, "When people first go onto a shopping center, they want information. In any kind of center, that is what they are looking for. Our job is to make the shopping experience easier."[10]

[7]Michael Hartnett, "On the Move Again: Shopping Center Industry Stages Strong Recovery," *Stores* (May 1996), p. 58.
[8]Ibid.
[9]See Susan Reda, "Mall Carts Are on a Roll," *Stores* (October 1996), pp. 96–97; "Developers Seek Real 'Special'ty Leasing," *Chain Store Age* (February 1996), p. 182; and Michael Hartnett, "Developers Push Innovative Approaches to Revive Lagging Mall-Based Business," *Stores* (May 1997), pp. 78–82.
[10]"Lower Prices, But Not Low Class," *Chain Store Age Executive* (March 1994), pp. 186, 188.

Table 10-1　CHARACTERISTICS OF TYPICAL NEIGHBORHOOD, COMMUNITY, AND REGIONAL TYPES OF U.S. PLANNED SHOPPING CENTERS

Features of a Typical Center	TYPE OF CENTER		
	Regional	**Community**	**Neighborhood**
Total site area (acres)	30–100+	10–30	3–10
Total sq. ft. leased to retailers	400,001–2,000,000+	100,001–400,000	30,000–100,000
Principal tenant	One, two, or more full-sized department stores	Branch department store (traditional or discount), variety store, and/or category killer store	Supermarket or drugstore
Number of stores	50–150 or more	15–25	5–15
Goods and services offered	Largest assortment for customers, focusing on goods that encourage careful shopping and services that enhance the shopping experience (such as a food court)	Moderate assortment for customers, focusing on a mix of shopping- and convenience-oriented goods and services	Lowest assortment for customers, emphasizing convenience-oriented goods and services
Minimum number of people living/working in trading area needed to support center	100,000+	20,000–100,000	3,000–50,000
Trading area in driving time	Up to 30 minutes	Up to 20 minutes	Fewer than 15 minutes
Location	Outside central city, on arterial highway or expressway	Close to one or more populated residential area(s)	Along a major thorough-fare in a single residential area
Layout	Mall, often enclosed with anchor stores at major entrances/exits	Strip or L-shaped	Strip
Percentage of all centers	5	32	63
Percentage of all centers' selling space	29	46	25
Percentage of all centers' retail sales	30	41	29

Source: Percentage data are from "NRB/Shopping Centers Today 1996 Shopping Center Census," *Shopping Centers Today* (April 1997), special section.

■　Some enclosed malls are opening themselves up. For instance, "Anaheim Plaza, renovated in the early 1970s to house department stores and small retailers, became one of the first enclosed malls in Orange County, California, with a prime location near Disneyland. But in the 1980s, it was outflanked by more modern malls. 'It had lost its glamour,' says Thomas Schriber of Newport Beach's Donahue Schriber, a real estate development company. So Anaheim Plaza's owner, a state pension fund, bulldozed most of the mall in 1994. In its place, it built a string of stores, opening onto the parking lot, including a Wal-Mart and single-category retailers such as CompUSA, Old Navy, Radio Shack, Petco, and Payless Shoes, among others."[11]

There are three major types of planned shopping centers: regional, community, and neighborhood. Their characteristics are displayed in Table 10-1, and they are described next.

[11]Mitchell Pacelle, "The Aging Shopping Mall Must Either Adapt or Die," *Wall Street Journal* (April 16, 1996), pp. B1, B16.

Regional Shopping Center ❑ A **regional shopping center** is a large, planned shopping facility appealing to a geographically dispersed market. It has at least one or two full-sized department stores (each with a minimum of 100,000 square feet) and 50 to 150 or more smaller retailers. A regional center has a very broad and deep assortment of shopping-oriented goods, as well as a number of services intended to enhance the consumer's experience at the center. The market for a typical regional center is 100,000+ people, who live or work up to 30 minutes driving time from the center. On average, people travel fewer than 20 minutes. See Figures 10-4 and 10-5.

The regional center is the result of a planned effort to re-create the shopping variety of a central city in suburbia. Some experts even credit the regional shopping center with becoming the social, cultural, and vocational focal point of an entire suburban area. Frequently, a regional center is used as a town plaza, a meeting place, a concert hall, and a place for a brisk indoor walk. Despite people's declining overall interest in shopping (which does pose a significant problem for retailers), according to Stillerman Jones & Company (a research firm), on a typical visit to one of the 1,920 U.S. regional centers, people spend an average of 68 minutes there.[12]

The first regional center opened in 1950 in Seattle, anchored by a branch of Bon Marche, a leading downtown department store. The Southdale Center (outside Minneapolis), built in 1956 for the Dayton Hudson Corporation, was the first fully enclosed, climate-controlled mall.

One current derivative form of regional center, known as the megamall, is particularly intriguing. A **megamall** is an enormous planned shopping center with 1 million+ square feet of retail space, multiple anchor stores, up to several hundred specialty stores, food courts, and entertainment facilities. Its goal is to heighten consumer interest in shopping and greatly expand the trading area. There are 380 U.S. megamalls, including the gigantic Mall of America (described at http://www.link.be/retail/mall.html) in Bloomington, Minnesota. The Mall of America has four anchor stores (Bloomingdale's, Macy's, Nordstrom, and Sears), over 450 specialty stores, a 14-screen movie theater, a health club, 52 restaurants and nightclubs, the world's largest indoor amusement park

Figure 10-4

Mall St. Matthews in Louisville, Kentucky: An Enclosed Regional Shopping Center

[12]Tim Cavanaugh, "Mall Crawl Palls," *American Demographics* (September 1996), pp. 14–16.

Figure 10-5

The Falls in Miami, Florida: An Open-Air Regional Shopping Center

(Knott's Camp Snoopy, created and managed by Knott's Berry Farm of California), and 12,000 parking spaces—all on 4.2 million square feet of space. Why build this megamall? The Mall of America has stores to fit every budget, from discount to moderate to up-scale. It attracts customers from Colorado to Washington, D.C., as well as from around the world—up to 200,000 shoppers in a single day![13]

Community Shopping Center ❑ A **community shopping center** is a moderate-sized, planned shopping facility with a branch department store (traditional or discount), a variety store, and/or a category killer store, in addition to several smaller stores (usually similar to those in a neighborhood center). It offers a moderate assortment of both shopping- and convenience-oriented goods and services to consumers from one or more nearby, well-populated, residential areas. About 20,000 to 100,000 people, who live or work within 10 to 20 minutes of the center, are served by this location.

Superior long-range planning is used for a community shopping center than for a neighborhood shopping center. For example, balanced tenancy is usually better enforced and cooperative promotion expenditures are more likely. Thus, store composition and the center's image are kept pretty consistent with pre-set goals.

A rapidly emerging type of community center is the **power center,** a shopping site with (a) up to a half-dozen or so category killer stores and a mix of smaller stores or (b) several complementary stores specializing in one product category. A power center usually occupies 200,000 to 400,000 square feet and is situated on a major highway or road intersection. Its goals are to be quite distinctive—thus providing consumers with a strong motivation to go there—and to better compete with regional shopping centers. There are about 2,000 U.S. power centers. For instance, Colorado's Brookhill development and New York's The Mall at Cross County are both category killer power centers.

---

[13]"All's Well at the Mall," *Sales & Marketing Management* (January 1997), pp. 58–59.

The 271,000-square-foot Brookhill has these anchor stores: Toys "Я" Us, Media Play, Pacific Linen, Lil' Things, Discovery Zone, Builders Square, and Sears Homelife Furniture. The 216,000-square-foot The Mall at Cross County features Sports Authority, T.J. Maxx, Kids "Я" Us, and LensCrafters. Each has many smaller stores, as well. The 200,000-square-foot Towne Center Village in Marietta, Georgia, is a specialized home furnishings power center. It features furniture, custom sofa, and Oriental rug stores.[14]

Neighborhood Shopping Center ❑ A **neighborhood shopping center** is a planned shopping facility with the largest store being a supermarket and/or a drugstore. Other retailers in the center often include a bakery, a laundry-dry cleaner, a stationery store, a barbershop and/or a beauty parlor, a hardware store, a restaurant, a liquor store, and a gas station. This center focuses on convenience-oriented goods and services for people living or working in the immediate vicinity. It serves 3,000 to 50,000 people who are within 15 minutes driving time (usually fewer than 10 minutes).

A neighborhood shopping center is usually arranged in a strip. When first developed, it is carefully planned, and tenants are balanced. Over time, the planned aspects of this center may diminish and newcomers may face fewer restrictions. For example, a liquor store may be allowed to replace a barbershop. In this case, there would be no barbershop. A center's ability to maintain balance depends on its continuing attractiveness to potential tenants (as expressed by the extent of the store vacancy rate).

In number, but not in selling space or sales, neighborhood centers account for nearly two-thirds of all U.S. shopping centers.

THE CHOICE OF A GENERAL LOCATION

The last part of Step 2 in location planning requires a retailer to select one of the three basic locational formats: isolated, unplanned district, or planned center. The decision depends on the firm's strategy and a careful evaluation of the advantages and disadvantages of each alternative.

Once this is done, the retailer then chooses a broadly defined site for its store(s), Step 3. Two decisions are needed here. First, the specific kind of isolated store, unplanned business district, or planned shopping center location must be picked. If a retailer wants an isolated store, it must decide whether to locate on a highway or side street. Should the retailer desire an unplanned business area, it must decide whether to locate in a CBD, an SBD, an NBD, or a string. A retailer seeking a planned area must determine whether to locate in a regional, community, or neighborhood shopping center; and whether to situate in a derivative form of shopping center such as a megamall or power center.

Here are the preferences of a variety of retailers:

■ Talbots, The Gap, The Body Shop, J.Crew, Sam Goody, and Williams-Sonoma are among the mall-based retailers now opening more stores in central and secondary business districts: "They've discovered that, these days, many shoppers would rather navigate their own village centers than the sprawling parking lots of regional malls."[15]

■ The Uni-Mart chain of convenience stores favors isolated locations in small towns: "We are their gas station, their restaurant, their drugstore, their newspaper stand."[16]

■ Deb Stores, which targets the fashion-conscious junior apparel female, likes enclosed regional shopping centers. As a rule, it does not consider strip centers.[17]

---

[14]Compiled by the authors from various sources on the Web. See also Susan Reda, "Do Power Centers Make Sense?" *Stores* (May 1995), pp. 20–26; and W. Paul O'Mara, Michael D. Beyard, and M. Dougal, *Developing Power Centers* (Washington, D.C.: Urban Land Institute, 1996).

[15]Pacelle, "More Stores Spurn Malls for the Village Square," p. B1.

[16]Randall Lane, "The Sleepier, the Better," *Forbes* (November 6, 1995), pp. 84, 88.

[17]*Deb Stores, Inc. 1995 Annual Report.*

■ Many of Consolidated Stores' chains have different location strategies. The Itzadeal! and All for One stores are smaller, closeout retail outlets that are in strip shopping centers in less-populated communities. Toy Liquidators uses factory outlet centers to appeal to serious bargain hunters, who view their trips as major shopping events. The Amazing Toy Store is in neighborhood centers in highly populated areas. Recently acquired K-B Toys (formerly Kay-Bee) is mostly in regional shopping centers.[18]

Second, a retailer must determine the general placement of its store(s). For an isolated store, this means selecting a specific highway or side street. For an unplanned district or planned center, this means designating a specific district (e.g., downtown Los Angeles or Pittsburgh) or center (e.g., Seminary South in Fort Worth, Texas, or Chesterfield Mall in Richmond, Virginia).

In Step 3, the retailer narrows down the decisions made in the first two steps and then chooses a general location. Step 4 requires the retailer to evaluate alternative specific sites, including their position on a block (or in a center), the side of the street, and the terms of tenancy. The factors to be considered in assessing and choosing a general location and a specific site within that location are described together in the next section because many strategic decisions are similar for these two steps.

LOCATION AND SITE EVALUATION

The assessment of every general location and the specific sites contained within them both require extensive analysis. Site selection is as crucial as the choice of a retail area, especially for stores relying on customer traffic patterns to generate business.

In any area, the optimum site for a particular store is called the **one-hundred percent location.** Since different kinds of retailers need different kinds of locations, a location labeled as 100 percent for one firm may be less than optimal for another. Thus, an upscale ladies' apparel shop would seek a location with different strengths from those desired by a convenience store. The specialty shop would benefit from heavy pedestrian traffic, closeness to major department stores, and proximity to other specialty stores. The convenience store would rather locate in an area with ample parking and heavy vehicular traffic. It does not need to be close to other stores.

Figure 10-6 contains a checklist for location and site evaluation. In choosing a location, a retailer would rate every alternative location (and specific site) on all of the criteria and develop an overall rating for each alternative. Two firms may rate the same location quite differently, depending on their stores' requirements. This figure should be used in conjunction with the trading-area data noted in Chapter 9, not instead of them.

Pedestrian Traffic

Probably the most crucial measures of a location's and site's value are the number and type of people passing by. Other things being equal, a site with the highest pedestrian traffic is often best.

Because everyone passing a location or site is not necessarily a good prospect for all types of stores, many retailers use selective counting procedures, such as counting only males and females carrying shopping bags. Otherwise, pedestrian traffic totals may include too many nonshoppers. As an example, it would be improper for an appliance retailer to count as prospective shoppers all the people who pass a downtown site on the way to work. In fact, much of the pedestrian traffic in a downtown location may be from people who are in the area for nonretailing activities.

A proper pedestrian traffic count should encompass these four elements:

■ Separation of the count by age and gender (children under a given age should not be counted).

---

[18]*Consolidated Stores 1996 Annual Report.*

Figure 10-6

A Location/Site Evaluation Checklist

	Rate each of the following criteria on a scale of 1 to 10, with 1 being excellent and 10 being poor.	
Pedestrian Traffic	Number of people	_____
	Type of people	_____
Vehicular Traffic	Number of vehicles	_____
	Type of vehicles	_____
	Traffic congestion	_____
Parking Facilities	Number and quality of parking spots	_____
	Distance to store	_____
	Availability of employee parking	_____
Transportation	Availability of mass transit	_____
	Access from major highways	_____
	Ease of deliveries	_____
Store Composition	Number and size of stores	_____
	Affinity	_____
	Retail balance	_____
Specific Site	Visibility	_____
	Placement in the location	_____
	Size and shape of the lot	_____
	Size and shape of the building	_____
	Condition and age of the lot and building	_____
Terms of Occupancy	Ownership or leasing terms	_____
	Operations and maintenance costs	_____
	Taxes	_____
	Zoning restrictions	_____
	Voluntary regulations	_____
Overall Rating	General location	_____
	Specific site	_____

- ■ Division of the count by time (this allows the study of peaks, low points, and changes in the gender of the people passing by the hour).
- ■ Pedestrian interviews (these let researchers find out the proportion of potential shoppers).
- ■ Spot analysis of shopping trips (these allow observers to verify the stores actually visited).

Vehicular Traffic

The quantity and characteristics of vehicular traffic must be examined, especially by retailers appealing to customers who drive there. Convenience stores, outlets in regional shopping centers, and car washes are examples of retailers that rely on heavy vehicular traffic. Automotive traffic studies are quite important in suburban areas, where pedestrian traffic is often limited.

As in the analysis of pedestrian traffic, some adjustments to the raw count of vehicular traffic should be made. For instance, some retailers count only homeward-bound traffic. Some exclude vehicles passing on the other side of a divided highway, and many firms omit out-of-state license plates in their counts. Data on traffic patterns are usually available from the state highway department, the county engineer, or the regional planning commission.

Besides traffic counts, a retailer should study the extent and timing of congestion (caused by heavy traffic, detours, narrow and poor roads, and so on). Vehicular customers will normally avoid heavily congested areas, and shop where driving time and driving difficulties are minimized.

Parking Facilities

Parking facilities must not be overlooked in assessing a location and specific sites in it. The vast majority of U.S. retail stores built since the end of World War II include some provision for nearby off-street parking. In many business districts, parking facilities are provided by individual stores, cooperative arrangements among stores, and municipal governments. In planned shopping centers, parking facilities are shared by all stores there. The number and quality of parking spots, their distances from store sites, and the availability of employee parking should all be evaluated.

It is hard to generalize about a retailer's needs for parking facilities because they depend on such factors as the trading area of the store, the type of store, the portion of shoppers using an automobile, the existence of other parking facilities, the turnover of spaces (which depend on the length of the shopping trip), the flow of shoppers throughout the day and the week, and parking by nonshoppers. Nonetheless, a shopping center normally requires about 4 or 5 parking spaces per 1,000 square feet of gross floor area; and whereas a supermarket usually requires 10 to 15 parking spaces per 1,000 square feet of gross floor area, a furniture store would need only 3 or 4.

Sometimes, free parking in shopping locations that are in or close to commercial areas creates problems. Commuters and employees of nearby businesses may park in these facilities, reducing the number of spaces available for shoppers. This dilemma can be lessened by the validation of shoppers' parking stubs and requiring payment from nonshoppers.

Another problem may occur if total selling space in a location goes up due to the addition of new stores or the expansion of current ones. Parking facilities may then be inadequate because space formerly allotted to parking might be given to the new stores or the extensions, and because parking needs rise to accommodate new employees, new shoppers, and longer shopping trips.

Double-deck parking or parking tiers are possible solutions to this problem. In addition to saving land, these types of parking shorten the distance from a parked car to a store. This is crucial when one recognizes that many customers of a regional shopping center may be unwilling to walk more than a few hundred feet from their cars to the center.

Having too large a parking facility may also cause some difficulties. If the facility is far from full, the location's image may suffer because an illusion of emptiness is created—and customers would wonder why. A parking lot may contain 150 cars, but if the capacity of the lot is 500 cars, it might appear that the lot is empty and the stores unpopular.

Transportation

The availability of mass transportation, access from major highways, and ease of deliveries must be examined in assessing a location and specific sites.

In a downtown area, closeness to mass transportation is important, particularly for people who do not own cars, commute to work there, or would not otherwise shop in an area with heavy traffic congestion and limited parking. The availability of buses, taxis, subways, trains, or other kinds of public transit must be investigated for any area not readily servicing vehicular traffic. Because most downtown shopping areas are at the hub of a mass transportation network, they allow people from all over a city to shop there.

Locations dependent on vehicular traffic should be rated on the basis of their access to major thoroughfares. As mentioned in the previous chapter, driving time is an important consideration for many people. In addition, drivers heading eastbound on a highway often do not like to make a U-turn to get to a store on the westbound side of that highway.

The transportation network should also be studied for its ability to convey delivery trucks to and from the store. Many thoroughfares are excellent for customer traffic but ban large trucks or cannot bear their weight.

Store Composition

An area's store composition should be studied. How many stores are there? How large are they? The number and size of stores should be consistent with the kind of location selected. For example, a retailer interested in an isolated site would want no stores nearby; a retailer interested in a neighborhood business district would want to locate in an area with 10 or 15 small stores; and a retailer interested in a regional shopping center would desire a location with more than 50 stores, including at least 1 or 2 large department store anchors (to generate customer traffic).

A firm should weigh its store's compatibility with adjacent or nearby stores in studying locations and sites. If the stores at a given location (be it an unplanned district or a planned center) complement, blend, and cooperate with one another, and each benefits from the others' presence, **affinity** exists. With a strong level of affinity, the sales of each store would be greater, due to the high level of customer traffic, than if the stores are apart from each other.

The practice of similar or complementary stores locating near each other is based on two major premises: (1) customers like to compare the offerings of similar stores as to price, style, selection, and service, and (2) customers like one-stop shopping (a variety of products is often bought from different stores on the same shopping trip). Thus, affinities can exist among competing stores, as well as among complementary stores. Since more people travel to shopping areas with large selections than to convenience-oriented areas, the sales of all stores are enhanced.

One measure of compatibility is the degree to which stores exchange customers. The stores in these categories are very compatible with each other and have high customer interchange:

■ Supermarket, drugstore, bakery, fruit-and-vegetable store, meat store.
■ Department store, apparel store, hosiery store, lingerie shop, shoe store, jewelry store.

As one expert said about affinity: "The department stores of Boulevard Haussmann in Paris, the outfitters of London's Oxford Street, the electrical retailers of Akihabara in Tokyo, and the theaters and cinemas of Broadway are among the better-known examples of this phenomenon. But the clustering of similar outlets is a truly universal trait, ranging from the hamburger alleys and automobile rows of most American cities to the pronounced clusters of goldsmiths and banana sellers in the marketplaces of the third world."[19]

[19]Stephen Brown, "Retail Location Theory: The Legacy of Harold Hotelling," *Journal of Retailing*, Vol. 65 (Winter 1989), p. 451.

A location's retail balance should also be considered. **Retail balance** refers to the mix of stores within a district or shopping center. Proper balance occurs when the number of store facilities for each merchandise or service classification is equal to the location's market potential, a wide range of goods and service classifications is provided to ensure one-stop shopping, there is an adequate assortment within any good or service category, and there is a proper mix of store types (balanced tenancy).

Specific Site

Besides the factors already detailed, the specific site should be reviewed on the basis of visibility, placement in the location, size and shape of the lot, size and shape of the building, and condition and age of the lot and building.

Visibility refers to a site's ability to be seen by pedestrian and vehicular traffic. A site on a side street or at the end of a shopping center does not have the same visibility as one on a major road or at the entrance of a shopping center. High visibility makes passersby aware a store exists and is open. Furthermore, some people hesitate to go down a side street or to the end of a center.

Placement in the location refers to a site's relative position in the district or center. A corner location may be desirable since it is situated at the intersection of two streets and has "corner influence." A corner site is usually more expensive to own or lease because it offers these advantages: greater pedestrian and vehicular passersby due to converging traffic flows from two streets, increased show window display area, and less traffic congestion by the use of two or more entrances. Corner influence is greatest in high-volume retail locations. That is why some Pier 1 stores, Tootsies apparel shops, and Kay jewelry stores occupy corner lots in shopping districts or corner spots in shopping malls. See Figure 10-7.

Some advantages of a corner location are reduced in a shopping center. For instance, traffic on the streets perpendicular to many neighborhood and community centers is usually sparse. Accordingly, fewer additional customers are attracted to a corner store. Also, because many stores in larger shopping centers have two entrances (one in the mall and one in the parking area), shoppers can go from parking spots to the main mall without using the designated walkways, stores have more window display space without the need for corner locations, and traffic flows to and through the center are eased.

Figure 10-7

Corner Influence and Tootsies

At the Phipps Plaza regional mall in Atlanta, Georgia, Tootsies' apparel store uses a corner exterior display window to attract passersby.

Placement decisions should be keyed to retailer needs. A convenience-oriented firm, such as a stationery store, would be very concerned about the side of the street, the location relative to other convenience-oriented stores, nearness to parking, access to a bus stop, and the distance from homes. A shopping-oriented retailer, such as a furniture store, would be more interested in the use of a corner site to increase window display space, proximity to wallpaper and other related retailers, accessibility of its pickup platform to consumers, and ease of deliveries to the store.

The size and shape of the lot should be evaluated. A department store requires significantly larger space than a boutique; and a department store may desire a square site, whereas the boutique may seek a rectangular one. Any site should be viewed in terms of the total space needed: parking, walkways, selling, nonselling, and so on.

When a retailer buys or rents an existing building, its size and shape should be examined. In addition, the condition and age of the lot and the building should be investigated. These characteristics would then be measured against the firm's needs.

Due to the saturation of stores in many desirable locations and the lack of leasing or ownership opportunities in others, some retailers have turned to more nontraditional sites—often to complement their established stores. Here are a few examples:

■ TGI Friday, Johnston & Murphy, and Bally are among the growing number of retailers with airport stores.
■ McDonald's now has outlets in hundreds of Wal-Marts and at dozens of Amoco and Chevron gas stations.
■ Some fast-food outlets share facilities to give customers better variety, as well as to share costs.

As one observer recently noted: "The development of retail outlets in nontraditional locations is largely a response to two things: changing consumer demands and fairly saturated local markets. Fast-food chains in particular have developed virtually every profitable piece of real estate in many markets, yet they still want to increase the number of opportunities for shoppers to see their brand name on the street. Fearing they'll be outnumbered by competitors, these expansion-minded retailers are finding alternatives to freestanding stores. The result is everything from a shopping mall inside Paris' Louvre museum to fast-food restaurants in gas stations. This strategy not only makes chain retailers even more visible, it also appeals to growing consumer demands for ease and convenience. Convenience isn't just about making a store easy to shop in. It's about helping the customer accomplish three or four things that they have to get done over a lunch break or after work. It's about meeting a whole range of needs. And alternative retail sites aren't just for fast-food restaurants. Even upscale retailers are finding new sites."[20]

Terms of Occupancy

Terms of occupancy—including ownership versus leasing, the type of lease, operations and maintenance costs, taxes, zoning restrictions, and voluntary regulations—must be evaluated for each prospective site.

Ownership Versus Leasing ❑ A retailer with adequate financial resources can either own or lease premises. Ownership is more common in small stores, in small communities, and/or at inexpensive locations. It has several advantages over leasing. There is no risk that an outside property owner will not renew a lease or will double or triple the rent when a lease expires. With ownership, monthly mortgage payments are stable. Operations are flexible; the retailer can engage in scrambled merchandising, break down walls, and so on. It is also likely that property value will appreciate over time, giving the retailer a tan-

[20]Shelly Reese, "Toilet Paper and a Big Mac," *American Demographics* (July 1996), pp. 14–15.

TECHNOLOGY IN RETAILING

How Computer-Generated Data Can Drive Down CAM Costs

A clause in many shopping center leases specifies that common area maintenance (CAM) costs (for such items as parking lot maintenance, exterior lighting, and common area cleaning) are incurred by the property owner and then charged back to retailer tenants, usually based on their size or sales. Although retail tenants have always questioned CAM charges, only recently have they been able to use computer software programs or data bases to evaluate these fees.

One such program has a separate Occupancy Cost Management (OCM) module. The OCM component enables a retailer to compare a property owner's submitted invoices against those specified in the retailer's lease. The program also identifies leases that specify maximum costs for certain elements, and leases that require property owners to send their retailer-tenants usage/expense information.

Sorrelco, a lease audit and consulting firm, maintains a data base of the CAM fees charged by several thousand shopping center developers throughout the United States. This data base lets a retail tenant quickly assess the fairness of CAM charges. As Sorrelco's president says, "There are 100 malls all over the country where charges for CAM [and other expenses] are excessive compared to similar facilities in adjacent counties or even adjacent cities." At one California mall, for example, a developer assessed its tenants $23 per square foot—$12 for CAM and $11 for store utilities, nearly twice the state average (according to data from Sorrelco).

Source: Julie Ritzer Ross, "New Systems Aid Stores in CAM Clashes," *Stores* (April 1996), pp. 75–76.

gible asset if it decides to sell the business. The disadvantages of ownership are the high initial costs, the necessary long-term commitment, and the inflexibility in changing sites. At Home Depot, about 70 percent of its store properties are owned by the retailer.[21]

If a retailer chooses to own the store premises, it must decide whether to construct a new facility or purchase an existing building. In weighing these alternatives, a retailer should consider the purchase price and maintenance costs, zoning restrictions, the age and condition of existing facilities, the adaptability of existing facilities to its needs, and the time to erect a new building. To encourage building rehabilitation in small towns (5,000 to 50,000 people), Congress enacted the Main Street program of the National Trust for Historic Preservation in 1980. Retailers in over 1,100 U.S. communities have benefited through their participation in this program (see http://www.nthp.org) by getting tax credits and low-interest loans.

Despite ownership advantages, most retailers lease store sites. For example, the great majority of store sites in central business districts and regional shopping centers are leased, largely due to the high property investments for ownership. Department stores tend to have renewable 30-year leases, supermarkets usually have renewable 20-year leases, and stores such as T.J. Maxx typically have 10-year leases with options to extend for one or more 5-year periods. Some leases give the retailer the right to end an agreement before the expiration date—under given circumstances and for a specified payment by the retailer.

Leasing enables retailers to minimize their initial investment, reduce their risk, acquire leases at prime locations that could not accommodate additional stores, gain immediate occupancy and customer traffic, and reduce their long-term commitment (if they so desire). Many retailers also feel they can open more outlets or spend more on other elements of their strategy mixes by leasing. Firms that lease also accept the disadvantages of this approach: the limits on operating flexibility, the restrictions on subletting and selling the business, possible nonrenewal problems, future rent increases, and not benefiting from the rising value of real estate.

[21] *Home Depot 1995 Annual Report.*

Some large retailers build new stores and then sell them to real-estate investors who lease the property back to the retailers on a long-term basis. This is called a **sale-leaseback.** Retailers using sale-leasebacks can construct stores to their specifications and have bargaining power in leasing terms, while they reduce their capital expenditures.

Tax-exempt industrial revenue bonds have also been used to finance retail facilities. In this arrangement, a state or municipality uses bond proceeds to build stores or warehouses and gives retailers long leases (with payments used to pay bond principal and interest). The practice reduces investment costs for retailers, but requires them to commit to a site for an extended period.

Types of Leases ❏ Inasmuch as most retailers lease (rent) store facilities, it is important to be familiar with several of the basic lease types used by property owners, including the straight lease, percentage lease, graduated lease, maintenance-increase-recoupment lease, and net lease. Property owners no longer rely solely on constant rent leases, partly due to their concern about interest rates and the related rise in many of their operating costs; thus, terms can become quite complicated.

The simplest, most direct arrangement is the **straight lease,** whereby a retailer pays a fixed dollar amount per month over the life of the lease. Rent usually ranges from $1 to $50 annually per square foot, depending on factors like the location's desirability and store traffic. At some sites, rents can be much higher (up to hundreds of dollars per square foot). On New York City's Fifth Avenue (from 49th to 57th Streets), the average yearly rent is $575 per square foot! And in Tokyo, Japan, on the Ginza, rent is $425 per square foot![22]

A **percentage lease** stipulates that rent is related to the retailer's sales or profits. This differs significantly from a straight lease, which provides for constant payments each month, regardless of revenues or earnings. For example, a drugstore may be required to pay 4 percent of sales, a toy store 6 percent, and a camera store 12 percent (with these figures being keyed to the space occupied and sales per square foot). A percentage lease enables a property owner to be protected against the effects of inflation, as well as to benefit when a store is successful; it also allows a tenant to view the lease as a variable cost, which means rent is lower when its performance is weak and higher when performance is good. The percentage rate varies by type of shopping district or center and by type of store.

Percentage leases have variations. In one, a minimum or maximum rent is noted:

■ Percentage lease with specified minimum—Low sales are partly the retailer's responsibility; thus, the property owner should receive some minimum payments (as in a straight lease) that at least partially cover the mortgage, taxes, and property maintenance.

■ Percentage lease with specified maximum—A very successful retailer should not pay more than a maximum rent. Superior merchandising, promotion, and pricing should reward the retailer.

A second variation is the sliding scale. In this percentage lease, the ratio of rent to sales changes as sales rise. A sliding-down scale has a retailer pay a lower percentage as sales go up; 5 percent of the first $100,000 in sales and 3 percent of all sales over $100,000 is an example. A sliding-down scale is an incentive to the retailer, while providing more rent for a property owner.

A **graduated lease** calls for precise rent increases over a specified period of time. Thus, rent may be $4,000 per month for the first five years, $4,800 per month for the next five years, and $5,600 per month for the last five years of a lease. Rental payments are known in advance by both the retailer and the property owner and are based on anticipated increases in sales and costs. There is no problem in auditing sales or profits, as

[22]Lisa W. Foderaro, "Survey Reaffirms 5th Ave. at Top of the Retail Rent Heap," *New York Times* (April 29, 1997), p. B8.

Table 10-2 EFFECTIVE ANNUAL RENT PER SQUARE FOOT, 1996 (SELECTED METROPOLITAN AREAS)

Metropolitan Area	Central Business District	Regional Mall	Community/ Neighborhood Shopping Center
Boston, Massachusetts	$40.00	$43.00	$16.00
Cedar Rapids, Iowa	10.80	19.50	9.00
Charleston, South Carolina	20.00	19.00	10.00
Cleveland, Ohio	28.00	24.00	12.00
Denver, Colorado	15.00	22.00	12.00
Harrisburg, Pennsylvania	10.00	28.00	12.00
Indianapolis, Indiana	25.00	35.00	11.00
Los Angeles, California	22.50	36.00	18.00
Louisville, Kentucky	12.00	18.00	11.00
Mercer County, New Jersey	12.00	25.00	14.00
Norfolk, Virginia	7.00	20.00	10.00
Orlando, Florida	20.00	35.00	12.00
St. Louis, Missouri	15.00	32.00	14.50

Note: Effective annual rent includes common-area charges.

Source: Various issues of *Chain Store Age.*

there is for percentage leases. A graduated lease is often used with small retailers having weak financial statements and controls.

A **maintenance-increase-recoupment lease** has a provision allowing for rent increases if a property owner's taxes, heating bills, insurance, or other expenses rise beyond a certain point. This provision most often supplements a straight rental lease agreement.

A **net lease** calls for all maintenance costs, such as heating, electricity, insurance, and interior repair, to be paid by the retailer, which is responsible for their satisfactory quality. A net lease frees the property owner from managing the facility and lets the retailer have control over store maintenance. It would be used to supplement a straight lease or a percentage lease.

Table 10-2 shows 1996 rent payments by location type for several cities.

Other Considerations ❑ After assessing ownership and leasing opportunities, a retailer must look at the costs of operations and maintenance. Mortgage or rental payments are only one part of a site's costs. The age and condition of a facility may cause a retailer to have high total monthly costs, even though the mortgage or rent is low. Furthermore, the costs of extensive renovations should be calculated.

Taxes must be evaluated, especially in an ownership situation. Long-run projections, as well as current taxes, must be examined. Differences in sales taxes (those that customers pay) and business taxes (those that the retailer pays) among alternative sites must be weighed. Business taxes should be broken down into real-estate and income categories. As of 1996, the highest state sales tax was in Mississippi and Rhode Island (7 percent), while Alaska, Delaware, Montana, New Hampshire, and Oregon had no state sales tax.

Zoning restrictions should be analyzed. There may be legal limitations pertaining to the kind of stores allowed, store size, building height, the type of merchandise carried, and other factors that have to be overcome (or another site chosen). For example, it took 12 years (1978 to 1990) for the Redmond Town Center in Washington state to receive all the approvals for construction to begin on this mixed-use shopping facility. Then, it took until 1997 for building to be completed. As one observer stated, "getting the land was the easiest part."[23]

[23]"Worth Its Wait," *Chain Store Age Executive* (June 1990), p. 32; and Richard Buck, "Four Eastside Cities Lead Big Boom in Retail," *Seattle Times* (April 29, 1996).

Overcoming Community Resistance to Shopping Center Development

David White, a shopping center developer from Vermont, once remarked, "I was on my way to the office, and noticed a bumper sticker on the car in front of me. It said, 'Make my day. Shoot a developer.'" Indeed, some retailing analysts suggest Northern New England (Maine, New Hampshire, and Vermont) may be the most anti-retail development area in the entire country.

Among the three Northern New England states, Vermont has had the most retail-related construction in recent years. While in past years, many firms ignored Vermont due to its small and rural population base, retailers have become more interested as opportunities for their expansion elsewhere have declined. Retailers generally start in Burlington, Vermont's most densely populated area.

In commenting about the difficulties in building in Vermont, White says, "It's not that it's not possible to do things. You have to understand the ethic, the issues, and respect them." In building retail facilities in Vermont, it helps to be a local builder or at least to work with one. For example, the planning commission knows that a builder with 40 or so years of experience in Vermont will keep its word. To secure building permits, builders have to anticipate and react to a citizen review process for all major retail developments. It also speeds acceptance of a project if a builder signals that it is ready to adhere to a municipality's requirements.

Source: Debra Hazel, "Building Against the Grain in Vermont," *Chain Store Age* (July 1996), pp. 113–114.

Voluntary restrictions, those not mandated by the government, should also be examined. These are most prevalent in planned shopping centers and may include required membership in merchant groups, uniform store hours, and cooperative security forces. For instance, leases for many stores in regional shopping centers have included clauses protecting anchor tenants (large department stores) from too much competition—especially from discounters. These clauses may involve limits on product lines, bans against discounting, fees for common services, and specifications as to acceptable store practices. Anchors have been given such protective clauses by developers since the latter need their long-term commitments to finance the building of centers.

Some shopping center practices have been limited by the Federal Trade Commission (FTC). As an illustration, the FTC discourages "exclusives"—whereby only a particular retailer in a shopping center can carry specified merchandise, and "radius clauses"—whereby a tenant agrees not to operate another store within a certain distance of the center.

Because of the overbuilding of retail facilities in many areas, some retailers are now in a better position to bargain over the terms of occupancy. This differs from city to city, and from shopping location to shopping location.

Overall Rating

The last task in selecting a general location, and the specific site within it, is to compute overall ratings. First, each location under consideration is given an overall rating based on its performance on all the criteria displayed in Figure 10-6. The overall ratings of alternative locations are then compared, and the best location is chosen. The same procedure is used to evaluate the alternative sites within the location.

It is often difficult to compile and compare composite evaluations because some attributes may be positive while others are negative. For example, the general location may be a good shopping center, but the site in the center may be poor; or an area may have excellent potential but it will take two years to build a store. Therefore, the attributes in Figure 10-6 need to be weighted according to their importance to the retailer. An overall rating should also include certain knockout factors, those that would preclude consideration of a site. Possible knockout factors are a short-duration lease (fewer than three years), no evening or weekend pedestrian traffic, and poor tenant relations with the landlord.

Summary

1. *To thoroughly examine the types of locations available to a retailer: isolated store, unplanned business district, and planned shopping center* After a retailer rates alternative trading areas, it decides which type of location is desirable, selects the general location, and chooses a particular site. There are three basic locations a firm should distinguish among.

An isolated store is freestanding, not adjacent to other stores. This type of location has several advantages, including no competition, low rent, flexibility, road visibility, easy parking, and lower property costs. There are also distinct disadvantages: difficulty in attracting traffic, no variety for shoppers, no shared costs, and zoning restrictions.

An unplanned business district is a shopping area where two or more stores are located together or nearby. Store composition is not based on long-range planning. Unplanned business districts can be broken down into four categories: central business district, secondary business district, neighborhood business district, and string.

An unplanned business district generally has such points as these in its favor: variety of goods, services, and prices; access to public transit; nearness to commercial and social facilities; and pedestrian traffic. Yet, this type of location's shortcomings have led to the growth of the planned shopping center: inadequate parking, older facilities, high rents and taxes in popular CBDs, discontinuity of offerings, traffic and delivery congestion, high theft rates, and some declining central cities.

A planned shopping center is centrally owned or managed and well balanced. It usually has one or more large (anchor) stores and many smaller stores. During the past several decades, the growth of the planned shopping center has been great. This is due to extensive goods and service offerings, expanding suburbs, shared strategy planning and costs, attractive locations, parking facilities, lower rent and taxes (except for most regional shopping centers), lower theft rates, popularity of malls (although some people are now bored with shopping centers), and lesser appeal of inner-city shopping. The negative aspects of the planned center include operations inflexibility, restrictions on merchandise lines carried, and anchor store domination. There are three shopping center forms: regional, community, and neighborhood.

2. *To note the decisions necessary in choosing a general retail location* First, the specific form of isolated store, unplanned business district, or planned shopping center location is determined, such as whether to locate on a highway or side street; in a CBD, an SBD, an NBD, or a string; or in a regional, community, or neighborhood shopping center. Then, the general location for a store is specified, such as singling out a particular highway, business district, or shopping center.

3. *To describe the concept of the one-hundred percent location* Extensive analysis is required when evaluating each general location and the specific sites contained within it. Most importantly, the optimum site for a given store must be determined. Such a site is called the one-hundred percent location, and it differs by store.

4. *To discuss several criteria for evaluating general retail locations and the specific sites within them* These factors should be studied: pedestrian traffic, vehicular traffic, parking facilities, transportation, store composition, the attributes of each specific site, and terms of occupancy. An overall rating would then be computed for each location and site, and the best one would be selected.

Affinity occurs when the stores at the same location complement, blend, and cooperate with one another; each benefits from the others' presence.

5. *To contrast alternative terms of occupancy* Terms of occupancy are critical in choosing a site. A retailer must opt whether to own or lease. If it leases, an agreement is negotiated by a straight lease, percentage lease, graduated lease, maintenance-increase-recoupment lease, and/or net lease. Operating and maintenance costs, taxes, zoning restrictions, and voluntary restrictions also need to be weighed.

Key Terms

isolated store (p. 312)
unplanned business district (p. 313)
central business district (CBD)
   (p. 313)
secondary business district (SBD)
   (p. 316)
neighborhood business district
   (NBD) (p. 317)
string (p. 317)
planned shopping center (p. 317)

balanced tenancy (p. 317)
regional shopping center (p. 322)
megamall (p. 322)
community shopping center (p. 323)
power center (p. 323)
neighborhood shopping center
   (p. 324)
one-hundred percent location
   (p. 325)
affinity (p. 328)

retail balance (p. 329)
terms of occupancy (p. 330)
sale-leaseback (p. 332)
straight lease (p. 332)
percentage lease (p. 332)
graduated lease (p. 332)
maintenance-increase-recoupment
   lease (p. 333)
net lease (p. 333)

Questions for Discussion

1. A bowling alley chain has decided to open outlets in a combination of isolated locations, unplanned business districts, and planned shopping centers. Comment on this strategy.

2. Why do gift stores often locate in shopping centers or business districts, while convenience stores, such as 7-Eleven, often operate at isolated sites?

3. From the retailer's perspective, compare the advantages of locating in unplanned business districts versus planned shopping centers.

4. Differentiate among the central business district, the secondary business district, the neighborhood business district, and the string.

5. Develop a brief plan to revitalize the neighborhood business district nearest your campus.

6. What is a megamall? What is a power center? How should other retailers react to a megamall or power center locating near them?

7. Evaluate the community shopping center nearest your campus.

8. What are some of the problems that planned shopping centers will probably have to address in the future? How should they respond?

9. Explain why a one-hundred percent location for Home Depot may not be a one-hundred percent location for a local hardware store.

10. What criteria should a small retailer use in selecting a general store location and a specific site within it? A large retailer?

11. What difficulties are there in using a rating scale such as that shown in Figure 10-6? What are the benefits?

12. How do the parking needs for a drugstore, a membership club, and a movie theater differ?

13. Under what circumstances would it be more desirable for a retailer to build a new store rather than to buy or lease an existing facility?

14. What are the pros and cons of a straight lease versus a percentage lease for a prospective retail tenant?

Web-Based Exercise:

NATIONAL TRUST FOR HISTORIC PRESERVATION

(http://www.nthp.org)

Questions

1. What is the purpose of the National Trust for Historic Preservation?
2. Describe the "Main Street" program.
3. How may a community take advantage of the "Main Street" program? What are the responsibil-

ities of the community and its retailers who want to participate in the program?

4. What can you learn from the case study section of this Web site?

Haddonfield, New Jersey (http://www.haddonfield.com/business), is known as one of the premier residential communities in southern New Jersey. *Philadelphia* magazine recently named Haddonfield as the "best place to live" in the region. Although the magazine did not rate Haddonfield on specific attributes, retail experts generally cite the community's charm (based on the successful preservation of its historic homes), the area's unique shopping opportunities, and its sense of community as major positive attributes. An additional attraction to Haddonfield is its linkage with surrounding areas through several highways and a high-speed mass transit system that connects the community to downtown Philadelphia.

While historic Haddonfield was originally settled by English immigrants in 1682, efforts to preserve the town's colonial heritage have gained momentum during the last 30 years. The Haddonfield Preservation Society, organized in 1966, was instrumental in passing an ordinance forbidding the alteration of historic buildings unless the changes were in keeping with the town's original architecture. Partly as a result of the group's efforts, Haddonfield became listed in the National Register of Historic places in 1982.

Downtown Haddonfield now has over 150 retail stores, in addition to a number of lawyers, accountants, and other professionals. Most of these retail businesses cater to the needs of the upper-income individuals who live and work within a ten-mile radius of the town. Some of Haddonfield's merchants specialize in luxury-type goods (such as fine jewelry, designer fashions, and fine art), others in meeting the convenience needs of the local population (such as hardware and film processing stores), and a third group caters to consumers who visit Haddonfield as part of a day trip. Most merchants are independents, but the area also has some national retail chains.

Retail space in Haddonfield is generally scarce. Stores that are vacant are usually in transition between owners. Retailers generally state that they are attracted to the area because of its high density of affluent consumers. While most customers live within a short distance of the shopping area, others travel longer distances due to the area's charm and specialized retailers.

Despite the overall attractiveness of the retail environment in Haddonfield, there are areas of concern. Almost all the merchants in Haddonfield would agree that parking is an issue that needs further attention. Strict ordinances that limit new construction, as well as a store's expansion and the use of sidewalk displays and signs, are also viewed as restrictive by some merchants. Lastly, as in any shopping district, retailers exercise autonomy in setting their own store hours. This affects the ability of an area to draw shoppers during early evening hours on weekdays, and on weekends when not all stores are open.

The Haddonfield retail community is polarized about how to best attract more shoppers. One group of retailers has sponsored such activities as craft shows, sidewalk sales, and carriage rides as a means of increasing sales to the mass market. These merchants have promoted the events in several ways, including advertisements on cable TV, a Web site (featuring ads from selected merchants, as well as a classified section), and brochures placed in the Philadelphia convention center. This merchant group has financed the promotions through the collection of dues from members, depending on each retailer's business and location. On the other hand, another group of merchants is advocating a less aggressive marketing effort. This group credits Haddonfield's historic preservation efforts with the revitalization of its shopping district. The group also wants to maintain the quietness of the community and its appeal to upper-income shoppers.

CASE 1
Shopping in Historic Haddonfield: Planning Within a CBD*

Questions

1. Classify downtown Haddonfield as a planned or an unplanned business district. Support your answer.

*This case was prepared and written by Andrew Cullen, Senior Consultant, The Pennmor Group, and Professor Carol Felker Kaufman, Rutgers University, Camden, New Jersey. The casewriters would like to acknowledge the participation and assistance of the Haddonfield government, community leaders, and business professionals in providing valuable insight in the preparation of this case.

CASE I
(Continued)

2. What are the pros and cons of Haddonfield for a national retail chain? What could a national chain like McDonald's do to enhance its ability to operate in historic sites like Haddonfield?
3. Given the opportunity to shape their marketing efforts, what would you suggest Haddonfield do next? (These can be discussed as alternative courses of action.)
4. Figure 10-6 contains a checklist for location and site evaluation. Using the criteria in the checklist, evaluate downtown Haddonfield's attractiveness as a potential site. Discuss the benefits and the limitations of using this scale.

CASE 2
The Mall of America[†]

The Mall of America (also called the Mega-Mall) is the largest regional shopping center in the United States, with 2.5 million gross leasable square feet. It is located on a 78-acre site near the Minneapolis airport, about 10 to 15 minutes from downtown Minneapolis-St. Paul. The mall (http://www.link.be/retail/mall.html), which opened in August 1992, cost over $700 million to build.

Unlike smaller regional shopping centers that are predominately retail, the Mall of America is a blend of entertainment, food, and retail facilities. Roughly one-half of the overall space in the mall is devoted to retail. In addition to its four department stores (R.H. Macy, Bloomingdale's, Nordstrom, and Sears) and over 400 specialty stores, the mall has a 7-acre "Camp Snoopy" amusement park (with 50 rides and attractions, including a roller coaster), a 14-screen movie theater, 45 restaurants, an 18-hole miniature golf course, 9 nightclubs, and even a wedding chapel. The unique combination of attractions has enabled Mall of America to become a tourist destination. The Automobile Club of America (AAA) recently rated the Mall of America as the third-hottest destination in the United States, behind only Disney World and the country-western village in Branson, Missouri.

During its planning and early construction stages, many critics were skeptical as to whether the Mall of America would be a success. Thus, to attract the four department store anchor tenants (stores that had never before been together in the same mall), the developer offered each store a "sweetheart" lease (with each anchor tenant paying either little or no rent during the first years of its lease). In addition, Macy's and Bloomingdale's were given $35 million and $40 million allowances, respectively, to entice them to open stores at the mall. According to one retail analyst, "Contracts like these were unheard of, even at very weak malls." The developer also made wide use of "bumpbacks," in which the front of retail space was rented out, with large vacant space in the back of these stores. Bumpbacks reduce the feel of vacancies to consumers, as well as to current and prospective retail tenants.

Now, however, even the worst skeptics have turned around due to the Mega-Mall's retail sales figures, the number of visitors, the length of a shopping stay, and retail occupancy statistics. The Mall of America has sales per square foot of $425 per year (versus an average of $200 to $400 for many regional malls), an average customer purchase of $91 (twice the average for all regional malls), 40 million visitors per year (more than Disney World and the Grand Canyon combined), and the average Mall of America visitor stays 3.5 hours (twice as long as the national length of stay for a regional mall). No wonder the mall has a 94 percent occupancy rate.

[†]The material in this case is drawn from Kenneth Labich, "What It Will Take to Keep People Hanging Out at the Mall," *Fortune* (May 29, 1995), pp. 102–106; "Restaurants and Institutions Road Trip: The Mall of America," *Restaurants & Institutions* (November 1, 1995), pp. 35–40; and Chad Rubel, "Three Malls Turn to Tourists—and Thrive," *Marketing News* (May 6, 1996), pp. 4–5.

CASE 2
(Continued)

An important concern for the Minneapolis-St. Paul economy is the impact of the Mall of America on the area's smaller retail shopping centers. A study by the mall's developer found that over 30 percent of the customer traffic to the mall comes from over 150 miles away, some from foreign countries. This increased tourist base has expanded overall retail sales in Minneapolis-St. Paul. The Mall of America is now also positioning itself as a convention center able to handle as many as 4,000 conventioneers at a time. The increased convention activity will also be a boon to restaurant and hotel businesses. A recent study by the mall's developer found that the mall contributes $1.4 billion annually to the Minnesota economy.

Many analysts see the Mall of America as a laboratory for stores that seek to involve customers in "hands-on" activities while shopping or to offer entertainment combined with eating facilities. For example, Oshkosh's location at the mall encourages shoppers to "try before they buy" at its skating rink, basketball court, and Rollerblade track—all situated in its Mall of America store. The mall also contains a Planet Hollywood and a Rainforest Cafe, two popular "eatertainment" restaurant facilities.

Questions
1. Compare the Mall of America to a traditional regional shopping center.
2. What are the pros and cons of having a Mall of America store location versus having one in a smaller regional shopping center for a specialty store retailer?
3. Describe the difficulties with the Mall of America's attracting so many tourists.
4. As a retailer in a nearby regional shopping center that did not have a Mall of America outlet, how would you compete against similar stores located in the Mall of America?

Video Questions on Mall of America

1. Discuss the pros and cons to retailer tenants of the Mall of America's unique combination of entertainment, food, and retail facilities.
2. Describe the Mall of America's promotional program.

Part Four ■ Comprehensive Case

Kirksville Retail Trade Assessment Project: Curing The Outshopping Phenomenon*

INTRODUCTION

With outshopping, residents of an area, often a small town, travel far distances to shop for selected goods and services. A number of reasons have been frequently cited for outshopping behavior. These include access to chain stores, the greater selection existing in a larger community, better availability of fashion-based merchandise, and lower prices. This case discusses a major research study on outshopping conducted by the Kirksville Chamber of Commerce, which hired a local marketing research firm to study why its local residents outshopped, which goods were most commonly purchased away from Kirksville, and how Kirksville could better retain its local customers' retail business. Although the names of all of the communities involved in the study have been disguised, the case is based on an actual situation.

BACKGROUND INFORMATION

Kirksville, Minnesota (population 4,200) was first settled in 1820. For most of its history, it was a self-sufficient, isolated rural community. Until recently, community residents prided themselves on the fact that successive generations of families lived, worked, and shopped only in Kirksville. However, over the past decade, the rapid growth of three adjacent communities has caused increased numbers of Kirksville residents to both work and shop there.

Kirksville is today situated in the midst of three larger communities. East Aurora has 67,000 people and is a 15-to-20 minute ride from Kirksville. Hamilton has 80,000 people and is a 50 to 55 minute drive from Kirksville. Marilla has 51,000 people and is 35 to 40 minutes from Kirksville. Each of these communities has a much broader retail base than Kirksville. In particular, East Aurora has a regional shopping center with over 60 stores (including several

*This case was prepared and written by Professor Keith C. Jones, Lynchburg College in Virginia, and Professor James Finch, University of Wisconsin, La Crosse. The authors would like to thank the Kirksville Chamber of Commerce for the funding of this project and case. The name of the community has been disguised.

Table 1 LISTING OF RETAIL BUSINESSES IN COMPETITIVE MARKETS

East Aurora (Professional and Agri-Business Population Base)
3 ShopKos
2 Kmarts
1 Target
1 Wal-Mart
1 Farm and Fleet (rural/farm-oriented discount chain)
1 Woolworth's (primary business district location)
1 primary business district of East Aurora featuring several specialty stores
1 secondary business district (approximately 20 stores)
7 shopping areas with strip stores consisting of various retailers
3 institutions of higher education
2 major grocery chains (multiple stores) and 2 grocery warehouse stores
1 regional shopping center with approximately 60 stores, 4 department store anchors (5 of the discount stores, 3 of the shopping areas, and the 2 grocery warehouse stores are all located in mall area)
4 auto dealers

Hamilton (Large Medical and Professional Population Base)
2 ShopKos
1 Kmart
1 Wal-Mart
1 regional shopping center with 80 stores and 2 anchor department stores
2 institutions of higher education
11 shopping areas with strip stores consisting of various retailers
1 primary business district (successful) featuring several specialty and department stores (larger and more upscale than those in the other communities)
3 major grocery chains (multiple stores) and 1 grocery warehouse store
1 Sam's Wholesale Club
5 auto dealers

Marilla (Agri-Business Population Base)
1 Kmart
1 Wal-Mart
1 Pamida
1 economically depressed primary business district with a limited number of specialty stores
1 small mall with 15 stores
2 institutions of higher education
1 Farm and Fleet
1 Big Bear (agricultural-based discount store)
2 major grocery chains (multiple stores)
2 auto dealers

department stores). Hamilton has a Sam's Wholesale Club. Marilla has both a Kmart and a Wal-Mart. See Table 1.

As a result, Kirksville has seen a gradual, but steady, drop in retail trade. Many merchants see the trend as irreversible, and some have contemplated closing their existing stores in Kirksville and moving to one of the nearby communities. In contrast to the other areas, Kirksville's central business district has less width and depth of retailers in virtually every category. See Table 2.

To respond to its declining position, the Kirksville Chamber of Commerce hired Tower Market Research (TMR) to analyze Kirksville's retail environment. Excerpts from TMR's interim report, *The Kirksville*

Retail Trade Assessment Project: Phase I, are provided next.

THE TRADE ASSESSMENT PROJECT

DATA COLLECTION TECHNIQUES AND RESPONDENTS

A phone survey was used to gather the data from Kirksville residents. It consisted of both open- and closed-ended questions. The responses from 133 Kirksville residents were obtained through a random sampling procedure, based on listings in the local Kirksville phone directory. Of those responding, 90.3 percent currently lived in Kirksville and 64.7 percent of the sample had lived in Kirksville more than 20 years. Most of the respondents (79.1 percent) indicated they were responsible for the household shopping. Other characteristics of the respondents are listed in Table 3.

PURCHASING HABITS OF RESPONDENTS

To assess the need for retailing improvements in Kirksville, the researchers studied respondents' town of purchase in several product categories, such as clothing, household goods, groceries, services, and other. Within the "other" category were sporting goods, farm equipment, farm hardware, and auto/truck sales. This "home shopping" (at Kirksville) and "outshopping" behavior is summarized in Table 4.

INFLUENCERS OF SHOPPING HABITS

After establishing respondents' locational purchasing habits, the researchers attempted to identify the factors that influenced their choice of shopping area. When respondents were asked to identify the first and second most critical factors in their selection of a shopping locale, price had the greatest number of mentions, followed by selection, convenience, product quality, loyalty, and one-stop shopping. See Table 5.

In comparing patronage at various locales, TMR found no significant relationship between price and patronage at any shopping location. However, significant relationships were found between convenience and selected shopping habits. Consumers who identified convenience as the most important factor influencing their shopping destination were more apt to buy clothing, shoes, and groceries in Kirksville. But, they expressed dissatisfaction with the times of day and days of the week that Kirksville stores were open.

Table 2 RETAIL-RELATED BUSINESSES IN KIRKSVILLE

Becker Agencies	Wagner Insurance
Bud's Used Cars	Wise Choice Restaurant
Country Rose Flowers and Gifts	Bob's Shoes and Repair
Danielson Insurance Agency	Weichert Motors
Deeine Motors	Bubbers Jewelry
Dewitz Shoes	Myron and Delores' Cafe
Ellingson Motors	Family Dental Center
Ewenique Boutique	Pine Cone Place (gift shop)
Frankie's Inn	Rask Dry Cleaners
H&R Block	B&M Service Center
Hardware Hank	The Cutting Edge-Beauty Salon
Hiawatha Valley Mental Health Center	Gift Mill
Hoskins Electric	Early Childhood Education
Jack's Bar and Diane's Diner	Schulze Plumbing and Heating
Ken's Small Engine	State Bank
Kirksville Argus (gas station)	Haugstad's Confectionery
Kirksville Bakery	Kirksville Plumbing and Heating
Kirksville Drug	Radio Shack
Kirksville Municipal Liquor Store	Togerson Paint and Floor Covering
Kirksville Veterinary Service	Von Arx Law Office
Kirksville Wheel and Alignment	Alberts Grocery Store
Laundromat	Gaustad Accounting
McCarthy Insurance Agency	Kirksville Oil Company
McCormick Funeral Home	Phyllis Shoppe-Ladies Fashion
Morey Real Estate Agency	Nelson Appliance Center
New Horizon Video Store	Mary Ann's Floral
Quillin's IGA	Dr. B's, Optometrist
Rippe, Hammell and Murphy Law Office	Helen's Beauty Salon
Schroeder Jewelry	Olie's Barber Shop
Schultz and Schultz Law Office	Ben Franklin
	Coast to Coast
Von Arx Furniture and Crafts	Sprague National Bank
	Rice Pharmacy
	Kirksville Chiropractic Center

Table 3 DEMOGRAPHIC DESCRIPTION OF KIRKSVILLE SURVEY GROUP

	Number Responding	Percentage of Respondents
Residence:		
Kirksville	121	90.3
Other	13	9.7
Total	134	100.0
Education:		
0–8th grade	16	12.0
9th–11th grade	7	5.3
High school graduate or G.E.D.	63	47.3
Vocation/technical school graduate	13	9.8
College graduate	34	25.6
Total	133	100.0
Respondents as major household shopper:		
Yes	106	79.1
No	28	20.9
Total	134	100.0
Length of residence in Kirksville:		
More than 20 years	86	64.7
11–20 years	26	19.5
6–10 years	11	8.3
1–5 years	10	7.5
Total	133	100.0
Average length of residence in the area:	32.11 years	
Size of Household:		
1	26	19.4
2	42	31.3
3	23	17.2
4	19	14.2
5	12	9.0
6 or more	12	9.0
Total	134	100.0

There are some minor rounding errors.

The length of residency in Kirksville also influenced the perceived importance of convenience in the shopping destination decision. It was regarded as much more important for those individuals who resided in Kirksville for more than 20 years.

RESIDENTIAL/WORK INFLUENCE

Where people reside and where they work often influence their perceptions of stores and their shopping habits (such as patronage). Of the respondents to this survey, 49 lived and worked in Kirksville, while 71 lived in Kirksville and worked elsewhere. See Table 6. If these two groups are compared, we find that those individuals who worked outside of Kirksville had a greater tendency to shop outside of Kirksville. Because these respondents shopped elsewhere for most of their products, their perceptions of Kirksville businesses were a direct result of their exposure to other stores and the opportunity to shop at these stores. See Table 7.

In making a site selection decision, a retailer must consider "accumulative attraction," which is the ability of other retailers in an area to draw similar types of customers to the location. TMR assessed accumulative attraction for the Kirksville business district by looking into what reasons, other than shopping, brought respondents to town. The top four reasons were to attend church activities, visit a banking institution, attend school events, and visit friends. See Table 8.

REVIEWING THE RESULTS

From the TMR survey, it is evident that most people shop outside of Kirksville. Two particular issues addressed by the study were the awareness of product offerings and preferred shopping hours. To measure

Table 4 OVERALL PURCHASING HABITS BY PRODUCT CATEGORY

NUMBER OF RESPONDENTS PURCHASING AT SPECIFIED LOCATION

PRODUCT CATEGORY	Kirksville	East Aurora	Hamilton	Marilla	Other	Kirksville and East Aurora
Men's clothing	4	100	0	0	10	7
Women's clothing	18	85	0	0	3	23
Children's clothing	3	72	1	0	3	6
Shoes	25	82	0	0	5	21
Appliances	64	47	0	0	3	10
Furniture	24	75	0	1	6	10
Carpeting	65	42	0	0	2	7
Hardware	106	16	0	0	1	7
Farm equipment	29	3	0	0	0	0
Farm hardware	31	4	0	1	0	3
Groceries	86	17	0	0	1	28
Barber/beauty shop	93	16	0	1	10	6
Auto repair	110	6	0	0	8	2
Sporting goods	29	51	1	0	2	5
Autos/trucks	88	17	0	2	4	7
Entertainment	51	47	0	0	1	18
Banking	94	16	0	0	13	8

Table 5 THE MOST IMPORTANT FACTORS INFLUENCING PATRONAGE DECISION

Factor	Percentage of Respondents Rating Factor First or Second in Importance
Price	75.2
Selection	32.3
Convenience	29.3
Product quality	19.5
Loyalty	7.5
One-stop shopping	3.0
Other	7.1

Percentages total to greater than 100.0 due to multiple answers.

Table 6 PLACE OF RESIDENCE AND EMPLOYMENT

	Number of Respondents	Percentage of Respondents
Work in Kirksville and live in Kirksville	49	36.8
Work in Kirksville and live elsewhere	5	3.8
Work elsewhere and live in Kirksville	71	53.4
Live elsewhere and work elsewhere	8	6.0
Total	133	100.0

Table 7 MOST IMPORTANT FACTOR INFLUENCING PATRONAGE DECISION, BASED ON PLACE OF RESIDENCY AND EMPLOYMENT

	LIVE AND WORK IN TOWN		LIVE IN TOWN ONLY	
	Number	Percentage	Number	Percentage
Price	26	53.1	34	47.9
Convenience	8	16.3	13	18.3
Selection	7	14.3	9	12.7
Product quality	3	6.1	7	9.9
Loyalty	1	2.0	4	5.6
One-stop shopping	0	0.0	1	1.4
Other	4	8.2	3	4.2
Total	49	100.0	71	100.0

awareness, respondents were asked if they felt their neighbors were aware of the merchandise mix offered by Kirksville retailers. Over 65 percent of the respondents believed people were very aware of the products offered. Only 18 percent thought people are not aware of the merchandise mix offered by Kirksville retailers.

With a majority of the population working outside of the Kirksville area, the issue takes on added importance. Of those responding to this question, two-thirds would like to see the Kirksville stores stay open later on Friday night. However, just one-third of the 134 respondents replied to this question, making responses to this question somewhat inconclusive.

Besides changes in store hours, respondents were asked what modifications existing Kirksville stores would have to undertake to encourage them to shop in Kirksville. There were three primary categories of responses. One called for improved selections. These respondents perceived Kirksville retailers as offering a limited variety of merchandise, particularly in these merchandise lines: men's, women's, young adults', and children's clothing; and gift selection. Respondents

Table 8 ACCUMULATIVE ATTRACTION

	Number of Responses	Percentage of Respondents (number = 134)
Church	53	39.6
Banking	46	34.3
School events	44	32.8
Visiting friends	41	30.6
Post office	35	26.1
Employment	35	26.1
Government	23	17.2
I'm never in town	3	2.2
Other	35	26.1

Percentages total to greater than 100.0 due to multiple answers.

also expressed a need for a fabrics/sewing/craft store, sporting goods, a discount store (Kmart and Wal-Mart were specifically mentioned), fast-food and other restaurants, and a hardware/farm supplies store.

The second category of responses pertained to customer service. A few individuals said they did not like the attitude exhibited by local store clerks. Some respondents commented that clerks did not say thank you, did not learn people's names, and were not available enough to assist the customer. Others remarked that Kirksville stores closed too early to go there after work (most Kirksville merchants closed at 5:00 P.M. on weekdays).

The third category of responses related to pricing. A number of the residents indicated that prices in Kirksville were perceived to be much higher than those in surrounding communities.

Questions

1. What are the positive and negative characteristics of the Kirksville retail environment?
2. What factors influence residents' store choice decisions?
3. Apply the concepts of primary, secondary, and fringe trading areas to Kirksville and its adjacent competitors.
4. How can Reilly's law of retail gravitation and Huff's law be applied to Kirksville?
5. What additional information would you like to have before making recommendations to the Kirksville Chamber of Commerce?
6. Based on the results reported in Phase I of the Kirksville Retail Trade Assessment Project, what recommendations would you make to the Chamber of Commerce?
7. As a prospective retailer, would you open a store in Kirksville? Explain your answer.

Part Five

In Part 5, the elements in managing a retail enterprise are discussed. The steps in setting up a retail organization and the special human resource management environment of retailing are first presented. Operations management is then examined—from both financial and operational perspectives.

Chapter 11 reports how a retailer can use an organization structure to assign tasks, policies, resources, authority, responsibilities, and rewards to satisfy the needs of the target market, employees, and management. It also shows how human resource management can be deployed to have that structure work properly. Human resource management consists of recruiting, selecting, training, compensating, and supervising personnel.

Chapter 12 focuses on the financial dimensions of operations management in enacting a retail strategy. These topics are discussed: profit planning, asset management—including the strategic profit model and other key business ratios, budgeting, and resource allocation.

Chapter 13 presents the operational aspects of operations management. These specific operating concepts are analyzed: store format and size, space allocation, personnel utilization, store maintenance, energy management, inventory management, store security, insurance, credit management, computerization, and crisis management.

11

Retail Organization and Human Resource Management

CHAPTER OBJECTIVES

1. To study the procedures involved in setting up a retail organization
2. To examine the various organizational arrangements utilized in retailing
3. To consider the special human resource environment of retailing
4. To describe the principles and practices involved with the human resource management process in retailing

According to a female director at J.C. Penney, more opportunities for women at that firm opened up starting in 1989. During that year, Penney relocated its home office from New York City to Dallas. Because many managers at all levels did not move to Dallas, a large number of positions became available. Also, at the same time, Penney began to reposition itself away from being a mass merchandiser and toward being a national department store focusing on women's fashion apparel. With that transition, "came the absolute need to better understand both women and minorities and for them to better understand us." Although Penney had many female executives before 1989, many were in entry- or middle-management positions. Furthermore, only a few minority members had been represented at any level of management.

To encourage workplace diversity, Penney enacted flexible staffing, instituted career pathing (to identify the steps needed to reach specific positions), and built a modern child care facility. It also established advisory teams to address the special needs of women and minority group members and to identify issues and barriers to advancement for them. Two particularly successful programs are Penney's mentoring group (with sponsored employees) and its networking program (where high potential women and minorities interact with senior executives at luncheon events).

Sensitivity training is seen as important in better understanding diversity at Penney. In a recent three-year period, 18,000 Penney associates participated in diversity/inclusion training, including the firm's top 120 senior executives who undertook a full week of training. Penney also sponsors about 25 women's and 16 multicultural conferences each year.

In 1995, Penney's chairman received the "Catalyst Award" (from a national nonprofit, women-in-business organization) for the firm's efforts in promoting female executives. Penney has been the only retailer to receive this award in its 30-year history. During the six-year period after Penney began its initiative, women represented 60 percent of the firm's entry-level managers, 31 percent of its middle-level managers, and 15 percent of its senior-level managers. One of Penney's four merchandise divisions is now headed by a woman, and the president of one of its four operating regions is African-American. Penney's goal is for women to represent 46 percent of every management level, with minorities representing 16 percent.[1]

---

[1] Gale Duff-Bloom, "Women in Retailing—Is There a Glass Ceiling?" *Arthur Andersen Retailing Issues Letter* (May 1996), pp. 1–4; and Marianne Wilson, "J.C. Penney Embraces Diversity," *Chain Store Age Executive* (June 1995), pp. 19–23.

There are three basic steps to managing a retail business properly: setting up an organization structure, hiring and managing personnel, and managing operations—both financially and nonfinancially. In this chapter, the first two steps are covered. Chapters 12 and 13 deal with operations management.

OVERVIEW

Through a **retail organization,** a firm structures and assigns tasks (functions), policies, resources, authority, responsibilities, and rewards so as to efficiently and effectively satisfy the needs of its target market, employees, and management. Figure 11-1 shows a variety of needs that a retailer should take into account when planning and assessing an organization.

SETTING UP A RETAIL ORGANIZATION

Figure 11-1

Selected Factors That Must Be Considered in Planning and Assessing a Retail Organization

TARGET MARKET NEEDS

Are there a sufficient number of personnel (salespeople, deliverypersons, cashiers, etc.) available to provide customer service at the appropriate levels?

Are personnel knowledgeable and courteous?

Are store facilities well maintained?

Are the specific needs of branch store customers met?

Are changing needs promptly addressed?

EMPLOYEE NEEDS

Are positions challenging enough?

Is there an orderly promotion program?

Is the employee able to participate in the decision making?

Are the channels of communication clear and open?

Are jobs satisfying?

Is the authority-responsibility relationship clear?

Does the firm promote from within?

Does each employee get treated fairly?

Is good performance rewarded?

MANAGEMENT NEEDS

Is it relatively easy to obtain and retain competent personnel?

Are personnel procedures clearly defined?

Does each worker report to only one supervisor?

Can each manager properly supervise and control the number of workers reporting to him (her)?

Do operating departments have adequate staff support (i.e., computerized reports, market research, and advertising)?

Are the levels of organization properly developed?

Are the organization's plans well integrated?

Are employees motivated?

Is absenteeism low?

Does the organization provide continuity so that personnel can be replaced in an orderly manner?

Is the organization flexible enough to adapt to changes in customer preference and/or regional growth patterns?

Figure 11-2

The Process of Organizing a Retail Firm

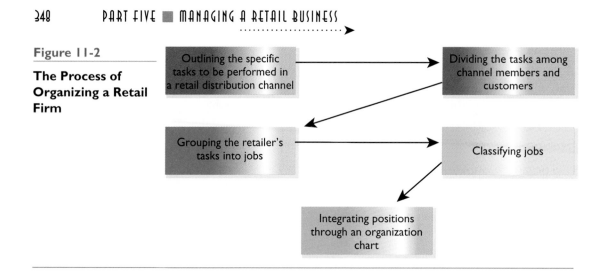

As a rule, a retailer cannot survive unless its organization structure satisfies the needs of the target market, regardless of how well employee and/or management needs are met. Thus, an organization structure that reduces costs by centralized buying but results in the firm's insensitivity to geographic differences in customer preferences would probably be improper.

Even though many retail firms carry out similar tasks or functions (such as buying, pricing, displaying, and wrapping merchandise), there are many ways of organizing to perform these functions and focus on the needs of customers, employees, and management. The process of setting up a retail organization is outlined in Figure 11-2 and described next.

Specifying Tasks to Be Performed

The general tasks to be performed in a retail channel of distribution must be enumerated. Among the typical tasks are

- Buying merchandise.
- Shipping merchandise.
- Receiving merchandise.
- Checking incoming shipments.
- Setting prices.
- Marking merchandise.
- Inventory storage and control.
- Preparing merchandise and window displays.
- Facilities maintenance (e.g., keeping the store clean).
- Customer research and exchanging information.
- Customer contact (e.g., advertising, personal selling).
- Facilitating shopping (e.g., convenient site, short checkout lines).
- Customer follow-up and complaint handling.
- Personnel management.
- Repairs and alteration of merchandise.
- Billing customers.
- Handling receipts and financial records.
- Credit operations.
- Gift wrapping.
- Delivery.
- Returning unsold or damaged merchandise to vendors.
- Sales forecasting and budgeting.
- Coordination.

Figure 11-3

The Division of Retail Tasks

Performer	Tasks
Retailer	Can perform all or some of the tasks listed in the preceding section, from buying merchandise to coordination.
Manufacturer or Wholesaler	Can perform few or many functions, such as: shipping, marking merchandise, inventory storage and control, display preparation, research, sales forecasting, etc.
Specialist(s)	Can include the following types: buying office, delivery firm, warehouse, marketing research firm, advertising agency, accountant, credit bureau, computer service firm. Each specializes in the performance of a particular task.
Consumer	Can assume responsibility for delivery, credit (cash-only sales), sales effort (self-service or direct marketing), product alterations (do-it-yourselfers), etc.

The proper performance of these activities, keyed to the strategy mix chosen, is necessary for effective retailing to occur.

Dividing Tasks Among Channel Members and Customers

Although the tasks just cited are often performed in a retail channel of distribution, they do not necessarily have to be performed by a retailer. Some can be undertaken by a manufacturer, a wholesaler, a specialist, or the consumer. Figure 11-3 shows the types of activities that could be carried out by each party. The following illustration indicates some of the criteria to be considered in allocating the tasks related to consumer credit.

A task should be carried out only if desired by the target market. Thus, unless a retailer, such as a convenience store, finds a number of customers disapprove of cash-only sales, it should not accept credit cards. For some firms, liberal credit policies may provide significant advantages over competitors. For others, a cash-only policy may reduce their overhead and lead to lower prices.

A task should be performed by the party with special competence and/or equipment. Credit collection may require a legal staff and a computer-based record-keeping system. These are usually affordable only by medium-sized or large retailers. Smaller retailers would rely on bank credit cards to overcome the lack of necessary resources.

The retailer should consider the loss of control over an activity when it is delegated to another party. A credit collection firm, pressing hard to receive payment on a past-due account, may antagonize a customer to the point of losing future sales for the retailer.

The retailer's institutional framework can have an impact on task allocation. Franchisees are readily able to get together to have their own credit bureau. Independents cannot do this as easily.

Task allocation should take into account the savings gained by sharing or shifting tasks. The credit function can be better performed by an outside credit bureau if it has specialized personnel, has ongoing access to financial data, uses tailored computer software, pays lower rent (due to an out-of-the-way site), and so on. Many retailers cannot attain these savings themselves.

Grouping Tasks into Jobs

After the retailer decides which functions to perform, its tasks are grouped into jobs. These jobs must be clearly defined and structured. These are some examples of grouping tasks into jobs:

Tasks	Jobs
Displaying merchandise, customer contact, gift wrapping, customer follow-up	Sales personnel
Entering transaction data, handling cash receipts, processing credit purchases, gift wrapping, inventory control	Cashier(s)
Receiving merchandise, checking incoming shipments, marking merchandise, inventory storage and control, returning merchandise to vendors	Inventory personnel
Window dressing, interior display setups, use of mobiles	Display personnel
Billing customers, credit operations, customer research	Credit personnel
Repairs and alterations of merchandise, resolution of customer complaints, customer research	Customer service personnel
Cleaning store, replacing old fixtures	Janitorial personnel
Personnel management, sales forecasting, budgeting, pricing, coordination of tasks	Management personnel

While grouping tasks into jobs, the retailer should consider using specialization. Under specialization, each employee is responsible for limited functions (as opposed to each employee's performing many diverse functions). Specialization has the advantages of clearly defined tasks, greater expertise, reduced training costs and time, and hiring personnel with narrow education and experience. Problems can result due to extreme specialization: poor morale (boredom), personnel not being aware of their jobs' importance, and the need for an increased number of employees.

The proper use of specialization involves assigning specific duties and responsibilities to individuals so a job position encompasses a relatively homogeneous cluster of work tasks. These tasks should have an essential and enduring purpose within the retail organization.

Once work tasks are grouped, job descriptions are constructed. These outline the job titles, objectives, duties, and responsibilities for every position. They are used as a hiring, supervision, and evaluation tool. Figure 11-4 contains a job description for a store manager.

Classifying Jobs

Jobs are then broadly categorized through a functional, product, geographic, or combination classification system. In a functional classification, jobs are divided among functional areas such as sales promotion, buying, and store operations. Expert knowledge is utilized.

Product classification divides jobs on a goods or service basis. For example, a department store can hire personnel for clothing, furniture, gift items, appliances, and so on. Product classification recognizes that differences exist in the personnel requirements for different products. Tighter control and responsibility are also possible.

Geographic classification is useful for multiunit stores operating in different locales. Personnel are adapted to local conditions. Job descriptions and qualifications are under the control of individual branch managers.

Figure 11-4

**A Job Description
for a Store Manager**

JOB TITLE: Store Manager for 34th Street Branch of Pombo's Department Stores

POSITION REPORTS TO: Senior Vice-President

POSITIONS REPORTING TO STORE MANAGER: All personnel working in the
34th Street store

OBJECTIVES: To properly staff and operate the 34th Street store

DUTIES AND RESPONSIBILITIES:

1. Personnel recruitment, selection, training, motivation, and evaluation
2. Merchandise display
3. Inventory storage and control
4. Approving orders for merchandise
5. Transferring merchandise among stores
6. Sales forecasting
7. Budgeting
8. Handling store receipts
9. Preparing bank transactions
10. Locking and unlocking store
11. Reviewing customer complaints
12. Reviewing computer data forms
13. Semiannual review of overall operations
14. Forwarding reports to top management

COMMITTEES AND MEETINGS:

1. Store Managers' Review Committee
2. Attendance at monthly meetings with Senior Vice-President
3. Supervision of weekly meetings with department managers

Some retailers, especially larger ones, use combinations of these three classifications. If a branch unit of a department store hires and supervises its own selling staff, but buying personnel for each product line are centrally hired and controlled by company headquarters, the functional, product, and geographic forms of organization are combined.

Developing an Organization Chart

In planning a retail organization, the firm should not look at jobs as individual units but as parts of the whole. The format of a retail organization must be planned in an integrated, coordinated way. Jobs must be defined and distinct; yet, interrelationships among positions must be clear. As a prominent retail executive once remarked, "A successful chief executive does not build a business. He or she builds an organization and the organization builds the business. It is done no other way."[2]

The **hierarchy of authority** outlines the job relationships within a company by describing the reporting relationships among employees (from the lowest level to the store manager or board of directors). Coordination and control are provided by this hierarchy.[3]

---

[2]*Levitz 1995 Annual Report.* See also Leonard L. Berry and Robert F. Lusch, "Making Corporate Performance 'Soar,' " *Marketing Management* (Fall 1996), pp. 13–23.

[3]See Linda K. Good, Thomas J. Page, Jr., and Clifford E. Young, "Assessing Hierarchical Differences in Job-Related Attitudes and Turnover Among Retail Managers," *Journal of the Academy of Marketing Science,* Vol. 24 (Spring 1996), pp. 148–156.

Table 11-1   PRINCIPLES FOR ORGANIZING A RETAIL FIRM

■ An organization should be concerned about its employees. Job rotation, promotion from within, participatory management, recognition, job enrichment, and so on, improve worker morale.

■ Employee turnover, lateness, and absenteeism should be monitored, as they may indicate personnel problems.

■ The line of authority should be traceable from the highest to the lowest positions. In this way, employees know to whom they report and who reports to them (chain of command).

■ A subordinate should only report to one direct supervisor. This avoids the problem of workers receiving conflicting orders (unity of command).

■ Responsibility should be associated with adequate authority. A person responsible for a given objective needs the power to achieve it.

■ Although a supervisor can delegate authority, he/she retains responsibility for the acts of subordinates. The delegation of authority cannot be an excuse for a manager's failing to achieve a goal. This concept requires a manager to actively evaluate the performance of subordinates while they are working to reach a goal.

■ There is a limit to the number of employees a manager can directly supervise (span of control).

■ The firm should strive to limit the number of organization levels. The greater the number of levels, the longer the time for communication to travel and the greater the coordination problems.

■ An organization has an informal structure aside from the formal organization chart. Informal relationships exercise power in the organization and may bypass formal relationships and procedures.

The levels in a retail organization are reflected by the number of positions separating the top official from the lowest employee. A firm with a large number of subordinates reporting to one supervisor has a **flat organization.** Some benefits of a flat organization are good communication, quicker handling of problems, and better employee identification with a job. The major problem tends to be too many employees reporting to one manager.

A **tall organization** has several levels of managers. This arrangement leads to close supervision and fewer employees reporting to each manager. The problems include a long channel of communication, an impersonal impression given to workers (regarding access to higher-level personnel within the organization), and inflexible rules.

With these factors in mind, a retailer develops an **organization chart,** which graphically displays the hierarchal relationships within the firm. Table 11-1 lists the principles to consider in establishing an organization chart. Figure 11-5 shows examples of functional, product, geographic, and combination organization charts.

ORGAN-IZATIONAL PATTERNS IN RETAILING

Retail organization structures differ by institutional type. For example, an independent retailer has a much simpler organization than a chain retailer. An independent does not have to manage units that may be distant from the main store, the owner-manager usually personally supervises all employees, and workers have ready access to the owner-manager in the event of any personal or work-related problems. In contrast, a chain must specify how tasks are to be delegated, coordinate multiple store operations, and establish common policies for all employees.

A discussion of organizational arrangements used by independent retailers, department stores, chain retailers, and diversified retailers follows.

Organizational Arrangements Used by Small Independent Retailers

Small independent retailers generally use simple organizational arrangements because they contain only two or three levels of personnel (the owner-manager and employees), and the owner-manager personally runs the business and oversees workers. There are

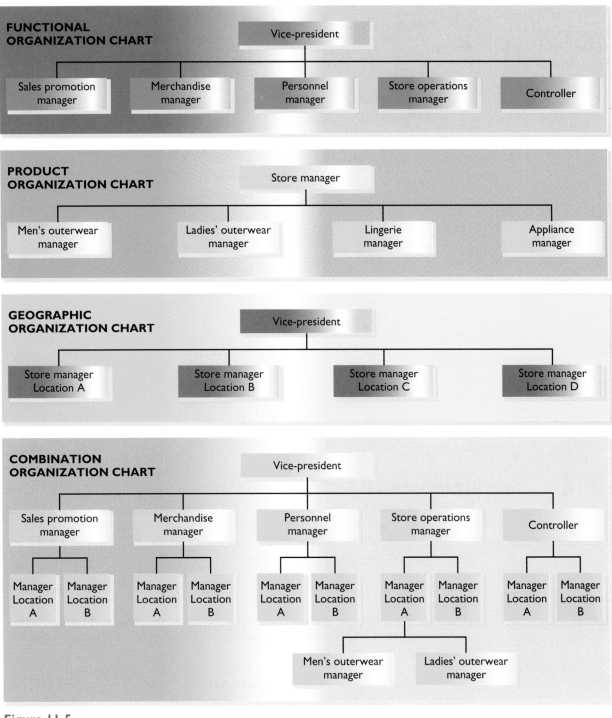

Figure 11-5

Different Forms of Retail Organization

few employees and little departmentalization (specialization), and there are no branch units. This does not mean, however, that fewer activities must be performed.

The small independent has little specialization of functions because there are many tasks to be performed relative to the number of workers available to do them. Thus, each worker must allot part of his or her time to several duties.

Figure 11-6

Organization Structures Used by Small Independents

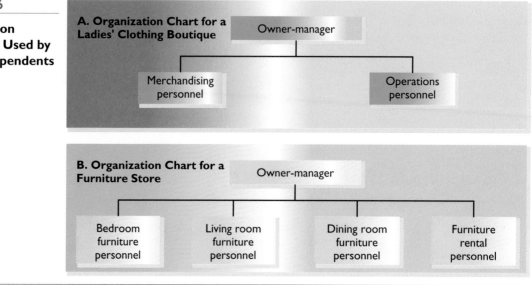

A. Organization Chart for a Ladies' Clothing Boutique

Owner-manager

Merchandising personnel | Operations personnel

B. Organization Chart for a Furniture Store

Owner-manager

Bedroom furniture personnel | Living room furniture personnel | Dining room furniture personnel | Furniture rental personnel

Figure 11-6 shows the organization structures of two small independents. In A, a boutique is organized on a functional basis: merchandising versus operations. Merchandising personnel are responsible for buying and selling goods and services, assortments, displays, and ads. Operations personnel are responsible for store maintenance and operations (such as inventory management and financial reports). In B, a furniture store is organized on a product-oriented basis, with the personnel in each category responsible for selected activities. All of the product categories get appropriate attention, and some expertise is developed. This expertise is particularly important since different skills are necessary to buy and sell each type of furniture.

Organizational Arrangements Used by Department Stores

More than 70 years after its introduction (in 1927), many medium and large department stores continue to use organizational arrangements that are a modification of the **Mazur plan,** which divides all retail activities into four functional areas: merchandising, publicity, store management, and accounting and control.[4] The functional areas include these tasks:

1. Merchandising—buying, selling, stock planning and control, planning promotional events.
2. Publicity—window and interior displays, advertising, planning and executing promotional events (in cooperation with merchandise managers), advertising research, public relations.
3. Store management—merchandise care, customer services (such as adjustment bureaus), purchasing store supplies and equipment, store maintenance, operating activities (such as receiving, checking, marking, and delivering merchandise, and overseeing warehouse), store and merchandise protection (such as insurance and security), training and compensating personnel, workroom operations.
4. Accounting and control—credit and collections, expense budgeting and control, inventory planning and control, record keeping.

These four areas are organized in terms of line (direct authority and responsibility) and staff (advisory and support) components. For instance, a controller and a publicity

[4]Paul M. Mazur, *Principles of Organization Applied to Modern Retailing* (New York: Harper & Brothers, 1927).

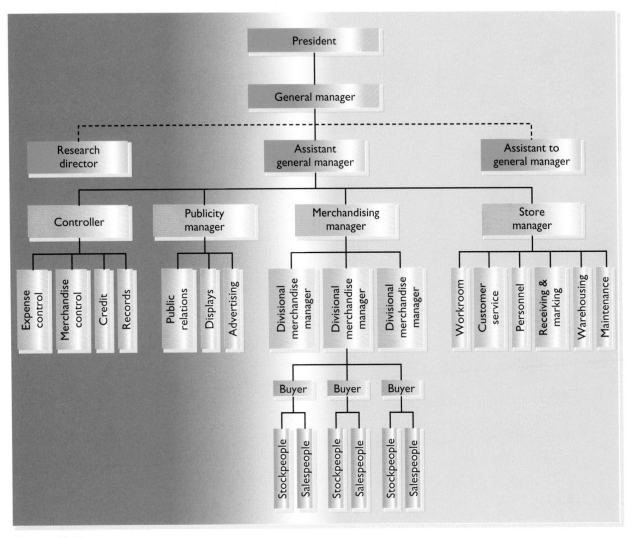

Figure 11-7

The Basic Mazur Organization Plan for Department Stores

Source: Adapted from Paul Mazur, *Principles of Organization Applied to Modern Retailing* (New York: Harper & Brothers, 1927), frontispiece. Reprinted by permission.

manager provide staff services to the merchandising divisions, but within these staff areas, personnel are organized on a line basis. This principle can be more clearly understood from an examination of Figure 11-7, which illustrates the basic Mazur plan.

As shown in Figure 11-7, the merchandising division is responsible for buying and selling activities and is headed by a merchandising manager. This person is often regarded as the most important area executive in the store and is responsible for supervising buyers, devising a financial control system for each department, coordinating department merchandise plans and policies (so a store has a consistent image among departments), and interpreting economic data and their effect on the store. In some stores, divisional merchandise managers are utilized, so the number of buyers reporting to a single manager does not become unwieldy.

The buyer, under the basic Mazur plan, has complete responsibility for controlling expenses and reaching profit goals within his or her department. The buyer's duties include preparing preliminary budgets, studying fashion trends, bargaining with vendors over price, planning the number of salespeople needed, and informing sales personnel about merchandise purchased and fashion trends. The grouping of buying and selling activities

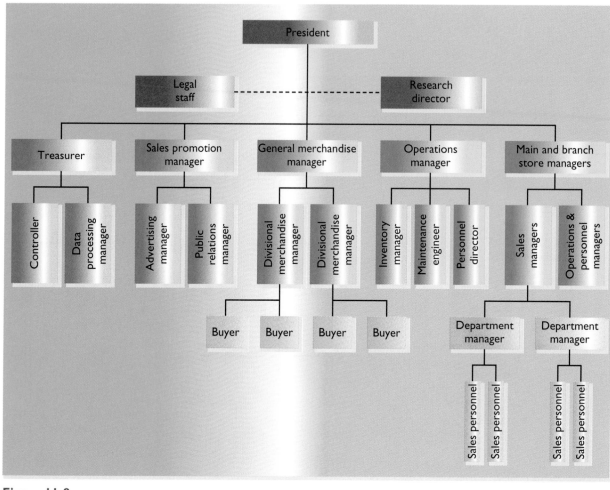

Figure 11-8

The Equal-Store Organizational Format Used by Many Chain Stores

into one job (buyer) may present a major problem. Since buyers are not constantly on the selling floor, control of personnel (training, scheduling, and supervision) may suffer.

The growth of branch stores has led to three derivative forms of the Mazur plan: the **mother hen with branch store chickens organization,** by which headquarters executives oversee and operate the branches; the **separate store organization,** by which each branch has its own buying responsibilities; and the **equal store organization,** by which buying is centralized and branches become sales units with equal operational status.

In the "mother hen" organization, most authority remains with managers at the main company store. Merchandise planning and buying, advertising, financial controls, store hours, and many other tasks are centrally managed. To a great extent, this organization standardizes the performance of all outlets. Branch store managers hire and supervise the employees in their stores and are responsible for making sure day-to-day operations conform to company policies. This organization works well if there are few branches and the buying preferences of branch customers are similar to customers of the main store. Yet, as the branch stores increase in number, the buyers, the advertising director, the controller, and others may become overworked and give too little attention to the branches. In addition, because the main store's personnel are physically removed from the branches, differences in customer preferences may easily be overlooked.

The "separate store" organization places merchandise managers directly in branch stores. Branches have autonomy for merchandising and operations decisions. Customer needs are quickly noted, but duplication by managers in the main store and the branches is possible. Coordination can also be a problem (such as maintaining a consistent image from outlet to outlet). Transferring stock between branches is more complex and more costly. This format is best if individual stores are large, branches are geographically separated, or local customer tastes vary widely.

With the "equal store" organization, department stores try to achieve the benefits of both centralization and decentralization. It is the most popular arrangement for multiunit department stores. Buying functions—such as forecasting, planning, buying, pricing, merchandise distribution to branches, and promotion—are centrally managed. Selling functions—such as presenting merchandise, selling, customer services, and store operations—are managed in each outlet. All outlets, including the main store, are treated equally; and buyers are freed from supervising main store personnel. Data gathering is critical because buyers have less customer and store contact, responsibility is more widely dispersed (and harder to pin down—buyers versus sales manager).

Organizational Arrangements Used by Chain Retailers

Chain retailers of various types often use a version of the equal-store organizational format explained in the preceding section and depicted in Figure 11-8. Although chain store organization structures may differ, they generally have these characteristics:

- There are a large number of functional divisions, such as sales promotion, merchandise management, distribution, store operations, real estate, personnel, and information systems.
- Overall authority and responsibility are centralized, with individual store managers responsible for sales.
- Many operations are standardized (fixtures, store layout, building design, merchandise lines, credit policy, and store service).
- An elaborate control system keeps management informed.
- A certain amount of decentralization enables branch stores to adapt better to local conditions and increases the store manager's responsibilities. For example, while some large chains standardize 80 percent to 90 percent of the merchandise carried by their outlets, store managers are free to fine-tune 10 percent to 20 percent of the mix to appeal to local markets—be they rural or urban, African-American or Hispanic, or high or low income. This is really a form of employee empowerment, but on the store manager level.

To further emphasize the last point above, consider the case of Colleen Downey, *Progressive Grocer's* 1996 Chain Manager of the Year. Although Downey (manager of the 40,000-square-foot Hen House supermarket outlet in a Kansas City suburb) has a strict series of operating rules to follow, she is also given the latitude to use her own initiative to adapt the chain's overall plan: "For the Thanksgiving turkey promotion, Downey used technology to solve a public relations problem that Hen House had in the past. Traditionally, Hen House sold only fresh turkeys. That meant taking orders and having 25 or 30 customers standing around at any one time waiting to be served. Downey and her staff devised a method of collecting data from customers and presenting them with a turkey personalized with their names, phone numbers, and the weight and price of the birds on the label. The program entailed the use of in-store Lotus software and Label Master equipment. It also called for a precise schedule of responsibilities for those in the fresh poultry department, as well as support personnel. 'We roped off an area with theater ropes and customers waited in line. As they reached the head of the line, three service people introduced a poultry teammate to each customer, and the poultry department employee went to the back room and brought out the turkey,' Downey said. The result was record sales. 'We probably had about 500 or 600 special orders,' she estimated."[5]

[5]Steve Weinstein, "Meeting the Challenge," *Progressive Grocer* (April 1996), p. 45.

Figure 11-9

The Organizational Structure of Toys "Я" Us (United States Only), Selected Positions

Source: Adapted by the authors from the *Toys "Я" Us 1996 Annual Report.*

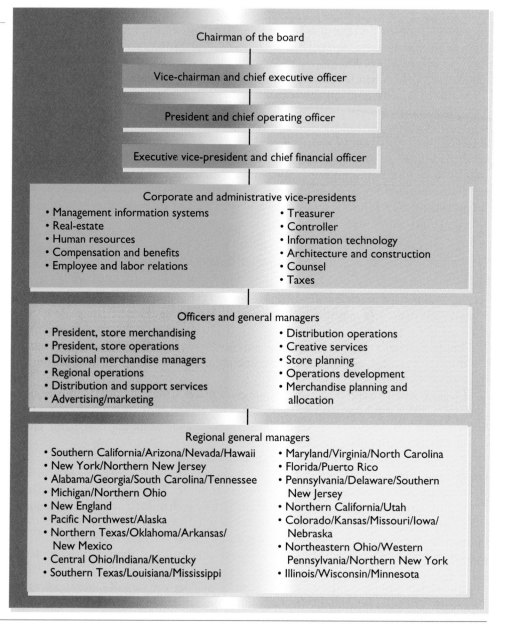

Chairman of the board

Vice-chairman and chief executive officer

President and chief operating officer

Executive vice-president and chief financial officer

Corporate and administrative vice-presidents
- Management information systems
- Real-estate
- Human resources
- Compensation and benefits
- Employee and labor relations
- Treasurer
- Controller
- Information technology
- Architecture and construction
- Counsel
- Taxes

Officers and general managers
- President, store merchandising
- President, store operations
- Divisional merchandise managers
- Regional operations
- Distribution and support services
- Advertising/marketing
- Distribution operations
- Creative services
- Store planning
- Operations development
- Merchandise planning and allocation

Regional general managers
- Southern California/Arizona/Nevada/Hawaii
- New York/Northern New Jersey
- Alabama/Georgia/South Carolina/Tennessee
- Michigan/Northern Ohio
- New England
- Pacific Northwest/Alaska
- Northern Texas/Oklahoma/Arkansas/New Mexico
- Central Ohio/Indiana/Kentucky
- Southern Texas/Louisiana/Mississippi
- Maryland/Virginia/North Carolina
- Florida/Puerto Rico
- Pennsylvania/Delaware/Southern New Jersey
- Northern California/Utah
- Colorado/Kansas/Missouri/Iowa/Nebraska
- Northeastern Ohio/Western Pennsylvania/Northern New York
- Illinois/Wisconsin/Minnesota

Figure 11-9 shows the organizational structure for the U.S. Toys "Я" Us store division of Toys "Я" Us, Inc. It is an equal-store format organized by function and geographic area.

Organizational Arrangements Used by Diversified Retailers

A **diversified retailer,** also known as a retail conglomerate or conglomerchant, is a multiline merchandising firm under central ownership. Like a chain, a diversified retailer has more than one outlet; however, unlike a typical chain, these outlets cover different types of retail operations. Here are two examples of diversified retailers:

■ Burlington Coat Factory operates six other retail businesses, besides its flagship Burlington Coat Factory discount apparel chain: Luxury Linens, Baby Depot, Totally 4 Kids, Cohoes (an upscale apparel chain), Decelle (an off-price chain), and Fit for Men (for "hard to fit" men). See Figure 11-10.

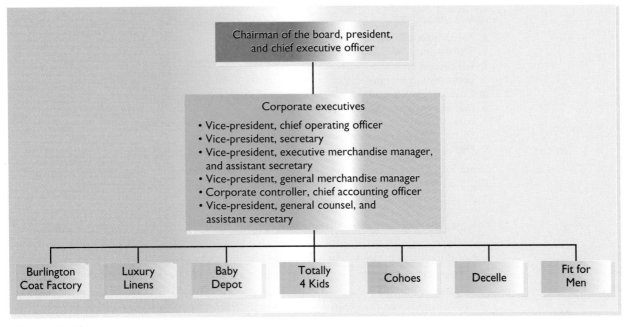

Figure 11-10

The Organizational Structure of Burlington Coat Factory

Source: Adapted by the authors from the *Burlington Coat Factory 1996 Annual Report.*

■ Japan's Aeon Group comprises superstores, supermarkets, discount stores, home centers, specialty and convenience stores, financial services stores, and restaurants. In addition to Japan, Aeon has facilities in 13 other countries. It is also a leading shopping center developer. Jusco, with $18 billion in annual sales, is the largest retailer in the Aeon group.

Due to their multiple strategy mixes, diversified retailers face atypical considerations in developing and maintaining an organization structure. First, interdivision control is needed. Operating procedures and clear goals must be communicated among divisions. Second, interdivision competition must be coordinated (e.g., Should a firm's department stores and discount stores carry the same brands?). Third, resources must be divided among different divisions. Fourth, potential image and advertising conflicts must be avoided. Fifth, management skills must be adapted to rather different operations. Accordingly, a diversified retailer usually has a very complex organization structure.

Human resource management involves the recruitment, selection, training, compensation, and supervision of personnel in a manner consistent with the retailer's organization structure and strategy mix. It is required of all retailers, with policies dependent on their line of business, the number of employees, the location of outlets, and other factors.

HUMAN RESOURCE MANAGEMENT IN RETAILING

Because good personnel are needed to develop and carry out retail strategies, and labor costs can amount to 50 percent or more of some retailers' operating expenses, the value of effective human resource management is clear. This is further illustrated through the following:

■ U.S. retailing now employs 21 million people and this will rise to 23 million by the year 2000; thus, there is a constant need to attract new employees—as well as to retain existing ones. For example, over 2 million fast-food workers are aged 16 to 20, and they

Table 11-2   THE TRUE COST OF EMPLOYEE TURNOVER

1. Recruiting and hiring new employees.
2. Training costs—including management time.
3. Full pay and benefits during training, before full productivity is reached.
4. Lost sales and alienated customers during off-site training.
5. Costs of mistakes made by new, inexperienced employees.
6. Loss of customers loyal to departing employees.
7. Loss of knowledge and experience built up by departing employees.
8. Lost or damaged relationships with suppliers.
9. Employee morale and customer perception of that morale.

Source: Terri Kabachnick, "Turning Against the Tide," *Arthur Andersen Retailing Issues Letter* (Center for Retailing Studies, Texas A&M University: September 1995), p. 3. Reprinted by permission.

must be regularly replaced since they stay in their jobs for only short times. In general, retailers need to reduce the turnover rate for their employees. When workers quickly, and in great numbers, exit a firm, the results can be disastrous. See Table 11-2.

■ The Lark is a five-store chain of upscale apparel shops that operates in low-income, minority neighborhoods in Gary, Indiana, and Chicago. "Because many black shoppers say they feel slighted or even mistrusted by sales help in mainstream stores, they are particularly receptive to retailers that treat them well." At The Lark, "good service begins with good treatment of employees, 90 percent of whom are black. Managers are paid $30,000 to $70,000 a year and salespeople $15,000 to $40,000. The Lark also offers employees health insurance, pays half the tuition for any outside education they seek, and has a $500 no-questions-asked loan policy should employees get in a jam. Of 75 employees, only two left in the last year."[6]

■ Dollar General has a progressive human resource mission, keyed to such principles as these: "We believe in the dignity of the person and the work. Our productivity is, therefore, attained by emphasizing strengths, not by dwelling on weaknesses. We believe that any success is short-lived if it does not involve mutual gain."[7]

■ The highest entry-level position at Home Depot is usually assistant store manager; store managers are typically not hired from outside the company. Although Home Depot is a large and growing chain, the firm's co-founders and other senior executives have been personally involved in the training of virtually every manager. They want to be sure the basic operating philosophy is clearly communicated to and carried out by all employees.

■ At Nordstrom, there is decentralized buying, and salespeople have considerable input. They can place special orders, decide when products are delivered, get extra merchandise if needed, and resolve customer problems.

■ At West Point Market, an Akron, Ohio, supermarket, new employees are given performance reviews every 30, 60, and 90 days—"both to give positive reinforcement and to pinpoint specific problems."[8]

The Special Human Resource Environment of Retailing

Retailers face a special human resource environment, which is characterized by a large number of inexperienced workers, long hours, highly visible employees, many part-time workers, and variations in customer demand. These factors often make the hiring, staffing, and supervision of employees a complicated process.[9]

---

[6]Robert Berner, "Urban Rarity: Stores Offering Spiffy Service," *Wall Street Journal* (July 25, 1996), pp. B1, B10.
[7]*Dollar General Corporation 1993 Annual Report.*
[8]Mary Ann Linsen, "Searching for Solutions," *Progressive Grocer* (May 1993), pp. 183–188.
[9]See Kal Lifson, "Turn Down Turnover to Turn Up Profit," *Chain Store Age* (November 1996), pp. 64–68; and Susan Reda, "Who Will Mind the Store?" *Stores* (March 1997), pp. 20–25.

At Beall's Department Stores: A Tough Employee Ethics Code

Beall's, a 174-unit outlet and department store chain based in Bradenton, Florida, is among the many retail firms that have a tough ethics code. Beall's ethics code is part of the 26-page handbook that must be signed by all employees when they are hired. Topics include drug abuse, the use of Beall's resources, sexual harassment, software privacy, conflict-of-interest situations, and fair marketing practices. A separate section of the code clearly states that "looking the other way, constitutes unspoken approval" of unethical activity.

The ethics code ends with guidelines to help employees determine whether any behavior falls outside Beall's rules. This portion of the handbook stresses whether an act is legal, balanced, and would "stand inspection." As Beall's divisional vice-president for loss prevention says, "by standing inspection we question to whether it would make the person proud of himself or herself; whether the employee would feel positive about it if his or her family knew of it; and how he or she might react to having the decision or action reported in a newspaper."

Besides the handbook guide, Beall's distributes questionnaires annually to all of its employees that reinforce the firm's ethical orientation. These questionnaires also provide employees with a means of documenting that they have not participated in any unethical behavior.

Source: Julie Ritzer Ross, "Retailers Toughen Ethics Codes to Curb Employee Abuses," *Stores* (July 1996), pp. 83–84.

The greatest personnel difficulty for many retailers is probably the relative inexperience of a lot of their workers. As previously noted, there is a need for a large labor force in retailing, and persons with little or no prior experience are frequently hired. For numerous new workers, a position in retailing represents their first "real" job. People are attracted to retailing because they find jobs near to their homes; and retail positions may require limited education, training, and skill (such as checkout clerks, wrappers, stock clerks, and some types of sales personnel). Also, the low wages paid for some positions call for the hiring of inexperienced people. Thus, high employee turnover and cases of poor performance, lateness, and absenteeism may be the result.

The long working hours generally encountered in retailing, including Saturdays and Sundays in various locales, turn off some prospective employees; and there is a strong trend toward longer store hours, because family shoppers and working women shoppers want stores with evening and weekend hours. Accordingly, some retailers must have at least two shifts of full-time employees.

In retailing, employees are highly visible to the customer. Therefore, when a retailer selects and trains personnel, special care must be taken with regard to their manners and appearance. Unfortunately, some small retailers may not recognize the importance of employee appearance (such as being neatly groomed and appropriately attired).

Due to the long hours of retail stores, firms often have to hire part-time personnel. In many supermarkets, over half the workers are part-time; and problems can arise accordingly. Part-time employees may be more apt to be lackadaisical, late, absent, or quit their jobs than full-time employees (who are more career-oriented). This means they must be closely monitored.

Last, variations in customer demand by day, time period, or season may cause personnel planning problems. For example, the majority of consumers make their major supermarket shopping trips on Thursday, Friday, or Saturday. So, how many employees should a supermarket have on the premises Sunday (or Monday) through Wednesday, and how many should be used Thursday through Saturday? Demand differences during the day (morning, afternoon, evening) and by season (fall, Christmas) also affect personnel planning.

As a rule, retailers should consider points such as these:

- Employee recruitment and selection procedures must be able to generate a sufficient number of applicants efficiently.
- Some training programs must be intensive and short in duration because many workers are inexperienced and temporary.
- Compensation must be perceived as "fair" by employees.
- Advancement opportunities must be available to employees who look at retailing as a career.
- Employee appearance and work habits must be explained and reviewed.
- Morale problems may result from the high rate of employee turnover and the large number of part-time workers.
- Full- and part-time employees may have conflicts, especially when part-time personnel are used to minimize overtime for full-time workers.

The Human Resource Management Process in Retailing

The **human resource management process** in retailing consists of these interrelated personnel activities: recruitment, selection, training, compensation, and supervision. The goals of this process are to obtain, develop, and retain employees.

When applying this process, diversity, labor laws, and employee privacy should all be kept in mind. Diversity involves two fundamental premises: (1) that employees be hired and promoted in a fair and open way, without regard to their gender, ethnic background, and other related factors; and (2) that in an increasingly diverse society, the workplace should be representative of such diversity. For example, at McDonald's, more than 50 percent of middle managers and greater than 25 percent of franchise operators are females and minority group members. At the Marriott Marquis hotel in New York, there are 1,700 employees, representing every race, hailing from 70 nations, and speaking 47 languages. Nationwide, women account for nearly 40 percent of all supermarket executives. Nonetheless, as the chair of the Conference Board's Council on Work Force Diversity recently said: "Corporate America can ill afford to be lulled into a false sense of comfort as to upward mobility gains. Despite progress made in the U.S. work force by white women and people of color over the past decade, we are far from having a critical mass in upper management positions. The glass ceiling is alive and well."[10]

There are several aspects of labor laws for retailers to address, such as these:

- Not hiring underage workers.
- Not paying workers "off the books."
- Not requiring workers to engage in illegal acts (such as bait and switch selling).
- Not discriminating in hiring or promoting workers.
- Not violating worker safety regulations.
- Not dealing with suppliers that disobey labor laws.

Retailers need to ask themselves: What privacy rights should employees have? There are both legal and ethical ramifications to their answers. Consider this view:

> Employers argue that in today's increasingly competitive economy, they have a right to choose the workers who best fit the job, and in order to make informed choices, they need information—information that can be acquired only through such procedures as background checks, credit checks, and drug tests. Once workers have been hired, the argument goes, monitoring is then essential to maintain and often improve productivity. Driving much of the expanded need for information are the growing

---

[10]"Diversity: Making the Business Case," *Business Week* (December 9, 1996), special advertising section; *McDonald's 1995 Annual Report*; Alex Markels, "How One Hotel Manages Staff's Diversity," *Wall Street Journal* (November 20,1996), pp. B1–B2; and Nicole Harris, "Revolt at the Deli Counter," *Business Week* (April 1, 1996), p. 32.

responsibilities of the employer in two important and costly areas: health insurance and liability. Health insurance costs have been eating into corporate profits at an exponential rate. Insuring high-risk workers, like smokers or skydivers, further drives up the cost of insuring everyone else. But to know which workers are high-risk requires still more information, whether from medical tests or personal questions and surveillance. A second justification for workplace monitoring is that employers face liability for the actions of their employees. Also, under the fast-growing tort of "negligent hiring," an employer can be sued for its failure to adequately check the past histories of its workers.

Today, a host of new privacy issues are coming over the horizon. Does an employer's need to ensure a safe workplace justify asking intrusive questions? Can an employee's personal life or sexual orientation be grounds for dismissal? What happens when privacy can be invaded by new technology and no law exists to cover a perceived injury? A robust economy is obviously in everyone's interest. Improving efficiency and performance contribute to that end. Careful selection and monitoring of workers are vital management tools that entail some intrusion into personal lives. But might we reach a point at which the workplace has become so dehumanizing that any increase in profit is not worth the sacrifice of privacy?[11]

In the next subsections, each activity in the human resource management process is discussed for retail sales and middle-management positions.

Recruitment of Retail Personnel ❑ **Recruitment** is the activity whereby a retailer generates a list of job applicants. Sources of potential employees include educational institutions, other channel members, competitors, advertisements, employment agencies, unsolicited applicants, and current and former employees who are looking for new positions or who recommend friends. Table 11-3 indicates the characteristics of these sources.

For entry-level sales jobs, retailers are apt to rely on educational institutions, ads, walk-ins (or write-ins), and employee recommendations. For middle-management positions, retailers are likely to use employment agencies, competitors, ads, and current employees.

Often during recruitment, the retailer's major goal is to generate a large list of potential employees, which will be sharply reduced during selection. However, retailers that accept applicants for further consideration only if they meet minimum background standards (such as education, experience) can save a lot of time and money during selection.

Selection of Retail Personnel ❑ The firm next selects new employees from among those recruited. The major goal at this stage is to match traits of potential employees with the requirements of the jobs being filled. The procedure should include job analysis and description, the application blank, interviewing, testing (optional), references, and a physical exam. The steps should be done in an integrated way.

Job analysis consists of gathering information about each job's functions and requirements: duties, responsibilities, aptitude, interest, education, experience, and physical condition. It is used to select personnel, set performance standards, and assign salary levels. For example, department managers at general merchandise stores often oversee other sales associates, serve as the main sales associates for their departments, have some administrative and analytical responsibilities, report directly to the store manager, are eligible to receive bonuses, and are paid from $20,000 to $35,000+ annually. Most have been with their firms for two or more years.

---

[11]Ellen Alderman and Caroline Kennedy, "Privacy," *Across the Board* (March 1996), pp. 32–33.

Table 11-3   RECRUITMENT SOURCES AND THEIR CHARACTERISTICS

Sources	Characteristics
1. Outside the Company	
Educational institutions	a. High schools, business schools, community colleges, universities, graduate schools
	b. Good for training positions; ensure minimum educational requirements are fulfilled; especially useful when long-term contacts with instructors are developed
Other channel members, competitors	a. Employees of wholesalers, manufacturers, ad agencies, competitors; leads from each of these
	b. Reduce extent of training; can evaluate performance with prior firm(s); must instruct in company policy; some negative morale if current employees feel bypassed for promotions
Advertisements	a. Newspapers, trade publications, professional journals, Web sites
	b. Large quantity of applicants; average applicant quality may not be high; cost/applicant is low; additional responsibility placed on screening; can reduce number of unacceptable applicants by noting job qualifications in ads
Employment agencies	a. Private organizations, professional organizations, government, executive search firms
	b. Must be carefully selected; must be determined who pays fee; good for applicant screening; specialists in personnel
Unsolicited applicants	a. Walk-ins, write-ins
	b. Wide variance in quality; must be carefully screened; file should be kept for future positions
2. Within the Company	
Current and former employees	a. Promotion or transfer of existing full-time employees, part-time employees; rehiring of laid-off employees
	b. Knowledge of company policies and personnel; good for morale; honest appraisal from in-house supervisor
Employee recommendations	a. Friends, acquaintances, relatives
	b. Value of recommendations depend upon honesty and judgment of current employees

Job analysis should lead to written job descriptions. A **traditional job description** contains each position's title, supervisory relationships (superior and subordinate), committee assignments, and the specific roles and tasks to be performed on an ongoing basis. Figure 11-4 showed a traditional job description for a store manager.

Yet, the use of the traditional job description alone has been criticized. This approach may limit the scope of a job, as well as its authority, responsibility, and decision-making power; be static and not let a person grow; limit activities to those listed; and not describe how positions are coordinated. Thus, to complement a traditional job description, many personnel experts advocate using a **goal-oriented job description,** that enumerates basic functions, the relationship of each job to overall goals, the interdependence of positions, and information flows. Figure 11-11 illustrates a goal-oriented job description.

An **application blank** is usually the first tool used to screen applicants; providing data on education, experience, health, reasons for leaving prior jobs, organizational memberships, hobbies, and references. It is relatively short, requires little interpretation, and can be used as the basis for probing in an interview. A refinement of this tool is the **weighted application blank.** Retailers utilizing such a form generally have analyzed the performance of current and past employees and determined the criteria (education, experience, and so on) best correlated with job success (as measured by longer tenure, higher sales volume, less absenteeism, and so on). Factors having a high relationship with success are given more weight than others, and a certain number of points are assigned to each factor. After weighted scores are given to all job applicants (based on data they provide), a minimum total score can become a cutoff point for hiring. An effective application blank aids a retailer in lowering turnover and identifying high achievers.

An application blank should be used in conjunction with a job description. Those meeting the minimum job requirements are processed further (interview). Those who do

Figure 11-11

A Goal-Oriented Job Description for a Management Trainee

Attributes Required	Ability	Desire	In the Retailing Environment
ANALYTICAL SKILLS: ability to solve problems; strong numerical ability for analysis of facts and data for planning, managing, and controlling.			Retail executives are problem solvers. Knowledge and understanding of past performance and present circumstances form the basis for action and planning.
CREATIVITY: ability to generate and recognize imaginative ideas and solutions; ability to recognize the need for and be responsive to change.			Retail executives are idea people. Successful buying results from sensitive, aware decisions, while merchandising requires imaginative, innovative techniques.
DECISIVENESS: ability to make quick decisions and render judgments, take action, and commit oneself to completion.			Retail executives are action people. Whether it's new fashion trends or customer desires, decisions must be made quickly and confidently in this ever-changing environment.
FLEXIBILITY: ability to adjust to the ever-changing needs of the situation; ability to adapt to different people, places, and things; willingness to do whatever is necessary to get the task done.			Retail executives are flexible. Surprises in retailing never cease. Plans must be altered quickly to accommodate changes in trends, styles, and attitudes, while numerous ongoing activities cannot be ignored.
INITIATIVE: ability to originate action rather than wait to be told what to do and ability to act based on conviction.			Retail executives are doers. Sales volumes, trends, and buying opportunities mean continual action. Opportunities for action must be seized.
LEADERSHIP: ability to inspire others to trust and respect your judgment; ability to delegate and to guide and persuade others.			Retail executives are managers. Running a business means depending on others to get the work done. One person cannot do it all.
ORGANIZATION: ability to establish priorities and courses of action for self and/or others; skill in planning and following up to achieve results.			Retail executives are jugglers. A variety of issues, functions, and projects are constantly in motion. To reach your goals, priorities must be set, work must be delegated to others.
RISK-TAKING: willingness to take calculated risks based on thorough analysis and sound judgment and to accept responsibility for the results.			Retail executives are courageous. Success in retailing often comes from taking calculated risks and having the confidence to try something new before someone else does.
STRESS TOLERANCE: ability to perform consistently under pressure, to thrive on constant change and challenge.			Retail executives are resilient. As the above description should suggest, retailing is fast-paced and demanding.

not are immediately rejected. In this way, the application blank provides a quick and inexpensive method of screening.

The interview seeks to obtain information that can be amassed only through personal questioning and observation. It lets the prospective employer determine the candidate's oral ability, note his or her appearance, ask questions keyed to the application blank, and probe into career objectives.

Several decisions about the interviewing process must be made: the level of formality, the number of interviews and the length of each, the physical location of interviews, the person(s) to do interviewing, the use of a relaxed or intense atmosphere, and the degree to which interviewing is structured. These decisions often depend on the interviewer's ability and a job's requirements.

Many, particularly smaller, retailers hire an applicant if he or she performs well during the interview. Other, usually larger, retailers use an additional selection device: testing. In this case, a candidate who does well during an interview is asked to complete psychological tests (which measure personality, intelligence, interest, and leadership skills) and/or achievement tests (which measure learned knowledge).

Such tests must be administered and interpreted by qualified people. Standardized exams should not be used unless they are proven as effective predictors of job performance. Because achievement tests deal with specific skills or information, such as industry knowledge, the ability to make a sales presentation, and insights into the principles of retailing, they are much easier to interpret than psychological tests; and direct relationships between knowledge and ability can be shown. In giving tests to job applicants, retailers must be careful not to violate any federal, state, or local law. For example, the federal Employee Polygraph Protection Act of 1988 bars firms from using lie detector tests in most retail hiring situations (drugstores are exempt from this law).

In conjunction with interviewing and testing, retailers often get references from applicants. The references can be checked either before or after the interview stage. The purposes of contacting references are to see how enthusiastically others recommend an applicant, check the applicant's honesty, ask a prior employer why the applicant left the job, and review the types of people who will vouch for an applicant. Mail and phone checks are inexpensive, fast, and easy.

When a candidate successfully completes the interview, testing, and reference check steps, many firms require a physical exam before giving a job. This is especially due to the physical activity, long hours, and tensions involved in some retailing positions. A clean bill of health would mean the candidate is offered a job. Again, federal, state, and local laws must be followed.

Each step in the selection process complements the others; together they give the retailer a total information package upon which to base personnel decisions. As a rule, retailers should use job descriptions, application blanks, interviews, and reference checks. The use of follow-up interviews, psychological and achievement tests, and physical exams depends on the nature of the retailer and the types of positions.

Inexpensive tools (like application blanks) are used in the early screening stages, whereas more expensive, in-depth tools (like interviews) are used after the applicant pool has been reduced a lot. Federal and state rules require that questions asked in the selection process be directly linked to job performance. Equal opportunity, nondiscriminatory practices must be enforced.

Training Retail Personnel ❏ When a new employee first joins the company, he or she should be exposed to a pre-training session. **Pre-training** is an indoctrination on the history and policies of the retailer and a job orientation on the hours, compensation, chain of command, and job duties. In addition, the new employee would be introduced to his or her co-workers.

Training programs are used to teach new (and existing) personnel how best to perform their jobs or how to improve themselves. Training can range from one- or two-day sessions on writing up sales forms, operating a cash register, personal selling techniques, or compliance with affirmative action programs to two-year programs for executive trainees on all aspects of the retailer and its operations. For example,

■   At Circuit City, new sales counselors complete a minimum two-week training program focusing on product knowledge, customer service, and store operations. Seven

Table 11-4 SELECTED TRAINING DECISIONS

1. When does training occur? (At the time of hiring and/or after being at the workplace?)
2. How long should training be?
3. What training programs are for new employees? For existing employees?
4. Who should conduct each training program? (Supervisor, co-worker, training department, or outside specialist?)
5. Where should training take place? (At the workplace or in a training room?)
6. What material (content) should be learned? How should it be taught?
7. Should audiovisuals be used?
8. How can the effectiveness of training be measured?

regional training facilities are used for classroom sessions taught by more than 40 professional trainers. A state-of-the-art video facility produces video, audio, and computer-based training materials. Formalized training for store, sales, and operations managers deals with human resource skills, sales management, and critical operating procedures. Individual development plans address personal training needs, giving associates advancement opportunities.[12]

■ Sears University was established in 1994. It offers regular education programs plus self-study options. In the first year of operation, 10,000 managers participated in hands-on programs ranging from one day to one week. In addition, each month, about 4,000 self-study courses are completed. Some programs provide managers with core skills in buying, merchandising, and human resource management. Others help participants function as strategic leaders. Courses are taught by seasoned line managers, training and development experts, and university faculty consultants.[13]

Effective retailers realize training is an ongoing activity. New equipment, changes in laws, and new product lines, as well as motivating current personnel, employee promotions, and employee turnover, necessitate not only training but retraining, as well. Thus, Federated Department Stores has a program called "clienteling," whereby sales associates are tutored on how to develop better long-term relationships with specific repeat customers. Core vendors of Federated are regularly involved in teaching sales associates about the features and benefits of new merchandise when it is introduced.[14]

Several training decisions need to be made, as shown in Table 11-4. Those decisions can be divided into three categories: identifying needs, devising appropriate training methods, and evaluation.

Immediate training needs for both new and existing employees can be identified by the retailer's measuring the gap between the skills those workers already have and the skills desired by the firm (for each job). Training should also prepare employees for possible job rotation, promotions, and emerging changes in the company. A five-year plan for personnel development would let a firm identify future needs and train workers accordingly. Both short- and long-run training needs can be unearthed by communications with top management, formal evaluations, informal observations, group discussions, employee requests, and employee performance.

After needs are identified, the best training method(s) for addressing them must be uncovered from among lectures, demonstrations, films, programmed instruction, conferences, sensitivity training, case studies, role playing, behavior modeling, and competency-based instruction. These techniques may be personalized; some may even be

[12]*Circuit City Stores, Inc. 1996 Annual Report.*

[13]*Sears 1995 Annual Report.*

[14]*Federated Department Stores, Inc. 1995 Annual Report;* and Robert M. Kahn, "Tailor-Made Training," *Sales & Marketing Management* (March 1997), pp. 66–72.

TECHNOLOGY IN RETAILING

Utilizing CD-ROM Workstations in Employee Training

Supermarkets such as Dominick's Finer Foods, Giant Foods, Finast, Furr's, Pathmark, and Ralphs are among the retail chains that now use CD-ROM workstations to train cashiers.

As the director of training and development at Finast said, "This [CD-ROM training] delivers consistent training, it reduces training costs, and our training time has been cut in half." Finast's training manager adds that the CD-ROM workstations "cut our training costs for cashiers in half." While it used to take 16 hours to train a cashier at the register, it now takes 8 hours with CD-ROMs. Furr's Supermarkets also reports significant reductions in cashier training time; and CD-ROM-based training has enabled Furr's to train as many as 25 cashiers in a four-day

period. Furr's expects a 20-month payback for its CD-ROM training system. Other supermarkets say CD-ROM training is more consistent than the prior training done by individual store managers.

Both Finast and Furr's use training packages developed by Strategic Systems Associates (SSA). SSA tailors its program to meet the specific needs of each supermarket. The standard SSA package provides cashiers with a tour of the cash register (such as the keyboard), as well as special procedures (such as the handling of food stamps). Trainees can repeat specific portions of the training program they do not fully understand.

Sources: "CD-ROM Workstations Ease Cashier Training," *Chain Store Age* (August 1996), pp. 54–56; and "Rita Lauds Spartan Stores for CD-ROM Course," *Chain Store Age* (September 1996), pp. 70, 74.

---

computerized (as many large firms are starting to do). The methods' characteristics are noted in Table 11-5. Retailers often use two or more techniques of training to reduce boredom and cover the material better.

For training to succeed, an environment conducive to learning must be created. As one expert noted: "A significant amount, perhaps 25 percent, of avoidable turnover is caused by new hires feeling uncomfortable, unwanted, and unsure of their abilities in the first few weeks on the job. The training of supervisors on how to accomplish this special attention and nurturance of new associates to get them 'over the hump' of the first few weeks has been very effective in reducing turnover."[15] These are essential principles for enacting a positive training environment:

- All people can learn if taught properly.
- A person learns better when motivated; intelligence alone is not sufficient.
- Learning should be goal-oriented.
- A trainee learns more when he or she participates and is not a passive listener.
- The teacher must provide guidance.
- Learning should be viewed as a process of steps rather than a one-time occurrence.
- Learning should be spread out over a reasonable period of time rather than be compressed.
- The learner should be encouraged to do homework or otherwise practice.
- Different methods of learning should be combined.
- Performance standards should be set and good performance recognized.
- The learner should feel a sense of achievement.
- The teacher should adapt to the learner and to the situation.

A training program must be systematically evaluated for effectiveness. Comparisons may be made between the performances of those who have received training and those who have not. They may also be made among employees receiving different types of training for the same job. When a retailer measures the success of a training program,

[15]Lifson, "Turn Down Turnover to Turn Up Profit," p. 68.

Table 11-5 THE CHARACTERISTICS OF RETAIL TRAINING METHODS

Method	Characteristics
Lecture	Factual, uninterrupted presentation of material; can use professional educator and/or expert in the field; no active participation by trainees
Demonstration	Good for showing equipment or sales presentation; exhibits relevance of training; active participation by trainees
Video	Animated; good for demonstration; can be used many times; no active participation by trainees
Programmed Instruction	Presents information in a structured manner; requires response from trainees; provides performance feedback; adjustable to trainees' pace; high initial investment
Conference	Useful for supervisory training; conference leader must encourage participation; reinforces training
Sensitivity Training	Extensive interaction; good for supervisors as a tool for understanding employees
Case Study	Actual or hypothetical problem presented, including circumstances, pertinent information, and questions; learning by doing; exposure to a wide variety of problems
Role Playing	Trainees placed into real-life situations and act out roles
Behavior Modeling	Trainees taught to imitate models shown on videotape or in role-playing sessions
Competency-Based Instruction	Trainees given a list of tasks or exercises that are presented in a self-paced format

evaluations should always be made in relation to stated training goals. In addition, training effects should be measured over several time intervals (such as immediately, 30 days later, 6 months later), and proper records maintained.

Compensation of Retail Personnel ❏ **Compensation** includes direct monetary payments (such as salaries, commissions, and bonuses) and indirect payments (such as paid vacations, health and life insurance benefits, and retirement plans). To motivate employees better, some retailers also have profit-sharing plans. Smaller retailers often pay salaries, commissions, and/or bonuses, with little emphasis on fringe benefits. Bigger firms generally pay salaries, commissions, and/or bonuses plus fringe benefits. Total compensation should be fair to both the retailer and its employees to be effective.

In 1996, a new federal minimum wage law went into effect (the first one in more than a decade). As of October 1, 1996, the minimum wage rose to $4.75 per hour from $4.25 per hour; and on September 1, 1997, the rate rose again, this time to $5.15 per hour. The law also set a lower "training wage" of $4.25 for teenagers during their initial 90 days of employment. The law is expected to have the most impact on retailers employing entry-level, part-time workers (which encompass millions of people). Yet, "The blow has been softer than it might have been on many employers because they already pay more than the new hourly rate since the labor market is so tight. Hugh Schmidt, a McDonald's franchisee in Vail, Colorado, says he starts workers at $6.50 an hour and bumps them to $7 right away because the slopes, hotels, and T-shirt shops all vie for the same people: 'Supply and demand matter more than what the minimum wage is.' "[16]

At some larger retailers, compensation levels for certain positions are set through collective-bargaining contracts. According to the U.S. Bureau of Labor Statistics, about 1.25 million retail employees are represented by labor unions, and union membership varies greatly. As an example, over 40 percent of supermarket chains employ unionized clerks, while only one-eighth of independent supermarkets have unionized clerks. Union contracts also frequently affect nonunion personnel, who ask for similar compensation.

[16]Christina Duff, "New Minimum Wage Makes Few Waves," *Wall Street Journal* (November 20, 1996), pp. A2, A14.

In a straight-salary plan, a worker is paid a fixed amount per hour, week, month, or year. Earnings are not directly tied to productivity. Advantages of a straight-salary plan are retailer control, employee security, and known expenses. Disadvantages are retailer inflexibility, limited worker incentive to increase productivity, and fixed costs. Lower-level retail personnel (such as clerks and cashiers) are usually paid salaries.

With a straight-commission plan, earnings are directly tied to productivity (such as sales volume). A fixed amount is not paid. Advantages of this plan are retailer flexibility, the tie to worker productivity, no fixed costs, and employee incentive. Disadvantages are the retailer's potential lack of control over the tasks employees perform, the risk of low earnings to employees, the instability of retail costs, and the lack of limits placed on worker earnings. Sales personnel for autos, real estate, insurance, furniture, jewelry, and other expensive items are often paid on straight commission—as are direct-selling personnel.

To combine the attributes of both salary and commission plans, some retailers pay their employees a salary plus commission. Shoe salespeople, major appliance salespeople, and some management personnel are among the employees paid in this manner. At times, bonuses are awarded as supplements to salary and/or commission. These are normally given for outstanding company or individual performance. At Finish Line stores, national, regional, district, and store managers receive fixed salaries and earn bonuses based primarily on the sales, payroll, and theft rate goals of the stores for which they are responsible.[17]

Sometimes, top retail management is paid by a "compensation cafeteria," whereby those executives can choose their own combination of salary, bonus, deferred bonus, fringe benefits, life insurance, stock options, and deferred retirement benefits.

One of the thorniest issues facing retailers today involves the benefits portion of employee compensation, especially as related to pensions and health care. Consider the following:

> The economy is growing. Profits are up. Wages are beginning to rise a bit. So why are so many Americans feeling pinched? The answer may lie less in paychecks than in pension plans and health insurance. As employers struggle to stay competitive, they're chipping away at benefits as never before. "A lot of firms simply no longer want to pay benefits," says Paul Tobias, chairman of the Cincinnati-based National Employee Rights Institute. Consider paid holidays. Fifteen years ago, virtually every medium and large private U.S. employer offered at least one paid holiday per year. Today, that has slipped to about 90 percent. In 1980, 95 percent of such employers offered some kind of health insurance; now, 80 percent do. The growing class of low-wage retail workers may be hard-pressed to pay for what benefits are available. At Wal-Mart stores, only 41 percent of its workers actually got health insurance through the company. Those who did paid at least a $60-a-month family-plan premium, with a $1,000 deductible. "If Wal-Mart isn't providing decent benefits, how can you expect smaller retailers to do better?" asks Greg Denier, a spokesperson for the 1.4 million member United Food & Commercial Workers Union. Wal-Mart says it hasn't raised premiums in three years. "We provide great benefits," adds a spokesperson.[18]

Supervision of Retail Personnel ❏ **Supervision** is the manner of providing a job environment that encourages employee accomplishment. The objectives of supervision are to oversee personnel, achieve good performance, maintain employee morale and motivation, control expenses, minimize redundancies, communicate company policies, and resolve problems. Supervision is provided through personal contact, meetings, and written reports between managers and subordinates.

---

[17]*Finish Line 1995 Annual Report.*
[18]Eric Schine, "Benefits Are Being Pecked to Death," *Business Week* (December 4, 1995), p. 42.

A key element of supervision is the continued motivation of employees. **Job motivation** is the drive within people to attain work-related goals. The role of supervision is to motivate employees to achieve company objectives and thereby harness human energy to the retailer's needs. As one astute grocery store owner noted, "We need to keep the staff happy because they're the first line of defense when customers come into the store."[19]

Several theories of motivation have been developed. Three of them are McGregor's Theory X and Theory Y, Herzberg's theory of satisfiers and dissatisfiers, and Theory Z (popularized by the Japanese and now in growing use in the United States).

Theory X is the traditional view of motivation and has been applied to lower-level retail positions:

■ Management is responsible for organizing money, materials, equipment, and people resources.

■ Personnel should be directed, motivated, controlled, and modified in accordance with the needs of the organization.

■ Management must actively intervene with personnel; otherwise, people are passive and resistant to organizational needs.

■ The average worker lacks ambition, dislikes responsibility, and prefers to be led.

■ The average worker is self-centered and resistant to change.[20]

Theory Y is a more modern view of motivation and applies to all levels of retail personnel:

■ Management is responsible for organizing money, materials, equipment, and people resources.

■ People are not by nature passive or resistant to organizational needs.

■ Motivation, potential for development, capacity for assuming responsibility, and readiness to achieve company goals are all present in people. Management must make it possible for people to recognize and develop their abilities.

■ The essential management task is to arrange the organizational environment so employees can achieve their own goals by directing their efforts toward company objectives.[21]

Theory X assumes employees must be closely supervised and controlled, and economic inducements motivate. Theory Y assumes workers can be self-managers and be given authority, motivation is social and psychological, and management is decentralized and participatory.

Herzberg's theory offers another perspective on motivation. It says the factors involved in producing job satisfaction and motivation (satisfiers) differ from those leading to job dissatisfaction (dissatisfiers). Factors that can cause job satisfaction are achievement, recognition for achievement, the job itself, responsibility, and growth or advancement. Factors that can lead to job dissatisfaction are worker unhappiness with company policies and their administration, the supervision method, interpersonal relations, work conditions, salary, and job security.[22]

---

[19]Phaedra Hise, "The Motivational Employee-Satisfaction Questionnaire," *Inc.* (February 1994), p. 73. See also Shankar Ganesan and Barton A. Weitz, "The Impact of Staffing Policies on Retail Buyer Job Attitudes and Behavior," *Journal of Retailing*, Vol. 72 (Spring 1996), pp. 31–56.

[20]Douglas McGregor, "The Human Side of Enterprise" in Warren G. Bennis and Edgar Schein (Editors), *Leadership and Motivation: Essays of Douglas McGregor* (Cambridge, Mass.: MIT Press, 1966).

[21]Ibid.

[22]Frederick Herzberg, "One More Time: How Do You Motivate Employees?" *Harvard Business Review*, Vol. 46 (January–February 1968), pp. 53–62.

Starbucks Sets Rules for Workers of Foreign Suppliers

Starbucks Coffee recently developed basic guidelines aimed at improving labor conditions for workers at its foreign coffee suppliers. The guidelines require that foreign suppliers compensate workers at levels that "address the basic needs of workers and their families." The code allows the use of child labor only when it does not "interfere with mandated education," and it addresses the need for suppliers to help workers gain "access to safe housing, clean water, and health facilities and services."

Many multinationals have codes of conduct involving manufacturing workers in foreign nations, but the Starbucks code is believed to be the first instance involving an agricultural commodity. Starbucks acknowledges being "prodded" into developing a human rights policy by protesters concerned about poor working conditions at Guatemala coffee plantations.

Although the code is seen by most observers as a positive development, Starbucks does not have any plans to punish suppliers that do not uphold the code. A Starbucks spokesperson acknowledged that, "It's going to take a long time to improve conditions for agricultural workers" and that child labor, poor sanitary conditions, and near-subsistence wages are common in many foreign countries. The Starbucks code can also be contrasted with labels used by German, Dutch, and British coffee importers that certify their beans were picked by workers that earned a fair share of coffee profits.

Source: G. Pascal Zachary, "Starbucks Asks Foreign Suppliers to Improve Working Conditions," *Wall Street Journal* (October 23, 1995), p. B4.

Theory Z adapts elements from Theory Y and Herzberg's theory, but advocates more employee involvement in defining their jobs and sharing decision making with management. There is mutual loyalty between the firm and its workers, and both parties enthusiastically cooperate for the long-term benefit of each.[23] Though Theory Z has been most widely used by manufacturers in the United States, retailer applications are growing. Here are examples:

> Starbucks treats its employees quite well. The pay—$6 to $8 an hour—is better than with most entry-level food-service jobs. The firm also offers health insurance to all employees, even part-timers. Then there are the stock options. The fact that most workers leave before a single share vests makes it an affordable proposition, but it's a generous policy. Yes, it's self-serving: The temperature of every latte and the cachet of the "Starbucks experience" are entirely in its workers' hands. Starbucks has enacted several methods for its Gen Xers to talk to headquarters: E-mail, suggestion cards, regular forums. And it acts quickly on issues important to young people, like using recycling bins and improving living conditions in coffee-growing nations.[24]

> Carol DeJardin and Gary Smith, owners of two Thriftway supermarkets (one in West Linn, Oregon, and the other in Williamette, Oregon), encourage their managers and employees to exercise initiative when it comes to operations and customer service. Together with DeJardin and Smith, managers set their own gross margins, sales volumes, and labor percentages. They also buy, hire, do employee reviews, and participate in decisions about whom to promote. Employees are urged to search for ways to improve the shopping experience, whether it means solving a problem, making good on an exchange of a product, or simply serving customers cheerfully. DeJardin and Smith have a name for this: "Positively Outrageous Service." At the same time,

[23]William Ouchi, *Theory Z* (Reading, Mass.: Addison-Wesley, 1981).
[24]Jennifer Reese, "Starbucks: Inside the Coffee Cult," *Fortune* (December 9, 1996), p. 196.

DeJardin and Smith try to treat employees royally. They provide union-scale wages, benefits, and profit-sharing. Work schedules are posted two weeks ahead of time, so workers can request changes.[25]

Unlike most retailers that might relocate a store manager or operations chief, Home Depot moves management teams from existing markets into new communities, transferring its corporate culture across the continent. Besides the store manager, there are as many as eight assistant managers and more than a dozen department supervisors who make the move. They do all the screening and interviewing, hiring the best applicants and making sure the new associates reflect the diversity of the community, while they are paid the best wages in the industry.[26]

It is critical that supervision motivates employees in a manner yielding job satisfaction, low turnover, low absenteeism, and high productivity.

[25]Stephen Bennett, "People Who Serve People," *Progressive Grocer* (March 1993), p. 58.
[26]*Home Depot 1995 Annual Report.*

Summary

1. *To study the procedures involved in setting up a retail organization* A retail organization structures and assigns tasks, policies, resources, authority, responsibilities, and rewards to efficiently and effectively satisfy the needs of a firm's target market, employees, and management. There are five steps in setting up an organization: outlining specific tasks to be performed in a distribution channel, dividing tasks among channel members and customers, grouping tasks into jobs, classifying jobs, and integrating positions by an organization chart.

Specific tasks include buying, shipping, receiving, checking, pricing, and marking merchandise; inventory control; display preparation; facilities maintenance; research; customer contact and follow-up; personnel management; merchandise repairs; finances and credit; gift wrapping; delivery; returns; forecasting; and coordination. These tasks may be divided among retailers, manufacturers, wholesalers, specialists, and customers.

Tasks are next grouped into jobs, such as sales personnel, cashiers, inventory personnel, display personnel, credit personnel, customer service personnel, janitorial personnel, and management. Then jobs are categorized by functional, product, geographic, or combination classifications. Finally, an organization chart graphically displays the hierarchy of authority and the relationship among jobs, and it coordinates personnel.

2. *To examine the various organizational arrangements utilized in retailing* Retail organization structures differ by institutional type. Small independents generally use simple organizations, with little specialization. Many department stores use a version of the Mazur plan, whereby they separate functions into four categories: merchandising, publicity, store management, and accounting and control. The equal-store format, a version of the Mazur plan, is used by numerous chain stores. Diversified firms have very complex organizations.

3. *To consider the special human resource environment of retailing* Retailers have a unique human resource environment due to the large number of inexperienced workers, long hours, highly visible employees, many part-time workers, and variations in customer demand.

4. *To describe the principles and practices involved with the human resource management process in retailing* This process comprises several interrelated activities: recruitment, selection, training, compensation, and supervision. In applying the process, diversity, labor laws, and employee privacy should be kept in mind.

Recruitment is the activity of generating job applicants. Sources include educational institutions, channel members, competitors, ads, employment agencies, unsolicited applicants, and current and former employees.

The selection of retail personnel requires thorough job analysis, creating job descriptions, using application blanks, interviews, testing (optional), reference checking, and physical exams. After personnel are selected, they go through pre-training (job orientation) and job training. Effective training revolves around identifying needs, devising proper methods, and evaluating the results. Training is usually necessary for continuing, as well as new personnel.

Employees are compensated by direct monetary payments and/or indirect payments. The alternative direct compensation plans are straight salary, straight commission, and salary plus commission and/or bonus. Indirect payments involve such items as paid vacations, health benefits, and retirement plans. The latter issues are now much more controversial.

Supervision and motivation are needed to gain good employee performance. Supervision can be provided through personal contact, meetings, and written reports. Motivation theories include McGregor's Theory X and Theory Y, Herzberg's satisfiers-dissatisfiers, and Theory Z.

Key Terms

retail organization (p. 347)
hierarchy of authority (p. 351)
flat organization (p. 352)
tall organization (p. 352)
organization chart (p.352)
Mazur plan (p. 354)
mother hen with branch store
  chickens organization (p. 356)
separate store organization
  (p. 356)
equal store organization (p. 356)

diversified retailer (p. 358)
human resource management
  (p. 359)
human resource management
  process (p. 362)
recruitment (p. 363)
job analysis (p. 363)
traditional job description (p. 364)
goal-oriented job description
  (p. 364)
application blank (p. 364)

weighted application blank (p. 364)
pre-training (p. 366)
training programs (p. 366)
compensation (p. 369)
supervision (p. 370)
job motivation (p. 371)
Theory X (p. 371)
Theory Y (p. 371)
Herzberg's theory (p. 371)
Theory Z (p. 372)

Questions for Discussion

1. Cite at least 5 objectives a small retailer should take into consideration when setting up its organization structure.
2. Why are employee needs important in developing a retail organization?
3. Are the steps involved in setting up a retail organization the same for small and large retailers? Explain your answer.
4. Present a 5-item checklist that could be used in assigning tasks to members in a retail channel of distribution.
5. How would the hierarchy of authority in a flat organization differ from that in a tall organization? What are the potential ramifications?
6. What are the pros and cons of analyzing a retailer on the basis of its organization chart?
7. Describe the greatest similarities and differences in the organization structures of small independents, department stores, chain retailers, and diversified retailers.

8. How would small and large retailers act differently for each of the following?
   a. Diversity.
   b. Recruitment.
   c. Selection.
   d. Training.
   e. Compensation.
   f. Supervision.
9. Why are the job description and the application blank so important in employee selection?
10. What problems can occur while interviewing and testing prospective employees?
11. Present a plan for the ongoing training of both existing lower-level and middle-management-level employees without making it seem punitive.
12. Describe the goals of a compensation plan (both direct and indirect components) in a retail setting.
13. Under what circumstances should Theory X be used? Theory Y?
14. Comment on Herzberg's theory of satisfiers and dissatisfiers, and contrast it with Theory Z.

Web-Based Exercise:

AMERICAN SOCIETY FOR TRAINING AND DEVELOPMENT

(http://www.astd.org)

Questions

1. Read one of the articles from the latest issue of *Training and Development* magazine that is available at this Web site. Apply this article to your college bookstore.
2. Review the training statistics contained in the Web site that relate to costs, training time, and size of training staffs. Prepare a brief report based on this data.

3. What types of retailers should have the highest training costs? The lowest training costs? Explain your answer.
4. Read a research paper on job analysis and classification at the Web site. (First select "Training Research," then "Job Analysis, Classification, and Personality," and then "Job Analysis/ Classification.") Relate this paper to a department store retailer.

CASE 1

The Department Store Debate Over Sales Commissions*

Macy's East recently changed the sales compensation program for its sales associates in women's sportswear, domestics, and accessories from a commission system (which was used since the late 1980s) to a compensation system that uses a base hourly rate plus a quarterly bonus. According to a spokesperson for Federated Department Stores, Macy's parent company, this form of compensation will "cultivate a more seasoned, better informed corps of sales personnel." However, Macy's will continue to compensate salespeople in furniture, men's tailored clothing, and shoes on a commission basis. Macy's shift to the use of a salary-based system is another development in the long-standing debate over the effect of sales compensation systems on both a store's profitability and the quality of customer service.

There are several conditions under which a salary-based compensation system works best. One consultant says a salary-based plan is most appropriate when a retailer can determine that its sales are due to its store location or its merchandise, rather than the efforts of the sales associate. A salary-based system also better ensures that customers are not sold more than what they need or that short-term sales are not rewarded at the cost of long-term customer satisfaction. In one well-publicized case, Sears auto service personnel misused their commission-based compensation system by selling unnecessary auto services to unsuspecting motorists. These incidents had a long-term effect on Sears' credibility. Lastly, a commission-based sales compensation plan might have a negative impact on employee morale. As one retail consultant remarked, "Unfortunately, most sales commission plans tend to put employees in competition with each other—a system that does not foster teamwork and can result in poor customer service." This competition may relate to which employee works more trafficked store hours, who contacts loyal customers, or the roles of part-time versus full-time salespeople. For example, since part-time salespeople generally work during peak sales periods and do not perform administrative responsibilities, they could be better compensated than full-time personnel on a commission plan.

Those who favor the use of sales commissions commonly cite the success of Nordstrom (which has used a storewide commission-based plan for years) and Bloomingdale's (which started using sales commissions in selected departments in 1989). Nordstrom's use of commissions has allowed the firm to hire better personnel and to

*The material in this case is drawn from Susan Reda, "Department Stores Debate Sales Commission System," *Stores* (November 1996), pp. 37–38.

CASE 1
(Continued)

motivate them through sales commissions. Unlike at other retailers where sales commission plans may result in lower customer service, Nordstrom has developed and instilled a corporate culture where customer service and salesperson incentives work hand-in-hand. Even though they are not paid for doing so, Nordstrom salespeople routinely deliver products to a customer's home or office, arrange for a merchandise exchange or credit, and contact select customers when their favorite designer's clothes first arrive at the store.

To ensure that Bloomingdale's commissioned sales force continues to perform customer service responsibilities and store maintenance tasks (such as straightening merchandise and cleaning fitting rooms), Bloomingdale's continually coaches its staff on the importance of these duties. According to Bloomingdale's vice-president of personnel and labor relations, to be effective, a commission rate should be at least 20 percent of a salesperson's base pay. However, a sales commission system also has to safeguard against an employee's getting additional compensation with little or no extra effort.

Like Macy's, Bloomingdale's has a straight commission plan for sales personnel in certain departments (such as men's, women's, and designer apparel; shoes; better handbags; and furniture). In contrast, sales personnel in departments such as housewares, tabletops, and domestics are paid on the basis of a salary.

Questions
1. Under what conditions would you recommend that a department store switch from a salary-based compensation plan to a commission-based plan?
2. Under what conditions would you recommend that a department store switch from a commission-based compensation plan to a salary-based compensation plan?
3. To reduce friction between its full- and part-time salespeople who were paid on commission, Bloomingdale's chose to only use full-time salespeople in commission-based departments. Evaluate this strategy.
4. What are the pros and cons of using both salary- and commission-based plans in the same store?

CASE 2
Supervalu:
Performance
Appraisal[†]

Supervalu (http://www.supervalu-intl.com) is the second-largest food U.S. wholesaler, after Fleming. Supervalu supplies about 4,100 supermarkets in 48 states with grocery and nongrocery items. It also operates about 280 company-owned stores.

Supervalu uses a management-by-objectives (MBO) process in evaluating its buyers and other key personnel. This process is based on (1) the establishment of clear priorities, (2) a results orientation, (3) an appreciation of the critical skills needed to succeed, and (4) joint discussions between employees and their managers. To reduce ambiguity, goals are quantified, whenever possible.

Advocates of MBO programs say this method of performance appraisal results in an employee having a good understanding of management's expectations, as well as an ability to judge his/her level of success. Furthermore, as an active participant in the creation of their own personal objectives, an employee is more likely to accept the goals as fair.

This case describes Supervalu's performance-appraisal process by focusing on Bill Edwards, a Supervalu buyer, and Teresa Harrison, his supervisor. The discussion covers one year—from their meeting to discuss suitable objectives for the upcoming year to the recent meeting in which Edwards was evaluated.

A year ago, as part of an MBO-based performance-appraisal process, Bill Edwards and Teresa Harrison mutually agreed to hold Edwards accountable for fulfilling these specific goals for the forthcoming year: improving gross profits, increasing inventory turnover, reducing the number of vendor complaints, and building and sustaining good vendor relations in his department. Each of these goals was quantified.

[†]The material in this case is drawn from data supplied by Supervalu.

Two incidents are noteworthy in portraying Edwards' performance during the year. In one incident, he initiated a meeting with one of Supervalu's major suppliers, to complain about late deliveries and back orders. Although Edwards ultimately resolved the problem, some ill will was created when he initially suggested that Supervalu temporarily switch vendors until the supplier could resolve the problem. In another situation, Edwards initially refused to immediately inspect damaged freight at a loading dock. Instead, he tried to get the loading dock supervisor to accept the freight "as is," arguing that ultimately it would be accepted in its damaged condition by his customers. Only after he was reminded that this was against company policy, did Edwards work out another solution to the problem.

About eleven months after their initial meeting (when Edwards and Harrison agreed on Edwards' goals for the year), Harrison began to prepare for his performance evaluation meeting. She gathered information from a variety of sources, including financial data from Edwards' department, letters from vendors, specific behavior that Harrison had observed, and information from Edwards' co-workers.

One letter she received indicated that Edwards had done "an outstanding job in getting products needed quickly" and that Edwards' "ideas are original and fresh." Another letter, however, was critical. It noted that "he has discounted the firm's needs, and has sidestepped Supervalu's management policies. Edwards has a success at any price mentality." Harrison decided to call Sara Karnsby, one of Edwards' co-workers, to inquire about his performance. Karnsby's evaluation of Edwards was somewhat mixed. These are some of the comments she made: "Bill's been a lot better lately, in that he has great ideas and is more organized. But he is still hard for us to deal with sometimes." "While Bill is light on detail work, he gets things done. His customers really like him."

In commenting about a particularly difficult problem associated with Bill Edwards, Sara Karnsby told Teresa Harrison about a major holiday promotion when Edwards did not get an order to a supplier on time. Edwards tried to cover up the problem by purchasing another firm's products, even though the alternate product did not meet the client store's high-quality standards.

At the annual performance evaluation, Edwards was very upset that he was only judged as "average" on overall performance. He said he had "made his numbers," worked hard, established relations with vendors, and demonstrated his creativity. While Harrison agreed with him that he had made his numbers, she was critical of his human relations skills. She was especially concerned about his relations with his co-workers and his vendors—and his domineering personality.

As part of the MBO process for the next year, Edwards and Harrison have agreed that his key area for development will involve building human relations skills. They plan to meet in two months to discuss what he has learned from attending a special training seminar on negotiating skills and how he will apply the material to his job.

Questions
1. Describe the pros and cons of an MBO system of employee assessment.
2. Describe the relationship between an MBO evaluation system and a goal-oriented job description.
3. How can this appraisal system be tied into the development and evaluation of management training programs?
4. Was Edwards fairly evaluated? Explain your answer.

Video Questions on Supervalu
1. Evaluate Supervalu's performance-appraisal system.
2. What other suggestions could Harrison have given Edwards?

12

Operations Management: Financial Dimensions

1. To define operations management
2. To discuss profit planning
3. To describe asset management, including the strategic profit model and other key business ratios
4. To look at retail budgeting
5. To examine resource allocation

Although 1995 was a poor year for many retailers that went out of business (such as Fayva, Jamesway, and Woodward) and for others that closed selected stores (such as Edison Brothers, Kmart, and Petrie Stores), it was a banner year for the industry's "undertakers"—retail liquidators. These firms thrive by selling the unsold inventory that exists after other retailers go under or shut certain stores. Liquidators buy leftover inventory, hold "going-out-of-business" sales, and hope to make a good profit (due to the low costs of merchandise to them). In 1995, retail liquidators sold about $3 billion to $5 billion of goods, roughly two times the 1994 level.

There are several large retail liquidators, such as Gordon Brothers, Schottenstein, Nassi Bernstein, and Alco. All of them are well known to retailers, but they have low visibility with consumers—despite their large size and importance. For example, Gordon Brothers, based in Boston, has liquidated 800 stores, including Jamesway (a regional discount store chain) and Fayva (a shoe chain). Schottenstein, based in Columbus, Ohio, has liquidated 362 Edison Brothers stores and 198 selected Petrie Stores.

Retail liquidators perform a key function for troubled retailers who are looking to stay in business. They pay cash up front for unsold inventories, thereby enabling retailer managers to focus all their energies on their chains' best stores. While a retailer can run its own "going-out-of business" sale, it is hard to price broken lots and out-of-season merchandise. Furthermore, much effort is needed to successfully run these sales.

The retail liquidating business is a complex one. Markdowns have to be properly timed to encourage shoppers to return and to maximize the retailer's revenues (markdowns generally start at 20 percent off and go to as high as 90 percent off in a store's final days). A store's employees (who will be out of work after the sale ends) need to be given incentives that favor their continuing to work during the liquidation rather than seek another job.

Two major problems affecting the liquidation industry are the increased competition and consumer reaction to retail liquidations. Due to increased competition, retail liquidators are forced to raise their offers for merchandise. However, the liquidator's profitability is limited because many consumers have grown accustomed to half-price sales at traditional retailers.[1]

[1]Lori Bongiorno, "Everything Must Go—To the Liquidators," *Business Week* (January 15, 1996), p. 52.

Once a retailer devises an organization structure and forms a human resource management plan, it concentrates on **operations management**—the efficient and effective implementation of the policies and tasks necessary to satisfy the firm's customers, employees, and management (and stockholders, if a publicly owned company).

The way retailers operate their businesses has a major impact on sales and profitability. For example, large inventory levels, long store hours, expensive fixtures, extensive customer services, and heavy advertising may encourage consumers to shop and lead to higher sales volume. But at what cost? If a store pays night-shift salaries 25 percent more than day-shift salaries, is being open 24 hours per day worthwhile (do the increased sales justify the costs and add to overall profit)?

This chapter covers the financial aspects of operations management, with emphasis on profit planning, asset management, budgeting, and resource allocation. The operational dimensions of operations management are explored in detail in Chapter 13.

A **profit-and-loss (income) statement** represents a summary of a retailer's revenues and expenses over a particular period of time, usually on a monthly, quarterly, and/or yearly basis. It lets the retailer review its overall and specific revenues and costs during similar periods (for example, January 1, 1997 to December 31, 1997, versus January 1, 1996 to December 31, 1996), as well as analyze profitability. By having frequent profit-and-loss statements, a firm can monitor its progress toward goals, update performance estimates, and revise strategies and tactics.

In comparing profit-and-loss performance over time, it is crucial that the same time periods be used (such as the fourth quarter of 1997 with the fourth quarter of 1996) due to seasonality considerations. The retailer should also note that some yearly periods may have an unequal number of weeks (such as 53 weeks in one fiscal year versus 52 weeks in another). In addition, retailers that have increased the number of stores or the square footage of existing stores between accounting periods should take into account the larger facilities in their analysis. Thus, yearly sales growth should reflect both the total revenue growth and the rise in same-store sales.

A profit-and-loss statement consists of these major components:

■ **Net sales**—The revenues received by a retailer during a given time period after deducting customer returns, markdowns, and employee discounts.
■ **Cost of goods sold**—The amount a retailer has paid to acquire the merchandise sold during a given time period. It is based on purchase prices and freight charges, less all discounts (such as quantity, cash, and promotion).
■ **Gross profit (margin)**—The difference between net sales and the cost of goods sold; it consists of operating expenses plus net profit.
■ **Operating expenses**—The cost of running a retail business.
■ **Net profit before taxes**—The profit earned after all costs have been deducted.

Table 12-1 shows an annual profit-and-loss statement for Donna's Gift Shop, an independent retailer. These observations can be made from the table:

■ Donna's net sales were $220,000—computed by deducting returns, markdowns on the items sold, and employee discounts from total sales.
■ Donna's cost of goods sold was computed by taking the total purchase amount for the merchandise sold, adding freight charges, and subtracting quantity, cash, and promotion discounts. The cost of goods sold was $120,000.
■ Donna's gross profit was $100,000, calculated by subtracting the cost of goods sold from net sales. This sum was used for operating and other expenses, with the remainder accounting for net profit and the payment of local, state, and federal taxes.

Table 12-1 DONNA'S GIFT SHOP, 1997 PROFIT-AND-LOSS STATEMENT		
Net sales	$220,000	
Cost of goods sold	$120,000	
Gross profit		$100,000
Operating expenses:		
Salaries	$50,000	
Advertising	3,300	
Supplies	1,100	
Shipping	1,000	
Insurance	3,000	
Maintenance	3,400	
Other	1,700	
Total	$63,500	
Other costs	$17,500	
Total costs		$ 81,000
Net profit before taxes		$ 19,000

- Donna's operating expenses included salaries, advertising, supplies, shipping, insurance, maintenance, and other operating costs—for a total of $63,500.
- Donna's unassigned costs were $17,500.
- Donna's net profit before taxes was $19,000, computed by deducting total costs of $81,000 from gross profit. This amount covered federal, state, and local taxes, as well as profits.

Overall, 1997 was a pretty good year for Donna; her personal salary was $35,000 and the store's before-tax profit was $19,000. A further analysis of Donna's Gift Shop's profit-and-loss statement will be conducted in the budgeting section of this chapter.

ASSET MANAGEMENT

Each retailer has various assets to manage and liabilities to control. This section presents the basic components of a retailer's balance sheet, and describes the strategic profit model and other key business ratios.

A **balance sheet** itemizes a retailer's assets, liabilities, and net worth at a specific point in time; it is based on the principle that assets = liabilities + net worth. Table 12-2 has a balance sheet for Donna's Gift Shop.

Assets are any items a retailer owns with a monetary value. Current assets consist of cash on hand (or in the bank) and items readily converted to cash in the short run, such as inventory on hand (or in transit to the retailer) and accounts receivable (amounts owed to the retailer by customers). Fixed assets comprise property, buildings (a retail store, a warehouse, and so on), store fixtures, and equipment such as cash registers and trucks; these are used in operations for a long time period. The major fixed asset for many retailers is real estate.

Unlike current assets, which are recorded on a balance sheet on the basis of cost, fixed assets are recorded on the basis of cost less accumulated depreciation. This may create some difficulties in asset management, as records may not accurately reflect the true value of a firm's assets. For instance, many retailing analysts use the term **hidden assets** to describe depreciated assets, such as store buildings and warehouses, that are reflected on a retailer's balance sheet at low values relative to their actual worth. In some instances, investors are enticed to acquire retailers because of the high value of these hidden assets.

Liabilities are any financial obligations a retailer incurs in operating a business. Current liabilities comprise payroll expenses payable, taxes payable, accounts payable

At European Car Dealers: How Do You Make Money?

Europe has about 90,000 car dealers versus about 23,000 in the United States, and 17,000 in Japan. As a result, the average European car dealer sells less than one-third the number of cars as its U.S. counterpart and one-half the number of the typical Japanese dealer. These low volumes require European dealers to have large profit margins per unit. According to one Europe-based consultant, "Sales and distribution costs currently account for one-third of the final retail price of a car. This ratio can't be sustained."

The competition in many European cities is now so intense that consumers can easily purchase some brands (particularly Ford and Opel models) at 15 percent off list price. Dealers cannot survive long-term by selling new cars at these price levels. Although several dealers have begun to push used and "nearly new" cars that have higher profit margins, alternate channels such as Internet-based sales by car rental firms have developed for these autos.

European dealers increasingly complain of being squeezed by manufacturers that are anxious to cut their costs, by consumers looking for a good deal, and by new laws that permit European Union citizens to purchase cars outside their home countries. Some analysts suggest that, because of these factors, thousands of European car dealerships could close by the end of this decade.

Source: Brandon Mitchener, "Europe's Car Dealers Face Tough Bargain," *Wall Street Journal* (June 28, 1996), p. B10F.

(amounts owed to suppliers), and short-term loans; these must be paid in the coming year. Fixed liabilities comprise mortgages and long-term loans; these are generally repaid over several years.

A retailer's **net worth** is computed as assets minus liabilities. It is also called owner's equity and represents the value of a business after deducting all financial obligations.

In operations management, the retailer's goal is to use its assets in the manner providing the best results possible. There are three basic, commonly accepted, ways to measure those results: net profit margin, asset turnover, and financial leverage. Each component is discussed next.

Net profit margin is a performance measure based on a retailer's net profit and net sales:

$$\text{Net profit margin} = \frac{\text{Net profit}}{\text{Net sales}}$$

Table 12-2 A RETAIL BALANCE SHEET FOR DONNA'S GIFT SHOP (AS OF DECEMBER 31, 1997)

Assets			**Liabilities**		
Current:			Current:		
Cash on hand	$ 13,300		Payroll expenses payable	$ 4,000	
Inventory	24,100		Taxes payable	9,000	
Accounts receivable	1,100		Accounts payable	21,400	
Total		$ 38,500	Short-term loan	700	
			Total		$ 35,100
Fixed (present value):					
Property	$125,000		Fixed:		
Building	42,000		Mortgage	$65,000	
Store fixtures	9,700		Long-term loan	4,500	
Equipment	1,700		Total		$ 69,500
Total		$178,400			
			Total liabilities		$104,600
Total assets		$216,900			
			Net Worth		$112,300
			Liabilities + net worth		$216,900

In the case of Donna's Gift Shop, the net profit margin was a little over 8.6 percent; for a gift shop, this is a very good percentage. To enhance its profit margin, a retailer could seek to either increase its gross profit as a percentage of sales or reduce its operating expenses as a percentage of sales.[2] The firm could seek to raise its gross profits through opportunistic buying, selling exclusive product lines, avoiding price competition by having excellent customer service, minimizing markdowns because of more focused buying, and selling a mix of goods with high profit margins. A retailer could reduce operating expenses by emphasizing self-service, lowering personnel costs (by better scheduling and automation), refinancing a mortgage to take advantage of lower interest rates, cutting energy costs, and so on. However, a firm would have to be careful not to lessen customer service to the extent that sales and profit would decline.

Asset turnover is a performance measure based on a retailer's net sales and total assets:

$$\text{Asset turnover} = \frac{\text{Net sales}}{\text{Total assets}}$$

At Donna's Gift Shop, asset turnover was very low, 1.0143, meaning the store averaged $1.01 in sales per dollar of total assets. To improve its asset turnover ratio, a firm would have to generate increased sales by the same level of assets or keep the same sales with a reduced asset base. A firm might increase sales by opening longer hours, accepting mail-order sales, training employees to cross-sell additional products to consumers, or stocking well-known national brands instead of local brands. None of these tactics requires the asset base to be expanded. Or a firm might maintain sales on a lower asset base by moving to a smaller store (less wasted space), simplifying fixtures (or having suppliers install and own fixtures), keeping a more basic inventory on hand, and negotiating with property owners for them to pay part of the costs of a renovation.

By looking at the relationship between a retailer's net profit margin and its asset turnover, **return on assets (ROA)** can be computed:

$$\text{Return on assets} = \text{Net profit margin} \times \text{Asset turnover:}$$

$$\text{Return on assets} = \frac{\text{Net profit}}{\text{Net sales}} \times \frac{\text{Net sales}}{\text{Total assets}}$$

$$= \frac{\text{Net profit}}{\text{Total assets}}$$

Thus, Donna's Gift Shop had an ROA of 8.8 percent, computed as:

$$= .0864 \times 1.0143 = 0.0876 = 8.8\%$$

This return on assets is below average for gift stores because the firm's good net profit margin does not adequately offset its low asset turnover.

Financial leverage is a performance measure based on the relationship between a retailer's total assets and net worth:

$$\text{Financial leverage} = \frac{\text{Total assets}}{\text{Net worth}}$$

Donna's Gift Shop had a financial leverage ratio of 1.9314. This means assets were just under double Donna's net worth, and total liabilities and net worth were almost equal. As a result, Donna's financial leverage was a little above average for U.S. gift stores (which are rather conservative as a group). Yet, the store is in no danger.

A retailer with a high financial leverage ratio has a lot of debt, while a ratio of 1 means it has no debt—assets equal net worth. If the ratio is too high, there may be too much focus on cost-cutting and short-run sales so as to make large interest payments on a periodic basis; net profit margins may suffer due to interest charges; and a firm may even be forced into bankruptcy if debts cannot be paid in an orderly way.[3] See Figure 12-1.

[2]See Douglas J. Tigert, "The Profit Wedge: Key to Successful Retailing," *Chain Store Age* (January 1995), pp. 46–59.
[3]See Michael Hartnett, "Chains Take Chapter 11 Path to New Beginnings," *Stores* (January 1996), pp. 22–23.

Figure 12-1

The Rise and Fall of Merry-Go-Round Enterprises

Merry-Go-Round (MGR) grew from one store in the 1960s to a 1,450-store chain — featuring young men's and women's clothing and accessories — in 44 states under the Merry-Go-Round, Cignal, Dejaiz, and Chess King names in the 1990s. However, to finance expansion, MGR was highly leveraged (meaning the debt-to-equity ratio was high) and this led to tough times. In 1993, it suffered huge losses, mostly from slow-moving merchandise. This placed MGR in "technical violation" of some credit agreements, which specified it had to comply with certain working capital allowances and its assets-to-current debt ratio had to be a minimum figure. Thus, MGR could not gain credit approval for spring 1994 orders; and vendors refused to ship goods. MGR then filed for Chapter 11 bankruptcy protection so it could continue in business without paying its existing creditors and get out of leases at poor store locations. Unfortunately, it could not overcome its excessive debt and went out of business in 1996.

Over the last 15 years or so, the use of the **leveraged buyout (LBO),** whereby a retail ownership change is mostly financed by loans from banks, investors, and others, has had a major effect on retail budgeting and cash flow. One study found that over half of the revenues of publicly owned food-based retailers came from firms with high levels of leverage.[4]

At times, because debts incurred in LBOs can be excessive, some large retailers have had to concentrate more on covering the interest on their debts than in investing in their businesses; have had to run sales to generate cash to cover operating costs and to buy new merchandise; and have had to sell stores to pay off debt. Among those whose operations in the 1990s have been affected by LBOs are Macy's, Ralphs, Stop & Shop, Montgomery Ward, Pathmark, Carter Hawley Hale, and Revco. In their weakened state, some of these firms have been acquired by others (such as Macy's acquisition by Federated Department Stores). Safeway, which was involved in an LBO, has done well by cutting costs, reducing prices, and improving customer service. Although its financial leverage remains high, its 1995 ratio of 6.53 was much lower than its 1992 ratio of 21.50.[5]

---

[4]Steve Weinstein, "The Legacy of Leverage," *Progressive Grocer* (June 1993), pp. 70–76.
[5]"The 50 Largest Retailing Companies," *Fortune* (May 31, 1993), p. 220; and "The Fortune 500 Largest U.S. Corporations," *Fortune* (April 29, 1996), pp. F3–F4.

On the other hand, if financial leverage is too low, a retailer may be too conservative. It may limit its ability to renovate existing stores and to expand to new markets. In general, leverage would be too low if owner's equity is relatively high, and that equity could be partly replaced by increasing short- and long-term loans or accounts payable. Some equity funds could be taken out of a business by the owner (stockholders, if a public firm).

The Strategic Profit Model

The mathematical relationship among net profit margin, asset turnover, and financial leverage is expressed by the **strategic profit model,** which results in a performance measure known as **return on net worth.** See Figure 12-2. The strategic profit model can be used in planning or controlling assets. For instance, a retailer could learn that the major cause of its poor return on net worth is less-than-satisfactory asset turnover or too low financial leverage.

According to the strategic profit model, a retailer can increase its return on net worth by raising its net profit margin, asset turnover, or financial leverage. Because these measures are multiplied to determine a firm's return on net worth, a doubling of any of them—as an example—would result in the doubling of a firm's return on net worth.

This is how the strategic profit model can be applied to Donna's Gift Shop:

$$\text{Return on net worth} = \frac{\text{Net profit}}{\text{Net sales}} \times \frac{\text{Net sales}}{\text{Total assets}} \times \frac{\text{Total assets}}{\text{Net worth}}$$

$$= \frac{\$19,000}{\$220,000} \times \frac{\$220,000}{\$216,900} \times \frac{\$216,900}{\$112,300}$$

$$= .0864 \times 1.0143 \times 1.9314$$

$$= .1692 = 16.9\%$$

Overall, Donna's return on net worth was about average for all gift stores.

Table 12-3 applies the strategic profit model to various retailers. In evaluating the data in this table, it is best to make comparisons among the firms within given retail institutional categories. For example, the net profit margins of clothing retailers such as The Gap, Inc. and The Limited, Inc. have historically been much higher than those of supermarket chains. Because the financial performance of individual retailers differs from year to year, caution is advised in studying these data.

A comparison of Service Merchandise and Toys "Я" Us shows Service Merchandise's 1995 return on net worth was far superior to that of Toys "Я" Us. Yet, an analysis of the components of the strategic profit model reveals Service Merchandise's better return on net worth was largely due to high financial leverage. If Service Merchandise's financial leverage was 1.96 (the same as for Toys "Я" Us) and its net profit margin and asset turnover were as indicated in Table 12-3, its return on net worth would only have been 5.07 percent (1.25% × 2.07 × 1.96). This would have placed it 0.77 percent above Toys "Я" Us' 4.30, instead of 8.70 percent ahead.

The data on the home improvement stores indicate that although Home Depot and Lowe's each had a 1995 return on net worth of 14 percent to 15 percent, the chains had different factors leading to their results. Home Depot's net profit margin and asset turnover were both better than Lowe's, but Lowe's financial leverage was greater than Home Depot's. Thus, for instance, Lowe's could seek a better net profit margin. Yet, in trying to improve its profit margin, Lowe's must be careful not to adversely affect asset turnover. Higher prices might lead to lower inventory turnover.

Figure 12-2

The Strategic Profit Model

Table 12-3 APPLICATION OF STRATEGIC PROFIT MODEL TO SELECTED RETAILERS, 1995 DATA

Retailer	Net Profit Margin	×	Asset Turnover	×	Financial Leverage	=	Return on Net Worth
General Merchandise							
Discount-Oriented							
Wal-Mart	2.93%		2.47		2.57		18.56%
Service Merchandise	1.25		2.07		5.02		13.00
Toys "Я" Us	1.57		1.40		1.96		4.30
Kmart	−1.65		2.25		2.92		−10.81
Department Stores							
J.C. Penney	3.91		1.25		2.91		14.24
Nordstrom	4.01		1.51		1.92		11.60
Dillard's	2.74		1.28		1.93		6.74
Federated	0.50		1.05		3.35		1.74
Specialty Clothing							
The Limited, Inc.	12.20		1.50		1.64		30.03
The Gap, Inc.	8.05		1.88		1.43		21.58
Home Improvement							
Home Depot	4.73		2.10		1.47		14.67
Lowe's	3.19		1.99		2.15		13.64
Food-Based							
Safeway	1.99		3.16		6.53		41.02
Albertson's	3.69		3.04		2.12		23.82
Winn-Dixie	1.97		4.75		2.00		18.71
Publix	2.56		3.70		1.58		14.99
American Stores	1.73		2.49		3.13		13.46
Giant Food	2.55		2.61		1.88		12.47
Vons	1.34		2.32		3.51		10.93

Note: There are small rounding errors in the last column.

Source: Computed by the authors from data in "The Fortune 500 Largest U.S. Corporations," *Fortune* (April 29, 1996), pp. F1–F19.

The Impact of Consumer Bankruptcies on Retailers

Since 1993, the rate at which consumers have filed for personal bankruptcy has continuously risen. For example, during the fourth quarter of 1995, the increase in consumer bankruptcy filings rose more than 20 percent above the number of filings for the corresponding quarter of 1994. Besides the bankruptcies, the consumer debt owed to the average creditor went from about $750 in 1991 to $1,800 in 1996.

Consumers can apply for bankruptcy protection under either Chapter 7 or Chapter 13 of the U.S. Bankruptcy Code. Chapter 7 is used by consumers who lack the financial resources to repay their debts; these consumers want a bankruptcy court to release them from their debt. Chapter 13 is used by consumers who are overextended and want to pay their creditors under a structured plan. Many retailers have seen double-digit increases in both forms of bankruptcy. As a result, many retailers have encountered sharp increases in bad debts.

One theory accounting for the increase in bankruptcies is that there is no longer a social stigma associated with bankruptcy. In other cases, consumers have used Bankruptcy Code rulings to avoid payment. Since bankruptcy courts will not discharge debts made within 90 days of a bankruptcy filing, these consumers stop adding debt 90 days prior to filing for bankruptcy.

Source: Patricia A. Murphy, "Federal Panel Mulls Reforms as Consumer Bankruptcy Rate Soars," *Stores* (May 1996), pp. 69–70.

Other Key Business Ratios

Other key business ratios may also be used to measure a retailer's success or failure in reaching particular performance standards. Such ratios have a strong impact on a firm's short- and long-run performance. Accordingly, here are the definitions of several key business ratios (besides those covered in the preceding discussion):

■ Quick ratio—cash plus accounts receivable divided by total current liabilities, those due within one year. It shows a retailer's liquidity. A ratio greater than 1 to 1 means the firm is liquid and therefore easily able to cover short-term liabilities.
■ Current ratio—total current assets (including cash, accounts and notes receivable, merchandise inventories, and marketable securities) divided by total current liabilities. A ratio of 2 to 1 or more is considered good.
■ Collection period—accounts receivable divided by net sales and then multiplied by 365. It measures the quality of accounts receivable (the amounts due, but not yet paid by customers). In general, when most sales are on credit, any collection period one-third or more over normal selling terms (such as 40.0 for 30-day credit arrangements) means slow-turning receivables.
■ Accounts payable to net sales—accounts payable divided by annual net sales. This compares how a retailer pays suppliers relative to volume transacted. A figure above the industry average may indicate a firm relies on suppliers to finance operations.
■ Overall gross profit—net sales minus the cost of goods sold and then divided by net sales. This net firmwide average takes markdowns, discounts, and shortages into account. It is used by retailers to cover both operating costs and net profit.[6]

Table 12-4 presents several median key business ratios—including net profit margin, asset turnover, and return on net worth—for a number of retailer categories. From this table, a hardware store manager or owner would learn that the industry average is an extremely poor quick ratio of 0.7; liquid assets are less than current liabilities. The current ratio of 3.2 is quite good, mostly because of the value of inventory on hand. The collection period of 19.0 days is moderate, considering that many small purchases are paid for by cash. Accounts payable of 5.1 percent of sales is good. The overall gross profit of 32.4 percent would be used to cover both operating costs and profit. The net profit margin of 2.6 percent is a rather low figure for nonfood retailing. The asset turnover ratio is conservative, 2.2, another indicator of the value of inventory. The return on net worth percentage of 9.6 is quite low. In sum, on average, hardware stores require high inventory and other investments and yield low to medium returns.

BUDGETING

Budgeting outlines a retailer's planned expenditures for a given time period based on its expected performance. In this way, a firm's costs can be linked to satisfying target market, employee, and management goals. For example, what should planned personnel costs be if a firm wants a certain level of customer service, such as no shopper waiting in a checkout line for more than ten minutes? What compensation level should be planned to motivate salespeople? What total planned expenses will let management generate satisfactory revenues and reach profit goals?

There are several reasons why a retailer should methodically devise a budget:

■ Expenditures are clearly related to expected performance, and costs can be adjusted as goals are revised. This enhances productivity.
■ Resources are allocated to the appropriate departments, product categories, and so on.

[6]*Industry Norms and Key Business Ratios: Desk-Top Edition 1995–96* (New York: Dun & Bradstreet, 1996).

Table 12-4 MEDIAN KEY BUSINESS RATIOS FOR SELECTED RETAILER CATEGORIES, 1995

Line of Business	Quick Ratio (times)	Current Ratio (times)	Collection Period (days)	Accounts Payable to Net Sales (%)	Overall Gross Profit (%)[a]	Net Profit Margin (%)	Asset Turnover (times)	Return on Net Worth (%)
Auto & home supply stores	0.9	2.4	24.1	6.5	34.1	2.3	2.8	11.3
Car dealers	0.2	1.3	5.5	0.8	12.5	1.4	4.4	25.2
Department stores	1.3	3.9	16.8	4.8	33.0	1.5	2.0	5.3
Direct-selling companies	0.9	1.6	29.8	3.2	43.8	4.7	3.5	22.5
Drug & proprietary stores	1.0	2.9	15.7	4.3	26.5	2.5	3.9	14.5
Eating places	0.6	1.2	4.0	3.1	52.1	3.7	3.2	21.9
Family clothing stores	1.0	4.8	12.4	4.4	34.6	4.1	2.0	10.0
Florists	1.0	1.9	21.5	4.2	50.8	3.9	3.2	20.6
Furniture stores	0.9	2.8	23.4	5.2	36.6	3.1	2.4	10.8
Gasoline service stations	0.8	1.6	6.6	2.9	18.3	1.3	5.2	15.8
Gift, novelty, & souvenir shops	0.7	3.2	5.8	4.2	41.6	4.6	2.2	17.6
Grocery stores	0.6	1.9	2.6	2.9	21.6	1.3	5.1	13.4
Hardware stores	0.7	3.2	19.0	5.1	32.4	2.6	2.2	9.6
Hobby, toy, & game shops	0.7	3.3	2.6	5.4	40.3	3.7	2.6	15.3
Jewelry stores	0.7	3.0	21.9	9.3	43.6	3.9	1.6	10.4
Lumber & other materials dealers	1.2	2.7	34.0	4.7	24.9	2.3	2.8	10.7
Mail-order firms	0.8	2.3	18.3	6.4	40.6	2.7	3.1	18.2
Men's & boys' clothing stores	0.7	3.4	11.0	5.4	38.3	3.2	2.1	11.0
Radio, TV, & electronics stores	0.6	2.1	12.4	5.4	33.9	3.3	3.0	17.5
Sewing & needlework stores	0.5	3.5	5.3	5.9	40.6	2.9	2.3	8.3
Shoe stores	0.5	3.3	5.1	6.3	36.8	3.9	2.3	13.6
Sporting-goods & bicycle stores	0.5	2.5	6.6	7.2	33.2	3.9	2.6	16.8
Variety stores	0.6	3.3	6.2	5.0	34.4	2.3	2.6	11.0
Vending machine operators	0.4	1.0	3.3	3.3	46.4	2.4	3.1	17.8
Women's clothing stores	0.9	3.8	11.3	4.1	36.2	3.6	2.6	12.2

[a]Gross margins are reported as means rather than medians and represent net figures, which take into account all deductions (such as markdowns, discounts, and shortages).

Source: *Industry Norms and Key Business Ratios: Desk-Top Edition 1995–96* (New York: Dun & Bradstreet, 1996), pp. 160–177. Reprinted by permission.

■ Expenditures for various departments, product categories, and so on are coordinated.

■ Because management plans in a structured and integrated manner, the goal of efficiency can be given more prominence.

■ Cost standards are set, such as advertising equals 5 percent of sales.

■ A firm prepares for the future rather than reacts to it.

■ Expenditures are monitored during a budget cycle. For example, if a firm allocates $50,000 to buy new merchandise over a budget cycle, and it has spent $33,000 on such items halfway through that cycle, it has planned expenditures of $17,000 remaining.

■ A firm can analyze the differences between its expected and actual costs and performance.

■ A firm's expected and actual costs and performance can be contrasted with industry averages. For instance, how do a specialty store chain's total net operating expenses as a percentage of sales compare to the industry average?

In setting a budget, a retailer should consider the effort and time involved in the process, recognize that expectations may not be fully accurate (due to unexpected consumer demand, competitors' tactics, and so on), and be willing to modify plans as needed. It should not let itself become overly conservative (or inflexible) or simply add a percentage to each current expense category to arrive at the next year's budget, such as increasing expenditures by 3 percent across the board based on an anticipated sales growth of 3 percent.

The budgeting process is shown in Figure 12-3 and described next.

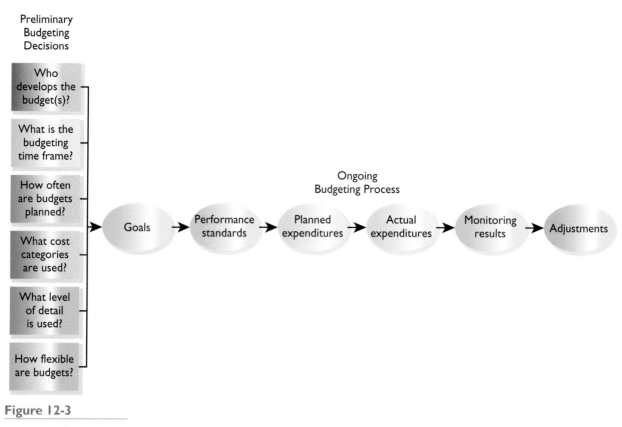

Figure 12-3

The Retail Budgeting Process

Preliminary Budgeting Decisions

A retailer must make six preliminary budgeting decisions.

First, the person(s) responsible for budgeting decisions is specified. Top-down budgeting places financial decisions with upper management; these decisions are then communicated down the line to succeeding levels of managers. Bottom-up budgeting requires lower-level executives to develop budget requests for their departments; these requests are then assembled, and an overall companywide budget is designed. With top-down budgeting, senior management centrally directs and controls budgets. With bottom-up budgeting, varied perspectives are included, managers are held accountable for their own decisions, and employee morale is enhanced. For these reasons, many firms combine aspects of the two approaches.

Second, the budgeting time frame is defined. Most firms set budgets with yearly, quarterly, and monthly components. Annual spending is then planned, while expected versus actual costs and performance are reviewed on a regular basis. As a result, a firm controls overall costs and responds to seasonal or other fluctuations. Sometimes, the time frame can be longer than a year or shorter than a month. For example, when a retailer decides to open a number of new stores over a five-year period, it specifies capital expenditures (property, construction, and other investment costs) for the entire five years. And when a supermarket chain such as Safeway orders milk, baked goods, and other perishable goods, it has daily or weekly budgets for each item.

Third, the frequency with which budgets are planned is determined. Though many retailers review their budgets on a regular, ongoing basis, the great majority of companies plan them once a year. In some firms, several months may be set aside each year for the budgeting process to be undertaken; this lets all participants have ample time to gather data and enables retailers to take their budgets through several drafts before giving final approval.

Fourth, cost categories are established:

- Capital expenditures involve major long-term investments in land, buildings, fixtures, and equipment. Operating expenditures include the short-term selling and administrative expenses of running a retail business.
- Fixed costs are those remaining relatively constant for the period of a budget, such as store security expenses and real-estate taxes, regardless of the retailer's performance. Variable costs are those related to the firm's performance over the budget period, such as sales commissions. If performance is high, these expenses often rise.
- Direct costs are incurred by specific departments, product categories, and so on, such as the earnings of department-based salespeople and cashiers. Indirect costs such as store windows and centralized cashiers are shared by multiple departments, product categories, and so on.
- Natural account expenses are reported by the names of the costs, such as salaries, and not assigned by their purpose. Functional account expenses are classified on the basis of the purpose or activity for which expenditures are made, such as cashier salaries.

Tables 12-5 and 12-6 show the expense categories set by the National Retail Federation. Note: Individual firms may use different categories from those in the tables, and for some retailers, certain categories may not be proper (such as executive office and central wrapping and packing expenses for a small retailer).

Fifth, the level of budgeting detail is ascertained. For example, should planned expenditures be allocated by department (such as produce), product category (such as fresh fruit), product subcategory (such as apples), or product item (such as McIntosh apples)? If a retailer has a very detailed budget, it must be sure every expense subcategory is adequately covered.

Sixth, the amount of flexibility in the budget is prescribed. On the one hand, a budget should be rigid enough to serve its purpose in guiding planned expenditures and linking costs to goals. On the other hand, a budget that is too inflexible would not let a retailer

Table 12-5	NATURAL ACCOUNT EXPENSE CATEGORIES
01	Payroll
03	Media costs
04	Taxes
06	Supplies
07	Services purchased
08	Other
09	Travel
10	Communications
11	Pensions
12	Insurance
13	Depreciation
14	Professional services
16	Bad debts
17	Equipment rentals
20	Real property rentals
90	Expense transfers (net)
92	Credits and outside revenues

Source: Alexandra Moran (Editor), *FOR 1996 Edition* (New York: Wiley, 1996).

adapt to changing market conditions, capitalize on unexpected opportunities, and/or minimize the costs associated with a strategy poorly received by the target market. Many retailers express their budget flexibility in quantitative terms. Thus, a buyer could be allowed to increase his or her quarterly budget by a certain maximum percentage if customer demand is higher than anticipated.

Ongoing Budgeting Process

After preliminary budgeting decisions are made, the retailer engages in the ongoing budgeting process shown in Figure 12-3:

- Goals are set. These goals are based on customer, employee, and management needs (as discussed in Chapter 11).
- Performance standards to achieve these goals are specified. Such standards include customer service levels, the compensation amounts needed to motivate employees and minimize personnel turnover, and the sales and profit levels needed to satisfy management. Frequently, the budget is related to a sales forecast, which is a projection of expected revenues for the next budget period. Forecasts are usually broken down by department or product category.
- Expenditures are planned in terms of performance goals. In **zero-based budgeting,** a firm starts each new budget from scratch and outlines the expenditures needed to reach that period's goals. All costs must be justified each time a budget is done. With **incremental budgeting,** a firm uses current and past budgets as guides and adds or subtracts from these budgets to arrive at the coming period's expenditures. Most retailers apply incremental budgeting because it is easier to use, less time-consuming, and less risky.
- Actual expenditures are made. The retailer pays rent and employee salaries, buys merchandise, places advertisements, and so on.
- Results are monitored. This involves two types of analysis. One, actual expenditures are compared with planned expenditures for each expense category previously specified by the retailer, and reasons for any deviations are reviewed. Two, the firm determines whether or not goals and performance standards have been met and tries to explain any deviations.
- The budget is adjusted. Major or minor revisions in the original budget are made, depending on how closely a firm has come to reaching goals. The funds allotted to some expense categories may be reduced, while greater funds may be provided to other categories.

Table 12-6 FUNCTIONAL ACCOUNT EXPENSE CATEGORIES[a]

010		Total property and equipment
	020	Buildings and equipment
	030	Furniture and fixtures
100		Total company management
	110	Executive office
	130	Branch management
	140	Internal audit
	150	Legal and consumer activities
200		Total accounting and management information
	210	Control management
	220	Sales audit
	230	Accounts payable
	240	Payroll
	280	Data processing
300		Total credit and accounts receivable
	310	Credit management
	330	Collection
	340	Accounts receivable and bill adjustment
	350	Cash office
	360	Branch store offices
400		Total sales promotion
	410	Sales promotion management
	420	Advertising
	430	Shows, special events, and exhibits
	440	Display
500		Total service and operations
	510	Services and operations management
	530	Security
	550	Telephones and communications
	560	Utilities
	570	Housekeeping
	580	Maintenance and repairs
600		Total personnel
	610	Personnel management
	620	Employment
	640	Training
	660	Medical and other employee services
	670	Supplementary benefits
700		Total merchandise receiving, storage, and distribution
	710	Management of merchandise receiving, storage, and distribution
	720	Receiving and marking
	730	Reserve stock shortage
	750	Shuttle services
800		Total selling and supporting services
	810	Selling supervision
	820	Direct selling
	830	Customer services
	840	Selling support services
	860	Central wrapping and packing
	880	Delivery
900		Total merchandising
	910	Merchandising management
	920	Buying
	930	Merchandising control

[a]These are also known as expense centers.

Source: Alexandra Moran (Editor), *FOR 1996 Edition* (New York: Wiley, 1996).

Table 12-7   DONNA'S GIFT SHOP, 1997 BUDGETED VERSUS ACTUAL PROFIT-AND-LOSS STATEMENT (IN DOLLARS)

	Budgeted		Actual		Variance[a]	
Net sales	$200,000		$220,000		+$20,000	
Cost of goods sold	$110,000		$120,000		−$10,000	
Gross profit		$90,000		$100,000		+$10,000
Operating expenses:						
Salaries	$ 50,000		$ 50,000		—	
Advertising	3,500		3,300		+$ 200	
Supplies	1,200		1,100		+$ 100	
Shipping	900		1,000		−$ 100	
Insurance	3,000		3,000		—	
Maintenance	3,400		3,400		—	
Other	2,000		1,700		+$ 300	
Total	$ 64,000		$ 63,500		+$ 500	
Other costs	$ 17,500		$ 17,500		—	
Total costs		$81,500		$ 81,000		+$ 500
Net profit before taxes		$ 8,500		$ 19,000		+$10,500

[a]Variance is a positive number if actual sales or profits are higher than expected or actual expenses are lower than expected. Variance is a negative number if actual sales or profits are lower than expected or actual expenses are higher than expected.

Table 12-7 compares budgeted (planned) and actual revenues, expenses, and profits for Donna's Gift Shop in 1997. The actual data come from Table 12-1, which was discussed earlier. The variance figures in Table 12-7 compare expected and actual results for each profit-and-loss item. Variances are positive numbers if actual performance is better than expected and negative numbers if performance is worse than planned. As the table indicates, net profit before taxes was $10,500 higher than anticipated. Actual sales turned out to be $20,000 higher than expected; thus, the cost of goods sold was $10,000 more than anticipated. Yet, because of solid cost controls, actual operating expenses were $500 lower than expected.

Table 12-8 recomputes the actual performance data in Table 12-7 to yield a percentage profit-and-loss statement for Donna's Gift Shop. A percentage profit-and-loss (income) statement summarizes a retailer's revenues and expenses for a specific period of time, with data expressed as percents of net sales. This statement lets a firm set goals and performance standards— and evaluate budgeted versus actual performance—on a perent-of-sales basis. As can be seen, actual net profit before taxes was 8.64 percent of sales; this compares very favorably to the planned level of 4.25 percent. Most of the increased net profit before taxes was due to actual operating costs being 40.75 percent of sales versus planned operating costs of 36.81 percent of sales.

In planning and applying a budget, a firm must carefully consider **cash flow,** which relates the amount and timing of revenues received to the amount and timing of expenditures made during a specific time period. In cash flow management, the intention is usually to make sure revenues are received prior to expenditures being made.[7] Otherwise, short-term loans may have to be taken or profits tied up in a business to pay off inventory expenses and so on. For seasonal businesses, this may be unavoidable. According to the Small Business Administration, underestimating costs and overestimating revenues, both of which affect cash flow, are the leading causes of new-business failures. Table 12-9 has two examples of cash flow.

[7]See Robert A. Mamis, "Money In, Money Out," *Inc.* (March 1993), pp. 96–103.

Table 12-8 DONNA'S GIFT SHOP, 1997 BUDGETED VERSUS ACTUAL PROFIT-AND-LOSS STATEMENT (EXPRESSED AS A PERCENT OF SALES)

	Budgeted		Actual	
Net sales	100.00		100.00	
Cost of goods sold	55.00		54.55	
Gross profit		45.00		45.45
Operating expenses:				
Salaries	25.00		22.73	
Advertising	1.75		1.50	
Supplies	0.60		0.50	
Shipping	0.45		0.45	
Insurance	1.50		1.36	
Maintenance	1.70		1.55	
Other	1.00		0.77	
Total	32.00		28.86	
Other costs	8.75		7.95	
Total costs		40.75		36.81
Net profit before taxes		4.25		8.64

Table 12-9 THE EFFECTS OF CASH FLOW

A. A retailer has rather consistent sales throughout the year. Therefore, the cash flow in any given month is positive. This means no short-term loans are needed, and the owner can withdraw funds from the firm if she so desires:

Linda's Luncheonette, Cash Flow for January

Cash inflow:		
Net sales		$11,000
Cash outflow:		
Cost of goods sold	$2,500	
Operating expenses	3,500	
Other costs	2,000	
Total		$ 8,000
Positive cash flow		$ 3,000

B. A retailer has highly seasonal sales that peak in December. Yet, to have a good assortment of merchandise on hand during December, it must order merchandise in September and October and pay for it in November. As a result, it has a negative cash flow in November that must be financed by a short-term loan. All debts are paid off in January, after the peak selling season is completed:

Dave's Party Favors, Cash Flow for November

Cash inflow:		
Net sales		$14,000
Cash outflow:		
Cost of goods sold	$12,500	
Operating expenses	3,000	
Other costs	2,100	
Total		$17,600
Negative cash flow		−$ 3,600
Short-term loan (to be paid off in January)		$ 3,600

**RESOURCE
ALLOCATION**

In allotting financial resources, a retailer should examine both the magnitude of various costs and productivity. Each has significance for asset management and budgeting.

The Magnitude of Various Costs

As we noted earlier, retail expenditures can be divided into capital and operating categories. **Capital expenditures** are the long-term investments in fixed assets. **Operating expenditures** are the short-term selling and administrative costs of running a business. Before making decisions, it is imperative to have a sense of the magnitude of various capital and operating costs. These examples illustrate this point.

In 1996, these were the average capital expenditures for erecting a single store for a range of retailers. The amounts include the basic building shell; heating, ventilation, and air-conditioning; lighting; flooring; fixtures; ceilings; interior and exterior signage; and roofing:

■ Supermarket—$2.9 million.
■ Department store—$8.4 million.
■ Full-line discount store—$3.5 million.
■ Apparel specialty store—$655,000.
■ Drugstore—$850,000.
■ Home center—$1.8 million.[8]

Thus, a typical home center chain must be prepared to invest $1.8 million to build each new outlet (which averaged 44,750 square feet industrywide in 1996) it opens. This does not include land and merchandise costs, and the total could be higher if a larger than average store is built.

Besides new-building construction costs, remodeling can also be expensive. Remodeling is prompted by competitive pressures, mergers and acquisitions, consumer trends, the requirement of complying with Title II of the Americans with Disabilities Act, environmental concerns, and other factors.

To reduce their investments, some retailers insist that real-estate developers help pay for building, renovating, and fixturing costs. These demands by retail tenants reflect the oversaturation of some areas, the increased retail space that is available due to the bankruptcy of some retailers (as well as mergers), and the increased interest by developers in gaining retailers that generate consumer traffic (such as category killers). For example, Oshman's Sporting Goods requires that developers contribute capital to its new-store locations. And 50-Off Stores, Inc., a general merchandise discounter, asks for construction allowances from landlords to help defray the costs of improvements to leased space.

Regarding operating expenses, these costs are usually expressed as a percentage of sales and range from an average of 22 percent in supermarkets to over 40 percent in some specialty stores. To succeed, a firm's operating costs must be in line with competitors'. May Department Stores has an edge over many rivals due to lower SGA (selling, general, and administrative expenses as a percentage of sales): May, 17 percent; J.C. Penney, 24 percent; Sears, 24 percent; Nordstrom, 26 percent; Proffitt's, 27 percent; and Federated, 30 percent.[9]

Resource allocation must also take opportunity costs into account. **Opportunity costs** involve forgoing possible benefits that may occur if a retailer could make expenditures in another opportunity rather than the one chosen. For example, if a supermarket chain decides to renovate ten existing stores at a total cost of $2.9 million, it would be unable to open a new outlet requiring a $2.9 million investment (excluding land and merchandise costs). Because financial resources are finite, firms often face either/or decisions. In this case, if the super-

[8]Estimated by the authors from Marianne Wilson, "Construction Costs Inch Downward," *Chain Store Age* (July 1996), pp. 81–84.
[9]Standard & Poor's, "Department Store SGA," *Stores* (October 1996), p. 108.

The ROI Challenge with Store Renovations

A recent study by the TRADE Retail Division of Deloitte & Touche found that the average payback time for a store renovation varies from a low of 19 months with family apparel stores such as Eddie Bauer and The Gap to 240 months (20 years) for large discount stores such as Wal-Mart and Kmart. Payback times are 27 months for small discount department stores and 65 months for women's apparel specialty stores.

The study used matched pairs of stores, with one store having been renovated two to three years before and the other having not been remodeled. Sales, gross margins, and other data on the renovated and non-renovated stores were compared for the time period from two years prior to the renovations to two years subsequent to them. Four to five chains were studied under each retail classification, and each chain was required to supply data on 4 to 12 pairs of stores. Retail participants were also asked to list their reasons for undertaking renovations.

Large discount stores had an average annual return of 6 percent or less on their store renovation investments, versus returns of 61 percent to 67 percent at family apparel specialty stores. While the large discount stores undertook renovations mostly in response to a new competitor, the family apparel stores generally carried out renovations to update their stores and to reposition their merchandise mix.

Source: Susan Reda, "Renovation's Returns," *Stores* (June 1995), pp. 22–24.

market chain expects to earn greater profits by renovating than by building a new store, the latter becomes a lost opportunity—at least for now.

Productivity

Due to erratic sales, mixed economic growth, rising labor costs, increasing competition, and other factors over the last several years, many retailers are now placing greater priority on improving **productivity,** the efficiency with which a retail strategy is carried out. The key question is: How can sales and profit goals be reached while keeping control over costs?

Productivity can be described in terms of costs as a percentage of sales, the time it takes a cashier to complete a transaction, the percentage of customers a salesperson sees in an average day who actually make purchases, profit margins, sales per square foot, inventory turnover, sales growth, and so on. For each of these measures, productivity goals would require a firm to apply its strategy as efficiently as possible.

Because different retail strategy mixes have distinct resource needs in terms of store location, fixtures, the level of personnel, and other elements, productivity measures must be related to norms for each type of strategy mix (like department stores versus full-line discount stores). Sales growth should also be measured on the basis of comparable seasons, using the same stores as in previous periods. Otherwise, the data will be affected by seasonality and/or the increased square footage of stores. For instance, the productivity of Builders Square stores can be evaluated by comparing its sales per square foot with key competitors. Thus, although its stores average about $16 million in annual sales, Home Depot stores average $41 million in the same size facility.[10] This suggests that Builders Square's asset management is weak relative to Home Depot.

Circuit City actually operates four different superstore prototypes with square footage and merchandise assortments tailored to population and volume expectations for specific trade areas: "With these formats, the company can productively penetrate virtually every market in the United States. The 'D' format was developed in fiscal 1995 to serve the most populous trade areas. Selling space in the 'D' format averages

[10]"State of the Industry," *Chain Store Age* (August 1996), Section Two, pp. 20A–21A.

23,000 square feet with total square footage averaging 42,242. 'D' stores offer the largest merchandise assortment of all the formats. The 'C' format constitutes the largest percent of the store base. Selling square footage in this format has been increased during the last several years, and new 'C' stores typically have about 17,000 square feet of selling space. Total square footage for all 'C' stores averages 33,828. The 'B' format often is located in smaller markets or in trade areas on the fringes of larger metropolitan markets. Selling space in these stores averages approximately 11,000 square feet with an average total square footage of 24,685. The 'B' stores offer a broad merchandise assortment that maximizes return on investment in these lower volume areas. The 'A' format serves the least populated trade areas. Selling space averages approximately 9,000 square feet, and total square footage averages 18,026. 'A' stores feature a layout, staffing levels, and merchandise assortment that create high productivity in the smallest markets."[11]

In general, productivity can be enhanced in two ways. A firm can improve employee performance, sales per foot of shelf space, and other factors by enhancing training programs, increasing advertising, and so on. And/or it can reduce costs by automating, requiring suppliers to do certain tasks, taking advantage of quantity discounts, seeking cheaper suppliers, being flexible in operations, and so on. An example would be a firm employing a small core of full-time workers during nonpeak times and supplementing them with many part-time workers during its peak periods.

Retailers need to consider that productivity must not be measured just from a cost-cutting perspective. Excessive cost-cutting can undermine customer loyalty. This happened a few years ago to Rally's, a Louisville, Kentucky, fast-food franchisor, when it sought to reduce operating costs by developing a new burger that was 20 percent smaller than its predecessor and consisted of frozen—rather than fresh—meat. Although the new burger recipe and Rally's reduction in advertising (from 8 percent of sales to 4.9 percent) helped the firm reduce costs as a percent of sales, sales slipped by 4 percent. At the same time, a competitor increased its market share by 5 percent. In addition, some franchisees decided to refuse to sell the smaller-size burger.[12]

These are two strategies that retailers have used to raise productivity:

■ Department stores such as Sears are paying more attention to space productivity. Sears has cleared hundreds of thousands of square feet of space in its stores, by moving some furniture departments into freestanding stores, converting space that was previously used by its affiliated home-improvement contractors to retail use, and better managing and displaying its merchandise categories.

■ Tuesday Morning Corporation, a seller of quality closeout merchandise, opens its stores for only four sales events each year. The stores are not in use when there are no sales events, other than to house inventory and to restock for the next sales event.[13] Operating costs are low because the stores save on labor expenses (part-time workers are used extensively), utilities, insurance, and so on. The firm further reduces its costs by locating in low-rent sites. The firm realizes it operates destination stores that are sought out by loyal customers.

As one supermarket industry analyst observed, "If you're not completely sure what your organizational goals ought to be or the costs associated with achieving those goals, and you have not devised accurate measurements to assess your progress either internally and/or with your trading partners, it's difficult to achieve the desired productivity."[14]

[11]*Circuit City 1996 Annual Report.*

[12]Claire Poole, "Easy on the Beef," *Forbes* (March 15, 1993), p. 74.

[13]See David P. Schulz, "Tuesday Morning Revamps Distribution System," *Stores* (June 1995), p. 50; and "Tuesday Morning Upgrade Raises Productivity," *Chain Store Age* (March 1996), pp. 36–37.

[14]Ryan Matthews, "The Final Frontier," *Progressive Grocer* (September 1996), p. 69.

Summary

1. *To define operations management* Operations management involves efficiently and effectively implementing the tasks and policies to satisfy the retailer's customers, employees, and management. This chapter covered the financial aspects of operations management. Operational dimensions are studied in Chapter 13.

2. *To discuss profit planning* The profit-and-loss (income) statement summarizes a retailer's revenues and expenses over a specific period of time, typically on a monthly, quarterly, and/or yearly basis. It consists of these major components: net sales, cost of goods sold, gross profit (margin), operating expenses, and net profit before taxes.

3. *To describe asset management, including the strategic profit model and other key business ratios* Each retailer has various assets and liabilities to manage. A balance sheet itemizes a retailer's assets, liabilities, and net worth at a specific point in time. Assets are any items with a monetary value owned by a retailer; some assets appreciate and may have a hidden value. Liabilities are financial obligations incurred in running a business. The retailer's net worth, also known as owner's equity, is computed as assets minus liabilities.

The results of asset management may be measured by reviewing a firm's net profit margin, asset turnover, and financial leverage. Net profit margin equals net profit divided by net sales. Asset turnover equals net sales divided by total assets. By multiplying the net profit margin by asset turnover, a retailer can determine its return on assets—which is based on net sales, net profit, and total assets. Financial leverage equals total assets divided by net worth. With leveraged buyouts (LBOs), firms may take on too much debt.

The strategic profit model incorporates asset turnover, profit margin, and financial leverage to yield a measure known as return on net worth. As an overall measure, with three specific components, it

allows a retailer to better plan or control its asset management.

These are among the other key ratios with which retailers should be familiar: quick ratio, current ratio, collection period, accounts payable to net sales, and overall gross margin.

4. *To look at retail budgeting* Budgeting outlines a retailer's planned expenditures for a given time period based on its expected performance; costs are linked to satisfying goals.

There are six preliminary decisions. First, responsibility is defined by top-down and/or bottom-up arrangements. Second, the time frame is specified. Third, the frequency of budget planning is set. Fourth, cost categories are established. Fifth, the level of detail is ascertained. Sixth, the amount of flexibility is determined.

The ongoing budgeting process then proceeds: goals, performance standards, planned expenditures, actual expenditures, monitoring results, and adjustments. With zero-based budgeting, each new budget starts from scratch; with incremental budgeting, current and past budgets serve as guides. The budgeted versus actual profit-and-loss (income) statement and the percentage profit-and-loss (income) statement are vital budgeting tools. In all budgeting decisions, the impact of cash flow, which relates the amount and timing of revenues received with the amount and timing of expenditures made, must be considered.

5. *To examine resource allocation* In resource allocation, both the magnitude of costs and productivity need to be examined. Costs can be divided into capital and operating categories; the amount of both must be regularly reviewed. Opportunity costs involve forgoing possible benefits that may occur if a retailer could invest in an opportunity other than the one chosen. Productivity is the efficiency with which a retail strategy is carried out; the goal is to maximize sales and profits while keeping costs in check.

Key Terms

operations management (p. 379)
profit-and-loss (income) statement (p. 379)
net sales (p. 379)
cost of goods sold (p. 379)

gross profit (margin) (p. 379)
operating expenses (p. 379)
net profit before taxes (p. 379)
balance sheet (p. 380)
assets (p. 380)

hidden assets (p. 380)
liabilities (p. 380)
net worth (p. 381)
net profit margin (p. 381)
asset turnover (p. 382)

Questions for Discussion

1. Describe the relationship of assets, liabilities, and net worth for a retailer. How is a balance sheet useful in examining these items?
2. A retailer has net sales of $650,000, net profit of $50,000, total assets of $550,000, and a net worth of $200,000.
   a. Calculate net profit margin, asset turnover, and return on assets.
   b. Compute financial leverage and return on net worth.
   c. Evaluate the financial performance of this retailer.
3. How can a supermarket increase its asset turnover?
4. Is too low a financial leverage necessarily bad? Why or why not?
5. Distinguish among these terms: quick ratio, current ratio, and collection period.
6. Under what circumstances would you recommend bottom-up budgeting rather than top-down budgeting?
7. What is zero-based budgeting? Why do most retailers utilize incremental budgeting, despite its limitations?

8. What is the value of a percentage profit-and-loss statement?
9. What are the disadvantages of a slow-turning accounts receivable?
10. How could a seasonal retailer improve its cash flow situation during periods when it must buy goods for future selling periods?
11. Distinguish between capital spending and operating expenditures. Why is this distinction important to retailers?
12. What factors should retailers consider when assessing opportunity costs?
13. What are several ways for these retailers to improve productivity?
    a. Muffler repair shop.
    b. Small toy store.
    c. Dry cleaner.
    d. Discount apparel store.
14. Comment on Tuesday Morning Corporation's strategy for maximizing its productivity.

Web-Based Exercise:

EDGAR (http://edgar.stern.nyu.edu)

Questions

1. What is EDGAR? Describe some of its features.
2. From the home page of the EDGAR Web site, select "Get Corporate SEC Filings." Then, enter "Boston Chicken, Inc." Describe what pops up on the screen.
3. Choose any two Boston Chicken, Inc. reports from the Web and explain what could be learned from these reports.
4. What could retailers ascertain by using the EDGAR Web site?

It was a month before the spring semester ended, and Lara Daly was thinking about summer jobs while waiting for her retailing class to begin. Daly turned to Tyler Morgan, a classmate and close friend and said, "I'm tired of the usual summer job where I don't get anything out of it except a few dollars an hour. I've only got one summer left before I graduate. This year, I want to be my own boss, get some real work experience, and make more money, too." "That's a great idea. Maybe we can do something together. Let's talk about it after class," Morgan replied.

The in-class discussion that day was on the strategic profit model. That material was so interesting that Daly and Morgan talked about it after class and continued their dialog through lunch together. They knew the strategic profit model concept was an important tool for evaluating a potential business opportunity. Morgan agreed to come up with an interesting retail opportunity which they would further review after the next retailing class.

So, Daly and Morgan met again two days later to discuss a proposed business venture. Daly noted that although she had $500 in the bank, this was her expense money for the fall semester; and she needed to be sure this money would be available at the beginning of the fall semester. Morgan also had $500 to invest; and he could secure a loan for up to $10,000 from his parents (at an interest rate of 6 percent per year), if necessary. Morgan explained to Daly that they both would be equally responsible for repayment of the $10,000, even if the business did not work out. With the loan and their personal savings, they had up to $11,000 for investing in a retail business.

One retail opportunity that seemed particularly attractive to Daly and Morgan was the resale of used cars. Morgan was aware of a local auto auction that specialized in repossessed cars (due to nonpayment of loans). If they were to pursue this venture, the partners would have to obtain a used car dealer's license (at a cost of $300). Regardless of the business venture they would undertake, Lara Daly and Tyler Morgan agreed to name their business, L & T Enterprises.

Daly and Morgan planned to purchase cars at the auction for an average amount of $3,000 and then to quickly resell them through classified ads (costing an average of $200 per car for a two-week ad) for $4,500. While they would "detail" (thoroughly clean, polish, and wax the interior and exterior) the cars and do some of the minor repairs themselves, they agreed to budget an average allowance of $500 per car for necessary parts and repairs.

Daly and Morgan decided to attend each of the four auto auctions held in their area over the summer. They would only bid on cars that were rather easy to sell (such as vans, four-wheel drive vehicles, and station wagons), had low mileage (less than 10,000 miles per year), and were "clean" (with only minor dents and pings), and that had not been involved in a major accident. They also planned to concentrate their bidding on 20 to 30 cars per auction, and to stop bidding on any car when its price was more than two-thirds its average retail value. Morgan thought they would be able to purchase between three and four cars at each of the four summer auctions.

The partners intended to detail, test, and repair each car within a week of taking title, and then to resell each car within two weeks of placing a classified ad for it. Thus, the expected turnaround time for selling each car would be three weeks after the auto's purchase. They could then go to the next auction with additional working capital.

Daly and Morgan wanted to have no more than four cars in inventory at any point in time. This meant that if they sold only two cars between auctions, at the next auction, they could purchase two additional cars. They both felt that restricting the number of cars they bought would assure that they could properly store all cars. This restriction would also facilitate closing L & T Enterprises before the start of classes and paying off their loan.

*This case was prepared and written by Professor William R. Swinyard, Brigham Young University.

CASE 1
(Continued)

Questions

1. Evaluate the auto brokerage business based on the strategic profit model.
2. Develop a projected profit-and-loss statement for L & T Enterprises based on the data presented in this case.
3. Are the financial assumptions used by Daly and Morgan realistic? Explain your answer.
4. Should Daly and Morgan pursue this business opportunity? Explain your answer.

CASE 2
Thomson's Computer Books[†]

Thomson's Computer Books has a reputation for stocking a wide selection of computer books and manuals, including hard-to-find books and technical material. Its customers generally are computer "nerds" who seek specialized texts that are not available elsewhere and consumers seeking computer manuals for current or older versions of major software packages. Many of the latter desire manuals that go beyond the documentation provided by software producers.

Thomson's two stores are about three miles apart in Plainview, a Midwestern city of 200,000 residents. Thomson's North location, consisting of 2,300 square feet, opened October 1, 1994. It is at the center of town in a high-traffic strip center. Four employees work there, three full-time and one part-time. The store has a toll-free number for out-of-town customers, and makes 36 percent of sales to people who live out-of-town (even out-of-state). By appealing to people in a four-state area, Mae and Bill Thomson have been able to lift the sales of this store. Thomson's North has a good following among purchasing agents in the Plainview business community as "the" source for hard-to-find items. Although 35 percent of sales are to institutions, Thomson's North is steadily building its retail traffic as people learn of it and discover its low prices.

Thomson's South store has 1,000 square feet and opened November 1, 1996. It is across the street from a community college with a small bookstore of its own. The neighborhood surrounding the community college is old and stable—a lower-middle-class residential area. One full-time employee works at the South store. Unlike Thomson's other shop, the South store has no real institutional business. The South store is located in a small strip center with four stores and eight parking spots. Although the South store did some fairly effective radio advertising when it opened, its recent advertising by flyers sent to previous customers and new radio spots has had little effect on store traffic or sales. Table 1 contains selected financial data for the two stores for January 1995 through May 1997. Table 2 shows a profit-and-loss statement for each store for 1996.

Bytes 'N Books (BNB) is Thomson's main competitor. It is in a strip shopping center in the central part of the city and has gross sales exceeding $1 million. BNB charges slightly higher prices and occupies 5,000 square feet. Like Thomson's North, BNB has a toll-free phone number for out-of-town customers. BNB also has a separate section for parents to leave their children to entertain themselves with educational software and video games while the parents shop elsewhere in the store. BNB's sales are 20 percent institutional and 80 percent retail. Unlike both Thomson's stores, BNB carries a full line of greeting cards, some stationery items, and some magazines.

Because 40 percent of Plainview's population owns computers or uses them on the job, Mae Thomson believes the sales potential for Thomson's Computer Books has not been fully reached.

Questions

1. Analyze the financial data in Tables 1 and 2.
2. What are the difficulties in evaluating the data in Tables 1 and 2?
3. What should Mae and Bill Thomson do next with the North and South stores? Give separate recommendations for the two stores.
4. Offer short-run and long-run financial goals for each Thomson's store. Explain your answer.

[†]This case was prepared and written by Professor Raymond A. Marquardt and Lynn Samsel, doctoral candidate, University of Nebraska–Lincoln.

CASE 2
(Continued)

Table 1   SELECTED FINANCIAL INFORMATION FOR THOMSON'S COMPUTER BOOKS—NORTH AND SOUTH STORES (JANUARY 1, 1995 TO MAY 31, 1997)

North Store	1995	1996	Five Months Ending May 31, 1997
Net sales	$309,876	$371,864	$137,594
Cost of goods sold	213,008	235,762	87,372
Gross profit	98,868	136,102	50,222
Operating expenses	124,555	127,376	54,804
Net profit (net loss)	(25,687)	8,726	(4,582)

South Store	1995	1996	Five Months Ending May 31, 1997
Net sales	—	$ 3,827	$ 8,998
Cost of goods sold	—	2,635	5,831
Gross profit	—	1,192	3,167
Operating expenses	—	7,568	9,250
Net profit (net loss)	—	(6,376)	(6,083)

Note: The North location opened on October 1,1994; the South store opened on November 1, 1996.

Table 2   PROFIT-AND-LOSS STATEMENTS FOR THOMSON'S COMPUTER BOOKS—NORTH AND SOUTH STORES (FISCAL YEAR 1996)

	North Store	South Store
Sales		
Software manuals/learning aids	$157,920	$ 526
Programming books	53,106	520
General computer books	50,214	1,225
Technical manuals	44,969	934
Wiring diagrams	19,448	264
Computer disks	12,859	217
Computer accessories	5,926	64
Miscellaneous	27,422	77
Total sales	$371,864	$ 3,827
Total cost of goods sold	235,762	2,635
Total gross profit	$136,102	$ 1,192
Operating Expenses		
Wages	$ 39,310	$ 1,954
Rent	31,880	1,045
Advertising and promotion	9,958	256
Freight and postage	6,340	45
Interest expense	5,242	—
Insurance	3,759	—
Taxes and permits	3,541	11
Telephone	3,425	186
Legal and accounting	3,180	332
Utilities	2,999	116
Operating supplies	1,760	165
Office expense	—	3,117
Miscellaneous	15,982	341
Total operating expenses	$127,376	$ 7,568
Total profit (loss)	$ 8,726	($6,376)

13
Operations Management: Operational Dimensions

Sports Authority is one of the leading retailers in terms of developing contingency plans for potential disasters. According to a vice-president at one insurance firm, "Only a well-thought-out emergency plan that assigns responsibilities to trained members of a team can ensure the most effective response, safeguarding staff members' health and safety while preserving company assets." In devising its response plan to natural disasters, Sports Authority has paid particular attention to both weather-related situations and fire. It focuses on weather due to the high incidence of natural disasters and on fire due to an experience at one of its outlets.

Before Hurricane Andrew approached the areas in which it had stores, Sports Authority executives already had prepared an emergency response plan. It included procedures for protection against possible looting and water damage, and for getting its stores running as soon as possible after the hurricane passed by. Although Sports Authority had some financial losses due to the hurricane, "the bill wasn't tremendous and not a dime was lost due to theft," said the vice-president for loss prevention and risk management of a major insurance company.

According to that insurance executive, the Occupational Safety & Health Administration (OSHA) requires that most businesses have emergency response plans covering such areas as evacuation and rescue. In addition, environmental regulations require retailers that stock or dispose of hazardous materials to have special plans.

An emergency response plan for a retailer should have five components:

- **Management commitment**—Managers must be held accountable for being prepared for potential emergencies. Emergency preparedness committees should be comprised of personnel from top management, operations, security, and human resources.
- **Identification of potential hazards**—Among the common hazards a retailer should be prepared for are fire, explosions, natural disasters, water leaks, and mechanical breakdowns.
- **Emergency response team**—Employees need to know which of the firm's resources can be used in an emergency, as well as the response times of local emergency personnel.
- **Employee training**—Appropriate personnel must be trained and regularly retrained.
- **Written plan**—An overall written emergency preparedness plan is needed. Part of the plan should include deciding exactly what constitutes an emergency. The plan should also have a table of contents and tabs so relevant portions can be quickly accessed.[1]

[1]Julie Ritzer Ross, "Preparing for the Worst: Emergency Preparedness Aids Disaster Recovery," *Stores* (May 1996), pp. 74–75.

As defined in Chapter 12, operations management is the efficient and effective imple- **OVERVIEW**
mentation of the policies and tasks that satisfy a retailer's customers, employees, and
management (and stockholders, if publicly owned). And while Chapter 12 examined the
financial dimensions of operations management, this chapter covers the operational
aspects.

For firms to ensure their long-run success, operational areas need to be managed as
well as possible. Thus, for example, a decision to change a store format or to introduce
new anti-theft equipment must be carefully reviewed since these acts could greatly affect
retail performance.

In running their businesses, retail executives make a wide range of operating decisions, **THE**
such as these: **OPERATIONAL DIMENSIONS OF OPERATIONS MANAGEMENT**

- What is the optimal format and size of a store?
- What is the relationship among shelf space, shelf location, and sales for each item in
  the store? How would total store sales change by varying space allocations and shelf
  locations?
- How can personnel best be matched to customer traffic flows? Would increased
  staffing improve or reduce productivity?
- What impact would the use of self-service versus sales personnel have on the sales of
  each product category?
- What effects do the uses of various building materials have on store maintenance?
- How can energy costs be better controlled?
- How can inventory be managed appropriately?
- How can inventory losses due to theft be reduced without disturbing most customers
  or employees?
- What levels of insurance are required?
- How can credit transactions be managed most effectively?
- How can computer systems improve operating efficiency?
- What kinds of crisis management plans should be in place?

In this chapter, we analyze these aspects of operations management: store format
and size, space allocation, personnel utilization, store maintenance, energy management,
inventory management, store security, insurance, credit management, computerization,
and crisis management.

Store Format and Size

With regard to store format, a firm should consider whether productivity would be
raised by such tactics as locating in a planned shopping center rather than in an unplanned business district, using prefabricated materials rather than customized ones in
construction, and/or applying certain kinds of store design and display layouts (as discussed in Chapter 17). As always, decisions must be related to the retail strategy mix. A
crucial store format decision for chain retailers is whether to use **prototype stores,**
whereby multiple outlets conform to relatively uniform construction, layout, and operations standards.

Prototype stores offer several benefits. They make construction and centralized
management control easier, reduce construction costs, let operating methods be standardized, facilitate the interchange of employees among outlets, allow fixtures and
other materials to be bought in quantity, and enforce a consistent chain image. Yet, a
strict reliance on prototypes may lead to inflexibility, failure to adapt to and/or capitalize on local customer needs, and too little creativity. Pep Boys (an auto accessory and

repair center chain), Radio Shack, Toys "Я" Us, Woolworth, fast-food outlets, and various supermarket chains are among those with prototype stores.

Together with prototype stores, some chains use **rationalized retailing** programs that combine a high degree of centralized management control with strict operating procedures for every phase of business. Most aspects of these chains' operations are performed in a virtually identical manner in a number of their outlets. Rigid control and standardization make this technique an easy one to enact and manage. In addition, a firm can add a significant number of units in a rather short time. Radio Shack and Toys "Я" Us both use rationalized retailing. They operate many stores that are similar in size, the number of items carried, store layout, merchandising, and sales approaches to others in that chain.

In their quest to be distinctive, and because of high rents and store saturation in many major metropolitan U.S. markets, various firms use one or both of two contrasting store-size approaches. On the one hand, such retailers as Home Depot, Barnes & Noble, and Sports Authority are opening category-killer-sized stores so they can try to dominate smaller-sized stores by having extensive assortments. To do this, food-based warehouse stores and large discount-oriented stores sometimes situate in secondary sites, where rents are much lower. These stores are confident they can draw customers from large trading areas. Cub Foods (a food-based warehouse chain), Wal-Mart, and others are engaged in this approach.

On the other hand, a number of retailers that believe large stores are not efficient in serving saturated (or small) markets or are now situated in high-rent areas have been opening smaller stores or downsizing existing ones. For instance,

■ Sears is in the midst of an "off the mall" strategy whereby it plans to open 800 Sears Dealer Stores by 1999. These stores have only 4,100 to 6,100 square feet of selling space and are located in such towns as Alamogordo, New Mexico (30,000 population), Charlevoix, Michigan (3,000 population), Peru, Illinois (9,000 population), Temple, Texas (46,000 population), and Warsaw, Indiana (11,000 population). The Dealer Stores are at least 20 miles from the nearest Sears department store, and are owned and operated by local entrepreneurs. The outlets feature appliances, power tools, auto batteries, consumer electronics, lawn and garden items, and repair and maintenance services.[2]

■ In 1996, Sports Authority debuted a new store format called Sports Authority Ltd. in Manhattan. Because of the high rents there, Sports Authority Ltd. outlets are between 12,000 and 17,000 square feet (far smaller than the typical Sports Authority store). Sports Authority Ltd. focuses on sports apparel and athletic footwear, as well as golf, tennis, and exercise equipment—and downplays hunting, fishing, and team sports gear.[3]

Space Allocation

Firms need to place considerable emphasis on allocating store space. They must use facilities as productively as possible and determine the amount of space and its placement for each product category. Sometimes, retailers decide to drop merchandise lines altogether because they occupy too much store space in relation to their sales and profit. That is why J.C. Penney eliminated home electronics, large sporting goods, and photographic equipment from its department stores.

With a **top-down space management approach,** a retailer starts with its total available store space (by outlet and for the overall firm, if a chain), divides the space into categories, and then works on in-store product layouts. This is in contrast to a **bottom-**

[2]David P. Schulz, "Home Centers Cultivate Rural Market," *Stores* (December 1995), pp. 29–30.
[3]"Sports Chains Plan for Long Term," *Discount Store News* (August 5, 1996), pp. 6, 117; and Tony Lisanti, "Retailers Hit the Big Cities, Big Time," *Discount Store News* (September 2, 1996), p. 11.

up space management approach, in which planning starts at the individual product level and then proceeds to the category, total store, and overall company levels.

Micro-merchandising is a strategy whereby a firm adjusts shelf-space allocations to respond to customer and other differences among local markets. Thus, Dominick's Finer Foods, a supermarket chain, allots shelf space to children's and adults' cereals on the basis of the demand patterns at its different stores; sales and inventory turnover have gone up accordingly. Wal-Mart adapts the space it allots to various product lines to reflect the demographics, weather, and popularity of different sporting activities at its various stores.

As noted in Chapter 3, an emerging technique that some firms, particularly supermarkets, are beginning to use to improve shelf-space productivity is **category management**—the process of managing a retail business that recognizes category groupings of products are strategic business units, so as to better meet consumer needs and achieve sales and profit goals. Category management orients retail managers toward the buying and selling decisions necessary to maximize the return on the assets assigned to them (including shelf space).[4] According to one expert, successful category management is predicated on these ten points:

1. Categories should be arranged as they would be if "consumers" had the option of stocking the shelf themselves.
2. Category configuration should be a function of time, space, and product utilization.
3. Category management should seek to drive multiple item purchases, not the selection of a single SKU from a like-item category set.
4. Category management is a fluid, dynamic, proprietary set of decisions, not a standard, universal, institutionalized practice.
5. The ultimate aim of category management is to create unique consumer value, not just bolster manufacturer-retailer sales.
6. A retailer's category management plan ought to be based on overall trading-area scenarios.
7. Category management is an exclusionary process—as much a way of deciding what not to sell as what to sell to everyone.
8. The fundamental data base for category management should be drawn from a pre-customer interface analysis of trading-area needs.
9. Category management is different things for suppliers and retailers. The goal of the supplier is to maximize purchases and margins within a given geographic area. The retailer's goal is to raise total store or store cluster profitability and productivity.
10. Category management is a strategy of differentiation.[5]

A fundamental notion in category management is that a firm must empower specific personnel to be responsible for the financial performance of every product category. As with micro-merchandising, category management means adapting a retailer's merchandising strategy in each store or region to best satisfy customers. Thus, "the advent of category management is shaking up the way many retailers approach merchandising. Items are no longer managed on their own. Now, many are managed in concert with the items around them to help a store make an improved pricing, promotion, or variety statement." At Giant Food, such responsibility goes to nine category managers, each of whom devises and implements business plans to maximize the profits within his or her product category. These managers oversee the relationships among

[4]See Ryan Matthews, "Category Management Grows Up," *Progressive Grocer* (November 1996), pp. 79–81; "Key Insights: Thoughts on 'Efficient' Category Management from a Food Industry Guru," *Progressive Grocer* (August 1996), pp. 32–34; "Category Management Gains, But Confusion Still Reigns," *Chain Store Age* (January 1996), pp. 112, 116; and "Category Management Is Working at Giant," *Chain Store Age* (March 1997), pp. 56, 62.
[5]"Toward a Revised Theory of Category Management," *Progressive Grocer* (August 1995), p. 36.

assortments, prices, promotions, and displays to achieve optimum returns. As of 1998, Giant Food expects to be fully converted to category management.[6]

In deciding the proper space allocation per product category, these are several of the crucial measures of performance to retailers. Comparisons can be made by studying company data from period to period and by looking at categorical statistics published in trade magazines:

- ■ Sales per linear foot of shelf space—annual sales divided by the total linear footage devoted to the product category.
- ■ Gross profit per linear foot of shelf space—annual gross profit divided by the total linear footage devoted to the product category.
- ■ Return on inventory investment—annual gross profit divided by average inventory at cost.
- ■ Inventory turnover—the number of times during a given period, usually one year, that the average inventory on hand is sold.
- ■ Days supply—the number of days of supply of an item on the shelf; it is a similar measure to inventory turnover.
- ■ Direct product profitability (DPP)—an item's gross profit less its direct retailing costs (such as warehouse and store support, occupancy, inventory, and direct labor costs, but not general overhead).

Currently, the companywide use of category management in retailing is in its relative infancy. Although a lot of firms are using the concept in selected product categories, only a small number of major U.S. retailers have fully integrated category management programs. According to one recent study, 68 percent of supermarkets, 50 percent of drugstores, 31 percent of apparel specialty stores, 29 percent of traditional department stores, and 29 percent of full-line discount stores indicated that they had engaged in at least some category management.[7]

Category management data can be analyzed with software such as Apollo from Information Resources Inc. (http://www.infores.com/public/solutions/retail/retail.htm), Spaceman from A.C. Nielsen (http://www.acnielsen.com/home/mss/mss-sfw.htm), and DecisionSuite from Information Advantage (http://www.infoadvan.com). A few retailers have even developed their own software. Category management programs typically base the allocation of space on sales, inventory turnover, and profits at the individual store level. Because data are store specific, space allocations can reflect actual purchases.

Figure 13-1 indicates how a firm could use category management to better merchandise liquid detergent. One axis relates to direct product profitability. For the supermarket in this example, $0.69 per item is the average DPP for all liquid detergents. Those with higher amounts would be placed in the top half of the grid; those with lower amounts would be placed in the lower half. The other axis classifies the detergents in terms of unit sales (an indicator of inventory turnover), with 12.3 items per week being the dividing line between slow- and fast-moving detergents. On the basis of this two-by-two grid, all detergents could be placed into one of four categories: high potential ("sleepers")—products with high profitability but low unit sales; winners—products with high profitability and high weekly sales; underachievers ("dogs")—products with low profitability and low weekly sales; and traffic builders—products with low profitability and high weekly sales. Specific strategies are recommended in this figure.

Here are just some of the other tactics being used to lift the productivity of store space: Many retailers have vertical displays, which occupy less room than horizontal displays; they may hang displays on store walls or from ceilings. Formerly free space is now

[6]Michael Garry and Glenn Snyder, "Turning Partnering into Reality," *Progressive Grocer* (September 1993), pp. 44–46; and *Giant Food 1996 Annual Report.*
[7]"Improved Inventory Management: The New Strategic Imperative," *Chain Store Age* (December 1996), Section Two, p. 6A.

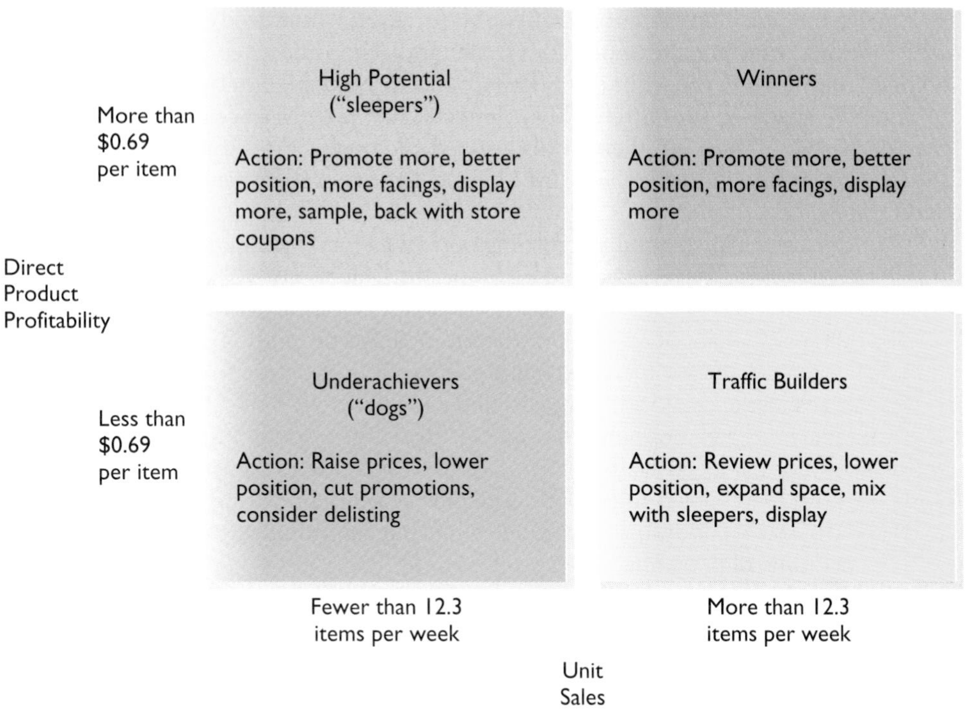

Figure 13-1

Applying Category Management to Heavy-Duty Liquid Detergent

Source: Walter H. Heller, "Profitability: Where It's Really At," *Progressive Grocer* (December 1992), p. 27. Copyright *Progressive Grocer.* Reprinted by permission.

	Fewer than 12.3 items per week	More than 12.3 items per week
More than $0.69 per item	**High Potential ("sleepers")** — Action: Promote more, better position, more facings, display more, sample, back with store coupons	**Winners** — Action: Promote more, better position, more facings, display more
Less than $0.69 per item	**Underachievers ("dogs")** — Action: Raise prices, lower position, cut promotions, consider delisting	**Traffic Builders** — Action: Review prices, lower position, expand space, mix with sleepers, display

Direct Product Profitability (vertical axis)

Unit Sales (horizontal axis)

Note: The criteria are based on the average profit and movement of the items in the product category of heavy-duty liquid detergent. The averages change for each product category.

devoted to vending machines and small point-of-sale displays; and product displays are being located in front of stores. Open doorways, mirrored walls, and vaulted ceilings give small, cramped stores the appearance of being larger. Some retailers allot up to 75 percent to 80 percent or more of their total floor space to selling; the rest is used for storage, rest rooms, and so on. Scrambled merchandising (involving high-profit, high-turnover items) occupies more square footage in a wider range of stores and greater space in mail-order catalogs than ever before. By staying open longer hours, retailers are also using space better.

Utilization of Personnel

From an operations perspective, the efficient utilization of retail personnel is important for several reasons. First, labor costs are high. For instance, in department stores, wages and benefits account for 46 percent of all operating costs; and in specialty stores, wages and benefits account for 43 percent of all operating costs.[8]

Second, high employee turnover leads to increased recruitment, training, and supervision costs. Third, poor personnel may not have good selling skills, mistreat customers, misring sales transactions, and make other costly errors. Fourth, productivity gains in technology have occurred much more rapidly than those in labor; yet, many retailers remain quite labor-intensive.

Fifth, labor deployment decisions are often subject to unanticipated fluctuations in customer demand. Thus, although retailers know they must increase sales personnel in peak sales periods and reduce them in slow periods, they may still be over- or understaffed if the weather changes, competitors run special sales, or suppliers increase promotion support.

[8]Alexandra Moran (Editor), *FOR 1996 Edition* (New York: Wiley, 1996), pp. 6, 9.

Finally, unionization places restrictions on firms with unionized employees. In these cases, working conditions, compensation, job tasks, overtime rates, performance measurement, termination procedures, seniority rights, promotion criteria, and other factors are generally specified in written labor contracts. Not only must retailers abide by the terms of these contracts, but their flexibility in deploying workers may be affected.

These are among the tactics being used by retailers to maximize personnel productivity:

■ Hiring process—By carefully screening potential employees before they are offered jobs, turnover can be reduced and better performance secured.

■ Workload forecasts—For each season, week, day, and time period, the needed number and type of personnel can be pre-determined. Accordingly, a drugstore may have one pharmacist, one cashier, and one stockperson in the store from 2 P.M. to 5 P.M. on Wednesdays and add a pharmacist and a cashier from 5 P.M. to 7:30 P.M. (to accommodate people shopping after work). In doing workload forecasts, personnel costs must be balanced against the possibilities of lost sales if customer waiting time is excessive. The key is to be both efficient (cost-oriented) and effective (service-oriented). Today, a number of retailers are using computer software to aid them in the scheduling of personnel.[9]

■ Job standardization and cross-training—Through **job standardization,** the tasks of personnel with similar positions in different departments, such as cashiers and stockpeople in clothing and candy departments, are kept rather uniform. With **cross-training,** personnel learn tasks associated with more than one job, such as cashier, stockperson, gift wrapper, and customer complaints handler. A firm can increase personnel flexibility and minimize the total number of employees needed at any given time by job standardization and cross-training. For example, if one department is slow, a cashier could be assigned to another that is busy; and a salesperson could also process transactions, help set up displays, and handle customer complaints. Cross-training can even reduce employee boredom.

■ Employee performance standards—Each employee must have clear performance standards and be accountable for meeting them. Cashiers can be judged on the basis of transaction speed and misrings; buyers can be judged on the basis of department revenues and the use of markdowns; and senior executives can be judged on the basis of the firm's reaching sales and profit goals. Personnel are usually more productive when they work toward specific goals.

■ Compensation—Financial compensation, promotions, and recognition can reward good performance. They serve to motivate employees better. Thus, a cashier will be motivated to reduce misrings if he or she knows there is a bonus for keeping mistakes under a certain percentage of all transactions processed.

■ Self-service—Personnel costs as a percentage of sales can be reduced significantly if self-service facilities are used, thus lessening the need for personnel. However, two points should be taken into account. First, self-service requires better in-store displays, well-known brands, ample assortments on the selling floor, and goods/services with simple features. Second, by reducing or eliminating sales personnel, some customers may feel they are receiving inadequate service; and there is no cross-selling (whereby customers are encouraged to buy complementary goods they may not have been thinking about).

■ Length of employment—Long-term employment can be encouraged. Generally, full-time workers who have been with a firm for an extended time are more productive than those who are part-time and/or who have worked at the firm for a short

[9]"Retailers See Quick ROI in Automated Labor Scheduling," *Chain Store Age* (November 1996), pp. 78, 82; "Time Tools: Labor-Scheduling Software Isn't Just for Store Managers Anymore," *Chain Store Age* (October 1996), pp. 1C–12C; and Julie Ritzer Ross, "Sorting Out Labor Scheduling Systems," *Stores* (March 1996), pp. 37–39.

Table 13-1   SELECTED STORE MAINTENANCE DECISIONS

■   What should the retailer's responsibility be for maintaining outside facilities? For instance, does a lease agreement make the retailer or the property owner accountable for snow removal in the parking lot?

■   Should store maintenance activities be performed by the retailer's own personnel or by outside specialists? Will that decision differ by type of facility (e.g., air-conditioning versus flooring) and by type of service (e.g., maintenance versus repairs)?

■   What repairs should be classified as emergencies? How promptly should nonemergency repairs be made?

■   How frequently is store maintenance required for each type of facility (e.g., daily vacuuming of floors versus weekly or monthly washing of exterior windows)? How often should special maintenance activities be done (e.g., waxing floors and restriping spaces in a parking lot)?

■   How should store maintenance vary by season and by time of day (e.g., when a store is open versus when it is closed)?

■   How long should existing facilities be utilized before acquiring new ones? What schedule should be followed?

■   What performance standards should be set for each element of store maintenance? Do these standards adequately balance costs against a desired level of maintenance?

time. The former are often more knowledgeable, are more anxious to see the retailer succeed, require less supervision, are popular with their customers, can be promoted to higher-level positions, and are more apt to accept and adapt to the special environment of retailing. Often, the high productivity associated with full-time, long-term workers far outweighs their relatively high compensation.

Store Maintenance

Store maintenance encompasses all the activities involved in managing a retailer's physical facilities. These are just some facilities that must be managed well: exterior—parking lot, points of entry and exit, outside signs and display windows, and common areas adjacent to a store (e.g., sidewalks); interior—windows, walls, flooring, climate control and energy use, lighting, displays and signs, fixtures, and ceilings. Table 13-1 shows several maintenance decisions.

The quality of store maintenance affects consumer perceptions of the retailer, the life span of facilities, and operating expenses. Consumers do not like to patronize stores that are unsanitary, decaying, or otherwise poorly maintained. This means regularly cleaning light fixtures, always replacing burned-out lamps, and periodically cleaning or repainting room surfaces to optimize light reflection. Some chains even go so far as to replace all lamps at the same time to assure constant color and light levels throughout the chain.

Ongoing and thorough maintenance can let a retailer use its current facilities for an extended period before having to invest in new ones. At home centers, for instance, the heating, ventilation, and air-conditioning equipment lasts an average of 13 years; flooring an average of 13 years; and interior signs an average of 6 years. But maintenance can be rather costly. In a typical year, a 35,000-square-foot home center spends over $10,000 on floor maintenance alone.[10]

Energy Management

Today, due to the rise in costs over the last two decades (although prices have stabilized in recent years), energy management is a vital consideration in store operations for many retailers. For firms with special needs, such as food stores and florists, energy management is especially critical. A typical outlet of a supermarket chain has annual energy costs amounting to about 1 percent of sales.

[10]Marianne Wilson, "Construction Costs Inch Downward," *Chain Store Age* (July 1996), pp. 81–84. See also "The Costs and Concerns of Management," *Chain Store Age* (April 1997), pp. SCM3–SCM7.

To better manage their energy resources, more firms now:

■ Use better-quality insulation materials in constructing and renovating stores to gain long-run monthly savings in energy bills.

■ Carefully adjust interior temperature levels over nonselling hours. In summer, air-conditioning is reduced at off-hours; in winter, heating is lowered at off-hours.

■ Use computerized systems, that can be programmed by store department and to fractions of a degree, to closely monitor temperature levels.

■ Have centralized computer-controlled systems, whereby operators can monitor and manipulate temperature, lighting, heat, and air-conditioning in multiple store units from a single office. Such systems even let the operators learn whether managers have left on lights in closed stores and turn those lights off from their consoles. Vast cost savings are possible.

■ Substitute high-efficiency bulbs and fluorescent ballasts for traditional lighting, thus reducing energy costs significantly.

■ Install "targeted desiccant" air-conditioning systems to better control humidity levels in specific store areas, such as refrigerated and freezer locations, thus minimizing moisture condensation.

Here is an example of how seriously retailers are taking energy management:

Eddie Bauer, the outdoor apparel retailer, has a new 225,000-square-foot headquarters building, in Redmond, Washington, with total systems integration [as shown in Figure 13-2]. "We were able to put what we wanted into the building that made sense from a technology standpoint. Whether it was more efficient HVAC (heating, ventilation, and air-conditioning) or lighting, we did it," said the manager of corporate planning and construction. The facility is distinguished by its floating or fly roof. It meets all Environmental Protection Agency standards as a "Green Building" with energy-efficient systems and a design that maximizes natural light. Climate control is provided by a rooftop/variable air volume (VAV) packaged air-conditioning system with building automation controls. Three large rooftop units supply cooling to series fan-powered VAV boxes with electric heat. Supply and exhaust fans are run by inverters to optimize energy consumption. To monitor and control system operation, the rooftops feature microprocessor-based unit control modules. The units are pre-programmed to operate on the economizer cycle when outdoor air temperature falls below 55° F. Using outdoor air for cooling in place of the refrigeration cycle reduces building operating costs significantly. The building automation system uses color graphics to convey information to building operators, which helps simplify service and maintenance. The units can diagnose and report a problem before it causes any discomfort to the occupants of the building.[11]

Inventory Management

A retailer employs **inventory management** to acquire and maintain a proper merchandise assortment while ordering, shipping, handling, and other related costs are kept in check. From an operations vantage point, inventory management has three interrelated phases: retailer to supplier, supplier to retailer, and retailer to consumer. See Figure 13-3.

First, a retailer places an order with a supplier based on a sales forecast and/or actual customer behavior. Both the number of items and their variety (such as assorted colors and materials) are requested in ordering. Order size and frequency depend on quantity discounts and inventory costs. Second, a supplier fills the retailer's order and sends merchandise to a warehouse or directly to the store(s). Third, the retailer receives merchandise, makes items available for sale (by removing them from shipping cartons, marking prices on them, and placing them on the selling floor), and completes customer transac-

[11]"Eddie Bauer Opts for Total System Integration," *Chain Store Age* (August 1996), p. 80.

Figure 13-2

Eddie Bauer's Corporate Headquarters

At its Redmond, Washington, headquarters, Eddie Bauer has an integrated, extremely efficient, energy system with a design that encourages natural light.

tions. Some transactions are not complete until items are delivered to the customer. The cycle starts anew when a retailer places another order.

These are some factors for retailers to consider in inventory management, from an operations perspective:

■ How can the handling of merchandise received from different suppliers be coordinated?
■ How much inventory should be on the selling floor versus in a warehouse or storage area?
■ How often should inventory be moved from nonselling to selling areas of a store?
■ What inventory functions can be done during nonstore hours rather than while a store is open?
■ What are the trade-offs between faster delivery times from suppliers and higher shipping costs?
■ What support is expected from suppliers in storing merchandise and/or setting up displays?
■ What level of in-store merchandise breakage is acceptable?
■ Which items require customer delivery? How should this be accomplished with regard to timing and responsibility?

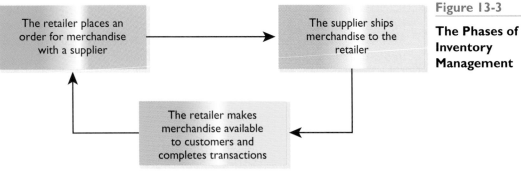

Figure 13-3

The Phases of Inventory Management

To improve inventory management results, a number of retailers now engage in quick response inventory planning—which, until a few years ago, was mostly used by manufacturers. With **quick response (QR) inventory planning,** a retailer reduces the amount of inventory it keeps on hand by ordering more frequently and in lower quantity. A QR system requires a retailer to have good relationships with suppliers, coordinate shipments, monitor inventory levels closely to avoid running out of stock, and regularly communicate with suppliers via electronic data interchange and other means.

For the retailer, a QR system reduces inventory costs, minimizes the space required for product storage, and lets the firm better match its orders with market conditions—by replenishing stock more quickly. For the manufacturer, a QR system can also improve inventory turnover and better match supply and demand by giving the vendor the data to track actual sales. These data were less available to the manufacturer in the past. In addition, a QR system that operates effectively makes it more difficult for a retailer to switch suppliers.

According to one study of retail operations executives, 48 percent of retailers are currently using a QR system to make purchases from vendors. Overall, the most active users of QR are department stores, full-line discount stores, specialty apparel stores, home centers, supermarkets, and drugstores.[12] Among the individual firms using QR with at least some products are Federated Department Stores, Cub Foods, Dillard's, Shaw's Supermarkets, Home Depot, The Limited, Inc., Dayton Hudson, Mercantile, Kmart, Sears, J.C. Penney, Giant Food, and Wal-Mart.

A QR system is most effective when used in conjunction with floor-ready merchandise, lower minimum order sizes, newly formatted store fixtures, and electronic data interchange. **Floor-ready merchandise** refers to items that are received at the store in condition to be put directly on display without any preparation by retail workers. Thus, with this approach, apparel manufacturers are responsible for pre-ticketing garments (with information specified by the retailer) and placing them on hangers. Similarly, Safeway supermarkets require that vendors put Safeway tags on fruit like apples and grapefruit, freeing produce clerks for other tasks.

Quick response also means suppliers need to rethink their minimum order sizes. For instance, while a minimum order size of 12 for a given size or color used to be required by sheet and towel makers, minimum order size is now as low as two units. Likewise, minimum order sizes for men's shirts have been reduced from six to as few as two units.[13]

The new minimum order sizes have led some retailers to refixture in-store departments. Prior to quick response, fixtures were often configured on the basis of a retailer's stocking full inventories. Today, retailers need to make an impact with smaller inventories.

Electronic data interchange, EDI (described in Chapter 8), lets retailers use QR inventory planning efficiently—by a paperless, computer-to-computer relationship between retailers and their vendors. Research studies suggest that retail prices could be reduced by an average of 10 percent or so with the industrywide usage of QR and EDI. These illustrations show the use of EDI and QR at specific retailers:

■ "When everything works smoothly, the most comprehensive systems chalk up sales at the register, send data to the warehouse to ensure shelves are restocked, advise the manufacturer that new orders will be coming, warn raw materials suppliers to ready new production, and even arrange shipping. About half of Kmart's sales now come from items in which the vendor itself manages every store's inventory by tapping into Kmart's sales computers. The idea is that such systems enable retailers and manufacturers to predict consumer demand accurately and adapt to surprises quickly, while minimizing expensive inventory."[14]

[12]"Retail Distribution and Logistics: Managing the Supply Chain," *Chain Store Age* (October 1996), Section Two, p. 16.
[13]Gary Robins, "Quick Response," *Stores* (March 1993), pp. 21–22.
[14]Michael M. Phillips, "Retailers Rely on High-Tech Distribution," *Wall Street Journal* (December 19, 1996), pp. A2, A6.

■ Costco has been "aggressive in getting our vendors online with EDI, and at this point at least 35 percent of our purchase orders and 25 percent of our invoices are being sent or received via EDI. But we deal with a lot of local commodity vendors that don't have the facilities or expertise for EDI, and we're not looking to force them. If a fax machine is a leading-edge technology to them, so be it. They can fax into our imaging system."[15]

■ Saks Fifth Avenue is expanding its "accrediting vendors on their logistical performance. Just as the vendors are audited for item marking, accuracy of invoices, completeness of orders, and, in some cases, compliance with floor-ready standards, they will in the future be measured on their ability to ship as committed. The bottom line is that this type of performance measurement will give Saks a way to manage the full supply chain from a logistical perspective. 'It allows us to accredit the various components in the supply chain. It allows us to accredit the vendor's ability to ship as they have committed to ship, as well as the carrier's ability to move the shipment, our organization's ability to process it, as well as the outbound shipment to the stores.'"[16]

Some retailers have gone further than QR planning and become more involved with **logistics**—the total process of moving goods from a manufacturer to a customer in the most timely and cost-efficient manner possible. Unlike other methods of inventory management, logistics regards transportation, storage, order processing, packaging, purchasing, and customer service as interdependent. It also oversees inventory management decisions as items travel through a retail supply chain (from manufacturer to warehouse to distribution center to store or, sometimes, even to consumers' homes). If a logistics system works well, firms reduce stockouts, hold down inventories, and improve customer service—all at the same time. See Figure 13-4.

Montgomery Ward uses a detailed logistics approach, based on GE Information Services' ASN Plus electronic software. According to GE Information Services (http://www.geis.com),

Implementing ASN Plus offers Montgomery Ward numerous benefits. The system allows the retailer to move goods to the selling floor more quickly, reduce handling costs, and lower inventory requirements. Suppliers also benefit from ASN Plus: it allows them to provide advance shipment notification and accurate bar-code labels, both required by Montgomery Ward. Additionally, suppliers can use ASN Plus to plan their material purchases more efficiently and resolve discrepancies before shipments arrive at their destinations. ASN Plus lets suppliers scan items while packing shipments, create bar-code container labels, and electronically notify a retailer of shipment contents prior to shipment receipt. When used with EDI software, ASN Plus can electronically verify shipment contents against purchase orders down to the carton content level, automate shipment labeling, and transmit accurate EDI advance shipment notices on demand.

In the supermarket sector of retailing, a number of firms are striving to apply their own form of logistics management, known as **efficient consumer response (ECR).** Through ECR, supermarkets are incorporating aspects of quick response inventory planning, electronic data interchange, and logistics planning. Here is how: "Phase one concentrates on initiating electronic data interchange programs aimed at efficient inventory replenishment. Even at this stage, results can be impressive with reductions of paperwork by more than half their previous levels. Phase two addresses continuous replenishment, which can help dramatically to reduce inventory levels even further. The last stage links retail sales all the way back to the manufacturer's ordering raw materials."[17]

Although U.S. supermarket retailers believe ECR may enable them to cut tens of billions of dollars in distribution costs, implementing it has not been easy. Many supermarkets are still

[15]"PriceCostco Imaging Complements EDI," *Chain Store Age* (May 1996), p. 222.

[16]Gary Robins, "Saks Speeds Up the Pace of Traffic," *Stores* (October 1995), pp. 70–71.

[17]R. Craig MacClaren, "Manufacturers Are Setting a Fast Pace for ECR," *Promo* (March 1994), p. 42. See also Julie Ritzer Ross, "Retailers Take the Lead in Implementing ECR," *Stores* (May 1996), pp. 30–33; and Ryan Mathews, "ECR: More Promise Than Performance," *Progressive Grocer* (April 1997), pp. 26–28.

Figure 13-4

Eckerd's: Effective Logistics at Work

unwilling to trade their ability to negotiate special short-term purchase terms with vendors in return for routine order fulfillment without special deals. And as one expert said, "For most companies, the first decision was whether or not to 'do' ECR, and obviously a large number of players have made the decision to move forward on ECR initiatives. Now the kinds of decisions being made involve operational issues, but those kinds of applications cost money. Things like continuous replenishment take inventory out of the pipeline, but require complex communication architectures like EDI. The other thing happening quite often is that when people are faced with the decision of, say, building a new store or doing other demand-side projects, the decision tree is fairly simple and straightforward. Implementing ECR is more abstract, more complex, and, because it is less tangible, requires more thought."[18]

Merchandising decisions are discussed thoroughly in Chapters 14 and 15.

Store Security

Store security relates to two basic issues: personal security and merchandise security. With regard to personal security, many consumers and employees feel less safe at retail establishments than they did just a few years ago.

[18]Ryan Mathews, "Is ECR Dead?" *Progressive Grocer* (September 1996), p. 29.

Consider these recent survey findings: Twenty percent fewer people now shop at night than in 1990. Many stores with early opening hours on Sunday do 40 percent of that day's business before noon due to people feeling more comfortable with daytime shopping. Nearly one-half of shoppers believe malls are not as safe as they were just a few years ago. One-sixth of people age 60 and older no longer go out at night. One-third of consumers have stopped going to malls they feel are unsafe or visit there only during specific hours.[19]

In sum, "despite the falling national crime rates, some people are still afraid to go shopping. Many stores that used to do a lot of business after dark are not doing so any more; and people are shopping fewer stores and for fewer hours. Parking areas are a major source of angst for people, who are far more scared of walking through a large parking lot than anything else about shopping."[20]

These are some of the practices retailers are utilizing to address the issue of personal safety:

■ Uniformed security guards provide a visible presence that is reassuring to customers and employees, and a warning to potential thieves and muggers. Some malls even have horse-mounted guards to further protect people. Alpha & Omega supplies horse-mounted guards for two dozen malls in Texas, New Mexico, California, New York, Missouri, and Illinois (at the rate of $27.50 to $45 an hour per rider).

■ Undercover security personnel are used to thwart criminal attempts that wait for uniformed guards to pass by.

■ Brighter lighting is used in parking lots, which are also patrolled more frequently by guards on foot and in vehicles. Also the guards more often work in teams to better head off potential problems.

■ TV cameras and other devices scan the in-store and outside areas frequented by customers and employees. 7-Eleven has a new in-store integrated cable TV and alarm monitoring system, complete with audio capabilities, in 1,600 outlets.

■ Some shopping areas have imposed curfews for teenagers. At the Mall of America in Minneapolis, on Friday and Saturday nights after 6:00 P.M., anyone younger than 16 years of age must be accompanied by a person who is at least 21 years old. This is a controversial, but thus far, successful tactic.

■ Access to store facilities (such as storage rooms) has been tightened.

■ Bank deposits are made more frequently—often by armed-security guards.[21]

Each year, $30 billion in U.S. retail sales are lost due to **inventory shrinkage** caused by employee theft, customer shoplifting, and vendor fraud. According to one study, employees account for 48 percent of the losses, customers 44 percent, and vendors 8 percent. Shrinkage ranges from 0.4 percent of sales at supermarkets to 2.5 percent of sales at sporting goods stores.[22] Thus, some merchandise security program is needed by all retailers.

To reduce theft, there are three key points to include in operating plans. First, loss prevention should be weighed as stores are designed and built. Thus, the placement of store entrances, dressing rooms, and delivery areas should be planned from a security

[19]Richard Halverson, "Crime Steals Shoppers' Confidence," *Discount Store News* (May 6, 1996), pp. 70, 72.
[20]Robert Langreth, "Shoppers' Concerns Over Safety Persist Despite Declining National Crime Statistics," *Wall Street Journal* (May 13, 1996), p. B4B.
[21]See James Ketelsen, "Mall Mounties," *Forbes* (June 17, 1996), pp. 84–85; "7-Eleven Expands Security Offensive," *Chain Store Age* (January 1996), p. 154; Susan Reda, "Mall of America Curfew Focuses on Teen Control Issue," *Stores* (December 1996), pp. 53–55; Susan Reda, "Armed Robbery Targets Retail," *Stores* (December 1995), pp. 16–18; and Claire Sykes, "Restaurant Survey Links Employee Theft, Other Counter-Productive Behaviors," *Stores* (May 1997), pp. 74–76.
[22]"Theft's Multibillion Dollar Impact on Retailers," *Chain Store Age* (January 1997), pp. 175, 178; "Retail Shrinkage," *Stores* (March 1996), p. 61; and Ryan Mathews, "Loss Prevention: It's Later Than You Think," *Progressive Grocer* (February 1997), pp. 69–72.

International Shoplifting Gangs Invade the United States

According to store security experts, highly-organized international shoplifting gangs steal over $1 billion in merchandise per year. As one detective who has worked with a special FBI task force remarked, "Stealing is what they do for a living. Their job for the whole day is to go out and take from as many stores as they can."

International theft rings generally favor malls, specialty stores (those staffed by two to three sales associates), and expensive apparel items. They tend to work in teams, with the leader entering the store alone and marking off desired merchandise (with paper clips or other objects). The leader then signals for other members to either enter the store or, if trouble is sensed, to proceed to another store. In one mode of operation, some ring members seek to divert the attention of store employees by getting them to walk across the store. Meanwhile, other members begin to empty entire racks of clothing and remove a store's security tags or stuff garments in specially-lined bags (that let them leave the store without security alarms detecting the theft).

Loss prevention experts urge retailers to train their employees to be aware of these practices, to closely follow suspicious shoppers, and to alert mall security staff as quickly as possible.

Source: Julie Ritzer Ross, "International Gangs Create Major New Shoplifting Threat," *Stores* (March 1996), pp. 35–36.

standpoint. Second, a combination of security measures should be enacted, like employee background checks, in-store guards, electronic security equipment, and merchandise tags. Third, retailers need to communicate the importance of loss prevention to employees, customers, and vendors, as well as the actions they will take to reduce losses (such as firing workers and prosecuting shoplifters).

Here are some activities that reduce losses due to merchandise theft:

■ Product tags, security guards, video cameras, point-of-sale computers, employee surveillance, and burglar alarms are each being used by more firms. Storefront protection is also popular.

■ Many general merchandise retailers and some supermarkets use **electronic article surveillance,** by which specially designed tags or labels are attached to products. The tags can be sensed by electronic devices that are placed at store exits. If the tags are not removed by store personnel or desensitized by electronic scanning equipment, an alarm goes off. Retailers now also have greater access to nonelectronic tags. These are tightly attached to products and must be removed by special detachers; otherwise the products are unusable. Dye tags will also permanently stain products, if not removed properly. See Figure 13-5.

■ A lot of firms are doing detailed background checks for every employee. At Canada's BiWay Stores, "Pre-employment is the most important of all the programs we have in place to reduce theft in the workplace."

■ Various retailers have employee training programs on the impact of losses and offer incentives for reducing them. Others distribute written policies on ethical behavior that are signed by all personnel, including owners and senior management. For example, Target Stores has enrolled managers at problem stores in a Stock Shortage Institute. Neiman Marcus has shown workers a film with interviews of convicted shoplifters in prison to highlight the problem's seriousness.

■ More retailers are apt to fire employees and prosecute shoplifters involved with theft. Courts are imposing stiffer penalties; and in some areas, store detectives are empowered by police to make arrests. In well over 40 states, there are civil restitution laws, whereby shoplifters must pay for stolen goods or face arrests and criminal trials. In most states, fines are higher if goods are not returned or they are damaged.

Figure 13-5

Sensormatic: The Leader in Store Security Systems

These aesthetically pleasing, acrylic pedestals (part of Sensormatic's Euro Pro Max system) provide an unobstructed vision of exits, as well as the ultimate electronic article surveillance system. An alarm goes off if a person tries to leave a store without a product's security tag being properly removed.

Shoplifters must also contribute to court costs. By imposing its own fines, Eckerd (the drugstore chain) saves time and immediately gets its merchandise back, rather than handing goods to police for evidence.

■ Some mystery shoppers are hired to watch for shoplifting, not just to observe shopping behavior for research purposes.[23]

Figure 13-6 presents a detailed list of tactics retailers can use to combat employee and shopper theft, by far the leading causes of losses.

When devising and enacting a store security plan, a retailer must assess the impact of such a plan on employee morale, shopper comfort, and vendor relations. As a J.C. Penney executive once remarked, "we want employees to pay attention to selling—not have them watching each other or wondering if someone's looking over their shoulder."[24] Likewise, by setting strict rules for fitting rooms (like limiting the number of garments brought in at one time) and/or placing chains on expensive furs and suede coats, a firm may cause some people to try on and buy less clothing—or visit another store.

Insurance

In retail operations, the purchase of insurance that covers the firm in case of losses due to fire, customer lawsuits regarding on-premises accidents, and other causes must be carefully planned. Among the types of such insurance bought by retailers are workers' compensation, public liability, product liability, property, and directors' and officers' liability. In addition, many retailers offer some type of health insurance option to their full-time employees; sometimes, the retailers pay the entire premiums, other times, employees pay part or all of the premiums.

[23]See Jill Jordan Sieder, "To Catch a Thief, Try This," *U.S. News & World Report* (September 23, 1996), p. 71; "Closing in on Front-End Shrink," *Progressive Grocer* (May 1996), pp. 12–13; Robert Berner, "For Certain Customers, This Department Store Has Five Metal Rings," *Wall Street Journal* (December 18, 1996), pp. A1, A8; "Pre-Job Screening Cuts Shrink at BiWay," *Chain Store Age* (May 1996), p. 98; and Julie Ritzer Ross, "Mystery Shoppers Gain as Loss Prevention Tool," *Stores* (November 1996), pp. 58–63.
[24]David J. Solomon, "Hotlines and Hefty Rewards: Retailers Step Up Efforts to Curb Employee Theft," *Wall Street Journal* (September 17, 1987), p. 37.

Figure 13-6

Ways Retailers Can Deter Employee and Shopper Theft

A. Employee Theft
- Using pencil-and-paper honesty tests, voice stress analysis, and psychological tests as employee screening devices.
- Developing a system of locking up trash to prevent merchandise from being thrown out and then retrieved.
- Verifying through use of undercover personnel whether all sales are rung up.
- Utilizing cameras and mirrors to monitor activities.
- Implementing central control of all exterior doors to monitor opening and closing.
- Properly identifying deliverypeople.
- Verifying receipts and goods taken out.
- Sealing all trucks after they are loaded with goods.
- Inspecting worker packages, tool boxes, lunch boxes.
- Dividing responsibilities (e.g., having one employee record sales; another making deposits).
- Giving rewards for spotting thefts.
- Having training programs.
- Vigorously investigating all known losses.
- Firing offenders immediately.

B. Shopper Theft While Store Is Open
- Using in-store detectives or uniformed guards.
- Prosecuting all individuals charged with theft.
- Using electronic article surveillance wafers, electromagnets, or stick-ons for high-value and theft-prone goods.
- Developing comprehensive employee training programs.
- Providing employee bonuses based upon overall reduction in shortages or based on value of recovered merchandise.
- Inspecting all packages brought into store.
- Utilizing self-closing/self-locking showcases for high-value items such as jewelry.
- Chaining down expensive samples, such as high-fidelity equipment, to fixtures.
- Placing goods with high value/small size in locked showcases.
- Attaching expensive clothing together.
- Alternating the direction of hangers on clothing near doors.
- Limiting the dollar value and quantity of merchandise displayed near exits.
- Limiting the number of entrances and exits to the store.
- Utilizing cameras and mirrors to increase visibility, especially in low-traffic areas.

C. Employee/Shopper Theft While Store Is Closed
- Conducting thorough check of the building at night to make sure no one is left in store.
- Locking all exits, even fire exits, at night.
- Utilizing ultrasonic/infrared detectors, burglar alarm traps, or guards with dogs when store is closed.
- Placing valuables in safe.
- Using shatterproof glass and/or iron gates on display windows to prevent break-ins.
- Making sure exterior lighting is adequate when store is closed.
- Periodically testing burglar alarms.

Insurance decisions are vital for several reasons. First, over the past decade, premiums have risen dramatically—in some cases, doubling. Second, some insurers reduced the scope of their coverage; they now require higher deductibles before paying claims and/or will not provide coverage on all aspects of operations (such as the professional liability of pharmacists). Third, there are fewer insurance carriers servicing retailers today than a decade ago; this limits the choices of retailers. Fourth, insurance against environmental risks (such as leaking tanks) is more important than in the past due to government regulations. Overall, at department stores and specialty stores, insurance costs (excluding health) amount to 1 percent of revenues.

As a result, a number of retailers have employed costly programs aimed at lessening their vulnerability to employee and customer claims due to dangerous or unsafe conditions and at holding down insurance premiums:

> They entail installing no-slip floors, carpeting, and rubber mats at entrances; frequent mopping and inspection of wet floors; training fixture designers to design risk-free fixtures; conducting frequent elevator and escalator maintenance checks; conducting fire drills; designing and constructing fire resistant stores, warehouses, and distribution centers; building separate structures to warehouse dangerous products; enacting appropriate employee training programs; and documenting that proper maintenance has been done, in the event of legal action. The list is as long as a retailer—or its insurance company—wants to make it.[25]

Credit Management

Credit management involves the policies and practices retailers follow in receiving payments from their customers. These are some of the major operational decisions to be made:

■ What form of payment is acceptable? A retailer may accept cash only; cash and personal checks; cash and credit card(s); cash and debit cards; or all of these.

■ Who administers the credit plan? The firm can have its own credit system and/or accept major credit cards (such as Visa, MasterCard, American Express, and Discover).

■ What are customer eligibility requirements to make a check or credit purchase? For a check purchase, identification such as a photo ID might be sufficient. For a credit purchase, a new customer would have to meet requirements as to age, employment, annual income, and so on; and an existing customer would be evaluated in terms of his or her outstanding balance and credit limit. A minimum purchase amount may also be specified for a credit transaction.

■ What are the tradeoffs between the cost of permitting credit transactions and the increased profits generated by credit sales?

■ What credit terms will be used? A retailer with its own plan must determine when interest charges will begin, what the rate of interest will be, and minimum monthly payments.

■ How are late payments or nonpayments to be handled? Some retailers with their own credit plans rely on outside collection agencies to follow up on past-due accounts.

In credit management, a retailer generally needs to balance the ability of credit to generate additional revenues against the cost of processing credit payments. The latter can include screening, transaction, and collection costs, as well as bad debts. If a firm completes all credit functions itself, it will incur these costs; if outside credit arrangements (such as Visa) are used, that firm covers the costs by its payments to the credit organization.

[25]Holly Klokis, "A Bad Break for Retailers," *Chain Store Age Executive* (June 1986), p. 16; and "Slip/Fall Liability for Upscale Retailer," *Chain Store Age Executive* (November 1992), p. 112.

According to a study of specialty stores, supermarkets, drugstores, convenience stores, department stores, and discount stores, the average sales transaction involving payment by check is 75 percent higher than one with payment in cash; and the average sales transaction involving payment by credit card is more than double the amount with payment in cash. Fifty percent of all retail transactions and 40 percent of all revenues entail cash payments, 22 percent of transactions and 25 percent of revenues entail check payments, and 28 percent of transactions and 35 percent of revenues entail credit-card and debit-card payments (with debit cards generating 2 percent of all sales at the stores surveyed). Among the retailers accepting credit-card payments, 30 percent have their own company card, 98 percent accept MasterCard and/or Visa, 80 percent accept Discover, and 53 percent accept American Express. Most handle two or more cards.[26]

Credit card fees paid by retailers generally range from 1.5 percent to 4.5 percent of sales for Visa, MasterCard, and Discover—depending mostly on the retailer's credit volume. American Express charges up to 5.5 percent of sales. MasterCard, Visa, and Discover also have transaction fees of 5 cents to 25 cents per charge and monthly statement fees of $5 to $25. American Express' rates includes these fees. In contrast, the costs of retailers' own credit operations as a percent of credit sales are 2.0 percent.[27]

Many supermarkets, gas stations, and drugstores—among others—have begun placing greater emphasis on some form of **debit-card system,** whereby the purchase price of a good or service is immediately deducted from a consumer's bank account and entered into a retailer's account by an appropriate computer terminal. The retailer's risk of nonpayment is eliminated and its costs are reduced with debit rather than credit transactions. For traditional credit cards, end-of-month billing is employed (with no interest charges if payments are made promptly); with debit cards, monetary account transfers are made at the time of the purchase—delayed billing carries interest charges from the day an item is bought. There has been, and will continue to be, some resistance to debit transactions by consumers who like the delayed-payment benefit of conventional credit cards. Some people may also dislike debit cards because of privacy or security issues (such as: Can a retailer look at a customer's bank balance? Can a retail clerk gain access to a customer's checking account by learning the person's access code?).

Regardless of the payment plan adopted, it is imperative for a retailer to communicate all policies clearly to both employees and customers. Credit is discussed further in Chapter 17 in the section on customer services.

Computerization

As we noted in Chapter 3, many retailers are improving their operations productivity by computerization; and with the declining prices of computer systems and related software, even more firms will do so in the near future. In this section, computerized checkouts and electronic point-of-sale systems, and other operations applications are presented.

The **computerized checkout** is used by many types of retailers (large and small), so they can efficiently process transactions and have strict inventory control. Firms are increasingly relying on UPC-based systems, whereby cashiers manually ring up sales or pass items over or past optical scanners. Computerized registers instantly record and display sales, customers get detailed receipts, and all inventory data are stored in a computer memory bank. See Figure 13-7.

This type of checkout lowers costs by reducing transaction time, employee training, misrings, and the need for price markings on items. In addition, retailers can increase their productivity because of better inventory control, reduced spoilage, and improved ordering. Firms also get in-depth data on an item-by-item basis, which aids in determining store layout and merchandise plans, setting the amount of shelf space per item, and automatically replenishing inventory.

[26]Ernst & Young, "Survey of Payment Methods," *Chain Store Age* (January 1996), Section Two.
[27]Rosalind Resnick, "Going Plastic," *Nation's Business* (July 1995), pp. 28–30.

ETHICS IN RETAILING

In Retail Scanning: How Accurate Is Accurate?

A supermarket's scanning accuracy affects the quality of price data that are derived from scanning, its profits, and consumer confidence in its honesty. The impact on profits occurs due to the costs of rescanning and the lost revenues when undercharging consumers. Research by the Pennsylvania Food Merchants Association (PFMA) found that regardless of a store's pricing accuracy, undercharges were 1.5 to 2 times more likely to occur than overcharges. The average amount undercharged was 39 cents, while the average overcharge was 30 cents.

Under new pricing guidelines set by the National Conference of Weights and Measures, retail scanners need to have at least a 98 percent accuracy level. Since the typical scan accuracy for supermarkets is somewhere between 94 percent and 99 percent, many supermarket operators still have to upgrade their scanning equipment and practices.

According to the *ECR Progress Report*, many grocery-related firms have now made accurate scanning data a top priority. This study found that 49 percent of wholesalers and 81 percent of the supermarket chains supplied by those wholesalers are at some stage of implementing a scanning data accuracy program. Among the supermarkets that have achieved scanning accuracy levels as high as 99.9 percent are Wegmans, H.E. Butt, and Martin's Super Markets.

Sources: Michael Garry, "Is Your Scanning Accurate?" *Progressive Grocer* (August 1995), pp. 55–57; and Julie Ritzer Ross, "Study Validates Industry Efforts to Improve Price Scanning Accuracy," *Stores* (January 1997), pp. 90–96.

There are two potential problems facing retailers using computerized checkouts. First, UPC-based systems will not reach peak efficiency until all manufacturers attach UPC labels to their merchandise; otherwise, retailers must incur labeling costs. Second, because UPC symbols are unreadable by humans, some states have enacted laws making price labeling on individual packages mandatory; others are considering such legislation. This lessens the labor savings of retailers that would like to post only shelf prices, rather than enter prices on all individual items.

Figure 13-7

The Value of Computerized Checkouts

Because of continuing technological advances (and the associated cuts in the prices of equipment), even the smallest stores are now able to computerize their operations, thus making them more efficient and responsive to consumers. Shown here is a Fina convenience store, which has a relatively inexpensive (but fully functional) computer terminal and the ability to electronically process credit card transactions.

Computerized Labor-Scheduling Systems Come to Supermarkets

The Food Marketing Institute recently conducted an *In-Store Systems Study*, in which 65 percent of the 216 supermarket firms surveyed said they planned to have computerized labor-scheduling systems in place by the beginning of 1996. Let's look at a few supermarkets that are using such systems.

Buttrey Food & Drug, formerly a division of American Stores, uses the People Planner time- and-attendance scheduler and forecaster by Information Marketing Businesses. During pilot tests of the software, front-end labor efficiencies improved about 10 percent. People Planner software tracks traffic patterns for front end, deli, pharmacy, and other departments, and schedules personnel accordingly for each department.

Safeway Stores uses the SuperSked labor-scheduling system by Management Robotics. SuperSked was chosen on the basis of the quality of its schedules, adherence to management policies and union rules, ease of learning and use, and ability to add new features. Due to better labor scheduling, Safeway has found that the software lets it reduce customer waiting lines and increase labor productivity.

Edwards Super Food Stores employs Timecorp Systems' Timecorp software to conduct its labor-scheduling activities. Edwards switched to an automated labor-management system after it found it was not uniformly forecasting and distributing its labor resources throughout all of its stores.

Source: Bruce Fox, "Labor Scheduling Gains in Supermarket Industry," *Chain Store Age* (December 1995), pp. 105–108.

There have been a number of recent technological developments related to computerized checkouts. These include wireless scanners that let workers scan heavy items without having to pick them up, radio frequency identification tags (RFID) which emit a unique radio frequency code when placed near an appropriate transmitter receiver (this is faster than UPC codes and more appropriate for harsh climates), and speech recognition (that can tally up an order for one hamburger and a diet Coke, for example, on the basis of a clerk's verbal order).[28]

Many retailers are and will continue expanding beyond the computerized checkout to an **electronic point-of-sale system,** which performs all the tasks of a computerized checkout and also verifies check and charge transactions, provides instantaneous sales reports, monitors and changes prices, sends intra- and interstore messages, evaluates personnel and profitability, and stores data. In most cases, a point-of-sale system would be used in conjunction with a firm's retail information system. The terminals in the electronic point-of-sale system can either stand alone (the "intelligent" type) or be integrated with an in-store minicomputer or a headquarters mainframe. In any case, keyboards, printers, scanners, wands, and screens can be used as needed by the retailer.

These are among the other basic ways in which retailers use computers in their operations:

■ To train, schedule, and compensate personnel.
■ To forecast sales and prepare budgets.
■ To coordinate inventory orders and handling, and manage distribution centers. See Figure 13-8.
■ To reduce checkout time and cashier misrings.
■ To communicate with suppliers.
■ To obtain current information.

[28]See "The Future of Bar Coding," *Chain Store Age* (January 1997), pp. 3C–11C; and Michael Garry, "POS: Open and Graphic," *Progressive Grocer* (July 1996), pp. 79–82.

Figure 13-8

CounterPoint Business Software from Synchronics

Efficient order entry helps retailers make customers happy and expedites the shipping and tracking of inventory. CounterPoint software enables retailers to monitor inventories, customer histories, accounts receivable, and purchasing data—as well as better place orders.

- ■ To preserve and retrieve credit records.
- ■ To generate and maintain data-base (mailing) lists.
- ■ To allocate shelf space and advertising expenditures.
- ■ To analyze performance.

Crisis Management

Despite their best intentions, retailers may sometimes be faced with crisis situations that need to be managed as smoothly as possible. Crises may be brought on by such events as an in-store fire or broken water pipe, bad weather breaking the store's front window, access to a store being partially blocked due to picketing by striking workers, a car accident in the parking lot, a burglary, a sudden illness by the owner or a key employee, storms that knock out a retailer's power, unexpectedly high or low consumer demand for a good or service, a sudden increase in a supplier's prices, a natural disaster like a flood or an earthquake, or other factors.

Although crises cannot always be anticipated, and some adverse effects may occur regardless of retailer efforts, several principles should be adhered to while devising operations management plans:

1. Contingency plans should be established for as many different types of crisis situations as possible. That is why retailers buy insurance, install backup lighting in anticipation of power failures, and prepare management succession plans in the event of sudden illnesses of key officers. For instance, a firm could have a checklist of steps to follow if there is an incident such as an in-store fire or a parking lot accident.
2. Essential information should be communicated to all affected parties, like the fire or police department, employees, customers, and the media, as soon as a crisis occurs.
3. There should be cooperation and not conflict among the involved parties.
4. Responses should be as quick as feasible; indecisiveness may worsen the situation.
5. The chain of command for decisions should be clear and the decision maker given adequate authority to act.

As one crisis management expert noted, "By all means, avoid involving your business in a crisis. But once you're in one, accept it, manage it, and try to keep your vision focused on the long term."[29]

[29]Norman R. Augustine, "Managing the Crisis You Tried to Prevent," *Harvard Business Review,* Vol. 73 (November–December 1995), pp. 147–158.

Summary

1. *To describe the operational scope of operations management* As defined in Chapter 12, operations management is efficiently and effectively enacting the policies needed to satisfy a retailer's customers, employees, and management. In contrast to Chapter 12, which dealt with financial aspects, this chapter covered operational facets. While running their firms, retail executives must make a wide range of operating decisions.

2. *To study several specific operational aspects of operations management* Store format and size considerations include the use of prototype stores and the size of stores. Firms operating prototype stores often do so under the aegis of rationalized retailing. Some retailers are emphasizing large, category-killer size stores; others are opening smaller, targeted stores.

In space allocation, retailers may deploy a top-down or a bottom-up approach. With micromerchandising, allocations are responsive to local needs. For category management, product groupings are set up as strategic business units to satisfy consumer needs, while maximizing profits. Among the performance measures for space allocation are sales per linear foot, gross profit per linear foot, return on inventory investment, inventory turnover, days supply, and direct product profitability.

Personnel utilization activities to improve productivity range from workload forecasts to job standardization and cross-training. Job standardization means the tasks of people with similar positions in different departments are kept rather uniform. Cross-training means people learn tasks associated with more than one job. A firm can elevate its personnel flexibility and minimize the total number of workers needed at any given time by these techniques.

Store maintenance includes all the activities involved in managing the retailer's physical facilities. The quality of store maintenance influences people's perceptions of the retailer, the life span of facilities, and operating expenses.

Energy management is a major operational concern for many retailers. At firms with special needs, energy management is crucial. To better control energy resources, retailers are doing everything from using better-quality insulation materials when building and renovating stores to substituting high-efficiency bulbs and fluorescent ballasts for traditional lighting.

Inventory management requires that retailers strive to acquire and maintain proper merchandise assortments while ordering, shipping, handling, and other related costs are kept in check. To improve performance, many firms are now engaged in quick response inventory planning, whereby they reduce the amount of inventory they keep on hand by ordering more often and in lower quantity. A QR system works best if used in conjunction with floor-ready merchandise, lower minimum order sizes, newly formatted store fixtures, and electronic data interchange. Some retailers are more actively involved with logistics—the total process of moving goods from a manufacturer to a customer in the most timely and cost-efficient manner possible. A number of supermarkets are trying to apply their own form of logistics management, known as efficient consumer response (ECR).

Store security techniques are needed to protect both personal and merchandise safety. Because of safety concerns, fewer people now shop at night and some avoid shopping areas they view to be unsafe. To improve personal safety, retailers are employing security guards, better lighting in parking lots, tightening access to store facilities, and other tactics. Inventory shrinkage is caused by employee theft, customer shoplifting, and vendor fraud. To reduce it, loss prevention must be planned as stores are designed and built; a combination of security measures should be enacted, like employee background checks and electronic security systems; and firms must communicate the importance of loss prevention to employees, customers, and vendors, as well as the actions they will take to reduce losses.

Insurance covers the retailer against losses arising from fire, customer lawsuits, and other causes. Among the types of insurance that retailers buy are workers' compensation, public liability, product liability, property, and directors' and officers' liability. In addition, many firms offer some type of health insurance option.

Credit management pertains to the policies and practices retailers follow in receiving customer payments. In general, credit and check payments mean larger transactions than cash payments. One-half of retail transactions are in cash, 22 percent by check, and 28 percent by credit card. Some retailers are placing greater emphasis on debit cards.

A growing number of retailers are computerizing elements of operations. Computerized checkouts and electronic point-of-sale systems are especially helpful. Electronic point-of-sale systems perform all the tasks of computerized checkouts; and also verify check and charge transactions, provide instant sales reports, monitor and change prices, send intra- and interstore messages, evaluate personnel and profitability, and store data.

Crisis management is needed to handle unexpected situations as smoothly as possible. There should be contingency plans; key information should be communicated to all affected parties; there should be cooperation among the involved parties; responses should be as quick as feasible; and the chain of command for decisions should be clear.

Key Terms

prototype stores (p. 403)
rationalized retailing (p. 404)
top-down space management
   approach (p. 404)
bottom-up space management
   approach (p. 404)
micro-merchandising (p. 405)
category management (p. 405)
job standardization (p. 408)

cross-training (p. 408)
store maintenance (p. 409)
inventory management (p. 410)
quick response (QR) inventory
   planning (p. 412)
floor-ready merchandise (p. 412)
logistics (p. 413)
efficient consumer response (ECR)
   (p. 413)

inventory shrinkage (p. 415)
electronic article surveillance
   (p. 416)
credit management (p. 419)
debit-card system (p. 420)
computerized checkout (p. 420)
electronic point-of-sale system
   (p. 422)

Questions for Discussion

1. What are the pros and cons of rationalized retailing? For which kind of firms is this most desirable?
2. Differentiate between the top-down and bottom-up space management approaches.
3. Discuss Figure 13-1.
4. Why would a retailer be interested in job standardization and cross-training for its employees?

5. Comment on this statement: "The quality of store maintenance efforts affects consumer perceptions of the retailer, the life span of facilities, and operating expenses."
6. Talk to two local retailers and ask them what they have done to maximize their energy efficiency. Present your findings.

7. Could a small retailer use a quick response inventory system? Why or why not?
8. Differentiate between logistics and inventory management.
9. Present a five-step plan for a retailer to reassure customers that it is safe to shop there.
10. Would you offer a reward to retail employees who report theft on the part of co-workers? Explain your answer.
11. A mom-and-pop store does not accept checks because of the risks involved. However, it does accept Visa and MasterCard. Evaluate this strategy.

12. As the owner of a local supermarket, how would you persuade customers to use debit cards (because you are interested in expanding business, but do not want to accept credit cards)?
13. What potential problems may result if a retailer relies on its computer to implement too many actions (such as employee scheduling or inventory reordering) automatically?
14. Outline contingency plans a retailer could have in the event each of these occurs:
    a. An in-store fire.
    b. Vandalism of the storefront.
    c. A manufacturer's product recall.
    d. The bankruptcy of a key supplier.

Web-Based Exercise:

INFORMATION RESOURCES INC. (http://www.infores.com)

Questions

1. Describe the "Logistics Replenishment" section of the IRI Web site. (http://www.infores.com/public/solutions/retail/rlogist.htm)
2. From the home page of the Web site, select "Products & Services Directory." Then access the material on IRI's "Apollo Professional" space management software. Evaluate its basic features.

3. What are the key differences between the "Apollo Professional" and the "Apollo TotalStore" software packages?
4. From the home page of the Web site, select "Products & Services Directory." Then access the material on IRI's "The Category Manager" software. Explain how it can be used by a small retailer.

CASE 1
Condiments: Category Management*

This case examines data on condiments from a category management perspective. The main purpose of category management is to determine the optimal assortment of condiments that will maximize sales opportunities and eliminate unnecessary duplication of products.

The condiments category is comprised of ketchup, barbecue sauce, mustard, steak sauce, Worcestershire sauce, cocktail sauce, and chili sauce. It currently accounts for $1.5 billion in annual U.S. sales. Within the category, ketchup accounts for 32 percent of sales, barbecue sauce for 26 percent, mustard for 19 percent, steak sauce for 14 percent, Worcestershire sauce for 4 percent, cocktail sauce for 3 percent, and chili sauce for 1 percent. Of the products within the category, ketchup is by far the largest, with about $480 million in annual sales. Ketchup is also found in 97 percent of U.S. households.

Let's look at some of the general characteristics of condiments buyers. These shoppers spend $1,500 more per year in grocery expenditures than the average household, and households with children are the largest buyers of condiments. Condiments buyers seek flavor and variety in their purchases. For example, customers, on average, stock different varieties within the same condiments groupings (such as multiple styles of mustard) in their homes at any point in time. Lastly, customers make 80 percent of their condiments purchases at regular prices.

Understanding consumer behavior relating to the purchase of condiments can help grocery retailers better plan their assortments of condiments, and consumer behavior

*The material in this case is drawn from data supplied by H.J. Heinz.

CASE 1
(Continued)

differs for each condiment category. For example, ketchup buyers first decide on whether to purchase a premium versus a value brand and then choose the product's size. On the other hand, mustard buyers focus first on the choice of flavor (such as yellow, Dijon, brown, spicy, or specialty), then on the package type (glass or plastic), and finally on package size. Each segment of the mustard market also appeals to a different target audience. Although yellow mustards appeal more to households with children, Dijon and specialty mustards appeal more to one- to two-person households.

The category can also be better managed by determining where each SKU is within a consumer's purchase tree. The purchase tree consists of three levels: core items, unique items, and unnecessary duplications. Core items have mass-market appeal, while unique items increase variety and selection to the mass market and further extend a product's shopper base to include additional segments sufficiently large to be profitable. In contrast, unnecessary duplications can be safely eliminated since they are viewed by shoppers as redundant with more popular products.

The use of the product tree concept may be illustrated by a supermarket chain stocking five separate choices of hickory-flavored barbecue sauce in each of two price tiers. By eliminating the slowest-selling item in each price tier (the unnecessary duplication), the chain can greatly increase its return on inventory investment and its inventory turnover, reduce its days of supply of inventory, and decrease total inventory costs. Even after the reduction in unnecessary duplication items, the chain would still offer two national brands and private-label choices.

One principle of category management is that the top-selling 50 percent of a firm's items in a category may comprise as much as 95 percent of the category's total sales. Thus, there are real benefits to constantly re-evaluating assortment decisions.

There are three vital considerations with regard to assortment decision making. First, stocking goods in a product subcategory should reflect the behavior of that subcategory's shoppers. For example, since package type is a much more important buying determinant to a mustard buyer than to a ketchup buyer, the former need to be offered multiple package types in each size. Second, retailers should leverage manufacturer research to improve category performance. Manufacturers such as H.J. Heinz have access to all sorts of data—consumer research, syndicated data, and demographic data—that they are willing to share with supermarkets. Third, retailers should study product-placement alternatives. One recent study showed that ketchup and mustard should be placed at opposite ends of an aisle (with steak sauce, Worcestershire sauce, and chili sauce located between them). This positioning maximizes the sales of steak sauce, Worcestershire sauce, and chili sauce. Another study recommends that high-profit items such as steak sauce be kept at eye level (versus ankle or knee level) to maximize its visibility.

Questions
1. List and describe three other measures of category performance that could be used, besides those cited in this case.
2. Explain the relationship among return on inventory investment, inventory turnover, days of inventory supply, and inventory costs.
3. What lessons in this case can be applied to another category such as lightbulbs?
4. How can a store manager differentiate among core, unique, and unnecessary duplication items?

Video Questions on Condiments Category Management
1. Comment on recent trends in the consumption of mustard, steak sauce, and barbecue sauce.
2. Explain the principles of product placement for condiments.

CASE 2
Sensormatic: Pilferage Control†

Although Sensormatic Electronics (http://www.sensormatic.com) makes a wide variety of electronic article surveillance (EAS) products (such as its Sensor Ink and Inktag products that mark thieves with ink and damage stolen goods), sophisticated cameras that monitor stores and warehouses, and unobtrusive labels (that can be hidden under a product's regular label), its most popular product is the Ultra-Max system—with 1 billion hard tags in use worldwide.

The Ultra-Max system uses raised plastic tags that resemble chicklet gum in both size and shape. Unlike other products, Ultra-Max tags can be reactivated if a customer returns a product to the store. Because Ultra-Max tags are clearly visible to shoppers, they are an active deterrent to theft. The Ultra-Max system is based on acousto-magnetic technology. When an Ultra-Max tag that has not been deactivated enters a magnetic field located near a store exit, the material inside the tag vibrates. This vibration then sets off an alarm. The success of the Ultra-Max system is based on its relative lack of false alarms, its ability to cover wide-area store exits (up to 9 feet between two pedestals), and the ease of deactivating the alarm by retail personnel.

One of the most vital emerging developments in pilferage control is source tagging, whereby manufacturers place anti-theft devices on products before shipment to retailers. At present, most EAS tags are attached to goods by retailers. However, source tagging relieves retailers of the labor expense of placing sensors on each product and increases sales of manufacturers' products. Without source tagging, many retailers would lock up small valuable products in glass cases that need to be opened by salesclerks. Although this practice results in lower pilferage costs, it also reduces revenues for both manufacturers and retailers.

The effectiveness of source tagging was recently proven in the industry's first apparel source-tagging test. In this field experiment, The Buckle (a retailer with 171 specialty apparel stores in the Midwest and Southwest) purchased its jeans from a vendor that sewed an Ultra-Max apparel source tag directly into garments as part of the manufacturing process. The apparel source tag was made of fabric and resembled other brand labels on the garment. The Buckle found that its inventory shrinkage results with source tagging were consistent with those obtained by the traditional hard tags the retailer itself installed.

Sensormatic has also worked with other retailers to increase the use of source tagging. In 1996, it signed an agreement with Kmart whereby Sensormatic would supply the retailer with its entire EAS requirements. Sensormatic and Kmart are also forming a joint source-tagging task force to implement source tagging among all of Kmart's vendors (including apparel, health and beauty care items, and food products).

There are several benefits to the use of source tagging to retailers: low costs, faster access to merchandise, and improved anti-pilferage performance. Since the EAS product is attached by the manufacturer as part of its usual production process, retailers no longer have to attach EAS products by hand. The use of source tagging further enables retailers to reduce order lead times as merchandise no longer has to go to a separate staging area for tagging. Lastly, source tagging offers better protection against professional shoplifters who override detection from Ultra-Max by placing stolen merchandise in foil-lined bags.

At present, more than 600 manufacturers use Sensormatic technology in their source-tagging efforts. These include A.T. Cross, Eastman Kodak, L'Oreal, Norelco, Panasonic, Toshiba, Waterman, and Zenith Electronics. Products protected by source tagging include music CDs, power tools, jewelry, cigarettes, and apparel items.

Another emerging development in pilferage control involves source integration, by which EAS labels are incorporated inside a product. Thus, EAS security cannot be

†The material in this case is drawn from *Sensormatic Electronics Corporation 1995 Annual Report; Sensormatic Electronics Corporation 10K for the Fiscal Year Ended June 30, 1995;* and company press releases.

removed by a consumer when removing a product's label or package. With source integration, retailers can more aggressively display merchandise or use fewer packaging materials. Several retail trade organizations, including the National Association of Chain Drug Stores, the National Association of Recording Merchandisers, and the Home Center Institute, have identified integrated source tagging as the ultimate EAS security form.

CASE 2
(Continued)

Questions
1. What are the advantages and disadvantages of source tagging versus tagging by retailers?
2. What are the obstacles to the increased use of source tagging?
3. How can a specialty store determine the value of source tagging for compact cameras?
4. Describe the pros and cons of source integration versus source tagging.

Video Questions on Ultra-Max
1. Describe the guidelines for installing Sensormatic labels.
2. Develop a procedure for a salesclerk to approach a customer who has set off a store alarm.

INTRODUCTION

Employee turnover in retailing is costly, frustrating, and time-consuming. But firms can't seem to stop the revolving door. Turnover is actually a symptom of a more fundamental problem that begins long before retailers notice employees coming and going at an alarming rate.

Turnover is the inevitable result of mismatching people to jobs, people to companies, and people to people. The term "human resources" is misleading. Just because you have humans working in your company doesn't mean you have resources. For people to be productive, they must believe in themselves and their contribution. People must feel that their talents and personalities are compatible with their work and their co-workers. They must believe that they can use the unique talents inherent in their individual human nature.

Basic skills and competencies were sufficient employment criteria in the age of assembly lines, when little creativity or judgment was required. Retailing—or any job in which interactive skills are a factor—requires a precise *matching* of individual styles to company, co-worker, and customer. But before you can match, you must be very clear what you're matching *to*. Interviews in which prospective employees are rated for their ability to "fit into" an organization are useless unless the organization and its people, culture, and customers are clearly defined.

Retention occurs long before hiring or interviewing. Employers who fail to profile the *nature* of a position create the potential for turnover themselves. Here's a story that illustrates what I mean: Three construction workers are taking their lunch breaks high over the city. "What have you got, Joe?" one asks. "Tuna," says Joe, "how about you?" "Turkey," answers the second guy, who then asks the third, "what about you, Nick?" "Baloney," Nick answers, "and I hate baloney. If I get it one more time, I'm gonna jump right off this building." The next day, they ask each other again. Nick opens his lunch box, unwraps the sandwich and screams, "BALONEY—AGAIN," then jumps off the building. The two remaining construction workers watch him descend to the pavement. "Shame," says the first one. "Yeah," agrees the second, "but the real shame is that he packs his own lunch."

When you hire someone, you're packing your own lunch. While retailers claim to hate the baloney of turnover, they keep serving it to themselves. Turnover isn't something to fix; it is something to avoid. The purpose of this case is to demonstrate that turnover, and its financial consequences, are not the problem. They are the result of failing to draw clear profiles of the employer, the job, and the prospective employee, and matching them for a better fit.

GOOD HIRING—GOOD BUSINESS

Can we really expect customer satisfaction without employee satisfaction? Can we continue to demand productive employees without bothering to define and communicate expectations? Can managers expect model employees when they've never taken the time to construct a model of the kind of company they are—or want to be? If you're unclear about what you want, and you don't know how to ask for it, you probably won't get it.

Not long ago, my firm conducted a survey of 860 employees from 32 varied retailers. The sample ranged from CEOs to middle managers to frontline employees. Here are some findings:

- Employee turnover is the single largest hidden cost in retailing.
- 76 percent of senior managers surveyed said that low productivity among staff—from middle management to frontline—is their single biggest job challenge.
- Turnover in excess of 100 percent annually is tolerated because it is thought to be inevitable.
- 72 percent of hiring managers have never acquired interviewing and profiling skills.
- Only 22 percent of the companies surveyed *measure* turnover and hold managers *accountable* for results.

*The material in this case was adapted by the authors from Terri Kabachnick, principal and founder of Terri Kabachnick & Company, "Turning Against the Tide," *Arthur Andersen Retailing Issues Letter* (Center for Retailing Studies, Texas A&M University: September 1995), pp. 1–6. Reprinted by permission.

- 83 percent of managers hire people they "like" rather than matching people to jobs.
- 82 percent of managers refer to frontline employees as "coverage."
- Less than one-third of the retailers surveyed use hiring tools such as interactive computer testing, job profiles, behavior and belief assessments, and selling/service profile assessments.
- Of the companies using behavior assessment technology to aid hiring, education, and retention, 96 percent reported significant decreases in turnover.

BELIEFS DETERMINE BEHAVIOR

Are strong beliefs in the company's core values necessary for productivity? Research indicates that consciously or subconsciously every decision we make or action we take is based on our beliefs. Core beliefs relevant to job requirements, such as belief in the importance of serving customers, are necessary to performing well. Beliefs provide the "why" behind a person's actions.

An example from our survey: Debra, a sales associate, secretly believes shoppers do not want to be "bothered." After all, she hates to be bothered by a salesperson when she shops. However, she knows she must approach customers to keep her job. Her manager reminds her of this almost daily. So, she approaches customers when the manager is there. If he's not, she doesn't. She feels she's right. In Debra's words: "If a customer needs me, she'll let me know." Beliefs govern our thoughts and thoughts govern our behavior.

Three years ago, I was working with a San Francisco firm. We were faced with two critical problems: high turnover and low productivity. During one discussion about these issues, the store manager used a young man named John, a sales associate in the men's sportswear department, as an example. With fourteen days left in his probationary period, John's productivity was below average and he was in danger of losing his job. I asked the store manager if I could speak with John, do a job profile on him, and assess his behavior. Both the manager and John agreed.

John's profile revealed that his short, stocky stature made him uncomfortable selling clothing to people who he perceived to be more stylish than himself. He felt awkward selling fashion and recommending styles and colors. The profile also revealed that John's product knowledge wasn't up to snuff due to his trouble in attending to facts and details. Departments such as fine jewelry or electronics would not suit him. John was enthusiastic and people-oriented; he was a persuasive seller and desired to work in an autonomous, creative atmosphere.

I recommended John be transferred to the card and gift department. He blossomed; within 30 days, he was ringing up three times his previous sales—selling cards. Within three months, John also developed an impressive clients' file—racking up sales of $362,000 in his first year. Knowing the price of greeting cards, you can determine how many cards John sold. When was the last time you were "sold" a greeting card? Stories of this sort are being repeated many times by executives and managers who have learned how to use employee profiles effectively.

Many retailers shrink from discussions about beliefs, values, talents, and "human nature." Afraid to open Pandora's Box, they retreat to the safety of training programs. Beliefs and values can be changed, but not through simple training. They are fundamental human issues, as individual—and difficult to change—as our personalities.

In our survey, retail managers were tested on 27 statements of belief. Here are today's eight most common self-sabotaging beliefs in retail:

1. I just don't have the time to deal with all the "soft stuff" (people issues). I have too many more important responsibilities.
2. Turnover won't stop. Why invest time and money on employees who'll leave soon anyway?
3. The more I compliment employees, the more money they want.
4. I don't mind answering employees' questions, but some of them are really stupid.
5. I don't have the time to listen to people who take forever making their point.
6. I don't understand this company. How can I keep my credibility as a manager and carry out policies with which I don't agree?
7. Retailing is a struggle—no matter what you do, someone will change it. So why bother being creative? Just follow the rules.
8. I know what's best, if only "my people" listened to me.

Managers at high-turnover retailers (over 75 percent) often feel employees are short term, and deserving of little management time and effort. They hire "coverage." Yet, employees are not coverage; they are individuals with unique beliefs, values, passions, talents, convictions, and styles. It is the mix that makes them good at some things, bad at others. Managers at retailers with healthy turnover (under 40 percent) believe every individual makes a difference. They look for people whose beliefs, values, and behavior match those of the firm and the job. They sell the *personal benefits* of working for the firm to potential hires. They communicate the message that although a job may be temporary, the candidate will be able to learn basic skills and lessons that will be useful. They teach and emphasize life and job skills.

One of my clients is Peebles, a successful Virginia-based retailer with 60-plus department stores. Management decided the key to reducing turnover and improving customer service was the "internal customer." Peebles began by developing a profile of the firm's beliefs, values, and behavior. It then profiled selected management positions including store manager, regional manager, merchandise manager, fashion buyer, and basics buyer. Peebles used a combination of style analysis, work environment, and personal interests and values instruments to study the behavior and beliefs needed for each job. The result was a profile of the person who would best fit Peebles and the job. Potential hires were then screened. Communication and behavior assessments helped determine *how* a person did his or her job. The values and beliefs assessments showed the *why* behind a person's actions. Successful profiling led to a firmwide program involving the total organization. Peebles has reduced turnover by 48 percent.

FISH GOTTA SWIM, BIRDS GOTTA FLY

None of us can escape our own human nature. "Fish gotta swim, birds gotta fly." It is the nature of fish to swim and birds to fly. If you're hiring birds to swim or fish to fly, you're going to have a turnover problem. All the training in the world isn't going to solve the problem. Prospective employees are unique, and every retailer has a distinct culture. Every retailer should have a template of the latter, a profile of the former, and a method for matching the two.

If a retailer hires a person to do a job that requires the same behavior a person brings to the job, several things happen. First, he or she focuses energy on completing the job. Second, he or she enjoys doing the job. When the behavior of the job does not match the natural behavior of the individual, that person expends a great deal of energy trying to adjust his or her behavior. This stressful process can cause sickness, drug or alcohol abuse, or behavioral problems—all of which increase benefit costs and absenteeism, as well as decrease service quality and productivity.

Dave was hired as an executive trainee for a Midwestern client. The company invested five years in training and developing Dave. He was then promoted to store manager. Within three months, Dave developed a series of health problems. He took more sick days in six months than in his entire five years with the company. His productivity and store sales dropped significantly. Management was stunned. How could an individual change so dramatically? In doing an assessment on Dave, I learned he was quality-oriented and preferred a systematic approach to work. Naturally patient, with good listening skills, he needed a paced environment in which work was completed with an emphasis on quality and procedure. I recommended a transfer to one of the firm's smaller stores with fewer employees. The move was made. Within one year, Dave's results were no sick days, reduced employee turnover, and a 22 percent sales increase.

Ask yourself: How much expense could our company save by matching people to the right jobs? What productivity and job satisfaction gains could we achieve? How do we get a handle on ourselves and on the nature of the people working for us, and the people we are looking to hire?

Four definitions are critical for effective recruiting, hiring, and retention:

1. **Self**—Who am I?
2. **Job**—What are the success requirements for the job?
3. **Organization**—What do we believe? What do we value? How do we behave?
4. **Employee/Applicant**—Who is this person really? What does he or she value? What does he or she believe? How does he or she think? How does he or she act?

The definitions were derived from assessment tools profiling applicants and employees, jobs, and firms. The result is a clearer definition of the right employee for a given retailer and a given job. The "right employee" definition serves as a profile; once you have it, you look for that person. How will you know if you have found him or her? Let's look at the definitions again.

SELF-DEFINITION

As a manager/employer, what is your behavior? Are you a specialist or generalist? Do you like to work through people or with them? What is your behavioral and communication style? How do you respond to your job environment? Are you task- or idea-oriented? Knowing how you communicate, manage, and lead lets you recognize, understand, and adapt to other styles.

JOB DEFINITION

Many employers expect employees to fit an ill-defined job. Example: "Sell to and service the customers so they are satisfied." Too much is assumed and too little known from this statement. If the job could talk, what would it say? A few examples:

- Make unpopular decisions in carrying out the job.
- Persist steadily at routine work.
- Manage diverse types of people.
- Follow detailed instruction; have patience.
- Be satisfied to stay at this job level.

These requirements are rated by assigning a value of 1 through 5 to each statement, where 1 means unimportant to the job and 5 means highly important. The job profile is then compared to the individual's profile to chart compatibility.

A job should be defined from several sources and differences reconciled. For example, using a job profile assessment, several firms asked a director of stores, a district manager, and a store manager to describe the behavior requirements of a store manager. The results showed significant differences. The most common disagreements were in the interpretation of job procedures, prioritizing duties, citing behavior needed for success, defining the time needed to complete tasks, and how to interact with co-workers and customers for successful results.

ORGANIZATION DEFINITION

What defines this firm's culture? How does the firm deal with problems and challenges? Is it aggressive? Leading edge? How does the company relate to employees and customers? Is there a high task emphasis? Are there tight controls? How are rules and procedures handled? Is there room for team participation, adaptability, and formal and informal areas of responsibility? Does the firm have direction? Does the status quo rule the day, or does the firm value innovation?

Most importantly, is everyone on the same page? Are top management, middle management, and frontline employees in sync with the firm's goals, strategies, and styles? Or do misalignments, mixed signals, and inconsistencies confuse, frustrate, and hamper productivity on all levels?

Consider this—an ineffective, nonproductive employee loses her job. She is hired by another company and becomes a top executive. In my research, this has happened often. The behavior profile of the firm is critical in successfully matching individuals to their job environment.

EMPLOYEE/APPLICANT DEFINITION

How can an employer gain insight into a person and get beyond what a person says in an interview? How can a manager measure the "skill versus will" factor? Where does experience fit?

Recent job behavior studies have dashed one long-held theory. Is past behavior a true indicator of future behavior? I believe not. Change the job and a person's behavior or "response to environment" changes. Employers need to understand individual preferences beyond what they learn via traditional information gathering. Human bias is removed by assessing communication styles, behavior, beliefs, values, and job perceptions. The assessment also gives answers to: What does an employee *need* to learn instead of what do we *want* to teach? What tools does a person need to be self-motivated and productive? Does a person "see" a job correctly?

The closer the match, the better a fit. The more *natural* the combination of employer, job, organization, and employee, the greater the chance for success. Productive people are almost always satisfied, which makes customer satisfaction another *natural* outcome.

DISCOVERING NEW TOOLS

Sophisticated tools and techniques that demystify profiling are available to firms wishing to turn the tide against turnover. Many methodologies exist. They adapt behavioral science research to the needs of the business community. However, not all are retailing specific, and some are time-consuming and expensive. Many instruments are also targeted to a higher grade level than the average store employee is comfortable answering. If properly administered and interpreted, many analytical tools, validated by business and government, can reduce the human bias prevalent in hiring. But retailers are surprisingly reluctant to abandon outdated assembly-line interviewing and hiring practices.

Recent technological advances in computer-driven testing have dramatically decreased the cost and time required for using these instruments on a firmwide basis. Price is down; accuracy is up. When designed, administered, and analyzed by a qualified person, with retail industry experience, many of the available profiling techniques can be customized with impressive results.

I have found a combination of two methodologies successful. One is the D.I.S.C. theory and language derived from the work of Dr. William Marston and

Walter Clark and validated in computerized reports by Bill Bonnstetter, president and CEO of Target Training International. The other is the Psych-K system from Robert Williams, president of Ki-Point Communications. The combination of methodologies provides rare insight into an applicant's behavior, beliefs, and values. For example, by using one or more of the menus available on the software, a report may show a person's perception of a job compared to the job's requirements.

Hiring isn't the only valuable use of individual profiling. Profiling *current* employees can decrease turnover and spark productivity:

1. Is the employee utilizing his or her natural skills?
2. What is the employee's productivity level compared to potential?
3. How is the team's productivity?
4. What education and/or job aids does this employee need to be effective?
5. Should this employee be counseled to consider work in a different environment?
6. Should the employee be repositioned or reclassified?
7. Is the employee ready for additional responsibilities?
8. What can the direct supervisor do to increase communication and job satisfaction?

To foster greater productivity, we must stop, examine, and change the tools we're using. Ironically, the major obstacle to heightened productivity is human nature itself. As the old saying goes, a man is chopping a big pile of wood. His job gets harder and the work gets slower as the ax gets duller. A bystander asks, "Why don't you stop to sharpen your ax?" To which, the woodchopper replies, "Can't. I've got too much wood to chop."

If we truly want to attack turnover at the root, we have to stop and make changes in our methodology. We have to take the time to sharpen the ax. My advice to the woodchopper is "I'll trade you that ax for a chain saw."

Questions

1. How does the case relate to this comment in Chapter 11? "Through a retail organization, a firm structures and assigns tasks (functions), policies, resources, authority, responsibilities, and rewards so as to efficiently and effectively satisfy the needs of its target market, employees, and management."
2. What organization structure would you recommend to reduce employee turnover? Why?
3. React to this statement in the case: "Turnover in excess of 100 percent annually is tolerated because it is thought to be inevitable."
4. Evaluate the self-sabotaging beliefs noted in the case.
5. How does high employee turnover adversely affect financial operations management?
6. Why is employee recruitment so important with regard to employee productivity?
7. Explain how profiling can improve employee productivity.

Part Six

Merchandise Management and Pricing

- In Part 6, the merchandise management and pricing aspects of the retail strategy mix are presented. Merchandise management consists of the buying, handling, and financial aspects of merchandising. Pricing decisions are crucial due to their impact on the financial aspects of merchandise management and their interaction with other retailing elements.

- Chapter 14 covers merchandise buying and handling. Each stage in the buying and handling process is described: organization, merchandise plans, information about customer demand, merchandise sources, evaluation methods, negotiations, concluding the purchase, merchandise handling, reordering, and re-evaluation.

- Chapter 15 concentrates on financial merchandise management. First, the cost and retail methods of accounting are introduced. The merchandise forecasting and budgeting process is presented next. Unit control systems are then discussed. The last part of the chapter integrates dollar and unit financial inventory controls.

- Chapter 16 deals with pricing. The outside factors affecting decisions are reviewed: consumers, government, suppliers, and competitors. A framework for developing a price strategy is described: objectives, broad policy, basic strategy, implementation, and adjustments.

Chapter 14

Buying and Handling Merchandise

CHAPTER OBJECTIVES

1. To examine nonfinancial merchandise planning and management

2. To outline the merchandise buying and handling process: organization, merchandise plans, information about customer demand, merchandise sources, evaluation methods, negotiations, concluding the purchase, merchandise handling, reordering, and re-evaluation

3. To discuss each element in the merchandise buying and handling process in detail

4. To place special emphasis on what merchandise a retailer should carry, how much to stock, when to stock items, and where to store items

With 1 million square feet of selling space spread over ten floors, Macy's Herald Square, New York store has always presented a challenge in terms of efficiently handling merchandise. Among the specific problems Macy's Herald Square has encountered were difficulties in moving goods throughout a ten-story building, vehicular traffic congestion in reaching the store with delivery trucks, and heavy in-store traffic levels (making it hard to stock items during hours the store was open). So, until recently, Macy's Herald Square often had a merchandise backlog, and an ongoing problem since some items did not get to the store until after sales dates had elapsed.

In 1995, Macy's Herald's Square hired a consulting firm to help accomplish two overall goals: Macy's wanted the proper assortment of stock to be available for sale earlier in the day. It also wanted sales managers to be able to spend more time on selling and customer service.

Today, Macy's Herald Square's new logistics strategy encompasses all aspects of merchandise handling. A major part of the strategy entails the use of several teams that now report to the director of operations. The receiving and delivery team unloads trailers and delivers merchandise to specific delivery zones. At each delivery zone, two other teams take over. The placement team handles goods in the housewares and other basic areas, while the processing team handles all goods that need to be folded as part of their display presentation and then tagged for security. Both the placement and processing teams work overnight.

Three other key components of the new logistics strategy are the use of the fill-in team, the recovery team, and the administrative team. The fill-in team comes into the store at mid-morning and is responsible for rounding out the merchandise based on sales made earlier in the day. The recovery team starts in the afternoon and is responsible for straightening displays, cleaning the fitting rooms, and refolding merchandise. The administrative team handles damaged goods, returns of unsold merchandise to vendors, and all price changes.

Under Macy's Herald Square's previous system, it took five to seven days to process and move merchandise from receiving to the selling floor; turnaround time under the new system has been reduced to 24 hours or less. Also with the new system, the number of stock associates at Herald Square has been reduced from 300 to 205. Based on this program's success, it has been rolled out to all of the more than 90 stores in the Macy's East division.[1]

[1] "New System Keeps the Goods Flowing at Macy's," *Chain Store Age* (September 1996), pp. 42–48.

Devising and enacting a merchandise plan is a key phase in a retail strategy. To succeed, **OVERVIEW**
a firm must have the proper assortments of goods and services when they are in demand
and sell them in a manner consistent with the overall strategy. **Merchandising** consists
of the activities involved in acquiring particular goods and/or services and making them
available at the places, times, and prices and in the quantity to enable a retailer to reach
its goals.

Even for the best firms, merchandising decisions can dramatically affect performance. This is illustrated by McDonald's struggles with the McLean Deluxe, which it
dropped during 1996:

> Say so long to the McLean Deluxe. The reduced-fat hamburger, that McDonald's
> rolled out in 1991 to quell those who said too much fast food was fat food, is being
> discontinued. It will be phased out in coming weeks, as inventories of the sandwich's patties run out. Although touted as nutritious (with 10 grams, it had half the
> fat of a McDonald's Quarter Pounder), the McLean never caught on with customers. Some of the fat was replaced with a seaweed derivative, giving the burger
> a different taste. It also cost more than other sandwiches, and McDonald's seldom
> promoted it. "I sell maybe one a day," a franchisee in Northern California said over
> the weekend. McDonald's doesn't intend to draw attention to the McLean's passing, but customers will be hearing a lot about this month's sandwich special: A
> double cheeseburger.[2]

In this chapter, the buying and handling aspects of merchandise planning and
management are discussed. Merchandising's financial side is described in Chapter 15.
Retail pricing is covered in Chapter 16. Planning for a service retailer is examined in
Chapter 19.

Figure 14-1 shows the **merchandise buying and handling process,** comprised of an **THE MER-**
integrated and systematic sequence of steps from establishing a buying organization **CHANDISE**
through regular re-evaluation. It is essential for each step to be used in merchandising. **BUYING AND**
HANDLING
Establishing a Formal or Informal Buying Organization **PROCESS**

The first stage is establishing a buying organization. Merchandising cannot be done
properly unless the buying organization is well defined—specifying who is responsible
for merchandise decisions, the tasks of these people, the authority to make decisions, and
the relationship of merchandising to overall retail operations. Figure 14-2 highlights the
range of buying-organization attributes from which retailers may choose.

With a **formal buying organization,** merchandising is viewed as a distinct retail
task and a separate department is set up. All or most functions involved in acquiring merchandise and making it available for sale (Figure 14-1, Steps 2 through 10) are then under the control of this department. A formal organization is most often used by larger
firms and involves distinct buying personnel. In an **informal buying organization,**
merchandising is not viewed as a distinct task. The same personnel handle both merchandising and other retail tasks; responsibility and authority are not always clear-cut.
Informal organizations generally occur in smaller retailers.

The major advantages of a formal buying organization are the clarity of responsibilities and authority and the use of full-time, specialized merchandisers. The major disadvantage is the cost of having a separate department. The key advantages of an informal

[2]Richard Gibson, "McDonald's Decides Its McLean Burger Fails to Cut the Mustard with Diners," *Wall
Street Journal* (February 5, 1996), p. B5.

Figure 14-1

The Merchandise Buying and Handling Process

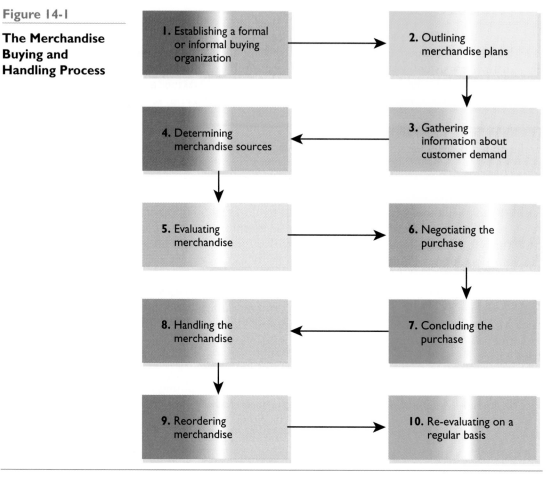

Figure 14-2

The Attributes of Buying Organizations

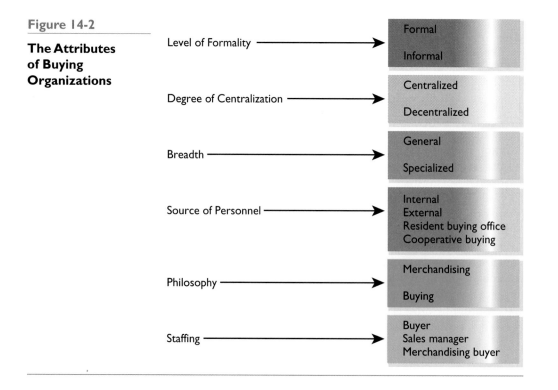

buying organization are the low costs and flexibility. The key disadvantages are less-defined responsibilities and authority, and the de-emphasis on merchandise planning.

Both structures exist in great numbers. It is not crucial for a firm to use a formal department. It is crucial that the firm recognizes the role of merchandising and ensures that responsibility, activities, authority, and the interrelationship with operations are aptly defined and enacted.

Multiunit retailers must also choose whether to have a centralized buying organization or a decentralized one. In a **centralized buying organization,** all purchase decisions emanate from one office. For instance, a chain may have eight stores, with all merchandise decisions made at the headquarters store. In a **decentralized buying organization,** purchase decisions are made locally or regionally. As an example, a 12-store chain may allow each outlet to select its own merchandise or divide the branches into geographic territories (such as four branches per region) with regional decisions made by the headquarters store in each territory.

Among the advantages of centralized buying are the integration of effort, strict controls, consistent image, proximity to top management, staff support, and discounts through volume purchases. Among the possible disadvantages are the inflexibility, time delays, poor morale at local stores, and excessive uniformity.

Decentralized buying offers these advantages: adaptability to local market conditions, quick order processing, and improved morale because branches have autonomy. The potential disadvantages are disjointed planning, an inconsistent image, limited management controls, little staff support, and the loss of volume discounts.

Many chains have combined the benefits of both formats by deploying a centralized buying organization while also giving regional or local store managers the power to revise orders or place their own orders:

> "If you can customize assortments in different locations, you're going to win in the retail business," says Jonathon Rand, merchandise information director, Apparel and Home Fashions Group, Sears. Every retailer struggles with the issue of inclusion: how to incorporate input from store operations people into assortment planning decisions at the corporate and local levels. Some companies, notably J.C. Penney and Nordstrom, use a local decision model, while specialty stores and mass merchants often have a centrally directed model. To improve local assortments, consider a hybrid of these two models, one that consolidates data collection into a central data warehouse, yet has the ability for both headquarters decision makers and regional operations people to manipulate data to meet their own needs. Headquarters buying staff typically have the most vendor leverage, and thus can most effectively source a majority of merchandise that meets consumer needs. But when individual stores have some purchasing flexibility, make sure that local purchases and inventories are visible in the corporate data base so results are known and actors are accountable. Local assortment proficiency is primarily a function of better communications between local stores and corporate headquarters.[3]

A choice must be made between a general buying organization and a specialized one. In a general organization, one or several people buy all of a firm's merchandise. Thus, the owner of a small hardware store may buy all the merchandise for his or her store. With a specialized organization, each buyer is responsible for a product category. For instance, a department store usually would have separate buyers for girls', juniors', and women's clothes.

The general approach is better if the retailer is small or there are few different goods/services involved. The specialized approach is better if the retailer is large or many goods/services are handled. Through specialization, knowledge is improved and

[3]Marie Beninati, Paul Evans, and Joseph McKinney, "A Blueprint for Local Assortment Management," *Chain Store Age* (February 1997), p. 30.

Figure 14-3

Michaels Stores' Inside Buying Organization

Michaels Stores is a growing chain of arts, crafts, and decorative products shops. Each of its outlets carries about 30,000 items that are selected by the firm's full-time buyers. Michaels has a corporate merchandising group to choose products from and negotiate purchase terms with about 1,000 vendors. Merchandising personnel often travel to meet with vendors. Shown here is a buying trip to the Orient.

responsibility well defined; however, costs are higher and extra personnel are normally required.

A retailer can choose an inside buying organization and/or an outside one. An **inside buying organization** is staffed by a retailer's own personnel and merchandise decisions are made by permanent employees of the firm. See Figure 14-3. With an **outside buying organization,** a company or personnel external to the retailer are hired, usually on a fee basis. Although most retailers use either an inside or an outside buying organization, some employ a combination of the two.

An outside organization is most frequently used by small or medium-sized retailers or those far from their sources of supply. In these cases, it is more efficient for the retailers to hire outside buyers than to use company personnel. An outside organization has clout in dealing with suppliers (because of purchase volume), usually services noncompeting retailers, offers marketing research expertise, and sometimes sponsors private-label goods. Outside buying organizations may be paid by retailers that subscribe to their services, or by vendors, which give commissions. Sometimes, an individual retailer decides to set up its own internal organization if it feels its outside group is dealing with direct competitors or the firm finds it can buy items more efficiently on its own.

A **resident buying office,** which can be an inside or outside organization, is used when a retailer wants to keep in close touch with key market trends and cannot do so through just its headquarters buying staff. Such offices are usually situated in important merchandise centers (sources of supply) and provide valuable data and contacts. There are a few large companies that operate outside resident buying offices in the United States, serving several thousand retailers. For example, Bloomingdale's, Bon Marche, and Saks Fifth Avenue (all of which also have their own inside buying organizations) use Minneapolis-based Associated Merchandising Corporation's worldwide network of buying offices to get more marketing research data, better identify emerging fashion trends, and obtain recommended sources of supply; and Doneger Group services 1,000 retail clients.[4]

Smaller, independent retailers are now involved with cooperative buying to a greater degree than ever before (to compete with bigger chains). Under **cooperative buying,** a group of independent retailers gets together to make quantity purchases from a supplier. Volume discounts are then achieved. It is most popular among food and hardware retail-

---

[4]Isadore Barmash, "Buying Offices: Once a Staple, Now Few Exist," *Shopping Center Today* (May 1997), pp. 76, 86.

Changing Distribution Systems in Japan

Distribution systems in Japan are undergoing a basic shift due to a combination of factors. These include deregulation, manufacturing developments, changing consumer behavior patterns, and economic forces. Let's look at each of these factors:

■ In the past, Japanese retailers were very heavily regulated. For example, to open, large stores had to secure approval from retail groups operated by local chambers of commerce. These approvals sometimes took up to eight years. Now, all store approval decisions must be acted on within one year. In addition, only very large stores must now seek permission.

■ The current relatively weak economic climate in Japan (caused by a slowdown in consumer expenditures and by higher unemployment) has forced some manufacturers to offer less variety and assortments in response to retailer demands for stronger-selling products.

■ Japanese consumers have become more cost-conscious. This has elevated the role of discount stores. Families are also now more prone to shop in suburban areas instead of downtown.

■ The Japanese recession has made warehouse and storage space less costly. As a result, some big chains have been able to bypass their wholesalers and build their own distribution centers. Lower land costs have also increased the use of central city locations by some retailers that at one time favored less-costly suburban locations. At a time when consumer shopping patterns are shifting, these retailers hope to lure consumers back downtown with reduced prices.

Source: John Fahy and Fuyuki Taguchi, "Reassessing the Japanese Distribution System," *Sloan Management Review*, Vol. 36 (Winter 1995), pp. 49–61.

ers. In some cases, retailers initiate the cooperative; in others, a wholesaler or manufacturer may form a cooperative as an attempt to cut operating costs. The National Retail Federation has a new Group Buying Service (http://www.nrf.com/services/group) to enable small and medium-sized retailers to "pool their purchasing power" for packaging, delivery, and similar goods and services that aid in everyday merchandising operations. It is not yet involved with actual merchandise buying.

Another decision involves a retailer's determining whether the buying organization is to be concerned with merchandising or buying. As noted at the beginning of the chapter, merchandising includes the broad range of activities involved in buying and selling goods and services, such as purchases, pricing, storage, and display. Buying includes only product purchases and not their sale. Many firms consider merchandising the foundation for their success, and buyers (or merchandise managers) engage in both buying and selling tasks. However, some retailers consider their buyers to be highly skilled specialists who should not be active in the selling function, which is done by other skilled specialists. One study of store managers at full-line discount stores found that most of them have great influence as to the way items are displayed, but have rather little influence regarding decisions as to whether to stock or promote particular brands.[5]

The advantages of a merchandising philosophy are that there is a smooth, integrated chain of command; the buyer's expertise is used in selling; responsibility and authority are clear (a buyer does not blame sales personnel for poor sales efforts and vice versa); the buyer ensures that items are properly displayed; costs are reduced (fewer staff specialists); and the buyer is close to consumers by his or her involvement with selling.

[5]"Areas Where Managers Feel They Have the Most Influence," *Discount Store News* (October 4, 1993), p. 29. See also Robert Berner, "How Gap's Design Shop Keeps Its Imitators Hustling," *Wall Street Journal* (March 13, 1997), pp. B1, B5.

The advantages of separate buying and selling functions are that similar skills are not needed for each task; the morale of in-store personnel goes up as they get more authority; selling is not viewed as a secondary function; salespeople are closer to customers than buyers; there can be specialists in each area; and buyers may not be good supervisors due to their time away from the store and the differences in managing buying and selling personnel.

Both philosophies are used, and the strengths of merchandising versus buying remain open to debate. An individual firm must evaluate which format is better for carrying out its own strategy.

The last decision in this stage of buying and handling merchandise centers on staffing the buying organization. What positions must be filled, and what qualifications should be required? Firms with a merchandising vantage point are most concerned with hiring good buyers. Firms that take a buying and selling perspective are interested in hiring both buyers and sales managers.

Many large retailers hire college graduates whom they place in extensive training programs and promote internally to positions as buyers and sales managers. A buyer must be attuned to the marketplace, must be assertive in bargaining with suppliers, must use buying plans (detailed shopping lists that completely outline purchases) extensively, and may have to travel to major marketplaces. A sales manager must be a good organizer, supervisor, and motivator. A merchandising buyer must possess the attributes of each.

Today, more retailers than ever feel the critical qualification for good buying personnel is their ability to relate to customers and methodically anticipate future needs. In addition, to some extent, buyers are involved with each of the remaining activities described in this chapter and many of those detailed in Chapter 15.

Outlining Merchandise Plans

Merchandise planning centers on four basic decisions: what merchandise to stock, how much merchandise to stock, when to stock merchandise, and where to store merchandise.

In making decisions, a firm needs to be sure it carries a distinctive merchandise mix, one that lets it stand out from competitors and that is consistent with its retail positioning. Consider this:

All businesses know about tight dollars and fierce competition. Retailers could write a book about it. Throughout the industry, too much supply is chasing too little demand—with myriad formats vying for the attention of a mature marketplace. Product differentiation, by and large, is minimal. Most of the time, price is king. The upshot of these realities is twofold. First, consumers hold the upper hand; it is a buyer's market. Second, firms have few ways to secure an increasingly desirable commodity: customer loyalty. The pie, after all, is not growing. Gaining a larger slice means identifying each person's specific product and service needs, and meeting them consistently and cost-effectively. Above all, customers feel entitled to exactly what they want for a price they are prepared to pay. If one retailer cannot deliver, there are many other choices. But the pressures of modern living also suggest that people will remain loyal to retailers that tailor products to meet specific needs. Loyalty can be propagated by better merchandise management.[6]

What Merchandise Is Stocked ❏ A retailer must first determine what quality of merchandise to carry. Should it carry top-line, expensive items and sell to upper-income customers? Or should it carry middle-of-the-line, moderately priced items and cater to middle-income customers? Or should it carry bottom-line, inexpensive items and attract lower-income customers? Or should it try to draw more than one market

[6]Beninati, Evans, and McKinney, "A Blueprint for Local Assortment Management," p. 28.

Table 14-1 FACTORS TO CONSIDER IN PLANNING MERCHANDISE QUALITY

Factor	Relevance for Planning
Target market(s)	Merchandise quality must be matched to the wishes of the desired target market(s).
Competition	A retailer can sell similar quality (follow the competition) or different quality (to appeal to a different target market).
Retailer's image	Merchandise quality must be directly related to the perception that customers have of the retailer.
Store location	The location affects the retailer's image and the number of competitors, which, in turn, relate to quality.
Stock turnover	High quality and high prices usually yield a lower turnover than low quality and low prices.
Profitability	High-quality merchandise generally brings greater profit per unit than low-quality merchandise; however, turnover may cause total profits to be greater for low-quality merchandise.
Manufacturer versus private brands	For many consumers, manufacturer (national) brands connote higher quality than private (dealer) brands.
Customer services offered	High-quality merchandise requires personal selling, alterations, delivery, and so on. Low-quality merchandise may not.
Personnel	Skilled, knowledgeable personnel are necessary for quality merchandise. Limited personnel (self-service) are needed for low-quality merchandise.
Perceived goods/service benefits	Low-quality merchandise attracts customers who desire functional product benefits (e.g., warmth, comfort). High-quality merchandise attracts customers who desire extended product benefits (e.g., status, services, style).
Constrained decision making	a. Franchise or chain operators have limited or no control over product quality. They either buy directly from the franchisor (chain) or must abide by quality standards. b. Independent retailers who buy from a few large wholesalers will be limited to the range of quality offered by those wholesalers.

segment by offering a variety in quality, such as middle- and top-line merchandise for middle- and upper-income shoppers? The firm must also decide whether to carry promotional merchandise (low-priced closeout items or special buys used to generate store traffic).

There are several factors to consider in deciding on merchandise quality: the desired target market(s), competition, the retailer's image, store location, stock turnover, profit margins, manufacturer versus private brands, customer services, personnel, the perceived goods/service benefits, and constrained decision making. See Table 14-1.

For example, Dollar General (the variety store chain) has an overall merchandising strategy that is very consistent with its approach to merchandise quality:

> Dollar General Corporation seeks profitable growth by providing value in consumable basic merchandise to low-, middle-, and fixed-income families. The Company sells this general merchandise at retail through a chain of more than 2,500 small, company-owned stores in 24 states. The Company's strategy is to offer quality merchandise at everyday low prices. Dollar General emphasizes even-dollar price points and believes its prices are usually below those of competitors. The majority of products are priced at $10 or less, with nearly 50 percent of the products priced at $1 or less. The most expensive items typically are priced at $35.[7]

Dollar General is so successful that its annual sales are nearly $2 billion. See Figure 14-4.

The second major decision a retailer makes on what merchandise to handle involves determining how innovative to be. Several factors should be examined: target market(s),

---

[7]*Dollar General Corporation 1996 Annual Report.*

Figure 14-4

Dollar General's Merchandising Philosophy

MERCHANDISING

We want our customers to make Dollar General their destination for everyday basics. To accomplish this, we have improved our selection of everyday items, ensured that goods in our stores are in-stock and implemented additional seasonal promotions.

goods/service growth potential, fashion trends and theories (if applicable), the retailer's image, competition, customer segments, responsiveness to consumers, investment costs, profitability, risk, constrained decision making, and dropping declining goods/services. See Table 14-2.

An innovative retailer, one that carries new goods and services and plans for upcoming trends, faces a great opportunity—distinctiveness (due to its being first in the market)—and a great risk—possibly misreading customer interests and being stuck with large inventories. By weighing each factor in Table 14-2 and preparing a thorough plan for merchandising new goods and services, a retailer should be able to capitalize on its opportunities and reduce its risks.

Here are two illustrations of distinctive merchandising strategies:

■ The Long John Silver's fast-food chain was one of the first firms to introduce a new line of "wrap" sandwiches, which mix such traditional ingredients as shrimp, chicken, or beef, with ethnic foods, sauces, and fillings—and wrap them in rolled flatbread, pita bread, or tortillas. As one industry consultant remarked, "This is probably the first truly new sandwich item to come along in I don't know when. There is a lot of sameness to the restaurant industry, so the fact that it is different in and of itself will generate a lot of trial. The products' near-limitless range of fillings offers retailers a golden positioning opportunity: a portable product for on-the-go consumers that is equally appealing to boomers watching their waistlines and Generation Xers bored with burgers. Wraps also allow chains, battered by price wars, to market a product with a higher perceived value and price point."[8]

[8]Bill McDowell, "Fast-Food Chains Warm Up to New 'Wrap' Sandwiches," *Advertising Age* (October 28, 1996), p. 55.

Table 14-2 FACTORS TO CONSIDER IN PLANNING MERCHANDISE INNOVATIVENESS

Factor	Relevance for Planning
Target market(s)	Evaluate whether the target market is conservative or progressive.
Goods/service growth potential	Consider each new offering on the basis of rapidity of initial sales, maximum sales potential per time period, and length of sales life.
Fashion trends	Understand vertical and horizontal trends, if selling fashion merchandise.
Retailer image	The kinds of goods/services a retailer carries are influenced by its image. The level of innovativeness should be consistent with this image.
Competition	Lead or follow competition in the selection of new goods/services.
Customer segments	Customers can be segmented by dividing merchandise into established-product displays and new-product displays.
Responsiveness to consumers	New offerings should be handled when they are requested by the target market.
Amount of investment	These types of investment are possible for each new good/service: product costs, new fixtures, and additional personnel (or further training for existing personnel).
Profitability	Each new offering should be assessed for potential profits (for the particular item, as well as the overall profits of the retailer).
Risk	The major risks involve the possible tarnishing of the retailer's image, investment costs, and opportunity costs.
Constrained decision making	Franchise and chain operators may be restricted in the new goods/services they can purchase.
Dropping declining goods/services	Older goods/services should be deleted if sales and/or profits are too low.

■ Hammacher Schlemmer is a 150-year-old chain of gift stores, but what gift stores! As its Web site noted, "It is our mission to enhance our customers' lives by bringing them unique products that either solve problems or further their lifestyles, and eliminate their need to comparison shop. Always innovative, the chain was the first to carry the steam iron, electric dry shaver, pop-up toaster, cordless telephone, and microwave oven." Today, Hammacher Schlemmer carries such products as these: $700 wine-storing refrigerators, $1,000 portable one-person saunas, $350 Bose Wave Radios, $30 decks of magnetic playing cards, $2,000 Ted Williams' autographed baseball bats, and $40 heated mittens. "These are the same kinds of products we have always offered. Unique, functional, and innovative."

The retailer should assess the growth potential for each new good or service it carries. Three growth elements are of special interest: the rapidity of initial sales, maximum sales potential per time period, and the length of selling life. How fast will a new good or service generate sales? What are the most sales (dollars and units) to be achieved in a season or a year? Over what time period will a good or service continue to sell?[9]

A useful tool for assessing growth potential when planning a retail strategy is the **product life cycle,** which shows the expected behavior of a good or service over its life. The traditional product life cycle has four stages: introduction, growth, maturity, and decline—as depicted and described in Figure 14-5.

During introduction, the retailer should anticipate a more limited target market, consisting of higher-income and more innovative consumers. The good or service will probably be supplied in one basic version, not a choice of alternatives. The manufacturer (supplier) may limit distribution to "finer" stores. Yet, new convenience items such as food and houseware products are normally mass distributed. Items that are initially distributed selectively

[9]See Pierre Desmet, "Merchandising and the Life Cycle of Books Sold by Mail," *Journal of Direct Marketing,* Vol. 9 (Summer 1995), pp. 61–71.

Figure 14-5

**The Traditional
Product Life Cycle**

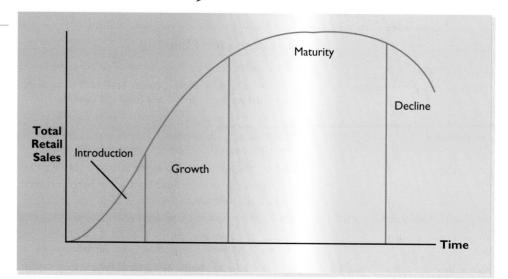

	Life Cycle Stage			
Strategy Variable	Introduction	Growth	Maturity	Decline
Target market	High-income innovators	Middle-income adopters	Mass market	Low-income and laggards
Good or service	One basic offering	Some variety	Greater variety	Less variety
Distribution intensity	Limited or extensive	More retailers	More retailers	Fewer retailers
Price	Penetration or skimming	Wide range	Lower prices	Lower prices
Promotion	Informative	Persuasive	Competitive	Limited
Supplier structure	Monopoly-oligopoly	Oligopoly-competition	Competition	Oligopoly

generally have a high (skimming) price strategy. Merchandise that is mass distributed typically involves low (penetration) pricing to encourage faster consumer acceptance. In either case, early promotion must be explanatory, geared to informing consumers. At this stage, there is only one or very few possible suppliers.

As innovative consumers buy a new good or service and recommend it to their friends, sales increase rapidly and the product life cycle enters the growth stage. The target market expands to include middle-income consumers who are somewhat more innovative than the average. Variations of the basic offering appear; width and depth of assortment expand. The number of retailers carrying the product increases. Price discounting is not widely employed, but a variety of retailers offer a large range of prices, customer services, and quality. Retail promotion is more persuasive and aimed at acquainting consumers with product availability and extended services. There is an increasing number of suppliers.

In maturity, sales reach their maximum level. The largest portion of the target market is reached during this period. Lower-, middle-, and upper-income shoppers select from very broad product offerings and options. All types of retailers (discount to upscale) carry the good or service in some form. Prestige retailers continue emphasizing brand names and customer services, but others enter into active price competition. Price is more prominently cited in promotional activities. For retailers and their suppliers, the maturity stage is the most competitive.

According to the traditional product life cycle, a good or service then enters decline, often brought on by two factors: the target market shrinks (due to product obsolescence, the availability of newer substitutes, and consumer boredom) and price cutting lessens profit margins. In decline, the target market may become the lowest-income consumer and laggards. Some retailers cut back on their variety (to reduce the space allotted to these items); others drop the good or service for profit and image reasons. At the retailers still carrying the items, lower prices are offered, and promotion is reduced and geared to price. There are fewer suppliers, as many turn to other items.

Not all goods and services conform to the traditional product life cycle just detailed. Some derivatives are shown in Figure 14-6. In a boom sales pattern, sales rise quickly and maintain a high level for a long period of time. Many cosmetics, pharmaceutical products, and rental services can be placed in this category.

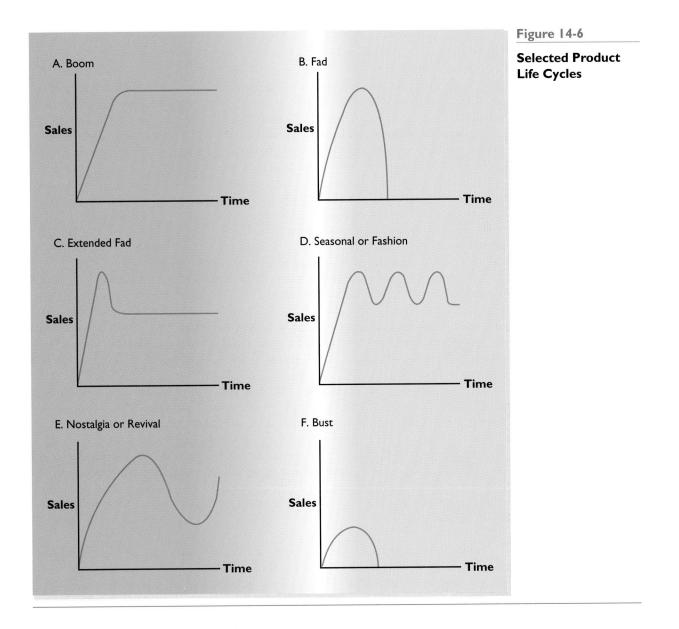

Figure 14-6

Selected Product Life Cycles

A fad curve occurs if a good or service generates a lot of sales, but only for a short time. The retailer must be careful not to overorder because of enthusiasm over high early sales. Often, toys and games are short-lived fads, such as the Tickle Me Elmo doll that flew off store shelves in late 1996 and early 1997. An extended fad is like a fad, except that residual sales continue for a longer period at a fraction of earlier sales. Clothing with designer insignias is an example of a product that can be classified as an extended fad.

A seasonal or fashion curve results for a good or service that sells well over nonconsecutive time periods. Seasonal items, such as ski equipment and air conditioner servicing, have excellent sales during one season per year. Since the strongest sales of seasonal items usually occur at the same time each year, retail planning is rather simple. Fashion products are much less predictable. Sales of items like bow ties or miniskirts are often high for a number of years, become unpopular for a while, and then become popular again. For these items, merchandise planning is harder.

With a nostalgia or revival curve, a seemingly obsolete good or service is revived. An innovative retailer will recognize potential in this area and merchandise accordingly. For example, direct marketers often use TV commercials to sell cassettes and compact discs featuring the music or artists who were previously successful. They also heavily promote "greatest hits" recordings featuring combinations of artists.

A bust product cycle is one in which a good or service is not successful at all (unlike a fad), and the retailer loses money and, sometimes, status. This happened with Pizza Hut's original attempt to sell a "light" pizza; despite extensive testing, the product did not do well and never made it into full distribution. Sometimes, retailers have to slash prices to sell a huge amount of excess inventory for an unpopular item. This takes place with books that are expected to be best-sellers but fail to attract enough readers.

An apparel retailer must be familiar with fashion trends and related theories. Such trends may be divided into vertical and horizontal categories; fashions may go through one or a combination of the two. A vertical trend occurs when a fashion is first accepted by an upscale market segment and undergoes changes in its basic form before it is sold to the general public. The fashion passes from the upper to the lower social classes through three vertical stages: distinctive (original designs, designer dress shops, custom-made, worn by high society); emulation (modification of original designs, finer stores, alterations, worn by the middle class); and economic emulation (simple copies of originals, discount and bargain stores, mass produced, mass marketed).

In recent years, horizontal fashion trends have grown in importance. A horizontal trend occurs when a new fashion is accepted by a broad spectrum of people upon introduction, while retaining its basic form. Within any social class, there are innovative customers who act as opinion leaders. New fashions must be accepted by these leaders, who then convince other members of the same social class (who are more conservative) to buy the items. Merchandise is sold across the class and not from one class down to another.

By understanding both theories and learning which is more appropriate for its positioning niche in the marketplace, a retailer can better predict fashion successes and the types of customers who will buy from it. Figure 14-7 contains a checklist for predicting fashion adoption.

In planning innovativeness, a retailer's emphasis is too often on new-product additions. Equally important are the decisions involved in dropping existing goods or services. Because of limited resources and shelf space, some items have to be dropped when others are added. Instead of intuitively removing existing offerings, the retailer should use structured guidelines:

■ Select items for possible elimination on the basis of declining sales, prices, and profits; the appearance of substitutes; and the loss of usefulness.
■ Gather and analyze detailed financial and other data about these items.

Figure 14-7

A Checklist for Predicting Fashion Adoption

		Yes	No
1.	Does the fashion satisfy a consumer need?	—	—
2.	Is the fashion compatible with emerging consumer life-styles?	—	—
3.	Is the fashion oriented toward the mass market? Toward a market segment?	— —	— —
4.	Is the fashion radically new?	—	—
5.	Are the reputations of the designer(s) and the retailers carrying the fashion good?	—	—
6.	Are several designers marketing some version of the fashion?	—	—
7.	Is the price range for the fashion appropriate for the target market?	—	—
8.	Will extensive advertising be used?	—	—
9.	Will the fashion change over time?	—	—
10.	Will consumers view the fashion as a long-term trend?	—	—

■ Consider nondeletion strategies such as cutting costs, revising promotion efforts, adjusting prices, and cooperating with other retailers.

■ After a deletion decision is made, do not overlook timing, parts and servicing, inventory, and holdover demand.

As an illustration, in 1995, Toys "Я" Us began to streamline the number of items carried in its stores by more than 20 percent. It felt the selection sometimes made shopping cumbersome for customers. By eliminating particular items, Toys "Я" Us is now able to have more in-depth merchandise displays; and even after deleting so many items, Toys "Я" Us still has a bigger selection than competitors'.[10]

How Much Merchandise Is Stocked ❑ Once a retailer decides what merchandise to carry, it must determine how much of that merchandise to stock. Thus, the width and depth of assortment are planned next. **Width of assortment** refers to the number of distinct goods/service categories with which a retailer is involved. **Depth of assortment** refers to the variety in any one goods/service category with which a retailer is involved. As mentioned in Chapter 5, product assortment can range from wide and deep (a department store) to narrow and shallow (a box store). Selected advantages and disadvantages of each type of assortment strategy are shown in Table 14-3.

Assortment strategies vary widely. For example, KFC's thousands of worldwide outlets emphasize chicken and related quick-service products. They do not sell hamburgers, pizza, or other popular fast-food items; these do not fit with KFC's merchandising approach. On the other hand, Wal-Mart's huge supercenters feature thousands of both general merchandise and food items. This is 7-Eleven's approach, as described at its Web site (http://www.7-11.com):

[10] *Toys "Я" Us 1996 Annual Report.*

Table 14-3   RETAIL ASSORTMENT STRATEGIES

Advantages	Disadvantages
Wide and Deep	
(many goods/service categories and a large assortment in each category)	
Broad market	High inventory investment
Full stocking of items	General image
High level of customer traffic	Many items with low turnover
Customer loyalty	Some obsolete merchandise
One-stop shopping	
No disappointed customers	
Wide and Shallow	
(many goods/service categories and a limited assortment in each category)	
Broad market	Low variety within product lines
High level of customer traffic	Some disappointed customers
Emphasis on convenience customers	Weak image
Less costly than wide and deep	Many items with low turnover
One-stop shopping	Reduced customer loyalty
Narrow and Deep	
(few goods/service categories and a large assortment in each category)	
Specialist image	Too much emphasis on one category
Good customer choice in category(ies)	No one-stop shopping
Specialized personnel	More susceptible to trends/cycles
Customer loyalty	Greater effort needed to enlarge the size of the trading area
No disappointed customers	Little (no) scrambled merchandising
Less costly than wide and deep	
Narrow and Shallow	
(few goods/service categories and a limited assortment in each category)	
Aimed at convenience customers	Little width and depth
Least costly	No one-stop shopping
High turnover of items	Some disappointed customers
	Weak image
	Limited customer loyalty
	Small trading area
	Little (no) scrambled merchandising

7-Eleven convenience stores in the United States and Canada serve about 6 million customers every day. Each store is focused on meeting the needs of convenience-oriented customers by providing a broad selection of fresh, high-quality goods and services at everyday fair prices, speedy transactions, and a clean, safe, and friendly shopping environment. Each store's selection of up to 3,000 different goods and services is tailored to meet the needs and preferences of local customers. 7-Eleven is well known for its Oscar Mayer "Big Bite" hot dogs, nachos, and pastries, as well as its famous semifrozen drink, "Slurpee," and a broad selection of fountain soft drink sizes and flavors. The company is currently expanding and upgrading the quality and variety of its food service through the daily preparation and delivery of fresh sandwiches, produce, dinner entrees, and bakery items in many locations. 7-Eleven stores have a number of convenient services designed to meet the unique needs of individual neighborhoods, including automated money orders, copiers, fax machines, ATMs, and, where available, lottery tickets and online games.

Retailers should consider several factors in planning the width and depth of assortment to carry. Sales and profit should be evaluated. If goods/service variety is increased, will overall sales go up? Will overall profits? Carrying ten varieties of cat food will not necessarily yield greater sales or profits than stocking four varieties. The retailer should be sure to look at the investment costs that occur with a large variety.

Space requirements must be examined. How much space is required for each good or service category? How much space is available? Because selling space is limited, it should be allocated to those goods and services generating the greatest customer traffic and sales. The turnover rate should also be considered in assigning shelf space.[11]

In planning, a distinction should be made among scrambled merchandising, complementary goods and services, and substitute goods and services. With scrambled merchandising, a retailer adds unrelated items to generate more customer traffic and lift profit margins (e.g., a florist adding umbrellas). Handling complementary goods/services lets the retailer sell basic items and related offerings (e.g., stereo and CDs, lawn service and tree spraying). Scrambled merchandising and complementary goods/services are both intended to increase the retailer's overall sales. Yet, carrying too many substitute goods/services (e.g., competing brands of toothpaste) may simply shift sales from one brand to another and have little impact on a retailer's overall sales.

For some firms, especially supermarkets, the proliferation of substitute products has created a difficult problem: how to offer consumers an adequate choice without tying up too much investment and floor space in one product category. For example, the shelves at the H.E. Butt supermarket in Austin, Texas, are stocked with 25 different kinds of citrus, 9 varieties of mushrooms, 12 types of potatoes, 2,200 different wines, 330 kinds of beer, 100 varieties of mustard, and 500 types of cheese. Yet, as one expert says, "If variety is healthy for a supermarket, too much duplication can harden its arteries."[12]

A retailer may sometimes have no choice about stocking a full assortment within a product line. A powerful supplier may insist that the retailer carry its entire line or else it will not distribute through the retailer at all. But large retailers—and smaller ones that belong to cooperative buying groups—are now standing up to suppliers; and many retailers stock their own brands next to manufacturers'. As retail chains (and buying groups) have gotten bigger, this phenomenon has grown. When retailers and manufacturers compete for shelf space allocated to various brands and for control over display locations, this is known as the **battle of the brands.**[13]

A retailer needs to determine the proper mix of manufacturer, private, and generic brands to carry. **Manufacturer (national) brands** are produced and controlled by manufacturers. They are usually well known, supported by manufacturer ads, somewhat pre-sold to consumers, require limited retailer investment, and often represent maximum product quality to consumers. These brands dominate sales in many product categories. Among the most popular manufacturer brands are Barbie, Liz Claiborne, Coke, Fisher-Price, Kodak, Levi's, Maybelline, Pepsi, Rubbermaid, and Sony. As a vice-president at VF (a leading maker of jeans, including Lee and Wrangler) recently remarked, "We are challenging the continued growth of private label by intensifying product innovation, magnifying our investment in marketing, and becoming much more assertive on in-store presentation. We recognize that the private-label business has effectively become another segment of the branded business."[14]

---

[11]See R. Craig MacClaren, "Out-of-Stocks Mean Out-of-Pocket," *Promo* (May 1996), p. 54.

[12]"Trying to Bag Business," *U.S. News & World Report* (February 26, 1996), p. 54; and Steve Weinstein, "How to Avoid Product Duplication," *Progressive Grocer* (July 1993), p. 103.

[13]See John A. Quelch and David Harding, "Brands Versus Private Labels: Fighting to Win," *Harvard Business Review*, Vol. 74 (January–February 1996), pp. 99–109; and Stephen J. Hoch, "How Should National Brands Think About Private Labels?" *Sloan Management Review*, Vol. 37 (Winter 1996), pp. 89–102.

[14]"National Brands Fight Back," *Stores* (February 1996), p. 69.

Private (dealer) brands contain names designated by wholesalers or retailers, are more profitable to retailers, are better controlled by retailers, are not sold by competing retailers, are less expensive for consumers, and lead to customer loyalty to retailers (rather than to manufacturers). Yet, with most private-label products, retailers must line up suppliers, arrange for physical distribution and warehousing, sponsor ads, create in-store displays, and absorb losses from unsold items. Retailers' interest in their own brands' sales is evident from these examples:

- Industrywide, private brands account for 20 percent of unit sales at supermarkets, 12 percent of unit sales at drugstores, and 11 percent of unit sales at mass merchandisers. At drugstores, one-quarter of stationery and school supply sales are from private brands, while vitamins represent the highest dollar volume for private brands sold there.[15]

- For retailers such as The Gap, Inc., The Limited, Inc., and McDonald's, their own private brands represent most of company revenues.

- At firms such as Sears, both private brands and manufacturer brands are strong. In fact, Sears has two of the best-known brands around: Craftsman (tools) and Kenmore (appliances), as well as smaller private brands like Canyon River Blues Glory (jeans). J.C. Penney also has a number of private brands to complement its manufacturer brand offerings, including City Streets, St. John's Bay, Worthington, Stafford, Original Arizona Jean Company, and Hunt Club. Federated Department Stores has expanded its private brand efforts, so "We can control our own destiny."[16]

- More retailers now view private brands as an integral part of a category management program: "Most grocery and drug retailers agree that private-brand products play a major role in category management by providing higher profits than national brands."[17] There are now many premium private brands, as well (such as A&P's Master Choice brand and Saks Fifth Avenue's SFA Collection).

- A greater number of firms are marketing private brands aggressively: "Private-label items are getting wake-up calls in the form of slick packaging, catchy names, broadcast ad campaigns, promotional programs—even in-store sampling. In other words, retailers are enthusiastically mimicking the sales tactics that makers of packaged goods have used for decades."[18]

According to one expert:

When *Women's Wear Daily* conducted a survey of the most recognizable brands in women's sportswear, Kmart's Jaclyn Smith Collection came in fourth, ahead of such fashion superstars as Calvin Klein and Ralph Lauren. Yet, when a survey studied buying habits before holidays, on the other hand, it found shoppers tended to shy away from house labels, preferring national brands when the stakes are high. The success of private brands has enabled them to share the shelf space and spotlight traditionally reserved for national brands. Once considered an unpretentious medium to pump up retail volume, it has undergone a transformation. Flexing their merchandising muscle, retailers across all channels have devised good quality/sound value private brands—many of which can go toe-to-toe with items marketed by

[15]"Private Label Business," *Stores* (March 1996), p. 60; "Weak Spots," *Promo* (October 1995), p. 1; and Faye Bookman, "Drug Chains Try Private Label Weapon Against Competition," *Stores* (March 1996), pp. 30–31.
[16]Alice Z. Cuneo, "Federated Stores Fashion Own Line of Branded Clothes," *Advertising Age* (September 2, 1996), p. 3.
[17]"Private Label Plays a Key Role in Category Management," *Promo* (July 1995), p. 50; and Ryan Mathews, "Safeway's Doctrine of the Select," *Progressive Grocer* (January 1997), p. 32.
[18]Stuart Elliott, "Advertising," *New York Times* (March 22, 1994), p. D23.

branded manufacturers. In doing so, they've not only enhanced profitability but also differentiated their offerings from competitors, enhanced their image, and reduced their dependence on branded manufacturers. But some analysts wonder if the popularity of store brands will wane, as it has in the past. There are natural limits on house brands' market share, they argue, and the supposed high profitability of the products has been exaggerated.[19]

Thus, despite the exciting possibilities, care must be taken by retailers in deciding how much emphasis to place on their own private brands. There are many consumers who are loyal to manufacturer brands and would shop elsewhere if those brands are not stocked.

Generic brands feature products' generic names as brands (such as canned peas or instant coffee); they are no-frills goods stocked by some retailers. These items usually receive secondary shelf locations, have little or no promotion support, are sometimes of less overall quality than other brands, are stocked in limited assortments, and have plain packages. Generics are controlled by retailers and are priced well below other brands. In U.S. supermarkets carrying them, generics have stabilized at less than 1 percent of sales. However, in the prescription drug industry, where the product quality of manufacturer brands and generics is similar, generics account for one-third of unit sales.

These factors also take on added importance if a retailer moves toward a wider and deeper merchandising strategy:

■ Risks, merchandise investments, damages, and obsolescence may increase dramatically.
■ Personnel may be spread too thinly, sometimes over dissimilar goods and services.
■ Both the positive and negative ramifications of scrambled merchandising may occur.
■ Inventory control procedures may be much more difficult; and overall merchandise turnover probably will slow down.

Assortment planning should incorporate a basic stock list (for staples), a model stock plan (for items such as fashion merchandise), and a never-out list (for best-sellers). Staple merchandise consists of the regular items carried by a retailer. To a supermarket, staples are such items as milk, bread, canned soup, and facial tissues. To a department store, staples are such items as luggage, cameras, glassware, and housewares. Because these items have relatively stable sales (sometimes seasonal) and their nature does not change much over time, a retailer can clearly outline the assortments for these items. A **basic stock list** specifies the inventory level, color, brand, style category, size, package, and so on for every staple item carried by the retailer.

Planning assortments for fashion merchandise, furniture, and other nonstandardized items is harder than for staples due to demand variations, style changes, and the number of sizes and colors to be carried. For these items, decisions are two-pronged. First, product lines, styles, designs, and colors are selected. Second, a **model stock plan** is used to order specific items, such as the number of green, red, and blue pullover sweaters of a certain design by size. With a model stock plan, many items of popular sizes and colors are ordered; and small amounts of less-popular sizes and colors are ordered to fill out the assortment. Thus, a specialty store may stock one Size 18 dress and six Size 10 dresses for each style carried.

A **never-out list** is used when a retailer plans stock levels for best-sellers. Items accounting for high sales volume are stocked in a manner that ensures they are always available. Products are added to and deleted from this list as their popularity and importance to the retailer change. Thus, before a new Stephen King novel is released, bookstores

[19]Susan Reda, "Private Label Transformation," *Stores* (January 1995), pp. 28–29.

order large quantities to be sure they can meet anticipated demand. After it disappears from newspaper best-seller lists, smaller quantities are kept.

For virtually all types of retailers, it is usually a good strategy to use a combination of a basic stock list, a model stock plan, and a never-out list. These lists may sometimes overlap.[20]

When Merchandise Is Stocked ❏ A retailer should next ascertain when each type of merchandise is to be stocked. For new goods and services, the retailer must decide when they are first displayed and sold. For established goods and services, the firm must plan the regular merchandise flow during the year.

To order merchandise properly, the retailer should forecast sales during the year and take into account various other factors: peak seasons, order and delivery time, routine versus special orders, stock turnover, discounts, and the efficiency of inventory procedures.

As noted earlier in the chapter, some goods and services have peak seasons during the year. For these items (e.g., winter coats and boat rentals), a retailer should plan large inventories during peak periods and less for the off-season. Because some people like to shop during the off-season, the retailer should not eliminate the items.

A retailer should plan purchases based on order and delivery time. How long does it take the firm to process an order? After the order is sent to the supplier, how long does it take to receive delivery of merchandise? By adding these two time periods together, the retailer can get a good idea of the lead time to restock its shelves. If it takes a retailer 7 days to process an order and the supplier an additional 14 days to deliver merchandise, the retailer should begin to order new merchandise at least 21 days before the old inventory runs out.

Planning differs for routine versus special orders. Routine orders involve restocking staples and other regularly sold items. Deliveries are received weekly, monthly, and so on. Planning and problems are thus minimized. Special orders involve merchandise that is not sold regularly. These orders require a lot of planning and close cooperation between retailer and supplier. Specific delivery dates are usually arranged. Custom furniture is a product requiring special orders.

Stock turnover (how quickly merchandise sells) greatly influences how often items must be ordered. Convenience items like milk and bread (which are also highly perishable) have a high turnover rate and must be restocked quite often. Shopping items like refrigerators and color TV sets have a lower turnover rate and are restocked less often.

In deciding when and how often to buy merchandise, a retailer should consider quantity discounts. Large purchases may mean lower per-unit costs. Using efficient inventory procedures, such as electronic data interchange and quick response planning procedures, would also decrease costs and order times while increasing merchandise productivity.

Where Merchandise Is Stored ❏ The last basic merchandise planning decision entails where items are handled. A single-unit firm usually must choose how much merchandise to place on the selling floor, how much to place in a stockroom, and whether to use a warehouse. A chain must also allocate items among stores.

Some retailers focus almost entirely on warehouses as central, or regional, distribution centers. Products are shipped from suppliers to these warehouses, and then allotted and shipped to individual outlets. Burlington Coat Factory's 420,000-square-foot New Jersey warehouse processes up to 125,000 pieces of merchandise a day and services stores nationwide; and Toys "Я" Us has 16 distribution centers, fourteen of which are owned

---

[20]See Julie Ritzer Ross, "Inventory Management Systems Cut Costs While Keeping Store Shelves Full," *Stores* (July 1997), pp. 78–80.

and two of which are leased; these centers average 443,000 feet in size and can house about 80,000 pallets (storage bins) of merchandise stacked fifty feet high.[21]

Other retailers, including many supermarket chains, do not rely as much on central or regional warehouses. Instead, they have at least some goods shipped directly from suppliers to individual stores. This is known as **direct store distribution (DSD);** and it works best with retailers that also utilize EDI. Direct store delivery "is a conduit for moving high-velocity, high-bulk, perishable, and specialty products from the manufacturer directly to the retail shelf." Industrywide, 27 percent of the average supermarket's sales are from items with DSD. As an example, Vons has high-volume products shipped directly to its supermarkets rather than to a Vons warehouse for further distribution.[22]

The advantages of central warehousing include efficiency in transportation and storage, mechanized processing of goods, improved security, efficient marking of merchandise, ease of returns, and smooth and coordinated merchandise flow. Central warehousing's key disadvantages are the excessive centralized control, the extra handling of perishables, the high operating costs for small retailers, and potential order-processing delays. In addition, centralized warehousing may reduce the capability of quick response systems by adding another stage in distribution. These are the pros and cons of DSD:

> On the one hand, DSD offers great promise, both as a way to ensure that fresh product is always on the shelf and as a significant step toward realizing the potential offered by micromarketing. Depending on the brand or brands he or she represents, a DSD vendor may be in a store as often as two or three times a week. This frequency should guarantee DSD-delivered products are among the freshest in the store, and the combined retail knowledge of DSD vendors ought to be—at least in a perfect world—an invaluable source of information to store managers. It should also open the door to the possibility of selling individual stores slightly differently in response to their unique consumer population. On the other hand, DSD is a distribution system that, in its current form at least, adds layers and layers of complexity to backroom receiving and vendor/distributor relations and can be the primary cause behind the generation of mountains of invoices and receiving documents.[23]

In allocating merchandise among its outlets, a retailer should consider the target market(s). Products should be carried by branch stores only if they address the tastes and needs of the customers served by those stores. The more geographically dispersed a retailer is, the more essential it is to pinpoint the differences in store product assortments.

Store size should also be studied in allotting products among branch stores. When the outlets' target markets are similar, the allotment should be based on sales. If Store A has sales of $1 million and Store B has sales of $2 million, Store B should receive twice as many items as A. However, refinements must be made when the target markets differ.

Gathering Information About Consumer Demand

After overall merchandising plans are set, information about the target market is needed. A retailer should gather data on consumer demand before buying or rebuying any merchandise. Information gathering, as related to retailing, was detailed in Chapter 8.

Good merchandise management depends on a retailer's ability to generate a rather accurate sales forecast. After all, the most vital merchandising functions for a retailer are anticipating and satisfying customer demand. Sales forecasting is discussed further in the next chapter.

---

[21]*Burlington Coat Factory 1996 Annual Report;* and *Toys "Я" Us 1996 Annual Report.* See also Julie Ritzer Ross, "Retail Industry Seen Lagging on Warehouse Management Systems," *Stores* (May 1997), pp. 30–33.
[22]"Understanding DSD," *Progressive Grocer* (November 1995), pp. 6–10.
[23]Ryan Mathews, "DSD: Toward a Unified Distribution System," *Progressive Grocer* (November 1995), p. 4.

TECHNOLOGY IN RETAILING

Mass Customization: A Fad or the Future of Retailing?

By using mass customization, innovative retailers can now customize their goods and services to individual customer specifications. If practiced well, mass customization offers each consumer the goods and services that are tailored to his or her needs at close to the same speed and cost as mass-produced goods and services. Custom Footwear and General Nutrition Corporation (GNC) are two retailers that have effectively used mass customization.

At Custom Footwear, whose first shoe store opened in Westport, Connecticut, each shopper's shoe size is determined on the basis of a computerized scanner that generates 13 measurements for each foot. These data are transmitted to a factory in Italy, where custom shoes are made to order. Not only do the shoes precisely fit a customer's feet, but the customer can choose among a wide variety of styles, colors, and leathers. The average price for a pair of shoes at Custom Footwear is $140.

The General Nutrition Corporation's new Alive! prototype store in Orlando lets customers have their daily vitamin supply needs packaged in "vita-paks," that are labeled with the customer's name. It takes five minutes to complete the entire process, which consists of keying the selection of vitamins (depending on each person's unique needs) into a computer, verifying the vitamin's potency level, and packaging the customized vita-pak.

Source: Susan Reda, "Mass Customization Retailing," *Stores* (June 1996), pp. 37–39.

In gathering data for merchandising decisions, a retailer has several possible information sources. The most valuable is the consumer. By researching the target market's demographics, life-styles, and potential shopping plans, a retailer can study consumer demand directly.

Other sources of information can be used when direct consumer data are unavailable or insufficient. Suppliers (manufacturers and/or wholesalers) usually do their own sales forecasts and marketing research (e.g., test marketing). They also know how much outside promotional support a retailer will get, and this affects sales. In closing a deal with the retailer, a supplier may present charts and graphs, showing forecasts and promotional support. Yet, the retailer should remember one significant point: it is the retailer that has direct access to the target market and its needs.

Retail sales and display personnel interact with consumers and can pass their observations along to management. A **want book (want slip)** system is a formal way to record consumer requests for unstocked or out-of-stock merchandise. The want book is used in smaller firms; want slips are used by larger retailers. These tools are very helpful to a retailer's buyers. Due to their involvement with consumers, personnel should be encouraged to offer feedback and not be shut off from making comments. Outside of customers, salespeople may provide the most useful information for merchandising decisions.

Buying personnel can learn a lot about consumer demand by visiting suppliers, talking with sales personnel, and observing customer behavior. Usually, buyers are responsible for complete sales forecasts and merchandise plans in their product categories; top management combines the forecasts and plans of individual buyers to obtain overall company projections.

Competitors are another information source. A conservative retailer may not stock an item until competitors do. Comparison shoppers, who look at the offerings and prices of competitors, may be employed. In addition, trade publications report on trends in each area of retailing and provide a legal way of gathering data from competitors. See Figure 14-8 for an example of a competition shopping report.

Other sources may offer useful pieces of information: government sources show unemployment, inflation, and product safety data; independent news sources conduct their own consumer polls and do investigative reporting; and commercial data can be purchased.

Figure 14-8

**A Competition
Shopping Report**

COMPETITION SHOPPING REPORT

Store #_____   Date_____

Dept. #_____   Qualified Competition Shopped:

                                     1._____
                                     2._____

Our Style No.	Mfr. Model or Style	Description	Our Price	1st Compet. Price	2nd Compet. Price	Store's Recom. Price	Buyer's Recom. Price

Item Seen at Our Competitor's Store Which We Should Carry:					
Manufacturer	Mfr. Model or Style	Description	Reg. or List Price	Sale Price	Buyer's Comments

_Signature of Shopper_____   Store Manager_____

Information should be gathered from several sources; one type of data may be insufficient. Whatever the amount of information acquired, the retailer should feel comfortable it is sufficient for it to be able to make decisions as accurately as possible. For routine merchandising decisions (e.g., staple products), limited information may be adequate. On the other hand, new-car sales can fluctuate widely and require extensive data for sales forecasts.

Determining Merchandise Sources

The next step in merchandise buying and handling is to determine the sources of merchandise. Three major possibilities exist:

■ Company-owned—A large retailer owns a manufacturing and/or wholesaling facility. A company-owned supplier handles all or part of the merchandise the retailer requests.

■ Outside, regularly used supplier—This supplier is not owned by the retailer but used regularly by it. The retailer knows the quality of the goods and services and the reliability of the supplier through firsthand experience.

■ Outside, new supplier—This supplier is not owned by the retailer and the retailer has not bought from it before. The retailer may be unfamiliar with the quality of the merchandise and the reliability of this supplier.

The basic types of outside suppliers (regularly used and new) are shown in Figure 14-9.

These two examples show the complexity in choosing suppliers. Sears buys products from several thousand primary suppliers in the United States alone, and a total of more than 10,000 suppliers overall. This means Sears constantly assesses potential vendors and the performance of existing ones. To improve its efficiency in dealing with suppliers, Sears has enacted an EDI linkup with its primary suppliers. It prepared a computer software program, which it has made available to suppliers at no charge.

The semiannual International Home Furnishings Market in High Point, North Carolina, is the world's largest wholesale furniture fair. Each fair lasts more than a week, takes place in over 150 separate buildings, involves 2,200 domestic and international home furnishings exhibitors, draws 70,000 people (over half of whom are retail buyers, including ones from 85 countries), and results in transactions worth several hundred million dollars.[24]

In choosing vendors, such criteria as these should be considered:

■ Reliability—Will a supplier consistently fulfill all written promises?
■ Price-quality—Who provides the best merchandise at the lowest price?
■ Order-processing time—How fast will deliveries be made?
■ Exclusive rights—Will a supplier give exclusive selling rights?
■ Functions provided—Will a supplier provide shipping, storing, and other functions, if needed?
■ Information—Will a supplier pass along any important goods/service data?
■ Ethics—Will a supplier fulfill all verbal promises?
■ Guarantee—Does a supplier stand behind its offerings?
■ Credit—Can credit purchases be made from a supplier? On what terms?
■ Long-run relations—Will a supplier be available over an extended period?
■ Reorders—Can a supplier promptly fill reorders?
■ Markup—Will markup (price margins) be adequate?
■ Innovativeness—Is a supplier's line innovative or conservative?
■ Local advertising—Does a supplier advertise in local media?
■ Investment—How large are total investment costs with a supplier?
■ Risk—How much risk is involved in dealing with a supplier?

Sometimes, retailers and their suppliers work well together. Other times, there are conflicts. As we have discussed throughout the book, the benefits of relationship marketing between retailers and their suppliers can be invaluable—well worth the effort that may be necessary to make the relationships work. For example, each year, Sears honors about 150 of its best suppliers for their ongoing supportive roles in Sears' success:

Whoever said it's lonely at the top wasn't on our Partners in Progress list. As Sears' success continues to soar, satisfied customers have returned again and again for our exceptional goods and services. In recognition of their outstanding contributions to Sears' commitment of total customer satisfaction, Sears honors superior suppliers as

[24]Clint Johnson, "Braced for a Slowdown," *Triad Business News* (July 14, 1995).

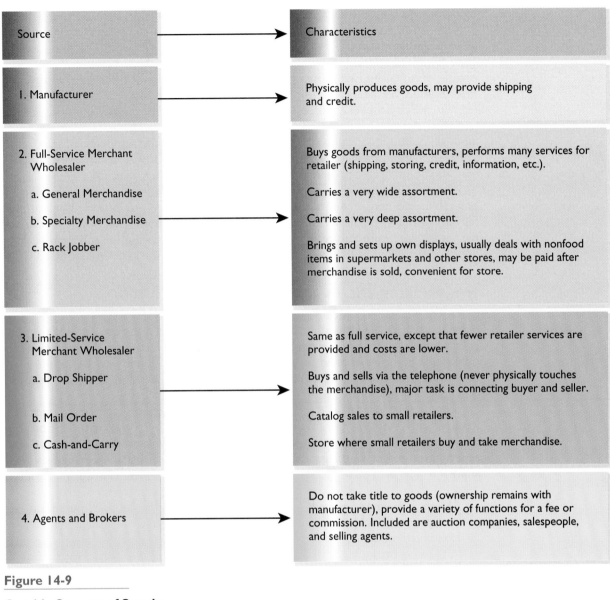

Figure 14-9

Outside Sources of Supply

"Partners in Progress." Selected from over 10,000 vendors, these companies lead the way in product innovation, quality, and service. They have helped bring Sears' private and distinctive brand-name products to millions of Sears customers nationwide. To this extraordinary group, we owe a very special and appreciative "Thanks."[25]

Evaluating Merchandise

Whatever source is chosen, the retailer needs a procedure for evaluating the merchandise under purchase consideration. Should each individual unit be examined, or can an item be bought by description?

Three types of evaluation are possible: inspection, sampling, and description. The technique depends on the item's cost, its attributes, and its regularity of purchase.

[25]"Whoever Said It's Lonely at the Top Wasn't on Our List," *Wall Street Journal* (March 27, 1996), p. B5.

Inspection occurs when every single unit is examined before purchase and after delivery. Jewelry and art are two examples of expensive, relatively unique purchases where the retailer carefully inspects all items.

A retailer uses sampling when it regularly buys a large quantity of breakable, perishable, or expensive items. Inspecting each piece of merchandise becomes inefficient in this situation. So, items are sampled for quality and condition. For example, a retailer ready to purchase several hundred light fixtures, bananas, or inexpensive watches does not inspect each fixture, banana, or watch. Instead, a number of units (a sample) is examined. The entire selection is purchased if the sample is satisfactory. An unsatisfactory sample might cause a whole shipment to be rejected (or a discount negotiated). Sampling may also occur on receipt of merchandise.

A retailer engages in description buying when a firm purchases standardized, nonbreakable, and nonperishable merchandise. The items are not inspected or sampled; they are ordered in quantity from a verbal, written, or pictorial description. For example, a stationery store can order paper clips, pads, typing paper, and so on from a catalog or order form. After it receives an order, only a count of those items is conducted.

Negotiating the Purchase

Once a merchandise source is chosen and pre-purchase evaluation is conducted, a retailer negotiates the purchase and its terms. A new or special order usually results in a negotiated contract. In this case, a retailer and a supplier carefully discuss all aspects of the purchase. On the other hand, a regular order or reorder often involves a uniform contract. In this instance, terms are standard or have already been agreed on, and the order is handled in a routine manner.

For off-price retailers and other deep discounters, negotiated contracts are normally required with every purchase. That is because these firms employ **opportunistic buying,** whereby special low prices are negotiated for merchandise whose sales have not lived up to expectations, end-of-season goods, items consumers have returned to the manufacturer or another retailer, and closeouts. Here's how Consolidated Stores (the closeout giant) puts it:

> [Deep discounters] provide a valuable service to manufacturers by purchasing excess products that generally result from production overruns, package changes, discontinued products, and returns. They take advantage of generally low prices in the off-season by buying and warehousing merchandise for future sale. In addition, to hold their market share in an increasingly competitive environment, manufacturers are introducing new products and new packaging on a more frequent basis. As a result, they want larger, more sophisticated deep discounters to buy bigger merchandise quantities and control distribution and advertising specific products.[26]

A number of purchase terms have to be specified, whether a negotiated or a uniform contract is involved. These include the delivery date, quantity purchased, price and payment arrangements, discounts, form of delivery, and point of transfer of title.

The delivery date and the quantity purchased must be clearly stated. A retailer should be able to cancel an order if either provision is not carried out satisfactorily. The retailer's purchase price, payment arrangements, and permissible discounts are also important. What is the retailer's cost per item (including handling charges)? What forms of payment are permitted (e.g., cash versus credit)? What discounts are permitted? Often, retailers' purchase prices are discounted for early payments (e.g., "2/10/net 30" means a 2 percent discount is given if the full bill is paid in ten days; the full bill is due in thirty days), trade activities (such as setting up displays), and quantity purchases. Stipulations are needed for the form of delivery (water, air, truck, rail, and so

---

[26]*Consolidated Stores Corporation 1996 Annual Report.*

on) and the party responsible for shipping charges (e.g., FOB factory—free on board—means a supplier places merchandise with the shipper, but the retailer pays the freight). Last, the point of transfer of title—when ownership changes from supplier to buyer—should be noted in a contract.

Concluding the Purchase

For many medium-sized and large firms, purchases are concluded automatically; computers are used to complete and process orders (based on electronic data interchange and quick response inventory planning), and each purchase is fed into the computer's data bank. Smaller retailers often conclude purchases manually; orders are written up and processed manually, and purchases are added to the store's book inventory in the same manner. However, with the rapid advances in computerized ordering software, even small retailers can sometimes place orders electronically—especially if they are tied to large wholesalers that supply them with EDI and QR capabilities.

Multiunit retailers must determine whether to use central, regional, or local approval to conclude purchases: Should central or regional management have the final okay in a purchase, or should the local manager have the final say? This issue was discussed earlier in the chapter. Advantages and disadvantages accrue to each approval technique.

As mentioned in the previous section, transfer of title should be carefully specified with the supplier. Several alternatives are possible:

1. The retailer takes title immediately upon purchase.
2. The retailer assumes ownership after merchandise is loaded onto the mode of transportation.
3. The retailer takes title when a shipment is received.
4. The retailer does not take title until the end of a billing cycle, when the supplier is paid.
5. The retailer accepts merchandise on consignment and does not own the items. The supplier is paid after merchandise is sold.

Gifts in Kind America: Helping Retailers Be Charitable AND Cut Logistics Costs

Retailers that are holding unsaleable merchandise in their backroom inventory areas may be able to benefit society, while at the same time save money. How? By giving these goods away to charitable organizations. One such organization, Gifts in Kind America, provides a variety of free services to retailers including shipping, warehousing, and distribution to charities, preparation of tax documentation, and public relations.

At Sears, for example, Gifts in Kind personnel regularly pick up apparel, hardware, tools, and soft goods from the retailer's five Chicago-based return centers. Disney's hundreds of stores also actively participate in the Gifts in Kind America program. Said a Disney spokesperson, "We realized that in partnering with Gifts in Kind America, we would enjoy the simplicity of funneling unneeded items through one organization, incur no costs, and contribute to the common good."

Besides the satisfaction of giving goods to the needy, retailer participants in these programs benefit from a reduction in long-term warehousing costs, lower transportation costs (these goods are no longer shipped to jobbers), and receive tax deductions on donated items. Gifts in Kind America also tailors its programs to meet the needs of its donors. Thus, some retailers want their goods distributed outside of their market areas, so as not to directly compete with their traditional merchandise. Other firms, such as Sears, have specified that Gifts in Kind America take special steps to guard against the return of donated merchandise at Sears stores for retail credit.

Source: Julie Ritzer Ross, "Retailers Use Charity Program to Cut Logistics Costs," *Stores* (March 1996), pp. 46, 48.

It is essential for a retailer to understand the differences among these alternatives, because its responsibilities and rights differ in each case.

A consignment or memorandum deal can be made if a vendor is in a weak position
and wants to persuade retailers to carry its items. In a **consignment purchase,** a retailer
has no risk because title is not taken; the supplier owns the goods until sold. In a **memorandum purchase,** risk is still low, but a retailer takes title on delivery and is responsible for damages. In both options, retailers do not pay for items until they are sold and
can return items.[27]

Handling the Merchandise

During this phase, a retailer physically handles merchandise, which involves such varied tasks as receiving and storing goods, price and inventory marking, setting up displays, figuring on-floor quantities and assortments, completing customer transactions,
arranging for customer delivery or pickup, processing returns and damaged goods,
monitoring pilferage, and controlling merchandise. It is in this stage that distribution
management is most critical, whether it entails retail distribution centers or direct store
delivery. Here is why:

> When the Nature Company decided to improve operations at the integrated ware-
> housing and transportation facility it shared with three other retailers, there wasn't
> time for re-engineering. With shipping dates for the crucial holiday season fast ap-
> proaching, the retailer could give its outside adviser, Garr Consulting, just 12 weeks
> to come up with a plan to help the distribution facility substantially reduce operat-
> ing costs while also improving productivity and cycle time. "We really had no choice
> but to jump in and make the changes, because there were problems to be addressed
> in every area of the business," said Fred Snyder, senior vice-president of distribution
> at the Nature Company. Garr began the overhaul in May. "There were several in-
> stances where we had to call an audible and try again until it worked," recalled Bill
> Killen, vice-president of Garr. "But we were staring down the barrel of the firm's
> peak selling season, beginning in August, so we kept going." A highly focused,
> pragmatic blueprint for change was applied to every aspect of the business, from
> distribution to transportation and management. By the time August arrived, the
> transformation was well in hand, and had begun to yield significant results. Less
> than a year after the process began, distribution costs had been reduced by 20 per-
> cent, and transportation expenses were down 2 percent. Order cycle time had been
> reduced from eight days to five days or fewer, and shipment quality had improved
> from an estimated 98 percent to 99.7 percent.[28]

According to a recent study of mass merchants, department stores, grocery stores,
specialty stores, and category-killer stores, about four-fifths of those retailers had at least
one distribution center. In contrast, one-quarter of the firms had at least some merchandise shipped by the vendor directly to the retailer (ranging from 10 percent of items at
specialty stores to 80 percent at category-killer stores).[29]

First, items are usually shipped from suppliers to warehouses, for storage and dis-
bursement, or directly to retailers' store(s). For example, Walgreen, the giant drugstore
chain, has fully automated warehouses to stock thousands of products and speed their
delivery to the stores. See Figure 14-10. On the other hand, rather than rely exclusively

---

[27]Paul W. Cockerham, "Consignment Gains Foothold in Supermarket Industry," *Stores* (April 1996),
pp. 36–39.
[28]Susan Reda, "Nature Company Takes Fast Track to Better Distribution," *Stores* (September 1996), p. 60.
[29]"Retail Distribution and Logistics: Managing the Supply Chain," *Chain Store Age* (October 1996),
Section Two.

Figure 14-10

Reaching New Heights at Walgreen

Advanced forklift technology allowed Walgreen to add another level of storage to its newest distribution center in Woodland, California. The $60 million, 335,000-square-foot facility opened in 1996 to support aggressive West Coast store expansion. Over the next several years, Walgreen will focus on technology upgrades and expansion to existing facilities to accommodate growth and keep on the leading edge of retail distribution.

on deliveries from suppliers, The Limited, Inc. orders some apparel by satellite, uses common and contract carriers to pick it up from manufacturers in the United States and Asia (with chartered jets making several flights a week); ships items to its own warehouses in Columbus, Ohio; and then delivers them to stores. At J.C. Penney, there are separate distribution centers for its store and catalog operations.

Next, prices and inventory information are marked on merchandise. Supermarkets estimate that price marking on individual items costs them an amount equal to their annual profits, and they look forward to the time when shelf prices will be sufficient. Price and inventory marking can be done in various ways. Small firms may hand-post prices and manually keep inventory records. Some retailers use their own computer-generated price tags and rely on pre-printed UPC data on packages to keep inventory records. Others buy tags, with computer- and human-readable price and inventory data, from outside suppliers. Still others expect vendors to provide source tagging.

The more information labels or tags possess, the more efficient the inventory control system. For example, with portable printers from Monarch Marking Systems, a retailer can use hand-held devices to print UPC-based labels; and the devices can be connected to a store's computer system. By utilizing Seagull Scientific Systems' Bar Tender for Windows software, retailers can easily print product tags that include a wide range of data. See Figures 14-11 and 14-12.

Store displays and on-floor quantities and assortments depend on the type of retailer and merchandise involved. Supermarkets typically have bin and rack displays and place most inventory on the selling floor. Traditional department stores have all kinds of interior displays (such as ensemble displays) and place a lot of inventory in the back room, off the sales floor. Displays and on-floor merchandising are discussed more fully in Chapter 17.

Figure 14-11

The Monarch 1130 Series Labeler

The 1130 Series labelers are a new family of identification and pricing solutions. They are simple and easy to use. They have ergonomic handle grips, lift-up covers for quick maintenance, label-viewing windows, and other features.

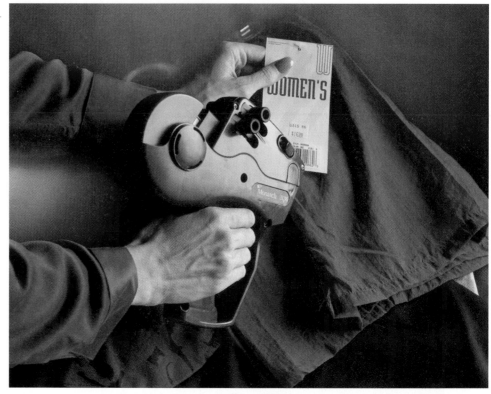

Merchandise handling is not complete until the customer buys and receives it from a retailer. This means order taking, credit or cash transactions, packaging, and delivery or pickup. Automation has improved retailer performance in each of these areas.

A procedure for processing returns and damaged goods is also needed. In particular, a retailer needs to determine which party is responsible for customer returns (the supplier or the retailer) and the provisions under which damaged goods would be accepted for refund or exchange (such as the length of time a warranty is honored).

As discussed in Chapter 13, monitoring and reducing inventory losses due to theft is an aspect of merchandise handling that has rapidly grown in significance. More retailers are taking aggressive actions to deal with this problem than before due to the high costs of merchandise theft.

Merchandise control involves evaluating revenues, profits, turnover, inventory shortages, seasonality, and costs for each goods/service category and item carried by a retailer. Control is generally achieved by developing and maintaining book (perpetual) inventory data, and then periodically conducting a physical inventory count to check the accuracy of the book figures. The latter usually must be adjusted to reflect damaged goods, pilferage, customer returns, and other factors. An in-depth discussion of this topic appears in Chapter 15.

Reordering Merchandise

A plan for reordering merchandise is necessary for those items the retailer purchases more than once. Four factors are critical in devising such a plan: order and delivery time, inventory turnover, financial outlays, and inventory versus ordering costs.

Order and delivery time must be determined. How long would it take for a retailer to process an order and a supplier to fulfill and deliver that order? It is possible that delivery time could be so lengthy that a retailer must reorder while a full inventory still exists. On the other hand, overnight delivery may be available for some items.

Figure 14-12

Bar Tender for Windows

Seagull Scientific Systems' Bar Tender for Windows printing software can be used to generate a wide variety of label designs.

The turnover rate for each type of merchandise must be calculated. How long would it take for a retailer to sell out its inventory? A fast-selling product allows a retailer to have two choices: order a surplus of items and spread out reorder periods, or keep a low inventory and order frequently (short order periods). A slow-selling item may let a retailer reduce its initial inventory level and spread out the reorder period.

The financial outlays under various purchase options must be considered. A large order, which provides a quantity discount, may require a large cash outlay. A small order, while more expensive per item, results in lower total costs at any one time (since less inventory is held).

Finally, inventory holding versus ordering costs must be weighed. The advantages of having a large inventory are customer satisfaction, quantity discounts in purchases, low per-item shipping charges, and ease of control and handling. The potential disadvantages are high investment costs; the greater possibility of obsolescence, deterioration, and damages; storage costs; insurance costs; and opportunity costs. The advantages of placing many orders and keeping a small inventory are the low investment costs, low opportunity costs, low storage costs, and low damages and obsolescence. The potential disadvantages are disappointing customers by being out of stock, higher per-unit costs, the impact of order-fulfillment delays, the need for partial shipments, extra service charges, and more complex control and handling. Retailers normally try to trade off these two costs by maintaining a large enough inventory to satisfy customers while not keeping a high surplus inventory. Quick response inventory planning reduces both inventory and ordering costs through closer retailer–supplier relationships.

Re-Evaluating on a Regular Basis

Once a well-integrated merchandise buying and handling strategy is in place, the retailer should not just enact its plan. It should be re-evaluated regularly, with management reviewing the buying organization (Step 1 in Figure 14-1), and that organization should review the buying and handling process (Steps 2 through 9). The overall procedure, as well as the handling of individual goods and services, should be monitored.

Summary

1. To examine nonfinancial merchandise planning and management Developing and instituting a merchandise plan is a key element in a successful retail strategy. Merchandising consists of the activities involved in a retailer's buying goods and services and making them available for sale.

2. To outline the merchandise buying and handling process This is an integrated, systematic way of acquiring and processing merchandise. It consists of ten steps: (1) setting up a buying organization; (2) outlining merchandise plans; (3) gathering data on consumer demand; (4) determining merchandise sources; (5) evaluating merchandise; (6) negotiating the purchase; (7) concluding the purchase; (8) handling merchandise; (9) reordering merchandise; and (10) re-evaluating regularly.

3. To discuss each element in the merchandise buying and handling process in detail Buying-organization decisions include the level of formality, degree of centralization, amount of specialization, inside versus outside personnel, cooperative efforts, merchandising versus buying, and staffing. A buying philosophy includes only the purchase of goods and services and not their sale; a merchandising philosophy entails both activities. Some firms separate buying and selling functions.

Merchandise plans involve the four basic decisions noted under this chapter's objective 4.

Data from customers, sources of supply, personnel, competitors, and others must be collected to help the retailer forecast and adapt to demand.

A retailer must choose firm-owned; outside, regularly used; and/or outside, new supply sources. Inspection, sampling, and/or description in merchandise evaluation must be planned.

Purchase terms may have to be negotiated in their entirety (such as with opportunistic buying) or uniform contracts may be used. The purchase must also be concluded (automatic-manual, management approval, and transfer of title).

Merchandise handling decisions include receiving and storing, price and inventory marking, displays, on-floor assortments, customer transactions, delivery or pickup, returns and damaged goods, monitoring pilferage, and control.

Reorder procedures depend on order and delivery time, inventory turnover, financial outlays, and inventory versus ordering costs.

Both the overall merchandising procedure and specific goods and services need to be regularly reviewed.

4. To place special emphasis on what merchandise a retailer should carry, how much to stock, when to stock items, and where to store items First, in choosing what items to handle, a retailer must pick the quality of merchandise (below average, above average, or medium) to stock and how innovative (progressive or conservative) to be. The product life cycle is useful for projecting the sales of a product over its life and the types of customers who purchase during different time periods.

Second, how much merchandise to stock is a decision involving width and depth of assortment. A product assortment can range from wide and deep to narrow and shallow. In planning an assortment, these factors should be reviewed: sales, profit, investment costs, space requirements, turnover, complementary and substitute products, manufacturer insistence, and the brand mix (manufacturer, private, and/or generic).

A third required decision is when merchandise is to be stocked. An accurate sales forecast is needed for efficient planning. Among the points to consider are peak seasons, order and delivery time, routine versus special orders, stock turnover, discounts, and the efficiency of inventory procedures.

A fourth decision concerns where merchandise is stored. The retailer must resolve whether to use warehouses or to have items shipped directly to its store(s). Merchandise also has to be allocated among store branches.

Key Terms

merchandising (p. 437)
merchandise buying and handling process (p. 437)
formal buying organization (p. 437)
informal buying organization (p. 437)
centralized buying organization (p. 439)
decentralized buying organization (p. 439)
inside buying organization (p. 440)

outside buying organization (p. 440)
resident buying office (p. 440)
cooperative buying (p. 440)
product life cycle (p. 445)
width of assortment (p. 449)
depth of assortment (p. 449)
battle of the brands (p. 451)
manufacturer (national) brands (p. 451)
private (dealer) brands (p. 452)

generic brands (p. 453)
basic stock list (p. 453)
model stock plan (p. 453)
never-out list (p. 453)
direct store distribution (DSD) (p. 455)
want book (want slip) (p. 456)
opportunistic buying (p. 460)
consignment purchase (p. 462)
memorandum purchase (p. 462)

Questions for Discussion

1. Why is good merchandising so critical to a retailer's success or failure?
2. What are the advantages and disadvantages of a centralized buying organization?
3. Under what circumstances could a retailer carry a wide range of merchandise quality without hurting its image? When should the quality of merchandise carried be quite narrow?
4. How innovative should each of these be in planning merchandise? Explain your answers.
   a. Supermarket.
   b. Women's shoe store.
   c. Small luggage store.
   d. Web-based florist.
5. How should a consumer electronics store use the product life cycle concept?
6. If you were a franchise operator, how would you feel about enforcing constrained decision making with regard to merchandise planning? Why?
7. Why are some retailers hesitant to drop fading goods and services?

8. Give examples of retailers fitting into each of these merchandise assortment plans.
   a. Narrow-shallow.
   b. Narrow-deep.
   c. Wide-deep.
9. How could a college store use a basic stock list, a model stock plan, and never-out lists?
10. What problems may occur if a retailer mistimes purchases?
11. What information should a specialty store gather before adding a new greeting card brand?
12. Cite the advantages and disadvantages associated with these merchandise sources for a small art gallery. How would your answers differ for a large art gallery chain?
    a. Company-owned.
    b. Outside, regularly used.
    c. Outside, new.
13. Devise a checklist a retailer could use to negotiate opportunistic buying terms with suppliers.
14. Which is more difficult, merchandise planning for a small bookstore or a book superstore? Explain your answer.

Web-Based Exercise:

DALLAS MARKET CENTER (http://www.dallasmarketcenter.com)

Questions

1. What is the Dallas Market Center?
2. What types of merchandise does it feature during the year?
3. What information can be acquired from this Web site?
4. Who would be the prime target markets for the Dallas Market Center?

CASE 1
The Negotiation Ratio*

Negotiation is the process used to resolve the terms under which retail buyers and suppliers conduct business. Although some may think suppliers offer products to retailers on a "take it or leave it" basis, the latter regularly negotiate with their suppliers on product prices, special discounts and incentives, buyback guarantees on unsold merchandise, and so on. This give and take especially occurs with larger retailers, with retailers that sell private brands, and in cases where retailers have high channel power relative to the suppliers.

Much negotiation in retailing is based on the power of the retailer relative to the supplier. In some cases, suppliers have increased their power by tightly controlling distribution in a given geographic area. Thus, Stearns and Foster commonly restricted the sale of its bedding products to the leading department stores in an area and Bulova generally limited the sale of its watches to "better quality" jewelry stores. In such cases, retail buyers are likely to work hard to keep these suppliers content. On the other hand, many large retail chains have increased their power.

A useful tool in analyzing buyer–seller relationships is the "negotiation ratio." The numerator of this ratio is the quantitative value (expressed in dollars) of the sum of benefits the buyer receives. The denominator is the cost of those benefits to the supplier. For example, a retailer may be offered a $1,000 cooperative advertising allowance as an alternative to a $1,000 price discount. In computing the negotiation ratio, in this instance, it is important to bear in mind that a retailer may view cooperative advertising as being worth less than $1,000 (due to restrictions placed by the manufacturer on an ad's use) and that a manufacturer may view the additional cost to be less than $1,000 (since the cooperative advertising allowance would be used to replace $1,000 in the manufacturer's current national advertising budget). Under most circumstances, a retailer would seek concessions and a manufacturer would be wise to offer a deal with the highest negotiation ratio (offering the greatest benefit to the retailer per dollar of cost to the supplier).

Let's see how the negotiation ratio could be used to evaluate a group of concessions or a supplier's marketing program. Suppose, for example, a supplier offers to reduce its prices by an additional 5 percent on all purchases during an 18-month period, guarantee to buy back unused merchandise equal to 10 percent of sales, and offer an extended warranty to the final consumer (a two-year versus the standard one-year warranty). In computing the value of these concessions, the buyer would need to make assumptions about the amount of purchases, the percent of unsold stock, and the value of the extended warranty to the final consumer. To complete the negotiation ratio, the supplier needs to determine the total costs of these concessions.

A supplier may also use the negotiation ratio as a way of fine-tuning its offer. It may find that a three-year warranty has less costs to the supplier but has higher perceived

---

*This case was prepared and written by Professors Roger Dickinson, University of Texas, Arlington, and William W. Keep, University of Kentucky.

value to a retail buyer than the buyback offer. The costs and benefits of other combinations can also be computed.

The negotiation ratio shares some of the weaknesses of other planning tools and processes. Its value depends on the accuracy of the buyer's and seller's assumptions regarding future outcomes (such as total sales within an 18-month period) and the value of alternative concessions (such as the value of a buyback guarantee versus an extended warranty). In addition, the ratio does not analyze the impact of a concession on future buyer–supplier relationships or on competitive conditions (competitors may demand the extended warranty if this is successfully marketed to final consumers). Furthermore, including additional variables and outcomes in multiple time periods increases the complexity of the negotiation ratio concept.

Questions
1. Discuss the pros and cons of the use of the negotiation ratio.
2. Describe how the negotiation ratio may be affected by a situation of high channel power by a supplier.
3. Compute a negotiation ratio for the $1,000 cooperative advertising allowance and the $1,000 price reduction example cited in this case. List your assumptions. (Note: There is more than one correct answer.)
4. Compute the negotiation ratio for the second example cited in this case with the additional 5 percent on all purchases during an 18-month period, the buyback guarantee, and the extended warranty. (Note: There is more than one correct answer.)

CASE 1 (Continued)

Distribution and Marketing Systems Inc. (DMSI) is an independent supplier of merchandise receiving, handling, warehousing, and transportation services for retailers. Its services are ideal for firms that do not want to invest scarce human and financial resources in distribution facilities. Many of DMSI's retail customers are growing rapidly, are in the process of downsizing, or feel a specialist can more efficiently fulfill distribution and logistics responsibilities. DMSI has a 250,000-square-foot distribution center in Charlotte, North Carolina. It ships goods from this site to 500 retail stores and distribution centers in the United States and Canada. Over one-quarter of all the goods it ships are manufactured within 24 hours driving time from Charlotte.

One of DMSI's major customers is Dick's Clothing and Sporting Goods, a retailer that doubled in size, to 40 stores, in just one year. Because Dick's did not have a distribution facility big enough to handle the growth, it chose to outsource logistics functions (including receiving, counting, pricing, picking, and ultimately shipping merchandise to Dick's main distribution center) to DMSI. Let's look at the information and merchandise flow for an order of Nike shoes received at DMSI's main distribution center for Dick's. This flow consists of eight steps:

1. Dick's receives a call from Nike that its order of shoes is ready to be shipped.
2. DMSI personnel assign a cost-effective motor carrier to ship the shoes from Nike's location in Memphis to DMSI's distribution center in Charlotte.
3. DMSI personnel unload the truck and verify the carton count against the shipping documentation.
4. DMSI personnel enter the receipt of the order in Dick's purchase-order tracking system.

CASE 2 Distribution and Marketing Systems Inc. (DMSI): Outsourcing Retail Distribution and Transportation Services[†]

†The material in this case is drawn from data supplied by DMSI.

CASE 2
(Continued)

5. Dick's personnel generate a pick list of sneakers for each of Dick's stores.
6. DMSI personnel sort the Nike sneakers by size and style.
7. DMSI personnel add price and security tags (and can even place merchandise on hangers if required by a retailer).
8. DMSI personnel pick the order for each store based on Dick's requirements.

This process is generally completed in less than four hours from receipt of the order at DMSI's distribution center.

According to DMSI, four factors account for its competitive edge over other firms providing similar functions: an efficient layout, the use of flexible labor scheduling, customized services for each client, and transportation advantages. DMSI's efficient layout is derived from its receiving goods on one side of the building and then shipping from the opposite side. As DMSI processes a shipment, each customer's goods move closer to the shipping station. This lets DMSI process twice as many goods in one-half the space of the average distribution center. DMSI's flexible labor scheduling means the required personnel are present when a shipment arrives. This speeds processing and delivery times. Personnel are also paid incentives on the basis of their order-filling and order-processing accuracy. They routinely meet or exceed 99.9 percent or better accuracy targets.

DMSI believes in customized services for each client. Every retailer's orders are processed in a part of the distribution center reserved exclusively for that retailer. In addition, DMSI personnel are dedicated to individual retailer clients. They are specifically trained to enter order-status information directly in the client's computer system through a connection at DMSI. Lastly, DMSI receives better than average shipping rates through quantity discounts, and continuously evaluates each motor carrier's performance and rewards future business based on a carrier's performance.

Questions

1. Under what conditions (other than those mentioned in the case) should a retailer outsource its merchandise handling?
2. Describe the pros and cons of outsourcing a retailer's distribution and transportation functions.
3. Evaluate DMSI's information/merchandise flow for Dick's.
4. What other competitive advantages does DMSI possess in comparison to a typical retailer?

Video Questions on DMSI

1. What are the advantages and disadvantages of Dick's using a single company-owned distribution center versus the use of direct store delivery by DMSI?
2. Develop five criteria that a retailer could use to evaluate DMSI.

15

Financial Merchandise Management

The cost method of inventory valuation tracks merchandise movement on an item-by-item basis in terms of actual cost. In contrast, the retail method of inventory valuation is an estimate of the value of merchandise (rather than tracking exact costs for thousands of individual items).

A major benefit of the cost method is its better accuracy than the retail method, due to the latter's estimating technique. The cost method also can be more easily integrated with direct product profitability. And, according to retail analysts, enhanced computer capabilities can aid the transition from the retail to the cost method of accounting. However, ingrained traditions, due to years of using the retail method, and the high costs of change are slowing the rate of conversion. A regional director of retail industry services at a Big Six accounting firm says 55 percent of general merchandise retailers use the retail method and 45 percent the cost method.

Montgomery Ward is an example of a large retailer still using the retail method, despite considering a switch to the cost method. After the firm considered switching to the cost method, its director of accounting said, "It's something we'd like to do, but there are a lot of systems involved and it can be a lot costly." Adds a vice-president at Musicland, a software retailer, "At some point in the future, we'll surely entertain the idea of changing. That will most likely be when we take a look at changing our systems." One key difficulty in enacting a change at Musicland is the integration of the retail method with the firm's ordering and inventory management systems.

In contrast, Waban, parent of BJ's Wholesale Club and the HomeBase home improvement chain, has used the cost method since both divisions started. Notes Waban's treasurer and chief financial officer, "There's no question it's [the cost method] more accurate. The retail method was devised as an estimating technique to deal with a large number of stock-keeping units."

Other retailers use the retail method predominantly, but also apply the cost method. For example, Costco uses the retail method for all departments except a few manufacturing-based areas such as the bakery. Dayton Hudson uses the retail method for all departments except pharmacies and groceries in its Target supercenters.[1]

CHAPTER OBJECTIVES

1. To describe the major aspects of financial merchandise planning and management
2. To explain the cost and retail methods of accounting
3. To study the merchandise forecasting and budgeting process
4. To examine alternative methods of inventory unit control
5. To integrate dollar and unit merchandising control concepts

---

[1] David P. Schulz, "Retailers Consider Switch to Cost Accounting," *Stores* (November 1995), pp. 50–51.

OVERVIEW

Through **financial merchandise management,** a retailer specifies exactly which products (goods and services) are purchased, when products are purchased, and how many products are purchased; both dollar and unit controls are employed. **Dollar control** involves planning and monitoring a retailer's financial investment in merchandise over a stated time period. **Unit control** relates to the quantities of merchandise a retailer handles during a stated time period. Dollar controls usually precede unit controls, as a retailer must plan its dollar investment before making assortment decisions.

Well-structured financial merchandise plans offer such benefits as these:

■ The value and amount of inventory in each department and/or store unit during a given period of time can be delineated. Stock is thus balanced, and fewer markdowns may be necessary.

■ The amount of merchandise (in terms of investment) a buyer can purchase during a given period can be stipulated. This gives a buyer direction.

■ A buyer can study the inventory investment in relation to planned and actual revenues. This improves the return on investment.

■ The retailer's space requirements can be partly determined by estimating beginning-of-month and end-of-month inventory levels.

■ A buyer's performance can be rated. Various measures may be used as performance standards.

■ A buyer can determine stock shortages, giving an estimate of bookkeeping errors and pilferage.

■ Slow-moving items can be classified—thus leading to increased sales efforts or markdowns.

■ A proper balance between inventory levels and out-of-stock conditions can be maintained.

This chapter divides financial merchandise management into four areas: methods of accounting, merchandise forecasting and budgeting, unit control systems, and financial inventory control. The hypothetical Handy Hardware Store is used to illustrate the concepts covered.

INVENTORY VALUATION: THE COST AND RETAIL METHODS OF ACCOUNTING

Retail inventory accounting systems can be complex because they entail a great deal of data (due to the number of items sold). A typical retailer's dollar control system must provide such data as the sales and purchases made by that firm during a budget period, the value of beginning and ending inventory, the extent of markups and markdowns, and merchandise shortages.

Table 15-1 shows a profit-and-loss statement for Handy Hardware Store for the period from January 1, 1997 through June 30, 1997. The sales amount represents total receipts over this time. Beginning inventory is computed by counting the merchandise in stock on January 1, 1997—recorded at cost. Purchases (at cost) and transportation charges (costs incurred in shipping items from the supplier to the retailer) are derived by adding the invoice slips for all merchandise bought by Handy in the period.

Together, beginning inventory, purchases, and transportation charges equal the cost of **merchandise available for sale.** Because Handy does a physical inventory twice yearly, ending inventory is figured by counting the merchandise in stock on June 30, 1997—recorded at cost (Handy codes items so costs can be derived for each item in stock). The **cost of goods sold** equals the cost of merchandise available for sale minus the cost value of ending inventory. Sales less cost of goods sold yields **gross profit,** while **net profit** is gross profit minus retail operating expenses.

Retailers usually have different data needs than manufacturers. The assortments are larger; costs cannot be printed on cartons unless coded (due to customer inspection).

Table 15-1   HANDY HARDWARE STORE PROFIT-AND-LOSS STATEMENT, JANUARY 1, 1997–JUNE 30, 1997

Sales		$208,730
Less cost of goods sold:		
Beginning inventory (at cost)	$ 22,310	
Purchases (at cost)	144,700	
Transportation charges	1,300	
Merchandise available for sale	$168,310	
Ending inventory (at cost)	45,250	
Cost of goods sold		123,060
Gross profit		$ 85,670
Less operating expenses:		
Salaries	$ 35,000	
Advertising	12,500	
Rental	8,000	
Other	13,000	
Total operating expenses		68,500
Net profit before taxes		$ 17,170

Stock shortages are higher; sales are conducted more often; and retailers require monthly, not quarterly, profit data.

Two inventory accounting systems are available to a retailer: the cost and retail methods of accounting. The cost accounting system values merchandise at cost plus inbound transportation charges. The retail accounting system values merchandise at current retail prices.

Next, the cost and retail inventory methods are examined on the basis of such factors as the frequency with which data are obtained, the difficulties in doing a physical inventory, the complexities in record keeping, the ease of settling insurance claims (if there is inventory damage), the extent to which stock shortages can be calculated, and the complexities of the systems.

ETHICS IN RETAILING

What Responsibility Do Large Retailers Have to Their Suppliers?

Department stores are increasingly placing special demands on suppliers and penalizing those that do not conform to the retailers' guidelines. Thus, if an apparel maker fails to adhere to these demands, it can receive a "chargeback," a deduction from its invoiced amount. Here are two examples of special regulations and chargebacks by department stores. Ames Department Stores has this chargeback schedule on a per shipment basis: $300 for an incorrect shipping label, $500 for incorrect shipping packing materials, and 5 percent of the shipment cost for late or early shipments. Younkers, a Midwest chain, deducts 2 percent from each merchandise invoice as an allowance for damaged goods.

Some small apparel makers have begun refusing to sell to department stores and now sell only to specialty stores and catalog retailers. These firms say that too high a percentage of their profits are eaten up by chargebacks. Others, such as Schwab Company, a children's clothing manufacturer, actively fight chargebacks by providing evidence they followed customer rules (such as Polaroid photographs of boxes showing proper placement of shipping labels).

Some retailing analysts feel the rules and chargebacks are a symptom of the high degree of channel power held by large department stores. These analysts believe that both the rules and chargebacks may even increase as a result of recent mergers among retailers.

Source: Christina Duff, "Big Stores' Outlandish Demands Alienate Small Suppliers," *Wall Street Journal* (October 27, 1995), pp. B1, B5.

The Cost Method

In the **cost method of accounting,** the cost to the retailer of each item is recorded on an accounting sheet and/or is coded on a price tag or merchandise container. When a physical inventory is conducted, every item's cost must be ascertained, the quantity of every item in stock counted, and the total inventory value at cost calculated.

One way to code merchandise cost is to use a ten-letter equivalency system, such as M = 0, N = 1, O = 2, P = 3, Q = 4, R = 5, S = 6, T = 7, U = 8, and V = 9. An item coded with the letters STOP would have a cost value of $67.23. The technique is useful as an accounting tool and for retailers that allow price bargaining by customers (profit per item is easy to compute).

A retailer can use the cost method while it does physical or book inventories. A physical inventory involves an actual merchandise count; a book inventory relies on record-keeping entries.

A Physical Inventory System Using the Cost Method ❑ In a **physical inventory system,** ending inventory is measured by an actual count of the merchandise still in stock at the close of a selling period; ending inventory is then recorded at cost. The retailer cannot compute gross profit until after ending inventory is valued. Thus, a firm using the cost method and relying on a physical inventory system can derive gross profit only as often as it conducts a full physical inventory. Since most retailers do so just once or twice a year, relying on a physical inventory system imposes limitations on merchandise planning.

By using only a physical inventory system, a firm could also be unable to compute inventory shortages (due to pilferage, unrecorded breakage, and so on) because ending inventory value is set by simply adding the costs of all items in stock. What the ending inventory level *should be* is not computed.

A Book Inventory System Using the Cost Method ❑ A **book inventory system** (also known as a **perpetual inventory system**) avoids the problem of infrequent financial analysis by keeping a running total of the value of all inventory on hand at cost at a given time. Therefore, end-of-month inventory values can be computed without a physical inventory, and frequent financial statements can be prepared. In addition, a book inventory lets a retailer uncover stock shortages by comparing projected inventory values with actual inventory values through a physical inventory.

A retailer maintains a perpetual system by regularly recording purchases and adding them to existing inventory value; sales transactions are then subtracted to arrive at the new current inventory value (all at cost). Table 15-2 shows a book (perpetual) inventory system for Handy Hardware for the period from July 1, 1997 through December 31, 1997. Note that the ending inventory in Table 15-1 becomes the beginning inventory in Table 15-2.

Table 15-2 assumes merchandise costs are rather constant and monthly sales at cost are easily computed. Yet, suppose merchandise costs rise. How would inventory then be valued? Two ways to value inventory are the FIFO (first-in-first-out) and LIFO (last-in-first-out) methods.

The **FIFO method** logically assumes old merchandise is sold first, while newer items remain in inventory. The **LIFO method** assumes new merchandise is sold first, while older stock remains in inventory. FIFO matches inventory value with the current cost structure—the goods remaining in inventory are the ones bought most recently, while LIFO matches current sales with the current cost structure—the goods sold first are the ones bought most recently. During periods of rising inventory values, LIFO offers retailers a tax advantage because lower profits are shown.

In Figure 15-1, the FIFO and LIFO methods of inventory valuation are illustrated for Handy Hardware's snow blowers for the period January 1, 1997 through December 31, 1997; the store carries only one model of snow blower. Handy has found that it sold

Table 15-2 HANDY HARDWARE STORE PERPETUAL INVENTORY SYSTEM, JULY 1, 1997–DECEMBER 31, 1997[a]

Date	Beginning-of-Month Inventory (at cost)	+	Net Monthly Purchases (at cost)	–	Monthly Sales (at cost)	=	End-of-Month Inventory (at cost)
7/1/97	$45,250		$ 20,000		$ 31,200		$ 34,050
8/1/97	34,050		14,000		19,200		28,850
9/1/97	28,850		13,800		14,400		28,250
10/1/97	28,250		22,000		14,400		35,850
11/1/97	35,850		25,200		20,400		40,650
12/1/97	40,650		7,950		30,600		18,000
		Total	$102,950		$130,200		(as of 12/31/97)

[a]Transportation charges are not included in computing inventory value in this table.

110 snow blowers in 1997 at an average retail price of $320. Handy knows it started 1997 with a beginning inventory of 15 snow blowers, which it had bought for $150 each. During January 1997, it bought 50 snow blowers at $175 each; from October to December 1997, Handy bought another 75 snow blowers for $225 apiece. Because Handy sold 110 snow blowers in 1997, as of the close of business on December 31, it had 30 units left in inventory.

Using the FIFO method, Handy would assume its beginning inventory and initial purchases were sold first. The 30 snow blowers remaining in inventory would have a cost

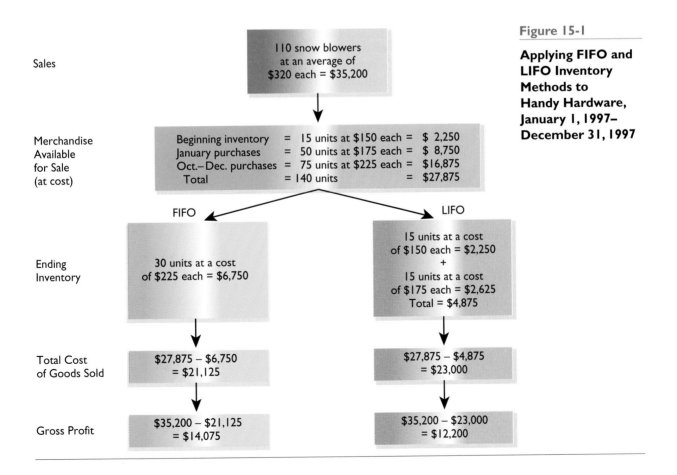

Figure 15-1

Applying FIFO and LIFO Inventory Methods to Handy Hardware, January 1, 1997– December 31, 1997

value of $225 each, resulting in a total cost of goods sold of $21,125 and a gross profit of $14,075. Using the LIFO method, Handy would assume the most recently purchased items were sold first and the remaining inventory would consist of beginning goods and early purchases. Of the snow blowers remaining in inventory, 15 would have a cost value of $150 each and 15 a cost value of $175 apiece, resulting in a total cost of goods sold of $23,000 and a gross profit of $12,200. The FIFO method presents a more accurate picture of the cost of goods sold and the true cost value of ending inventory. The LIFO method indicates a lower profit, leading to the payment of lower taxes, but an understated ending inventory value at cost.

The retail method of inventory, which combines FIFO and LIFO concepts, is explained later in this chapter. A fuller discussion of FIFO and LIFO may be found in a basic accounting text.

Disadvantages of Cost-Based Inventory Systems ❑ Cost-based physical and book systems have significant disadvantages. First, both require a retailer to assign costs to each item in stock (and to each item sold). During periods when merchandise costs are changing, cost-based inventory valuation systems are most useful only for retailers with low inventory turnover, limited assortments, and high average prices. Examples of firms with these attributes are car dealers, furriers, furniture stores, and major-appliance dealers.

Second, neither cost-based method provides for adjusting inventory values to reflect style changes, end-of-season markdowns, or sudden surges of demand (which may raise prices). Thus, the ending value of inventory, based on the cost of the merchandise, may not reflect its actual worth. This discrepancy could be quite troublesome if the ending inventory value is used in computing required insurance coverage or in filing insurance claims for losses.

Despite these factors, retailers making the products they sell—such as bakeries, restaurants, and furniture showrooms—often keep records on a cost basis. A department store with these operations (or others involving manufacturing) could use the cost method for them and the retail method for other departments. Also, as noted in the chapter's opening vignette, with the advent of sophisticated computer systems, the cost method is being adopted by more firms than in the past.

The Retail Method

With the **retail method of accounting,** closing inventory value is determined by calculating the average relationship between the cost and retail values of merchandise available for sale during a period. Though the retail method overcomes the disadvantages of the cost method, it requires detailed record keeping. Also it is more complex because ending inventory is first valued in retail dollars and then converted to cost in order to compute gross margin (gross profit).

There are three basic steps to determine an ending inventory value by the retail method:

1. Calculating the cost complement.
2. Calculating deductions from retail value.
3. Converting retail inventory value to cost.

Calculating the Cost Complement ❑ The value of beginning inventory, net purchases, additional markups, and transportation charges are all included in the retail method. Beginning inventory and net purchase amounts (purchases less returns) are recorded at both cost and retail levels. Additional markups represent the extra revenues received by a retailer when it increases selling prices over the period covered, due to inflation or unexpectedly high demand. Transportation charges are the retailer's costs for

Table 15-3 HANDY HARDWARE STORE, CALCULATING MERCHANDISE AVAILABLE FOR SALE AT COST AND AT RETAIL, JULY 1, 1997–DECEMBER 31, 1997

	At Cost	At Retail
Beginning inventory	$ 45,250	$ 69,600
Net purchases	102,950	170,263
Additional markups	—	8,200
Transportation charges	1,746	—
Total merchandise available for sale	$149,946	$248,063

shipping the goods it buys from suppliers to the retailer. Table 15-3 shows the total merchandise available for sale at cost and at retail for Handy Hardware during the period from July 1, 1997 through December 31, 1997, based on cost data from Table 15-2.

By using Table 15-3 data, the average relationship of cost to retail value for all merchandise available for sale by Handy Hardware in the six-month period can be computed. This concept is called the **cost complement:**

$$\text{Cost complement} = \frac{\text{Total cost valuation}}{\text{Total retail valuation}}$$

$$= \frac{\$149,946}{\$248,063}$$

$$= 0.6045$$

Because the cost complement is 0.6045 (60.45 percent), on average, 60.45 cents of every retail sales dollar is made up of Handy Hardware's merchandise cost.

Calculating Deductions from Retail Value ❏ The ending retail value of inventory must reflect all deductions from the total merchandise available for sale at retail. Besides customer sales, deductions would include markdowns (such as special sales and reduced prices on discontinued, end-of-season, and shopworn goods), employee discounts, and stock shortages (due to pilferage, unrecorded breakage, and so on). Although sales, markdowns, and employee discounts can be recorded throughout an accounting period, a physical inventory is needed to learn about stock shortages.

From Table 15-3, it is known that Handy Hardware had a retail value of merchandise available for sale of $248,063 in the period from July 1, 1997 through December 31, 1997. This was reduced by sales of $211,270 and recorded markdowns and employee discounts of $7,017. The ending book value of inventory at retail as of December 31, 1997, was $29,776. See Table 15-4.

After a physical inventory is taken, stock shortages are simple to compute under the retail method. A firm would just compare the retail book value of ending inventory with

Table 15-4 HANDY HARDWARE STORE, COMPUTING ENDING RETAIL BOOK VALUE, AS OF DECEMBER 31, 1997

Merchandise available for sale (at retail)		$248,063
Less deductions:		
Sales	$211,270	
Markdowns	5,817	
Employee discounts	1,200	
Total deductions		218,287
Ending retail book value of inventory		$ 29,776

Table 15-5	HANDY HARDWARE STORE, COMPUTING STOCK SHORTAGES AND ADJUSTING RETAIL BOOK VALUE, AS OF DECEMBER 31, 1997	
Ending retail book value of inventory		$29,776
Physical inventory (at retail)		28,235
Stock shortages (at retail)		1,541
Adjusted ending retail book value of inventory		$28,235

the actual physical ending inventory value at retail. If the book inventory exceeds the physical inventory, a stock shortage exists. Table 15-5 shows the results of a physical inventory by Handy Hardware. The shortages are $1,541 (at retail), and book value is adjusted accordingly. Although Handy recognizes that the shortages are from pilferage (by customers and/or employees), bookkeeping errors (not recording markdowns, employee discounts, and breakage), and overshipments not billed to customers, it cannot learn the proportion of shortages caused by each of these factors.

Occasionally, a physical inventory may reveal a stock overage, which represents the excess of physical ending inventory value over book value. An overage may be due to errors in doing a physical inventory or in maintaining a book inventory. If overages occur, the ending retail book value of inventory must be adjusted upward.

Inasmuch as a retailer must conduct a physical inventory to compute stock shortages (overages), and a physical inventory is taken only once or twice a year, shortages (overages) are often estimated for monthly merchandise budgets.

Converting Retail Inventory Value to Cost ❏ The retailer must next convert the adjusted ending retail book value of inventory to cost so as to compute dollar gross profit (gross margin). The ending inventory at cost equals the adjusted ending retail book value multiplied by the cost complement. For Handy Hardware, this would be:

$$\text{Ending inventory} = \text{Adjusted ending retail book value} \times \text{Cost complement}$$
$$\text{(at cost)}$$
$$= \$28,235 \times .6045$$
$$= \$17,068$$

The preceding equation does not yield the exact ending inventory value at cost for Handy but approximates it based on the average relationship between cost and the retail selling price for all merchandise available for sale.

The adjusted ending inventory at cost can be used to find gross profit. See Table 15-6. For Handy Hardware, the July 1, 1997 through December 31, 1997 cost of goods sold was $132,878, resulting in gross profit of $78,392. By deducting operating expenses of $69,500, Handy sees the net profit before taxes for this six-month period was $8,892.

Advantages of the Retail Method ❏ Several strengths of the retail method are evident in comparing the cost and retail accounting methods:

■ The retail method is easier to use when taking a physical inventory. The chances of making errors in valuing merchandise are reduced since the physical inventory is recorded at retail value and costs do not have to be decoded.
■ Because undertaking a physical inventory is simpler, it can be completed more frequently. This lets a retailer be more aware of slow-moving items and stock shortages and take appropriate corrective actions.
■ The physical inventory method at cost requires a physical inventory to prepare a profit-and-loss statement. In contrast, the retail method lets a firm devise a profit-

Table 15-6 HANDY HARDWARE STORE PROFIT-AND-LOSS STATEMENT, JULY 1, 1997–DECEMBER 31, 1997

Sales		$211,270
Less cost of goods sold:		
Total merchandise available for sale (at cost)	$149,946	
Adjusted ending inventory (at cost)[a]	17,068	
Cost of goods sold		132,878[b]
Gross profit		$ 78,392
Less operating expenses:		
Salaries	$ 35,000	
Advertising	12,500	
Rental	8,000	
Other	14,000	
Total operating expenses		69,500
Net profit before taxes		$ 8,892

[a]Adjusted ending inventory (at cost) = Adjusted retail book value × Cost complement = $28,235 × .6045 = $17,068

[b]Cost of goods sold = Monthly sales (at cost) + Transportation charges + Stock shortages (at cost) = $130,200 + $1,746 + $932 = $132,878

and-loss statement based on book inventory figures, which can be adjusted to include estimated stock shortages between physical inventories. A book inventory system is better than a physical system at cost because frequent statements are needed if a firm is to study profit trends by department.

■ A complete record of ending book values is quite important in determining the proper level of insurance coverage and in settling insurance claims. The retail book method gives a firm an estimate of inventory value throughout the year. Since physical inventories are usually taken when merchandise levels are low, the book value at retail allows firms to plan insurance coverage for peak periods and shows the values of the goods on hand (in case there is a claim adjustment). The retail method is accepted in insurance claims.

Limitations of the Retail Method ❏ The greatest weakness of the retail method is the bookkeeping burden of recording a lot of cost- and price-related data. Ending book inventory figures can be correctly computed only if these items are accurately noted: the value of beginning inventory (at cost and at retail), purchases (at cost and at retail), shipping charges, markups, markdowns, employee discounts, transfers from other departments or stores, returns, and sales. Though personnel are freed from the burden of taking many physical inventories, ending book value at retail may be inaccurate unless all required data are precisely recorded. With computerization, this potential problem is lessened.[2]

A second limitation of the retail method is that the cost complement is an average figure based on the total cost of merchandise available for sale and its total retail value. It is possible for the resultant ending cost value of inventory to only approximate the true cost of items on hand. This is especially true if fast-selling items have different markups from slow-selling items and/or if there are wide variations among the markups of goods within a single department.

Familiarity with the retail and cost methods of inventory is essential for understanding the financial merchandise-management material described in the balance of this chapter.

[2]See Patricia A. Murphy, "Audit Recovery Firms Find Big Savings from Tiny Mistakes," *Stores* (November 1996), pp. 51–52.

Accounting Software Programs: Not Just for Big Retailers Anymore

The availability of accounting software packages for the supermarket industry has grown very rapidly in the past few years. Priced as low as $400 (and as high as $150,000 for a complex multistore package), many of these software packages include general ledger, accounts receivable, accounts payable, payroll, bank reconciliation, and inventory management functions. Several even connect point-of-sale data with accounting functions. Though most of the programs are designed for use in a wide variety of industries, most can be customized for use by particular retail sectors.

Hames Corporation, a two-store, Alaskan-based chain, uses the generalized accounting software system developed by Passport Software of Glenview, Illinois, to perform general ledger, accounts receivable, payroll, and check reconciliation functions. The system is so versatile that it is also used for accounting functions in Hames' liquor, home, sporting goods, and clothing stores.

Market Basket Foods, a 38-store supermarket chain based in Nederland, Texas, uses specialized accounting software developed by FMS of Pasedena, Maryland. The software provides Market Basket with specialized management reports such as customer account synopses, as well as sales per square foot and labor hours per department summaries. In addition to providing Market Basket's accounting software, FMS has also served as a controller for a small independent supermarket or provided a hardware-software time sharing.

Source: Terry Hennessy, "Staying in Control," *Stores* (April 1995), pp. 73–76.

MERCHANDISE FORECASTING AND BUDGETING: DOLLAR CONTROL

As mentioned in the chapter overview, dollar control means planning and monitoring a firm's inventory investment over time. Figure 15-2 shows the dollar control process for merchandise forecasting and budgeting, comprising six stages: designating control units, sales forecasting, inventory-level planning, reduction planning, planning purchases, and planning profit margins.

It is essential that the sequential nature of this process be followed since a change in any one stage affects all the stages after it. For instance, if a retailer's sales forecast is too low, it may run out of items because it does not plan to have enough inventory on hand during a selling season and its planned purchases will also be too low.

Designating Control Units

Merchandise forecasting and budgeting require the selection of **control units,** the merchandise categories for which data are gathered. Such classifications must be narrow enough to isolate opportunities and problems with specific merchandise lines. A retailer wishing to control goods within departments must record data on dollar allotments separately for each category.

As an example, knowing that total markdowns in a department are 20 percent above last year's level is less valuable than knowing the specific merchandise lines in which large markdowns are being taken. A retailer can broaden its control system by summarizing the categories that comprise a department. However, a broad category cannot be broken down into components. This means it is better to err on the side of too much information than too little.

It is also helpful to select control units consistent with other internal company data and with trade association data, if possible. Intrafirm comparisons are meaningful only when classification categories are stable over time. A classification system that shifts over time does not permit comparisons between periods. Valid external comparisons can be made only if control categories are similar for a given retailer and its trade association(s).

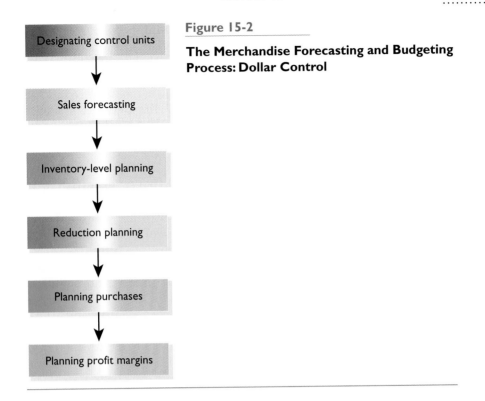

Figure 15-2

The Merchandise Forecasting and Budgeting Process: Dollar Control

Control units may be set up on the basis of departments, classifications within departments, price line classifications, and standard merchandise classifications. A discussion of each follows.

At the very least, retailers should keep financial records in terms of specified departmental categories. Even a small firm like Handy Hardware needs to acquire data on a departmental basis (such as tools and equipment, supplies, housewares, and so on) for buying, inventory control, and markdown decisions. The broadest practical division is the department, which enables a retailer to assess the performance of each general merchandise grouping or buyer.

To obtain more financial data than available through departmental categories, **classification merchandising** can be used, whereby each specified department is subdivided into further categories for related types of merchandise. Thus, in planning merchandise for its tools and equipment department, Handy Hardware can keep financial records not only on the overall performance of that department but also on the individual performance of such categories as lawn mowers/snow blowers, power tools, hand tools, and ladders.

One special form of classification merchandising involves **price line classifications,** whereby retail sales, inventories, and purchases are analyzed by retail price category. This analysis is quite valuable if a firm offers the same type of product at vastly different prices to different target markets (such as Handy Hardware carrying $20 power tools for do-it-yourselfers and $135 power tools for contractors). Retailers with deep assortments most often use price line control. As a case in point, a men's clothing store may want to differentiate between sports jackets selling in the $89–$119 range and those in the $179–$219 range. Such diverse categories of sports jackets are usually sold to different customers or to the same customers for different purposes.

To best contrast its financial data with industry averages, a firm's merchandise categories should conform to those cited in trade publications. The National Retail Federation devised a **standard merchandise classification** to list the most common merchandise-reporting categories—for a wide range of retailers and products. It annually produces *Merchandising and Operating Results of Retail Stores,* using its classifications. More specific classifications are also popular for some retailers. Published each year is *Progressive Grocer's* "Supermarket Sales Manual," based on standard classifications for that industry.

Once each appropriate dollar control unit is set, all transactions—such as sales, purchases, transfers, markdowns, and employee discounts—must be recorded under the proper classification number. For instance, if house paint is denoted as Department 25 and brushes as 25-1, all transactions must carry these category designations.

Sales Forecasting

A retailer estimates its expected future revenues for a given time period by **sales forecasting.** Sales forecasts may be companywide, departmental, and/or for individual merchandise classifications. Perhaps the most important step in any financial merchandise-planning process is accurate sales forecasting. Because of its effect on subsequent steps, an incorrect estimate of future sales throws off the entire process.[3]

Firmwide and departmentwide sales of larger retailers are often forecast by the use of statistical techniques such as trend analysis, time series analysis, and multiple-regression analysis. A discussion of these techniques is beyond the scope of this text. It should be noted that few small retailers use those methods; they rely more on "guesstimates," projections based on experience.

Sales forecasting for merchandise classifications within departments (or price lines) generally relies on more qualitative techniques, even for larger firms. One way of forecasting sales for these narrower categories is first to project sales on a companywide basis and by department, and then to break down these figures judgmentally into merchandise classifications.

Sales forecasts must carefully anticipate and take into account external factors, internal company factors, and seasonal trends. Among the external factors that could affect a retailer's future sales are consumer demographic and life-style trends, competitors' actions, the state of the economy, changes in the tastes of the target market, and new supplier offerings. For example, *Chain Store Age* regularly monitors changes in consumer buying behavior.[4] Among the internal company factors that could impact a retailer's future sales are additions and deletions of merchandise lines, changes in promotion and credit policies, changes in business hours, opening new outlets, and remodeling existing stores. With a number of retailers, seasonal variations must be considered in developing monthly or quarterly sales forecasts. For instance, Handy Hardware's yearly snow blower sales should not be estimated from December sales alone.

A retailer can develop a sales forecast by examining past trends and projecting future growth (based on external and internal factors). Table 15-7 shows such a forecast for Handy Hardware. It should be regarded as an estimate, subject to revisions. That is why a financial merchandise plan needs some flexibility. The firm should be aware that some factors may be particularly hard to incorporate in devising a forecast, such as merchandise shortages, consumer reactions to new products, strikes by suppliers' personnel, the rate of inflation, and new government legislation.

After a yearly forecast is derived, it should be broken into quarterly or monthly planning periods. In retailing, monthly sales forecasts are usually required. Thus, jewelry stores know December typically accounts for a very strong one-fifth of annual sales, while drugstores know December usually provides one-tenth or so of annual sales (slightly above the monthly average).

To acquire more specific estimates, a retailer could use a **monthly sales index,** which is calculated by dividing each month's actual sales by average monthly sales and

[3]See Thomas J. Blischok, "Preparing for Christmas Cheer," *Chain Store Age* (July 1996), pp. 53–56, 62; and Christina Duff, "Estimating Sales for Christmas Is Art, Not Science," *Wall Street Journal* (November 27, 1996), pp. B1, B3.

[4]Michael P. Niemira, "Consumer Spending: What's Hot, What's Not," *Chain Store Age* (July 1996), p. 36.

Table 15-7 HANDY HARDWARE STORE, A SIMPLE SALES FORECAST USING PRODUCT CONTROL UNITS

Product Control Units	Actual Sales 1997	Projected Growth/ Decline (%)	Sales Forecast 1998
Lawn mowers/ snowblowers	$100,000	+10.0	$110,000
Paint and supplies	64,000	+3.0	65,920
Hardware supplies	54,000	+8.0	58,320
Plumbing supplies	44,000	−4.0	42,240
Power tools	44,000	+6.0	46,640
Garden supplies/ chemicals	34,000	+4.0	35,360
Housewares	24,000	−6.0	22,560
Electrical supplies	20,000	+4.0	20,800
Ladders	18,000	+6.0	19,080
Hand tools	18,000	+9.0	19,620
Total year	$420,000	+ 4.9	$440,540

multiplying the results by 100. Table 15-8 shows Handy Hardware's 1997 actual monthly sales and monthly sales indexes. The data indicate the store is seasonal, with peaks in late spring and early summer (for lawn mowers, garden supplies, house paint and supplies, and so on), as well as December (for lighting fixtures, snow blowers, and gifts).

According to Table 15-8, average monthly 1997 sales were $35,000 ($420,000/12). Thus, the monthly sales index for January is 67 [($23,400/$35,000) × 100]; other monthly indexes are computed similarly. Each monthly index shows the percentage deviation of that month's sales from the average month's. A May index of 160 means May sales are 60 percent higher than the average month. An October index of 67 means sales in October are 33 percent below the average.

Once monthly sales indexes are determined, a retailer can forecast monthly sales, based on a yearly sales forecast. Table 15-9 shows how Handy Hardware's monthly sales can be forecast if the next year's (1998's) average monthly sales are expected to be $36,712. May sales are projected at $58,739 ($36,712 × 1.60); October sales at $24,597 ($36,712 × 0.67).

Table 15-8 HANDY HARDWARE STORE, 1997 SALES BY MONTH

Month	Actual Sales	Monthly Sales Index[a]
January	$ 23,400	67
February	20,432	58
March	24,000	69
April	32,800	94
May	56,098	160
June	51,900	148
July	52,280	149
August	31,400	90
September	23,452	67
October	23,400	67
November	33,442	96
December	47,396	135
Total yearly sales	$420,000	
Average monthly sales	$35,000	
Average monthly index		100

[a]Monthly sales index = (Monthly sales/Average monthly sales) × 100

Table 15-9 HANDY HARDWARE STORE, 1998 SALES FORECAST BY MONTH

Month	Actual Sales 1997	Monthly Sales Index	Monthly Sales Forecast for 1998[a]		
January	$ 23,400	67	$36,712 ×	.67 =	$ 24,597
February	20,432	58	36,712 ×	.58 =	21,293
March	24,000	69	36,712 ×	.69 =	25,331
April	32,800	94	36,712 ×	.94 =	34,509
May	56,098	160	36,712 ×	1.60 =	58,739
June	51,900	148	36,712 ×	1.48 =	54,334
July	52,280	149	36,712 ×	1.49 =	54,701
August	31,400	90	36,712 ×	.90 =	33,041
September	23,452	67	36,712 ×	.67 =	24,597
October	23,400	67	36,712 ×	.67 =	24,597
November	33,442	96	36,712 ×	.96 =	35,244
December	47,396	135	36,712 ×	1.35 =	49,561
Total sales	$420,000		Total sales forecast		$440,540[b]
Average monthly sales	$35,000		Average monthly forecast		$36,712

[a]Monthly sales forecast = Average monthly forecast × (Monthly index/100). In this equation, the monthly index is computed as a fraction of 1.00 rather than 100.

[b]There is a small rounding error.

Inventory-Level Planning

Following its derivation of a sales forecast, a retailer must plan the inventory levels for that period. Inventory must be sufficient to meet sales expectations, allowing a margin for error. Among the techniques to plan inventory levels are the basic stock, percentage variation, weeks' supply, and stock-to-sales methods.

With the **basic stock method,** a retailer carries more items than it expects to sell over a specified period. This gives a firm a cushion if sales are higher than anticipated, shipments are delayed, or customers want to select from a variety of items. It is best when inventory turnover is low or sales are erratic during the year. Beginning-of-month planned inventory equals planned sales plus a basic stock amount:

Basic stock (at retail) = Average monthly stock at retail − Average monthly sales

Beginning-of-month planned inventory level (at retail) = Planned monthly sales + Basic stock

If Handy Hardware, with an average monthly 1998 sales forecast of $36,712, wants to have extra stock on hand equal to 10 percent of its average monthly sales forecast (or $3,671) and expects January 1998 sales to be $24,597:

Basic stock (at retail) = ($36,712 × 1.10) − $36,712

= $40,383 − $36,712 = $3,671

Beginning-of-January planned inventory level (at retail) = $24,597 + $3,671 = $28,268

With the **percentage variation method,** the beginning-of-month planned inventory level during any month differs from the planned average monthly stock by only one-half of that month's variation from estimated average monthly sales. This method is recommended when stock turnover is more than six times a year or relatively stable, since it results in planned monthly inventories that are closer to the monthly average than other techniques:

Beginning-of-month
planned inventory level = Planned average monthly stock at retail × ½ [1 + (Estimated monthly sales/
(at retail)   Estimated average monthly sales)]

If Handy Hardware plans average monthly stock of $40,383 and November 1998 sales are expected to be 4 percent less than average monthly sales of $36,712, the store's planned inventory level at the beginning of November 1998 would be:

Beginning-of-November
planned inventory level   = $40,383 × ½ [1 + ($35,244/$36,712)]
(at retail)
            = $40,383 × ½ (1.96) = $39,575

For Handy Hardware, the percentage variation method is not a good one to use due to its variable sales. With that method, Handy would plan a beginning-of-December 1998 inventory of $47,450 (based on planned average monthly stock of $40,383), less than it expects to sell.

The **weeks' supply method** involves forecasting average sales on a weekly basis, so beginning inventory is equal to several weeks' expected sales. It assumes the inventory carried is in direct proportion to sales. Thus, too much merchandise may be stocked in peak selling periods and too little during slow selling periods:

Beginning-of-month
planned inventory level = Average estimated × Number of weeks
(at retail)   weekly sales   to be stocked

If Handy Hardware forecasts average weekly sales of $5,478.54 during the period from January 1, 1998 through March 31, 1998, and it wants to stock 13 weeks of merchandise (based on expected turnover in the first part of 1998), beginning inventory would be $71,221:

Beginning-of-January
planned inventory level = $5,478.54 × 13 = $71,221
(at retail)

With the **stock-to-sales method,** a retailer wants to maintain a specified ratio of goods-on-hand to sales. A stock-to-sales ratio of 1.3 means that if Handy Hardware plans sales of $34,509 in April 1998, it should have $44,862 worth of merchandise (at retail) available during the month. Like the weeks' supply method, the stock-to-sales ratio tends to adjust inventory levels more drastically than changes in sales require.

Yearly industrywide stock-to-sales ratios are provided by such sources as *Merchandising and Operating Results of Retail Stores* (New York: Wiley [for the National Retail Federation]), *Industry Norms and Key Business Ratios* (New York: Dun & Bradstreet), and *Annual Statement Studies* (Philadelphia: Robert Morris Associates). A retailer can thus compare its ratios with other firms'.

Reduction Planning

Besides forecasting sales, a firm should estimate the extent of its expected **retail reductions,** which represent the difference between beginning inventory plus purchases during the period and sales plus ending inventory. Planned reductions should encompass anticipated markdowns (price reductions to stimulate merchandise sales), employee and other discounts (price reductions given to employees, senior citizens, clergy, and others), and stock shortages (caused by pilferage, breakage, and bookkeeping errors). It is essential for a retailer to estimate and plan reductions, not just wait for them to occur:

Planned reductions = (Beginning inventory + Planned purchases) − (Planned sales + Ending inventory)

A retailer's reduction planning revolves around two key factors: estimating expected total reductions for the budget period and assigning the estimates by month. A firm should study the following in planning total reductions:

- Past experience with reductions.
- Markdown data for similar retailers.
- Changes in company policies.
- Merchandise carryover from one budget period to another.
- Price trends.
- Stock-shortage trends.

Past experience is a good starting point in reduction planning. This information can then be compared with that of similar firms—by reviewing available data on markdowns, discounts, and stock shortages in trade publications. For instance, a retailer having more (higher) markdowns than competitors could investigate and correct this situation by adjusting its buying practices and price levels or training sales personnel better.

In assessing past reductions, a retailer must consider its own procedures. Policy changes in a budget period often affect the quantity and timing of markdowns. If a firm expands its assortment of seasonal and fashion merchandise, this would probably lead to a rise in necessary markdowns.

Merchandise carryover, price trends, and stock-shortage trends also affect planning. If such items as gloves and antifreeze are held in stock during off seasons, markdowns are usually not needed to clean out inventory. However, the carryover of fad merchandise merely postpones reductions. Price trends of product categories impact on retail reductions. For example, many full home-PC systems are now available for $1,000 or so, down considerably from earlier prices. This means higher-priced PCs have to be marked down some to be saleable.

A firm can use its recent stock-shortage trends (determined by comparing book and physical inventory values over prior budget periods) to project future reductions due to employee, customer, and vendor theft; breakage; and bookkeeping mistakes. Generally, about one-quarter of all stock shortages in retailing are the result of clerical and handling errors. If a firm has total stock shortages amounting to less than 2 percent to 4 percent of annual sales, it is usually deemed to be doing well. Figure 15-3 shows a checklist for firms to reduce shortages from clerical and handling errors. Suggestions for reducing shortages arising from theft were covered in Chapter 13.

After determining total reductions, they must be planned by month because reductions as a percentage of sales are not the same during each month. Stock shortages may be much higher during busy periods, when stores are more crowded and transactions happen more quickly.

Planning Purchases

The formula for calculating planned purchases for a period is

$$\text{Planned purchases} \atop \text{(at retail)} = \begin{array}{l} \text{Planned sales for the month} + \text{Planned} \\ \text{reductions for the month} + \text{Planned} \\ \text{end-of-month stock} - \text{Beginning-of-month stock} \end{array}$$

Answer yes or no to each of the following questions. A no answer to any question means corrective measures must be taken.

Buying

1. Is the exact quantity of merchandise purchased always specified in the contract?
2. Are purchase quantities recorded by size, color, model, etc.?
3. Are special purchase terms clearly noted?
4. Are returns to the vendor recorded properly?

Marking

5. Are retail prices clearly marked on merchandise?
6. Are the prices marked on merchandise checked for correctness?
7. Are markdowns and additional markups recorded by item number and quantity?
8. Does a cashier check with a manager if a price is not marked on an item?
9. Are the prices shown on display shelves checked for consistency with those marked on the items themselves?
10. Are old price tags removed when an item's price is changed?

Handling

11. After receipt, are purchase quantities checked against contract specifications?
12. Is merchandise handled in a systematic manner?
13. Are goods separated by merchandise classification?
14. Are all handling operations monitored properly (e.g., receiving, storing, distribution)?
15. Is enough merchandise kept on the selling floor (to reduce excessive handling)?
16. Are items sold in bulk (such as produce, sugar, candy) measured accurately?
17. Are damaged, soiled, returned, or other special goods handled separately?

Selling

18. Do sales personnel know correct prices or have easy access to them?
19. Are markdowns, additional markups, etc., communicated to sales personnel?
20. Are misrings by cashiers made on a very small percentage of sales?
21. Are special terms noted on sales receipts?
22. Do sales personnel confirm that all items are rung up by cashiers?
23. Are employee discounts noted?
24. Is the addition on sales receipts done mechanically or double checked if computed by hand?
25. Are sales receipts numbered and later checked for missing invoices?

Inventory Planning

26. Is a physical inventory conducted at least annually?
27. Is a book inventory maintained throughout the year?
28. Are the differences between physical inventory counts and book inventory always accounted for?
29. Are sales and inventory records reviewed regularly?

Accounting

30. Are permanent records on all transactions kept?
31. Are both retail and cost data maintained?
32. Are all types of records monitored for accuracy?
33. Are inventory shortages compared with industry averages to determine acceptability of performance?

How Profitable Are Private Brands in Europe?

A European research project, titled "Retail Competition in the Fast-Moving Consumer Goods Industry: The Case of France and the UK," set out to contrast the retail strategies of three major grocery chains in France (which stressed low prices and manufacturer brands) with three of Great Britain's leading chains (which emphasized fresh produce and private brands).

The study found that food retailers in the two nations have very different approaches to their private-brand strategies. Store brands were introduced in France only as recently as the 1970s as "no-frills" alternatives to manufacturer brands; and French supermarkets are barred from using TV advertising for private brands. In contrast, some British retailers have

used private brands for over 100 years; they are very popular there. British retailers also can legally advertise private brands on TV.

The research project further determined that private labels can greatly increase a retailer's profitability. For a typical grocery product, such as canned milk, gross margins on manufacturer brands are less than 10 percent, while the margins on private brands are between 10 percent and 20 percent (even though private brands are less costly to the final consumer). Successful private brands also generate and sustain customer loyalty. Manufacturer brands, on the other hand, stimulate store traffic when priced at low levels and appeal to brand loyal shoppers.

Source: "A European Case Study," *Progressive Grocer* (November 1995), pp. 8–9.

If Handy Hardware projects June 1998 sales to be $54,334 and total planned reductions to be 5 percent of sales, plans end-of-month inventory at retail to be $36,000, and has a beginning-of-month inventory at retail of $40,000, planned purchases for June are

Planned purchases
(at retail) = $54,334 + $2,717 + $36,000 − $40,000 = $53,051

Because Handy Hardware expects 1998 merchandise costs to be about 60 percent of retail selling price, it is planning to purchase $31,831 of goods at cost in June 1998:

$$\begin{aligned} &\text{Planned purchases at retail} \\ \text{Planned purchases} = &\times \text{Merchandise costs as a} \\ \text{(at cost)} \quad &\text{percentage of selling price} \\ = &\$53,051 \times 0.60 = \$31,831 \end{aligned}$$

Open-to-buy is the difference between planned purchases and the purchase commitments already made by a buyer for a given time period, often a month. It represents the amount the buyer has left to spend for that month and is reduced each time a purchase is made. At the beginning of a month, a firm's planned purchases and open-to-buy are equal if no purchases have been committed prior to the start of that month. Open-to-buy is recorded at cost.

At Handy Hardware, the buyer has made purchase commitments for June 1998 valued in the amount of $27,500 at retail. Accordingly, Handy's open-to-buy at retail for June is $25,551:

$$\begin{aligned} \text{Open-to-buy} \quad &= \text{Planned purchases for the month} \\ \text{(at retail)} \quad &- \text{Purchase commitments for that month} \\ &= \$53,051 - \$27,500 = \$25,551 \end{aligned}$$

To calculate the June 1998 open-to-buy at cost, $25,551 is multiplied by Handy Hardware's merchandise costs as a percentage of selling price:

$$\text{Open-to-buy} \atop \text{(at cost)} = {\text{Open-to-buy at retail} \atop \times \text{Merchandise costs as a}} \atop \text{percentage of selling price}$$
$$= \$25,551 \times 0.60 = \$15,331$$

The open-to-buy concept has two significant strengths. First, it assures the retailer that a specified relationship between stock on hand and planned sales is maintained, which avoids overbuying and underbuying. Second, it lets a firm adjust merchandise purchases to reflect changes in sales, markdowns, and so on. For instance, if Handy Hardware revises its June 1998 sales forecast to $60,000, it automatically increases planned purchases and open-to-buy by $5,666 at retail and $3,400 at cost.

From a strategic perspective, it is usually advisable for a retailer to keep at least a small open-to-buy figure for as long as possible. This enables the firm to take advantage of special deals, purchase new models when introduced, and fill in items that sell out. An open-to-buy limit sometimes must be exceeded due to underestimates of demand (low sales forecasts).

Planning Profit Margins

In developing a merchandise budget, a retailer is quite interested in profitability (expressed by dollar and percentage profit margins) and thus must consider anticipated net sales, retail operating expenses, profit, and retail reductions in pricing merchandise:

$$\text{Required initial} \atop \text{markup percentage} = \frac{{\text{Planned} \atop \text{retail expenses}} + {\text{Planned} \atop \text{profit}} + {\text{Planned} \atop \text{reductions}}}{\text{Planned net sales} + \text{Planned reductions}}$$

The required markup figure is an overall company average; individual items may be priced according to demand and other factors, as long as the firm's average is sustained. A more complete markup discussion is contained in Chapter 16. The concept of initial markup is introduced at this point for continuity in the description of merchandise budgeting.

Handy has an overall 1998 sales forecast of $440,540 and expects annual operating expenses to be $145,000. Reductions are projected to be $22,000. The total net dollar profit margin goal is $30,000, amounting to 6.8 percent of sales. Therefore, its required initial markup is 42.6 percent:

$$\text{Required initial} \atop \text{markup percentage} = \frac{\$145,000 + \$30,000 + \$22,000}{\$440,540 + \$22,000} = 42.6\%$$

$$\text{Required initial} \atop \text{markup percentage} \atop \text{(all factors} \atop \text{expressed as a} \atop \text{percentage of} \atop \text{net sales)} = \frac{32.9\% + 6.8\% + 5.0\%}{100.0\% + 5.0\%} = 42.6\%$$

Figure 15-4 summarizes the merchandise forecasting and budgeting process. It expands on Figure 15-2 by including the bases for each decision stage.

Figure 15-4

The Merchandise Forecasting and Budgeting Process: Dollar Control

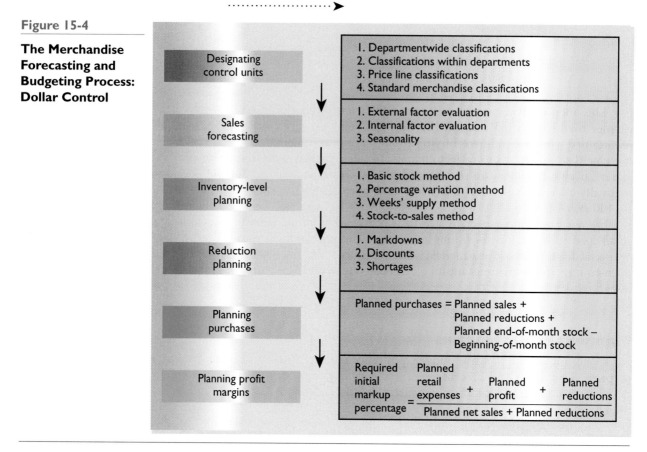

UNIT CONTROL SYSTEMS

Unit control systems deal with quantities of merchandise in units rather than in dollars. Information typically contained in unit control systems includes

■ The identification of items selling well and those selling poorly.
■ A focus on opportunities and problem areas in terms of price, color, style, size, and so on.
■ The computation (if a perpetual inventory system is used) of the quantity of goods on hand. This minimizes overstocking and understocking.
■ An indication of inventory age, highlighting candidates for markdowns or special promotions.
■ A determination of the optimal time to reorder merchandise.
■ A review of experiences with alternative sources (vendors) when problems arise.
■ The level of inventory and sales for each item in each store branch. This improves the transfer of goods between branches and alerts salespeople as to which branches have desired products. Also, less stock can be held in each store, reducing costs.

Physical Inventory Systems

A physical-inventory unit-control system is similar to a physical-inventory dollar-control system. But a dollar control system is concerned with the financial value of inventory, while a unit control system looks at the number of units by item classification. With unit control, the retailer gives someone the task of monitoring inventory levels, either by visual inspection or actual count.

In a typical visual inspection system, merchandise is placed on pegboard (or similar) displays, with each item numbered on the back of its package or on a stock card. Minimum inventory quantities are clearly noted for items, and sales personnel are responsible to reorder when the number of items on hand reaches the minimum level. Accuracy occurs only if merchandise is placed in numerical order on the displays (and sold accordingly). The system is used in the houseware and hardware displays of various discount, variety, and hardware stores.

Although a visual inspection system is easy to maintain and inexpensive, it has two shortcomings. First, it does not provide data on the rate of sales of individual items. Second, minimum stock quantities may be arbitrarily defined and not drawn from in-depth analysis.

The other physical inventory system, actual counting, requires a firm to regularly compile the number of units on hand. A stock-counting system records—in units—inventory on hand, purchases, sales volume, and shortages during specified periods. For example, Handy Hardware could use the system for its insulation tape:

Number of Rolls of Tape for the Period December 1, 1997–December 31, 1997

Beginning inventory, December 1, 1997	50
Total purchases for period	35
Total units available for sale	85
Closing inventory, December 31, 1997	30
Sales and shortages for period	55

A stock-counting system requires more clerical work than a visual system, but it lets a firm obtain sales data for given periods and stock-to-sales relationships as of the time of each count. A physical system is not as sophisticated as a perpetual inventory system, and its use is more justified with low-value items having predictable sales rates.

Perpetual Inventory Systems

A **perpetual-inventory unit-control system** keeps a running total of the number of units handled by a retailer through ongoing record-keeping entries that adjust for sales, returns, transfers to other departments or stores, receipt of shipments, and other transactions. All additions to and subtractions from beginning inventory are recorded.

Perpetual (book) inventory systems can be done manually, use merchandise tags processed by computers, or rely on point-of-sale devices such as optical scanning equipment. Technological advances have greatly aided retailers in applying computer-based perpetual inventory systems.

A manual system requires employees to gather data by examining sales checks, merchandise receipts, transfer requests, and other documents. The data are then coded and tabulated.

A merchandise-tagging system relies on pre-printed tags attached to each item in stock. These tags include data by department, classification, vendor, style number, date of receipt, color, and material. When an item is sold, one copy of the merchandise tag is removed and sent to a tabulating facility, where the coded information is analyzed by computer. Because pre-printed merchandise tags are processed in batches, they can be used by small- and medium-sized retailers (which subscribe to independent service bureaus) and by branches of chains (with data being processed at a central location).

Point-of-sale systems, manufactured by firms such as IBM, Digital Equipment Corporation, and NCR, feed data from merchandise tags or product labels directly to in-store computer terminals for immediate data processing. Computer-based systems are quicker, more accurate, and of higher quality than manual systems. And because of the

Figure 15-5

How Does a UPC-Based Scanner System Work?

Courtesy Giant Food Inc.

When the checker passes an item with the UPC symbol over a scanning device, the symbol is read by a low-energy laser.
The UPC symbol is found on many supermarket products and looks like this.

Each product has its own unique identification number. For example, the first five digits, 11146, represent the manufacturer, Giant in this case. The second five digits represent the specific items; 01345 identifies 24 ounce iced tea mix.
Note that the price is not in the symbol. The symbol identifies the product, not the price.

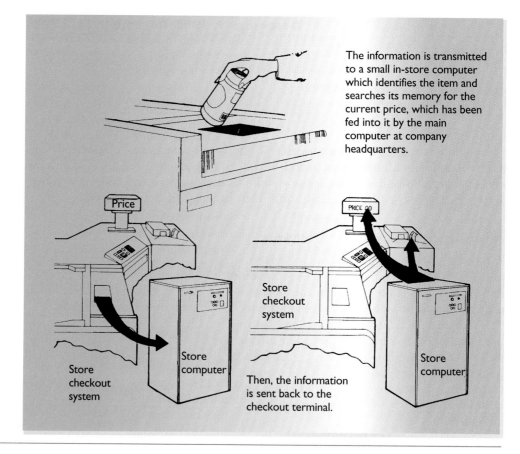

The information is transmitted to a small in-store computer which identifies the item and searches its memory for the current price, which has been fed into it by the main computer at company headquarters.

access to PCs, computerized checkout equipment, and service bureaus, costs are reasonable for smaller retailers.

Newer point-of-sale systems can be easily networked, have battery backup capabilities (in case of power interruptions), and use industry-standard components (enabling retailers to better choose printers, keyboards, and monitors). Many point-of-sale systems use optical scanners, that transfer data from merchandise to computers by wands or stationary devices that interact with sensitized strips on the items. Figure 15-5 shows how UPC bar coding works. As discussed earlier in the text, the Universal Product Code (UPC) is the dominant format for coding data onto merchandise.

A retailer does not have to use a perpetual system for all of its inventory. Many firms combine perpetual and physical systems, whereby key items (accounting for a large proportion of sales) are controlled by a perpetual system and other items are controlled by a physical inventory system. In this way, attention is properly placed on the retailer's most important products.

Up to this point, dollar and unit control concepts have been discussed as separate entities. Yet, in practice, they are directly linked.[5] The decision on how many units to buy at a given time affects and is affected by dollar investments, inventory turnover, quantity discounts, warehousing and insurance costs, and so on.

Three aspects of financial inventory control are described next: stock turnover and gross margin return on investment, when to reorder, and how much to reorder.

FINANCIAL INVENTORY CONTROL: INTEGRATING DOLLAR AND UNIT CONCEPTS

Stock Turnover and Gross Margin Return on Investment

Stock turnover represents the number of times during a specific period, usually one year, that the average inventory on hand is sold. It can be measured by store, product line, department, and vendor. High stock turnover has several virtues. Inventory investments are productive on a per-dollar basis. Merchandise on the shelves is fresh. Losses due to changes in styles and fashion are reduced. Costs associated with maintaining inventory (such as interest, insurance, breakage, and warehousing) are lessened.

Stock turnover can be computed in units or dollars (at retail or cost):

$$\text{Annual rate of stock turnover (in units)} = \frac{\text{Number of units sold during the year}}{\text{Average inventory on hand (in units)}}$$

$$\text{Annual rate of stock turnover (in retail dollars)} = \frac{\text{Net yearly sales}}{\text{Average inventory on hand (at retail)}}$$

$$\text{Annual rate of stock turnover (at cost)} = \frac{\text{Cost of goods sold during the year}}{\text{Average inventory on hand (at cost)}}$$

The choice of a turnover formula depends on the retailer's accounting system.

In computing stock turnover, the average inventory level for the entire period covered in the analysis needs to be reflected. Turnover rates are invalid if the true average is not used, as occurs if a firm mistakenly views the inventory level of a peak or slow month as the yearly average.

Table 15-10 shows overall stock turnover rates for various retailer types. Gasoline service stations and grocery stores have very high rates. They rely on sales volume for their success. Jewelry, shoe, clothing, and hardware stores have very low rates. They require larger profit margins on each item sold and maintain a sizable assortment for customers.

A retailer can raise stock turnover by a number of different strategies, such as reducing its assortment, eliminating or having minimal inventory for slow-selling items, buying in an efficient and timely way, applying quick response inventory planning, and using reliable distributors.

Despite the advantages of high turnover, there are instances in which it can have adverse effects. Purchasing items in small amounts could increase merchandise costs

[5]See "Improved Inventory Management: The New Strategic Imperative," *Chain Store Age* (December 1996), Section Two.

Table 15-10   ANNUAL MEDIAN STOCK TURNOVER RATES FOR SELECTED TYPES OF RETAILERS

Type of Retailer	Annual Median Stock Turnover Rate (Times)
Auto and home supply stores	6.9
Department stores	4.5
Family clothing stores	3.7
Furniture stores	4.8
Gasoline service stations	38.7
Grocery stores	19.0
Hardware stores	4.4
Household appliance stores	6.2
Jewelry stores	2.6
Lumber and other building materials dealers	7.2
Men's and boys' clothing stores	3.7
New and used car dealers	6.5
Shoe stores	3.7
Women's clothing stores	5.1

Source: Industry Norms & Key Business Ratios: Desk-Top Edition 1995–96 (New York: Dun & Bradstreet, 1996), pp. 160–177.

because quantity discounts may be lost and transportation charges may rise. Since a high turnover rate could be due to low width and/or depth of assortment, some customer sales may be lost. High turnover could lead to low profits if prices must be lowered to move inventory quickly. A retailer's return on investment depends on both turnover and profit per unit.

Gross margin return on investment (GMROI) shows the relationship between the gross margin in dollars (also known as total dollar operating profits) and the average inventory investment (at cost) by combining profitability and sales-to-stock measures:

$$\text{Gross margin return on investment (GMROI)} = \frac{\text{Gross margin in dollars}}{\text{Net sales}} \times \frac{\text{Net sales}}{\text{Average inventory at cost}}$$

$$= \frac{\text{Gross margin in dollars}}{\text{Average inventory at cost}}$$

In this formula, the gross margin in dollars is defined as net sales minus the cost of goods sold. The gross margin percentage (a profitability measure) is derived by dividing the dollar gross margin by net sales. A sales-to-stock ratio is provided by dividing net sales by average inventory at cost. [Note: A sales-to-stock ratio may be converted to stock turnover by multiplying that ratio by (100 − Gross margin percentage)/100.]

GMROI is a useful concept for several reasons:

■ It shows how different retailers can prosper with different gross margins and sales-to-stock ratios. For example, a conventional supermarket may have a gross margin percentage of 20 and a sales-to-stock ratio of 22, resulting in a GMROI of 440 percent (20% × 22). A department store may have a gross margin percentage of 44 and a sales-to-stock ratio of 10, resulting in a GMROI of 440 percent (44% × 10). The GMROIs of the two stores are the same due to the trade-off between profitability per item and turnover.

■ It is a good indicator of a manager's performance because it focuses on factors controlled by that person. Interdepartmental comparisons can also be made.

■ It is simple to plan and understand, and data collection is easy.
■ A retailer can determine if GMROI performance is consistent with other company goals, such as its image and cash flow.

It is vital for the gross margin percentage and the sales-to-stock ratio to be examined individually when using the GMROI formula. If only the overall GMROI is studied, performance may be assessed improperly. Some retailing experts have also suggested that the basic GMROI formula described here be expanded to include accounts receivable, accounts payable, and inventory carrying costs.

When to Reorder

One way to control inventory investment is to set stock levels at which new orders must be placed. Such a stock level is called a **reorder point.** Determining a reorder point depends on order lead time, usage rate, and safety stock. **Order lead time** is the period from the date an order is placed by a retailer to the date merchandise is ready for sale (received, price-marked, and put on the selling floor). **Usage rate** refers to average sales per day, in units, of merchandise. **Safety stock** is the extra inventory kept on hand to protect against out-of-stock conditions due to unexpected demand and delays in delivery. It is planned according to the firm's policy toward running out of items (service level).

This is the formula if a retailer does not plan to carry safety stock, believing customer demand is stable and its orders are promptly filled by suppliers:

Reorder point = Usage rate × Lead time

If Handy Hardware sells 10 paintbrushes a day and needs 8 days to order, receive, and display them, it has a reorder point of 80 brushes. It would reorder brushes once inventory on hand reaches 80. By the time brushes from that order are placed on shelves (8 days later), stock on hand will be zero, and the new stock will replenish the inventory.

This strategy is correct only when Handy has a perfectly steady customer demand of 10 paintbrushes daily and it takes exactly 8 days for all stages in the ordering process to be completed. Yet, this does not normally occur. If customers buy 15 brushes per day during a given month, Handy would run out of stock in 5 ⅓ days and be without brushes for 2 ⅔ days. Similarly, if an order takes 10 days to process, Handy would have no brushes for 2 full days, despite correctly estimating demand. Figure 15-6 shows how stockouts may occur if safety stock is not planned.

For a retailer interested in maintaining safety stock, the reorder formula becomes:

Reorder point = (Usage rate × Lead time) + Safety stock

As a rule, retailers should include safety stock in merchandise planning because demand is rarely constant from day to day or week to week and deliveries from suppliers can be delayed.

Suppose Handy Hardware decides to plan safety stock of 30 percent for paintbrushes; its reorder point is

Reorder point = (10 × 8) + (.30 × 80) = 80 + 24 = 104

Handy still expects to sell an average of 10 brushes per day and receive orders in an average of 8 days. A safety stock of 24 extra brushes is kept on hand to protect against unexpected demand or a late shipment.

For retailers dealing with staples (products with small sales variations during the year or their primary selling season), a procedure is available for estimating safety stock. It is based on the Poisson probability distribution, as illustrated in Table 15-11. According to this method, if Handy estimates its paintbrush basic reorder point to be 80

Figure 15-6

How Stockouts May Occur

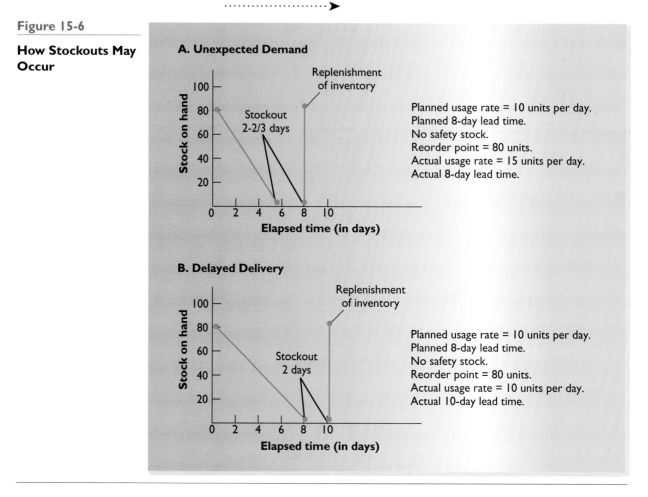

for the spring and summer, it would plan a safety stock of 21 to have a 99 percent probability of not running out of stock; 14 to have a 95 percent probability of not running out of stock; and 9 to have an 80 percent probability of not running out of stock. This means Handy would take a 20 percent chance of being out of stock by planning a reorder point of 89 (including safety stock).

As Table 15-11 shows, the safety stock required is proportionately greater for low-turnover items than for high-turnover items. At the 99 percent level, safety stock for a retailer with an estimated basic reorder point of 40 is 37.5 percent (15/40) of that reorder point. At the same level, safety stock for a retailer with an estimated basic reorder point of 400 is 11.5 percent (46/400) of that reorder point.

By combining a perpetual inventory system and reorder point calculations, a merchandise ordering process can be programmed into a computer and reordering done automatically when stock-on-hand reaches the reorder point. This is referred to as an **automatic reordering system.** However, intervention by a buyer or a store manager must be possible, especially if monthly sales fluctuate greatly.

How Much to Reorder

The decision as to how much to order affects how often a retailer orders merchandise. A firm placing large orders generally reduces ordering costs but increases inventory-holding costs. A firm placing small orders often minimizes inventory-holding costs while ordering costs may rise (unless electronic data interchange and a quick response inventory system are used).

Table 15-11 SAFETY STOCK LEVELS REQUIRED TO OBTAIN VARIOUS PROBABILITIES OF NOT RUNNING OUT OF STAPLES

Estimated Basic Reorder Point	Retail Stock Policy Chance of Not Running Out of Stock (%)	Safety Stock Needed to Achieve Stock Policy	Required Reorder Point[a]
25	99	$2.3 \sqrt{\text{Estimated reorder point}}$ $= 2.3 \sqrt{25} = 12$	37
40	99	$2.3 \sqrt{40} = 15$	55
80	99	$2.3 \sqrt{80} = 21$	101
100	99	$2.3 \sqrt{100} = 23$	123
200	99	$2.3 \sqrt{200} = 33$	233
400	99	$2.3 \sqrt{400} = 46$	446
25	95	$1.6 \sqrt{\text{Estimated reorder point}}$ $= 1.6 \sqrt{25} = 8$	33
40	95	$1.6 \sqrt{40} = 10$	50
80	95	$1.6 \sqrt{80} = 14$	94
100	95	$1.6 \sqrt{100} = 16$	116
200	95	$1.6 \sqrt{200} = 23$	223
400	95	$1.6 \sqrt{400} = 32$	432
25	80	$\sqrt{\text{Estimated reorder point}}$ $= \sqrt{25} = 5$	30
40	80	$\sqrt{40} = 6$	46
80	80	$\sqrt{80} = 9$	89
100	80	$\sqrt{100} = 10$	110
200	80	$\sqrt{200} = 14$	214
400	80	$\sqrt{400} = 20$	420

[a]Required reorder point = Estimated basic reorder point + Safety stock

Economic order quantity (EOQ) is the quantity per order (in units) that minimizes the total costs of processing orders and holding inventory. Order-processing costs include computer time, order forms, labor, and handling new goods. Holding costs include warehousing, inventory investment, insurance, taxes, depreciation, deterioration, and pilferage. EOQ calculations can be done by both large and small firms.

As Figure 15-7 shows, order-processing costs drop as the quantity per order (in units) goes up because fewer orders are needed to buy the same total annual quantity, and inventory-holding costs rise as the quantity per order goes up because more units must be held in inventory and they are kept for longer periods. The two costs are summed into a total cost curve.

Mathematically, the economic order quantity is

$$EOQ = \sqrt{\frac{2DS}{IC}}$$

where

EOQ = quantity per order (in units)
$\quad D$ = annual demand (in units)
$\quad S$ = costs to place an order (in dollars)
$\quad I$ = percentage of annual carrying cost to unit cost
$\quad C$ = unit cost of an item (in dollars)

Figure 15-7

Economic Order Quantity

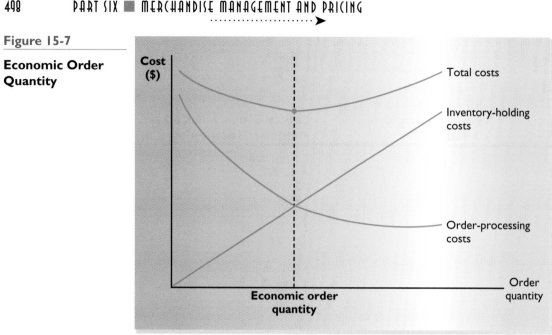

Handy estimates it can sell 150 power-tool sets per year. They cost $90 each. Breakage, insurance, tied-up capital, and pilferage equal 10 percent of the costs of the sets (or $9 each). Order costs are $25 per order. The economic order quantity is

$$EOQ = \sqrt{\frac{2(150)(\$25)}{(0.10)(\$90)}} = \sqrt{\frac{\$7,500}{\$9}} = 29$$

The EOQ formula must often be modified to take into account changes in demand, quantity discounts, and variable ordering and holding costs.

Summary

1. *To describe the major aspects of financial merchandise planning and management* Financial merchandise management stipulates which products are bought by the retailer, when they are bought, and what quantity is bought. Dollar control involves planning and monitoring the inventory investment made during a given period, while unit control relates to the quantities of merchandise handled in that period. Financial merchandise management encompasses methods of accounting, merchandise forecasting and budgeting, unit control systems, and integrated dollar and unit controls.

2. *To explain the cost and retail methods of accounting* The two accounting techniques available to retailers are the cost and retail methods of inventory valuation. Physical and book (perpetual) procedures are possible with each. Physical inventory valuation requires actu-

ally counting merchandise at prescribed intervals. Book inventory valuation relies on accurate bookkeeping and a smooth flow of data.

The cost method obligates a retailer to maintain careful records for each item bought or code its cost on the package. This must be done to find the exact value of ending inventory at cost. Many firms use the LIFO accounting method to approximate that value, which lets them reduce taxes by having a low ending inventory value. With the retail method, closing inventory value is based on the average relationship between the cost and retail value of merchandise available for sale. This more accurately reflects market conditions, but is more complex.

3. *To study the merchandise forecasting and budgeting process* Merchandise forecasting and budgeting is a form of dollar control with six stages: designating control units, sales forecasting, inventory-level planning, reduction planning, planning purchases, and planning profit margins. Adjustments at any point in the process require all later stages to be modified accordingly.

Control units are merchandise categories for which data are gathered. They must be narrow enough to isolate problems and opportunities with specific product lines. Sales forecasting—whereby expected future sales are estimated for a given time period—may be the key stage in the merchandising and budgeting process because its accuracy affects so many other stages. Through inventory-level planning, a firm sets merchandise quantities for specified periods; techniques include the basic stock, percentage variation, weeks' supply, and stock-to-sales methods. Reduction planning estimates expected markdowns, discounts, and stock shortages. Planned purchases are keyed to planned sales, reductions, ending inventory, and beginning inventory. Profit margins are related to a retailer's planned net sales, operating expenses, profit, and reductions.

4. *To examine alternative methods of inventory unit control* A unit control system involves physical units of merchandise. Critical unit control data include designating best-sellers and poor sellers, the quantity of goods on hand, inventory age, reorder time, and so on. A physical-inventory unit-control system may use visual inspection or a stock-counting procedure. A perpetual-inventory unit-control system keeps a running total of the number of units a firm handles through ongoing record-keeping entries that adjust for sales, returns, transfers, new items received, and so on. A perpetual system can be applied manually, by merchandise tags processed by computers, or by point-of-sale devices.

5. *To integrate dollar and unit merchandising control concepts* The aspects of financial inventory control that integrate dollar and unit control concepts are stock turnover and gross margin return on investment, when to reorder, and how much to reorder. Stock turnover represents the number of times during a specified period that the average inventory on hand is sold. Gross margin return on investment shows the relationship between the gross margin in dollars (total dollar operating profits) and average inventory investment (at cost). A reorder point calculation—when to reorder—includes the retailer's usage rate, order lead time, and safety stock. The economic order quantity—how much to reorder—aids a retailer in choosing how large an order to place, based on both ordering and inventory costs.

Throughout this chapter, several mathematical merchandising equations are introduced and illustrated.

Key Terms

financial merchandise management (p. 472)
dollar control (p. 472)
unit control (p. 472)
merchandise available for sale (p. 472)
cost of goods sold (p. 472)
gross profit (p. 472)
net profit (p. 472)
cost method of accounting (p. 474)
physical inventory system (p. 474)
book inventory system (perpetual inventory system) (p. 474)
FIFO method (p. 474)

LIFO method (p. 474)
retail method of accounting (p. 476)
cost complement (p. 477)
control units (p. 480)
classification merchandising (p. 481)
price line classifications (p. 481)
standard merchandise classification (p. 481)
sales forecasting (p. 482)
monthly sales index (p. 482)
basic stock method (p. 484)
percentage variation method (p. 485)
weeks' supply method (p. 485)
stock-to-sales method (p. 485)

retail reductions (p. 485)
open-to-buy (p. 488)
perpetual-inventory unit-control system (p. 491)
stock turnover (p. 493)
gross margin return on investment (GMROI) (p. 494)
reorder point (p. 495)
order lead time (p. 495)
usage rate (p. 495)
safety stock (p. 495)
automatic reordering system (p. 496)
economic order quantity (EOQ) (p. 497)

Questions for Discussion

1. What kinds of retailers can best use a perpetual inventory system involving the cost method?
2. Because the FIFO method of costing inventory seems more logical than the LIFO method by assuming the first merchandise purchased is the first merchandise sold, why do more retailers use LIFO?
3. Explain the cost complement concept in the retail method.
4. Contrast the basic stock method and the stock-to-sales supply method of merchandise planning.
5. Present two situations in which it would be advisable for a retailer to take a markdown, instead of carrying over merchandise from one budget period to another.

6. What are the pros and cons of a high stock turnover?

7. How does an automatic reordering system work? What are its advantages and disadvantages?

8. Why is the formula for economic order quantity shown in this chapter an oversimplification?

9. A retailer has yearly sales of $475,000. Inventory on January 1 is $200,000 (at cost). During the year, $400,000 of merchandise (at cost) is purchased. The ending inventory is $225,000 (at cost). Operating costs are $65,000. Calculate the cost of goods sold and net profit, and set up a profit-and-loss statement. There are no retail reductions in this problem.

10. A retailer has a beginning monthly inventory valued at $40,000 at retail and $28,000 at cost. Net purchases during the month are $120,000 at retail and $70,000 at cost. Transportation charges are $4,000. Sales are $120,000. Markdowns and discounts equal $28,000. A physical inventory at the end of the month shows merchandise valued at $10,000 (at retail) on hand. Compute the following:
    a. Total merchandise available for sale—at cost and at retail.
    b. Cost complement.
    c. Ending retail book value of inventory.
    d. Stock shortages.
    e. Adjusted ending retail book value.
    f. Gross profit.

11. The sales of a full-line discount store are listed here. Calculate the monthly sales indexes. What do they mean?

January	$ 80,000	July	$ 80,000
February	90,000	August	120,000
March	90,000	September	140,000
April	120,000	October	100,000
May	120,000	November	160,000
June	100,000	December	240,000

12. If the planned average monthly stock for the discount store in Question 11 is $160,000, how much inventory should be planned for August if the retailer uses the percentage variation method? Comment on this retailer's choice of the percentage variation method.

13. The discount store in Questions 11 and 12 knows its cost complement for all merchandise purchased last year was 0.64; it projects this figure to remain constant. For the current year, it expects to begin and end December with inventory valued at $60,000 at retail and estimates December reductions to be $8,000. The firm already has purchase commitments for December worth $120,000 (at retail). What is the open-to-buy at cost for December?

14. A retailer sells an average of 20 standard touch-tone telephones per day and desires a safety stock of 40 phones. If it takes seven days for an order to be placed and received by the retailer, what is its reorder point? Explain your answer.

Web-Based Exercise:

DUN & BRADSTREET (http://www.dnb.com)

Questions

1. Review the Web site's section on "Managing Finances Effectively" (from the "Small Business Services" selection). Present ten tips for a local computer retailer to better manage cash flow.

2. Review the Web site's section on "Managing Finances Effectively" (from the "Small Business Services" selection). Develop ten tips for a used car retailer on better managing cash flow.

3. Describe how a local apparel shop can make better credit decisions (see the Web site's "Credit" option).

4. Describe how a local jeweler can better manage past due collections (see the Web site's "Collections" section).

McKesson Corporation (http://www.mckesson.com) is the largest distributor of pharmaceutical and health-care products in the United States and Canada. McKesson works with more than 5,000 independent members of its Valu-Rite voluntary cooperative pharmacy organization, as well as hospitals and health-care networks. McKesson is a recognized leader in financial merchandise management with its CareMax, OmniLink, and Acumax systems.

Through CareMax, independent pharmacies affiliated with McKesson can reduce product purchase costs by as much as 50 percent on selected prescription drugs, over-the-counter drugs, and health and beauty aids. Besides enabling the pharmacies to better compete against chain pharmacies, the CareMax system lets them improve customer service by mailing refill reminder notices to individual patients (based on the initial purchase quantity and the recommended dosage for each prescription). According to McKesson's senior vice-president of marketing and product management, CareMax "unites independent pharmacies, expands their access to managed care patients, and helps them enhance patient care."

OmniLink provides a link between each pharmacy's in-store computer system and McKesson's computer data center for the customers who are serviced by managed care providers. Through OmniLink, a pharmacist can immediately determine if a dispensed drug is approved for reimbursement by a customer's insurance plan, whether it must dispense a generic drug, and whether the submitted price is within the insurance plan's reimbursement guidelines. According to McKesson, this system increases a store's income by between $6,000 and $12,000 per year.

The third system, Acumax Plus, is designed to track inventory at McKesson's Denver distribution center. It tracks every item in that warehouse from the time of its receipt through its shipment from the warehouse to a customer. Whenever an item is moved within the warehouse, Acumax Plus automatically tracks its new location, and updates the inventory quantity. The scanned bar-code data are transmitted by radio signal to McKesson's mainframe computer.

Acumax Plus has four key components: a wrist mounted computer/scanner from Symbol Technologies, software from Worldwide Chain Store systems, an IBM AS/400 mainframe computer, and modified operations systems (for order-processing, inventory management, and distribution operation applications) that were developed by McKesson. Acumax Plus handles these inventory management tasks: receiving, putaway, replenishment, cycle counting, returns, inventory lookup, picking, checking, staging, and invoicing.

Acumax Plus improves financial merchandise management productivity through the use of date-and-time stamping, merchandise verification, and picking location modeling. It automatically records a date-and-time stamp for all inventory functions. This allows McKesson's management to evaluate an inventory picker's productivity. Acumax Plus also automatically verifies the merchandise picked against ordered goods so that mispicks and order quantities can be easily noted and corrected. Acumax even provides directions to the next picking location, when a picker is at the previous location. Due to these features, Acumax has reduced mispicks and stock shortages in its Denver distribution center by well over 50 percent.

As McKesson's senior vice-president of distribution says, "With Acumax Plus, we've achieved order-filling and inventory accuracy levels of more than 99 percent, helping us ensure that the right product arrives at the right time and place for both our customers and their patients." Under McKesson's older nonautomated system, the firm used to take two physical inventories a year. Inventory management accuracy is now so strong that it no longer plans to take physical inventories.

CASE 1
McKesson's Computerized Financial Merchandise Management Systems for Retailers*

*The material in this case is drawn from *McKesson Corporation 1996 Annual Report;* and Sharon L. Oswald and William R. Boulton, "Obtaining Industry Control: The Case of the Pharmaceutical Industry," *California Management Review,* Vol. 38 (Fall 1995), pp. 138–151.

CASE 1
(Continued)

Questions

1. What type of control units should McKesson use in its inventory planning? Explain your answer.
2. How can McKesson use the data from CareMax, OmniLink, and Acumax systems in its sales forecasting?
3. Which inventory-level planning system should McKesson use? Why?
4. Should McKesson never take another physical inventory? Explain your answer.

Video Questions on McKesson

1. How well do you think Acumax Plus simplifies inventory management for McKesson? Why?
2. Show how McKesson can use the Acumax Plus system to determine if a retailer was shipped insufficient quantities.

CASE 2
Saks Fifth Avenue: Store Versus Catalog Financial Merchandise Management†

This case focuses on Saks Fifth Avenue and its financial merchandise management at its stores and at its Folio catalog division. In the past, the Folio division's recurring problem was that store-based merchants used one system to buy goods, while Folio's telemarketers used another system to record orders. Unfortunately, the two systems did not properly interface. The stores and the catalog division sold different merchandise, and each had different merchandise-handling systems. As a result, telemarketers were not provided with access to up-to-date information on stock availability. Furthermore, Saks' buyers could not update the telemarketers as to when a hot-selling fashion would become available for sale.

The retailer was essentially tracking inventory movement with one system, while another independent system tracked the financial value of the inventory. According to Saks' director of applications systems for the Folio Group, this unit had two systems that did not properly interface: a limited order-processing system and a merchandising system that also could not properly handle customer phone and mail-based orders.

An added concern was that Saks' retail inventory management system was based on the retail method (which was appropriate for its store-based operations), while the cost method was more appropriate for the catalog unit. Although Saks' stores took markdowns on a consistent basis, its Folio operation offered different discounts to individual buyers. For example, it commonly offered a special discount to new catalog customers, a 10 percent savings on their first mail order. In addition, while Saks' store prices were consistent, prices at its catalog division often varied based on the date of the catalog. Some consumers, realizing the variability in prices, often purchased items from different catalogs on the same order.

As a short-run solution to these problems, Saks personnel attempted to manually enter data from one system to another. However, as Saks' director of applications systems noted, "People ended up keying in out-of-date, unreliable information. We were double-keying information, like purchase order insertion dates. It made it difficult for the merchants to reorder, to forecast, and to see accurate return rates. And on the phones, the telemarketers still couldn't answer all the customers' questions."

After much research and deliberation, Saks executives decided to install Mozart, a fully integrated order-management computer system especially designed for catalog retailers. Mozart can reflect special discounts, allow multiple prices for the same item, and provide credit authorization for phone orders. It also links Saks' warehouse and financial systems so telemarketers can determine whether there are adequate quantities of an

---

†The material in this case is drawn from "Information Is in Fashion at Saks," *Chain Store Age* (November 1996), pp. 11A–13A.

ordered item on hand, at the time the order is placed. The system alerts the telemar- **CASE 2**
keters to suggest alternatives (such as a different color or style) if a good is temporarily *(Continued)*
out-of-stock and provides a list of cross-selling opportunities (such as recommending a
suitable fashion accessory for a dress). Mozart even notes opportunities to trade up the
customer to a slightly more costly alternative. Lastly, the system lets a sales associate
provide the promised in-stock date for goods that are currently out-of-stock.

Perhaps the most important benefit to the Mozart system is that a telemarketer can
now handle all of a customer's questions without the need to put a person on hold or
to transfer the customer's call to another department. Thus, Saks customers receive the
level of customer service they have the right to expect regardless of whether they deal
with an in-store sales associate or a telemarketer: "Access to a broad range of up-to-
date merchandise data has made our telemarketers into problem solvers. That makes
both the telemarketer and the customer feel a lot better."

Questions

1. Evaluate Saks' old financial merchandise system.
2. What are the pros and cons of Saks' new Mozart system?
3. Why do you think the retail method is more appropriate for Saks' stores and the cost
   method is more appropriate for its Folio catalog operation?
4. How can Saks integrate an automatic reordering system into its new financial merchandise management system?

Chapter 16

Pricing in Retailing

CHAPTER OBJECTIVES

1. To describe the role of pricing in a retail strategy and to show that pricing decisions must be made in an integrated and adaptive manner

2. To examine the impact of consumers; government; manufacturers, wholesalers, and other suppliers; and current and potential competitors on pricing decisions

3. To present a framework for developing a retail price strategy: objectives, broad policy, basic strategy, implementation, and adjustments

According to retailing analysts, one recent trend in new-car pricing, the "no-dicker sticker" (in which car dealers adhere to fixed prices and permit no bargaining) is already in decline. During 1994, almost 2,000 of the nation's 23,000 new-car dealers used a one-price strategy; however, by the middle of 1996, only 1,000 to 1,200 dealers were still utilizing this strategy.

Although car dealers initially assumed that bargaining lowered buyer confidence, dealers now understand that many buyers either enjoy the negotiation process and/or feel they can get a better price by negotiating. Furthermore, the "no-dicker sticker" dealers often found that fixed pricing made them vulnerable to competitors that undercut their fixed prices by $100 or so.

With negotiated pricing, dealers are free to charge higher prices to unsophisticated buyers—called "hitting a home run" by new-car salespeople. The salespeople are also encouraged to negotiate for the highest prices since their compensation is based on the gross profit of each car they sell. At fixed-price dealers, cars are sold at a uniform markup (often the average price paid by buyers or the full list price at Saturn dealers). Because fixed-price salespeople do not have to negotiate price, they can spend more time with each customer or handle more customers. Training and advertising expenses are also lower in fixed-price dealerships.

In contrast to industry trends, Saturn dealers continue to use fixed pricing. This pricing strategy is required as part of the dealer's franchise contract with General Motors. While fixed pricing has been quite successful at Saturn, it has not caught on at other General Motors dealerships. At Chevrolet, for example, many dealers tried fixed pricing for only a few weeks before switching back to negotiated pricing. According to a Chevrolet executive, at least half of the dealers that tried fixed prices for six months or more (the minimum period recommended by General Motors) have switched back to negotiated pricing.

General Motors is now working with its dealers on a value-pricing program. With value pricing, heavily advertised cars are equipped with popular options and offered to customers at significant discounts from traditional list prices. Because the dealers purchase value-priced cars at lower costs and these models are offered at significant reductions, there is little flexibility in negotiating prices for these cars.[1]

---

[1]Keith Bradsher, "Sticker Shock: Car Buyers Miss Haggling Ritual," *New York Times* (June 13, 1996), pp. D1, D23.

A retailer has to price goods and services in a way that achieves profitability for the firm **OVERVIEW** and satisfies customers, while adapting to various constraints. Pricing is a crucial strategic variable due to its direct relationship with a firm's goals and its interaction with other retailing-mix elements. A pricing strategy must be consistent with the retailer's overall image (positioning), sales, profit, and return-on-investment goals. There are three basic pricing options for a retailer. Each has different advantages and disadvantages:

■ A discount orientation uses low prices as the major competitive advantage of the firm—which will trade off a low-status image, fewer shopping frills, and low per-unit profit margins in return for a target market of price-based customers, low operating costs, and high inventory turnover. Off-price retailers and discount department stores are in this category.

■ With an at-the-market orientation, the firm has average prices, and it offers solid service and a nice atmosphere to middle-class customers. Profit margins are moderate to good, and average to above-average quality products are stocked. A firm may find it hard to expand the price range of the products sold, and it may be squeezed by retailers positioned as discounters or prestige stores. Traditional department stores and many drugstores are in this category.

■ An upscale orientation is where a prestigious image represents the firm's major competitive advantage. The firm is willing to trade off a smaller target market, higher operating costs, and lower inventory turnover in return for customer loyalty, distinctive services and product offerings, and high per-unit profit margins. Upscale department stores and specialty stores are in this category.

As mentioned several times throughout *Retail Management,* one of the keys to successful retailing is providing a good value (in the mind of the consumer), regardless of the pricing orientation chosen. Every customer, whether spending $4.00 for an inexpensive ream of paper or $40 for a ream of embossed, personalized stationery, wants to feel he or she is receiving a good value for the money. Consider the following:

Pricing something at $9.99 versus $10 is generally associated with discounters. It puts the focus on the first digit. The implication is that this retailer is trying to save me money. You sell a Packard-Bell PC for $1,999.95. There's just a five-cent difference between the price and $2,000. But people place the emphasis on the other number. In contrast, Nordstrom and other high-end retailers often price in even numbers. That lends an aura of quality to the product.[2]

The interaction of price with other retailing-mix elements can be shown by Tie Town, a hypothetical off-price retailer. Its two partners have set a broad strategy consisting of

■ A target market of price-conscious men.
■ Selling inexpensive ties (in the $9 to $12 range).
■ A limited range of merchandise quality (end-of-season ties and overruns).
■ Self-service.
■ An outlet mall location.
■ A deep assortment.
■ Quantity purchases at discount from suppliers.
■ An image of efficiency and variety.

[2]Gene Koprowski, "The Price Is Right," *Marketing Tools* (September 1995), p. 60. See also Robert J. Dolan, "How Do You Know When the Price Is Right?" *Harvard Business Review,* Vol. 73 (September–October 1995), pp. 174–183.

TECHNOLOGY IN RETAILING

The Smart Card: A New Payment System for Retailers

The "smart card" looks just like a credit card, but has a computer chip embedded in it. The chip stores the card's initial cash value (which can be purchased in $10, $20, $50, $100, and higher denominations) and keeps track of its balance.

Consumers use the smart card by inserting it into a special terminal at the point of sale. This terminal completes the transaction after determining if the card has a large enough balance. Unlike with a traditional credit card, the consumer does not have to sign an invoice and the merchant does not have to receive credit authorization. Furthermore, the smart card is being marketed as an alternative to cash.

As part of a large-scale experiment with the smart card, Visa International (through three participating banks) offered consumers and athletes smart cards in conjunction with the 1996 Summer Olympics held in Atlanta. In total, about 50 different merchants representing over 15,000 locations in Atlanta accepted the Visa smart card during the Olympics.

One stumbling block to widespread smart card acceptance is the investment required by merchants for terminals (from $200 to $1,000 per terminal) and bank processing fees. However, according to research conducted by Visa, a retailer accepting the smart card as a payment option may be able to increase its sales by 5 percent to 40 percent.

Source: Patricia A. Murphy, "Smart Cards Begin First Major U.S. Test," *Stores* (July 1996), pp. 76–78.

Chapter 16 divides retail pricing into two major sections: the external factors affecting a price strategy and developing a price strategy.

EXTERNAL FACTORS AFFECTING A RETAIL PRICE STRATEGY

Before describing how a retail price strategy is developed, it is necessary to explore the external factors affecting price decision making. Consumers, government, manufacturers and wholesalers, and competitors each have an impact on the pricing strategy of a retailer, as shown in Figure 16-1. Sometimes, these factors may have only a minor effect; in other cases, they may severely restrict a retailer's options in setting prices.

The Consumer and Retail Pricing

There is often a relationship between price and consumers' purchases and perceptions. Thus, retailers should understand the price elasticity of demand that they face.[3]

The **price elasticity of demand** relates to the sensitivity of customers to price changes in terms of the quantities they will buy. If relatively small percentage changes in price result in substantial percentage changes in the number of units purchased, price elasticity is high. This occurs when the urgency for a purchase is low or acceptable substitutes exist. However, if large percentage changes in price have small percentage changes in the number of units bought, demand is considered inelastic. This occurs when purchase urgency is high or there are no acceptable substitutes (as takes place with store or retailer loyalty). Unitary elasticity occurs in instances where percentage changes in price are directly offset by percentage changes in quantity.

Price elasticity is computed by dividing the percentage change in the quantity demanded by the percentage change in the price charged:

[3]See Stephen J. Hoch, Byung-Do Kim, Alan L. Montgomery, and Peter E. Rossi, "Determinants of Store-Level Price Elasticity," *Journal of Marketing Research*, Vol. 32 (February 1995), pp. 17–29; and Saroja Subrahmanyan and Robert Shoemaker, "Developing Optimal Pricing and Inventory Policies for Retailers Who Face Uncertain Demand," *Journal of Retailing*, Vol. 72 (Spring 1996), pp. 7–30.

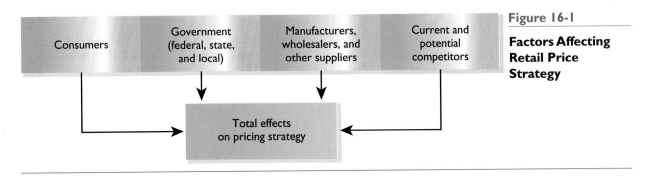

Figure 16-1

Factors Affecting Retail Price Strategy

$$\text{Elasticity} = \frac{\dfrac{\text{Quantity 1} - \text{Quantity 2}}{\text{Quantity 1} + \text{Quantity 2}}}{\dfrac{\text{Price 1} - \text{Price 2}}{\text{Price 1} + \text{Price 2}}}$$

Because the quantities bought generally decline as prices go up, elasticity tends to be a negative number.

Table 16-1 shows the calculation of price elasticity for a 1,000-seat movie theater (with elasticities converted to positive numbers). The table demonstrates that the quantity demanded (tickets sold) declines at every price level from $4.00 to $8.00; fewer customers patronize the theater at $8.00 than at $4.00. Demand is inelastic from $4.00 to $5.00; total ticket receipts increase since the percentage change in price is greater than the percentage change in tickets sold. Demand is unitary from $5.00 to $6.00; total ticket receipts are constant since the percentage change in tickets sold exactly offsets the percentage change in price. Demand is elastic from $6.00 to $8.00; total ticket receipts decline since the percentage change in tickets sold is greater than the percentage change in price.

For this example, total ticket receipts are highest at $5.00 or at $6.00. But what about total theater revenues? If patrons spend an average of $2.50 each at the concession stand, the best price is $5.00 (total overall revenues of $6,390). The theater is most interested in total revenues generated since operating costs are the same whether there are 852 or 710 patrons. But as a rule, retailers should evaluate the costs, as well as the revenues, from serving additional customers.

In retailing, computing price elasticity is difficult for two reasons. First, as in the case of the movie theater, demand for individual events or items may be hard to predict. One

Table 16-1 A MOVIE THEATER'S ELASTICITY OF DEMAND

Price	Tickets Sold (Saturday night)	Total Ticket Receipts	Elasticity of Demand[a]
$4.00	1,000	$4,000	
			E = 0.72
5.00	852	4,260	
			E = 1.00
6.00	710	4,260	
			E = 1.77
7.00	540	3,780	
			E = 2.23
8.00	400	3,200	

Computation example = [(1,000 − 852)/(1,000 + 852)]/[($4.00 − $5.00)/($4.00 + $5.00)] = 0.72

[a]Expressed as a positive number.

week, the theater may attract 1,000 patrons to a movie, and the next week it may attract 400 patrons to a different movie. Second, retailers such as supermarkets and department stores sell thousands of items and could not possibly compute elasticities for every one. As a result, many firms rely on average markup pricing, competition, tradition, and industrywide data to indicate price elasticity.

Consumer price sensitivity varies by market segment, based on shopping orientation. Here are several of them:

■ Economic consumers—They perceive competing retailers as similar to one another and shop around for the lowest possible prices. This segment has grown dramatically in recent years.
■ Status-oriented consumers—They perceive competing retailers as quite different from one another. They are more interested in prestige brands and customer services than in price.
■ Assortment-oriented consumers—They seek retailers with strong assortments in the product categories being considered. They look for fair prices.
■ Personalizing consumers—They shop where they are known. There is a strong personal bond with retail personnel and the firm itself. These shoppers will pay slightly above-average prices.
■ Convenience-oriented consumers—They shop only because they must. They want nearby locations and long hours, and may shop by catalog. These people will pay higher prices.

After identifying potential segments, retailers decide which of them form their target market.

The Government and Retail Pricing

While studying the impact of government on planning a pricing strategy, it must be kept in mind that three levels of government exist: federal, state, and local. Although many significant laws are federal, some of these laws apply only to interstate commerce. A retailer operating exclusively within the boundaries of one state may not be restricted by some federal legislation.

Government activity entails seven main areas: horizontal price fixing, vertical price fixing, price discrimination, minimum price levels, unit pricing, item price removal, and price advertising.

Horizontal Price Fixing ❏ **Horizontal price fixing** involves agreements among manufacturers, among wholesalers, or among retailers to set certain prices. Such agreements are illegal according to the Sherman Antitrust Act and the Federal Trade Commission Act, regardless of how "reasonable" resultant prices may be. It is also illegal for retailers to reach agreements with one another regarding the use of coupons, rebates, or other price-oriented tactics.

Although few large-scale legal actions have been taken in recent years, the penalties for horizontal price fixing can be severe. For example,

■ The managers of three supermarkets (First National, Fisher Foods, and Stop & Shop) met weekly in parking lots late at night and jointly decided what "specials" each would offer and at what prices. When they were caught, their supermarkets were fined a total of $1.7 million, and four executives were fined $100,000 each. The executives also got suspended jail sentences and were placed on five years' probation.[4]

[4]Michael A. Duggan, "United States v. First National Supermarkets," *Journal of Marketing*, Vol. 47 (Fall 1983), pp. 127–128.

■ Four supermarket chains (Waldbaum's, Pathmark, King Kullen, and LAMM) had a private agreement to limit their use of double and triple coupons. With such coupons, the chains matched or exceeded the coupon values offered by manufacturers with their own discounts. After their tactics were uncovered, the firms were ordered to pay fines totaling $830,000.[5]

■ The U.S. Department of Justice accused the National Automobile Dealers Association (which represented 84 percent of the country's car dealers) of violating antitrust laws by encouraging members to undertake steps to limit price competition in selling to consumers. The association settled out of court, signing a consent decree—effective for 10 years—that would prohibit it from urging members to enact pricing or advertising programs that would restrict competition. It also agreed not to punish dealers for their pricing policies.[6]

Vertical Price Fixing ❑ **Vertical price fixing** occurs when manufacturers or wholesalers are able to control the retail prices of their goods and services. Until 1976, this practice was allowed in the United States due to a belief that manufacturers and wholesalers had the right to protect their brands' reputations and that these reputations could be diluted through indiscriminate price cutting by retailers. Vertical price fixing was also viewed as protecting smaller and full-service retailers against discounters (which could not have prices below those set by manufacturers and wholesalers).

However, this practice was criticized by consumer groups and many manufacturers, wholesalers, and retailers as being anticompetitive, keeping prices artificially high, and allowing inefficient retailers to stay in business. As a result, the Consumer Goods Pricing Act, which ended the interstate use of fair trade practices and resale price maintenance, was enacted. At present, retailers cannot be required to adhere to list prices developed by manufacturers and wholesalers.

Manufacturers and wholesalers today can legally control retail prices only by one of these methods: they can screen retailers; they can set realistic list prices; they can pre-print prices on products (which retailers do not have to use); they can set regular prices that are accepted by consumers (such as 50 cents for a newspaper); they can use consignment selling, whereby the supplier owns items until they are sold and assumes costs normally associated with the retailer; they can own retail facilities; and they can refuse to sell to retailers advertising discount prices in violation of written policies. The supplier has a right to announce a general policy regarding dealer pricing and can refuse to sell to those that do not comply with it, but it cannot use coercion or conspire with other dealers to prohibit a retailer from advertising low prices.

Many discount retailers nonetheless believe that, in the 1980s, the Federal Trade Commission and the Department of Justice did not adequately protect their right to compete on the basis of price. From 1981 through 1990, the FTC did not bring any actions to curb vertical price fixing, even though numerous discount retailers said they were denied access to product lines and consumers had been forced to pay higher prices as a result.

During the 1990s, the FTC has become more involved in this area, settling complaints filed against Nintendo, Kreepy Krauly (a maker of swimming pool cleaning devices), and others. In addition, for several years, a number of the nation's state attorneys general have actively policed manufacturers that engage in vertical price fixing, such as getting Stride Rite to agree to pay $7.2 million to New York consumers to avoid charges of price fixing on its popular Keds sneakers. Similar settlements were made with Nintendo (a $25 million fine) and Mitsubishi Electric (an $8 million fine).[7]

[5]"Four Supermarket Concerns Are Fined Total of $830,000," *Wall Street Journal* (November 27, 1984), p. 64.
[6]Stephen Labaton, "Car Dealers' Group Settles U.S. Antitrust Suit," *New York Times* (September 21, 1995), p. D7.
[7]Joseph Pereira, "Stride Rite Agrees to Settle Charges It Tried to Force Pricing by Retailers," *Wall Street Journal* (September 28, 1993), p. A5; and Joe Davidson, "Rules Allowing Manufacturers to Fix Prices with Distributors Are Rescinded," *Wall Street Journal* (August 11, 1993), p. A3.

Price Discrimination ❏ The **Robinson-Patman Act** bars manufacturers and wholesalers from discriminating in price or sales terms in selling to individual retailers if these retailers are purchasing products of "like quality" and the effect of such discrimination would be to injure competition. The intent of the Robinson-Patman Act is to stop large retailers from using their power to gain discounts not justified by cost savings achieved from big orders. It is feared that, without the Robinson-Patman Act, smaller retailers could be driven out of business because of noncompetitive final prices due to significantly higher merchandise costs.

There are exceptions to the Robinson-Patman Act that allow justifiable price discrimination if

■ Products are physically different.
■ The retailers paying different prices are not competitors.
■ Competition is not injured.
■ Price differences are due to differences in the supplier's costs.
■ Market conditions change—whereby costs rise or fall, or competing suppliers shift their prices.

Discounts are not illegal, as long as a supplier follows the preceding rules, makes discounts available to competitive retailers on an equitable basis, and offers discounts sufficiently graduated so small (as well as large) retailers can qualify. Discounts for cumulative purchases (total orders during the year) and for multistore purchases by chains may be difficult to justify. In 1996, a private lawsuit brought by drugstores against pharmaceutical manufacturers resulted in a $351 million settlement. The drugstores had been paying higher prices than managed care organizations and mail-order firms for prescription drugs.[8]

Although the Robinson-Patman Act seems to restrict sellers more than buyers, retailers do have specific liabilities under Section 2(F) of the Act: "It shall be unlawful for any person engaged in commerce, in the course of such commerce, knowingly to induce or receive a discrimination in price which is prohibited in this section." From a strategic perspective, a retail buyer must try to receive the lowest prices charged to any competitor in its class; yet, it must also be careful not to bargain so hard that discounts cannot be justified by one of the acceptable exceptions.[9]

Minimum-Price Laws ❏ About half the states have **minimum-price laws** that prevent retailers from selling certain items for less than the cost plus a fixed percentage to cover overhead. Merchandise costs are defined in various ways; often, they are purchase or replacement costs, whichever are less.

Minimum-price laws aim to protect small retailers from **predatory pricing,** in which large retailers seek to destroy competition by selling goods and services at very low prices, thus causing small retailers to go out of business. Besides general laws, many states have acts setting minimum prices for specific products. For instance, New Jersey and Connecticut laws require the retail price of liquor to be not less than the wholesale cost (including taxes and delivery charges).

With **loss leaders,** retailers price selected items below cost to lure more customer traffic for those retailers. Firms such as supermarkets often use loss leaders to increase overall sales and profits under the assumption that people will buy more than one item once drawn to a store. Although loss leaders are restricted by some minimum-price laws, because this approach is usually consumer-oriented, the laws are rarely applied (as long as there is no predatory pricing).

---

[8]Robert Langreth, "Settlement Cleared in Pharmacies' Suit Over Price Fixing, But Debate Lingers," *Wall Street Journal* (June 24, 1996), p. B5.
[9]See Bryan Gruley and Joseph Pereira, "FTC Antitrust Case Accuses Toys "Я" Us," *Wall Street Journal* (May 23, 1996), pp. A3, A6; and Joseph Pereira and Bryan Gruley, "Toys "Я" Us Says It Will Challenge FTC," *Wall Street Journal* (May 22, 1996), p. A3.

In one recent, widely watched case, three independent pharmacies in Conway, Arkansas, filed a predatory pricing suit claiming Wal-Mart had sold selected products below cost in an attempt to reduce competition. During 1993, Wal-Mart was found guilty in an Arkansas court, ordered to pay $289,407 in damages to the pharmacies, and ordered to stop selling health and beauty aids and over-the-counter drugs at prices below cost in its Conway store. This was the first time Wal-Mart was unable to settle a predatory pricing case out of court. Wal-Mart agreed it had priced selected products below cost to meet or beat rivals' prices, but not to harm small competitors. After Wal-Mart appealed the verdict to the Arkansas Supreme Court, it was overturned. In 1995, that court ruled Wal-Mart had not engaged in predatory pricing because the three pharmacies were still profitable and "competition appears to be thriving."[10]

Unit Pricing ❑ The proliferation of package sizes has led to **unit-pricing** laws in many states. The aim of such legislation is to let consumers compare the prices of products available in many sizes. Food stores are most affected by unit-price rules, and in many cases, these stores must express both the total price of an item and its price per unit of measure. Thus, a 6.5-ounce can of tuna fish priced at 99 cents would also have a shelf label showing this is $2.44 per pound. With unit pricing, a person could learn that a 12-ounce can of soda selling for 35 cents (2.9 cents per ounce) is costlier than a 67.6-ounce (2-liter) bottle of soda selling for $1.49 (2.2 cents per ounce).

The intent of unit-pricing laws is to give basic information to consumers who feel price is a crucial decision factor and to provide added data for those people who consider brand-name or other factors as most important. Although early research studies questioned the effectiveness of unit pricing, later findings have indicated it is advantageous for both retailers and consumers.

Not all retailers must comply with unit-pricing laws. Generally, there are exemptions for retailers with low-volume sales or for those operating only one outlet. In addition, grocery items are much more heavily regulated than nongrocery items. The costs to affected retailers include computing per-unit prices, printing product and shelf labels, and keeping computer records. These costs are influenced by the way prices are attached to goods (by the supplier or the retailer), the number of items in a store subject to unit pricing, the frequency of price changes, sales volume, and the number of stores in a chain. A number of supermarket chains have reported that the costs of unit pricing are not excessive, whereas smaller food stores report that costs are high.

Unit pricing can be a good strategy for retailers to follow, even when not required by law. For instance, Giant Food has found its unit-pricing system more than pays for itself in terms of decreased price-marking errors, better inventory control, and improved space management.

Item Price Removal ❑ The boom in computerized checkout systems has led many firms, especially supermarkets, to advocate **item price removal**—whereby prices are marked only on shelves or signs and not on individual items. Scanning equipment reads pre-marked codes on product labels and enters price data at the checkout counter. This practice is banned in several states and local communities.

Supermarkets say item price removal would significantly reduce labor costs and let them offer lower prices. Opponents feel this would lead to more errors against consumers and make it harder for shoppers to verify prices as they are rung up. Giant Food uses item price removal in its supermarkets—with little consumer resistance and considerable cost

[10]Louise Lee, "Arkansas Court Rules Wal-Mart Didn't Use Illegal Pricing Practices," *Wall Street Journal* (January 10, 1995), p. B10; and Norman W. Hawker, "Wal-Mart and the Divergence of State and Federal Predatory Pricing Law," *Journal of Public Policy & Marketing*, Vol. 15 (Spring 1996), pp. 141–147. See also Joseph P. Guiltinan and Gregory T. Gundlach, "Aggressive and Predatory Pricing: A Framework for Analysis," *Journal of Marketing*, Vol. 60 (July 1996), pp. 87–102.

savings. Giant maintains accurate, highly visible shelf prices and gives items free to consumers if the prices processed by its electronic cash registers (equipped with scanners) are higher than those posted on shelves.

Price Advertising ❑ The FTC has guidelines for price advertising. These guidelines deal with advertising price reductions, advertising prices in relation to competitors' prices, and bait-and-switch advertising.

FTC guidelines generally state that a retailer cannot claim or imply a price has been reduced from some former level (such as a manufacturer's list or suggested list price) unless the former price was an actual, bona fide one at which the retailer offered a good or service to the public on a regular basis during a reasonably substantial, recent period of time.

When a retailer claims its prices are lower than those of other firms, FTC guidelines say it must make certain price comparisons pertain to competitors selling large quantities in the same trading area. A particularly controversial, but basically legal, practice is price matching: "If a store pledges to match a competitor's advertised prices, it isn't promising that all its prices are the lowest in town. What's more, such stores expect only a small percentage of shoppers to try to collect on price-matching promises. Critics question the fairness of a policy which lets retailers cut special deals with only the most conscientious comparison shoppers."[11]

Bait advertising, or **bait-and-switch advertising,** is an illegal practice in which a retailer lures a customer by advertising goods and services at exceptionally low prices; then, once the customer contacts the retailer (by entering a store or calling a toll-free 800 number), he or she is told the good/service of interest is out of stock or of inferior quality. A salesperson tries to convince the customer to purchase a better, more expensive substitute that is available. In bait advertising, the retailer has no intention of selling the advertised item. In deciding whether a promotion constitutes bait advertising, the FTC can consider how many sales were made at the advertised price, whether a sales commission was paid on sale items, and the total amount of sales relative to advertising costs.

Manufacturers, Wholesalers, and Other Suppliers— and Retail Pricing

Manufacturers, wholesalers, and other suppliers have an impact on a retail pricing strategy. In instances where suppliers are unknown or products are new, retailers may seek price guarantees to ensure that inventory values and profits are maintained. **Price guarantees** protect retailers against possible price declines. Suppose a new supplier sells a retailer radios having a final list selling price of $30 and guarantees the price to a retailer. If that retailer is unable to sell the radios at this price, the manufacturer pays the difference. Should the retailer have to sell the radios at $25, the manufacturer gives a rebate of $5 per radio. Another type of price guarantee is one in which a supplier guarantees to a retailer that no competitor will be able to buy an item for a lower price. If anyone does, the retailer will get a rebate. The relative power of the retailer and its suppliers determines whether such guarantees are provided.

There are often conflicts between manufacturers (and other suppliers) and their retailers in setting final prices since each would like some input and control. Manufacturers usually want to have a certain image and to let all retailers, even ones that are rather inefficient, earn profits. In contrast, most retailers want to set prices based on their own image, goals, and so forth.

---

[11]Francine Schwadel, "Are Price-Matching Policies Largely PR?" *Wall Street Journal* (March 16, 1989), p. B1. See also Larry D. Compeau, Dhruv Grewal, and Diana S. Grewal, "Adjudicating Claims of Deceptive Advertised Reference Prices: The Use of Empirical Evidence," *Journal of Public Policy & Marketing,* Vol. 14 (Fall 1994), pp. 312–318; and Nikhil Deogun, "Winn-Dixie Policy Faces Review by FTC," *Wall Street Journal* (December 23, 1996), p. B6.

A supplier can control prices by using an exclusive distribution system, refusing to sell to price-cutting retailers, or having its own retail facilities. A retailer can gain control by being important to its suppliers as a customer, threatening to stop carrying suppliers' lines, stocking private brands, or selling gray market goods.

Many manufacturers set the selling prices to their retailers by estimating final retail prices and then subtracting required retailer and wholesaler profit margins from these figures. In the men's haberdashery industry, the common retail markup (gross profit) is 50 percent of the final selling price. Thus, a man's shirt retailing at $30 can be sold to the retailer for no more than $15. If a wholesaler is involved, the manufacturer's price to the wholesaler must be far less than $15.

Retailers sometimes carry manufacturers' brands and place high prices on them so rival brands (such as private-label merchandise) can be sold more easily. This is called **selling against the brand** and is disliked by manufacturers since sales of their brands are apt to decline. Some retailers also sell **gray market goods,** brand-name products purchased in foreign markets or goods transshipped from other retailers. Manufacturers particularly dislike gray market goods because they are often sold at low prices by unauthorized dealers. Firms such as Givenchy now limit gray market goods on the basis of copyright and trademark infringement.

A retailer also has suppliers other than manufacturers and wholesalers. These include employees, fixtures manufacturers, landlords, and outside parties (such as advertising agencies). Each of them has an effect on price because of their costs to the retailer.

Competition and Retail Pricing

The degree of control an individual firm has over prices often depends on the competitive environment it faces. In a market-pricing situation, there is a lot of competition; and because people have a large choice as to the retailer to patronize, they often seek the lowest prices. Thus, firms price similarly to each other and have low control over price. Supermarkets, fast-food firms, and gas stations are in very competitive industries and tend to sell similar goods and services; they thus use market pricing. Demand for specific retailers may be weak enough so that a number of customers would switch to a competitor if prices are raised much.

In administered pricing, firms seek to attract consumers on the basis of distinctive retailing mixes. If strong differentiation from competitors can be reached, a retailer can control the prices it charges. This occurs when people consider image, assortment, personal service, and other factors to be more important than price and will pay above-average prices for the goods and services of distinctive retailers. Traditional department stores, fashion apparel stores, and upscale restaurants are among those that seek to have unique offerings and have some control over their prices.

Because most price-oriented strategies can be easily and quickly copied, the reaction of competitors is predictable when the leading firm is successful. Therefore, a retailer should view price strategy from a long-run, as well as a short-run, perspective. If the competitive environment becomes too intense, a price war may erupt—whereby various retailers continually lower prices below regular amounts and sometimes below merchandise costs to attract consumers away from competitors. Price wars are sometimes difficult to end and can lead to low profits, losses, or even bankruptcy for some competitors.

As shown in Figure 16-2, there are five steps (objectives, policy, strategy, implementation, and adjustments) in a retail price strategy. Like any other strategic activity, pricing begins with clear goals and ends with an adaptive or corrective mechanism. Pricing policies must be integrated with the total retail mix; this occurs in the second step of price planning. The process can be complex due to the often erratic nature of demand and the number of items carried by many retailers; and all aspects of the process are affected by the external factors already noted.

DEVELOPING A RETAIL PRICE STRATEGY

Figure 16-2

A Framework for Developing a Retail Price Strategy

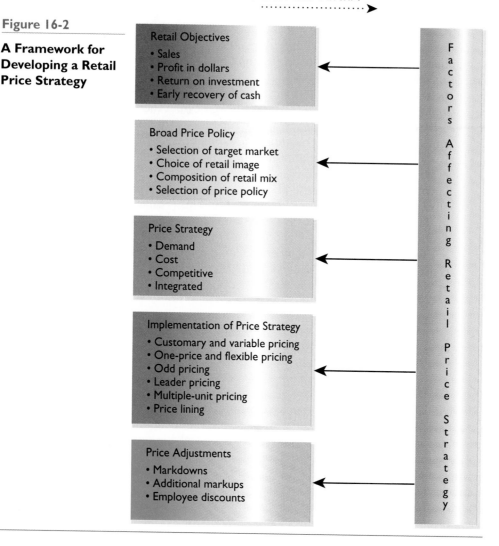

Retail Objectives
• Sales
• Profit in dollars
• Return on investment
• Early recovery of cash

Broad Price Policy
• Selection of target market
• Choice of retail image
• Composition of retail mix
• Selection of price policy

Price Strategy
• Demand
• Cost
• Competitive
• Integrated

Implementation of Price Strategy
• Customary and variable pricing
• One-price and flexible pricing
• Odd pricing
• Leader pricing
• Multiple-unit pricing
• Price lining

Price Adjustments
• Markdowns
• Additional markups
• Employee discounts

Factors Affecting Retail Price Strategy

Retail Objectives and Pricing

A retailer's pricing strategy must reflect its overall goals, and financial goals can be stated in terms of sales and profits. Besides its broad objectives, a retailer needs to set more specific pricing goals to avoid such potential problems as confusing people by having too many prices, spending excessive time bargaining with customers, employing frequent sales to stimulate customer traffic, having inadequate profit margins, and placing too much emphasis on price in the strategy mix.

Overall Objectives and Pricing ❏ Sales goals are often stated in terms of revenues and/or unit volume. An example of a sales goal and a resultant pricing strategy is a car dealer's desire to achieve large revenues by setting low prices and selling a high unit volume. This aggressive price strategy is known as **market penetration.** It is proper if customers are highly sensitive to price, low prices discourage actual and potential competition, and retail costs do not rise as much as sales volume increases.

Profit-in-dollars objectives are sought when a retailer concentrates on total profit or profit per unit. With a **market skimming** strategy, a firm charges premium prices and attracts customers less concerned with price than service, assortment, and status. Though this approach typically does not maximize sales, it does achieve high profit per unit. It is appropriate if the market segment a retailer defines as its target market

Table 16-2 TIE TOWN: DEMAND, COSTS, PROFIT, AND RETURN ON INVESTMENT[a]

Selling Price (in $)	Quantity Demanded (in units)	Total Sales Revenue (in $)	Average Cost of Merchandise (in $)	Total Cost of Merchandise (in $)	Total Nonmerchandise Costs (in $)	Total Costs (in $)
9.00	57,000	513,000	7.60	433,200	52,000	485,200
10.00	52,000	520,000	7.85	408,200	47,000	455,200
11.00	40,000	440,000	8.25	330,000	44,000	374,000
12.00	30,000	360,000	8.75	262,500	40,000	302,500

Selling Price (in $)	Average Total Costs (in $)	Total Profit (in $)	Profit/Unit (in $)	Markup at Retail (in %)	Profit/Sales (in %)	Average Inventory on Hand (in units)
9.00	8.51	27,800	0.49	16	5.4	6,000
10.00	8.75	64,800	1.25	22	12.5	6,500
11.00	9.35	66,000	1.65	25	15.0	7,000
12.00	10.08	57,500	1.92	27	16.0	8,000

Selling Price (in $)	Inventory Turnover (in units)	Average Investment in Inventory at Cost (in $)	Inventory Turnover (in $)	Return on Investment (in %)
9.00	9.5	45,600	9.5	61
10.00	8.0	51,025	8.0	127
11.00	5.7	57,750	5.7	114
12.00	3.8	70,000	3.8	82

Note: Average cost of merchandise reflects quantity discounts. Total nonmerchandise costs include all retail operating expenses.

[a] Numbers have been rounded off.

Table 16-3 DERIVATION OF TIE TOWN DATA

Column in Table 16-2	Source of Information or Method of Computation
Selling price	Trade data, comparison shopping, experience
Quantity demanded (in units) at each price level	Consumer surveys, trade data, experience
Total sales revenue	Selling price × Quantity demanded
Average cost of merchandise	Contacts with suppliers, quantity discount structure, estimates of order sizes
Total cost of merchandise	Average cost of merchandise × Quantity demanded
Total nonmerchandise costs	Experience, trade data, estimation of individual retail operating expenses
Total costs	Total cost of merchandise + Total nonmerchandise costs
Average total costs	Total costs/Quantity demanded
Total profit	Total sales revenue − Total costs
Profit per unit	Total profit/Quantity demanded
Markup (at retail)	(Selling price − Average cost of merchandise)/Selling price
Profit as a percentage of sales	Total profit/Total sales revenue
Average inventory on hand	Trade data, merchandise turnover data (in units), experience
Inventory turnover (in units)	Quantity demanded/Average inventory on hand (in units)
Average investment in inventory (at cost)	Average cost of merchandise × Average inventory on hand (in units)
Inventory turnover (in $)	Total cost of merchandise/Average investment in inventory (at cost)
Return-on-inventory investment	Total profit/Average investment in inventory (at cost)

is insensitive to price, new competitors are unlikely to enter the market, and additional sales will greatly increase retail costs.

Return on investment and early recovery of cash are two other profit-based goals. Return on investment is sought if a firm stipulates that profit must be a certain percentage of its investment, such as 20 percent of inventory investment. Early recovery of cash is used by retailers that may be short on funds, wish to expand, or be uncertain about the future. A market skimming strategy is often applied by retailers with return on investment or early recovery of cash as a goal.

Tie Town, the off-price tie shop introduced at the beginning of the chapter, may be used to illustrate how a retailer could set sales, profit, and return-on-investment goals. Tie Town sells inexpensive ties (avoiding competition with department and haberdashery stores), has a single selling price for all ties (to be set for the next year from within the range of $9 to $12), minimizes operating costs, maximizes self-service, and carries a large selection to generate traffic.

Table 16-2 contains data gathered by Tie Town pertaining to demand, costs, profit, and return-on-inventory investment at prices from $9 to $12. It must select the most appropriate price within that range. Table 16-3 shows how Tie Town arrived at the figures in Table 16-2.

From Table 16-2, several conclusions concerning the best price for Tie Town can be drawn:

- A sales goal would lead to a price of $10. Total sales are highest ($520,000).
- A dollar profit goal would lead to a price of $11. Total profit is highest ($66,000).
- A return-on-investment goal would also lead to a price of $10. Return-on-inventory investment is 127 percent.

Discount Retailing in South Korea Is Ready to Soar

Some retailing analysts believe that high prices in South Korea and a changed legislative environment there have combined to generate significant opportunities for discounters. Prices for many products are now more expensive in Seoul than in New York, Los Angeles, London, and sometimes even Tokyo. The Korean government is also making it easier for foreign and local businesspeople to open new retail outlets. In the past, the government sought to protect its smaller, less efficient retailers.

Discount retailing is spreading fast in South Korea, where Costco has already opened stores. The first outlet (operated as a joint venture with the Shinsegae Department Store) has 100,000 members (as compared with its typical U.S. store's 45,000 member base). Costco plans to open a total of 10 stores in South Korea as of the year 2000. To appeal to Korean nationalism, 75 percent of Costco's sales there are from Korean-made products.

In contrast, E-Land, a Korean-based apparel firm with discount outlets in Korea, does not carefully monitor country of origin. According to a company director, "Customers have a right to the best product and price. That's more important than misguided nationalism." E-Land intends to open more than 100 of its "next generation" department stores by the year 2000. These stores are a cross between a department and a warehouse store.

Source: Gale Eisenstodt, "Park Gui-Sook's Reading List," *Forbes* (September 11, 1995), pp. 73–76.

■ Although a large quantity can be sold at $9, that price would lead to the least profit ($27,800).
■ A price of $12 would yield the highest profit per unit and as a percentage of sales, but total dollar profit is not maximized at this price.
■ High inventory turnover would not necessarily lead to high profits.

As a result, Tie Town's partners have decided a price of $11 would let them earn the highest dollar profits, while generating good profit per unit and profit as a percentage of sales.

Specific Pricing Objectives ❑ Table 16-4 provides a list of specific pricing goals other than sales and profits. Although a number of objectives are enumerated in the table, each firm must determine their relative importance given its particular situation—and plan accordingly. Furthermore, some goals may be incompatible with one another, such as "to not encourage customers to become overly price-conscious" and a " 'we-will-not-be-undersold' philosophy."

Table 16-4 SELECTED SPECIFIC PRICING OBJECTIVES

■ To maintain a proper image.
■ To not encourage customers to become overly price-conscious.
■ To be perceived as fair by all parties (including suppliers, employees, and customers).
■ To be consistent in setting prices.
■ To increase customer traffic during slow periods.
■ To clear out seasonal merchandise.
■ To match competitors' prices without starting a price war.
■ To promote a "we-will-not-be-undersold" philosophy.
■ To be regarded as the price leader in the market area by consumers.
■ To provide ample customer service.
■ To minimize the chance of government actions relating to price advertising and antitrust matters.
■ To discourage potential competitors from entering the marketplace.
■ To create and maintain customer interest.
■ To encourage repeat business.

Broad Price Policy

Through a broad price policy, a retailer generates a coordinated series of actions, a consistent image (especially vital for chain and franchise units), and a plan including short- and long-run considerations (thereby balancing immediate and long-term goals). In this stage, a firm must be sure its price policy is interrelated with the target market, the retail image, and the other elements of the retail mix.

A broad price policy translates price decisions into an integrated framework. For example, a firm must decide whether prices should be established for individual items, interrelated for a group of goods and services, or based on an extensive use of special sales. These are some of the price policies from which a retailer could choose:

■ No competitors will have lower prices; no competitors will have higher prices; or prices will be consistent with competitors'.
■ All items will be priced independently, depending on the demand for each; or the prices for all items will be interrelated to maintain an image and ensure proper markups.
■ Price leadership will be exerted; competitors will be price leaders and set prices first; or prices will be set independently of competitors.
■ Prices will be constant over a year or season; or prices will change if merchandise costs change.

Price Strategy

A price strategy can be demand, cost, and/or competitive in orientation. In **demand-oriented pricing,** a retailer sets prices based on consumer desires. It determines the range of prices acceptable to the target market. The top of this range is called the demand ceiling, the maximum consumers will pay for a good or service.

With **cost-oriented pricing,** a retailer sets a price floor, the minimum price acceptable to the firm so it can reach a specified profit goal. A retailer usually computes merchandise and retail operating costs and adds a profit margin to these figures.

For **competition-oriented pricing,** a retailer sets its prices in accordance with competitors'. Price levels of key competitors and how they affect the firm's sales are studied.

As a rule, retailers should use a combination of all three approaches in enacting a price strategy. The approaches should not be viewed as operating independently of one another.

Demand-Oriented Pricing ❏ Demand-oriented pricing is often used by retailers having sales or market share goals. It seeks to estimate the quantities customers would demand at various price levels and concentrates on the prices associated with stated sales goals. Whereas cost-oriented pricing relies on costs, a demand-oriented approach looks more at customer demand.

In using demand-oriented pricing, it is critical to understand the psychological implications. The term **psychological pricing** refers to consumer perceptions of retail prices. Two aspects of psychological pricing are the price-quality association and prestige pricing.

The **price-quality association** is a concept stating that many consumers feel high prices connote high quality and low prices connote low quality. This association is particularly important if competing firms or products are hard to judge on bases other than price, consumers have little experience or confidence in judging quality (as with a new retailer or product), buyers perceive large differences in quality among retailers or products, and brand names are an insignificant factor in product choice. Though various studies have documented the price-quality relationship, research also indicates that if other quality cues, such as retailer or product features and the stocking of well-known brands, are introduced, these factors may be more significant than price in a person's judgment of overall retailer or product quality.

Prestige pricing, in which it is assumed consumers will not buy goods and services at prices considered too low, is based on the price-quality association. According to this concept, consumers may feel too low a price means quality and status are poor. In addition, some people look for prestige pricing in selecting retailers and do not patronize with prices perceived as too low. Saks Fifth Avenue and Neiman Marcus do not generally carry the least expensive versions of items because their customers may believe them to be inferior.

Prestige pricing does not apply to all shoppers. Thus, the target market must be considered before a retailer reaches a decision here. Some people may be economizers and always shop for bargains; and neither the price-quality association nor prestige pricing may be applicable for them.

Cost-Oriented Pricing ❑ One form of cost-oriented pricing, markup pricing, is the most widely practiced retail-pricing technique. In **markup pricing,** a retailer sets prices by adding per-unit merchandise costs, retail operating expenses, and desired profit. The difference between merchandise costs and selling price is the retailer's **markup.** If a retailer buys a desk for $200 and wants to sell it for $300, the extra $100 is needed to cover retail operating expenses and profit. The markup is 33⅓ percent at retail or 50 percent on cost.

The markup percentage depends on such factors as a product's traditional markup, the manufacturer's suggested list price, inventory turnover, the competition, rent and other overhead costs, the extent to which a product must be altered or serviced, and the selling effort required.

Markups can be computed on the basis of retail selling price or cost, but are typically calculated in terms of retail selling price. There are several reasons for this. First, retail expenses, markdowns, and profit are always stated as a percentage of sales. Thus, if markups are expressed as a percentage of sales, they are quite meaningful. Second, manufacturers quote their selling prices and trade discounts to retailers as percentage reductions from retail list prices. Third, retail selling-price data are more readily available than cost data. Fourth, profitability statistics appear to be smaller if expressed on the basis of retail price instead of cost; this can be useful when dealing with the government, employees, and consumers.

A **markup percentage** is calculated as

$$\text{Markup percentage (at retail)} = \frac{\text{Retail selling price } - \text{ Merchandise cost}}{\text{Retail selling price}}$$

$$\text{Markup percentage (at cost)} = \frac{\text{Retail selling price } - \text{ Merchandise cost}}{\text{Merchandise cost}}$$

The difference is in the denominator. For both formulas, merchandise cost is the per-unit invoice and freight cost to a retailer, less per-unit trade or quantity discounts.

Table 16-5 shows a range of markup percentages at retail and at cost. As markups go up, the disparity between the percentages grows. Suppose a retailer buys a watch for $20 and considers whether to sell it for $25, $40, or $80. The $25 price yields a markup of 20 percent (at retail) or 25 percent (at cost), the $40 price yields a markup of 50 percent (at retail) or 100 percent (at cost), and the $80 price yields a markup of 75 percent (at retail) or 300 percent (at cost).

The markup concept has various applications in pricing and purchase planning. These illustrations detail its usefulness:

■   A discount clothing store can buy a shipment of men's jeans at $12 each and wants a 30 percent markup at retail. What retail price should the store charge to achieve this markup?

Table 16-5   MARKUP EQUIVALENTS

Percentage at Retail	Percentage at Cost
5.0	5.3
10.0	11.1
15.0	17.6
20.0	25.0
25.0	33.3
30.0	42.9
35.0	53.8
40.0	66.7
45.0	81.8
50.0	100.0
60.0	150.0
75.0	300.0
80.0	400.0
90.0	900.0

$$\frac{\text{Markup percentage}}{\text{(at retail)}} = \frac{\text{Retail selling price} - \text{Merchandise cost}}{\text{Retail selling price}}$$

$$0.30 = \frac{\text{Retail selling price} - \$12.00}{\text{Retail selling price}}$$

$$0.30\,(\text{Retail selling price}) = \text{Retail selling price} - \$12.00$$

$$0.70\,(\text{Retail selling price}) = \$12.00$$

$$\text{Retail selling price} = \$17.14$$

The store should charge $17.14 to achieve a 30 percent markup at retail.*

■ A stationery store desires a minimum 40 percent markup at retail. If it feels envelopes should retail at 79 cents per box, what is the maximum price the firm can pay for the envelopes?

$$\frac{\text{Markup percentage}}{\text{(at retail)}} = \frac{\text{Retail selling price} - \text{Merchandise cost}}{\text{Retail selling price}}$$

$$0.40 = \frac{\$0.79 - \text{Merchandise cost}}{\$0.79}$$

$$\$0.79 - \text{Merchandise cost} = (0.40)\,(\$0.79)$$

$$\$0.79 - \text{Merchandise cost} = \$0.316$$

$$\text{Merchandise cost} = \$0.79 - \$0.316$$

$$\text{Merchandise cost} = \$0.474$$

To achieve at least a 40 percent markup, the retailer cannot pay more than 47.4 cents per box of legal-sized envelopes.[†]

*Selling price may also be computed by transposing the markup formula into

$$\text{Retail selling price} = \frac{\text{Merchandise cost}}{1 - \text{Markup}} = \frac{\$12.00}{1 - 0.3} = \frac{\$12.00}{0.7} = \$17.14$$

[†] Merchandise cost may also be computed by transposing the markup formula into

$$\text{Merchandise cost} = (\text{Retail selling price})\,(1 - \text{Markup})$$

$$\text{Merchandise cost} = (\$0.79)\,(1 - 0.40) = (\$0.79)\,(0.60) = \$0.474$$

■ A sporting-goods store has been offered a closeout purchase on an imported line of bicycles. The per-unit cost of each bicycle is $105, and the bikes should retail for $160 each. What markup at retail will the store obtain?

$$\text{Markup percentage (at retail)} = \frac{\text{Retail selling price} - \text{Merchandise cost}}{\text{Retail selling price}}$$

$$\text{Markup percentage} = \frac{\$160.00 - \$105.00}{\$160.00}$$

$$\text{Markup percentage} = \frac{\$55.00}{\$160.00}$$

$$\text{Markup percentage} = 34.4$$

The store will receive a markup of 34.4 percent on these bikes.

Markup may also be determined by examining planned retail operating expenses, profit, and net sales:

$$\text{Markup percentage (at retail)} = \frac{\text{Planned retail operating expenses} + \text{Planned profit}}{\text{Planned net sales}}$$

Suppose a florist estimates retail operating expenses (rent, salaries, electricity, cleaning, bookkeeping, and so on) to be $55,000 per year. The desired profit is $50,000 per year, including the owner's salary. Net sales are forecast to be $250,000. The planned markup is

$$\text{Markup percentage (at retail)} = \frac{\$55,000 + \$50,000}{\$250,000} = 42$$

Because potted plants cost the florist an average of $8.00 each, the retailer's selling price per plant is

$$\text{Retail selling price} = \frac{\text{Merchandise cost}}{1 - \text{Markup}}$$

$$\text{Retail selling price} = \frac{\$8.00}{1 - 0.42} = \$13.79$$

The florist will need to sell about 18,129 plants at $13.79 apiece to achieve its sales and profit goals. To reach these goals, all plants must be sold at the $13.79 price.

Because it is highly unusual for a retailer to sell all items in stock at their original prices, it is necessary to understand and compute initial markup, maintained markup, and gross margin. **Initial markup** is based on the original retail value assigned to merchandise less the costs of the merchandise. **Maintained markup** is based on the actual prices received for merchandise sold during a time period less merchandise cost. Maintained markups are related to actual prices received; so it can be hard to estimate them in advance. The difference between initial and maintained markups is that the latter reflect adjustments from original retail values caused by markdowns, added markups, shortages, and discounts.

The initial markup percentage depends on planned retail operating expenses, profit, reductions, and net sales:

$$\text{Initial markup percentage (at retail)} = \frac{\begin{array}{c}\text{Planned retail operating expenses} \\ + \text{Planned profit} + \\ \text{Planned retail reductions}\end{array}}{\begin{array}{c}\text{Planned net sales} + \\ \text{Planned retail reductions}\end{array}}$$

If planned retail reductions are zero, the initial markup percentage is equal to planned retail operating expenses plus profit, both divided by planned net sales. This results in the markup formula just explained.

To return to the florist example, suppose the firm projects that its retail reductions will be 20 percent of estimated sales, or $50,000. To reach its goals, the initial markup will have to be

$$\text{Initial markup percentage (at retail)} = \frac{\$55,000 + \$50,000 + \$50,000}{\$250,000 + \$50,000} = 51.7$$

and the original selling price will be

$$\text{Retail selling price} = \frac{\text{Merchandise cost}}{1 - \text{Markup}} = \frac{\$8.00}{1 - 0.517} = \$16.56$$

This means the original retail value of 18,129 plants will be about $300,000. Retail reductions of $50,000 will result in net sales of $250,000. Therefore, the retailer must begin selling plants at $16.56 apiece if its goal is to have an average selling price of $13.79 per plant and a maintained markup of 42 percent.

The maintained markup percentage can be viewed as

$$\text{Maintained markup percentage (at retail)} = \frac{\text{Actual retail operating expenses} + \text{Actual profit}}{\text{Actual net sales}}$$

or

$$\text{Maintained markup percentage (at retail)} = \frac{\text{Average selling price} - \text{Merchandise cost}}{\text{Average selling price}}$$

Gross margin is the difference between net sales and the total cost of goods sold. The total cost figure, as opposed to the gross cost figure, adjusts for cash discounts and additional expenses:

$$\text{Gross margin (in \$)} = \text{Net sales} - \text{Total cost of goods}$$

For the florist, gross margin (which is the dollar equivalent of maintained markup) is approximately $250,000 − $145,000 = $105,000. The total cost of goods is merchandise cost times the number of units purchased.

Although a retailer must set an overall companywide markup goal, markups for categories of merchandise or even individual products may differ. In fact, markups can vary significantly. For instance, in full-line discount stores, maintained markup as a percentage of sales ranges from 16.5 percent for consumer electronics to 41.5 percent for jewelry/watches.[12]

A **variable markup policy,** whereby a retailer purposely varies markups by merchandise category, achieves four major purposes:

1. It recognizes that the costs associated with separate goods/service categories may fluctuate widely. Some items require extensive alterations (such as clothing) or installation (such as carpeting). Even within a product line like women's clothing, expensive fashion items require higher end-of-year markdowns than inexpensive items. Therefore, the more expensive line would receive a higher initial markup

2. It allows for differences in product investments. For instance, in a major-appliance department, where the retailer orders regularly from a wholesaler, lower markups would be needed than in a fine jewelry department, where the retailer would have to maintain a complete stock of merchandise.

[12]"Productivity '96: Performance Breakdown," *Discount Store News* (August 5, 1996), p. 46.

3. It accounts for differences in sales efforts and merchandising skills. Selling a food processor may mean a substantial sales effort, whereas selling a blender may involve significantly less effort and skill.
4. It may enable a retailer to generate more customer traffic by advertising certain products at especially attractive prices. This entails leader pricing, which is discussed later in the chapter.

One emerging method for planning variable markups is **direct product profitability (DPP).** With DPP, a retailer finds the profitability of each category or unit of merchandise by computing adjusted per-unit gross margin and assigning direct product costs for such expense categories as warehousing, transportation, handling, and selling. In this way, the proper markup for each category or item can be set. DPP is gaining popularity with supermarkets, discount stores, and other retailers. The major problem is the complexity of assigning costs accurately.

Figure 16-3 shows how DPP works. In this example, each of two items has a retail selling price of $20. With Item A, the retailer has a merchandise cost of $12. Its per-unit gross margin is $8. Because the firm gets a $1 per-unit allowance (rebate) for setting up a special display for Item A, its adjusted gross margin is $9. Total direct retail costs for Item A are estimated at $5. Thus, the direct product profit for Item A is $4, or 20 percent of sales.

With Item B, the retailer has a merchandise cost of $10. Its per-unit gross margin is $10, and there are no special discounts or allowances. Since Item B requires a greater selling effort, its total direct retail costs are $6. And its direct profit is $4, or 20 percent of sales. To attain the same direct profit per unit, Item A has a markup of 40 percent (per-unit gross margin/selling price) and Item B has a markup of 50 percent.

For many reasons, cost-oriented (markup) pricing is popular among retailers. It is fairly simple, especially as a retailer can apply a standard markup for a category of products much more easily than it can estimate demand at various price levels; the firm also can adjust prices according to changes in demand or segment a market. Markup pricing has an inherent sense of equity in that the retailer earns a fair profit. In addition, when retailers have similar markups, price competition is significantly reduced. Last, markup pricing is efficient if it takes into account the competition, seasonal factors, and difficulties in selling specific merchandise categories.

Competition-Oriented Pricing ❑ In competition-oriented pricing, a retailer uses competitors' prices as a guide, rather than demand or cost considerations. A competition-oriented firm might not alter its prices to react to changes in demand or costs unless competitors alter theirs. Similarly, such a retailer might alter its prices when competitors do, even if demand or cost factors remain the same.

A competition-oriented retailer can price below the market, at the market, or above the market. Table 16-6 outlines the conditions influencing a firm's choice. It is clear from this table that pricing must be integrated with the overall strategy mix. A firm with a strong site, superior customer service, good assortments, favorable image, and exclusive brands could set prices above competitors. Yet, above-market pricing is not suitable for a retailer that has an inconvenient site, relies on self-service and best-sellers, is a fashion follower, and stresses private-label merchandise.

A competition-oriented pricing approach could be used for several reasons. It is rather simple; there are no calculations of demand curves or concern with price elasticity. The ongoing market price is assumed to be fair for both the consumer and the retailer. Pricing at the market level does not disrupt competition and therefore does not usually lead to retaliation.

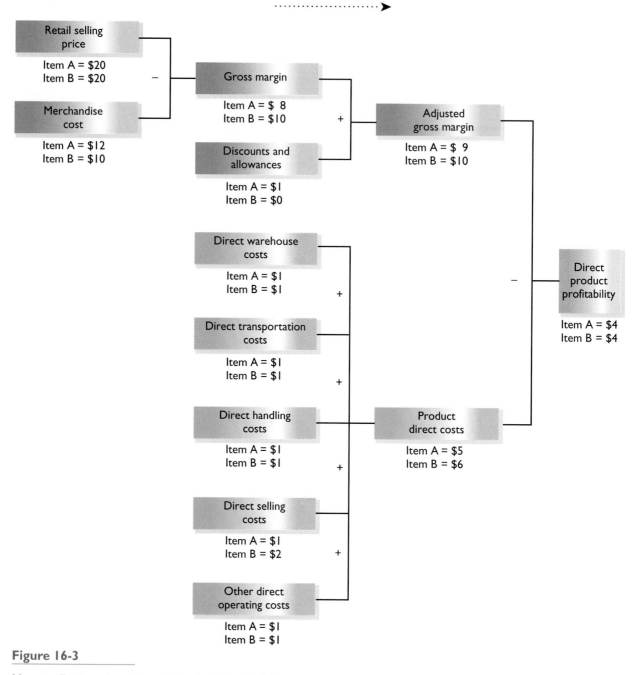

Figure 16-3

How to Determine Direct Product Profitability

Integration of Approaches to Price Strategy ❑ The three approaches for setting a retail price strategy should be integrated, so demand, cost, and competition are all taken into account. To do this, a firm should answer questions such as these before enacting a price strategy:

■ If prices are reduced, will revenues increase greatly? (Demand orientation)
■ Should different prices be charged for a product, based on negotiations with customers, seasonality, and so on? (Demand orientation)
■ Will a given price level allow a traditional markup to be attained? (Cost orientation)

Table 16-6 COMPETITION-ORIENTED PRICING ALTERNATIVES

ALTERNATIVE PRICE STRATEGIES

Retail Mix Variable	Pricing Below the Market	Pricing At the Market	Pricing Above the Market
Location	Poor, inconvenient site	Close to competitors, no locational advantage	Absence of strong competitors, convenient to consumers
Customer service	Self-service, little product knowledge on part of salespeople, no displays	Moderate assistance by sales personnel	High levels of personal selling, delivery exchanges, etc.
Product assortment	Concentration on best-sellers	Medium assortment	Large assortment
Atmosphere	Inexpensive fixtures, little or no carpeting or paneling, racks for merchandise	Moderate atmosphere	Attractive, pleasant decor with many displays
Role of fashion in assortment	Fashion follower, conservative	Concentration on accepted best-sellers	Fashion leader
Special services	Not available	Not available or extra charge to customers	Included in price
Merchandise lines carried	Private labels, name-brand closeouts, small manufacturers	Name brands	Exclusive name brands

■ What price level is necessary for a product requiring special costs in purchasing, selling, or delivery? (Cost orientation)

■ What price levels are competitors setting? (Competitive orientation)

■ Can a firm set higher prices than competitors due to its image? (Competitive orientation)

By no means is this list complete, but it demonstrates how a retailer can integrate demand, cost, and competitive price orientations. Figure 16-4 illustrates an integrated approach.

Figure 16-4

Integrated Pricing at Perry Drug Stores

Perry's price strategy is targeted at price-conscious customers, is tied to a low-cost operating structure, and takes competitors' prices into account ("Compare & Save"). In its "Perry Lowers Prices" campaign, the objective is to assure customers of the firm's price competitiveness while continuing to build on its strengths of convenient locations, a broad product mix, and responsive customer care.

Implementation of Price Strategy

Implementing a price strategy involves a variety of separate but interrelated specific decisions in addition to those broad concepts already discussed. A checklist of selected decisions is shown in Table 16-7. In this section, many of the specifics of pricing strategy are detailed.

Customary and Variable Pricing ❏ **Customary** pricing is used when a retailer sets prices for goods and services and seeks to maintain them for an extended period. Prices are not altered during this time. Examples of goods and services with customary prices are newspapers, candy, pay phones, arcade games, vending-machine items, and foods on restaurant menus. In each of these cases, a retailer seeks to establish customary prices and have consumers take them for granted.

A version of customary pricing is **everyday low pricing (EDLP),** in which a retailer strives to sell its goods and services at consistently low prices throughout the selling season. Under EDLP, the retailer sets low prices initially; and there are few or no advertised specials, except on discontinued items or end-of-season closeouts. The retailer reduces its advertising and product relabeling costs, while the manufacturer reduces the added production and shipping costs caused by erratic sales levels. EDLP also increases the credibility of the retailer's prices to the consumer. On the other hand, with EDLP, manufacturers tend to eliminate the special trade allowances designed to encourage retailers to offer price promotions during the year. Wal-Mart, Toys "Я" Us, and Ikea are among the retailers successfully utilizing EDLP.

In many instances, a retailer cannot or should not use customary pricing. A firm *cannot* maintain constant prices if its costs are rising. A firm *should not* maintain constant prices if customer demand varies. Under **variable pricing,** a retailer alters its prices to coincide with fluctuations in costs or consumer demand. Variable pricing may also provide excitement due to special sales opportunities for customers.

Cost fluctuations can be seasonal or trend-related. Seasonal fluctuations affect retailers selling items whose production peaks at certain times during the year. Thus, supermarket and florist prices vary over the year due to the seasonal nature of many agricultural and floral products. When items are scarce, their costs to the retailer go up. Trend-related fluctuations refer to the steady upward (or downward) spiral of costs to the retailer. If costs continually rise (as with luxury cars) or fall (as with PCs), the retaile must change prices permanently (unlike with seasonal fluctuations, which cause temporary changes).

Demand fluctuations can be place- or time-based. Place-based fluctuations exist for retailers selling seat locations (such as concert sites) or room locations (such as hotels). Different prices can be charged for different locations; for example, tickets close to the stage command higher prices. If variable pricing is not followed, location is based on a policy of first come, first served. Time-based fluctuations occur if consumer demand

---

Table 16-7   A CHECKLIST OF SELECTED SPECIFIC PRICING DECISIONS

1. How important is price stability? How long should prices be maintained?
2. Is everyday low pricing desirable?
3. Should prices change if costs and/or customer demand vary?
4. Should the same prices be charged of all customers buying under the same conditions?
5. Should customer bargaining be permitted?
6. Should odd pricing (e.g., $5.99) be used?
7. Should leader pricing be utilized to draw customer traffic? If yes, should leader prices be above, at, or below costs?
8. Should consumers be offered discounts for purchasing in quantity?
9. Should price lining be used to provide a price range and price points within that range?
10. Should pricing practices vary by department or product line?

differs by hour, day, or season. Demand for a movie theater is greater on Saturday than on Wednesday; demand for an airline is greater during December than February. Thus, prices should be lower during periods of low demand.

It is possible to combine customary and variable pricing. For instance, a theater can charge $3 every Wednesday night and $7 every Saturday. An airline can lower prices by 20 percent during off seasons.

One-Price Policy and Flexible Pricing ❏ Under a **one-price policy,** a retailer charges the same price to all customers buying an item under similar conditions. A one-price policy may be used in conjunction with customary pricing or variable pricing. In the latter case (variable pricing), all customers interested in a particular section of seats or arriving at the same time would pay the same price. This system is easy to manage, does not require skilled salespeople, makes shopping more convenient and quicker for consumers, permits self-service, puts consumers under less pressure, and is tied to the retailer's established price goals. Throughout the United States, one-price policies are the rule for most retailers, and bargaining over price is usually not permitted.

In contrast, **flexible pricing** allows consumers to bargain over selling prices, and those consumers who are good at bargaining obtain lower prices than those who are not. Many jewelry stores, auto dealers, housepainters, flea markets, and consumer electronics stores use flexible pricing. Retailers using this approach do not clearly post bottom-line prices; consumers need prior knowledge to bargain successfully. Flexible pricing encourages shoppers to spend more time in the store, gives an impression the retailer is discount-oriented, and generates high margins for customers who do not like haggling. It requires high initial prices and qualified salespeople.

Odd Pricing ❏ With **odd pricing,** retail prices are set at levels below even dollar values, such as $0.49, $4.98, and $199. The assumption is that people feel these prices represent discounts or that the amounts are beneath consumers' price ceilings. Realtors hope consumers setting a price ceiling of less than $150,000 will be attracted to houses selling for $149,500. From this perspective, odd pricing is a form of psychological pricing. See Figure 16-5.

Originally, odd prices were used to force salesclerks to give change on each purchase, thus preventing them from pocketing receipts without ringing up sales. Odd prices are now accepted as part of the U.S. system of retailing and are used more for psychological reasons.

Odd prices that are 1 cent or 2 cents below the next highest even price (e.g., $0.29, $0.99, $2.98) are most common up to the $10.00 level. Beyond that point and up to $50.00, 5-cent reductions from the highest even price (e.g., $19.95, $49.95) are more usual. For higher-priced merchandise, odd endings are in dollars (e.g., $399, $4,995).

Despite the widespread use of odd pricing in retailing, there has been little research on its psychological effects.[13]

Leader Pricing ❏ In **leader pricing,** a retailer advertises and sells selected items in its goods/service assortment at less than the usual profit margins. The goal is to increase customer traffic for the retailer in the hope of selling regularly priced goods and services in addition to the specially priced items. Leader pricing is different from bait-and-switch, in which sale items are not sold.

Leader pricing often involves frequently purchased, nationally branded, high-turnover goods and services because it is easy for customers to detect low prices and they generate high customer patronage. Supermarkets, home centers, discount department stores, toy stores, drugstores, and fast-food restaurants are just some of the retailers that utilize leader pricing to draw shoppers.

[13]See Robert M. Schindler and Thomas M. Kibarian, "Increased Consumer Sales Response Through the Use of 99-Ending Prices," *Journal of Retailing,* Vol. 72 (Summer 1996), pp. 187–199.

Figure 16-5

Odd Pricing: A Popular Retailing Tactic

There are two kinds of leader pricing: loss leaders and sales at lower than regular prices (but higher than cost). As noted earlier in this chapter, loss leaders are regulated on a statewide basis under minimum-price laws.

Multiple-Unit Pricing ❑ With **multiple-unit pricing,** a retailer offers discounts to customers who buy in quantity. For example, by selling items at two for $0.75 or six for $2.19, a retailer would attempt to sell more products than at $0.39 each. See Figure 16-6.

There are two reasons for using multiple-unit pricing. First, a retailer could seek to have customers increase their total purchases of an item. However, if customers buy multiple units to stockpile them, instead of consuming more, the firm's overall sales would not increase. Second, multiple-unit pricing could let a retailer clear out slow-moving and end-of-season merchandise.

Price Lining ❑ Rather than stock merchandise at all different price levels, retailers often employ **price lining** and sell merchandise at a limited range of price points, with each point representing a distinct level of quality. With price lining, retailers first determine their price floors and ceilings in each product category. They then set a limited number of price points within the range. As an example, department stores generally carry good, better, and best versions of merchandise that are consistent with their overall price policy—and set individual prices accordingly.

Price lining benefits both consumers and retailers. It lessens shopping confusion for consumers. If the price range for a box of handkerchiefs is $6 to $15 and the price points are $6, $9, and $15, consumers would know that distinct product qualities exist. However, should a retailer have prices of $6, $7, $8, $9, $10, $11, $12, $13, $14, an the consumer may be confused about product qualities and differences.

For retailers, price lining greatly aids the merchandise buying and handling process. Retail buyers can seek out only those suppliers carrying products at appropriate prices,

Figure 16-6

Multiple-Unit Pricing

The one-cent sale shown here is a form of multiple-unit pricing. The intent is to increase consumer patronage by bundling the purchase price of two items together.

and the buyers can keep in mind final selling prices in negotiating with suppliers. Retailers can automatically disregard products not fitting within price lines and thereby reduce inventory investment. Also, stock turnover is greatly increased by limiting the models carried.

Four difficulties do exist with price lining. First, depending on the price points selected, a price-lining strategy may have gaps between prices that are perceived as too large by consumers. Thus, a parent shopping for a graduation gift might find a $30 briefcase to be too inexpensive and a $120 briefcase to be too expensive. Second, inflation can make it tough to maintain price points and price ranges. When costs rise, retailers can either eliminate lower-priced items or reduce markups. Third, markdowns or special sales may disrupt the balance in a price line, unless all items in that line are reduced proportionally. Fourth, price lines must be coordinated for complementary product categories, such as blazers, skirts, and shoes.

Price Adjustments

Price adjustments allow retailers to use price as an adaptive mechanism. Markdowns and additional markups may be necessary in reacting to such factors as competition, seasonality, demand patterns, merchandise costs, and pilferage. Figure 16-7 shows a price change authorization form.

A **markdown** from the original retail price of an item may be used to meet the lower price of another retailer, adapt to inventory overstocking, clear out shopworn merchandise, reduce assortments of odds and ends, and increase customer traffic. An **additional markup** is an increase in a retail price above the original markup that is used when demand is unexpectedly high or costs are rising. In today's competitive marketplace, markdowns are applied by retailers much more frequently than additional markups.

Figure 16-7

A Price Change Authorization Form

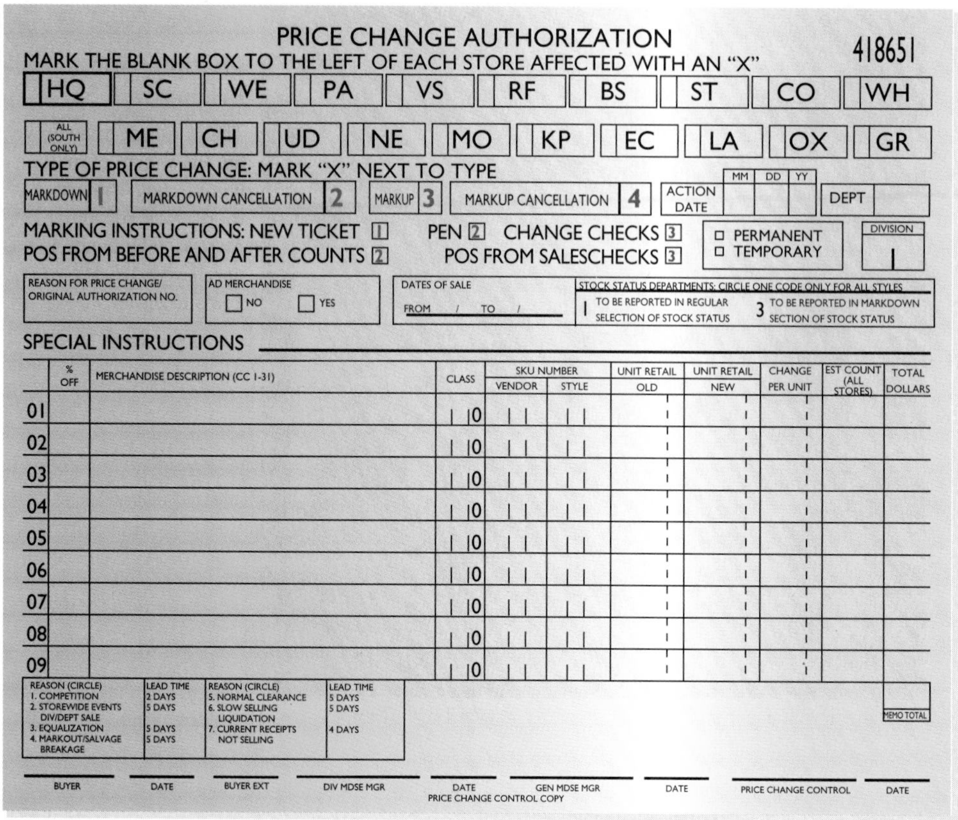
PRICE CHANGE AUTHORIZATION 418651

MARK THE BLANK BOX TO THE LEFT OF EACH STORE AFFECTED WITH AN "X"

HQ SC WE PA VS RF BS ST CO WH

ALL (SOUTH ONLY) ME CH UD NE MO KP EC LA OX GR

TYPE OF PRICE CHANGE: MARK "X" NEXT TO TYPE

MARKDOWN 1 MARKDOWN CANCELLATION 2 MARKUP 3 MARKUP CANCELLATION 4 ACTION DATE MM DD YY DEPT

MARKING INSTRUCTIONS: NEW TICKET 1 PEN 2 CHANGE CHECKS 3 □ PERMANENT □ TEMPORARY DIVISION 1

POS FROM BEFORE AND AFTER COUNTS 2 POS FROM SALESCHECKS 3

REASON FOR PRICE CHANGE/ ORIGINAL AUTHORIZATION NO. | AD MERCHANDISE □ NO □ YES | DATES OF SALE FROM / TO / | STOCK STATUS DEPARTMENTS: CIRCLE ONE CODE ONLY FOR ALL STYLES 1 TO BE REPORTED IN REGULAR SELECTION OF STOCK STATUS 3 TO BE REPORTED IN MARKDOWN SECTION OF STOCK STATUS

SPECIAL INSTRUCTIONS

	% OFF	MERCHANDISE DESCRIPTION (CC 1-31)	CLASS	SKU NUMBER VENDOR	SKU NUMBER STYLE	UNIT RETAIL OLD	UNIT RETAIL NEW	CHANGE PER UNIT	EST COUNT (ALL STORES)	TOTAL DOLLARS
01			10							
02			10							
03			10							
04			10							
05			10							
06			10							
07			10							
08			10							
09			10							

REASON (CIRCLE)	LEAD TIME	REASON (CIRCLE)	LEAD TIME
1. COMPETITION	2 DAYS	5. NORMAL CLEARANCE	5 DAYS
2. STOREWIDE EVENTS DIV/DEPT SALE	5 DAYS	6. SLOW SELLING LIQUIDATION	5 DAYS
3. EQUALIZATION	5 DAYS	7. CURRENT RECEIPTS NOT SELLING	4 DAYS
4. MARKOUT/SALVAGE BREAKAGE	5 DAYS		

MEMO TOTAL

BUYER DATE BUYER EXT DIV MDSE MGR DATE GEN MDSE MGR DATE PRICE CHANGE CONTROL DATE

PRICE CHANGE CONTROL COPY

A third price adjustment, discounts to employees, is mentioned here since such discounts may affect the computation of markdowns and additional markups. Also, although these discounts are not an adaptive mechanism, they influence morale. Some firms give employee discounts on all items and also let workers buy sale items before are made available to the general public.

Computing Markdowns and Additional Markups ❑ Markdowns and additional markups can be calculated in dollars (total dollar markdown or markup) or percentages. Two ways of determining a markdown are the markdown percentage and the off-retail percentage.

The **markdown percentage** is the total dollar markdown as a percentage of net sales (in dollars) and is computed as

$$\text{Markdown percentage} = \frac{\text{Total dollar markdown}}{\text{Net sales (in \$)}}$$

A difficulty with this formula is that net sales must reflect additional markups and employee discounts (along with dollar markdowns). Also, the formula does not enable a retailer to learn the percentage of items that are marked down as compared to those sold at the original price.

A complementary measure is the **off-retail markdown percentage,** which looks at the markdown for each item or category of items as a percentage of original retail price:

$$\text{Off-retail markdown percentage} = \frac{\text{Original price} - \text{New price}}{\text{Original price}}$$

Do Consumers Trust Retail "Sale" Advertising?

An experiment was recently conducted in which college students were exposed to one of 12 different versions of a retail price advertisement for a fashion T-shirt. The 12 ads differed in terms of the rationale of the price (no rationale, an "excess inventory" rationale, and a "volume purchase" rationale), the reference price used (either no reference price or a $20 reference price), and the selling price of the product (either $9.99 or $14.00).

After seeing the ads, the subjects were asked to report on their perceptions of the value of the advertised deal. They were also asked about their attitude toward the offer and their perceptions of the retailer's credibility.

The study found that advertising a product at a much lower than expected price (50 percent lower versus 25 percent lower) may make an offer more attractive without reducing the retailer's credibility. It also suggests that including the $20.00 regular price did not have a major effect on the consumer's perception of the offer or retailer (since this price was the typical price charged by local retailers). Lastly, respondents were more favorable when the offer was presented with a volume-purchase explanation (in terms of the attitude toward the offer, the perceived value of the offer, and their judgment of retailer credibility) than when the offer price was presented with an inventory reduction rationale or no rationale at all.

Source: George S. Bobinski, Jr., Dena Cox, and Anthony Cox, "Retail 'Sale' Advertising, Perceived Retailer Credibility, and Price Rationale," *Journal of Retailing,* Vol. 72 (Fall 1996), pp. 291–306.

With this formula, the markdown percentage for every item can be computed, as well as the percentage of items marked down.

Suppose a gas barbecue grill sells for $100 at the beginning of the summer and is reduced to $70 at the end of the summer. The off-retail markdown is 30 percent [($100 − $70)/$100]. If 100 grills are sold at the original price and 20 are sold at the sale price, the percentage of items marked down is 17 percent, and the total dollar markdown is $600.

The **additional markup percentage** looks at total dollar additional markups as a percentage of net sales, while the **addition to retail percentage** measures a price rise as a percentage of original price:

$$\text{Additional markup percentage} = \frac{\text{Total dollar additional markups}}{\text{Net sales (in \$)}}$$

$$\text{Addition to retail percentage} = \frac{\text{New price} - \text{Original price}}{\text{Original price}}$$

Retailers need to be aware that price adjustments affect their markups per unit and that significantly more customers would have to be attracted at reduced prices to attain a total gross profit equal to that at higher prices. The impact of a markdown or an additional markup on total gross profit may be ascertained through this formula:

$$\begin{array}{l}\text{Unit sales required to} \\ \text{earn the same total} \\ \text{gross profit with a} \\ \text{price adjustment}\end{array} = \frac{\text{Original markup (\%)}}{\text{Original markup (\%)} +/- \text{Price change (\%)}} \times \begin{array}{l}\text{Expected unit} \\ \text{sales at} \\ \text{original price}\end{array}$$

At a specialty store, suppose a Sony Walkman with a cost of $50 has an original retail price of $100, which is a markup of 50 percent. The firm expects to sell 500 units over the next year, leading to a total gross profit of $25,000 ($50 × 500). How many units would the retailer have to sell if it reduces the price to $85 or raises it to $110 and still e

$$\text{Unit sales required} \atop \text{(at \$85)} = \frac{50\%}{50\% - 15\%} \times 500 = 1.43 \times 500 = 714$$

$$\text{Unit sales required} \atop \text{(at \$110)} = \frac{50\%}{50\% + 10\%} \times 500 = 0.83 \times 500 = 417$$

A retailer's judgment regarding price adjustments would be affected by its operating expenses at various sales volumes and customer price elasticities.

Markdown Control ❏ Through markdown control, a retailer evaluates the number of markdowns, their proportion of sales, and their causes. This control must be such that buying plans can be altered in later periods to reflect markdowns. A good way to evaluate their causes is to have retail buyers record the reasons for each markdown and examine these reasons regularly. Possible buyer notations are "end of season," "to match the price of a competitor," "worn merchandise," and "obsolete style."

Markdown control lets a firm monitor its policies, such as the way items are stored and late acceptance of fashion shipments. Careful planning may also enable a retailer to avoid some markdowns by running more ads, training workers better, shipping goods more efficiently among branch units, and returning items to vendors. Table 16-8 cites ten ways to control markdowns.

The need for markdown control should not be interpreted as meaning that all markdowns can or should be minimized or eliminated. In fact, too low a markdown percentage may indicate that a retailer's buyers have not assumed enough risk in purchasing goods. See Figure 16-8.

Timing Markdowns ❏ Although there is some disagreement among retailers as to the best timing sequence for markdowns, much can be said about the benefits of implementing an early markdown policy. First, this policy offers merchandise at reduced

Table 16-8 TEN WAYS TO CONTROL MARKDOWNS

1. Adhere to a buying plan in terms of the quantities to be ordered, and the timing of receipt of merchandise. Do not buy too much merchandise to secure an additional quantity discount or promotional allowance. Learn to say "no" to vendors' salespeople.

2. Be an important customer. Limit the number of vendors with which you deal. Bargain for the right to exchange slow-selling merchandise during the season, if necessary.

3. Evaluate the reasons for slow-selling merchandise. Can additional displays or sales incentives quicken the sales pace?

4. Carefully study the impact of special purchases on the sale of traditional merchandise.

5. Be careful in size selection. It may be wise to risk being out of stock, for example, in very small and very large sizes versus having to take drastic markdowns.

6. Maintain a perpetual inventory of large-ticket items to avoid large markdowns.

7. Limit spoilage by properly caring for and displaying perishable or breakable goods, and by using appropriate packaging and containers.

8. Monitor layaway payments. Beware of an item being held back for a long period of time and then not being wanted by a customer. Request partial pre-payments to hold a layaway item.

9. Make sure that salespeople are properly motivated and trained.

10. Staple merchandise can generally be carried over to next year. The carrying costs must be weighed against the size of the necessary markdown, potential increases in price next year, shelf space occupied, shipping costs, etc.

Source: Adapted by the authors from William Burston, *A Checklist of 38 Ways of Controlling Markdowns* (New York: National Retail Federation, n.d.).

Figure 16-8

Parisian's Approach to Markdowns

Besides having traditional sales to boost the turnover of merchandise, Parisian has a separate room for clearance items. Customers know exactly where to look for these goods and the selling floor is not cluttered by old or discontinued merchandise.

prices when demand is still fairly active. Second, an early markdown policy requires lower markdowns to sell products than markdowns late in the selling season. Third, early markdowns free selling space for new merchandise. Fourth, a retailer's cash flow position can be improved.

The main advantage of a late markdown policy is that a retailer gives itself every opportunity to sell merchandise at original prices. Yet, the advantages associated with an early markdown policy cannot be achieved under a late markdown policy.

Retailers can also use a staggered markdown policy, whereby prices are discounted throughout the selling season. One totally pre-planned staggered markdown policy for reducing prices through a selling season involves an **automatic markdown plan.** In such a plan, the amount and timing of markdowns are controlled by the length of time the merchandise remains in stock. Filene's Basement applies markdowns under this timetable:

Length of Time in Stock	Percentage Markdown (from Original Price)
12 selling days	25
18 selling days	50
24 selling days	75
30 selling days	Given to charity

Such a plan ensures fresh stock and early markdowns.

A storewide clearance, usually conducted once or twice a year, is another way to time markdowns. Often a storewide clearance takes place after peak selling periods like Christmas and Mother's Day. The goal is to clean out merchandise before taking a physical inventory and beginning the next season. The advantages of a storewide clearance over an automatic (staggered) markdown policy are that a longer period is provided for selling merchandise at original prices; frequent markdowns can destroy a consumer's confidence in a retailer's regular pricing policy: "Why buy now, when it will be on sale next week?" An automatic policy may also encourage a steady stream of bargain hunters who are not potential customers for the firm's regular merchandise, while clearance sales limit bargain hunting to once or twice a year.

Retailers should be concerned about too frequent a use of markdowns. In the past, many retailers would introduce merchandise at high prices and then mark down prices on many items by as much as 60 percent to increase store traffic and improve inventory turnover. This caused customers to wait for price reductions and treat initial prices with skepticism. Today, a great number of retailers lower initial markup percentages, run fewer sales, and apply fewer markdowns than before. Nonetheless, one of the biggest problems facing some retailers is that they have gotten consumers too used to buying when items are discounted:

Remember all the nifty bargains you found shopping last year? So do retailers. And they vow never again. Retailers have countered slowing demand with constant discounting, trying to spur demand by giving up profits. Now, after one of their least profitable years, they are ruling out another avalanche of sales and markdowns. To make more money, they are deploying an array of merchandising gimmicks to wean shoppers off their addiction to deep discounts. There's just one catch: Shoppers' addiction to the steal lingers on. "An OK sale is 25 percent. A good sale is 40 percent. But if you can wait, you can do even better than that," says Barbara Meyer, a Chicago resident and loyal customer of Marshall Field, a local retailing institution. "I know everyone has to make their money, but I just feel somehow taken when I pay full price." Deirdre Flaherty, a management consultant, agrees: "There are certain stores where I would feel horribly guilty buying anything at full price because everything eventually goes on sale."

To reacquaint such shoppers with the joy of paying full price, some big retailers are conducting what amounts to a mass effort at behavior modification. Dayton Hudson is halving the number of sales "events" at its department stores. Shopping mall stores, from women's clothier Ann Taylor to kid-clothes merchan Gymboree, are trying to encourage full-price purchases by displaying fewer clothes. "If there's a jacket you love and you see only six on a rack, you're m likely to pay full price for it," says Ann Taylor's chief executive. Even Federated Department Stores, whose Macy's and Bloomingdale's stores have thrived by offering good deals, says it plans to abandon high-low pricing over the next five years and gradually switch to an everyday-low-pricing strategy, also called "value pricing." Though unthinkable a few years ago, the move is crucial to Federated's plans. "We are looking for more credible day-in-and-day-out prices," declares Federated's chief executive.[14]

[14]Laura Bird, "Apparel Stores Seek to Cure Shoppers Addicted to Discounts," *Wall Street Journal* (May 29, 1996), p. A1.

Summary

1. *To describe the role of pricing in a retail strategy and to show that pricing decisions must be made in an integrated and adaptive manner* Pricing is crucial to a retailer because of its interrelationship with overall objectives and the other components of the retail strategy mix. A price strategy must be integrated an responsive—and provide a good value to customers.

2. *To examine the impact of consumers; government; manufacturers, wholesalers, and other suppliers; and current and potential competitors on pricing decisions* Before devising a price strategy, a retailer must study the factors affecting pricing. Sometimes, the factors have a minor effect on a retailer's pricing discretion; other times, they severely limit pricing options.

With regard to consumers, retailers should be familiar with the price elasticity of demand and the different market segments that are possible. Government restrictions deal with horizontal and vertical price fixing, price discrimination, minimum prices, unit pricing, item price removal, and price advertising. Manufacturers, wholesalers, and other suppliers be required to provide price guarantees (if they are in a position of weakness) and there may be conflicts about which party controls retail prices. The competitive environment may foster market pricing, which could lead to price wars, or administered pricing.

3. *To present a framework for developing a retail price strategy* Such a framework consists of five stages:

objectives, broad price policy, price strategy, implementation of price strategy, and price adjustments.

Retail pricing goals can be chosen from among sales, dollar profits, return on investment, and/or early recovery of cash. After they are chosen, a broad policy is set and a coordinated series of actions is outlined, consistent with the retailer's image and oriented to the short and long run.

A price strategy integrates demand, cost, and competitive concepts. Each of these orientations must be understood separately and jointly. Psychological pricing, markup pricing, alternative ways of computing markups, gross margin, direct product profitability, and pricing below, at, or above the market are among the key aspects of strategy planning.

When enacting a price strategy, several specific tools can be used to supplement the broad base of the strategy. Retailers should be familiar with and know when to use customary and variable pricing, one-price policies and flexible pricing, odd pricing, leader pricing, multiple-unit pricing, and price lining.

Price adjustments may be necessary for a retailer to adapt to various internal and external conditions. Adjustments include markdowns, additional markups, and employee discounts. It is important that adjustments are controlled by a budget, the causes of markdowns are noted, future company buying reflects earlier errors or adaptations, adjustments are properly timed, and excessive discounting be avoided.

Key Terms

price elasticity of demand (p. 506)
horizontal price fixing (p. 508)
vertical price fixing (p. 509)
Robinson-Patman Act (p. 510)
minimum-price laws (p. 510)
predatory pricing (p. 510)
loss leaders (p. 510)
unit pricing (p. 511)
item price removal (p. 511)
bait advertising (bait-and-switch advertising) (p. 512)
price guarantees (p. 512)
selling against the brand (p. 513)
gray market goods (p. 513)
market penetration (p. 514)
market skimming (p. 514)
demand-oriented pricing (p. 518)

cost-oriented pricing (p. 518)
competition-oriented pricing (p. 518)
psychological pricing (p. 518)
price-quality association (p. 518)
prestige pricing (p. 519)
markup pricing (p. 519)
markup (p. 519)
markup percentage (p. 519)
initial markup (p. 521)
maintained markup (p. 521)
gross margin (p. 522)
variable markup policy (p. 522)
direct product profitability (DPP) (p. 523)
customary pricing (p. 526)
everyday low pricing (EDLP) (p. 526)

variable pricing (p. 526)
one-price policy (p. 527)
flexible pricing (p. 527)
odd pricing (p. 527)
leader pricing (p. 527)
multiple-unit pricing (p. 528)
price lining (p. 528)
markdown (p. 529)
additional markup (p. 529)
markdown percentage (p. 530)
off-retail markdown percentage (p. 530)
additional markup percentage (p. 531)
addition to retail percentage (p. 531)
automatic markdown plan (p. 533)

Questions for Discussion

1. Why is it important for retailers to understand the concept of price elasticity even if they cannot compute it?
2. Comment on each of the following from the perspective of a small retailer:
   a. Horizontal price fixing.
   b. Vertical price fixing.
   c. Price discrimination.
   d. Minimum-price law.
   e. Item price removal.
3. Why do some retailers sell gray market goods?
4. Give an example of a price strategy that integrates demand, cost, and competitive criteria.
5. Explain why markups are usually computed as a percentage of selling price rather than of cost.
6. A floor tile retailer wants to receive a 35 percent markup (at retail) for all merchandise. If one style of tile retails for $9 per tile, what is the maximum that the retailer would be willing to pay for a tile?
7. A car dealer purchases multiple-disc CD players for $150 each and desires a 40 percent markup (at retail). What retail price should be charged?
8. A photo store charges $11.00 to process a roll of slides; its cost is $7.00. What is the markup percentage (at cost and at retail)?
9. A retailer has planned operating expenses of $110,000, a profit goal of $60,000, and planned reductions of $31,000 and expects annual sales to be $600,000. Compute the initial markup percentage.
10. At the end of the year, the retailer in Question 9 determines that actual operating expenses are $120,000, actual profit is $42,000, and actual sales are $600,000. What is the maintained markup percentage? Explain the difference in your answers to Questions 9 and 10.
11. What are the advantages and disadvantages of the direct product profitability concept?
12. What are the pros and cons of everyday low pricing to a retailer? To a manufacturer?
13. What is the difference between markdown percentage and off-retail percentage?
14. A retailer buys merchandise for $35. At an original retail price of $55, it expects to sell 1,000 units.
    a. If the price is marked down to $47, how many units must the retailer sell to earn the same total gross profit it would attain with a $55 price?
    b. If the price is marked up to $65, how many units must the retailer sell to earn the same total gross profit it would attain with a $55 price?

Web-Based Exercise:

SAMPLESALE (http://www.samplesale.com)

Questions

1. Describe the SampleSale Web site.
2. Evaluate this Web site from a consumer perspective. From a retailer perspective.
3. Why do you think the SampleSale Web site generally does not mention regular and current prices for specific items? Comment on this.
4. As a store-based retailer, under what conditions would you *not* want to be listed on a Web site such as SampleSale? Explain your answer.

CASE 1
Dahl's Fair Practices*

Dahl's operates 14 supermarkets, 11 in Des Moines, Iowa, and 3 in Kansas City, Missouri. The company's pricing strategy can be best defined as "everyday regular prices," with 150 core items priced competitively. Although Dahl's market share on food in Des Moines has been estimated to be as high as 40 percent, it faces tough competition from Hy-Vee, which has a similar market share. In addition, its pharmacy operations must compete with Walgreen, a number of independent drug stores, three Kmarts, and two Wal-Marts.

Dahl's pricing practices are governed by a fair-practices statement clarifying its relationships with suppliers and customers. Table 1 shows its expectations with regard to suppliers. Dahl's fair-practices statement effectively meets goals such as these: By eliminating the usual "give-and-take" of negotiations, Dahl's and its suppliers save time and money. Dahl's knows it is getting the lowest legal price for products in each market area. It is given access to the same offers as other classes of retailers. For example, compliance with fair practices means that suppliers offer the same value-sized packages of goods to supermarkets that they offer to membership chains, and forward buying and diverting abuses are not allowed.

With forward buying, retailers receive special discounts, such as "$5 off the invoiced price per case," for buying a given quantity of merchandise. In return for the discounts, retailers agree to buy the manufacturers' products over a specified period, provide suitable shelf space, and pass on the savings to final consumers through sales prices. However, an abuse takes place if supermarkets (or other retailers) buy three weeks of merchandise during the last week of a promotion and then charge their customers the full retail price for three additional weeks beyond the promotion.

In diverting, manufacturers provide special discounts to retailers to gain market share in specific market areas. Yet, an abuse occurs when retailers buy a large quantity and then resell much of it to retailers located outside the markets where special promotions are offered. Firms that divert can profit by pocketing the difference between their cost and the resale price to other retailers. For manufacturers, diverting results in their being unable to meet regional sales goals and their loss of control. Thus, a manufacturer's specially priced goods aimed at the Milwaukee market could end up in a New York store that is not a recognized manufacturer's account.

Questions
1. Comment on Table 1 from Dahl's perspective.
2. Comment on Table 1 from the perspective of Dahl's suppliers.
3. What is the impact of everyday low pricing on forward buying?
4. How can a manufacturer control diverting?

Video Questions on Dahl's
1. What portions of Dahl's fair-practices statement are governed by the Robinson-Patman Act?
2. Can a membership chain retailer legally get a lower price than Dahl's? Explain your answer.

*The material in this case is drawn from *Dahl's Food Fairness Statement* (Des Moines, Iowa: n.d.); and "Getting Out and About," *Supermarket Business* (March 1995), pp. 85–87.

CASE 1
(Continued)

Table 1   SELECTED PRICING STRATEGIES AND TACTICS COVERED BY DAHL'S FAIR-PRACTICES STATEMENT

■ Dahl's wants to be viewed by all suppliers as a customer that handles business dealings professionally, equitably, and fairly.

■ Dahl's expects manufacturers, their sales agents, and distributors to observe the spirit and the letter of the Robinson-Patman Act. For example, Dahl's will not request special prices, allowances, or services from manufacturers or their sales agents if they know such prices, allowances, or services would force the manufacturer to unlawfully discriminate against other customers within the same market area.

■ Dahl's expects all suppliers to deal fairly with the company.

■ Manufacturers should not make distinctions among competing distributor customers within the same market area based on the "class of trade" or distributor format in the same market area. Thus, if a manufacturer develops prices, terms, promotions, deals, or packs for a particular class or distributor format, the manufacturer should inform ALL competing distributor customers within the same market area of the special offer and grant them an opportunity to qualify for the offer.

■ Dahl's plans to carefully review all its policies and practices to be sure they will be applied equitably to all suppliers. It does not want any of its suppliers to have an unfair advantage over its competitors.

■ According to Dahl's, this statement "has been read and understood by all members of our organization. (All executives, all store managers, and all department managers.) Individually and collectively, we are committed to its ongoing implementation."

■ The retailer abuses of forward buying and diverting (that have been used by some firms to obtain profits at the expense of suppliers) are not allowed.

CASE 2
Mr. 2nd's: Thriving on Closeouts[†]

In early 1996, Grossman's, a home improvement retailer specializing in lumber and building material products, closed its 60 or so remaining Grossman's stores and decided to concentrate on three businesses: Mr. 2nd's Bargain Outlet, Contractors' Warehouse, and Builder's Mart. Mr. 2nd's Bargain Outlet (http://www.bargain-outlets.com) specializes in the sale of closeout home improvement-related goods such as rebuilt power tools, rebuilt major appliances (particularly washers, dryers, and refrigerators), off-grade lumber, ready-to-assemble furniture, and seasonal goods. There are now 25 Mr. 2nd's outlets, some in former Grossman's locations. The 15 Contractors' Warehouse stores are aimed at home builders, general contractors, and other home care professionals. Grossman's has a 50 percent ownership interest in Builder's Mart, a Mexican retailer with a store format and strategy similar to Contractors' Warehouse.

As a closeout retailer, Mr. 2nd's does not have a consistent selection of merchandise. In some cases, merchandise quantities are in such short supply that these goods are offered in only one market area; in other cases, goods are available chainwide on a limited time basis. If they can be acquired at the right price, the chain carries seasonal items (such as gas grills and picnic sets) out of season. According to the vice-president and general merchandise manager for Mr. 2nd's, "We buy what we can get. We'll make a bulk buy if it's a deal. We buy opportunistically." This means Mr. 2nd's is prepared to purchase varying quantities of a product from a wide variety of sources. Its major purchasing criterion is whether the product can be priced low enough at retail to be a real bargain to consumers, as well as profitable for the retailer.

While some of Mr. 2nd's merchandise is bought from distributors and brokers specializing in factory surplus and seconds, other merchandise comes from vendor buybacks (in which suppliers purchase the remaining stock of competitors' products to secure retail shelf space for their own products) or from manufacturer overstocks (due to canceled orders from other retailers or manufacturers' inaccurate demand forecasting).

[†] The material in this case is drawn from David P. Schulz, "Mr. 2nd's Pursues Closeout Strategy," *Stores* (July 1996), pp. 68–70; and *Grossman's 10K for the Fiscal Year Ended December 31, 1995.*

As a price-oriented retailer, Mr. 2nd's pays close attention to both its costs and target market. Thus, although the chain carefully watches its rental costs, it also avoids low-rent industrial park locations that are difficult for its retail customers to find. To reduce its advertising costs, Mr. 2nd's new sites are generally in existing or adjacent market areas served by the firm's existing newspaper media. The chain also advertises consistently on the back page of the Sunday comics section. This strategy locks out this space from competitors and results in its quantity discounts from the media. Mr. 2nd's has a no-frills, self-service low overhead format. This strategy is ideally suited for its target market of do-it-yourself consumers who are seeking a cost-effective alternative to traditional home improvement centers. Many of these customers are loyal shoppers who seek out the chain's bargain prices despite its varying merchandise selection.

Grossman's distinguishes between the merchandise offerings for Mr. 2nd's and Contractors' Warehouse. This means Mr. 2nd's is not an outlet store for the Contractors' Warehouse division. Because each of these chains operates in different U.S. regions—Mr. 2nd's stores are in the Northeast and Contractors' Warehouse stores are in the West and Midwest, the transfer of merchandise between these units would not be economical.

Mr. 2nd's recently began marketing selected merchandise through its Web site. By using this site, the firm can extend its geographic reach beyond the Northeast at low cost.

Questions

1. Evaluate Mr. 2nd's pricing strategy.
2. Is Mr. 2nd's pricing strategy well-integrated? Explain your answer.
3. Should Mr. 2nd's charge the same price for merchandise at its stores and through its Web site? Explain your answer.
4. Comment on this statement: "Mr. 2nd's major purchasing criterion is whether the product can be priced low enough at retail to be a real bargain to consumers, as well as profitable for the retailer."

INTRODUCTION

Competition has forced many supermarkets to look closely at their food-service pricing strategy. The result? The industry is sharply divided over what works best for bakeries and delis.

Battered by discounters in the grocery aisles, painted by the national media as the underdog in a losing battle against other formats, and seeing profitability slip in a number of areas, supermarket operators are looking for some salvation in the bakery and deli. But even there, where gross margins average from 45 percent to 53 percent, firms are learning that they have to tailor their marketing as never before. "I believe pricing and competition in bakeries and delis will become more fierce," says Bob Baxley, the director of deli and food service at HEB (H. E. Butt), San Antonio, Texas. "With the technological advances in information systems, we will be armed with better and more timely information to help us focus on opportunities to improve both sales and profits."

SETTING A CLEARLY DEFINED STRATEGY

Having a clearly defined pricing strategy is critical to the success of bakeries and delis. "The company that tries to be all things to all people is going to lose," says Carol Christison, the executive director, International Dairy-Deli-Bakery Association, based in Madison, Wisconsin.

Some firms try to draw more customers into the food-service areas with everyday low prices (EDLP), while others concentrate on service, convenience, or special signature items. There is a growing debate, however, over the effectiveness of applying long-time grocery pricing strategies to food-service areas.

"The corporate mission will dictate pricing," according to Christison. "You are going to have loss leaders, whether they are nickel cookies or specials on Tide detergent. But you cannot apply the overall grocery model to the food-service area. The bottom line is that the perception by the consumer is different."

Others defend using traditional grocery pricing, saying aggressive pricing strategies are still the best road to profitability. "I really don't see a great deal of change," says Charlie Myers, group vice-president for bakery/deli operations at Fleming, based in Oklahoma City. "Our pricing philosophy is much the same, using EDLP and specials to create excitement. We offer value on key products to generate gross profit through a blended average."

Then, of course, there are the industry experts who say price is way down on the list of what attracts customers to the supermarket bakery and deli. "Convenience is high, then variety and taste," says Edward McLaughlin, Cornell University professor of marketing and the food industry marketing program. "Price runs about fourth on the list" for supermarket bakeries and delis.

Industry consultants agree that grocery pricing won't be what attracts more customers to bakeries and delis. In fact, they recommend charging more for some items. "We work with retailers to develop the specialty items to counter that traditional type of grocery marketing," says Howard Solganik, a consultant with Solganik & Associates.

Most of the deli and bakery competition is not the supermarket down the street, he says, but other food-service operations. And in that arena, low prices aren't nearly as important as improving the perception of supermarket quality. "Look at Boston Market prices," says Solganik. In general, food stores "are still selling chickens too cheaply because they are too scared to raise customers' expectations. The supermarkets are afraid customers might say, 'Wow, for $6, this must be a good chicken.'"

Buck Jones, an industry consultant with Jonessco Enterprises, says grocery pricing strategies that were devised 15 or 20 years ago need to be changed to meet

*The material in this case was adapted by the authors from Terry Hennessy, of *Progressive Grocer*, "Is the Price Right?" *Progressive Grocer* (November 1995), pp. 107–116. Copyright *Progressive Grocer*. Reprinted by permission.

growing competition from other food-service operators and, more importantly, to meet customers' evolving needs. "The main difference is that restaurants market food, and we sell as we would sell groceries. As such, customers perceive them quite differently. If we want to continue to sell groceries—piling them up and selling them cheap—that's fine; but grocery selling is quite different from food selling. Food selling depends on convenience, getting the customer in and out, and developing side dishes."

PUSHING SUPERMARKETS TO THINK DIFFERENTLY ABOUT PRICING

Learning from successful companies is essential. Minneapolis-based Fairway Foods, which supplies 150 in-store bakery operations and 19 corporate stores in the upper Midwest, is pushing store operators to do just that. "We have been trying to get the stores to wake up a bit, get a little sharper," says Tim Ulschmid, bakery director. "We want them to look at what some of the retail bakeries are doing. To be successful they have to be doing something right." At one Fairview-supplied store in a small Minnesota town, management decided the bakery would only sell what it baked that day, concentrating on freshness. Ulschmid applauds the effort: "Sometimes in-store bakeries shoot themselves in the foot by seeing how long they can keep items on shelves."

In the San Francisco Bay area, the delis and bakeries in Andronico's half-dozen stores don't even try to compete on many prices. "Our delis are not comparable to chain delis in offerings," says president Bill Andronico. "We are not positioning ourselves to be in the center of pricing pressure. On certain bakery items, there is a little pressure. We do some signature items in-house, but bring in all the bread. On the lunch meat side, we try to deal on the higher end of the quality spectrum. Chains don't compete. It's too expensive and there is not enough street traffic to justify it for them." The niche seems to be working for Andronico's, which has added new stores.

No one—professors, consultants, or retailers—is suggesting that pricing isn't important. Even at Andronico's, the company pays attention to competitors' prices on branded and commodity items. "It's a mixed thing for us," says Andronico. "If it's branded, we need to be aware of prices from competitors. We are always walking the line between sales and gross margin. We are always trying to maximize gross profit dollars."

While some of the decisions on pricing strategies have to do with corporate culture, a large part of the equation has to do with economic factors. "If the economy is pressing hard on people's shoulders, they tend to be more price-conscious," says Peter Houstle, executive vice-president of the Retailer's Bakery-Deli Association. "However, if you press too hard on price, someone else will come out with quality. The classic example is the freestanding bread bakeries. That proves there are people who are willing to pay $3 a loaf for bread."

Fleming's Charlie Myers agrees supermarkets must have their fingers on the pulse of the market. "It is important to be able to communicate to consumers that you have what they want. In food service, you must be able to provide them with an acceptable alternative. Competition is not just a supermarket down the street or around the corner. It is also fast-food and delivery operations."

Several experts cite Boston Market as a prime example of a deli competitor that came into a market dominated by supermarkets and won a healthy portion of the business simply by knowing what consumers wanted. "For years, supermarkets felt they could not go over $4 to $5 for barbecue chicken," says Jones. "Then Boston Market came in and charged $8 to $9."

CHANGING CONSUMER PERCEPTIONS

The entry of Boston Market and others has actually helped raise people's perceptions, says Jones; and that can help supermarkets—if they embrace the new marketing strategy that goes along with the price. "We need to look at why customers are willing to go there and spend $8 for a roasted chicken and at what things we aren't providing"—including making it easy for customers to get in and out, providing a full meal selection, and keeping the food looking fresh all the time.

Comparing price—while touting quality—doesn't hurt, either. In one of the more creative ads pitting price and quality against major competitors, WiseWay Super Centers ran a full-page newspaper ad with the screaming headline: "Kick The Bucket." The ad compared WiseWay's $3.98 roasted chicken with the same meal for more than $7 at KFC.

"The point," says WiseWay President Don Weiss, "was that compared with KFC and Boston Market, our store was a tremendous value." Weiss is aiming advertising squarely at the emerging food-service competition, not other supermarkets' delis and bakeries. "We are different from other supermarkets, as far as quality.

But all supermarkets as a class are less expensive," he says. "We must convince customers we have comparable quality to Boston Market and the others."

Baxley of H.E. Butt agrees that supermarkets must launch a full-scale assault to change the perceptions by customers: "The supermarket industry must deal with the onslaught of prepared meal choices being offered by all competition, including all styles of restaurants, as well as other meal distribution channels."

Jeff Kollmeyer, a spokesperson for eight-store Smitty's Supermarkets in Missouri, believes supermarkets must make sure they are competitive while they develop signature items: "You cannot afford to ignore competition; you have to evolve or other stores will copy you and take customers." While the major marketing factors in bakeries and delis are both quality and variety, more and more expect the price to be much more competitive. "There are some who will accept that they have to pay a bit more for the product quality, but that margin has been shrinking."

The whole trick to success is building on a solid foundation, according to industry experts. "When you look back at successful food operations," says Jones, "they started with a basic product, built a customer following, and then began expanding. KFC started with the original chicken recipe, McDonald's with a hamburger and fries, and Boston Market with roasted chicken. "You need to learn the disciplines and controls before you begin to expand. It's ridiculous to think you can start with a full variety."

Jones suggests that supermarket operators look through their menu of Mexican food, chicken, roast beef, and hamburgers, and then pick one or two to make signature items. Although Boston Market and KFC have already built an image of quality food service, they can't match supermarket prices. So once customers feel supermarket deli quality matches the Boston Markets of the world, supermarkets will have taken a giant step in addressing the advantages of some of their toughest competitors. "Pricing is important. But the typical supermarket marketing has been to reduce prices. These new entrants into food marketing should teach us to market differently—not just based on price."

In an effort to do a better job of marketing and managing the deli and bakery, some supermarket operators are turning to category management. In a recent study, IDDA asked grocers to rate 100 topics; and the top five all dealt with category management. "The food-service department is different than the grocery department," says Christison, "and you can't apply the grocery marketing and management plan to the deli. The idea is to manage strategic business units individually to produce the enhanced business results by focusing on delivering consumer value."

Not only does Christison recommend managing the categories differently, she suggests micromarketing to provide the best possible customer service: "You just can't make sweeping generalizations. When you go into upscale stores, for example, you often run into the mortgage poor, people who have poured all their money into the biggest house they can afford. In this market, you would sell gourmet macaroni and cheese, which is all they could afford. It comes down to micromarketing, taking marketing down to the smallest possible unit. There is no such thing as one-size-fits-all in the grocery business. That's why upscale shoppers go to Sam's Club."

HOW CONSUMERS VIEW SUPERMARKETS

According to recent research by *Progressive Grocer*, the shopper enjoyment rating of supermarkets (on a 10-point scale, with 1 being "least enjoyable" and 10 being "most enjoyable") was 6.33. In comparison, mass merchants were rated 6.82, specialty food stores were rated 6.80, membership clubs were rated 6.38, fast-food restaurants were rated 6.01, and convenience stores were rated 4.50. Here are some other findings from *Progressive Grocer's* "64th Annual Report of the Grocery Industry" (April 1997, various pages):

- Virtually all consumers patronized supermarkets, averaging $71 in expenditures per week.
- 68 percent of consumers patronized mass merchants, averaging $33 in expenditures per week.
- 64 percent of consumers patronized fast-food restaurants, averaging $14 in expenditures per week.
- 40 percent of consumers patronized chain drugstores, averaging $17 in expenditures per week.
- 40 percent of consumers patronized convenience stores, averaging $13 in expenditures per week.
- 27 percent of consumers patronized membership clubs, averaging $58 in expenditures per week.
- 10 percent of consumers patronized specialty food stores, averaging $18 in expenditures per week.

Over the last two decades, consumers' overall reasons for shopping at supermarkets have modified somewhat. However, since 1974, the three major reasons for patronizing supermarkets have remained the same (although their order has changed): cleanliness, low prices, and prices clearly labeled. See Table 1.

Finally, a recent survey by Cornell University compared the reasons why consumers buy bakery goods at supermarkets with the reasons why they purchase the same products at local bakeries and mem-

Table 1   WHAT SUPERMARKET SHOPPERS WANT

Factor	1995 Ranking	1985 Ranking	1974 Ranking
Cleanliness	1	1	1
Low prices	2	3	3
All prices clearly labeled	3	2	2
Accurate price scanning	4	Not asked	Not asked
Accurate, pleasant checkout clerks	5	5	4
Freshness data marked on products	6	4	6
Good produce	7	6	5
Convenient store location	8	8	10
Good meat	9	11	7
Good layout for fast, easy shopping	10	10	13
Unit pricing signs on shelves	11	13	22
Helpful personnel in service departments	12	15	12
Good dairy	13	14	11
Short wait for checkout	14	9	15
Shelves usually well-stocked	15	7	8
Good deli	31	31	32
Has in-store bakery	33	33	31

Source: "63rd Annual Report of the Grocery Industry," *Progressive Grocer* (April 1996), p. 43. Copyright *Progressive Grocer.* Reprinted by permission.

bership clubs. Selected results from that survey are shown in Table 2.

The message of the Cornell survey, says Edward McLaughlin, Cornell University professor of marketing and the food industry marketing program, is that supermarkets should be concentrating on what's important to their customers—and price is definitely down the list in the bakery. "Supermarket shoppers are not making bakery purchases based on price," he says. "The top reasons in our survey had much more to do with the selection and quality than the price.

TABLE 2   CONVENIENCE COUNTS FOR SUPERMARKETS

1. A whopping 81 percent of respondents listed convenience as the key reason for buying at supermarkets, compared with 28 percent citing the same reason for local bakeries and 17 percent for membership clubs.
2. For variety, membership clubs were the favorite for 25 percent of those surveyed. Local bakeries were second with 19 percent and supermarkets third with 17 percent.
3. Local bakeries, not surprisingly, were favored for taste with 48 percent. Supermarkets and membership clubs finished in a dead heat for second, with 17 percent each.
4. Membership clubs clobbered supermarkets in the price category, with 58 percent saying they shopped at the clubs because of price, while only 13 percent shopped in supermarkets for the same reason. Supermarkets can take some consolation in the fact that local bakeries did even worse in the price category. No one, evidently, goes to the local bakery for deals.

Source: Cornell University.

One key awareness that needs to be heightened is consumers' concern about health and quality."

Questions

1. How can a supermarket devise a unique merchandising philosophy?
2. Comment on this statement from a merchandising perspective: "It is important to be able to communicate to consumers that you have what they want. In food service, you must be able to provide them with an acceptable alternative. Competition is not just a supermarket down the street or around the corner. It is also fast-food and delivery operations."
3. From a merchandising perspective, what are the advantages and disadvantages of supermarkets with regard to membership clubs, specialty food stores, fast-food restaurants, and convenience stores?
4. Present a plan for supermarkets to employ both physical inventories and a book inventory system.
5. How can supermarkets improve their pricing strategies?
6. Relate these concepts to supermarket pricing.
   a. Price-quality association.
   b. Maintained markup.
   c. Variable markup policy.
   d. Everyday low pricing.
   e. Odd pricing.
   f. Leader pricing.
7. Analyze the data in Table 1.

Part Seven

Communicating with the Customer

- In Part 7, the elements involved in a retailer's communicating with its customers are discussed. First, the role of a retail image and how it is developed and maintained are covered. Various aspects of a promotional strategy are then detailed.

- Chapter 17 shows the importance of communications for a retailer. The significance of image in the communications effort and the components of a retailer's image are explained. The creation of an image depends heavily on a retailer's atmosphere—which is comprised of all of its physical characteristics, such as the store exterior, the general interior, layouts, and displays. The impact of customer services on a firm's image and the value of community relations are also studied.

- Chapter 18 focuses on promotional strategy, specifically how a retailer can inform, persuade, and remind its target market. The first part of the chapter deals with the four basic types of retail promotion: advertising, public relations, personal selling, and sales promotion. The second part describes the steps in a promotional strategy: objectives, budget, mix of forms, implementation of mix, and review and revision of the plan.

17

Establishing and Maintaining a Retail Image

CHAPTER OBJECTIVES

1. To show the importance of communicating with customers
2. To examine the concept of retail image
3. To describe how a retailer's image is related to the atmosphere it creates via its exterior, general interior, layout, and displays
4. To consider the impact of customer services and community relations on a retailer's image

Liz Little and her sister, Barbara Lock, are co-owners of V. Richards, an independent supermarket in Milwaukee, specializing in perishables (including pre-pared meals), gourmet grocery items, and catering. V. Richards is no ordinary supermarket. It is one of the few listed in an AAA travel guide as a tourist location! It was also one of the first grocery stores to hire a chef, and is one of the rare supermarkets ever featured in a positive story on the ABC network news show 20/20.

V. Richards recently underwent a $500,000 re-modeling project that increased its size from roughly 10,000 square feet to over 16,500 square feet—by taking over two adjoining stores. As a result of the extra space, all of its grocery shelves were reset, the aisles were widened, and additional selling area was provided for gourmet food products. The remodeling also expanded the cooler and freezer space, as well as the size of the kitchen. In addition, the store added a coffee/wine bar built in the form of an Italian piazza. It has marblelike linoleum, attractive metal gates, and trellises.

One of the cornerstones of the store is its prepared foods section. In the past, V. Richards pre-packaged its prepared foods to give consumers self-service convenience. Today, it has special delicatessen personnel to serve customers based on their specific needs for foods that are displayed in the store. This individualized service reduces waste (before, unsold pre-packaged products were discarded after one day to maintain V. Richards' exacting freshness standards) and better enables the store to differentiate its fresh, made-in-the-store entrees from factory-made entrees sold by nearby competitors. The personalized service gives the counter personnel time to explain the ingredients used, how to prepare and serve meals at home, and what salads and breads should accompany the chosen entrees.

The gourmet quality of foods carries over to many of the grocery items. For example, based on a shopper's recommendation, the store now carries a tomato paste packaged in a squeeze tube (whereas traditional tomato paste is in a can) that is popular in Europe.

In the weeks following the remodeling, V. Richards' sales revenues increased by 12 percent to 14 percent. The partners expect sales to permanently grow by 20 percent. Within a five-year period, the sisters are planning to add other stores.[1]

---

[1] Michael Garry, "Sister Act," *Progressive Grocer* (August 1996), pp. 30–36.

A retailer needs a well-devised and well-executed communications strategy to properly **OVERVIEW** position itself in customers' minds. As such, to attract customers, each firm must present information about itself to the target market, and this information must be interpreted by the target market in the manner intended. Once customers are attracted, it is then imperative for the retailer to create a proper shopping mood for them. A variety of physical and symbolic cues can be used to do this. For instance,

> Kohl's has achieved annual revenue and earnings increases of around 20 percent for a decade by targeting middle-income shoppers with a merchandise assortment that is 80 percent well-known brands, including Levi Strauss, Nike, Bugle Boy, Maidenform, Hanes, and Jockey, and 20 percent private label. By offering dominant assortments of moderate-priced apparel and soft home products, it has gone directly against traditional department stores, while also outpacing discount store competitors. Kohl's stores have a department store ambience, complete with enticing layouts, fixtures, and signs. But the similarities end there. Kohl's avoids mall sites in favor of more cost-conscious strip centers and has central checkout counters rather than registers in each department, thus letting it keep operating costs at levels comparable to those of discount stores. Kohl's reduces prices on branded items by 25 percent to 55 percent when they are advertised. As one major vendor noted, "As soon as you walk through the doors, you immediately understand this is a chain that stands behind national brands. The fixtures and point-of-sale displays call out brand statements in an impactful way, giving customers confidence that there will be breadth and depth to the offering and that what is advertised will be in stock."[2]

In this chapter, establishing and maintaining a retail image are described. The use of atmosphere, storefronts, store layouts, displays, customer services, and community relations are enumerated, as they relate to communicating with customers. Chapter 18 concentrates on the common promotional tools available to retailers in reaching their customers: advertising, public relations, personal selling, and sales promotion.

Please note that although the discussion in this chapter focuses more on store-based retailers, the overall principles also apply to nonstore-based firms. As an example, for mail-order retailers, storefronts are the covers of each catalog, and the layouts and displays are the interior pages devoted to product categories and the individual items and brands within them.

As defined in Chapter 2, *image* refers to how a retailer is perceived by consumers and others; and *positioning* refers to a firm's devising its strategy in a way that projects an image relative to its retail category and its competitors, and that elicits consumer responses to this image. To succeed, a firm must communicate a distinctive, clear, and consistent image. Once its image is established in consumers' minds, a retailer is placed in a niche relative to competitors. It is rather difficult to break out of that niche if it is firmly implanted in people's minds. **THE SIGNIFICANCE OF RETAIL IMAGE**

To further amplify, let us add these descriptions of retail image. It is

> the way in which a retailer is defined in a shopper's mind, partly by its functional qualities and partly by an aura of psychological attributes.[3]

---

[2]Susan Reda, "Kohl's Expands with Hybrid of Discount Store Efficiency, Department Store Ambience," *Stores* (February 1997), p. 50.

[3]Pierre Martineau, "The Personality of the Retail Store," *Harvard Business Review*, Vol. 36 (January–February 1958), p. 47.

a subjective phenomenon resulting from acquiring knowledge of a retailer as it is perceived relative to other firms, in accordance with a consumer's unique cognitive framework.[4]

unable to be all things to all people. Different groups of consumers might place different importance on various retail attributes. Retailers may thus emphasize different image attributes as part of their marketing strategy, and ideally, the image attributes stressed by the firm should be those to which the target market attaches the most importance.[5]

critical whenever a retailer enters a new market or analyzes its situation in a current market, and the firm considers how it is perceived relative to others in the trading area. Is the firm perceived as being the same (undifferentiated), generally the same but having some distinguishing feature (differentiated), or filling a unique market niche (subtyped)?[6]

related to both individual retailers and the shopping areas in which they are located. Once a shopping center is in place, consumers learn about its physical and tenant attributes through marketing communications, word of mouth, and so on, and ultimately, by visiting the center for their own personal shopping experience. Thus, it is these physical and tenant characteristics that generate the consumers' image of a shopping center on various image dimensions.[7]

Components of a Retail Image

Numerous factors contribute to a retailer's image, and it is the totality of these factors that forms an overall image. In different settings, it has been stated that a retail image is composed of

■ Quality, prices, and assortment.[8]
■ Fashionability, salespersonship, outside attractiveness, and advertising.[9]
■ Client mix, institutional maturity, product offerings, site convenience, shopping pleasure, ease of transactions, promotion emphasis, integrity, and image strength and clarity.[10]
■ Location, prices, facilities' cleanliness, ease of credit, product quality, shopping excitement, customer sophistication, personnel friendliness, congestion, and other factors.[11]

[4]Elizabeth C. Hirschman, "Retail Research and Theory" in Ben N. Enis and Kenneth J. Roering (Editors), Review of Marketing (Chicago: American Marketing Association, 1981), p. 119.

[5]Jan-Benedict E. M. Steenkamp and Michel Wedel, "Segmenting Retail Markets on Store Image Using a Consumer-Based Methodology," Journal of Retailing, Vol. 67 (Fall 1991), p. 301.

[6]Susan M. Keaveney and Kenneth A. Hunt, "Conceptualization and Operationalization of Retail Store Image: A Case of Rival Middle-Level Theories," Journal of the Academy of Marketing Science, Vol. 20 (Spring 1992), p. 172.

[7]Adam Finn and Jordan J. Louviere, "Shopping Center Image, Consideration, and Choice: Anchor Store Contribution," Journal of Business Research, Vol. 35 (March 1996), p. 241. See also Melanie Conty, "Image Is Everything," Shopping Center Today (May 1997), p. 222.

[8]Don L. James, Richard M. Durand, and Robert A. Dreves, "The Use of a Multi-Attribute Attitude Model in a Store Image Study," Journal of Retailing, Vol. 52 (Summer 1976), p. 30.

[9]Ronald B. Marks, "Operationalizing the Concept of Store Image," Journal of Retailing, Vol. 52 (Fall 1976), p. 44.

[10]Edgar A. Pessemier, "Store Image and Positioning," Journal of Retailing, Vol. 56 (Spring 1980), pp. 96–97.

[11]Linda L. Golden, Gerald Albaum, and Mary Zimmer, "The Numerical Comparative Scale: An Economical Format for Retail Image Measurement," Journal of Retailing, Vol. 63 (Winter 1987), p. 404.

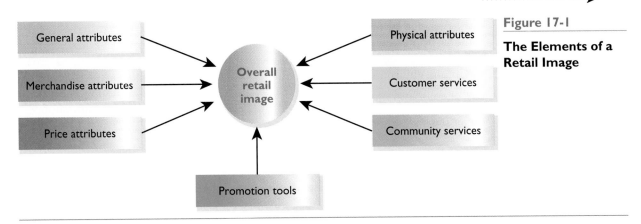

Figure 17-1

The Elements of a Retail Image

- Time, treatment, efficiency, price, physical, and technology factors.[12]
- Ambient factors, design factors, social factors, and merchandise and service quality.[13]

From the preceding groupings, we can derive a detailed summary of the components of a retailer's image:

1. Characteristics of the target market.
2. Retail positioning.
3. Store location and geographic coverage.
4. Merchandise assortment.
5. Price levels.
6. Attributes of physical facilities (atmosphere).
7. Customer services.
8. Community service.
9. Mass advertising and public relations.
10. Type and extent of personal selling.
11. Sales promotions.

Items 1 through 5 and their relation to image have been examined in earlier chapters in the text. Items 6 through 11 are the focal points for the discussion involving communications with the consumer in this and the next chapter. Figure 17-1 contains a breakdown of the elements of a retail image (incorporating Items 1 through 11).

The Dynamics of Creating and Maintaining a Retail Image

Creating and maintaining a retail image is a complex, multistep, ongoing process. It is a way of applying market segmentation and differentiating a firm from its competitors. It encompasses far more than a store's "atmosphere," which is discussed shortly. Furthermore, with so many consumers having little time for shopping and others having less interest in it, retailers must work harder to *entertain* shoppers than ever before:

The way a store looks goes beyond its fixturing, lighting, carpeting, and decor treatments. It is the result of a vision from the men and women charged with translating

---

[12]Joe Peritz, "Retailers Who Keep Score Know What Their Shoppers Value," *Marketing News* (May 24, 1993), p. 9.

[13]Julie Baker, Dhruv Grewal, and A. Parasuraman, "The Influence of Store Environment on Quality Inferences and Store Image," *Journal of the Academy of Marketing Science*, Vol. 22 (Fall 1994), pp. 328–339; and Barry J. Babin and William R. Darden, "Good and Bad Shopping Vibes: Spending and Patronage Satisfaction," *Journal of Business Research*, Vol. 35 (March 1996), pp. 201–206.

the message behind the merchandise (or the brand) into a format that will draw the customer. That's not easy in today's overstored, competitive marketplace. Architects, store planners, and designers are under great pressure to create winning environments that not only sell merchandise but also attract and entertain people. Such designs take the retail experience beyond buying and selling transactions—evoking a mood, an image, or an attitude to keep busy shoppers coming back for more.[14]

Let's look at three examples. Tiffany & Co. is a 155-year-old upscale retailer of jewelry, tableware, time pieces, gift items, and "extraordinary objects for everyday life." It realizes now "is no time for resting on one's laurels. Shoppers expect superior value and excellent service." The firm "can meet, and usually exceed, these expectations—so it has refined and intensified its efforts to clearly convey that message. Ads in major papers and magazines more specifically communicate product value to consumers in over a dozen countries." In addition, Tiffany does research and distributes various informative booklets: "Our intent is to heighten awareness, build confidence, attract more shoppers, and keep them coming back for more." And "as always, we will host consumer attractions and press briefings where our newest stores are opening and when new products are launched. Our stores have never been more outgoing and inviting."[15]

Finish Line is a chain with more than 250 stores in nearly 30 states. These 3,000- to 4,100-square-foot stores sell footwear, activewear, and related accessories for men, women, and children in a lively, engaging format. Its prices are competitive. Yet, "while the majority of merchandise is sold at our regular retail prices, we conduct consistent promotions which generally revolve around themes such as back-to-school, holiday seasons, and vendor weeks. In addition, we frequently promote individual items." The firm advertises through many media—including radio, TV, newspapers, and outdoor. "We also contribute to mall merchant association funds which will advertise both the mall and individual stores within the mall."[16] Figure 17-2 highlights the Finish Line store in Indianapolis' Circle Centre.

Bristol Farms Gourmet Specialty Foods Markets is a small, but growing, Southern California chain that operates stores as if they were theaters: "The upscale grocery stores feature music, live entertainment, exotic scenery, free refreshments, a video-equipped amphitheater, famous-name guest stars, and full audience participation." As Jodi Taylor, the firm's director of advertising and marketing, says, "We try very hard not to be a supermarket." Along with a mix of hard-to-obtain specialty foods, upscale grocery products, gourmet food service, and catering abilities, Bristol Farms uses "an aggressive brand of customer service that does without store directories or floor plans to bring shoppers and staffers into personal contact as frequently as possible. The desire to be an 'unsupermarket,' as founder Irv Gronsky refers to Bristol Farms, has led to its image as a store to which people come not just to shop, but to see and be seen." Taylor notes, "People come here to feel good, to learn about food, and to sample new things. It isn't just a shopping trip. We have had people tell us that when they get depressed they come up here and walk through the store because it makes them feel good. We have also had people meet at cooking classes and in the stores. We try to create an air of excitement all the time." The firm constantly runs demonstrations—"and sampling is an integral part of the marketing program. In fact, company policy calls for employees to permit customers to sample absolutely anything, from produce, meats, seafood, and specialty foods to packaged grocery products." The design of each Bristol Farms store "reflects the flavor of the area and local population it serves. The 18,000-square-foot Rolling Hills Estates market has a rustic look and wood-plank floors in accord with the large number

---

[14]"The Image Makers," *Chain Store Age* (April 1996), p. 44.
[15]*Tiffany & Co. 1992* and *1995 Annual Reports.*
[16]*Finish Line 1995 Annual Report.*

Figure 17-2

The Appealing Image of Finish Line

The basketball hoop depicted here measures 12 feet around by 4 feet deep.

of ranches and the rolling countryside nearby. In more traditional South Pasadena, the 22,000-square-foot store's decor emphasizes subdued greens, beiges, and other muted tones." Newspaper ads are placed in the *Los Angeles Times* every other week. According to Jodi Taylor, "They are not real price-pushy, but more about what we have available."[17]

Of particular concern to chain retailers and franchisors is maintaining a consistent image among all branches and units. However, despite the best planning, a number of factors may vary widely among branch stores and have an effect on image. These factors include management and employee performance, consumer profiles, competitors, convenience in reaching the stores, parking, safety, the ease of finding merchandise, and the qualities of the surrounding area.

Sometimes, retailers with good images receive negative publicity. This must be countered in order for them to maintain their desired standing with the public. For example, this was reported in *Business Week:*

> Bloomingdale's trademark Manhattan aura has worn thin, especially west of the Hudson. "The mystique hasn't been transferable" from New York, says consultant Alan Millstein. The stores were "either too avant-garde or too humdrum. And many times, their prices were too high." After a much-hyped 1989 launch, sales at the cathedral-like Bloomie's in downtown Chicago dropped off; ditto at the Mall of America outside Minneapolis. Bloomie's closed its Dallas store in 1990 after disappointing sales. As a result, large windows flood Bloomingdale's new Skokie, Illinois, store with natural light, and aisles are wide enough for two baby carriages. A cappuccino bar beckons near the Dana Buchman collection. There's glitz, yes, but without so much plum, black, and neon. Most important, it feels friendly. Customer focus groups had told Bloomie's execs they wanted a New York store without uppity

[17]Howard Riell, "Upscale Grocery Chain Grows with Service, 'Air of Excitement,' " *Stores* (March 1995), pp. 26–27.

salespeople. In fact, disappointing service had driven the erosion in Bloomingdale's reputation, says Chris Ohlinger, president of Service Industry Research Systems in Cincinnati, which tracks consumer perceptions of retailers. "When you encourage high expectations, a disappointment in service is a catastrophe." That's why 50 trained "selling experts" are scattered throughout the Skokie Bloomie's, supplementing the regular sales staff. Message: Service beats glitz. Maybe even in the Big Apple.[18]

ATMOSPHERE

A retailer's image depends heavily on the atmosphere it establishes. For a store-based retailer, **atmosphere** (also known as **atmospherics**) refers to the store's physical characteristics that are used to develop an image and draw customers. For a nonstore-based firm, the physical characteristics of such strategic-mix factors as catalogs, vending machines, and Web sites affect its image. This section looks at atmosphere from a store-based retailing perspective.

The sights, sounds, smells, and so forth of a store contribute greatly to the image projected to consumers. It is important that "atmosphere" be understood as the psychological feeling a customer gets when visiting a store or as the personality of the store, whereas "retail image" is a much broader and all-encompassing term relative to the tools a retailer uses to position itself.

Many people form impressions of a store before entering (due to location, storefront, and other factors) or just after entering (due to merchandise displays, the width of aisles, and other things). These people could judge a store prior to closely examining merchandise and prices. Store atmosphere may thus influence people's enjoyment of shopping, their time spent browsing and examining a retailer's offerings, their willingness to converse with personnel and to use such facilities as dressing rooms, their tendency to spend more money than originally planned, and their likelihood of future patronage.

Atmosphere (atmospherics) can be divided into these key elements: exterior, general interior, store layout, and displays. Figure 17-3 contains a detailed breakdown of these elements.

Exterior

The exterior characteristics of a store have a powerful impact on its image and should be planned accordingly.

A **storefront** is the total physical exterior of the store itself. It includes the marquee, entrances, windows, lighting, and construction materials. Via its storefront, a retailer can present a conservative, trendy, lavish, discount, or other image to the consumer. A firm should not underestimate the significance of the storefront as a determinant of image, particularly for new customers. When passing through an unfamiliar business district or shopping center, consumers often judge a store by its exterior.

There are various alternatives for a retailer to consider in planning its basic storefront. Here are a few of them:

- A modular structure—This is a one-piece rectangle or square that may attach several stores.
- A prefabricated (prefab) structure—This utilizes a store frame built in a factory and assembled at the store site.

[18]Susan Chandler and Ann Therese Palmer, "Bloomie's Tries to Lose the Attitude," *Business Week* (November 13, 1995), p. 52.

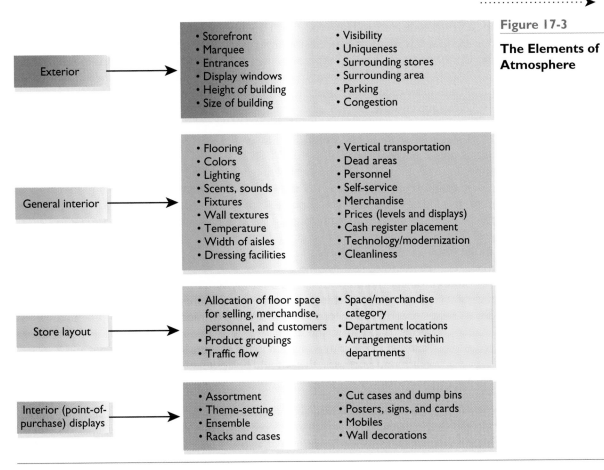

Figure 17-3

The Elements of Atmosphere

Exterior
- Storefront
- Marquee
- Entrances
- Display windows
- Height of building
- Size of building
- Visibility
- Uniqueness
- Surrounding stores
- Surrounding area
- Parking
- Congestion

General interior
- Flooring
- Colors
- Lighting
- Scents, sounds
- Fixtures
- Wall textures
- Temperature
- Width of aisles
- Dressing facilities
- Vertical transportation
- Dead areas
- Personnel
- Self-service
- Merchandise
- Prices (levels and displays)
- Cash register placement
- Technology/modernization
- Cleanliness

Store layout
- Allocation of floor space for selling, merchandise, personnel, and customers
- Product groupings
- Traffic flow
- Space/merchandise category
- Department locations
- Arrangements within departments

Interior (point-of-purchase) displays
- Assortment
- Theme-setting
- Ensemble
- Racks and cases
- Cut cases and dump bins
- Posters, signs, and cards
- Mobiles
- Wall decorations

ETHICS IN RETAILING

Storefront Security Gates: Safe Haven or Eyesore?

Many city-based retailers see solid-metal security gates as added protection against crime, but urban planners typically view these gates as more of a contributor to blight than a solution. The use of these gates began to flourish after inner-city rioting in the late 1960s and early 1970s, when insurance carriers either required or offered discounts to retailers installing such gates.

In reaction to the ugliness of solid-metal gates, some communities have enacted laws banning gates that are not at least 50 percent see-through. The sponsors of such laws say solid-metal gates contribute to a bunker mentality, deter window shopping, make it more difficult for police to inspect store interiors, and make it harder for firefighters to spot and fight blazes.

However, retailers with solid-metal gates worry that the newer mesh-based gates would make their stores more vulnerable to break-ins. They also do not want to install or switch to the newer gates due to cost factors; these gates cost at least $1,000 each (and are 10 percent to 15 percent more expensive than the solid gates). Also the retailers think it is comparatively easy to break a store window and pull goods out of the opening with a mesh gate.

One way to increase the usage of mesh gates is for municipalities to offer financial incentives to retailers that switch to such gates.

Source: Mitchell Pacelle, "Ugly Storefront Security Gates Are Bashed by Cities," *Wall Street Journal* (July 17, 1996), p. B1.

- ■ A prototype store—This is used by franchisors and chains. Because a consistent atmosphere is sought, uniform storefronts are constructed.
- ■ A recessed storefront—In this case, the store is one of many at its locale. To lure people, the storefront is recessed from the level of other stores. Customers have to walk in a number of feet to examine the storefront.
- ■ A unique building design—For example, round structures are distinctive.

In addition to the actual storefront, atmosphere can be enhanced by trees, fountains, and benches placed in front of the store. These intensify the consumer's feelings about shopping and about the store by establishing a relaxed environment.

A **marquee** is a sign used to display the store's name. It can be painted or a neon light, printed or script, and alone or mixed with a slogan (trademark) and other information. To be effective, the marquee should stand out and attract attention. Image is influenced because a marquee can be gaudy and flashy or subdued and subtle. The most widely known marquee in the world is the McDonald's golden arch, which some communities consider too overpowering.

Store entrances should be designed carefully, and three major decisions made. First, the number of entrances is determined. Many small stores have only one entrance. Large department stores may have four to eight or more entrances. A store hoping to draw vehicular and pedestrian traffic should have at least two entrances (one in front to lure pedestrians, another in the rear—adjacent to the parking lot). Because front and back entrances serve different purposes, they should be designed separately. One factor limiting the number of entrances is potential pilferage. Some urban stores have closed off entrances to reduce the size of their security forces.

Second, the type of entrance(s) is chosen from among many options. The doorway is selected: revolving; electric, self-opening; regular, push-pull; or climate-controlled. The latter is an open entrance with a curtain of warm or cold air, set at the same temperature as inside the store. This entry makes a store inviting, reduces pedestrian traffic congestion, and lets customers see inside the store. Entrance flooring is picked: cement, tile, or carpeting. Lighting is ascertained: traditional or fluorescent, white or colors, and/or flashing or constant.

Third, the walkways are considered. A wide, lavish walkway creates a very different atmosphere and mood from a narrow, constrained one. In the construction of the storefront, ample room must be provided for the walkways. Large window displays may be attractive, but customers would not be pleased if there is insufficient space for a comfortable entry into the store.

Display windows serve two main purposes: to identify the store and its offerings, and to induce people to enter. They give a lot of information about a store. By showing a representative merchandise offering, a store can create an overall mood. By showing fashion or seasonal goods, a store can show that it is contemporary. By showing sale items, a store can lure price-conscious consumers. By showing eye-catching displays that have little to do with its merchandise offering, a store can attract pedestrians' attention. By showing public service messages (e.g., a window display for the Jerry Lewis Telethon), the store can indicate its concern for the community.

Considerable planning is needed to develop good display windows. Thus, many retailers hire specialists to set up their displays properly. Decisions include the number, size, shape, color, and themes of display windows—and the frequency of changes per year. Some firms, especially ones in shopping malls, do not use display windows for the side of the building facing the parking lot; there are solid building exteriors. Those firms feel vehicular patrons are not lured by expensive outside display windows, but they do invest in display windows for storefronts inside the malls.

The exterior building's height and the size also contribute to a store's atmosphere. Building height can be disguised or nondisguised. Disguised building height occurs if part of a store—or shopping center—is beneath ground level. As a result, the building is not intimidating to people who are turned off by a large, impersonal structure. Nondisguised building height occurs if an entire store, or center, can be seen by pedestrians (all floors are at ground level or higher). Because overall building size cannot really be disguised, the target market should be researched to see how people feel about visiting different-sized facilities. An intimate boutique image cannot be generated with a block-long building. Nor can a department store image be linked to a small site.

Few retailers can succeed without good exterior visibility for their stores and/or shopping centers. This means pedestrian and/or vehicular traffic can clearly see the storefront or marquee. A store located behind a bus stop has poor visibility for vehicular traffic and pedestrians across the street. Many retailers near highways use billboards for visibility since drivers quickly pass by.

Visibility is gained through a combination of exterior features. The goal is to have the store appear unique, make it stand out, and catch the consumer's eye. A distinctive store design, an elaborate marquee, recessed open-air entrances, decorative windows, and different building height and building size are one grouping of storefront features that could attract consumers by their uniqueness. In the process, a retail image is reinforced.

Uniqueness, although it provides excellent visibility, may not be without shortcomings. An example is the multilevel "shopping-center in-the-round." Because such a center and its stores (which often occupy up to a square city block) are round-shaped, parking is provided on each floor level to make the walking distances of customers very short. However, a rectangular center would provide greater floor space on a lot of the same size; convenient on-floor parking may minimize customer shopping on other floors; added entrances increase chances for pilferage; many people dislike inclined and circular driving; and architectural costs are higher for unique buildings.

As a retailer plans a store exterior, the surrounding stores and the surrounding area should both be studied. Each contributes to the store's image, regardless of the retailer's distinctive storefront and building. The surrounding stores present image cues to consumers due to the stores being innovative or conservative, high or low priced, personal service or self-service, and so on. An overall area image rubs off on the individual firm because people tend to have a general perception of a shopping center or a business district. Thus, an individual storefront should be distinctive but not contradictory to the overall image of the site.

The surrounding area includes the demographics and life-styles of those living near a store. A store's image is affected by the neighborhood in which it is located. An unfavorable atmosphere would exist if vandalism and crime are high, people living near the store are not part of the target market, and the area is rundown.

Parking facilities can add to or detract from a store's atmosphere. Plentiful, free, nearby parking (with large spaces) creates a more positive atmosphere than scarce, costly, distant parking (with tiny spaces). Some potential shoppers may never enter a store if they drive around looking for parking and, not finding it, go elsewhere or return home. Other customers may run in and out of a store to finish shopping before the parking meter expires. In rating parking facilities, retailers should remember that many people have a limit on the distance they will walk from a parking spot to the most distant stores in a shopping district or center and others dislike multilevel garages.

Allied with the potential parking problem is that of congestion. A store's atmosphere would be diminished if its parking lot, sidewalks, and/or entrances are jammed. Consumers who feel crushed in the crowd generally spend less time shopping and are in poorer moods than those who feel comfortable.

Figure 17-4 shows some of the exciting things retailers are doing with their store exteriors, as does this example:

From supermarkets to specialty stores, retailers are putting an increased emphasis on store exteriors. And with good reason. Architects have long argued that, in an overstored environment, a well-executed facade can provide a crucial competitive

Figure 17-4

Using Store Exteriors to Generate Shopper Interest

Dillard's, Parisian, and the Bayside shopping district (in Florida) have visually appealing and inviting exteriors.

advantage. And now many retailers are seeking to maximize that advantage. The Gap, Inc. says it views the storefront as its outward packaging—a visible symbol of its brand identity. As such, it is negotiating with landlords to build Old Navy facades to its own detailed specifications.[19]

General Interior

Once customers are inside a store, there are numerous elements affecting their perceptions of it. At Crate & Barrel, the award-winning home products chain, this means: "The look—sparkling, clean, and contemporary—has a subtle, unique drama to it. Each individual element, from lighting to graphics to mass display techniques, is totally in sync." Each Crate & Barrel store has at least one full-time design and display employee; the flagship Manhattan store has six.[20]

The general interior elements of atmosphere are cited in Figure 17-3 and illustrated in Figure 17-5. They are described next.

Flooring can be made of cement, wood, linoleum, carpet, and so on. A plush, thick carpet creates one kind of atmosphere, and a cement floor causes another. Because people use cues to form store perceptions, flooring materials and designs are important. Thus, 95 percent of supermarkets have vinyl floors and 94 percent of department stores have carpeted floors. And LensCrafters (the optical chain) now uses maple wood flooring and blue carpeting in its stores to give a softer, warmer look: "The idea was to create a customer-friendly environment."[21]

Colors and lighting affect a store's image. Bright, vibrant colors contribute to a different atmosphere than light pastels or plain white walls. Lighting can be direct or indirect, white or colors, constant or flashing. For instance, a teen-oriented apparel boutique could use bright colors and vibrant, flashing lights to foster one atmosphere, and a maternity dress shop could use pastel colors and indirect lighting to form a different

Figure 17-5

The Warm Interior of Fuddruckers

At Fuddruckers, a moderate-priced food chain, the general store interior is planned meticulously—down to the NCR 7450 touch-screen point-of-sale system on the checkout counter.

[19]"Storefronts Show Advantage of Curb Appeal," *Chain Store Age* (November 1996), pp. 102–103.
[20]"Consistency Is Key at Crate & Barrel," *Chain Store Age* (April 1996), pp. 65, 70.
[21]"Types of Flooring Used," *Chain Store Age* (July 1996), p. 96; and Marianne Wilson, "LensCrafters Polishes Image with Style," *Chain Store Age* (October 1996), pp. 144–145.

atmosphere. Camelot Music stores have "spots of light sweep across the sales floor, stopping to highlight predetermined featured areas. The lighting in one area may fade out, only to pop up a few seconds later in another area."[22]

Scents and sounds influence the customer's mood and contribute to the atmosphere produced.[23] A restaurant can use food scents to increase people's appetites. A cosmetics store can use an array of perfume scents to attract shoppers. A pet store can let its animals' natural scents and sounds woo customers. A beauty salon can play soft music or rock, depending on its target market. Slow-tempo music in supermarkets encourages people to move more slowly. A housewares store can play chopping and sizzling sounds to stimulate cookware customers.

Store fixtures can be planned not only on the basis of their utility but also because of their aesthetics. Pipes, plumbing, vents, beams, doors, storage rooms, and display racks and tables should be considered in the interior decorating. A store seeking a high-price, high-quality image disguises and decorates its fixtures. A store seeking a low-price, low-quality image might leave fixtures exposed; this is inexpensive and portrays the desired image. At the Lake Buena Vista, Florida, World of Disney store, "fixturing incorporates Disney imagery and makes inventive use of different shapes, surfaces, and materials, while allowing maximum flexibility of merchandise presentation. Among the highlights is a finish in metal with gold 'pixie' dust."[24]

Wall textures can enhance or diminish a store's image. Prestigious stores often use fancy, raised wallpaper. Department stores are more likely to use flat wallpaper, while discount stores may have barren walls. Upscale stores might also have elaborate chandeliers, while discount stores would have simple lighting fixtures.

The customer's mood is affected by the temperature of the store and its way of achieving it. A person would be uncomfortable if there is insufficient heat in the winter and coolness in the summer. This can hasten his or her trip through the store. In another vein, the store's image is influenced by the use of central air-conditioning, unit air-conditioning, fans, or open windows.

The width of the aisles has an impact on retail image. Wide, uncrowded aisles create a better atmosphere than narrow, crowded ones. People shop longer and spend more if they are not pushed and shoved while walking or looking at merchandise. In Boston, although the basement in Filene's department store has many bargains, overcrowding keeps some customers away.

Dressing facilities can be elaborate, plain, or nonexistent. A prestigious store uses carpeted, private dressing rooms. An average-quality store uses linoleum-floored, semi-private rooms. A discount store uses small stalls or has no dressing facilities at all. For some apparel customers, dressing facilities (and their maintenance) are a major factor in store selection. To them, atmosphere and type of dressing facility are closely intertwined.

Multilevel stores must have some form of vertical transportation. The choices are elevator, escalator, and/or stairs. Larger stores may have a combination of all three. Traditionally, the operator-run elevator has been used in finer stores and stairs in discount stores. Today, escalators are quite popular and gaining stature. They provide consumers with a quiet ride and a panoramic view of the store. Finer stores decorate their escalators with fountains, shrubs, and trees. The placement and design of vertical transportation determine its contribution to atmosphere. Stairs remain important for discount and smaller stores.

[22]"Camelot Comes Alive with Color," *Chain Store Age* (April 1996), p. 90.

[23]See Cyndee Miller, "Scent as a Marketing Tool: Retailers—and Even a Casino—Seek Sweet Smell of Success," *Marketing News* (January 18, 1993), pp. 1–2; and J. Duncan Herrington and Louis M. Capella, "Effects of Music in Service Environments: A Field Study," *Journal of Services Marketing*, Vol. 10 (Number 2, 1996), pp. 26–41.

[24]"Disney Takes Flight as Retail Store of the Year," *Chain Store Age* (February 1997), p. 5RSOY. See also "Disney's Fifth Avenue Showplace," *Chain Store Age* (March 1997), pp. 112–114.

Light fixtures, wood or metal beams, doors, rest rooms, dressing rooms, and vertical transportation can cause **dead areas** for the retailer. These are awkward spaces where normal displays cannot be set up. In some cases, it is not possible for such areas to be deployed profitably or attractively. However, generally, retailers have learned to use dead areas better. For example, mirrors can be attached to exit doors. Vending machines can be located near rest rooms. Ads can be placed in dressing rooms. The most creative use of a dead area involves the escalator. For a long time, retailers considered it an ugly fixture in the middle of the store. Now, it is viewed differently. An escalator lets shoppers view each floor of the store, and sales of impulse items go up when placed at the entrance or exit of the escalator. Many retailers plan escalators so customers must get off at each floor and pass by appealing displays.

The number, manner, and appearance of store personnel reflect a store's atmosphere. Polite, well-groomed, knowledgeable personnel generate a positive atmosphere. Ill-mannered, poorly groomed, unknowing personnel engender a negative one. A store using self-service minimizes its personnel and creates a discount, impersonal image. A store cannot develop a prestigious image if it is set up for self-service.

The goods and services a retailer sells influences its image. Top-line items yield one kind of image, and bottom-line items yield another. The mood of the customer is affected accordingly.

Store prices contribute to image in two ways. First, price levels yield a perception of retail image in consumer minds. Second, the way prices are displayed is a vital part of atmosphere. Prestigious stores have few or no price displays and rely upon discrete price tags; sales are not emphasized. Discount stores accentuate price displays and show prices in large print. The placement of cash registers is also associated with the pricing strategy a firm uses. Prestigious stores place cash registers in inconspicuous areas such as behind posts or in employee rooms. Discount stores locate their cash registers centrally and have big signs pointing them out.

The technology used by the store and the modernization of its building and fixtures also affect its image. A store with state-of-the-art technology, such as computerized cash registers and automated inventory procedures, impresses people with its operations efficiency and speed. A store with slower, older technology may have long lines and impatient shoppers. A store with a modern building (new storefront and marquee) and new fixtures (lights, floors, and walls) fosters a more favorable atmosphere than one with older facilities. These overall observations can be made about store modernization:

■ Renovations are easier, faster, and less costly than building or opening new stores.
■ Improving store appearance, updating facilities, expansion, and the need to reallocate space are the main reasons for remodeling.
■ It results in strong sales and profit increases after completion.
■ Almost all stores are kept open during a renovation.

Last, but certainly not least, there must be a plan for keeping the store clean. No matter how impressive a store's exterior and interior may be, an unkempt store will be perceived poorly by customers. Consider this commentary: "Cleanliness is one of the most important things in a store. It sets the tone. Housekeeping is many things; keeping showcases clean; keeping bases clean where they are rapped by the vacuum cleaner. Everybody thinks of a store as the place where the merchandise is. But are your toilet facilities taken care of properly? Are trash baskets empty? It's not merely going through with a vacuum cleaner. It's cleaning doors, countertops, dust on top of seven-foot units."[25]

[25]Jules Abend, "Neat and Clean," *Stores* (November 1983), p. 15.

Store Layout

At this point, the specifics of store layout are planned and set up.[26]

Allocation of Floor Space ❑ Each store has a total square footage of floor space available and must allot it among selling, merchandise, personnel, and customers. **Selling space** is the area set aside for displays of merchandise, interactions between salespeople and customers, demonstrations, and so on. A firm like a supermarket or other self-service firm often allots a large amount of space to selling.

Merchandise space is the area where nondisplayed items are kept in stock or inventory. A traditional shoe store is a good example of a retailer whose merchandise space takes up a large percentage of total space.

Store personnel often require space for changing clothes, lunch and coffee breaks, and rest rooms. Firms may try to minimize **personnel space** by insisting on off-the-job clothes changing and other tactics. Because floor space is so valuable, that part allotted to personnel is usually controlled strictly. However, when planning personnel space, a retailer should consider employee morale and personal appearance.

Customers also require space, and it contributes greatly to a store's atmosphere. **Customer space** can include a lounge, benches and/or chairs, dressing rooms, rest rooms, a restaurant, vertical transportation, a nursery, parking, and wide aisles. Discount retailers generally skimp on these areas; those with upscale images provide their customers with adequate amounts of space for many or all of these factors.

A retailer cannot go further in its store-layout planning until floor space is properly allocated among selling, merchandise, personnel, and customers. Without that allocation, the firm would have no conception of the space available for displays, signs, rest rooms, and so on.

Today, a growing number of retailers are using planograms to allocate their store space. A **planogram** is a visual (graphical) representation of the space to be allotted to selling, merchandise, personnel, and customers—as well as to product categories. It also lays out their placement in a store. A planogram may be drawn by hand or generated by computer software, such as the Pegman software (http://www.intactix.com/pegman.html) shown in Figure 17-6.

Classification of Store Offerings ❑ A store's offerings are next classified into product groupings. Four types of groupings and combinations of them can be employed: functional, purchase motivation, market segment, and storability. With **functional product groupings,** a store's merchandise is categorized and displayed by common end uses. For example, a men's clothing store might carry these functional groups: shirts, ties, cuff links, and tie pins; shoes, shoe trees, and shoe polish; T-shirts, undershorts, and socks; suits; and sports jackets and slacks.

Purchase-motivation product groupings appeal to the consumer's urge to buy a product and the amount of time he or she is willing to spend in shopping. A committed customer with time to shop will visit the upper floors and extremities of a store; a disinterested customer with little time to shop will gravitate to displays on the first floor, near exits. A firm can capitalize on this by grouping products by purchase motivation. Look at the first floor of a department store. Items there tend to be impulse products and other relatively quick purchases. On the third floor of a department store are items encouraging and requiring more thoughtful shopping.

With **market-segment product groupings,** various products appealing to a given target market are placed together. Examples are a clothing store's dividing products into juniors', misses', and ladies' clothing categories; a music store's separating CDs into rock, jazz, classical, R&B, country and western, gospel, and other music sections; an art

---

[26]For more detailed information, see Michael J. Lopez, *Retail Store Planning & Design Manual,* Second Edition (New York: Wiley, 1995).

Figure 17-6

Pegman Space Management Software

Pegman is designed to optimize the use of in-store space. It lets retailers graphically depict products on-screen in sections or categories, linked to inventory and financial information. The retailers can set displays, assess them based on financial and aesthetic goals, and determine the impact on sales if changes are made.

gallery's placing paintings in different price groups; and a toy store's having distinct display areas for children and adult games.

For products needing special handling, **storability product groupings** may be used. A supermarket has freezer, refrigerator, and room-temperature sections. A florist keeps some flowers in a refrigerator and others at room temperature; so do a bakery and a fruit store.

Many retailers have a combination of product groupings and plan store layouts accordingly. In addition to the considerations just covered, provisions must be made for minimizing shoplifting and pilferage. This means positioning vulnerable product groupings away from corners and doors.

Determination of a Traffic-Flow Pattern ❑ The traffic-flow pattern of the store is then determined. There are two basic traffic-flow options available to retailers: straight and curving. With a **straight (gridiron) traffic flow,** displays and aisles are placed in a rectangular or gridiron pattern, as shown in Figure 17-7. With a **curving (free-flowing) traffic flow,** displays and aisles are placed in a free-flowing pattern, as shown in Figure 17-8.

A straight traffic pattern is most often used by food retailers, discount stores, hardware stores, and other convenience-oriented retailers (like stationery stores). It has several advantages:

- An efficient atmosphere is created.
- More floor space is devoted to product displays.
- People can shop quickly; regular customers especially desire clearly marked, distinct aisles and develop a routine way of walking through the store.
- Inventory control and security are simplified.
- Self-service is easy, thereby reducing labor costs.

The disadvantages of a gridiron pattern are the impersonal atmosphere, the more limited browsing by customers, and the rushed shopping behavior.

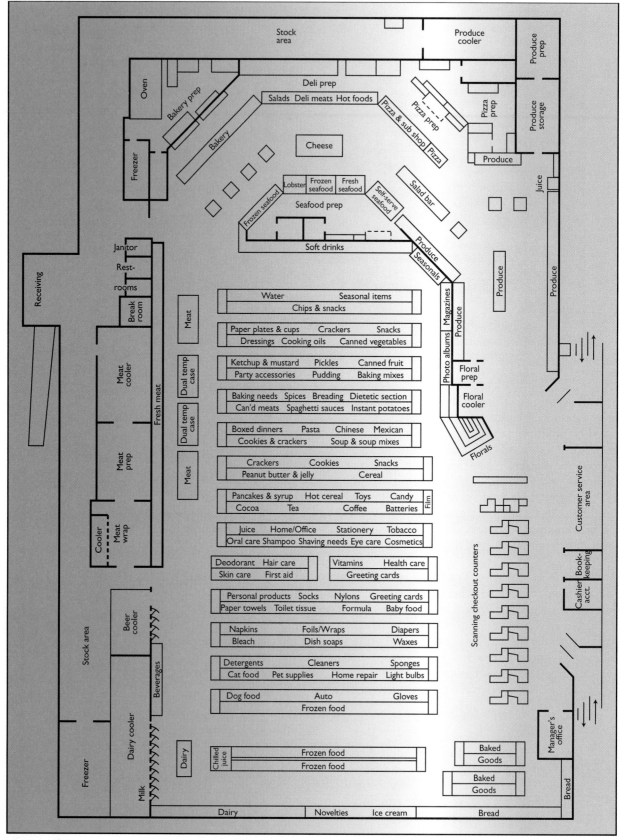

Figure 17-7

How a Supermarket Uses a Straight (Gridiron) Traffic Pattern

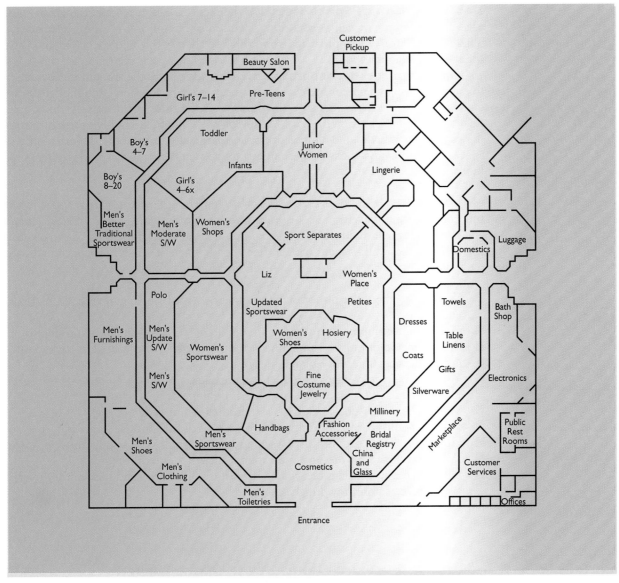

Figure 17-8

How a Department Store Uses a Curving (Free-Flowing) Traffic Pattern

A curving traffic pattern is most often used by boutiques, department stores, clothing stores, and other shopping-oriented stores. There are several benefits of this approach:

■ A friendly atmosphere is presented.
■ Shoppers do not feel rushed and will browse around.
■ People are encouraged to walk through the store in any direction or pattern they desire.
■ Impulse or unplanned purchases are enhanced.

The disadvantages of a free-flowing pattern are the possible customer confusion, the wasted floor space, the difficulties in inventory control and security, the higher labor intensity, and the potential loitering. Also free-flowing displays often cost more than standardized gridiron displays.

Determination of Space Needs ❏ The space for each product category is now ascertained. Selling, as well as nonselling, space must be considered in any calculations. There are two different approaches from which to choose: the model stock method and the space-productivity ratio.

Under the **model stock approach,** a retailer determines the amount of floor space to carry and display a proper merchandise assortment. Apparel stores and shoe stores are among those using the model stock method. With the **sales-productivity ratio,** a retailer assigns floor space on the basis of sales or profit per foot. Highly profitable product categories receive large chunks of space; marginally profitable categories get less space. Food stores and bookstores are among the retailers using space-productivity ratios in planning floor space.

Mapping Out In-Store Locations ❏ Department locations are mapped out at this point. For multilevel stores, the procedure includes assigning departments to floors and laying out the individual floors. What product categories should be placed on each floor? What should the layout of each floor be? A single-level store is concerned with only the second question. Here are some of the issues to be considered:

■ What items should be placed in the basement, on the first floor, on the second floor, and so on?
■ How should groupings be placed relative to doors, vertical transportation, and so on?
■ Where should impulse or unplanned product categories be located relative to categories that consumers pre-plan to buy?
■ Where should convenience products be situated?
■ How should associated product categories be aligned?
■ Where should seasonal and off-season products be placed?
■ Where should space-consuming categories such as furniture be located?
■ How close should product displays and stored inventory be to each other?
■ What travel patterns do consumers follow once they enter the store?
■ How can consumer lines be avoided near the cash register, and how can the overall appearance of store crowding be averted?

Ikea in Manhattan: Flexibility in Store Design

When Ikea announced its first store opening in high-rent New York City, many retail analysts questioned the firm's ability to use a 7,400-square-foot location to merchandise its 12,000 items. Ikea's answer was that it planned to use this site as a showcase for selected merchandise, as well as a staging point for a weekend shuttle bus to take shoppers to a nearby full-sized Ikea outlet located in Elizabeth, New Jersey.

The Manhattan store has become successful on its own due to its flexible and innovative design. According to the store's designer, although the outlet only stocks about 300 items at one time, it has been "able to adapt to any product category as though that category were the only one Ikea maintains." By ap-plying modular construction techniques, the store walls, video displays, lighting, and signage can all be easily reconfigured.

Every 8 to 12 weeks, Ikea plans to concentrate on another product line to build excitement. For example, when the store first opened, the "Ikea Cooks" theme was used to focus on the sale of kitchen cabinets, cookware, and kitchen accessories—and the audio system featured the sounds of boiling water and dicing knives. After two months, this was replaced with an "Ikea Plays" theme geared to children's furniture and toys.

Source: Paul W. Cockerham, "Ikea Holds Manhattan Outpost with Flexible Store Design," *Stores* (February 1996), pp. 65–66.

As an example, according to research conducted by card maker American Greetings (http://www.greetingcard.com), although just 40 percent of the people who enter a stationery store walk through its greeting-card department, 90 percent of those who do pass through that department typically buy at least one greeting card. Thus, the placement of the greeting-card department within the store has a great impact on card sales.

Arrangement of Individual Products ❏ The last step in store layout planning is to arrange individual products within departments. Various criteria may be used in positioning products. For instance, the most profitable items and brands could get favorable spots where consumer traffic is heavy; and products may be arranged by package size, price, color, brand, level of personal service required, and/or customer interest.

End-aisle display positions, eye-level positions, and checkout-counter positions are the most apt to increase sales for individual items. Continuity of locations is also important; shifts in store layout may decrease sales. The least desirable display position is often knee or ankle level, because consumers do not like to bend down.

Individual firms should do research to learn the sales impact of different product positions. However, it must be kept in mind that manufacturer and retailer goals often differ. A manufacturer wants its brand's sales to be maximized and pushes for eye-level, full-shelf, end-aisle locations. On the other hand, a retailer wants to maximize total store sales and profit, regardless of brand.

Self-service retailers have special considerations. Besides using a gridiron layout to minimize customer confusion, aisles, displays, and merchandise must be clearly marked. A large selling space, with on-floor assortments, is necessary. Cash registers must be plentiful and accessible. It is hard to sell complex and/or expensive items through self-service.

Consider some of the tactics deployed by supermarkets:

■ Sixty percent begin with produce, most of the rest with flowers. "The idea is to tantalize the customer, to draw you in with eye-catching displays and a promise of bounty and freshness."

■ "Cereal theory" means placing boxes on lower shelves, which are at eye level for children.

■ People buy more soup if the varieties are not shelved in alphabetical order.

■ Store brands do better when located to the left of manufacturer brands. "After seeing the name brand, the eye—habituated by a lifetime of reading—will automatically move left (as it would on a new page) to compare prices."

■ Since "the best viewing angle is 15 degrees below the horizontal, the choicest display level has been measured at 51 to 53 inches off the floor."[27]

Interior (Point-of-Purchase) Displays

Once the store's layout is fully detailed, a retailer devises its interior displays. Each **point-of-purchase (POP) display** provides consumers with information, adds to store atmosphere, and serves a substantial promotional role. In this section, several types and forms of displays are described. Most retailers use a combination of some or all of these kinds of displays.

An **assortment display** is one in which a retailer exhibits a wide range of merchandise for the customer. With an open assortment, the customer is encouraged to feel, look at, and/or try on a number of products. Greeting cards, books, magazines, and apparel are the kinds of products for which firms use open assortments. In recent years, food stores have expanded the placement of items such as fruit, vegetables, and candy in open displays. With a closed assortment, the customer is encouraged to look at a variety of

[27]Jack Hitt, "The Theory of Supermarkets," *New York Times Magazine* (March 10, 1996), pp. 56-61, 94, 98.

Figure 17-9

A Closed Display at Neiman Marcus

This upscale retailer uses closed displays for items such as sunglasses to encourage customers to interact with salespeople, thus enhancing the shopping experience.

merchandise but not touch it or try it on. Computer software and CDs are pre-packaged items a shopper is not allowed to open before buying. Jewelry is usually displayed in closed glass cases that must be unlocked by store employees. See Figure 17-9.

A **theme-setting display** depicts a product offering in a thematic manner and lets a retailer portray a specific atmosphere or mood. Firms often change their displays to reflect seasons or special events; some even have employees dress to fit the occasion. All or part of a store may be adapted to a theme, such as Washington's Birthday, Columbus Day, Valentine's Day, the Fourth of July, or another concept. Each special theme is enacted to attract customer attention and make shopping more enjoyable (and not a chore).

An **ensemble display** has become very popular. Instead of grouping and showing merchandise in separate categories (e.g., shoe department, sock department, pants department, shirt department, sports jacket department), complete ensembles are displayed. Thus, a mannequin could be dressed in a matching combination of shoes, socks, pants, shirt, and sports jacket, and these items would be readily available in one department or adjacent departments. Customers are pleased with the ease of a purchase and like being able to envision an entire outfit.

A **rack display** is often used by apparel retailers, houseware retailers, and others. The racks have a primarily functional use: to hang or present the products neatly. The major problems are possible cluttering and customers' returning items to the wrong place (thus disrupting the proper size sequence). Current technology allows retailers to use sliding, disconnecting, contracting/expanding, lightweight, attractive rack displays. See Figure 17-10. A **case display** is employed to exhibit heavier, bulkier items than racks hold. Records, books, pre-packaged goods, and sweaters are typically contained in case displays.

A **cut case** is an inexpensive display, in which merchandise is left in the original carton. Supermarkets and discount stores frequently set up cut-case displays. These cases do not create a warm atmosphere. Neither does a **dump bin,** which is a case that houses piles of sale clothing, marked-down books, or other products. Instead of neat, precise displays, dump bins contain open assortments of roughly handled items. The advantages of cut cases and dump bins are reduced display costs and a low-price image.

Figure 17-10

A Rack Display at Parisian

This chain employs rack displays so as to neatly present items, offer customers a hands-on experience, and maximize floor space.

Posters, signs, and cards can be used to dress up all types of displays, including cut cases and dump bins. These tools provide information about in-store product locations and stimulate customers to shop. A mobile, a type of hanging display with parts that move, especially in response to air currents, serves the same purpose—but is more appealing to the eye and stands out. Wall decorations also enhance a store's atmosphere and add to displays; they are particularly useful with thematic and ensemble displays. Today, walls may even feature video monitors.

CUSTOMER SERVICES

As defined in Chapter 1, customer services are the identifiable, but sometimes intangible, activities taken on by a retailer in selling its basic goods and services. The attributes of personnel who interact with customers (such as politeness and knowledge), as well as the number and variety of customer services offered by a firm, have a strong impact on and contribute to the image created. For instance, "Outside the First Chicago bank branch in tony Lake Forest, Illinois, Shaun Borden threatened to take his 'six-figure' account to another bank. 'I don't like the attitude of First Chicago,' said the president of Swiss Financial Securities Inc., a brokerage firm. Borden was steamed by the bank's plan to slap thousands of people whose balances were under $2,500 with a fee of $3 for visiting a teller when they could have used an ATM. Borden wasn't in that category, but perception counts—and his was that the bank unfairly jacked up its fees."[28]

[28]Russell Mitchell and Richard A. Melcher, "Thanks for Your Deposit. That'll Be $3," *Business Week* (May 15, 1995), p. 46.

On the other hand, "At Eaton's in Canada, there is a system of 26 different points of service, including checkouts, direct marketing, parking lots, and credit card acceptance. A point system measures service effectiveness. Phone calls to Eaton's should be answered in two rings, for example, and anyone who answers a phone must be able to provide directions to the store." And Target Stores cashiers "are authorized to take the customer's word, within reason, on the price of an unmarked item. The strategy keeps checkout lines moving swiftly and reinforces the customer's point of view."[29]

Planning the appropriate customer-services strategy can be complicated because retailers often face situations such as these:

> Of the many things American shoppers dislike about retail stores, few inspire vitriol like poor customer service. In a survey of 4,000 consumers by Yankelovich Partners, a research firm, department and discount stores tied for 11th in rankings of customer service out of a list of 20 types of firms—well behind the U.S. Postal Service, restaurants, and local phone companies. How can this be, during an era in which almost all retailers say obsessively good service is a cornerstone of business? The answer is that during this era of consolidation and retrenchment, retailers—department stores in particular—have been even more obsessive about cutting costs, systematically slicing away at the very areas on which service depends.

> Though experts say quality service depends, first and foremost, on sales help being available at the drop of a hat, retailers in the early 1990s sharply reduced staffing on the sales floor. Numbers are hard to come by, but analysts variously estimate the cuts at 10 percent to 30 percent. Now some firms, concluding they sliced too deeply, are siphoning money from other activities to expand frontline sales staffs. Also, after a long period in which department stores were especially esteemed for training buyers and executives in the fine points of merchandising, today, the retail industry spends less time training its employees than any other major business sector, according to the American Society for Training and Development. Finally, even as many other industries embrace pay-for-performance systems, retailers have been slow to experiment with new ways to motivate workers and focus attention on the customer. Some have scaled back sales commissions as a means of cutting costs.

> Of course, there are exceptions and some retailers generally succeed in transmitting their service philosophy through the ranks. Customers can count on fawning attention in the lingerie department at Neiman Marcus; and the clerks at Old Navy discount stores are quick to check the stockroom by their chic headsets. Wal-Mart has reaped top rankings from discount shoppers for service. Sears, after a decade of poor customer-service ratings, beefed up the sales force, among other things, and has witnessed a turnaround. But long after Nordstrom—with its liberal return policies and famously accommodating help—became recognized as the new standard for retail service, few rivals have adopted its higher commissions or put as much authority in the hands of sales associates. Instead, shoppers often face low-paid, ill-trained clerks who make assumptions about service that would appall executives.[30]

To apply customer services properly, a firm must first outline an overall service strategy and then plan individual services. Figure 17-11 shows one way a retailer may view customer services.

---

[29]Susan Reda, "Seven Keys to Better Service," *Stores* (January 1996), p. 34.

[30]Jennifer Steinhauer, "What Ever Happened to Service?" *New York Times* (March 4, 1997), pp. D1–D2.

	High	Low
High	***Patronage builders—*** High-cost activities that are the primary factors behind customer loyalties. Examples: transaction speed, credit, gift registry	***Patronage solidifiers—*** The "low-cost little things" that increase loyalty. Examples: courtesy (referring to the customer by name and saying thank you), suggestion selling
Low	***Disappointers—*** Expensive activities that do no real good. Examples: weekday deliveries for two-earner families, home economists	***Basics—*** Low-cost activities that are "naturally expected." They don't build patronage, but their absence could reduce patronage. Examples: free parking, in-store directories

Value of Service to Customer

Figure 17-11

Classifying Customer Services

Source: Adapted by the authors from Albert D. Bates, "Rethinking the Service Offer," *Retailing Issues Letter* (December 1986), p. 3. Reprinted by permission.

Developing a Customer Services Strategy

In developing a customer services strategy, a retailer has to make decisions involving the range, level, choice, price, measurement, and retention of its services.

What services are primary and what services are ancillary for a particular retailer? **Primary customer services** are those considered basic components of the retail strategy mix; they must be provided. Examples are credit for a furniture retailer, new-car preparation for an auto dealer, and a liberal return policy for a gift shop. These services form an essential part of those retailers' strategy mixes, and they could not stay in business without them.

TECHNOLOGY IN RETAILING

Rainforest Cafe: A State-of-the-Forest Restaurant

The Rainforest Cafe is an example of the new wave of theme restaurants that combine elements of environmentally based education/theater with restaurants: "The concept of the Rainforest Cafe is built around the five senses and what we call the five E's— entertainment, environment, education, earning a return on our investment, and our employees." The restaurants typically contain aquariums, live parrots, a waterfall, a mechanical crocodile, a thunderstorm with lightning, and a talking tree (that provides guests with messages about the environment as they wait for a table). In line with its environmental emphasis, the Rainforest Cafe does not serve beef raised on deforested land or fish caught in nets.

Besides the restaurant itself, each Rainforest Cafe contains a retail shop with over 500 items, including three-dimensional animals, a glow-in-the-dark cave, and a jungle house. The retail shop sells Rainforest T-shirts and embroidered products. Despite the large area devoted to merchandise, only 26 percent of the Rainforest Cafe's revenues actually come from its retail sales. Rainforest plans to soon license its eight animal characters for use on selected merchandise.

Although some of the new Rainforest Cafes are isolated, most are part of major tourist attraction shopping malls with high customer traffic, such as Mall of America and Woodfield Mall and Gurnee Mills Mall (both in Illinois). These sites let Rainforest Cafe utilize the malls' established base of shoppers.

Sources: Chad Rubel, "New Menu for Restaurants: Talking Trees and Blackjack," *Marketing News* (July 29, 1996), pp. 1, 16; and "Rainforest Cafe: Welcome to the Jungle," *Chain Store Age* (March 1997), pp. 94–96.

Figure 17-12

Ancillary Services: Going Above and Beyond the Norm

To upgrade their customer service, some supermarkets have installed self-service NCR Price Verifiers, which enable shoppers to check the prices of items they have selected—before they go to the checkout center.

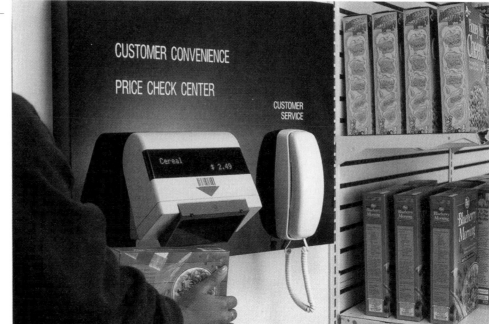

Ancillary customer services are extra elements that enhance a retail strategy mix. A retailer could cater to its target market adequately without these services, but using them enhances its competitive standing. Examples are home delivery for a supermarket, an extra warranty for an auto dealer, gift wrapping for a toy store, and credit for a flea market vendor.

It is vital for each retailer to determine which customer services are primary and which are ancillary for its own situation. Primary services for one retailer, such as delivery, may be ancillary for another. Remember: Primary services have to be provided; ancillary services are not required but improve a firm's image.[31] See Figure 17-12.

What level of customer services is proper to complement a firm's image? An upscale retailer would define more services as primary than a discounter because consumers expect that firm to supply a wide range of services as part of its basic strategy mix. This is not true of a discounter. In addition, the performance of services would be different. Thus, customers of an upscale retailer may expect elaborate gift wrapping, valet parking, a restaurant, and a ladies' room attendant, while customers of a discounter may expect cardboard gift boxes, self-service parking, a lunch counter, and an unattended ladies' room. In these instances, the customer service categories are the same; the level of the services is not.

Should there be a choice of customer services? Some firms let customers select from among various levels of service; others provide only one level. A retailer may honor several credit cards or only its own. Trade-ins may be allowed on some items or all. Warranties may have optional extensions or fixed lengths. A retailer may offer one-month, three-month, and six-month payment plans or insist on a one-month payment period.

Should customer services be free? Two factors are causing a number of retailers to charge for some services: increased costs and consumer behavior. Delivery, gift wrapping, and other services are labor intensive, and their costs are steadily rising. Furthermore, it has been found that people are more apt to be at home for a delivery or a service call if a fee is imposed. Without a fee, retailers may have to attempt a delivery

---

[31]See "More Retailers Seek Value Incentives to Stir Patronage," *Discount Store News* (April 14, 1997), pp. 3, 62.

two or three times to find someone at home. In settling on a free or fee-based strategy, a firm must determine which services are primary (these are often free) and which are ancillary (these may be offered for a fee); competitors and profit margins should be watched closely, and the target market should be studied. In setting fees, a retailer must also decide if its goal is to break even or to make a profit on the services.

How can a retailer measure the benefits of providing customer services against their costs? The purpose of customer services is to attract and retain consumers, thus maximizing sales and profits. This means ancillary services should not be offered unless they raise a firm's total sales and profits. Unfortunately, little research on the benefit-cost ratios of various services has been done. Thus, a retailer should plan ancillary services based on its experience, competitors' actions, and customer comments; and when the costs of providing these services increase, higher prices should be passed on to the consumer.

How can customer services be terminated? Once a retailer establishes its image, consumers are likely to react negatively to any reduction of services. Nonetheless, inefficient and costly ancillary services may have to be discontinued. In dropping customer services, a firm's best strategy is to be forthright—explaining why services are being terminated and how the customer will benefit by lower prices and so on. Sometimes, a firm may choose a middle ground, charging for previously free services and allowing those who want the services to continue to receive them.

Planning Individual Services

Once a broad customer service plan is outlined, individual services are planned. For example, a department store may offer all these services: credit, layaway, gift wrapping, a bridal registry, parking, pay phones, a restaurant, a beauty salon, carpet installation, dressing rooms, clothing alterations, customer rest rooms and sitting areas, the use of baby strollers, home delivery, and fur storage. The range of typical customer services is shown in Table 17-1 and described next.

Table 17-1 TYPICAL CUSTOMER SERVICES

Credit

Delivery

Alterations and installations

Packaging (gift wrapping)

Complaints and returns handling

Gift certificates

Trade-ins

Trial purchases

Special sales for regular customers

Extended store hours

Mail and telephone orders

Miscellaneous

■ Bridal registry	■ Rest rooms
■ Interior designers	■ Restaurant
■ Personal shoppers	■ Baby-sitting
■ Ticket outlets	■ Fitting rooms
■ Parking	■ Beauty salon
■ Water fountains	■ Fur storage
■ Pay telephones	■ Shopping bags
■ Baby strollers	■ Information

Today, most retailers let their customers make credit purchases. Even some supermarkets and fast-food chains—two of the last major holdouts—now allow credit card transactions, and many firms accept personal checks with proper identification. Whereas smaller and medium-sized retailers rely on bank cards and companies such as American Express to process purchases made on credit, larger retailers often have their own credit systems and credit cards. In greater numbers, larger retailers have also begun to accept outside credit cards in addition to their own.

Credit's role in retail purchases can be seen through the following:

■ Visa, MasterCard, American Express, Discover, and Carte Blanche are just some of the major credit cards accepted by various retailers.
■ 40 percent to 60 percent of department and specialty store purchases are on credit. Consumers' use of credit rises greatly as the amount of a purchase goes up.[32]
■ Annually, tens of millions of people use a Sears credit card when shopping at one of the chain's stores.
■ More retailers are offering co-branded cards to increase customer loyalty. See Figure 17-13.
■ Computerization has eased the credit process and made it more efficient, thus encouraging more retailers to accept some form of credit system.

Retailer-generated credit cards have four key advantages. One, the retailer saves the sales fee it would have to pay for outside card sales. Two, people are encouraged to shop with a given firm because its card is usually not accepted elsewhere. Three, contact can be maintained with customers and information learned about them. Four, attractive card design contributes to overall company image. There are also disadvantages to retailer credit cards: startup costs are high, the firm must worry about unpaid bills and slow cash flow, credit checks and follow-up tasks must be performed, and customers without the firm's card may be discouraged from buying.

Figure 17-13

Co-Branding: A Growing Retail Credit Tool

The Phillips 66 MasterCard offers a two percent rebate on any purchase made at a Phillips 66 service station and a one percent rebate on other purchases.

---

[32]See "Credit: The More You Pay, the More You Owe?" *Chain Store Age* (November 1996), p. 140.

Bank and other commercial credit cards allow small- and medium-sized retailers to offer credit, generate added business for all types of retailers, appeal to tourists and mobile shoppers, provide advertising support from the sponsor, reduce bad debts, eliminate startup costs for the retailer, and provide data. Yet, these cards do charge a service fee per transaction (based on the sales volume of the retailer) and do not engender retailer loyalty.

As noted, both retailer and commercial credit cards enhance the retailer's information capabilities. They provide data on credit sales (such as the size of the average transaction and the merchandise bought), customer demographics (such as place of residence and income), and branch store performance (such as credit versus cash sales by product category).

All bank cards and most retailer cards involve revolving accounts. With a **revolving credit account,** a customer charges items and is billed monthly on the basis of the outstanding cumulative balance. An **option credit account** is a form of revolving account; no interest is assessed if a person pays a bill in full when it is due. See Table 17-2, Example 1. However, should a person make a partial payment, he or she is assessed interest monthly on the unpaid amount. See Table 17-2, Examples 2 and 3.

The customer receives a credit limit with a revolving account, and his or her total balance cannot exceed this limit. Several states let retailer and commercial credit cards charge up to 2 or more percent interest per month (an annual rate of 24 percent or more) on unpaid balances.

Table 17-2 HOW A REVOLVING CREDIT ACCOUNT WORKS

Example 1: Revolving Account (no interest paid)

Purchases in June	$100.00	
End-of-month bill		$100.00
Payment		$100.00
Balance due		$ 0.00

Example 2: Revolving Account (interest paid)

Purchases in June	$100.00	
End-of-month bill		$100.00
Payment		$ 50.00
Balance due		$ 50.00
Purchases in July	$ 0.00	
Balance from June	$ 50.00	
One month's interest	$ 0.75	
(at 1½ % per month)		
Total end-of-month bill		$ 50.75
Payment		$ 50.75
Balance due		$ 0.00

Example 3: Revolving Account (interest paid)

Purchases in June	$400.00	
End-of-month bill		$400.00
Payment		$100.00
Balance due		$300.00
Purchases in July	$400.00	
Balance from June	$300.00	
Interest on balance	$ 4.50	
Total end-of-month bill		$704.50
Payment		$200.00
Balance due		$504.50
Purchases in August	$ 0.00	
Balance from July	$504.50	
Interest on balance	$ 7.57	
Total end-of-month bill		$512.07
Payment		$512.07
Balance due		$ 0.00

Some credit card firms (such as American Express) and some retailers emphasize open credit accounts. With an **open credit account,** a consumer must pay the bill in full when it is due. Partial, revolving payments are not permitted. A person with an open account also has a credit limit.

Under a **monthly payment credit account,** the consumer pays for a purchase in equal monthly installments. Interest is usually charged. As an illustration, suppose a person buys a $300 camera and pays for it over 12 months. Equal monthly payments of $27.50 ($25 principal and $2.50 interest) yield a total cost of $330 for the camera. The true interest rate is 18.46 percent on the average monthly balance.[*]

Deferred billing enables customers to make purchases and not pay for them for several months, without interest. This may be a holiday or other promotion tool. Thus, Christmas shoppers could be encouraged to buy in November and December and not pay until March.

A **layaway plan** allows customers to give a retailer deposits to hold products. When customers complete payment, they take the items. In the meantime, they do not have to worry about the firm's running out of stock.

COD (collect on delivery) lets customers have products delivered to them before payment is made. The bill must be paid in full when merchandise is received. Direct marketers sometimes use COD.

As the preceding indicate, retailers have wide flexibility in picking a credit strategy. The one that best fits the firm's image, customers, and needs should be selected. Although the trend to credit card usage continues, some firms (such as a number of gas stations) have moved in the opposite direction and ended credit card transactions to reduce costs and prices. In the proper setting (such as off-price chains), discounts for cash also seem feasible.

For the retailer whose products and/or customers require that items be delivered, there are three considerations in setting up delivery service: the method of transportation, ownership versus rental of equipment, and timing. The shipping method can be car, van, truck, train, boat, mail, and/or plane. The costs and appropriateness of the methods depend on the merchandise involved.

Large retailers often find it economical to own delivery vehicles. This also enables them to advertise their company names, have control over delivery schedules, and have their employees handle deliveries. Small retailers serving limited trading areas may use their own personal vehicles. However, many small, medium, and even large retailers use a delivery firm such as United Parcel Service or utilize commercial truckers when consumers reside away from a delivery area, transportation is used sporadically, and shipments are not otherwise efficient (because less than full truckloads would be sent).

Last, the timing of deliveries must be planned. The retailer must decide how quickly orders are to be processed and how often deliveries are to be made to different geographic areas. For example, will customers residing in a Baton Rouge, Louisiana, suburb receive deliveries daily, once a week, or monthly?

For certain firms, alterations and installations are primary services, and treated accordingly—though more retailers now charge fees. However, many discounters have stopped offering alterations of clothing and installations of heavy appliances on both a free and a fee basis. They feel the services are too ancillary to their business and not worth the effort. Other retailers offer only basic alterations: shortening pants, taking in the waist, and lengthening jacket sleeves. They do not adjust jacket shoulders or width. Some appliance retailers may hook up washing machines but not do plumbing work. Various clothing chains have central alteration systems to lower costs.

Within a store, packaging (gift wrapping)—as well as complaints and returns handling—can be centrally located or decentralized. Centralized packaging counters and

---

[*]The computation for this is ($30 interest)/[(1/2)($300 initial principal + $25 last month's principal)] = ($30)/[(1/2)($325)] = ($30)/($162.50) = 18.46 percent.

complaints and returns departments have several advantages: they may be situated in otherwise dead spaces; the main selling areas are not cluttered; specialized personnel can be used; and a common store policy is enacted. The advantages of decentralized facilities are that shoppers are not inconvenienced; people are kept in the selling area, where a salesperson may resolve problems or offer different merchandise; and extra personnel are not required. In either case, a clear policy as to the handling of complaints and returns must be stated. The axiom "The customer is always right" should be followed when possible. Unfortunately, customers are often not convinced this policy is in effect.

Gift certificates encourage new and existing customers to shop with a given retailer. Many firms require gift certificates to be spent and not redeemed for cash. Trade-ins also induce new and regular shoppers to patronize a retailer. People get the feeling of a bargain. Trial purchases let shoppers test products before purchases become final, thus reducing risks. If customers like the products, they are kept and paid for; if customers dislike them, they can be returned. Some mail-order retailers allow trial purchases.

Retailers are increasingly offering special services to regular customers. Special sales, not open to the general public, are run to increase customer loyalty. Extended hours, such as evenings and weekends, are provided. This lengthens in-store shopping time and decreases rushing. Mail and telephone orders placed by regular customers are handled for convenience. All of these tactics give a firm an image of caring among its most important customers.

Other useful customer services, some of them discussed previously, include a bridal registry, interior designers, personal shoppers, ticket outlets, free (or low-cost) and plentiful parking, water fountains, pay phones, baby strollers, rest rooms, a restaurant, babysitting, fitting rooms, a beauty salon, fur storage, shopping bags, and in-store information counters. The latter should not be undervalued; confused customers are less apt to be satisfied and/or to complete their shopping trips. A retailer's willingness to offer some or all of these services indicates to its customers its concern for them and is a strong contributor to image.

In particular, firms need to consider the impact of excessive self-service. Here are the observations of an executive at one supermarket chain:

> We're doing more self-service. But, by the same token, we do so with caution. It must be done carefully and by neighborhood—not just to make things simple for the home office. You need a good balance between service and self-service, depending on the neighborhood.[33]

And at Nordstrom, the award-winning Seattle-based chain:

> Legendary service has been the key to gaining customers in new markets. Salespeople commonly write thank-you notes or make home deliveries to customers. Each store employs a concierge stationed near the entrance to help customers with special requests. Such amenities have won Nordstrom loyalty and affection.[34]

COMMUNITY RELATIONS

The manner in which retailers interact with the communities around them also has an impact on their image and performance. Firms can enhance their images by actions such as:

---

[33]Mary Ann Linsen, "Service Vs. Self-Service: A Balancing Act," *Progressive Grocer* (November 1993), p. 92.
[34]Dori Jones Yang and Laura Zinn, "Will 'The Nordstrom Way' Travel Well?" *Business Week* (September 3, 1990), p. 83.

■ Making sure that stores are barrier-free for disabled shoppers.
■ Showing a concern for the environment, such as recycling trash and cleaning streets.
■ Supporting charities.
■ Participating in antidrug programs.
■ Employing area residents.
■ Running special sales for senior citizens and other groups.
■ Sponsoring Little League and other youth activities.
■ Cooperating with neighborhood planning groups.
■ Donating money and/or equipment to schools.

7-Eleven is a top corporate sponsor of the Muscular Dystrophy Association, participates in Mothers Against Drunk Driving (MADD) public awareness programs, and supports organizations that promote literacy and multicultural understanding. Wal-Mart, Kmart, and Consolidated Stores are among the numerous retailers participating in some type of antidrug program. Safeway and Giant Food are just two of the many supermarket chains that give money and/or equipment to schools in their neighborhoods.

As with any aspect of retail strategy planning, community relations efforts can be undertaken by retailers of any size and format. Here's an illustration.

The Village Market in Wilton, Connecticut—which has 16,000 residents—is a full-service independent supermarket owned by Peter Keating, who was a long-time employee. Although many other independent supermarkets have succumbed to the competition from large chains, food-based superstores, and membership clubs, the Village Market has been quite successful due to its customer services (it accepts credit cards) and societally oriented niche.

The firm donates $20,000 per year to local groups, ranging from the Little League to the local YMCA. It also matches funds that civic groups receive in their fund-raising efforts for items like a Wilton grade school piano and cheerleaders' uniforms. Peter Keating has even coached the local Brownie troop on how to sell cookies. The Village Market does not limit its community involvement to just child-oriented programs. For example, it actively promotes the local food bank. Each year, the store collects three to four tons of food from its customers and employees for the needy. The company also regularly offers free water and free use of its freezers to community residents when local power fails.[35]

[35]Andrew H. Malcolm, "Grocer Thrives with Personal Touches," *New York Times* (January 29, 1993), p. B5.

Summary

1. *To show the importance of communicating with customers* Customer communications are crucial for a retailer (store- or nonstore-based) to position itself in customers' minds. Various physical and symbolic cues can be used when communicating.

2. *To examine the concept of retail image* Creating and maintaining the proper image, the way a firm is perceived by its customers, is an essential aspect of the retail strategy mix. The components of a firm's image are its target market characteristics, retail positioning, store location, merchandise assortment, price levels, physical facilities, customer services, community service, mass advertising and publicity, personal selling, and sales promotions. Accordingly, a retail image requires a multistep, ongoing process. For chains, it is essential that there be a consistent image among branches.

3. *To describe how a retailer's image is established through the use of atmosphere via its exterior, general interior, layout, and displays* A retailer's image depends heavily on the atmosphere (atmospherics) projected. For a store-based retailer, atmosphere is defined as the physical attributes of the store utilized to develop an image; it is composed of the exterior, general interior, store layout, and displays. For a nonstore-based firm, the physical attributes of such strategic mix factors as catalogs, vending machines, and Web sites affect its image.

The store exterior is comprised of the storefront, marquee, entrances, display windows, building height and size, visibility, uniqueness, surrounding stores and area, parking, and congestion. It sets a mood or tone before a prospective customer even enters a store.

The general interior of a store encompasses its flooring, colors, lighting, scents and sounds, fixtures, wall textures, temperature, width of aisles, dressing facilities, vertical transportation, dead areas, personnel, self-service, merchandise, price displays, cash register placement, technology/modernization, and cleanliness. The interior of an upscale retailer is far different from that of a discounter—portraying the image desired, as well as the costs of doing business.

In laying out a store's interior, six steps are followed. One, floor space is allocated among selling, merchandise, personnel, and customers; and adequate space is provided for each, based on a firm's overall strategy. More firms now use planograms to allot store space. Two, product groupings are set, based on function, purchase motivation, market segment, and/or storability. Three, traffic flows are planned, using a straight or curving pattern. Four, space per product category is computed through a model stock approach or sales-productivity ratio. Five, departments are located. Six, individual products are arranged within departments.

Interior (point-of-purchase) displays provide information for consumers, add to store atmosphere, and have a promotional role. Interior display possibilities include assortment displays, theme displays, ensemble displays, rack and case displays, cut case and dump bin displays, posters, mobiles, and wall decorations.

4. *To consider the impact of customer services and community relations on a retailer's image* Customer services are the identifiable, but mostly intangible, activities offered by a retailer in selling its basic goods and services. As a firm outlines its customer services strategy, several decisions must be made: What services are primary and ancillary? What level is needed to complement the company's image? Should a variety be presented? Should fees be charged? How can service effectiveness be measured? How can unprofitable services be terminated? Customer services include credit, delivery, alterations and installations, packaging, complaints and returns handling, gift certificates, trade-ins, and so on.

When forming a credit strategy, a retailer must decide whether to have its own credit plan and/or accept outside credit cards. It must also choose which of these tactics to utilize: revolving accounts, option accounts, open accounts, monthly payment accounts, deferred billing, layaway plans, and COD.

Customers are likely to react favorably to retailers showing community interest and involvement in such activities as establishing stores that are barrier-free for disabled persons, supporting charities, and running special sales for senior citizens.

Key Terms

atmosphere (atmospherics) (p. 552)
storefront (p. 552)
marquee (p. 554)
dead areas (p. 559)
selling space (p. 560)
merchandise space (p. 560)
personnel space (p. 560)
customer space (p. 560)
planogram (p. 560)
functional product groupings (p. 560)
purchase-motivation product groupings (p. 560)
market-segment product groupings (p. 560)

storability product groupings (p. 561)
straight (gridiron) traffic flow (p. 561)
curving (free-flowing) traffic flow (p. 561)
model stock approach (p. 564)
sales-productivity ratio (p. 564)
point-of-purchase (POP) display (p. 565)
assortment display (p. 565)
theme-setting display (p. 566)
ensemble display (p. 566)
rack display (p. 566)
case display (p. 566)

cut case (p. 566)
dump bin (p. 566)
primary customer services (p. 569)
ancillary customer services (p. 570)
revolving credit account (p. 573)
option credit account (p. 573)
open credit account (p. 574)
monthly payment credit account (p. 574)
deferred billing (p. 574)
layaway plan (p. 574)
COD (collect on delivery) (p. 574)

Questions for Discussion

1. Why is it sometimes difficult for a retailer to convey its image to consumers? Give a local example of a retailer with a fuzzy image.
2. How could a stationery store project an upscale retail image? How could a used-car dealer project such an image?
3. Define the concept of *atmosphere.* How does this differ from that of *image?*
4. Which aspects of a store's exterior are controllable by a retailer? Which are uncontrollable?
5. What are the advantages and disadvantages of self-service?
6. How would the following differ for a luxury hotel and a discount motel?
   a. Flooring.
   b. Lighting.
   c. Fixtures.
   d. Personnel.
   e. Level of self-service.
7. What are meant by selling, merchandise, personnel, and customer space?
8. Present a planogram for a nearby convenience store.
9. Develop a purchase-motivation product grouping for a gift store.
10. Which stores should *not* use a straight (gridiron) layout? Explain your answer.
11. Why would a retailer use the sales-productivity ratio instead of the model stock approach in determining space needs? What are the limitations of the sales-productivity ratio?
12. For each of these services, give an example of a retailer that would consider it primary and a retailer that would consider it ancillary.
    a. Delivery.
    b. Credit.
    c. Alterations.
    d. Personal shoppers.
13. Distinguish among revolving, open, and monthly credit accounts. What are the pros and cons of each?
14. Why should a retailer contribute to a charity or pay to sponsor a Little League team?

Web-Based Exercise:

TRADER JOE'S (http://www. traderjoes.com)

Questions

1. Write a short report describing Trader Joe's overall image based on this Web site. Include quality, price, assortment, physical, and technical factors. If you are familiar with a Trader Joe's store, compare the image description based on the Web site with that of the store. If not, would you want to shop there? Why or why not?
2. How does this Web site convey an atmosphere for Trader Joe's?
3. Evaluate Trader Joe's "Choosing and Using Our Products" section.
4. Comment on the customer services provided by Trader Joe's.

**CASE I
Goodings:
Atmosphere
at the Flagship
Store***

Gooding's is a supermarket chain that fits its stores to their locations. Unlike its unit in Disney World that caters to tourists, Gooding's flagship supermarket in an affluent section of Orlando appeals to residents who live within three miles of that store. The income level of these residents is two times that of the average metropolitan Orlando resident.

The term "flagship" generally denotes the largest or newest retail unit in a chain, but Gooding's flagship store possesses neither of these qualities. Although the store has been remodeled twice (most recently in 1994), it is more than 15 years old. Gooding's newer units are 60,000 square feet in size (and include such service facilities as a dry cleaner,

*The material in this case is drawn from data supplied by Gooding's.

bank, and cellular phone store), while this store is 47,000 square feet in size (34,000 square feet of this is selling space) and does not have any of these service facilities.

What clearly makes this unit Gooding's flagship store is its selection of high-quality products (such as meats, produce, prepared foods, and baked goods), set in a most pleasing atmosphere. Its merchandising and atmosphere are both aimed at its demanding high-income consumers.

One retailing analyst described the Orlando store's philosophy as "try something new" or "a combination of intrigue and temptation." For example, the store offers customers both traditional cuts of prime beef and unusual foods (such as ostrich, caribou, kangaroo, wild boar, and pheasant). Although one may think that the products are offered for image purposes only, the store sells large quantities of these meats. The produce department also offers unusual fruits and vegetables, in addition to standard varieties. Gooding's has worked hard to make this a destination department, despite its being located in the rear of the store. The prepared foods department is also far from a typical "me-too" department. On a typical day, 20 varieties of chilled salads and entrees are offered, including such specialties as smoked chicken ravioli, curried Dijon chicken salad, and roasted red peppers. Fresh Caesar salad is individually prepared and served for consumers during the store's peak hours. Lastly, all of the store's bakery items, including croissants, are "baked from scratch" on the premises.

The store's atmosphere is most unusual for a supermarket. It has a full sushi bar, an espresso bar, and a seafood department with live fish housed in large fish tanks. All food service personnel wear a chef's hat to underscore the food's high quality and the store's cleanliness. In addition, the store has a working fountain and seating area, and much of the store is carpeted.

The flagship store is financially successful (its weekly sales volume is over $400,000 compared with a weekly break-even volume of $275,000). Nonetheless, the store's manager feels it is unfairly viewed as high-priced by some consumers. The store's upscale products and image have contributed to this image. To change this perception, the store recently discontinued its double-couponing strategy. Instead, it now promotes the "10,000 new low prices in Orlando" theme.

Another issue for Gooding's is the high degree of competition in the Orlando supermarket business. Because Orlando has experienced high population growth, Publix, Winn-Dixie, and Albertson's all operate supermarkets in Orlando. Winn-Dixie has remodeled all of its stores. Albertson's (a chain based in Boise, Idaho) has a new warehouse distribution center in Florida, signaling to Florida's other supermarket chains that Albertson's plans a major presence in Florida. In 1994, Albertson's even opened a supermarket in the same shopping center as Gooding's flagship store. Fortunately, it has had little impact on the flagship store's sales.

Questions

1. Gooding's has been employee-owned since 1988. What impact does employee ownership have on a store's atmosphere?
2. What are the pros and cons of Gooding's strategy of placing its produce department in the rear of the store?
3. Evaluate Gooding's "10,000 new low prices in Orlando" theme with the use of double couponing from a store image perspective.
4. What services should Gooding's flagship store consider to reinforce its current image?

Video Questions on Gooding's

1. Evaluate Gooding's sales by department in terms of its image.
2. Present specific suggestions to improve Gooding's poor in-store pizza department.

CASE 2
Personal Shopping Comes of Age[†]

Personal shoppers are retail employees who provide a broad range of services for their customers. These services typically include assembling selected items for client approval, offering advice on appropriate fashion accessories, selecting gifts for friends and relatives, and even wrapping and mailing items. To attract better customers, personal shoppers in stores such as Neiman Marcus have begun to sponsor fashion shows and wardrobe clinics. At other stores, personal shoppers advise customers on the proper clothing for a vacation trip based on the weather forecast and the dress code at selected restaurants.

Until recently, personal shoppers were used mostly by upscale department stores as a special accommodation for their very best customers. The use of personal shoppers has now expanded to middle-range department stores (such as Macy's and Marshall Field) and to a much broader range of shoppers. Most retailers with personal shoppers feel this extra customer service is a way of generating and maintaining shoppers. It can also motivate and retain a firm's best salespeople.

Retailers report that the most frequent users of personal shoppers are females. They are often busy executives who are time-pressed or need direction as to what types of clothing are apropos for work. For example, 80 percent of Saks Fifth Avenue's clients of its personal shoppers are career women; and Nordstrom knows the overwhelming majority of its personal shopper clients are time-constrained working women. However, Nordstrom has also found that another important market segment is men who need help in keeping up with fashion trends.

Although there are several possible career paths for personal shoppers, many start out as successful store-based salespeople who were ultimately promoted to the back room or the personal shopping department. A good personal shopper earns $50,000 per year; a top one can make an annual six-figure income. Because commissions and bonuses are key components in a personal shopper's income (the average commission is 8 percent of sales), a personal shopper needs to be trained to think in terms of long-term client relationships. Thus, a skillful personal shopper would not encourage a customer to spend more than necessary. This may mean encouraging a client to keep an older but still stylish suit or to buy a pair of contrasting slacks to get more mileage from a new blazer. These strategies generate buyer confidence and encourage repeat business.

A regular client at a Neiman Marcus or a Saks Fifth Avenue may spend between $1,000 and $2,000 during a seasonal wardrobe event, while the best clients at these stores may spend as much as $10,000 or more in a week. As a result, keeping wealthy clients happy is so important to personal shoppers, that most of them will gladly handle special requests. Typically, these clients and their spouses are offered complimentary full-day makeovers, free refreshments, access to hard-to-find items, and in-home wardrobe consultation services.

It is imperative that all retailers employing personal shoppers monitor their actions carefully since poor performance can lead to the loss of their best customers. Many firms advise clients to clearly communicate with personal shoppers as to their budget limits, color and designer preferences, and whether they wish to be sent clothing on an "on approval" basis, without being notified in advance. This communication avoids misunderstandings between the personal shopper and the client.

Despite comprehensive safeguards, there is high potential for abuse by personal shoppers who may receive an especially high commission from a retailer for selling goods of a specific designer or from a personal shopper who needs to meet a monthly sales quota. Because some personal shoppers can charge items on their clients' credit cards without the clients' signature, the latter may receive unordered goods from shoppers seeking to temporarily inflate their own sales commissions.

[†]The material in this case is drawn from Amy Myers Jaffe, "Retailing's New Strategy: I Can Get It for You Personal," *New York Times* (August 13, 1995), Section 3, p. 8.

Questions

1. Under what conditions is a personal shopper a primary customer service? An ancillary customer service?
2. Develop a list of appropriate personal shopper services for a $1,000 a year clothing customer and for a $6,000 a year clothing customer.
3. Develop a strategy to curb potential abuses among personal shoppers.
4. How would you train personal shoppers to think in terms of long-term customer relationships?

18

....
Promotional Strategy

As part of its comprehensive promotion strategy, McDonald's effectively uses partnerships with such firms as United Airlines, Walt Disney, Twentieth Century Fox, and Saban Entertainment. These partnerships provide a "win-win" situation—with McDonald's deriving increased sales and its partners obtaining greater awareness for featured goods and services through the retailer's worldwide distribution and promotional activities.

McDonald's United Airlines relationship started with the latter's use of McDonald's Friendly Skies Meals program. United now also features the "McDonald's Magical Radio," an in-flight audio channel for children—which includes free headsets, copies of McDonald's *Fun Time* magazine, and in-flight music from Kid Rhino records.

McDonald's ten-year alliance with Disney gives McDonald's the exclusive fast-food industry rights to promote Disney movies, videos, and theme park rides. McDonald's is involved with 14 to 17 Disney-related promotions per year. The McDonald's partnership follows Disney's five-year partnership with Burger King. That relationship resulted in Burger King's having significant sales increases because of tie-in promotions with Disney's *The Lion King, Pocahontas, Aladdin, Toy Story,* and *Beauty and the Beast.* Some analysts were quite surprised at Disney's dropping Burger King as a partner, since the co-sponsored promotions had been so successful.

As part of its agreement, McDonald's is paying Disney $100 million in royalty and licensing fees. In addition, McDonald's will pay promotional monies as the "presenting sponsor" of Disney's new Animal Kingdom theme park, expected to open in 1998. McDonald's has also agreed to make Disney its exclusive studio and to commit virtually its entire promotional calendar to Disney; and McDonald's is precluded from future deals with such entertainment giants as Universal Studios and Warner Bros. Although McDonald's has the right to refuse a tie-in deal on any Disney movie, Disney then may offer that tie-in to any other fast-food chain other than Burger King, Pizza Hut, Taco Bell, and KFC.

In its partnership with Twentieth Century Fox and Saban Entertainment, McDonald's has tie-ins to the popular Power Rangers toys and accompanying movies. In 1996, a joint promotion featured in-store merchandising materials, TV ads, and pre-event publicity. McDonald's customers were offered a Power Ranger toy at cost ($1.59) with a purchase of a Happy Meal or a large sandwich. This promotion resulted in the sale of over 25 million Power Ranger Zord sets.[1]

---

[1] Michael Wilke, "McDonald's Gets in Tune with United Airlines," *Advertising Age* (May 20, 1996), p. 29; Blair R. Fischer, "Disney Cooks Deal with McDonald's," *Promo* (May 1996), pp. 10–11; Thomas King, "Mickey May Be the Big Winner in Disney-McDonald's Alliance," *New York Times* (May 29, 1996), p. B2; and "McDonald's/ Mighty Morphin Power Rangers," *Promo* (March 1996), p. R6.

Retail promotion is broadly defined as any communication by a retailer that informs, **OVERVIEW** persuades, and/or reminds the target market about any aspect of that firm. This chapter deals with developing and enacting a promotional strategy. In the first part of the chapter, elements of promotion (advertising, public relations, personal selling, and sales promotion) are detailed. The second part centers on the strategic aspects of promotion: objectives, budget, mix of forms, implementation of mix, and review and revision of the plan.

Advertising, public relations, personal selling, and sales promotion are the four elements **ELEMENTS OF** of promotion. Each is discussed here in terms of goals, advantages and disadvantages, **THE RETAIL** and basic forms. Although these elements are described individually, a good promotional **PROMO-** plan normally integrates them—based on the overall strategy of the retailer. A movie **TIONAL MIX** theater concentrates more on advertising and sales promotion (point-of-purchase displays to prompt food and beverage sales), while an upscale independent specialty store stresses personal selling.

Retailers spend significant sums on promotion efforts. For example, in a typical department store, about 3 percent of sales is spent on advertising and 8 percent to 10 percent on personal selling and support services.[2] In addition, most department store chains invest heavily in sales promotions (such as special events) and employ internal or external public relations offices to generate favorable publicity and respond to media requests for information.

This is the ambitious promotion plan of HMV Record Stores:

The goal is to build a brand identity for HMV as the chain continuously "serving music"—a play on the slogan, "His master's voice," from which the company derived its name. "What I felt was needed was a creative direction in all our U.S. markets," said Alan McDonald, vice-president for marketing at HMV U.S.A. His reference was to the stores HMV U.S.A., a unit of the British firm Thorn EMI, has in cities such as Atlanta, Boston, New York, Philadelphia, and Washington, as well as the Rock-and-Roll Hall of Fame and Museum in Cleveland. "We'd been saying very little other than running ads with HMV logos," McDonald said, "and even the logos differed from one ad to the other." Along with "co-op advertising"—funds record firms give HMV U.S.A. for campaigns centering on specific artists and albums—the retailer's annual budget is $4 million. But before spending anything, McDonald wanted data on the retail music market, particularly on the frequent buyers of CDs (now the dominant music format). Such consumers account for almost 75 percent of all CD sales. HMV, according to research, was recognized for strengths in service, selection, and prices. Those factors became the focus of a newspaper and magazine ad campaign, along with the concept that "although you'll find video at our stores, music is what we're about, as against CD-ROMs, video games, books, fragrances, or clothing"—items rivals sell. Other parts of the campaign include bus stop posters, flyers with discount coupons, and sponsorship of events like the Central Park concert series in Manhattan. To hit the tourist market in Manhattan, HMV has run a free shuttle bus between hotels and Grand Central Terminal. The bus is painted pink and covered with HMV logos, and riders can obtain discount coupons.[3]

[2]Schonfeld & Associates, "Advertising-to-Sales Ratios, 1996," *Advertising Age* (July 1, 1996), p. 11; and Alexandra Moran (Editor), *FOR 1996 Edition* (New York: Wiley, 1996), pp. 8–9.
[3]Stuart Elliott, "Advertising," *New York Times* (July 2, 1996), p. D7.

Table 18-1 SELECTED U.S. ADVERTISING-TO-SALES RATIOS BY TYPE OF RETAILER

Type of Retailer	Advertising Dollars as Percentage of Sales Dollars[a]	Advertising Dollars as Percentage of Margin[b]
Apparel and accessories stores	2.5	7.6
Auto and home supply stores	1.1	2.9
Department stores	3.1	9.5
Drug and proprietary stores	1.3	4.7
Eating places	4.0	18.0
Family clothing stores	2.8	9.0
Furniture stores	5.9	13.3
Grocery stores	1.1	4.0
Hobby, game, and toy shops	1.7	5.5
Hotels/motels	4.1	10.5
Lumber and building materials	1.0	3.5
Mail-order firms	9.9	26.4
Movie theaters	3.1	17.2
Photofinishing labs	2.9	5.4
Radio, television, and consumer electronics stores	3.3	14.7
Record and tape stores	3.3	7.1
Shoe stores	4.0	12.6
Variety stores	1.7	7.4

[a]Advertising dollars as percentage of sales = Advertising expenditures/Net company sales

[b]Advertising dollars as percentage of margin = Advertising expenditures/(Net company sales − Cost of goods sold)

Source: Schonfeld & Associates, "Advertising-to-Sales Ratios, 1996," *Advertising Age* (July 1, 1996), p. 11. Reprinted by permission. Copyright Crain Communications Inc.

Advertising

Advertising is paid, nonpersonal communication transmitted through out-of-store mass media by an identified sponsor. Four aspects of the definition merit further clarification:

1. Paid form—This distinguishes advertising from publicity (an element of public relations), for which no payment is made by the retailer for the time or space used to convey a message.
2. Nonpersonal presentation—In advertising, a standard message is delivered to the entire audience, and it cannot be adapted to individual customers (except when the World Wide Web is involved).
3. Out-of-store mass media—These include newspaper, radio, TV, World Wide Web, and other mass communication channels, rather than personal contacts. In-store communication (such as displays and audio announcements) are considered sales promotion.
4. Identified sponsor—Advertising clearly divulges the name of the sponsor, unlike publicity.

Sears has the highest annual dollar advertising expenditures among U.S. retailers—$1.2 billion. About 3.9 percent of its U.S. sales is spent on ads. In contrast, many firms have higher advertising-to-sales ratios, despite lower dollar spending; these include McDonald's (5.5 percent of systemwide U.S. sales) and Circuit City (4.9 percent). On the other hand, Wal-Mart spends just 0.4 percent of sales on ads, relying more on word of mouth and everyday low prices.[4] Table 18-1 shows 1995 advertising-to-sales ratios for a number of retailing categories.

[4]"100 Leading National Advertisers," *Advertising Age* (September 30, 1996), various pages.

Differences Between Retailer and Manufacturer Advertising Strategies ❏ Although the definition cited applies to all advertising, it is important to examine some of the key differences between retailer and manufacturer advertising strategies. First, retailers usually have more geographically concentrated target markets than manufacturers. This means they can adapt better to local needs, habits, and preferences than manufacturers. However, retailers typically are unable to utilize national media as readily as manufacturers. For example, only the largest retail chains and franchises can advertise on national TV programs. An exception is direct marketing (including the World Wide Web) because trading areas for even small firms can be geographically dispersed.

Second, retail ads emphasize immediacy. Individual items are placed for sale and advertised during specific, short time periods. Timely purchases are sought. In contrast, manufacturers are more often concerned with developing favorable attitudes toward products or the company and not with short-run sales increases.

Third, many retailers stress prices in ads, whereas manufacturers usually emphasize several product attributes. In addition, retailers often display a number of different products in one ad, whereas manufacturers tend to minimize the number of products mentioned in a single ad.

Fourth, media rates tend to be lower for retailers than for manufacturers. Because of this factor and the desire of many manufacturers and wholesalers for wide distribution, the costs of retail advertising are sometimes shared by manufacturers or wholesalers and retailers. Two or more retailers may also share costs. This is known as **cooperative advertising.**

Objectives ❏ Retail advertising may be tied to a wide variety of specific goals, including

■ Short-term sales increases.
■ Greater customer traffic.
■ Developing and/or reinforcing a retail image.
■ Informing customers about goods and services and/or company attributes. See Figure 18-1.
■ Easing the job for sales personnel.
■ Developing demand for private brands.

A retailer would select one or more goals and base advertising efforts on it (them).

Advantages and Disadvantages ❏ The major advantages of advertising are that

■ A large audience is attracted. Also, for print media, circulation is supplemented by the passing of a copy from one reader to another.
■ The costs per viewer, reader, or listener are low.
■ A large number of alternative media are available. Therefore, a retailer can match a medium to the target market.
■ The retailer has control over message content, graphics, timing, and size (or length), so a standardized message in a chosen format can be delivered to the entire audience.
■ In print media, a message can be studied and restudied by the target market.
■ Editorial content (a TV show, a news story, and so on) often surrounds an ad. This may increase its credibility or the probability it will be read.
■ Because a customer can become aware of a retailer and its goods and services before shopping, self-service or reduced-service operations are possible.

The major disadvantages of advertising are that

■ Because the message is standardized, it is inflexible (except for the World Wide Web, whose interactive nature can be tailored to people's needs). The retailer cannot focus on the needs of individual customers.

Figure 18-1

**Retail Advertising:
Presenting
Information to
Consumers**

Local Market

The First Factory Outlet Mall in Puerto Rico

SAN JUAN

The total population of Puerto Rico is 3.7 million. More than 1.75 million shoppers, many who are affluent, live within a 25 mile radius of this site. The site is prominently located on Highway 3, only a quarter of a mile east of the intersection of Highways 3 and 188. It will have superb visibility and accessibility to the greater San Juan metro area.

1990 Census	Within 10 mile radius	Within 15 mile radius	Within 25 mile radius
Population	394,485	1,005,631	1,770,280
Households	115,186	317,988	543,101
Average Age	31.6	33.2	32.5

For more information, contact Steve Aronow, John Ellis, Ron Simkin, Jay Tillman, or Ed Woods at (901) 762-7366.

■ Some types of advertising require large investments. This may eliminate the access of small retailers to certain media (such as TV).
■ Media may reach large geographic areas, and for retailers, waste may occur. Thus, a small supermarket chain may find only 40 percent of a paper's readers reside in its trading area.
■ Some media require an extremely long lead time for placing ads. This reduces the retailer's ability to advertise fad items or to react to some current events themes.
■ Some media have a high throwaway rate. For instance, circulars and mail ads may be discarded without being read.
■ Ads often are brief. This means a 30-second TV commercial or quarter-page newspaper ad cannot contain much information.

How Do Retailers Advertise in Indonesia?

When Wal-Mart opened its first store in Jakarta, Indonesia, during the later months of 1996, it began a competitive battle with PT Matahari Putra Prima (Matahari), the leading Indonesian competitor with a very similar retail strategy to Wal-Mart. Although Wal-Mart's global sales are 85 times those of its new rival, Matahari has a 40 percent market share of Indonesia's department store sales. Over the past several years, Matahari's annual sales have grown by 40 percent, while the firm has maintained solid profit margins of 6 percent of revenues.

A local Indonesian agency is handling Wal-Mart's advertising. The campaign stresses the firm's everyday low pricing strategy and its one-stop shopping appeal. Wal-Mart is also using a "smiley face" image (similar to one used in the 1970s in the United States) on its promotional handouts, in newspaper inserts, and in circulars that are mailed to consumer households.

In response to Wal-Mart's market entry and expansion plans, Matahari has stepped up its own advertising budget to $15 million. According to a Matahari spokesperson, "We want to stop them [Wal-Mart] now, before they get too big." Its new TV commercials (30- and 60-second spots) promote Matahari as the retailer that Indonesians can count on. Matahari hopes its 98 percent name recognition among Indonesian consumers will continue to be a major competitive advantage.

Source: Rebecca Fannin, "Wal-Mart to Do Battle with Indonesian Giant," *Ad Age International* (July 1996), pp. 12–14.

These are broad generalities about the entire field of advertising. The pros and cons of specific media are described next.

Media ❑ Retailers can choose from among papers, phone directories, direct mail, radio, TV, the World Wide Web, transit, outdoor, magazines, and flyers/circulars. A summary of the attributes of these media appears in Table 18-2.

Papers can be classified as dailies, weeklies, and shoppers. Among retailers, the paper is the most preferred medium, having the advantages of market coverage, short lead time, reasonable costs, flexibility, longevity, graphics, and editorial association (ads near columns or articles). Disadvantages include the possible waste (circulation to a wider geographic area than that containing the target market), the competition among retailers, the black-and-white format, and the appeal to fewer senses than TV. To maintain their dominant position, many papers have redesigned their graphics, and some have now run a limited number of color ads. Free-distribution shopper papers (also known as "penny savers")—delivered to all consumer households in a geographic area—are growing in use, sometimes at the expense of other types of papers.

Phone directories (the White and Yellow Pages) are key advertising media. In the White Pages, retailers get free alphabetical listings along with all other phone subscribers, commercial and noncommercial. The major advantage of the White over the Yellow Pages is that customers who are familiar with a retailer's name are not distracted by seeing competitors' names. The major disadvantage, in contrast with the Yellow Pages, is the alphabetical rather than type-of-business listing. Thus, a customer unfamiliar with repair services in his or her area will usually look in the Yellow Pages under "Repair" and choose a listed firm.

With the Yellow Pages, retailers pay for alphabetical listings (and larger display ads, if desired) in their business categories. Most retailers advertise in the Yellow Pages. The advantages include their widespread usage by people who are ready to shop or purchase and their long life (one year or more). The disadvantages are that retailer awareness is not stimulated and there is a lengthy lead time for new ads. Since the breakup of AT&T, retailers have had multiple Yellow Pages firms vying for their business—sometimes at lower rates.

Table 18-2   ADVERTISING MEDIA COMPARISON CHART

Medium	Market Coverage	Particular Suitability	Major Advantages	Major Disadvantages
Daily papers	Single community or entire metro area; local editions may be available.	All larger retailers.	Wide circulation, short lead time.	Nonselective audience, heavy ad competition.
Weekly papers	Single community usually; may be a metro area.	Retailers with a strictly local market.	Targeted readers, local identification.	Limited audience, little ad creativity.
Shopper papers	Most households in one community; chain shoppers can cover a metro area.	Neighborhood retailers and service businesses.	Targeted readers, low costs.	Small audience, a giveaway and not always read.
Phone directories	Geographic area or occupational field served by the directory.	All types of goods and service-oriented retailers.	Attract consumers who are ready to shop or purchase, permanent message.	Limited to active shoppers, long lead time needed.
Direct mail	Controlled by the retailer.	New and expanding firms, those using coupons or special offers, mail order.	Targeted readers, personalized and aimed at good prospects, can be tied to data base.	High throwaway rate, low image to many consumers.
Radio	Definable market area surrounding the station.	Retailers focusing on identifiable segments.	Relatively low costs, good market coverage.	No visual effect, must be used regularly to be of value.
TV	Definable market area surrounding the station.	Retailers of goods and services with wide appeal.	Dramatic impact, wide market coverage.	High cost of time and production, audience waste.
World Wide Web	Global.	All types of goods and service-oriented retailers.	Wide market coverage, interactive, low costs, multimedia capabilities.	Privacy issues, need for continuous updating, hard to measure results.
Transit	Urban or metro community served by transit system.	Retailers near transit routes, especially those appealing to commuters.	Targeted audience, repetition and length of exposure.	Clutter of ads, distracted or uninterested audience.
Outdoor	Entire metro area or single neighborhood.	Amusement and tourist-oriented retailers, well-known firms.	Dominant size, frequency of exposure.	Clutter of ads, distracted or disinterested audience.
Local magazines	Entire metro area or region, zoned editions sometimes available.	Restaurants, entertainment-oriented firms, specialty shops, mail-order firms.	Special-interest audience, creative options.	Long lead time, less sense of immediacy.
Flyers/circulars	Single neighborhood.	Restaurants, dry cleaners, service stations, and other neighborhood firms.	Very targeted audience, low costs.	High throwaway rate, poor image.

Direct mail is the medium whereby retailers send catalogs or ads to customers through the U.S. mail or private delivery firms. Some of its advantages are the targeted audience, tailor-made format, controlled costs, quick feedback, and potential tie-ins (such as retailers with their own credit cards including ads with monthly billing statements). Computerized data bases have greatly improved the efficiency of direct-mail advertising. Among the disadvantages of direct mail are the high throwaway rate ("junk mail"), poor image to some consumers, low response rate, and outdated mailing lists (addressees may have moved).

Radio is used by a variety of retailers. The advantages are the relatively low costs, its value as a medium for car drivers and riders, its ability to use segmentation, its rather short lead time, and its wide reach. The disadvantages include no visual impact, the need for repetition, the need for brevity, and waste. The use of radio by retailers has gone up in recent years.

TV, although increasing in importance due to the rise of national and regional firms, is far behind papers in retail advertising expenditures. Among the advantages of TV are the dramatic effects of video messages, the large market coverage, creativity, and program affiliation (for regular sponsors). The disadvantages of TV include the high minimum costs, the audience waste, the need for brevity, the need for repetition, and the limited availability of popular time slots for nonregular sponsors. Because cable TV is more focused than conventional stations, it appeals to a growing number of local retailers.

From an advertising perspective, retailers are utilizing the World Wide Web to provide information to customers about store locations, to describe the products carried, to let people order catalogs, and so forth. Some firms are also selling products from their Web sites. Retailers have two opportunities to reach customers via the Web: by advertising on browsers (such as Netscape and Internet Explorer) and other firms' Web sites and by communicating with customers at their own sites. As noted in Chapter 6, retailer participation in this kind of advertising is growing quickly.

Transit advertising is used in areas with mass-transit systems. Ads are displayed on buses and in trains and taxis. They have the advantages of a captive audience, a mass market, a high level of repetitiveness, and a geographically defined market. Disadvantages are the ad clutter, a distracted or uninterested audience, a lack of availability in small areas, restricted travel paths, and graffiti. Besides the transit ads already mentioned, retailers often advertise on their delivery trucks.

Outdoor (billboard) advertising is sometimes used by retailers. Posters and signs may be displayed in public places, on buildings, and alongside highways. Advantages are the large size of the ads, the frequency of exposure, the relatively low costs, and the assistance in directing new customers. Disadvantages include the clutter of ads, a distracted or uninterested audience, the limited information, and some legislation banning outdoor ads.

Magazines are growing more significant for retailers due to three factors: the rise in national and regional retailers, the creation of regional and local editions, and the use by mail-order firms. Advantages of magazines are their tailoring to specific markets, the creative options, editorial associations, the longevity of messages, and the use of color. Among the disadvantages are the long lead time, less sense of consumer urgency, and waste.

Flyers/circulars are also a major advertising medium. Single-page (flyers) or multiple-page (circulars) ads can be distributed in parking lots or right to consumer homes. Advantages include a very targeted audience, low costs, flexibility, and speed. Among the disadvantages are the high level of throwaways, the poor image to some consumers, and clutter. Flyers are good for smaller retailers, while circulars are used by larger ones.

Types ❏ Advertisements can be classified by content and payment method. See Figure 18-2.

Ads may be pioneering, competitive, reminder, or institutional. *Pioneer ads* have awareness as a goal and offer information (usually on new firms or locations). *Competitive ads* have persuasion as a goal. *Reminder ads* are geared to loyal customers and stress the attributes that have made the retailers successful. *Institutional ads* strive to keep retailer names before the public without emphasizing the sale of goods or services. Public service messages are institutional in nature.

In placing ads, retailers may pay their own way and/or seek cooperative ventures. For the retailers paying their own way, the major advantages are control and flexibility. The major disadvantages are the costs and efforts required. Cooperative ventures are those where two or more parties share the costs and the decision making. It is estimated that more than $10 billion is spent annually on U.S. cooperative advertising, most through vertical agreements. Newspapers are much preferred over other media for cooperative ads related to retailing.

Figure 18-2

Types of Advertising

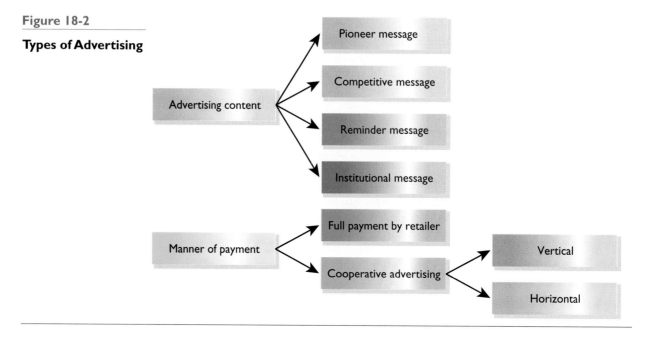

In a **vertical cooperative-advertising agreement,** a manufacturer and a retailer or a wholesaler and a retailer share an ad.[5] Each party's duties and responsibilities are usually specified contractually. Retailers are typically not reimbursed until after ads are run and invoices are provided to the manufacturer or the wholesaler. Vertical cooperative advertising is subject to the Robinson-Patman Act; manufacturers and other suppliers must offer similar arrangements to all retailers on a proportional basis. The advantages of a vertical agreement to a retailer are its reduced ad costs, the assistance in preparing advertisements, greater coverage of the market, and less expenditure of the retailer's time. Disadvantages to a retailer include less control, flexibility, and distinctiveness. Some retailers have been concerned about the requirements they must satisfy to be eligible for support and the emphasis on the supplier's name in ads. Manufacturers and other suppliers are responding by being more flexible and understanding of their retailers' concerns. For instance, in the American Express cooperative program, restaurants can choose from among dozens of border designs and copy blocks (which can be tailored to a wide variety of cuisines). Restaurants can also insert their own logos and add other copy.

With a **horizontal cooperative-advertising agreement,** two or more retailers share an ad. A horizontal agreement is most often undertaken by small, noncompeting retailers (such as independent hardware stores); retailers situated together in a shopping center; and franchisees of the same franchising firm. The advantages and disadvantages are similar to those in a vertical agreement. Two further benefits are the increased bargaining power of retailers in dealing with the media and the synergies of multiple retailers working together.

While planning a cooperative advertising strategy, retailers should consider such questions as these:

■ What ads qualify, in terms of merchandise and special requirements?
■ What percentage of advertising is paid by each party?
■ When can ads be run?
■ What media can be used?

[5]See Raju Narisetti, "Joint Marketing with Retailers Spreads," *Wall Street Journal* (October 24, 1996), p. B6.

■ Are there special provisions regarding message content?
■ What documentation is required for reimbursement?
■ How does each party benefit?
■ Do cooperative advertisements obscure the image of individual retailers?

Public Relations

Public relations entails any communication that fosters a favorable image for the retailer among its publics (consumers, investors, government, channel members, employees, and the general public). It may be nonpersonal or personal, paid or nonpaid, and sponsor controlled or not controlled. **Publicity** is any nonpersonal form of public relations whereby messages are transmitted through mass media, the time or space provided by the media is not paid for, and there is no identified commercial sponsor.

The basic distinction between advertising and publicity is the nonpaid nature of the latter. Because of this difference, publicity messages are not as readily controllable by a retailer. A story about a new store opening may not appear at all, appear after the fact, or not appear in the form desired. Yet, to consumers, publicity is often deemed more credible and important than ads. Thus, advertising and publicity (public relations) should be complements, not substitutes, for each other. Many times, publicity could precede advertising.

Two leading retail practitioners of public relations are the Taco Bell and Wendy's fast-food chains. Here's how one industry expert reviewed a recent campaign from Taco Bell:

In case you were out of town, Taco Bell ran April Fools' Day ads in seven major papers announcing the purchase of the Liberty Bell to help reduce the federal budget deficit. (Never mind that the Liberty Bell is owned by the city of Philadelphia.) What a coup! What guts! Such creative timing! Frankly, I can't recall a single publicity stunt that accomplished so much positive exposure with little effort and expense. It serves to remind us of the cost-effective power of a professionally planned PR event. Especially one with bold spirit and fearless timing.

Full-page ads appeared in New York, Chicago, Los Angeles, Washington, D.C., Philadelphia, and Dallas, and in *USA Today*, proudly announcing the Liberty Bell purchase and urging other corporations to do likewise. Ad copy noted that the bell would be renamed the "Taco Liberty Bell" and rotated for public viewing between its traditional home in Philadelphia and Taco Bell's corporate headquarters in Irvine, California. Naturally, that lit up phone lines in Philadelphia, Washington, D.C., and elsewhere. More than 2,000 calls were made to Taco Bell's customer service hotline. Radio call-in shows all over the country were buzzing with the news. Later that day, Taco Bell issued a news release, confessing to the hoax and announcing a $50,000 donation for restoration of the Liberty Bell. It was all in good fun. Even those quickly angered had to crack a smile when they realized the prank. By evening, Tom Brokaw was describing the stunt on *NBC Nightly News*. The next morning, the mayor of Philadelphia was challenging Taco Bell's marketing manager on *CBS Morning News* to come up with more cash than $50,000. In all, more than 400 TV mentions were logged, including virtually every major metro market. Add this to thousands of newspaper stories and radio mentions, and you've got total exposure for Taco Bell worth millions of dollars for a media cost of $300,000 or so.[6]

[6]Bob Lamons, "Taco Bell Rings in New Age of Publicity Stunts," *Marketing News* (May 20, 1996), p. 15.

Figure 18-3

Wendy's Creative Public Relations Via the World Wide Web

Wendy's uses its colorful and informative Web site (http://www.wendys.com), illustrated in Figure 18-3, as a prime public relations vehicle:

Welcome to Wendy's Cyberspace home! Explore Wendy's House for interesting information on Wendy's International, Inc., menu and nutritional information, adoption information important for everyone to know, and a complete multimedia history of the famous Wendy's advertising campaigns including some hilarious clips of founder Dave Thomas. No need to be quiet in this <u>Library</u>. Check here for historical information including clips from Wendy's famous advertising campaigns. Glad you came. C'mon in to the <u>Sitting Room</u> to find out about adoption. Want to know why Dave Thomas is so supportive of adoption? The answer is here. We get down to business in <u>Dave's Office</u>. Information about Wendy's International from annual reports and quarterly SEC filings to the International franchise program are located here. Everybody knows Dave. Find out a little more about him in the <u>Parlor</u>. Yum! Something's cooking in the <u>Kitchen</u>! Peek in here for nutritional and other product information. You'll want to explore the whole house—visit regularly—'cause we just never know what Dave is going to come up with next!

Objectives ❑ Public relations seeks to accomplish one or more of these goals:

■ To increase awareness of the retailer and its retailing strategy mix.
■ To maintain or improve a company's image.
■ To show the retailer as a contributor to the public's quality of life.
■ To demonstrate innovativeness.
■ To present a favorable message in a highly believable manner.
■ To minimize total promotion costs.

Advantages and Disadvantages ❑ The major advantages of public relations are that

■ An image can be presented or enhanced.
■ An objective source presents the message for the retailer, providing credibility (e.g., a good review of a restaurant).
■ There are no costs for the message's time or space.
■ A mass audience is addressed.
■ Carryover effects are possible (for example, if a store is perceived as community-oriented, the value it offers is more apt to be perceived as good).
■ People pay more attention to news stories than to clearly identified ads.

The major disadvantages of public relations are that

■ Some retailers do not believe in spending any funds on image-related communication.
■ With publicity, there is little retailer control over the message and its timing, placement, and coverage by a given medium.
■ It may be more suitable for short-run rather than long-run planning.
■ Although there are no media costs for publicity, there are costs for a public relations staff, planning activities, and the activities themselves (such as store openings).

Types ❑ Public relations (publicity) can be categorized as expected or unexpected, and image enhancing or image detracting.

Expected public relations occurs when a retailer plans activities in advance and strives to have the media report on them, or anticipates that certain events will result in media coverage. Community services, such as donations and special sales; parades on holidays (such as the Macy's Thanksgiving Day Parade); the sales of new goods and services; and the opening of a new store are activities a retailer hopes will gain media coverage. The release of quarterly sales figures and publication of the annual report are events a retailer can anticipate will be covered by the media.

Unexpected publicity takes place when the media report on a retailer's performance without its having advance notice of the coverage. TV and newspaper reporters may visit restaurants and other retailers anonymously—rating their performance and quality. A fire, an employee strike, or other newsworthy events may be cited. Investigative stories on company practices may appear.

There is positive publicity when the media report on the firm in a favorable manner, with regard to the excellent nature of its retailing practices, its efforts on behalf of its community, and so on. However, the media may also provide negative publicity about a firm. For instance, with a store opening, the media could describe the location in less than glowing terms, criticize the store's effects on the environment, and otherwise be critical. The retailer has no control over the message; and the media may not cover this or any other publicity event. That is why public relations must be viewed as a component of the promotion mix, not as the whole mix.

Personal Selling

Personal selling involves oral communication with one or more prospective customers for the purpose of making sales. The level of personal selling utilized by a retailer depends on the image it wants to convey, the types of products sold, its level of self-service, and its interest in long-term customer relationships—as well as expectations of customers.[7]

At J.C. Penney, this means stepped-up training programs for sales associates. Why? First, higher levels of selling are needed to reinforce its transition to a more fashion-oriented department store. Unlike discounters that rely on self-service merchandising, Penney wants to stress the advice given by its sales staff. Second, Penney wants to stimulate greater cross-selling, whereby sales associates recommend related-item purchases to customers. Effective cross-selling increases the average sales transaction. Third, Penney wants sales associates to better "save the sale," by suggesting to customers who are returning merchandise to try different colors, styles, or quality. Fourth, through top-notch personal selling, Penney believes it can foster further customer loyalty. Table 18-3 highlights Penney's tips for its sales associates.

[7]See Sharon E. Beatty, Morris Mayer, James E. Coleman, Kristy Ellis Reynolds, and Jungki Lee, "Customer-Sales Associate Retail Relationships," *Journal of Retailing*, Vol. 72 (Fall 1996), pp. 223–247.

Table 18-3 J.C. PENNEY'S TIPS FOR SALES ASSOCIATES

1. Greet the customer to make him or her feel welcome. This sets the tone for the customer's visit to your department.
2. Listen to customers to determine their needs.
3. Know your merchandise. For example, describe the quality features of Penney's private brands.
4. Know merchandise in related departments, as well. This can increase sales, as well as lessen a customer's shopping time.
5. Learn to juggle several shoppers at once.
6. Pack the customer's merchandise carefully. Ask if the customer would want the merchandise on a hanger to prevent creasing.
7. Constantly work at keeping the department looking its best.
8. Refer to the customer by his or her name; this can be gotten from the person's credit card.
9. Stress Penney's "hassle-free" return policy.

Source: J.C. Penney.

Objectives ❏ Among the goals of personal selling are to

■ Persuade customers to make purchases (because they often enter a store after acquiring some information through advertising).
■ Stimulate sales of impulse items or products related to customers' basic purchases.
■ Complete transactions with customers.
■ Create awareness of items marketed through in-home selling and telemarketing.
■ Feed back information to company decision makers.
■ Provide adequate levels of customer service. See Figure 18-4.
■ Improve and maintain customer satisfaction.

Advantages and Disadvantages ❏ The major advantages of selling are related to the nature of personal contact:

■ A salesperson can adapt a message to the needs of the individual customer.
■ A salesperson can be flexible in offering ways to address customer needs.
■ The attention span of the customer is higher than with advertising.
■ For store-based retailers, there is little or no waste; most people who walk into a store are potential customers.
■ Customers respond more often to personal selling than to ads.
■ Immediate feedback is provided.

The major disadvantages of personal selling are that

■ Only a limited number of customers can be reached at a given time.
■ The costs of interacting with each customer can be high.
■ Customers are not initially lured into a store through personal selling.
■ Self-service may be discouraged.
■ Some customers may not perceive salespeople as helpful and knowledgeable, but rather as too aggressive.

Types ❏ Most types of retail sales positions can be categorized as either order taking or order getting. An **order-taking salesperson** is involved in routine clerical and sales functions, such as setting up displays, placing inventory on the shelves, answering simple questions, filling orders, and ringing up sales. This type of selling most often occurs in stores that have a strong mix of self-service with some personnel on the floor.

Figure 18-4

Personal Selling: When Self-Service Isn't Appropriate

Despite the greater emphasis on self-service retailing, many products (such as Lancombe cosmetics) lend themselves to a more personal approach, where salespeople can present information and answer questions.

An **order-getting salesperson** is actively involved with informing and persuading customers, and in closing sales. This is the true "sales" employee. Order getters usually sell higher-priced or complex items, such as real estate, autos, apparel, appliances, and consumer electronics. On average, they are much more skilled and better paid than order takers.

In some instances, a manufacturer may help finance the personal selling function by providing **PMs** (defined as promotional money, push money, or prize money) for retail salespeople selling that manufacturer's brand. PMs are in addition to the compensation received from the retailer. Many retailers are concerned about this practice because it encourages their sales personnel to be loyal to the manufacturer, and salespersons may be less responsive to actual customer desires (if customers desire brands not yielding PMs).

Retail salespeople may operate in a store, visit consumers' homes or places where consumers work, and/or engage in telemarketing.

Functions ❑ Store-based sales personnel may be responsible for all or many of these tasks: greeting customers, determining customer wants, showing merchandise, giving a sales presentation, demonstrating goods and/or services, answering objections, and closing the sale. See Figure 18-5. Nonstore-based sales personnel may also have to generate customer leads (by knocking on doors in residential areas or calling people who are listed in a local phone directory).

Upon entering a store or a department in it (or being contacted at home), a customer would be greeted by a salesperson. Typical in-store greetings are

"Hello, may I help you?"

"Good morning [afternoon]. If you need any help, please call upon me."

"Hi, is there anything in particular you are looking for?"

With any greeting, the salesperson seeks to put the customer at ease and build rapport.

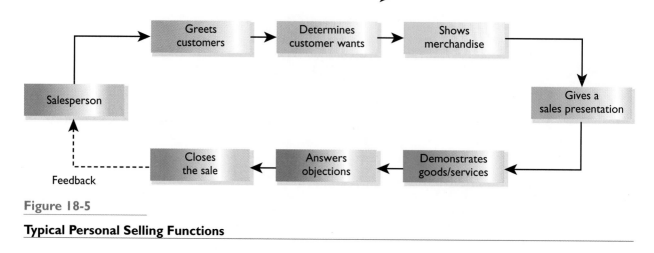

Figure 18-5

Typical Personal Selling Functions

The salesperson next learns what the customer wants. From the perspective of the retailing concept, a salesperson could not succeed without ascertaining customer wants:

- Is the person just looking, or is there a specific good or service in mind?
- For what purpose is the item to be used (such as gift or personal)?
- Does the person have a price range in mind?
- What other information can the person provide to help the salesperson?

At this point, a salesperson may show or present products. Based on customer wants, he or she would select the good or service most apt to satisfy that customer. The salesperson may decide to trade up (discuss a more expensive version) or present a substitute (especially if the retailer does not carry or is out of the requested item).

The salesperson now makes a sales presentation to motivate the customer to purchase. The two most common ones are the canned sales presentation and the need-satisfaction approach. The **canned sales presentation** is a memorized, repetitive speech given to all customers interested in a particular item. It is most effective when sales force turnover is high and customers require little assistance. The **need-satisfaction approach** is based on the principle that each customer has a different set of wants; thus, a sales presentation should be geared to the demands of the individual customer. This approach is being utilized more and more in retailing.

In a sales presentation, a demonstration may be useful. It would show the actual utility of an item and allow customer participation. Demonstrations are often used to sell stereos, autos, TV sets, health club memberships, dishwashers, video games, and watches.

A customer may raise questions during the selling process, and the salesperson must address them. After all questions are answered, the salesperson then closes the sale. This involves getting the customer to conclude a purchase. Typical closing lines are

"Will you take it with you or have it delivered?"

"Cash or charge?"

"Would you like this gift-wrapped?"

"Have you decided on the color, red or blue?"

For the personal selling process to be completed effectively, salespeople must be enthusiastic, knowledgeable about their firm and its offerings, interested in their customers, and able to communicate effectively. Table 18-4 contains a selected list of ways retail sales can be lost through poor personal selling and how to avoid these problems.

Table 18-4   SELECTED REASONS WHY RETAIL SALES ARE LOST—AND HOW TO AVOID THEM

■ *Poor qualification of the customer:* Information should be obtained from the customer so a salesperson can gear a presentation to the prospective buyer.

■ *Salesperson does not demonstrate the good or service:* A good sales presentation should be built around the item shown in use; benefits can then be easily visualized.

■ *Failure to put feeling into the presentation:* The salesperson should be sincere and consumer-oriented in his or her presentation.

■ *Poor knowledge:* The salesperson should know the major advantages and disadvantages of his or her goods and services, as well as competitors', and be able to answer questions.

■ *Arguing with a customer:* The salesperson should avoid arguments in handling customer objections, even if the customer is completely wrong.

■ *No suggestion selling:* The salesperson should attempt to sell related items (such as service contracts, product supplies, and installation) along with the basic product.

■ *Giving up too early:* If an attempt to close a sale is unsuccessful, it should be tried again.

■ *Inflexibility:* The salesperson should be creative in analyzing alternative solutions to a customer's needs, as well as in adapting his or her message to the requirements of the individual customer.

■ *Poor follow-up:* The salesperson should be sure an order is correctly written, merchandise arrives at the agreed-on time, and the customer is satisfied.

Sales Promotion

Sales promotion encompasses the paid communication activities other than advertising, public relations, and personal selling that stimulate consumer purchases and dealer effectiveness. Included are displays, contests, sweepstakes, coupons, frequent-shopper programs, prizes, samples, demonstrations, referral gifts, and other limited-time selling efforts outside of the ordinary promotion routine. Considerable information on sales promotion is available from *Promo* magazine (http://www.mediacentral.com/promo), including annual data by category.

The value and complexity of sales promotion are clear from this *Promo* commentary:

Shoppers are explorers. They're on safari, hunting for bargains, new products, and different items to add excitement to their everyday lives. Three of every four are open to new experiences as they browse the aisles of supermarkets and search for bargains at drugstores and mass merchandisers. This translates into an opportunity to make a measurable impact just when they're free of distractions and most receptive to new ideas. More than ever, research reveals what promotion-savvy firms have known for years: the last best chance to make a difference is in the store. But how best to reach and motivate customers? Shopping behavior changes as people enter different types of stores. Example: of those who browse the aisles at a supermarket, only 19 percent become browsers at a chain drug or discount store. Three out of five supermarket browsers turn into destination shoppers when they enter a chain drugstore, and two-fifths become destination shoppers in mass merchandise stores. The upshot: firms need to work harder to get shoppers' attention in a drug or discount store by using more intrusive promotion techniques such as displays or special signage. But while shopping styles vary by type of store in general, there are exceptions based on product category. For categories such as shampoos and pain relievers, which are bought more frequently at drugstores and mass merchandisers, more browsing takes place than at supermarkets. Thus, at the supermarket, it's the shampoos and pain relievers that need more intrusive promotion techniques to stop the base runners, while at drug and discount stores, it's the food items that need to use them.[8]

[8]"Special Report: Impact in the Aisles," *Promo* (January 1996), pp. 25, 28.

Objectives ❏ Sales promotion goals include

■ Increasing short-run sales volume.
■ Maintaining customer loyalty.
■ Emphasizing novelty.
■ Supplementing other promotion tools.

Advantages and Disadvantages ❏ The major advantages of sales promotion are that

■ It often has eye-catching appeal.
■ The themes and tools can be distinctive.
■ The consumer may receive something of value, such as coupons or free merchandise.
■ It helps draw customer traffic and maintain loyalty to the retailer.
■ Impulse purchases are increased.
■ Customers can have fun, particularly with contests and demonstrations.

The major disadvantages of sales promotion are that

■ It may be difficult to terminate certain promotions without adverse customer reactions.
■ The retailer's image may be hurt if trite promotions are used.
■ Sometimes frivolous selling points are stressed rather than the retailer's product assortment, prices, customer services, and other factors.
■ Many sales promotions have only short-term effects.
■ It should be used only as a supplement to other promotional forms.

Types ❏ Figure 18-6 describes the major types of sales promotions. Each is described here.

Point-of-purchase promotion consists of in-store displays designed to increase sales. The effect of these displays on retail image was discussed in Chapter 17. From a promotional perspective, the displays may remind customers, stimulate impulse behavior, allow self-service to be applied, and reduce a retailer's promotion costs when manufacturers provide displays. The long-run impact of point-of-purchase promotions must be carefully studied. For instance, in some product categories, total sales may not rise if special displays are used; instead, customers could stockpile items and purchase less when the special displays are removed. See Figure 18-7.

These examples show the extent of point-of-purchase display use:

■ Virtually all retailers deploy some type of POP displays.
■ The Point-of-Purchase Advertising Institute (POPAI) estimates that manufacturers and retailers together annually spend $12 billion on in-store displays.
■ According to Donnelley Marketing, retailers spend one-sixth of their total promotional budgets on in-store promotions.
■ Display ads appear on shopping carts in the majority of U.S. supermarkets. Also thousands of supermarkets have in-store electronic signs above their aisles promoting well-known brands.
■ Retailers use about two-thirds of all displays provided by manufacturers.[9]

Contests and sweepstakes are similar in nature; they seek to attract and retain customers by participation in events that can lead to substantial prizes. A contest requires a customer to demonstrate some skill in return for a reward. A sweepstakes requires only participation, with the lucky winner chosen at random. The disadvantages of contests

---

[9]*Promo's Annual Sourcebook '97,* pp. 11–12; and *18th Annual Survey of Promotional Practices* (Oakbrook Terrace, Illinois: Donnelley Marketing).

Type	Description
Point-of-purchase	Window, floor, and counter displays that allow a retailer to remind customers and stimulate impulse purchases. Sometimes, the displays are supplied by manufacturers.
Contests	Customers compete for prizes by completing a contest (game), such as a crossword puzzle, a slogan, or a football lottery. Winning is at least partially based on a correct answer (skill).
Sweepstakes	Similar to a contest, except that participants merely fill out application forms and the winner is picked at random (chance). No skill is involved. Direct-mail retailers use this tool quite often.
Coupons	Retailers advertise special discounts for customers who redeem advertised coupons. Customers clip coupons from print media or POP displays, and redeem them with the retailer.
Frequent-shopper programs	Customers are given points or discounts based on the dollar amounts of their purchases. The points are accumulated to acquire goods or services.
Prizes	Similar to frequent-shopper programs, except that the retailer gives prizes immediately, such as glasses, silverware, and others. Usually, one piece of a set is obtained with each purchase.
Samples	Free tastes or smells of items are given to customers.
Demonstrations	Products are shown cleaning up floors, mixing foods, and so on. Services are also demonstrated (e.g., judo instructions).
Referral gifts	Presents or gifts are given to current customers when they bring in new customers.
Matchbooks, pens, calendars, shopping bags, etc.	Items that contain the retailer's name are given to customers.
Special events	Include fashion shows, autograph sessions with book authors, art exhibits, and holiday activities (such as children's rides).

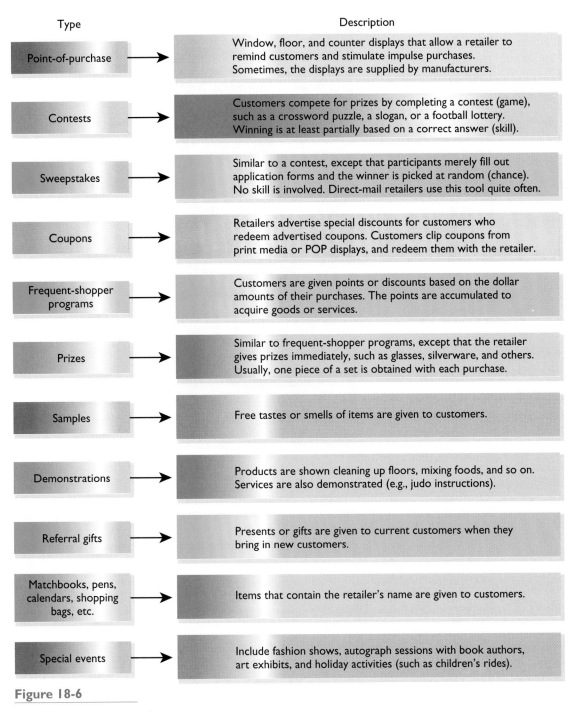

Figure 18-6

Types of Sales Promotion

and sweepstakes are their costs, customer reliance on these tools as the reason for continued retailer patronage, the effort required of consumers, and entries by nonshoppers. Together, manufacturers and retailers spend over $200 million each year on contests and sweepstakes.

Coupons are used to present discounts from the regular selling prices of manufacturer and retailer brands. Each year, 325 billion coupons are distributed in the United States, with grocery products accounting for nearly four-fifths of that amount. U.S. consumers

Figure 18-7

Point-of-Purchase Displays: Wooing the Customer in the Store

POP displays are intended to gain the consumer's attention—and get the person to stop and look at a product. This display for Virtual i-glasses! invites passersby to try out the innovative PC accessory.

actually redeem 7 billion coupons, resulting in their saving $4 billion; retailers receive $600 million to $700 million for handling redeemed coupons. Coupons are offered to consumers by freestanding inserts in Sunday papers and placements in daily papers, direct mail, Web sites, regular magazines, and Sunday newspaper magazines. They are also placed in or on packages and dispensed from electronic in-store machines.[10] See Figure 18-8.

There are four important advantages of coupons. First, in many cases, manufacturers pay to advertise and redeem coupons. Second, coupons are very helpful to an ongoing ad campaign and increase store traffic. According to surveys, 99 percent of consumers use coupons at least once during the year. Third, the use of coupons increases the consumer's perception that a retailer offers good value. Fourth, ad effectiveness can be measured by counting redeemed coupons.

The disadvantages of coupons include their possible negative effect on the retailer's image, consumers shopping only if coupons are available, low redemption rates, the clutter of coupons, retailer and consumer fraud, and handling costs. Just 2 percent of coupons are redeemed by consumers due to the large number of them that are received by each American household.

As described in Chapter 3, frequent-shopper programs foster customer relationships by awarding special discounts or prizes to people for their continued patronage. In most such programs, customers must accumulate a certain number of points (or their

[10]See Daniel Shannon, "Still a Mighty Marketing Mechanism: Reports of Couponing's Demise Overstate the Case," *Promo* (April 1996), pp. 84–90; Shelly Reese, "Declining Use, Costs Spur Hard Look at Coupons," *Stores* (March 1997), pp. 28–29; and Julie Ritzer Ross, "Internet Seen Offering Opportunities, Risks for Coupon Distribution," *Stores* (February 1997), pp. 36-37.

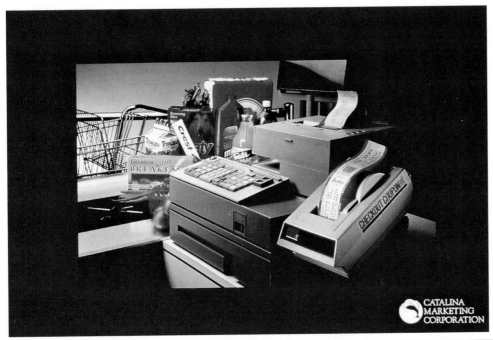

Figure 18-8

The Latest in Coupon Distribution: In-Store Dispensers

With the system shown, a frequent shopper gives his or her membership card to the cashier who scans in purchases. The transactions are added to the person's data base (account) and result in custom coupons that are printed at the checkout counter.

CATALINA MARKETING CORPORATION

equivalent), which are redeemed for cash or prizes. Some programs are very successful. At Vons, the California supermarket chain, more than 4 million shoppers belong to its VonsClub. Here is how it works:

> A customer swipes a magnetic card through a card reader at checkout and automatically receives discounts on items Vons has chosen to promote that week. At the same time, a computer collects detailed and comprehensive data about the items purchased by the cardholder on that store visit and combines them in the data base with life-style information it has already obtained about the customer. This data base then is used to form Vons' marketing efforts.[11]

Among the advantages of frequent-shopper programs are the loyalty bred (customers can accumulate points only by patronizing a specific firm or firms), the "free" nature of awards to many consumers, and the competitive edge for a retailer that is similar to others. On the other hand, a number of consumers feel frequent-shopper programs are not really free and therefore would rather shop at lower-priced stores without these programs; it may take customers a while to gather enough points to get meaningful gifts; and profit margins may be smaller if retailers with frequent-shopper programs try to price competitively with firms that do not have these programs.

Prizes are similar to frequent-shopper programs; but instead of points, prizes are given with each purchase. Prize giveaways are most effective when sets of glasses, silverware, dishes, place mats, and so on are distributed one at a time to shoppers. These encourage loyalty. The problems are the cost of the prizes, the difficulty of termination, and the possible impact on image.

As a complement to personal selling, free samples (such as a taste of a cake or a smell of a perfume) and/or demonstrations (such as cooking lessons) may be used. $600 million is spent annually on sampling and demonstrations in U.S. stores—mostly at

[11]Leah Haran, "With 4M+ Cards, VonsClub Helps Target Shoppers," *Advertising Age* (October 16, 1995), p. 24.

supermarkets, membership clubs, specialty stores, and department stores.[12] They are effective because customers become involved and impulse purchases increase. Loitering and costs may be problems.

Referral gifts are used to encourage existing customers to bring in new customers. Direct marketers, such as book and record clubs, often use this tool. It is a technique that has no important shortcomings and recognizes the value of friends in influencing purchasing decisions.

Items such as matchbooks, pens, calendars, and shopping bags may be given to customers. They differ from prizes since they promote retailers' names and are not part of a set. These items should be used as supplements. The advantage is longevity. There is no real disadvantage.

Retailers may use special events to generate consumer enthusiasm. Events can range from store grand openings to fashion shows to art exhibits. When Toys "Я" Us opens stores, it has giveaways and activities for children, and there is always a guest appearance by the firm's Geoffrey the giraffe (a human in a costume). Generally, in planning a special event, the potential increase in consumer awareness and store traffic needs to be weighed against that event's costs.

PLANNING A RETAIL PROMOTIONAL STRATEGY

To communicate successfully with customers, retailers should plan their overall promotional strategy carefully. A systematic five-step approach to promotional planning is depicted in Figure 18-9 and explained next.

Determining Promotional Objectives

Broad promotional objectives include increasing sales, stimulating impulse and reminder buying, raising customer traffic, getting leads for sales personnel, presenting and reinforcing the retailer image, informing customers about the attributes of goods and services, popularizing new store sites, capitalizing on manufacturer support, offering customer service and enhancing customer relations, and maintaining customer loyalty.

In developing a promotional strategy, a retailer must determine which of these goals are most important. It is necessary for the firm to state its goals clearly in order to give direction to the selection of promotional types, media, and messages.

Goals must be stated as precisely as possible. Thus, increasing company sales is not a specific enough goal. However, increasing sales by 20 percent is directional, quantitative, and measurable. With such an objective, a firm could devise a thorough promotional plan and evaluate its success.

Establishing an Overall Promotional Budget

Several procedures are available for setting the size of a promotion budget. Five techniques are discussed here.

With the **all-you-can-afford method,** a retailer first allots funds for each element of the retail strategy mix except promotion. Whatever funds are left over are placed in a promotional budget. This is the weakest of the budgeting techniques. Its shortcomings are that little significance is placed on promotion as a retail strategy-mix variable; expenditures are not linked to goals; and if little or no funds are left over, the promotion budget is too small or nonexistent. The method is used predominantly by small, conservative retailers.

The **incremental method** of promotion budgeting relies on previous budgets for the allocation of funds. A percentage is either added to or subtracted from one year's budget to determine the next year's. For instance, if this year's promotion

[12]*Promo's Annual Sourcebook '97,* p. 21.

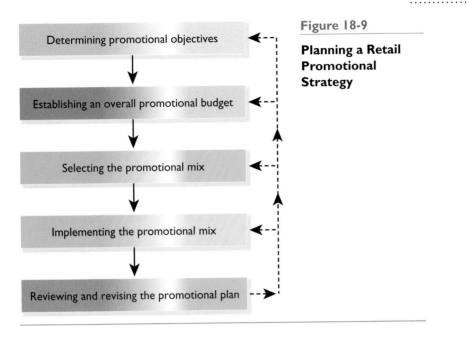

Figure 18-9

Planning a Retail Promotional Strategy

budget is $10,000, next year's budget would be calculated by adding or subtracting a percentage to or from that amount. A 10 percent rise means that next year's budget would be $11,000. This technique is useful for a small retailer. A reference point is used. The budget is adjusted based on the firm's feelings about past successes and future trends. It is easy to use. Yet, key disadvantages do exist. The budget is rarely tied to specific goals. Intuition or "gut feelings" are used. Evaluating promotional effectiveness is hard.

For the **competitive parity method,** a retailer's budget is raised or lowered based on the actions of competitors. Thus, if the leading firm in an area raises its promotion budget by 8 percent, competitors in the area could follow suit. This method has utility for small and large firms. The advantages are that it uses a comparison point and is market-oriented and conservative. The disadvantages are that it is a following, not a leading, philosophy; it may be difficult to get data on competitors; and it is assumed that competing firms are similar (in terms of the number of years in business, size, target market, location, merchandise, prices, and so on). This last point is particularly critical: competitors may actually need quite different promotional budgets.

In the **percentage-of-sales method,** a retailer ties its promotion budget to sales revenue. First, the firm develops a promotion-to-sales ratio. During each succeeding year, the ratio of promotion dollars to sales dollars then remains constant, while the dollar amount varies. For instance, a firm could set promotion costs at 10 percent of sales. If this year's sales are expected to be $100,000, there is a $10,000 promotion budget. If next year's sales are projected at $140,000, a $14,000 budget is planned. The benefits of this procedure are the use of sales as a base, its adaptability, and the correlation of promotion with sales. The shortcomings are that there is no relation to goals (as an example, for an established firm, an increase in sales may not require an increase in promotion); promotion is not used to lead sales, but follow them; and promotion drops during poor sales periods when increases might be beneficial. This technique provides too many promotional funds in periods of high sales and too few funds in periods of low sales.

Under the **objective-and-task method,** a retailer clearly defines its promotional goals and then prepares a budget to satisfy these goals. For example, a retailer may decide its goal is to have 70 percent of the people in its trading area know its name by the end of a one-month promotion campaign, up from 50 percent currently. To do so, it calculates what tasks and costs are required to achieve that goal:

Objective	Task	Cost
1. Gain awareness of working women.	Use eight quarter-page ads (in four successive Sunday editions of two area papers).	$12,000
2. Gain awareness of motorists.	Use forty 30-second radio ads during prime time on local radio stations, at $200 each.	8,000
3. Gain awareness of pedestrians.	Give away shopping bags— 5,000 bags at $1.00 each.	5,000
	Total budget	$25,000

The objective-and-task method is the best overall budgeting technique. Among its advantages are that goals are clearly stated; expenditures are related to completing goal-oriented tasks; it is adaptable; and success (or failure) can be assessed. The major shortcoming is the complexity in setting goals and specific tasks, especially for small retailers.

When deciding how to plan their promotion budgets, retailers should weigh the strengths and weaknesses of each method in relation to their own requirements and constraints. To assist firms in their budgeting efforts, there is now computer software available.[13]

Selecting the Promotional Mix

After a budget is set, a retailer must determine its promotional mix: the combination of advertising, public relations, personal selling, and sales promotion. A firm with a rather limited budget may rely on store displays, flyers, targeted direct mail, and publicity to generate customer traffic, while a firm with a big promotion budget may rely more on newspaper and TV ads.

The choice of promotional mix is often affected by the type of retailer involved. Table 18-5 shows how selected small firms vary in terms of their promotion mixes— such as coin-operated laundries emphasizing Yellow Page directories and flyers; and health food stores relying on local papers, as well as point-of-purchase displays. In supermarkets, product sampling, continuity programs (such as frequent-shopper promotions), theme sales, bonus coupons, half-price sales, and register-tape plans are the techniques used most. However, the use of sales promotions varies greatly between independent and chain outlets. At upscale stores, there is more attention to personal selling and less to advertising and sales promotion relative to discounters.

Retailers often use an assortment of promotional forms to reinforce each other. Thus, a melding of media advertising and point-of-purchase displays may be more effective in getting across a message than one form alone.

In reacting to a retailer's communication efforts, a consumer often goes through a sequence of steps called the **hierarchy-of-effects model,** which leads him or her from awareness to knowledge to liking to preference to conviction to a purchase.[14]

[13]See Julie Ritzer Ross, "Decision Support System Helps Mercantile Take Customer-Focused Approach to Promotion," *Stores* (March 1997), pp. 51–52.

[14]Peter D. Bennett (Editor), *Dictionary of Marketing Terms,* Second Edition (Chicago: American Marketing Association, 1995), p. 129.

Are Restaurants Low in Fat or High in Bologna?

The Federal Trade Commission (FTC) has been investigating whether some major restaurant chains have made misleading claims about the fat content of such popular dishes as Chili's "Guiltless Veggie Pasta" and Big Boy's "Health Smart Grilled Chicken Mozzarella." In the case of Chili's, the FTC asked the company to provide "all substantiation, including testing, reports, studies, research, experiments" and other data in support of Chili's "Guiltless" dishes. The FTC made a similar request of Big Boy for its "Health Smart" dishes.

The Center for Science in the Public Interest (CSPI), a consumer group, also conducted its own laboratory analysis of samples of Chili's "Guiltless Fajitas" and Big Boy's "Health Smart Chicken 'n'

Vegetable Stir Fry." The CSPI found the chicken fajitas had 30 grams of fat per serving (versus the claimed 17 grams on the menu), and the Big Boy's chicken had 27 grams of fat per serving (versus the claimed 18 grams).

In response to the inquiries by the FTC and CSPI, a spokesperson for Big Boy stated that if the meals "are prepared according to specifications, all the dishes come back at, or lower than, what we claim in terms of fat." Elias Brothers Restaurants Inc., which owns the trademark for Big Boy, says the company checks its recipes through in-house nutritionists and the staff at a local hospital.

Source: Laurie McGinley, "FTC Probes Fat-Content Claims Made by Some Restaurant Chains," *Wall Street Journal* (April 30, 1996), p. B8.

Different promotional mixes are needed in each step. See Figure 18-10. Ads and public relations are most effective in developing awareness, and personal selling and sales promotion are most effective in changing attitudes and stimulating desires. This is especially true for expensive, complex goods or services.

Table 18-5 THE PROMOTION MIXES OF SELECTED SMALL RETAILERS

Type of Retailer	Favorite Media	Emphasis on Personal Selling	Special Considerations	Promotional Opportunities
Apparel store	Weekly papers; direct mail; radio; Yellow Pages; exterior signs.	High.	Cooperative ads available from manufacturers.	Fashion shows for community groups and charities.
Auto supply store	Local papers; Yellow Pages; POP displays; exterior signs.	Moderate.	Cooperative ads available from manufacturers.	Direct mail.
Bookstore	Local papers; shoppers; Yellow Pages; radio; exterior signs.	Moderate.	Cooperative ads available from publishers.	Author-signing events.
Coin-operated laundry	Yellow Pages; flyers in area; local direct mail; exterior signs.	None.	None.	Coupons in newspaper ads.
Gift store	Weekly papers; Yellow Pages; radio; direct mail; exterior signs.	Moderate.	None.	Special events; Web ads.
Hair grooming/ beauty salon	Yellow Pages; mentions in feature articles; exterior signs.	Moderate.	Word-of-mouth communication key.	Participation in fashion shows; free beauty clinics.
Health food store	Local papers; shoppers; direct mail; POP displays; exterior signs.	Moderate.	None.	Display windows.
Restaurant	Newspapers; radio; Yellow Pages; outdoor; entertainment guides and theater programs; exterior signs.	Moderate.	Word-of-mouth communication key.	Write-ups in critics' columns; special events.

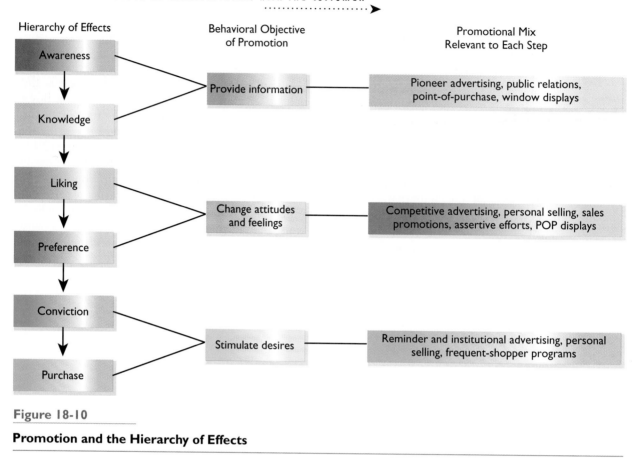

Figure 18-10

Promotion and the Hierarchy of Effects

Implementing the Promotional Mix

The implementation of a promotional mix involves choosing which specific media to use (such as, Newspaper A and Newspaper B), the timing of promotion, the content of messages, the makeup of the sales force, specific sales promotion tools, and the responsibility for coordination.

Consider this example,

> Around Valentine's Day, customers of Oakland Pointe Shopping Center in Pontiac, Michigan, could get Hershey's kisses for free after buying $25 worth of goods. It was all part of a promotion to encourage shoppers to visit other stores at the neighborhood center. Slowly, neighborhood and community center owners are coming around to the idea of marketing their properties to increase customer response. For many strip center managers, the goal is to encourage cross shopping, far less common at neighborhood centers than regional malls. "When you go to a strip center, you're destination-oriented. My challenge as a marketing consultant is to give you a reason to explore the other tenants," says Lois Fletcher, president of Traffic, a firm that specializes in strip center marketing. Among the methods she uses are bag stuffers, always on high quality stock, to introduce the promotions available at a center for the next week. Whenever possible, Fletcher uses the goods or services at that center. A promotion, at Novi (Michigan) Town center, involved giving away stuffed animals from one tenant at other stores for a $50 purchase. According to Ernie Reno, vice-president of marketing for center operator Linder Properties, "Everything is geared to involving as many merchants as we can." Reno also is ju-

dicious with his ad dollars, preferring very local, smaller papers to dailies and standalone inserts. Such activities have now given him a data base of 20,000 names at Oakland Pointe. With few exceptions, direct mail is prohibitively expensive, he says. William Sulzbacher, president of Baita Property Services, isn't so sure. "We started out believing it was cost prohibitive, but we found a way to make direct mail work," he says. Retailers can put their own messages on Baita's direct mail pieces, which could include different sections good at different times. The goal, Sulzbacher says, is to draw people to a center's stores two or three times with the same piece. Another Linder promotion is to let tenants draw from a percentage of a center's marketing funds to run their own ads, as long as the center's logo and identification is on the ad. "It's about three times more expensive to get new customers than to keep the old. So I concentrate on the existing base and get the customer to come more frequently," Reno says.[15]

Media Decisions ❑ The choice of specific media is based on a wide variety of elements, including overall costs, efficiency (the cost to reach the target market), lead time, and editorial content. Overall costs are important because the extensive use of an expensive medium may preclude implementing a balanced promotional mix. In addition, a firm may not be able to repeat a message in a costly medium, and ads are rarely effective when shown only once.

A medium's efficiency relates to the cost of reaching a given number of target customers. Media rates are typically expressed in terms of cost per 1,000 readers, watchers, or listeners:

$$\text{Cost per thousand} = \frac{\text{Cost per message} \times 1,000}{\text{Circulation}}$$

A newspaper with a circulation of 400,000 and a per-page rate of $10,000 has a per-page cost per thousand of $25.

In this computation, total circulation is used to measure efficiency. Yet, because a retailer usually appeals to a limited target market, only the relevant portion of circulation should be considered. Thus, if 70 percent of a newspaper's readers are target customers for a particular firm (and the other 30 percent live outside its trading area), the real cost per thousand is

$$\begin{aligned}
\text{Cost per thousand} \atop \text{(target market)} &= \frac{\text{Cost per page} \times 1,000}{\text{Circulation} \times \dfrac{\text{Target market}}{\text{Circulation}}} \\[2mm]
&= \frac{\$10,000 \times 1,000}{400,000 \times 0.70} = \$35.71
\end{aligned}$$

Different media require different lead times. For instance, a newspaper ad can be placed shortly before publication, whereas a magazine ad sometimes must be placed months in advance. In addition, the retailer must decide what kind of editorial content it wants near its ads (such as a sports story, the comics, a personal-care column, or a feature story).

Timing of the Promotional Mix ❑ Ad decisions must take reach and frequency into account. **Reach** is the number of distinct people exposed to a retailer's ads in a specific period. **Frequency** is the average number of times each person who is reached is exposed to a retailer's ads in a specific period.

---

[15]"Looking for Big Results, Without Big Dollars," *Chain Store Age* (May 1996), pp. 84–85.

A retailer can advertise extensively or intensively. Extensive media coverage often means ads reach many people but with relatively low frequency. Intensive media coverage generally means ads are placed in selected media and repeated frequently. Repetition is important, particularly for a retailer seeking to develop an image or sell new goods or services.

In enacting its promotional mix, a retailer must consider peak seasons and whether to mass or distribute efforts. When peak seasons occur, all elements of the mix are usually utilized; in slow periods, promotional efforts are typically reduced. A **massed promotion effort** is used by retailers, such as Avon, that promote mostly in one or two seasons. A **distributed promotion effort** is used by retailers, such as McDonald's, that promote throughout the year.

Even though they are not really affected by seasonality as much as many other retailers, massed advertising is practiced by supermarkets, the majority of which use Wednesday as the day to place major weekly newspaper ads. This placement takes advantage of the fact that a high proportion of consumers conduct their major shopping trip on Thursday, Friday, or Saturday.

Sales force size can vary by time (morning versus evening), day (weekdays versus weekends), and month (December versus January). Sales promotions also vary in their timing. Store openings and holidays are especially good times for sales promotions (and public relations).

Content of Messages ❏ Whether written or spoken, personally or impersonally delivered, message content is important. In advertising, themes, wording, headlines, the use of color, size, layout, and placement must be selected. Publicity releases need to be written. In personal selling, the greeting, the sales presentation, the demonstration, and the closing need to be applied. With sales promotion, the firm's message must be composed and placed on the promotional device.

To a large extent, the characteristics of the promotional form influence the message. A shopping bag often contains no more than a retailer's name; a billboard (seen while driving at 55 miles per hour) is good for visual effect, but can hold only limited written material; and a salesperson may be able to maintain a customer's attention for a while, thus expanding the content of the message that is conveyed. Some shopping centers now use a glossy magazine format to communicate a community-oriented image, introduce new stores to consumers, and promote the goods and services carried at stores in the center.

In advertising and public relations, distinctiveness can be an aid to a retailer due to message proliferation. Thus, cluttered ads displaying many products suggest a discounter's orientation, while fine pencil drawings and selective product displays suggest a specialty store focus.

More retailers have recently become involved in **comparative advertising,** whereby messages compare their offerings with those of competitors. Comparative ads can help position a retailer in relation to competitors, increase awareness of the firm, maximize the efficiency of a limited budget, and provide credibility. Yet, such ads provide visibility for competitors, may confuse people, and may lead to legal action by competitors. Fast-food and off-price retailers are among those using comparative ads.

Makeup of Sales Force ❏ Qualifications for sales personnel must be detailed, and these personnel must be recruited, selected, trained, compensated, supervised, and monitored. Personnel should also be classified (such as order takers versus order getters) and assigned to the appropriate departments. An in-depth discussion regarding human resource management was provided in Chapter 11.

Sales Promotion Tools ❏ The specific sales promotion tools must be chosen from among those cited in Figure 18-6. The combination of tools depends on short-run (and changing) goals and the other components of the promotion mix. If possible, cooperative ventures with manufacturers or other suppliers should be sought. Tools inconsistent with the retailer's image should never be used.

Fiesta Mart: Planning and Analyzing Promotions with Promoman

TECHNOLOGY IN RETAILING

Promoman is an example of promotional planning computer software that better enables firms to plan and analyze promotion strategies. This program, developed by Nielsen, provides retailers with a forecast of promotion-driven sales based on up to 52 weeks of past sales data. It also lets a retailer forecast the effect of a promotion on the sales of other products in the category.

Programs such as Promoman are becoming increasingly more important to retailers. In the past, manufacturers often provided their retailers with up-front allowances for their promotions. Today, however, more manufacturers are compensating retailers on a pay-for-performance basis (tied to actual sales). Retailers thus need to select the right type of goods for promotions.

Fiesta Mart, a 34-store supermarket chain based in Houston, is one of a number of retailers that uses Promoman. The program tells the firm's buyers how much added business to expect from each advertised item and what gross margins to anticipate (after taking competitors' pricing into account).

Although Promoman is costly (its list price is $150,000), single-source information providers such as Nielsen, IRI, and EMS are often willing to barter the software in exchange for scanner data. According to one study, promotion analysis software has a definite positive impact on bottom-line profitability.

Source: Michael Garry, "Computing Promotions," *Progressive Grocer* (July 1995), pp. 95–96.

Responsibility for Coordination ❑ Regardless of the retailer's size or organizational form, someone within the firm must have authority over and responsibility for the promotion function. Larger retailers often assign this job to a vice-president of promotion, who oversees display personnel, works with the firm's ad agency, supervises the retailer's own advertising department (if there is one), and supplies branch outlets with the necessary in-store materials. Personal selling is usually under the jurisdiction of the store manager in a large retail setting.

For a promotional strategy to succeed, its components have to be coordinated with other retail mix elements. Sales personnel must be informed of special sales and know product features; featured items must be received, marked, and displayed; and bookkeeping entries must be made.

Often, a shopping center or a shopping district runs theme promotions, such as "back to school." In those instances, someone must have responsibility for coordinating the activities of all retailers participating in the event.

Reviewing and Revising the Promotional Plan

An analysis of the success of a promotion plan depends on the objectives sought, and that analysis is simplified if the goals are clearly stated in advance (as suggested in this chapter). Revisions would be made for promotional tools not achieving their pre-set goals.

Here are some ways to test the effectiveness of a promotional effort:

Examples of Retail Promotion Goals	Approaches for Evaluating Promotion Effectiveness
Inform current customers about new credit plans; acquaint potential customers with new offerings.	Study company and product awareness before and after promotion; evaluate extent of audience.
Develop and reinforce a particular image; maintain customer loyalty.	Study image through surveys before and after public relations and other promotion efforts.
Increase customer traffic; get leads for salespeople; increase revenues above last year's; reduce customer returns from prior year's.	Evaluate sales performance and the number of inquiries; study customer intentions to buy before and after promotion; study customer trading areas and average purchases; review coupon redemption.

Figure 18-11

MindTrack: A Futuristic Way of Studying Advertising Effectiveness

As in other aspects of retailing, sophisticated technology is also making its way into the measurement of promotion effectiveness. One newly launched application is MindTrack, which is depicted in Figure 18-11:

Advanced Neurotechnologies, Inc. has designed a brainwave-to-computer interface that measures direct emotional response to virtually any communication medium. Consumers may not know, may not be able to express, or may not be willing to reveal their emotions verbally. Research that requires participants to push a button or turn a dial is subject to cognitive processing of emotion, too. MindTrack samples brainwaves hundreds of times per second while the consumer is exposed to a message. The rapid monitoring precludes cognitive interference, and reactions are obtained without verbal communication. MindTrack measures emotional dimensions and core emotion states established in advertising research literature for attitude formation, recall, persuasion, and purchase intent. The basic emotional dimensions of brainwave activity are pleasure/displeasure, arousal/sluggishness, and submission/dominance to the message.[16]

Although it may sometimes be tough to assess promotion efforts (for instance, increased revenues might be due to a variety of factors, not just promotion), it is still crucial for retailers to systematically study and adjust their promotional mixes when appropriate.[17]

[16]Kelly Shermach, "Respondents Get Hooked Up and Show Their Emotions," *Marketing News* (August 28, 1995), p. 35.
[17]See Thomas Robinson, "The Age of Accountability," *Marketing Tools* (June 1996), pp. 4–8.

Summary

1. *To explore the scope of retail promotion* Retail promotion involves any communication by a retailer that informs, persuades, and/or reminds the target market about any aspect of the retailer through ads, public relations, personal selling, and sales promotion.

2. *To study the elements of retail promotion: advertising, public relations, personal selling, and sales promotion* Advertising involves any paid, nonpersonal communication and has the advantages of a large audience, low costs per person, many alternative media, and other factors. Its disadvantages include message inflexibility, high absolute costs, and the wasted portion of the audience. Key advertising media are papers, phone directories, direct mail, radio, TV, the World Wide Web, transit, outdoor, magazines, and flyers/circulars. Of special significance are cooperative ads, by which a retailer shares the costs and message with manufacturers, wholesalers, or other retailers.

Public relations encompasses communication that fosters a favorable image for a retailer among its publics. It may be nonpersonal or personal, paid or nonpaid, and sponsor controlled or not controlled. Publicity is the nonpersonal, nonpaid form of public relations. The advantages of public relations include the awareness created, the enhanced image presented, the objectivity of the source to the consumer, and no costs for messages. Disadvantages include the lack of control over messages, the short-run nature, and the nonmedia costs. Publicity can be expected or unexpected, and positive or negative.

Personal selling involves oral communication with one or more potential customers and is critical for persuasion and in closing sales. Some advantages are the adaptability, flexibility, and immediate feedback. Some disadvantages are the small audience, high per-customer costs, and the inability to help lure customers into the store. Order-taking (routine) and/or order-getting (creative) selling personnel can be employed. Sales functions include greeting the customer, determining wants, showing merchandise, making a sales presentation, demonstrating goods and/or services, answering objections, and closing the sale.

Sales promotion comprises the paid communication activities other than advertising, public relations, and personal selling. Among the advantages are that it may be eye-catching, unique, and valuable to the customer. Among the disadvantages are that it may be hard to end, have a negative effect on image, and rely on frivolous selling points. Types of sales promotion include POP displays, contests and sweepstakes, coupons, frequent-shopper programs, prizes, samples, demonstrations, referral gifts, matchbooks, pens, calendars, shopping bags, and special events.

3. *To discuss the strategic aspects of retail promotion: objectives, budgeting, the mix of forms, implementing the mix, and reviewing and revising the plan* First, goals are stated in specific and measurable terms. Second, an overall promotion budget is set on the basis of one of these techniques: all you can afford, incremental, competitive parity, percentage of sales, or objective and task.

Third, the promotional mix is outlined, based on the firm's budget, the type of retailing involved, the coverage of the media, and the stage in the hierarchy-of-effects model. Fourth, the promotional mix is enacted. Included are decisions involving specific media, promotional timing, message content, sales force composition, particular sales promotion tools, and the responsibility for coordination. Last, the retailer systematically reviews and adjusts the promotional plan, consistent with its pre-set goals.

Key Terms

retail promotion (p. 583)
advertising (p. 584)
cooperative advertising (p. 585)
vertical cooperative-advertising
  agreement (p. 590)
horizontal cooperative-advertising
  agreement (p. 590)
public relations (p. 591)
publicity (p. 591)

personal selling (p. 593)
order-taking salesperson (p. 594)
order-getting salesperson (p. 595)
PMs (p. 595)
canned sales presentation (p. 596)
need-satisfaction approach (p. 596)
sales promotion (p. 597)
all-you-can-afford method (p. 602)
incremental method (p. 602)

competitive parity method (p. 603)
percentage-of-sales method (p. 603)
objective-and-task method (p. 603)
hierarchy-of-effects model (p. 604)
reach (p. 607)
frequency (p. 607)
massed promotion effort (p. 608)
distributed promotion effort (p. 608)
comparative advertising (p. 608)

Questions for Discussion

1. Are there any retailers that should *not* use advertising? Explain your answer.
2. How would an advertising plan for a small retailer differ from that of a large retail chain?
3. How do manufacturer and retailer cooperative advertising goals overlap? How do they differ?
4. How may a PC retailer try to generate positive publicity?
5. Give three examples each of order-taking salespeople and order-getting salespeople. Under which circumstances should each type be used?
6. How can advertising, public relations, personal selling, and sales promotion complement each other for a retailer?
7. Are there any retailers that should *not* use sales promotion? Explain your answer.
8. What are the pros and cons of coupons?
9. Develop sales promotions for each of the following:
   a. A revitalized central business district.
   b. An existing restaurant now open on Sunday for the first time.
   c. A new small appliance retailer.
   d. A new membership club in a moderate-sized suburb.
10. Which method of promotional budgeting should a small retailer use? A large retailer? Why?
11. Explain the hierarchy-of-effects model from a retail perspective. Apply your answer to a new travel agency.
12. Describe the difference between frequency and reach in retail advertising. Which is more important? Why?
13. Develop a checklist for a traditional department store to coordinate its promotional plan.
14. For each of these promotional goals, explain how to evaluate promotional effectiveness:
    a. Increase customer traffic by 10 percent.
    b. Develop an innovative image.
    c. Maintain customer loyalty.

Web-Based Exercise:

WILSON INTERNET SERVICES (http://www.wilsonweb.com/commerce)

Questions

1. Evaluate Wilson's Web Page Planning Worksheet. (http://www.wilsonweb.com/worksheet/pageplan.htm)
2. What are the pros and cons of locating a retail Web site in an Internet mall? (http://www.wilsonweb.com/articles/mall.htm)
3. Comment on Wilson's shopping cart program. (http://www.wilsonweb.com/commerce/store-sys.htm)
4. Compute the costs of developing a Web site for a shoe retailer specializing in sandals based on data at Wilson's site. Discuss two alternative Web configurations. (http://www.wilsonweb.com/packages/pkg-tabl.htm)

CASE I
Basically Bagels: Promotion Mix Planning to Grow and Strengthen a Business*

Ron and Kathy Lieberman decided to open a bagel bakery/restaurant after being unable to find freshly baked bagels and fresh appetizing supplies (such as cut-to-order smoked white fish and homemade cream cheese) near their home. After more than three years of planning, they opened their store, Basically Bagels, in a Wilkes-Barre, Pennsylvania, suburb. Although Ron and Kathy both knew the retail site they chose was poor (in terms of pedestrian and vehicle traffic and road visibility), they chose it based on the low rent. The Liebermans realized they would need to devise and enact an effective promotional program to generate and sustain store traffic at the site.

*This case was prepared and written by Professor Anne Heineman Batory, Wilkes University and Professor Stephen S. Batory, Bloomsburg University of Pennsylvania.

The initial promotional strategy for the store's grand opening fully met its goals. The local cable TV station and the local newspaper provided excellent coverage. As a result, the store was very busy during its first three weeks of operation. Unfortunately, sales soon slackened off. The owners attributed this to two factors: a reduction in the novelty effect for a new store and the store's air-conditioning system being inadequate during the hot and humid summer season.

For two years, the Liebermans' attempts to expand sales were unsuccessful. This was despite running coupons (such as buy 12 bagels—get 6 free) and using the shop as a broadcast site for a popular local radio station. However, the coupons did not generate added revenues because most redeemers were current customers. While the Liebermans were initially excited about the on-site broadcast that featured a popular disk jockey, it had virtually no effect on store traffic or sales.

Two key events occurred during the third year of Basically Bagels' operation that led to the successful turnaround of the firm. First, the Liebermans began selling a line of gift baskets (as an alternative to fruit baskets), besides their usual bagels and appetizing products. The gift baskets consisted of special bagels (with a long shelf life), cream cheese spreads, specialty coffees, and other gourmet products housed in an attractive wicker basket. The baskets were promoted by a one-page, threefold flyer that was mailed to community residents and businesses.

The second positive event was a bartering agreement negotiated between the Liebermans and WKRZ, the area's leading radio station. Through this agreement, the radio station received bagel baskets and other merchandise (primarily for use in listener contests) as full payment for Basically Bagels' spot advertising. The long-term use of these ads and contests resulted in continued reinforcement of the store and its high-quality products.

After being at their original location for over eight years, the Liebermans still advertise on WKRZ and participate in contests aimed at the station's listeners. Basically Bagels has also begun to use local cable TV advertising (with spot commercials on general news and business news programs) and to run a commercial on an early-morning news program of a local TV network affiliate.

Although Basically Bagels no longer offers coupons or price promotions, it gives its customers its own form of a "Baker's Dozen" (14 bagels for the cost of a dozen) to increase sales volume. It has instituted a frequent-buyer club for specialty coffee and bagel products to raise consumer loyalty. In this program, customers receive the eleventh cup of coffee or the eleventh specialty bagel free of charge. Recently, Basically Bagels expanded its hours of operation by having an "After Hours" evening cafe with specialty coffees and pastries.

Basically Bagels has begun to refine the promotion of its gift baskets. The gift basket catalog is now a glossy, full-color catalog that is professionally prepared; and the gift baskets are to be marketed on the firm's new Web site. With these promotional vehicles, Basically Bagels plans to sell its gift baskets beyond its normal trading area. Basically Bagels also now promotes its bagel baskets as a bereavement token in tactful ads placed in the obituary section of the town's paper.

The success of Basically Bagels has not gone unnoticed. Several competitors, including both local bakers and units of nationally based franchises, have entered the Wilkes-Barre suburban market. Ron and Kathy Lieberman know that it is time again to re-examine their store's overall promotional strategy.

Questions
1. Evaluate Basically Bagels' overall promotional strategy.
2. What additional promotional media should now be considered? Explain your answer.
3. What is the role of public relations for Basically Bagels?
4. How should Ron and Kathy revise their promotional strategy based on the emergence of competitors?

CASE 2
Flushing Fine Furniture†

Thirty-three years ago, Alex Brewster, a master carpenter who specialized in building custom-made furniture, bought a three-story warehouse in Flushing, New York. He renovated the ground floor as a showroom, the middle floor as a storage area, and the top floor as a cabinetry shop. Alex and his carpenters initially concentrated on making custom-made cabinets, living room display cases, and bookcases; later on, they added custom-made dining room and bedroom sets.

Despite the lack of a detailed promotional plan or a high level of promotional expenditures, Flushing Fine Furniture (FFF) was popular from the onset. Most shoppers were repeat customers or came on the basis of recommendations of friends and relatives. For its first fifteen years of business, FFF's sole advertising efforts consisted of occasional small ads in a local shopper paper and a simple listing in three local Yellow Pages directories.

In 1980, Brewster realized he needed to reposition FFF away from custom-made furniture due to long lead times and high costs. The lead time from ordering to delivery had reached 12 weeks. This was longer than many customers were willing to wait. Producing custom-made furniture was also costly since mass production technology could not be used. Brewster concluded that what people now wanted was high-quality, stylish furniture that was sold in a pleasant environment. He also reasoned that by stopping production of custom-made furniture, he could expand his retail showroom from one to three floors.

After selling all of its existing inventory, FFF reopened as a retailer of branded bedroom, living room, and dining room sets. It represented more than 400 furniture manufacturers, displayed furniture in room settings, and offered free decorating advice to customers. Between 1980 and 1990, sales doubled from $10 million to $20 million. Brewster's daughter Susan joined FFF in 1988 as an interior design consultant and his son Robert joined as a part-time salesperson, while earning his bachelor's degree at a local college. After completing his master's degree in marketing in 1995, Robert became director of marketing.

After examining the store's sales figures, Robert discovered that between 1990 and 1995, furniture sales were pretty flat, at $22 million per year. He also believed that major furniture was a high-involvement shopping good and people were willing to travel long distances to find what they wanted. The household furniture business also had become much more competitive with the opening of an Ikea, a Huffman-Koos, and an Ethan Allen furniture chain store within several miles of FFF. In addition, FFF's competition included several major department stores with excellent furniture departments, such as Macy's and Bloomingdale's. Virtually all of these firms have large advertising budgets and regularly advertise furniture sales in daily newspapers (sometimes with freestanding inserts) and use local radio and TV commercials.

As a result, Robert questioned his father's resistance to media advertising and FFF's lack of a promotional plan. He decided to develop a tentative promotional plan for his father for review. In developing the plan, Robert deliberately sought to avoid traditional print and broadcast media because they were extensively used by FFF's larger competitors. He wanted to consider using innovative media such as the World Wide Web, video catalogs, and CD-ROMs.

Robert wanted to explore several Web-based promotional alternatives. These included joining a home-based shopping mall that would lead to sharing advertising costs and site visits with appliance, lighting, and kitchen and bath renovators. Another possibility would be for FFF to develop its own Web site by retaining a professional Web expert.

Robert also considered devising a catalog in either a VHS or CD-ROM format. He estimated the development cost of an attractive VHS video catalog at between $25,000

†This case was prepared and written by Professor Larry Goldstein, Iona College.

CASE 2
(Continued)

and $50,000; and copies would run between $1 and $2 each, depending on quality and length. While Robert did not know the development and per copy costs of a CD-ROM catalog, he was intrigued by its long shelf life and the high trial rate among computer owners who have multimedia capabilities. This group also has very favorable demographics for FFF.

Questions

1. What promotional opportunities did Alex Brewster overlook? How could he have capitalized on these opportunities?
2. Do you think FFF was correct to avoid using the broadcast and print media for advertising?
3. Is going online appropriate for FFF? Explain your answer.
4. Evaluate the concept of video and CD-ROM catalogs for FFF.

CASE 3
Selling at Bon Marche[‡]

Bon Marche (http://www.federated-fds.com), the 42-store division of Federated Department Stores, with $900 million in 1995 sales, is one of the leading department store chains in the Pacific Northwest. Bon Marche's philosophy is to guarantee shopper satisfaction in terms of merchandise and customer service. This is done at four different levels: anticipating customer needs, merchandise presentation, handling returns and problems, and exceptional opportunities.

At Bon Marche, anticipating customer needs usually means focusing on the little extras that shoppers might not even anticipate occurring at another chain. These might include offering to take a product to the gift wrap area to save the customer time or suggesting to a busy shopper that a product could be delivered to the person's home as an added convenience.

In presenting merchandise, sales associates are taught to know the features of every item sold, as well as their comparative benefits. Their product knowledge makes shoppers feel more secure, increases the chances that shoppers pick the proper items, reduces returns, and lessens customers' total time commitment.

Although many consumers feel uncomfortable entering a department to return an item, Bon Marche specifically trains sales associates to put them at ease. Its sales associates are taught to accept for repair or replacement those products that are not properly functioning, as well as to exchange wrong colors, sizes, or styles for the appropriate ones.

Salespeople often have exceptional opportunities to capitalize on Bon Marche's "I guarantee it" philosophy. Examples include a sales associate's making a special delivery to a consumer in an emergency situation or installing equipment in a consumer's home.

One sales manager for men's clothing at a branch of Bon Marche developed procedures for effective selling based upon the "I guarantee it" philosophy. These procedures are shown in Table 1. The sales manager intends to submit this material to a Bon Marche vice-president for review and possible chainwide adoption.

Questions

1. Evaluate the selling procedures outlined in Table 1. How would you improve these procedures?
2. How would you change these procedures to accommodate a semiannual sale that attracts shoppers who wait for this event?

[‡]The material in this case is drawn from Bon Marche correspondence.

CASE 3
(Continued)

Table I   SUGGESTED PROCEDURES FOR EFFECTIVE APPAREL SELLING

■ When meeting new customers, salespeople should explain the long-term relationship sought by Bon Marche. Customer height and weight, as well as color, style, and texture preferences, should be ascertained and noted in the sales associate's log book. The desired price range for various items should also be recorded. Company policies, such as alteration costs, should be fully described.

■ Sales associates should try to set appointments with loyal customers. Undivided attention can then be given to individual customers, the sales associates can assemble selections in advance of appointments, and customers can allocate adequate time for an in-store visit.

■ All sales associates should be honest in appraising the style, color, and fit of garments.

■ Sales associates should be aware of the opportunities available through cross-selling. For example, a sports jacket purchase could lead to the purchase of slacks and a tie.

■ Sales associates should stay with customers throughout the in-store experience. Nonetheless, shoppers should be allowed to browse throughout the store, if they so desire. Salespeople should be available at shoppers' requests.

■ Sales associates are expected to be present when customers return to pick up altered garments to verify the fit. This is another opportunity to ensure client satisfaction and to suggest other items (in a subtle way).

■ Customers should be encouraged to trade up to better-quality garments as they go through their career cycles.

■ Regular customers should be contacted in advance of special sales to alert them to the opportunity to purchase at 10 percent to 50 percent off usual Bon Marche prices.

3. How should a department manager respond to a sales associate who has the highest volume in the department yet refuses to abide by the procedures in Table 1? Explain your answer.

4. As a newly hired sales associate in Bon Marche's camera department, you are concerned about devising an appropriate sales presentation, as well as offering superior customer service. State four different types of customer needs that are common for the $59 to $500 camera equipment you are responsible for selling. Offer a presentation for each type of need.

Video Questions on Bon Marche

1. Should Bon Marche salespeople use the canned sales presentation or the need-satisfaction approach? Why? Would your answer be the same for a discount clothing store? Why?

2. Cite five exceptional opportunities for a sales associate in Bon Marche's china department.

Part Seven ■ Comprehensive Case

Using Consumer Life-Style Analysis to Revamp Retail Space*

INTRODUCTION

Which color actually triggers the salivary glands to create a desire for sugar? Which shade of gold can generate a customer purchase response for fast food? What can parking lots tell retailers about how to design their interior space? Businesses with a handle on the combinations of colors, shapes, and textures that influence buying decisions can sell by design.

Residential and commercial designers have long used elements such as color to create an emotional response in their customers—light walls to foster a sense of openness, for example. But these have been essentially subjective choices rooted in basic principles of interior design, not defined by or linked to a particular marketing discipline. Increasingly, designers are examining how certain aspects of their work may impact purchase responses in consumers. These design theories evolve out of an assumption that the way individuals respond to colors and shapes is not arbitrary but learned, inherited, and dependent on a variety of identifiable characteristics including life-style patterns. This helps turn left-brain marketing information into right-brain design solutions. In the future, the designer's tools of color, shape, and texture will take on the added dimension of marketing through life-style analysis.

In his 1896 book, *The Principles of Light and Color*, Edwin D. Babbit explored the potential of light and colors as a "power to vitalize, heal, refine, and delight." His studies spawned a kind of chromatic acupuncture in which colors were placed in strategic locations to cure a variety of ailments ranging from toothaches (indigo) to baldness (orange).

A far more practical view was suggested by Faber Birren in his 1950 work, *Color Psychology and Color Therapy*. Birren focused on "functional color" and

how "it differs from so-called interior decoration in that personal preferences or emotional attitudes are denied for well-ordered scientific practice." Birren's "color prescriptions" have had far-reaching impact on everything from the creation of Yellow Pages (to relieve monotony for phone operators) to brightly colored accent walls in factories that grab attention and therefore help reduce industrial accidents caused by inattentiveness. These efforts were largely confined to the industrial sector. But more recent studies have explored how various forms, symbols, and logos affect consumer response to company and brand names.

The Lifecode process takes these insights a step further, by identifying and quantifying the design characteristics best suited for specific target audiences. It uses design elements coupled with customer life-style profiles to trigger the targeted emotional reactions required for customers to see and feel the benefit of owning a product. In place of advertising headlines and art-directed eye flow in a magazine ad, this system employs visual cues such as chair shapes, window patterns, floor surfaces, and traffic flow to create a three-dimensional ad at the point of purchase.

The Lifecode process evolved out of the most unlikely of settings, a neighborhood bowling center. Step into the world of Olathe Lanes East in the Kansas City suburb of Olathe, Kansas. Other than the familiar sound of crashing pins, there's very little that would make Ralph Kramden of *The Honeymooners* classic TV show feel at home. Everything about this facility runs counter to previous industry wisdom. It was created as the result of a simple observation made in a parking lot.

A TALE OF TWO BOWLING CENTERS

In January 1990, shortly after an early-morning electrical fire had reduced the thriving Olathe Lanes East bowling facility to little more than a concrete pad and a pile of melted steel, the owner, Charlie Boyd, contacted our company to rebuild the lanes. He really

*The material in this case was adapted by the authors from Barbara J. Eichhorn, president of BJ's Lifecode Merchandising/Design, "Selling by Design: Using Life-Style Analysis to Revamp Retail Space," *American Demographics* (October 1996), pp. 45–48. Reprinted by permission.

wanted us to just rebuild the lanes as quickly as possible, with virtually no changes from its previous decor. However, after a couple of meetings, I noticed something that prompted me to dig a little deeper.

Following the fire, Boyd and his staff had rerouted all of the league and recreational activity to his other facility, Olathe Lanes West, less than three miles away. When I pulled into the parking lot of this center on Tuesday or Thursday, it was filled with Fords and Chevrolets, pickup trucks and older cars—no imports. But on Wednesday and Friday, the lot was filled with BMWs, Cadillacs, sport vans, and other upscale vehicles. It was obvious the lanes actually had two entirely different sets of customers despite their physical proximity. Even though Boyd believed that "bowlers are bowlers," he couldn't disagree with what he saw in his own parking lot. He agreed to let us take a more in-depth look at his customer base.

At that time, we were not familiar with Claritas' PRIZM profiles or other widely available geodemographic cluster systems that identify the life-style makeup of neighborhoods. We built our own profiles from scratch using a questionnaire loosely based on Maslow's Hierarchy of Needs and the VALS 2 psychographic scheme from SRI International. We asked basic questions about where customers lived, as well as their attitudes and buying styles. See Figure 1.

We found substantial differences between the groups of men and women who were regulars at each of the Olathe Lanes' facilities. They varied in income, education, shopping preferences, and even the food they ate and beer they drank. Equally important, we discovered the underlying differences in their motivations for coming to the lanes.

Olathe Lanes East customers came for relaxation and exercise. The priority wasn't just on bowling; the activity could just as easily have been billiards or swimming. This was true for both the women and children (who represented about 65 percent of customers) and the men. Women in particular patronized Olathe Lanes East primarily for exercise and personal fulfillment. They liked to socialize, too, but this was not their most important motivation. Many already belonged to other groups, such as country clubs and charity organizations. Men came to the East Lanes to escape workday tension, to relax away from their management careers. They were not specifically interested in being competitive (or bowling for that matter); they wanted to unwind.

The customers at Olathe Lanes West had a distinctly different profile. Some women's groups came two or three times a week, and their primary motivation was to meet and interact with friends. The men responded in much the same way—this was a gathering place for friends. Yet, competition was intense. Many of the league bowlers in this facility were employed in repetitive task jobs. The lanes were a place to compete with their peers and excel.

At this point, we asked what we believe is the single most critical question before initiating a design project: "What is your goal for rebuilding this business?" Usually the response is rather lengthy and comes straight out of the firm's mission statement, but Boyd answered very quickly and, I thought, very honestly. He said, "Simple. I want to make a profit." "Okay," I replied. "And what inside a bowling center makes the most profit?"

Boyd's answer was not surprising to anyone associated with the entertainment industry. His biggest potential for profit in the bowling facilities was not through bowling, but through food and beverage sales. This insight shifted the focus from building a bowling alley that happens to sell food, to, in effect, creating a 160-seat food facility with a recreational component—in this case, bowling—attached to it.

SETTING UP FOR CHANGE

Bowling center design has operated under the same paradigms for decades. Most facilities from the 1950s and 1960s were constructed on two or three tiers, with an upper-level concourse and steps leading down to the lanes. Small scoring desks surrounded by a seating area sport a few cupholders, but very little surface area. This design evolved in part because centers wanted to discourage food in the bowling area, a strategy that doesn't make the best sense for a business that sees most of its profits from food and beverage sales.

The redesign of Olathe Lanes East eliminated seating tiers, placing all services, concessions, and lanes on a single level. Another major change was to install the largest tables that could fit in the areas behind the lanes, because as restaurant operators know, customers tend to fill the table space available with food and drink. The food court and bar became the centerpiece of the facility.

Next, we turned our attention to theme and decor. Based on the profile research we eventually did on both facilities using the PRIZM life-style segmentation system, we confirmed what we surmised. Customers at Olathe Lanes East fell almost entirely into three upscale clusters: Young Suburbia (38 percent), Pools and Patios (30 percent), and Furs and Station Wagons (23 percent).

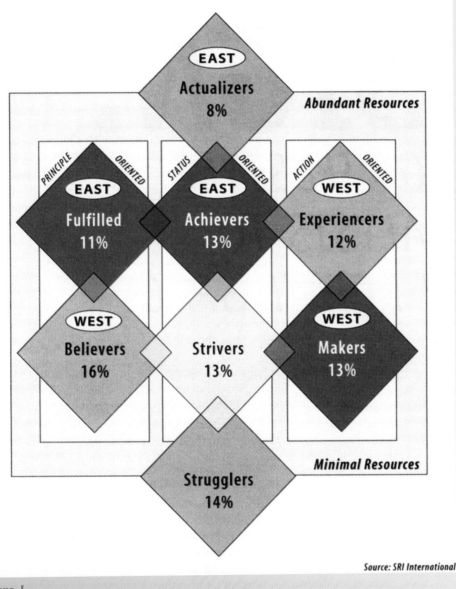

EAST VS. WEST

Source: SRI International

EAST
Actualizers
8%

Abundant Resources

PRINCIPLE   ORIENTED
STATUS   ORIENTED
ACTION   ORIENTED

EAST
Fulfilled
11%

EAST
Achievers
13%

WEST
Experiencers
12%

WEST
Believers
16%

Strivers
13%

WEST
Makers
13%

Minimal Resources

Strugglers
14%

Figure 1

VALS 2 Segmentation Applied to Bowling Center Customers at Olathe Lanes East and West

Actualizers have the most resources. They are successful and sophisticated. They like the finer things in life. *Fulfilled* are principle-oriented and have abundant resources. They are mature, satisfied, comfortable, and reflective. *Believers* are principle-oriented, with lower resources. They follow routines organized around homes, families, and social or religious groups. *Achievers* are status-oriented, with the second highest resources. They are committed to their jobs and families, and satisfied with them. *Strivers* are status-oriented, with lower resources. Their values are similar to achievers, but with fewer resources. They are unsure of themselves. *Experiencers* are action-oriented and are acquiring resources. They are young and enthusiastic, and seek variety and excitement. *Makers* are action-oriented, with lower resources. They live in a traditional context of family, work, and physical recreation. *Strugglers* have the least resources (too few for a self-orientation). They are poor, older, and low in skills.

Note: The percentages in the figure refer to the distribution of the overall U.S. population.

We selected an Art Deco motif for the facility, a style popular in the area and seen in many Kansas City municipal structures. It not only suggests a certain sophistication appealing to the target group, it also fits stylistically with bowling and echoes some of the history of the sport. For example, it enabled us to work with black-and-white formats, as well as a complex color scheme favored by upper-socioeconomic-status patrons involving teal and bordeaux.

Rather than using sharp edges and angles that suggest tension and motion, everything was softened to create a relaxing atmosphere. The icons of Art Deco lend themselves well to shapes that create the best backdrop for this customer profile. The cloud and circle shapes predominant in Deco design became curves and balls in the redesigned facility. From chair backs to curved walls, virtually all counter tops and signs reflect the round smoothness of the bowling balls and pins themselves. Wood accents in mahogany add to the quality image, as do the faux marble top and beveled mirrors in the rest rooms. The new upscale look of the rest rooms has had an even more practical benefit; customers take better care of them. Wear and tear and graffiti had necessitated annual repainting in the old facility. In six years, these new rest rooms have required no major maintenance.

Some people equate higher noise levels with having more fun, but noise is not music to these particular life-style groups. Nine different decorative sound-refracting materials minimize the decibel level usually associated with noisy automated pinsetters. The newly designed Brunswick high-tech bowling equipment adds to the upscale look. Other structural elements include the use of concourse skylights and floor-to-ceiling windows, often seen in the homes of Young Suburbia and Furs and Station Wagons, our target markets. These dispel the popular image of bowling alleys as dimly lit places and create a personalized, open, active environment.

Every aspect of the 82 design surfaces in the facility is linked to customer life-style data. The result is a completely coordinated design style that flows from area to area. The effect is one that might be associated more closely with a fine restaurant than a bowling alley.

Following the grand reopening of Olathe Lanes East, Charlie asked us to redesign his West facility. Despite the fact that this bowling center draws business from essentially the same six-mile radius as the East Lanes, Furs and Station Wagons are replaced by four predominantly blue-collar groups: Blue Collar Nursery (17 percent), Middle America (39 percent),

Blue Chip Blues (13 percent), and Shotguns and Pickups (9 percent).

The redone West Lanes feature a folksy, outdoors style tied thematically to the Southwest. The predominant scheme is peach stucco with blue-green accents. The dark mahogany of the East center gave way to natural oak; and the soothing half-round shapes gave way to squares and energetic triangles. Figure 2 shows the before-and-after looks of Olathe Lanes East and West.

STRIKING SUCCESS

By the end of the first year in the new facility, Olathe Lanes East reported that food and beverage sales had increased by more than two-and-a-half times per line bowled over the traditional bowling blueprints and color scheme. Together, the two facilities, which the owner had considered extremely successful prior to the redesign, showed a substantial increase in total profitability. Each customer base favored their center's atmosphere over the other's.

The key reason why the bowling alleys' sets of patrons had become so divergent is a major interstate highway that passes between the two. Over time, vastly different growth patterns developed on either side of the I-35 corridor. The life-style gap became significantly greater than the three miles that physically separate the facilities. When a customer base changes, retail stores often fail to retarget their exterior facade and interior space for the new folks in town.

Not every project succumbs to such simple analysis as the two distinct customer groups described in this case. In an assignment for the Frigidaire Corporation, we faced the challenge of redesigning an appliance store in Chambersburg, Pennsylvania, that sold large appliances to an older conservative group (Middle American, 22 percent; Coalberg/Corntown, 20 percent) and stereo systems to younger liberal groups (Towns and Gowns, 17 percent; New Homesteaders, 10 percent). The solution was to create two distinctly different looks within the same facility and construct a traffic flow enabling customers to quickly find their particular area of interest. Icons that suggest love and belonging, important to the first two cluster groups, include huge grapevine wreaths shaped like hearts in the washer/dryer department. Mirrored ceilings with flashing purple neon lights in the stereo section appeal to the younger shoppers.

The results of this successful design mix confirm it is possible to address different customer life-styles—even within the same establishment. It also points up

Figure 2

Olathe Lanes East and West: Before and After

Before their redesign, the Olathe Lanes East and West looked alike (above center). After, East customers relax with soothing curves (lower left), while West patrons enjoy energetic triangles (lower right).

the importance of designing retail space with customer life-styles in mind. In the instance of the two bowling centers, a traditional 1950s design still worked to some extent, but the new space proved much more profitable.

The development of the Olathe Lanes facilities changed our business from one driven by traditional interior design into one driven by marketing. Today, we begin every project by looking at customer life-styles rather than design trends. If other marketing messages are crafted based on insights into customer wants and needs, so should the ultimate destination: the place of purchase. Any retail environment— restaurant, appliance store, bank, or mall—can benefit by treating its exterior and interior as ready-made ads for the business. The goal is to create an environment that invites people to come in and stay (and spend) a while. It can be just as important to customize a store's color and design elements as it is to customize the product mix. Whether you're selling furniture or clothing, you need to know if your customers are the leather or lace type—or both.

Questions

1. Before reading this case, how would you have described the image and atmosphere of a bowling alley? Explain your answer.
2. Now that you have read the case, how would you describe the image and atmosphere of a bowling alley? Explain the differences from your answer to Question 1.
3. Draw and label a planogram for a proposed bowling alley near your school.
4. What customer services should be primary and which ancillary for a bowling alley? Why?
5. Discuss the advertising you would recommend for Olathe Lanes East and West.
6. What role should public relations play at Olathe Lanes East and West? Why?
7. What sales promotion activities are appropriate for the revamped Olathe Lanes East and West? Explain your answer.

Part Eight

- In Part 8, two aspects of retailing that are crucial in anticipating, planning for, and responding to the future are detailed.

- Chapter 19 focuses on how firms offering rented-goods, owned-goods, and nongoods services can develop and enact proper strategies, as well as prepare for the future. These retailers must address the intangibility of service offerings, the inseparability of services from their providers, the perishability of services, and the variability of service performance.

- Chapter 20 ties together the elements of a retail strategy that have been described throughout the text. The chapter examines planning and opportunity analysis, productivity, performance measures, and scenario analysis. The value of data comparisons (benchmarking) is assessed. Strategic control via the retail audit is covered.

Chapter 19

Planning by a Service Retailer

CHAPTER OBJECTIVES

1. To examine the scope of service retailing
2. To show how service retailing differs from goods-oriented retailing
3. To apply strategy concepts to service retailing: situation analysis, objectives, target marketing, overall strategy, implementation, and re-evaluation
4. To evaluate uncontrollable factors as they pertain to service retailers

Walt Disney is now offering adult education classes at its new Disney Institute, in Orlando, Florida. Some of the courses offered at the Institute (such as computer animation, storytelling, and home video) "mime the Disney heritage," according to the vice-president in charge of the Institute; others cover cooking, sports, and gardening. With the Institute, Walt Disney is seeking to reach aging baby boomers and retirees, people who its traditional theme parks do not reach.

Many retailing analysts see the Disney Institute (along with such ventures as a cruise line, the Mighty Ducks professional ice hockey team, and a new planned city called Celebration) as part of the firm's overall diversification strategy. Yet, Disney sees this as a logical extension of the "edutainment" business. As a result of this philosophy, Institute courses tend to introduce people to a field of study, as opposed to providing in-depth, technically based instruction. As the director of the Institute's Life-Styles program says, "If you want to study photography in depth, go to the Nikon Institute."

Although Disney uses working professionals as instructors at the Institute, it is still very much concerned with its overall image. All instructors, like the "cast-member" employees at its theme parks, are required to be well-groomed with short and neat hair, and even to wear a Disney uniform. Says one instructor who has complained about the uniform, "You think people want to see what a real photographer or a filmmaker looks like, not a Pirates of the Caribbean character."

The grounds of the Disney Institute, with pastel-colored concert halls and classrooms, are based on the Chautauqua Institution, an upstate New York adult-learning complex that concentrates on the performing arts, politics, and philosophy. After Michael Eisner, Walt Disney's chairman, visited Chautauqua in 1985, he planned to create a similar environment to "enhance and improve quality of life in the Disney fashion." It took him a decade to do so.

As compared to its Florida theme parks that attract about 33 million visitors annually, Disney expects the Institute with its 457 rooms to attract close to 100,000 people annually. The cost for the three-day minimum stay ranges from $429 per person to $1,653, depending upon the room and meal plans chosen. While observers do not think the Institute will contribute greatly to Disney's profitability (due to its small scale), they expect it to add to merchandise revenues, attract new visitors to the amusement parks, and help fill hotel rooms.[1]

---

[1] Lisa Bannon, "Disney Decides World Isn't So Small, Creating Education Resort for Boomers," *Wall Street Journal* (March 1, 1996), pp. B1, B5.

Service retailing in the United States and elsewhere in the world is growing steadily and **OVERVIEW**
represents a very large portion of overall retail trade. Although the total revenues from
service retailing are hard to estimate because key government data do not separate retail
services from business services, the dimensions of service retailing can be seen from the
following.

In the United States, consumers spend three-fifths of their after-tax income on such
services as travel, recreation, personal care, education, medical care, and housing. Three-
quarters of the labor force is employed in the service sector. Consumers spend billions of
dollars each year to rent such products as power tools and party goods (coffee urns, silverware, wine glasses, etc.). People annually spend $125 billion to maintain and repair
their cars. There are 90,000 beauty salons and barber shops, 56,000 laundry and cleaning outlets, 43,000 hotels and motels, 22,000 video-rental stores, and 15,000 sports and
recreation clubs. During the past 25 years, the prices of services have risen more than the
prices of many goods. Due to technological advances, automation has substantially reduced manufacturing labor costs; but many services remain rather labor-intensive due to
their personal nature.[2]

Tens of millions of domestic and foreign travelers annually visit amusement parks
around the world, such as Walt Disney World, Disneyland, Universal Studios Florida,
Universal Studios Hollywood, and Sea World in the United States; Disneyland Paris
in France; and Tokyo Disneyland in Japan. About 15 million Americans visit foreign
countries each year as tourists, while 17 million foreign tourists visit the United
States.[3]

At shopping centers, from the world's largest regional mall—the West Edmonton
Mall in Canada—to the smallest neighborhood shopping center, service retailers such as
restaurants, beauty salons, and others play a key role in drawing customer traffic and
providing a positive shopping atmosphere. See Figure 19-1.

As noted in Chapter 5, **service retailing** encompasses rented goods, owned goods,
and nongoods. With rented-goods services, consumers lease physical products for a
specified period of time. With owned-goods services, consumers own physical products
that are repaired, maintained, or altered. With nongoods services, consumers receive
personal expertise from service providers; physical goods are not involved or have a small
role in the business.

Service retailing's growth and the differences in strategic planning for a service retailer and a goods retailer make this a topic to be thoroughly studied. In the future, the
service sector will continue to expand. Opportunities will be plentiful for those who
know how to anticipate and plan for them. Consider these two examples:

■ The car-rental business is a tough one. It is seasonal, consumers often have specifications in mind (such as a sedan, convertible, or van), and vacationers and business
travelers may require different rental locations. A car-rental firm also needs a host of
facilitating services, such as providing data about terms, having a reservation system, handling a car's checkout and return, processing bills, and handling complaints. One car-rental firm that is both an innovator and a leader in service quality
is Hertz (http://www.hertz.com). Its successful strategy is largely based on the array of services offered. These include the #1 Club Gold program for frequent customers, express return, delivery service to hotels, emergency roadside assistance,
special services for physically challenged customers, and more. Hertz is highly computerized. See Figure 19-2.

[2]*Statistical Abstract of the United States 1996* (Washington, D.C.: U.S. Department of Commerce, 1996),
various pages.
[3]Ibid.

Figure 19-1

The Diversity of Service Retailing at the West Edmonton Mall

■ Multiplex movie theaters have revolutionized that industry, and virtually killed off the single-screen theater and drive-ins. Multiplexes are doing well for several reasons. They offer a large variety of movies. The most popular movies are shown on two to three "screens," which enables customers to choose from among 10 to 20 different viewing times during the day. Family members can watch separate "screens" and still be in the same theater. From a cost perspective, multiplexes are efficient because seating capacities can be adjusted on the basis of audience size; and multiplexes encourage people to stay longer at shopping centers.[4]

Service retailing can also be quite challenging:

Like interactive TV, flying cars, Esperanto, and Roger Clinton, home delivery is a recurring idea that has never quite fulfilled its promise. Maybe this time, though.

[4]See Neal Templin, "Multiplying Multiplexes," *Wall Street Journal* (February 28, 1997), p. B12.

Figure 19-2

Hertz: The Rental Car Leader

Due to its extensive array of customer services and its convenient locations around the world, Hertz has been the market-share leader in its industry for years.

Surveys reveal that among household chores, many people rate grocery shopping only slightly less onerous than cleaning. Home delivery is already on the rise. An annual survey conducted by America's Research Group, in Charleston, South Carolina, revealed that 9 percent of respondents used a home-delivery service in 1996, up from 6.9 percent in 1995. Estimates suggest home delivery might eventually capture as much as 20 percent of the money spent on groceries each year. So the stakes are high. In more genteel days, it was common for small stores to deliver grocery orders. Other firms delivered milk and meat. But those and similar services faded as supermarkets subsumed smaller stores and small towns became sprawling suburbs. Two major trends helped to reawaken interest in home delivery. Starting in the mid-1970s, the growing ranks of working women had less time to grocery shop, but they could order in by phone, so companies such as Domino's Pizza flourished. The second trend, the growth of home PCs, beginning a decade later, enabled shoppers to place orders more complex than a large pepperoni with extra cheese—a week's worth of groceries, for instance. Today, a number of firms, including Peapod, based in Chicago, fill the bags at local supermarkets, and deliver them to people's homes. Peapod has an exclusive relationship with one retail chain in each market. In Chicago, it's Jewel-Osco; in Northern California, it's Safeway; and Peapod also has deals with Stop & Shop in Boston and Kroger in Columbus, Ohio. Peapod provides consumers with software that lets them create customized shopping lists, view prices and specials, and place orders. The software even lets users view nutritional labels, sort groceries by price or nutritional content, find recipes, and send E-mail. While Peapod allows customers to order at any time, it doesn't deliver on Mondays.[5]

STRATEGY CONCEPTS APPLIED TO SERVICE RETAILING

The unique aspects of services, which influence a retail strategy, are (1) the intangible nature of many services makes a consumer's choice of competitive offerings tougher than with goods; (2) the service provider and his or her services are sometimes inseparable (thus localizing marketing efforts); (3) the perishability of many services prevents storage and increases risks; and (4) the human nature of many services makes them more variable.

The intangible (and possibly abstract) nature of services makes it harder for a firm to develop a clear consumer-oriented strategy, particularly as many retailers (such as opticians,

---

[5]Joshua Macht, "Errand Boy," *Inc.* (November 1996), p. 62.

Characteristics of
Service Retailing

Selected Strategic Implications

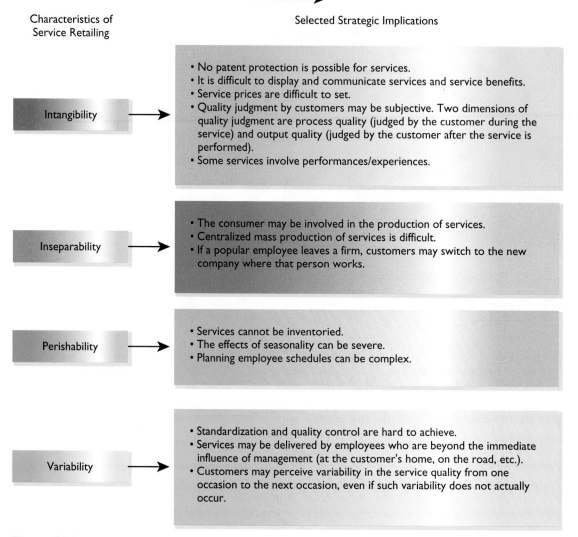

• No patent protection is possible for services.
• It is difficult to display and communicate services and service benefits.
• Service prices are difficult to set.
• Quality judgment by customers may be subjective. Two dimensions of quality judgment are process quality (judged by the customer during the service) and output quality (judged by the customer after the service is performed).
• Some services involve performances/experiences.

• The consumer may be involved in the production of services.
• Centralized mass production of services is difficult.
• If a popular employee leaves a firm, customers may switch to the new company where that person works.

• Services cannot be inventoried.
• The effects of seasonality can be severe.
• Planning employee schedules can be complex.

• Standardization and quality control are hard to achieve.
• Services may be delivered by employees who are beyond the immediate influence of management (at the customer's home, on the road, etc.).
• Customers may perceive variability in the service quality from one occasion to the next occasion, even if such variability does not actually occur.

Figure 19-3

Characteristics of Service Retailing That Differentiate It from Goods Retailing and Their Strategic Implications

Source: Adapted by the authors from Valarie A. Zeithaml, A. Parasuraman, and Leonard L. Berry, "Problems and Strategies in Service Marketing," *Journal of Marketing,* Vol. 49 (Spring 1985), p. 35. Reprinted by permission of the American Marketing Association.

repairpeople, and landscapers) start service businesses on the basis of their product expertise. The inseparability of the service provider and his or her services means the owner-operator is often indispensable and good customer relations are pivotal. Perishability presents a risk that in many cases cannot be overcome. Thus, revenues from an unrented hotel room are forever lost. Variability means service quality may differ for each shopping experience, store, or service provider. See Figure 19-3.

Figure 19-4 shows one way to classify service retailers. An individual firm should precisely identify the combination of attributes in this figure that it possesses (or wants to possess) and act accordingly. A service retailer can usually be described in terms of each category in Figure 19-4. A car-rental firm may be classed as rented goods (level of tangibility), nonprofessional (service provider skill), equipment-based (level of labor intensity), low contact (level of customer contact), profit-oriented (goal), and rather nonregulated (level of regulation). Yet, no classification system is

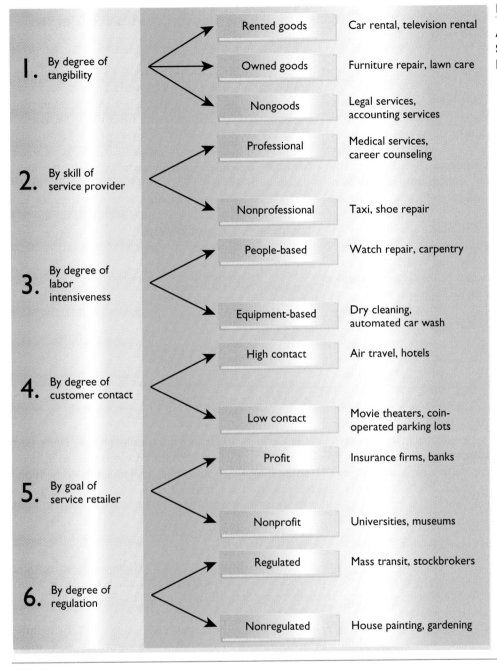

Figure 19-4

A Classification System for Service Retailers

ironclad. If a problem occurs (such as a rental car's not functioning properly or a promised car's being unavailable), a low-contact car-rental firm might become a high-contact firm.

Although service-oriented retailing differs from goods-oriented retailing, strategic planning should be conducted by the same overall procedure:

1. The situation is analyzed, including a definition of the service category.
2. The objectives of the firm are enumerated and ranked.
3. Consumer characteristics and needs are identified.
4. The overall strategy is outlined.

Service Quality: Consumer Perceptions in Mexico Versus the United States

A research project recently examined whether there are differences in perceived service quality between Mexican and U.S. consumers. Respondents were asked to rate their agreement or disagreement to a series of 50 statements regarding service quality. The questionnaire included items on the degree of service, an overall service rating, service quality in Mexico and the United States, the degree of service necessary to a regular customer, and store ratings.

The study was administered in a Mexican city approximately 150 miles from the U.S. border and in a U.S. city of comparable size and distance from the Mexican border. Four different types of retail businesses were studied in each area: a bank, a grocery store, an apparel specialty store, and a department store. Twenty-five shoppers were interviewed at each site in each city.

The study found that there are significant differences in perceived quality between Mexican and U.S. consumers. On 27 of 33 questions, the Mexican respondents rated service quality higher than the comparable U.S. respondents. Service quality factors of importance also differed between the two groups. Mexican respondents said availability, a full offering, goods and services functioning as advertised, and confidence in the support staff were most important. U.S. respondents said personalized service and ease of purchasing were most important.

Source: Paul Herbig and Alain Genestre, "An Examination of the Cross-Cultural Differences in Service Quality: The Example of Mexico and the USA," *Journal of Consumer Marketing,* Vol. 13 (Number 3, 1996), pp. 43–53.

5. The strategy is implemented.
6. The strategy is regularly re-evaluated and adjusted.

In particular, a service retailer must understand its organizational mission, effectively select opportunities, set clear goals, cater to consumer needs, be cost effective, be distinctive, determine how to set prices, communicate with customers, and plan for competition.

Table 19-1 notes how firms can plan for the differences between service and goods retailing.

Situation Analysis

While developing a service strategy, a firm must determine if rented-goods, owned-goods, or nongoods services are involved because planning is different for each type of service. The service category must then be more narrowly defined, as these illustrations show:

■ Is a retailer interested in opening a barber shop and giving haircuts? Or should a men's personal-care salon be opened, with such services as haircutting, manicures, facial massages, hair coloring, and facial-care advice?

■ Is a firm going to operate an upscale resort hotel? Or should a discount motel chain be started?

■ Should a prospective dry cleaner focus on clothing or household products? Or both?

These examples indicate the range of options available to potential service retailers and demonstrate the necessity of defining the service category.

A firm should choose its service category before making any other strategic decisions. Too narrow a definition of the service category runs the risk of attracting a small target market and ignoring related services that may be vital to customer satisfaction. For example, a retailer that repairs TVs may also get a lot of requests from customers to repair VCRs. If the firm defines its offering too narrowly (and decides not to repair

Table 19-1 SPECIAL MANAGERIAL CONSIDERATIONS FOR SERVICE RETAILERS IN SEVEN KEY STRATEGIC AREAS

Service Retailing as Compared with Goods Retailing	Managerial Adjustments Needed by Service Retailers
a. Store organization More specialized supervision is needed. More specific search for service employees is needed. Lower employee turnover is needed. Higher pay for skilled craftspeople than for merchandising personnel is needed.	Separate management for service areas will be required. Nontraditional sources for identification of employees must be used. Frequent salary and performance reviews must be carried out. Pay levels will need to be adjusted upward over periods of longevity for service employees.
b. Service production More involvement in producing the service is needed. More emphasis on quality control is needed. There is more need to monitor consumer satisfaction. There is more need to refine scheduling of employees. Quality must be consistent among all outlets.	Production skills will need to be obtained by supervisors. Supervisors must be able to assess the quality of a service performed for a customer. Prior customers should be researched to measure their satisfaction with the service. Maximizing service employees' time requires matching consumer purchasing with the employees' ability to produce the service. Standards for consistency of the service must be set and continually evaluated; central training may be required for workers in multiple-branch operations.
c. Pricing Services vary in cost; therefore, pricing is harder. There is more difficulty in price competition or promotion based on price.	Prices may be quoted within a range instead of an exact figure before the purchase. Services should be promoted in terms of criteria other than price.
d. Promotion Value is more difficult for consumers to determine. It is difficult to display services within a store. Visual presentation is more important. Cross-selling with goods is important. It is more difficult to advertise in catalogs.	Consumers need to be convinced of value through personal selling. In-store signing or a service center is required to notify customers of services' availability. Before-and-after photographs may be possible with some services. Testimonials may be possible with other services. A quota or bonus for goods-oriented salespersons who suggest services will lead to increased service selling. Conditions for the sale and for away-from-the-store performance must be specified.
e. Complaints It is harder to return a service. A customer is more sensitive about services involving a person (rather than a good).	Policies must be established for adjusting the service purchased by a dissatisfied customer. Specific guarantees and policies about adjustments must be established; new types of insurance must be added to cover liabilities.
f. Controls There is a greater opportunity to steal customers.	Employees' assurances of loyalty must be established. Protection of store loyalty must be sought.
g. Measuring performance Capital expenditures vary widely for different services. Small or no inventories are required to offer services. Higher labor costs exist for services. Some services support the sale of goods. Cost accounting is more important.	Return on net worth may not be the most important measurement of the value of a service to the retailer. Turnover, markdown controls, and other goods-related controls are not as appropriate. Profit after labor costs replaces the gross margin used by goods retailing. Sales-supporting services should be assessed differently from revenue-producing ones. Job-specific records are required to assess the profits of each sale.

Source: Adapted by the authors from J. Patrick Kelly and William R. George, "Strategic Management Issues for the Retailing of Services," *Journal of Retailing,* Vol. 58 (Summer 1982), pp. 40–42. Reprinted by permission.

VCRs), it misses out on an opportunity to expand sales and it takes a chance of losing the TV-repair business from these customers. On the other hand, too broad a definition of the service category (such as equipment repair) could result in a nonspecialist image and may mean a larger operation and greater investment than desired.

When selecting a service category, personal abilities, financial resources, and time resources should be matched to the requirements of the business. The personal abilities required of a service-oriented retailer are usually quite distinct from those of a goods-oriented retailer:

■ With service retailing, the major value provided to the customer is some type of service, not the ownership of a physical product.

■ Specific skills may be required, and the skills may not be transferable from one type of service to another. For example, TV repairpeople, beauticians, and accountants cannot easily change businesses or transfer skills. The owners of appliance stores, cosmetics stores, and toy stores (all goods-oriented firms) would have an easier time changing and transferring their skills to another area.

■ More service operators must possess licenses or certification to run their businesses. Barbers, real-estate brokers, dentists, attorneys, plumbers, and others must pass exams in their fields.

■ Owners of service businesses must enjoy their jobs and have the aptitude for them. Because of the close personal contact with customers, these elements are essential and difficult to feign.

The financial resources necessary for a service-oriented retailer often differ significantly from those of a goods-oriented retailer. The major ongoing cost for service retailers is often labor. Whereas the opening of a service station demands a high capital investment, the compensation for mechanics is the largest ongoing cost of doing business. For goods retailers, the major ongoing investment is inventory.

Many service retailers can thus operate on lower overall investments and succeed on less yearly revenues than goods retailers. A service station can function with one gas attendant and one skilled mechanic. A tax-preparation firm can succeed with one accountant. A watch repair business needs one repairperson. In each case, the owner may be the only skilled worker. Costs can be held down accordingly. On the other hand, a goods retailer needs an adequate assortment and supply of inventory, which may impose financial obligations, require storage, and be costly.

At times, this distinction between service and goods retailing is not as great as expected since suppliers may let their goods-oriented retailers receive items on consignment or offer low-interest credit terms. Furthermore, some service retailing requires not only an initial capital investment but also other substantial ongoing nonlabor costs. An amusement park, a car wash, and a laundromat all have high electricity and maintenance costs.

In choosing a service category, it is crucial for all costs to be computed. The owner's labor should not be viewed as cost-free since he or she could earn wages as someone else's employee (and because the owner needs a steady income to maintain a given life-style).

The time resources of a prospective retailer should be weighed in terms of the requirements of alternative business opportunities. Some businesses, like a self-service laundromat or a movie theater, require low time investments. Other businesses, like house painting or a travel agency, require large time investments because personal service is the key to profitability. More service retailers fall into the high rather than the low time-investment category.

Setting Objectives

Besides the sales, profit, and image goals sought by goods-oriented retailers, service-oriented retailers should set other objectives due to their unique characteristics. These include increasing service tangibility, matching demand and supply, standardizing services, making services more efficient, and fostering customer relationships.

Service tangibility can be increased by stressing service-provider reliability, promoting a continuous slogan (for instance, "Avon calling"), describing specific service accomplishments (such as a car tune-up's improving gas consumption by one mile per gallon), and offering warranties (such as some hotels giving automatic refunds to unhappy guests). American Airlines (http://www.americanair.com) offers an AAccess program at its Web site, whereby customers can select flights and make their reservations interactively. The AAccess program is a tangible representation of American Airlines and its logos. See Figure 19-5.

Demand and supply can be better matched by offering similar services to market segments with different demand patterns (such as Manhattan tourists and residents), new services with demand patterns that are countercyclical from existing services (such as cross-country skiing during the winter at Denver golf resorts), new services that complement existing ones (such as beauty salons adding tanning booths), special deals during nonpeak times (such as midweek movie theater prices), and new services not subject to existing capacity constraints (such as a ten-table restaurant starting a home-delivery service).

Standardizing services reduces their variability, makes it easier to set prices, and improves efficiency. Services can be standardized by

■ Clearly defining each of the tasks involved.
■ Determining the minimum and maximum times needed to complete each task.
■ Selecting the best order for tasks to be done.
■ Noting the optimum time and quality of the entire service.

Standardization has been successfully applied to such firms as quick-auto-service providers (oil change, tune-up, and muffler repair firms), legal services (for wills, house closings, and similar proceedings), and emergency-medical-care centers. If services are standardized, there is often a trade-off: more consistent quality and convenience in exchange for less of a personal touch.

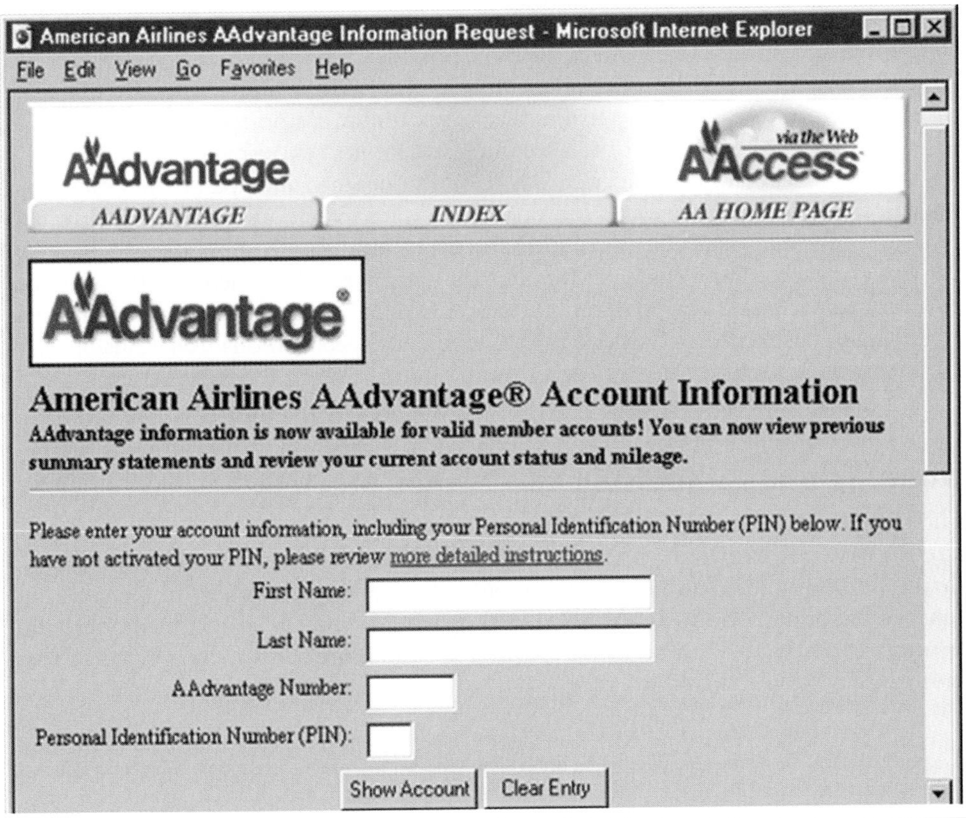

Figure 19-5

AAccess: A Technique for Making a Service More Tangible

Through its Web-based AAccess program, American Airlines lets the members of its frequent-flyer program learn about flights and make reservations. By prominently displaying its logos, thoroughly explaining the AAccess program on the PC monitor, and enabling customers to operate interactively, American Airlines is making itself more tangible (and desirable).

An important tool in standardizing labor-intensive services is a **service blueprint,** which systematically lists all the functions to be performed and the average time expected for each one's completion. Figure 19-6 shows a service blueprint for a quick-oil-change firm's employees to follow. The blueprint identifies employee and customer activities (in order), as well as expected average performance times for each activity. Among the advantages of a service blueprint are that it helps standardize services (within a location and between locations), isolates points where the service may be weak or prone to failure (Do employees actually check transmission, brake, and power-steering fluid levels in one minute?), outlines a plan that can be evaluated for completeness (Should the customer be offered options for oil grades?), evaluates personnel needs (Should one employee change the oil and another wash the windshield?), and helps recommend productivity improvements (Should the customer or an employee drive a car into and out of the service bay?).

Besides standardizing services, retailers may be able to make services more efficient by automating them, thereby substituting machinery for labor. For instance, attorneys are increasingly using computerized word processing for common paragraphs in wills and house closings. This means more consistency in the way documents look, time savings, and neater—more error-free—documents. Among the service firms that have automated at least part of their operations are banks, car washes, bowling alleys, airlines, phone services, real-estate brokers, and hotels.

Even more than goods retailers, most service firms recognize that long-term customer relationships are essential to their well-being. After all, service retailing is much more dependent on personal interactions and word-of-mouth communication:

> Relationship marketing benefits the customer, as well as the firm. For continuously or periodically delivered services that are personally important, variable in quality, and/or complex, many customers will desire to be "relationship customers." High-involvement services also hold relationship appeal to customers. Medical, banking, insurance, and hairstyling services illustrate some or all of the significant factors—importance, variability, complexity, and involvement—that would cause many customers to desire continuity with the same provider, a proactive service attitude, and customized service delivery. All are potential benefits of relationship marketing. The intangible nature of services makes them difficult for customers to evaluate prior to purchase. The heterogeneity of labor-intensive services encourages customer loyalty when excellent service is experienced. Not only does the auto repair firm want to find customers who will be loyal, but customers want to find an auto repair firm that evokes their loyalty. Relationship marketing allows service providers to be more knowledgeable about customer requirements and needs. Knowledge of the customer combined with social rapport built over a series of service encounters facilitate the tailoring or customizing of service to the customer's specifications. Relationship marketing does not apply to every service situation. However, for those services distinguished by the characteristics discussed here, it is a potent marketing strategy.[6]

Defining and Examining the Target Market

The target market must be defined and examined, and the consumer and the service offering carefully matched. Consumer demographics, life-styles, and decision making should all be studied. In this way, the retailer can develop a strategy in a logical and consistent manner. To illustrate, a barber shop would typically attract customers who are more conservative, less affluent, less mobile, and more convenience-oriented than those drawn to a personal-care salon.

---

[6]Leonard L. Berry, "Relationship Marketing of Services—Growing Interest, Emerging Prospects," *Journal of the Academy of Marketing Science,* Vol. 23 (Fall 1995), pp. 237–238.

Expected Average Time per Activity

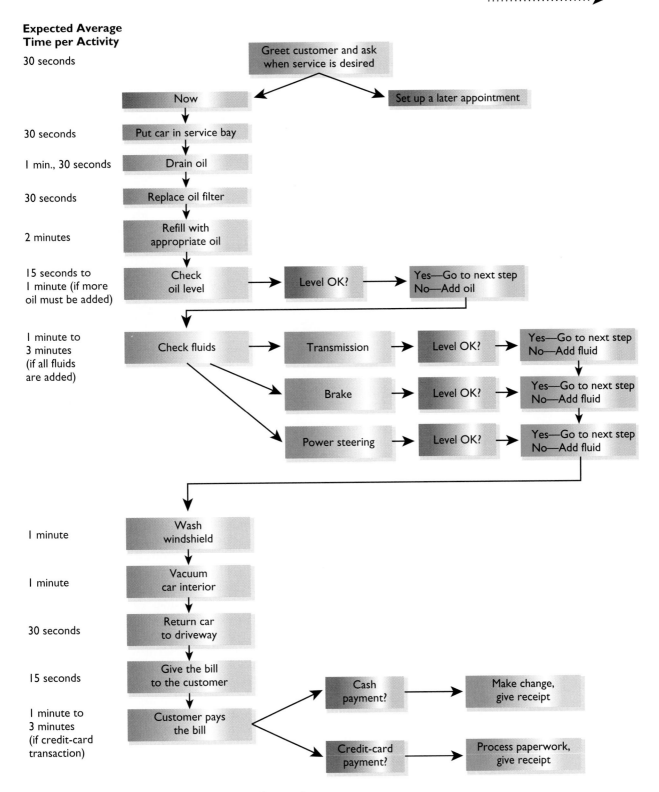

Total expected time = 10 minutes to 14 minutes, 45 seconds.

Figure 19-6

A Service Blueprint for a Quick-Oil-Change Firm's Employees

Figure 19-7

Public Fax Machines at Airports: For the Time-Pressured Traveler

Service retailers can use segmentation and/or mass-marketing approaches. These examples show the variety of target market alternatives available:

■ Different car-rental firms appeal to distinct market segments. Hertz and Avis have outlets at airport terminals; their convenient locations enable them to target full-service customers with above-average prices. Thrifty Rent-A-Car has outlets at sites near airports; it is more oriented to discount-oriented travelers. Snappy Rental specializes in replacement cars for people who need them because of insurance coverage after an accident.

■ Public fax machines are used by two kinds of customers. There are those who cannot afford a fax machine or who do not send enough faxes to make a purchase worthwhile. These people go to retailers such as pharmacies, copy centers, and convenience stores that charge a moderate fee to send a fax. There are those who have fax facilities at the office or at home, but are always on the move. They look for machines at airports and hotels, and pay a larger fee to send a fax. See Figure 19-7.

■ Family Golf, a chain of "golf centers" in ten states, encourages golfers to bring along their spouses and children: "Family Golf's facilities generally have two tiers of hitting tees—heated in winter—accommodating up to 100 swingers. They also have clubhouses with locker rooms and private party rooms, snack bars or restaurants, well-stocked pro shops, and instructors certified by the Professional Golf Association. There are practice putting greens and sand traps and, for less serious duffers, 18-hole, tastefully landscaped miniature golf courses. By marketing to families, Family Golf has greatly broadened its base of potential customers. Tagalong spouses and children usually spend at least a few bucks on snacks or miniature golf. Once at the range, if they do hit a bucket of balls, there's a good chance they'll sign up for lessons and start pricing a set of clubs in the pro shop. As the firm's founder says, 'Golf is a very intimidating game. We try to make it easy to learn without getting discouraged.' "[7]

■ Renters Choice caters to consumers who want to acquire high-ticket items, but cannot afford to purchase them: "Paulette Mitchell, who earns her living as a home-care nurse, dreamed of owning a big-screen TV. But where would she get $3,032 all at once? Charge it to her credit card? Mitchell didn't have one. After becoming entangled in debt a couple of years back, she'd sworn off credit cards. Thanks to Renters Choice, she

[7]John R. Hayes, "The Guilty Golfer," *Forbes* (June 17, 1996), pp. 90, 92.

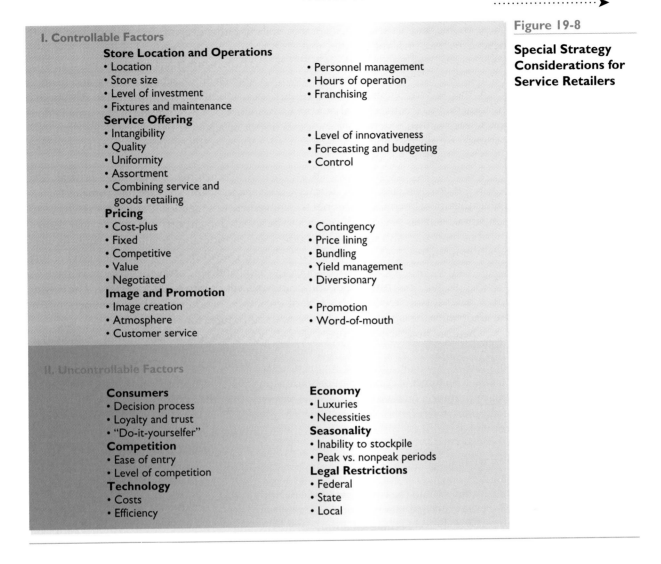

Figure 19-8

Special Strategy Considerations for Service Retailers

I. Controllable Factors

Store Location and Operations
- Location
- Store size
- Level of investment
- Fixtures and maintenance

Service Offering
- Intangibility
- Quality
- Uniformity
- Assortment
- Combining service and goods retailing

Pricing
- Cost-plus
- Fixed
- Competitive
- Value
- Negotiated

Image and Promotion
- Image creation
- Atmosphere
- Customer service

- Personnel management
- Hours of operation
- Franchising

- Level of innovativeness
- Forecasting and budgeting
- Control

- Contingency
- Price lining
- Bundling
- Yield management
- Diversionary

- Promotion
- Word-of-mouth

II. Uncontrollable Factors

Consumers
- Decision process
- Loyalty and trust
- "Do-it-yourselfer"

Competition
- Ease of entry
- Level of competition

Technology
- Costs
- Efficiency

Economy
- Luxuries
- Necessities

Seasonality
- Inability to stockpile
- Peak vs. nonpeak periods

Legal Restrictions
- Federal
- State
- Local

got her TV anyway. Now ensconced in her modest Dallas living room is a 52-inch RCA rear-projection set. Every Tuesday she goes to a Renters Choice store in a Dallas strip center and pays $40 cash, plus tax and insurance. If she keeps this up, she'll eventually own the TV. Her total price: $6,065.10—an effective annual interest rate of 55 percent. Usury? Not to Mitchell, who earns $30,000 a year. The extra cost enables her to enjoy the set now, not in the distant future. She's paying with money she would have dribbled away. 'I throw away money all the time,' says Mitchell."[8]

Outlining Overall Strategy

In planning the overall strategy for a service business, the full range of controllable factors (store location and operations, service offering, pricing, and image and promotion) and uncontrollable factors (consumers, competition, technology, economic conditions, seasonality, and legal restrictions) must be studied. Figure 19-8 contains a list of the special considerations facing service retailers in each of these areas. They are detailed in the sections that follow.

Controllable Factors: Store Location and Operations ❑ The store location and operations aspects of strategy must be outlined. The importance of store location to service retailers varies greatly. Sometimes, as with TV repairs, house painting, and lawn care, the service is "delivered" to the appropriate site. The firm's location becomes the

[8]Christine Foster, "You Want It, You Rent It," *Forbes* (February 10, 1997), p. 104.

client's home, and the actual office of the retailer is rather insignificant. Many clients might never even see a firm's office; they make contact by phone or personal visits, and customer convenience is optimized. In these instances, the firm incurs travel expenses, but it also has low (or no) rent and does not have to maintain store facilities, set up displays, and so on.

Other service retailers are visited on "specific-intent" shopping trips. Although a customer may be concerned about the convenience of a location, he or she usually does not select a skilled practitioner such as a doctor or a lawyer based on the location. It is common for doctors and attorneys to have offices in their homes or near hospitals or court buildings, respectively.

For some service retailers that are visited by customers, location is critical. Car washes, travel agencies, movie theaters, hotels, and health spas are just some of the retailers that must be concerned about the convenience of their locations. That is why some car-rental agencies pay premium rents to be situated in airports rather than near them.

The store size and level of investment are considerably smaller for many service-oriented retailers than for goods-oriented ones. A small store can often be used because little or no room is needed for displaying merchandise. A travel agency may have 12 salespeople and book millions of dollars in trips, yet fit into a 500-foot store. The investment factor further relates to the lack of inventory. In addition, phone transactions can further reduce the significance of store size and fixtures for service retailers.

There are times when fixtures—as well as facilities maintenance—may be more crucial for service-oriented firms than goods-oriented ones. Since the sale of tangible, branded goods (which can be compared among different firms) is not the major focus of service retailing, a customer may base part of his or her opinion of a firm on the visible store fixtures and appearance. To revisit the travel agency example, the desks, carpeting, light fixtures, computers, wall plaques, and cleanliness level could all be used by a client to develop a perception of the firm—although these items are not part of the promotion mix.

Some aspects of personnel management can be hard, and maybe frustrating, for a service firm:

- When should the firm be staffed? Are there peak business hours?
- How can customer waiting time be minimized?
- What should permanent employees do during the time when no customers appear?
- How can employee performance be measured? How should the performance of technical personnel with high customer contact be evaluated?
- How can productivity be increased?
- How should employees be paid (salary, commission, or some combination)?
- If an employee quits or is fired, will customers follow him or her to another firm?

Due to the personal nature of many service firms, these and other human resource issues must be weighed before a strategy is enacted or revised. And trade-offs related to various service levels must be assessed.[9] Thus, "Seeking to improve their financial performance, most airlines are putting fewer attendants on board aircraft. The result: Passengers wait longer for meals and beverages; meal carts clog aisles longer; dirty trays stack up; and getting the little extras of life aloft—a pillow, a magazine, water—is often a do-it-yourself experience."[10]

---

[9]See Julie Baker and Michealle Camerson, "The Effects of the Service Encounter on Affect and Consumer Perception of Waiting Time: An Integrative Review and Research Propositions," *Journal of the Academy of Marketing Science*, Vol. 24 (Fall 1996), pp. 338–349; Michael D. Hartline and O. C. Ferrell, "The Management of Customer-Contact Service Employees: An Empirical Investigation," *Journal of Marketing*, Vol. 60 (October 1996), pp. 52–70; David E. Bowen and Edward E. Lawler III, "Empowering Service Employees," *Sloan Management Review*, Vol. 36 (Summer 1995), pp. 73–84; and Scott W. Kelley, Timothy Longfellow, and Jack Malehorn, "Organizational Determinants of Service Employees' Exercise of Routine, Creative, and Deviant Discretion," *Journal of Retailing*, Vol. 72 (Summer 1996), pp. 135–157.

[10]James S. Hirsch, "With Fewer Attendants Aboard Jets, Mood of Passengers Turns Turbulent," *Wall Street Journal* (July 23, 1993), pp. B1, B5.

Decisions on operating hours should be made in conjunction with personnel management—and the hours planned in terms of customer, not employee, convenience. A shoe repair store should be open in the early morning, and a savings bank should have evening and/or Saturday hours. Although a shoe repair store can have one worker open the store in the morning to receive broken or worn shoes, as the work will be done later, a savings bank must plan to have enough employees during evening and/or weekend hours to handle all customer services as people wait.

Franchised services are still expanding. Blockbuster, Fantastic Sams, Jazzercise, Century 21 Real Estate, Jenny Craig, Holiday Inn, Lawn Doctor, Kampgrounds of America, and Mail Boxes, Etc. are just some of the franchises engaged in service retailing. The greatest potential problem facing these chains relates to the level of uniformity in the services provided by different franchisees. For example, Blockbuster must ensure that franchisees offer similar video assortments at comparable prices. Fantastic Sams must provide consistent haircutting services at all locales. Jazzercise must be sure there are professional, knowledgeable fitness instructors at every studio. Century 21 must weed out unethical brokers and insist on certain performance standards.

As with goods-oriented franchising, if any unit in a service franchise performs poorly, the whole franchise would suffer. Because service-oriented franchising is more intangible, extra care needs to be given to positioning the company in a clear and consistent way. Employee training and supervision take on great importance.

Controllable Factors: Service Offering ❏ A goods-oriented firm, carrying items such as perfume or cars or TVs, sells tangible products that can be seen, smelled, touched, heard, and, sometimes, tasted. A service firm handling rentals and/or repair services deals with tangible items, but its service is still intangible. A nongoods service firm, such as an accounting firm, has the most intangibility to overcome in marketing itself to consumers because its services often cannot be seen, smelled, touched, heard, or tasted.

Even though an airline rents seats to passengers, the quality of the service it offers depends on such intangibles as customer perceptions about flight attendant courtesy, aircraft cleanliness, the smoothness of the flight, the firm's record for being on time, and baggage-handling speed. As the SAS airline president once remarked, "We have thousands of 'moments of truth' out there every day."

This is how a service retailer, a travel agency, might deal with the intangibility of its offering. The agency can stress the expertise of its agents and the types of travel arrangements handled. Agents can be trained so they are aware of all available vacation packages—and their options—and able to design customized trips. The agency can foster good relationships with popular airlines and hotels to provide one-stop shopping for customers. To present its service offering as tangibly as possible, the agency can use fast PCs to acquire airline and other information and to process orders (to demonstrate knowledge and efficiency), place certificates around the office (to indicate the training received by employees, the awards recognizing the firm's past performance, and testimonials from satisfied clients), have an assortment of colorful and well-written brochures (to show hotel accommodations, sightseeing excursions, and so on), and offer specific vacation packages (with the names of the hotels and airlines, all package components, and prices).

As with a goods-oriented firm, a service-oriented firm must consider the quality of its offering. Airlines always compete on the basis of "no frills" versus "extra service," trying to please various market segments. They know many students want no-frills flights, whereas businesspeople are often more concerned about the time of departure, and tourists desire in-flight services.

Quality may also be hard to plan due to differing customer perceptions of the same service. A tax-preparation service may be patronized because the consumer desires accurate mathematical computation, an opportunity for financial savings, advice, convenience, or freedom from responsibility. Different market segments can be lured by each of these perceived benefits. Figure 19-9 shows ten factors consumers may use to rate the quality of a service.

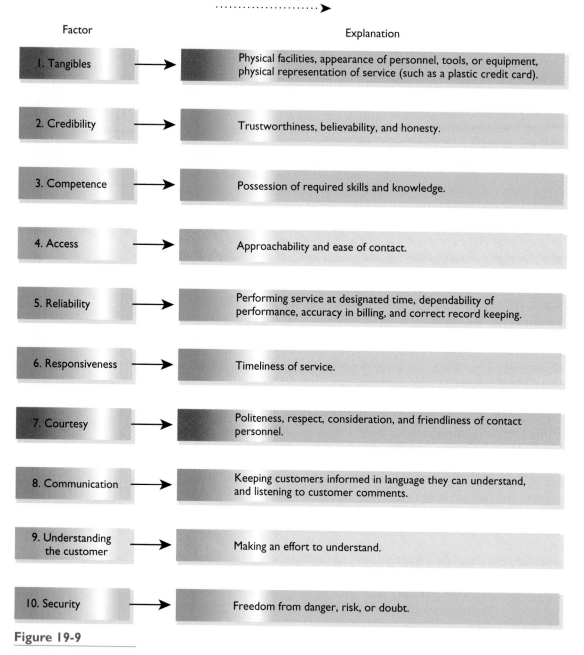

Factor | Explanation

1. Tangibles → Physical facilities, appearance of personnel, tools, or equipment, physical representation of service (such as a plastic credit card).

2. Credibility → Trustworthiness, believability, and honesty.

3. Competence → Possession of required skills and knowledge.

4. Access → Approachability and ease of contact.

5. Reliability → Performing service at designated time, dependability of performance, accuracy in billing, and correct record keeping.

6. Responsiveness → Timeliness of service.

7. Courtesy → Politeness, respect, consideration, and friendliness of contact personnel.

8. Communication → Keeping customers informed in language they can understand, and listening to customer comments.

9. Understanding the customer → Making an effort to understand.

10. Security → Freedom from danger, risk, or doubt.

Figure 19-9

Ten Factors Consumers Use to Determine Service Quality

Source: Adapted by the authors from Valarie A. Zeithaml, A. Parasuraman, and Leonard L. Berry, *Delivering Quality Service: Balancing Customer Perceptions and Expectations* (New York: Free Press, 1990), pp. 21–22. Free Press is a division of Simon & Schuster. Reprinted by permission.

As a service retailer selects a level of service quality, its target market, competition, image, location, number of customer transactions, profitability, use of national versus private brands, services offered, personnel, perceived customer benefits, and constrained decision making should be kept in mind. An added factor (of greater importance than to a goods-oriented retailer), the uniformity of the service offering provided by the same firm, must be thoroughly planned.

Customers want to receive the same service level each time a particular retailer is patronized. Thus, employees' appearance, skills, attitude, and performance must be consistent. Customer loyalty is predicated on this assumption. If a person eats at a restaurant where it usually takes an hour to complete dinner, this person would probably be dissatisfied with a visit taking two hours to finish dinner (due to slow service). On the other hand, if a restaurant normally has two-hour service, its regular customers would not be unhappy with the length of the meal.

The width and depth of the service assortment, while different from a goods-oriented retailer, must be planned. Two illustrations can show this. Width of assortment for a car-rental agency may consist of cars, trucks, vans, and/or camper-trailers. Depth of assortment would be the models within any line (such as cars) and the range of services (such as daily, weekly, and monthly rentals; automatic and manual transmissions; and air-conditioned and non-air-conditioned). In Florida, some car-rental firms stress one product line (cars) and offer smaller economy cars only. This is a narrow-shallow service assortment that is popular with the budget-oriented vacationer.

Sports arenas also make assortment decisions involving the events they will exhibit. Madison Square Garden in New York utilizes a wide-deep strategy. The assortment is wide because all types of sports and nonsports events are exhibited, including basketball and hockey games, tennis tournaments, boxing and wrestling matches, rodeos, circuses, dog shows, the Ice Capades, political conventions, rock concerts, and trade shows. There is depth of assortment because a number of basketball teams, hockey teams, tennis stars, and others play there. In addition, tickets are priced over a wide range and available on a daily, seasonal (one sport), and all-events basis.

Because of the growth of service retailing, many traditional firms are now uniting service and goods retailing. These are among the companies offering retail services in the same stores where they sell merchandise:

■ Some Stop 'N Go convenience stores offer fax services.
■ Various department stores own and operate restaurant facilities.
■ Many supermarkets sell film processing and have ATMs.
■ Costco has a travel agency to serve people who belong to its membership clubs.
■ A number of stationery stores and drugstores sell lottery tickets.

In some cases, traditional goods-oriented retailers lease sections of their stores to service operators, such as banks, opticians, beauty parlors, and jewelry appraisers, and to professionals like dentists and lawyers. Various traditional retailers also have arrangements with finance companies (most auto dealers do this) and repairpeople (a number of appliance stores do this) and receive commissions for performing the sales function for them.

A retailer combining goods and services in one setting must follow a consistent strategy. The goods and services should complement each other, be a logical extension for the retailer, and not adversely affect the firm's image. The coalitions just cited adhere to these guidelines. Combination goods/service retailing will continue expanding in the future. In 1990, 921 U.S. supermarkets had in-store full-service banks; by 1996, there were 4,400 such supermarkets: "Advocates of supermarket banking hail it as a 'win-win-win' proposition. Busy shoppers save time using convenient supermarket bank branches that offer extended hours. Banks get access to a steady stream of shoppers—between 15,000 and 30,000 individuals each week. And supermarkets receive a guaranteed source of income and rent from the bank, regardless of how well groceries sell."[11] See Figure 19-10.

Service-oriented retailers' innovation planning is much different from goods-oriented retailers and sometimes unpredictable. A rented-goods retailer must anticipate which new models or styles will be popular. For example, which movies will be the most desirable videos to be rented during the next 12 months? Which car models will customers prefer to rent?

[11]"Supermarket Banking Booms," *Stores* (February 1997), p. 16; and Lynette Khalfani, "Supermarket Banking Gets More Popular," *Wall Street Journal* (December 16, 1996), p. B10B. See also Tamsin Carlisle, "Gamble by World's Biggest Mall Pays Off," *Wall Street Journal* (March 7, 1997), pp. B1, B6.

Good Times Ahead for In-Store Banking

A recent study by the National Commerce Bankcorporation (NCBC) confirms the importance of banking in a supermarket to consumers. Seventy percent of the respondents to the survey stated that they use the bank branch located in the supermarket and regard it as a key component of the store. The majority of respondents even view in-store banks as more important than the supermarket's bakery, delicatessen, and floral department.

Thousands of supermarkets currently offer full-service bank branches, and retailing analysts expect this number to grow to 6,000 by the year 2000. Some new sites will be 100-square-foot "mini-branches," which can be used to process simple transactions. These mini-branches will appear in smaller supermarket units.

One of the latest supermarket chains to add in-store banking is Pathmark Stores. Pathmark plans to open 70 Summit Bank branches in its New Jersey and Eastern Pennsylvania stores over the next several years. According to Pathmark's treasurer, the firm's primary reason for its partnership with Summit is to forge a relationship with the 1 million or so households already served by the bank: "We've already seen that if offered a choice between a store without a bank and one with a place where they can take care of all banking and grocery chores, most people today will pick the latter because they are so pressed for time."

Source: Julie Ritzer Ross, "Despite Cultural Pitfalls, In-Store Banking Surges," *Stores* (June 1996), pp. 34–36.

Figure 19-10

Supermarket Banking: Cost-Effective and Customer-Oriented

Central Carolina Bank operates full-service branches in various supermarkets, including the Harris Teeter store in Cary, North Carolina, that is shown here. Central Carolina Bank branches in supermarkets are typically open 60 to 65 hours per week (compared to 41 hours at a traditional bank outlet). Each supermarket branch has a manager, assistant manager, and four sales and service specialists. Virtually every service at traditional banks is available at the supermarket branches, except safe deposit boxes.

A service retailer handling repairs and improvements must deal with two types of innovation planning. First, techniques for repairing or improving new merchandise must be learned. There is normally enough time to prepare for new items (such as large-screen rear-projection TVs) since these goods often have factory warranties for 90 days up to 1 year or longer. Second, new techniques must be devised and marketed to service existing items (such as a new way to tune up a car or treat the lawn). Customers must be sold on the techniques, which may mean overcoming some resistance.

A nongoods-service firm has the toughest job in planning new services since it deals with the most intangibles. Accordingly, an accountant must determine which financial planning services to offer clients; and a dance studio must decide the classes and programs to add and which to drop.

Forecasting and budgeting are central to any retailer's plans, but these tasks take on greater significance for a service firm due to the perishability of its services and the need to plan employee schedules carefully. Daily, weekly, monthly, and yearly sales must be forecast as accurately (and realistically) as possible. For established firms, past sales data often yield good estimates for the future when combined with an analysis of competition, the target market, and the economy. With strong customer loyalty, repeat sales can be foreseen. New firms must look at demographics and other factors but will rely essentially on estimates (usually keyed to the hours of work expected by the owner-operator) subject to large errors. The budget must be constructed in terms of projected sales and the level of service quality to be offered, and it must allow for an acceptable profit.

A clear control mechanism is necessary in evaluating and revising the service firm's strategy. Compared to a goods-oriented retailer, a service-oriented firm has one area simplified and another magnified. Inventory control, including pilferage, is simple for non-goods retailers. For repair and rental retailers, inventory complexity is still usually less than for goods retailers, though the rental retailer may face some sloppy or malicious customers. On the other hand, service-oriented firms may be hard pressed to gauge productivity. After all, a fast worker may be haphazard, incomplete, or messy. To overcome this difficulty, performance standards must be set, and, equally critical, service employees must be compared with one another on their overall performances.

Controllable Factors: Pricing ❏ Too often, "Pricing mismanagement plagues service industries because many service firms ignore the special challenge of pricing intangible products. Three distinct but related concepts for service pricing can help firms capture and communicate value through their pricing":

- *Satisfaction-based pricing,* which recognizes and reduces customer perceptions of uncertainty that service intangibility magnifies. It involves service guarantees, benefit-driven pricing, and flat-rate pricing.
- *Relationship pricing,* which encourages long-term relationships with valuable customers. It entails long-term contracts and price bundling.
- *Efficiency pricing,* which shares cost savings with customers that arise from the firm's efficiently executing service tasks. It is related to the concept of cost leadership.[12]

In setting prices, a service firm has several options to consider. These include cost-plus, fixed, competitive, value, negotiated, contingency, price lining, bundling, yield management, and diversionary. Many of these methods may be combined.

In **cost-plus pricing,** a retailer uses its costs of providing services as the basis for prices. The firm adds its costs to desired profit margins to derive selling prices. This is straightforward for such service firms as coin-operated laundromats. Fifty-five percent to 60 percent of revenues could cover the lease; 17 percent to 20 percent the repair, service,

[12]Leonard L. Berry and Manjit S. Yadav, "Capture and Communicate Value in the Pricing of Services," *Sloan Management Review,* Vol. 37 (Summer 1996), pp. 41–51.

and collections expenses; 10 percent the purchase of new washing and drying machines; 8 percent the operating costs; and 5 percent to 10 percent the expected net profit.

Yet, for many service retailers, service costs are not so simple to determine. How, for instance, does a self-employed repairperson determine labor costs? The easiest way is to find out the wages earned by a comparable repairperson working as an employee. But besides labor costs, materials, rent, taxes, and other factors must be included in calculations.

Cost-plus pricing has many disadvantages. It is not market-oriented; the price consumers are willing to pay for a given service is not ascertained. Idle time is seldom included in this technique. Total per-sale costs are tough to compute. Cost cutting is rarely pursued actively.

Fixed pricing exists in situations where a branch of government has some degree of control and retailers must conform to a stated price structure. In some cities, parking lot rates are set by law. Congress sets postage stamp rates. Taxi prices are often government approved.

Fixed pricing produces mixed results. Advantages include the elimination of price wars, the protection of small firms, and consumer safeguards. Disadvantages include the lack of retailer control over a key strategic factor, inflexibility, and possible complacency.

Competitive pricing is a marketing-oriented strategy whereby a service retailer sets its prices on the basis of the prices charged by competitors. If a neighborhood theater charges $4 per ticket for a movie that has been in circulation for three months, a theater showing first-run movies might charge $6.50. Similarly, two hotels with comparable facilities and sites, serving the same target market, would most likely have similar prices. Competitive pricing is the simplest, and probably the most effective, method for pricing services (because costs can usually be adjusted to accommodate prices). As always, pricing must be consistent with the overall strategy.

The use of competitive pricing is easy, responsive to the marketplace, and adaptive to the environment. It is conservative because a retailer goes along with competitors. Yet, a firm might improperly assume its costs, positioning, and service offering are the same as its competitors'.

With **value pricing,** prices are set on the basis of fair value for both the service provider and the consumer. For this approach to be effective, service firms must be in a strong competitive situation and have relative control over prices. Value pricing is common for such service professionals as doctors and lawyers. They set fees based on the value of their time and the services performed.

Negotiated pricing occurs when a retailer works out pricing arrangements with individual customers because a unique or complex service is involved and a one-time price must be agreed upon. Unlike cost-plus, fixed, or competitive pricing (whereby each consumer pays the same price for a standard service), each consumer may pay a different price under negotiated pricing (depending on the nature of the unique service). A moving company charges different fees, depending on the distance of the move, who packs the breakable furniture, the use of stairs versus an elevator, access to highways, and the weight of such furniture as a piano.

Under negotiated pricing, a firm can respond to each consumer with tailor-made proposals. It is crucial that negotiated prices be competitive with those of other service firms and include a detailed cost analysis. This method can be time-consuming and expensive (because an estimate must usually be given to a consumer). Negotiated pricing is inefficient for standard, recurrent services.

Contingency pricing is an arrangement whereby the retailer does not get paid until after the service is performed and payment is contingent on the service's being satisfactory. A real-estate broker earns a fee only when a house purchaser (who is ready, willing, and able to buy) is presented to the house seller. Several brokers may show a house to prospective buyers, but only the broker who actually sells the house earns a commission.

In some cases, such as real estate and lawn care, consumers prefer contingency payments; they want to be assured the service is properly performed. This pricing technique presents some risks to a retailer since considerable time and effort may be spent without payment. A real-estate broker may show a house 25 times, may not sell it, and therefore is not paid.

Price lining is used by service retailers providing a wide selection of services. A range of prices is matched to service levels. A travel agent handling European vacations can use price lining by creating several packages—with trips to Spain, France, and Italy priced from $1,750 to $7,500 per person. At each package price, a different combination of travel features is offered (from no frills to top of the line). A country club can use price lining by creating different types of membership: golf, tennis, and pool; golf and pool; golf only; tennis and pool; tennis only; and pool only. Each membership category is priced differently.

Price lining, as a supplement to one of the other pricing methods already mentioned, lets a retailer expand its target market and create a differentiated service offering. The latter point is important because many consumers relate price to quality. Therefore, price lining helps a retailer foster a diversified service image.

A service firm may offer bundled and/or unbundled prices to customers. With **bundled pricing,** a retailer provides a number of services for one basic price. A $60 air conditioner tune-up could include in-home servicing, vacuuming the unit, replacing the air filter, unclogging tubing, lubricating the unit, and checking air circulation. This approach helps standardize a service offering and makes bookkeeping simpler. However, it is unresponsive to different customer needs.

As an alternative, many service firms use **unbundled pricing,** whereby they charge separate prices for each service provided. A TV-rental retailer could charge separate prices for the television rental, home delivery of the set, and a monthly service contract. This enables the retailer to link prices more closely with actual costs, present consumers with service choices, and perform only the services specifically requested. On the other hand, unbundled pricing may be harder to manage and may result in people buying fewer services than they would purchase under bundled pricing. If a retailer uses both bundled and unbundled pricing, it engages in a form of price lining.

In **yield management pricing,** a service firm determines the combination of prices that yield the highest level of revenues for a given time period. It is widely used in the airline and hotel industries. For instance, a crucial airline decision involves how many first-class, full-coach, intermediate-discount, and deep-discount tickets to sell on each flight. Through yield management pricing, an airline would offer fewer discount tickets for flights during peak periods than for ones in nonpeak times. The airline has two goals: to try to fill as many seats as possible on every flight and to sell as many full-fare tickets as it can ("You don't want to sell a seat for $119 when a person will pay $500"). Yield management pricing is efficient and consumer-oriented, but it may be too complex for small service retailers and it often requires sophisticated computer software.

Diversionary pricing is a practice used by deceptive service firms. In this case, a low price is stated for one or a few services (which are emphasized in promotion) to give the illusion that all prices are low. However, the prices of services that are not advertised are higher than the average. The intent is to attract consumers to the low-priced service and then entice them to purchase the high-priced ones, as well. A service station may promote an inexpensive tune-up to give the impression that all prices are low and then have high prices on repairs.

Because price and image are so closely related for a service retailer, it is imperative that a cohesive pricing strategy be enacted. The methods described in this section provide good insights into the options available. The difficulties lie in assessing demand and measuring service costs.

Controllable Factors: Image and Promotion

❏ Proper positioning is particularly crucial to a service retailer's success. People will patronize a retailer only if a unique and desirable image is created and reinforced. Every restaurant presents an image, whether it be clean and efficient, rustic, romantic, or a gourmet's delight. Each movie theater presents an image by virtue of its prices, selection of movies, cleanliness, parking, and waiting lines. Dry cleaners develop their images through the quality of cleaning, speed, and prices.

The most important element in a service retailer's image is the customer's perception of how well the basic service is performed. A clear image can be easily created by a rental firm because tangible goods are involved; the consumer perceives a well-defined offering, which can be compared with that of other retailers. A repair or nongoods retailer may find it harder to carve out a distinct place in the market due to the intangibility of its offering (making it tougher for people to comparison shop). Thus, a repair or nongoods firm must generate an image based on a stated set of criteria (keyed to the factors cited in Figure 19-9), which are communicated to customers.

In generating an image, an appropriate atmosphere must be established. A clean and efficient restaurant image is aided by waxed floors, regularly washed windows, functional booths and tables, and counter service. A rustic image is fostered by early American furniture, lanterns, wooden fixtures, and pioneer attire for waiters and waitresses. A romantic restaurant has secluded booths, candlelight, and soft music. A gourmet's delight has the local newspaper critic's column in the window, a lavish dessert display near the front door, and freshly cooked meals.

A movie theater's image is affected by its having extra cashiers on busy nights, separating smokers and nonsmokers (or not permitting smoking at all), cleaning popcorn and other debris from floors, and projecting a clear picture and sound. A dry cleaner's image is influenced by using an easy-opening front door, having a clean countertop, displaying prices and cleaning data, and arranging clean clothes neatly on hangers.

A key part of atmosphere is store design. This includes the storefront, interior layout, and displays. The design must be constructed in a manner that is consistent with and adds to the service firm's image and atmosphere. Thus, in a dentist's office, cleanliness, good lighting, roominess, and reading materials in the reception area all contribute to patients' perceptions.

The level of customer service has a strong impact on image. Personal care, delivery, parking, credit, and phone sales are some supplemental customer services for a service firm to consider. A self-service laundromat is perceived differently from a laundry service that picks up, cleans, and returns clothes. A restaurant with metered, on-street parking is viewed as distinct from one with valet parking. A diet center with deferred billing has an image unlike one insisting on full payment before a class begins. A taxi service operating by phone is not the same as one requiring the patron to stand in the middle of the street and wave. At a hotel, "front desk, housekeeping, and parking employee performance have significant effects on perceived quality, whereas front desk and room service employee performance have significant effects on perceived value."[13]

Some service firms rarely use mass promotion. Seldom do barber shops, dry cleaners, repair retailers, housepainters, laundromats, taxis, parking lots, or interior decorators advertise in media other than the Yellow Pages or neighborhood papers. They tend to be small and localized and to rely on loyal customers and/or convenient sites. Other service firms do rely heavily on promotion. These include hotels, motels, health spas, banks, and travel agents. They are usually larger and have a wider geographic market. In addition, multiple outlets are common.

Until the late 1970s, many professional associations did not let members advertise. Since then, the U.S. courts and the Federal Trade Commission have ruled that attorneys, physicians, pharmacists, optometrists, opticians, accountants, and others may advertise. Today, when advertising, professionals are expected to exhibit high standards of ethics, explain when services should be sought, and state what they can realistically provide to clients.

---

[13]Michael D. Hartline and Keith C. Jones, "Employee Performance Cues in a Hotel Service Environment: Influence on Perceived Service Quality, Value, and Word-of-Mouth Intentions," *Journal of Business Research*, Vol. 35 (March 1996), pp. 207–215.

Virtually all types of service retailers stress personal selling in their promotion mixes. For instance, barbers, dry-cleaning attendants, repairpeople, painters, taxi drivers, and parking lot attendants are each involved in a selling function, as well as in providing the primary service. So are hotel and motel personnel, health spa employees, bank tellers, and travel agents. Again, it must be mentioned that it is often personal attention that wins customers for service retailers.

Service retailers sometimes supplement their communication efforts with sales promotions. A health spa may offer a free month's membership for new enrollees. An airline may offer extra discounts for frequent passengers. A cruise ship may run coupon offers. Premiums or prizes may be given by banks, movie theaters, and car-rental firms.

Due to its good performance, a service retailer hopes to gain positive **word-of-mouth communication,** which occurs when one consumer talks to others. If a satisfied customer refers his or her friends to that retailer, this can build into a chain of customers. No service retailer can succeed if it receives extensive negative word-of-mouth communication (for example, "The hotel advertised that everything was included in the price. Yet it cost me $35 to play golf"). Such comments would cause the retailer to lose substantial potential business.

A service-oriented retailer, more than its goods-oriented counterpart, must have positive word-of-mouth to attract new customers and retain existing ones. Most service firms credit word-of-mouth referrals with generating most new customers/clients/patients. As two experts noted:

> The personal, independent source of information—advice of a family member, friend, or associate—is by far the preferred source of information for all service categories. The personal, advocate source—information from the service providers' representatives—is less preferable than the independent source and slightly but significantly preferable to information contained in advertising or promotional messages.[14]

Uncontrollable Factors: Consumers ❏ A service retailer must understand and respond to consumers, who go through some form of decision process in selecting and buying services. The way in which consumers use the process depends on the cost of the service, its newness, the recurrence of the purchase, and other factors. Due to the intangible nature of many services, it is imperative that each element in the decision process be studied by the retailer: stimulus, problem awareness, information search, evaluation of alternatives, purchase, and post-purchase behavior. In addition, the relation of purchase behavior to consumer demographics and life-styles should be studied.

The thriving service retailer relies on the continued patronage and trust of customers, because many customers exhibit high levels of loyalty once they have selected a beautician, a dentist, a plumber, an accountant, a service station, or other service provider. This loyalty is usually much greater than for a goods-oriented firm because customers can easily switch among retailers selling the same merchandise. It is not as easy to switch among repair or nongoods retailers; satisfaction with these firms is due to a total offering that is hard to compare. In addition, loyal customers have a bond with their current service provider that may be impossible for a competitor to break.

Once a service firm becomes established, business should be good as long as a consumer orientation is maintained. In this situation, a new beautician, dentist, plumber, accountant, or service station would find it difficult to break into the market.

One customer type is often beyond the reach of some service retailers: the do-it-yourselfer. And the number of do-it-yourselfers in the United States is growing, as service costs increase. The do-it-yourselfer does a car tune-up, paints the house, mows the

[14]Pamela L. Alreck and Robert B. Settle, "The Importance of Word-of-Mouth Communications to Service Buyers" in David W. Stewart and Naufel J. Vilcassim (Editors), *1995 AMA Winter Educators' Conference* (Chicago: American Marketing Association, 1995), p. 193.

lawn, makes all vacation plans, and/or sets up a darkroom for developing film. Goods-oriented discount retailers do well by selling supplies to these people, but service retailers suffer since the major service (labor) is done by the customer. Market segmentation is thus desirable, and perhaps even necessary, to avoid the do-it-yourself segment or to serve it by offering low prices for basic services.

Uncontrollable Factors: Competition ❏ Ease of entry differs for rental businesses versus repair and nongoods businesses. Because a rental retailer must often invest a large amount in the items rented (such as cars), the investment may limit entry into the market. On the other hand, a repair or nongoods firm usually relies on labor (often his or her own) and tools, which lowers investment costs. This makes entry easier. An exception occurs if extensive education and licensing provisions restrict entry.

Where easy entry exists, the level of competition is high. In particular, small firms arise, and they can be profitable if they appeal to specific target markets. Numerous small travel agencies, restaurants, and film processors flourish. Where entry is difficult, the level of competition is low. There are few bowling alleys, amusement parks, and country clubs in any geographic area.

When a prospective service retailer chooses a site, the existing and potential competition should be measured. The locale selected should have sufficient traffic and growth potential to accommodate the new firm. A location with one profitable car wash may become a site with two unprofitable car washes if a second firm opens and shares business with the first; and a car wash cannot easily be moved once it is built.

Uncontrollable Factors: Technology ❏ A service retailer has various technological options available in operating a business. A hotel can use an expensive computerized reservation system or older, less costly manual reservation procedures. A taxi service can feature old Yellow Cabs or new-model Chevrolets or Fords. A car wash can clean vehicles by hand or by large machines. A gardener can use hand-operated cutting shears or elaborate automatic tools.

A business relying on older technology must provide superior personal service and rely on a loyal customer following. A firm depending on newer methods can eventually lower costs and do a more efficient and consistent job, which, in turn, results in an improved image and lower prices than those of competitors. A modern reservation system eliminates duplication, provides accurate information, and aids in strategy planning. A new, more compact taxi gets good gas mileage and is inexpensive to maintain. An automatic car wash has the capacity to clean and wax up to 100 or more cars per hour and leaves the cars sparkling. A gardener with automatic tools handles twice as many customers and does a more consistent job.

Uncontrollable Factors: The Economy ❏ A service retailer should consider the effect of the economy on business. Because a number of services can be classified as luxuries, they are apt to be affected by economic conditions. If the economy is poor, air travel, overseas vacations, restaurants, lawn-care firms, and others are adversely influenced. Laundromats, beauty salons, dry cleaners, and others are less affected since for many consumers, they are necessities rather than luxuries.

In adapting to uncertain economic conditions, a service retailer can reduce sales fluctuations by offering an assortment of services and de-emphasizing the luxury aspects of them. It is important that business conditions be anticipated and included in strategy planning.

Uncontrollable Factors: Seasonality ❏ Some service retailers face seasonal demand for their services. Country clubs are most popular in the late spring, the summer, and the early fall. Many tourist hotels are busiest on weekends and holidays. Landscapers work most often in the fall and spring. Local buses and trains are most crowded during the morning and evening commuter rush hours.

Green Marketing and Service Retailers

When people talk about reducing the environmental impact of production and/or consumption, they generally confine their discussion to goods. Service organizations, however, such as those that provide transportation and health care, can also have a significant impact on the environment. For example, airlines consume significant quantities of energy, and physicians utilize a variety of components from tongue depressors to high-tech equipment.

By designing and enacting environmentally based programs, a service organization can make a major difference in its environmental impact. For example, McDonald's reduced its waste by 3 million pounds per year just by changing the materials in its beverage straws and by removing corrugated dividers from its shipping cartons for its cold drinking cups.

If they use the "3R's formula" for environmental management (reusing, recycling, and reducing), service organizations can better protect the environment. Thus, a hotel can reuse scarce resources by reclaiming water used for grounds-keeping purposes, increase its recycling efforts by collecting beverage containers from its restaurants, and reduce natural resource usage by closing off a floor to stop energy consumption there during a slow season. The same concept can be applied to a retail bank that has refillable and *not* disposable pens (reusing), collects the paper discarded in its daily operations (recycling), and shortens the size of client statements (reducing).

Source: Stephen J. Grove, Raymond P. Fisk, Gregory M. Pickett, and Norman Kangun, "Going Green in the Service Sector: Social Responsibility Issues, Implications, and Implementation," *European Journal of Marketing*, Vol. 30 (Number 5, 1996), pp. 55–66.

The greatest problem for these service firms is an inability to stockpile resources. If a country club has the capacity to handle 500 people, it cannot admit 750 people on Friday because there were 250 on Thursday. A hotel cannot fill 1,000 rooms with 6,000 holiday visitors, even though half the rooms were empty during midweek. A landscaper cannot serve two customers at the same time in the spring to make up for idle time in the winter. Buses and trains cannot sell 20,000 tickets for 5,000 seats during the rush hour to make up for a lack of passengers at other times.

Service businesses have to be oriented toward satisfying demand during peak periods. Employees must be scheduled accordingly and long-range planning based on realistic forecasting (including peak and nonpeak periods). Special services and offers can attract customers during nonpeak times. Country clubs can introduce indoor activities. Hotels can offer low prices and added services (such as the free use of a golf cart or free drinks at a show) for midweek patrons. Landscapers can offer snow removal and other winter services. Buses and trains can offer fare discounts and tie-ins with restaurants and theaters for off-hour riders.

Uncontrollable Factors: Legal Restrictions ❑ All service retailers should be familiar with the federal, state, and local restrictions under which they must operate. On the federal level, various agencies, such as the Federal Aviation Administration and the Federal Deposit Insurance Corporation, oversee service firms. In addition, many national self-governing bodies set guidelines for their members. These groups include the American Bar Association, the American Medical Association, and the American Institute of Certified Public Accountants.

In recent years, the federal government has pursued a policy of deregulating transportation, banking, communications, and other service industries. This has increased the flexibility of firms in preparing and carrying out their strategies. It has also led to the greater use of such marketing practices as consumer research.

On the state level, these are some of the restrictions facing service retailers: insurance companies and their rates are approved; licensing exams are administered and qualifications set for various professionals; utility rates are approved; trade schools are certified;

and advertising messages may be limited. Most state bar associations do not allow law firms to use movie stars, famous athletes, or former clients as spokespersons.

At the local level, the service retailer must be aware of zoning, operating, and other laws. Each municipality has different limitations (such as whether service professionals are allowed to operate home offices in residential areas), and this should be considered in selecting a location.

Implementing a Service Strategy

After a general strategy is outlined, the service retailer must put it into action. The tactics followed must conform to the overall strategy and an integrated plan enacted. In addition, the strategy should be fine-tuned whenever necessary. Here are a variety of examples involving the implementation of service strategies.

Retail strategies used by service professionals vary greatly. On the one hand, there are many doctors, lawyers, dentists, and others who do not believe in retailing tactics or use them. They do not view themselves as involved with service retailing, think activities such as advertising are demeaning, deplore competitive tactics, and do not understand all the elements in strategic retail planning. These professionals believe their skills market themselves.

On the other hand, there are a growing number of service professionals who are quite involved in retail strategies in response to the competition in their fields. For example, the number of U.S. dentists has grown dramatically since 1970. Yet, over this period, due to better prevention measures (such as fluoride toothpaste and fluoridated water), the number of cavities has dropped significantly. Many dentists have adapted to the situation by using such tactics as advertising in local papers, offering free initial examinations, locating in neighborhood shopping districts or shopping centers, and adding new products for adults (such as "invisible" braces).

Rented-goods retailing has expanded as the costs of buying merchandise have risen sharply. Annually, U.S. consumers spend billions of dollars renting appliances, tools, household goods, computers, TVs, pre-recorded videos, and other items. Car leasing is also popular, with a third of new vehicles being leased. As Ford notes at its financing Web site (http://www.fordcredit.com):

There are many great reasons to choose a Red Carpet Lease:

- *Little or No Down Payment*—A typical lease doesn't require a large down payment. The only up-front money you will need is the first month's lease payment and a refundable security deposit (usually equal to the first month's payment rounded up to the nearest $25).
- *Low Monthly Payment*—You're not paying for the whole value of a vehicle, just the portion of the vehicle's value you will use plus a lease charge to the leasing company. As a result, you will be able to enjoy lower monthly payments than if you had financed the vehicle.
- *A New Car More Often*—To get affordable payments, some people finance their cars for four years or more. For about the same payment, you can lease a new car every two or three years. You get the best years of a car's life before maintenance and repair bills add up.
- *More Car for the Money*—Say you only have a fixed amount of money you can spend on your car every month. If you shop makes and models, you'll find lease dollars will go further than purchase dollars. That's because you only pay for the best portion of your car's life. Leasing gives the opportunity to upgrade from a "no options" car to a more fully loaded model, or from a smaller car to a larger one, or even up to a luxury model.
- *Ford Auto Club Membership*—Every lessee will automatically get a complimentary Ford Auto Club membership, which includes benefits such as emergency roadside service, emergency travel expense reimbursement, custom trip rout-

ing, and 24-hour toll-free access. The Auto Club membership is in effect for the term of your lease.

■ *A Generous Mileage Allowance*—A standard lease allows you to drive 15,000 miles per year at no extra cost. This is based on the needs of the average driver. It does not mean you are limited to 15,000 miles per year. If you anticipate you'll drive more than 15,000 miles per year, additional mileage may be built into your lease.

■ *Unused Extra Mileage Refund*—If you decide to purchase extra mileage at the front end of your lease and do not use it all (or do not exercise the Purchase Option), you will be issued a refund for your unused prepaid mileage if the total is greater than $1.00.

■ *Built-In Gap Protection*—You have the added assurance of "gap" protection. Should your leased vehicle be stolen or destroyed in an accident, Ford Credit will waive the difference, or "gap," between your insurance check and your lease's payoff price. With this waiver, you are only responsible for the insurance deductible and past-due payments.

■ *Warranty Protection*—All Ford and Mercury vehicles have a 36-month/36,000-mile limited warranty. Lincoln vehicles have a similar 48-month/50,000-mile warranty.

The U.S. household goods moving industry has undergone major changes due to deregulation. Before the Household Goods Transportation Act, interstate shippers could only haul used household goods at rates controlled by federal regulators. Today, carriers can ship a wide range of goods, offer various services, and control their prices.

Private storefront postal services rent mail boxes, receive and forward letters and packages, and pack boxes. They offer customers longer hours, quicker service, more flexibility, and greater assistance with mailing problems than the U.S. Postal Service. They all offer packaging materials, multiple modes of shipping, and other standard services. Some have telex and fax machines and provide word processing, phone answering, and copying services. Because of their level of service, these firms have shipping prices far above those charged by the Postal Service and such nongovernmental carriers as United Parcel Service and Federal Express. The largest private postal service is Mail Boxes, Etc., headquartered in San Diego; it has more than 3,100 franchised outlets throughout the United States and a number of other countries.[15]

Re-evaluating the Service Strategy

Once a service strategy is in full operation, it should be monitored. Figure 19-11 shows a simple form for assessing a service firm's strategy. It could be used by virtually any service firm.

Both the overall service strategy and its individual components should be re-evaluated regularly and adjustments made as needed. A service firm can then quickly and accurately adapt to changes in the uncontrollable environment (consumers, competition, technology, economy, seasonality, and legal restrictions). The retail audit, described in Chapter 20, is as useful a tool for a service retailer as for a goods retailer.

During the last several years, there has been more interest in measuring the quality of service retailing.[16] The most well-known measurement tool is **SERVQUAL,** which

---

[15]"18th Annual Franchise 500," *Entrepreneur* (January 1997), pp. 296–297.

[16]See Linda L. Price, Eric J. Arnould, and Patrick Tierney, "Going to Extremes: Managing Service Encounters and Assessing Provider Performance," *Journal of Marketing*, Vol. 59 (April 1995), pp. 83–97; Pratibha A. Dabholkar, Dayle I. Thorpe, and Joseph O. Rentz, "A Measure of Service Quality for Retail Stores: Scale Development and Validation," *Journal of Marketing Science*, Vol. 24 (Winter 1996), pp. 3–16; and Samart Powpaka, "The Role of Outcome Quality as a Determinant of Overall Service Quality in Different Categories of Services Industries: An Empirical Investigation," *Journal of Services Marketing*, Vol. 10 (Number 2, 1996), pp. 5–25.

Figure 19-11

Assessing a Service Retailer's Strategy

Answer YES or NO to each of these statements:	YES	NO
1. There is a clearly defined mission for the firm.	___	___
2. There are stated long-term and short-term goals.	___	___
3. Key environmental trends are studied on a regular basis.	___	___
4. A target market has been identified and its characteristics are known.	___	___
5. The unique dimensions of service retailing are understood, with regard to		
a. Intangibility	___	___
b. Inseparability	___	___
c. Perishability	___	___
d. Variability	___	___
6. The strategic plan takes into account each of the factors noted in item 5.	___	___
7. Employees understand their special relationship with customers.	___	___
8. Customer service is stressed.	___	___
9. There are ongoing efforts to communicate the firm's image.	___	___
10. The pricing approach is keyed to the target market and the services and positioning of the firm.	___	___
11. A service blueprint is used to maximize productivity.	___	___
12. a. High-caliber personnel are hired and trained.	___	___
b. Employee turnover is low.	___	___
13. Service value is properly conveyed to customers.	___	___
14. Customer referrals are encouraged and rewarded.	___	___
15. Complaints are promptly resolved–to the customer's satisfaction.	___	___
16. The actions of competitors are monitored.	___	___
17. New services are added, so the firm's offering does not become stale.	___	___
18. A significant amount of time is spent in planning.	___	___

NOTE: ANSWERING NO TO ANY OF THE STATEMENTS MEANS THE SERVICE RETAILER HAS A DEFICIENCY THAT NEEDS TO BE CORRECTED.

lets retailers assess the quality of their service offerings by asking customers to react to a series of statements in five areas of performance (drawn from Figure 19-9):

■ *Reliability*—(1) Providing services as promised. (2) Dependability in handling service problems. (3) Performing services right the first time. (4) Providing services at the promised time. (5) Maintaining error-free records.
■ *Responsiveness*—(6) Keeping customers informed about when services will be done. (7) Prompt service. (8) Willingness to help customers. (9) Readiness to act on customer requests.
■ *Assurance*—(10) Employees who instill customer confidence. (11) Making customers feel safe in their transactions. (12) Employees who are consistently courteous. (13) Employees who have the knowledge to answer customer questions.
■ *Empathy*—(14) Giving customers individual attention. (15) Employees who deal with customers in a caring way. (16) Having the customer's best interest at heart. (17) Employees who understand the needs of their customers. (18) Convenient business hours.

■ *Tangibles*—(19) Modern equipment. (20) Visually appealing facilities. (21) Employees who have a neat, professional appearance. (22) Visually appealing materials associated with the service.[17]

Regardless of the re-evaluation method, this should be kept in mind by service retailers:

> Although the focus of many service firms is the continual improvement of service delivery, even the most customer-oriented culture and the strongest quality program will not entirely eliminate mistakes during service delivery. Unfortunately, one negative service encounter can undermine an extraordinary record of superior service, lowering evaluations of service quality and causing customers to search for other service providers. Yet, service organizations that are prepared to correct mistakes and handle customer concerns may be able to successfully differentiate themselves from competitors by implementing effective service recoveries. Service recovery refers to the actions a service provider takes in response to service failure.[18]

[17]A. Parasuraman, Valarie A. Zeithaml, and Leonard L. Berry, "Alternative Scales for Measuring Service Quality: A Comparative Assessment Based on Psychometric and Diagnostic Criteria," *Journal of Retailing*, Vol. 70 (Fall 1994), pp. 201–230. See also Valarie A. Zeithaml, A. Parasuraman, and Leonard L. Berry, *Delivering Quality Service* (New York: Free Press, 1990), pp. 23–33; A. Parasuraman, Leonard L. Berry, and Valarie A. Zeithaml, "Refinement and Reassessment of the SERVQUAL Scale," *Journal of Retailing*, Vol. 67 (Winter 1991), pp. 420–450; and Valarie A. Zeithaml, A. Parasuraman, and Leonard L. Berry, "Reassessment of Expectations as a Comparison Standard in Measuring Service Quality: Implications for Further Research," *Journal of Marketing*, Vol. 58 (January 1994), pp. 111–124.

[18]Scott W. Kelley and Mark A. Davis, "Antecedents to Customer Expectations for Service Recovery," *Journal of the Academy of Marketing Science*, Vol. 22 (Winter 1994), p. 52.

Summary

1. *To examine the scope of service retailing* This form of retailing represents a sizable share of overall retail revenues and will continue expanding in the future. It encompasses a wide variety of businesses.

Service retailing can be divided into three broad categories: rented goods, owned goods, and nongoods. With each, the customer receives a service but does not obtain ownership of a physical product.

2. *To show how service retailing differs from goods-oriented retailing* While the basic principles of planning and enacting a strategy are the cornerstones of any successful retail business, there are some major differences between service-oriented and goods-oriented firms. These distinctions exist largely due to the intangibility, inseparability, perishability, and variability associated with many services.

Service retailers can be classified in terms of their tangibility, service provider skill, labor intensiveness, customer contact, goals, and the degree of regulation.

3. *To apply strategy concepts to service retailing* In conducting a situation analysis, the service category must be defined. Personal abilities, financial resources, and time resources should be weighed in the category selection. Next, goals are set to reflect service tangibility, demand and supply, standardization (the use of a service blueprint can be quite helpful here), and the efficiency of services. The target market is then specified and described.

The overall strategy is outlined, consistent with the service category and target market. With the general strategy, the retailer must consider various controllable factors. Store location and operations factors include location, store size, the level of investment, fixtures and maintenance, personnel management, hours, and type of ownership. Service-offering factors include intangibility, quality, uniformity, assortment, combinations of goods and services, innovativeness, forecasting and budgeting, and control. Pricing techniques include cost-plus, fixed, competitive, value, negotiated, contingency, price lining, bundling, yield management, and diversionary. Image and promotion factors include image creation, atmosphere, customer services, promotion, and word-of-mouth.

After a service-retailing strategy is carefully outlined, it must be applied as prescribed. The strategy is then regularly monitored and adjusted as necessary. SERVQUAL is one technique for measuring the quality of service retailing.

4. *To evaluate uncontrollable factors as they pertain to service retailers* While devising a strategy, the service retailer must also analyze relevant uncontrollable factors. Consumers, competition, technology, the economy, seasonality, and legal restrictions should each be investigated. The strategy should plan for and adapt to these variables.

Key Terms

service retailing (p. 625)
service blueprint (p. 634)
cost-plus pricing (p. 643)
fixed pricing (p. 644)
competitive pricing (p. 644)
value pricing (p. 644)

negotiated pricing (p. 644)
contingency pricing (p. 644)
price lining (p. 645)
bundled pricing (p. 645)
unbundled pricing (p. 645)

yield management pricing (p. 645)
diversionary pricing (p. 645)
word-of-mouth communication
 (p. 647)
SERVQUAL (p. 651)

Questions for Discussion

1. What are the unique aspects of service retailing? Give an example of each.
2. It is often stated that many service retailers are not consumer-oriented. Why do you think this comment is made? Is it accurate?
3. Should dental, accounting, and other services be considered a part of retailing? Why or why not?
4. In what kinds of service retailing are personal skills most important? In what kinds are they least important?
5. For each of the following, name several alternative final-consumer market segments to which they can appeal.
   a. Laundromat.   d. Plumber.
   b. Bank.   e. Amusement park.
   c. Fitness club.   f. Appliance repair service.
6. What reasons can you give for the growth of franchised services?
7. Apply the concepts cited in Figure 19-9 to a new sports stadium near your college.

8. Why is personnel management especially difficult in service retailing?
9. Present an example of each type of pricing:
   a. Cost-plus.   e. Negotiated.
   b. Fixed.   f. Contingency.
   c. Competitive.   g. Bundled.
   d. Value.   h. Diversionary.
10. Explain the concept of atmosphere from a service-retailer perspective.
11. Discuss the importance of word-of-mouth to a service retailer.
12. Does the consumer use the decision process differently for services than for goods? Explain your answer.
13. What alternative strategies can service retailers use to deal with the do-it-yourselfer?
14. How could a dentist use SERVQUAL to assess service quality?

Web-Based Exercise:

CLUB MED (http://www.clubmed.com)

Questions

1. Describe Club Med's multiple target markets based on the Web site.
2. Evaluate Club Med's overall service offering.
3. What are the pros and cons of Club Med's pricing strategy from the perspective of a guest? From the perspective of Club Med?

4. What is Club Med's "Good Deals" program? How may it be improved?

The Shoreline Foundation is a group with 1,100 members, in Guilford, Connecticut, that has used borrowed facilities (such as a neighboring school, scout camp, or retirement community pool) for swimming, exercise, day camp, and after-school enrichment programs. Virtually all members live in one of four suburban communities: Branford, North Branford, Guilford, and Madison. Members come from one of two demographic groupings: older adults or families with children.

After raising the necessary funds, Shoreline's directors have decided to build their own facility. Although they have identified a site, they need to decide what type of facility best meets the needs of their members and the residents of the surrounding communities. A professor teaching a marketing research class at a nearby college agreed to do Shoreline's research as a class project. About 1,300 questionnaires were sent to foundation members and other relevant groups in the target area. Responses were coded by town, and 174 usable responses were received within two weeks of the mailing (the deadline for incorporating responses into the data base).

Table 1 summarizes the survey results. The first two questions allowed multiple responses. Question 1 obtained data on selected pool and other activities by household members. Question 2 dealt with the planned frequency of use for the pool and the other facilities. Questions 3–6 asked when facilities would be used, maximum commuting time, maximum yearly membership dues, and likelihood of joining. Questions 7–9 provided data on place of residence, gender of respondent, and the respondent's current membership category.

An analysis of the questionnaires by the class revealed that respondents who would use the facility for multiple seasons were willing to pay more than those who planned to use the facility for a single season. In general, the greatest differences in responses were between individual and family member segments; those willing to pay a higher annual fee were family members who planned to use the facility multiple times per week. Family members also differed from individual members by age (family-member respondents had an average age of 48 years; the average age of individual-member respondents was 68), annual fee they were willing to pay (family members would pay $400 versus $250 for individual members), and maximum commuting time (individuals would commute up to 18 minutes; families would commute a maximum of 16 minutes).

There were several significant differences among respondents by place of residence. Guilford/Madison respondents would pay up to $400; the maximum fee for other respondents was $300. Guilford/Madison residents were also less likely to use the facility in the summer (55 percent versus 63 percent for other residents). Lastly, Guilford/Madison residents were on average "very likely" to join, whereas other respondents were "likely" to join.

CASE 1
Planning a Pool & Wellness Facility*

Questions
1. Evaluate the data in Table 1.
2. Define the target market for the Pool & Wellness facility based on the data in Table 1.
3. Develop a fee schedule for the Pool & Wellness facility. Your schedule should reflect individual and family memberships and summer only memberships.
4. What additional data does Shoreline need to plan its facility better? Where can it be obtained?

*This case was prepared and written by Professor Patricia M. Anderson, Quinnipiac College, based on input from the trustees and staff of the Shoreline Foundation in Guilford, Connecticut, and MBA students Eric Blumenthal, Dyan Grant Enright, Tim Elliott, Cathy Laydon, Dale Norton, and Brenna McVety.

Table 1 RESPONSES TO QUESTIONS ABOUT A SHORELINE POOL & WELLNESS FACILITY

1. What pool activities would you and/or your household members participate in at the planned facility? Please answer for yourself and household. If you will not use pool, skip to question 2.

| | Men | Women | Children/Young Adults | | | | Total |
			Preschool	Elem.	Jr. High	High School	
Swim Lessons	5	19	28	76	12	4	144
Swim Teams	2	4	5	46	16	16	89
Swim Laps	64	66	2	13	8	8	161
Recreational Swim	87	101	19	81	36	23	347
Aquatic Therapy	18	38	0	0	0	0	56
Mild Exercise	20	46	1	2	1	1	71
Vigorous Exercise	87	0	0	1	3	3	94
Water Sports	10	7	2	18	16	10	63

2. How often would you and/or your household members participate in these activities at the planned facility?

| | Monday–Friday | | Sat.–Sun. | 1–2 days | 1–2 days | Total |
	1–2 days	3–5 days	(weekends)	a month	a year	
Pool Activities	103	78	93	22	1	297
Land Aerobics	24	24	16	5	2	71
Open Gym (basketball)	36	21	36	11	1	105
Equipment Room—Nautilus	44	46	42	12	4	148
Wellness Programs	35	13	15	12	2	77
Multipurpose room for:						
Adult Meetings	9	2	4	12	6	33
After School—ages 4–12	44	0	14	8	1	67
Teens—ages 13–18	13	11	23	8	3	58

3. When would you or your household members use the facility you described in questions 1 and 2?
   (97) Summer; (149) Fall; (149) Winter; (142) Spring; Weekdays (M–F): (37) 6–9 A.M.; (60) 9:00 A.M.–Noon; (33) Noon–4 P.M.; (87) 4–7 P.M.; (44) 7–10 P.M.; Weekends (S–S): (31) 6–9 A.M.; (57) 9 A.M.–Noon; (68) Noon–4 P.M.; (48) 4–7 P.M.; (19) 7–10 P.M. *Note:* 48 would go 3 seasons; 87, 4 seasons; 43 chose one time slot; 87 chose two.

4. The most time you would commute to the facility is: (16) 10 minutes; (89) 15 minutes; (51) 20 minutes; (9) > 20 minutes.

5. The most you would pay per year to use this "Pool & Wellness" facility is:
   (16) under $250; (74) $250–$300; (58) $301–$400; (15) $401–$500; (136) family membership; (36) individual membership. (Respondent chose one.)

6. How apt are you and/or your household members to join this facility? (95) Very; (51) Likely; (19) Somewhat; (1) Not very; (2) Not at all.

7. You live in: (25) Branford; (16) North Branford; (79) Guilford; (32) Madison; (20) Other.

8. Gender: (21) Male; (98) Female; (24) Both (Some answered for household).
   Age: 16 to 40: 26%; up to 47: 51%; up to 64: 75%; up to 96: 100%.

9. Membership category? (86) Day Camp; (35) Aquatic Fitness; (4) Swim Lessons; (7) Enrichment Programs; (4) Walking Club; (12) Other.

Throughout *Retail Management,* a number of individual factors pertaining to the devel- **OVERVIEW**
opment of retail strategies have been examined. Chapter 20 focuses on integrating and
controlling the retail strategy. It ties together the material detailed previously, shows why
retailers need to plan and enact coordinated strategies, and describes how to assess success or failure.

By doing this, a firm can take a proper view of the retailing concept, like Syms (a
leading off-price apparel chain) has done. According to founder Sy Syms
(http://www.symsclothing.com):

"An Educated Consumer Is Our Best Customer" started in my first store. It was a
small store in the financial district of Manhattan. We eventually were forced to relocate when they started construction on the World Trade Center. It was only one employee and me. We weren't into suits and more expensive things yet, mostly shirts,
ties, undershorts, and the like. Our 'target market' was the young clerks and beginning sales trainees of the financial houses nearby. They would come out onto the
street for their lunch hour. If the weather was nice, they'd get a sandwich and walk
around in the sunshine. They'd come into my store and browse around; we hoped
they wouldn't drip on our merchandise. Competition was fierce because there were
five or six other stores just like ours all within one or two blocks. The prevailing philosophy of retailing for the previous 30 or 40 years at least was "CAVEAT EMP-
TOR" . . . buyer beware. If you bought a new car and something went wrong, tough
on you. If your suit's colors ran at the dry cleaners, it was your lookout; if you bought
anything and it didn't work, fell apart, or was no good, it was YOUR lookout.
Manufacturers and the retailers who sold the goods had information about the products offered, but they kept it to themselves. You bought what was there, like it or not,
good or bad. Information was never offered, even though it existed. But, along came
the consumer movement, consumer reporting publications, government oversight
and things began to change.

In my store, I'd sensed that I could make ourselves different and better than all of our
competitors if we offered our customers information about the things they wanted to
buy. Just information. We had the information; now we would give it to the people
who could use it, whether they asked for it or not. At first, customers looked at us
strangely, almost as though we came from another planet. No one had ever done that
before—offering information—and even BEFORE a customer bought. But it
worked straight off. Soon, we had a cadre of loyal customers who told their friends
about our store. We did business. We did good business. We did great business. And
we grew from that, keeping the philosophy of imparting information wherever we
went, however and wherever we expanded. When my daughter Marcy formally
joined the firm, she pointed out its importance as philosophical/commercial linkage,
created the phrase you now know, and we promulgated it everywhere. I'm proud to
say that it has become one of the most well-known and well-respected business
phrases. There's a reason it is written in six languages on the facade of our New York
store: The phrase is known in many languages now. But, it's more than a phrase, a
philosophy, a slogan. It has become a force, our force, a synergy. It energizes every
one of our stores, everyone in our stores, our ads, our corporate concept, even this
Web site. It still works, because an educated consumer is STILL our best customer
and we'll gratefully continue to deliver information to educate and enlighten them.

It is vital for a retailer to view strategic planning as an integrated and ongoing process— **INTEGRATING**
not as a fragmented and one-time-only concept. As Figure 20-1 shows, Kay Jewelers **THE RETAIL**
knows that well. **STRATEGY**

At Kay Jewelers, the beauty of fine jewelry is combined with the business of merchandising. The "Kay Exclusive" jewelry design process profiled here shows the special Kay Jewelers approach to every aspect of merchandising, from initial design to final sale.

1. Merchandise Positioning.

Kay Jewelers buyers strive to anticipate consumers' desires. Our buyer notes that diamond and precious gem combinations are increasingly sought after, and suggests a necklace and earring set.

2. Design Proposal.

A designer is given the parameters: a pear-shaped sapphire and round diamond combination in a necklace and earrings. More than a dozen preliminary sketches are assessed by the buyer and top management.

3. Preliminary Casting.

Designs selected for execution are carved in wax, a mold is made, and the jewelry is casted by artisans. With input from management, fine-tuning decisions are made about weight, polishing, angles, etc.

4. Test Marketing.

Kay Jewelers executives agree on a test market. Past experience shows that test marketing as few as 25 pieces over just six weeks can yield very accurate estimates, used to project chainwide distribution and sales figures.

5. Manufacturing.

Kay's purchasing agents buy gems and precious metals strictly for projected need and do not maintain substantial inventories of raw materials vulnerable to wide fluctuations in market value. Kay realizes cost efficiencies by subcontracting jewelry manufacture to outside goldsmiths.

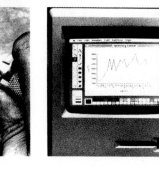

6. Quality Control.

Inspectors examine each item for gold content, quality of finish, gold and diamond weights, and proper setting. The items are scrutinized again in the store before they are put into inventory.

7. Retail Showcasing.

When the new merchandise arrives in the stores, the excitement among store personnel guarantees that it will be featured prominently in displays.

8. Advertising/Promotion

The public hears about the "Kay Exclusive Line" through advertising in print and on the radio. It is emphasized that these pieces are Company designs, meet high standards of quality, and are backed by Kay's warranties.

9. Warranty.

The new design carries our lifetime guarantee, the most extensive in the business, of a trade-in allowance at least 25% greater than the original purchase price after five years. Customers also are protected from the loss of a diamond from its setting.

10. Inventory Control.

Kay Jewelers salespeople tally all purchases on in-store point-of-sale terminals. Within 24 hours, a printout of sales results by specific item allows us to make accurate reordering and forecasting decisions.

This "Kay Exclusive" item, (pictured at left), a diamond and sapphire earring and necklace set, illustrates the step-by-step process through which fashion trends are transformed into new designs and increased sales.

Figure 20-1

Kay Jewelers' "Facets of a Sale"

Figure 20-2

Elements of a Retail Strategy

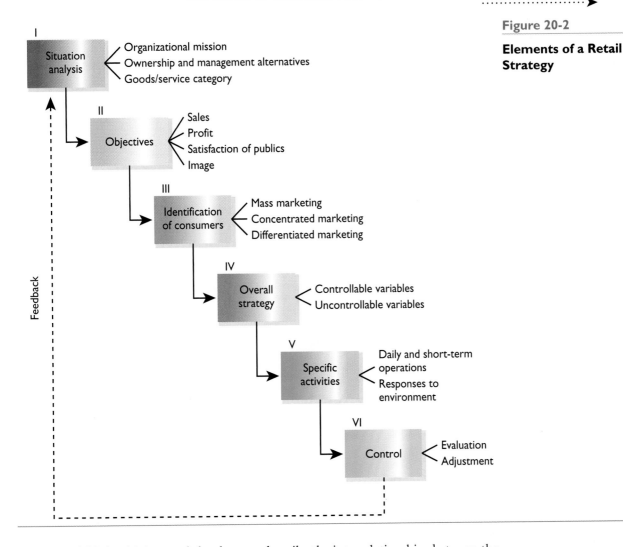

One of this book's key goals has been to describe the interrelationships between the various stages in enacting a retail strategy and demonstrate the need to operate in an integrated format. Figure 20-2, reproduced from Chapter 2, shows the overall development of a retail strategy and how steps are interconnected and integrated. Figure 20-3 highlights the integrated strategy of Gymboree, the California-based children's apparel chain. In 1996, *Chain Store Age* cited Gymboree as the leading "high performance retailer" among all publicly held U.S. firms.[2]

In particular, four fundamental factors need to be considered in devising and enacting any integrated retail strategy: planning procedures and opportunity analysis, defining productivity, performance measures, and scenario analysis. These factors are discussed next.

Planning Procedures and Opportunity Analysis

Planning procedures can be optimized by several coordinated activities. Senior executives should first outline the firm's overall direction and goals. This provides written guidelines for middle- and lower-level managers, who should get input from all types of internal and external sources. These managers are thus encouraged to generate ideas at an early stage. Top-down (by upper managers) and bottom-up or horizontal (by middle- and lower-level managers) plans then can be combined. Last, specific plans should be

[2]Marianne Wilson, "Gymboree Grows Up," *Chain Store Age* (November 1996), pp. 47–52.

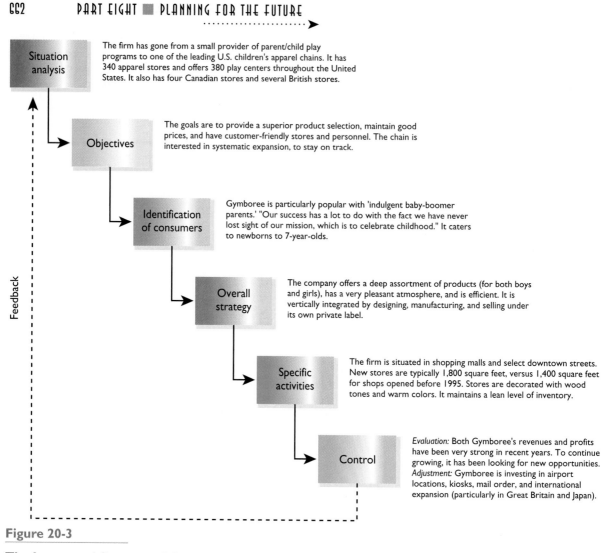

Situation analysis

The firm has gone from a small provider of parent/child play programs to one of the leading U.S. children's apparel chains. It has 340 apparel stores and offers 380 play centers throughout the United States. It also has four Canadian stores and several British stores.

Objectives

The goals are to provide a superior product selection, maintain good prices, and have customer-friendly stores and personnel. The chain is interested in systematic expansion, to stay on track.

Identification of consumers

Gymboree is particularly popular with 'indulgent baby-boomer parents.' "Our success has a lot to do with the fact we have never lost sight of our mission, which is to celebrate childhood." It caters to newborns to 7-year-olds.

Overall strategy

The company offers a deep assortment of products (for both boys and girls), has a very pleasant atmosphere, and is efficient. It is vertically integrated by designing, manufacturing, and selling under its own private label.

Specific activities

The firm is situated in shopping malls and select downtown streets. New stores are typically 1,800 square feet, versus 1,400 square feet for shops opened before 1995. Stores are decorated with wood tones and warm colors. It maintains a lean level of inventory.

Control

Evaluation: Both Gymboree's revenues and profits have been very strong in recent years. To continue growing, it has been looking for new opportunities. *Adjustment:* Gymboree is investing in airport locations, kiosks, mail order, and international expansion (particularly in Great Britain and Japan).

Feedback

Figure 20-3

The Integrated Strategy of Gymboree

Source: Marianne Wilson, "Gymboree Grows Up," *Chain Store Age* (November 1996), pp. 47–52.

enacted, including checkpoints and dates. In doing this, planning is more systematic and reflects input from multiple parties. Figure 20-4 shows the "Organizational Operational Excellence" policy recently introduced at Kmart, after in-depth planning that included input from many parties in the company.

Opportunities need to be carefully examined with regard to their impact on overall strategy, and not in an isolated manner. Thus, the Woolworth Corporation closed the remaining U. S. Woolworth variety stores due to their poor performance. It has high hopes for its various shoe chains, sporting goods stores, and apparel stores. The variety stores no longer fit in Woolworth's mix of retail businesses.

While evaluating opportunities, retailers should utilize some form of **sales opportunity grid,** which rates the promise of new goods, services, procedures, and/or store outlets across a variety of criteria. In this way, opportunities may be evaluated on the basis of the integrated strategies the retailers would follow if the opportunities are pursued.

Table 20-1 shows a sales opportunity grid for a large supermarket that wants to decide which of two brands of salad dressing to carry. The store manager has specified the integrated strategy to be followed for each brand; Brand A is established,

Figure 20-4

**Kmart's New
Employee Pledge**

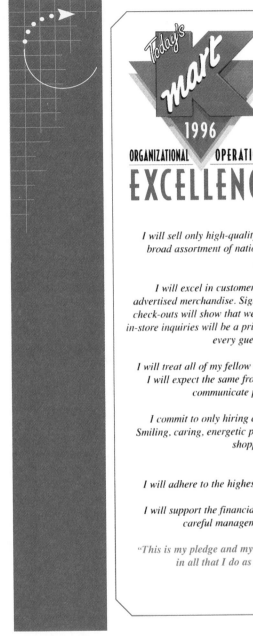

"I believe that Kmart is a great company and will become a leader in the retail arena. In my every word and deed, I will strive for excellence."

I will put our customers first, every day and in every way.

I will do everything in my power to operate the best store in town — a safe, clean, orderly, bright, sparkling store that attracts families with children.

I will sell only high-quality, on-trend merchandise priced at great value, a broad assortment of national brands, complemented with outstanding proprietary goods.

I will excel in customer service. I will be in-stock on all regular and advertised merchandise. Signing and pricing will be accurate. Friendly, fast check-outs will show that we care about our customers' time. Telephone and in-store inquiries will be a priority. And, I pledge "Satisfaction Guaranteed" to every guest who honors us with a visit.

I will treat all of my fellow associates fairly, professionally, with respect, and I will expect the same from them. I will be a team player and honestly communicate praise or criticism for our actions.

I commit to only hiring and retaining people who enjoy our profession. Smiling, caring, energetic people who want to contribute to our customers' shopping experiences and our associates' morale.

I will adhere to the highest principles of integrity in all of my interactions.

I will support the financial health of our business through responsible and careful management of the resources entrusted to me.

"This is my pledge and my commitment, to personally strive for excellence in all that I do as a proud member of the Kmart team."

whereas Brand B is new. Due to its newness, the manager believes initial sales of Brand B would be lower, but total first year sales would be similar. The brands would be priced the same and occupy identical floor space. Brand B would require more display costs but would offer the store a larger markup. Brand B would return a greater total gross profit ($781 to $613) and net profit ($271 to $193) than Brand A by the end of the first year. On the basis of the overall grid in Table 20-1, the store manager would choose Brand B. Yet, if the supermarket is more concerned about immediate profit, Brand A might be chosen because it is expected to take Brand B a while to gain consumer acceptance.

Table 20-1 A SUPERMARKET'S SALES OPPORTUNITY GRID FOR TWO BRANDS OF SALAD DRESSING

	BRAND	
Criteria	**A (established)**	**B (new)**
Retail price	$1.29/8-ounce bottle	$1.29/8-ounce bottle
Floor space needed	8 square feet	8 square feet
Display costs	$10.00/month	$20.00/month for 6 mos.
		$10.00/month thereafter
Operating costs	$0.12/unit	$0.12/unit
Markup	19%	22%
Sales estimate		
During first month		
Units	250	50
Dollars	$323	$65
During first six months		
Units	1,400	500
Dollars	$1,806	$645
During first year		
Units	2,500	2,750
Dollars	$3,225	$3,548
Gross profit estimate		
During first month	$61	$14
During first six months	$343	$142
During first year	$613	$781
Net profit estimate		
During first month	$21	−$12
During first six months	$115	−$38
During first year	$193	$271

Example 1:
Gross profit estimate = Sales estimate − [(1.00 − Markup percentage) × (Sales estimate)]
Brand A gross profit estimate during first six months = $1,806 − [(1.00 − 0.19) × ($1,806)] = $343

Example 2:
Net profit estimate = Gross profit estimate − (Display costs + Operating costs)
Brand A net profit estimate during first six months = $343 − ($60 + $168) = $115

Defining Productivity in a Manner Consistent with the Strategy Chosen

As noted in Chapters 12 and 13, productivity refers to the efficiency with which a retail strategy is carried out; and it is in any retailer's interest to reach sales and profit goals while keeping control over costs. The most productive strategies are those that are well integrated as to target market, location(s), and operations, merchandising, pricing, and communications efforts.

A retailer must be careful in enacting its strategy. On the one hand, it does not want to incur unnecessary expenses. Thus, a firm would not want to have eight salespeople working at one time if four of them could satisfactorily handle all customers. Likewise, it would not want to pay a high rent for a site in a regional shopping center if customers would be willing to travel a few miles farther to a less-costly site. On the other hand, a retailer would not want to lose customers due to insufficient sales personnel to handle the rush of shoppers during peak hours. Also it would not want to be in a low-rent location if this could lead to a significant fall in customer traffic.[3]

[3]See Wagner A. Kamakura, Thomasz Lenartowicz, and Brian T. Ratchford, "Productivity Assessment of Multiple Retail Outlets," *Journal of Retailing*, Vol. 72 (Winter 1996), pp. 333–356.

Figure 20-5

Optimizing Retail Productivity

How can **you** make store automation easy and profitable?

The Easy1™ Multi-Media Point of Sale System from INTELL*i*LINK is a complete "front register to back office" store automation system.

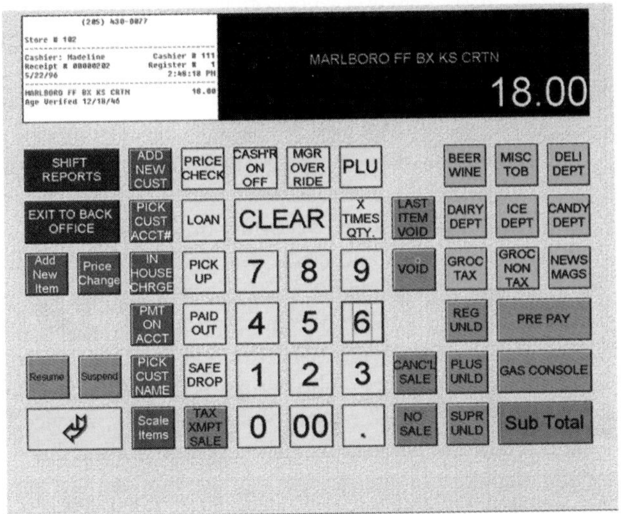

A sample touch screen keyboard for a typical convenience store is shown. Other vertical markets easily addressed by Easy1™ include beverage, grocery, hardware, cash - n - carry and pet stores, pharmacies and discount tobacco shops.

The Easy1™ can **reduce** store cost, **increase** customer satisfaction, and **improve** employee productivity.

If you want to increase store profits, you MUST make some changes!

To create the Easy1™, we did *NOT* use old technology and make limited improvements. Instead, we started with a clean slate and engineered a totally new concept. We believe it is the most advanced and yet easy to use system available today.

Software operating on a *Windows NT™* platform offers unique functionality and eliminates hardware and software "compatibility" problems that frequently occur in other point of sale systems.

The Easy1™ point of sale system features state-of-the-art touch screen technology and performs transactions two to three times faster than traditional cash registers... and is much easier to use.

Making changes means making decisions. The key to making better decisions is to have better information, and the better your information, the higher your profits.

Potential areas of profitability growth using store automation have been targeted by national wholesale and retail associations for years.

This often means neither the least expensive strategy nor the most expensive one may be the most productive strategy, since the former approach might not adequately service customers and the latter might be wasteful. The most productive approach applies a specific integrated retail strategy (such as a full-service jewelry store) as efficiently as possible. See Figure 20-5.

A productive strategy for an upscale firm should be far different from that for a discounter. An upscale retailer would not succeed with self-service operations, and it would be unnecessary (and inefficient) for a discounter to have a large sales staff. This was demonstrated by the demise of Garfinckel's—an 85-year-old, Washington, D.C.-based, upscale department store chain that lost its appeal to affluent shoppers. As a former customer said before Garfinckel's went out of business: "A store like Nordstrom has wonderful service, so I'm willing to pay higher prices. Hecht's and Woodie's have variety at good prices, but you do more self-shopping. I didn't want to go to Garfinckel's, pay high prices, and still have self-shopping."[4]

[4]Edmund L. Andrews, "First Altman's, Now Garfinckel's," *New York Times* (June 28, 1990), pp. D1, D6.

Spiegel (http://www.spiegel.com) is one of the pre-eminent U.S. retailers. It is also an example of a firm with a well-integrated, productive strategy. Here are some reasons why:

The mission is as clear as today's retail environment is complex. Through our catalogs and stores, we seek to provide the best specialty shopping experience around. *Bar none.* In pursuing this mission, Spiegel's management and employees are committed to these imperatives: (1) Know the customer. Our primary customer, the busy, working woman, is our most valued asset. We must understand her needs, desires, and demands; and adapt our offerings and strategies to changes in her purchasing attitudes. (2) Apply state-of-the-art knowledge. We believe in the prudent application of the latest business information, systems, and technology to improve our customer understanding and gain a competitive advantage. (3) Offer real value. We recognize today's working woman is a sophisticated shopper who demands real value. We strive to satisfy this need by offering an optimal combination of style, quality, service, and price in all product lines. (4) Build brand personality. Although the national and proprietary brands featured in our catalogs and stores address different tastes and needs, we work to ensure that collectively these brands make Spiegel synonymous in consumers' minds with the best specialty shopping experience. (5) Be a low-cost operator. We allocate human and financial resources in a disciplined manner across our businesses to control costs and achieve real value for customers. These imperatives guide our management team as it formulates strategies to carry out the company's mission in today's increasingly competitive marketplace. They also provide a framework for employees as they implement these strategies through an ongoing process of research, response, and follow through. Most important, they keep Spiegel focused on the needs of our customers and shareholders as we strive to strengthen our position as a leader in specialty retailing.[5]

Performance Measures

By determining the relevant **performance measures**—the criteria used to assess effectiveness—and setting standards (goals) for each of them, a retailer can better develop and integrate its strategy. Among the performance measures frequently used by retailers are total sales, average sales per store, sales by goods/service category, sales per square foot, gross margins, gross margin return on investment, operating income, inventory turnover, markdown percentages, employee turnover, financial ratios, and profitability.

To properly gauge the effectiveness of a strategy, a firm should use **benchmarking,** whereby the retailer sets its own standards and measures performance based on the achievements of its sector of retailing, specific competitors, high-performance firms, and/or the prior actions of the company itself. Retailers of varying sizes and in different goods or service lines can acquire a lot of data from such sources as the Internal Revenue Service, Small Business Administration, *Progressive Grocer, Stores, Chain Store Age, Discount Store News,* Dun & Bradstreet, the National Retail Federation, Robert Morris Associates, and annual reports. This information enables the retailers to compare their performance with others.[6] Tables 20-2 to 20-8 have a wide range of data that may be used by individual firms to set their own performance standards.

Table 20-2 contains revenue, expense, and income data for small retailers in 20 different business categories. The cost of goods sold as a percentage of revenues is highest for gas stations and grocery stores, gross profit is greatest for barber shops and dentists, operating expenses are the most for coin laundries and motels, and net income is highest for barber shops and dentists.

[5]*Spiegel, Inc. 1992 Annual Report,* p. 1.
[6]See Julie Ritzer Ross, "Benchmarking: Improving Performance Through Standards of Comparison," *Stores* (November 1996), pp. 53–54; Hokey Min and Hyesung Min, "Competitive Benchmarking of Korean Luxury Hotels Using the Analytic Hierarchy Process and Competitive Gap Analysis," *Journal of Services Marketing,* Vol. 10 (Number 3, 1996), pp. 58–72; Gregory B. Murphy, Jeff W. Trailer, and Robert C. Hill, "Measuring Performance in Entrepreneurship Research," *Journal Business Research,* Vol. 36 (May 1996), pp. 15–23; and "Using the Numbers," *Progressive Grocer* (May 1996), pp. 117–123.

Table 20-2 BENCHMARKING BY ANNUAL OPERATING STATEMENTS OF TYPICAL SMALL RETAILERS (EXPRESSED IN TERMS OF REVENUES = 100%)

Type of Retailer	Total Revenues	Cost of Goods Sold	Gross Profit	Total Operating Expenses	Net Income
Apparel stores	100	66.7	33.3	29.2	4.1
Auto parking	100	32.9	67.1	59.1	8.0
Auto repair shops	100	53.9	46.1	33.7	12.4
Barber shops	100	4.1	95.9	41.3	54.6
Bars/drinking places	100	54.3	45.7	41.2	4.5
Beauty salons	100	20.0	80.0	54.0	26.0
Bicycle stores	100	69.8	30.2	24.5	5.7
Coin laundries	100	11.3	88.7	85.1	3.6
Dentists	100	8.5	91.5	49.6	41.9
Drugstores	100	69.0	31.0	22.5	8.5
Eating places	100	53.0	47.0	41.4	5.6
Gas stations	100	84.0	16.0	12.2	3.8
Gift stores	100	63.2	36.8	34.0	2.8
Grocery stores	100	83.1	16.9	14.4	2.5
Hardware stores	100	74.8	25.2	20.9	4.3
Motels	100	12.9	87.2	84.4	2.8
Photography studios	100	29.0	71.0	54.8	16.2
Real-estate brokers	100	9.1	90.9	52.2	38.7
Repair services	100	40.1	59.9	41.5	18.4
Used-car dealers	100	83.5	16.5	14.3	2.2

Source: U.S. Internal Revenue Service.

Table 20-3 reports industry performance data for supermarkets of all sizes, indicating sales for each product category sold. Meat and seafood, produce, and dairy products account for the largest amount of overall store revenues. The highest sales growth is with baby foods, the in-store bakery, and soup. Pharmacy products and video rental are now important enough to be reported as separate categories; a few years ago, they were not.

Table 20-4 reveals the level of customer satisfaction with leading department/discount stores, supermarkets, hotels and motels, and restaurants/fast-food firms. It is based on an ongoing survey, comprising 15 factors, that yields the American Customer Satisfaction Index (ACSI):

- Overall expectation of quality.
- Expectation regarding customization.
- Expectation regarding reliability (how often things go wrong).
- Overall evaluation of experience.
- Evaluation of customization experience.
- Evaluation of reliability experience.
- Rating of quality given the price.
- Rating of price given the quality.
- Overall satisfaction.
- Expectancy disconfirmation (performance falling short or exceeding expectations).
- Performance versus the customer's ideal.
- The customer's level of complaining.
- Repurchase likelihood.
- Price tolerance (increase) given a repurchase.
- Price tolerance (decrease) to induce repurchase.[7]

[7]Claes Fornell, Michael D. Johnson, Eugene W. Anderson, Jaesung Cha, and Barbra Everitt Bryant, "The American Customer Satisfaction Index: Nature, Purpose, and Findings," *Journal of Marketing*, Vol. 60 (October 1996), pp. 7–18. See also "Americans Are More Finicky Than Ever," *Fortune* (February 3, 1997), pp. 108–110.

Table 20-3   BENCHMARKING SUPERMARKET SALES BY PRODUCT CATEGORY (1995 DATA)[a]

	PERFORMANCE MEASURE		
Product Category	**Dollar Sales (Millions)**	**Percent of Overall Sales**	**Annual Sales Growth 5 Years (Percent)[b]**
Baby foods	$ 2,802.47	0.90	6.10
Baking needs	5,501.31	1.76	0.75
Beer & wine	7,412.43	2.38	4.39
Breakfast foods	10,199.02	3.27	4.24
Candy & gum	3,447.78	1.11	3.43
Canned fish	1,653.78	0.53	−2.49
Canned fruit	1,271.56	0.41	−0.48
Canned vegetables	3,061.25	0.98	−0.08
Coffee & tea	5,408.86	1.74	3.77
Cookies & crackers	6,250.92	2.01	1.22
Desserts & toppings	807.04	0.26	2.34
Juice (grocery)	4,182.55	1.34	4.49
Nuts & dried fruit	1,542.22	0.49	−0.68
Pasta	2,464.35	0.79	3.49
Pickles & olives	1,305.68	0.42	1.99
Prepared foods	2,302.94	0.74	2.73
Rice & dried vegetables	1,394.01	0.45	1.91
Sauces & dressings	6,451.65	2.07	4.37
Snacks	6,373.01	2.04	3.15
Soft drinks & mixes	12,866.58	4.13	3.14
Soup	2,940.38	0.94	4.96
Spices & extracts	1,273.24	0.41	2.13
Spreads & syrups	1,996.59	0.64	−0.82
Total grocery edibles	**92,909.62**	**29.81**	**2.88**
Household supplies	8,473.54	2.72	−0.96
Paper, plastic, film, & foil	9,912.39	3.18	0.08
Pet foods	5,087.77	1.63	−0.90
Tobacco products	7,096.08	2.28	−4.59
Total grocery nonfoods	**30,569.78**	**9.81**	**−1.55**
Bakery foods, packaged	9,171.79	2.94	3.12
Dairy products	25,406.32	8.15	1.58
Deli	9,861.13	3.16	4.60
Florals	572.55	0.18	2.34
Frozen foods	16,632.45	5.34	1.69
Ice cream	4,743.65	1.52	2.73
In-store bakery	5,903.45	1.89	5.67
Meat & seafood	49,544.49	15.90	1.62
Produce	31,490.07	10.10	3.28
Total perishables	**153,325.90**	**49.18**	**2.40**
General merchandise	**12,355.40**	**3.96**	**2.39**
Health and beauty aids	**12,672.78**	**4.07**	**2.74**
Pharmacy	**5,308.17**	**1.70**	**NA**
Video rental	**1,296.92**	**0.42**	**NA**
Unclassified[c]	**3,261.43**	**1.05**	**NA**
Total supermarket	**$311,700.00**	**100.00**	**2.78**

NA means not available.

[a] There are small rounding errors in the table.

[b] Five-year compounded average annual growth rate.

[c] Because the items in this category change, the growth rate is not computed.

Source: "1995 Supermarket Sales Manual," *Progressive Grocer* (July 1996), p. 34. Reprinted by permission.

Table 20-4 BENCHMARKING BY THE AMERICAN CUSTOMER SATISFACTION INDEX (RANKED BY 1996 SCORES)

Retailer	1994 Index Score	1996 Index Score
Department/Discount Stores	**77**	**75**
Nordstrom	84	83
Wal-Mart	80	81
J.C. Penney	79	77
Dayton Hudson (discount stores)	77	76
Dayton Hudson (department stores)	—	76
Meijer (discount stores)	—	76
May	74	75
Sears	73	75
Dillard's	75	74
Montgomery Ward	72	72
Kmart	74	72
Federated	71	71
Supermarkets	**76**	**75**
Publix	82	82
Meijer's (supermarkets)	77	79
Supervalu	77	77
Albertson's	75	77
Food Lion	78	76
Kroger	78	76
Winn-Dixie	76	75
American Stores	71	73
Safeway	72	73
A&P	68	67
Hotels and Motels	**75**	**72**
Promus (Embassy Suites, etc.)	82	83
Hyatt	76	77
Marriott	80	77
Hilton	75	75
Ramada	70	70
Restaurants/Fast-Food Firms	**69**	**70**
Wendy's	72	73
Domino's Pizza	67	70
Little Caesars	72	69
KFC	67	68
Pizza Hut	69	66
Taco Bell	66	66
Burger King	66	65
McDonald's	63	63

Sources: University of Michigan Business School and American Society for Quality Control. Reprinted by permission.

ACSI addresses these two questions: "Are customer satisfaction and evaluations of quality improving or declining in the United States? Are they improving or declining for particular sectors of industry, for specific industries, and for specific companies?" ACSI is based on a scale of 0 to 100, with 100 being the highest possible score. A national sample of nearly 50,000 respondents participates in phone interviews, with at least 100 interviews of current customers for each of the 200 firms studied (http://www.acsi.asqc.org). According to Table 20-4, the highest 1996 scores achieved by any of the retailers listed were the 83 for Nordstrom and Promus (the hotel chain); the lowest were the 63 to 66 for McDonald's, Burger King, Taco Bell, and Pizza Hut.

ETHICS IN RETAILING: Boosting Profits by Addressing Customer Complaints

Research conducted by Burke Customer Satisfaction Associates found that the more shoppers are "connected" with a retailer, the more apt they are to complain to that firm if things go wrong. According to the director of research and development at Burke, in general, other consumers do not complain because they do not want to spend the time or feel the retailer will not act on their complaints.

The study, based on interviews with 1,179 department store shoppers, found that when people feel committed to a store, they would rather complain than just patronize a new retailer. Those most likely to complain are also older. For example, 61 percent of those age 55 and older would definitely voice a com-

plaint, versus 50 percent of all adult shoppers and only 39 percent of those under age 35. Older people more often expect retailers to take a corrective action as a result of their complaints. When retailers do, they boost their profits further since the once-again happy customers become even more loyal.

J.C. Penney is one of the numerous retailers that takes complaints very seriously. According to a corporate spokesperson, in any of its 1,250 stores, "only the store manager has the final authority to say 'no' to a customer complaint." Penney recognizes that resolving problems goes a long way toward strengthening customer loyalty.

Source: Tibbett L. Speer, "They Complain Because They Care," *American Demographics* (May 1996), pp. 13–14.

Table 20-5 shows performance data for ten leading department store chains. Here are just a few of the conclusions reached by studying this table: Neiman Marcus and Nordstrom have by far the highest annual sales per store, with the annual per-store sales for the ten chains ranging from $9 million to $64 million. As a percentage of sales, department store operating results are mixed, ranging from deficits at Bon Ton Stores and Proffitt's to very strong results at May Department Stores. May Department Stores, Neiman Marcus, and Carson Pirie Scott have the strongest operating income return on assets. Yet, May has had middle-of-the-road comparable store sales increases. Overall, no firm is the leader in all the categories depicted, which means different strategies can succeed.

Table 20-6 displays the performance for several leading consumer electronics chains. An analysis of the table reveals that the approaches in this industry segment also vary widely: Best Buy and Circuit City are by far the leading firms in annual sales. Yet, Circuit City has been much more profitable than Best Buy. The number of stores in the chains listed range from 1 to 419. Sales per store and store size differ dramatically. Although J&R Music World generates $233 million in sales through its one outlet, Rex/AV Affiliates has annual per-store sales of only $2.2 million and its stores average 7,000 square feet. Yearly sales per square foot range from $2,750 for BrandsMart USA to $235 for Luskin's. For those publicly reporting profits, pre-tax earnings as a percentage of sales tend to be low—reflecting the discount orientation of consumer electronics firms and intense price cutting.

In reviewing the performance of other retailers, a firm should be sure to look at the *best practices* in retailing—whether they involve companies in its own sector of business or in other sectors: "It's really a simple proposition, best practices. Find someone who does a great job, observe and monitor them, benchmark their results, and apply the most appropriate techniques they use. From the enterprise that scrutinizes a best practice in one territory or store and tries to clone it to the rest of its organization, to the merchant that scrupulously studies the best of its competitors, the value of analyzing, adopting, or adapting best practices is a management technique that cannot be overestimated."[8]

[8]"Best Practices in Retailing," *Chain Store Age* (November 1995), pp. 49–108.

Table 20-5 BENCHMARKING DEPARTMENT STORES (1995 DATA)[a]

Company	Average Sales Per Store ($)	Operating Income as a Percentage of Sales[b]	Operating Income as a Percentage of Assets	Percentage Change in Annual Comparable Store Sales
Bon Ton	8,866,526	−1.0	−1.9	0.2
Carson Pirie Scott	18,848,904	8.1	12.7	2.7
Dayton Hudson	21,776,836	5.7	5.6	−1.0
Dillard's	25,344,916	6.6	8.2	2.0
Federated	28,500,972	4.4	4.6	2.7
May	31,839,394	13.4	13.9	2.5
Mercantile	28,865,922	6.7	9.5	1.2
Neiman Marcus	64,008,441	7.9	13.5	6.4
Nordstrom	53,422,299	4.5	6.8	−0.7
Proffitt's	12,760,746	−0.9	−1.5	3.0

[a] In a few instances, companywide data (rather than just department store data) are used in the table.

[b] Operating income = Sales − Cost of goods sold − Selling, general, and administrative expenses (including depreciation and amortization).

Source: "State of the Department Store Industry," *Chain Store Age* (August 1996), p. 25A. Reprinted by permission. Copyright Lebhar-Friedman, Inc., 425 Park Avenue, New York, NY, 10022.

Since 1989, *Chain Store Age* has annually published a best practices listing of "high-performance retailers." These are publicly owned U.S. firms that perform well above average on a **retail performance index,** which encompasses five-year trends in revenue growth and profit growth, and a six-year average return on assets. Due to its importance for publicly held firms, return on assets is weighted twice as much as either revenue growth or profit growth in the retail performance index. An overall performance index of 100 is considered average. Table 20-7 shows the leading high-performance retailers for 1995. A review of the table reveals there are various ways to be a high-performance retailer. For example, Gymboree (the overall leader) is not first in any of the categories shown. However, it ranks among the top six firms in each category. On the other hand, Dollar Tree (the second-best high-performance retailer) leads in return on assets, but is seventh in revenue growth and twelfth in profit growth. By learning which are the high-performance retailers in different industry categories, a prospective or existing company can study the strategies of those retailers and try to emulate their best practices.

Finally, by benchmarking its own internal performance and conducting gap analysis, a retailer can measure its results and plan for the future. Through **gap analysis,** a company can compare its actual performance against its potential performance, and then determine the areas in which it must improve. Table 20-8 indicates Home Depot's financial performance for the period from 1993 through 1995. The data in the table may be used to benchmark Home Depot in terms of its own performance. For instance, in comparison with 1993, Home Depot reduced its general and administrative expenses as a percentage of sales and increased the size of the average customer transaction in 1995. It maintained the same level of gross margin and pre-opening expenses as a percentage of sales. However, net earnings as a percentage of sales fell, as did the current ratio and inventory turnover. These results were due to "gaps" that Home Depot must correct to regain its financial momentum.

Scenario Analysis

With **scenario analysis,** a retailer projects the future by examining the key factors that will affect its long-run performance and then prepares contingency ("what if") plans

Table 20-6 BENCHMARKING CONSUMER ELECTRONICS CHAINS (1995 DATA)

Chain	1995 Sales (millions)	Number of Stores (as of 1/96)	Estimated 1995 Sales/Store	Average Store Size (sq. ft.)	Estimated 1995 Sales/ Square Foot	1995 Pre-tax Earnings (millions)[a]	Pre-tax Earnings as Percentage of 1995 Company Sales
Best Buy	$7,200	251	$ 28,685,000	45,000	$ 637	$ 48.0	0.7
Circuit City	7,030	419	16,778,000	30,000	559	179.4	2.6
The Wiz	1,100	53	20,755,000	30,000	692	NA	NA
The Good Guys	889	73	12,178,000	20,000	609	24.1	2.7
Yes	859	90	9,544,000	12,000	795	NA	NA
Sun Television & Appliance	806	47	17,149,000	24,000	715	14.3	1.8
Rex/AV Affiliates	442	199	2,221,000	7,000	317	24.1	5.5
Tops Appliances	421	9	46,777,000	42,000	1,114	NA	NA
BrandsMart USA	330	3	110,000,000	40,000	2,750	NA	NA
Campo Electronics	295	31	9,516,000	15,000	634	NA	NA
J&R Music World	233	1	233,000,000	150,000	1,553	NA	NA
Luskin's	120	30	4,000,000	17,000	235	NA	NA

NA means data not available.
[a] Includes interest expenses, corporate expenses, and other unusual items.

Source: Computed by the authors from "Discount Industry Annual Report," *Discount Store News* (July 1, 1996), pp. 41, 81. Reprinted by permission. Copyright Lebhar-Friedman, Inc., 425 Park Avenue, New York, NY, 10022.

Table 20-7 BENCHMARKING HIGH-PERFORMANCE RETAILERS

Company	Compound Annual Revenue Growth, 1990–1995	5-Year Revenue Growth Index	Compound Annual Profit Growth, 1990–1995	5-Year Profit Growth Index	Average Annual Return on Assets, 1990–1995	6-Year Return on Assets Index	Retail Performance Index[a]
Gymboree	57.84	604	109.10	1,225	13.77	401	658
Dollar Tree	41.88	437	61.79	694	20.52	597	581
Micro Warehouse	60.28	629	100.37	1,127	8.65	252	565
Leslie's Poolmart	17.13	179	149.84	1,682	4.28	125	528
Circuit City	24.32	254	124.42	1,397	6.82	198	512
Bed Bath & Beyond	34.97	365	30.66	344	20.45	595	475
Urban Outfitters	28.87	302	47.63	535	17.46	508	463
Catherine's	19.08	199	118.13	1,326	4.16	121	442
Baby Superstore	50.42	526	70.58	792	6.27	182	421
Staples	59.34	620	69.94	785	3.77	110	406
Kohl's	20.64	216	86.66	973	6.99	203	399
Office Depot	53.39	558	68.81	773	4.31	126	395
Whole Foods Market	46.04	481	62.83	705	5.19	151	372
West Marine	27.71	289	45.19	507	11.34	330	364
Consolidated Stores	17.36	181	69.93	785	7.74	225	354
The Buckle	20.11	210	9.87	111	18.22	530	345
Auto Zone	21.90	229	42.90	482	11.48	334	345
The Gap	17.85	186	19.63	220	16.61	483	343
Ultimate Electronics	45.23	472	45.84	515	6.54	190	342
Dollar General	21.98	230	43.14	484	11.02	321	339
Total Retailing Median	**9.58**	**100**	**8.91**	**100**	**3.44**	**100**	**100**

[a] Retail performance index = [Revenue growth index + Profit growth index + 2 (Return on assets index)]/4

Source: Management Horizons, "High Performance Retailers 1990–1995," *Chain Store Age* (November 1996), p. 48. Reprinted by permission. Copyright Lebhar-Friedman, Inc., 425 Park Avenue, New York, NY, 10022.

Table 20-8 HOME DEPOT: INTERNAL BENCHMARKING AND GAP ANALYSIS

	1993	1994	1995
Statement of Earnings Data			
Net sales (in 000s)	$9,238,763	$12,476,697	$15,470,358
Earnings before taxes (in 000s)	$736,871	$979,751	$1,195,303
Net earnings (in 000s)	$457,401	$604,501	$731,523
Gross margin (% of sales)	27.7	27.9	27.7
General and administrative expenses (% of sales)	2.0	1.8	1.7
Pre-opening expenses (% of sales)	0.4	0.4	0.4
Net earnings (% of sales)	5.0	4.8	4.7
Balance Sheet Data and Financial Ratios			
Total assets (in 000s)	$4,700,889	$5,778,041	$7,354,033
Working capital (in 000s)	$993,963	$918,724	$1,255,487
Merchandise inventories (in 000s)	$1,293,477	$1,749,312	$2,180,318
Current ratio (times)	2.02	1.76	1.89
Inventory turnover (times)	5.9	5.7	5.5
Return on average equity (%)	17.9	19.3	17.4
Customer and Store Data			
Number of states	23	28	31
Number of stores	264	340	423
Square footage at year end (in 000s)	26,383	35,133	44,356
Number of customer transactions (in 000s)	236,101	302,181	370,317
Average sale per transaction	$39.13	$41.29	$41.78
Comparable-store sales increase (%)	7	8	3
Weighted-average sales per square foot	$398	$404	$390

Source: Home Depot 1995 Annual Report.

based on alternative scenarios (such as low, moderate, and high levels of competition in the firm's trading area). Scenario analysis is not an easy task. Consider these points:

Home sales are booming—and so are bankruptcies. Dealers are besieged with demand for 36-inch TVs decked out with stereo VCRs and satellite dishes, but used-car lenders are running out of gas. The mail brings 401(k) statements brimming with paper profits to high-income zip codes and dunning notices from credit card issuers to poor ones. Welcome to the schizoid credit market, where your forecast for consumer spending—indeed, for the entire economy—depends on the end of the income scale you study. Alarmists note that record-high consumer debt-to-income ratios and credit card write-offs are sending out recession signals and tremble over just how long household spending can continue to power the economy.[9]

Will cyberspace win out over retail space? Will consumers of the future prefer shopping the Internet over shopping the store? As Microsoft CEO Bill Gates notes, "No one knows, for any age group of consumers or any type of product, how quickly consumers will find the Internet to be a major way to gather information and make choices about what they buy. I think you will see quite a divide, where young people

[9]Mike McNamee and Richard A. Melcher, "Message from the Mall," *Business Week* (March 24, 1997), p. 30.

Are Canadian Pharmacies the Wave of the Future?

Increasingly, U.S.-based chain retailers are studying successful Canadian pharmacy chains to better plan their own futures. In Canada, the 2,000 pharmacy chain stores have had strong competition from the country's 4,600 independent stores. The chains have also had to deal with such restrictive government policies as a ban on the sale of tobacco (in Ontario pharmacies) and the low prescription reimbursement fees set by managed care providers.

One closely watched retailer is Shoppers Drug Mart (Shoppers), Canada's largest pharmacy chain. Let's look at several key facets of Shoppers' overall retail strategy:

■ Cosmetics constitutes 9 percent of Shoppers' total sales, as compared with 4 percent to 5 percent of sales at a typical U.S. pharmacy. The firm relies on its use of cosmeticians and a full assortment of private-brand beauty items.

■ Although it has centralized purchasing, distribution, and accounting systems, store managers have the authority to use micro-marketing.

■ The pharmacists are an essential aspect of the firm's strategy. Instead of just being seen as drug dispensers, they are viewed by the company as medication counselors. This increases loyalty among consumers, as well as by the health-care providers.

■ It extensively stocks private brands for its vitamins and over-the-counter medications.

Source: Faye Brookman, "Canadian Chains Stress Innovation in Tough Competitive Environment," *Stores* (June 1996), pp. 42–44.

accustomed to being out on the Internet won't think of doing a lot of shopping without first checking information on it. Even if they go to the store later, they'll inform themselves before they go. On the other hand, older shoppers may never dive into this thing." By the year 2005, however, "people in their 30s and 40s will have grown up in an era where the computer is just how you do things."[10] (See Figure 20-6.)

The Limited, Inc.'s chairman Leslie Wexner likes to talk about building bridges to the 21st century. His bridge is more than just a political figure of speech; it is taking tangible form as a massive shopping, business, entertainment, and residential complex being built not far from The Limited's headquarters in Columbus, Ohio. Construction is progressing on the project, called Easton, which Wexner believes will serve as a model for retail development in the future. The mixed use mega-development consists of nearly 4 million square feet of retail space, 4 million to 5 million square feet of office facilities, and more than 1 million square feet of lodging and conference facilities, restaurant, entertainment venues, and residential living units. According to Wexner, "Far more than just another mall, Easton will serve as a bridge to the 21st century; as a place where people can live, work, shop, and be entertained within a carefully planned community that will function as if it had existed and grown as a town over many years."[11]

J.C. Penney will be celebrating its one-hundredth anniversary in April 2002. In preparation, it has spent several years doing scenario analysis. The result is a well-conceived plan:

■ *Top Ten Markets:* Penney is committed to being a major player in the biggest U.S. markets: Chicago, Dallas/Fort Worth, Detroit, Los Angeles, Miami, New York/New Jersey, Philadelphia, San Francisco, Seattle, and Washington, D.C. "These are complex markets, and we're filling them out."

[10]Bruce Fox, "Gates and Panel Debate the Future of Retailing," *Chain Store Age* (June 1996), pp. 57–58.
[11]Susan Reda, "Limited's Wexner Plans 'Bridge' to 21st Century with Massive Ohio Project," *Stores* (March 1997), p. 63.

Figure 20-6

Are You Ready for Cyberspace Retailing?

As reported in *Futurist* magazine, through NTT's Web-based InterSpace, "Tower Records offers a virtual music store where customers can 'meet' each other in front of the store, go in and preview CDs and videos in the store, and purchase their choices interactively from a real sales associate."

- *Speed to Market:* "This is the all-encompassing one, getting things to market quicker, and the development of our private label." To do this, one of the company's most critical goals is to decrease product development and distribution times.
- *Diversifying Growth:* "When you're a $21 billion company, just 5 percent sales growth is a $1 billion increase." Thus, Penney will place more emphasis on drugstores. It now operates Thrift Drug, Eckerd Drug, and other chains—a total of 2,800 stores. To leverage the Eckerd name, all the drugstores will be changed to that name. Penney is also going to open more freestanding home stores and fine jewelry stores, and increase its Web activity.
- *Customer Service:* Motivating salespeople to be more customer-service oriented is another goal. "It's a perennial one. We've put a full-court press on it in terms of attitude."
- *SG&A (Selling, General, & Administrative Costs):* "In a business always challenged on its bottom line, we are always looking at our cost structure. Now that technology is almost a given, the competitive edge is what you do with it. A lot of our efforts entail using technology better to be better merchants, serve our customers better and improve SG&A."
- *Economic Value Added:* Penney's goal is that each dollar of capital it spends should yield a gain to stockholders. "It's a philosophy used at many firms to increase shareholder value. We're putting a full-court press on this, too. This management has the responsibility to current and future associates to make this company stronger in 2002 than today."[12]

[12]Debra Hazel, "Pitching Penney into the 21st Century," *Chain Store Age* (January 1997), pp. 51–59.

After a retail strategy is devised and put into action, it must be continuously assessed and necessary adjustments made. A vital evaluation tool is the **retail audit,** which is the systematic examination and evaluation of a firm's total retailing effort or some specific aspect of it. The purpose of a retail audit is to study what a retailer is presently doing, appraise how well the firm is performing, and make recommendations for future actions.

CONTROL: USING THE RETAIL AUDIT

An overall company audit should investigate a retailer's objectives, strategy, implementation, and organization. First, goals would be reviewed and evaluated for their clarity, consistency, and appropriateness. Second, the firm's strategy and its methods for deriving it would be analyzed. Third, how well the strategy has been implemented and actually received by customers would be reviewed. Fourth, the organizational structure would be analyzed; lines of command, types of organization charts, and other factors are the kinds of data studied in this phase.

Good auditing includes several elements: Audits are conducted regularly. In-depth analysis is involved. Data are amassed and analyzed systematically. An open-minded, unbiased perspective is maintained during the audit process. There must be a company willingness to uncover weaknesses that must be corrected, as well as strengths that must be exploited. After an audit is done, the appropriate decision makers must be responsive to the recommendations made in the audit report.

Undertaking an Audit

There are six steps in retail auditing. See Figure 20-7 for an overview of the process:

1. Determining who does the audit.
2. Determining when and how often the audit is conducted.
3. Determining areas to be audited.
4. Developing audit form(s).
5. Conducting the audit.
6. Reporting to management.

Determining Who Does the Audit ❏ In conducting a retail audit, one or a combination of three parties can be utilized: a company audit specialist, a company department manager, and an outside auditor. The advantages and disadvantages of each are noted here.

A company audit specialist is an internal employee whose prime responsibility is the retail audit. The advantages of this person include the auditing expertise, the thoroughness, the level of knowledge about the firm, and the ongoing nature (no time lags). Disadvantages include the costs (very costly for small retailers that do not need full-time auditors) and the limited independence of these auditors.

A company department manager is an internal employee whose prime responsibility is operations management, but he or she may also be asked to participate in the retail audit. The advantages of this source are that added personnel expenses are not needed and that such a manager is knowledgeable about the firm and has a full understanding of day-to-day operations. Disadvantages include the manager's time away from the primary job, the potential lack of objectivity, time pressure, and the complexity of conducting companywide audits.

An outside auditor is a person who is not a permanent employee of the retailer but who works as a consultant (usually for a fee). Advantages include the auditor's broad experience, objectivity, and thoroughness. Disadvantages include the high costs per day or hour (however, for small retailers, it may be cheaper to hire expensive, per diem consultants than to employ full-time auditors; the opposite is usually true for larger firms), the time lags while a consultant gains familiarity with the company, the failure of some retailers to use outside specialists on a continuous basis, and the reluctance of some employees to cooperate with outsiders.

Figure 20-7

The Retail Audit Process

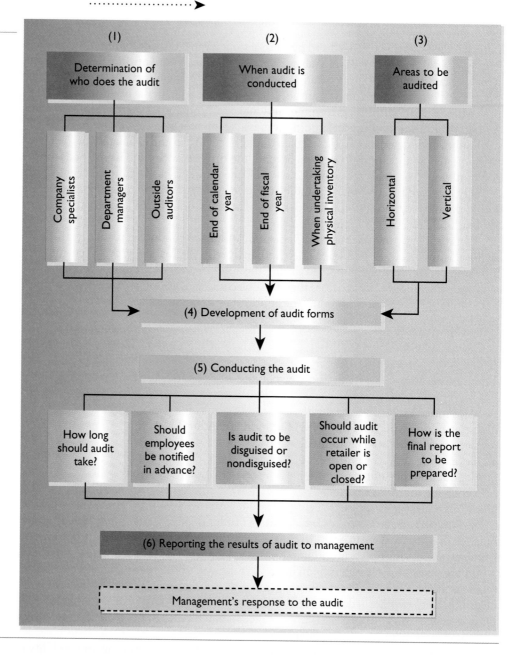

Determining When and How Often the Audit Is Conducted ❑ Logical times for conducting an audit are at the end of the calendar year, at the end of the company's annual reporting year (fiscal year), or at the point of a complete physical inventory. Each of these is appropriate for evaluating a retailer's operations during the previous period.

An audit must be enacted at least annually, although some retailers desire more frequent analysis. It is important that the same period(s), such as January–December, be studied each year if meaningful comparisons, projections, and adjustments are to be made.

Determining Areas to Be Audited ❑ A retail audit typically includes more than financial analysis; it reviews various aspects of a firm's strategy and operations. It can also be used during successful and unsuccessful periods to identify strengths and weaknesses. There are two basic types of audits—horizontal and vertical.

Are Kinko's Plans for the Future a Net(work) Plus?

Kinko's is a growing chain that provides both photocopying and printing services, as well as in-store PC rental facilities and other services. Although its early stores were targeted almost totally at college students (that is why most outlets were located near college campuses), Kinko's now also appeals to small-business owners and those who work from home. Unlike most traditional copying and printing shops, the vast majority of Kinko's stores are open 24 hours a day.

Kinko's has decided to add Internet-access capabilities to its existing services. This new service is aimed at traveling executives, small-business and home business owners, and college students. Thus, at Kinko's units in Seattle, Houston, Philadelphia, and elsewhere, customers can send and receive E-mail, conduct research on the World Wide Web, and even download software. These services do not require that the user have an Internet account. Some of Kinko's stores also have personnel to help customers set up a home page.

Because Kinko's has expanded beyond its traditional college student market, it faces added competition from such large firms as Office Max and Staples. These firms offer copying facilities and printing services, as well as sell a wide variety of business equipment and supplies. However, they are not open 24 hours a day, do not have in-store PC rental facilities, and do not provide Internet access.

Source: Laurie Flynn, "Kinko's Adds Internet Services to Its Copying Business," *New York Times* (March 18, 1996), p. D5.

A **horizontal retail audit** involves analyzing a retail firm's overall performance, from its organizational mission to goals to customer satisfaction to basic retail strategy mix and its implementation in an integrated, consistent way. Since this audit studies the interrelation of many strategic elements and their relative importance, it may also be considered a "retail strategy audit."

A **vertical retail audit** involves analyzing—in depth—a retail firm's performance in one area of its strategy mix or operations, such as the credit function, customer service, merchandise assortment, or interior displays. A vertical audit is focused and specialized in nature.

The two audits should be used in conjunction with one another because a horizontal audit often reveals areas that merit further investigation by a vertical audit.

Developing Audit Forms ❑ To be orderly and thorough, a retailer should use detailed audit forms. An **audit form** lists the area(s) to be examined and the exact information required in evaluating each area. Audit forms usually resemble questionnaires, and they are completed by the auditor.

Without audit forms, the analysis becomes more haphazard and subjective, and it is not standardized. Important questions may be omitted or poorly worded. The biases of the auditor may show through. Most significantly, questions may differ from one audit period to another, which could limit comparisons over time.

Examples of retail audit forms are presented shortly.

Conducting the Audit ❑ After the auditor is selected, the timing of the audit is determined, the areas of analysis chosen, and audit forms constructed, the audit itself is undertaken.

Management should specify in advance how long the audit will take and conform to this timetable. Prior notification of employees depends on management's perception of two factors: the need to compile some data in advance to increase efficiency and save time versus the desire to get a true picture and not a distorted one (which may occur if there is too much prior notice).

A disguised audit is one in which a firm's employees are not aware an audit is taking place. It is useful if the auditor investigates an area like personal selling and wishes to act out the role of a customer to elicit employee responses. A nondisguised audit is one in which a firm's employees know an audit is being conducted. This is desirable if employees are asked specific operational questions and help in gathering data for the auditor.

The decision as to whether to perform an audit when the firm is open or closed depends on the type of data required. Some audits should be done while a retailer is open, such as analyses of parking lot adequacy, in-store customer traffic patterns, the use of vertical transportation, and customer relations. Other audits should be done while a retailer is closed, such as analyses of the condition of fixtures, inventory levels and turnover, financial statements, and employee records.

The format for the audit report must be determined. It can be formal or informal, brief or long, oral or written, and a statement of findings or a statement of findings plus recommendations. The report has a better chance of acceptance if presented in the format desired by management.

Reporting Audit Findings and Recommendations to Management

❏ The last step in the audit process is presenting findings and recommendations to management. It is the responsibility of management, not the auditor, to determine what adjustments (if any) to make. It is essential that the proper company executives read the report thoroughly, consider each point made, and enact the needed strategy changes.

Management should treat each audit seriously and react accordingly. It is a serious mistake if only lip service is paid to findings. A firm's long-term success is predicated on its evaluating the present and adapting to the future. No matter how well an audit is performed, it is a worthless exercise if not taken seriously by management.

Responding to an Audit

After management studies the audit findings, appropriate actions should be taken. Areas of strength should be continued and areas of weakness revised. All actions must be consistent with the retail strategy and recorded and stored in the retail information system.

For example, TJX Companies, Inc., the parent company of several off-price apparel chains, places great reliance on its retail audits. Here is what it stated in one recent annual report:

The TJX Companies, Inc. is the largest off-price apparel retailer in North America. The Company operates 587 T.J. Maxx stores, the recently acquired Marshalls chain of 496 stores, and Winners Apparel Ltd., a Canadian off-price family apparel chain with 52 stores. TJX is developing HomeGoods, a U.S. off-price home fashion chain with 22 stores, and T.K. Maxx, an off-price family apparel concept in the United Kingdom, which has 9 stores. The Company also operates Chadwick's of Boston off-price women's fashion catalog. The Company strives to provide value to customers by offering brand names, fashion, quality, and price. For fiscal 1996, Company stores derived 31.4 percent of sales from the Northeast, 21.4 percent from the Midwest, 28.2 percent from the South, 1.5 percent from the Central States, 13.0 percent from the West, and 4.5 percent from Canada. As a result of the Marshalls acquisition, the Company added Marshalls stores to its existing base of T.J. Maxx off-price family apparel stores as of January 27, 1996. Management believes it will realize improved operating efficiencies for the combined entity through the integration of many administrative and operational functions, as well as increased purchasing leverage. In addition, with the acquisition of Marshalls, the Company will be able to decrease the amount of excess retail square footage in the competitive off-price retail sector by closing underperforming stores. The Company expects to close about 30 T.J. Maxx stores during fiscal 1997 and 170 Marshalls stores over the next two years. The Company plans to retain the independent identities of T.J. Maxx and Marshalls, including certain elements of merchandising, product assortment, and store appearance. The majority of sales volume is done through the T.J. Maxx and Marshalls stores. T.J. Maxx operates in 48 states, with an average store size of 28,000 gross square feet, while Marshalls operates in 38 states and Puerto Rico, with an average store size of 32,000 gross square feet. T.J. Maxx and Marshalls sell a broad range of brand-name family apparel, accessories, shoes, domestics, giftware, and jewelry at prices generally 20 percent to 60 percent below department and specialty store regular prices. Winners Apparel Ltd., which was acquired in fiscal 1991, is a Canadian off-price family apparel retailer. HomeGoods, an off-price business the Company began testing in fiscal 1993, sells domestics, giftware, and other home fashions. T.K. Maxx, the Company's newest venture, operates off-price apparel stores in the United Kingdom. Chadwick's of Boston sells, through a mail-order catalog, women's career and casual fashion apparel priced significantly below department store regular prices.[13]

Possible Difficulties in Conducting a Retail Audit

There are several potential obstacles that may occur in conducting a retail audit. A retailer should be aware of them:

- An audit may be costly to undertake.
- An audit may be quite time-consuming.
- Performance measures may be inaccurate.
- Employees may feel threatened and not cooperate as much as desired.
- Incorrect data may be collected.
- Management may not be responsive to the findings.

At the present time, many retailers—particularly smaller ones—do not understand or perform systematic retail audits. But as these retailers move toward the year 2000, this must change if they are to analyze themselves properly and plan correctly for the future.

ILLUSTRATIONS OF RETAIL AUDIT FORMS

In this section, a management audit form for retailers and a retailing performance checklist are presented. These forms demonstrate how both small and large retailers can inexpensively, yet efficiently, conduct retail audits.

An internal or external auditor (or department manager) would complete one of the forms in a thorough, periodic way and then discuss the findings with management. The examples noted are both horizontal audits. A vertical audit would be an in-depth analysis of any one area in the forms.

A Management Audit Form for Small Retailers

The *Management Audit for Small Retailers* was prepared by the Small Business Administration. This booklet, although written for small firms, provides a series of questions and discussions applicable to all retailers. It comprehensively details the components of a retail audit.

Figure 20-8 shows selected questions from each of the areas covered in the *Management Audit for Small Retailers*. It should be viewed as a single, overall horizontal audit, not as fragmented pieces. "Yes" is the desired answer to every question. For those questions answered negatively, the firm should determine the causes for the responses and adjust strategy accordingly.

[13]*TJX Companies, Inc. 1996 Annual Report.*

A Look at Yourself and Your Ability to Grow

_____ 1. Do you keep abreast of changes in your field by subscribing to leading trade and general business publications?

_____ 2. Do you plan for a profit (your net income) above a reasonable salary for yourself as manager?

_____ 3. Are you an active member of a trade association?

Customer Relations

_____ 4. Do you purposely cater to selected groups of customers rather than to all groups?

_____ 5. Do you have a clear picture of the retail image you seek to implant in the minds of your customers?

_____ 6. Do you evaluate your own performance by asking customers about their likes and dislikes and by shopping competitors to compare their assortments, prices, and promotion methods with your own?

Personnel Management and Supervision

_____ 7. Do employees in your firm know to whom they each report?

_____ 8. Do you delegate as much authority as you can to those immediately responsible to you, freeing yourself from unnecessary operating details?

_____ 9. Do you seek your employees' opinions of stock assortments, choice of new merchandise, layout, displays, and special promotions?

_____ 10. Do you apply the concept of "management by objectives," that is, do you set work goals for yourself and for each employee for the month or season ahead and at the end of each period check the actual performance against these goals?

Merchandise Inventory Control

_____ 11. Do you keep sales, inventory, and purchase records by types of merchandise within your departments?

_____ 12. Do you control your purchases in dollars by means of an open-to-buy system?

_____ 13. For staple and reorder items, do you prepare a checklist (never-out list) that you frequently check against the actual assortment on hand?

_____ 14. Do you make certain that best-sellers are reordered promptly and in sufficient volume and that slow-sellers are processed swiftly for clearance?

_____ 15. Are you taking adequate safeguards to reduce shoplifting and pilferage in your store?

Budgetary Control and Productivity

_____ 16. In controlling your operations, do you frequently compare actual results with the budget projections you have made; and do you then adjust your merchandising, promotion, and expense plans as indicated by deviation from these projections?

_____ 17. Do you study industry data and compare the results of your operation with them?

_____ 18. Do you think in terms of ratios and percentages, rather than exclusively in dollars-and-cents?

_____ 19. Do you use a variety of measures of performance, such as:

_____ a. Net profit as a percent of your net worth?

_____ b. Stockturn (ratio of your sales to the value of your average inventory)?

_____ c. Gross profit margin per dollar of cost investment in merchandise (dollars of gross margin divided by your average inventory at cost)?

_____ d. Sales per square foot of space (net sales divided by total number of square feet of space)?

_____ e. Selling cost percent for each salesperson (remuneration of the salesperson divided by that person's sales)?

Buying

_____ 20. Are you continually searching the market for the most suitable merchandise, prices, and sources rather than relying too much on established sources?

_____ 21. When reordering new items that have shown volume potential, do you make it a point to order a sufficient number?

_____ 22. Do you keep up assortments through important selling seasons, such as Christmas and Easter, in spite of the probability of markdowns on the remainders?

_____ 23. For goods having a short selling season (such as straw hats), do you pre-determine the following dates: (a) when first orders are to be placed, (b) when retail stocks are to be complete, (c) extent of peak selling period, (d) start of clearance, and (e) final cleanup?

_____ 24. Do you take advantage of all available discounts—trade, quantity, seasonal, and cash—and do you include them on your written orders?

Figure 20-8

A Management Audit Form for Small Retailers

Source: This is adapted from John W. Wingate and Elmer O. Schaller, *Management Audit for Small Retailers* (Washington, D.C.: Small Business Administration, Small Business Management Series No. 31, Third Edition, 1977).

Pricing

_____ 25. Do you figure markup as a percentage of retail selling price rather than as a percentage of costs?

_____ 26. Do you set price lines or price zones?

_____ 27. Do the prices you set provide adequate markups within the limits of competition?

_____ 28. In retail pricing of new items and in evaluating their cost quotations, are you guided by what you think the typical customer will consider good value?

_____ 29. Before you mark down goods for clearance, do you consider alternate supplementary ways of moving them—such as special displays, repackaging, or including them in a deal?

Advertising and Sales Promotion

_____ 30. Do you advertise consistently in at least one appropriate medium: newspapers, direct mail, flyers, local television, or radio?

_____ 31. Does each of your ads specifically "sell" your firm in addition to the merchandise advertised?

_____ 32. Do you regularly and systematically familiarize your salespeople with your plans for advertised merchandise and promotions?

_____ 33. Do you consult your suppliers about dealer aids helpful to the promotion of their merchandise in your store?

_____ 34. Do you use "co-op" ads with other merchants in your community?

_____ 35. Do you conduct a continuing effort to obtain free publicity in the local press or broadcast media?

Display

_____ 36. Are your window displays planned to attract attention, develop interest, create desire, and prompt a customer to enter your store for a closer inspection?

_____ 37. Do you give as much attention to your interior display as to your windows?

Equipment and Layout

_____ 38. Are goods that the customers may not be specifically looking for but are likely to buy on sight (impulse merchandise) displayed near your store entrances and at other points that have heavy traffic?

_____ 39. Are your cash registers well located?

_____ 40. Are nonselling and office activities kept out of valuable selling space?

_____ 41. Do you receive, check, and mark incoming goods at central points rather than on the selling floor?

Cash and Finance

_____ 42. Does someone other than the cashier or bookkeeper open all mail and prepare a record of receipts that will be checked against deposits?

_____ 43. Do you deposit all of each day's cash receipts in the bank without delay?

_____ 44. Do you calculate your cash flow regularly (monthly, for example) and take steps to provide enough cash for each period's needs?

_____ 45. Have you established, in advance, a line of credit at your bank, not only to meet seasonal requirements but also to permit borrowing at any time for emergency needs?

Credit

_____ 46. Do you have a credit policy?

_____ 47. Are your bad-debt losses comparable with those of other similar retailers?

_____ 48. Periodically, do you review your accounts to determine their status?

Insurance

_____ 49. Is your company's insurance handled by a conscientious and knowledgeable agent?

_____ 50. Have you updated your insurance needs to insure adequate protection for buildings, equipment, merchandise, and other assets, as well as for public liability?

Accounting Records

_____ 51. Do you have your books balanced and accounts summarized each month?

_____ 52. Do you use a modern point-of-sale register for sales transactions and modern equipment to record accounts receivable?

_____ 53. Do you keep data on sales, purchases, inventory, and direct expenses for different types of merchandise?

Taxes and Legal Options

_____ 54. To be sure you are not overpaying your taxes, do you retain a tax accountant to review your accounting records and prepare your more complicated tax returns?

_____ 55. Do you retain a good lawyer to confer with on day-to-day problems that have legal implications?

Planning for Growth

_____ 56. Over the past few years, have you done much long-range planning for growth?

_____ 57. When you find that change is called for, do you act decisively and creatively?

_____ 58. Do you make most of your changes after thoughtful analysis rather than as reactions to crises?

_____ 59. Are you grooming someone to succeed you as manager in the not too distant future?

Figure 20-8

(Continued)

A Retailing Performance Checklist

Figure 20-9 contains another type of audit form, a retailing performance checklist, which can be used to assess overall strategy performance. Included is each component of a retail strategy.

The checklist can also be used by small and large retailers alike. Its purpose is to identify strengths and weaknesses, so a strategy can be adapted. Unlike the yes-no answers in Figure 20-8, the checklist lets a retailer rate its performance in each area, thus providing more in-depth information. A total score is not computed. Because all items are not equally important, a simple summation would not present a meaningful score.

Figure 20-9

A Retailing Performance Checklist

Rate your firm's performance for each of the following criteria on a scale of 1 to 5, with 1 being excellent and 5 being poor.

I. Development of strategy
   1. Adherence to the philosophy of business   _____
   2. Clear objectives   _____
   3. Consistent objectives and image   _____
   4. Distinctive positioning   _____
   5. Well-defined goods and/or service offerings   _____
   6. Well-defined and ongoing budget   _____
   7. Proper use of research   _____
   8. Thorough short-run planning   _____
   9. Thorough long-run planning   _____
   10. Reactions to external environment   _____
   11. Well-established evaluation criteria   _____
   12. Adjustments in strategy   _____

II. The consumer
   1. Well-defined target market   _____
   2. Consistency with image   _____
   3. Size of target market   _____
   4. Knowledge of consumer needs   _____
   5. Demographic trends for target market   _____

III. Store location
   1. Consistency with image   _____
   2. Size of trading area   _____
   3. Popularity of trading area   _____
   4. Access to vehicular traffic   _____
   5. Access to mass transportation   _____
   6. Parking facilities   _____
   7. Composition of existing stores   _____
   8. Affinity with existing stores   _____
   9. Turnover of stores   _____
   10. Visibility of store   _____
   11. Condition of building   _____
   12. Terms of occupancy   _____
   13. Store hours   _____
   14. Store facilities   _____
   15. Maintenance of facilities   _____

IV. Retail organization and human resource management
   1. Clarity of retail organization   _____
   2. Appropriateness of retail organization   _____
   3. Adaptability of retail organization   _____
   4. Employee recruitment   _____
   5. Employee selection   _____
   6. Employee training   _____
   7. Employee compensation   _____
   8. Employee supervision   _____
   9. Employee motivation   _____
   10. Opportunities for advancement   _____

Figure 20-9

(Continued)

V. Operations management
    1. Return on assets _____
    2. Return on net worth _____
    3. Appropriateness of budgeting style _____
    4. Cash flow _____
    5. Store size _____
    6. Space allocation _____
    7. Employee turnover _____
    8. Store maintenance _____
    9. Inventory management _____
    10. Store security _____
    11. Use of insurance _____
    12. Credit management _____
    13. Level of computerization _____
    14. Crisis management _____

VI. Merchandising
    1. Buying organization _____
    2. Appropriateness of merchandise quality _____
    3. Level of innovativeness _____
    4. Width of assortment _____
    5. Depth of assortment _____
    6. Availability of manufacturer brands _____
    7. Availability of private brands _____
    8. Knowledge of merchandise sources _____
    9. Caliber of merchandise sources _____
    10. Purchase terms _____
    11. Reordering procedures _____
    12. Use of dollar control systems _____
    13. Use of unit control systems _____
    14. Inventory valuation procedures _____
    15. Accuracy of records _____
    16. Merchandise forecasting and budgeting process _____
    17. Stock turnover _____
    18. Gross margin return on investment _____

VII. Pricing
    1. Consistency with other retail strategy mix factors _____
    2. Awareness of consumer sensitivity to price _____
    3. Awareness of and compliance with government restrictions _____
    4. Relations with suppliers _____
    5. Competitive pricing environment _____
    6. Use of thorough, systematic approach to pricing _____
    7. Use of demand-, cost-, and competition-based
       pricing techniques _____
    8. Adaptability _____
    9. Use of price lining _____
    10. Level of markdowns _____

VIII. Communications
    1. Appropriateness of image _____
    2. Customer perception of image _____
    3. Storefront(s) _____
    4. Cleanliness of facilities _____
    5. Traffic flow _____
    6. Width of aisles _____
    7. Use of dead space _____
    8. Displays _____
    9. Customer service _____
    10. Amount of promotion _____
    11. Amount of advertising _____
    12. Quality of advertising _____
    13. Uses of public relations _____
    14. Amount of personal selling _____
    15. Quality of sales force _____
    16. Uses of sales promotion _____

Summary

1. *To demonstrate the importance of integrating a retail strategy* This chapter shows why it is necessary for retailers to plan and apply coordinated strategies, and describes how to assess success or failure. The stages of a retail strategy must be viewed as an ongoing, integrated system of interrelated steps—not as a fragmented, one-time-only concept.

2. *To examine four key factors in the development and enactment of an integrated retail strategy: planning procedures and opportunity analysis, defining productivity, performance measures, and scenario analysis* Planning procedures can be optimized by adhering to a series of specified actions, from situation analysis to control. Opportunities need to be studied in terms of their impact on overall strategy, and not in an isolated way. The sales opportunity grid is a good tool for comparing various strategic options.

   To maximize productivity when enacting their strategies, retailers need to define exactly what productivity represents to them. Though firms should be as efficient as possible, this does not necessarily mean having the lowest possible operating costs (which may lead to customer dissatisfaction), but rather keying spending to the performance standards required by a retailer's chosen strategy mix and niche in the market (such as upscale versus discount).

   By picking the proper performance measures and setting standards for them, a retailer can better integrate its strategy. Measures include total sales, average sales per store, sales by goods/service category, sales per square foot, gross margins, gross margin return on investment, operating income, inventory turnover, markdown percentages, employee turnover, financial ratios, and profitability. The *Chain Store Age* retail performance index combines sales growth, profit growth, and return-on-assets measures.

   With scenario analysis, a retailer projects the future by examining the major factors that will impact on its long-term performance and then prepares contingency plans keyed to alternative scenarios. It is not easy to do.

3. *To show how industry and company data can be used in strategy planning and analysis (benchmarking)* A firm should utilize benchmarking, whereby it sets its own standards and measures performance based on the achievements of its sector of retailing, specific competitors, high-performance companies (best practices), and/or its own prior actions. Plentiful data are available to do this. Through gap analysis, a retailer can compare its actual performance against its potential performance, and then see areas in which it must improve.

4. *To explain the principles of a retail audit, its utility in controlling a retail strategy, the difference between horizontal and vertical audits, and the possible difficulties with auditing* A retail strategy needs to be regularly monitored, evaluated, and fine-tuned or revised. The retail audit is one way to accomplish this control function. It is a systematic, thorough, and unbiased review and appraisal. Through an audit, a firm's goals, strategy, implementation, and organization can each be investigated.

   The retail audit process has six steps: determining who does the audit; determining when and how often it is conducted; setting the areas to be audited; developing audit forms; conducting the audit; and reporting results and recommendations to management. After the right executives read the audit report, necessary revisions in strategy should be made.

   In a horizontal audit, a retailer's overall strategy and performance are assessed. In a vertical audit, one element of a firm's strategy is evaluated in detail. Among the potential difficulties of auditing may be the costs, the time commitment, the inaccuracy of performance standards, the poor cooperation from some employees, the collection of incorrect data, and an unresponsive management. A number of firms do not do audits; as a result, they may have problems evaluating their positions and planning for the future.

5. *To provide examples of audit forms* Two audit forms are presented in the chapter: a management audit for retailers and a retailing performance checklist.

Key Terms

sales opportunity grid (p. 662)
performance measures (p. 666)
benchmarking (p. 666)
retail performance index (p. 671)

gap analysis (p. 671)
scenario analysis (p. 671)
retail audit (p. 677)

horizontal retail audit (p. 679)
vertical retail audit (p. 679)
audit form (p. 679)

Questions for Discussion

1. Why is it so imperative for a firm to view its strategy as an integrated and ongoing process?
2. Present an integrated strategy for Gymboree to increase sales by 12 percent annually for each of the next three years. Refer to Figure 20-3 in your answer.
3. Develop a sales opportunity grid for a neighborhood stationery store planning to add lottery tickets to its product line.
4. Comment on this statement: "Often neither the least expensive strategy nor the most expensive strategy may be the most productive strategy." Does this mean off-price stores should upgrade their strategies? Explain your answer.
5. Cite five performance measures commonly used by retailers, and explain what can be learned by studying each.
6. What is benchmarking? Present a five-step procedure to do retail benchmarking.
7. What do you think are the pros and cons of the retail performance index described in this chapter and highlighted in Table 20-7?
8. How are the terms *gap analysis* and *scenario analysis* interrelated?
9. Distinguish between horizontal and vertical retail audits. Develop a vertical audit form for a retailer selling furniture.
10. What are the attributes of good retail auditing?
11. Distinguish among these auditors. Under what circumstances would each be preferred?
    a. Outside auditor.
    b. Company audit specialist.
    c. Company department manager.
12. Under what circumstances should a disguised audit be used?
13. How should management respond to the findings of an audit? What can happen if the findings are ignored?
14. Why do many retailers not conduct any form of retail audit? Are these reasons valid? Explain your answer.

Web-Based Exercise:

NEIMAN MARCUS (http://www.neimanmarcus.com)

Questions

1. As described at its Web site, is Neiman Marcus' overall retail strategy well integrated? Explain your answer.
2. Evaluate the questionnaire in the "customer lounge" section of the Neiman Marcus Web site.
3. What performance measures should Neiman Marcus use to assess the effectiveness of its Web site?
4. Present a ten-item horizontal retail audit form for the Neiman Marcus Web site.

CASE 1
Fleming Companies: Strategic Planning in Action*

Since its purchase of Scrivner, Inc. (a $6 billion food distribution company) in 1994, Fleming Companies (http://www.fleming.com) has become the largest U.S. wholesale grocery distributor, with sales nearing $20 billion. It handles food and general merchandise products for more than 3,500 independently owned supermarkets in 42 states, the District of Columbia, and several nations. It operates 35 supply centers to provide retailer customers with merchandise in a variety of product categories (such as dairy, frozen foods, meats, bakery, delicatessen, and fresh produce). It also operates 300 of its own stores (accounting for one-sixth of total revenues).

Fleming's current objectives are to balance its earnings and re-engineering costs, to improve productivity, to leverage its size to create marketing opportunities, to increase sales to new and existing customers, and to improve the earnings of its company-owned stores. Let's look at its strategies and degree of success on each of them.

*The material in this case is drawn from *Fleming Companies 1995 Annual Report*; and Louise Lee, "Texas Grocer's Award in Suit Reveals a Maze of Wholesale Pricing," *Wall Street Journal* (May 1, 1996), pp. A1, A4.

CASE 1
(Continued)

Balance Earnings and Re-engineering Costs   Fleming's strategic plan recognizes the need to re-engineer at least one-third of the volume from its supply centers in order to see a measurable impact on productivity. Although Fleming personnel have been able to re-engineer 40 percent of its volume, the effort took management's attention away from other vital activities. Fleming also underestimated the difficulty in getting retailers to fully understand the new systems.

Improve Productivity   Fleming is not only concerned with reducing its costs, it also wants to lower costs in the entire supply chain (from manufacturer to retailer). It wants to eliminate duplication in the supply system. Part of its productivity improvements can be seen from its eliminating 2,800 jobs, the increase in truckload utilization by 4 percent, and its closing or selling 2 million square feet of underutilized warehouse space.

Leverage Size to Create Marketing Opportunities   Fleming has begun using category management techniques by working more closely with key vendors. It has started centrally buying perishables (it is now the largest single customer of America's top five produce growers). It recently introduced a new premium-quality private brand, Marquee Premium.

Increase Sales to New and Existing Customers   In an attempt to better serve its customers, Fleming has shifted from a geographic-based organization structure to a market segment-based format. These segments are independents (east and west), IGA (east and west), price impact, conventional voluntary, Piggly Wiggly, chains, alternative format, military, international, and convenience store. Each segment is now serviced by a special Fleming team that understands the unique product and servicing requirements of that type of business. Fleming has also established a national sales organization to aggressively pursue new business.

Improve Earnings of Company-Owned Stores   Fleming hopes to make its own retail stores highly profitable by turning these units into the most progressive users of technology. Its company-owned stores already routinely use computer-based advanced front-end scanning, inventory management and pricing, receiving, time and attendance record keeping, and electronic funds transfer systems. Its present strategic plan calls for increasing the percentage of revenues from company-owned stores to 25 percent. Fleming wants this approach to result in its getting more promotional dollars from manufacturers and having a steadier base of customers.

One diversion for Fleming is a lawsuit in which David's Supermarkets has sued the firm on the basis of what David's claims is the wholesaler's unfair pricing system. The suit alleges that Fleming did not pass on manufacturer rebates to all its retailer customers and that Fleming asked some makers of private brands to boost prices beyond what they intended to charge. Although a state judge initially ordered Fleming to pay David's $211.2 million in damages, this judgment was later thrown out and a new trial ordered. As such, Fleming's chairman and chief executive officer, chief financial officer, and attorneys will devote much of their attention to the new trial, while other executives continue to work on Fleming's core business: the buying and selling of groceries.

Questions
1. Evaluate Fleming's overall retail strategy.
2. List and explain ten performance measures Fleming could use to assess the success of its strategy.
3. Explain how Fleming can further utilize computers in implementing its programs.
4. Develop a plan for Fleming to evaluate the fairness of its pricing system through use of a vertical retail pricing audit.

Video Questions on Fleming
1. Describe how experts see retail distribution changing over the next ten years. How can Fleming adapt to each of these changes?
2. Describe the difficulties in managing a business for the long term while having stable earnings.

Founded in 1994, Beverages and More! is a rapidly growing and successful chain of category-killer beverage and gourmet snack food stores in the San Francisco area. The heart of each of its 18,000-square-foot stores is the superior wine and beer selection.

While a traditional California supermarket carries 30 or so Chardonnay wines, Beverages and More! carries over 300 (from a variety of vineyards and vintages). Wines account for 40 percent of the chain's total sales, and beers and spirits comprise another 40 percent. The typical Beverages and More! store stocks over 300 microbrews, 300 imported beers, and over 1,200 spirits. Gourmet food, nonalcoholic beverages, and general merchandise make up 15 percent of sales; the other 5 percent is from cigars. Four-foot-high glass cases equipped with humidifiers display the cigars near each store entrance. Most of them are imported from the Caribbean.

Several new product categories are being added to the Beverages and More! product mix. These include some 500 types of cheeses, fresh pasta, olives, deli salads, dips, and gourmet deli meats. A test of frozen appetizers and desserts is in process. These new items are expected to boost the proportion of overall revenues attributed to food to around 25 percent.

Prices at Beverages and More! have remained relatively low due to the chain's low purchase costs and low overhead. Because the firm purchases huge amounts of its goods, it is able to take advantage of quantity discounts and its buying clout with vendors. Furthermore, Beverages and More! generates additional savings by insisting that most vendors deliver their goods directly to the chain's stores, as opposed to a distribution center. Direct store delivery reduces costs due to the elimination of certain warehousing and shipping expenses.

The chain's primary market is 35- to 54-year-olds, who are affluent and college educated. Males presently account for 60 percent of the firm's total revenues. In contrast, 90 percent of the customers of a typical liquor store are male. Beverages and More! appeals both to consumers who shop the store regularly and seek a wide selection and low prices, and those who visit the stores to stock up for parties and holiday gatherings. The average transaction size at a Beverages and More! store is over $30.

Beverages and More! recently launched Club Bev, a frequent shoppers program. With Club Bev, each purchase by a member is scanned; and the chain then enters the information into its data base. The data base is used to develop targeted newsletters that reflect individual consumer purchase histories. Thus, the newsletter for a cigar smoker has a different editorial content than a newsletter oriented toward a cheese buyer.

Even though the chain is very young, Beverages and More! has ambitious expansion plans. It hopes to enter other areas of California in the near future. After that, it will consider other markets—possibly the East Coast.

CASE 2
Beverages and More!: Devising and Enacting an Integrated Retail Strategy[†]

Questions
1. What are the competitive advantages and disadvantages of Beverages and More! in comparison with traditional beverage stores? In comparison with traditional gourmet food stores?
2. Do you think that Beverages and More!'s retailing strategy is well integrated? Explain your answer.
3. Present a five-year plan for Beverages and More! to expand into other regions of the United States. What potential risks does it face? How would you overcome them?
4. Describe a customer-service vertical retail audit for Beverages and More!

[†]This case was prepared and written by Professor Howard W. Combs, San Jose State University. The material in this case is drawn from John Arrizza, "Speaking Easy About Beverages and More!" *Direct Marketing* (April 1995), pp. 66–69; Clifford Carlsen, "Killer on the Loose," *San Francisco Times* (December 23, 1994), pp. 1–3; Michael Garry, "The Best Revenge," *Progressive Grocer* (July 1996), pp. 70–76; Joyce Rouston, "Beverages and More! Steve Boone Is Back," *Market Watch* (June 1995), pp. 70–74; Ann Wozencrafi, "Liquor Barn Creator Back in New Store," *Contra Costa Times* (June 22, 1994), pp. 1–5.

Part Eight
Comprehensive Case

Toys "Я" Us: Analysis of a Global Strategy*

INTRODUCTION

Toys "Я" Us (http://www.tru.com) is the largest toy retailer in the world and still growing. In 1996, it operated about 1,200 stores worldwide (including Kids "Я" Us stores, all of which are domestic). See Table 1. Toys "Я" Us reported an unbroken record for both sales and earnings from its inception as a public firm until 1996. While net sales rose from $8.7 billion in fiscal 1995 to $9.4 billion in fiscal 1996, net earnings fell from $532 million in 1995 to $148 million in 1996. See Table 2.

Toys "Я" Us accounts for about 25 percent of total U.S. retail toy sales, the largest market share for any specialty retailer. This is quite remarkable considering Toys "Я" Us does not have stores in every major geographic area. As of early 1996, the firm had outlets in 48 states (and Puerto Rico), but operated fewer than 10 stores each in 26 of these states (and in Puerto Rico).

Although Toys "Я" Us presently owns the Kids "Я" Us and Babies "Я" Us chains in the United States, this case focuses on the domestic and international strategies of Toys "Я" Us stores.

COMPANY BACKGROUND AND HISTORY

Charles Lazarus, founder and current chairman of Toys "Я" Us, Inc., began his retailing career in 1948 by selling baby furniture in Washington, D.C. He soon found customers asking him for toys, which he

*The material in this case is drawn from Michael Hartnett, "New Toys "Я" Us Concepts Focus on Improving the Shopping Experience," *Stores* (March 1996), pp. 26–27; "Change at the Checkout," *Economist* (March 4, 1995), pp. 1–18; Bob Davis, "To All U.S. Managers Upset by Regulations: Try Germany or Japan," *Wall Street Journal* (December 14, 1995), pp. A1, A9; Richard Halverson, "TRU Goes Forth with Baby, Mega Concepts," *Discount Store News* (May 20, 1996), pp. 1, 40; Joseph Pereira, "Toys "Я" Us is Betting Big on Baby Stores," *Wall Street Journal* (October 3, 1996), pp. B1, B4; Joseph Pereira, "Toys "Я" Us to Close 25 Stores and Take a $270 Million Charge in Restructuring," *Wall Street Journal* (February 2, 1996), p. A3; *Toys "Я" Us, Inc. 1996 Annual Report;* and Steve Gelsi, "Toys Story," *Adweek* (February 3, 1997), pp. 14–15.

began to stock. Unlike baby furniture, toys encouraged repeat store visits by customers. So, at that point, Lazarus established the firm's unique approach to retailing by developing a supermarket-style format with wide aisles, self-service merchandising, shopping carts, and centralized cashiers.

In 1966, Lazarus sold his toy store operation, which he had expanded to two outlets, to Interstate Stores for $7.5 million in cash. Unfortunately, poor management and overexpansion in discount stores forced Interstate into bankruptcy in 1974 and brought Lazarus back into control of the company. By 1978, he had returned the firm to solid ground in both profitability and sales growth, and he subsequently changed the company name to Toys "Я" Us.

Toys "Я" Us' overall philosophy of business is "to capitalize on our position as the low-cost retailer in the toy business by continuing to aggressively price our merchandise in order to obtain large market share gains." It is known as a very efficient retailer in controlling expenses. It uses gravity-feed racks in U.S. toy stores to reduce the labor expenses associated with stocking diapers and baby formula, electronic data interchange to communicate with key suppliers, UPC scanning to maximize inventory turnover and minimize stockouts (both domestically and internationally), systematic labor scheduling to allocate workers properly, and shelf labeling (rather than item marking) to reduce labor costs.

THE DOMESTIC STRATEGY OF TOYS "Я" US

These are some of the ingredients of Toys "Я" Us' domestic strategy:

■ Although over one-half of annual store sales are made in the fourth quarter (particularly during the six weeks before Christmas), the firm maintains a year-round inventory of toys. In contrast, most department stores reduce or even close their toy department directly after Christmas. As a re-

Table 1 NET SALES, NET INCOME, AND NUMBER OF STORES FOR TOYS "Я" US, INC., FISCAL YEARS ENDING JANUARY 28, 1990 THROUGH FEBRUARY 3, 1996

	1996	1995	1994	1993	1992	1991	1990
Operations							
Net Sales ($ millions)	9,427	8,746	7,946	7,169	6,124	5,510	4,788
Net Income ($ millions)	148	532	483	438	340	326	321
Number of Stores at Year End							
Toys "Я" Us—United States	653	618	581	540	497	451	404
Toys "Я" Us—International	337	293	234	167	126	97	74
Kids "Я" Us—United States	213	204	217	211	189	164	137

Source: Toys "Я" Us, Inc. 1996 Annual Report.

sult, Toys "Я" Us has a high level of customer loyalty and can obtain early indications of the popularity of new toys.

▨ Many orders are placed in February (an off season for toy manufacturers) to secure better purchase terms from vendors. Thus, the firm often gets advantageous terms (including up to 12 months to pay for purchases).

▨ Customers are offered an extensive selection, involving thousands of items.

▨ Items are arranged in stores according to blueprints, and most store units use similar displays and layouts. The standard U.S. prototype store occupies 46,000 square feet of space, with 30,000- and 20,000-square-foot stores located in smaller markets. In addition, stores typically employ vertical merchandising with 16-foot-high displays. This all facilitates operations and eases shopping for customers.

▨ Most stores are either freestanding units or situated in strip shopping centers.

▨ The firm's size gives it delivery priority on fast-selling merchandise which may be in short supply.

▨ It has an aggressive pricing policy, although it is not a discounter. In the past, everyday low pricing was used, but the firm now relies more on a seasonal catalog with discount coupons for select items.

▨ A sophisticated computerized inventory management system records data on an item-by-item basis and compares actual against projected sales. Shelf space for items with better than expected sales performance is then expanded, while items with poorer than anticipated results are marked down and receive less shelf space in the future.

▨ The company has been adding new domestic toy stores at the rate of roughly 35 per year. In adding new stores, it operates on a regional basis using a "hub-and-spoke" distribution system, which

TABLE 2 NET SALES, COSTS AND EXPENSES, AND NET INCOME DATA FOR TOYS "Я" US, INC., FOR FISCAL YEARS ENDING JANUARY 29, 1994 THROUGH FEBRUARY 3, 1996 (IN MILLIONS)

	2-3-96	1-28-95	1-29-94
Net Sales	$9,426.9	$8,745.6	$7,946.1
Costs and Expenses:			
Cost of sales	$6,592.3	$6,008.0	$5,494.7
Selling, advertising, general, and administrative	1,894.8	1,664.2	1,497.0
Restructuring and other charges	396.6	—	—
Depreciation and amortization	191.7	161.4	133.4
Interest expense	103.3	83.9	72.3
Interest and other income	(17.4)	(16.0)	(24.1)
Total	$9,161.3	$7,901.5	$7,173.3
Earnings before income taxes	$265.6	$844.1	$772.8
Income taxes	117.5	312.3	289.8
Net income	$ 148.1	$ 531.8	$ 483.0

Source: Toys "Я" Us, Inc. 1996 Annual Report.

enables the firm to efficiently expand. Stores in a new region are served by either a newly opened distribution center or a nearby distribution center. As of February 1996, Toys "Я" Us had 17 U.S. warehouses/distribution centers.

- Unlike competitors, the company owns and maintains its own fleet of trucks. It firmly believes this arrangement provides the maximum flexibility to meet seasonal peak loads.

Toys "Я" Us continually fine-tunes its overall toy-based strategy. Among its most recent strategy modifications are the streamlining of the number of items carried, "Concept 2000," and the acquisition of Baby Superstore Inc. As part of a strategic inventory repositioning strategy, Toys "Я" Us has reduced the number of items carried to 11,000 (from as many as 16,000) at each of its U.S.-based toy stores. This allows the retailer to better display key merchandise in more central sections of stores.

"Concept 2000" is the floor plan for all new and remodeled 46,000-square-foot stores in the United States. As part of the revised layout, stores will have wider aisles, icons so shoppers can better locate merchandise, and special Lego Shops, Learning Centers, and a video game section. The stores will also have areas that change by season such as Warner Kids Shops and special presentations of Barbie dolls.

In 1996, Toys "Я" Us acquired Baby Superstore, a 70-store chain with everything from pacifiers to cribs, in a stock swap valued at $410 million. Toys "Я" Us planned to expand the chain to 105 stores by the end of 1997. Retail analysts feel Toys "Я" Us can improve Baby Superstore's performance by applying its sophisticated inventory management system to that chain.

THE OVERALL FOREIGN STRATEGY OF TOYS "Я" US STORES

Toys "Я" Us executives view the U.S. market for toys as much more saturated than foreign markets. Accordingly, for several years, the firm has opened more stores outside the United States than within it. Forty-five stores were opened in international markets in 1996, versus 35 in the United States. Table 3 shows the number of Toys "Я" Us international stores by nation, as well as country data.

According to Larry Boutz, head of Toys "Я" Us' global division, "We look forward to the day when our international division will be at least the same size as the one in the U.S. Our corporate goal is to create a large multinational retail company. It's a fact that in parts of Europe, Asia, and Latin America where we want to be operating, total middle-class wealth and population are greater than in the U.S. The world is just much bigger than our own country. So, looking at the mere mathematics of it, it makes all the sense in the world." Besides using direct ownership for foreign expansion, Toys "Я" Us also applies both franchising (in such countries as Israel, Saudi Arabia, United Arab Emirates, Indonesia, South Africa, and Turkey) and 50 percent joint venture agreements (in Hong Kong and Taiwan).

Many industry experts expect Toys "Я" Us' foreign operations to be more profitable as economies of scale are reached. According to one observer, of Toys "Я" Us' 20 foreign operations, only two markets (Canada and Great Britain) have the economies of scale to allow them to have profits comparable to those in the United States.

Toys "Я" Us uses a similar marketing strategy throughout the world. It consists of selling diapers and baby formula at low prices to build store loyalty at an early age, strong local management, large warehouse-style stores, efficient distribution systems, state-of-the-art technology, aggressive marketing, a self-service strategy with shopping carts, and low prices. According to Charles Lazarus, "We can go anywhere that has a supermarket, 'cause it's the same kind of shopping experience."

These are some of the basic elements of Toys "Я" Us' foreign strategy:

- The foreign stores are quite similar to the U.S. stores. The firm uses freestanding buildings and suburban sites for both U.S. and foreign operations. International stores also follow prototype store designs like those used in the United States.
- Despite its standardized operations, the firm caters to local preferences. As Boutz describes the product mix, "It's heavily local with a broad overview from our global vendors and ourselves. We have a delicate mix of local goods, as much as 30 or 40 percent, to support the local toy industry, as well as a heavy multinational dose from such suppliers as Hasbro, Mattel, Lego, Nintendo, Sega, and Procter & Gamble."
- It generally expands in one market area at a time. The company seeks adequate distribution facilities to service stores and be able to advertise efficiently in each foreign market.
- Infant items are discounted in both the U.S. and foreign stores. The firm assumes first-time mothers who are attracted will remain as steady customers throughout their toy-purchasing life cycle.

Table 3 TOYS "Я" US INTERNATIONAL LOCATIONS (AS OF FEBRUARY 3, 1996) AND SELECTED DEMOGRAPHIC DATA (LATEST AVAILABLE)

	Toys "Я" Us Int'l. Stores	Population Estimate Mid-1996	GDP per Capita	Annual Real Economic Growth Rate
Australia	21	18,300,000	$20,720	6.4 %
Austria	7	8,000,000	19,400	2.1
Belgium	3	10,100,000	26,740	1.9
Canada	58	29,900,000	19,215	3.0
Denmark	1	5,200,000	19,860	4.5
France	37	58,300,000	26,200	−0.7
Germany	57	83,500,000	28,250	1.9
Great Britain	50	58,500,000	17,980	4.2
Hong Kong	4	6,300,000	24,530	5.5
Israel	1	5,200,000	13,880	6.8
Japan	37	125,600,000	41,020	0.4
Luxembourg	1	400,000	22,000	1.0
Malaysia	4	20,000,000	4,027	8.0
Netherlands	9	15,500,000	17,940	2.0
Portugal	3	9,900,000	10,190	2.3
Singapore	4	3,400,000	19,940	10.1
Spain	26	38,900,000	13,120	1.8
Sweden	3	8,900,000	18,580	2.4
Switzerland	4	7,100,000	22,080	1.8
Taiwan	6	21,300,000	12,439	6.1
United Arab Emirates	1	3,100,000	22,470	2.9
Total Stores	337			

Sources: Toys "Я" Us, Inc. 1996 Annual Report; and 1997 Information Please Almanac (Boston: Houghton Mifflin Co., 1997), various pages.

▪ It has begun an international catalog program similar to that in the United States.

Of all the foreign markets where there are Toys "Я" Us stores, Germany and Japan have presented some of the greatest challenges to the firm. There are tight government regulations with which it must cope in terms of zoning, labor, and promotional rules. These regulations are more demanding than those in the United States.

THE MARKET ENVIRONMENT FOR TOYS "Я" US IN GERMANY

When Toys "Я" Us first announced its interest in German expansion in 1987, it had problems with toy makers that refused to sell to it in response to their fear of the retailer's power. In addition, small retailers warned German parents that Toys "Я" Us' impersonal self-service style could potentially create safety hazards, since the correct operation of toys and other items would not be explained. Ironically, the chain's presence in Germany resulted in an expansion of the overall toy market. Prior to its entry, Germans used to buy toys for children only at Christmas time. The toy market is now year-round.

The German market remains a tough one, particularly due to strong zoning restrictions, strict laws for promotion, and the power of labor unions. For example, one German law prohibits any retailer from building a store larger than 15,000 feet in areas outside the core of a city. The official reasons for this regulation are to protect Germany's small independent retailers in suburban areas from large chain stores and to encourage city construction and growth. In practice, the restriction makes it harder for retailers such as Toys "Я" Us to find large urban locations for their units.

Germany heavily controls retail sales practices. Under its rebate law, retailers can offer sales only twice a year. In addition, due to union pressure, store hours are limited. They can only be open $68\frac{1}{2}$ hours per week and must close at 6:30 P.M. on weekdays and at 2 P.M. on Saturdays. Sunday hours are banned.

Despite these obstacles, analysts still look favorably at opportunities in Germany due to the rise in disposable income, the strength of the German mark, and the poor state of retail facilities in the eastern part of the country.

THE MARKET ENVIRONMENT FOR TOYS "Я" US IN JAPAN

For several reasons, Toys "Я" Us faces a unique marketplace in Japan. The retail toy market there is comprised of thousands of mom-and-pop operations. These outlets generally have less than 325 square feet of floor space and buy merchandise through wholesalers. In contrast, Toys "Я" Us operates 54,000-square-foot stores there and buys direct from manufacturers. Furthermore, Japan (like Germany) restricts retail hours and advertising strategies. Although stores in Japan may stay open until 8 P.M., they are required to close 24 days a year for "holiday" purposes. Stores also cannot give discount coupons since these incentives violate laws intended to protect consumers from "confusion."

Toys "Я" Us has conquered many of the obstacles presented by Japan. It reduced local opposition by operating its stores as a joint venture with Fujita & Co., a Japanese trading company. Fujita, which owns 20 percent of the Japanese Toys "Я" Us, chooses store sites and is responsible for selecting a local manager to run each store. As in Germany, many Japanese landlords were initially reluctant to lease stores to Toys "Я" Us, fearing this action would upset local clients. Many property owners now give preferential lease terms to Toys "Я" Us based on the traffic it generates. Furthermore, few Japanese toy manufacturers were initially willing to risk offending wholesalers by selling directly to Toys "Я" Us. Eventually, they capitulated. According to the president of Japan's *Toy Magazine,* "Toys "Я" Us is too successful to ignore."

CONCLUSION

Despite a generally upbeat outlook, Toys "Я" Us still faces these challenges: complications in profit planning, a low stock price, and increased competition in foreign markets.

Profit planning is especially difficult at Toys "Я" Us due to the importance of fourth-quarter sales. This quarter generates about 80 percent of the firm's total yearly profits. Besides the impact of the state of the economy, Toys "Я" Us' sales and profit performance is dependent on the existence of a hot video game, doll, or other toy that is in sufficient supply for the retailer to benefit.

Poor same-store sales results, particularly in the United States, have kept Toys "Я" Us' stock price at similar levels to that in the early 1990s. During the same period, the U.S. stock market soared. The low stock price has hurt employee morale because they are eligible for the firm's stock option plan.

Lastly, Toys "Я" Us' prosperity in foreign markets has not gone unnoticed by large U.S. retailers (such as Wal-Mart) that are searching for expansion opportunities. Toys "Я" Us clearly needs to constantly re-evaluate its short- and long-term plans, both nationally and internationally, to sustain the level of success it experienced in the past.

Questions

1. Evaluate Toys "Я" Us' "Concept 2000."
2. What synergies exist between Toys "Я" Us and Baby Superstore?
3. What are the advantages and disadvantages of Toys "Я" Us' strategy of simultaneously pursuing domestic and foreign growth?
4. Comment on Toys "Я" Us' use of standardization in its foreign efforts.
5. Develop a ten-year plan for Toys "Я" Us to pursue in Germany and Japan.
6. What are the benefits of the Japanese market to Toys "Я" Us in contrast to the U.S. market?
7. What lessons can Toys "Я" Us learn from its experiences in Germany and Japan that can be applied to other foreign markets?

Appendix A

Careers in Retailing

A person looking for a career in retailing has two broad possibilities: owning a business or working for an employer. One alternative does not preclude the other. Many people open their own retail businesses after getting experience as employees. A person can also choose franchising, which has elements of both entrepreneurship and managerial assistance. Franchising was discussed in Chapter 4.

Regardless of the specific retail career path chosen, recent college graduates often gain personnel and profit-and-loss responsibilities faster in retailing than in any other major industry. For instance, after an initial training program, an entry-level manager supervises personnel, works on in-store displays, interacts with customers, and reviews sales and other data on a regular basis. An assistant buyer helps in planning merchandise assortments, interacting with suppliers, and outlining the promotion effort. Typically, new merchandise selections must be made at least once every four to six months.

OWNING A BUSINESS

Owning a retail business is popular, and many opportunities exist. Four-fifths of retail outlets are sole proprietorships, and many of today's retail giants began as independents. Wal-Mart, J.C. Penney, Kmart, Filene's, Toys "Я" Us, McDonald's, Sears, and Lillian Vernon illustrate this:

> If you haven't heard of Lillian Vernon, you've been living outside the reach of the U.S. Postal Service. Vernon, a veteran retailer, personifies the American dream. She parlayed $2,000 in wedding money and a $495 advertisement in a 1951 issue of *Seventeen* into a public company that posted $238 million in sales in 1996. Since opening, Lillian Vernon Corp. has flooded the market with nearly one-half billion catalogs. The firm specializes in mom-and-apple-pie merchandise—colorful holiday paraphernalia and personalized doodads of every sort.[1]

People too often overlook the possibility of owning a retail business. Many times, initial investments can be quite modest (several thousand dollars). Direct marketing, direct selling, and service retailing often require relatively low initial investments—as do various franchises. Financing may also be available from banks, manufacturers, store-fixture firms, and equipment companies. Chapter 2 contained a discussion of starting and operating a retail business.

OPPORTUNITIES AS A RETAIL EMPLOYEE

Retailing is a major employer. In the United States, about 21 million people work for traditional retailers. This does not include millions of others employed by firms such as banks, insurance companies, and airlines. By any measure, more people work in retailing than in any other industry.

[1]Jane Applegate, "The Maven of Mail Order," *PriceCostco Connection* (February 1997), p. 23.

Retail career opportunities are plentiful because of the number of new retail businesses opening each year and the labor-intensive nature of retailing. Nationally, thousands of new outlets open every year in the United States. Furthermore, certain segments of retailing are growing at particularly rapid rates. Thus, general merchandise retailers such as Wal-Mart and Kmart plan to open as many as 500 megastores (each being 200,000 square feet in size) by the year 2000.

The increases in employment due to new store openings and the sales growth of retail formats (such as power retailing) also mean there are significant opportunities for personal advancement for talented retail personnel. For instance, each time a chain opens a new outlet, there is a need for a store manager and other management-level people.

Selected retailing positions, career paths, and compensation ranges are described next.

Types of Positions in Retailing

Retailing employment is not confined to buying and merchandising. Career opportunities with retailers also encompass advertising, public relations, credit analysis, marketing research, warehouse management, data processing, personnel management, accounting, and real estate. See Table 1 for a list and description of various retailing positions. From the table, one can see the range of career options available. However, some highly specialized positions may be available only in large retail firms.

To a certain extent, the type of position a person seeks should be matched with the type of retailer likely to have such a position. For example, chain stores and franchises may have real-estate divisions. Department stores and chain stores may have large personnel departments. Mail-order firms may have large advertising production departments. If one is interested in travel, a buying position or a job with a retailer having geographically dispersed operations should be sought.

Career Paths in Retailing

For new college graduates, the executive training programs of larger retailers offer good learning experiences and the potential for substantial advancement. These firms often offer careers in merchandising and nonmerchandising areas.

Here is how a new college graduate could progress through a career path at a typical department store or specialty store chain: He or she usually begins with a training program (which may last for a period ranging from three months to a year or more) on how to run a merchandise department. That program often involves both on-the-job and classroom experiences. On-the-job training usually includes working with merchandise records, reordering stock, planning displays, and supervising salespeople. Classroom activities normally include learning how to evaluate vendors, analyze computer reports, forecast fashion trends, and administer store policy.

At the completion of initial training, the employee becomes an entry-level operations manager (often called a sales manager, assistant department manager, or department manager—depending on the firm) or an assistant buyer. An entry-level manager or assistant buyer works under the direction of a seasoned department (group) manager or buyer and analyzes sales, assists in purchasing goods, handles reorders, and helps in setting up displays. The entry-level manager supervises personnel and learns store operations; the assistant buyer is more involved in purchases than operations. Depending on a retailer's philosophy, either person may follow the same type of career path, or the entry-level operations manager may progress up the store management ladder and the assistant buyer up the buying ladder.

During this time, responsibilities and duties depend on the department (group) manager's or buyer's willingness to delegate and teach. They also depend on the autonomy given to that manager (buyer) to plan and enact a strategy. In a situation where a

Table 1 SELECTED POSITIONS IN RETAILING

Job Title	Description
Accountant (internal)	Records and summarizes the retailer's transactions. Verifies reports. Provides financial information, budgets, forecasts, and comparison reports.
Advertising manager	Develops and implements a retailer's advertising program. Determines media, copy, and message frequency. Recommends advertising budget and choice of advertising agency.
Assistant buyer	Works under the direction of a buyer, usually in a specific product category. Assists in sales analysis, order handling, buying, and setting up displays.
Assistant department manager	Works under the supervision of a department manager. Assists in managing personnel, controlling inventory, and other store operations.
Assistant store manager	Helps in implementing merchandising strategy and policies; interviews, hires, and trains sales personnel; takes inventory; and orders supplies.
Auditor (internal)	Analyzes data, interprets reports, verifies accuracy of data, and monitors adherence to the retailer's regular policies and practices.
Buyer	Devises and controls sales and profit projections for a product category (generally for all stores in a chain); plans proper merchandise assortment, styling, sizes, and quantities; negotiates with and evaluates vendors; and supervises in-store displays.
Catalog manager	Selects merchandise for inclusion in catalogs, works with vendors, orders catalogs, and monitors order fulfillment (particularly timely shipments).
Commercial artist	Creates illustrations, layouts, and types of print to be used in the retailer's advertisements and catalogs, as well as on private-label packages.
Credit manager	Supervises the retailer's credit process, including credit eligibility, credit terms, late payment fees, and consumer credit complaints.
Data-processing manager	Oversees daily operations of a retailer's computer facility. Generates appropriate accounting, credit, financial, inventory, and sales reports. Recommends computer hardware and software for the retailer.
Department manager	Responsible for a department's merchandise displays, analyzing merchandise flow, and the training and direction of the sales staff. Assists buyers in selecting merchandise for branch stores.
District store manager	Responsible for management personnel, sales generation, merchandise presentation, expense control and customer services in all stores in district.
Divisional merchandise manager	Plans, manages, and integrates buying for an entire merchandise division (composed of many departments).
Fashion coordinator	Directs buyers in evaluating fashion trends. Oversees fashion shows.
Fashion director	Responsible for developing and maintaining a retailer's overall fashion perspective.
Franchisee	Purchases a business from a franchisor. Benefits by common format, joint ads, and troubleshooting of franchisor. Decisions constrained by franchisor.
Franchisor	Develops a business format and image, then licenses the right to utilize this format and name to independent businesspeople. Oversees franchises, maintains operating standards, and receives royalty fees.
Group manager	Manages a number of department managers in different merchandise classifications. Trains, supervises, and evaluates these department managers.
Management trainee	First position for most college graduates entering retailing. Involves company orientation, classroom and on-the-job training, and close contact with buyers and group managers. Leads to department manager or assistant buyer.
Marketing research director	Acquires and analyzes relevant and timely data to assist executives in making important decisions. Very involved in methodology and data collection.
Merchandise administrator	Coordinates and evaluates the work of buyers in several related merchandise classifications (in a division).
Merchandise analyst	Plans and evaluates merchandise allocation to stores to ensure items are shipped at the right time, in proper amounts, and in the right assortment. Sets assortment strategy based on trends. Monitors reorder systems.
Merchandise manager	Coordinates selling efforts among different departments (merchandise categories). Acts as liaison between store managers and buyers. Similar to group manager, but there are expanded merchandise responsibilities.

Continued

Table 1 (CONTINUED)

Job Title	Description
Operations manager	Responsible for receiving, checking, marking, and delivering merchandise; customer service; workroom operations; personnel; and maintaining the physical plant of the retailer.
Personnel manager	Devises a personnel policy. Analyzes long-run personnel needs. Recruits, selects, and trains employees. Works on compensation scales and supervision rules.
Public relations director	Keeps the public aware of the retailer's positive accomplishments. Measures public attitudes. Seeks to maintain a favorable image of the company.
Real-estate director	Evaluates retail sites. Negotiates lease or purchase terms. Works with builder on construction projects.
Salesperson	Enables customers to make proper choices. Handles minor complaints. Stocks some merchandise and sets up some displays. Notes understocked items. May also serve as a cashier.
Sales promotion manager	Plans and enacts special sales, themes, and sales promotion tools (such as contests).
Security supervisor	Responsible for minimizing pilferage among employees and customers. Recommends security systems and procedures. Manages a retailer's security personnel.
Senior vice-president for merchandising	Responsible for developing and evaluating all of the merchandise categories for performance. Has direct accountability for growth and profit.
Store manager	Oversees all store personnel and operations in a given outlet. Coordinates activities with other units in a chain. Responsible for customer service; implements merchandising and human resource policies.
Warehouser	Stores and moves goods within a retailer's warehouse. Maintains inventory records and rotates stock.

manager or buyer has authority to make decisions, the entry-level manager or assistant buyer will usually be given more responsibility. If a firm has centralized management, a manager (buyer) is more limited in his or her responsibilities, as is the entry-level manager or assistant buyer. Further, an assistant buyer will gain more experience if he or she is in a firm near a wholesale market center and can make trips to the market to buy merchandise.

The next step in a department store or specialty store chain's career path is a promotion to department (group) manager or buyer. This position can be viewed as entrepreneurial, the running of a business. The manager or buyer selects merchandise, develops a promotional campaign, decides which items to reorder, oversees departmental personnel, and/or supervises record keeping. For some retailers, *manager* and *buyer* are synonymous terms. For others, the distinction is as just explained for entry-level positions. Generally, a person is considered for promotion to manager or buyer after two years.

Large department store and specialty store chains have additional levels of personnel to plan, supervise, and control merchandise departments. On the store management side, there can be group managers, store managers, branch vice-presidents, and others. On the buying side, there can be divisional managers, merchandising vice-presidents, and others.

At many firms, advancement is indicated by specific career paths. This lets employees monitor their performance, know the next career step, and progress in a systematic, clear manner. Selected career paths at Federated Department Stores, PetsMart (a chain of pet supply stores), and Pep Boys (an auto supply and service chain) are shown in Figures 1 through 3. At each succeeding step on the career ladders, a manager gains additional responsibility and authority.

Over the last several years, retailing career opportunities for women have risen dramatically. Women now account for about two-fifths of all retailing executives. Opportunities for women to own retail businesses have also increased in recent years. Since 1989, the number of women owning McDonald's franchises has more than tripled. Furthermore, the number of female-owned proprietorships in wholesaling and retailing has gone up more than 50 percent since 1980.

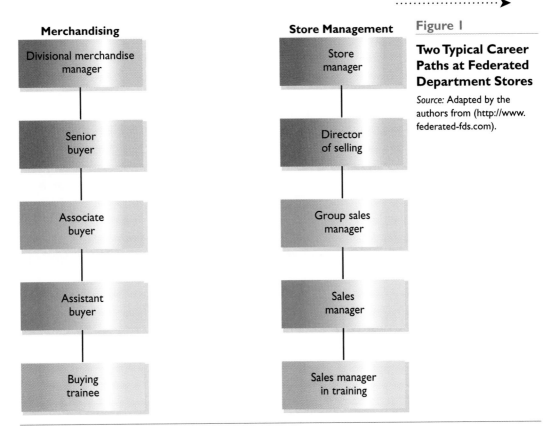

Merchandising

- Divisional merchandise manager
- Senior buyer
- Associate buyer
- Assistant buyer
- Buying trainee

Store Management

- Store manager
- Director of selling
- Group sales manager
- Sales manager
- Sales manager in training

Figure 1

Two Typical Career Paths at Federated Department Stores

Source: Adapted by the authors from (http://www.federated-fds.com).

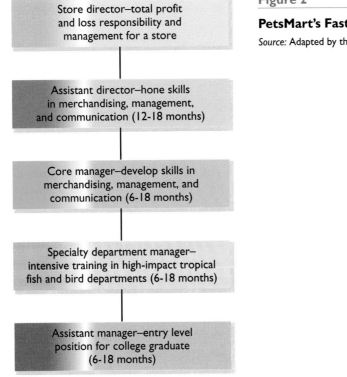

- Store director–total profit and loss responsibility and management for a store
- Assistant director–hone skills in merchandising, management, and communication (12-18 months)
- Core manager–develop skills in merchandising, management, and communication (6-18 months)
- Specialty department manager– intensive training in high-impact tropical fish and bird departments (6-18 months)
- Assistant manager–entry level position for college graduate (6-18 months)

Figure 2

PetsMart's Fast-Track Career Ladder

Source: Adapted by the authors from (http://www.petsmart.com).

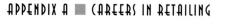

Figure 3

Pep Boys' Executive Career Ladder

Source: Pep Boys. *Reprinted by permission.*

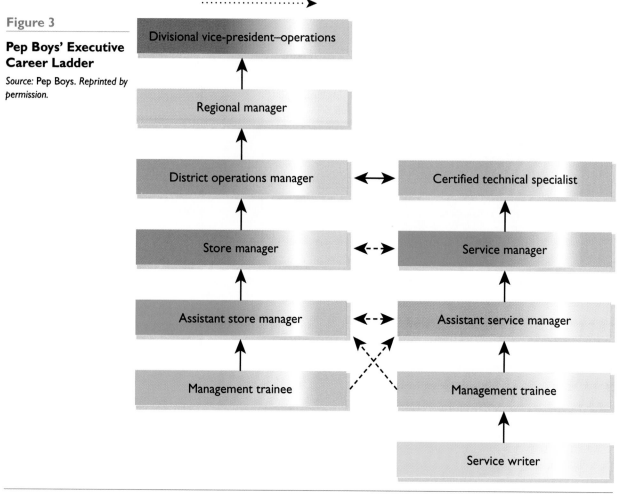

Compensation Ranges in Retailing

Table 2 lists compensation ranges for personnel in a number of retailing positions.

GETTING YOUR FIRST POSITION AS A RETAIL PROFESSIONAL The search for career opportunities, interview preparation, and the evaluation of the options open to you are key steps in getting your first professional position in retailing. It is essential that you devote sufficient time to these steps so your job hunt progresses as quickly and as smoothly as possible.

Searching for Career Opportunities in Retailing

Various sources should be consulted in searching for career opportunities. These sources should include your school's placement office, company directories and Web sites, classified ads in your local newspapers, and networking (with professors, friends, neighbors, and family members).

Here are some hints to consider in searching for career opportunities in retailing:

■ Do not "place all your eggs in one basket." Do not rely too much on a friend or relative to get you a job. A friend or relative may be able to get you an interview, but not a guaranteed job offer.

Table 2 TYPICAL COMPENSATION RANGES FOR PERSONNEL IN SELECTED RETAILING POSITIONS

Position	Compensation Range
Department manager—soft-line retailer	$ 15,000–$ 27,000+
Store management trainee	$ 17,000–$ 28,000+
Assistant buyer	$ 17,000–$ 35,000+
Department manager—department store	$ 17,000–$ 35,000+
Department manager—mass merchandiser	$ 17,000–$ 35,000+
Store manager—specialty store, home center, drugstore	$ 17,000–$ 55,000+
Market research junior analyst	$ 19,000–$ 30,000+
Department manager—hard-line retailer	$ 19,000–$ 35,000+
Store manager—soft-line retailer	$ 21,000–$ 45,000+
Buyer—specialty store, home center, drugstore, department store	$ 24,000–$ 50,000+
Warehouse director	$ 24,000–$ 90,000+
Market research analyst	$ 25,000–$ 40,000+
Buyer—discount store	$ 27,000–$ 50,000+
Market research senior analyst	$ 30,000–$ 50,000+
Market research assistant director	$ 30,000–$ 65,000+
Buyer—national chain	$ 32,000–$ 70,000+
Security director	$ 32,000–$ 70,000+
Store manager—department store	$ 35,000–$ 75,000+
Senior human resources executive	$ 35,000–$ 140,000+
Market research director	$ 35,000–$ 75,000+
Divisional merchandise manager	$ 45,000–$ 85,000+
Senior advertising executive	$ 45,000–$ 110,000+
Operations director	$ 50,000–$ 90,000+
General merchandise manager—drugstore, home center	$ 50,000–$ 90,000+
Senior real-estate executive	$ 50,000–$ 120,000+
General merchandise manager—specialty store, department store	$ 55,000–$ 100,000+
General merchandise manager—discount store, national chain	$ 65,000–$ 125,000+
Senior financial executive	$ 65,000–$ 200,000+
Senior merchandising executive	$ 75,000–$ 250,000+
President	$150,000–$ 800,000+
Chairman of the board	$150,000–$10,000,000+

Source: Estimated by the authors from various publications.

■ Treat your career search in a serious and systematic manner. Plan in advance and do not wait until the recruiting season at your school has started to generate a list of potential retail employers.

■ Use directories with lists of retailers. These include *Careers in Retailing* from *Discount Store News;* the College Placement Council's annual guide; the yearly *Peterson's Business & Management Jobs; Hoover's Handbook of American Business,* which profiles over 500 U.S. companies of all kinds; *Standard & Poor's Register;* and the Yellow Pages in your area. Also consult *Retail Management's* Web site.

■ Rely on the "law of large numbers." In sending out resumés, you may have to write to at least 10 to 20 retailers to get just two to four interviews.

■ Make sure your resumé and accompanying cover letter highlight your most distinctive qualities. These may include school honors, officer status in a key organization, appropriate work experience, special computer expertise, and the proportion of college tuition you paid for yourself. Figure 4 shows a sample resumé geared to an entry-level position in retailing.

■ Show your resumé to at least one professor for his or her reaction. Be receptive to the constructive comments made. Remember, your professor's goal is to help you get the best possible first job.

JENNIFER MARCUS
17 HART DRIVE
WEST HARTFORD, CONNECTICUT 06117
(203) 555-7416

Employment Objective:	Assistant Buyer Position, Formal Training Program Desired
Education:	Bachelor of Business Administration, December 1997
	Hofstra University Hempstead, New York 11550-1090
	Major: Marketing Minor: Psychology
	Class Rank: Top 10%
Scholarships and Awards:	Hofstra University Distinguished Scholar Academic Award
	Dean's List for 6 semesters
	Cum laude graduate
Extracurricular Activities:	Vice-President, Retail Management Society, Spring 1996-Fall 1997
	Responsible for recruitment of members, arranging for guest
	speakers, and budget preparation and control
	Member, American Marketing Association
Computer Skills:	Proficient in Word Perfect; working knowledge of Lotus and SPSS
Work Experience:	
January 1996-present	Assistant to Store Manager, Fashion World
	200 Main Street, Hempstead, New York
	Responsible for setting up displays, providing product information to
	the sales staff, interacting with certain vendors, and handling returns
January 1994-December 1995	Cashier, Thrifty Drug Stores
	Green Fields Shopping Center, Valley Fields, New York
	Responsible for customer transactions, processing credit card sales,
	and restocking shelves
	Paid half of tuition expenses by working 20 hours per week while
	attending college
Personal:	Willing to relocate
	Hobbies include photography and personal computers
References:	Will be furnished upon request

Figure 4

A Sample Resumé

Preparing for the Interview

The initial and subsequent interviews for a retail position, which may last for 20 to 30 minutes or longer, play a large part in determining if you are offered a job. For that reason, it is necessary that you prepare properly for all interviews. Consider the following hints:

■ Adequately research each firm. Be aware of its goods/service category, current size, overall retail strategy, competitive developments, and so on.

■ Anticipate such questions as these and plan general responses in advance: "Tell me about yourself." "Why are you interested in a retailing career?" "Why do you want a job with us?" "What are your major strengths?" "What are your major weaknesses?" "What do you want to be doing five years from now?" "Are you willing to relocate?" "Which college courses did you like most?" "Which courses did you like least?" "What would your previous employers say about you?" In pre-interview preparation, role-play your answers to these questions with someone. Listen to his or her comments.

■ Get ready for every interview as if it is the most important one you will be having. Otherwise, you may not be properly prepared if the position turns out to be more desirable than you originally felt. Also, keep in mind that you represent both your college and yourself at all interviews you go on.

■ Be prepared to raise your own pertinent questions when asked to do so in the interview. Such questions should relate to career paths, training programs, and opportunities for advancement.

■ Dress appropriately and be well groomed.

■ Verify the date and place of the interview. Be prompt.

■ Have a pen and pad available to record key information after the interview has been completed.

■ Write a note to the interviewer within a week after the interview to thank him or her for spending time with you and to express a continuing interest in the company.

Evaluating Retail Career Opportunities

Job seekers often place too much emphasis on initial salary or the firm's image (as to fashion orientation or target market) in assessing career opportunities. Many other factors should be considered.

There are several key issues to ponder while deciding what career opportunity to pursue. These questions should be linked to the attributes of each specific job offer you may receive:

■ What activities do you like undertaking?

■ What are your personal strengths and weaknesses?

■ What are your current and long-term goals?

■ Do you want to work for an independent, a chain, or a franchise operation?

■ Does the opportunity offer an acceptable and clear career path?

■ Does the opportunity include a formal training program?

■ Will the opportunity enable you to be rewarded for good performance?

■ Will you have to relocate?

■ Will each promotion in the company result in greater authority and responsibility?

■ Is the compensation level fair relative to other offers?

■ Can a superior employee move up the career path significantly faster than an average one?

■ If ownership of a retail firm is a long-term goal, which opportunity provides the best preparation?

B

About the Web Site That Accompanies *Retail Management*

(http://www.prenhall.com/rm_student)

Accompanying *Retail Management: A Strategic Approach* is a Web site that includes everything from career data to a comprehensive listing of company sites on the World Wide Web. Once you have connected to the Internet, it is designed to run on your Web browser (such as Netscape or Internet Explorer).

The Web site is user-friendly, interactive, real-world-based, and keyed to the concepts covered in *Retail Management.* In this appendix, we describe how to use the Web site and present an overview of each of its six components.

DIRECTIONS FOR USE

To utilize the Web site, you need to be connected to the Internet and have access to a Web browser such as Netscape or Internet Explorer. You will also need a printer if you want to reproduce material for your own reference or for class submissions.

Follow these steps:

- After booting up your computer, connect to the Internet and access your Web browser.
- From within your browser, enter the Web site by going to the OPEN menu at the top of the browser screen and typing the address (http://www.prenhall.com/rm_student).
- Print any file by going to the FILE menu at the top of the screen and clicking on the word PRINT. (You can also click on the printer icon on the menu bar.) You can print one screen or all the screens in a file.
- The first time you use the Web site (or if you have questions later on), be sure to read the information at the home page. You should print this material for later reference.
- From the menu screen, you can click your mouse on the icon of any of the components of the Web site. You then enter into that specific program.
- All descriptions, instructions, exercise questions, and so forth appear at the home page or in the programs and can be quickly and simply accessed and printed.

WEB SITE COMPONENTS

Interactive Study Guide

There is a detailed study guide for *Retail Management.* It enables you to review concepts and prepare for exams. There are chapter summaries, chapter-by-chapter listings of key terms, and 20 multiple choice, 20 true-false, and 15 fill-in questions per chapter (with answers and text page references). By looking up the text page references, you can study the topics that are giving you trouble. Also you can look at the glossary section to further brush up on key terms.

Web Site Directory

This section lists hundreds of retailing-related Web sites, divided by topic. The sites range from search engines to government agencies, retail firms to trade associations, and so forth. There are special groupings by retailer type (such as department stores and apparel firms).

Glossary

The glossary includes all of the key terms cited in *Retail Management*. The terms may be accessed alphabetically by typing in the relevant words.

Career Information

There is advice on resumé writing, how to take an interview, jobs in retailing, retail career ladders, and a comprehensive listing with the names and addresses of retail employers (over 500 companies). There are materials from the U.S. Bureau of Labor Statistics' *1996–97 Occupational Outlook Handbook,* real company career paths, and more. We even include a template from Syms (a leading off-price apparel chain) on how to build a resumé.

Computer Exercises

Sixteen text-based exercises, noted by a computer symbol throughout *Retail Management,* can be downloaded from our Web site. Look at our site's home page for more information on installing and running the exercises. The program is complete with help screens, instructions, and questions. The exercises are divided by part:

■ **Part 1**
   1. Store Positioning (Chapter 2)

■ **Part 2**
   2. Franchising (Chapter 4)
   3. Wheel of Retailing (Chapter 5)
   4. Scrambled Merchandising (Chapter 5)
   5. Direct Marketing (Chapter 6)

■ **Part 3**
   6. Attitude Survey (Chapter 8)

■ **Part 4**
   7. Reilly's Law (Chapter 9)
   8. Buying Power Index (Chapter 9)
   9. Trading Area Saturation (Chapter 9)

■ **Part 5**
  10. Strategic Profit Model (Chapter 12)
  11. Key Business Ratios (Chapter 12)
  12. Budgeting and Cash Flow (Chapter 12)

■ **Part 6**
  13. Retail Method of Accounting (Chapter 15)
  14. Open-to-Buy (Chapter 15)

■ **Part 7**
  15. Seasonal Promotional Planning (Chapter 18)

■ **Part 8**
  16. Sales Opportunity Grid (Chapter 20)

Real-World Software Packages

You can download demonstration versions of four actual software packages used by retailers. Look at the site's home page for more information on installing and running the software packages. These packages are all being marketed to retailers today:

- *Atlas from Claritas.* It gives a graphic tour of an Atlas software GIS system.
- *B-Coder from TAL Enterprises.* It shows how bar codes can be generated and printed out by retailers.
- *PCensus-USA from Tetrad.* It shows how demographic data can be tied to a GIS system. There are data from the 1990 Census and updates from Equifax National Decision Systems (which classifies households into 50 market segments).
- *PSearch-USA from Tetrad.* It enables retailers to locate counties, census tracts, block groups, or zip codes with particular life-style and demographic profiles.

Additional Markup An increase in a retail price above the original markup that is used when demand is unexpectedly high or when costs are rising.

Additional Markup Percentage Looks at total dollar additional markups as a percentage of net sales:

$$\frac{\text{Additional markup}}{\text{percentage}} = \frac{\text{Total dollar additional markups}}{\text{Net sales (in \$)}}$$

Addition to Retail Percentage Measures a price rise as a percentage of original price:

$$\text{Addition to retail percentage} = \frac{\text{New price} - \text{Original price}}{\text{Original price}}$$

Advertising Any paid, nonpersonal communication transmitted through out-of-store mass media by an identified sponsor.

Affinity Exists when the various stores at a given location complement, blend, and cooperate with one another, and each benefits from the others' presence.

All-You-Can-Afford Method A promotional budgeting technique in which a retailer first allots funds for each element of the retail strategy mix except promotion. Whatever funds are left over are placed in a promotional budget.

Analog Model A computer site-selection tool in which potential sales are estimated on the basis of existing store revenues in similar areas, the competition at a prospective location, the new store's expected market shares at that location, and the size and density of the location's primary trading area.

Ancillary Customer Services Extra elements that enhance a retail strategy mix. They do not have to be provided.

Application Blank The first tool used to screen applicants. It provides data on education, experience, health, reasons for leaving prior jobs, organizational memberships, hobbies, and references.

Assets Any items a retailer owns with a monetary value.

Asset Turnover A performance measure based on a retailer's net sales and total assets. It is equal to net sales divided by total assets.

Assortment Display An interior display in which a retailer exhibits a wide range of merchandise for the customer. It may be open or closed.

Atmosphere Refers to a store's physical characteristics that are used to develop an image and draw customers.

Atmospherics *See* Atmosphere.

Attitudes (Opinions) The positive, neutral, or negative feelings a person has about the economy, politics, goods, services, institutions, and so on.

Audit Form Lists the area(s) to be examined and the exact information required in evaluating each area.

Automatic Markdown Plan Controls the amount and timing of markdowns on the basis of the length of time merchandise remains in stock.

Automatic Reordering System Orders merchandise when stock-on-hand reaches a pre-determined reorder point. An automatic reorder can be generated by a computer on the basis of a perpetual inventory system and reorder point calculations.

Bait Advertising An illegal practice whereby a retailer lures a customer by advertising goods and services at exceptionally low prices; then, once the customer contacts the retailer, he or she is told the good/service of interest is out of stock or of inferior quality. A salesperson tries to convince the customer to purchase a better, more expensive substitute that is available. The retailer has no intention of selling the advertised item.

Bait-and-Switch Advertising *See* Bait Advertising.

Balanced Tenancy Occurs when stores in a planned shopping center complement each other in the quality and variety of their product offerings. The kind and number of stores are linked to the overall needs of the surrounding population.

Balance Sheet Itemizes a retailer's assets, liabilities, and net worth at a specific point in time; it is based on the principle that assets equal liabilities plus net worth.

Basic Stock List Specifies the inventory level, color, brand, style category, size, package, and so on for every staple item carried by the retailer.

Basic Stock Method An inventory-level planning tool wherein a retailer carries more items than it expects to sell over a specified period:

Basic stock = Average monthly stock at retail − Average monthly sales

Battle of the Brands When retailers and manufacturers compete for shelf space allocated to various brands and for control over display locations.

Benchmarking Occurs when the retailer sets its own standards and measures performance based on the achievements of its sector of retailing, specific competitors, high-performance firms, and/or the prior actions of the company itself.

Bifurcated Retailing Denotes the decline of middle-of-the-market retailing due to the popularity of both mass merchandising and positioned retailing.

Book Inventory System Keeps a running total of the value of all inventory on hand at cost at a given time. This is done by regularly recording purchases and adding them to existing inventory value; sales transactions are then subtracted to arrive at the new current inventory value (all at cost).

Bottom-Up Space Management Approach Exists when planning starts at the individual product level and then proceeds to the category, total store, and overall company levels.

Box (Limited-Line) Store A food-based discounter that focuses on a small selection of items, moderate hours of operation (compared to supermarkets), few services, and limited national brands.

BPI *See* Buying Power Index.

Budgeting Outlines a retailer's planned expenditures for a given time period based on its expected performance.

Bundled Pricing Involves a retailer providing a number of services for one basic price.

Business Format Franchising An arrangement in which the franchisee receives assistance on site location, quality control, accounting systems, startup practices, management training, and responding to problems—besides the right to sell goods and services.

Buying Power Index (BPI) A measure of a geographic area's market characteristics, expressed as:

BPI = 0.5 (the area's percentage of U.S. effective buying income)
+ 0.3 (the area's percentage of U.S. retail sales)
+ 0.2 (the area's percentage of U.S. population)

Canned Sales Presentation A memorized, repetitive speech given to all customers interested in a particular item.

Capital Expenditures Retail expenditures that are long-term investments in fixed assets.

Case Display Employed to exhibit heavier, bulkier items than racks hold.

Cash Flow Relates the amount and timing of revenues received to the amount and timing of expenditures made during a specific time period.

Category Killer Store An especially large specialty store featuring an enormous selection in its product category and relatively low prices. It draws consumers from wide geographic areas.

Category Management A relationship-oriented technique that some firms, especially supermarkets, are beginning to use to improve shelf-space productivity.

CBD *See* Central Business District.

Census of Population Supplies a wide range of demographic data for all U.S. cities and surrounding vicinities. Data are organized on a geographic basis.

Central Business District (CBD) The hub of retailing in a city. It is the largest shopping area in that city and is synonymous with the term "downtown." The CBD exists where there is the greatest concentration of office buildings and retail stores.

Centralized Buying Organization Occurs when a retailer has all purchase decisions emanating from one office.

Chain Multiple retail units under common ownership that engage in some level of centralized (or coordinated) purchasing and decision making.

Channel Control Occurs when one member of a distribution channel can dominate the decisions made in that channel by the power it possesses.

Channel of Distribution Comprises all of the businesses and people involved in the physical movement and transfer of ownership of goods and services from producer to consumer.

Class Consciousness The extent to which a person desires and pursues social status.

Classification Merchandising Allows firms to obtain more financial data by subdividing each specified department into further categories for related types of merchandise.

COD (Collect on Delivery) Lets customers have products delivered to them before payment is made.

Cognitive Dissonance Doubt that occurs after a purchase is made, which can be alleviated by customer after-care, money-back guarantees, and realistic sales presentations and advertising campaigns.

Collect on Delivery *See* COD.

Combination Store Unites supermarket and general merchandise sales in one facility, with general merchandise typically accounting for 25 percent to 40 percent of total store sales.

Community Shopping Center A moderate-sized, planned shopping facility with a branch department store, a variety store, and/or a category killer store, in addition to several smaller stores. About 20,000 to 100,000 people, who live or work within 10 to 20 minutes of the center, are served by this location.

Comparative Advertising Messages comparing a retailer's offerings with those of competitors.

Compensation Includes direct monetary payments (such as salaries, commissions, and bonuses) and indirect payments (such as paid vacations, health and life insurance benefits, and retirement plans).

Competition-Oriented Pricing An approach in which a retailer sets its prices in accordance with competitors'.

Competitive Advantages The distinct competencies of a retailer relative to competitors.

Competitive Parity Method A promotional budgeting technique by which a retailer's budget is raised or lowered based on the actions of competitors.

Competitive Pricing A marketing-oriented strategy whereby a service retailer sets its prices on the basis of the prices charged by competitors.

Computerized Checkout Enables retailers to efficiently process transactions and have strict inventory control. In a UPC-based system, cashiers manually ring up sales or pass items over or past optical scanners. Computerized registers instantly record and display sales, customers get detailed receipts, and all inventory data are stored in a computer memory bank.

Concentrated Marketing Selling goods and services to one specific group.

Consignment Purchase Items not paid for by retailer until they are sold. The retailer can return unsold merchandise. Title is not taken by the retailer until the final sale is completed.

Constrained Decision Making Excludes franchisees from or limits their involvement in the strategic planning process.

Consumer Behavior Involves the process by which people determine whether, what, when, where, how, from whom, and how often to purchase goods and services.

Consumer Cooperative A retail firm owned by its customer members. A group of consumers invests in the company, receives stock certificates, elects officers, manages operations, and shares the profits or savings that accrue.

Consumer Decision Process The stages a consumer goes through in buying a good or service: stimulus, problem awareness, information search, evaluation of alternatives, purchase, and post-purchase behavior. Demographics and life-style factors affect this decision process.

Consumerism Involves the activities of government, business, and independent organizations that are designed to protect individuals from practices infringing upon their rights as consumers.

Contingency Pricing An arrangement whereby the retailer does not get paid until after the service is performed, and payment is contingent on the service's being satisfactory.

Control The phase in the evaluation of a firm's strategy and tactics in which a semiannual or annual review of the company takes place.

Controllable Variables Those aspects of business that the retailer can directly affect (such as hours of operation and sales personnel).

Control Units Merchandise categories for which data are gathered.

Convenience Store A food-oriented retailer that is well located, is open long hours, and carries a moderate number of items. It is small, has average to above-average prices, and average atmosphere and customer services.

Conventional Supermarket A departmentalized food store that emphasizes a wide range of food and related products; sales of general merchandise are rather limited.

Cooperative Advertising Occurs when a manufacturer or wholesaler and a retailer, or two or more retailers, share advertising costs.

Cooperative Buying The procedure used when a group of independent retailers gets together to make quantity purchases from a supplier.

Core Customers Consumers with whom retailers should seek to nurture long relationships. They should be singled out in a firm's data base.

Corporation A retail firm that is formally incorporated under state law. It is a legal entity apart from individual officers (or stockholders).

Cost Complement The average relationship of cost to retail value for all merchandise available for sale during a given time period.

Cost Method of Accounting Requires the retailer's cost of every item to be recorded on an accounting sheet and/or coded on a price tag or merchandise container. When a physical inventory is conducted, every item's cost must be ascertained, the quantity of every item in stock counted, and the total inventory value at cost calculated.

Cost of Goods Sold The amount a retailer has paid to acquire the merchandise sold during a given time period. It equals the cost of merchandise available for sale minus the cost value of ending inventory.

Cost-Oriented Pricing An approach in which a retailer sets a price floor, the minimum price acceptable to the firm so it can reach a specified profit goal. A retailer usually computes merchandise and retail operating costs and adds a profit margin to these figures.

Cost-Plus Pricing Occurs when a retailer adds its costs to desired profit margins to derive selling prices.

Credit Management Involves the policies and practices retailers follow in receiving payments from their customers.

Cross-Training Enables personnel to learn tasks associated with more than one job.

Culture A distinctive heritage shared by a group of people. It influences the importance of family, work, education, and other concepts by passing on a series of beliefs, norms, and customs.

Curving (Free-Flowing) Traffic Flow Presents displays and aisles in a free-flowing pattern.

Customary Pricing A pricing strategy whereby a retailer sets prices for goods and services and seeks to maintain them for an extended period.

Customer Loyalty (Frequent Shopper) Programs Intended to reward a retailer's best customers, the ones with whom it wants to form long-lasting relationships.

Customer Service Refers to the identifiable, but sometimes intangible, activities undertaken by a retailer in conjunction with the basic goods and services it sells.

Customer Space The area required by shoppers that contributes greatly to a store's atmosphere. It can include a lounge, benches and/or chairs, dressing rooms, rest rooms, a restaurant, vertical transportation, a nursery, parking, and wide aisles.

Cut Case An inexpensive display, in which merchandise is left in the original carton.

Data Analysis The stage in the research process which assesses secondary and/or primary data and relates it to the defined issue or problem.

Data-Base Management The procedure used to gather, integrate, apply, and store information related to specific subject areas. It is a key element in a retail information system.

Data-Base Retailing A way of collecting, storing, and using relevant information on customers.

Data Warehousing A new advance in data-base management whereby copies of all the data bases in a company are maintained in one location and can be assessed by employees at any locale.

Dead Areas Awkward spaces where normal displays cannot be set up.

Dealer Brands *See* Private Brands.

Debit-Card System A computerized system whereby the price of a good or service is immediately deducted from a consumer's bank account and entered into a retailer's account.

Decentralized Buying Organization Lets purchase decisions be made locally or regionally.

Deferred Billing Enables customers to make purchases and not pay for them for several months, without interest.

Demand-Oriented Pricing An approach by which a retailer sets prices based on consumer desires. It determines the range of prices acceptable to the target market.

Demographics Objective and quantifiable population data that are easily identifiable and measurable.

Department Store A large retail unit with an extensive assortment (width and depth) of goods and services that is organized into separate departments for purposes of buying, promotion, customer service, and control.

Depth of Assortment Refers to the variety in any one goods/service category with which a retailer is involved.

Destination Retailer A retailer to whom consumers will make a special shopping trip. The destination may be a store, a catalog, or a Web site.

Destination Store A retail outlet with a trading area much larger than that of a competitor with a less unique appeal to customers. It offers a better merchandise assortment in its product category(ies), promotes more extensively, and creates a stronger image.

Differentiated Marketing Aiming at two or more distinct consumer groups, with different retailing approaches for each group.

Direct Marketing A form of retailing in which a customer is first exposed to a good or service through a nonpersonal medium and then orders by mail or phone—sometimes, by computer.

Direct Product Profitability (DPP) Calculated when a retailer finds the profitability of each category or unit of merchandise by computing adjusted per-unit gross margin and assigning direct product costs for expense categories such as warehousing, transportation, handling, and selling. It equals an item's gross profit less its direct retailing costs.

Direct Selling Includes both personal contact with consumers in their homes (and other nonstore locations such as offices) and phone solicitations initiated by a retailer.

Direct Store Distribution (DSD) Exists when retailers have at least some goods shipped directly from suppliers to individual stores. It works best with retailers that also utilize EDI.

Discretionary Income Money left after paying taxes and buying necessities.

Disguised Survey A technique in which the respondent is not told the real purpose of a research study.

Distributed Promotion Effort Used by retailers that promote throughout the year.

Diversification The way in which retailers become active in business outside their normal operations—and add different goods and/or service categories.

Diversified Retailer A multiline merchandising firm under central ownership. It is also known as a retail conglomerate or conglomerchant.

Diversionary Pricing A practice used by deceptive service firms. A low price is stated for one or a few services (emphasized in promotion) to give the illusion that all prices are low.

Dollar Control Involves planning and monitoring a retailer's financial investment in merchandise over a stated time period.

Downsizing Exists when unprofitable stores are closed or divisions are sold off by retailers dissatisfied with their performance.

DPP *See* Direct Product Profitability.

DSD *See* Direct Store Distribution.

Dual Vertical Marketing System Involves firms involved in more than one type of distribution arrangement. This enables those firms to appeal to different consumers, increase revenues, share some of their costs, and maintain a good degree of control over their strategy.

Dump Bin A case display that houses piles of sale clothing, marked-down books, or other products.

Ease of Entry Occurs for retailers due to low capital requirements and no, or relatively simple, licensing provisions.

EBI *See* Effective Buying Income.

Economic Base Refers to an area's industrial and commercial structure—the companies and industries that residents depend on to earn a living.

Economic Order Quantity (EOQ) The quantity per order (in units) that minimizes the total costs of processing orders and holding inventory:

$$EOQ = \sqrt{\frac{2DS}{IC}}$$

where

EOQ = Economic order quantity (in units)
D = Annual demand (in units)
S = Costs to place an order (in dollars)
I = Percentage of annual carrying cost to unit cost
C = Unit cost of an item (in dollars)

ECR *See* Efficient Consumer Response.

EDI *See* Electronic Data Interchange.

Editor & Publisher Market Guide Provides considerable economic base data for cities on a yearly basis. It also contains statistics on population size and total households by city.

EDLP *See* Everyday Low Pricing.

Effective Buying Income (EBI) Personal income (wages, salaries, interest, dividends, profits, rental income, and pension income) minus federal, state, and local taxes and nontax payments (such as personal contributions for social security insurance). It is commonly known as disposable personal income.

Efficient Consumer Response (ECR) A form of logistics management through which supermarkets are incorporating aspects of quick response inventory planning, electronic data interchange, and logistics planning.

Electronic Article Surveillance Involves attaching specially designed tags or labels to products.

Electronic Banking Involves both the use of automatic teller machines (ATMs) and the instant processing of retail purchases.

Electronic Data Interchange (EDI) Lets retailers and suppliers regularly exchange information through their computers with regard to inventory levels, delivery times, unit sales, and so on, of particular items.

Electronic Point-of-Sale System Performs all tasks of a computerized checkout and also verifies check and charge transactions, provides instantaneous sales reports, monitors and changes prices, sends intra- and interstore messages, evaluates personnel and profitability, and stores data.

Employee Empowerment A method of improving customer service in which workers have discretion to do what they believe is necessary—within reason—to satisfy the customer, even if this means bending some company rules.

Ensemble Display An interior display whereby coordinated merchandise is grouped and displayed together.

EOQ *See* Economic Order Quantity.

Equal Store Organization Centralizes the buying function. The branches become sales units with equal operational status.

Ethics Let a retailer act in a trustworthy, fair, honest, and respectful manner with each of its constituencies.

Evaluation of Alternatives The stage in the decision process where a consumer selects one good or service to buy from a list of alternatives.

Everyday Low Pricing (EDLP) A version of customary pricing, whereby a retailer strives to sell its goods and services at consistently low prices throughout the selling season.

Exclusive Distribution Takes place when suppliers enter into agreements with one or a few retailers that designate the latter as the only companies in specified geographic areas to carry certain brands and/or product lines.

Experiment A type of research in which one or more elements of a retail strategy mix are manipulated under controlled conditions.

Extended Decision Making Occurs when a consumer makes full use of the decision process, usually for expensive, complex goods and services with which the consumer has had little or no experience.

External Secondary Data Available from sources outside a firm.

Factory Outlet A manufacturer-owned store selling that firm's closeouts, discontinued merchandise, irregulars, canceled orders, and, sometimes, in-season, first-quality merchandise.

Family Life Cycle Describes how a traditional family evolves from bachelorhood to children to solitary retirement.

Feedback Signals or cues as to the success or failure of part of a retail strategy.

FIFO Method Logically assumes old merchandise is sold first, while newer items remain in inventory. It matches inventory value with the current cost structure.

Financial Leverage A performance measure based on the relationship between a retailer's total assets and net worth. It is equal to total assets divided by net worth.

Financial Merchandise Management Occurs when a retailer specifies exactly which products are purchased, when products are purchased, and how many products are purchased.

Fixed Pricing Exists in situations where a branch of government has some degree of control and retailers must conform to a stated price structure.

Flat Organization A firm with many subordinates reporting to one supervisor.

Flea Market Has many retail vendors offering a range of products at discount prices in plain surroundings. Many flea markets are located in nontraditional sites not normally associated with retailing. They may be indoor or outdoor.

Flexible Pricing A strategy that allows consumers to bargain over selling prices; those consumers who are good at bargaining obtain lower prices than those who are not.

Floor-Ready Merchandise Items that are received at the store in condition to be put directly on display without any preparation by retail workers.

Food-Based Superstore A retailer that is larger and more diversified than a conventional supermarket but usually smaller and less diversified than a combination store. It caters to consumers' complete grocery needs and offers them the ability to buy fill-in general merchandise.

Formal Buying Organization Views the merchandise-buying function as a distinct retail task; a separate department is set up.

Franchising Involves a contractual arrangement between a franchisor (a manufacturer, a wholesaler, or a service sponsor) and a retail franchisee, which allows the franchisee to conduct a given form of business under an established name and according to a given pattern of business.

Free-Flowing Traffic Flow *See* Curving Traffic Flow.

Frequency The average number of times each person who is reached is exposed to a retailer's ads in a specific period.

Frequent Shopper Programs *See* Customer Loyalty Programs.

Fringe Trading Area Includes the customers not found in primary and secondary trading areas. These are the most widely dispersed customers.

Full-Line Discount Store A type of department store characterized by (1) a broad merchandise assortment; (2) centralized checkout service; (3) merchandise normally sold by self-service with minimal assistance; (4) no catalog order service; (5) private-brand nondurable goods and well-known manufacturer-brand durable goods; (6) hard goods accounting for a much greater percentage of sales than at traditional department stores; (7) a relatively inexpensive building, equipment, and fixtures; and (8) less emphasis on credit sales than in full-service stores.

Functional Product Groupings Categorize and display a store's merchandise by common end uses.

Gap Analysis Enables a company to compare its actual performance against its potential performance, and then determine the areas in which it must improve.

Generic Brands No-frills goods stocked by some retailers. These items usually receive secondary shelf locations, have little or no promotion support, are sometimes of less overall quality than other brands, are stocked in limited assortments, and have plain packages.

Geographic Information Systems (GIS) Combine digitized mapping with key locational data to graphically depict such trading-area characteristics as the demographics of the population, data on customer purchases, and listings of current, proposed, and competitor locations.

Geographic Mapping A technique used by retailers in evaluating the trading area of a store. With it, a firm learns the distances people are apt to travel to get to a store, the population density of the geographic area surrounding the store, and the travel patterns and times from various sites.

GIS *See* Geographic Information Systems.

GMROI *See* Gross Margin Return on Investment.

Goal-Oriented Job Description Enumerates a position's basic functions, the relationship of each job to overall goals, the interdependence of positions, and information flows.

Goods Retailing Focuses on the sale of tangible (physical) products.

Goods/Service Category A retail firm's line of business.

Graduated Lease Calls for precise rent increases over a specified period of time.

Gravity Model A computer site-selection model based on the premise that people are drawn to stores that are closer and more attractive than competitors'.

Gray Market Goods Brand-name products purchased in foreign markets or goods transshipped from other retailers. They are often sold at low prices by unauthorized dealers.

Gridiron Traffic Flow *See* Straight Traffic Flow.

Gross Margin The difference between net sales and the total cost of goods sold. Also known as Gross Profit.

Gross Margin Return on Investment (GMROI) Shows the relationship between total dollar operating profits and the average inventory investment (at cost) by combining profitability and sales-to-stock measures:

$$\text{GMROI} = \frac{\text{Gross margin in dollars}}{\text{Net sales}} \times \frac{\text{Net sales}}{\text{Average inventory at cost}}$$

$$= \frac{\text{Gross margin in dollars}}{\text{Average inventory at cost}}$$

Gross Profit The difference between net sales and the cost of goods sold. Also known as Gross Margin.

Herzberg's Theory Says the factors involved in producing job satisfaction and motivation (satisfiers) differ from those leading to job dissatisfaction (dissatisfiers).

Hidden Assets Depreciated assets, such as store buildings and warehouses, that are reflected on a retailer's balance sheet at low values relative to their actual worth.

Hierarchy of Authority Outlines the job relationships within a company by describing the reporting relationships among employees. Coordination and control are provided.

Hierarchy-of-Effects Model The sequence of steps a consumer goes through in reacting to a retailer's communication efforts that leads him or her from awareness to knowledge to liking to preference to conviction to a purchase.

Horizontal Cooperative-Advertising Agreement Enables two or more retailers (usually small, situated together, or franchisees of the same company) to share an ad.

Horizontal Price Fixing Involves agreements among manufacturers, among wholesalers, or among retailers to set prices. This is regardless of how "reasonable" resultant prices may be.

Horizontal Retail Audit Involves analyzing a retail firm's overall performance, from its organizational mission to goals to customer satisfaction to basic retail strategy mix and its implementation in an integrated, consistent way.

Household Life Cycle Incorporates life stages of both family and nonfamily households.

Huff's Law of Shopper Attraction Delineates trading areas on the basis of the product assortment carried at various shopping locations, travel times from the consumer's home to alternative shopping locations, and the sensitivity of the kind of shopping to travel time.

Human Resource Management Involves the recruitment, selection, training, compensation, and supervision of personnel in a manner consistent with the retailer's organization structure and strategy mix.

Human Resource Management Process Consists of these interrelated personnel activities: recruitment, selection, training, compensation, and supervision. The goals are to obtain, develop, and retain employees.

Image Represents how a given retailer is perceived by consumers and others.

Implementation The stage in the research process during which recommendations are put into practice.

Impulse Purchases Occur when consumers purchase products and/or brands they had not planned on buying before entering a store, reading a mail-order catalog, seeing a TV shopping show, tuning to the World Wide Web, and so on.

Income Statement *See* Profit-and-Loss Statement.

Incremental Budgeting The process whereby a firm uses current and past budgets as guides and adds or subtracts from these budgets to arrive at the coming period's expenditures.

Incremental Method A promotional budgeting technique by which a percentage is either added to or subtracted from one year's budget to determine the next year's.

Independent A retailer that owns only one retail unit.

Infomercial A program-length TV advertisement (most often, 30 minutes in length) for a specific good or service that airs on cable television or on broadcast television at a fringe time. It is particularly worthwhile for products that benefit from visual demonstrations.

Informal Buying Organization Does not view merchandising as a distinct retail function; the same personnel handle both merchandising and other retail tasks.

Information Search Consists of two parts: determining the alternative goods or services that will solve the problem at hand (and where they can be bought) and ascertaining the characteristics of each alternative. Search may be internal or external.

Initial Markup (at Retail) Based on the original retail value assigned to merchandise less the merchandise costs, expressed as a percentage of the original retail price:

$$\text{Initial markup percentage (at retail)} = \frac{\text{Planned retail operating expenses + Planned profit + Planned retail reductions}}{\text{Planned net sales + Planned retail reductions}}$$

Inside Buying Organization Staffed by a retailer's own personnel; merchandise decisions are made by permanent employees of the firm.

Intensive Distribution Takes place when suppliers sell through as many retailers as possible. This arrangement usually maximizes suppliers' sales; and it enables retailers to offer many brands and product versions.

Internal Secondary Data Available within a company.

Internet A global electronic superhighway of computer networks that use a common protocol and are linked by telecommunications lines and satellite.

Inventory Management Involves a retailer seeking to acquire and maintain a proper merchandise assortment while ordering, shipping, handling, and related costs are kept in check.

Inventory Shrinkage Involves employee theft, customer shoplifting, and vendor fraud.

Isolated Store A freestanding retail outlet located on either a highway or a street. There are no adjacent retailers with which this type of store shares traffic.

Issue (Problem) Definition A step in the marketing research process that involves a clear statement of the topic to be studied.

Item Price Removal A practice whereby prices are marked only on shelves or signs and not on individual items. This practice is banned in several states and local communities.

Job Analysis Consists of gathering data about each job's functions and requirements: duties, responsibilities, aptitude, interest, education, experience, and physical condition.

Job Motivation The drive within people to attain work-related goals.

Job Standardization Keeps the tasks of personnel with similar positions in different departments, such as cashiers and stockpeople in clothing and candy departments, rather uniform.

Layaway Plan Allows customers to give a retailer deposits to hold products. When customers complete payments, they take the items.

LBO *See* Leveraged Buyout.

Leader Pricing Occurs when a retailer advertises and sells selected items in its goods/service assortment at less than usual profit margins. The goal is to increase customer traffic in the hope of selling regularly priced goods and services in addition to the specially priced items.

Leased Department A department in a retail store—usually a department, discount, or specialty store—that is rented to an outside party.

Leveraged Buyout (LBO) An ownership change that is mostly financed by loans from banks, investors, and others.

Liabilities Any financial obligations a retailer incurs in operating a business.

Life-Styles The ways in which individual consumers and families (households) live and spend time and money.

LIFO Method Assumes new merchandise is sold first, while older stock remains in inventory. It matches current sales with the current cost structure.

Limited Decision Making Occurs when a consumer uses each of the steps in the purchase process but does not need to spend a great deal of time on each of them.

Limited-Line Store *See* Box Store.

Logistics The total process of moving goods from a manufacturer to a customer in the most timely and cost-efficient manner possible.

Loss Leaders Items priced below cost to lure more customer traffic. Loss leaders are restricted by state minimum-price laws.

Maintained Markup (at Retail) Based on the actual prices received for merchandise sold during a time period less merchandise cost, expressed as a percentage:

$$\text{Maintained markup percentage (at retail)} = \frac{\text{Actual retail operating expenses} + \text{Actual profit}}{\text{Actual net sales}}$$

or

$$\frac{\text{Average selling price} - \text{Merchandise cost}}{\text{Average selling price}}$$

Maintenance-Increase-Recoupment Lease Has a provision allowing for rent increases if a property owner's taxes, heating bills, insurance, or other expenses rise beyond a certain point.

Manufacturer (National) Brands Produced and controlled by manufacturers. They are usually well known, are supported by manufacturer ads, are somewhat pre-sold to consumers, require limited retailer investment, and often represent maximum product quality to consumers.

Markdown A reduction from selling price to meet the lower price of another retailer, adapt to inventory overstocking, clear out shopworn merchandise, reduce assortments of odds and ends, and increase customer traffic.

Markdown Percentage The total dollar markdown as a percentage of net sales (in dollars):

$$\text{Markdown percentage} = \frac{\text{Total dollar markdown}}{\text{Net sales (in \$)}}$$

Marketing Research in Retailing Entails the collection and analysis of information relating to specific issues or problems facing a retailer.

Marketing Research Process Embodies a series of activities: defining the issue or problem to be studied, examining secondary data, generating primary data (if needed), analyzing data, making recommendations, and implementing findings.

Market Penetration A pricing strategy in which a retailer seeks to achieve large revenues by setting low prices and selling a high unit volume.

Market-Segment Product Groupings Place various products appealing to a given target market together.

Market Skimming A pricing strategy wherein a firm charges premium prices and attracts customers less concerned with price than service, assortment, and status.

Markup The difference between merchandise costs and retail selling price.

Markup Percentage (at Cost) The difference between retail price and merchandise cost expressed as a percentage of merchandise cost:

$$\text{Markup percentage (at cost)} = \frac{\text{Retail selling price} - \text{Merchandise cost}}{\text{Merchandise cost}}$$

Markup Percentage (at Retail) The difference between retail price and merchandise cost expressed as a percentage of retail price:

$$\text{Markup percentage (at retail)} = \frac{\text{Retail selling price} - \text{Merchandise cost}}{\text{Retail selling price}}$$

Markup Pricing A form of cost-oriented pricing in which a retailer sets prices by adding per-unit merchandise costs, operating expenses, and desired profit.

Marquee A sign used to display a store's name and/or logo.

Massed Promotion Effort Used by retailers that promote mostly in one or two seasons.

Mass Marketing Selling goods and services to a broad spectrum of consumers.

Mass Merchandising A positioning approach whereby retailers offer a discount or value-oriented image, a wide and/or deep merchandise assortment, and large store facilities.

Mazur Plan Divides all retail activities into four functional areas: merchandising, publicity, store management, and accounting and control.

Megamall An enormous planned shopping center with 1-million-plus square feet of retail space, multiple anchor stores, up to several hundred specialty stores, food courts, and entertainment facilities.

Membership Club Aims at price-conscious consumers, who must be members to shop.

Memorandum Purchase Occurs when items are not paid for by the retailer until they are sold. The retailer can return unsold merchandise. However, it takes title on delivery and is responsible for damages.

Merchandise Available for Sale Equals beginning inventory, purchases, and transportation charges.

Merchandise Buying and Handling Process Comprised of an integrated and systematic sequence of steps from establishing a buying organization through regular re-evaluation.

Merchandise Space The area where nondisplayed items are kept in stock or inventory.

Merchandising Consists of the activities involved in acquiring particular goods and/or services and making them available at the places, times, and prices and in the quantity to enable a retailer to reach its goals.

Mergers Involve the combination of separately owned retail firms.

Micro-Merchandising A strategy whereby a firm adjusts shelf-space allocations to respond to customer and other differences among local markets.

Minimum-Price Laws State regulations preventing retailers from selling certain items for less than the cost plus a fixed percentage to cover overhead. These laws restrict predatory pricing and loss leaders.

Model Stock Approach A method of determining the amount of floor space to carry and display a proper merchandise assortment.

Model Stock Plan The planned composition of fashion goods, which reflects the mix of merchandise available based on expected sales. The model stock plan indicates product lines, colors, and size distributions.

Monthly Payment Credit Account Requires the consumer to pay for a purchase in equal monthly installments. Interest is usually charged.

Monthly Sales Index A measure of sales seasonality that is calculated by dividing each month's actual sales by average monthly sales and then multiplying the results by 100.

Mother Hen with Branch Store Chickens Organization Exists when headquarters executives oversee and operate the branches. This works well if there are few branches and the buying preferences of branch customers are similar to customers of the main store.

Motives The reasons for consumers' behavior.

Multidimensional Scaling A statistical technique that allows attitudinal data to be collected for several attributes in a manner that allows data analysis to produce a single overall rating of a retailer (rather than a profile of individual characteristics).

Multiple-Unit Pricing A policy whereby a retailer offers discounts to customers who buy in quantity.

Mystery Shoppers People hired by retailers to pose as customers and observe their operations, from sales presentations to how well displays are maintained to in-home service calls.

National Brands *See* Manufacturer Brands.

NBD *See* Neighborhood Business District.

Need-Satisfaction Approach A sales technique based on the principle that each customer has different wants; thus, a sales presentation should be geared to the demands of the individual.

Negotiated Pricing Occurs when a retailer works out prices with individual customers because a unique or complex service is involved and a one-time price must be agreed upon.

Neighborhood Business District (NBD) An unplanned shopping area that appeals to the convenience-shopping and service needs of a single residential area. The leading retailer is typically a supermarket, a large drugstore, or a variety store and it is situated on the major street(s) of its residential area.

Neighborhood Shopping Center A planned shopping facility with the largest store being a supermarket and/or a drugstore. It serves 3,000 to 50,000 people who are within 15 minutes' driving time (usually fewer than 10 minutes).

Net Lease Calls for all maintenance costs, such as heating, electricity, insurance, and interior repair, to be paid by the retailer—which is responsible for their satisfactory quality.

Net Profit Equals gross profit minus retail operating expenses.

Net Profit Before Taxes The profit earned after all costs have been deducted.

Net Profit Margin A performance measure based on a retailer's net profit and net sales. It is equal to net profit divided by net sales.

Net Sales The revenues received by a retailer during a given time period after deducting customer returns, markdowns, and employee discounts.

Net Worth Computed as a retailer's assets minus its liabilities.

Never-Out List Used when a retailer plans stock levels for best-sellers. Items accounting for high sales volume are stocked in a manner that ensures they are always available.

Niche Retailing Enables retailers to identify customer segments and deploy unique strategies to address the desires of those segments.

Nondisguised Survey A technique in which the respondent is told the real purpose of a research study.

Nongoods Services The area of service retailing in which intangible personal services (rather than goods) are offered to consumers—who experience services rather than possess them.

Nonprobability Sample An approach in which stores, products, or customers are chosen by the researcher—based on judgment or convenience.

Nonstore Retailing Utilizes strategy mixes that are not store-based to reach consumers and complete transactions. It occurs via direct marketing, direct selling, and vending machines.

Objective-and-Task Method A promotional budgeting technique by which a retailer clearly defines its promotional goals and then prepares a budget to satisfy these goals.

Objectives The long-run and short-run performance targets that a retailer hopes to attain. Goals can involve sales, profit, satisfaction of publics, and image.

Observation A form of research in which present behavior or the results of past behavior are observed and recorded. It can be human or mechanical.

Odd Pricing A strategy in which retail prices are set at levels below even-dollar values, such as $0.49, $4.98, and $199.

Off-Price Chain Features brand-name apparel and accessories, footwear, linens, fabrics, cosmetics, and/or housewares and sells them at everyday low prices in an efficient, limited-service environment.

Off-Retail Markdown Percentage The markdown for each item or category of items as a percentage of original retail price:

$$\text{Off-retail markdown percentage} = \frac{\text{Original price } - \text{ New price}}{\text{Original price}}$$

One-Hundred Percent Location The optimum site for a particular store. A location labeled as 100 percent for one firm may be less than optimal for another.

One-Price Policy A strategy wherein a retailer charges the same price to all customers buying an item under similar conditions.

Open Credit Account Requires a consumer to pay his or her bill in full when it is due.

Open-to-Buy The difference between planned purchases and the purchase commitments already made by a buyer for a given time period, often a month. It represents the amount the buyer has left to spend for that month and is reduced each time a purchase is made.

Operating Expenditures The short-term selling and administrative costs of running a business.

Operating Expenses The cost of running a retail business.

Operations Management The efficient and effective implementation of the policies and tasks necessary to satisfy a firm's customers, employees, and management (and stockholders, if a publicly owned company).

Opinions *See* Attitudes.

Opportunistic Buying Negotiating special low prices for merchandise whose sales have not lived up to expectations, end-of-season goods, items consumers have returned to the manufacturer or another retailer, and closeouts.

Opportunities The marketplace openings that exist because other retailers have not yet capitalized on them.

Opportunity Costs Involve forgoing possible benefits that may occur if a retailer could make expenditures in another opportunity rather than the one chosen.

Option Credit Account A form of revolving account that allows partial payments. No interest is assessed if a person pays a bill in full when it is due.

Order-Getting Salesperson Actively involved with informing and persuading customers, and in closing sales. This is a true "sales" employee.

Order Lead Time The period from the date an order is placed by a retailer to the date merchandise is ready for sale (received, price-marked, and put on the selling floor).

Order-Taking Salesperson Involved in routine clerical and sales functions, such as setting up displays, placing inventory on the shelves, answering simple questions, filling orders, and ringing up sales.

Organizational Mission A retailer's commitment to a type of business and to a distinctive role in the marketplace. It is reflected in the firm's attitudes to consumers, employees, suppliers, competitors, government, and others.

Organization Chart Graphically displays the hierarchal relationships within a firm.

Outshopping When a person goes out of his or her hometown to shop.

Outside Buying Organization A company or person external to the retailer that is hired to fulfill the buying function, usually on a fee basis.

Overstored Trading Area A geographic area with so many stores selling a specific good or service that some retailers will be unable to earn an adequate profit.

Owned-Goods Services The area of service retailing in which goods owned by consumers are repaired, improved, or maintained.

Parasite Store An outlet that does not create its own traffic and that has no real trading area of its own.

Partnership An unincorporated retail firm owned by two or more persons, each of whom has a financial interest.

Perceived Risk The level of risk a consumer believes exists regarding the purchase of a specific good or service from a specific retailer, whether or not that belief is factually correct.

Percentage Lease Stipulates that rent is related to the retailer's sales or profits.

Percentage-of-Sales Method A promotional budgeting technique whereby a retailer ties its promotion budget to sales revenue.

Percentage Variation Method An inventory-level planning method where beginning-of-month planned inventory level during any month differs from planned average monthly stock by only one-half of that month's variation from estimated average monthly sales. Under this method:

Beginning-of-month planned inventory level (at retail) = Planned average monthly stock at retail × 1/2 [1 + (Estimated monthly sales/ Estimated average monthly sales)]

Performance Measures The criteria used to assess retailer effectiveness. They include total sales, average sales per store, sales by goods/service category, sales per square foot, gross margins, gross margin return on investment, operating income, inventory turnover, markdown percentages, employee turnover, financial ratios, and profitability.

Perpetual Inventory System *See* Book Inventory System.

Perpetual-Inventory Unit-Control System Keeps a running total of the number of units handled by a retailer by ongoing record-keeping entries that adjust for sales, returns, transfers to other departments or stores, receipt of shipments, and other transactions. It can be done manually, use tags processed by computers, or rely on point-of-sale devices.

Personality The sum total of an individual's traits, which make that individual unique.

Personal Selling Involves oral communication with one or more prospective customers for the purpose of making sales.

Personnel Space The area required for employees for changing clothes, lunch and coffee breaks, and rest rooms.

Physical Inventory System Involves an actual counting of merchandise. A retailer using the cost method of inventory valuation and relying on a physical inventory system can derive gross profit only as often as it conducts a full physical inventory.

Planned Shopping Center Consists of a group of architecturally unified commercial establishments built on a site that is centrally owned or managed, designed and operated as a unit, based on balanced tenancy, and surrounded by parking facilities.

Planogram A visual (graphical) representation of the space to be allocated to selling, merchandise, personnel, and customers—as well as to product categories.

PMs A manufacturer's payments for retail salespeople selling that manufacturer's brand. PMs are in addition to the compensation received from the retailer.

Point of Indifference The geographic breaking point between two cities (communities), so that the trading area of each can be determined. At this point, consumers would be indifferent to shopping at either area.

Point-of-Purchase (POP) Display An interior display that provides consumers with information, adds to store atmosphere, and serves a substantial promotional role.

POP Display *See* Point-of-Purchase Display.

Positioning Enables a retailer to devise its strategy in a way that projects an image relative to its retail category and its competitors, and elicits consumer responses to that image.

Post-Purchase Behavior Further purchases or reevaluation based on a purchase.

Poverty of Time Occurs when greater striving for financial security leads to less rather than more free time since the alternatives competing for consumers' time rise considerably.

Power Center A shopping site with (a) up to a half-dozen or so category killer stores and a mix of smaller stores or (b) several complementary stores specializing in a product category.

Power Retailer The status reached by a company that is dominant in some aspect of its strategy. Consumers view the company as distinctive enough to become loyal to it and go out of their way to shop there.

Predatory Pricing Involves large retailers that seek to destroy competition by selling goods and services at very low prices, thus causing small retailers to go out of business. The practice is restricted by federal and state laws.

Prestige Pricing Assumes consumers will not buy goods and services at prices deemed too low. It is based on the price-quality association.

Pre-training An indoctrination on the history and policies of the retailer and a job orientation on the hours, compensation, chain of command, and job duties.

Price Elasticity of Demand Relates to the sensitivity of customers to price changes in terms of the quantities they will buy:

$$\text{Elasticity} = \frac{\dfrac{\text{Quantity 1} - \text{Quantity 2}}{\text{Quantity 1} + \text{Quantity 2}}}{\dfrac{\text{Price 1} - \text{Price 2}}{\text{Price 1} + \text{Price 2}}}$$

Price Guarantees Protect retailers against possible price declines. If a retailer cannot sell an item at a given price, the manufacturer pays it the difference between planned retail and actual retail selling prices.

Price Line Classifications Enable retail sales, inventories, and purchases to be analyzed by retail price category.

Price Lining (1) A practice whereby retailers sell merchandise at a limited range of price points, with each price point representing a distinct level of quality.

Price-Lining (2) Used by service retailers providing a wide selection of services. A range of prices is matched to service levels.

Price-Quality Association A concept stating that many consumers feel high prices connote high quality and low prices connote low quality.

Primary Customer Services Those considered basic components of the retail strategy mix; they must be provided.

Primary Data Collected to address the specific issue or problem under study. These data can be gathered internally or externally through surveys, observations, experiments, and simulation.

Primary Trading Area Encompasses 50 percent to 80 percent of a store's customers. It is the geographic area closest to the store and possesses the highest density of customers to population and the highest per-capita sales.

Private (Dealer) Brands Contain names designated by wholesalers or retailers, are more profitable to retailers, are better controlled by retailers, are not sold by competing retailers, are less expensive for consumers, and lead to customer loyalty to retailers.

Probability (Random) Sample An approach whereby every store, product, or customer has an equal or known chance of being chosen for study.

Problem Awareness The stage in the decision process where the consumer not only has been aroused by social, commercial, and/or physical stimuli, but also recognizes the good or service under consideration may solve a problem of shortage or unfulfilled desire.

Problem Definition *See* Issue Definition.

Productivity The efficiency with which a retail strategy is carried out.

Product Life Cycle Shows the expected behavior of a good or service over its life. The traditional cycle has four stages: introduction, growth, maturity, and decline.

Product/Trademark Franchising An arrangement in which franchised dealers acquire the identities of their suppliers by agreeing to sell the latter's products and/or operate under suppliers' names.

Profit-and-Loss (Income) Statement Represents a summary of a retailer's revenues and expenses over a particular period of time, usually on a monthly, quarterly, and/or yearly basis.

Prototype Stores Occur with an operations strategy that requires multiple outlets in a chain to conform to relatively uniform construction, layout, and operations standards.

Psychological Pricing Refers to consumer perceptions of retail prices.

Publicity Any nonpersonal form of public relations whereby messages are transmitted through mass media, the time or space provided by the media is not paid for, and there is no identified commercial sponsor.

Public Relations Entails any communication that fosters a favorable image for the retailer among its publics (consumers, investors, government, channel members, employees, and the general public).

Purchase Act An exchange of money or a promise to pay for ownership or use of a good or service. Purchase variables include the place of purchase, terms, and availability of merchandise.

Purchase-Motivation Product Groupings Appeal to the consumer's urge to buy a product and the time he or she is willing to spend in shopping.

QR Inventory Planning *See* Quick Response Inventory Planning.

Quick Response (QR) Inventory Planning Enables a retailer to reduce the amount of inventory it keeps on hand by ordering more frequently and in lower quantity.

Rack Display An interior display that hangs or presents products neatly.

Random Sample *See* Probability Sample.

Rationalized Retailing A strategy involving a high degree of centralized management control combined with strict operating procedures for every phase of business.

Reach The number of distinct people exposed to a retailer's ads in a specified period.

Recommendations The stage in the research process during which the alternative approach to best solve a problem or issue is presented.

Recruitment The activity whereby a retailer generates a list of job applicants.

Reference Groups Influence people's thoughts and/or behavior. They may be classified as aspirational, membership, and dissociative.

Regional Shopping Center A large, planned shopping facility appealing to a geographically dispersed market. It has at least one or two full-sized department stores and 50 to 150 or more smaller retailers. The market for this center is 100-plus people, who live or work up to 30 minutes' driving time from the center.

Regression Model A computer site-selection model that develops a series of mathematical equations showing the association between potential store sales and various independent variables at each location under consideration.

Reilly's Law of Retail Gravitation The traditional means of trading area delineation that establishes a point of indifference between two cities or communities, so the trading area of each can be determined.

Relationship Retailing Exists when retailers seek to establish and maintain long-term bonds with customers, rather than act as if each sales transaction is a completely new encounter with them.

Rented-Goods Services The area of service retailing in which consumers lease and use goods for specified periods of time.

Reorder Point The stock level at which new orders must be placed:

Reorder point = (Usage rate × Lead time)
+ Safety stock

Resident Buying Office An inside or outside buying organization that is usually situated in important merchandise centers (sources of supply) and provides valuable data and contacts.

Retail Audit The systematic examination and evaluation of a firm's total retailing effort or some specific aspect of it. Its purpose is to study what a retailer is presently doing, appraise how well the firm is performing, and make recommendations for future actions.

Retail Balance Refers to the mix of stores within a district or shopping center.

Retail Information System Anticipates the information needs of retail managers; collects, organizes, and stores relevant data on a continuous basis; and directs the flow of information to the proper retail decision makers.

Retailing Consists of those business activities involved in the sale of goods and services to consumers for their personal, family, or household use.

Retailing Concept Comprises these four elements: customer orientation, coordinated effort, value-driven, and goal orientation.

Retailing Effectiveness Checklist Lets a firm systematically assess its preparedness for the future.

Retail Institution Refers to the basic format or structure of a business. Institutions can be classified by ownership, store-based retail strategy mix, service versus goods retail strategy mix, and nonstore-based retail strategy mix.

Retail Life Cycle A theory asserting that institutions—like the goods and services they sell—pass through identifiable life-cycle stages: innovation, accelerated development, maturity, and decline.

Retail Method of Accounting A way by which the closing inventory value is determined by calculating the average relationship between the cost and retail values of merchandise available for sale during a period.

Retail Organization How a firm structures and assigns tasks (functions), policies, resources, authority, responsibilities, and rewards so as to efficiently and effectively satisfy the needs of its target market, employees, and management.

Retail Performance Index Encompasses five-year trends in revenue growth and profit growth, and a six-year average return on assets.

Retail Promotion Any communication by a retailer that informs, persuades, and/or reminds the target market about any aspect of that firm.

Retail Reductions Represent the difference between beginning inventory plus purchases during the period and sales plus ending inventory. They should encompass anticipated markdowns, employee and other discounts, and stock shortages.

Retail Strategy The overall plan guiding a retail firm. It has an influence on the firm's business activities and its response to market forces, such as competition and the economy.

Return on Assets (ROA) A performance ratio based on a retailer's net sales, net profit, and total assets:

$$\frac{\text{Return}}{\text{on assets}} = \frac{\text{Net profit}}{\text{Net sales}} \times \frac{\text{Net sales}}{\text{Total assets}} = \frac{\text{Net profit}}{\text{Total assets}}$$

Return on Net Worth (RONW) A performance measure based on a retailer's net profit, net sales, total assets, and net worth:

$$\frac{\text{Return on}}{\text{net worth}} = \frac{\text{Net profit}}{\text{Net sales}} \times \frac{\text{Net sales}}{\text{Total assets}} \times \frac{\text{Total assets}}{\text{Net worth}}$$

Revolving Credit Account Allows a customer to charge items and be billed monthly on the basis of the outstanding cumulative balance.

ROA *See* Return on Assets.

Robinson-Patman Act Bars manufacturers and wholesalers from discrimination in price or sales terms in selling to individual retailers if these retailers are purchasing products of "like quality" and the effect of such discrimination would be to injure competition.

Routine Decision Making Takes place when a consumer buys out of habit and skips steps in the purchase process.

Safety Stock The extra inventory kept on hand to protect against out-of-stock conditions due to unexpected demand and delays in delivery.

Sale-Leaseback The practice of retailers building new stores and then selling them to real-estate investors who lease the property back to the retailers on a long-term basis.

Sales Forecasting Lets a retailer estimate expected future sales for a given time period.

Sales Opportunity Grid Rates the promise of new goods, services, procedures, and/or store outlets across a variety of criteria.

Sales-Productivity Ratio A method for assigning floor space on the basis of sales or profit per foot.

Sales Promotion Encompasses the paid marketing communication activities other than advertising, public relations, and personal selling that stimulate consumer purchases and dealer effectiveness.

Saturated Trading Area A geographic area having a proper amount of retail facilities to satisfy the needs of its population for a specific good or service, as well as to let retailers prosper.

SBD *See* Secondary Business District.

Scenario Analysis Lets a retailer project the future by examining the key factors that will affect its long-run performance and then preparing contingency plans based on alternate scenarios.

Scrambled Merchandising Occurs when a retailer adds goods and services that are unrelated to each other and to the firm's original business.

Secondary Business District (SBD) An unplanned shopping area in a city or town that is usually bounded by the intersection of two major streets. It has at least a junior department store, a variety store, and/or some larger specialty stores—in addition to many smaller stores.

Secondary Data Those that have been gathered for purposes other than addressing the issue or problem currently under study.

Secondary Trading Area A geographic area with an added 15 percent to 25 percent of a store's customers. It is located outside a primary trading area, and customers are more widely dispersed.

Selective Distribution Takes place when suppliers sell through a moderate number of retailers. This allows suppliers to have higher sales than in exclusive distribution and lets retailers carry some competing brands.

Self-Fulfillment A life-style concept whereby people express their growing sense of uniqueness through goods and services purchases.

Selling Against the Brand The practice of retailers carrying manufacturers' brands and placing high prices on them so rival brands (such as private-label goods) can be sold more easily.

Selling Space The area set aside for displays of merchandise, interactions between salespeople and customers, demonstrations, and so on.

Semantic Differential A disguised or nondisguised survey technique, whereby a respondent is asked to rate one or more retailers on several criteria; each criterion is evaluated along a bipolar adjective scale.

Separate Store Organization Treats each branch as a separate store with its own buying responsibilities. Customer needs are quickly noted, but duplication by managers in the main store and the branches is possible.

Service Blueprint Systematically lists all the service functions to be performed and the average time expected for each one's completion.

Service Retailing Involves transactions between companies or individuals and final consumers where the consumers do not purchase or acquire ownership of tangible products. It encompasses rented goods, owned goods, and nongoods.

SERVQUAL Lets retailers assess the quality of their service offerings by asking customers to react to a series of statements in five areas of performance: reliability, responsiveness, assurance, empathy, and tangibles.

Simulation A type of experiment whereby a computer-based program is used to manipulate the elements of a retail strategy mix rather than test them in a real setting.

Single-Source Data Collection Occurs when a research firm develops a sample of consumer households, determines their demographic and life-style backgrounds by surveys, observes television viewing behavior by in-home cable hookups to the firm's computers, and monitors shopping behavior by having people make purchases in designated stores.

Situation Analysis The candid evaluation of the opportunities and potential problems facing a prospective or existing retailer.

Social Class An informal ranking of people in a culture based on their income, occupation, education, dwelling, and other factors.

Social Responsibility Occurs when a retailer acts in the best interests of society—as well as itself. The challenge is to balance corporate citizenship with a fair level of profits.

Sole Proprietorship An unincorporated retail firm owned by one person.

Sorting Process Involves the retailer's collecting an assortment of goods and services from various sources, buying them in large quantity, and offering to sell them to consumers in small quantities.

Specialog Enables a firm to cater to specific needs of customer segments, emphasize a limited number of items, and reduce its catalog production and postage costs.

Specialty Store A general merchandise retailer that concentrates on selling one goods or service line.

Standardization A strategy of directly applying a domestic market retail strategy to foreign markets.

Standard Merchandise Classification A detailed list of common merchandise-reporting categories devised by the National Retail Federation. Its use lets retailers contrast their financial data with industry averages.

Stimulus A cue (social or commercial) or a drive (physical) meant to motivate or arouse a person to act.

Stock-to-Sales Method An inventory-level planning technique wherein a retailer wants to maintain a specified ratio of goods-on-hand to sales.

Stock Turnover Represents the number of times during a specific period, usually one year, that the average inventory on hand is sold. Stock turnover can be computed in units or dollars (at retail or cost):

$$\text{Annual rate of stock turnover (in units)} = \frac{\text{Number of units sold during year}}{\text{Average inventory on hand (in units)}}$$

$$\text{Annual rate of stock turnover (in retail dollars)} = \frac{\text{Net yearly sales}}{\text{Average inventory on hand (at retail)}}$$

$$\text{Annual rate of stock turnover (at cost)} = \frac{\text{Cost of goods sold during the year}}{\text{Average inventory on hand (at cost)}}$$

Storability Product Groupings Classify and display products needing special handling and storage together.

Storefront The total physical exterior of a store. It includes the marquee, entrances, windows, lighting, and construction materials.

Store Loyalty Exists when a consumer regularly patronizes a particular retailer (store or nonstore) that he or she knows, likes, and trusts.

Store Maintenance Encompasses all the activities involved in managing a retailer's physical facilities.

Straight Lease Requires the retailer to pay a fixed dollar amount per month over the life of a lease. It is the simplest, most direct leasing arrangement.

Straight (Gridiron) Traffic Flow Presents displays and aisles in a rectangular or gridiron pattern.

Strategic Profit Model Expresses the mathematical relationship among net profit margin, asset turnover, and financial leverage. It can be used in planning or controlling a retailer's assets.

Strategy Mix A firm's particular combination of these factors: store location, operating procedures, goods/services offered, pricing tactics, store atmosphere and customer services, and promotional methods.

String An unplanned shopping area comprising a group of retail stores, often with similar or compatible product lines, located along a street or highway.

Supercenter A special type of combination store that blends an economy supermarket with a discount department store.

Supermarket A self-service food store with grocery, meat, and produce departments and minimum annual sales of $2 million. This retail category includes conventional supermarkets, food-based superstores, combination stores, box (limited-line) stores, and warehouse stores.

Supervision The manner of providing a job environment that encourages employee accomplishment.

Survey A research technique whereby information is systematically gathered from respondents by communicating with them.

Survey of Buying Power Reports current demographic data on metropolitan areas, cities, and states. It also provides such information as total annual retail sales by area, annual retail sales for specific product categories, annual effective buying income, and five-year population and retail sales projections.

Tactics Actions that encompass a retailer's daily and short-term operations.

Tall Organization A format with several levels of managers. It leads to close supervision and fewer employees reporting to each manager.

Target Market The customer group that a retailer seeks to attract and satisfy.

Terms of Occupancy Include ownership versus leasing, the type of lease, operations and maintenance costs, taxes, zoning restrictions, and voluntary regulations.

Theme-Setting Display An interior display that depicts a product offering in a thematic manner and lets a retailer portray a specific atmosphere or mood.

Theory X The traditional view of motivation that assumes employees must be closely supervised and controlled. It has been applied to lower-level retail positions.

Theory Y A more modern view of motivation that assumes workers can be self-managers and be given authority, motivation is social and psychological, and management is decentralized and participatory. It applies to all levels of retail personnel.

Theory Z Advocates more employee involvement in defining their jobs and sharing decision making with management. It adapts elements from Theory Y and Herzberg's theory.

Threats Environmental and/or marketplace factors that can adversely affect retailers if they do not react to them (and sometimes, even if they do).

Top-Down Space Management Approach Exists when a retailer starts with its total available store space (by store and for the overall firm, if a chain), divides the space into categories, and then works on in-store product layouts.

Total Retail Experience Consists of all the elements in a retail offering that encourage or inhibit consumers during their contact with a given retailer.

Trading Area A geographic area containing the customers of a particular firm or group of firms for specific goods or services.

Trading-Area Overlap Occurs when the trading areas of stores in different locations encroach upon one another. In the overlap area, the same customers are served by both stores.

Traditional Department Store A department store where merchandise quality ranges from average to quite good, pricing is moderate to above average, and customer service levels of help range from medium to high.

Traditional Job Description Contains each position's title, supervisory relationships (superior and subordinate), committee assignments, and the specific roles and tasks to be performed on an ongoing basis.

Training Programs Used to teach new (and existing) personnel how best to perform their jobs or how to improve themselves.

Unbundled Pricing Involves a retailer's charging separate prices for each service offered.

Uncontrollable Variables Those aspects of business to which the retailer must adapt (such as competition, the economy, and laws).

Understored Trading Area A geographic area having too few stores selling a specific good or service to satisfy the needs of its population.

Unit Control Relates to the quantities of merchandise a retailer handles during a stated time period.

Unit Pricing A practice required by many states, whereby retailers (mostly food stores) must express price in terms of both the total price of an item and its price per unit of measure.

Universal Product Code (UPC) A classification for coding data onto products by a series of thick and thin vertical lines. It lets retailers record data instantaneously as to the model number, size, color, and other factors when an item is sold, and to transmit the data to a computer monitoring unit sales, inventory levels, and other factors. The UPC is not readable by humans.

Unplanned Business District A type of retail location where two or more stores situate together (or in close proximity) in such a way that the total arrangement or mix of stores in the district is not the result of prior long-range planning.

UPC See Universal Product Code.

Usage Rate Refers to average sales per day, in units, of merchandise.

Value Delivery System Comprises all of the activities needed to develop, produce, deliver, and sell and service particular goods and services.

Value Pricing Occurs when prices are set on the basis of fair value for both the service provider and the consumer.

Variable Markup Policy A strategy whereby a retailer purposely varies markups by merchandise category.

Variable Pricing A pricing strategy wherein a retailer alters its prices to coincide with fluctuations in costs or consumer demand.

Variety Store A retail store that handles a wide assortment of inexpensive and popularly priced goods and services, such as stationery, gift items, women's accessories, health and beauty aids, light hardware, toys, housewares, confectionery items, and shoe repair.

Vending Machine A retailing format that involves the coin- or card-operated dispensing of goods and services. It eliminates the use of sales personnel and allows around-the-clock sales.

Vertical Cooperative-Advertising Agreement Enables a manufacturer and a retailer or a wholesaler and a retailer to share an ad.

Vertical Marketing System Consists of all the levels of independently owned businesses along a channel of distribution. Goods and services are normally distributed through one of three types of systems: independent, partially integrated, and fully integrated.

Vertical Price Fixing Occurs when manufacturers or wholesalers are able to control the retail prices of their goods and services.

Vertical Retail Audit Involves analyzing—in depth—a retail firm's performance in one area of its strategy mix or operations.

Video Catalog A retail catalog that appears on a CD-ROM disk and is viewed on a computer monitor.

Video Kiosk A freestanding, interactive computer terminal that displays products and related information on a video screen; it often uses a touchscreen for people to make selections.

Want Book (Want Slip) A notebook or slip in which store employees record consumer requests for unstocked or out-of-stock merchandise.

Warehouse Store A food-based discounter offering a moderate number of food items in a no-frills setting.

Weeks' Supply Method An inventory-level planning method wherein beginning inventory is equal to several weeks' expected sales. It assumes the inventory carried is in direct proportion to sales. Under this method:

$$\begin{array}{l}\text{Beginning-of-month} \\ \text{planned inventory level} \\ \text{(at retail)}\end{array} = \begin{array}{l}\text{Average estimated weekly} \\ \text{sales} \times \text{Number of weeks to} \\ \text{be stocked}\end{array}$$

Weighted Application Blank A form whereby criteria that best correlate with job success are given more weight than others. After weighted scores are given to all job applicants, a minimum total score can be used as a cutoff point for hiring.

Wheel of Retailing A theory stating that retail innovators often first appear as low-price operators with a low-cost structure and low profit-margin requirements. Over time, these innovators upgrade the products they carry and improve their facilities and customer services. They then become vulnerable to new discounters with lower cost structures.

Width of Assortment Refers to the number of distinct goods/service categories with which a retailer is involved.

Word-of-Mouth Communication Occurs when one consumer talks to others.

World Wide Web (WWW) One way of assessing information on the Internet, whereby people work with easy-to-use Web addresses (sites) and pages. Users see words, colorful charts, pictures, and video, and hear audio—turning their PCs into interactive multimedia centers.

WWW *See* World Wide Web.

Yield Management Pricing Used when a service firm determines the combination of prices that yield the highest level of revenues for a given time period.

Zero-Based Budgeting The practice followed when a firm starts each new budget from scratch and outlines the expenditures needed to reach that period's goals. All costs must be justified each time a budget is done.

Photo Credits

Chapter 1
Fig. 1-1 (page 5) Weis Markets, Inc. Reprinted by permission. **Fig. 1-2 (page 9)** U.S. Bureau of Engraving and Printing. **Fig. 1-7 (page 17)** Lands' End, Inc. Reprinted by permission. **Fig. 1-8 (page 17)** Lands' End, Inc. Reprinted by permission. **Fig. 1-10 (page 20)** John Petrey/John Petrey Studios. Reprinted by permission. **Fig. 1-11 (page 21)** Carson, Pirie, Scott & Co. Reprinted by permission.

Chapter 2
Fig. 2-2 (page 31) Photo reprinted by permission of John B. Gifford. **Fig. 2-6 (page 42)** Reprinted by permission of John B. Gifford. **Fig. 2-7 (page 43)** Reprinted by permission from *Chain Store Age.* Copyright Lebhar-Friedman, Inc., 425 Park Avenue, New York, NY, 10022. **Fig. 2-8 (page 44)** Reprinted by permission from *Chain Store Age.* Copyright Lebhar-Friedman, Inc., 425 Park Avenue, New York, NY, 10022.

Chapter 3
Fig. 3-1 (page 63) Innovative Computer Consultants, Inc. Reprinted by permission. **Fig. 3-3 (page 70)** Reprinted by permission of Stores Automated Systems, Inc. **Fig. 3-4 (page 71)** Reprinted by permission of Stores Automated Systems, Inc. **Fig. 3-5 (page 73)** SpectraLink Corporation. Reprinted by permission. **Fig. 3-6 (page 74)** Reprinted by permission of Retail Technologies International. **Fig. 3-9 (page 87)** Toys "Я" Us. Reprinted by permission.

Chapter 4
Fig. 4-2 (page 107) The Talbots, Inc. Reprinted by permission. **Fig. 4-4 (page 112)** Reprinted by permission of Barry Berman. **Fig. 4-6 (page 114)** Reprinted by permission.

Chapter 5
Fig. 5-4 (page 141) Phillips Petroleum Company. Reprinted by permission. **Fig. 5-5 (page 144)** Reprinted by permission of John B. Gifford. **Fig. 5-6 (page 149)** Reprinted by permission of John B. Gifford. **Fig. 5-7 (page 155)** Reprinted by permission of Phillips-Van Huesen. **Fig. 5-8 (page 158)** Ace Hardware. Reprinted by permission.

Chapter 6
Fig. 6-1 (page 165) John Petrey/John Petrey Studios. Reprinted by permission. **Fig. 6-2 (page 166)** Spiegel. Reprinted by permission. **Fig. 6-3 (page 172)** L.L. Bean. Reprinted by permission. **Fig. 6-5 (page 180)** Reprinted by permission of Mary Kay Cosmetics. **Fig. 6-6 (page 186)** Reprinted by permission from *Inc.* Magazine. Copyright Goldhirsh Group, Inc., 38 Commercial Wharf, Boston, MA, 02110.

Chapter 7
Fig. 7-1 (page 202) Reprinted by permission of John B. Gifford. **Fig. 7-4 (page 211)** Reprinted by permission of Giant Food. **Fig. 7-8a (page 226)** Reprinted by permission of Nash Finch. **Fig. 7-8b (page 226)** Reprinted by permission of Ames Department Stores. **Fig. 7-8c (page 226)** Reprinted by permission of Ross Stores, Inc.

Chapter 8
Fig. 8-3 (page 239) Reprinted by permission of Retail Technologies International. **Fig. 8-4 (page 241)** Reprinted by permission of MicroStrategy, Inc. **Fig. 8-5a (page 245)** Reprinted by permission of Symbol Technologies. **Fig. 8-5b (page 245)** Reprinted by permission of Symbol Technologies. **Fig. 8-5c (page 245)** Reprinted by permission of Symbol Technologies. **Fig. 8-5d (page 245)** Reprinted by permission of Symbol Technologies. **Fig. 8-7 (page 255)** Reprinted by permission of Food Lion. **Fig. 8-8 (page 256)** Reprinted by permission of *Chain Store Age.* Copyright Lebhar-Friedman, Inc., 425 Park Avenue, New York, NY 10022. **Fig. 8-11 (page 261)** Reprinted by permission of Gadd International Research, Inc.

Chapter 9
Fig. 9-2a (page 280) U.S. Bureau of the Census. Reprinted by permission. **Fig. 9-2b (page 281)** U.S. Bureau of the Census. Reprinted by permission. **Fig. 9-3a (page 282)** Reprinted by permission of Decisionmark (Proximity). **Fig. 9-3a (page 283)** Reprinted by permission of Caliper Corporation (Maptitude). **Fig. 9-3a (page 284)** Reprinted by permission of Tetrad Computer Applications (PCensus). **Fig. 9-5 (page 287)** Reprinted by the permission of Donnelley Marketing, Inc.

Chapter 10
Fig. 10-1 (page 313) Reprinted by permission of McDonald's Corporation. **Fig. 10-2a (page 316)** Reprinted by permission of the Rouse Company. **Fig. 10-2b (page 316)** Reprinted by permission of the Rouse Company. **Fig. 10-4 (page 322)** Reprinted by permission of the Rouse Company. **Fig. 10-5 (page 323)** Heitman Retail Properties. Reprinted by permission. **Fig. 10-7 (page 329)** Reprinted by permission of John B. Gifford.

Chapter 12
Fig. 12-1 (page 383) Merry-Go-Round Enterprises, Inc. Reprinted by permission.

Chapter 13

Fig. 13-2 (page 411) Eddie Bauer. Reprinted by permission. Photo credit to Ann Hopping/Callison Architecture, Inc. **Fig. 13-4 (page 413)** Reprinted by permission of Eckerd Corporation. **Fig. 13-5 (page 417)** Reprinted by permission of Sensormatic Electronics Corporation. **Fig. 13-7 (page 421)** Reprinted by permission of American Petrofina. **Fig. 13-8 (page 423)** Reprinted by permission of Synchronics, Inc.

Chapter 14

Fig. 14-3 (page 440) Michaels Stores. Reprinted by permission. **Fig. 14-4 (page 444)** Dollar General Corp. Reprinted by permission. **Fig. 14-10 (page 463)** Walgreen Company. Reprinted by permission. **Fig. 14-11 (page 464)** Reprinted by permission of Monarch Marking Systems. **Fig. 14-12 (page 465)** Reprinted by permission of Seagull Scientific Systems, author of "Bar Tender" label printing software.

Chapter 16

Fig. 16-4 (page 525) Perry Drug Stores. Reprinted by permission. **Fig. 16-5 (page 528)** Reprinted by permission of John B. Gifford. **Fig. 16-6 (page 529)** Reprinted by permission of John B. Gifford. **Fig. 16-8 (page 533)** Reprinted by permission of John B. Gifford.

Chapter 17

Fig. 17-2 (page 551) Finish Line. Reprinted by permission. **Fig. 17-4a (page 556)** Reprinted by permission of Dillard. **Fig. 17-4b (page 556)** Parisian photo. Reprinted by permission of John B. Gifford. **Fig. 17-4c (page 556)** Bayside photo. Reprinted by permission of Rouse Company. **Fig. 17-5 (page 557)** Reprinted by permission of NCR Corporation. NCR is a copyright of NCR Corporation. **Fig. 17-6 (page 561)** MarketWare Corp. Reprinted by permission. **Fig. 17-9 (page 566)** Reprinted by permission of John B. Gifford. **Fig. 17-10 (page 567)** Reprinted by permission of John B. Gifford. **Fig. 17-12 (page 570)** Reprinted by permission of NCR Corporation. NCR is a copyright of NCR Corporation. **Fig. 17-13 (page 572)** Reprinted by permission of Phillips Petroleum Company.

Chapter 18

Fig. 18-1 (page 586) Belz Factory Outlet World. Reprinted by permission. **Fig. 18-3 (page 592)** Wendy's International. Reprinted by permission. **Fig. 18-4 (page 595)** Reprinted by permission of John B. Gifford. **Fig. 18-7 (page 600)** Reprinted by permission of Virtual i-O, Inc. **Fig. 18-8 (page 601)** Reprinted by permission of Catalina Marketing Corporation. **Fig. 18-11 (page 610)** Reprinted by permission of Advanced Neurotechnologies, Inc.

Part 7 Case

Fig. 1 (page 619) SRI International. Reprinted by permission of *American Demographics*. **Fig. 2a (page 621)** Reprinted by permission of BJ's Merchandising/Design. **Fig. 2b (page 621)** Reprinted by permission of BJ's Merchandising/Design. **Fig. 2c (page 621)** Reprinted by permission of BJ's Merchandising/Design.

Chapter 19

Fig. 19-1a (page 626) Reprinted by permission of Triple Five Corporation. Photos by The Postcard Factory. **Fig. 19-1b (page 626)** Reprinted by permission of Triple Five Corporation. Photos by The Postcard Factory. **Fig. 19-1c (page 626)** Reprinted by permission of Triple Five Corporation. Photos by The Postcard Factory. **Fig. 19-1d (page 626)** Reprinted by permission of Triple Five Corporation. Photos by The Postcard Factory. **Fig. 19-2 (page 627)** Reprinted by permission of the Hertz Corporation. **Fig. 19-5 (page 633)** American Airlines. Reprinted by permission. **Fig. 19-7 (page 636)** Reprinted by permission of John B. Gifford. **Fig. 19-10 (page 642)** Reprinted by permission of CCB Central Carolina Bank and Trust Company.

Chapter 20

Fig. 20-1 (page 660) Kay Jeweler's, Inc. Reprinted by permission. **Fig. 20-4 (page 663)** Kmart Corporation. Reprinted by permission. **Fig. 20-5 (page 665)** Reprinted by permission of Intellilink Services. **Fig. 20-6 (page 676)** InterSpace is reprinted by permission of NTT.

Name Index

Subject Index

An asterisk before a term indicates Glossary entry.

An asterisk before a term indicates Glossary entry.

An asterisk before a term indicates Glossary entry.

An asterisk before a term indicates Glossary entry.

An asterisk before a term indicates Glossary entry.

An asterisk before a term indicates Glossary entry.

An asterisk before a term indicates Glossary entry.

An asterisk before a term indicates Glossary entry.

An asterisk before a term indicates Glossary entry.

An asterisk before a term indicates Glossary entry.

An asterisk before a term indicates Glossary entry.

An asterisk before a term indicates Glossary entry.

An asterisk before a term indicates Glossary entry.

An asterisk before a term indicates Glossary entry.

An asterisk before a term indicates Glossary entry.